26th Pacific Asia Conference on Language, Information and Computation 2012

(PACLIC 26)

Bali, Indonesia
7-10 November 2012

ISBN: 978-1-62748-393-3

Printed from e-media with permission by:

Curran Associates, Inc.
57 Morehouse Lane
Red Hook, NY 12571

Some format issues inherent in the e-media version may also appear in this print version.

Printed by Curran Associates, Inc. (2013)

Association for Computational Linguistics
209 N. Eighth Street
Stroudsburg, Pennsylvania 18360

Phone: 1-570-476-8006
Fax: 1-570-476-0860

acl@aclweb.org

Additional copies of this publication are available from:

Curran Associates, Inc.
57 Morehouse Lane
Red Hook, NY 12571 USA
Phone: 845-758-0400
Fax: 845-758-2634
Email: curran@proceedings.com
Web: www.proceedings.com

Welcome Message from Honorary Chairs

On behalf of the Organizing Committee of the 26th Pacific Asia Conference on Language, Information and Computation (PACLIC 26), we would like to extend our warm welcome to all of the participants and speakers, and in particular, we would like to express our sincere gratitude to our invited speakers.

This international conference is organized by the Faculty of Computer Science, Universitas Indonesia and is supported by the I-MHERE DIKTI project. We are very keen to host a conference about language processing fields which involves many researchers in this Asia Pacific region. We believe that this international conference will open up the opportunities for sharing and exchanging original research ideas and opinions, getting inspiration for future research, and broadening knowledge about various new topics and approaches in language study. We hope that in this conference, the attendees would have the opportunity to meet with new people and discuss the opportunity to collaborate together.

We chose to organize PACLIC 26 in Bali so that aside from attending this interesting conference, you can also enjoy the scenery and the culture of Bali. We realize that there might not be enough time to see all the nice places in Bali, but we hope that you can bring home some good memories.

We would like to express our sincere appreciation to the members of the Program Commitee for a fruitful reviews of the submitted papers, as well as the Organizing Commitee for the time and energy they have devoted to editing the proceedings and arranging the logistics of holding this conference. We would like to give an appreciation to the authors who have submitted their excellent works to this conference. Last but not least, we would like to extend our gratitude to the Ministry of Education and Culture of the Republic of Indonesia and the Dean of the Faculty of Computer Science at Universitas Indonesia for their continued support towards the PACLIC 26 conference.

Have a nice time in Bali and enjoy the conference.

Honorary Chairs:

Mirna Adriani (Universitas Indonesia)
I Wayan Arka (ANU / Universitas Udayana)

Welcome Message from Program Co-Chairs

Welcome to Bali! This is the first time that the PACLIC conference is being held in Indonesia, and we are very excited about this fact. By all accounts, Indonesia is a linguistic treasure trove, with over 700 living languages today according to the Ethnologue report. Moreover, with an increasing number of its 240 million population active on the Internet via the Web and social networks, clearly these are exciting times to be engaging in computational approaches towards the languages of Indonesia.

However, this PACLIC conference in 2012 is special for other reasons, most notably the commemoration of 25 years of the conference series. Over the years, the conference has developed into one of the leading conferences in the fields of theoretical and computational linguistics, extending beyond the Asia-Pacific region. This year, the specific research topics that the papers focus on can be classified into the following: discourse & pragmatics, grammar & syntax, information extraction, information retrieval, lexical semantics, machine translation, parsing, sentiment analysis, text summarization & paraphrasing, and word sense disambiguation & distributional semantics. Moreover, there is an interesting mix of both theoretical and computational approaches to almost all of the aforementioned topics.

We received paper submissions representing immense diversity, with authors from 29 countries or regions, namely Australia, Bahrain, Belgium, Canada, China, Czech Republic, Denmark, Egypt, France, Germany, Hong Kong, India, Indonesia, Japan, Korea, Macau, Malaysia, Pakistan, Philippines, Qatar, Singapore, Slovakia, Sri Lanka, Taiwan, Thailand, Tunisia, United Kingdom, United States, and Vietnam. To ensure that all accepted papers met the high quality standard of the PACLIC conference, all papers were sent to three reviewers. Of the 117 submissions that we received, 39 papers (33%) were accepted for oral presentation, and another 18 papers (15%) were accepted for poster presentation. We believe this has yielded an interesting, diverse, and high-quality collection of papers, and are confident that the conference will be successful as a result.

A successful conference is the result of many peoples efforts and contributions. Aside from the efforts of the authors who will be presenting their current work, thanks must be given to the tremendous efforts made by the program committee members in their paper reviews. Besides the oral and poster paper presentations, the conference is enriched by several invited speakers. Firstly there is a Special Session commemorating 25 years of PACLIC, which brings together Prof Kiyong Lee from Korea University, Prof Yuji Matsumoto from the Nara Institute of Science and Technology, and Prof Benjamin T'sou from the Hong Kong Institute of Education, three figures who have been instrumental in the formation of the PACLIC tradition. We have also scheduled invited talks from Prof I Wayan Arka from ANU & Universitas Udayana and Prof Tim Baldwin from the University of Melbourne. The expertise in the respective fields of all five speakers will undoubtedly provide us with new insights for research. On behalf of the program committee, we express our heartfelt thanks to them all. We would also like to thank the steering committee for their guidance, and the local organizing committee at Universitas Indonesia for their dedicated efforts and their excellent coordination with all parties, which has ensured that this conference will be a successful event.

Finally, we wish that you will all enjoy the conference presentations and resulting discussions between old and new friends, and also have some time to enjoy the wondrous setting that is the island of Bali.

Program Co-Chairs:
Ruli Manurung (Universitas Indonesia)
Francis Bond (Nanyang Technological University)

PACLIC 26 Organizers

Steering Committee:

Jae-Woong Choe, Korea University
Yasunari Harada, Waseda University
Chu-Ren Huang, Hong Kong Polytechnic University
Rachel Edita Roxas, De La Salle University-Manila
Maosong Sun, Tsinghua University
Benjamin T'sou, City University of Hong Kong
Min Zhang, Institute for Infocomm Research

Honorary Chairs:

Mirna Adriani, Universitas Indonesia
I Wayan Arka, ANU/Universitas Udayana

Program Committee:

Co-Chairs:

Ruli Manurung, Universitas Indonesia
Francis Bond, Nanyang Technological University
Shu-Kai Hsieh, National Taiwan University
Donghong Ji, Wuhan University
Olivia Kwong, City University of Hong Kong
Seungho Nam, Seoul National University
Ryo Otoguro, Waseda University
Rachel Edita Roxas, De La Salle University-Manila

Members:

Wirote Aroonmanakun, Chulalongkorn University
Timothy Baldwin, University of Melbourne
Stephane Bressan, National University of Singapore
Hee-Rahk Chae, Hankuk University of Foreign Studies
Hsin-Hsi Chen, National Taiwan University
Eng Siong Chng, Nanyang Technological University
Siaw-Fong Chung, National Chengchi University
Beatrice Daille, University of Nantes
Mary Dalrymple, Oxford University
Danilo Dayag, De La Salle University

Andrew Spencer, University of Essex
Jian Su, Institute for Infocomm Research
I-Wen Su, National Taiwan University
Keh-Yih Su, Behavior Design Corporation
Henry S. Thompson, University of Edinburgh
Takenobu Tokunaga, Tokyo Institute of Technology
Josef van Genabith, Dublin City University
Aline Villavicencio, Universidade Federal do Rio Grande do Sul
Haifeng Wang, Baidu
Houfeng Wang, Peking University
Hui Wang, National University of Singapore
Jiun-Shiung Wu, National Chiayi University
Jae II Yeom, Hongik University
Satoru Yokoyama, Tohoku University
Min Zhang, Institute for Infocomm Research
Qiang Zhou, Tsinghua University
Michael Zock, Laboratoire d'Informatique Fondamentale de Marseille, C.N.R.S.
Chengqing Zong, Chinese Academy of Sciences

Local Organizing Committee:

Bayu Distiawan, Universitas Indonesia
Muhammad Hilman, Universitas Indonesia
Samuel Louvan, Universitas Indonesia
Lelya Rimadhiana, Universitas Indonesia
Clara Vania, Universitas Indonesia

The First Workshop on Generative Lexicon for Asian Languages (GLAL)

Organizers:

Shu-Kai Hsieh (Institute of Linguistics, National Taiwan University)
Zuoyan Song (School of Chinese Language and Literature, Beijing Normal University)
Kyoko Kanzaki (National Institute for Japanese Language and Linguistics)

Program Committee:

Toni Badia(Universitat Pompeu Fabra, spain)
Christian BASSAC (Universit de Lyon2, France)
Pierrette Bouillon (ETI/TIM/ISSCO, Switzerland)
Nicoletta Calzolari (CNR-ILC, Italy)
Ann Copestake (University of Cambridge, UK)
Christiane Fellbaum (Princeton University, USA)

Catherine Havasi(MIT,USA)
Chu-Ren Huang (The Hongkong Polytechnic University, China)
Hitoshi Isahara (NICT, Kyoto, Japan)
Chungmin Lee(Seoul National University, Seoul, Korea)
Alessandro Lenci (Universita di Pisa, Pisa, Italy)
Kentaro Nakatani(Kounan University, Japan)
Seungho Nam (Seoul National University, Seoul, Korea)
Fiammetta Namer (ATILF-CNRS, University of Nancy, France)
Naoyuki Ono (Tohoku University, Sendai, Japan)
Laurent Prvot (Aix-Marseille Universit & CNRS, France)
James Pustejovsky (Brandeis University, USA)
Anna Rumshisky (Brandeis University, USA)
Patrick Saint-Dizier (CNRS, Toulouse, France)
Koichi Takeuchi(Okayama University, Japan)
Hongjun Wang (Peking University, Beijing, China)
Nianwen Xue (Brandeis University, Waltham, MA USA)
Yulin Yuan (Peking University, Beijing, China)
Seohyun Im (Brandeis University, USA)

Organized by :

Faculty of Computer Science
Universitas Indonesia

Sponsored by :

I-MHERE Project
Directorate General of Higher Education
Ministry of Education and Culture
Republic Indonesia

Table of Contents

1. Invited Talks

2. Regular Papers

3. The First Workshop on Generative Lexicon for Asian Languages

Invited Talk 1

All Possible Worlds to Small Worlds: A Story of How We Started and Where We Will Go Doing Semantics

Kiyong Lee, Korea University Seoul

Bio

Kiyong Lee is Professor emeritus of linguistics, Korea University, Seoul. He has been convenor of an ISO working group for the development of semantic annotation schemes since June 2004. He was invited as Visiting Professor to Department of Korean, Tenri University, Nara, Japan, in 1999-2000 and also as Visiting Professor to the Department of Chinese, Translation and Linguistics, City University of Hong Kong, on three different occasions. He was a keynote speaker on formal semantics at the 18th Congress of Linguists (July 21-26, 2008) in Seoul. He was awarded a prize for academic excellence from the National Academy of Sciences, Korea, on the basis of a three-volume book on Semantics: Formal, Possible Worlds, and Situation Semantics, and also a book award for his Computational Morphology from the Ministry of Culture and Tourism, Korea, in 2002. Since he graduated with an A.B. degree from Saint Louis University, St. Louis, MO, USA, in 1963, Kiyong Lee has taught Latin, English, Philosophy, and Linguistics at four different universities full-time and at over 20 universities part-time. As a Fulbright student, he also received a Ph.D. in Linguistics from the University of Texas, Austin, TX, USA, in 1974 and did research work as a Fulbright scholar at CSLI, Stanford University, Palo Alto, CA, USA, and as a DAAD scholar at the Computational Linguistics Lab, University of Erlangen, Germany. Kiyong Lee has been president of the Linguistics Society of Korea (1990-1992) and that of the Korean Society of Cognitive Science (1989-1990). He was also one of the founding members of the Korean Society for Language and Information and the first representative of its precursor, named the Seoul Workshop on Formal Grammar Theory. He has thus helped organize and host several PACLICs in Korea and abroad since its inception in December 1981.

Invited Talk 2

All Possible Worlds to Small Worlds: A Story of How We Started and Where We Will Go Doing Semantics

Yuji Matsumoto

Bio

Yuji Matsumoto is now a professor of Computational Linguistics in the Graduate School of Information Science, Nara Institute of Science and Technology. He got his PhD degree from Kyoto University in 1990. He has experienced a researcher at Electrotechnical Laboratory, a deputy chief of the first laboratory at New Generation Computer Technology Research Center, an Associate professor at Kyoto University, before getting the current position. He is now the Vice-President of the Asian Federation of Natural Language Processing, and the President of ACL SIGDAT, and a Advisory Board member of ACL SIGNLL. He is a Fellow of Information Processing Society of Japan, and the Association for Computational Linguistics.

Invited Talk 3

Developing a Deep Grammar of Indonesian within the ParGram Framework: theoretical and implementational challenges

I Wayan Arka, Australian National University/Udayana University

Bio

I Wayan Arka is affiliated with the Australian National University (as a Fellow in Linguistics at School of Culture, History and Language, College of Asia and the Pacific) and Udayana University Bali (English Department and Graduate Program in Linguistics). His interests are in descriptive, theoretical and typological aspects of Austronesian and Papuan languages of Indonesia. Wayan is currently working on a number of projects: NSF-funded research on voice in the Austronesian languages of eastern Indonesia (2008-2011), ARC-funded projects for the development of computational grammar for Indonesian (2008-2011) and the Languages of Southern New Guinea (2011-2014).

Invited Talk 4

Idiomaticity and Classical Traditions in Some East Asian Languages
Benjamin Tsou, The Hong Kong Institute of Education

Bio

Benjamin Tsou has been doing research on corpus linguistics and sociolinguistics via the on-going Linguistic Variation in Chinese Speech Communities project (http://livac.org) which focuses on the characteristics and evolving use of Chinese media language in Beijing, Hong Kong, Macau, Shanghai, Singapore and Taipei, involving the sophisticated processing and analysis of more than 450 million Chinese characters since 1995. His group has been tracking new and different neologistic developments as well as underlying sociolinguistic changes, and has also worked on the alignment and comparison of English-Chinese bilingual texts in the legal and technical domains. His research on the Language Atlas of China and his textbook on sociolinguistics have won awards from the Chinese Academy of Social Sciences and the Chinese Ministry of Education respectively.

Professor Tsou is the Chiang Chen Chair Professor of Linguistics and Language Sciences and the Director of the Research Centre on Linguistics and Language Information Sciences at The Hong Kong Institute of Education. He is a member of Acadmie Royale des Sciences dOutre-Mer of Belgium. He serves on the Standing Committee of the Executive Board of the Chinese Information Processing Society of China, and is the founding President of the Asian Federation of Natural Language Processing and of the Linguistic Society of Hong Kong. He publishes widely and is also a member of numerous editorial boards. Professor Tsou received his Ph.D from the University of California, Berkeley, and MA from Harvard University.

Invited Talk 5

Social Media: Friend or Foe of Natural Language Processing?
Tim Baldwin, University of Melbourne, Australia

Bio

Timothy Baldwin is an Associate Professor and Deputy Head of the Department of Computing and Information Systems, The University of Melbourne, and a contributed research staff member of the NICTA Victoria Research Laboratories. He has previously held visiting positions at the University of Washington, University of Tokyo, Saarland University, and NTT Communication Science Laboratories. His research interests cover topics including social media, deep linguistic processing, multiword expressions, computer-assisted language learning, information extraction, web mining and machine learning, with a particular interest in the interface between computational and theoretical linguistics. Current projects include web user forum mining, biomedical text mining, and intelligent interfaces for Japanese language learners. He is President of the Australasian Language Technology Association in 2011-2012. Tim completed a BSc(CS/Maths) and BA(Linguistics/Japanese) at the University of Melbourne in 1995, and an MEng(CS) and PhD(CS) at the Tokyo Institute of Technology in 1998 and 2001, respectively. Prior to commencing his current position at The University of Melbourne, he was a Senior Research Engineer at the Center for the Study of Language and Information, Stanford University (2001-2004).

From All Possible Worlds to Small Worlds: A Story of How We Started and Where We Will Go Doing Semantics

Kiyong Lee
Korea University, Seoul
ikiyong@gmail.com

Abstract

This is a short story of how we have evolved over the last 40 years, doing semantics. It could partially overlap with a history of PACLIC which is commemorating the 25th year or a quarter of a century of its founding. The story tells how we semanticists of natural language moved from all possible worlds to small worlds, now living in and with a tiny mobile world.

1 Introduction

The story goes back to the early 1970s with generative semantics and the dawning of Montague semantics. The beginning was concerned with big open worlds, all possible worlds, for truth meant, in the eyes of philosophers, being true in all possible worlds. And linguists inherited their notion of truth in constructing a formal theory of natural language semantics. In the 1980s, however, the focus of linguistic semantics changed from necessary or possible truth to something more contingent or informative, namely various sorts of information obtainable from small worlds, called *situations*. A new trend developed in the 1990s towards the computational modeling of semantic theories, based on so-called *real* language data or large corpora such as BNC (the British National Corpus). This required various situations of language use to be constrained with an idealized set of conditions. Then around the turn of the second millennium, semanticists have followed a data-driven approach to the construction of their model-theoretic semantics, which requires a large amount of language resources or raw corpora tagged with a variety of information, both morphosyntactic and semantic. As a result, some semanticists including myself have proposed doing semantics using annotated language resources, which was known as *annotation-based semantics*.

My story will narrate how our colleagues have reacted to all these changes. Not being an historian, however, the speaker dares not guarantee his view to be fair and objective. Instead, it will be very subjective and introspective. Hence, it will simply be head-driven without being data-driven. I, as an old member of the PACLIC community, justify this narrowly defined role of an invited speaker because I trust that other PACLIC founding members, Benjamin T'sou and Akira Ikeya, will balance whatever might be one-sided in my talk.

2 The 1970s: Truth and All Possible Worlds

Every decade has its own exciting moments. To me, the 1970s must have been the most exciting decade in my life. In the summer of 1971, I went as a Fulbright student to the University of Texas at Austin, hoping to specialize in machine translation and the theory of translation. When I got there, there was no trace of such a thing as machine translation with all the projects and the people gone away and with nothing left of MT. Professor Winfred P. Lehmann, an outstanding historical linguist and a pioneer in machine translation, who had initiated the Texas MT project, was still at Austin, running the Department of Linguistics and making the Department rank Number 2 nationwide or globally in the area of linguistics along with UCLA after MIT around 1970.

So I ended up the Department of Linguistics, writing a doctoral thesis in an area that had just begun, known as *Montague grammar*, much later *Montague semantics*.

Till early 1970s, semantics has failed to be recognized as a proper part of linguistics arguably because it could not be evaluated quantitatively or its data was not measurable or simply because it could not be a subject matter of empirical science. At Austin, Texas, however, we had a wonderful group of linguists who would become forerunners of formal semantics: Emmon Bach, Stanley Peters, Bob Wall, Lauri Karttunen, and David Dowty, but none of them offered any course in semantics, when I arrived there. Emmon taught syntax and I loved his way of raising issues and urging his students to think, although most of my classmates didn't agree with my pleasure of sitting in his class. Stanley taught mathematical linguistics, while Bob was gone on his sabbatical. Lauri was supposed to create a course in semantics or pragmatics, but he hadn't had any students till or just before the summer of 1973 when Texas would be hosting the first Performadillo conference with its theme on pragmatic presupposition and *implicature*, a term coined by H.P. Grice (1967). David Dowty was in the last years of his graduate study, finishing up his dissertation (Dowty, 1972) on aspectual features (e.g., progressive) of predicates based on generative semantics, if I remember correctly.

One day in 1972 or so, Stanley Peters came back from a conference on the West Coast, USA, with a thick typescript written by Barbara Partee. This was Barbara's first introduction to Montague grammar with its focus on the categorial grammar-based syntax, for her first effort was to synthesize Montague and generative grammars. As his research assistant, my sole assignment was to read that typescript. I was, however, more interested in the formalization of semantics with a type-theoretic lambda calculus and so-called *model-theoretic semantics* mainly because they sounded more challenging or because these were the things that I had not known about. At that time, however, there was no one around who could help me understand all this stuff. I exchanged a couple of letters with Barbara Partee and her replies were great. Bob Wall, who was my dissertation supervisor, had set up a course in intensional logic specifically to help me with a student named Tom Hester, who had studied philosophy. Stanley Peters gave me two tutorial courses, one of which was modal logic, using Hughes and Cresswell's (1968) wonderful book on modal logic. Those courses were tutorial because no one else wanted to study such a thing as modal logic or anything that had to do with mathematics or logic. What I have learned from these courses became a basis for me to go through Montague's PTQ (Montague, 1973), EFL (Montague, 1970a), and UG (Montague, 1970b) almost by myself.

My paper, entitled "Negation in Montague Grammar", was accepted for presentation at the Tenth Meeting of the Chicago Linguistic Society in 1974. My presentation was a disaster, I think, because it consumed most of the allocated time explaining one single translation:

(1) **everyone** $\Rightarrow \lambda P \forall x[human(x) \rightarrow P(x)]$.

The formula looked worse because it still had the capped $\hat{u}$ for the (individual) concept or intension of an individual variable u or the de-capped $\check{x}$ of an individual concept variable. So I didn't have enough time to explain how to treat quantified sentences like:

(2) a. Everyone didn't come
  b. Not everyone knows everything.

in Montague's PTQ or any other more interesting issues involving negation. Nevertheless, Bob Wall as my supervisor devoted himself and his whole summer to help me to finish my doctoral thesis and receive a Ph.D. within three years after coming to Texas. I was just in time to get back to my university in Korea to resume my professorial responsibilities, for I had only three years' leave of absence from my university in Korea. When my family and I arrived in Tokyo on our way home to Korea, a telegram had been waiting, telling me to get back right away.

Here I should mention Roland Hausser, for he and I have been working together all our life since our Texas days. He and I have helped each other to finish our doctoral theses and we are still proud of ourselves being two of the three first ones, including Michael Bennett, to write a doctoral thesis on Montague grammar. That was August, the hottest summer month, of 1974 in Texas, while Michael was enjoying his cool summer in California. Roland discussed quantification in the framework of Montague grammar, whereas I explicated PTQ and treated some English constructions as a non-native speaker. Unfortunately none of us had an opportunity to join the inner group of Montague grammarians, for both Roland and I had to leave the United States and found it hard to travel back to the States, while Michael passed away early in his career because of his ill health.

Happily back in Korea, I found a nice group of excellent linguists trained in the United States. Among them were three semanticists: Suk-Jin Chang from Illinois at Urbana-Champaign, In-Seok Yang from Hawaii, and Chungmin Lee from Indiana. They had received their Ph.D.'s in 1973 or a year earlier, but that was too early for them to have enough time to work on Montague grammar. Instead, they followed the group of generative semanticists such as Jim McCawley, George Lakoff, Paul Postal, and Haj Ross. Nevertheless, they have been the most influential persons in Korea to persuade me and, five years later, Ik-Hwan Lee, who also received his Ph.D. from Texas in 1979, to propagate Montague grammar in Korea.

In the winter of 1975, In-Seok Yang organized a small workshop supported by the Fulbright Commission in Korea and invited me to conduct a one-week or ten-day seminar on Montague grammar, using my dissertation as a textbook. For that workshop, a dozen of us stayed at a Fulbright hermitage at the Academy House in the north-eastern mountain ranges of Seoul. With a larger group of linguists, this seminar was resumed six months later again with its focus on Montague.

After these seminars, Professor Yang proposed the founding of the Linguistic Society of Korea. With his nomination, Professor Suk-Jin Chang was then elected its first president. Meanwhile, Korea invited Emmon Bach, Barbara Partee, and David Dowty to give lectures on Montague grammar. At that time Barbara was fully occupied with importing Chomsky's transformations into Montague grammar, as exemplified by two of her papers, "Some extensions of transformational extensions of Montague grammar" (1973) and "Montague grammar and transformational grammar" (1975). When I was asked to comment on her lecture given at Seoul National University, I had to state regretfully that my post-lecture comments were to be replaced with a series of questions that I had already asked during her lecture. I was afraid to keep asking questions or making negative comments because I personally preferred to do Montague grammar or any other grammar without any transformations.

Montague grammar was not a fully developed grammar of natural language, for it did not have any phonological component nor a lexical component. It did, however, contain a small list of interpretation rules, called *meaning postulates*, the original idea of which had been proposed by Rudolf Carnap (1952). Montague (1973) introduced them as constraints on a set of possible worlds or models that delineate so-called *admissible* worlds. Natural language semanticists such as David Dowty caught on this notion of meaning postulate and developed it to a full set of lexical decompositions, as had been discussed in generative semantics with examples like the verb **kill** being decomposed into a logical form

(3) $\exists\{M, x, y\}[M(x)\, cause'[become'[\neg alive'(y)]$.

These endeavors were well represented by Dowty's (1979) *Word Meaning and Montague Grammar* or his earlier work (1976) "Montague grammar and the lexical decomposition of causative verbs". In contrast, Partee's (1976) *Montague Grammar* represented other efforts to extend Montague grammar. Michael Bennett's "A variation and extension of a Montague fragment of English" and Rich Thomason's "Some extensions of Montague grammar" both of which are included in Partee (1976), are good examples of how Montague grammar was explicated and extended.

The decade of 1970s was dominated by Chomsky's transformational grammar. Partee's (1973) "Some transformational extensions of Montague grammar" or Bach's (1979) "Montague grammar and classical transformational grammar" were typical examples of how Montague grammarians responded to Chomskyan linguistics. In our PACLIC group, however, we were freer to accept non-transformational approaches to syntax or grammar in general. GPSG, HPSG, and LFG were well accepted both in Japan and Korea. As I mentioned earlier, Takao Gunji produced JPSG for Japanese.

Byung-Soo Park started to turn his Kyunghee University into the oriental mecca of HPSG, while Soo-Song Shin of the German Department of Seoul National University was a strong believer in LFG.

Before moving over to the next decade, I should explain why I have called the 1970s as the decade of truth and all possible worlds. When we inherited truth-conditional model-theoretic semantics from philosophers and logicians, we also inherited their concerns: the notions of truth and possible worlds or models. For them, meaning meant truth or truth with respect to some model or a possible world in a model, while validity meant truth in all possible worlds in a model or in all models. The interpretation of negation, disjunction, quantification, and modality all involve truth and possible worlds or circumstances. Montague's PTQ itself hardly talks about truth or possible worlds. In other papers, however, Montague claims that the aim of semantics is to formulate truth conditions and entailment relations.

Most linguists of natural language semantics are fully aware of what Montague or formal semantics should be concerned with. In those early years, however, we had not been exposed to many of the important works by analytic philosophers or philosophers of ordinary language. We knew almost nothing about Alonzo Church's lambda calculus nor of his type theory, and very little about Alfred Tarski's truth-conditional semantics or Rudolph Carnap's meaning and necessity. We read little about David Lewis and Gilbert Harman, one or both of whom said that the construction of logical forms or semantic representations, as done by generative semanticists, was not doing real semantics, but playing with Markerese or some artificial language, while generative semanticists were trying to apply or enrich first-order quantificational logic to represent ambiguity or inferences in natural language. McCawley (1981)'s famous book *Everything that Linguists Have Always Wanted to Know about Logic (but were Ashamed to Ask)*, however, was a result of such efforts to help linguists to learn logic and do semantics. Montague (1970a) himself stated that natural language semantics could be developed without going through the process of translating natural language to some formal language, an intermediate language, as shown in EFL (Montague, 1970a). Nevertheless, to do semantics or formal semantics, linguists had to learn all sorts of logics, higher-order logics and modal logics for both epistemic and deontic modalities.

While trying to cohabit with philosophers in the universe of all possible worlds, formal semanticists of natural language or Montagovian semanticists were mostly occupied with the translation of some fragments of English or some other languages into intensional logic with a type-theoretic lambda calculus. One minor, but most important revision of intensional logic was to get rid of the type of *individual concepts*, as illustrated by Montague's example (a):[1]

(4) a. The temperature is 30, but it's rising.
b. My son tries to go up the tree [literal], while my blood pressure is going up [metaphoric].

Here, *the temperature* was treated in PTQ as denoting an extensional entity of type *individual*, tagged `<e>`, while the *it* was treated as denoting an intensional entity of type called *individual concept*, tagged `<s,e>`. K. Lee (1981) tried to save the notion of individual concepts unsuccessfully, for the inclusion of individual concepts simply complicated the representation of semantic content in general. While the notion of intension or the distinction between extension and intension, the ambiguity between *de re* and *de dicto*(opaque) readings played no central role in the analysis of natural language, the λ-operator with the β reduction has become a powerful descriptive tool and remains as such to this day. This little tool helps to treat such linguistic phenomena as:

(5) a. Deletion: `John tried PRO to fly.`
$\lambda PP(j)(\lambda x[x\, tried\, \lambda y[y\, to\, fly]])$

b. Coordination:
`John`$_i$ `sings and x`$_i$ `dances well.`
$\lambda PP(j)(\lambda x[x\, sings\, and\, x\, dances\, well])$

c. *wh*-constructions:
`Who do you think t loves Mary?`
$\lambda x[do\, you\, think\, x\, loves\, Mary]$

d. Quantification:
`John and every student of his`

[1]Comparing (a) with (b), we could have treated Montague's example (a) much differently.

`wanted PRO to run a marathon.`
$\lambda P\exists x[P(j)\wedge x = j\wedge\forall y[student(y,x)\rightarrow P(y)]]$
$(\lambda z[want(z,\lambda w[run\_marathon(z)])])$

e. Coreference:
`John`$_i$ `loves his`$_i$ `mother.`
$\lambda PP(j)$
$(\lambda x\exists y[loves(x,y)\wedge mother\_of(y,x)])$

and many other interesting phenomena in language. Knowingly or unknowingly, the little lambda operation (λ) allowed those abstract entities, called PRO and *trace*, to be introduced into syntax or the extended version of Chomsky's generative transformational grammar.

While finding it difficult to construct a model-theoretic semantics of fragments of natural language, we linguists have found it easier to accommodate Frege's notion of compositionality. This was so, especially because we have known about recursivity in generative syntax, introduced by Noam Chomsky, or when we were playing with the BASIC programming language, as in the following:[2]

(6) a. PS rules
S $\rightarrow$ NP VP
NP $\rightarrow$ NP S

b. Home Rules
#1. Wife, the Boss.
#2. Go to #1.

and also the notion of projection rules for semantic combination, introduced by Katz and Fodor (1963). We were fascinated with the so-called *homomorphism*, structural resemblance or one-to-one correspondence between the syntactic rules and their corresponding interpretation (semantic) rules or the rules of translating a natural language to a formal language such as intensional logic. We thus extended Montague's PTQ to other fragments of English or other languages. I myself tried to construct something called AMG, Augmented Montague Grammar, to accommodate case marking phenomena in Korean. Many of my colleagues were more ambitious and successful to extend categorial grammar as an alternative to Chomsky's generative grammar, then based on his *Aspects* theory called the *Standard Theory* or later called the *Extended Standard Theory*. Montague grammarians could not follow Chomsky, when his theory became *Revised Extended Standard Theory* with an acronym *REST*. Our late Professor In-Seok Yang jokingly predicted that time had come for Chomsky to rest with his 1982's *Government and Binding* theory that might apply to the conditions and rules of dictatorial regimes as well as of linguistic theories. I should, however, note that our European colleagues around Amsterdam were more successful in constructing model-theoretic semantics or doing real semantics for natural language. One prominent contribution was made by Daniel Gallin's work (1975) *Intensional and Higher-order Modal Logic with Applications to Montague Semantics*. Most of their efforts, however, were known later, in the 1980s and 1990s. Theo Janssen's work on Montague grammar, for instance, was published in 1983. I should also mention Harry Bunt's work (1985), *Mass Terms and Model-Theoretic Semantics* that discussed the distributivity of quantified events with examples such as:

(7) The two old men swallowed a beer and lifted the piano upstairs.

This and other similar examples are still discussed among semanticists.

3 The 1980s: Situations and Small Worlds

Again I will begin to talk about the 1980s by narrating what started to happen around me in Korea. In mid-summer 1981, the First Seoul International Conference on Linguistics (SICOL-1981) was held in Seoul. It was organized by Professor In-Seok Yang, the third president of the Linguistic Society of Korea. He was that very person who set up the first workshop on Montague Grammar in Korea and probably was the most energetic administrator who turned into a brilliant linguist with a lot of humor that was often misunderstood. When she was visiting Korea, he embarrassed Barbara Partee, asking her if she could remember him sitting in her class packed with a large audience in an LSA institute, held in LA ten years before. Susumo Kuno could

[2] The second example is taken from a plaque hanging on the wall of a country house belonging to a colleague of mine. He said that he bought it at a souvenir shop somewhere in New England.

not pardon his joke on his non-Oxonian Cambridge accent during his lecture at Seoul National University.

To this first SICOL, several world-known or aspiring linguists were invited. Among them were George Lakoff, Haj Ross, and Gerald Gazdar. By then George Lakoff had given up anything formal, including generative semantics. Instead, he talked about metaphors and also about *Women, Fire, and Dangerous Things*. Before coming to Seoul, John R. Ross, more often called *Haj*, had produced a landmark work in syntax, an MIT dissertation, entitled *Constraints in Variables in Syntax*. When I attended the LSA Linguistic Institute held at the University of North Carolina, Chapel Hill, in the summer of 1972, he taught Ivan Sag, me, and others Squish Grammar, a non-discrete grammar, with the fuzzy notion of nouniness. The title of his talk at SICOL-1981 was "Human Linguistics", but against our expectation it was focused on complicated and very sad human relations among the MIT linguists headed by Noam Chomsky. These relations were sad and bad, for eventually Haj had to pack up and leave MIT. Our small group in Korea was prepared to listen to Gazdar (1979) talking about his new book on formal pragmatics, but he talked about something else, which turned out to be the beginning of GPSG. We also had the honor of meeting the two most important persons from Japan: Professors Kazuko Inoue and Akira Ikeya. Both of them were much impressed by the organization of SICOL and also by linguistic activities in Korea especially because Professor Inoue was in charge of hosting the International Congress of Linguists in the ensuing year in Japan, while Professor Ikeya was much more interested in importing or inviting Korean linguists to Japan.

With the support of Professor Inoue, Ikeya sensei immediately proposed to start a series of binational joint working group meetings focusing on formal linguistic theories and other related issues. As a result, Korea agreed to host its first Korea-Japan joint workshop, entitled *The First Seoul Workshop on Formal Grammar Theory*, in January 1982. Ik-Hwan Lee, the first Secretary of our Korean group, which later became KSLI (the Korea Society for Language and Information), organized this first meeting at International House, Ewha Womans University. Roland Hausser was invited from the University of Munich, Germany, to give the first keynote lecture at this first meeting.

For these pre-PACLIC meetings, I remember going to Kyoto University (February 1983), Matsuyama University (December 1984), and Sophia University in Tokyo in those early years. I missed the meeting that was held in Japan in December 1989, for I just had a major medical operation at that time. We had a real symposium over soju or sake, while discussing Montague, categorial grammar or lambda calculus. In Kyoto, we had the honor of meeting Prof. Makoto Nagao at his Kyoto University Lab and listened to him perhaps with the demonstration of his famous example-based machine translation (EBMT). EBMT was publicly opened to the world in 1984. In Matsuyama, Geoff Pullum was invited, who was one of the authors of Generalized Phrase Structure Grammar. Byung-Soo Park and Hwan-Mook Lee attended that meeting, each presenting a paper. I was also there too. Before or around that time, Byung-Soo and I promised to coauthor a book on GPSG and I wrote a few chapters, but we never managed to publish a book, for HPSG moved in too fast. That book could have been the first KPSG, corresponding to JPSG proposed earlier by Takao Gunji. I forgot the names of all those wonderful people, whom I met in Kyoto and Matsuyama and would like to thank again, but I still remember the young lady then from Hiroshima, named Mizuho Hasegawa, who later became a dean (of academic affairs) at a women's university in Tokyo or its vicinity.

Going back to earlier years, Ikeya sensei with the support of Professor Arata Ishimoto, organized the Second Colloquium on Montague Grammar and Related Topics in March 1982.[3] At this workshop, Takao Gunji (1982) presented a paper, entitled "Dynamic Universe of Discourse and Implicatures", analyzing the semantics of donkey-sentences. I don't remember exactly when, but Professor Ikeya introduced me to Professor Arata Ishimoto, the first president of the Logico-Linguistic Society of Japan. He then invited me to come to Japan and stay at the guest house of his Science University of Tokyo to work together for over a week. We worked on

[3] See Ishimoto (1982).

the law of identity and the copular verb "be" in the framework of Montague Grammar, but unfortunately didn't manage to produce a joint paper.

By this time, a couple of things have changed particularly in the field of formal semantics. Montague grammar began to be called *Montague semantics*. It wasn't a grammar in a real sense, for it lacked both phonology and morphology. It also had very little to say about the lexicon. Furthermore, the categorial grammar that was adopted in Montague's PTQ wasn't Montague's invention. Instead, it had a long Polish tradition in mathematical logic, especially attributed to Kazimierz Ajdukiewicz at Adam Mickiewicz University in Poznań (See Ajdukiewicz (1935) and other contributions by Bar-Hillel (1953), and Lambek (1958). Through Hwan-Mook Lee, who was teaching at the University of Warsaw, I had the honor of visiting this university and sitting on a leather-made worn-out, but glorious chair of Ajdukiewicz in his old office. There I was invited by Professor Jacek Fisiak to give a talk at his School of English. Although it wasn't his invention, Montague made linguists like me work on categorial grammar. His real contribution was, however, most recognized in the area of making formal semantics applicable to the semantics of natural language. Dowty, Wall, and Peters's (1981) great book that introduced Montague's work was thus entitled *Introdction to Montague Semantics*.

Besides its emphasis on Frege's principle, called the *principle of compositionality*, Montague semantics helped understand the three basic characteristics of formal semantics: it should be characterized as a (1) truth-conditional, (2) model-theoretic, and (3) possible worlds semantics. What is true or false has become the core of meaning or the starting point of discussing what is meant by a sentence. This feature was understood as part of the correspondence theory of meaning that relates language to the world. That a sentence is true means that there is a world or situation in which what is meant or described by that sentence holds. A model theory allows the construction of some situations in which such a sentence holds to be true or false. Then a possible worlds semantics is needed to treat the meaning of sentences involving modality or factuality. Consider worn-out archaic sentences like:

(8) a. `If I were a bird, then I could fly.`

b. `I wish I were a millionaire.`

c. `I believe that the earth is a square.`

or more mundane sentences from E.L. James #1 *New York Times* bestseller, *Fifty Shades of Grey* like:

(9) a. `If this guy is over thirty, then I'm a monkey's uncle.`

b. `Just because you can doesn't mean that you should.`

To interpret sentences like these, we have to go beyond the actual world where we live and think of some other possible worlds in which I could be a bird and fly or be a millionaire or a monkey's uncle and in which the earth could be a square. We should also be thinking of what we can do and what we should or must do. As attested by Partee (2004)'s book *Compositionality in Formal Semantics*, many of the great semantics works have been following all these principles of semantics, making great contributions in the area of natural language semantics, based on formal semantics in the short history of Montague semantics.

As we began to understand what Montague semantics was, we also began to understand its limitations. First, higher-order intensional logic was not of much help, for it failed to properly interpret propositional attitudes involving verbs like *believe*, *assert*, *know*, and *wish* and so-called *propositions* expressed by them. In Montague Semantics, a proposition is defined to be a function from worlds or indexes to truth values and a valid proposition maps every world or index to a truth value. Hence all of the valid propositions such as:

(10) a. (p=Law of Identity) `If John is an idiot, then he is.`

b. (q=Law of Excluded Middle) `Either Mary is a genius or she is not.`

denote one identical function, at least in a bivalent logic. As a result, statements like:

(11) a. `Mia believes that p.`

b. `Mia believes that q.`

where p and q are understood to be valid propositions, are understood to convey the identical beliefs. Ordinary linguists, however, know that they are about two different persons and that they carry different information.

Second, consisting of a single non-empty set of individuals as its domain of discourse, classical model-theoretic semantics does not help to resolve paradoxes such as the Liar's paradox or a restricted quantification. Epimenides, a Cretan, supposedly said:

(12) All Cretans are liars.

and also we often say, even if there are many people around:

(13) No one is here.

while a model theory fails to exclude the speaker from the domain of the discourse or that non-empty set of individuals in a model.

Third, the universe of possible worlds is too big to comprehend. David Lodge's *Small World* is, on the other hand, quite interesting, for humans can talk about and do a lot of things in a small world. The basic difference between the possible worlds view and the small world view is like seeing the whole universe from the top down with the eyes of God or a tiny part of the world from the bottom up with the near-sighted eyes of the created beings. This difference can be easily understood if you accept the action theory of language use. All these issues came up to the surface when Jon Barwise and John Perry of Stanford University published a book, entitled *Situations and Attitudes* in 1983 or much earlier with some other people. Their subsequent work was known to be *Situation Theory* and *Situation Semantics*, an application of situation theory to the semantics of natural language, to be acronymed *STASS*.

By mid-80s, CSLI (Center for the Study of Language and Information) was founded by these philosophers and others in linguistics, psychology, and computer science at Stanford University and at the research centers surrounding the university, namely Xerox PARC and SRI International. It soon became the center of formal semantics as well as formal and computational works in language and the mind, attracting a lot of scholars home and abroad. Accelerated by the fame of the Silicon Valley, the place was occupied with computer scientists, computational linguists, psychologists, and all the people who were called *cognitive scientists* or scientists of *symbolic systems*. When I got there as a one-year visiting scholar in December 1986, I found such renowned persons as well as friends such as Martin Kay, David Israel, Jerry Hobbs, Terry Winograd, Stanley Peters, Lauri Karttunen, Joan Bresnan, Ron Kaplan, Ivan Sag, Roland Hausser, Kris Halvorsen, Peter Sells, Craig Roberts, Mary Dalrymple, Carl Pollard, Dan Flickinger, and others from Hewlett-Packard, Zerox PARC, and SRI International as well as various departments at the university. There was Syun Tutiya, a young philosopher, from Tokyo and later a large group of computer scientists from Japan including Hideyuki Nakashima, Yasuhiro Katagiri and Koiti Hasida. At its peak, CSLI reports and other publications were more in demand than those publications by MIT, Academic Press, or Springer. CSLI also had the strong funding and other support from the Systems Development Foundation and the Fifth Generation enterprises in Japan to host workshops and also to build its own beautiful mission-style building near the medical center of the university.

Perhaps the first large-scale workshop was held in Half-Moon Bay not far from Santa Cruz along California Highway 1 soon after the Christmas holidays in 1986 or in January 1987. I was there to witness how the STASS activities would start developing in the following decade and how the STASS meetings would continue to be held in Asilomar, California, (March 1989) and also in Loch Rannoch, Scotland, (September 1990), till Jon Barwise left for Bloomington, Indiana, and sadly died of cancer to our great loss. Being a mathematical logician, Jon was most interested in constructing his own unique theory of situations, so he has been working with mathematical logicians such as Peter Aczel, Gordon Plotkin, and Keith Devlin. At the same time, possibly persuaded by linguists such as Robin Cooper, he was also interested in representation issues in Situation Theory and Situation Semantics. They jointly published two articles entitled "Simple Situation Theory and its graphical representation" (1991) and "Extended Kamp Notation" (1993). One of my books, written in Korean and published in Korea, was a collection of my papers based on Situation Semantics, entitled *Situation Semantics*, that partially tells what Situation Semantics is. Unfortunately these days no one talks about Situation Theory or Situation Semantics. Nevertheless I believe it has had a great impact on the development of formal semantics of natural language, especially dealing with some dynamic or computational aspects or pragmatic-oriented issues that arise in the ordinary use of language.

The STASS group was interested in Kamp's (1981) DRT (Discourse Representation Theory) not simply because of its representation scheme. It found in DRT a way of constructing an interpretation model bottom-up, without bringing in all of the imaginable possible worlds most of which are found irrelevant for the interpretation of a fragment of language under analysis. Even the interpretation of the notorious *donkey sentences* can be fully represented in a small box with some linkings with a small set of entities referred to, called *discourse referents*. The combination of STASS representation of various types of situations such as *described*, *discourse*, *resource*, and *background* situations with DRT boxes was shown to work beautifully for the treatment of many complicated sentences. Cooper and Kamp (1991) thus managed to coauthor a paper entitled "Negation in Situation Semantics and Discourse Representation Theory", showing how they can implement each other or benefit from each other.

Apparently the first joint efforts between Barwise and Kamp failed to produce anything significant mainly because neither the earlier theory of Situation Theory nor the 1981 DRT was adequately developed to be able to deal with issues involving negation or some other issues. Kamp (1981) treated implication, but not negation. By late 1980s, Situation Theory was able to deal with two types of negation, one of which can be interpreted as *denial*, for a proposition as a truth-value carrier could be considered as consisting of a situation s, an infon i, often called *soas* (state of affairs), and a *support relation* $\models$ that links them. This was then represented as below:

(14) Proposition p: $(s \models i)$,
such that p is true if there is a situation s which supports the infon i that carries a basic unit of information, but otherwise it is false.

The type of negation, which can be interpreted as a denial, is then represent as:

(15) Denial or Negative Proposition:$(s \not\models i)$

The infon also carried information on its polarity, either positive and negative.[4] So we may have a negative infon as represented as below:

(16) Negative Inform: $\ll bald, Socrates, 0\gg$,
which carries the information about Socrates not being bald.

This information could have been correct of Socrates when he was still a young man.

Such a treatment of negation in Situation Theory could have been amalgamated into the new version of DRT, presented in Kamp and Reyle (1994), which was forthcoming at the time when Cooper and Kamp (1991) jointly worked on negation. This paper, however, dealt with negative infons only with an example:

(17) John doesn't own a car.

This does not entail that there is no situation whatsoever in which John owns a car because the existence of a car is restricted to a particular set of cars, say Hyundai-made Korean cars, by a resource situation, as proposed in Situation Theory. The same interpretation can be uphold in Kamp and Reyle (1994). Details of this amalgamation work should be left for discussion in some other occasion in the future.

During all these fast-evolving years, I found myself stuck with a pre-terminal stage cancer. I could participate in most of the STASS activities, but to my regret failed to submit any papers and have them included in the STASS proceedings and to make my name known forever. At any rate, my colleagues in Korea thought that I would die soon and they decided to lengthen my life by electing me president of the Linguistic Society of Korea and also of the Korean Society for Cognitive Science. They then persuaded me to organize the 1991 Seoul International

[4]0 stands for the negative polarity.

Conference on Linguistics and also to organize the first international conference on cognitive science in Seoul. Hans Kamp was invited to SICOL-1991, but I am afraid he didn't say a word on DRT. This announced the end of the 1980s and the beginning of the 1990s.

4 The 1990s: Data-driven, Statistics-bound, and Computational

Despite my ill-health and poor publication records, I managed to get invited to travel and give talks here and there. Professor Arnim von Stechow invited me to come to Tübingen to give a talk. I was reluctant to accept the invitation and make such a long trip to Europe, but the Korean students, Jung-Goo Kang and Byongrae Ryu, there in Tübingen, Germany, and Professor Roland Hausser in Erlangen, Germany, persuaded me to accept his invitation and come to Germany. Roland also invited me to his university in Erlangen. Since then I frequented Germany, visiting Saarbrücken and Erlangen. In Saarbrücken, I met Hans Uszkoreit briefly and then Manfred Pinkal for lunch. Manfred wanted to hear about Situation Semantics from me, almost thinking that I had been its originator, and we had a wonderful discussion. He then suddenly remembered his afternoon class and left me alone in the faculty dining room.

While traveling here and there in Germany, Great Britain, Japan, Columbus, Ohio, and also making regular visits to Palo Alto, California, I began to realize that the focus of formal semantics was changing from strictly mathematico-logical issues to something more computational. In the early 1990s, Kris (Per-Kristian) Halvoresen, then of Xerox PARC, for instance, gave a tutorial on Computational Semantics during the LSA Linguistic Institute, held in Santa Cruz in the summer of 1991. And fortunately around that time I was able to work with Ron Kaplan at Xerox PARC and began to do something that you may call computational, for I was trying to implement Korean on his LFG workbench and hoped that I could use it to test my toy programs for Computational Semantics. There were, however, a couple of practical problems that hindered the continuation of any serious work in Computational Semantics. One simple, but serious problem had to do with the importing of Hangul characters and fonts into the system, for Korea was still arguing which coding system it should adopt beyond industrial applications and no full-fledged Unicode had been developed by then. Another practical problem was that the LISP-based system required too much memory for ordinary workstations, not to mention personal desktops or laptops, to run anything really significant. Ron tried to install a new version of the LFG Workbench on my newly-purchased expensive workbench remotely from Palo Alto, but every endeavor just ended in frustration only. The Internet was also too slow then in both U.S.A. and Korea. Remember that this was twenty some years ago and I was still a young man reaching to be sixty.

In the summer of the same year, namely 1991, I also attended an ACL conference held at UC Berkeley. There everybody saw that a number of accepted papers in the area of corpus work rapidly increased, in contrast to the predominance of accepted papers in the the area of logical programming or AI-oriented researches in the previous years. Till then few accepted papers had dealt with corpora and any statical findings from data in corpora, for the so-called stochastic approach was not welcome on the American scene of linguistics. At least twice I was invited to review NSF grant applications in the 90s, but nothing theoretical or formal was successful in securing any grant in those years. Every national grant had to account for its technological or social applicability and usefulness for the nation or its communities that paid taxes. This trend was more so in the area of communications using spoken data. Unlike written texts, spoken data was more manageable to the statistical approach, for humans seem to discern sound differences in a more probabilistic way. Years later, namely during the 2004 LREC in Lisbon, where he was giving an acceptance speech for the Antonio Zampolli award, I remember Fredrick Jelinek saying "Every time I fire a linguist the performance of the speech recognizer goes up" and he indeed fired linguists at his IMB Research Center.

In December 1995, almost 13 years after the first Korea-Japan joint workshop, our PACLIC was born in Hong Kong at the hands of our venerable Benjamin T'sou. The conference was officially named *The Tenth Pacific Asia Conference on Language, Information and Computation.* According to the Call for Abstracts for this conference, organizers of two conferences, the Asian Conference on Language, Information and Computation (ACLIC) and the Pacific Asia Conference on Formal and Computational Linguistics (PACFoCoL), agreed to merge their conferences to PACLIC and number this merged conference the 10th. Strictly speaking or if you prefer PACLIC to be recognized to be older, we can rightly claim that PACLIC dates back to the winter of 1982 when Ikeya sensei and Ik-Hwan Lee, secretary of the Korean group, organized the first J-K joint workshop in Seoul that I just mentioned. Hence, we should be celebrating not the 25th anniversary, but the 30th anniversary of PACLIC this year. Remember that in our Asian society the older the more respected, wrongly believing that the older are the wiser.

From the beginning, the scope of this group, which I mean to be the whole PACLIC group, has gone beyond language and information, comprising the area of computation in general and NLP in particular. We have thus invited computer scientists to form the core of our group. From Korea, we have always had Key-Sun Choi of KAIST, who once organized a J-K joint workshop in Wonju as Secretary of the Korean hosting group. We also had Hyuk-Chul Kwon, now full professor of computer science at Pusan National University, always occupying a seat on the second row right after professors in our tutorial classes as a graduate student of SNU. Professors Kilnam Chon, who was known to be the father of Internet in Korea, of CS Department, KAIST, and Yungtaek Kim, who was the godfather of NLP and MT in Korea, have been the strong supporters of our KSLI, the Korean Society of Language and Information. I expect Professor Ikeya, Benjamin, and my good old friend Chu-Ren to make a long list of their colleagues working for the organization of PACLICs in the past and the present.

By the end of the decade of 1990s, computation definitely got into the core of linguistics. ACL and COLING got flourishing, gathering up a huge crowd for each of their conferences. Publishers were looking for books prefixed with the magic word *computational*. Oxford University Press published a book, entitled *Computational Approaches to the Lexicon*, edited by B.T.S. Aktkins and A. Zampolli, in 1994. A year later, namely in 1995, Cambridge University Press published *Computational Phonology: A Constraint-based Approach* by Steven Bird. Books on computational morphology came out much earlier: in 1991, the MIT Press published *Computational Morphology* by G.D. Richie et al. and, in 1992, *Morphology and Computation* by R.W. Sproat. Kiyong Lee couldn't wait too long to publish his own, so he published a prize-winning book, entitled *Computational Morphology*, but written in Korean. Patrick Blackburn and Johan Bos published two books on computational semantics: *Representation and Inference for Natural Language: A First Course in Computational Semantics* (1995) and *Working with Discourse Representation Theory: An Advanced Course in Computational Semantics* (1996), both of which were published by CSLI Publications, Stanford.

My ambition has been to write a book on Computational Semantics and then to end my life. This was so because I published three books on semantics in 1988: *Language and the World: Formal Semantics*, *Tense and Modality: Possible Worlds Semantics*, and *Situation and Information: Situation Semantics*, all of which were again written in Korean and also prize-winning. I had thought this could be a pioneering work at least in Korea, but then learned that the term *Computational Semantics* appeared far back in the mid-1970s: Eugene Charniak and Yorick Wilks edited a book, entitled *Computational Semantics: An Introduction to Artificial Intelligence and Natural Language Comprehension*, in 1976 and a course on Computational Semantics was offered at the Institute for Semantic and Cognitive Studies in Switzerland in 1975, while I was still working on Categorial Grammar and Lambda Calculus.

In the late 1990s, computational stuff started popping up in PACLICs, too. Most of the papers in PACLIC 10 (1995) were computational. Chungmin Lee presented a wonderful paper on polarity phenomena and Ik-Hwan Lee another great situation-theoretic paper on generic expressions with examples such as *The dog barks* and *Dogs bark*, but I am afraid papers on pure linguistic theories were attracting less attention than in the earlier decades. On the other hand, papers like "HMM Parmeter Learning for Japanese Morphological Analyzer" (Koichi Takeuchi and Yuji Matsumoto), "Using Brackets to Improve Search for Statistical Machine Translation"(Dekai Wu and Cindy Ng), and "Predication of Meaning of Bisyllabic Chinese Compound Words Using Back Propagation Neural Network"(Lua Kim Teng) attracted the audience. Kiyong Lee also presented a computational paper "Recursion Problems in Concatenation: A Case of Korean Morphology", but to his great disappointment he had almost no audience, for it had no statistical formulas or tables, thus being understood as one of the classical morphology papers.

Papers related to Computational Semantics or Lexical Semantics also began to appear in PACLICs. PACLIC 14, held in 2000 at Waseda University, Tokyo, for instance, had papers like: Chu-Ren Huang and Kathleen Ahrens, "The Module-Attribute Representation of Verbal Semantics", Samuel W.K. Chan, Benjamin K. T'sou, and C.F. Choy, "Textual Information Segmentation by Cohesive Ties", and to your disappointment, my own "Developing Database Semantics as a Computational Model". In contrast, we had a keynote lecture by Masayoshi Shibatani gave a keynote lecture, which was far from being computational. The title of his lecture was "Language Typology and the Comparison of Languages" (abstract) and I was asked to introduce him and chair his lecture. He emphasized that his work was real linguistics because it was totally data-driven and that I agreed. Pleased with my chairing and support, Professor Shibatani invited me and a few others to an expensive udong house near Waseda University. He then invited my wife and me to his castle-like two-story mansion, located somewhere deep in the valleys of the Okayama Prefecture, where Momotaro-san, born of a big peach floating on the river, conquered Oni, or Japanese devils, with his faithful company of a pheasant, a monkey, and a dog. Shibatani sensei and I promised to meet again when I would develop a computational semantics based on his Mindanao dialects of the Philippines.

5 The 2000s: Linked with Bits of Information, Distributed Partial Information

As the second millennium reached, too many things were happening all over. Here were a few things that happened around me. In the summer of 2002, I retired from my university and began to build a house in the country where I could retire and be a farmer. When I retired, my colleagues were, I thought, really happy to see me go, but kept me teaching for two more years in their Department of Linguistics, which I could no longer claim to be ours or mine, although I helped found it. My good old friends Ik-Hwan Lee and Minhaeng Lee at Yonsei University invited me to their university to teach Computational Semantics, Computational Morphology or something like that. Key-Sun Choi of KAIST also put me to work for ISO. Alex Fang of City University of Hong Kong invited me to do writing at his university as a visiting professor three times and I still owe him a monograph on ISO annotation schemes to finish. So I have had very little time to take care of my country house and the two doggies from one of my neighbors, whom I seldom see around, but all the trees there have grown up for themselves, while all the books, the papers, the diskettes, and the notes were piled up unsorted. Thanks to you the PACLIC Steering Committee members and the PACLIC 26 organizers in Bali, I managed to recollect myself and revive my short memory of the past, the past 40 years. Having said enough to bore you with my private chatting, I just like to end my talk by telling you a bit about a kind of Computational Semantics, called *Annotation-based Semantics*.

Annotation-based semantics was initiated by several people. Among them are Ian Pratt-Harttman, Harry Bunt, Graham Katz, James Pustejovsky, and Kiyong Lee myself. We all agree that such a semantics guarantees a *robust* system. It should not fail to operate when applied to the processing of natural language texts, although they usually contain a large number of syntactically ill-formed strings of words and indexical or other expressions that are interpretable only contextually. Ordinary linguistic semantics fails to process information from materials presented in a tabular form, maps, and pictures. Annotation-based semantics, however, continues to work successfully, that is, in a robust way, because all of the appropriate pieces of information taken from those media are annotated and represented in a machine-readable format before they are formally interpreted.

Annotation-based semantics can also control the flow of information. Sometimes we get too much or too little information to take an appropriate action.

To inform the local organizers of PACLIC 26 of my flight schedule, I wrote to Ruli the following email, asking if I should book a hotel myself. Part of the email relevant for the flight schedule can be annotated in XML, a machine-readable language, using two ISO-supported annotation schemes, ISO-Space (2012) and ISO-TimeML (2012), as follows:

(18) a. Email Text:

`Dear Ruli,`
`I'll be` **arriving at Bali/Denpasar by KE629 at 00:05 Thursday 1 November** `and leaving by KE634 at 02:05 Monday 12 November. Should I book a hotel myself? Best, Kiyong`

b. Annotation:

```
<isoSpace xml:id="a1">
<PLACE xml:id="pl1"
type="PROVINCE" country="ID"
form="NAM"/>
<PLACE xml:id="pl2" type="PPLC"
cvt="CITY" province="#pl1"
country="ID" form="NAM"
latLong="8°39'S 115°13'E"/>
<QSLINK xml:id="qsl1"
figure="#pl2" ground="#pl1"
relation="IN"/>
<ADJUNCT xml:id="a1"
type="flight" value="KE629"/>
<MOTION xml:id="m1"
motion_class="PATH/MANNER"
motion_type="REACH"/>
<MOVELINK xml:id="mvl1" source=""
goal="#pl2" goal_reached="YES"
means="KE629"/>
</isoSpace>
<isoTimeML xml:id="a2">
<TIMEX3 xml:id="t1" type="TIME"
value="2012-11-01T00:05"/>
<TIMEX3 xml:id="t2" type="DATE"
value="2012-11-W4T00:05"
corres="#t1"/>
<TLINK xml:id="tl1"
eventID="#m1" relatedToTime="#t1"
relType="IS_INCLUDED"/>
</isoTimeML>
```

c. Interpretation:

$\exists\{e, x, y, z, w\}[move(e) \wedge named(x, Seoul) \wedge named(y, Denpasar) \wedge named(z, Bali) \wedge IN(y, z) \wedge named(w, KE629) \wedge source(x, e) \wedge goal(y, e) \wedge means(w, e) \wedge [\tau(e) \subseteq t] \wedge calYear(t) = 2012\ calMonth(t){=}November\ calDay(t){=}01\ dateTime(t){=}00{:}05\ weekDay(t){=}Thursday]$

You may say that annotation and interpretation make things more complicated. The fact is, however, that what we seem to know very little contains a very long list of complicated pieces of information. Till I analyzed this tiny fragment of a text, for instance, I had thought that Bali was a tiny island somewhere in the Indian Ocean. I didn't know at all that Bali was a province of Indonesia and that Denpasar was its capital city. The first three lines of the annotation contain this information. Nevertheless, the interpretation here conveys only part of the information conveyed by the two sets of annotations above: one set contains spatial information, whereas the other set contains temporal information.

Information may be provided in a tabular form. Here is a daily bus schedule, presented in a table format. Some relevant part of the information can also be annotated and represented in XML, followed by its interpretation.

(19) a. Daily Bus Schedule:

`Bus#1048 05:30am, Bus#950 05:45, Bus#055 06:00, Air-Bus#10 06:15, ..., Bus#1049 23:45.`

b. Annotation:

```
<isoTimeML xml:id="a3">
(1) <TIMEX3 xml:id="t1"
type="SET" value="PT15M"
quant="EVERY" scopes="#e1"/>
(2) <TIMEX3 xml:id="t2"
type="PERIOD" value="DAY"
beginPoint="XXXX-XX-XXT05:30"
endPoint="XXXX-XX-XXT23:45"
qaunt="EVERY" scopes="#t1"/>
(3) <EVENT xml:id="e1"
type="TRANSITION" pred="DEPART"/>
(4) <TLINK xml:id="tl1"
eventID="#e1" relatedToTime="#t1"
relType="IS_INCLUDED"/>
(5) <TLINK xml:id="tl2"
timeID="#t1" relatedToTime="#t2"
relType="IS_INCLUDED"/>
</isoTimeML>
```

c. Interpretation:

$$\sigma_{a3} :=$$

$$\forall t_2[[day(t_2) \rightarrow \exists t_3[interval(t_3)=[T05{:}30, T23{:}45] \wedge t_3 \subseteq t_2]] \rightarrow \forall t_1[length(t_1)=(15, minute) \rightarrow [depart(e) \wedge bus(x) \wedge Arg(1, x, e) \wedge (t_1 \subseteq t_3) \wedge (\tau(e) \subseteq t_1)]]]$$

This says that a bus leaves every 15 minutes from 5:30 in the morning to 23:45 in the evening everyday.

What is being said in a plain language is much easier for us to understand, for this is the basic linguistic ability of humans. But to represent in a formal language gets complicated. To show how we derive such a complex piece of information in a compositional manner requires a much more complex process of combining its component pieces of information, each of which is represented by each XML element. Computational semanticists, however, attempt to formulate each step of such processes so that the computer can be trained to perform the process of annotating and interpreting various pieces of information conveyed by various types of media, for instance, not only still photos, but moving pictures. Inderjeet Mani and James Pustejovsky's most recent book, *Interpreting Motion: Grounded Representations for Spatial Language*, clearly shows what we, linguists and computer scientists, should be doing to develop the semantics of motion and space in general and the specification of semantic annotation and interpretation in particular. Harry Bunt's lecture, "The Semantics of Semantic Annotation", which was presented in PACLIC 21 (2007), Seoul, is an excellent example of showing how to interpret semantic annotations.

6 Concluding Remarks

C.S.Lewis is quoted, supposedly saying that he was told not to trust Catholics, as he began his early life, nor to trust linguists, as he began his career of teaching English at Oxford. Two of his best friends among his informal literary discussion group *Inklings* were, however, Catholic linguists: Hugo (H.V.D.) Dyson and J.R.R. Tolkien, the author of the novel *the Lord of the Rings*. They were philologists and made things easy to understand. Present-day linguists, on the other hand, are proud of writing or talking like Noam Chomsky, who wrote *Syntactic Structures* in terse English and made us memorize each page of it, or like Richard Montague, who published "Universal Grammar" and developed higher-order logics for natural language semantics. If linguists or semanticists keep talking or writing like them, then they may not have any followers who trust them. I once presented a paper, entitled "A Simple Syntax for Complex Semantics", which was supposedly a keynote speech for PACLIC 16 in February 2002. I concluded that talk by saying that a syntax must be kept simple for complex semantics, for the complexity of syntax is a theory and that of semantics, a reality. Fortunately, generative syntax took its path to minimalism (See Chomsky (1993).), while we have also seen a semantics like Copestake at al. (2005)'s Minimal Recursion Semantics (MRS).

I was surprised to learn that *small world* is a mathematical notion. It forms a network with nodes most of which are not directly connected, but connected with some distances. We thus get information about ourselves or our surrounding environment not from our neighbors right next door, but from those third persons at a distance who are situated in better perspective. It is still a robust structure with distributed bits of information, for the whole structure is preserved even when some of its parts collapse, thus providing objective validity. This picture seems to well represent the current situation of the world in which we live by exchanging information in the most efficient way with a tiny mobile gadget. Seen as a theory of action, the meaning of semantics can be understood with respect to such a small or tiny world rather than with respect to all possible worlds that are inconceivable or keep asking for the proof of their logical consistency or mathematical completeness. We need new semantics that can interpret all those signals that are sent out from those small worlds and also translate those interpretations in our metalanguage that is still bound to be a system consisting of sequences of discrete linearized symbols.

Reflecting on the past quarter of a century of the PACLIC meetings, I hope that our PACLIC will remain as a small world and that all its members would be closely connected with one another. I have attended most of the biennial conferences of LREC (Language Resources and Evaluation Conferences), namely those meetings in Las Palmas (2002), Lisbon (2004), Marakech (2008), Malta (2010), and Istanbul (2012). I also attended several meetings of ACL or LSA. I am afraid that these meetings have kept growing with so many plenary and parallel sessions, poster sessions, and satellite workshops and also with so many participants. This year's LREC, held in Istanbul, for instance, had over 1,300 participants. One big problem is that one gets either totally lost in the crowd or completely exhausted with so many contacts. As the cost for organizing such big conferences rises, participants have to pay a larger amount of the registration fee, sometimes reaching one thousand dollars. This was the case with an IEEE-sponsored workshop that I attended to read a paper a year ago. With so many official events and personal appointments, some papers are presented with almost no audience and some posters are just standing there. As a result, I predict that all these big conferences will eventually break up into smaller groups and that these small groups will grow up to become big organizations, with a cycle of growth and breaking up necessarily repeating. I thus repeat my hope that PACLIC will remain a small world so that all of us can enjoy close comradeship in pursuing our academic work and exchanging every bit of our knowledge or doubt with each other as we may be doing at a meeting like this wonderful conference in Bali.

Acknowledgments

For the completion of this story, I have a long list of people to whom I owe many thanks: Barbara Partee whose writing "Reflections of a Formal Semanticist as of Feb 2005" inspired me to adopt her style; two non-linguists, Don Diltz, a real estate brokerage manager in San Francisco and an old colleague of mine, whom I have known for 43 years since January 1969 while teaching English together at Chonbuk National University, Jeonju, Korea, and Tyrone Cashman, a philosopher and environmentalist living at the foot of Mount Tamalpais near Sausalito, California, who has been my friend and spiritual guide since summer 1957; Suk-Jin Chang, who has been the real leader of our PACLIC group in Korea and proofread the penultimate version of this talk; Roland Hausser, who retired from his professorship at the University of Erlangen to his inherited mansion at Bayreut, Germany; Hwan-Mook Lee, professor emeritus of Chonnam National University of Korea; Chongwon Park, who is chair of the English Department, University of Minnesota at Duluth; Alex C. Fang of City University of Hong Kong, and Ghang and Ryun, who are my family members. I also thank Chu-Ren Huang, Jae-Woong Choe, and Ruli Manurung of the PACLIC Steering Committee members and all the colleagues in the small world.

References

Aczel, Peter, David Israel, Yasuhiro Katagiri, and Stanley Peters (eds.). 1993. *Situation Theory and its Applications III*. CSLI Lecture Notes No. 37. CSLI Publications, Palo Alto, CA.

Ajdukiewicz, Kazimierz. 1935. Die syntaktische konnexität. In Storrs McCall (ed.), *Polish Logic (1920-1939)*, translated from *Studia Philosphica* 1, 1-27. Oxford University Press, Oxford.

Bach, Emmon. 1979. Montague grammar and classical transformational grammar. In S. Davis and M. Mithun (eds.), *Linguistics, Philosophy, and Montague Grammar*, pp. 3-49. University of Texas Press, Austin.

Bar-Hillel, Yehoshua. 1953. A quasi-arithmetical notation for syntactic description. *Language* 29, 47-58.

Barwise, Jon, and Robin Cooper. 1991. Simple situation theory and its graphical representation. In Jerry Seligman (ed.), *Partial and Dynamic Semantics III*. DYANA Deliverable R2.1.C. Center for Cognitive Science, University of Edinburgh.

Barwise, Jon, Jean Mark Gawron, Gordon Plotkin, and Syun Tutia (eds.). 1991. *Situation Theory and its Applications Volume 2*. CSLI Lecture Notes N0. 26. CSLI Publications, Palo Alto, CA.

Barwise, Jon, and Robin Cooper. 1993. Extended Kamp notation. In Peter Aczel, David Israel, Yasuhiro Katagiri, and Stanley Peters (eds.), *Situation Theory and its Applications III* pp. 29-54. CSLI Lecture Notes Number 37. CSLI Publications, Palo Alto, CA.

Beesley, Kenneth R., and Lauri Karttunen. 2003. *Finite-State Morphology*. CSLI Publications, Palo Alto, CA.

Bennett, Michael. 1974. *Some Extensions of a Montague Fragment of English*, UCLA Ph.D. Dissertation.

Bennett, Michael. 1976. Variation and extension of a Montague fragment. In Partee (1976), pp. 119-163.

Bunt, Harry. 1985. *Mass Terms and Model-Theoretic Semantics*. Cambridge University Press, Cambridge.

Bunt, Harry. 2007. The semantics of semantic annotation. In *Proceedings of the 21st Pacific Asia Conference on Language, Information and Computation*. Seoul National University (November 1-3, 2007), Seoul.

Bunt, Harry (ed.). 2012. *Proceedings of The Joint ISA-7, SRSL-3 and I2MRT Workshop on Interoperable Semantic Annotation.* The Eighth International Conference on Language Resources and Evaluation (LREC 2012) Satellite Workshop, Istanbul.

Bunt, Harry (ed.). 2012. *Proceedings of The Eighth ISO-ACL SIGSEM Joint Workshop on Interoperable Semantic Annotation (ISA-8).* PisA.

Carnap, Rudolph. 1952. Meaning postulates. *Philosophical Studies* 3(5), 65-73.

Chomsky, Noam. 1957. *Syntactic Structures.* Mouton, the Hague.

Chomsky, Noam. 1965. *Aspects of the Theory of Syntax.* The MIT Press, Cambridge, MA.

Chomsky, Noam. 1981. *Lectures on Government and Binding.* Foris Publications, Dordrecht.

Chomsky, Noam. 1993. A minimalist program for linguistic theory. *MIT Occasional Papers* No. 1. Distributed by MIT Working Papers in Linguistics, Cambridge.

Cooper, Robin, and Hans Kamp. 1991. Negation in situation semantics and discourse representation theory. In Barwise et al. (1991) (eds.), pp. 311-334.

Copestake, Ann, Dan Flickinger, Carl Pollard, and Ivan A. Sag. 2005. Minimal recursion semantics: an introduction. *Research on Language and Computation* 3, 281-332. Springer, Berlin (2006).

Davidson, Donald, and Gilbert Harman (eds.). 1972. *Semantics of Natural Language.* D. Reidel, Dordrecht.

Dowty, David R. 1972. *Studies in the Logic of Verb Aspect and Time Reference in English.* University of Texas at Austin Ph.D. dissertation.

Dowty, David R. 1976. Montague grammar and the lexical decomposition of causative verbs. In Partee (ed.) (1976), pp. 201-245.

Dowty, David R. 1979. *Word Meaning and Montague Grammar.* D. Reidel, Dorderecht.

Gallin, Daniel. 1975. *Intensional and Higher-order Modal Logic with Applications to Montague Semantics.* North-Holland, Amsterdam.

Gazdar, Gerald. 1979. *Pragmatics: Implicature, Presupposition and Logical Form.* Academic Press, New York.

Gazdar, Gerald, Ewan H. Klein, Geoffrey K. Pullum, and Ivan A. Sag. 1985. *Generalized Phrase Structure Grammar.* Blackwell, Oxford.

Gilbert, Douglas, and Cyde S. Kilby. 2005. *C.S. Lewis: Images of His World.* Lion Hudson PLC, Wilkinson House. Translated into Korean by Seokmuk Chung, Gachi Changjo Publishing, Seoul.

Grice, H.P. 1967. Logic and conversation. William James Lectures, Harvard University. Reprinted in P. Cole and J. Morgan (1975) (eds.), *Syntax and Semantics, 3: Speech Acts*, pp. 41-58. Academic Press, New York.

Gunji, Takao. 1982. Dynamic universe of discourse and implicatures. In Arata Ishimoto (ed.), I:1-24.

ISO/TC 37/SC 4/WG 2. 2012. *ISO NP 24617-7:2012(E) Language resource management - Semantic annotation framework - Part 7: Spatial information (ISO-Space).* The International Organization for Standardization, Geneva.

ISO/TC 37/SC 4/WG 2. 2012. *ISO 24617-1:2012(E) Language resource management - Semantic annotation framework - Part 1: Time and events (SemAF-Time, ISO-TimeML).* The International Organization for Standardization, Geneva.

Hausser, Roland. 1974. *Quantification in an Extended Montague Grammar.* Ph.D. dissertation, University of Texas at Austin.

Hughes, G.E., and M.J. Cresswell. 1968. *An Introduction to Modal Logic.* Methuen and Co., London.

Ishimoto, Arata (ed.). 1982. *Formal Approaches to Natural Language: Proceedings of the Second Colloquium on Montague Grammar and Related Topics.* Tokyo Working Group of Montague Grammar. March 1982.

Kamp, Hans. 1981. A theory of truth and semantic representation. In J. Groenendijk et al. (eds.), *Formal Methods in the Study of Language.* Mathematical Centre, University of Amsterdam, Amsterdam.

Kamp, Hans, and Uwe Reyle. 1994. *From Discourse to Logic: Introduction to Model-theoretic Semantics of Natural Language, Formal Logic and Discourse Representation Theory.* Kluwer Academic Publishers, Dordrecht.

Katz, Graham. 2007. Towards a denotational semantics for TimeML. In Schilder, Frank, Graham Katz, and James Pustejovsky (eds.), pp. 88-106.

Katz, Jerry J., and Jerry A. Fodor. 1963. The structure of semantic theory. *Language* 39, 170-210.

Lakoff, George. 1987. *Women, Fire, and Dangerous Things: What Categories Reveal about the Mind.* University of Chicago Press, Chicago.

Lakoff, George, and Mark Johnson. 1980. *Metaphors We Live By.* University of Chicago Press, Chicago.

Lambek, Joachim. 1958. The mathematics of sentence structure. *American Mathematical Monthly* 65, 154-170.

Lee, Eunryoung, and Aesun Yoon (eds.). 2011. *Recent Trends in Language and Knowledge Engineering.* Hankookmunhwasa, Seoul.

Lee, Ik-Hwan. 1979. *Korean Particles, Questions, and Complements: a Montague Grammar Approach.* Ph.D. dissertation, University of Texas at Austin.

Lee, Kiyong. 1974a. Negation in Montague grammar. Proceedings of the Chicago Linguistic Society (CLS) 10, 378-79.

Lee, Kiyong. 1974b. *The Treatment of Some English Constructions in Montague Grammar*. Ph.D. dissertation, University of Texas at Austin.

Lee, Kiyong. 1981. A superstar * convention in Montague Grammar. *Linguistics* 19, 495-512. Originally presented a SICOL-1981 (The First Seoul International Conference on Linguistics).

Lee, Kiyong. 1995. Recursion problems in concatenation: a case of Korean morphology. In Benjamin K. T'sou and Tom B.Y. Lai (eds.), *Proceedings of the 10th Pacific Asia Conference on Language, Information and Computation*, pp. 215-224. City University of Hong Kong (December 27-28, 1995), Hong Kong.

Lee, Kiyong. 2000. Developing database semantics as a computational model. In Akira Ikeya and Masahito Kawamori (eds.), *Proceedings of the 14th Pacific Asia Conference on Language, Information and Computation*, pp. 231-241. Waseda University (February 15-17, 2000), Tokyo.

Lee, Kiyong. 2002. Special lecture: A simple syntax for complex semantics. In Ik-Hwan Lee, Yong-beom Kim, Key-sun Choi, and Minhaeng Lee (eds.), *Proceedings of the 16th Pacific Asia Conference on Language, Information and Computation*, pp. 2-27. The Korean Society for Language and Information (January 31- February 2, 2002, Jeju), Korea.

Lee, Kiyong. 2004. Invited talk: Processing and representing temporally sequential events. In Hiroshi Masuichi, Tomoko Ohkuma, Kiyoshi Ishikawa, Yasunari Harada, and Kei Yoshiot (eds.), *Proceedings of the 18th Pacific Asia Conference on Language, Information and Computation*, pp. 9-14. Waseda University (December 8-10, 2004), Tokyo.

Lee, Kiyong. 2006. Multilinguality in temporal annotation: A case of Korean. In Tingting He, Maosong Sun, and Qunxiu Chen (eds.), *Proceedings of the 20th Pacific Asia Conference on Language, Information and Computation*, pp. 13-20. Tsinghua University Press (Huazhong Normal University, November 1-3, 2006), Wuhan.

Lee, Kiyong. 2008. Invited Lecture: Formal semantics for interpreting temporal annotation. In Piet van Sterkenbur (ed.), *Unity and Diversity of Languages* 97-108. John Benjamins, Amsterdam.

Lee, Kiyong. 2011. A compositional interval semantics. In Lee and Yoon (eds.), pp. 122-156.

Lee, Kiyong. 2012. Interoperable spatial and temporal annotation schemes. In Bunt (ed.) (2012a), pp. 61-68.

Lee, Kiyong, Jonathan Webster, and Alex Chengyu Fang. 2010. eSpatialML: an event-driven spatial annotation framework. In *Proceedings of the 24th Pacific Asia Conference on Language, Information and Computation*, pp. Tohoku University (4-7 November, 2010), Sendai.

Lee, Kiyong, and Harry Bunt. 2012. Counting time and events. In Bunt (ed.) (2012), pp. 34-41.

Mani, Inderjeet, and James Pustejovsky. 2012. *Interpreting Motion: Grounded Representations for Spatial Language*. Oxford University Press, Oxford.

Lewis, David. 1970. General semantics. *Synthese* 22: 18-67. Reprinted in Davidson and Harman (eds.) (1972), *Semantics of Natural Language*, pp. 169-218. D. Reidel, Dordrecht.

Lodge, David. 1984. *Small World: An Academic Romance.* Secker & Warburg.

McCawley, James D. 19981. *Everything that Linguists Have Always Wanted to Know about Logic (but were Ashamed to Ask).* Chicago University Press, Chicago.

Montague, Richard. 1970a. English as a formal language. In Richmond H. Thomason (ed.) (1974).

Montague, Richard. 1970b. Universal grammar. In Richmond H. Thomason (ed.) (1974), pp. 222-46.

Montague, Richard. 1973. The proper treatment of quantification in ordinary English. In Richmond H. Thomason (ed.) (1974), 247-70.

Partee, Barbara H. 1973. Some transformational extensions of Montague grammar. *Journal of Philosophical Logic* 2, 509-534. Reprinted in Partee (1973), pp. 51-786.

Partee, Barbara H. (ed.) 1976. *Montague Grammar.* Academic Press, New York.

Partee, Barbara H. (ed.) 2004. *Compositionality in Formal Semantics: Selected Papers by Barbara Partee.* Blackwell, Malden, MA.

Pratt-Hartmann, I. 2007. From TimeML to Interval Temporal Logic. In J. Geertzen, E. Thijsse, H. Bunt, and A. Schffrin (eds.), *Proceedings of The Seventh International Workshop on Computational Semantics*, pp. 166-180. Tilburg.

Pustejovsky, James, Jessica Littman, and Roser Saur[$\acute{i}$]. 2007. Arguments in TimeML: events and entities. In Frank Schilder, Graham Katz, and James Pustejovsky (eds.) (2007), pp. 107-127.

Pustejovsky, James, Kiyong Lee, Harry Bunt, and Laurent Romary. 2010a. ISO-TimeML: A standard for annotating temporal information in language. in *Proceedings of LREC 2010, the Seventh International Conference on Language Resources and Evaluation*, 394-397. Malta.

Pustejovsky, James, Kiyong Lee, Harry Bunt, and Laurent Romary. 2010b. Revised version of Pusejovsky et al. (2010a), a manuscript submitted to the journal *Language Resources and Evaluation.*

Pustejovsky, James, Jessica. L. Moszkowicz, and Marc Verhagen. 2012. The current status of ISO-Space. *Proceedings of the Joint ISA-7, SRSL-3 and I2MRT Workshop on Interoperable Semantic Annotation*, 70-77. LREC 2012 Satellite Workshop, Istanbul.

Pustejovsky, James, Jessica. L. Moszkowicz, and Marc Verhagen. 2012. The current status of ISO-Space. *Proceedings of the Eighth ISO-ACL SIGSEM Joint Workshop on Interoperable Semantic Annotation (ISA-8)*, 70-77.

Ritchie, G.D., G.J. Russell, A.W. Black, and S.G. Pulman. 1991. *Computational Morphology*. The MIT Press, Cambridge.

Schilder, Frank, Graham Katz, and James Pustejovsky (eds.). 2007. *Annotating, Extracting and Reasoning about Time and Events*. Springer, Berlin.

Thomason, Richmond H. (ed.). 1974. *Formal Philosophy: Selected Papers of Richard Montague*. Yale University Press, New Haven, CT.

Thomason, Richmond H. 1976. Some extensions of Montague Grammar. In Partee (ed.) (1976), pp. 77-117.

Developing a Deep Grammar of Indonesian within the ParGram Framework: Theoretical and Implementational Challenges

I. Wayan Arka
Australian National University/Udayana University
wayan.arka@anu.edu.au

Abstract

This paper discusses theoretical and implementational challenges in developing a deep grammar of Indonesian (IndoGram) within the lexical-functional grammar (LFG)-based Parallel Grammar (ParGram) framework, using the Xerox Linguistic Environment (XLE) parser. The ParGram project involves developing and processing computational grammars in parallel to test the LFG's theoretical claims of language universality, while at the same time testing its robustness to handle typologically quite different languages. Two relevant cases are discussed: voice-related morphosyntactic derivation and crossed-control dependency in Indonesian. It will be demonstrated that parallelism should be taken as a matter of degree, that it cannot always be maintained for good language-specific reasons and that the participation of IndoGram has also contributed to the rethinking and improvement of certain parallelism standards.

1 Introduction*

This paper discusses theoretical and implementational challenges to developing a deep grammar of Indonesian (IndoGram) within the Parallel Grammar (ParGram) framework. Using the Xerox Linguistic Environment (XLE) parser (Maxwell and Kaplan 1993; Crouch et al. 2007) with lexical-functional grammar (LFG) (Bresnan 1982, 2001; Dalrymple 2001) as the underlying linguistic theory, the IndoGram project joins the research and development program of broad-coverage grammars from a typologically wide range of languages. The approach (Butt et al 1999, 2002) involves developing and processing computational grammars in parallel to test the LFG's theoretical claims of language universality, while at the same time testing its robustness to handle typologically quite different languages.

While parallelism is preferred, it is demonstrated that this cannot always be strictly maintained for good language-specific reasons. It is also shown that the participation of IndoGram has contributed to the richness of linguistic phenomena to be handled within the ParGram project and to the rethinking and improvement of certain parallelism standards. Two relevant cases are discussed: voice-related morphosyntactic derivation and crossed control dependency.

The paper is structured as follows. An overview of the ParGram project is first presented in section 2. Linguistic analyses of voice alternations and crossed-control constructions and their XLE implementation are given in sections 3 and 4 respectively, followed by some discussion in section 5. Conclusions are given in section 6.

2 The (Indonesian) ParGram project: an overview

The Parallel Grammar (ParGram) project is an international collaborative research project for the development of large-scale computationally tractable grammars and lexicons of the world's (major) languages. Members include the corporate research laboratories of the Palo Alto Research

* Research reported in this paper was supported by the author's ARC Discovery Grant DP DP0877595 (2009–2011).

Center (PARC) (USA) and Fuji Xerox (Japan), as well as Stanford University, Oxford University, Manchester University, the Universities of Stuttgart and Konstanz, (Germany), the University of Bergen (Norway), the University of Essex (UK) and Langue et dialogue (France).

Current ParGram analyses (Butt et al 1999, 2002) are the result of over fifteen years of research and discussion based on data from a typologically wide range of languages (English, German, French, Japanese, Norwegian, Urdu, Welsh and Malagasy). The approach (Butt et al 1999, 2002) is to develop and process grammars in parallel. Similar analyses and technical solutions, wherever possible, are given for similar structures in each language. Parallelism has the computational advantage that the grammars can be used in similar applications and that machine translation (Frank 1999) can be simplified. However, ParGram also allows flexibility where parallelism is not maintained when different analyses are desirable and justified for good language-specific reasons. An encouraging result from ParGram work is the ability to bundle grammar-writing techniques into transferable knowledge and technology from one language to another, which means that new grammars can be bootstrapped in a relatively short amount of time (Kim et al 2003).

The underlying syntactic framework for ParGram is lexical-functional grammar (LFG), a stable and mathematically well-understood constraint-based theory of linguistic structure (Kaplan 1982; Dalrymple 2001; Bresnan 2001). Two important structures are assumed in LFG: constituent structure (*c-structure*; *c-str*) and functional structure (*f-structure*; *f-str*). The *c-structure* representation captures surface (overt) linguistic expressions that vary across languages. It is modelled in phrase structure trees that show structural dominance and precedence relations of units. *F-structure* captures abstract relations of predicate argument structures and related features such as tense. This is where cross-linguistic similarity or universality is represented. Thus, the equivalent sentences of English *Wayan will help Mary* in Indonesian and Tagalog are, respectively, *Wayan akan menolong Mary* and *Tatulong si Wayan kay Mary*. Indonesian is more like English in its *c-str*, whereas Tagalog is quite different, as seen in (1)a-b. However, they all share the same *f-str*, as shown in (1)b.[1]

(1). a. *c-str*: Indonesian b. *c-str*: Tagalog c. *f-str* for both (a) and (b)

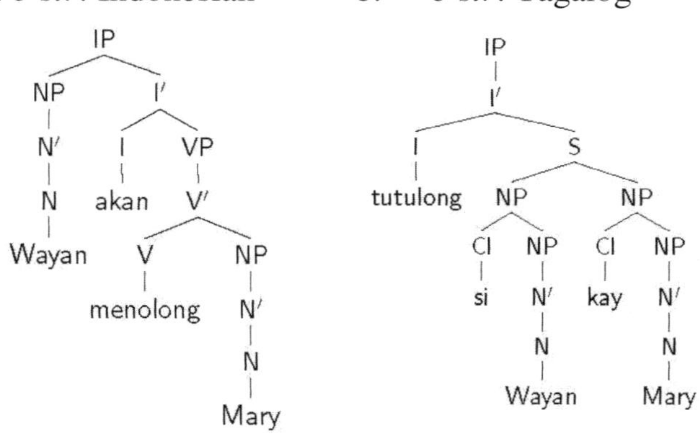

$$\begin{bmatrix} \text{PRED} & \text{`HELP}\langle\text{SUBJ, OBJ}\rangle\text{'} \\ \text{TENSE} & \text{FUTURE} \\ \text{SUBJ} & \begin{bmatrix}\text{PRED} & \text{`WAYAN'}\end{bmatrix} \\ \text{OBJ} & \begin{bmatrix}\text{PRED} & \text{`MARY'}\end{bmatrix} \end{bmatrix}$$

ParGram is built on the XLE platform (Maxwell and Kaplan 1993; Crouch et al. 2007), developed and maintained at PARC, which implements LFG theory. It outputs *c-structures* (trees) and *f-structures* as the syntactic analysis. The actual *c-str* and *f-str* output parse of a specific sentence from a given language contains richer information, however, as seen in (2) below.

Since *f-str* is the locus for cross-linguistic parallelism, it is of great significance in ParGram. It is the *f-str* that is used in a range of computational applications, e.g. in machine translation, sentence condensation and question answering. The ParGram project dictates the type of *f-str* analysis and the form of the features used in the grammars (Butt and King 2007).

[1] Abbreviations: 1, 2, 3 (first, second, third person); APPL (applicative); ARG (argument), ART (article); AV (actor voice); FUT (future); ITR (intransitive); MIDD (middle voice); OBJ (object); OBL (oblique); PASS (passive); PRED (predicate, a semantic form in LFG); pl (plural); PROG (progressive); s (singular), REL (relativiser); SUBJ (grammatical subject), TR (transitive); U (undergoer); UV (undergoer voice).

(2).

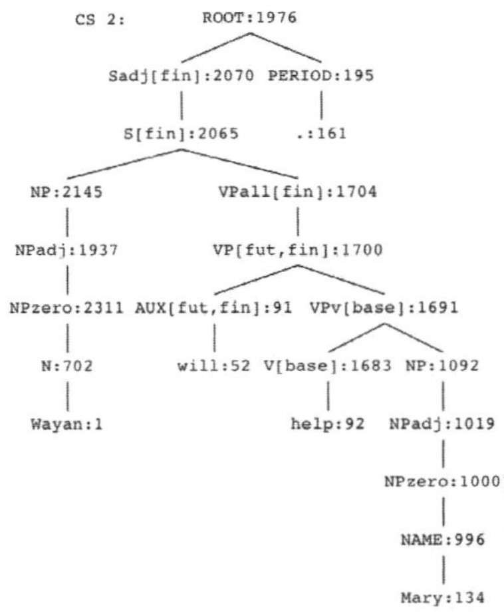


```
                 PRED       'help<[1:Wayan], [134:Mary]>'
                               1 PRED  'Wayan'
                             702 CHECK [LEX-SOURCE guesser]
                 SUBJ       2311
                            1937 NTYPE [NSYN proper]
                            2145 CASE nom, NUM sg, PERS 3
             161                 PRED  'Mary'
             195                 CHECK [LEX-SOURCE morphology]
              92             134
            1683                       NSEM [PROPER [NAME-TYPE first_name, PROPER-TYPE name]]
            1691 OBJ         996 NTYPE
              52            1000       NSYN proper
              91            1019
            1700            1092 CASE obl, GEND-SEM female, HUMAN +, NUM sg, PERS 3
            1704 CHECK      [SUBCAT-FRAME V-SUBJ-OBJ]
            2065
            2070 TNS-ASP    [MOOD indicative, PERF -_, PROG -_, TENSE fut]
            1976 CLAUSE-TYPE decl, PASSIVE -, VTYPE main
```

3 Morphosyntactic alternations: voice and applicative/causative alternations

Current research in Austronesian (AN) linguistics has led to good understanding of voice systems in this language family, of which Indonesian is a member. Austronesian voice systems are generally richer than those encountered in Indo-European languages like English. English shows only a two-way system: active-passive alternations, e.g. *John kissed Mary* vs. *Mary was kissed by John*. Indonesian, like other AN languages of the Philippines/Taiwan, shows a multi-way system. There is more than one non-actor voice. In the AN languages of the Philippines and Taiwan, there is no clear structure that can be analysed as passive. In Indonesian, however, one of the non-actor voices, namely the structure with *di*-verb plus a PP agent as in (3)c, can indeed be analysed as a true passive equivalent to the English passive. The agent is grammatically oblique, expressed by a PP (like in English), optional (indicated by the brackets) and pragmatically not prominent.

(3). a. *Aku akan menanam pohon itu*
1s FUT AV.plant tree that
'I will plant the tree'.

b. *Pohon itu akan ku=tanam*
tree that FUT 1s=UV.plant
'The tree, I will plant'.

c. *Pohon itu akan di-tanam (oleh mereka).*
tree that FUT PASS- plant by them
'The tree will be planted (by them)'.

Unlike Indo-European languages, the voice-system in Indonesian is symmetrical in a morphological and syntactic sense. Morphologically, they are symmetrical, as all voice types – AV (active/actor voice), UV (undergoer voice)[2] and PASS (passive voice) – are equally marked, e.g. from the root *tanam* 'plant', we can derive AV, UV, volitional/accidental PASS verbs and MIDD(le) verbs, as shown in (4). Syntactically, they are symmetrical in the sense that, unlike the voice alternations in English, the system allows both the actor and undergoer of a transitive verb to be equally linked to SUBJ without demoting any of them. Consequently, the voice alternation does not affect the transitivity. Thus, (3)b is as transitive as (3)a, and is syntactically not passive.

[2] UV is a type of voice where the Undergoer argument is the grammatical subject (hence, like passive) but the Actor argument is still highly prominent, obligatorily present showing up as a core argument. Note that in passive the Actor argument is optional and not a core argument.

(4). *tanam*

menanam	*ku-∅-tanam*	*di-tanam*	*ter-tanam*	*ber-tanam*
meN-tanam	'1s=UV-plant'	'PASS-plant'	PASS-plant	MIDD-plant
'AV-plant				

The unusual nature of the voice system in Indonesian and other AN languages poses descriptive, typological and theoretical challenges, and have led to controversy in linguistics. This also gives rise to an implementational problem in ParGram which is discussed further below. Descriptively, how to label different non-actor voices is not straightforward. Authors from different schools of linguistics analyse and label them differently. For certain linguists (Cole, Hermon, and Yanti 2008), structures like (3)b-c are analysed as passives, despite a clear difference in the syntactic status of the A argument. In my analysis (Arka and Manning 2008), sentences (3)b-c are syntactically distinct structures, with the first being active-like and translatable as active in languages like English (Purwo 1989). There are good linguistic reasons to label them differently. In this paper, I adopt my own analysis to capture the symmetricality of the Indonesian voice system, while at the same time allowing passivisation of the English type to exist in the system.

From a typological-theoretical point of view, the voice type exhibited by Indonesian adds to the richness of voice, and any theory should be able to account for this. That is, our theory should be such that it is able not only to capture the English type of voice, but also to predict the Indonesian-type voice with its expected properties. I argue that an argument structure–based theory of voice within LFG can handle this in a precise way, as further discussed below. I also demonstrate that the analysis is computationally implementable. In addition, the causative-applicative derivation by *-i/-kan* further adds to the complexity of the voice system in Indonesian. That is, a verb can have voice morphology as well as *-i/-kan*, which constrains alternations. For example, the root *tanam* 'plant' without *-i* has its patient argument appearing as object in the actor voice, or as subject in the passive voice, as in (3)a and (3)c, respectively. With the applicative *-i,* it is the locative argument (*sawah*) that is the object in the AV sentence (5)a, and the subject in the passive sentence (5)b. The underlying theme *padi* becomes a second object or an oblique (possibly marked by *dengan*), as seen in (5).

(5). a.

Mereka	*menanami*	*sawah-nya*	*(dengan)*	*padi.*
3pl	AV.plant-APPL	rice.field-3POSS	with	rice

'They planted their rice field with rice'.

b.

Sawahnya	*ditanami*	*(dengan)*	*padi*	*oleh*	*mereka.*
rice.field-3POSS	PASS-plant-APPL	with	rice	by	3pl

'Their rice field was planted with rice'.

c. ?* *Padi ditanami sawahnya oleh mereka.*
FOR: ?? 'The rice was planted (with) rice field'.

The challenge in the analysis and its implementation is to ensure the right output when both voice and applicative morphology are present. We want to have the applicative with *-i* applied first before the passive with *di-* as in (6)a. That is, the locative argument is first introduced into the second position by . This locative argument is then linked to SUBJ when the agent argument is removed or demoted by the passive from the first place in the argument structure list. (The linking mechanism picks up the most prominent argument from the *a-str* list as SUBJ.) That is, applicative and voice derivations must be applied in that order. Otherwise, we would get an unacceptable sentence where the theme (*padi* 'rice'*)* becomes the passive SUBJ as in (5)c. The incorrect derivation can be schematised in (6)b.

(6). a. *tanam* 'plant<ag , th>'
↓
tanam-i 'plant-APPL <ag , <u>loc</u> | th>'
↓
di-tanam-i 'PASS-plant-APPL<<u>loc</u>| ag th>'
SUBJ

b. * *tanam* 'plant<ag , th>'
↓
di-tanam 'PASS-plant<th|agt>'
↓
di-tanam-i 'PASS-plant-APPL<th, loc|ag>'
SUBJ

We handle this by proposing an analysis where *-i* is a three-place predicate, as shown in (7). Affixation with *-i* involves complex predicate composition, with argument fusion of the matrix and embedded arguments. Importantly, *-i* comes with a thematically a locative (LOC)-related argument (i.e., possibly goal or source, in addition to locative) in the second argument (ARG2). ARG2 is either new, or fused with the LOC argument of the base wherever possible. ARG1 is thematically higher than ARG2, though not necessarily an agent. This representation allows us to capture both causative and applicative uses of *-i*, as well as other uses; see the different types of fusion exemplified in (10)–(14).

(7). *A-str* of -i and its associated semantic roles

'$PRED_1$ < ARG_1 , ARG_2 , $PRED_2$ < _ , ...>>'
(A) ($U:_{LOC}$) where argument(s) of $PRED_1$ fuse(s) with arguments of $PRED_2$

Thus, the root *tanam* 'plant' affixed with *-i* gives rise to *tanami* with *a-str* showing the fusion, as seen in (8). This *a-str* becomes the input for voice linking. The AV links the most prominent ARG (namely ARG1) to SUBJ (9)a. In contrast, the PASS voice demotes ARG1 to oblique and makes the locative ARG SUBJ (9)b.

(8).
'3pl' 'garden' 'mango'
-i <ARG1, ARG2 'plant < _ , _ >'>'
(U:loc) (ag) (th)

(9). a. AV:
'3pl' 'garden' 'mango'
SUBJ OBJ OBJ2/OBL
-i <ARG1, ARG2 'plant < _ , _ >'>'
(U:loc) (ag) (th)

b. PASS:
'garden' 'mango' '3pl'
SUBJ OBJ2/OBL OBL
-i < ARG2 'plant < _ , _ > < _ >'
(U:loc) (ag) (th)

Another property of the suffix *-i* that complicates the analysis is that *-i* is multifunctional. It shows applicative and causative polysemy. For example, *-i* in *panasi* is causative 'hot-cause', whereas *-i* in *tiduri* is applicative (i.e. 'sleep on [loc]'). In addition, the stems are possibly intransitive or transitive, not necessarily verbal, as shown in Table 1.

The resulting subcategorisation frames of *-i* affixation are not uniform. There are at least four types. Each of them is briefly discussed and exemplified below; see Arka et al. 2009 for a detailed discussion.

Roots	*Derived -i verbs*	*Roots*	*Derived -i verbs*
air (N) 'water'	*air-i* 'water'	*lompat* 'jump' (V_{ITR})	*lompat-i* 'jump over'
kulit (N) 'skin'	*kulit-i* 'peel'	*tidur* 'sleep' (V_{ITR})	*tidur-i* 'sleep on'
gula (N) 'sugar'	*gula-i* 'put sugar in'	*diam* 'stay' (V_{ITR})	*diam-i* 'dwell in'
ketua '(N) chair (of an organisation)	*ketua-i* 'chair or lead in a meeting/organisation'	*tulis* 'write' (V_{TR})	*tulis-i* 'write on something'.
panas (A) 'hot'	*panas-i* 'heat (water)'	*kirim* 'send' (V_{TR})	*kirim-i* 'send'
basah (A) 'wet'	*basah-i* 'dampen'	*siram* 'spray' (V_{TR})	*siram-i* 'spray with'
lengkap (A) 'complete'	*lengkap-i* 'complete'	*cium* 'kiss' (V_{TR})	*cium-i* 'kiss repeatedly'
jauh 'far' (A)	*jauh-i* 'make oneself far from'	*pegang* 'hold' (V_{TR})	*pegang-i* 'hold tightly'

Table 1: the suffix *-i* with its stems in different lexical categories

Type 1. Type 1 involves derived monotransitive *-i* verbs undergoing a valence-changing applicativisation effect. With a two-place intransitive base (with a goal/locative second argument) such as *jatuh* 'fell (on)to X', *datang* 'come to X' and *lewat* 'pass at X', the result is a strictly monotransitive *-i* verb[3]. This is exemplified by (10)a-b. The derived structure of *menjatuhi* (10)b can be represented as (10)c. The fusion of arguments is indicated by a line connecting the two arguments. This *-i* derivation involves a double fusion.

(10). a. *Mangga yang besar jatuh ke rumah-nya*
mango REL big fall to house-3s
'A big mango fell onto his house'.

b. *Mangga yang besar men-jatuh-i rumah-nya* (**menjatuhkan*)
mango REL big AV-fall-i house-3s
'A big mango fell onto his house'.

c. 'mango' 'house'
SUBJ OBJ
-i <ARG1, ARG2 'jatuh < _ (_)>'
(U:loc)

Type 2. This type is associated with three-place predicates with a displaced theme such as *kirim* 'send' and *suguh* 'serve'. The derived *-i* verb can either be ditransitive with the displaced theme being OBJ2, or three-place monotransitive with the displaced theme realised as OBL instrument. An example showing the derived ditransitive structure is shown in (11).

(11). a. *Engkau menyuguh-i aku minuman lezat*
2s AV.serve-i 1s drink tasty
'You served me a very tasty drink'.

[3] There is evidence that the goal/locative of *jatuh* 'fall' or *datang* 'come' is an oblique-like argument (i.e. associated with the conceptual unit of [PATH] of the verbs) although it is not required to be overtly present on the surface syntax. A (general) goal/locative adjunct cannot typically take -i in Indonesian:

i) a. *Ia tinggal di Jakarta*
3s live LOC Jakarta
'S/he lives in Jakarta;.

b. * *Ia meninggal-i Jakarta*
3s AV.live-i Jakarta
FOR 'S/he lives in Jakarta'.

ii) a. *Ali menangis di kamar*
Ali AV.cry LOC room
'Ali cried in the room'.

b. * *Ali menangisi kamar*
Ali AV.cry-I room
FOR: 'Ali cried in the room.'

b.

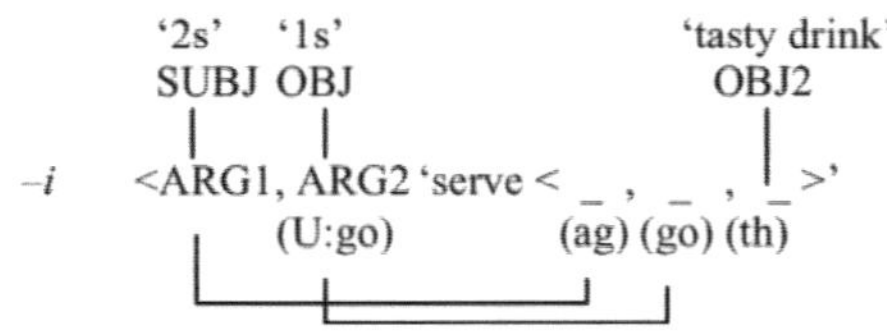

Type 3. There is no valence change in this type of *-i* derivation, e.g. *pukul* 'hit' (transitive)→ *pukuli* (transitive) 'hit repeatedly', where *-i* signifies repetition or intensification.

(12). a. *Ia* *memukul-i* *saya*
3s AV.hit-i 1s
'S/he was hitting me, s/he hit me repeatedly'.

b.

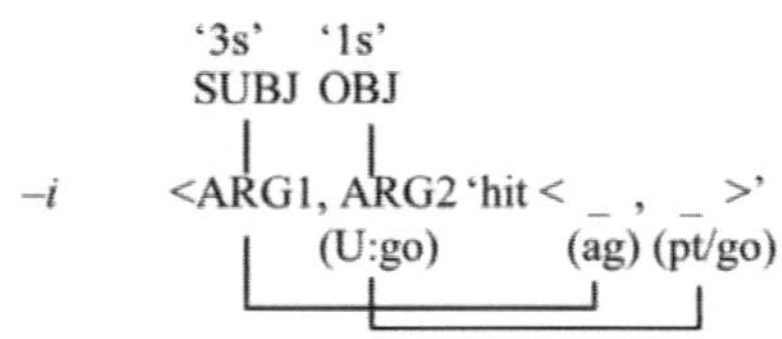

Type 4. This is the type of *-i* affixation resulting in causativisation. The *-i* verbs can be monotransitive (13)b (with the displaced theme showing up as an oblique instrument marked by *dengan*), or ditransitive (13)c (with the displaced theme being OBJ2). Type 4 *-i* structures involve single fusion, as depicted in (13)d, the only difference being the realisations of the unfused embedded displaced theme[4].

(13). a. *Air itu sedang meng-alir ke sawah.* SUBJ OBJ
water that PROG AV-flow to rice.field 'flow < _ , _ >'
'The water is flowing to the rice field'. (th) (loc)

b. *Dia meng-alir-i sawah=nya dengan air itu.*
3s AV-flow-*i* rice.field=3sg with water that
'S/he flooded his/her rice field with the water'.

c. *Dia meng-alir-i sawah=nya air itu.*
3s AV-flow-*i* rice.field=3sg water that
'S/he flooded his/her rice field with the water'.

d.

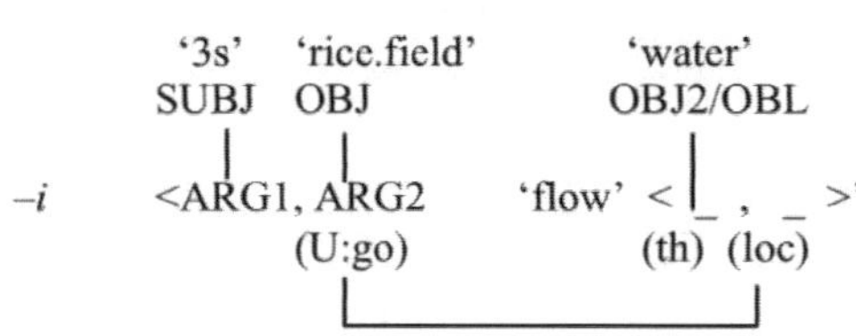

Type 4 *-i* includes those *-i* verbs with nonverbal roots, e.g. *sakit* 'sick', *panas* 'hot' and *kotor* 'dirty'. This is exemplified in (14)a. The fusion of the theme-locative argument shown in (14)b captures the meaning that *jalan* 'road' is understood as the surface of the road.

---

[4] In fact, the *a-str* of the type (13)d allows for double fusion if ARG1 is not filled in with an agent. Thus, the following is acceptable. The water flows because of its natural force.

Air itu mengalir-i sawahnya
water that AV.flow-I rice.field
'The water flooded his/her rice field'.

(14). a. *Jangan* *kotor-i* *jalan* *itu*
NEG dirty-i road that
'Don't (you) make (the surface of) the road dirty'.

b.
'you' 'road'
SUBJ OBJ
| |
–*i* <ARG1, ARG2 'dirty' < _ >'
(U:loc) (th)

As seen, the types involve different kinds of argument fusion, single or double. They are constrained by the semantics of the root. The general rule for *-i* composition appears to be that arguments of thematically similar types tend to fuse. Thus, the actor-like ARG1 of the matrix PRED tends to fuse with the actor-like ARG1 of the embedded PRED. Likewise, the undergoer-like ARG2 of the matrix PRED fuses with the undergoer-like ARG2 of the embedded PRED.

The properties of *-i* are now well understood. We are pleased to report that we have successfully implemented a novel unified argument structure–based analysis to capture those properties. The analysis and implementation make use of the idea of predicate composition (Alsina 1996; Butt 1995) and the restriction operator (Butt and King 2006 ; Butt, King, and Maxwell III 2003; Kaplan and Wedekind 1993). The main components of the implementation in XLE can be briefly described as follows.

The grammar consists of phrase structure and sublexical rules with certain relevant annotations, e.g. showing grammatical functions (SUBJ, OBJ and ADJUNCT) as in (15), or templates indicated by @ as in (16). The voice and applicative/causative templates are given in (17)a and (17)b, respectively. For the time being, as seen in (17)a, we still maintain the classic (simpler) analysis of voice alternations as lexical rules, rather than principled alternations based on a mapping theory (Arka 1993; Bresnan 2001). Note that the nesting of the templates with the @APPL template inside the @VOICE template in (16) is meant to capture the idea that applicativisation applies before voice alternation. This is to obtain the intended result as discussed earlier (cf. example (5), representation (6)).

(15). a. S → NP VP
(↑SUB)= ↓

b. VP → V' PP
↓ ∈(↑ADJUNCT)

c. V' → (NP) V (NP)
(↑OBJ)= ↓ (↑OBJ)= ↓

(16). a. V → V_VOICE_BASE V_ STEM' V_SFX_BASE

b. V_STEM' → {V_STEM-APPL_I _ V_I_BASE
@(VOICE @(APPL_I VApp_I))
|
V_STEM-CAUS_I V_I_BASE
@(VOICE @(CAUS_I VCaus_I)) }.

(17).

<table>
<tr><th>a. Voice template</th><th>b. Applicative/causative template</th></tr>
<tr><td>VOICE(_SCHEMATA) =
{ _SCHEMATA
@ACTOR-VOICE
| _SCHEMATA
@UNDERGOER-VOICE
(↑ OBJ) →(↑ SUBJ)
(↑ SUBJ) → (↑ OBJ)
|_SCHEMATA
@PASSIVE-VOICE
(↑ OBJ) → (↑ SUBJ)
{ SUBJ) → NULL
| (↑SUBJ) → (↑ OBL)
| (↑SUBJ) → (↑ OBJ) } }.</td><td>{(↑ PRED) = 'V_Appl_i <(↑ SUBJ) (↑ OBJ) %PRED3>'
↑\PRED\GF = ↓\PRED\GF [Type 1: IntrRoot → Vtr]
{ (↓ SUBJ) = (↑ SUBJ)
(↓ OBL-LOC)=(↑ OBJ) |
(↓ SUBJ) = (↑ SUBJ)
(↓ OBL-LOC) = (↑ OBJ) [Type 2: TrRoot → Vtr]
(↓ OBJ)= (↑ OBL-INST)
(↑ OBL-INST CASE)=c obl-inst |
(↓ SUBJ) = (↑ SUBJ) [Type 3: TrRoot → Vtr]
(↓ OBJ)=(↑ OBJ)
(↑ TNS-ASP PROG)=+
~(↑ OBL-INST) "just for the iterative meaning of –i" }
(↓ PRED)=(↑ PRED ARG3) |
(^ PRED) = 'V_Appl_i <(↑ SUBJ)(↑ OBJ) (↑ OBJ2) %PRED4>'
↑ \PRED\GF= ↓ \PRED\GF
(↓ SUBJ) = (↑ OBJ) [Type 4: IntrRoot → Vtr]
(↓ OBL-LOC) = (↑ OBJ)
(↓ OBJ)= (↑ OBJ2)
(↓ PRED)=(↑ PRED ARG4) }
(↑ APPLICATIVE)= +.</td></tr>
</table>

The grammar also consists of a lexicon containing both free words and affixes. They are listed with their own entries. Sample entries are given in (18) below.

(18). Sample entries: free forms

a.	*sawah*	N	XLE	@(CN rice field).
b.	*mereka*	PRON	XLE	@(PPRO 3 pl).
c.	*tanam*	V	XLE	@(VOICE @(TRANS plant)).

Sample entries: bound forms

e.	+I	V_I .		
f.	AV+	V_VOICE		@(VOICE-TYPE AV).
g.	UV+	V_VOICE		@(VOICE-TYPE UV).
h.	PASSdi+	V_VOICE	XLE	@(VOICE-TYPE PASSIVE).

The Indonesian grammar is equipped with a tokeniser and morphological analyser (Mistica et al. 2009; Femphy et al. 2008). It was built using XFST (Xerox Finite State Transducer) (Beesley and Karttunen 2003). The grammar can therefore identify morphemes of words with a complex morphological make-up and collect their grammatically relevant information for the purpose of further processing. For example, the sentence *Sawah ditanami padi* 'A rice field planted with rice' consists of three words, with one word, namely *ditanami*, morphologically complex. The sentence can be correctly parsed. The input string (19)a is first broken into tokens by the tokeniser. The output is then fed into the morphological analyser so that the words *sawah*, *padi* and *ditanami* can be analysed and assigned morpheme and category tags, as in (19)b. Since the relevant tags and forms are listed in the lexical entries, e.g. PASSdi+ (for *di-*) and +I (for the suffix *-i*) (see (18)), the XLE grammar can pick up the tags, and use the information to assign the word a hierarchical structure based on the sublexical rules formulated in (16). In addition, given the functional constraints carried by the morphemes and the structures (cf. template calls signalled by @ in the entries and in the sublexical rules), the grammar can also build functional structures involving predicate composition for the *-i* verb. Other words of the sentence input are parsed in a similar way, and the grammar can unify all information and constraints for the whole sentence. The output *c-* and *f-structures* are displayed in (20). Note that the voice prefix *di-* is higher in the structure than the applicative *-i*. The AVM (attribute-value matrix) diagram shows that the applicative suffix *-i* is a matrix predicate, taking the *a-str* of the base *tanam* as an argument in its *a-str*. The subject is removed by the passivisation (indicated by 'NULL').

(19). a. Input string: *Sawah ditanami padi.*

b. Morphologically analysed string: *Sawah*+Noun PASSdi+*tanam*+I+Verb *padi*+Noun

(20). (a)

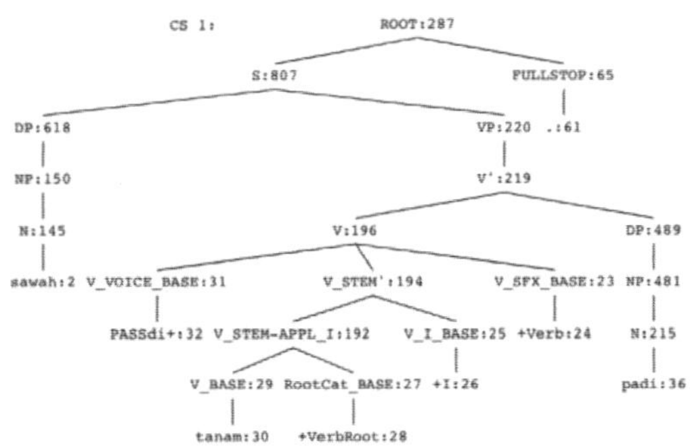

(b)

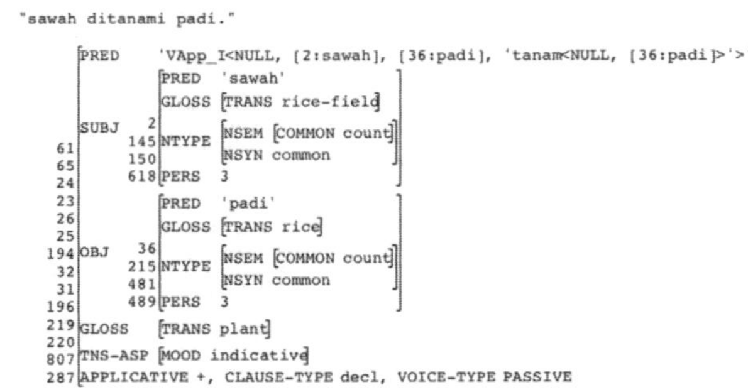

4 Crossed-control structures in Indonesian

Our grammar can also intelligently handle the ambiguity and complexity of dependency relations, in particular the so-called crossed-control construction (CCC), exemplified by (21). The term 'control' here refers to a referential dependency between the unexpressed (controlee) argument and expressed (controller) argument. Sentence (21) is ambiguous between the ordinary-control reading in (21)a and the crossed-control reading in (21)b. In the first reading, represented in (22)a, the unexpressed argument of *dicium* (i.e. 'kissee', indicated by a dash) is SUBJ and understood as the matrix argument, *saya* (the 'wanter', controller). In the second reading, represented in (22)b, the wanter is the kisser, not expressed by the matrix SUBJ but by the embedded OBL argument. Of particular interest in this paper is the second, crossed control, reading.

(21). *Saya mau/ingin [_ di-cium oleh Ibu]*
1s want PASS-kiss by Mother
a. 'I wanted to be kissed by Mother'. (Ordinary Control Reading)
b. 'Mother wanted to kiss me'. (Crossed Control Reading)

(22).	a. **Ordinary control reading**: SUBJ = [_] SUBJ OBL ['wanter' ['kissee' 'kisser']] 'I' 'mother'	b. **Crossed control reading:** SUBJ = [_]SUBJ OBL ['wanter' ['kissee' 'kisser']] 'I' 'mother'

Note that reading (21)b is not possible in other languages like English. In English, the sentence *I wanted to be kissed by Mother* can never mean the 'wanter' is the 'kisser' (i.e. 'Mother wanted to kiss me').

CCCs are not restricted to intransitive verbs like *ingin/mau* 'want'. Matrix transitive verbs such as *coba* 'try', *ancam* 'threaten' and *tolak* 'refuse' also show crossed-control reading. Consider (23), where the matrix verb and the embedded verbs are transitive, both allowing AV-PASS voice alternations. A crossed-control reading is observed in (23)b – the trier/actor is the killer (*temannya*), whereas the matrix subject *dia* is the patient of *kill.*

(23). a. *Teman-nya* *men-coba* [_ *membunuh* *dia*].
friend-3POSS AV-try AV.kill 3s
'His friend(s) tried to kill him'.

b. *Dia* *dicoba* [_ *di-bunuh* *(oleh)* *teman-nya.*
3s PASS-try PASS-kill by friend-3POSS
'His friend(s) tried to kill him'.

More examples from an online newspaper are given in (24). All the embedded verbs are in the passive, but the agents are understood as the matrix actor. For example, the syntactic subject of *berusaha* 'attempt' (24)a is inanimate (*politik lokal*). Its logical subject/actor, the attempter, is the embedded oblique argument (*pusat*).

(24). a. *Politik* *lokal* *di* *Indonesia* *selalu* ***berusaha dikendalikan oleh pusat.***[5]
politics local in Indonesia always try PASS-control by central
'The central government always tries to control the local politics'.

b. *Ternyata* *skuter* *model* *Eropa* ***nekat*** ***dijual*** ***disana oleh...Honda***[6]
in fact scooter model Europe insist PASS-sell there by Honda
'It turns out that Honda insisted on selling the European model of the scooter there'.

c. *rancangan* *peraturan* *daerah* *...akhirnya* ***di-tolak***
bill regulation local finally PASS-reject

untuk ***di-sahkan*** *oleh* *DPRD* *Gresik*[7]
to PASS-pass by loca.legislative.assembly Gresik

'The DPRD of Gresik finally rejected to pass the local draft bill'.

The crossed-control reading is constrained by voice type, particularly when both matrix and embedded verbs are transitive. First of all, the crossed control reading is not possible when the matrix verb is in AV. Thus, sentence (25) is strange in its ordinary-control reading (i), and it can never mean (ii) (i.e. the crossed-control reading). Any theory or analysis of control constructions should be able to handle the blocking constraint of the crossed-control reading by the AV. This is further discussed in section 5.

(25). *Dia* *mencoba* *di-cium* *oleh artis* *itu.*
3s AV.try PASS-kiss by artist that
i) 'He tried to be kissed by the artist'. (ordinary-control reading)
ii) *'The artist tried to kiss him'. (crossed-control reading)

In addition, for the crossed-control reading to be possible, the verbs should have harmonious non-actor voice types. In (23)b, both have passive *di-*. In (26)a-b below, both have undergoer voice (UV). Note that the actor pronominal *kau* appears once, either on the matrix or on the embedded verb. Mixing the non-actor voices, PASS and UV, results in bad sentences (26)c-d.

(26). a. *Dia* *kau=coba* [_ _ *bunuh*]
3s 2SG=UV.try UV.kill
'You tried to kill him/her'.

[5] http://politik.kompasiana.com/2012/04/12/politik-lokal-di-indonesia-dari-otokratik-ke-reformasi-politik/.
[6] http://fanderlart.wordpress.com/2009/09/24/dual-keen-eyes-ga-laku-ya-di-vietnam/.
[7] http://gresik-satu.blogspot.de/2012/04/2-ranperda-usulan-eksekutif-ditolak.html.

b. *Dia* *coba* [_ *kau=bunuh*]
3s UV.try 2s=UV.kill
'You tried to kill him/her'.

c. * *Dia dicoba* [*kau=bunuh*]

d. **Dia kau=coba* [_ *dibunuh*]

The pattern seen in (26) serves as evidence for the analysis that CCCs involve syntactic argument sharing. That is, the two arguments ('controller' and 'controlee') must be of the same type syntactically. Mixing voice types results in the two having different argument types: OBL in passive and OBJ in UV; (26)c and d are bad due to the violation of this argument sharing constraint.

At first, it might look like a puzzle: How is it possible that the actor of the matrix verb (e.g. *ibu* 'mother') is not realised on the matrix structure, but rather controlled by the argument of the embedded verb? The reverse is cross-linguistically common. The challenge is to get a precise linguistic analysis of the CCC capturing the properties so far discussed and then to implement this. Any analysis of CCC should be consistent with, or built on, the existing theory of control so that the analysis should also naturally work for the ordinary-control structures. In this paper, the analysis and the implementation stem from a lexically based LFG theory of control, where the notion of syntactic *a-str* and argument sharing is important.

The proposal is that the CCC should be analysed as a serial verb construction (SVC), forming a complex predicate, which licenses 'raising' and argument sharing; this enables an argument to be realised only once in the surface syntax. Cross-linguistically, this is a well-known property of SVCs. One piece of evidence that the verb *ingin/coba* and the complement VP form a tight SVC unit and therefore allow crossed-control reading comes from the fact that the reading disappears when some material intervenes (observed by Purwo 1984) as in (27), or else the sentence is ungrammatical, as in (28).

(27). *Si Yem* *ingin* ***supaya*** *dicium si Dul.*
ART Yem want in.order.to PASS-kiss ART Dul
i. 'Yem wanted to be kissed by Dul'.
ii. NOT FOR: 'Dul wanted to kiss Yem'. (Purwo XX)

(28). * *Politik* *lokal di* *Indonesia* *selalu* ***berusaha*** ***agar*** ***dikendalikan***
politics local in Indonesia always try in.order.to PASS-control
oleh ***pusat.***
by central
'The central government always tries to control the local politics in Indonesia'.
(i.e. FOR the same meaning as in (24)a)

The SVC analysis of CCCs can be described as follows. First, verbs come with rich information in their lexical entries. Some of the information may be by default inherited from their class or type. Control verbs like *mau* 'want' and *coba* 'try' have their entries represented in (29). The SUBJ control equation of (↑SUBJ)=(↑XCOMP SUBJ) is the default ordinary control. The equation means that the matrix SUBJ is the same as the embedded clause's SUBJ. It is a semantically based control relation (Foley and Van Valin 1984; Sag and Pollard 1991). That is, with the orientation verb *mau* 'want' and commitment verb *coba* 'try', the controller/doer of the action wanted or tried is the wanter/trier. Other types of verbs, e.g. the influence type such as *suruh* 'ask', would have a different specification, namely OBJ control. That is, in the 'asking' event, it is the 'askee' (OBJ) that is the controller/doer of the action being asked.

(29). a. *mau* V (↑PRED) = 'want<(↑SUBJ)(↑XCOMP)>'
'exp' 'proposition'
(↑SUBJ)=(↑XCOMP SUBJ)

b. *coba* V (↑PRED) = 'try<(↑SUBJ)(↑XCOMP)>'
'agt' 'proposition'
(↑SUBJ)=(↑XCOMP SUBJ)

Second, an SVC is a structure with a complex VP with more than one V in it, as shown in (30). It has its own *a-str* structure specification, which is not always exactly the same as the *a-str* specifications of the component predicates that make it up.

(30).

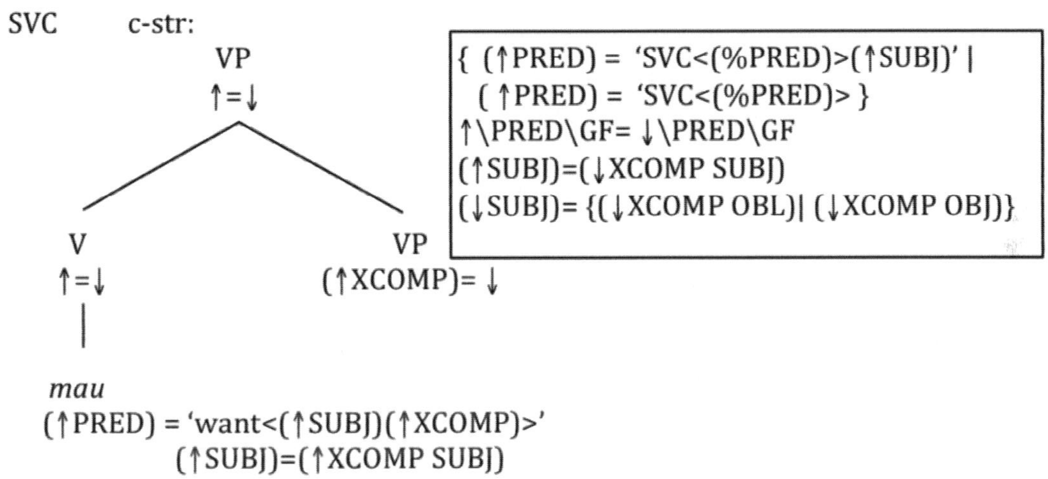

The SVC analysis is also implemented in XLE by means of a restriction operator, as is the case of applicativisation discussed earlier.

The mechanism of how the analysis works can be described as follows. When a control verb is inserted into a VP[SVC] structure, the information of the verb's predicate argument structure is altered due to its composition with other component parts of the SVC. Importantly, the SVC has its own predicate, possibly imposing sharing with raising constraints. The SVC's predicate restriction is partially shown in the box in (30). The specification says that the SVC's predicate takes the whole control predicate and possibly allows a nonthematic SUBJ position (indicated by being outside the angle brackets). This allows the control verb's underlying SUBJ (i.e. the wanter), indicated by (↓SUBJ), to be shared with the embedded complement (XCOMP)'s agent-OBL (or OBJ). Thus, when the verb *mau* occupies the terminal note V, the SVC would take the whole PRED *mau*, but would make the experiencer of *mau* (i.e. the underlying subject annotated as (↓SUBJ) in the box) the same as the embedded XCOMP OBL. In addition, the SVC's SUBJ is a raised argument (i.e. nonthematic matrix SUBJ, shared with the XCOMP SUBJ).

In what follows, we demonstrate that the grammar can parse sentences with both crossed-control and ordinary-control reading. The intransitive *mau* is first exemplified below, followed by the transitive *coba*.

4.1 *Mau* 'want'

The *c-str* and *f-str* output parses for the crossed-control reading (b) of sentence (21) with *mau* are given in (31). The *f-str* shows that the SVC takes the whole *a-str*/subcategorisation (SUBCAT) frame of *mau* and assigns nonthematic matrix SUBJ, *saya* (tag 4). This matrix SUBJ is shared with the embedded XCOMP SUBJ. It is a thematic SUBJ (i.e. patient) of the XCOMP; hence, the sharing captures the raising effect. The grammar can correctly identify *saya* as the subject of the whole SVC structure, even though *saya* is not an argument of the matrix verb *mau*. It also shows that *ibu* 'mother' (tag 39) is the underlying (thematic) subject of *mau* (i.e. the first argument of *mau*), not the syntactic (SUBJ) argument of the SVC: It shows up only as the OBL of the XCOMP.

(31). *c-str* *f-str*

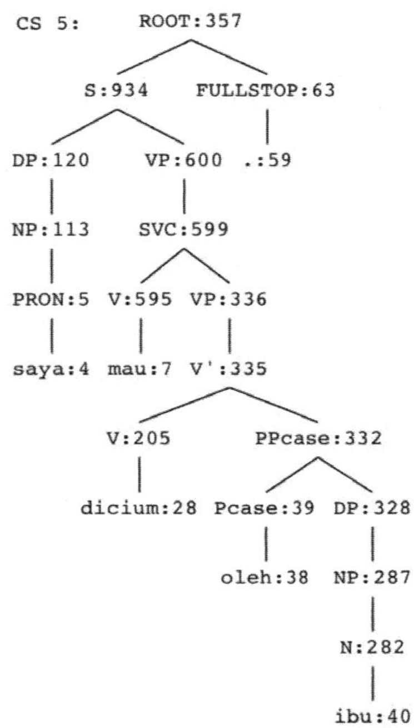

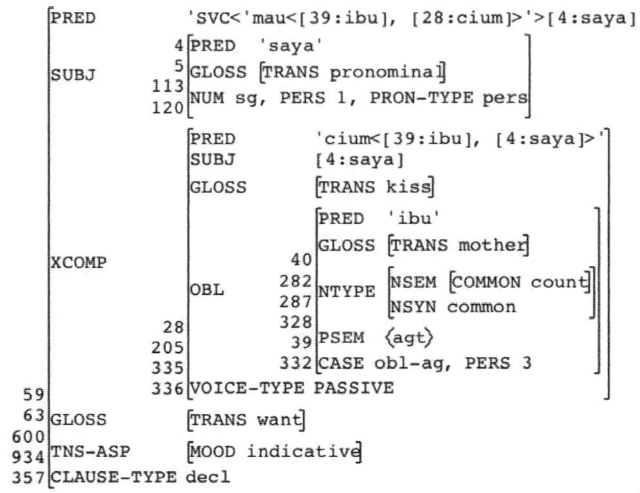

The grammar can also capture the ordinary-control reading, e.g. (21)b. This is the reading equivalent to the English sentence *I want to be kissed by mother*, where the wanter is the controller and the kissee. The *c-str* and *f-str* parses are shown in (32).

(32). *c-str* *f-str*

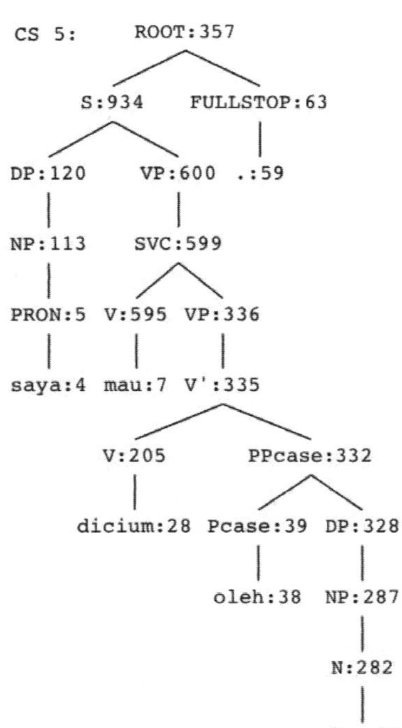

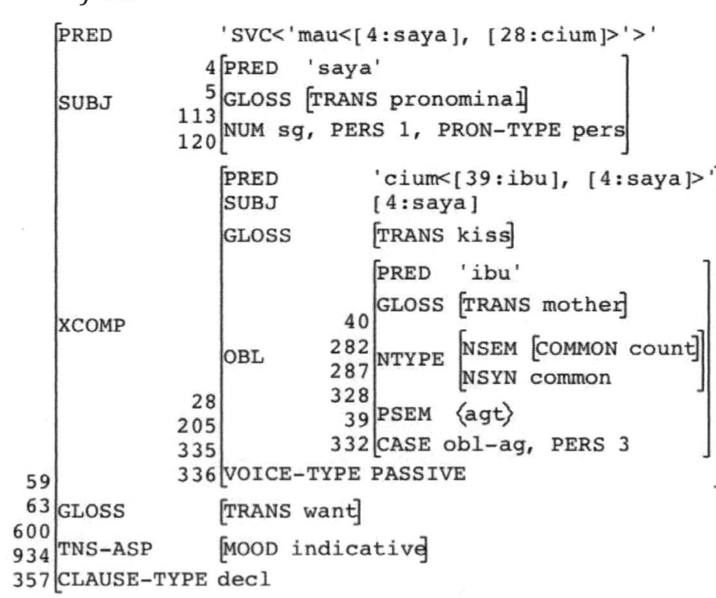

An important point of analysis and implementation to note here is the status of the wanter argument. Unlike in the crossed-control reading in (31), the wanter *saya* (tag 4) is syntactically the matrix thematic SUBJ of *mau*, as well as SUBJ of the SVC controlling the embedded SUBJ, the kissee. That is, there is no raising of the XCOMP SUBJ to a nonthematic position in the ordinary-control reading. This is a critical point not made explicit in the earlier raising analysis of the Indonesian 'want' in Polinsky and Potsdam (2008). As intended, the argument *ibu* 'mother' (tag 40) is parsed by the grammar only as the (agent) argument of the embedded verb *cium* 'kiss', realised as an OBL.

4.2 Transitive *coba* 'try'

Unlike *mau/ingin* 'want', which is strictly intransitive, the verb *coba* is transitive, allowing the possibility of different voice marking: *men-coba* 'AV-try' vs. *di-coba* 'PASS-try' exemplified in (23). It is only when used passively do we find the crossed-control reading, as seen in (23)b. As noted earlier, the AV matrix verb does not allow a crossed-control reading, as shown in example (25).

The *c-str* and *f-str* parses of the crossed reading (23)b are given in (33). As shown, the grammar correctly analyses the subject of the matrix verb *dia* (tag 4) as a non-thematic SUBJ of the verb *coba*, placed outside the angle brackets in the *f-str*. That is, *dia* is not the trier; rather, it is the SUBJ/patient of the embedded verb *bunuh,* raised to the matrix SVC's SUBJ. The logical subject (actor) of the verb *coba* 'try', namely *teman*, is correctly analysed as OBL, as realised in the embedded verb (tag 29).

For the ordinary-control reading of *coba*, exemplified by (23)a, the trier is the controller, realised as matrix SUBJ. The analysis is that the SVC just takes the whole SUBCAT frame of *mencoba* where the actor/trier is already linked to SUBJ, and there is no need for an embedded argument to raise to a nonthematic argument. In short, a nonthematic argument is not needed. The grammar can capture this analysis as intended, as seen in the *f-str* parse output in (34). That is, the matrix SUBJ *teman* (tag 6) is the trier/actor, controlling the SUBJ of the embedded verb *membunuh* 'kill'. All arguments are thematic: No SUBJ argument is represented outside the angle brackets.

(33). *c-str* *f-str*

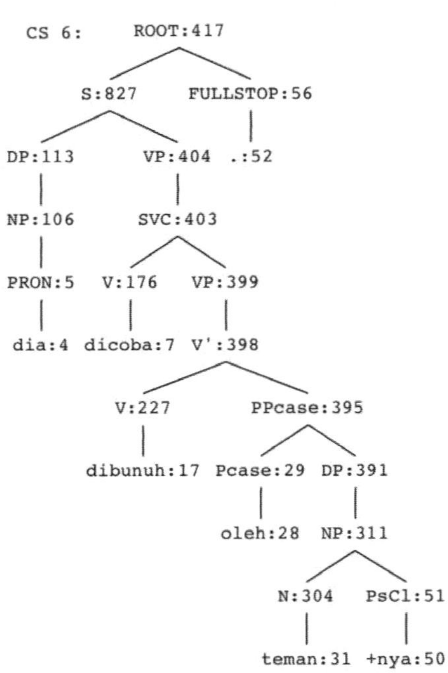

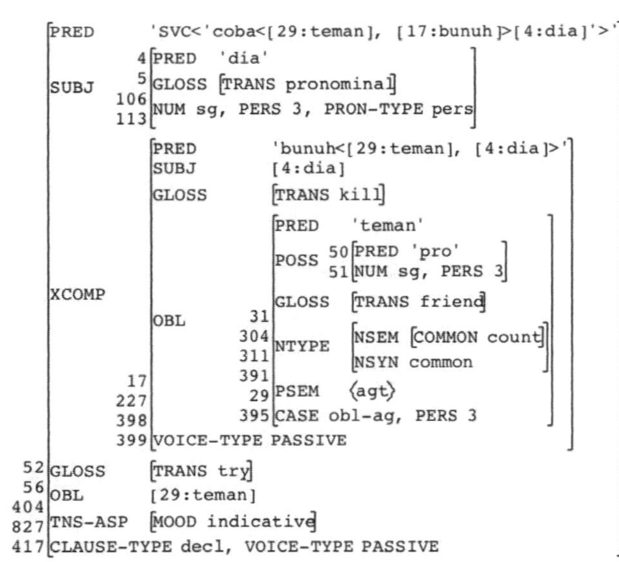

(34). *c-str* *f-str*

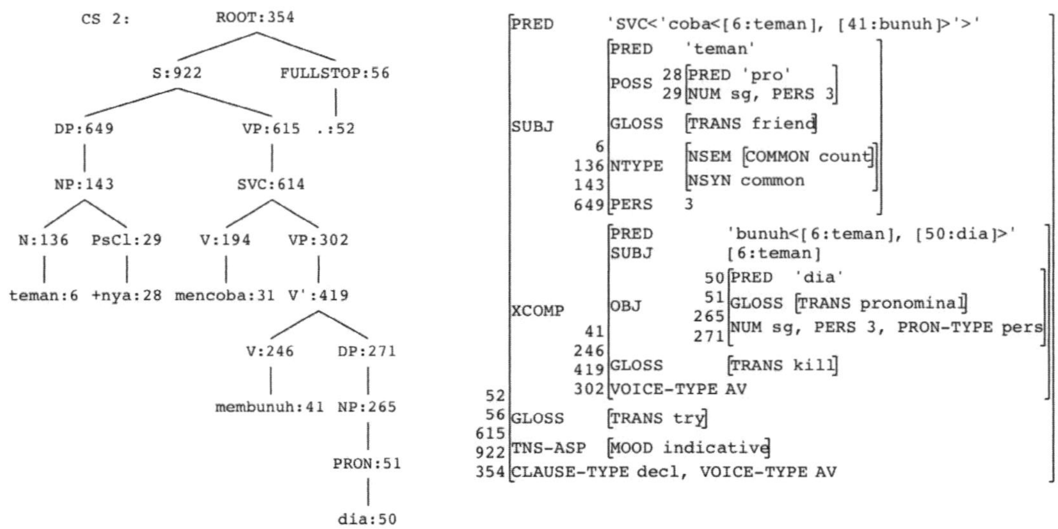

To sum up, our Indonesian grammar has the ability to handle not only the standard or ordinary-control construction of the type found in English, but also the complex crossed-control constructions involving voice alternations.

5 Discussion

The goal of the ParGram project was to have a common grammar development platform and a unified methodology of grammar writing to develop large-scale (parallel) grammars for typologically different languages (Butt and King 2007). Such an endeavour is, in fact, at the heart of the lively debate in linguistics with respect to the two opposing ideals given in (35), and is therefore a constant challenge both from a theoretical perspective in linguistics and from a practical standpoint in its implementation in ParGram.

(35). a. The generativist-universalist ideal: Having explicit formal representations of universal linguistic properties/features within some kind of generative system;

b. The descriptivist-typologist ideal: Capturing language-specific, possibly distinctive genius and/or typologically different patterns.

In this section, I briefly discuss further theoretical points and challenges on the basis of voice alternations and CCCs in Indonesian presented in this paper.

On voice, grammatical function (GF) and features

The *f-str* representation is supposed to capture a universal level of language analysis, showing parallelism or universalism. Indonesian grammar has brought in the richness of voice systems of AN languages, and raised theoretical and implementational challenges in incorporating it into the ParGram framework.

Linguistically, as discussed in section 3, a symmetrical voice system as exemplified by Indonesian is typologically distinct from the nonsymmetrical type shown by English. Any theory of syntax should be able to capture both this distinct property and other shared properties with English. In LFG, the theory of voice adopted in this paper makes use of the notion of a syntactic argument structure distinct from surface grammatical functions (GFs) such as SUBJ and OBJ, and voice alternations are handled by a linking theory (Manning 1996; Arka and Manning 2008; Arka 2003).

Before IndoGram joined the group, there was a simple feature of voice, namely [PASSIVE +/–] to capture voice in English-like languages. Surely this feature cannot satisfy the descriptive-typological ideal because Indonesian has a multi-way voice system. A new voice feature should be introduced, namely [VOICE-TYPE], whose value can be one of these in Indonesian: *actor-voice, undergoer-voice, passive-voice* and *middle-voice*. Thus, the parallelism is captured by having the same feature attribute VOICE-TYPE, whereas typological variation is captured by allowing different languages having to have different voice values.

A serious theoretical issue is the nature of parallelism in relation to GFs. The relevant question to raise here is how tenable it is to adopt GFs such as SUBJ and OBJ as universal functions residing in the *f-str*. Given the descriptive-typological ideal, how should these GFs labels be interpreted? They are assumed to be 'universal' in LFG. Should we qualify the notion of universalism, particularly given the nature of voice types and related GFs in Austronesian languages like Indonesian? I argue that we should. One reason for this is the fact that the notion of OBJ, for example, is broader in Indonesian (and other AN languages like Tagalog and Balinese) than in English. OBJ in these languages can be linked not only to the undergoer as in AV, but also to actor as in UV. An OBJ-actor is not possible in Indo-European languages like English. In other words, while we use the same GF labels such as OBJ, their exact grammatical space across languages is not the same. In addition, the status of a GF in the grammar is not exactly the same across languages. While both Indonesian and English have SUBJ, SUBJ in English is obligatory, as seen in the existence of dummy/expletive 'it' as in *it rained, it's hot,* etc.; in contrast, SUBJ is not obligatory in Indonesian. Therefore, the grammatical space of GFs and the related voice types in Indonesian are not the same as in English. The UV structures, for instance, have no exact parallel in English.

To capture both universalist-typologist ideals (35), the notion of parallelism should not be taken in its strict sense. The same GF with its related structure and features might be assigned a slightly different interpretation in different languages.

On the implementation of linking and different layers of syntactic representation

The existing ParGram platform makes use of the earlier conception of LFG, where surface constituency (*c-str*) and rich the syntactic functional (*f*-)structure are distinguished. The latter contains syntactic and semantic information. In this earlier conception of LFG, GFs such as SUBJ and OBJ are primitive/basic notions listed in the entries. LFG theory has developed, particularly with the emergence of mapping theories. It is theoretically necessary, as evidenced from languages that exhibit voice alternations such as Indonesian, to recognise the surface SUBCAT frame containing SUBJ/OBJ as distinct from the argument structure level containing syntactic-thematic information such as core/non-core, actor/non-actor in order to capture the principled syntax-semantics interface in relation to the universalist and typologist's ideal. We now have a good analysis of how linking works across languages, including AN languages like Indonesian.

The challenge is how to implement recent analyses within ParGram's XLE framework, cast in an earlier version of LFG. One particular question is how to capture the notion of deep(er) *a-str*, where actor (ACT) and undergoer (UND) are relevant. Note that in the earlier LFG version implemented in XLE, the deep *a-str* (<ACT, UND>) and surface syntactic *a-str* are conflated in the SUBCAT frame, e.g. the verb *bawa* 'bring' would have the SUBCAT frame of 'bawa<SUBJ OBJ>', with SUBJ and OBJ interpreted as both as SUBJ/actor and OBJ/undergoer by default.

The tricky part is capturing principled argument alternations (i.e. alternative linking) as in voice and applicativisation/causativisation. As discussed in sections 3–4, we have made use of the restriction operator in the implementation, manipulating the SUBCAT list in the *f-str*, e.g. in applicativisation and CCC analysis. In this way, we can talk about the underlying arguments

SUBJ/actor/experiencer that become (surface) OBL in crossed reading constructions[8]. However, if we look further afield at other Austronesian languages of eastern Indonesia (and the Papuan languages of Indonesia), there seems to be good reason to keep the idea of deep SUBJ/OBJ (i.e. ACT/UND) without distinguishing between surface and underlying relations. These languages show no voice alternations. If we maintain the idea of linking in these languages, then the linking is fixed (i.e. actor is always SUBJ and undergoer is always OBJ). Again, the interpretation of SUBJ in these languages is slightly different from that in Indonesian and English, where SUBJ can carry any semantic role. In short, the parallelism/universality of very basic notions of GFs remains an issue theoretically if more AN languages are taken into account in the ParGram project.

Handling constraints interaction and ambiguity

As the grammar becomes larger, the rules and related constraints become more complex. Handling constraint interactions between parts of the grammar poses a challenge in the analysis and implementation. The grammar often produces multiple parses. The IndoGram experience suggests that most of these are not wanted, but certain others are. However, as we know, natural language is full of ambiguity. Certain ambiguity that is attested should be recognised by our grammar. This is the case with the ambiguity of the ordinary and crossed-control reading in (36), when the subject is animate, *dia* '3SG'.

(36). *Dia/pintu itu mau di-tendang oleh John.*
3s/door that want PASS-kick by John
i) a. He wanted or was willing to be kicked by John. (ordinary control)
b. #The door wanted to be kicked by John. (ordinary control)
ii) John wanted to kicked him/the door. (cross-reading)

A deep intelligent grammar should be able not only to recognise the ambiguity but also to select one reading (i.e. disambiguate) (36) when the subject is inanimate, *pintu itu* 'the door'. The inanimate subject renders only the crossed-control reading (36)ii. This does not appear to be a big challenge, but nouns should be semantically tagged with 'animacy'. At the moment, our Indonesian grammar has no ability to sort out this kind of animacy-based disambiguation.

Indeed, the interaction between lexical class properties and syntactic behaviour is important in the grammar of Indonesian. One task not yet fully implemented in the IndoGram project at the moment (despite a good linguistic analysis) is the semantically driven causative-applicative polysemy. For example, the same suffix *-i* can appear as a causative (as in *sakit-i* 'make hurt') or an applicative (as in *datang-i* 'come to X') depending on the semantic type of the root, whether it is agentive/motion or patientive. In principle, the analysis is implementable: Roots need to be tagged appropriately with their semantic classes, and then the morphosyntactic components of the grammar recognise the tags and respond accordingly in the parsing process. This is one of the items in progress at the moment that needs further work.

Grammatical constraints also interact with the pragmatic information structure. For example, focussing the control verb by fronting it also results in disambiguation, as illustrated by (37)a-b. The declarative sentence (37)a is ambiguous between the two readings of control. However, fronting/focussing the verb with the focus marker *kah*, as in (37)b, gives rise to only one reading, namely the ordinary-control reading. In addition, there is also a slight nuance of temporal difference, with the fronted *maukah* focussing on present/future event in (37)b.

---

[8] One problem with this is that, with the current setup of XLE, the implementation can typically only parse, but not generate.

(37). a. *Kau mau dicium oleh orang itu?* (ambiguous:
2s want PASS-kiss by person that both ordinary and crossed reading)
i) 'Did/do you want to be kissed by the person?
ii) 'Did the person want to kiss you?'

b. *Mau=kah kau di-cium oleh orang itu?* (unambiguous)
want=KAH 2Ss PASS-kiss by person that (ordinary reading only)
'Do you want to be kissed by the person?'

We have a good explanation based on the theory of control developed in this paper as to why the crossed-control reading disappears in (37)b: Fronting the matrix verb in effect breaks up the SVC structure. The argument fusion of (↓SUBJ)=(↓XCOMP OBL) is licensed only by an SVC structure, and is therefore inapplicable here. The verb *mau* is the main matrix verb imposing the lexical semantic control specified in its entry, that is, the experiencer is SUBJ, i.e. (↑SUBJ)=(↑XCOMP SUBJ). Our grammar has not yet able to capture this pragmatic-syntactic constraint interaction, however; while we have a good analysis of the disappearance of the crossed-control effect, some more work needs to be done to implement the analysis, and this is not always easy.

6 Concluding remarks

Developing a large-scale, deep, intelligent grammar is expensive in terms of both time and resources, mainly due to the complexity of natural languages. This complexity has been illustrated by discussing how to handle two types of structures – voice alternations and crossed-control constructions – in our computational development of IndoGram within the ParGram project. We are primarily concerned with theoretically well-grounded analyses of the structures which meet the universalist and descriptivist-typologist ideals in linguistics.

We are also concerned with implementational issues such as efficient and intelligent parsing. We want the grammar to be able to give us the most wanted parse(s), reducing unintended ones. However, at the same time, we want the grammar to be able to recognise and maintain natural ambiguity, as demonstrated in cases of multiple readings associated with control structures. For this, and for other cases such as the causative-applicative polysemy of *-i*, the grammar needs to able to check the semantics of lexical items.

There is also a challenge to the complexity of the grammar due to its interaction with pragmatics. We have demonstrated that focussing by fronting the control verb renders an unambiguous control reading.

While there has been progress in our understanding of how lexical classes play a role in the grammar, and how the grammar interacts with pragmatics, much of the precise interplay among them is still unknown. This is indeed a real challenge, particularly in a project that aims to produce a deep intelligent large-coverage grammar.

References

Arka, I Wayan. 1993. *The -kan causative in Indonesian*. MPhil Thesis, University of Sydney, Sydney.

———. 2003. *Balinese morphosyntax: a lexical-functional approach*. Canberra: Pacific Linguistics.

Arka, I Wayan, Mary Dalrymple, Meladel Mistica, Suriel Mofu, Avery Andrews, and Jane Simpson. 2009. A linguistic and computational morphosyntactic analysis for the applicative -i in Indonesian. Paper read at The Proceedings of the LFG 09 Conference, http://csli-publications.stanford.edu/LFG/14/lfg09toc.html, at Cambridge.

Arka, I Wayan, and Christopher Manning. 2008. "Voice and grammatical relations in Indonesian: a new perspective." In *Voice and grammatical relations in Austronesian Languages*, edited by P.K. Austin and S. Musgrave, 45-69. Stanford: CSLI.

Beesley, Kenneth R., and Lauri Karttunen. 2003. *Finite State Morphology*. Stanford: CSLI.

Bresnan, Joan. 1982. *The mental representation of grammatical relations*. Cambridge, Massachusetts: the MIT Press.

———. 2001. *Lexical functional syntax*. London: Blackwell.

Butt, Miriam, and Tracy Holloway King. 2006 "Restriction for morphological valency alternations: the Urdu causative." In *Intelligent Linguistic Architectures: Variations on Themes.* , edited by Ronald M. Kaplan. Stanford: CSLI.

———. 2007. "Urdu in a Parallel Grammar Development Environment." In *Language Resources and Evaluation: Special Issue on Asian Language Processing: State of the Art Resources and Processing* edited by T. Takenobu and C.-R. Huang, 191–207.

Butt, Miriam, Tracy Holloway King King, and John T Maxwell III. 2003. Complex predicates via restrictions. Paper read at the proceedings of the LFG'03 Conference, CSLI, http://csli-publications.stanford.edu/LFG/8/lfg03.html.

Cole, Peter, Gabriella Hermon, and Yanti. 2008. "Voice in Malay/Indonesian." *Lingua* (118):1500-1553.

Crouch, D., M. Dalrymple, R. Kaplan, T. H. King, J. Maxwell, and P. Newman. 2007. "XL E Documentation."Available on-line at http://www2.parc.com/isl/groups/nltt/xle/doc/xletoc.html.

Dalrymple, Mary. 2001. *Lexical Functional Grammar, Syntax and semantics*. San Diego: Academic Press.

Femphy, P, R Mahendra, R Manurung, and I W Arka. 2008. Two-level Morphological analysis for Indonesian. Paper read at Proceedings of the 2008 Australasian Language Technology Association Workshop (ALTA 2008), at Hobart, Australia.

Foley, William A., and Robert D. Van Valin. 1984. *Functional syntax and universal grammar*. Cambridge: Cambridge University Press.

Kaplan, Ronald M., and Jürgen Wedekind. 1993. "Restriction and correspondence-based translation." *Proceedings of the Sixth European Conference of the Association for Computational Linguistics*:193–202.

Manning, Christopher D. 1996. *Ergativity: argument structure and grammatical relations*. Stanford: CSLI.

Maxwell, John T, and Ronald M. Kaplan. 1993. "The Interface between Phrasal and Functional Constraints." *Computational Lingusitics* no. 19:571–589.

Mistica, Meladel, I Wayan Arka, Timothy Baldwin, and Avery Andrews. 2009. *Double Double, Morphology and Trouble: Looking into Reduplication in Indonesian*. Edited by Luiz Pizzato and Rolf Schwitter, *Australasian Language Technology Workshop (ALTW 2009), Sydney, Australia, pp. 44—52.* UNSW, Sydney: http://www.alta.asn.au/events/alta2009/alta-2009-proceedings.html.

Polinsky, Maria, and eric Potsdam. 2008. "The syntax and semantics of wanting in In donesian. ." *Lingua* no. 118:1617–1639.

Purwo, Bambang Kaswanti. 1989. "Voice in Indonesian : A Discourse Study." In *Serpih -serpih telaah pasif bahasa Indonesia*, edited by B.K. Purwo, 344-442. Jogyakarta: Kanisius.

Purwo, Bambang Kaswanti 1984. *Deiksis dalam bahasa Indonesia. Jakarta: Balai Pustaka.*

Sag, Ivan, and Carl Pollard. 1991. "An integrated theory of complement control." *Language* no. 67:63-113.

PACLIC-26
Bali, November 8-10, 2012

Idiomaticity and Classical Traditions in Some East Asian Languages[1]

Benjamin K. Tsou
Research Centre on Linguistics and Language Information Sciences,
The Hong Kong Institute of Education
btsou99@gmail.com

1. Introduction

A mark of erudition in verbal communication is the use of idiomatic language employing metaphors and figurative speech. Its study is important not only for linguistic research but also for the study of language, rhetorics, literacy studies and cultural history, and the relationship amongst them.

The rhetorical distinction between literal and metaphorical meanings and so semantic and discoursal opacity often associated with idioms is universal. But the format of idioms can stand out, and the means by which the expressions are formed, often drawing on the use of notable objects or events relevant to the native society concerned are often culture bound. These objects and events can often be drawn from relatively closed sets.

Idioms are commonly used in metaphors and figurative speech in all languages and in daily communication. They have not only attracted the attention of specialists interested in language, rhetorics and literary studies (Black 1962, Makkai 1972, Xiang 1979), but even visiting national leaders to China from USA and Japan in recent years have cited them in their speeches. In the last few decades, several major areas associated with idioms and metaphors have become noticeable: (a) Syntax and Semantics, e.g. Chafe's well-known 1968 paper on syntactic decomposability issues of frozen idioms; (Katz and Postal (1963) and Jackendoff (1995)); (b) Cognitive studies, e.g. Gibbs (1980, 1985, 1987), Nippold et al. (1989), Zuo (2006), Zhang (1984); and (c) Cultural studies, e.g. Lakoff (1987) [gender], Tang (2007) [food related items], Nall (2008) [numbers], Fontecha and Catalan (2003) [animals], Liu (1984), Fan (2007) [color terms], Mo (2001) [Chinese culture and idioms]. There are also notable anthologies on the relevant approaches, e.g. Everaert (1989, 1992, and 1995).

We note that when some salient linguistic features are found to be shared across two languages, the question often arises as to whether their origin might be due to: (a) shared genetic affinity, or (b) borrowing across language boundaries. Furthermore, they could be also (c) universal features if shared by all other languages, or (d) typological linguistic features if shared by structurally similar natural languages, as well as (e) areal or regional features if they are found only in a particular geographical region. Moreover, they are not mutually exclusive.

[1] This research is supported by the Research Grants Council Committee of the University Grants Council of Hong Kong ((1) General Research Fund (GRF) Project No. 844012 "Quadrasyllabic Idiomatic Expressions (QIEs) in Chinese and neighboring Languages: An Investigation into Linguistic and Cultural History" and (2) GRF Project No.148908 "A Quantitative and Qualitative Comparison of Word Formation in Modern Standard Chinese and Early Modern Chinese"). I am grateful for comments leading up to this paper from co-investigators in the two projects: Andy Chin, Hintat Cheung, and particularly Shin Kataoka who has drawn my attention to many of the examples in this paper.

On the other hand, when two related languages have dissimilar terms to express similar objects or events, then the difference could well represent salient non-linguistic variations. For example, the word for government in Indonesia is *Pemerintah* and in Malay *Kerajaan*. In the latter case of Malay, the word reflects the structure of government involving constitutional monarchy (as indicated by "*Rajah*") whereas the case of Indonesian reflects an organization structure presided over by a leader. The form *Selamat* means "hello" in Indonesia and Malaysia, originating from Semitic languages: Arabic S*alam* "peace" e.g. *Salaam Alaikum* "peace be with you" and Hebrew *Shalom* (peace). But in the Philippine languages, it means "thank you". This shift of meaning may not be unreasonable if we consider the broader context of language contact interaction in which we find the universal and customary conversation opening and closing moves, which are the same in Islamic societies (*Salaam Alaikum*), in stark contrast to English (with *hello-hi* and *goodbye* respectively) and other languages. In the exchange of identical but multifunctional pragmatic expressions during the opening and closing communicative moves among participants, a possible semantic switching taking place could be understandable.

In Asia, two long standing major classical traditions have been recognized:

(I) Sanskrit base [Indosphere[2]]

Devanagari, on which the Sanskrit writing system is based, has influenced the writing systems of Indosphere languages of the South Asian subcontinent, Burmese, Thai, Lao, Tibetan etc, but not Indonesia and Malaysia in which once dominant Hindu Kingdoms in the Indonesian archipelago have given way to Islamic sultanates, with exceptions to be found in Bali, for example. In these languages, there has not been much evidence of the Indic past in non-materialistic terms, other than loan words, while Jawi, the script derived from Arbic, still survives.

(II) Sinitic base [Sinosphere]

Its emblematic logographic writing system has greatly influenced the historical development of Sinosphere writing systems in Japan, Korea, Vietnam, and among other ethnic groups like the Nasi etc, on which the associated classical traditions, including the Chinese classical language have had significant impact. Thus their students to this day are often exposed to literary classics of Chinese origin such as the *Chronicles of Three Kingdoms* (三國演義) and *Water Margin* or *All Men and Brothers* (水滸傳). This tradition bears interesting comparison with the lesser trend of students in Thailand, Laos, and Cambodia (but not Indonesia or Malaysia) studying the Indic epic Ramayama. One distinctive feature of languages associated with Sinosphere is the importance given to relatively unique idiomatic expressions such as 不三不四 [not-3-not-4] "improper", similar to English "neither fish nor fowl" but with stronger negative connotations. For example, civil servants in Japan, Korea and Vietnam, in order to gain promotion, have to take language examinations in which there are expectations on familiarity with such expressions. This is often seen as a difficult and arduous task because of the drastic typological linguistic differences between Japanese, Korean and Vietnamese on the one hand, and Chinese on the other hand. Thus, considerable efforts have to be made by the civil servant aspiring to promotion.

It is interesting to note that whereas Korea and Japan, for example, have adopted the Chinese logographic writing system, and have even incorporated it into basically at one time or another

---

[2] Matisoff (1990) proposed the terms *Sinosphere* and *Indosphere* to distinguish between two major and often superimposed cultural traditions within Asia.

bimodal writing systems. On the other hand, related languages such as Mongolians and Manchus switched to the Chinese language when they conquered all of China, rather than imposed their own language as the native language, with possible adaptation or adoption of the logographic script. There were some minor unsuccessful attempts such as that by the Kitan Kingdom (契丹) which developed a demotic script, and the use of Phags-Pa script of the Mongols, which though squarish in shape and written from right to left, was much more influenced by the writing system of the Tibetans who have shared Lamaism as a common religion.

2. Background on Quadrasyllabic Idiomatic Expressions (QIEs) of Chinese origin

Idioms have (a) relatively stable and unusual parallel phonological, syntactic and/or semantic patterns, (b) semantic sophistication (metonymy, hyponymy, locus classicus, etc.), requiring background knowledge and draws on (c) metalinguistic ability to differentiate between metaphorical literate versus literal meanings and projected positive or negative sentiments, as in the above English example of "neither fish or fowl" and 不三不四 [not-3-not-4] "improper", or logical deduction, such as "(as) poor as a church mouse" in English[3]. While similar structures are found in different idiomatic expressions, one unusual type of idiomatic expressions with origins in Sinosphere stands out from the others and they have pervasive presence in the region.

It would be rewarding to systematically explore: (a) The extent of spread of such similar idiomatic expressions in the region; (b) The sociolinguistic and historical status and extent of Chinese as a "High" or "Supreme" status language (Tsou and You 2007) in the relevant language communities, including the significance of the logographic writing systems or its absence; and (c) The degree of structural compatibility between the relevant regional languages and Chinese, and how it might influence horizontal transfer. There is considerable value to examining their emergence, alteration, innovation, or selection in the context of cultural equilibrium or punctuated equilibrium (Aikhenvald and Dixon 2001) and in terms of a hierarchy of borrowable elements (Curnow 2001) to shed light on the development and expansion of Sinosphere. More details on the structure of this type of Chinese idiomatic expressions are given below.

Even though the Chinese language has the tendency to be monosyllabic and its writing system morpho-syllabic, a large portion of its words consist of disyllables which can be aggregated as longer linguistic expressions.

The following table provides a comparison of very likely equivalent English and Chinese idiomatic expressions:

1. I'm all ears	洗耳恭聽 [wash-ear-polite-listen]
2. Strike while the iron is hot	打鐵趁熱 [strike-iron-during-heat]
3. Take the rough with the smooth	逆來順受 [negative-come-positive-take]
4. Walls have ears	隔牆有耳 [through-wall-have-ears]
5. Advice most needed is least heeded	忠言逆耳 [honest-words-negative to-ears]
6. After a storm comes a calm	否極泰來 [negative-extreme-calm-come]
7. An eye for an eye	以眼還眼 [take-eye-respond-eye]
8. Birds of a feather flock together	物以類聚 [thing-take-class-gather]

[3] This is because in puritanical times, churches would have been good examples of frugality and so there would not have been much leftover for the resident mice there.

9. Blood is thicker than water	血濃於水 [blood-thick(er)-than-water]
10. Do in Rome as the Romans do	入鄉隨俗 [enter-village-follow-custom]
11. Don't cry over spilt milk	覆水難收 [upset-water-hard-recover]
12. A man may dig his grave with his teeth	禍從口出 [calamity-from-mouth-come]

Table 1. Some Equivalent English and Chinese Idiomatic Expressions

It is quite clear from the above comparison that the English expressions are of uneven length but Chinese are quadrasyllabic (and quadra-logographic) expressions of even length.

The use of QIE in Chinese is pervasive in many domains of discourse and language use. For examples:

(13) *Greetings*: 好久不見 [very-long-no-see] "long time no see", 不見不散 [no-see-no-disperse] "wait until we meet"
(14) *Slogans*: 安全第一 [safe-whole-number one] "safety is top priority", 酒後勿駛 [drink-after-don't-drive] "don't drive if you drink"
(15) *Movie names*: 窈窕淑女 [slim-fit-gentle-lady] "My Fair Lady", 浩劫重生 [calamity-again-alive] "Cast Away"
(16) *Advertisement* (*Real Estate*): 全海靚裝 [all-sea-beautiful-renovation] "full seaview", 樓皇氣派 [building-emperor-air-atmosphere] "imperial bearing"

Chinese QIEs are relatively distinct linguistic structures, standing out from regular language, comparable to the use in English of Latin or Latinate expressions *Lacuna/ lacunae*; *Caveat emptor*. Specifically, some defining characteristics of QIEs may be summarized as follows:

a) Four syllables or logographs
b) Relatively fixed structure and patterns
c) Figurative meaning and semantic opacity

The quadrasyllabic structure draws on a basic disyllabic propensity in Chinese, reflecting, for example, a common reduplicative tendency in addressing close relatives:

媽 *ma* → 媽媽 *ma-ma* "mother"
爸 *ba* → 爸爸 *ba-ba* "father"
姐 *jie* → 姐姐 *jie-jie* "sister"

The quadrasyllabic propensity is further evidenced by contractions from pentasyllabic expressions, for examples:

(17) 傻人有傻福 → 傻有傻福
[Silly-person-has-silly-blessing] → [silly-has-silly-blessing]
"Innocence is blessing"

(18) 新瓶裝舊酒 → 新瓶舊酒
[New-bottle-contains-old-wine] → [new-bottle-old-wine]
"New wine in old bottle"

(19) 事後諸葛亮 → 事後孔明
[Event-after-Zhu-ge-liang[4]] → [event-after-Kong-ming]
"Wisdom in hindsight"

Quadrasyllabic expressions can result from systematic compression of well-known lines from the classics, as can be seen from examples derived through such compression of verse taken from *The Book of Odes* 詩經 (10th – 7th B.C.):

	A		B	+ C
(20)	夢寐以求 [dream-sleep-to-seek] "desiring in dreams"	←	窈窕淑女，	寤寐求之
(21)	愛莫能助 [love-cannot-able-help] "unable to help"	←	維中人甫舉，	之愛莫助之
(22)	人才濟濟 [person-talent-crowd-crowd] "bountiful talents"	←	濟濟多士，	文王以寧

It can be seen from the above examples that QIEs are pervasive and deeply entrenched within the *Chinese cultural tradition* since historical times.

QIEs contain relatively stable patterns of syntactic, semantic and phonetic parallelism, full or partial syllabic reduplication (i.e. phonetic parallelism) which are universal in language, such as *pera pera* meaning "fluent" in Japanese, and can cover alliteration, rhyming, and onomatopoeia e.g. *hanky-panky* in English, *xilihuala* 稀里啦 "noisy, messy" in Mandarin, *bingling-bamlam* "noisy" in Cantonese. However there can be more complex syntactic and semantic parallelism (e.g. synonymy) as well as antithetical parallelism (Tsou 1968) (e.g. contrasting or antonym pairs as in 天長地久 [sky-long-earth-lasting] "perpetual" or 水火不容 [water-fire-not-contain] "incompatible"). The rich and complex instances of parallelism are quite extensive.

QIE's complex semantic content is usually much greater than the aggregated meaning of the constituent morphemes and disyllabic words. They typically carry deeper connotations than their simple paraphrases, and can involve, if not project, awareness of shared cultural background and familiarity with Classical Chinese, for example: 三顧茅蘆 [three-glance-thatch-cottage], literally meaning "(paying) three visits to the thatched cottage". This QIE conveys an earnest invitation to someone to assume important responsibility, and is based on King Liu Bei's 劉備 three famous attempts to draw his chief strategist Kong Ming 孔明 (3rd Century AD) out of self-imposed isolation, as recorded in the *Chronicles of Three Kingdoms*.

[4] *Zhu-ge-liang* 諸葛亮 and *Kong-ming* 孔明 are names of the same minister whose wisdom is legendary from the *Chronicles of the Three Kingdoms*. In everyday language, quadrasyllabic, pentasyllabic expressions or expressions of other length may be found but the more frequent use of the former, especially in more formal discourse, would signify erudition.

QIEs involve discoursal opacity, which entails metalinguistic ability to differentiate between literal and metaphorical usage, which in turn can draw on logical deduction and can project positive or negative polar sentiments as rhetorical devices. For instance, the QIE 孤男寡女 [lonely-man-single-woman] "unmarried couple" has negative connotations arising from Confucian disdain for interaction among unmarried male and female. It is found among inappropriate sentences composed by secondary school students drawn from the author's previous fieldwork in China: "丈夫死後，他們娘倆孤男寡女，相依為命過著艱難的生活" , literally *"after the death of her husband, the widow and son, being "**lonely man and single woman**", relied on each other and lived a hard life*". In such an example, metalinguistic ability is absent to distinguish between literal and metaphorical meanings as well as the negative connotations, and there are hints of malapropism.

The traditional and extensive native Chinese literature on QIEs has been preoccupied with whether QIEs are words or set phrases, and with the proper classification of such expressions (Liu 1984; Zhou 1994, 1997; Xu 1997) into subcategories. For example:

- *Idioms* 成語, often involving Locus Classicus, e.g. No. (11) 覆水難收 [poured-water-hard to-recall] "irreversible case", which is based on a Han dynasty wife, who had left a poor husband, and who later could not reinstate herself as his wife after he passed the Imperial examination and became a high official. In this QIE, the conclusion of irreversibility could also be logically deduced without Locus Classicus;
- *Common sayings* 熟語, e.g. 不三不四 [not-three-not-four] "improper";
- *Colorful terms* 諺語, e.g. 你死我活 [you-die-I-live] "(fighting) fiercely", 混水摸魚 [muddy-water-catch-fish] "opportunistic"; and
- *Idiomatic riddles* 歇後語, e.g. 和尚打傘 [Buddhist-priest-hold-umbrella] implies 無法無天 [no-*hair (law)* (homophonic)-no-sky]. Here *hair* and *law* are homonyms in Chinese, and *sky*, the symbol of justice in Chinese culture, is blocked by the umbrella, therefore "a lawless society". Here, the first QIE is paired with a second, which is often unexpressed but appreciated after the puns are resolved.

3. QIEs in some East Asian languages

In comparison to tone and monosyllabicity, these QIEs are much more representative of a likely unique linguistic trait of the Chinese language and are much more emblematic of Sinitic civilization. Their use in Chinese has much more significant rhetorical and sociolinguistic status when compared with the parallel use for foreign expressions in English and other European languages. Their judicious use provides an indication of desirable erudition and cultured status of the user and, as maybe expected, they are commonly found in socio-culturally elevated speech registers. Such expressions have been imported and calqued in Japanese, Korean, and Vietnamese, etc (i.e. QIE-prone languages) with which Chinese has had intensive contact. Moreover they are found in great abundance among the non-Sinitic languages of Southwest China, such as the Zhuang-Dong and Loloish and there is overlap with Southern Chinese dialects, especially Cantonese.

Examples given below are taken from other Asian languages, constituting distinctive and often autonomous linguistic expressions, which stand out from the usual language but which are integrated with the full discourse structure, much as the Latin expressions in English, as mentioned earlier.

(23) QIE examples from Japanese:

a) **山紫水明** (さんしすいめい)
b) **人事不省** (じんじふせい)
c) **解衣推食** (かいいすいしょく)
d) **蘭摧玉折** (らんさいぎょくせつ)
e) **広大無辺** (こうだいむへん)
f) **以夷制夷** (いいせいい)
g) **前人未踏** (ぜんじんみとう)
h) **遠慮会釈** (えんりょえしゃく)

(24) QIE examples from Korean:

a) 각골명심 (刻骨铭心)
b) 간담상조 (肝胆相照)
c) 객반위주 (客反为主)
d) 가담항설 (街谈巷说)
e) 거안사위 (居安思危)
f) 견리망의 (见利忘义)
g) 거안제미 (举案齐眉)
h) 격물치지 (格物致知)

(25) QIE examples from Vietnamese

a) đồng bệnh tương lân (同病相憐)
b) ngư ông đắc lợi (漁翁得利)
c) tụ tinh hội thần (聚精會神)
d) thủy trung lao nguyệt (水中撈月)
e) hữu danh vô thực (有名無實)
f) phu xướng phụ tùy (夫唱婦隨)
g) nhập gia tùy tục (入家隨俗)
h) Đả thảo kinh xà (打草驚蛇)

(26) QIE examples from Zhuang

a) Dem gyaeuj dem rieng (添枝加葉)
b) Dub gu fong rek (挖肉補瘡)
c) Duh caeg sim diuq (做賊心虛)
d) Bae naj yawj laeng (瞻前顧後)
e) Nyaeb sip haeuj rwz (自討苦吃)
f) Sam sim song hoz (三心兩意)
g) Langh bit roengz raemx (正中下懷)
h) Ep meuz gwn meiq (強人所難)

(27) QIE examples from Cantonese

a) 九牛一毛 [9-ox-1-hair] "a drop in the ocean"
b) 人山人海 [people-mountain-people-sea] "a large crowd"
c) 人頭豬腦 [human-head-pig-brain] "a stupid person"
d) 九唔搭八 [9-not-match-8] "completely nonsensical"
e) 朝行晚拆 [morning-set-night-demount] "industrious"
f) 秤不離舵 [libra-not-leave-rudder] "inseparable"
g) 逆來順受 [negative-come-positive-take] "take the rough with the smooth"

It can be seen from the above examples that these languages are part of the logographic cultural circle in Sinosphere with varying degrees of overlapping cultural traits, and with the presence of QIEs.

According to Shibatani (1990), about 60% of entries in a modern Japanese dictionary are estimated to be Sino-Japanese. QIEs (yojijukugo 四字熟語) are also an integral part of Sino-Japanese, reflecting a millennium of contact since the adaptation of the Chinese logographic writing system. They are part of the syllabus for the national language Kokugo 国語 and even for high school and university entrance exams as well as civil-service exams. Interestingly, as early as 1007, Minamoto Tamenori had already compiled a book of idioms *Sezoku Genbun* 世俗諺文 for Japanese students. Korean and Vietnamese also have many QIEs of Chinese origin, which are called 사자성어 四字成語 and thành ngữ Hán 成語漢 respectively.

It is not surprising that Japanese, Korean, and Vietnamese speakers would encounter significant challenge to comprehend Chinese QIEs because of typological differences from their own languages, e.g. opposite order of [Object + Verb] and [Attribute + Head] Therefore the common adaptation of QIEs in Japanese and Korean present an unusual opportunity to study how and, more importantly, why typologically different languages might overcome such severe linguistic barriers. Given such linguistic handicap, there is a need to consider the sociolinguistic history and nature of language contact China has had with Japan and Korea.

Structural accommodation is necessary in the indigenization of some Chinese QIEs in Japanese, Korean and Vietnamese and their calques. We could note below 3 kinds of processes: (a) Manipulation of word order: Japanese and Korean are SOV languages. Some QIEs with SVO order have become SOV in Japanese and Korean: e.g. Chinese 不省人事 [not-recognize-people-matter] "fully unconscious" (VO) becomes 人事不省 [people-matter-not-recognize] (OV) in Japanese. Also Chinese 露出馬腳 [expose-out-horse-leg] "betray oneself" (VO) becomes □□□□ (馬腳露出) [horse-leg- expose-out] (OV) in Korean; (b) Paraphrase: 俟河之清 [wait- Yellow river-attrib-clarity] "wait for something that never happens" in Minamoto's 1009 book appears now in contemporary Japanese only after syntactic accommodation (reversal): 河清を俟つ [river-clarity+acc. marker+wait]. Vietnamese has [HEAD+ATT.] whereas Chinese has the reverse order. Chinese QIE 井底之蛙 [well-bottom-attrib-frog] "a person with limited vision" [ATT.+HEAD] has two manifestations in Vietnamese: (i) tỉnh ñế chi oa (井底之蛙) (original Chinese), but also (ii) ếch ngồi ñáy giếng (蛙坐底井) [frog-sit-bottom-well] "indigenized"; and (c) Innovation: Original extensions of QIEs are found in Japanese, Korean, Vietnamese languages: e.g. ichigoichie 一期一会 [one-cycle-one- meeting] "an encounter with someone only occurs once in life" (Japanese), 문전옥답 (門前沃畓) [gate-front-abundant-field] "well-off family" (Korean), or tình nhập lý (入情入理) [enter-feeling-enter-logic] "reasonable" (Vietnamese). These examples suggest a hypothesis that *structural incompatibility may be accommodated in purposeful indigenization by restructuring.

On the other hand, there is relatively low adoption of QIEs among typologically similar, if not genetically related, Mongolian (e.g. Tanaka 2005), Manchu and Uyghur, which shows great contrast with QIE-prone Japanese and Korean and invites explanation. It is noteworthy that these QIE-resistant languages had made short-lived attempts to develop different writing systems, ranging from the Tibetan inspired Mongolian 'Phags-pa' script (Coblin 2006) and Uyghur inspired Jurchen Script (Kane 2009), which showed Chinese influence mostly by being written vertically down and from right to left, with essentially mono-syllabic symbols. The reasons for the demise of these scripts deserve extensive studies in the context of this project.

Furthermore, in the south and as noted, there are many QIE-prone non-Sinitic languages which have not seriously adopted Chinese logographic writing system, or any sustained writing tradition (e.g. Li in Hainan, Bai in Yunnan and Zhuang in Guangxi). We note that QIE-prone Zhuang and related languages have internal rhyme and show evidence of related rhyming metathesis which bear interesting comparison with Cantonese lexical metathesis not found in northern dialects. This complex and unusual feature allows us to consider whether QIEs may not be a readily borrowed feature but could be a possible shared genetic linguistic feature between Cantonese-Yue and Zhuang, which will need to be fully examined and tested. Spoken Cantonese lexicon contains many native QIEs, in addition to those shared with Mandarin. Of special interest would be constituent switching or lexical metathesis found in Cantonese QIEs.

(28) A1 A2+ B1 B2 => A1 B1+ A2 B2
揀擇飲食[choose-select-eat-drink] =>
揀飲擇食[choose-eat-select-drink]
"picky on food"

(29) A1 A2+ B1 B2 => A1 B2+ B1 A2
朝拆晚行 [a.m.-dissemble-p.m.-assemble] =>
朝行晚拆 [a.m.-assemble-p.m.-dissemble]
"for convenience"

(30) A1 A2 => A1 + XY + A2
事實 [fact] =>
事不離實 [matter-NOT-LEAVE-substance]
"factually speaking"

In No. (28), near-synonyms or hyponyms (*drink*, *eat*) have been juxtaposed and a play on the normal Cantonese phrase 揀食 [choosy-food] "picky on food" by switching to the unusual 揀飲 [choosy-drink] "picky on drink". No. (29) shows the interesting result of clear metathesis, which would be illogical to the discerning hearer because in cramped living quarters (as in Hong Kong), a collapsible bed should be dissembled in the morning and reassembled at night (and not the reverse order indicated by the surface structure). In No. (30), a disyllabic word 事實 [matter-substance] "truth" has been paraphrased quadrasyllabically with infixing morphemes 事不離實 [**matter**-not-leave-**substance**] thereby leading to the semi-productive creation of a new QIE. It is also an analogic derivation from a traditional Cantonese rhyming paired QIEs drawing on the similie: 公不離婆 [husband-not-leave-wife] (**like**) 秤不離砣 [scale-not-leave-weight] "the husband and wife being together like the scale and its weight" i.e. "showing a close and intimate relationship" where 婆 (po) and 砣 (to) are rhymes.

4. The internal structure of QIEs

Chafe (1968) draws on the famous example of English idiom: ***kick the bucket*** and shows that it shares the same part of speech as its idiomatic counterpart '***to die***'. Thus the sentence "the bucket was kicked by him" can only have the literal meaning but not the metaphorical meaning of dying because 'to die' is intransitive just as *waterloo* would be a mother noun like its literal counterpart *defeat*. Similarly, Chinese QIE can also assume different parts of speech accordingly. For examples,

(31) as noun:

你們都是+ABCD
[you-are-all-ABCD] (ABCD = 烏合之眾 [dirty-group's-gang] "motley crew")

就像+ABCD+一様
[just-like-ABCD] (ABCD = 井底之蛙 [well-bottom's-frog] "frog under the well")

(32) as adjective:

V 得+ABCD
[V-until-ABCD] (ABCD = 落花流水 [fall-flower-flow-water] "like fallen flowers")

這麼+ABCD
[so-ABCD] (ABCD = 粗心大意 [thick-heart-big-meaning] "careless")

(33) as verb:

一定+ABCD
[definitely-ABCD] (ABCD = 盡力而為 [all-effort-to-do] "with all (his) might")

你應該+ABCD
[you-should-ABCD] (ABCD = 再接再厲 [re-take-re-sharpen] "continue on and on")

They are finite possibilities for the internal morphological and syntactic structures of QIE.

(34)
a) ABCD = ABC+D / AB+CD = NP
b) ABCD = A+B+CD / AB+C+D = SV
c) ABCD = AB+CD = VP sequence
d) ABCD = AB+CD = coordination
e) ABCD = AB+CD = subordination

It follows from the above that 3 kinds of linguistic knowledge are evident in QIEs: i.e. (a) *structural parallelism*; (b) *semantic saliency*; (c) *discoursal opacity*.

Table 2 below provides some examples of structural parallelism:

(35)**千 山 萬 水** '1K-mountain-10K-waters'		千-萬、山-水	
(36)不**明**不**白** 'not-bright-not-clear'	不-不	明-白	
(37)**如霜似雪** 'like-frost-like-snow'	如-似	霜-雪	
(38)先**苦**後**甜** 'first-bitter-later-sweet'			先-後、苦-甜
(39)無**拘**無**束** 'no-arrest-no-restrict'	無-無、拘-束		
	Synonymy	Hypernymy	Antonymy

Table 2. Examples of structural parallelism

It can be seen that 如-似 [like-similar] "similar to" and 拘-束 [arrest-restrict] "control" are synonymous and 不-不 [no-no] and 無-無 [without-without], being reduplications, are extreme cases of synonymy. By comparison, 山-水 [mountain-water] share the hypernym "terrestrial objects", 明-白 [bright-clear] "clarify" share the hypernym "cognition", 霜-雪 [frost-snow] share the hypernym "weather". Furthermore, 先-後 [precede-follow] "sequence" and 甜-苦 [bitter-sweet] "life's extremes" are antonymous. It can be seen that the rhetorical devices used involve synonymy, hyponymy and antonymy and are commonly deployed in the projection of discoursal opacity.

More specifically, the relevant internal linguistic features may be further analyzed as in the following:

a. Hypernymy

(40) 三五成群 [3-5-become-crowd] "in small groups"
(41) 三六九等 [3-6-9-etc] "in different groups"
(42) 三教九流 [3-religion-9-branch] "the riff raff"
(43) 三心兩意 [3-heart-2-mind] "undecided"
(44) 張三李四 [Zhang-3-Li-4] "any Tom, Dick or Henry"

b. Classical language usage

(45) 三年五載 [3-year-5-year] "in-a-few-years"
(46) 三思而行 [3-think-then-act] "think before acting"
(47) 三差五錯 [3-error-5-mistake] "any deviation"

c. Culture bound

(48) 三生有幸 [3-incarnation-have-luck] "forever indebted"
(49) 三從四德 [3-obedience-4-virtue] "traditional loyalty (for women)"

d. Locus Classicus
(50) 三過其門 [3-pass-his-door] "devoted to duty" (51) 朝三暮四 [morning-3-evening-4] "indecision" (52) 舉一反三 [propose-1-reply-3] "good logical deduction" (53) 孟母三遷 [Mencius-mother-3-move] "moving to better environment"
e. Synonymy
(54) 三回四次 [3-times-4-occasions] "many times" (55) 說三道四 [say-3-call-4] "mumbling insignificant things"
f. Word Morphology
(56) 三差五錯 [3-error-5-mistake] "any deviation" (差-錯) (57) 三災八難 [3-calamity-8-difficulty] "disaster" (災-難) (58) 三長兩短 [3-long-2-short] "accident" (長-短)
g. Homonymy (phonetic/semantic replication or rhyme)
(59) 三三五五 [3-3-5-5] "in small groups" (cf. 不三不四)
h. Antonymy
(60) 三長兩短 [3-long-2-short] "accident" (61) 朝三暮四 [morning-3-evening-4] "Indecision" (62) 三好兩歉 [3-good terms-2-apologies] "inconsistent relationship"

Table 3. Eight major linguistic features associated with QIE

Table 3 singles out eight special features of QIEs drawn from LIVAC[5]. From more than 30K entries found there, 130 entries, involving the numeral 3, are used as examples:

a) The *hypernymic* relation is by far most commonly drawn on to convey metaphorical meaning. Thus, No. (42) 三教九流 [3-religon-9-branches] signifying too many diversified sects is used to project the image of disorganized 'riff raff'. In No. (44) *Zhang* 張 and *Li* 李, being common manifestations of the hypernym *surname*, alternate with the hypothetical given names: sequential numbers 3 and 4, which belong to the hypernym of *number*.

[5] The LIVAC (Linguistic Variations in Chinese Speech Communities) [http://livac.org] synchronous corpus has been based at the Research Centre on Linguistics and Language Information Sciences of The Hong Kong Institute of Education since 2010. It continuously draws on the analysis of texts from representative Chinese newspapers and electronic media of major Chinese communities in Beijing, Hong Kong, Shanghai, Singapore, Taipei from 1995. By 2012, 450 million characters of texts have been analyzed and 1.5M words have been culled from them in the corpus.

b) *Classical Chinese* knowledge is needed. For examples, No. (45) 三年五載 (MSC), No. (47) 三差五錯 (MSC), where 載 and 差 are semi-bound nouns in Modern Standard Chinese, but free morpheme in Classical Chinese.

c) *Culture bound*. No. (48) 三生有幸 refers to multiple sequential reincarnations and so extended duration of gratitude. No. (49) 三從四德 refers to traditional obedience for women toward her father, her husband, and her son, a reflection of customary culture of loyalty of the past.

d) *Locus Classicus*. In addition to Chinese cultural tradition, some items are drawn from historical events (compared to *Achilles' heel*, *Waterloo* (defeat) etc). In No. (53) 孟母三遷, the mother of the sage Mencius 孟子 moved three times in order to ensure her son kept good company. No. (50) 三過其門 refers to Xiayu 夏禹 who was Minister in charge of flood control and who was so devoted to duty that he did not stop by even when passing by his own home.

e) *Synonymy* – terms with equivalent meaning are used as a way to reinforce the thrust of the semantic content, e.g. 說三道四 [say-3-call-4] "mumbling insignificant things"

f) *Morphological structure* of Modern Standard Chinese where the distinction between free and semi-bound morphemes exists, e.g. 三差五錯, 三災八難 where 差 and 災 are semi-bound morphemes in MSC.

g) *Homophony* - Identity in terms of phonological and semantic content is a simplistic reinforcement of the parallelism in structure.

h) *Antonymy* - Ability to binary opposite distinction (in addition to lateral similarity as in synonymy, and hierarchical similarity (in most cases of hyponymy) is important to complement the linguistic, cultural, and cognitive skills.

The internal morphology of QIE can be represented as a coordinate and parallel structure.

(63)

A   B

1 2 3 4
任 重 道 遠
(duty-heavy) (Road-far)
"important and arduous mission"

The following table provides a breakdown of the different internal grammatical patterns in QIEs.

Types	%
Coordinative	35.0
Attributive	21.5
Subject-predicate	17.5

Verb-object	15.0
Other	11.0
Total	100.0

Table 3. Distribution of structural types

Following the common preference of structural parallelism, some likely and interesting structural variations between underlying and surface forms are noted.

Thus, variations in terms of permutation or metathesis could involve different comparable syntactic units and revisions in argument structure from a base structure, consider:

(64) 養妻活兒 [sustain-wife-alive-child]

"to maintain family"

(65) 養活妻兒 [sustain-alive-wife-child]

The structural ambiguities in (64) and (65) can be structurally represented as (66) and (67) below:

(66) A1 B1 + A2 B2 ⇒

養 妻 活 兒

sustain wife alive son

V N V N

(67) A1 A2 + B1 B2 ⇒

養 活 妻 兒

V Result. N N

In (66), the static verb 活 "alive" has apparently become a causative verb "to cause to be alive" with 兒 "son" as object, in parallel with verb-object 養妻 [sustain-wife] because of structural parallelism, and poetic license, but in actual fact it could be also the simple metathesis between resultative verb 活 "alive" in the disyllabic verb 養活 [feed-alive] "sustain" with the first object 妻 "wife" of the disyllabic compound 妻兒 [wife-son] "family" in the underlying No. (67). Such a case invites the hypothesis that the path of production of the QIE may be different from the path of cognition. Preliminary investigation shows that Southerners like Cantonese quite readily accept categorial shift between *stative verb* and *transitive verb* for 活 "alive, cause to be alive" and so they readily accept No. (66). But Northerners tend to see exceptional poetic license in No. (66), which they would normally not accept.

Another relevant pair of examples can be seen in No. (68) and No. (69).

(68) 魚沉雁落 [fish-sink-duck-down]

"unusual beauty"

(69) 沉魚落雁 [sink-fish-down-duck]

No. (68) and No. (69) refer to the understood exposure to unrivaled beauty which could cause fish to sink (to hide out of shame) and likewise wild geese to descend from flight (to hide). This situation has been rendered more graphic and dynamic with the normally intransitive static verbs 沉

"sink" and 落 "fall" in No. (68) projecting dynamic development as transitive verbs before the objects 魚 "fish" and 雁 "wild geese" as objects respectively in No. (69), where rhetorical if not poetic license has been exercised.

Our preliminary analysis from the above common Chinese QIEs involving numerals indicate that a gradation exists amongst five top cognitive skills associated with the eight features discussed earlier.

(1) Hyponymic relation
(2) Classical language usage
(3) Culture bound
(4) Locus classicus
(5) Similarity relationship (synonym and homonymy)

It would be useful to compare language acquisition among children with language attrition among language handicapped adults, such as those who suffer from Alzheimer's disease in relation to the attributes noted here, especially to see if there are complementary trends between the two situations.

5. Conclusion[6]

The eight linguistic and rhetorical features of QIEs and the indulgence in syntactic ambiguities and rhetorical niceties encouraged by poetic license are related to those often employed in traditional Chinese verse and prosaic discourse. The parallel relationship between similar linguistic elements, and the binary opposition of linguistic elements as well as their manipulation in QIEs are fundamental in Chinese literary traditions, culminating in the famous *Regulated Verse* 律詩 form and in rhetoric discourse, as in *The Literary Mind and Carving of Dragons* 文心雕龍 (5th Century AD). As such, they are an integral part of poetics: It is noted that "The poetic resources concealed in the morphological and syntactic structure of language, briefly the poetry of grammar, and its literary product, the grammar of poetry, have been seldom known to critics and mostly disregarded by linguists but skillfully mastered by creative writers" (Jacobson, 1961). Given the popularity of original and derived QIEs in the region (even for native Chinese speakers), but the immense complexity in structure and consequently the efforts needed to overcome linguistic hurdles by peoples within Sinosphere, a natural question can be readily posed: why should such cognitive handicaps be retained, even after the traditional cultures in Sinosphere have been challenged if not partially replaced by Western ones?

References

Aikhenvald, Alexandra Y. and R. M. W. Dixon (eds.) 2001. *Areal Diffusion and Genetic Inheritance: Problems in Comparative Linguistics*. Oxford: Oxford University Press.
Chafe, Wallace L. 1968. "Idiomaticity as an Anomaly in the Chomskyan Paradigm." *Foundations of Language*, 4, 109-127.
Coblin, W. South. 2006. *A Handbook of 'Phags-pa Chinese*. Honolulu: University of Hawai'i Press.
Curnow, T.J. 2001. "What Language Features Can Be 'Borrowed'? In Aikhenvald and Dixon (eds.), 412-436.

[6] On the basis of the analysis of QIEs, an unprecedented *Chinese QIE Crossword Puzzle Games* 成語填字坊 has been developed and available through The Research Centre of Linguistics and Language Information Sciences of The Hong Kong Institute of Education and other platforms: (1) web: http://www.rclis.ied.edu.hk/crossword/, (2) Android: http://chilin.no-ip.org/android/; (3) iOS: http://chilin.no-ip.org/iphone/.

Everaert, Martin, E.-J. van der Linden, A. Schenk,. and R. Schreuder. (eds.) 1995. *Idioms: Structural and Psychological Perspectives*. Hillsdale, NJ: Erlbaum.
Everaert, Martin, et al. 1989. *Proceedings of the First Tilburg Workshop on Idioms*. Tilburg: ITK.
Everaert, Martin, et al. 1992. *Proceedings of IDIOMS.* Tilburg: ITK.
Fan, Shiyan. 2007. *Colors in Idioms*. MA thesis. Liaoning Normal University.
Fillmore, Charles, Paul Kay and Catherine O'Connor (1988). Regularity and Idiomaticity in Grammatical Constructions: The Case of let alone. *Language* 64: 501–38.
Fontecha, Almudena F. & Rosa M. J. Catalán. 2003. Semantic Derogation in Animal Metaphor: A Contrastive-Cognitive Analysis of Two Male / Female Examples in English and Spanish. *Journal of Pragmatics*, 35, 5: 771-797.
Gibbs, R. 1980. "Spilling the beans on understanding and memory for idioms in conversation." *Memory and Cognition*, 8: 449-456.
Gibbs, R. 1985. "On the process of understanding idioms." *Journal of Psycholinguistic Research*, 14; 465-472.
Gibbs, R. 1987. "Linguistic factors in children's understanding of idioms." *Journal of Child Language*, 14: 569-586.
Goldberg, A. & Suttle, L. (2010). *Construction Grammar*. Wiley.
Jackendoff, R. 1995. *Semantics and Cognition*. Cambridge, MA: MIT Press.
Jakobson, R. 1961. Closing Statement: Linguistics and Poetics. In Sebeok (ed), *Style in Language*. Cambridge: Mass., The M. J. T. Press.
Jakobson, R. 1981. *Selected Writings, Volume III: Poetry of Grammar and Grammar of Poetry*. The Hague: Mouton, 18-51.
Jakobson, R. 1990. "Two Aspects of Language and Two Types of Disturbances." In Linda Waugh and Monique Monville-Burston. *On Language.* Cambridge, MA: Harvard University Press.
Kane, Daniel. 2009. *The Kitan Language and Script.* Leiden; Boston: Brill.
Katz, Jerrold J. and Paul M. Postal. 1963. "Semantic Interpretation of Idioms and Sentences Containing Them." M.I.T. R.L.E., *Quarterly Progress Report*, 70, 275-82.
Lakoff, G. 1987. *Women, Fire and Dangerous Things: What Categories Reveal about the Mind.* Chicago: Chicago University Press.
Langacker, Ronald (1987, 1991). *Foundations of Cognitive Grammar.* 2 vols. Stanford: Stanford University Press
Liu, Shuxin. 1984. "Fixed Expressions and Its Classification." *Yuyan Yanjiu Luncong*, 2.
Matisoff, James A. (1990). On Megalocomparison. *Language* 66.1, p. 113.
Mo, Pengling. 2001. *Chinese Idioms and Chinese Culture.* Nanjing: Jiangsu Jiaoyu Chubanshe.
Nall, Timothy M. 2008. *Analysis of Chinese Four-character Idioms Containing Numbers: Structural Patterns and Cultural Significance*. Unpublished PhD thesis. Ball State University.
Nippold, M.A. & S.T. Martin. 1989. "Idiom interpretation in isolation versus context: A developmental study with adolescents." *Journal of Speech and Hearing Research*, 32: 59-66.
Shibatani, Masayoshi. 1990. *The Languages of Japan*. Cambridge: Cambridge University Press.
Tang, Chihsia. 2007. "A Comparative Study of English and Chinese Idioms with Food Names." *UST Working Papers in Linguistics*, 3: 83-93.
Tsou, B.K. 1968. Some Aspects of Linguistic Parallelism and Chinese Versification. In Charles E.Gribble (ed.) *Studies Presented to Professor Roman Jakobson By His Students*. Cambridge, Mass:Slavica Publishers.
Tsou, B.K., T. Lee, H. Cheung, and P. Tung. 2006. *HKCOLAS: Hong Kong Cantonese Oral Language Assessment Scale*. Hong Kong: Language Information Sciences Research Center, City University of Hong Kong and Department of Health, HKSAR.
Tsou, B.K. and R.J. You. 2007. *A Course in Sociolinguistics*. Taipei: Wunan.

Xiang, Guangzhong. 1979. "Idioms and Ethnic and Cultural Tradition." *Zhongguo Yuwen*, 2.
Xu, Yaomin 1997. "Definitions and Classification of Idioms." *Zhongguo Yuwen*, 1.
Zhang, Zonghua 1984. "Semantics of Idioms." *Cichu Yanjiu*, 4.
Zhou, Jian 1994. "Typicality and Atypicality of Idioms." *Yuwen Yanjiu*, 3.
Zhou, Jian 1997. "On Typicality of Idioms." *Nankai Journal*, 2.
Zuo, Zhijun 2006. *Acquisition of Chinese Idioms: From the Perspective of Cognition.* MA thesis. Ocean University of China.

Things between Lexicon and Grammar
(Extended Abstract)

Yuji Matsumoto
Graduate School of Information Science
Nara Institute of Science and Technology (NAIST)
matsu@is.naist.jp

A number of grammar formalisms were proposed in 80's, such as Lexical Functional Grammars, Generalized Phrase Structure Grammars, and Tree Adjoining Grammars. Those formalisms then started to put a stress on lexicon, and were called as lexicalist (or lexicalized) grammars. Representative examples of lexicalist grammars were Head-driven Phrase Structure Grammars (HPSG) and Lexicalized Tree Adjoining Grammars (LTAG). While grammars and lexicons were two major linguistic resources of syntactic processing of natural languages, lexicons began to play an important role in language processing.

Things have changed from early 90's, when large scale language resources became available and corpus-based research started to dominate almost all aspects of natural language processing (NLP). Part-of-speech taggers and syntactic parsers are the most well-studied topics in corpus-based research. Various parsers, based either on phrase structure grammars or on dependency structures, have been developed, applying various machine learning techniques on syntactically annotated corpora. State-of-the-art parsers developed in this way have achieved very good performance. Those trends are also beneficial to lexicalist grammars since parsing with those grammar formalisms is amenable to phrase structure-based parsing through abstraction of grammatical schemata or a derivation process with those grammar formalism (i.e., a derivation tree) can be considered to correspond to a word dependency tree.

Recent trends in NLP have started to target diversely spread areas that require semantic and pragmatic information. Some areas like social media analysis, such as twitter or blog text analysis, have a more preference to getting semantic or sentiment information than syntactic information. Though this trend is attracting people's attention and is getting growing importance, still syntactic analysis keeps to play an important role. Simple extension of annotated corpora and lexical statistics will not be able to skyrocket parsers' performance. Improvement of parsing accuracy especially that of long sentences requires to tackle problems that are not on the current main stream of parser development.

In this talk, I will take up three issues that lie between grammars and lexicons: Coordination structures, multiword expressions and complex sentence patterns. I will first give a brief overview of syntactic processing in past two/three decades, then will talk about the issues one by one especially about our experiences related with them. Finally, I will consider future directions of sentence analysis taking those into account.

Coordination Structures

Coordination Structures are well-known and notorious phenomena observed in all languages, and especially in long sentences. Not only pairs of phrases of the same category but also pairs of any sequences or words that are *similar* in some sense can be coordinated. No grammar formalisms, except for Categorial Grammars, can give a comprehensive account and appropriate representation for coordination structures.

There is a proposal to use dynamic programming matching to find coordination structures as they tend to consist of similar sequences of words or phrases. One problem, however, is: When they are coordinated, some constructions such as noun phrases or sequences of complements for a predicates usually have similar structures, other constructions such as verb phrases or compound sentences may have very different structures. Another problem is: A coordination structure may be embedded in another coordination structure while they cannot overlap each other.

I will give our experiences to handle embedded coordination structures and our experiments to see how coordination structure information helps improve parsing accuracy. Through those, I will talk about our findings.

Multiword Expressions

Multiword expressions (MWEs) are those consisting of multiple words that have non-compositional and/or idiosyncratic interpretations. Some of them, which appear in fixed forms, should be registered in a dictionary. However, there are other types of MWEs that have syntactic flexibilities. There are a series of workshops devoted to MWEs (`http://multiword.sourceforge.net/`).

Although construction of MWE lexicons and MWE annotated corpora is done in some languages such as French and Swedish, no large scale English MWE lexicon and MWE annotated corpus have been developed. Some of the MWEs have non-standard POS patterns and behave unpredictably from the constituent words, many of them should be registered in dictionaries for language processing.

I will give an overview of language analysis research with MWEs, and will give our current attempt to construct an English MWE dictionary and its application to Part-of-speech tagging.

Complex Sentence Patterns

Simple sentences in a language have a rather uniform construction. However, there are a variety of structures in complex sentences in any language. Subordinate structures and embedded clauses are typical structures of complex sentences, and those structures could be produced in a recursive manner, making an analysis of such structures very difficult. There are also some complex sentence patterns that are difficult to define in existing grammar formalisms. Such complex sentences are also very difficult to parse in existing parsing algorithms since they usually parse a sentence in a bottom-up manner assuming some type of locality.

I will talk about our recent experiments to find subordinate and embedded clause patterns in an auto-parsed English corpus. Although there are a huge number of complex sentence patterns, once they are attempted to merge into a smaller number of patterns by ignoring redundant phrases and punctuations we found that a small number of complex sentence patterns can have a very wide coverage of whole complex sentences. I will introduce the results of our experiments and will discuss further possibilities of extracting wider types of complex sentence patterns.

Considerations and Conclusions

The issues in sentence analysis discussed in this article are the remaining "things" we need to tackle between standard grammars and lexicons. The main difficulty related with these issues is that they are intermingling phenomena with the standard syntactic analysis. Knowing coordination structures, multiword expressions and complex sentence patters in advance in a given sentence is definitely useful to sentence parsing, while identifying those structures requires some syntactic analysis.

A natural conclusion is joint analysis of syntactic parsing and those specific constructions. There have been a number of proposals for joint processing of different levels of language processing, such as joint POS tagging and phrase/NE chunking, joint POS tagging and parsing, joint syntactic and semantic parsing, and so on. It is important and valuable to seek for methods of joint processing of syntax and the constructions taken up in this article.

Another important topic is how to acquire and represent the knowledge or expressions in a comprehensible and reusable format since those phenomena should be analyzed not only an independent manner but also in an integrated module in other language processing systems and tools. The know-how of extraction, construction and representation of those resources should be transferable over languages.

Acknowledgments

I would like to express my sincere appreciation to the staff and students in our laboratory for their cooperation and valuable discussions.

Social Media: Friend or Foe of Natural Language Processing?

Timothy Baldwin
The University of Melbourne, VIC 3010, Australia
tb@ldwin.net

Abstract

In this talk, I will outline some of the myriad of challenges and opportunities that social media offer for natural language processing. I will present analysis of how pre-processing can be used to make social media data more amenable to natural language processing, and review a selection of tasks which attempt to harness the considerable potential of different social media services.

There is no question that social media are fantastically popular and varied in form — ranging from user forums, to microblogs such as Twitter, to social networking sites such as Facebook — and that much of the content they host is in the form of natural language. This would suggest a myriad of opportunities for natural language processing (NLP), and yet much of the applied research on social media which uses language data is based on superficial analysis, often in the form of simple keyword search. This begs the question: Are NLP methods not suited to social media analysis? Conversely, is social media data too challenging for modern-day NLP? Alternatively, are simple term search-based methods sufficient for social media analysis, i.e. is NLP *overkill* for social media? In exploring these questions, I attempt to answer the overarching question of whether social media data is the friend or foe of NLP.

I approach the question first from the perspective of what challenges social media language poses for NLP. The most immediate answer is the infamously free-form nature of language in social media, encompassing spelling inconsistencies, the free-form adoption of new terms, and regular violations of English grammar norms. Unsurprisingly, when NLP tools are applied directly to social media data, the results tend to be miserable when compared to data sets such as the Wall Street Journal component of the Penn Treebank. However, there have been recent successes in adapting parsers and POS taggers to social media data (Foster et al., 2011; Gimpel et al., 2011). Additionally, lexical normalisation and other preprocessing strategies have been shown to enhance the performance of NLP tools over social media data (Lui and Baldwin, 2012; Han et al., to appear). Furthermore, social media posts tend to be short and the content highly varied, meaning it is difficult to adapt a tool to the domain, or harness textual context to disambiguate the content. There is also the engineering challenge of real-time processing of the text stream, as much of NLP research is carried out offline with only secondary concern for throughput. As such, we might conclude that social media data is a foe of NLP, in that it challenges traditional assumptions made in NLP research on the nature of the target text and the requirements for real-time responsiveness.

However, if we look beyond the immediate text content of social media, we quickly realise that there are various non-textual data sources that can be used to enhance the robustness and accuracy of NLP models, in a way which is not possible with static text corpora. For example, simple information on the author of a post can be used to develop author-adapted models based on the previous posts of the same individual (at least for users who post sufficiently large volumes of data). Links in the post can be used to disambiguate the textual content of the post, whether in the form of URLs and the content contained in the target document(s), hashtags and the content of other similarly-tagged posts, threading structure in web user forums, or addressee information and the content of posts from that individual. Simple timestamp information may provide insights into what timezone the user is likely to be based in, allowing for adjustment of language priors for use in language identification. User-declared metadata may also provide valuable information on the probable interpretation of a given post, e.g. knowing that a person is from Australia may allow for adjustment of lexical or word–POS priors. Multimodal content such as images or videos included in the post may also provide valuable insights into the likely interpretation for particular words. Social network information may also allow for user-specific adjustment of language priors of various types. In this sense, the rich context that permeates social media can very much be the friend of NLP, in providing valuable assistance in disambiguating content.

Turning to the question of why the majority of social media analysis makes use of simple language analysis such as word counts for a canned set of query terms, I suggest that the cause is largely because of the constraints imposed on the user by different social media APIs, and also the relative accessibility of such simple techniques, as compared to full-strength NLP. I go on to claim that "the tail has been wagging the dog" in social media research, in the sense that while impressive results have been achieved for particular application types, the choice of application has been constrained by what is achievable with relatively simple keyword analysis. For example, searching for keywords relating to earthquakes or influenza allows for impressive results to be achieved in earthquake detection or influenza outbreak analysis (Sakaki et al., 2010; Ritterman et al., 2009). However, this style of approach presupposes a highly-constrained, predetermined information need which is expressible in a small number of relatively unambiguous query terms. In applications such as trend analysis, the information need is more open-ended and it is unreasonable to expect that a static set of keywords will capture new trends. Even for highly-constrained information needs, there may not be a high-precision set of query terms which provide the necessary information. While it is certainly not the case that full-blown NLP is needed in all social media applications, it is equally not correct to say that NLP is overkill for all social media analysis. Rather, the emergence of more mature, robust NLP technologies tailored to social media data will enable new opportunities for social media analysis, earning new friends for NLP in the process.

References

Jennifer Foster, Ozlem Cetinoglu, Joachim Wagner, Joseph Le Roux, Joakim Nivre, Deirdre Hogan, and Josef van Genabith. 2011. From news to comment: Resources and benchmarks for parsing the language of web 2.0. In *Proc. of the 5th International Joint Conference on Natural Language Processing (IJCNLP 2011)*, pages 893–901, Chiang Mai, Thailand.

Kevin Gimpel, Nathan Schneider, Brendan O'Connor, Dipanjan Das, Daniel Mills, Jacob Eisenstein, Michael Heilman, Dani Yogatama, Jeffrey Flanigan, and Noah A. Smith. 2011. Part-of-speech tagging for Twitter: Annotation, features, and experiments. In *Proc. of the 49th Annual Meeting of the Association for Computational Linguistics: Human Language Technologies (ACL HLT 2011)*, pages 42–47, Portland, USA.

Bo Han, Paul Cook, and Timothy Baldwin. to appear. Automatically constructing a normalisation dictionary for microblogs. *ACM Transactions on Intelligent Systems and Technology*.

Marco Lui and Timothy Baldwin. 2012. langid.py: An off-the-shelf language identification tool. In *Proc. of the 50th Annual Meeting of the Association for Computational Linguistics (ACL 2012) Demo Session*, pages 25–30, Jeju, Republic of Korea.

Joshua Ritterman, Miles Osborne, and Ewan Klein. 2009. Using prediction markets and Twitter to predict a swine flu pandemic. In *Proceedings of the 1st International Workshop on Mining Social Media*, November.

Takeshi Sakaki, Makoto Okazaki, and Yutaka Matsuo. 2010. Earthquake shakes Twitter users: real-time event detection by social sensors. In *Proc. of the 19th International Conference on the World Wide Web (WWW 2010)*, pages 851–860, Raleigh, USA.

Towards a Semantic Annotation of English Television News - Building and Evaluating a Constraint Grammar FrameNet

Eckhard Bick

Institute of Language and Communication, University of Southern Denmark
Campusvej 55, DK 5230 Odense M
eckhard.bick@mail.dk

Abstract

This paper presents work on the semantic annotation of a multimodal corpus of English television news. The annotation is performed on the second-by-second-aligned transcript layer, adding verb frame categories and semantic roles on top of a morphosyntactic analysis with full dependency information. We use a rule-based method, where Constraint Grammar mapping rules are automatically generated from a syntactically anchored Framenet with about 500 frame types and 50 semantic role types. We discuss design decisions concerning the Framenet, and evaluate the coverage and performance of the pilot system on authentic news data.

1 Introduction and methodological focus

Because the communicative information contained in a multi-modal corpus is distributed across different channels, it is much more difficult to process automatically than a classical text corpus. Large multi-modal corpora, in particular, constitute a challenge to quantitative-statistical exploration or even comparative qualitative studies, because they may be too big for complete inspection, let alone extensive manual mark-up. In some types of multi-modal corpora, however, such as a film-subtitle corpus, or the television news corpus that is the object of this study, aligned transcripts or captions offer at least a partial solution, because this textual layer can be used to search the corpus and extract matching sections for closer inspection, comparison or even quantitative analysis.

The UCLA Communications Studies Archive (UCLA CSA) is a so-called monitor corpus of television news, where newscasts from a large number of channels are recorded daily in high-quality video mode, amounting to ~ 150.000 hours of recorded news, and growing by 100 programs a day (DeLiema, Steen & Turner 2012). To date only English language channels have been targeted, but the author's institution has plans to join the project with matching data for first the Scandinavian languages and German, then further European languages. This paper focuses on the linguistic annotation of the time-stamp-aligned textual layer of the corpus. Optimally, such annotation should address the following issues

- robustness in the face of spoken language data
- low error rate for basic morphosyntactic annotation
- conservation/integration of non-linguistic meta-annotation (speaker, source, time ...)
- unified tag system across languages to facilitate comparative studies
- a semantic annotation layer to support higher-level communicative studies

A well-established annotation format is the assignment of feature-attribute pairs to word tokens, expressed as tag fields and convertible to xml structures. A list of tokens with tags guarantees that all information is local and easy to filter or search, with meta-information carried along on separate lines between tokens. For the tagging/parsing task as such we have chosen the Constraint Grammar (CG) formalism (Karlsson et al. 1995, Bick 2000) which has proven robust enough for a large variety of corpus annotation task, including speech annotation (Bick 2012). An added advantage is the fact that comparable CG systems, with similar tag sets and annotation conventions, already exist not only for English, but also for many other European languages, among them almost all Germanic and Romance languages (http://visl.sdu.dk/constraint_grammar.html). CG systems are modular, hierarchical sets of rule-based grammars targeting different linguistic levels, and while higher level analysis can be performed within the same formalism, it is a challenging task. Thus, most of the existing CG systems perform only morphosyntactic and dependency annotation, with some notable exceptions in the area of NER and semantic role annotation. The system that comes closest to the task at hand, is the Danish DanGram system which implements a framenet-based verbal classification and semantic role annotation (Bick 2011), with a category inventory of ~500 verb frames and ~50 semantic roles. For our present task, we have attempted to port lexical material from this system, and adopted its verb classification scheme, which in turn was inspired by the VerbNet classes proposed by Kipper et al. (2006), ultimately with roots in (Levine 1993), and a smaller and thus more tractable granularity than PropBank (Palmer et al. 2005). Our semantic role inventory, following the one implemented for Portuguese by (Bick 2007), is also much smaller than PropBank's, the rationale being that medium-sized category sets allow for a reasonable level of abstraction compared to the underlying lexical items, and by roughly matching the granularity of other linguistic abstractions (syntactic function inventory, PoS/morphological categories) are well suited to be integrated with the latter in automatic disambuguation systems.

2 Frame role distinctors: valency, syntactic function and semantic classes

In this vein, the distinctional backbone of our frame inventory are syntactic valency frames like <vt> (monotransitive), <vdt> (ditransitive), <to^vp-forward> (prepositional transitive with the preposition "to" and a verb-incorporated 'forward'-adverb). Each of these valency frames is assigned at least one (or more[1]) verb senses, each with its own semantic frame. Depending, for instance, on the number of obligatory arguments, several valency or semantic frames may share the same verb sense, but two different verb senses will almost always differ in at least one syntactic or semantic aspect of their argument frame - guaranteeing that all senses can in principle be disambiguated exploiting a parser's argument tags and dependency links.

Currently, the EngGram FrameNet (EFN) contains 7820 verb sense for 4774 verb types, with 10.800 valency frames. For each frame, we provide a list of arguments with the following information:

1. Thematic role (Table 1)
2. Syntactic function (Table 2)
3. Morphosyntactic form (Table 4)
4. for np's, a list of typical semantic prototypes to fill the slot (Table 3)
5. An English language gloss / skeleton sentence

For about 2/3 of the frames, a best-guess link to a BFN verb sense is also provided, based on semi-automatic valency matches on EngGram-parsed BFN example sentences.

Our FrameNet uses ca. 35 core thematic roles (or case/semantic roles, Fillmore 1968), with a further 10-15 adverbial roles that are added by the semantic tagger based on syntactic context without the need of a verb frame entry (e.g. subclause function based on conjunction type). These roles are far from evenly distributed in running text. Table 1 provides some live corpus data, showing that the top 5 roles account for over half of all role taggings in running text. Note that the distribution is for all roles, not just verb frame roles, since the semantic tagger also tags some semantic relations based on nominal or adjectival valency *(e.g. abolition of X, full of Y).*

Table 1: Top 25 Semantic (Thematic) Roles

	Thematic Role	**in corpus**
§TH	Theme	21.91%
§ATR	Attribute	13.76%
§AG	Agent	7.07%
§LOC	Location	6.78%
§LOC-TMP	Point in time	5.44%
§PAT	Patient	4.20%
§DES	Destination/Goal	3.56%
§MES	Message	3.13%

[1]In 717 cases, there is more than one role combination for the same sense with the same valency, and in 11.2% multiple verb senses share the same valency frame, reflecting cases where semantic prototype or other slot filler information is needed to make the distinction.

§COG	Cognizer	3.00%
§SP	Speaker	2.58%
§BEN	Beneficiary	2.48%
§ID	Identity	2.16%
§TP	Topic	1.97%
§ACT	Action	1.91%
§INC	Incorporated particle	1.91%
§EXP	Experiencer	1.73%
§RES	Result	1.49%
§STI	Stimulus	1.37%
§FIN	Purpose	1.31%
§EV	Event	1.56%
§CAU	Cause	0.98%
§ORI	Origin	0.97%
§REC	Recipient	0.80%
§EXT-TMP	Duration	0.74%
§INS	Instrument/Tool	0.62%

Other roles: §COND condition, §COM co-agent, §HOL whole, §VOC vocative, §COMP comparison, §SOA state of affairs, §MNR manner, §PART part, §VAL value, §ASS asset, §EXT extension, §PATH path, §DON donor, §CONT contents, §CONC concession, §REFL reflexive, §POSS possessor, §EFF effect, §ROLE role, §MAT material, §ROLE role, §DES-TMP temp. destination, §ORI-TMP temp. origin

Even in a case-poor language like English, we found some clear likelihood relations between thematic roles and syntactic functions (table 2). Thus, agents (§AG, §COG, §SP) are typical subject roles, while patients (§PAT), messages (§MES) and results (§RES) are typical direct object roles, and recipients (§REC) and beneficiaries (§BEN) call for dative object function.

Table 2: Major syntactic Functions with most likely roles

	Function
@SUBJ	Subject
TH (44.5%) > AG (21.3%) > COG (9.6%) > SP (8.1%) > EXP (5.2%)	
@ACC	Direct object
TH (26.9%) > PAT (11.6%) > MES > RES > STI > ACT	
@DAT	Dative object
BEN (52.8%) > REC (41.9%)	
@PIV, @SA, @OA,@ADVL	Prepositional complements
LOC (30.1%), DES (11.9%) > PAT (10.0%) > BEN > TP > ORI > ATR > COM > COMP	
@SC	Subject complem.
ATR (95.7%) > RES	
@OC	Object complem.
ATR (80.7%) > RES	

The prototypical verb frame consists of a full verb and its nominal, adverbial or subclause complements. Like most other languages, however, English has also verb incorporations that are not, in the semantical sense, complements. The simplest kind are adverb incorporates, which we mark in the valency frame, but not in the argument list:

give up - <vi-up>, turn off - <vt-off>

More complicated are support verb constructions, where the semantic weight and - to a certain degree - valency reside in a nominal element, typically a noun that syntactically fills a (direct or prepositional) object slot, but semantically orchestrates the other complements. While adverb incorporates are marked as such by the EngGram parser already at the syntactic level (@MV<), noun or adjective incorporates receive an ordinary syntactic tag (@ACC, @SC), but are marked with an empty §INC (incorporate) role tag at the semantic level. This is why, currently, about 14.6% of EFN valency entries include incorporated material, but the percentage of non-adverbial incorporates is still small (about a 1/10 of all incorporations).

The examples below also show the corresponding valency tags, where 'vt' means *transitive* and 'vi' *intransitive.* Governed prepositions are prefixed (e.g. <of^...>) and incorporated material is postfixed (e.g. <...-stock>)

take place - <vt-place>,
take stock of - <of^vt-stock>

Some of the constructions can be rather complex and involve dependents of an incorporated noun, prepositional phrases or a combination of particles and adverbs:

take it out on - <on^vp-it-out>,
lay in waiting - <vi-in=waiting>
call in sick - <vi-in_sick>,
take care of - <of^vp-care>

One could argue that the real frame arguments (like the noun expressing what is catered for in *take care of*) should be dependency-linked to the §INC noun *care* and the frame class marked on the latter, but for consistency and processing reasons we decided to center all dependency relations on the support verb in these cases, and also mark the frame name on the verbal element of support constructions.

3 Frame annotation

One would assume that using argument information from our verb frame lexicon on the one hand and a functional dependency parser on the other, it should in theory be possible to annotate running text with verb senses and frame elements, simply by checking verb-argument dependencies for function and semantic class. To prove this assumption, we implemented our annotation module in the Constraint Grammar formalism, choosing this particular approach in part because that made it easier to exploit the DanGram-parser's existing CG annotation tags, but also to allow for later manual fine-tuning of rules and contextual exceptions – something that would be impossible in a probabilistic system based on machine learning. In our view, this is a clear methodological advantage, and also saved us the cost of hand-annotating a training corpus. And though the creation of EFN itself does involve manual work in its own right, we prefer this method not only because. for a linguist, it is more satisfying to express lexical knowledge directly in a lexicon format, rather than indirectly through manual corpus annotation, but also because the latter is, as a method, less effective, since it will mean repetitive work for some verbs and coverage problems for others, due to the sparse data problem inherently linked to the limited size of hand-annotated corpora.

As a first step, we adapted a converter program (framenet2cgrules.pl, Bick 2011) that turned each frame into a verb sense mapping rule - a relatively simple task, since argument checking amounts to simple LINKed dependency contexts in the CG formalism. The somewhat simplified rule example below targets the verb "tune":

SUBSTITUTE (V) (<v:for^vtp> <fn:adjust> <r:SUBJ:AG> <r:ACC:PAT>)
TARGET ("tune" V)
IF (c @SUBJ LINK 0 <H>) .... *find daughter dependent (c) subject, check its class*
OR (0 PAS/INF) ... *though this isn't necessary for passives and infinitives*
OR (0 PCP1 + @ICL-N<PRED LINK p <H>) ... *for postnominal gerund clauses, check their mother dependent (p, parent) for human class*
AND IF (c @ACC LINK 0 <mach> OR <V>) ... *find accusative daughter (c), check its class*
OR (0 PAS LINK c @SUBJ LINK 0 <pass-acc> LINK 0 <mach> OR <V>) ... *for passives, check subject class instead*
OR (0 <acc-ellipsis> LINK 1 (*) LINK *-1 @FS-N< BARRIER NON-V ... *in an object-less (<acc-ellipsis>) relative clause (FS-N<)*
LINK p <rel-acc> LINK 0 <mach> OR <V>) ... *find the mother (p) and check its class for machine or vehicle*
OR (0 PAS + @ICL-N< LINK p <mach> OR <V>) ... *do the same for postnominal passive clauses*

In this rule, apart from the <fn:adjust> framenet class (implicitly: sense), argument relation tags (<r:....>) are added indicating an AG role (agent) for the subject and a PAT (patient) role for the object, IF the former is human (<H>) and the latter a vehicle (<V>) or machine (<mach>). In the definition section of the grammar, such semantic noun sets are expanded to individual semantic prototype classes (table 3), individual words or a combinations of category tags.

LIST <H> = <H.*>r <hum> <inst> <org> <media> <party> <civ> <Lciv> <Ltown> <Lcountry> <Lregion> "anybody" "anyone" "everybody" "everyone" "who" "one" 1S 2S 2S/P 1P 2P (<fem> PERS) (<mask> PERS) (<masc> PERS) ("he" PERS) ("she" PERS) ("they" PERS) (<heur> <Proper>) ;

Table 3: Semantic prototypes

	Semantic (prototype) noun class
<H>	Human: <Hprof>, <Hfam>, <Hnat> <Hideo> ....
<cc>	concrete object: <cc-stone>, <cc-rag>, <cc-cord> ...
<act>	Action: <act-s> speech-act, <act-do> ... cp. -CONTR: <event> <process>
<L>	Location: <Lh> human place, <Ltop>, <Lwater>, <Labs>, <Lsurf> surface ...
<A>	Animal: <Azo> land animals, <Aorn> birds, <Aich> fish ...
<sem>	Semanticals: <sem-r> book, <sem-l> song, <sem-c> concept , <sem-s> speech ...
<food>	Food: <food>, <food-c>, <food-m>, <fruit> ...
<tool>	Tools: <tool-nus>, <tool-cut> ...
<cm>	Substance: <cm-liq> liquid, <cm-gas>, <cm-chem> ..

<mon>	money
<sit>	situation
<V>	vehicle (<Vground>,<Vair> ...)
<conv>	convention
<HH>	Group: <org>, <media>, <inst> institutions
<an>	anatomical (body part): <anmov>, <anorg>, <anzo>, <anbo> ...
.....	(about 200 classes)

Apart from semantic classes, the frame mapping rules in step one may exploit word class or phrase type (table 4). With noun phrases being the default, special context conditions will be added for finite or non-finite clausal arguments, adverbs and pronouns. Special cases are the 'pl' plural marker (implying np at the same time), and the 'lex' category used for incorporated “as is” tokens.

The second step consisted of the assignment of thematic roles to arguments. Current CG compilers do not allow mappings on multiple (argument) contexts, but with GrammarSoft's open-source CG3 compiler it is possible to unify tag variables with regular-expression string matches, so rules were written to match argument functions with head verb's new <r:....> tags in order to retrieve (and map) the correct thematic role from the latter.

```
MAP KEEPORDER (VSTR:§$1) TARGET @SUBJ
    (*p V LINK -1 (*) LINK *1 (<r:.*>r) LINK 0 PAS
    LINK 0 (<r:ACC:\(.*\)>r)) ;
```

The rule above is a simple example, retrieving a thematic role variable from the verb's accusative argument tag (<r:ACC.:..>) and mapping it as a VSTR expression onto the subject in case the verb is in the passive voice. Complete rules will also contain negative contexts (omitted here), for instance ruling out the presence of objects for intransitive valency frames.

The following rule is a generalisation over the @FUNC set (defined in the grammar as objects, predicatives etc. Note that pp roles are mapped on the noun argument of the preposition (@P<) rather than the (semantically “empty”) preposition itself, in spite of the latter being the immediate (syntactic) dependent of the verb. In our CG formalism, such a multi-step dependency relation is expressed as '*p' (open scope parent relation, ancestor relation). The TMP: tags are intermediate tags used for string matches. Thus the additional TMP:§$2 role tag will be used by rules handling coordination of same-role arguments.

```
MAP KEEPORDER (VSTR:<TMP:§$2> VSTR:§$2)
    TARGET @FUNC OR @P< OR @>>P OR <mv>
    (0 (<TMP:.*?\([A-Z\-]+<?\).*?>?>r) LINK *p V
    LINK 0 (VSTR:<r:$1:\(.*\)>r)) ;
```

While helping to distinguish between verb senses with the same syntactic argument frame, using semantic noun classes as context restrictions raises the issue of circularity in terms of corpus example extraction, and also reduces overall robustness of frame tagging, not least in the presence of metaphor. Therefore, all frame mapping rules are run twice - first with semantic noun class restrictions in place, then - if necessary - without. This way “skeletal-syntactic” (semantics-free) argument structures can still be used as a backup for frame assignment, allowing corpus-based extension of semantic noun class restrictions.

In a vertical, one-word-per-line CG notation, the frame-tagger adds <fn:sense> and <v:valency> tags on verbs, and §ROLE tags on arguments. Free adverbial adjuncts are only partially covered, a few by the frames themselves, but most by separate, frame-independent mapping rules exploiting local grammatical information such as preposition type and noun class. The example demonstrates a frame sense distinction for the English verb *lead*. Dependency arcs are shown as #n->m ID-links.

```
European  [European] <*> <jnat> ADJ POS @>N #11->12
powers  [power] <HH> N P NOM §AG=LEADER
    @SUBJ> #12->13
should  [shall] <aux> V IMPF @FS-<ACC #13->8
be  [be] <vch> <aux> V INF @ICL-AUX< #14->13
leading  [lead] <mv> <v:vt> <fn:run_obj>
    <fnb:73:Leadership> V PCP1 @ICL-AUX< #15->14
the  [the] <def> ART S/P @>N #16->18
Western  [Western] <jideo> <jgeo> ADJ POS @>N
    #17->18
response  [response] <event> <act-s> N S NOM
    §ACT=ACTION @<ACC #18->15
to  [to] PRP @N< #19->18
Russia's  [Russia] <*> <Proper> <Lcountry> N S GEN
    §AG @>N #20->21
invasion  [invasion] <act> N S NOM @P< #21->19
of  [of] PRP @N< #22->21
Georgia  [Georgia] <*> <Proper> <Lcountry> N S
    NOM §PAT @P< #23->22
```

In the example, BFN tags were added to EFN tags, in the form of double role tags, and <fnb:..> frame tags. Independently of the verbal frame lexicon, the semantic tagger was able to assign an §AG tag to *Russia,* based on the semantic prototype of <act> provided by EngGram with it's head noun *invasion.* However, the §PAT tag is a (wrong) default tag – with a true, nominal <fn:invade> frame, it should have been §DES (destination). A future noun frame lexicon should also cover *response,* assigning §CAU (or §STI) to its argument daughter *invasion.*

The second example contains another sense of *lead*, that of *cause*, with §CAU (cause) and §RES (result) as frame arguments. Note the <TRO...> meta tag line providing a time stamp for video alignment. Similar meta mark-up, not shown here, is maintained for speaker, source, topic, news channel etc.

A [a] <*> <indef> ART S @>N #1->3
blown [blown] ADJ POS @>N #2->3
tire [tire] <cc-tube> N S NOM **§CAU=CAUSE** @SUBJ> #3->4
may [may] <aux> V PR @FS-STA #4->0
have [have] <v.contact> <vtk+ADJ> <aux> V INF @ICL-AUX< #5->4
led [lead] <mv> **<v:to^vp> <fn:cause> <fnb:5:Causation>** V PCP2 AKT @ICL-AUX< #6->5
to [to] PRP @<PIV #7->6
<TR0="20080808170708.458">
this [this] <dem> DET S @>N #8->10
deadly [deadly] ADJ POS @>N #9->10
scene [scene] <sem-w> N S NOM **§RES=RESULT** @P< #10->7

Yet another sense of *lead* is that of a path leading somewhere (the *meander*-frame), with §AG and §DES (destination) argument roles. Note that in this third example, the subject agent is not a dependent of *lead* – rather it is the head of the non-finite relative clause in which *lead* is the main verb. We mark such referred roles with an R- prefix (§R-PATH). Also, the first frame in the example illustrates the phenomenon of transparent np's: The direct dependent of *control* is the syntactic object *'all'*, but semantically this is a transparent (<norole>) modifier part of the argument np, so we raise the semantic function to its 'of X' granddaughter, marking *'roads'* as §BEN (beneficiary) of the *run_obj (control)* frame. Finally, this is an example of how two roles are necessary on the same token *(roads),* which fill a semantic argument slot in two different frames.

They [they] <*> PERS 3P NOM @SUBJ> **§AG=CONTROLLING_ENTITY** #1->2
control [control] <mv> **<v:vt> <fn:run_obj> <fnb:1799:Control>** V PR -3S @FS-STA #2->0
all [all] <quant> **<norole>** INDP S/P @<ACC #3->2
of [of] PRP @N< #4->3
the [the] <def> ART S/P @>N #5->6
roads [road] <Lpath> N P NOM @P< **§R-PATH=PATH §BEN=DEPENDENT_ENTITY** #6->4
leading [lead] <mv> **<v:va+DIR> <fn:meander> <fnb:61:Path_shape>** V PCP1 @ICL-N< #7->6
into [into] PRP @<SA #8->7
that [that] <dem> DET S @>N #9->10
town [town] <Lciv> N S NOM @P< **§DES** #10->8

N=noun, V=verb, ADV=adverb, INDP=independent pronoun, ART=article, DET=determiner, KC=coordinating conjunction, PRP=preposition, @SUBJ=subject, @ACC=accusative object, @ADVL=adverbial, @PIV=prepositional object, @SA=subject adverbial, @CO=coordinator, @>N prenominal, @N<=postnominal, @FS=finite clause, @ICL=non-finite clause, @STA=statement, §AG=agent, §PAT=patient, §RES=result, §CAU=cause, §DES=destination

4 Evaluation

4.1 Coverage

The reason for using a custom-made Danish-derived FrameNet (EFN) rather than the Berkeley FrameNet (BFN, Baker et al. 1998, Johnson & Fillmore 2000) were not only the better integration of the latter with CG tags and valency frames, but also coverage issues (Palmer & Sporleder 2011). In order to quantify BFN coverage for our speech/news domain, we used an annotated sub-corpus of about 145050 words (of these 19900 punctuation tokens). Due to fall-back strategies, almost all (99.5%) of the 20,343 main verbs in the corpus had been assigned an EFN frame, indicating good basic lexical coverage of the domain. We then checked both the verbs and the frames against BFN v. 1.5. For 26.4% of verb types and 4.1% of verb tokens BFN did not have any frame entry at all[2]. To measure frame coverage, we used BFN frame classes mapped from the assigned EngGram frame categories, checking if the frame in question was associated with a BFN sense for the verb in question. If the verb's valency instantiation matched a valency found in a BFN example sentence, that particular frame had to be one of the EngGram frame classes, making matches more likely. At least with our somewhat heuristic

[2] Examples were *betray, campaign, guarantee, involve, limit* etc.

matching technique, BFN did not have a matching frame in its frame inventory for a given verb in 33.6% of frame instances and for 33.4% of the 1647 frame types in the corpus. This finding supports the analysis by Erk & Padó (2006) that BFN has an unbalanced coverage problem for word senses, with fewer senses per word than the German FrameNet, because it is built one frame at a time, not one verb at a time.

4.2 Performance

To evaluate the coverage and precision of our frame tagger, we annotated a chunk of 882.500 tokens from the UCLA CSA television news corpus, building on an EngGram dependency annotation (Bick 2009) as input, and using only the rules automatically created by our FrameNet conversion program, with no manual rule changes, rule ordering or additions.

Out of 120,843 words tagged as main verbs, 99.9% were assigned a verbal frame sense, though 20.18% of the assigned categories were default senses for the verb in question because of the lack of surface arguments to match for sense-disambiguation. 18.6% of frames were subject-less infinitive and gerund constructions, but of these, 57,2% did have other, non-subject arguments to support frame assignment. The corpus contained 2473 verb lexeme types, and the frame tagger assigned 5840 different frame types, and 4234 verb sense types. Type-wise, this amounts to 2.36 frames, and 1.71 senses per verb type (similar to the distribution in the frame lexicon itself), but token-wise ambiguity is about double that figure, as we will discuss later in this chapter.

Table 4: Frame slot distribution and surface expression probabilities

	frame slots	expressed surface arguments with frame roles	percentage of filled slots
SUBJ	95194	65780 (1061 PCP1 @ICL-N<)	69.1% (da 51.45)
ACC	41765	36629 (978 PAS @ICL-N<)	87.7% (da 77.03)
DAT	1470	1005	68.4% (da 53.72)
PIV	9049	5275	58.3% (da 99.23)
SC	17690	17670	99.9% (da 100.00)
OC	657	446	67.9% (da 100.00)
SA	2809	2762	98.3% (da 100.00)
OA	2231	2021	90.6% (da 100.00)
ADVL	29	27	93.1% (da 100.00)

Table 4 contains a break-down of surface expression percentages for individual argument types. Subject (SUBJ), dative objects (DAT) and prepositional objects appear to be the least obligatory categories, though the latter is lower than it would be in the face of a more unabridged valency lexicon, since the frame mapping grammar also allows pp adverbials to match PIV object slots, to cover cases where the EngGram valency lexicon lacked an entry that the frame mapping grammar did have. It should also be born in mind that both subjects and object slots may be filled not by direct daughters of the main verb, but – for instance – by the heads of non-finite postnominal or finite relative clauses. In these cases, the frame mapping grammar may encounter a slot filler without leaving a mark on the syntactic function counter used for to compute the above table. Predicative arguments (SC), of verbs like *be* and *become*, are 100% expressed, as are valency-bound adverbials (SA). and prepositional arguments (PIV) have almost as high an expression rate simply because most verbs have alternative valency frames of lower order (intransitive or monotransitive accusative) that the tagger would have chosen in the absence of a PIV argument. In other words, PIV arguments are strong sense markers, and their absence will sooner lead to false-positive senses of lower valency-order than to PIV-senses without surface PIV. Among the safest markers for frame senses are incorporated particles (§INC), as in *give up, take place etc.*, which are almost 100% obligatory for the valency pattern in question, and which the frame mapping grammar therefore will try to match these before more general verbal complementations.

On a random 5000-word chunk of the frame-annotated data, a complete error count was performed for all verbs. All in all, there were 629 main verb tags, of which 13 should have been auxiliaries and one had been wrongly verb-tagged by the parser *(even)*. Our frame tagger assigned 624 frames, missing out on only 4 regular verbs *(2 x vetted, unquote, harkens)*, and (wrongly) tagging the false-positive verb. This suggests a very good coverage in simple lexical terms (99.6%). In 20.7% of cases, the frame tagger assigned a default frame, usually a low-order valency frame without incorporates[3]. Of 615 possible frames, 495 were correctly tagged, yielding the following correctness figures:

Table 5: Performance of the frame sense tagger on television news

	Recall	Precision	F-score
total	80,49 (da 85.05)	79.32% (da 85.20)	79.91
ignoring pos/aux errors	80.49%	81.01%	80,75

These figures are an encouraging result, despite the "weak" (inspection-based) evaluation method. The performance falls 5 percentage points short of the results achieved for our point of departure, the Danish FrameNet (Bick 2011), but it has to be borne in mind that the current English system is work in progress, as indicated in rough terms by the smaller lexicon size of the new, derived framenet. More important than lexicon size as such, is granularity – the coverage of frequent verbs in term of valency frames and incorporations – and here the method of trying to port frames across languages was bound to miss out on many English constructions simply because translations tend to be many-to-one, i.e. conflating several rarer SL constructions to one or few more general TL constructions. Using ML techniques, the best participating systems in the SemEval 2007 frame identification task (Baker, Ellsworth & Erk 2007) achieved F-scores between 60% and 75%, though because of the stricter evaluation system any direct comparison will have to wait for future work based on a category mapping scheme, using the same data. Shi & Mihalcea (2004), also using FrameNet-derived rules, report an F-score of 74.5% for English, while Gildea & Jurafsky (2002), using statistical methods, report F-scores of 80.4% and 82.1% for frame roles and abstract thematic roles, respectively. For copula and support verb constructions, not included in the earlier evaluations, Johansson & Nugues (2006) report tagging accuracies for English of 71-73%, respectively, but a comparison is hard to make, since we only looked at support constructions that our FrameNet does know, with no idea about the theoretical lexical "coverage ceiling".

A qualitative look at the errors shows that the underlying part-of-speech tagging was very robust – thus only 2 verb class errors were found, one false positive and one false negative. The confusion of auxiliary and main verb for *be* and *have*, however, did play a certain role (10% of false positive frames), and so did incomplete valency frames or wrong syntactic attachments, resulting in missing slot fillers for the frame-mapping rules. Some of these underlying errors were ultimately domain-dependent and due to non-standard language in our (spoken) corpus. Thus, half of the auxiliary/main verb-confusion occurred due to missing words *(have bombing* instead of *have been bombing)* or unfinished sentences or retractions *(I don't - I think my people ...)*. Ignoring these errors, i.e. assuming correct tagging input, would influence precision, in particular, and raise the overall F-score by 1-2 percentage points[4].

A break-down of error types revealed that about 40% of all false positive errors (but only 8% of all frames) were cases where the human "gold sense" was not (yet) on the list of possible senses in the our EFN database. As one might expect, default mappings accounted for a higher percentage (26.4%) among error verbs than in the chunk as a whole (20.2%), and contributed to almost a third of the "frame-not-in-lexicon" cases.

Frequent verbs have a high sense ambiguity, and verbs with a high sense ambiguity were more error-prone than one-sense verbs, as can be seen from the table below. Thus, the verbs occurring in our evaluation chunk had 4.7 potential senses per verb (6.54 for the ambiguous ones), and the verbs accounting for frame tagging errors had a theoretical 10.26 senses each. While these numbers and their proportions closely matched the findings for Danish, there is a marked difference in the "sense density" for the verb lexica as such, reflecting the fact that the larger size of the Danish

[3] The default frame is not currently based on statistics, but decided upon when converting the framenet lexicon into a Constraint Grammar, as the first intransitive or monotransitive valency frame by order of appearence in the lexicon,. Other valency categories may also be default-rated, but need a special manual tag (atop="1"). Similarly, frames can be downgraded by assigning them higher atop numbers – in effect meaning they will only be used if all context slot conditons are present in the sentence. This way, the ultimate ranking of frames, and the decision on a default frame is fully controllled by the lexicographer.

[4] Given the syntactic and semantic knowledge base of our system, it would be feasible to design rules for identifying "false" main verbs at a later stage, to remedy this problem.

Framenet in terms of verb types is achieved by including the Zipf tail of verbs – i.e. rare verbs with one or few readings – while the overall sense count is not so different. Concluding from this, one can assume that an enlargement of EFN in terms of verb types will decrease rather than increase the ambiguity strain on tagging performance.

Table 6: Sense ambiguity per verb

	Verb type count	**theoretical sense count**	**senses / verb**	**sense type count in chunk (as tagged)**
EFN framenet lexicon	4774	10800	2.26 (da 1.46)	-
verb types in chunk	205	964	4.7 (da 4.21)	244
sense ambiguous	140	916	6.54 (da 6.77)	193
frame error verbs	56	576	10.26 (da 10.08)	78

5 Conclusions and Outlook

We have shown that a robust semantic tagger for English television news can be built by converting a valency-anchored frament into Constraint Grammar mapping rules, turning syntactic and semantic selection restrictions into dependency-linked context conditions. Though the system has a reasonable lexical coverage and frame sense recall for verbs, a great deal of work needs to be done on nominal frames and verbo-nominal incorporations. Also, evaluation should be carried out for semantic role tagging accuracy in addition to verb senses, optimally in a standardized evaluation environment.

References

Bick, Eckhard. 2000. *The Parsing System Palavras - Automatic Grammatical Analysis of Portuguese in a Constraint Grammar Famework,* Aarhus: Aarhus University Press

Bick, Eckhard. 2009. "Introducing Probabilistic Information in Constraint Grammar Parsing". *Proceedings of Corpus Linguistics 2009, Liverpool* (ucrel.lancs.ac.uk/publications/cl2009/)

Bick, Eckhard. 2007. Automatic Semantic Role Annotation for Portuguese. In: *Proceedings of TIL 2007* (Rio de Janeiro, July 5-6, 2007). ISBN 85-7669-116-7, pp. 1713-1716

Bick, E. & H. Mello & A. Panunzi & T. Raso (2012), The Annotation of the C-ORAL-Brasil through the Implementation of the Palavras Parser. In: Calzolari, Nicoletta et al. (eds.), *Proceedings LREC2012 (Istanbul, May 23-25)*. pp. 3382-3386. ISBN 978-2-9517408-7-7

Baker, C., Ellsworth, M., & Erk, K. 2007. SemEval-2007 Task 19: Frame Semantic Structure Extraction. Proceedings of (SemEval-2007), ACL 2007, pages 99-104

Baker, Collin F., Fillmore, J. Charles & John B. Lowe. 1998. The Berkeley FrameNet project. In Proceedings of the COLING-ACL, Montreal, Canada

DeLiema, David & Francis Steen & Mark Turner. 2012. Language, Gesture and Audiovisual Communication: A Massive Online Database for Researching Multimodal Constructions. Lecture. 11th Conceptual Structure, Discourse and Language Conf., Vancouver, May 17-20.

Erk, Katrin & Sebastian Padó. 2006. SHALMANESER – A Toolchain for Shallow Semantic Parsing. Proceedings of LREC 2006

Gildea, D. and D. Jurafsky. 2002. Automatic Labeling of Semantic Roles, Computational Linguistics, 28(3) 245-288.

Johansson, Richard & Pierre Nugues. 2006. Automatic Annotation for All Semantic Layers in FrameNet. *Proceedings of EACL 2006*. Trento, Italy.

Johnson, Christopher R. & Charles J. Fillmore. 2000. The FrameNet tagset for frame-semantic and syntactic coding of predicate-argument structure. In *Proceedings of* ANLP-NAACL 2000, April 29-May 4, 2000, Seattle WA, pp. 56-62.

Karlsson, Fred, Atro Voutilainen, Juha Heikkilä, and Arto Anttila. 1995. *Constraint Grammar: A Language-Independent System for Parsing Unrestricted Text.* Natural Language Processing, No

4. Mouton de Gruyter, Berlin and New York

Kipper, Karin & Anna Korhonen, Neville Ryant, and Martha Palmer. 2006. Extensive Classifications of English verbs. *Proceedings of the 12th EURALEX*. Turin, Sept. 2006.

Levin, Beth. 1993. *English Verb Classes and Alternation, A Preliminary Investigation*. The University of Chicago Press.

Palmer, Alexis & Caroline Sporleder. 2011. Evaluating FrameNet-style semantic parsing: the role of coverage gaps in FrameNet. *Proceedings of COLING '10. Pp 928-936.* ACL.

Palmer, Martha, Dan Gildea, Paul Kingsbury. 2005. The Proposition Bank: An Annotated Corpus of Semantic Roles. *Computational Linguistics, 31:1.*, pp. 71-105, March, 2005.

Shi, Lei & Rada Mihalcea. 2004. Open Text Semantic Parsing Using FrameNet and WordNet. In HLT-NAACL 2004, Demonstration Papers. pp. 19-22

Compositionality of NN Compounds: A Case Study on [N_1+Artifactual-Type Event Nouns]

Shan Wang[1, 2] **Chu-Ren Huang**[1] **Hongzhi Xu**[1]

[1]Dept. of Chinese and Bilingual Studies, The Hong Kong Polytechnic University, Hung Hom, Kowloon, Hong Kong

[2] Department of Computer Science, Volen Center for Complex Systems, Brandeis University

{wangshanstar, churenhuang, hongz.xu} @gmail.com

Abstract

Generative Lexicon theory (GL) establishes three mechanisms at work when a predicate selects an argument, i.e. pure selection, accommodation and type coercion. They are widely used in verbal selection of nouns in the entity domain. However, little attention has been devoted to the compositionality of [N_1+event noun] type NN compounds. This paper extends the usage of these mechanisms in two ways: 1) the eventive nominal head selection of a nominal modifier, and 2) their use in the eventive domain, through the case study on [N_1+比賽*bǐsài* 'competition']. Moreover, it reveals a new compositional mechanism sub-composition. It also discovers the domain contribution in type coercion. This work enriches the study on compositionality and GL.

1 Introduction

Event nouns in Mandarin Chinese have generated extensive interest (Han 2007, 2011; Liu 2004; Ma 1995; Wang & Huang 2011a, 2011b, 2012a, 2012c, 2012d). However, little research has concerned about the compositional mechanisms at work in [N_1+event noun] type $[N_1N_2]_N$ compounds.

Generative Lexicon theory (GL) provides a rich compositional representation through generative devices (Pustejovsky 1993, 2001, 2006, 2011; Pustejovsky & Jezek 2008). Under a tripartite system of the domain of individuals, including natural types, artifactual types and complex types (Pustejovsky 2001, 2006; Pustejovsky & Jezek 2008), GL establishes three mechanisms at work when a predicate selects an argument.

1) Pure Selection (Type Matching): the type a function requires is directly satisfied by the argument;

2) Accommodation: the type a function requires is inherited by the argument;

3) Type Coercion: the type a function requires is imposed on the argument type. This is accomplished by either:

(i) Exploitation: taking a part of the argument's type to satisfy the function;

(ii) Introduction: wrapping the argument with the type required by the function.

Following Pustejovsky (2001, 2006) and Pustejovsky & Jezek (2008), Wang & Huang (2012e) establish a type system for event nouns, including natural types, artifactual types, natural complex types and artifactual complex types. The current paper only focuses on *artifactual-type event nouns* and explores the compositional mechanisms of nominal modification to these nouns in NN compounds. Furthermore, the domain information contribution to the reading of a NN compound is surveyed.

2 Data Collection

The data of this study are mostly extracted from Chinese Gigaword (second edition)[1] and Sinica Corpus[2] accessed through Chinese Word Sketch Engine[3], with a few examples collected online through the search engines *Google* and *Baidu*.

[1] http://www.ldc.upenn.edu/Catalog/catalogEntry.jsp?catalogId=LDC2009T14

[2] http://db1x.sinica.edu.tw/kiwi/mkiwi/

[3] http://158.132.124.36/, http://wordsketch.ling.sinica.edu.tw/

3 Compositional Mechanisms of [N_1 + Artifactual-Type Event Nouns]

The internal structure of NN compounds has been widely investigated (Jackendoff 1975; Laurie Bauer 2008; Packard 2004; Warren 1978). In recent years, some research uses GL to analyze the relation between N_1 and N_2 (Johnston & Busa 1996; Lee et al. 2010; Qi 2012). The research using the GL gives a compositional treatment to capture the N_1 and N_2 relations, but it only concerns the situation when N_1 is a qualia role of N_2. It does not explain cases when N_2 is a qualia role of N_1. Moreover, it does not give a generalization for the qualia modification relation.

The following section analyses the compositional mechanisms of NN compounds. To make the discussion more concentrate, Section 3.2 and 3.3 use [N_1+比賽 *bǐsài* 'competition'] as a case study. To introduce a new way of compositionality, *sub-composition*, Section 3.4 uses a wider range of data.

3.1 Interpreting 比賽 *bǐsài* 'competition'

A 比賽 *bǐsài* 'competition' is an activity in which one try to win against the opponents. Its semantic type system is depicted below.

$$\left[\begin{array}{l}\text{比賽 } \textit{bǐsài} \text{ 'competition'} \\ \text{ARGSTR} = \left[\begin{array}{l}\text{D-ARG}_1 = \text{x: individual} \\ \text{D-ARG}_2 = \text{y: individual} \\ \text{D-ARG}_3 = \text{z: organizer} \\ \text{D-ARG}_4 = \text{r: rule}\end{array}\right] \\ \text{EVENTSTR} = [\text{E}_1 = \text{e}_1\text{: process}] \\ \text{QUALIA} = \left[\begin{array}{l}\text{FORMAL} = \text{a: activity} \\ \text{CONSTITUTIVE} = \{\text{x, y, z, r, c}\} \\ \text{TELIC} = [\text{e}_1 \text{ satisfies r} \rightarrow (\text{x} \vee \text{y}) \text{ win}] \\ \text{AGENTIVE} = \text{organize (z, a)}\end{array}\right]\end{array}\right]$$

A competition usually sets rules so that the participant who has the best performance will be the winner. Therefore, the purpose of 比賽 *bǐsài* 'competition', which is the telic role, is to win with some rules satisfied during the competing process e_1.

A competition could be either on the process of an event that participants involved in or the resultative product made during an event. In an [N_1+比賽 *bǐsài* 'competition'] compound, N_1 specifies the subject of the competition. That is, it signifies the process on which people are judged or the product that people create in a competition. Wang & Huang (2012b) classify nouns into pure event nouns, nominals (event nominals and result nominals) and entity nouns. Following this classification, the following will examine which kinds of nouns fit the N_1.

If the competition is about the process, then the competition is based on the behavior of participants during the event. Three kinds of N_1 fit this case: 1) pure event nouns: 體操 *tǐcāo* 'gymnastics', 馬術 *mǎshù* 'horsemanship', 雜技 *zájì* 'acrobatics', 圈操 *quāncāo* 'hoop gymnastics'; 2) event nominals: 舉重 *jǔzhòng* 'weightlifting', 賽艇 *sàitǐng* 'boat racing', 攀巖 *pānyán* 'rock climbing'; 3) entities: 龍舟 *lóngzhōu* 'dragon boat', 帆船 *fānchuán* 'yacht'[4].

If the competition is about the final product, then the rule to decide the winners will be based on the quality of the product. Two kinds of N_1 fit such as a case: 1) event nominals: 攝影 *shèyǐng* 'photography'; 2) entities: 書畫 *shūhuà* 'painting and calligraphy', 航模 *hángmó* 'model airplane'.

Summarizing, this section has illustrated the semantic type system of 比賽 *bǐsài* 'competition'. A competition can be either on the process or result. If the competition is about the process, N_1 can be a pure event noun, an event nominal or an entity. If the competition is about the result, N_1 can be an event nominal or an entity (coerced to be an event). To achieve the goal of a competition (the telic role), usually to win, one should satisfy some rules.

---

[4] 龍舟 *lóngzhōu* 'dragon boat' and 帆船 *fānchuán* 'yacht' can be treated either as an entity or activity in themselves. Here we treat them as an entity which is coerced to be an event through qualia exploitation. This is discussed in Section 3.3 in more details.

3.2 Pure Selection

When N_1 is an event nominal, the head 比賽 *bǐsài* 'competition' selects N_1 through pure selection. Because the verbal morpheme in the nominal N_1 already specifies what event it is. Examples are shown in Table 1 and Table 2.

Words	*Pinyin*	English	Frequency	Saliency
攝影	*shèyǐng*	photography	1074	51.01
舉重	*jǔzhòng*	weightlifting	957	48.31
賽艇	*sàitǐng*	boat racing	314	47.85
攀巖	*pānyán*	rock climbing	80	31.35
調酒	*tiáojiǔ*	wine mixing	13	20.26

Table 1: VO Type Event Nominals in Gigaword

For instance, in Table 1, within the N_1 攝影 *shèyǐng* 'photography', the verbal morpheme 攝 *shè* 'take a photograph of' is embedded in the photographing action.

Words	*Pinyin*	English	Frequency	Saliency
雙打	*shuāngdǎ*	doubles	1775	62.01
單打	*dāndǎ*	singles	1799	59.5

Table 2: Adj-V Type Event Nominals in Gigaword

Similarly, in Table 2, the verbal morpheme 打 *dǎ* 'play' in both 雙打 *shuāngdǎ* 'doubles' and 單打 *dāndǎ* 'singles' already specify the playing event.

3.3 Type Coercion through Qualia Exploitation of N_1

3.3.1 N_1 as an Entity

If N_1 is an entity, there will be two possibilities: 1) the competition is dependent on the process of a potential event that is related to the entity; 2) the competition is dependent on the final product N_1, where a potential event is also involved which is an agentive role of the entity. In both cases, we would like to say that there is type coercion from the entity to their potential events.

3.3.1.1 Type Coercion with Ordered Events (Type Coercion with Event Combination)

Pustejovsky (2000) finds that the qualia provide three relations: <, o and >. According to temporal properties, the partial orderings of qualia roles are: Agentive < Formal, Constitutive o Formal, and Formal < Telic. In [N_1+比賽 *bǐsài* 'competition'], N_1 can involve in more than one event. Type coercion of N_1 includes the combination of ordered events from different qualia roles. When N_1 is an entity, it sometimes requires the pre-existence of a creation event, which comes from the agentive role of N_1. The entity is produced through the creation event. 比賽 *bǐsài* 'competition' is to compare the quality of different products. The product quality can be decided according to either the formal or telic role.

In an art competition, what is being compared is the design, shape, color, etc., which are the formal role of the objects. These forms exist after the creation of the objects, which is the agentive role. Table 3 shows some examples.

Words	*Pinyin*	English	Frequency	Saliency	Qualia Roles
冰雕	*bīng diāo*	ice sculpture	73	35.35	agentive (做 *zuò* 'make') +formal
沙雕	*shā diāo*	sand sculpture	33	27.96	agentive (做 *zuò* 'make') +formal
花燈	*huā dēng*	lantern	59	26.56	agentive (做 *zuò* 'make') +formal
書畫	*shū huà*	painting and calligraphy	79	19.99	agentive (創作 *chuàngzuò* 'create') +formal

Table 3: Examples of Type Coercion with Ordered Events in Gigaword: Agentive > Formal

For instance, in table 3, 冰雕比賽 *bīngdiāo bǐsài* 'ice sculpture competition' involves an event of making ice sculpture (the agentive role), and then the quality of 冰雕 *bīngdiāo* 'ice sculpture' (the formal role) is compared to determine the winner.

In a competition of an application field, what is compared is the function of the objects, which is the telic role. The function exists after the creation of the objects. Examples are as shown in Table 4.

Words	*Pinyin*	English	Frequency	Saliency	Qualia Roles
航模	*háng mó*	model airpl	33	28.38	agentive (做 *zuò* 'make') +telic

		ane			
模型	*móxíng*	model	111	22.48	agentive (做 *zuò* 'make') +telic

Table 4: Examples of Type Coercion with Ordered Events: Agentive > Telic

For example, in Table 4, 航模比賽 *hángmó bǐsài* 'model airplane competition' first requires the creation of a model airplane (the agentive role), and then the function of different models (the telic role) is compared.

3.3.1.2 Type Coercion with one Individual Event

In 水餃比賽 *shuǐjiǎo bǐsài* 'dumpling competition', 水餃 *shuǐjiǎo* 'dumpling' can be coerced to three events, eating, making, or tasting through the telic role, agentive role, and formal role respectively, as illustrated below.

水餃 *shuǐjiǎo* 'dumpling'
EVENTSTR = [$E_1 = e_1$: process; $E_2 = e_2$: process; $D\text{-}E_3 = e_3$: state]
ARGSTR = [$ARG_1 = x$: human; $ARG_2 = y$: dumplings]
QUALIA = [TELIC = eat (e_2, x, y); AGENTIVE = make (e_1, x, y); FORMAL = taste (e_3, y)]

水餃比賽 *shuǐjiǎo bǐsài* 'dumpling competition' has three readings through type coercion of dumplings' different qualia roles: 1) through the telic role: x wins if x eats most dumplings; 2) through the agentive role: x wins if x makes most dumplings; 3) through the formal role: x wins if x's dumplings tastes best. These readings indicate that the context for 水餃比賽 *shuǐjiǎo bǐsài* 'dumpling competition' is that if you meet some rules, then you win. This can be depicted below:

Telic role for 水餃比賽 *shuǐjiǎo bǐsài* 'dumpling competition': R → [φ] win

R: rules

For 水餃比賽 *shuǐjiǎo bǐsài* 'dumpling competition', [φ] is competing by eating or making or tasting. That is, 水餃 *shuǐjiǎo* 'dumpling' can be coerced to any of the three events. Reading 1) and 2) have only one event involved respectively, while reading 3) comprises of an agentive event and the following formal role related event.

3.3.2 N_1 as a Pure Event Noun

Similar to N_1 as a entity in Section 3.3.1, when N_1 is a pure event noun, coercion is still at work. That is because just like an entity, an artifactual event comes into being (the agentive role) for some purpose (the telic role). Different from the diversity of N_1-as-an-entity coercion (including ordered events or an individual event), in [N_1+比賽 *bǐsài* 'competition'], N_1-as-a-pure event noun coercion normally only has one coerced event through the agentive role.

For example, in 體操比賽 *tǐcāo bǐsài* 'gymnastics competition', the coerced event 'perform gymnastics' is through exploiting the agentive role of 體操 *tǐcāo* 'gymnastics'. During a gymnastics competition, the existence of the gymnastics is the same as the process of the performance. Other examples of such N_1 include 馬術 *mǎshù* 'horsemanship', 雜技 *zájì* 'acrobatics', and 圈操 *quāncāo* 'hoop gymnastics'.

Summarizing, pure selection and type coercion have been used in verbal selection of nouns in the entity domain (Pustejovsky 1993, 2001, 2006, 2011; Pustejovsky & Jezek 2008). Section 3.2 and 3.3 have extended their usage in two ways: 1) nominal head selection of a nominal modifier, and 2) their use in the eventive domain, though a case study on [N_1+比賽 *bǐsài* 'competition']. The results are shown in Table 5.

[N_1+比賽 *bǐsài* 'competition']	**比賽 *bǐsài* 'competition': Process or Result**	**Compositional Mechanism: Pure Selection or Type Coercion**
Pure Event Noun+比賽 *bǐsài* 'competition'	Process	Type Coercion
Event Nominal+比賽 *bǐsài* 'competition'	Process or Result	Pure Selection
Entity+比賽 *bǐsài* 'competition'	Process or Result	Type Coercion

Table 5: Interpreting 比賽 *bǐsài* 'competition'

Table 5 shows that a competition can be either about the process or the result. For a process competition, N_1 can be a pure event noun, an event nominal or an entity. For a result competition, N_1 can be an event nominal or an entity. When N_1 is an event nominal, pure selection is usually at work, while when N_1 is a pure event noun or an entity, type coercion happens.

3.4 Sub-Composition

Pustejovsky (1995, 2012) introduces co-compostion. A typical example is *bake the cake*. The operation of co-composition results in a qualia structure for the VP that reflects aspects of both constituents. These include: 1) the governing verb *bake* applies to its complement; 2) the complement co-specifies the verb; 3) the composition of qualia structures results in a derived sense of the verb, where the verbal and complement agentive roles match, and the complement formal quale becomes the formal role for the entire VP.

This section introduces a new way of compositionality, *sub-composition*, through exploring [N_1+Artifactual-Type Event Noun]. There are two types of sub-composition: 1) N_1 as an argument and N_2 as a function, and 2) N_1 as a function and N_2 as an argument.

$$y = f(x)$$

A function f is a relationship which links a set of input and a set of potential output. The input x is called a variable or an argument, while the output y is named as a dependent variable. The requirement of a function is that each variable should have and only have exactly one output.

We define the qualia role of a word as a function. Pustejovsky (1995) analyses how lexical items encode semantic information in the qualia structure. This structure has four roles, each with some values. 1) The constitutive role is about the relation between an object and its constituents or parts. Its role values include material, weight, parts and component elements. 2) The formal role can distinguish an object within a larger domain. Orientation, magnitude, shape, dimensionality, color, and position are its role values. 3) The telic role is about the purpose and function of the object. 4) The agentive role describes factors involved in the origin of an object, such as creator, artifact, natural kind, and causal chain.

We treat the four qualia roles as the four functions of a word:

f_1 : FORMAL

f_2: CONSTITUTIVE

f_3: TELIC

f_4: AGENTIVE

In some cases, there is a verb in the telic or agentive role. For example, the telic role of 選拔賽 *xuǎnbásài* 'selection contest' is [*TELIC=select(x)*], where x is an argument that is selected. Therefore the function of 選拔賽 *xuǎnbásài* 'selection contest' is f_i:[*TELIC=select(x)*]. For convenience, we will hide the predicate '*select*' and use the qualia role to represent the function, i.e. f_i:*TELIC(x)*.

In a sub-compositional NN compound, either N_1 or N_2 can be a function, remaining the other as an argument (variable). The following section examines both Argument-Function Type and Function-Argument Type [N_1+Artifactual-Type Event Noun].

3.4.1 Argument-Function Type [N_1+ Artifactual-Type Event Noun]

Qualia structure encodes the lexical information of a lexical item. When N_1 has qualia modification to an NN, N_1 is the argument and N_2 is function.

1) $f_{i, N2}$: FORMAL

$N_1N_2 = N_2[\text{FORMAL}(N_1)]$

泰式拳擊 *tàishì quánjí* 'Thai-style boxing'

λx∃y [boxing (x) ∧ Tai-style(y) ∧ a style of (y, x)]

$$\begin{bmatrix} \text{拳擊 } \textit{quánjí} \text{ 'boxing'} \\ \text{QUALIA} = [\text{FORMAL} = \text{style}] \end{bmatrix}$$

A style is a formal role of boxing. Thus in the compound 泰式拳擊 *tàishì quánjí* 'Thai-style boxing', the N_1 泰式 *tàishì* 'Thai-style' is the formal role of the N_2 拳擊 *quánjí* 'boxing'. This compound can be represented as Boxing [FORMAL (Tai-Style)].

2) $f_{i, N2}$: CONSTITUTIVE

$N_1N_2 = N_2$[CONSTITUTIVE (N_1)]

闖關遊戲 *chuǎngguān yóuxì* 'crashing-through-barrier game'

λx∃y [game (x) ∧ crashing-through-barriers (y) ∧ subevent-of (y, x)]

遊戲 *yóuxì* 'game'
EVENTSTR= [E_1=e_1:process={$subevent_1$,$subevent_2$, ……}]
QUALIA = CONSTITUTIVE = e_1

A 遊戲 *yóuxì* 'game' is an activity that is composed of some subevents. In the above compound, the N_1 闖關 *chuǎngguān* 'crashing through a barrier' is a subevent of the N_2 遊戲 *yóuxì* 'game', so this compound can be represented as Competition [CONSTITUTIVE (Crashing-through-Barriers)].

3) $f_{i, N2}$: TELIC

$N_1N_2 = N_2$ [TELIC (N_1)]

慶功儀式 *qìnggōng yíshì* 'celebrating-victory ceremony'

λx∃y [ceremony (x) ∧ celebrating-a-victory (y) ∧ purpose-of (y, x)]

A ceremony is a formal event held with certain purpose. In the compound 慶功儀式 *qìnggōng yíshì* 'celebrating-victory ceremony', the N_1 慶功 *qìnggōng* 'celebrating a victory' states the aim of the N_2 儀式 *yíshì* 'ceremony', so N_1 is the telic role of N_2. This compound can be represented as Ceremony [TELIC (Celebrating-a-Victory)].

4) $f_{i, N2}$: AGENTIVE

$N_1N_2 = N_2$[AGENTIVE (N_1)]

職業病 *zhíyè bìng* 'occupational disease'

λx∃y [disease (x) ∧ occupation (y) ∧ cause (y, x)]

A disease is an illness caused by some reasons. In the compound 職業病 *zhíyè bìng* 'occupational disease', the N_1 職業 *zhíyè* ''occupation' is the cause of the N_2 病 *bìng* 'disease', so N_1 acts as the agentive role of N_2. This compound can be represented as Disease [AGENTIVE (Occupation)].

1)-4) illustrate four types of argument-function type N_1N_2, with N_1 as an argument and N_2 as a function. N_1 is a qualia role of N_2 and thus has qualia modification to N_2.

3.4.2 Function-Argument Type [N_1 + Artifactual-Type Event Noun]

When N_2 is a qualia role of N_1, N_1 is the function and N_2 is the argument.

1) $f_{i, N1}$: FORMAL

$N_1N_2 = N_1$[FORMAL (N_2)]

校慶活動 *xiàoqìng huódòng* 'school celebration activity'

λx∃y[activity(x) ∧ school-celebration (y) ∧ a kind of (y, x)]

校慶 *xiàoqìng* 'school celebration'
QUALIA = [FORMAL = activity]

The N_1 校慶 *xiàoqìng* 'school celebration' is a kind of activity, so it has a formal role 'activity', which is the N_2 活動 *huódòng* 'activity'. This compound can be represented as School-Celebration [FORMAL (Activity)].

2) $f_{i, N1}$: CONSTITUTIVE

$N_1N_2 = N_1$[CONSTITUTIVE (N_2)]

運動會開幕式 *yùndònghuì kāimùshì* 'sports meet opening ceremony'

λx∃y[opening ceremony (x) ∧ sports meet (y) ∧ part of (x, y)]

運動會 *yùndònghuì* 'sports meet'
QUALIA=[CONSTITUTIVE={opening ceremony, ……}]

運動會 *yùndònghuì* 'sports meet' is an event that includes many subevents, such as the opening ceremony, competitions and the closing ceremony. Therefore, in the compound 運動會開幕式 *yùndònghuì kāimùshì* 'sports meet opening ceremony', the N_2 開幕式 *kāimùshì* 'opening ceremony' is a constituent of the N_1 運動會 *yùndònghuì* 'sports meet'. This compound can be represented as Sports-Meet [CONSTITUTIVE (Opening-Ceremony)].

3) $f_{i, N2}$: TELIC

$N_1N_2 = N_1$[TELIC (N_2)]

火車運輸 *huǒchē yùnshū* 'train transportation'

λx∃y[transportation (x) ∧ train (y) ∧ purpose-of (x, y)]

火車 *huǒchē* 'train'
ARGSTR = [D-ARG_1 = z: entity]
QUALIA = [FORMAL = r: vehicle
TELIC = transport (r, z)]

火車 *huǒchē* 'train' is a vehicle that is usually used for transportation, carrying people and goods from one place to another. Thus, in the compound 火車運輸 *huǒchē yùnshū* 'train transportation', the N_2 運輸 *yùnshū* 'transportation' is the telic role of the N_1 火車 *huǒchē* 'train'. This compound can be represented as Train [TELIC (Transportation)].

4) $f_{i, N2}$: AGENTIVE

$N_1N_2 = N_1[\text{AGENTIVE } (N_2)]$

電影拍攝 *diànyǐng pāishè* 'movie shooting'

$\lambda x \exists y[\text{shooting } (x) \wedge \text{movie } (y) \wedge \text{produce } (x, y)]$

電影 *diànyǐng* 'movie'
ARGSTR = [D-ARG$_1$ = z: human]
QUALIA = [FORMAL = r: event·physobj
AGENTIVE = shoot (z, r)]

電影 *diànyǐng* 'movie' is produced by the shooting action. Hence in the compound 電影拍攝 *diànyǐng pāishè* 'movie shooting', the N_2 拍攝 *pāishè* 'shooting' is the agentive role of the N_1 電影 *diànyǐng* 'movie'. This compound can be represented as Movie [AGENTIVE (Shooting)].

It is common that NN compounds are ambiguous. For example, 火車運輸 *huǒchē yùnshū* 'train transportation' may have these readings: 1) trains are used for transportation; and 2) trains are a means of transportation.

Section 3.4.2 of this paper has dealt with the reading 1), treating it as a Function-Argument relation. The semantic representation is Train [TELIC (Transportation)]. For reading 2), the N_1 火車 *huǒchē* 'train' is taken as the formal role of N_2 運輸 *yùnshū* 'transportation'. Thus this is an Argument-Function relation, and this compound can be represented as Transportation [FORMAL (Train)].

In sum, this section has introduced a new mechanism of compositionality *sub-composition*. The structure N_1N_2 has two ways of sub-composition: 1) argument-function, when N_1 has qualia modification to N_2; and 2) function-argument, when N_2 is a qualia role of N_1. Because NN compounds are often ambiguous, they can have various relations according to different readings.

4 Domain Relevance of Type Coercion

Wang & Huang (2011a) has established the relation between type coercion and domain information. They reveal that type coercion can be dependent on a specific domain, because 1) intuitively, each domain often establishes a different type of event convention and NN compounds are always domain specific terms; 2) domain information can help to predict coercion types. Following this analysis, we argue that the coerced event is also domain relevant for eventive NN. We further observe that some domains have well-known conventional events, while some others do not. The former leads to a most probable and default reading, while the latter results in ambiguity. This point can be explained by the examples 足球比賽 *zúqiú bǐsài* 'football competition' and 湯圓比賽 *tāngyuán bǐsài* 'rice ball competition'.

Through qualia exploitation, both 足球 *zúqiú* 'football'[5] and 湯圓 *tāngyuán* 'rice ball' have the events demonstrated by the telic and agentive role. 足球 *zúqiú* 'football' has the playing event and producing event, while 湯圓 *tāngyuán* 'rice ball' has the eating event and making event as illustrated below.

足球 *zúqiú* 'football'
ARGSTR = [D- ARG$_1$ = y: manufacturer
D-ARG$_2$ = z: human]
QUALIA = [FORMAL = x: ball
TELIC = play (z, x)
AGENTIVE = produce (y, x)]

[5] In Mandarin Chinese, 足球 *zúqiú* 'football' can be treated either as an activity or an entity. When it is treated as an activity, 足球比賽 *zúqiú bǐsài* 'football competition' combines through pure selection and there is no type coercion. When it is treated as an entity, there is type coercion through qualia exploitation. In this section, we treat it in the second way.

湯圓 *tāngyuán* 'rice ball'
ARGSTR = [D-ARG$_1$ = y: individual
D-ARG$_2$ = z: individual]
QUALIA = [FORMAL = x: food
TELIC = eat (y, x)
AGENTIVE = make (z, x)]

Corpus data support the above analysis. Table 6 demonstrates [Verb+ 足球 *zúqiú* 'football'] in Gigaword. 踢 *tī* 'kick', 玩 *wán* 'play with', 打 *dǎ* 'play', 踢過 *tīguò* 'kick-experiential ASPECT', and 踢入 *tīrù* 'kick into' are the telic role of 足球 *zúqiú* 'football' , while 製 *zhì* 'make', 縫製 *féngzhì* 'sew', and 生產 *shēngchǎn* 'produce' are the agentive role.

Words	Pinyin	English	Frequency	Saliency	Qualia Role
踢	*tī*	kick	199	74.33	telic
玩	*wán*	play with	37	36.25	telic
打	*dǎ*	play	15	17.04	telic
踢過	*tīguò*	kick-experiential ASPECT	2	15.04	telic
踢入	*tīrù*	kick into	1	8.18	telic
製	*zhì*	make	4	11.46	agentive
縫製	*féngzhì*	sew	2	10.83	agentive
生產	*shēngchǎn*	produce	7	7.51	agentive

Table 6: 足球 *zúqiú* 'football' as Objects in Gigaword

Table 7 shows [Verb+湯圓 *tāngyuán* 'rice ball'] in Gigaword. 吃 *chī* 'eat', 品嚐 *pǐncháng* 'taste', 食用 *shíyòng* 'eat and use', and so on are the telic role of 湯圓 *tāngyuán* 'rice ball', while 製作 *zhìzuò* 'make', 包 *bāo* 'wrap', and 搓 *cuō* 'knead', and so on are the agentive role.

Words	Pinyin	English	Frequency	Saliency	Qualia Role
吃	*chī*	eat	152	56.04	telic
品嚐	*pǐncháng*	taste	10	24.5	telic
食用	*shíyòng*	eat and use	9	20.73	telic
吃到	*chīdào*	Eat-RVC	3	14.22	telic
煮食	*zhǔshí*	cook and eat	2	14.17	telic
享用	*xiǎngyòng*	enjoy	3	12.96	telic
吃吃	*chīchī*	eat eat	1	8.27	telic
嚐	*cháng*	taste	1	6.18	telic
共用	*gòngxiǎng*	share	1	5.06	telic
享受	*xiǎngshòu*	enjoy	1	3.48	telic
製作	*zhìzuò*	make	18	24.15	agentive
包	*bāo*	wrap	9	21.89	agentive
搓成	*cuōchéng*	knead-RVC	2	17.73	agentive
搓搖出	*cuōyáochū*	knead and shake out	1	13.06	agentive
搓	*cuō*	knead	1	13.06	agentive
捏	*niē*	pinch	2	12.32	agentive
搓出	*cuōchū*	knead-RVC	1	11.45	agentive
搓好	*cuōhǎo*	knead well	1	11.45	agentive
做	*zuò*	make	7	9.61	agentive
搓揉	*cuōróu*	knead and rub	1	9.07	agentive
自製	*zìzhì*	self-made	1	4.77	agentive
製成	*zhìchéng*	make-RVC	1	4.77	agentive

Table 7: 湯圓 *tāngyuán* 'rice ball' as Objects in Gigaword

However, as modifiers of 比賽 *bǐsài* 'competition', their activated coercions are different. 足球比賽 *zúqiú bǐsài* 'football competition' has a strong convention of occurring in the sports domain, so the most possible reading comes from the telic role. That is, a competition of playing football rather than producing a football. By contrast, 湯圓比賽 *tāngyuán bǐsài* 'rice ball competition' does not show a preference for either the telic or agentive event, which renders both eating and making rice balls as possible readings.

This finding is confirmed by corpus data of Gigaword Corpus. We set window size as 5 tokens between N$_1$ and N$_2$. The result is indicated in Table 8.

NN	Telic Event	Agentive	To

			Event		tal Hi ts
	Hit s	Freq uenc y	H i t s	Freq uenc y	
足球比賽 *zúqiú bǐsài* 'football competition'	443 2	100.0 0%	0	0.00 %	44 32
湯圓比賽 *tāngyuán bǐsài* 'rice ball competition'	2	28.57 %	5	71.43 %	7

Table 8: Coerced Event Difference in Gigaword

In Table 8, 足球比賽 *zúqiú bǐsài* 'football competition' has 4432 occurrences, with all of them indicating telic events and none as agentive events. 湯圓比賽 *tāngyuán bǐsài* 'rice ball competition' has seven hits in total, with two as telic events and five as agentive events, so this compound do not show strong tendency towards any of the two events.

5 Conclusions and Future Work

This paper discovers that [N_1+Artifactual-Type Event Noun] type compounds usually get a syntagmatic relation through three mechanisms: pure selection, type coercion and sub-composition.

In GL, pure selection and type coercion have been used when a predicate selects an argument (Pustejovsky 1993, 2001, 2006, 2011; Pustejovsky & Jezek 2008). This paper extends their usage in two directions: 1) nominal head selection of a nominal modifier, and 2) their usage in the nominal event domain, though the case study on [N_1+比賽 *bǐsài* 'competition'].

Moreover, this paper proposes a new compositional mechanism *sub-composition.* It is a relation between a function and an argument. The four qualia roles are treated as four functions. Two kinds of [N_1+ artifactual-type event noun] type [N_1N_2] compounds are composed through *sub-composition*: 1) N_1 as an argument and N_2 as a function, and 2) N_1 as a function and N_2 as an argument. In type 1), N_1 is a qualia role of N_2, and thus N_1 has enriched the function behavior; in type 2), N_2 is a qualia role of N_1, and thus N_2 has enriched the function behavior. Because a NN compound is often ambiguous, it may have several kinds of relations. The theorem for *sub-composition* can be generalized as follows.

> In order for α and β to combine as [αβ], you need to extract some sub-elements from α or β depending on which is the function. If [αβ] is an argument-function relation, then [αβ] = β [f_i (α)]. If [αβ] is a function-argument relation, then [αβ] = α [f_i (β)].

Following Wang & Huang (2011a), this paper further demonstrates that some domains have strong conventional events, while some others do not. The former gives a default reading, while the latter brings about ambiguity.

This research has not only enriches the study on compositionality and GL, but also reveals the domain information contribution in type coercion. In future work, we would extend the compositional mechanisms discussed here in two directions: 1) their usage to other types of event nouns, i.e., natural types, natural complex types and artifactual complex types, and 2) their usage to other constructions, such as 'adjective + noun'.

Acknowledgements

We are very grateful to Prof. James Pustejovsky for sharing his ideas during the discussions on this project. The remaining errors are ours. This research is funded by The Student Attachment Program of The Hong Kong Polytechnic University.

References

Han, Lei. 2007. The Selection of Event Nouns and Classifiers——A Case Study of *yǔ. Journal of East China Normal University (Philosophy and Social Sciences),* 39 (3). P64-68.

Han, Lei. 2011. Classification and Categorization of Event Nouns. *Paper presented at The 6th International Conference on Contemporary Chinese Grammar (ICCCG-6)*, I-Shou University, Kaohsiung, Taiwan.

Jackendoff, Ray. 1975. Morphological and Semantic Regularities in the Lexicon. *Language,* 51 (3). P639-671.

Johnston, Michael & Federica Busa. 1996. *Qualia Structure and the Compositional Interpretation of*

Compounds. Proceedings of the ACL SIGLEX workshop on breadth and depth of semantic lexicons, P77-88. Santa Cruz, California.

Laurie Bauer. 2008. When is a Sequence of Two Nouns a Compound in English? *English Language and Linguistics* 2 (1). P65-86.

Lee, Chih-yao, Chia-hao Chang, Wei-chieh Hsu & Shu-kai Hsieh. 2010. *Qualia Modification in Noun-Noun Compounds: A Cross-Language Survey*. Proceedings of the 22nd Conference on Computational Linguistics and Speech Processing (ROCLING-2010), P379-390. National Chi Nan University, Puli, Nantou, Taiwan.

Liu, Shun. 2004. A Study of Temporality of Common Nouns. *Language Teaching and Linguistic Studies* (4).P25-35.

Ma, Qingzhu. 1995. *Verbs with denotational Meaning and Nouns with Statement Meaning*. Research and Exploration of the Grammar. Beijing: The Commercial Press.

Packard, Jerome L. 2004. *The Morphology of Chinese: A Linguistic and Cognitive Approach*. Cambridge: Cambridge University Press.

Pustejovsky, James. 1993. *Type Coercion and Lexical Selection*. Semantics and the Lexicon, ed. by James Pustejovsky, P73-94. Dordrecht, The Netherlands: Kluwer Academic Publishers.

Pustejovsky, James. 1995. *The Generative Lexicon*. Cambridge, MA: MIT Press.

Pustejovsky, James. 2000. *Events and the semantics of opposition*. Events as grammatical objects: the converging perspectives of lexical semantics and syntax, ed. by Carol Tenny & James Pustejovsky, P445-482. Stanford: CSLI Publications.

Pustejovsky, James. 2001. *Type Construction and the Logic of Concepts*. The Language of Word Meaning, ed. by Pierrette Bouillon & Federica Busa, P91-123: Cambridge University Press.

Pustejovsky, James. 2006. Type Theory and Lexical Decomposition. *Journal of Cognitive Science* 7 (1). P39-76.

Pustejovsky, James. 2011. Coercion in a General Theory of Argument Selection. *Linguistics* 49 (6). P1401–1431

Pustejovsky, James. 2012. *Co-compositionality in Grammar*. The Oxford Handbook of Compositionality, ed. by Markus Werning, Wolfram Hinzen & Edouard Machery, P371-382. New York: Oxford University Press.

Pustejovsky, James & Elisabetta Jezek. 2008. Semantic Coercion in Language: Beyond Distributional Analysis. *Distributional Models of the Lexicon in Linguistics and Cognitive Science, special issue of Italian Journal of Linguistics/Rivista di Linguistica.*

Qi, Chong. 2012. *The Semantic Relations of Internal Construction in NN Modifier-Head Compounds.* The 13th Chinese Lexical Semantics Workshop (CLSW-13), ed. by Yanxiang He & Donghong Ji, P211-215. Wuhan University, China.

Wang, Shan & Chu-Ren Huang. 2011a. Domain Relevance of Event Coercion in Compound Nouns. *Paper presented at The 6th International Conference on Contemporary Chinese Grammar (ICCCG-6)*, I-Shou University, Kaohsiung, Taiwan.

Wang, Shan & Chu-Ren Huang. 2011b. Event Classifiers and Their Selected Nouns. *Paper presented at The 19th Annual Conference of the International Association of Chinese Linguistics (IACL-19)*, Nankai University, Tianjin, China.

Wang, Shan & Chu-Ren Huang. 2012a. A Constraint-based Linguistic Model for Event Nouns. *Paper presented at Forum on 'Y. R. Chao and Linguistics', Workshop of The 20th Annual Conference of the International Association of Chinese Linguistics (IACL-20)*, The Hong Kong Institute of Education, Hong Kong.

Wang, Shan & Chu-Ren Huang. 2012b. *A Preliminary Study of An Event-based Noun Classification System.* The 13th Chinese Lexical Semantics Workshop (CLSW-13), ed. by Yanxiang He & Donghong Ji, P4-9. Wuhan University, China.

Wang, Shan & Chu-Ren Huang. 2012c. Qualia Structure of Event Nouns in Mandarin Chinese. *Paper presented at The Second International Symposium on Chinese Language and Discourse* Nanyang Technological University, Singapore.

Wang, Shan & Chu-Ren Huang. 2012d. Temporal Properties of Event Nouns in Mandarin Chinese. *Paper presented at The 57th Annual International Linguistic Association Conference (ILA-57)* New York, USA

Wang, Shan & Chu-Ren Huang. 2012e. Type Construction of Event Nouns in Mandarin Chinese. *Paper presented at The First Workshop on Generative Lexicon for Asian Languages (GLAL-1), Workshop of The 26th Pacific Asia Conference on Language, Information and Computation (PACLIC-26)*, Bali, Indonesia.

Warren, Beatrice. 1978. *Semantic Patterns of Noun-Noun Compounds*. Göteborg: Acta Universitatis Göthoburgensis.

Automatic Domain Adaptation for Word Sense Disambiguation Based on Comparison of Multiple Classifiers

Kanako Komiya
Tokyo University of Agriculture and Technology
2-24-16 Naka-cho, Koganei
Tokyo, 184-8588 Japan
kkomiya@cc.tuat.ac.jp

Manabu Okumura
Tokyo Institute of Technology
4259 Nagatsuta Modori-ku
Yokohama 226-8503 Japan
oku@pi.titech.ac.jp

Abstract

Domain adaptation (DA), which involves adapting a classifier developed from source to target data, has been studied intensively in recent years. However, when DA for word sense disambiguation (WSD) was carried out, the optimal DA method varied according to the properties of the source and target data. This paper proposes automatic DA based on comparing the degrees of confidence of multiple classifiers for each instance. We compared three classifiers for three DA methods, where 1) a classifier was trained with a small amount of target data that was randomly selected and manually labeled but without source data, 2) a classifier was trained with source data and a small amount of target data that was randomly selected and manually labeled, and 3) a classifier was trained with selected source data that were sufficiently similar to the target data and a small amount of target data that was randomly selected and manually labeled. We used the method whose degree of confidence was the highest for each instance when Japanese WSD was carried out. The average accuracy of WSD when the DA methods that were determined automatically were used was significantly higher than when the original methods were used collectively.

1 Introduction

Classifiers in standard supervised machine learning have been trained for data in domain A using manually annotated data in domain A, e.g., to train classifiers for newswires using newswires. However, classifiers for data in domain B have sometimes been necessary when there have been no or few manually annotated data, and there have only been manually annotated data in domain A, which has been related to domain B. Domain adaptation (DA) involves adapting the classifier that has been trained from data in domain A (source domain) to data in domain B (target domain). This has been studied intensively in recent years.

However, the optimal method of DA varied according to the properties of the data in the source domain (the source data) and the data in the target domain (the target data) when DA for word sense disambiguation (WSD) was carried out.

There are many methods of DA for WSD but we assume that the optimal method varies according to each instance. This paper proposes automatic DA based on comparison of the degrees of confidence of multiple classifiers for each instance when Japanese WSD is performed. Our experiments show that the average accuracy of WSD when the DA methods that were determined automatically were used was significantly higher than when the original methods were used collectively.

This paper is organized as follows. Section 2 reviews related work on DA and Section 3 explains how a DA method is automatically determined. Sections 4 and 5 describe the methods and the data we used, respectievly. We present the results in Section 6 and discuss them in Section 7. Finally, we conclude the paper in Section 8.

2 Related Work

The DA problem can be categorized into three types depending on the information for learning, i.e., supervised, semi-supervised, and unsupervised approaches. A classifier in a supervised approach is developed from a large amount of labeled source data and a small amount of labeled target data with the aim of classifying target data better than a classifier developed only from the target data. A classifier in a semi-supervised approach is developed from a large amount of labeled source data and unlabeled target data with the aim of classifying target data better than a classifier developed only from the source data. Finally, a classifier is developed from a large amount of labeled source data with the aim of classifying target data accurately in an unsupervised approach. We focused on the supervised DA for WSD in this paper.

Many researchers have investigated DA within or outside the area of natural language processing. Chan and Ng (2006) carried out the DA of WSD by estimating class priors using an EM algorithm. Chan and Ng (2007) also conducted the DA of WSD by estimating class priors using the EM algorithm, but this was supervised DA using active learning.

In addition, Daumé III (2007) worked on the supervised DA. He augmented an input space and made triple length features that were general, source-specific, and target-specific. This was easy to implement, could be used with various DA methods, and could easily be extended to multi-DA problems.

Daumé III et al. (2010) extended the work in (Daumé III, 2007) to semi-supervised DA. It inherited the advantages of the supervised version and outperformed it by using unlabeled target data.

Agirre and de Lacalle (2008) worked on the semi-supervised DA for WSD. They applied singular value decomposition (SVD) to a matrix of unlabeled target data and a large amount of unlabeled source data, and trained a classifier with them. Agirre and de Lacalle (2009) worked on the supervised DA using almost the same method, but they used a small amount of labeled source data instead of the large amount of unlabeled source data.

Jiang and Zhai (2007) demonstrated that performance increased as examples were weighted when DA was applied. This method could be used with various other supervised or semi-supervised DA methods. In addition, they tried to identify and remove source data that misled DA, but they concluded that it was only effective if examples were not weighted.

Zhong et al. (2009) proposed an adaptive kernel approach that mapped the marginal distribution of source and target data into a common kernel space. They also conducted sample selection to make the conditional probabilities between the two domains closer.

Raina et al. (2007) proposed self-taught learning that utilized sparse coding to construct higher level features from the unlabeled data collected from the Web. This method was based on unsupervised learning.

Tur (2009) proposed a co-adaptation algorithm where both co-training and DA techniques were used to improve the performance of the model. The research by (Blitzer et al., 2006) involved work on semi-supervised DA, where they calculated the weight of words around the pivot features (words that frequently appeared both in source and target data and behaved similarly in both) to model some words in one domain that behaved similarly in another. They applied SVD to the matrix of the weights, generated a new feature space, and used the new features with the original features.

McClosky et al. (2010) focused on the problem where the best model for each document is not obvious when parsing a document collection of heterogeneous domains. They studied it as a new task of *multiple source parser adaptation*. They proposed a method of parsing a sentence that first predicts accuracies for various parsing models using a regression model, and then uses the parsing model with the highest predicted accuracy. The main difference is that their work was about parsing but ours discussed here is about Japanese WSD. They also assumed that they had labeled corpora in heterogeneous domains but we have not. We determined the best DA method for each instance.

Harimoto et al. (2010) measured the distance between domains to conduct DA using a suitable corpus in parsing. In addition, van Asch and Daelemans (2010) reported that performance in DA could be predicted depending on the similarity between source and target data using automatically annotated corpus in parsing. They focused on how corpora were selected for use as source data according to the distance between domains, but here we have focused on how to select a method of DA depending on the degrees of confidence of multiple classifiers.

The closest work to this work is our previous work: (Komiya and Okumura, 2011) which determined an optimal DA method using decision tree learning given a triple of the target word type of WSD, source data, and target data. It discussed what features affected how the best method was determined. The main difference was that (Komiya and Okumura, 2011) determined the optimal DA method for each triple of the target word type of WSD, source data, and target data, but this paper determined the method for each instance.

3 Automatic determination of DA method for each instance

We assumed that the optimal method would vary according to each instance. The DA method is automatically determined for each instance as follows:

(1) Train multiple classifiers based on various methods,

(2) Compare the degrees of confidence of multiple classifiers for each instance,

(3) Employ the classifier whose degree of confidence is the highest for the instance.

The degrees of confidence we used here are the predicted values that indicate how confident classification is and are often used to select instances to be labeled in active-learning. We focused on the fact that these degrees of confidence are output from classifiers as the probability, and we can carry out ensemble learning by comparing them.

We would be able to determine the best DA method automatically using ensemble learning based on the degrees of confidence for each instance. Hence, we expected the average accuracy of WSD, when DA methods that were determined automatically were used for each instance, to be higher than when the original methods were used collectively. Navigli (2009) introduced this method as ensemble method for WSD and called it *probability mixture*. We used the *probability mixture* assuming that each classifier is trained for each DA method, rather than for each WSD method.

4 DA methods for WSD

Three methods were used as the DA methods for WSD in this study. All the methods except *Similarity Filtering* were adapted from (Komiya and Okumura, 2011) and *Similarity Filtering* was adapted from (Komiya and Okumura, 2012).

- *Target Only*: Train a classifier with a small amount of target data that is randomly selected and manually labeled but without source data.
- *Random Sampling*: Train a classifier with source data and a small amount of target data that is randomly selected and manually labeled.
- *Similarity Filtering*: Train a classifier with source data and a small amount of target data that is randomly selected and manually labeled. Only the source data that are sufficiently similar to the target data are selected by filtering and used.

The source data were selected as follows in *Similarity Filtering*. Here, the instances in the source and target data are represented as a vector in the WSD feature space. Each instance of WSD represents a word token whose word sense should be disambiguated.

(1) For every instance of target data $\forall t_i \in T$, calculate $sim_{i,j}$, i.e., the cosine similarity to every instance of source data $\forall s_j \in S$.

(2) For every instance of source data $\forall s_j \in S$, find $t_{j,nearest}$, i.e., the nearest instance in all the target data.

(3) For every instance of source data $\forall s_j \in S$, determine if it will be included in the training data set. Only source data s_j whose $sim_{j,nearest}$ is higher than 0.8 are used for the training data in this paper.

Ten instances of the target data were randomly selected and manually labeled in all the experiments.

Libsvm (Chang and Lin, 2001), which supports multi-class classification, was used as the classifier for WSD. We trained three classifiers and employed the classifier whose degree of confidence was the highest. A linear kernel was used according to the results obtained from preliminary experiments. Seventeen features were introduced to train the classifier.

- Morphological features
  - Bag-of-words
  - Part-of-speech (POS)
  - Finer subcategory of POS
- Syntactic feature
  - If the POS of a target word is a noun, the verb which the target word modifies
  - If the POS of a target word is a verb, the case element of 'ヲ' (wo, objective) for the verb
- Semantic feature
  - Semantic classification code

Morphological features and a semantic feature were extracted from the surrounding words (two words to the right and left) of the target word. POS and finer subcategory of POS can be obtained using a morphological analyzer. We used ChaSen [1] as a morphological analyzer, the Bunruigoihyo thesaurus (National Institute for Japanese Language and Linguistics, 1964) for semantic classification codes (e.g. The code of 'program' is 1.3162.), and CaboCha [2] as a syntactic parser. Five-fold cross validation was used in the experiments.

5 Data

Three data which are the same as (Komiya and Okumura, 2011) were used for the experiments: (1) the sub-corpus of white papers in the Balanced Corpus of Contemporary Japanese (BCCWJ) (Maekawa, 2008), (2) the sub-corpus of documents from a Q&A site on the WWW in BCCWJ, and (3) Real World Computing (RWC) text databases (newspaper articles) (Hashida et al., 1998). DAs were conducted in six directions according to different source and target data. Word senses were annotated in these corpora according to a Japanese dictionary, i.e., the Iwanami Kokugo Jiten (Nishio et al., 1994). It has three levels for sense IDs, and we used the fine-level sense in the experiments. Multi-sense words that appeared equal or more than 50 times in both source and target data were selected as the target words in the experiment. There were 24 word types for white papers ⇔ Q&A site, 22 for white papers ⇔ newspaper articles, and 26 for Q&A site ⇔ newspaper articles. Twenty-eight word types were used in the experiments in total. Table 1 lists the minimum, maximum, and average number of instances of each word type for each corpus and Table 2 summarizes the number of instances of WSD for all combinations of corpora. Table 3 shows the list of target words.

Genre	Min.	Max.	Ave.
BCCWJ white papers	58	7,610	2074.50
BCCWJ Q&A site	82	13,976	2300.43
RWC newspaper	50	374	164.46

Table 1: Minimum, maximum, and average number of instances of each word type for each corpus

Source data	Target data	No. of instances
Q&A site	white paper	49,788
Q&A site	newspaper	4,276
white paper	Q&A site	60,930
white paper	newspaper	4,034
newspaper	Q&A site	63,805
newspaper	white paper	49,283
Total		232,116

Table 2: The number of instances of WSD for all combinations of corpora

(Komiya and Okumura, 2011) found that the optimal method of DA varied depending on each 'case' (i.e., a triple of the target word type of WSD, the source data, and the target data). Here, we have assumed that it varies according to each instance.

6 Results

Table 4 lists the micro and macro averaged accuracies of WSD for the whole data set and Tables 5 and 6 summarize the micro and macro averaged accuracies of WSD according to the corpora and DA methods, respectively. [3] The DA methods in bold are

[1] http://sourceforge.net/projects/masayu-a/

[2] http://sourceforge.net/projects/cabocha/

[3] The macro-averaged accuracies were always lower than micro-averaged accuracies in the three tables. We think this

Number of senses	Target words (in Japanese)	Sense example in English
2	場合	case
	自分	self
3	事業	project
	情報	information
	地方	area
	社会	society
	思う	suppose
	子供	child
4	分かる	understand
	考える	think
5	含む	contain
	使う	use
	技術	technique
6	関係	connection
	時間	time
	一般	general
	現在	present
	作る	make
7	今	now
8	前	before
10	持つ	have
11	進む	advance
12	見る	see
14	入る	enter
16	言う	say
21	出す	serve
22	手	hand
	出る	leave

Table 3: The list of target words

our proposed methods. *RS and TO* selected the DA method for each instance from *Random Sampling* and *Target Only*, *RS and SF* selected it from *Random Sampling* and *Similarity Filtering*, *SF and TO* selected it from *Similarity Filtering* and *Target Only*, and *All* selected it from *Random Sampling*, *Target Only*, and *Similarity Filtering* in Tables 4, 5, and 6. We used the -b option of libsvm when the method was *Random sampling*, *Target Only*, and *Similarity Filtering* to train a model for probability estimation. *MFS*, which is most frequent sense of fully annotated target data, *Source Only*, which is standard supervised learning only with the source data, *Self*, which is standard supervised learning with the whole target data, assuming that fully annotated data were obtained and could be used for learning, *oracle(i)*, which is oracle(instance) assuming that the system knows the optimal DA method for each instance, and *oracle(c)*, which is oracle(case) assuming that the system knows the optimal DA method given a 'case', were tested as references.

DA method	Micro	Macro
Random Sampling	79.85%	73.39%
Target Only	79.66%	72.09%
Similarity Filtering	78.47%	71.24%
RS and TO	***83.50 %**	***75.60%**
RS and SF	***81.22 %**	**74.09%**
SF and TO	***80.97 %**	**72.87%**
All	***82.96 %**	***74.77%**
MFS	77.05%	72.23%
Source Only	76.61%	69.82%
Self	92.82%	84.10%
oracle(i)_RS and TO	89.15%	83.31%
oracle(i)_RS and SF	89.15%	81.81%
oracle(i)_SF and TO	86.71%	79.82%
oracle(i)_All	91.74%	85.81%
oracle(c)_RS and TO	84.57%	77.73%
oracle(c)_RS and SF	84.03%	76.41%
oracle(c)_SF and TO	81.67%	75.17%
oracle(c)_All	85.14%	78.25%

Table 4: Average accuracies of WSD for the whole data set

The underline in these three tables means the highest accuracy for each combination of the source and target corpus and the bold means the proposed method outperformed the original methods. For example, the accuracy of *RS and TO* is in bold when it outperformed *Random Sampling* and *Target Only*. The asterisk means the difference between accuracies of the proposed and original methods is statistically significant according to a chi-square test. The level of significance in the test was 0.05.

7 Discussion

Table 4 indicates that our proposed method of automatic DA based on comparison of multiple classifiers always outperformed the original methods

is because the tasks with many data tend to give high accuracy.

Source data	Q&A site	Q&A site	white paper	white paper	newspaper	newspaper
Target data	white paper	newspaper	Q&A site	newspaper	Q&A site	white paper
DA method	Accuracy					
Random Sampling	87.21%	73.95%	83.97%	72.09%	76.61%	72.66%
Target Only	88.35%	66.46%	75.74%	67.75%	74.46%	84.57%
Similarity Filtering	88.20%	71.14%	70.04%	70.45%	75.04%	84.77%
RS and TO	**88.54%**	72.80%	*83.03%	**72.48%**	***78.10%**	***87.81%**
RS and SF	***88.65%**	73.20%	*80.14%	**72.46%**	***77.83%**	*80.86%
SF and TO	***90.17%**	70.39%	*74.53%	**70.72%**	***75.78%**	***88.09%**
All	***89.96%**	72.54%	*80.66%	**72.63%**	***77.22%**	***87.90%**
MFS	78.81%	67.35%	76.70%	68.59%	75.88%	78.74%
Source Only	80.64%	73.46%	83.37%	71.02%	75.50%	66.36%
Self	95.98%	78.09%	91.75%	79.57%	90.69%	96.07%
oracle(i)_RS and TO	91.09%	83.33%	90.59%	85.32%	83.18%	93.96%
oracle(i)_RS and SF	92.21%	81.48%	87.65%	79.35%	85.20%	94.47%
oracle(i)_SF and TO	93.85%	76.75%	83.70%	81.46%	81.42%	91.34%
oracle(i)_All	94.41%	84.87%	92.38%	87.63%	87.22%	95.06%
oracle(c)_RS and TO	88.58%	75.80%	85.41%	76.67%	76.66%	88.62%
oracle(c)_RS and SF	89.40%	75.28%	84.02%	73.53%	79.42%	86.21%
oracle(c)_SF and TO	89.83%	71.75%	76.35%	74.07%	76.66%	87.98%
oracle(c)_All	89.87%	75.84%	85.43%	77.09%	79.46%	88.80%

Table 5: Micro-averaged accuracies of WSD according to the corpora and the DA methods

when the average accuracies for all the directions of DA were compared. All the differences between micro-averaged accuracies of the proposed and original methods were statistically significant according to a chi-square test. When macro-averaged accuracies were compared, some differences were no longer significant due to the decrease of the samples of the test. Tables 5 and 6 denoted the same tendencies.

Table 4 also shows the micro and macro averaged accuracies of all the proposed method outperformed baseline methods, *Source Only* and *MFS*, as well as the three original methods. Particularlly, our proposed methods have beaten *MFS*, the baseline which needs fully annotated target data although our methods do not need them.

In addition, Tables 5 and 6 indicate that the automatic DA method based on comparison of multiple classifiers outperformed the original methods in four directions except when the source data were a Q&A site and the target data were newspapers and when the source data were white papers and the target data were a Q&A site. [4] These results mean that our proposed method is not always effective for every combination of all corpora but it is generally effective.

However, the results of *oracle(i)* are much better than those of the proposed methods. This indicates that the degree of confidence does not always predict the correct answer.

In addition, Table 4 shows the accuracy of *All*, i.e., the proposed method where the DA method was selected from three methods, is not the highest; the accuracy of *RS and TO*, the proposed method where the DA method was selected from two methods, is higher than this. According to Tables 5 and 6, the accuracies of *All* are not always the highest as seen in Table 4. In fact, the highest accuracy varies according to the combination of the source and target corpora and even depending on how they were averaged (micro vs. macro). Tables 5 and 6 show that

[4]However, *RS and TO* gives the highest accuracy when the source data were white papers and the target data were a Q&A site in Table 6.

Source data	Q&A site	Q&A site	white paper	white paper	newspaper	newspaper
Target data	white paper	newspaper	Q&A site	newspaper	Q&A site	white paper
DA method	Accuracy					
Random Sampling	84.45%	71.06%	72.56%	69.54%	69.25%	73.74%
Target Only	83.74%	63.76%	68.99%	67.31%	68.04%	82.18%
Similarity Filtering	83.85%	68.17%	58.75%	69.20%	67.16%	81.62%
RS and TO	**84.48%**	69.40%	**73.21%**	**71.04%**	***72.04%**	***84.64%**
RS and SF	**84.64%**	69.99%	*68.53%	**70.12%**	***72.18%**	79.73%
SF and TO	**85.69%**	67.08%	*63.59%	**69.44%**	**68.84%**	**84.07%**
All	**85.70%**	68.84%	*69.25%	**70.73%**	**71.41%**	**83.91%**
MFS	78.21%	66.28%	71.46%	70.27%	69.81%	77.58%
Source Only	75.27%	70.71%	70.66%	68.07%	67.86%	65.96%
Self	91.13%	74.79%	85.24%	78.59%	84.23%	91.53%
oracle(i)_RS and TO	88.32%	79.80%	82.55%	83.09%	77.66%	89.75%
oracle(i)_RS and SF	89.27%	78.61%	74.69%	76.89%	79.94%	92.36%
oracle(i)_SF and TO	89.83%	72.85%	77.19%	79.33%	74.81%	86.39%
oracle(i)_All	91.92%	81.39%	84.22%	85.56%	82.25%	90.53%
oracle(c)_RS and TO	85.71%	72.78%	76.44%	75.10%	73.07%	84.41%
oracle(c)_RS and SF	86.61%	72.36%	72.71%	71.66%	73.14%	82.72%
oracle(c)_SF and TO	85.89%	68.74%	70.39%	73.39%	69.71%	84.52%
oracle(c)_All	87.08%	72.88%	76.53%	75.82%	73.34%	85.06%

Table 6: Macro-averaged accuracies of WSD according to the corpora and the DA methods

only one combination for each table had the highest accuracy with *All* (white paper ⇒ newspaper in Table 5 and Q&A site ⇒ white paper in Table 6). They indicate that the accuracy does not always increase with the augmentation of the methods to be compared.

We think the reasons why *RS and TO* outperformed *All* are as follows. First, it is because the accuracy of *Similarity Filtering* was not as high as that of the other two methods according to Table 4. The accuracies of *RS and SF*, and *SF and TO* were also lower than that of *RS and TO*. Therefore, it seems that the accuracy of *All* decreased because the accuracy of the third method, *Similarity Filtering*, was lower than that of the others.

Moreover, we think that *RS and TO* achieved the highest accuracy because the two DA methods, *Random Sampling* and *Target Only*, were sufficiently different. In contrast, *Similarity Filtering* is similar to *Target Only* when the source and target data are not similar to each other and it is similar to *Random Sampling* when the source and target data are similar to each other. In other words, the DA method *Similarity Filtering* is intermediate between *Random Sampling* and *Target Only* and is similar to either of them in some way. We think that the experiments revealed that the accuracy of WSD increases when the DA methods are selected from those that are sufficiently different to one another.

Furthermore, we think that the property of *Target Only* affected the high accuracy of *RS and TO*. The accuracy of *Target Only* is very high especially when the percentage of occurrences of the most frequent sense is high as Khapra et al. (2010) stated that "Sense distributions of words are highly skewed and depend heavily on the domain at hand. This fact makes it very difficult for WSD approaches to beat the corpus baseline." On the other hand, the method *Target Only* will never be able to output the correct word sense for the instances whose word senses do not appear in the training data. Thus, the method with more training data, i.e., *Random Sampling*, should be used for these instances. We think the accuracy of *RS and TO* is high because the degree of confidence of *Target Only* is low for the instances whose word senses do not appear in the training data (because their features are not similar to those of instances in the training data) .

We compare these results with those of Komiya and Okumura (2011). Even though we cannot have a direct comparison because the svm-predict -b 0 and -b1 (with/without probability estimation) give different accuracy values, the best result of the proposed method (83.50) is comparable to that of Komiya and Okumura (2011) (83.50). In addition, oracle(i) always outperformed oracle(c) in all the experiments, which indicates that our assumption where the optimal method of DA varies according to each instance seems to be better than that of Komiya and Okumura (2011) where it varies according to each 'case'. Even though the degree of confidence does not always predict the correct answer, we think the proposed method is sufficiently useful because it is much simpler than the previous method.

Finally, this paper compared only three methods, *Target Only*, *Random Sampling*, and *Similarity Filtering*, and we used the method whose degree of confidence was the highest for each instance. It remains unanswered and should be investigated in the future how effective this method is when the DA methods used changes or when the number of DA methods increases.

8 Conclusion

This paper proposed automatic DA based on comparing the degrees of confidence of multiple classifiers for each instance. We compared three classifiers for three DA methods, *Target Only*, *Random Sampling*, and *Similarity Filtering* and used the method whose degree of confidence was the highest for each instance. *Target Only* was a method where a classifier was trained with a small amount of target data that was randomly selected and manually labeled but without source data, *Random Sampling* was a method where a classifier was trained with source data and a small amount of target data that was randomly selected and manually labeled, and *Similarity Filtering* was a method where a classifier was trained with selected source data that were sufficiently similar to the target data and a small amount of target data that was randomly selected and manually labeled. The average accuracy of WSD when the DA methods that were determined automatically were used was significantly higher than when the original methods were used collectively. However, the experiment revealed that the accuracy of *All*, the proposed method where the DA method was selected from the three methods, was not the highest. The accuracy of *RS and TO*, i.e., the proposed method where the DA method was selected from the two methods, was higher than this. We think that the accuracy of WSD increases when the DA methods are selected from the methods that are sufficiently different. Even though the degree of confidence does not always predict the correct answer, we think the proposed method is sufficiently useful. It remains unanswered and should be investigated in the future how effective this method is when DA methods used changes or when the number of DA methods increases.

Acknowledgments

We would like to thank the reviewers for very constructive and detailed comments. This research is supported be Grants-in-Aid for Scientific Research, Priority Area "Japanese Corpus".

References

Eneko Agirre and Oier Lopez de Lacalle. 2008. On robustness and domain adaptation using svd for word sense disambiguation. In *Proceedings of the 22nd International Conference on Computational Linguistics*, pages 17–24.

Eneko Agirre and Oier Lopez de Lacalle. 2009. Supervised domain adaption for wsd. In *Proceedings of the 12th Conference of the European Chapter of the Association of Computational Linguistics*, pages 42–50.

John Blitzer, Ryan McDonald, and Fernando Pereira. 2006. Domain adaptation with structural coppespondence learning. In *Proceedings of the 2006 Conference on Empirical Methods in Natural Language Processing*, pages 120–128.

Yee Seng Chan and Hwee Tou Ng. 2006. Estimating class priors in domain adaptation for word sense disambiguation. In *Proceedings of the 21st International Conference on Computational Linguistics and 44th Annual Meeting of the Association for Computational Linguistics*, pages 89–96.

Yee Seng Chan and Hwee Tou Ng. 2007. Domain adaptation with active learning for word sense disambiguation. In *Proceedings of the 45th Annual Meeting of the Association of Computational Linguistics*, pages 49–56.

Chih-Chung Chang and Chih-Jen Lin, 2001. *LIBSVM: a library for support vector machines*. Software available at http://www.csie.ntu.edu.tw/ cjlin/libsvm.

Hal Daumé III, Abhishek Kumar, and Avishek Saha. 2010. Frustratingly easy semi-supervised domain adaptation. In *Proceedings of the 2010 Workshop on Domain Adaptation for Natural Language Processing, ACL 2010*, pages 23–59.

Hal Daumé III. 2007. Frustratingly easy domain adaptation. In *Proceedings of the 45th Annual Meeting of the Association of Computational Linguistics*, pages 256–263.

Keiko Harimoto, Yusuke Miyao, and Jun'ichi Tsujii. 2010. Kobunkaiseki no bunyatekiou ni okeru seido teika youin no bunseki oyobi bunyakan kyori no sokutei syuhou, in japanese. In *Proceedings of NLP2010*, pages 27–30.

Koichi Hashida, Hitoshi Isahara, Takenobu Tokunaga, Minako Hashimoto, Shiho Ogino, and Wakako Kashino. 1998. The rwc text databases. In *Proceedings of the First International Conference on Language Resource and Evaluation*, pages 457–461.

Jing Jiang and ChengXiang Zhai. 2007. Instance weighting for domain adaptation in nlp. In *Proceedings of the 45th Annual Meeting of the Association of Computational Linguistics*, pages 264–271.

Mitesh Khapra, Sapan Shah, Piyush Kedia, and Pushpak Bhattacharyya. 2010. Domain-specific word sense disambiguation combining corpus based and wordnet based parameters. In *Proceedings of the 5th International Conference on Global Wordnet (GWC2010)*.

Kanako Komiya and Manabu Okumura. 2011. Automatic determination of a domain adaptation method for word sense disambiguation using decision tree learning. In *Proceedings of the 5th International Joint Conference on Natural Language Processing, IJCNLP 2011*, pages 1107–1115.

Kanako Komiya and Manabu Okumura. 2012. Automatic selection of domain adaptation method for wsd using decision tree learning. In *Journal of NLP (In Japanese), In press*.

Kikuo Maekawa. 2008. Balanced corpus of contemporary written japanese. In *Proceedings of the 6th Workshop on Asian Language Resources (ALR)*, pages 101–102.

David McClosky, Eugene Charniak, and Mark Johnson. 2010. Automatic domain adaptation for parsing. In *Proceedings of the 2010 Annual Conference of the North American Chapter of the Association for Computational Linguistics*, pages 28–36.

National Institute for Japanese Language and Linguistics. 1964. *Bunruigoihyo*. Shuuei Shuppan, In Japanese.

Roberto Navigli. 2009. Word sense disambiguation: A survey. *ACM Comput. Surv.*, 41(2):1–69.

Minoru Nishio, Etsutaro Iwabuchi, and Shizuo Mizutani. 1994. *Iwanami Kokugo Jiten Dai Go Han*. Iwanami Publisher, In Japanese.

Rajat Raina, Alexis Battle, Honglak Lee, Benjamin Packer, and Andrew Y. Ng. 2007. Self-taught learning: Transfer learning from unlabeled data. In *ICML '07: Proceedings of the 24th international conference on Machine learning*, pages 759–766.

Gokhan Tur. 2009. Co-adaptation: Adaptive co-training for semi-supervised learning. In *Proceedings of the IEEE International Conference on Acoustics, Speech and Signal Processing, 2009. ICASSP 2009.*, pages 3721–3724.

Vincent van Asch and Walter Daelemans. 2010. Using domain similarity for performance estimation. In *Proceedings of the 2010 Workshop on Domain Adaptation for Natural Language Processing, ACL 2010*, pages 31–36.

Erheng Zhong, Wei Fan, Jing Peng, Kun Zhang, Jiangtao Ren, Deepak Turaga, and Olivier Verscheure. 2009. Cross domain distribution adaptation via kernel mapping. In *Proceedings of the 15th ACM SIGKDD international conference on Knowledge discovery and data mining*, pages 1027–1036.

Calculating Selectional Preferences of Transitive Verbs in Korean

Sanghoun Song
Department of Linguistics
University of Washington
Box 354340 Seattle, WA 98195-4340, USA
sanghoun@uw.edu

Jae-Woong Choe
Department of Linguistics
Korea University
145 Anam-ro Seongbuk-gu Seoul, 136-701 Korea
jchoe@korea.ac.kr

Abstract

This study calculates the selectional preference strength between transitive verbs and their co-occurring objects, and thereby investigates how much they are co-related to each other in Korean. The selectional preference strength is automatically measured in a bottom-up way, and the outcomes are evaluated in comparison with a manually constructed resource that indicates which verb takes which class(es) of nouns as its dependents. The measurement offered by this study not only can be used to improve NLP applications, but also has a theoretic significance in that it can play a role as distributional evidence in the study of argument structure.

1 Introduction

Selectional Preference Strength (henceforth, SPS) refers to the degree of correlation between two co-occurring linguistic items. This study, exploiting some Korean language resources and employing the Kullback-Leibler Divergence model formulated by Resnik (1996), aims to calculate SPS between transitive verbs and the classes of co-occurring nouns that function as objects.

As far as we know, there has been no previous study to calculate SPS in Korean. Now that several Korean resources constructed on a comprehensive scale are currently available, it would be very interesting to conduct a systematic analysis of SPS in Korean and to see what kind of significant patterns and results can be found through such analysis. This research is an endeavour in that direction, and reports some results of our analysis of SPS between predicates and their object argument, which is based on language resources like treebanks, wordnets, and electronic dictionaries. We also expect that our analysis would make a meaningful contribution to our understanding of the semantic interaction between verbal items and argument structure in Korean.

This paper is structured as follows. Section 2 discusses why it is necessary to look into SPS in NLP, and offers a brief explanation of the background knowledge. Section 3 covers the computational model that this study employs, and Section 4 measures SPS using a Korean wordnet (i.e. KorLex) and a development corpus (i.e. the *Sejong* Korean Treebank). The results are evaluated quantitatively as well as qualitatively in Section 5. This paper closes in Section 6 with a brief look at our further work to help NLP systems perform better.

2 Background

The Korean language, as is well-known, is an agglutinative language with a large number of grammatical function morphemes. It also has features like the right-headness, scrambling, and virtually free deletion of any element from a sentence. On the more semantic side, Korean shows the usual restriction between a predicate and its selection of arguments. The sentence pair in (1) exemplifies the syntactic and semantic behaviours in Korean. The verb *masi* 'drink' can take as its object only a small set of nouns which can roughly defined as the 'drinkable', while rejecting a whole lot of other nouns. While *maykcwu* 'beer' would be a typical object, *chayk* 'book' is inappropriate as the object of the verb.

(1) a. *maykcwu-ul masi-ta*
beer-OBJ drink-DECL
'... drink beer.'

b. *#chayk-ul masi-ta*
book-OBJ drink-DECL
'# ... drink book.'

Notice that the two sentences are of the same morphological and syntactic configuration. It is thus clear that parsing sentences depends heavily on lexical semantics of the words involved. The major question addressed in this study is how we can capture the preferences that hold between a predicate and its arguments in Korean in a systematic way. Following Resnik (1996), this study contends that the questions can be properly answered by SPS, which defines the relationship between a verb and the entire noun class hierarchy.

2.1 Selectional Preference Strength

SPS, an information theoretic concept modeled by Resnik (1996), can be defined as a kind of relative entropy, which indicates how much interrelationship an entity has with another entity. The basic notion of SPS is exemplified in two structurally similar Q/A pairs (Resnik, 1996, pp. 127).

(2) a. Experimenter: Could a cow be green?

b. Subject: I think they're usually brown or white.

(3) a. Experimenter: Could an idea be green?

b. Subject: No, silly! They're only in your head.

Green cows do not necessarily exist in the real world, but we can figure them out by drawing a picture. In contrast, since we can hardly come up with 'a green idea', the question in (3) sounds strange.[1] That means 'cow' which is a kind of animals has a closer relationship with 'green' than 'idea' that comes under an abstraction. If we use a scale to represent the difference between the two relational pairs, we can say $\{\text{cow} \circ \text{green}\} > \{\text{idea} \circ \text{green}\}$, given that $\circ$ stands for the relational property. Here we can define the relational property that an operator $\circ$ represents as Selectional Preference, and the values that each relation has can be computed as numbers; for example, $\{\text{cow} \circ \text{green} = 100\}$, $\{\text{idea} \circ \text{green} = 5\}$.

Furthermore, we can make the relationship more abstractive. If we switch one item with another which conveys a similar meaning, almost the same preference goes for the other pair. For instance, elements in {green, purple}, {cow, dove}, and {idea, opinion} respectively are in the sister relations with each other within the lexical hierarchy (i.e. WordNet), whereby they are in complementary distribution as shown in (4).

(4) a. a green cow / a purple cow / a green dove

b. #a green idea / #a purple idea / #a green opinion

That means each element in each (4a-b) has the very similar or even the same relational values; for example, $\{\text{cow} \circ \text{green}\}$ is near equivalent to both $\{\text{dove} \circ \text{green}\}$ and $\{\text{cow} \circ \text{purple}\}$. With reference to the English WordNet, 'cow' belongs reflexively to 'animals', 'object', and 'physical entity', whose hierarchy differs from that of 'idea'. In a nutshell, the so-called Selectional Preferences hinges on the semantic properties that a class of words shares.

2.2 Data

Basically three types of resources are required to calculate SPS: (i) a lexical hierarchy (e.g. WordNet), (ii) a development corpus, and (iii) comparable data for evaluation.

As discussed in the previous subsection, a lexical hierarchy that represents the kinship of words as a tree (or graph) structure plays an essential role in measuring SPS. Several Korean lexical hierarchies have been created so far, which include KorLex[2], U-WIN[3], CoreNet[4], etc. This study, among them, makes exclusive use of KorLex for two reasons. First, KorLex contains a table that connects each synset with the corresponding synset on the English WordNet. This mapping table would be of great merit, when we plan to extend the current work to multilingual studies in the future. Second, there exists a table that links lexical items in the

[1] This paper does not take metaphorical expressions into consideration. For example, 'green' sometimes refers to a social issue related to the protection of the environment as exemplified as 'the green movement'. The current work is not concerned with those kinds of expressions.

[2] `http://korlex.cs.pusan.ac.kr`

[3] `http://nlplab.ulsan.ac.kr/club/u-win`

[4] `http://semanticweb.kaist.ac.kr/home/index.php/CoreNet`

Sejong electronic dictionary with each corresponding meaning of the synsets on KorLex (Park et al., 2010). Given that the *Sejong* electronic dictionary consists of a wide coverage of lexical items with a fine-grained linguistic description, if we take advantage of the table, we can systematically design further studies on the syntax/semantics interfaces.

A development corpus (preferably, naturally occurring texts) also play a critical part in computing SPS because there should be a data-oriented observation that shows which verbs take which nouns as the objects. A more in-depth and accurate analysis of the corpus can be expected to result in a better understanding of the syntax and semantics of the language. In particular, because the linguistic generalization of this study has to be drawn relying on the occurrence of functional tags (e.g. SBJ, OBJ), texts annotated at the syntactic layer (i.e. treebanks) are much more preferred. There are two available treebanks for Korean; one is the *Sejong* Korean Treebank, and the other is the Penn Korean Treebank. This study takes the former, mainly because the former is about three times larger than the latter. This study uses Xavier (Song and Jeon, 2008) as a tool to exploit the *Sejong* Korean Treebank.

This study makes a comparative analysis with the *Sejong* electronic dictionary for the purpose of evaluation, which has been manually encoded by linguists. The dictionary specifies the linguistic features of each argument in the XML format. For example, the second argument of *masi* 'drink', playing the theme role, has the selectional restriction (tagged within '<sel_rst ... >') as 'beverages'. Comparing the selectional preferences of the current work with the selectional restrictions given in the *Sejong* electronic dictionary, this study offers a quantitative evaluation (i.e. precision, recall, and f-measure).

3 Model

The verb and its argument(s) would be one of the representative categorical pairs that display Selectional Preferences clearly. Particularly, the classes of nouns that function as objects have been studied in many ways and in many languages because resolving objects performs a significant role in ambiguity resolution as well as syntactic parsing. For instance, Resnik (1995), who conducts several experiments using WordNet and English corpora such as BNC, compares the semantic characteristics of object nouns of 'drink' and 'find'. It is borne out by the experimental result that the object nouns of 'drink' cluster densely together, while those of 'find' are very scattered. The same goes for Korean as presented in (5).

(5) a. *maykcwu/khephi/#chayk-(l)ul masi-ta*
beer/coffee/book-OBJ drink-DECL

b. *chayk/sinmwun/#maykcwu-(l)ul ilk-ta*
book/newspaper/beer-OBJ read-DECL

c. *maykcwu/chayk-(l)ul chac-ta*
beer/book-OBJ find-DECL

3.1 Lowest Common Subsumer

Computational models for measuring similarity between words are roughly divided into two major types. One makes use of the definition of dictionaries (a.k.a. Lesk algorithm (Lesk, 1986)), and the other employs the Lowest Common Subsumer (hereafter, LCS) between two words. This study employs the latter because more algorithms have been implemented on the basis of it. LCS, according to Resnik (1995), means the lowest ancestor node that simultaneously subsumes its children nodes, by which the distance between the children can be measured. For instance, in a hierarchical tree (6), the LCS of 'a' and 'a′' is 'A', that of 'b' and 'b′' is B, and that of 'a' and 'b' is C.

(6)
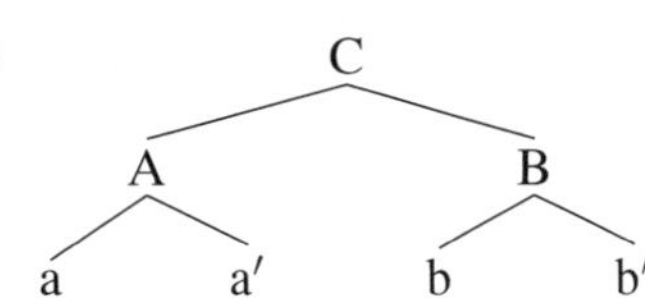

With reference to KorLex, (5) can be abstractly converted into (7). Each number in parenthesis in (7) stands for the index of LCS of the words given in (5), which denotes 'beverage', 'production', and 'entity', respectively.

(7) a. (07406270)-OBJ *masi* 'drink'

b. (03856368)-OBJ *ilk* 'read'

c. (00001740)-OBJ *chac* 'find'

3.2 Power Set

LCS is virtually located by creating a power set for each verbal item. A power set means a set whose elements are all the subsets of a given set, which can be conceptualized as a lattice structure. Given that a set S consists of three elements such as {a, b, c}, the lattice structure which represents the power set is sketched out in (8a), and thereby the power set of the set S is calculated as (8b), ignoring an empty set.

(8) a.

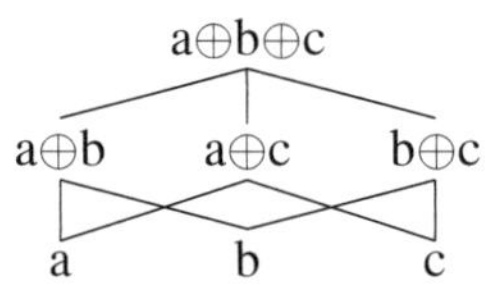

b. {{a}, {b}, {c}, {a,b} {a,c}, {b,c}, {a,b,c}}

If it is observed that a verbal item *v* takes three elements {a, a′, b} as its object nouns, the verb involves seven mappings to subsets of the set as shown in (9) with respect to a relational operator ∘ that defines SPS and another operator • that represents the LCS of the operands.[5] Note that {(a•a′) = A, (a•b) = C, (a′•b) = C}, as sketched out in (6).

(9) a. $v \circ$ a

b. $v \circ$ a′

c. $v \circ$ b

d. $v \circ$ (a•a′) = $v \circ$ A

e. $v \circ$ (a•b) = $v \circ$ C

f. $v \circ$ (a′•b) = $v \circ$ C

g. $v \circ$ (a•a′•b) = $v \circ$ C

If we make an assumption that the verb *v* is *masi* 'drink' and the three elements (i.e. a, a′, and b) are *maykcwu* 'beer', *khephi* 'coffee', and *chayk* 'book' respectively, we can obtain five relations as given in (10).[6] The numbers in parenthesis are the same as the ones given before.[7]

(10) a. *masi* 'drink' ∘ *maykcwu* 'beer' (07411192, 07411517)

b. *masi* 'drink' ∘ *khephi* 'coffee' (07452170, 14434748)

c. *masi* 'drink' ∘ *chayk* 'book' (02768681, 02769059)

d. *masi* 'drink' ∘ beverage (07406270)

e. *masi* 'drink' ∘ entity (00001740)

[5]The operator • satisfies the associative law.

[6]Note the different usages between 'w' and just w. The former represents a word, while the latter does a synset.

[7]A single word can be included in different synsets. For example, 'coffee' has two meanings; one is a kind of beans, and the other is a kind of beverages. Thus, words (i.e. 'w') can have multiple synsets as shown in (10a-c).

3.3 Hill Climbing

The cardinality of a power set of a set that includes *n* elements is represented as 2^n-1, excluding ϕ. That implies the cardinality grows exponentially. For example, if a verbal item takes 100 different nouns as its objects, $2^{100}-1$ subsets will be examined, which is too huge to calculate within a common development environment.[8] Thus, it is highly necessary to devise a means to overcome the problem in calculation.

This study, for this purpose, makes use of hill climbing, which refers to a computational technique that attempts to solve the whole problem by incrementally associating the partial solutions. Though it sounds like an ad-hoc method, if we are able to repeat it until no further improvements can be found, the better solution to the problem can be offered.[9]

Our model to compute LCS starts hill climbing with two parameters *m* and *n*, if the number of object nouns is more than *n*. Our model randomly chooses *n* elements out of the whole elements, and calculates LCS of the subset consisting of *n* elements. This procedure is iterated *m* times whereby the set of LCSs grows incrementally. For example, if a verbal item takes 100 nouns such as $\{a_1, a_2, ..., a_{100}\}$, (11) is one of the instances that our model can create, given that *m*=4, *n*=3.

(11) $\{a_3, a_{29}, a_{71}\}$
$\{a_{14}, a_{55}, a_{86}\}$
$\{a_{26}, a_{49}, a_{90}\}$
$\{a_{13}, a_{65}, a_{77}\}$

If we use parameters big enough to cover the greater part of the whole elements (for this study, *m*=30, *n*=16), we can obtain fairly plausible results.

3.4 Kullback-Leibler Divergence

The algorithm that this study makes use of is largely adapted from the Kullback-Leibler Divergence model presented in Resnik (1996), which plays a part to discriminate which LCS is the most significantly relevant to the given verbal item. (12)

[8]Actually, it is observed that some frequently used verbs such as *mek* 'eat' take more than 100 nouns.

[9]In particular, it is merited in the cases in which the ultimate conclusions are not likely to be drawn with an ordinary approach.

measures each strength that a verbal item has, in which *S* means 'strength', *v* stands for a 'verb', and *c* is short for a 'class' of nouns in the given lexical hierarchy.

(12)

$$S(v, c_i) = \frac{P(c_i|v) \log \frac{P(c_i|v)+1}{P(c_i)}}{\Sigma\, P(c|v) \log \frac{P(c|v)+1}{P(c)}}$$

Consequently, LCSs acquired in the previous two subsections can be ordered by SPSs the formula (12) defines. The top-ranked one among them (i.e. the LCS that has the strongest Selectional Preference with *v*) is called the Association Strength (hereafter, AS), which distributionally represent the semantic properties of the verbal item.

4 Calculation

This study establishes the following guidelines to conduct an experiment of calculating SPS. First, the calculation is performed in a bottom-up way (i.e. a data-oriented approach), mainly because there already exists a resource constructed in a top-down way (i.e. the *Sejong* electronic dictionary). Second, we try to measure SPS on a large scale exploiting as much data as we can. Korean, as aforesaid, already has various types of linguistic resources, but there are few secondary products based on the resources. Third, the system is implemented with an eye towards running in an automatic way, which facilitates applying the whole procedure to the future work that deals with other resources or other relational pairs (e.g. verbs and subjects).

4.1 Procedures

The first step of the current work is to make a list of verbal items with reference to the development corpus. In the *Sejong* Korean treebank, there are two types of verbal items in terms of annotation formats. The first one is tagged with 'VV', which includes common verbs. The second one is formatted as [NNG + *ha*], in which NNG belongs to verbal nouns and *ha* functions as a light verb. The first one contains 1,447 verbal entries, the second one does 1,313 entries; thus in total 2,760 verbal entries are included on the list.

The second step is to extract nouns which are dependent on the verbal items. The Xavier module extracts object nouns of the verbal entries from the *Sejong* Korean treebank, which are tagged as 'NP_OBJ'. After that, nouns that do not appear on KorLex are excluded, because it is not possible to calculate their SPS without any information from the lexical hierarchy. In this way, a total of 6,948 types and 42,099 tokens of nouns are acquired. Then the type/token ratio is 16.5%, and each verbal item takes 2.52 types of 15.25 nouns as its objects on average.[10]

Table 1: Basic Measures

# of verbal entries	2,760
# of verbs	1,447
# of verbal nouns	1,313
# of tokens of objects	42,099
# of types of objects	6,948
# of collected LCSs	32,557

The next step is to collect LCSs of each verbal item, building upon the model presented in the previous section. 2,561 verbal items have one or more LCS(s). 32,557 LCSs are collected, which means each verb involves 11.8 LCSs on average. The statistical measures presented so far are summarized in Table 1.

The final step is to measure SPS, and determine the strongest one (i.e. AS) for each verbal item, whose average and standard deviation are .0667 and .0756 respectively.

4.2 Outcomes

The outcomes acquired thus far are analyzed from two viewpoints. The first one is about whether frequency has a distributional effect on the outcomes or not. The second one is to look at the representative cases in which SPS can be obviously *vs.* hardly captured, and to set up a working hypothesis building upon the findings.

4.2.1 Frequency

This subsection deals with the relevance between frequency and Selectional Preferences. The analysis will be made in terms of four factors that can potentially have a correlation with each other. The first two are concerned with verbal items; one is (i-a) the frequency of verbal items themselves and (i-b) the type/token ratio of object nouns of verbal items. The other two include (ii-a) the size of LCSs and

[10]For this reason, we use *n*=16 in hill climbing.

Figure 1: frequency (i-a) *vs.* # of LCSs (ii-a)

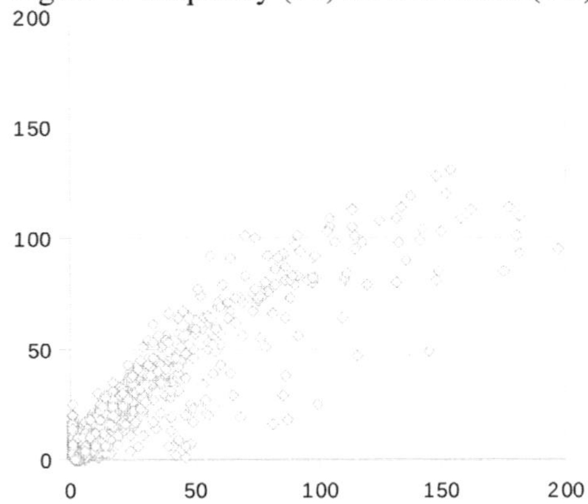

Figure 3: t/t (i-b) *vs.* # of LCSs (ii-a)

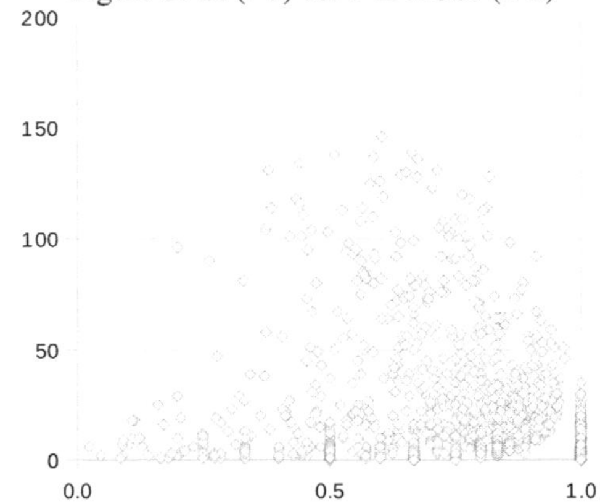

Figure 2: frequency (i-a) *vs.* AS (ii-b)

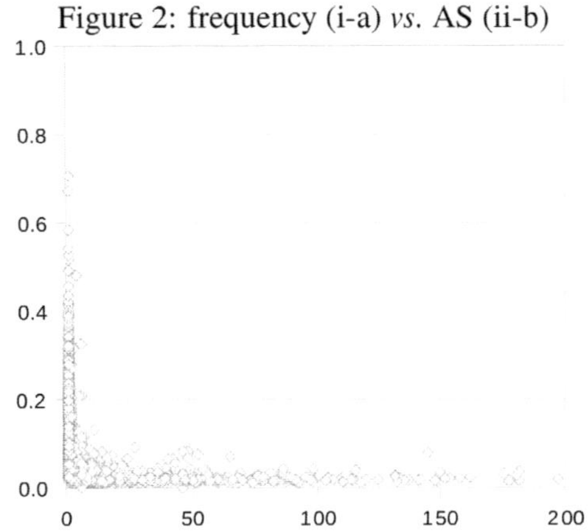

Figure 4: t/t (i-b) *vs.* AS (ii-b)

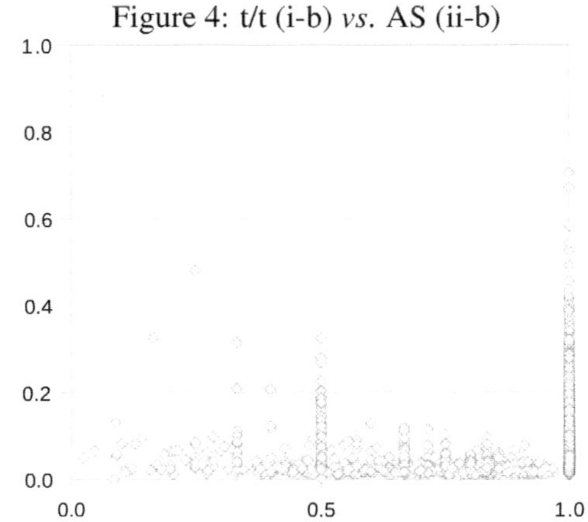

(ii-b) the value of each AS.

Figure 1, first, indicates the correlation between (i-a) the frequency on the X-axis and (ii-a) the number of LCSs on the Y-axis, in which each diamond represents (i-a, ii-a) on the coordinates. As can be expected, the high frequent items also show a high size of LCSs. Table 2 contains cases of the high, middle, and low frequent items that also show the corresponding sizes of LCSs.

Table 2: frequency *vs.* LCSs

verbs	freq	LCSs	synset (index)
ilwu 'achieve'	181	110	status (00024568)
ilk 'read'	180	101	production (03856368)
cwucangha 'claim'	46	48	knowledge (00020729)
ssis 'wash'	44	45	body parts (04924211)
koylophi 'bother'	6	5	human (00006026)
sunginha 'accredit'	3	1	action (00026194)

Figure 2 stands for the correlation between (i-a) frequency and (ii-b) the value of AS, which implies that verbal items that very less frequently appear can have full range of values, whereas the ASs of most other items, namely the higher frequent ones, are under .1.

Next, Figure 3 and Figure 4 illustrate the correlation between (i-b) the type/token ratio of object nouns and (ii-a) plus (ii-b), respectively. At a glance, Figure 3 and Figure 4 imply that there seems to be no clear relevance between (i-b) and (ii-a/b), except that the smaller the type/token ratio is, the less variety of nouns are used as the objects.

4.2.2 Strengths

Figure 5 to 7 indicate the distributional properties of SPSs of verbal items in (5). Figure 5 stands in stark contrast to Figure 7, and Figure 6 is somewhere between them. In each figure, the number of bars is the same as the number of LCSs, which represents how many synsets have SPS with the verbal item. The more bars a chart has, the more LCSs are collected with respect to the verbal item. On the other hand,

Table 3: SPS

verb	SPS	AS (index)
masi 'drink'	.04	beverage (07406270)
ilk 'read'	.028	production (03856368)
chac 'find'	.0218	entity (00001740)

the height of bars stands for SPS, which means the taller a bar is, the more preferably the class of nouns (on the X-axis) co-occur with the verbal item. There are not so many bars on Figure 5, but they are relatively taller than those on Figure 6 and Figure 7. That means *masi* 'drink' has a tighter relation with only a few number of synsets (i.e. LCSs). In contrast, there are quite a number of bars on Figure 7, mostly short, which implies *chac* 'find' can co-occur with a wide variety of nouns but their relationships are quite looser.

The verbal items exemplified in (5) have Association Strengths as given in Table 3. Among the verbal items that occur more than 10 times, the most typical *masi*-like items (i.e. high SPSs with few LCSs) and the most typical *chac*-like items (i.e. low SPSs with many LCSs) are exemplified in Table 4 and Table 5, respectively. The difference between *masi* 'drink' and *chac* 'find' can also be found in the list of candidates that are not selected as the AS, which are given in Table 6 and Table 7, respectively. The closely associated synsets with *masi* are relatively concrete and specific, whereas those with *chac* are the higher ones in the lexical hierarchy, namely, more abstractive and comprehensive.

Figure 5: SPSs of *masi* 'drink'

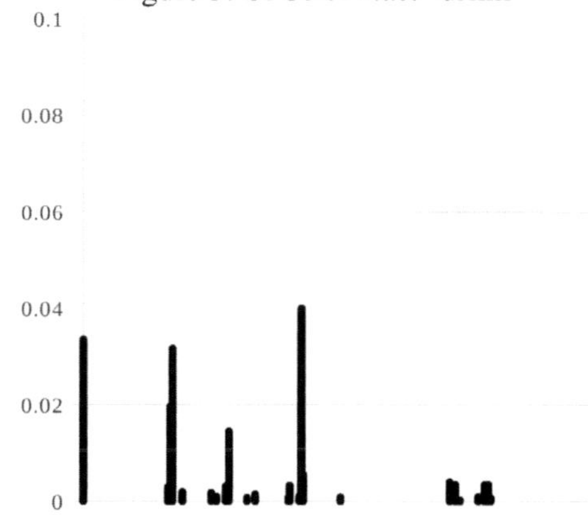

Figure 6: SPSs of *ilk* 'read'

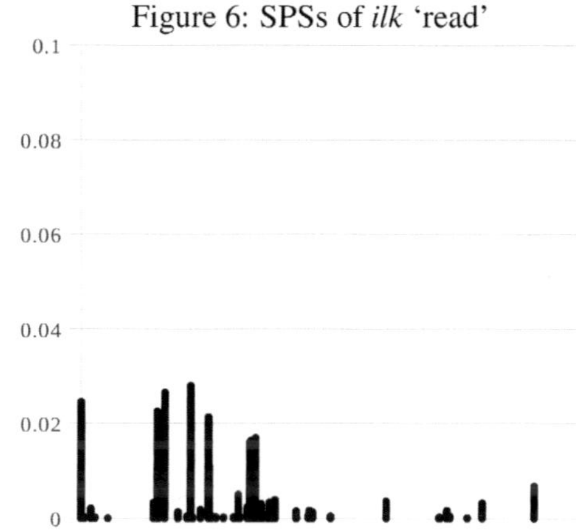

Figure 7: SPSs of *chac* 'find'

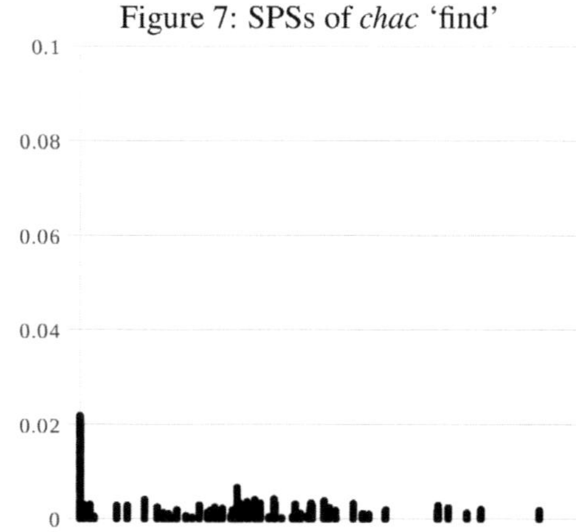

Table 4: high SPSs with fewer LCSs

verbs	t/t	LCSs	SPS	AS (index)
kkwul 'kneel'	.09	2	.132	kneel (02375920)
chwu 'dance'	.13	6	.083	dance (00498636)
sso 'shoot'	.57	6	.082	arms (04387884)

Table 5: low SPSs with many LCSs

verbs	t/t	LCSs	SPS	AS (index)
tul 'carry'	.38	131	.014	linguistic unit (05901081)
phiha 'avoid'	.75	100	.012	entity (00001740)
pwuthi 'stick'	.53	94	.011	mentality (00020333)

Figure 8 indicates the relationship between the number of LCSs and the value of SPSs of the corresponding verbal items. For example, the diamond corresponding to masi 'drink', whose LCSs are small but whose SPS values are relatively high, lies around the upper left area. In contrast, the mark for *chac* 'find', which has many LCSs and small values of SPSs, lies on the lower right corner. Figure 8 implies that verbal items that yield more than about ten LCSs show a tendency not to have so strong preference with co-occurring nouns.

Table 6: Other SPSs of *masi*

synset (index)	SPS
alcoholic drinks (07408983)	.0345
nutrient (00018827)	.0335
medicine (03129572)	.0316
ingredient (00017572)	.0295
ornament (03054637)	.0195

Table 7: Other SPSs of *chac*

synset (index)	SPS
object (00016236)	.0175
abstraction (00020486)	.0141
mentality (00020333)	.0136
knowledge (00020729)	.0112
relation (00027929)	.0107

Figure 8: # of LCSs *vs.* SPS

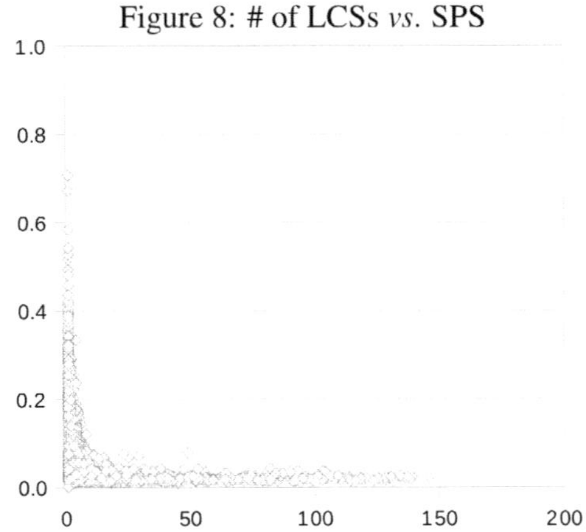

5 Evaluation

5.1 Quantitative Evaluation

The quantitative evaluation in this study is based on the comparison of the results with the *Sejong* electronic dictionary, which consists of 32,714 verbs plus 6,998 adjectives. The dictionary covers various linguistic levels, including selectional restrictions of verbal items. The comparative analysis of this study checks out how well the SPS values of this study matches with the lexical information.

The quantitative measurements that this study uses are precision, recall, and f-measure, which are respectively formulated as follows. Precision means the fraction of extracted instances which has a relevance with the corresponding item, whereas recall means the fraction of relevant instances which are extracted. F-measure associates these two measures simultaneously to show the compatibility.

(13) a.

$$precision = \frac{tp}{tp + fp}$$

b.

$$recall = \frac{tp}{tp + fn}$$

c.

$$f\text{-}measure = \frac{2 \times precision \times recall}{precision + recall}$$

If a certain class of nouns is specified for the object position of a predicate in the *Sejong* electronic dictionary, and is also computed as one of the LCSs of the corresponding verbal items, the value tp (i.e. true positive) increases. If a class of nouns appears in the results of this study but not in the dictionary, the value fp (i.e. false positive) increases. Finally, if a class of nouns is specified only in the *Sejong* electronic dictionary, the value fn (i.e. false negative) becomes greater by that much. The distinction among them is presented in the Table 8 for the ease of exposition.

Table 9 gives the evaluation measurement conducted by formula (13) and Table 8. It turns out the measures are pretty low, the f-measures being around 10%, which means that the two resources match with each other rather poorly. We suspect the poor results are mainly due to the difference in the lexical hierarchies assumed in KorLex and the *Sejong* electronic dictionary in the first place. It is true that the lexical hierarchies can be built upon different theoretical assumptions. The ontologies in the *Sejong* electronic dictionary and KorLex are much different from each other (Bae et al., 2010), so a proper comparison and evaluation should be done after the mapping between the two heterogeneous

Table 8: True/False Positive/Negative

	Sejong	**¬*Sejong***
LCSs	tp	fp
¬LCSs	fn	tn

Table 9: Quantitative Evaluation

precision	12.98%
recall	8.99%
f-measure	10.62%

ontologies is properly established. Bae et al. (2010) is an endeavour in that direction, but we could not include it in the current work. Another reason for the poor evaluation results, which is basically the same problem as the first, is that the terms used in both ontologies are different from each other in many cases. For instance, the concept 'abstraction' can be specified as an 'abstractive concept' in one resource and as just an 'abstraction' in the other; actually, KorLex takes the former, and the *Sejong* electronic dictionary takes the latter. The evaluation in this study was based on the surface match, and thus could not accommodate the mismatch in the terms used, which means when the mismatches are well taken care of, the f-measures would increase that much. Suffice it to say at the moment that the results given in Table 9 can be taken as a baseline values for the future studies.

5.2 Qualitative Evaluation

For a qualitative evaluation of this study, a manual checkup was done on some of the results of this study. We point out three issues that are found in the process, which need to be properly addressed in the future study.

First, it is discovered that homonyms sometimes have an adverse effect on the outcomes. For example, it is reported that *ketepwuthi* 'roll up' has a strong preference with a homonym *phal*, which can convey a meaning of either 'eight' or 'arm' in Korean. Although it is much more natural that 'roll up' has a relevance to 'arm' rather than 'eight' in the sense of 'roll up one's sleeves', the outcomes provide only *phal* 'eight' as the AS of *ketepwuthi*. This problem would be solved, if some sense-tagged texts are available as the development corpus, which has been partially studied by Park et al. (2010).

Second, causative forms which often bring about argument alternations are not taken into account in the process of extracting object nouns from the development corpus (i.e. the *Sejong* Korean Treebank). The causative forms in Korean, which are in the format of '*-key/tolok ha*', need to be analyzed from a fine-grained syntactic standpoint (Alsina et al., 1996), because NPs with theme-roles may not be in situ in the constructions.[11] The variation in form-meaning mapping in Korean causatives needs to be deeply explored in a corpus-oriented way, which we would like to reserve for another inquiry.

Finally, two closely relevant words sometimes exist far from each other within the hierarchy, which eventually causes a problem. For example, *michi* 'exert' takes two major types of nouns; one is *yenghyang* 'influence' and the other is *yenghyanglyek* 'power of influence'. It is obvious that these two words are closely relelated to each other, but they are not in the sister relation with each other in KorLex; the former is specified as an action, while the latter is a kind of abstractive concept. Since the verbal item *michi* 'exert', for this reason, cannot be preferably associated with these two words in the current processing model, we cannot construct the pattern like 'exert an influence on' from our results.[12]

6 Conclusion

In this paper, we calculated the SPS between verbal items and the classes of their co-occurring nouns. The SPS has been automatically measured with reference to two Korean language resources; (i) KorLex as the lexical hierarchy of noun classes, and (ii) the *Sejong* Korean Treebank as the development corpus. The acquisition model is grounded upon the LCS that represents the closest common ancestor node for the given two nodes within the hierarchy. The SPS is defined by Kullback-Leibler Divergence, which depends on the collection of LCSs. The results are evaluated with reference to the *Sejong* electronic dictionary which has been manually constructed.

This study, on the other hand, has certain limitation, especially in the evaluation process. It needs to

[11] We had tried to get rid of the form '*-key/tolok ha*' from the observed data and conducted the experiment from the beginning again, but we learned that there were more causative forms that involve argument alternations, other than '*-key/tolok ha*'. For example, an auxiliary *cwu*, whose original meaning comes from 'give', sometimes behaves like a causative marker and alters the argument structure.

[12] The two words, of course, are not always in the same distributional condition. For example, a verb *cwu* 'give' does not tend to co-occur with *yenghyanglyek* 'power of influence', while it does with *yenghyang* 'influence'. Given that KorLex has been constructed with some reference to those kinds of relational properties (i.e. collocations), it is not unusual that two or more words apparently related to each other sometimes come under different nodes in the hierarchy (Aesun Yoon, personal communication).

be done on the basis of resources that would overcome some clear limitations of the evaluation process adopted in this study. However, in spite of the limitations, we believe the results reported in this study can have some implications for future studies, including extending the results to other grammatical functions like subject, or making use of other Korean ontologies like U-WIN or CoreNet.

Acknowledgments

We thank Professor Aesun Yoon for her valuable comments and suggestions, though it should be noted that we could not fully accommodate them in this paper. We also thank three anonymous reviewers for helpful feedback. After the final version was submitted, we found out that there was a critical mistake in our handling of a key file name during the calculation, which resulted in incorrect figures and tables in that version. Therefore, in this minimally corrected version, as we did in the actual presentation of our paper during the conference, we substituted the corrected figures (Fig. 1-4, 8) for the wrong ones, and made due changes in some related tables and discussion. We thank the Program committee for allowing us to remedy our earlier mistake at the final moment. Of course, all remaining errors and infelicities are our own.

References

Alex Alsina, Joan Bresnan, and Peter Sells. 1996. Complex Predicates: Structure and Theory. In Alex Alsina, Joan Bresnan, and Peter Sells, editors, *Complex Predicates*, pages 1–12. CSLI Publications, Stanford.

Sun-Mee Bae, Kyoungup Im, and Aesun Yoon. 2010. Mapping Heterogenous Ontologies for the HLP Applications – Sejong Semantic Classes and KorLexNoun 1.5 –. *Korean Journal of Cognitive Science*, 21:95–126.

Michael Lesk. 1986. Automatic Sense Disambiguation Using Machine Readable Dictionaries: How to Tell a Pine Cone from an Ice Cream Cone. In *Proceedings of the 5th annual international conference on Systems documentation*, pages 24–26. ACM.

Heum Park, Aesun Yoon, Woo Chul Park, and Hyuk-Chul Kwon. 2010. Considerations on Automatic Mapping Large-Scale Heterogeneous Language Resources: Sejong Semantic Classes and KorLex. In *Proceedings of the Eighth Workshop on Asian Language Resouces*, pages 14–21, Beijing, China, August. Coling 2010 Organizing Committee.

Philip Resnik. 1995. Using Information Content to Evaluate Semantic Similarity. In *Proceedings of the 14th International Joint Conference on Artificial Intelligence*, pages 448–453.

Philip Resnik. 1996. Selectional Constraints: An Information-theoretic Model and its Computational Realization. *Cognition*, 61(1-2):127–159.

Sanghoun Song and Jieun Jeon. 2008. The Xavier Module - Information Processing of Treebanks. In *Proceedings of the International Conference of Cognitive Science (ICCS 2008)*, Seoul, South Korea.

Extracting and Visualizing Semantic Relationships from Chinese Biomedical Text

Qingliang Miao, Shu Zhang, Bo Zhang, Yao Meng, Hao Yu
Fujitsu R&D Center Co., Ltd.
{qingliang.miao, zhangshu, zhangbo, mengyao, yu}@cn.fujitsu.com

Abstract

In this paper, we study how to automatically extract and visualize food (or nutrition) and disease relationships from Chinese publications of Nutritional Genomics. Different from previous approaches that mostly apply handcrafted rules or co-occurrence patterns, we propose an approach using probabilistic models and domain knowledge. In particular, we first utilize encyclopedia to construct a domain knowledge base, and then develop a sentence simplification model to simplify complicated sentences we meet. Afterwards, we treat relation extraction issue as a sequence labeling task and adopt Conditional Random Fields (CRFs) models to extract food and disease relationships. Finally, these relationships are visualized. Experimental results on real-world datasets show that the proposed approach is effective.

1 Introduction

Advancements in biomedical science has led to large volume of published research articles, especially in Nutritional Genomics, an emerging interdisciplinary that studies the relationship between human genome, food and diseases (Hakenberg *et al.*, 2010; Sharma *et al.*, 2010; Tsuruoka *et al.*, 2011). For example, many researches in Nutritional Genomics study the relationships between "green tea", "soy", "fish oil" and "tumor diseases". Mining and drawing a full picture of these relationships can be adopted in many practical fields, such as public health services, drug discovery, etc. However, due to the considerable number of unstructured data, it is unrealistic to go through and obtain the panoramas of relationships manually. Consequently, automatically relation extraction and visualization techniques become ever more important and necessary. Some prior work has studied how to extract food and disease relationships from English biomedical text (Yang *et al.,* 2011). On Chinese biomedical text, however, there is relatively little investigation conducted on food and disease relation mining. In this paper, we focus on extracting and visualizing food and disease relationship from Chinese biomedical text.

S1 "金雀异黄素能够影响恶性黑色素瘤的体外生长，并抑制紫外线诱导的DNA氧化损伤。"
"Genistein could affect the growth of malignant melanoma in vitro and inhibit ultraviolet light -induced oxidative DNA damage."
S2 "研究表明绿茶能够预防人肝癌细胞HepG2。"
"It suggests that green tea could prevent Human hepatoma cell HepG2."

Figure 1: Example of relation-bearing sentences in Chinese and their English translation.

Figure 1 shows two examples of Chinese biomedical sentences and their English translation. The objective of semantic relationship mining is to extract all the binary semantic relationships between food and diseases, such as <金雀异黄素, 影响, 黑色素瘤> (<genistein, affect malignant melanoma>), <绿茶, 预防, 人肝癌细胞 HepG2> (<green tea, prevent, human hepatoma cell HepG2>).

In order to facilitate the explanation, we first introduce two basic terminologies of relation-bearing sentences.

Definition 1: Multiple Relation-bearing Sentence

Multiple relation-bearing sentence (*MRS*) contains more than two entities and mutual relationships.

Take Sentence 1 for example, there is one food entity—genistein, and two disease entities—malignant melanoma and DNA damage, and two relationships. Generally speaking, MRS could be represented by the following patterns, where *M-M*, *O-M* and *M-O* respectively represent many-to-many, one-to-many and many-to-one relationships. Table 1 below shows the multiple relation patterns, where *e* represents entity, *r* represents relation words/phrase.

Pattern	Multiple relation patterns
M-M	$\{e_1, e_2, \ldots, e_m, r, e_1', e_2', \ldots, e_n'\}$ $\{e_1, e_2, \ldots, e_m, (r_1), e_1', (r_2), e_2', \ldots, (r_n), e_n'\}$
O-M	$\{e, r, e_1', e_2', \ldots, e_n'\}$ $\{e, (r_1), e_1', (r_2), e_2', \ldots, (r_n), e_n'\}$
M-O	$\{e_1, e_2, \ldots, e_m, r, e'\}$

Table 1: Multiple relation patterns.

Definition 2: Single Relation-bearing Sentence

Single relation-bearing sentence (SRS) contains two entities and one relationship. Take Sentence 2 for example, we can see there are two entities (one food entity and one disease entity) and one relationship.

Mining semantic relationships from Chinese biomedical text is very challenging, because the sentence structure is complicated and most of the sentences contain multiple relationships. According to our statistic analysis of 3000 sentences from Chinese biomedical text, about 66% of the sentences are multiple relation-bearing sentences. Worse still, fewer biomedical resources such as USDA food database[1] and UMLS Meta thesaurus[2] are available in Chinese. Due to the complicated structure of multiple relation-bearing sentences, traditional methods could not perform effectively to extract food and disease relationships. Consequently, we have to simplify them, and then adopt extraction models to obtain food and disease relationships.

The remainder of the paper is organized as follows. In the following section we review the existing literature on semantic relation extraction. Then, we introduce the proposed approach in section 3. We conduct comparative experiments and present the results in section 4. At last, we conclude the paper with a summary of our work and give our future working directions.

2 Related Work

In the field of semantic relation mining, there are three dominant methods, namely, rule-based, pattern-based and learning-based methods (Finkelstein-Landau, M. and E. Mori, 1999; Bach and Badaskar, 2007; Weikum and Theobald, 2010; Zweigenbaum *et al.,* 2007). Next we will introduce these methods respectively.

Rule-based methods utilize predefined rules to extract relationships based on part of speech information (Weikum and Theobald, 2010). For example, if we want *isInstanceOf* relation, we can design extraction rules like <NP_0 such as {NP_1, NP_2,...NP_n}>. Some more sophisticated methods exploit syntactic information. For example, Fundel et al., first used a lexicalized parser to generate the dependency trees of each sentence, and then adopted four extraction rules to find protein and gene interactions (Fundel *et al.,* 2007). Rinaldi *et al.,* (2007) also utilized dependency parsing and lexicon to extract protein and gene relationships. However, rule-based methods mainly rely on handcraft rules, and suffer from low recall due to the sparseness of extraction rules. In addition, rule-based methods that incorporate syntactic information can be computationally costly in larger corpus.

Due to the sparseness issue in handcraft rules, pattern-based methods aim to construct comprehensive rules automatically (Hearst, 1992). Specifically, they are based on the duality of relationships, and usually adopt bootstrapping paradigm. For example, Brin (1998) proposed a pattern-based relation extraction system named DIPRE, which starts with a small set of seed facts for one or more relations of interest. Then it automatically looks for linguistic patterns in underlying sources as indicators of facts. Finally it utilizes these patterns to identify new fact candidates as further hypotheses to populate relationships. Agichtein and Gravano (2000) proposed a system called Snowball, which adopts similar strategy with DIPRE. However, Snowball does not use exact match, but a similarity function to group similar patterns instead. Snowball's

[1] http://ndb.nal.usda.gov/ndb/foods/list

[2] http://www.nlm.nih.gov/pubs/factsheets/umlsmeta.html

flexible matching system allows for slight variations in token or punctuation. In pattern-based methods, the initial patterns may shift during iterative processes, consequently it is inevitable to bring in noise. Girju and Moldovan (2002) extract lexico-syntactic patterns that refer to the causal relation.

Machine learning-based methods such as SVM and CRFs (Bundschus *et al.*, 2008; Lafferty *et al.*, 2001) can also be used in relationship extraction. Some work views relation extraction as classification issue, and adopt kernel features to train extraction models (Bunescu and Mooney, 2005; Zelenko *et al.*, 2003). Others treat relation extraction as a sequence labeling issue, and adopt HMM or CRFs to extract relationships. Bundschus et al., (2008) adopted CRFs model to extract treatment and disease relationships. However, effective learning features of these supervised approaches are derived from syntax parsers. Unfortunately, due to the complicated structure of biomedical sentences, few parsers perform well in Chinese biomedical sentences. When the sentence structure is complicated or the sentence contains multiple relationships, traditional methods cannot perform well (Jonnalagadda *et al.*, 2009).

3 The Proposed Approach

In this section, we will first introduce the architecture of the mining system, and then illustrate how to build domain knowledge base. After that, sentence simplification model will be introduced. In the end, we will explain how to utilize CRFs model to extract food and disease relationship on the basis of sentence simplification.

3.1 System Architecture

Figure 2 shows the architecture of the mining system. The inputs are unstructured biomedical texts, and the outputs are food and disease relationships. The system consists of four modules: (1) biomedical data server (BDS); (2) knowledge mining engine (KME); (3) relationship mining engine (RME); and (4) relationship visualization engine (RVE).

BDS collects biomedical texts by crawling scientific literature website such as *wanfang.com.* Then, web pages are cleaned to remove HTML tags, after that, abstracts in biomedical articles are extracted and splitted into sentences according to punctuations. Finally, word segmentation and part of speech tagging are conducted.

KME utilizes encyclopedia and biomedical corpus to construct knowledge base. Firstly, KME extracts food and disease entities from encyclopedia. Treating food and disease entities as anchor, KME adopts association rules to discover relation words from biomedical corpus. Finally, KME combines entities with relation words to construct domain knowledge base.

RME is the key part of the system, which includes three steps. Firstly, RME utilizes CRFs models and domain knowledge to extract food and disease entities. Secondly, it uses food and disease entities as anchors to simplify multiple relation-bearing sentences. Finally, CRFs models equipped with domain knowledge and other learning features are trained to extract relation words from simplified biomedical sentences.

RVE visualizes food and disease relationships. Figure 3 illustrates the visualization results of green tea and tumor disease relationships.

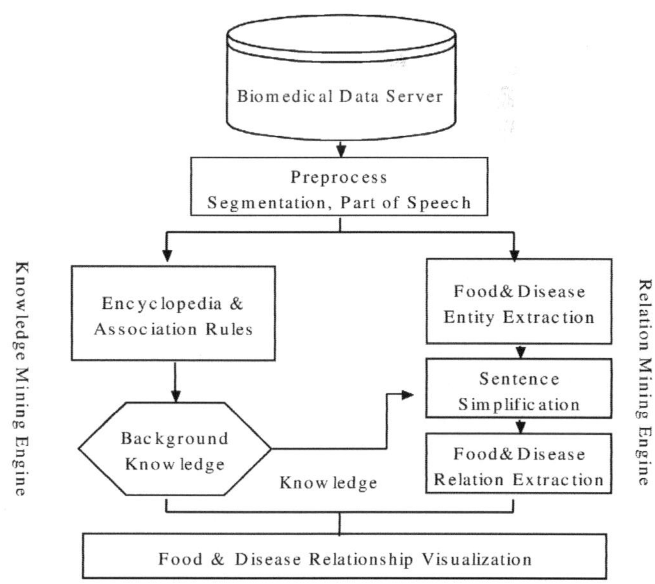

Figure 2: Flowchart of the proposed approach.

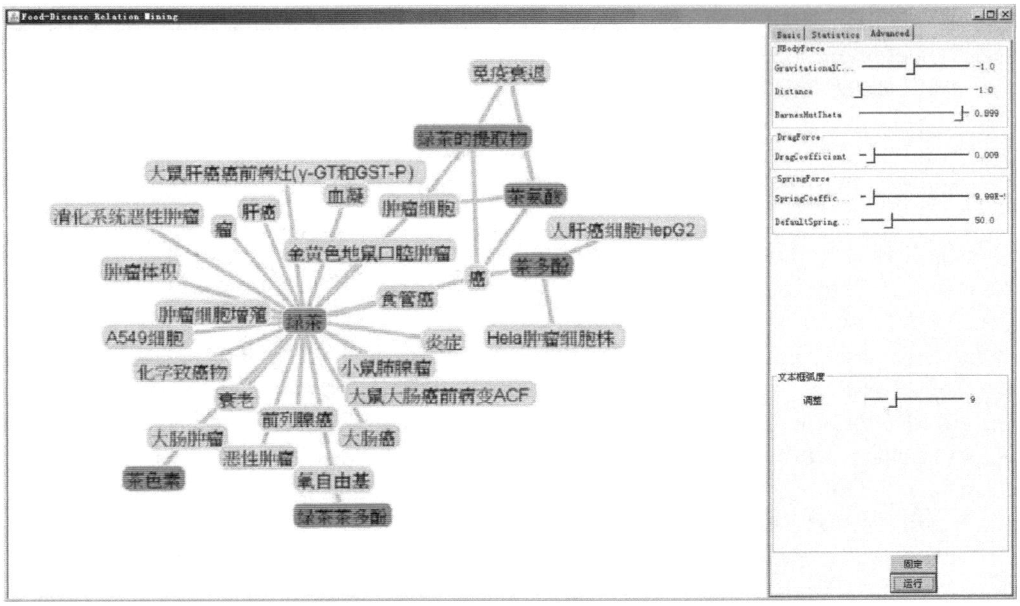

Figure 3: Food and disease relationship visualization results, red nodes represent green tea and its extractions, while green ones represent tumor disease entities.

3.2 Knowledge Base Construction

To construct a knowledge base, we need to extract food and disease entities and relation words. In particular, we first extract food and disease entities from three original data sources: *Wikipedia* Chinese version, *Baidu Baike*, and *Hudong Baike*. In these encyclopedias, concepts belonging to the same class are organized together. Therefore, we select 11 related categories such as "健康饮食(healthy food)", "营养学(nutrition)" and "疾病(disease)". After that, we collect food and disease entities from these 11 categories and assign each entity a Uniform Resource Identifier (URI). The URI is defined according to the following schema "*kb/category/entityName*". In the schema, field "*category*" is used to alleviate homonyms issues. For example, in our knowledge base, the URI of "apple" is defined as "*kb/fruit/apple*" instead of "*kb/company/apple*".

Through analyzing the content of each page, we extract 5 types of contents to construct domain knowledge, "*Title*", "*Alias*", "*Category*", "*Redirect*", "*Related Term*". Besides the above 5 types of contents, we also extract "*Function*" and "*Primary Constituent*" for food entities. We use Dublin Core (DC) metadata and Simple Knowledge Organization System (SKOS) to manage these contents. We will explain them in details as follows:

Title:

The titles in Hudong Baike are used as labels for the corresponding food and disease entities directly. Field "*entityName*" in URI is the same as title, which is represented by *dc:title*.

Alias:

In Wikipedia, editors may use alias to represent the same entity. For example, [[樱| 樱桃]] ([[cherry| prunus]]) will produce a link to \樱桃 while the displayed anchor is \樱. We call the displayed anchors as the aliases and represent them using *skos:exactMatch*.

Category:

Categories describe the subjects of a given entity, and we use *dcterms:subject* to present categories for the corresponding entities. *skos:broader* and *skos:narrower* are used to represent hyponymy relationships.

Redirection:

Encyclopedias usually use redirections to solve the synonymous problem. Redirection relations are described by *skos:closeMatch* to connect two entities.

```
<?xml version="1.0" encoding="UTF-8"?>
<rdf:RDF
    xmlns:rdf="http://www.w3.org/1999/02/22-rdf-syntax-ns#"
    xmlns:owl="http://www.w3.org/2002/07/owl#"
    xmlns:skos="http://www.w3.org/2004/02/skos/core"
    xmlns:dc="http://purl.org/dc/elements/1.1/"
    xmlns:dcterms="http://purl.org/dc/terms/"
    xmlns:xsi="http://www.w3.org/2001/XMLSchema-instance">
      <rdf:Description rdf:about="http://kb/food/soy_isoflavones">
          <dc:title>soy_isoflavones</dc:title>
          <skos:exactMatch>http://kb/food/isoflavones</skos:exactMatch>
          <dcterms:subject>food</dcterms:subject>
          <skos:relatedMatch>http://kb/food/soybean_saponin</skos:relatedMatch>
          <kb:function>http://kb/disease/osteoporosis</kb:function>
          <kb:constituent>http://kb/food/daidzin</kb:constituent>
          <kb:relationWord>http://kb/relationWord/prevent</kb:relationWord>
      </rdf:Description>
</rdf:RDF>
```


Figure 4: A snippet of domain knowledge base.

Related Term:

In Hudong Baike and Baidu Baike, there are related entities of a given entity. For example, related entities of "大豆异黄酮 (soy isoflavones)" are "大豆皂苷(soybean saponin)", "葛根异黄酮 (pueraria isoflavones)". *skos:relatedMatch* is used to represent Related Terms.

Function:

Function represents therapeutic efficacy of corresponding food. For example, "大豆异黄酮 (soy isoflavones)" has effect on "骨质疏松 (osteoporosis)" and "乳腺癌 (breast cancer)". *kb:function* is used to represent Function.

Primary Constituent:

Primary constituent of a given food are represented by *kb:constituent*, for example the primary constituent of "大豆异黄酮(soy isoflavones)" includes "大豆甙(daidzin)", "大豆甙元(daidzein)" and "染料木甙(genistin)".

After concepts extraction, we utilize food and disease entities as anchor to extract relation words from biomedical corpus. In relation-bearing sentences, relation words are usually verbs, verb or prepositional phrases, such as "prevent", "reduce mortality" and "with the increased risk of", etc. Specifically, we use extraction patterns like "*<F verb D>*"; "*<F verb phrase D>*" and "*<F prepositional phrase D>*" to extract relation words. "*F*" and "*D*" represent food and disease entity, respectively. After relation words extraction, we filter out relation words those less than 5 times. We also assign a URI *kb/relationWord/word* to each relation word and use *kb:relationWord* to represent relations.

Finally, we use Resource Description Framework (RDF) to describe the knowledge base. Due to the limited space, Figure 4 shows a snippet of domain knowledge base.

3.3 Sentence Simplification

As discussed above, the characteristic complexity of the sentences in biomedical text challenges the relationship mining task. Recently, researchers have paid attention to simplifying sentences (Bach *et al.,* 2011; Jonnalagadda *et al.,* 2009). However, these approaches usually use syntax information as learning features or to generate rules. This is a chicken and egg problem. Inspired by (Bach *et al.,* 2011), we develop a new sentence simplification model without using syntax parser. Moreover, ours uses domain knowledge to incorporate more constrains to reduce the search space and computational complexity. Benefits of this sentence simplification model are twofold: 1) Sentence structure is simplified, second, 2) Since we can obtain more simple sentences that contain only one-one relationship, it alleviates the data sparseness problem.

For a given multiple relation sentence, let *SF* and *SD* be food and disease entity set and *SV* be verb set. By combination, we have $n=|SF|*|SV|*|SD|$ simple sentences in candidate set *C*. *HSS* uses Function (1) and (2) to find out $m=|SF|*|SD|$ qualified simple sentences as the simplified results. Where s_i is simple sentence candidate and c is the complicated sentence. w^T is the weight vector, which needs to be estimated from training data. $f(s_i)$ is the feature function vector.

$$\arg\max \sum_{i=1}^{m} p(s_i \mid c)$$

$$p(s_i \mid c) = \frac{\exp(w^T f(s_i))}{\sum_{j=1}^{n} \exp(w^T f(s_j))}, s_i \in C$$

Besides the word count and distance features in (Bach *et al.*, 2011), we adopt several other learning features such as semantic features to model where the verb is semantic related to the relation words in domain knowledge base; entity class features to ensure that subject and object of simple sentences are food and disease entities; context features to model the part-of-speech information in relation words' contexts.

The workflow of the sentence simplification model is as follows: First, we extract all the food and disease entities by CRFs model and domain knowledge, and then we combine the food and disease entities with verbs to form simple sentence candidates. If we get *n* entities and *m* verbs, we can obtain *n*m*(n-1)* simple sentence candidates. Finally, we use the constraints to find true simple sentences.

Figure 5 illustrates an example of the sentence simplification procedure. In Figure 5, the initial sentence contains two disease entities "HepG2" and "gastric cancer", one food entity "green tea" and two verbs "suggest" and "prevent". Therefore, we have *3*2*2=12* simple sentence candidates as shown in Figure 5. Through semantic feature and entity class feature constraints, sentences using verb "suggest" as predicate verbs and sentences using disease entities as subject are filtered out from the candidate set. Finally, two sentences in shaded rectangles are obtained as single relation-bearing sentences.

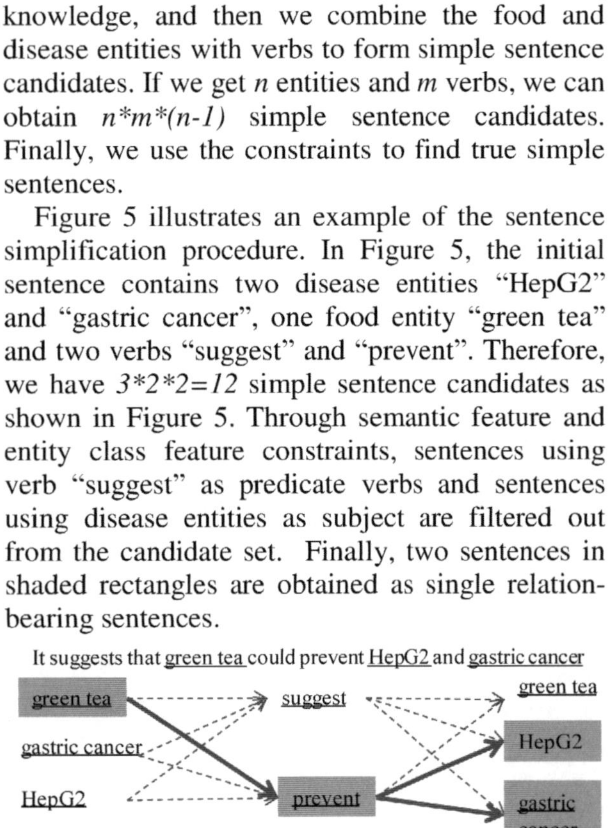

Figure 5: Workflow of the sentence simplification model.

3.4 Semantic Relation Mining

3.4.1 Extraction Model

We adopt CRFs models to extract relation words, because CRFs models are considered to be effective to solve the sequence labeling problem (Lafferty *et al.*, 2011). In addition, we can adopt flexible and abundant features such as lexical features, linguistic features and contextual clues to the process of CRFs model learning. Given a simple sentence of tokens, $x=x_1x_2...x_n$, we need to generate a sequence of labels $y=y_1y_2...y_n$. We define the set of possible label values as BIO to represent relation word.

We use a linear-chain CRF based on an undirected graph $G=(V, E)$, where V is the set of random variables. $Y=\{Y_i|1\leq i\leq n\}$ and $E=\{(Y_{i-1},Y_i)| 1\leq i\leq n\}$ is the set of edges forming a linear chain. For a given sentence x, the conditional probability of a sequence of labels y is defined as follows:

$$p(y \mid x) = \frac{1}{Z(X)} \exp\left\{ \sum_{e \in E,k} \lambda_k f_k(e, y|_e, x) + \sum_{v \in V,k} \mu_k g_k(v, y|_v, x) \right\}$$

$$Z(x) = \sum_y \exp\left\{ \sum_{e \in E,k} \lambda_k f_k(e, y|_e, x) + \sum_{v \in V,k} \mu_k g_k(v, y|_v, x) \right\}$$

where f_k and g_k are binary feature indicator functio ns and λ_k and μ_k are weights assigned for each featu re functions. $Z(x)$ is a normalization factor of all st ate sequences.

3.4.2 Features Sets

One character that makes CRFs so attractive is that they transform the sequence labeling problem into finding an appropriate training feature set. In this paper, we define the following training features for each token/word x_i in an input sentence x.

Word Features:

We use two types of word features: unigram and bigram as learning features. In particular, we first remove stop words and then extract every single word as unigram feature and every two adjacent words as bigram feature. Bigram features can capture useful relation information, such as "reduce risk" and "decreased mortality", etc.

Part of Speech Features:

As relation words are mainly verbs, prepositional and verb phrases, part of speech might also play an important role in contributing to relation extraction.

In particular, we adopt Stanford tagger[3] to produce part of speech features.

Lexical Features:

In addition to word features and part of speech features, the model could also benefit from domain knowledge. In this research, we incorporate domain knowledge in the form of lexical features. For each token x_i, we include a binary feature that indicates whether or not the token is in our domain knowledge base.

4 Experiments

In this section, we first describe the dataset used in the experiments and then we report our experiment results to demonstrate the effectiveness of our approach.

4.1 Datasets and Evaluation Criteria

Since there is no open and available dataset for food and disease relationship mining task available in Chinese, we collect experimental dataset from *wanfang.com* and annotate it by three interns. We collected 3108 relation-bearing sentences, and used them as Dataset 1 to evaluate the performance of food and disease entity extraction. We randomly selected 706 sentences as Dataset 2 to evaluate the performance of food and disease relation extraction. The statistics of the annotated results are shown in Table 2.

In order to verify the degree of agreement among three annotators, we adopted Fleiss' Kappa (Sim and Wright, 2005) to evaluate the consistency of annotated results. The Fleiss' Kappa of Dataset 1 and Dataset 2 are 0.87 and 0.82, which shows strong consistency. To construct the final gold standard, we adopted the following procedure. For sentences that have received the same labels from all three annotators, we assigned this agreed-upon label. For a small number of sentences that have received different assessments, we had all three annotators go through these sentences and discuss their assessments with each other in a face-to-face meeting. We then used their consensual assessment as the final label.

Based on the above manually constructed gold standard, *precision*, *recall* and *F-Measure* are used in our experiments to evaluate the proposed approach, in which *precision* is defined as the ratio between the number of correctly extracted entities/relationships and the total number of entities/relationships extracted by the system, while *recall* is calculated as the number of correctly extracted entities/relationships divided by the total number of entities/relationships in the original sentences and *F-measure* is the weighted harmonic mean of the *precision* and *recall*.

$$F - measure = \frac{2\, precision * recall}{precision + recall}$$

	#Sentence	#Entities	#Relationships
Dataset 1	3108	2035	/
Dataset 2	706	629	1485

Table 2: Statistics of the datasets.

4.2 Food and Disease Entity Extraction Results

We use Dataset 1 to evaluate food and disease entity extraction performance. Specifically, we randomly select 50% as training data and the rest as testing data and repeat the experiment 10 times. We adopt CRFs as extraction models. Table 3 shows the average *precision*, *recall* and *F-measure*. From Table 3, we can see that CRFs model achieves promising results. Since sentence simplification model exploits entity type information as anchors to simplify multiple relation-bearing sentences, effective entity extraction model is very important for relation extraction.

	Precision	Recall	F-measure
Food Entity	98.7	84.6	91.1
Disease Entity	99.2	84	91

Table 3: Food and disease entity extraction results.

4.3 Food and Disease Relation Extraction Results

We implement a pattern-based method using strategy (Brin, 1998) and Yang's method as baselines. Table 4 shows the average *precision*, *recall* and *F-measure*. From Table 4, we can see

[3] http://nlp.stanford.edu/software/tagger.shtml

FDRM outperforms both PB and Yang's method, and FDRM increases *precision*, *recall* and *F-measure* by 2.4%, 2.3% and 2.4% respectively.

Method	Ave Precision	Ave Recall	Ave F-measure
PB	0.681	0.689	0.677
Yang	0.738	0.747	0.732
FDRM	0.762	0.77	0.756

Table 4: Food and disease relation extraction results.

Figure 6 shows the *F-measure* in 10 experiments. From Figure 6, we can see that FDRM outperforms the baselines across all experiments.

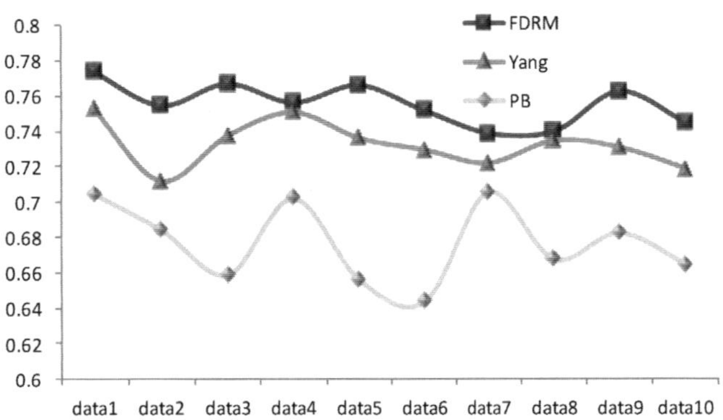

Figure 6: Relation mining results on F-measure.

We also conduct pairwise *t*-test to evaluate the improvement is significant or not. The *p*-values of FDRM and Yang, PB are 1.6E-04 and 3.75E-06 respectively and indicate the improvement is significant.

5 Conclusion

In this study, we propose a hybrid approach to extract and visualize food and disease relationships from Chinese biomedical text. As part of our work, we construct a domain knowledge base and develop a sentence simplification model. Experimental results on real-world datasets show the approach is promising. In addition, we find some interesting relationships, such as "<fresh milk, increase risk, lung cancer>". We believe that this study is just the first step in food and disease relationship mining and much more work needs to be done to further explore the issue. In our ongoing work, we will utilize more sophisticated nature language processing techniques such as co-reference resolution in the mining process. And we also plan to analyze polarity and strength of food and disease relationships.

References

Agichtein, E., and Gravano, L. 2000. Snowball: Extracting relations from large plain-text collections. *Proceedings of the 5th ACM International Conference on Digital Libraries*, pp.85-94.

Bach, N., and Badaskar, S. 2007. A review of relation extraction, *Literature review for Language and Statistics II.*

Bach, N., Gao, Q., Vogel, S., and Waibel, A. 2011. TriS: A statistical sentence simplifier with log-linear models and margin-based discriminative training, *Proceedings of the 5th International Joint Conference on Natural Language Processing*, pp. 474-482.

Brin, S. 1998. Extracting patterns and relations from the World Wide Web. *Proceedings of the World Wide Web and Databases*, 1590(2), pp. 172-183.

Bundschus, M., Dejori, M., Stetter, M., Tresp, V., and Kriegel, H.P. 2008. Extraction of semantic biomedical relations from text using conditional random fields, *BMC Bioinformatics*, Vol. 9.

Bunescu, R. C., and Mooney, R. J. 2005. Subsequence kernels for relation extraction. *In Advances in Neural Information Processing Systems*, pp. 171-178.

Finkelstein-Landau, M. and E. Mori. 1999. Extracting semantic relationships between terms: Supervised vs. unsupervised methods. *Proceedings of the Int. Workshop on Ontological Engineering on the Global Information Infrastructure,* pp. 71-80.

Fundel K., Kuffner R., and Zimmer R. 2007. RelEx-relation extraction using dependency parse trees, *Bioinformatics*, 23:365-71.

Girju, R. and Moldovan, D. 2002. Text mining for causal relations. *Proceedings of the FLAIRS Conference*, pp. 360-364.

Hakenberg, J., Leaman, R., Vo, N.H., Jonnalagadda, S., Sullivan, R., Miller, C., Tari, L., Baral, C., and Gonzalez, G. 2010. Efficient extraction of protein-protein interactions from full-text articles, *IEEE/ACM Transactions on Computational Biology and Bioinformatics*, 7(3).

Hearst, M. A. Automatic acquisition of hyponyms from large text corpora. 1992. *Proceedings of the 14th COLING*, pp. 539-545.

Jonnalagadda, S., and Gonzalez, G. 2009. Sentence simplification aids protein-protein interaction extraction, *Proceedings of the 3rd International Symposium on Languages in Biology and Medicine*.

Lafferty, J., McCallum, A., and Pereira, F. 2001. Conditional random fields: probabilistic models for segmenting and labeling sequence data. *Proceedings of the 18th International Conference on Machine Learning*.

Rinaldi, F., Schneider, G., Kaljurand, K., Hess, M., Andronis, C., Konstandi, O., and Persidis, A. 2007. Mining of relations between proteins over biomedical scientific literature using a deep-linguistic approach, *Artificial Intelligence in Medicine*, 39(2):127-36.

Sharma, A., Swaminathan, R., and Yang, H. 2010. A verb-centric approach for relationship extraction in biomedical text. *Proceedings of the fourth IEEE International Conference on Semantic Computing, Pittsburg*.

Sim, J., and Wright, C. C. 2005. The Kappa statistic in reliability studies: Use, interpretation, and sample size requirements, *In Physical Therapy*, 85(3), pp. 257-268.

Tsuruoka, Y., Miwa, M., Hamamoto, K., Tsujii, J., and Ananiadou, S. 2011. Discovering and visualizing indirect associations between biomedical concepts. *Bioinformatics*, 27(13), pp. i111-i119.

Weikum, G., and Theobald, M. 2010. From information to knowledge: harvesting entities and relationships from web sources. *Proceedings of the 29th ACM SIGMOD-SIGACT-SIGART Symposium on Principles of Database Systems of Data*, pp, 65-76.

Yang, H., Swaminathan, R., Sharma, A., Ketkar, V., and Silva, J.D. 2011. Mining biomedical text towards building a quantitative food-disease-gene networks, *book chapter in Learning structures and schemas from documents.*

Zelenko, D., Aone, C., and Richardella. 2003. A. Kernel methods for relation extraction. *Journal of Machine Learning Research*.

Zweigenbaum P., Demner-Fushman D., Yu H., and Cohen K.B. 2007. Frontiers of biomedical text mining: current progress, *Briefings in Bioinformatics*. 8(5). pp. 358-375.

Entity Set Expansion using Interactive Topic Information

Kugatsu Sadamitsu, Kuniko Saito, Kenji Imamura and **Yoshihiro Matsuo**
NTT Media Intelligence Laboratories, NTT Corporation
1-1 Hikarinooka, Yokosuka-shi, Kanagawa, 239-0847, Japan
{sadamitsu.kugatsu, saito.kuniko, imamura.kenji, matsuo.yoshihiro}
@lab.ntt.co.jp

Abstract

We propose a new method for entity set expansion that achieves highly accurate extraction by suppressing the effect of semantic drift; it requires a small amount of interactive information. We supplement interactive information to re-train the topic models (based on interactive Unigram Mixtures) not only the contextual information. Although the topic information extracted from an unsupervised corpus is effective for reducing the effect of semantic drift, the topic models and target entities sometimes suffer grain mismatch. Interactive Unigram Mixtures can, with very few interactive words, ease the mismatch between topic and target entities. We incorporate the interactive topic information into a two-stage discriminative system for stable set expansion. Experiments confirm that the proposal raises the accuracy of the set expansion system from the baselines examined.

1 Introduction

The task of this paper is entity set expansion in which the lexicons are expanded from just a few seed entities (Pantel et al., 2009). For example, the user inputs the words "Apple", "Google" and "IBM", and the system outputs "Microsoft", "Facebook" and "Intel". Many set expansion and relation extraction algorithms are based on bootstrapping algorithms (Thelen and Riloff, 2002; Pantel and Pennacchiotti, 2006), which iteratively acquire new entities from corpora. These algorithms suffer from the general problem of "semantic drift". Semantic drift moves the extraction criteria away from the initial criteria demanded by the user and so reduces the accuracy of extraction.

Recently, topic information is being used to alleviate semantic drift. Topic information means the genre of each document as estimated by statistical topic models. Sadamitsu et al. (2011) proposed a bootstrapping method that uses unsupervised topic information estimated by Latent Dirichlet Allocation (LDA) (Blei et al., 2003) to alleviate semantic drift. They use a discriminative method (Bellare et al., 2006) in order to incorporates topic information. They showed that the use of topic information improves the accuracy of the extracted entities.

Although unsupervised topic information has been confirmed to be effective, the topic models and target entity sometimes demonstrate grain mismatch. To avoid this mismatch, we refine the topic models to match the target entity grain. Deciding the entity grain from only positive seeds is difficult (Vyas et al., 2009). For example, the positive seed words are "Prius" and "Civic". In this situation, whether "Cadillac" is positive or negative depends on the user's definition. If the user thinks that "*Japanese car*" is positive grain, "Cadillac" should be placed into the negative class but if "*car*" is the positive grain it should be placed into the positive class. Note that we use the term "class" to refer to a set of entities denoted as C_P.

We control the topic models using not only positive seed entities but also a very small number of negative entities as distinguished from the output of the preliminary set expansion system. To implement this approach, we need topic models that offer controllability through the addition of negative words and high response speed for re-training. We utilize a variation of interactive topic models: interactive Unigram Mixtures (Sadamitsu et al., 2012). In a later section, we show that proposed method improves the accuracy of a set expansion system.

2 Set expansion using Topic information

2.1 Basic bootstrapping methods with discriminative models

In this section, we describe the basic method adopted from Bellare et al. (2006) since it offers easy handling of arbitrary features including topic information. At first, N_{ent} positive seed entities and N_{attr} seed attributes are given. The set of positive entity-attribute tuple, T_P, is obtained by taking the cross product of seed entity lists and attribute lists. Tuples T_P are used as queries for retrieving some documents, those that include a tuple present in T_P. Document set $D_{ent,attr}$ that includes the tuple $\{ent, attr\}$ is merged as an example to alleviate the sparseness of features.

Candidate entities are restricted to just the named entities that lie in close proximity to the seed attributes. Discriminative models are used to calculate the discriminative positive score, $s(ent, attr)$, of each candidate tuple, $\{ent, attr\}$. Their system extracts N_{new} new entities with high scores at each iteration as defined by the summation of $s(ent, attr)$ for all seed attributes (A_P); the condition is

$$\sum_{attr \in A_P} s(ent, attr) > 0. \qquad (1)$$

Note that we do not iteratively extract new attributes because our purpose is entity set expansion.

2.2 Bootstrapping with Topic information

The discriminative approach is useful for handling arbitrary features. Although the context features and attributes partly reduce entity word sense ambiguity, some ambiguous entities remain. For example, consider the class "*car*" with the attribute of "*new model*". A false example is shown here: "A *new model* of *Android* will be released soon. The attractive smartphone begins to target new users who are ordinary people." The entity "*Android*" belongs to the "*cell-phone*" class, not "*car*", but appears with seed attributes or contexts because many "*cell-phones*" are introduced in "*new model*" as occurs with "*car*". By using topic, i.e. the genre of the document, we can distinguish "*Android*" from "*car*" and remove such false examples even if the false entity appeared with positive context strings or attributes.

Sadamitsu et al. (2011), the most relevant work to our current study, can disambiguate entity word senses and alleviate semantic drift by extracting topic information from LDA and adding it as discriminative features. The topic models can calculate the posterior probability $p(z|d)$ of topic z in document d. For example, the topic models give high probability to topic z ="*cell-phone*" in the above example sentences[1]. This posterior probability is effective for discrimination and is easily treated as a global feature of discriminative models. The topic feature value $\phi_t(z, ent, attr)$ is calculated as follows,

$$\phi_t(z, ent, attr) \propto \sum_{d \in D_{ent,attr}} p(z|d). \qquad (2)$$

They also use topic information for selecting negative examples which are chosen far from the positive examples according to the measure of topic similarity.

There are other similar works. Paşca and Durme (2008) proposed clustering methods that are effective in terms of extraction, even though their clustering target is only the surrounding context. Ritter and Etzioni (2010) proposed a generative approach to allow extended LDA to model selection preferences. Although their approach is effective, we adopt the discriminative approach and so can treat arbitrary features including interactive information; moreover, it is applicable to bootstrapping methods.

3 Set expansion using Interactive Topic Information

3.1 Interactive Topic Information

Although topic information is effective for alleviating semantic drift, unsupervised topic information raises several problems. For example, Sadamitsu et al. (2011) reported that their set expansion system reached only 50% in the fine grained class "*car*";

[1] z is a random variable whose sample space is represented as a discrete variable, not explicit words.

an analysis showed that the nearest topic was mixed with "*motorcycle*". These classes are hard to distinguish even when both context and topic information are used simultaneously because they have similar context and topic information. One reason for the ineffectiveness of topic information is that the topics in topic models have grain sizes that are inappropriate for the target class in set expansion. Even when we use seed entities for modeling the semi-supervised topic models, as in (Andrzejewski et al., 2009), estimating the appropriate grain size is difficult because of a lack of information about other topics and contra-examples.

In order to control grain size in topic models, this section introduces interactive topic models that permit free control via human interaction. This interaction also includes some negative examples which are very effective in modifying the topic models. Topic model modification is now possible with the recent proposal of the Interactive Topic model (ITM) (Hu and Boyd-graber, 2011), which is based on LDA with the Dirichlet Forest prior (Andrzejewski et al., 2009). ITM makes it possible to accept the alterations input by users and to revise the topic model accordingly. Although ITM can modify a topic model, the calculation cost is high because it uses Gibbs sampling. The factor of processing overhead is very important because the user must wait for system feedback before interaction is possible. If user-interactivity is to be well accepted, we need to raise the response speed.

3.2 Interactive Unigram Mixtures

To obtain faster response, we utilize interactive Unigram Mixtures (IUMs) (Sadamitsu et al., 2012). This section details IUMs. IUMs are based on the simplest topic model, Unigram Mixtures (UMs) (Nigam et al., 2000) which are defined as

$$p(D) = \prod_{d=1}^{D} \sum_{z} p(z) \prod_{v} p(v|z)^{n(v,d)}, \quad (3)$$

where D is a set of documents, d a document, z a hidden topic of a document, v is word type, $n(v,d)$ is the word count of v in document d. $p(z)$ and $p(v|z)$ are the model parameters of UMs. Their approach is to use the standard EM algorithm to estimate UMs. The estimation is achieved by comput-

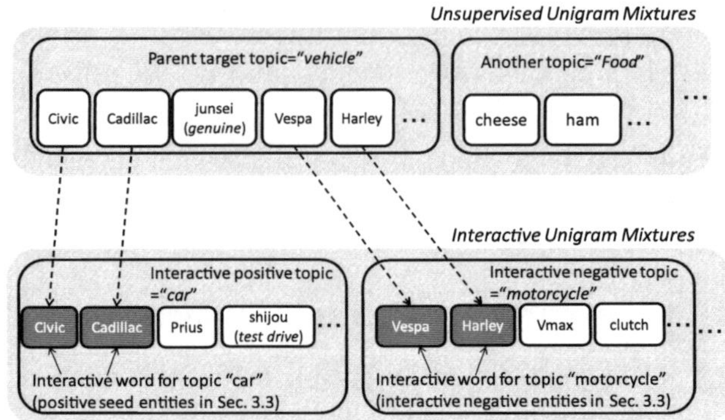

Figure 1: The abstract of interactive Unigram Mixtures with their characteristic topic words. The words in colored boxes are supervised words and the words in white boxes are the characteristic words extracted automatically. Note that, some characteristic topic words are not entity words.

ing the following formulae,

$$p(v|z) = \frac{\sum_d n(v,d)p(z|d)}{\sum_v \sum_d n(v,d)p(z|d)} \quad (4)$$

$$p(z) = \frac{\sum_d p(z|d)}{|D|}, \quad (5)$$

where $p(z|d)$ is called the posterior probability of topic z for document d. For UMs, posterior probability $p(z|d)$ is calculated in E-step by the following formula,

$$p(z|d) = \frac{p(z)\prod_v p(v|z)^{n(v,d)}}{\sum_z p(z)\prod_v p(v|z)^{n(v,d)}}. \quad (6)$$

UMs are not only faster than Gibbs sampling because only the standard EM algorithm is used, but they also make it easy to employ parallel processing (e.g. Map-Reduce).

IUMs are extended UMs and control each topic by utilizing a small set of interactive supervised words. Interactive updating involves using the interactive supervised words to re-model target topics as the set of child topics; for example, the interactive supervised words {Harley, Vespa} and {Civic, Cadillac} are used in order to re-model the target parent topic "*vehicle*" and construct the child topics "*motorcycle*" and "*car*", respectively, as shown in Figure 1. Note that, the words in white boxes in Figure 1 are example of characteristic topic words extracted by a score function such as $p(v|t)/p_{uni}(v)$, where

$p_{uni}(v)$ is a unigram model parameter for all documents. Note that, some characteristic topic words are not entity words because topic models describe all of words not only entity words (e.g. *"clutch"* in the "*motorcycle*" class).

In IUMs, we can focus on just a single parent topic which includes a subset of all documents e.g. *vehicle*. After creating unsupervised UMs, each document is clustered in topic z if its posterior probability satisfies $p(z|d) \geq 0.5$. Most documents meet this condition because UMs are uni-topic models unlike LDA, which offers multi-topic models. IUMs can be updated faster by this hard constraint because they process only the subset of documents.

In order to construct controlled topic models using very few supervised words, IUMs use supervised posterior probability $p_s(z|d_s)$. $p_s(z|d_s)$ is the probability of topic z according to document d_s that includes supervised words and is calculated as

$$p_s(z|d_s) = \frac{n_{d_s}(z)}{N_{d_s}}, \qquad (7)$$

where $n_{d_s}(z)$ is the number of supervised words in document d_s that belong to topic z. N_{d_s} is the number of supervised words that belong to any topic, $N_{d_s} = \sum_z n_{d_s}(z)$. $p_s(z|d_s)$ is used instead of the E-step in estimating UMs (Eq. 6). For example, we consider two documents, $\{Civic, Cadillac\} \in d_{s1}$ and $\{Civic, Vespa\} \in d_{s2}$. The supervised posterior probability of d_{s1} and d_{s2} is calculated as $p_s(z = \text{"Car"}|d_{s1}) = 1$ and $p_s(z = \text{"Car"}|d_{s2}) = 0.5$, $p_s(z = \text{"Motorcycle"}|d_{s2}) = 0.5$, respectively. These hypotheses can expand the supervised information from the word level to the document level.

The supervised posterior probability, $p_s(z|d_s)$, is too radical to be believed completely, so it is interpolated from the calculated posterior probabilities by the standard E-step in later iterations in the EM algorithms. The interpolated posterior probability $p_i(z|d_s)$ is calculated as

$$p_i(z|d_s) = w \cdot p_s(z|d_s) + (1 - w) \cdot p_c(z|d_s). \qquad (8)$$

In the initial EM iteration, the interpolation weight w is set to 1, which means that only the supervised posterior probability is used. Interpolation weight w is decreased with each iteration. In early iterations, w takes a high value to permit model learning to closely approach the supervised structure. In later iterations, w is given a low value to adjust the total balance of model parameters from the perspective of probabilistic adequacy.

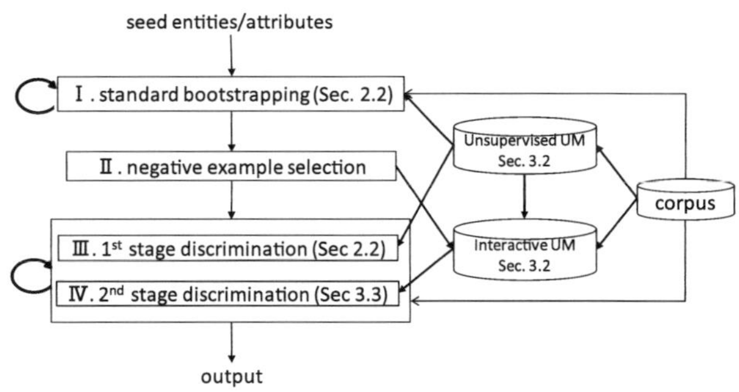

Figure 2: The structure of our system.

We note that the initial parameters are very important for modeling interactive topics appropriately. If the initial parameters are given at random, the model might converge on an inadequate local minima. To avoid this, the initial parameters are set to the parent topic model parameters.

3.3 Applying interactive Unigram Mixtures to set expansion

In this section we describe how to apply IUMs to set expansion in agreement with user's intuition. Our system's diagram is shown in Figure 2.

After the preliminary standard set expansion ("I" in Figure 2) outputs some entities, we can choose interactive negative entities "E_{IN}" (e.g. "Harley, Vespa" in previous sections) found by either automatic methods (McIntosh and Curran, 2009) or manual selection ("II" in Figure 2). Because this paper focuses on interactive control, it is out of scope as to which approach, automatic method or manual selection, should be used. In this paper, we choose few negative entities manually (in our experiments, we select two entities for each negative class). We choose not only E_{IN} but also their class names "C_{IN}" (e.g. "*motorcycle*" in previous sections) and treat them as negative "attributes" in the same way as seed attributes. IUMs are modeled using very little interactive information (E_{IN}, C_{IN}) as well as initial positive seed entities and attributes (E_P, A_P) as the supervised words for each child topic of target parent topic z_p. The target parent topic z_p is the one that

Table 1: Seed entities and seed attributes. The words surrounded by bracket are translation English. The words without brancket are appeared in Katakana or English itself.

class	seed entities	seed attributes
Car	Civic, Swift, Vitz, Corolla, Fit, Lexus, That's, Wagon R, Passo, Demio	kuruma (*car*), CM, shashu (*car line*),shinsha (*new car*), nosha (*delivering a car*), shingata (*new model*), engine, sedan, bumper, shaken (*automobile inspection*)
Dorama	Kita no Kuni kara, Tokugawa Yoshinobu, Mito Koumon, Nodame Cantabile, Dragon Sakura, Hana yori Dango, Furuhata Ninzaburo, ROOKIES, Aibou, Asunaro hakusho	dorama, meisaku (*master piece*), sakuhin (*product*), zokuhen (*sequel*), kantoku (*director*), shuen (*leader actor*), shutsuen (*appearance*), getsu-9 (*dorama started by Monday 9PM*), shichouritsu (*audience rate*), rendora (*miniseries*)
Soccer	Urawa Red Diamonds, Verdi, Avispa Fukuoka, Yokohama F Marinos, Barcelona, Real Madrid, Intel, Rome, Liverpool	soccer, J-League (*soccer league in Japan*), 1-bu (*Division 1*),goal

gives the highest $score(z)$,

$$z_p = \arg\max_z score(z), \quad (9)$$

$$score(z) = \sum_{v \in E_P} \frac{p(z)p(v|z)}{\sum_{z'} p(z')p(v|z')}, \quad (10)$$

where $p(z), p(v|z)$ are unsupervised UMs model parameters. Finally, the posterior probability calculated by IUMs is used as topic features as per the description in Sec 2.2.

Also we utilizes interactive negative entities not only for re-estimating the topic model but also for training the discriminative models as negative examples. Since there are only few interactive negative entities, we expand them by assuming that an entity co-occurring with an interactive negative class (C_{IN}) can be taken as negative entity "$E_{IN'}$". To summarize, interactive negative entity-attribute tuples "T_{IN}" are defined as in

$$T_{IN} = E_{IN} \times (C_{IN} + A_P) + E_{IN'} \times C_{IN},$$

where $\times$ indicates cross product. T_{IN} and T_P (described in Sec.2.1) are used as training data for discriminative models, negative and positive examples, respectively.

For using interactive information effectively, we adapt two stage discrimination. The first stage is the same as the original set expansion system with unsupervised topic model (described in Sec. 2.2); it achieves coarse grain general selection ("III " in Figure 2). In the second stage, the system trains a discriminative model using the same number of positive and negative tuples selected from T_P and T_{IN} respectively with interactive topic information calculated by IUMs ("IV" in Figure 2). The system uses the trained discriminative model in the second stage to re-score the selected candidates from the first stage.

Although the single step discriminative approach can be utilized by using T_{IN} in the first stage as the supervised data, this would degrade discrimination performance. The discriminative models could not train fine and coarse grain simultaneously as same as UMs. In preliminary experiments on the one stage method, we confirmed that the system outputs many inadequate entities belonging to wrong topics in the sense of coarse grain.

McIntosh (2010) proposed the method most similar to ours. In McIntosh (2010), only negative entities are clustered based on distributional similarity. We cluster not only the entities themselves but also their topic information.

Vyas and Pantel proposed an interactive method for entities refinement and improved accuracy of set expansion (Vyas and Pantel, 2009). They utilized the similarity method (SIM) and feature modification method (FMM) for refinement of entities and their local context features.

As far as we know, our proposal represents the first interactive method designed for the set expansion task with topic information. By incorporating interactive topic information, we can expect that the accuracy is improved since an improvement is achieved with unsupervised topic information.

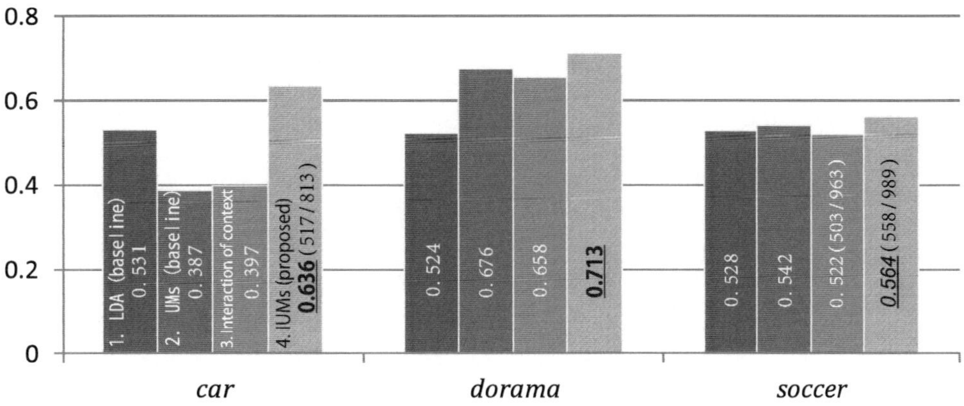

Figure 3: Results for the three classes "*car*", "*dorama*" and "*soccer team*". Bold font indicates that the difference in accuracy between proposal and best of baseline is significant by binomial test with $P < 0.05$ and italic font indicates $P < 0.1$.

4 Experiments

4.1 Experimental Settings

The experimental parameters follow those of the experiments in Sadamitsu et al. (2011). We used 30M Japanese blog articles crawled in May 2008. The documents were tokenized, chunked, and labeled with IREX 8 named entity types (Fuchi and Takagi, 1998; Suzuki et al., 2006), and transformed into context features. The context features were defined using the template "(head) *ent.* (mid.) *attr.* (tail)". The words included in each part were used as surface, part-of-speech, and named entity label features with added position information. Maximum word number of each part was set at 2. The features have to appear in both the positive and negative training data at least 5 times.

In the experiments, we used three classes, "*car*", "*dorama*" and "*soccer team*" since they often suffer semantic drift. The adjustment numbers for the basic setting are $N_{ent} = 10, N_{attr} = 10, N_{new} = 100, |C_{IN}| = 2$. Note that, for confirmation in a more severe situation, we set $N_{attr} = 4, |C_{IN}| = 1$ in "*soccer*" class. After running 10 Bootstrapping iterations, we obtained 1000 entities in total. The seed entities and attributes for each class are shown in Table 1

SVM^{light} (Joachims, 1999) with a second order polynomial kernel was used as the discriminative model. Unsupervised UMs and unsupervised LDA were used for training 100 mixture topic models. Parallel LDA, which is LDA with MPI (Liu et al., 2011), was used for training and inference for LDA. For training IUMs, we set the mixture number of child topics to 5, that covers both interactive and other unsupervised topics about each class. The other unsupervised topics, $(5 - (|C_{IN}| + |C_P|))$, catch the other structure in the parent topic z_p, where $|C_P|$ always equal to 1.

Four settings were examined.

- First is a baseline method using unsupervised topic information with LDA (without interaction); it is described in Sec. 2.2.
- Second is similar to first but the topic models, LDA, are replaced by unsupervised UMs.
- Third is the second setting with the addition of the set of interactive tuples, T_{IN}, for re-training discriminative models using only context information. This setting allows confirmation of just the IUMs effect by comparison to fourth setting which also models interactive topic information.
- Fourth, proposed, is the third setting with the addition of the IUMs learned from the set of interactive tuples, T_{IN}.

Each extracted entity is labeled with *correct* or *incorrect* by two evaluators based on the results of a commercial search engine. Some of the results

Table 2: Examples of extracted entities (first column) and characteristic topic words extracted from UMs and IUMs (fourth column). This table also shows interactive supervised positive and negative classes (second column) and their supervised entities (third column). The words with underline are incorrect extracted entity in the first column and incorrect characteristic topic words in the fourth column.

Extracted entities baseline(UM)&proposed(IUM)	Interactive classes (C_P&C_{IN})	Interactive entities (E_P&E_{IN})	Extracted topic words from each topic
Class = *"car"* *baseline*: Sylvia, Harley, E700 *proposed*: Sylvia, 117 coupe, nubi250 (car navigation system)	parent posi. (z_p)	(*=seed entities*)	tosou (*paint*), secchaku (*bond*), plug, junsei (*genuine*)
	interactive posi. C_P=*car*	(*=seed entities*)	turbo, kuruma (*car*), wheel, shijou (*test drive*)
	interactive nega.1 C_{IN_1}=*motorcycle*	Harley, CB400	baiku (*motorcycle*), plug, bolt, clutch
	interactive nega.2 C_{IN_2}=*train*	E700, E531 (*train names*)	kado (*movable*), ganpura (*plamodel of robot*), puramo (*plamodel*), Bandai (*plamodel company*)
Class = *"dorama"* *baseline*: Prison Break, Iron Man, Konan *proposed*: Prison Break, Shinsengumi!, Tokudane! (news program)	parent posi. (z_p)	(*=seed entities*)	Juri Ueno, Masami Nagasawa, (actoresses), Cannes, Hachiwan Diver (*anime title*)
	interactive posi. C_P="*dorama*"	(*=seed entities*)	Juri Ueno, Masami Nagasawa, Last Friends (*dorama title*), shichouritsu (*viewer rate*)
	interactive nega.1 C_{IN_1}= *movie*	Kung Fu Panda Iron Man	Cannes, Masami Nagasawa, Akunin (*movie title*), shishakai (*preview*)
	interactive nega.2 C_{IN_2}="*anime*"	Konan, Negima (*anime titles*)	TV Tokyo (*broadcasting many animes*), OVA (*original video anime*), Oricon, Yatta-man (*anime title*)
Class = *"soccer"* *baseline*: A Madrid, Giants *proposed*: A. Madrid, Manchester C, Football Association (not team)	parent posi. (z_p)	(*=seed entities*)	Chelsea, toushu (*pitcher*), anda (*hit*), shitten (*loss a point*)
	interactive posi. C_P="*soccer*"	(*=seed entities*)	Manchester United, DF, FW, FC Tokyo (soccer team name)
	interactive nega. C_{IN}="*baseball*"	Giants, Tigers (*baseball teams*)	anda (*hit*), toushu (*pitcher*), kai omote (*top of*), shikyuu (*ball four*)

(1231 entities) were double checked and the κ score for agreement between evaluators was 0.843.

4.2 Results

Figure 3 compares the accuracy of the four methods. If the number of extracted examples is lower than 1000, i.e. Eq. 1 was unsatisfied, the figure shows the number of extracted examples and the correct number in brackets. At first, we compare two baseline methods, first and second bar, that use different unsupervised topic models. The result is that "UMs" are superior to "LDA" in "*dorama*" but inferior in "*car*". They yield more variability than "LDA". One reason for this is that UMs are uni-topic models which leads to over-fitting. Uni-topic models describe most documents by one topic. For uni-topic models, setting a small number of topics (topic grain size is large) suits large topics rather than than small topics because the latter would have to be merged to match the grain size. Conversely, setting a large number of topics suits small topics rather than large topics because the latter would have to split. This restriction can degrade accuracy significantly. LDA smoothes the topics due to its multi-topic modeling. The third setting shows that the interactive tuples T_{IN} used for re-modeling with only context information is not effective. We consider this result indicates that context is not effective in terms of discrimination with fine grain, because at this grain positive context is similar to negative context. Proposed, on the other hand, offers improved accuracy in all classes significantly. These results show the effectiveness of the interactive method that uses topic information. The interactive methods are more effective than the selection of topic model type.

To confirm whether our proposal works properly, we show characteristic topic words extracted from IUMs with interactive classes (C_P, C_{IN}) and entities (E_P, E_{IN}) in Table 2. Because each topic z is not explicitly understandable, we use the characteristic topic words which are representative words for each topic z. The characteristic topic words are ranked by a score function $p(v|t)/p_{uni}(v)$.

- The first column shows target classes and the resulting entities yielded by using set expansion of baseline with UM and proposed method with IUM.
- The second column shows the parent positive topic (z_p) selected by Eq.(9), seed class (C_P) and the interactive supervised classes (C_{IN}) as interactive topic information.
- The third column shows the seed entities (E_P) and the interactive supervised negative entities (E_{IN}).
- The fourth column shows the characteristic topic words of each topic. In this experiment, we extracted 4 topic words from the words listed in top 10.

Table 2 shows that the characteristic topic words are strongly related to the interactive positive (negative) classes and their entities. For example, in the parent positive topic of "*dorama*" class in Figure 2, there are some characteristic topic words, "Juri Ueno", "Masami Nagasawa" (*actresses*), "Cannes" and "Hachiwan Diver (*anime title*)". The words with underline are inadequate topic words for "*dorama*" class. After applying IUM, in the interactive positive topic, the topic words are refined as adequate words, "shichouritsu (*viewer rate*)" and a dorama title. IUMs also model appropriately for the interactive negative topic "*movie*" whose extracted topic words are "Cannes" and "shishakai (*preview*)".

On the other hand, in the "*motorcycle*" class which is the first interactive negative class for "*car*" class, topic words include "plug", "bolt" and "clutch". Although these words are not uniquely "*motorcycle*" words, they tend to appear with "*motorcycle*" class in the corpus used. There are many inadequate characteristic topic words extracted for the "*train*" class, which is the second negative class of the "*car*" class. The characteristic topic words are placed into the "*plamodel*" (plastic model) topic. We consider that the "*train*" words were extracted by the "*plamodel*" topic via semantic drift. This situation is assumed as an example of human's mispredication for a negative topic. Even if IUMs model a class (*plamodel*) different from user prediction topic (*train*), interactive topic information is also effective for alleviating semantic drift. As a result, "*car*" class as the interactive positive topic, its topic words are more pure like "turbo" and "shijou (*test drive*)" than in the parent positive topic.

A similar observation is confirmed from the "*soccer*" class. Because the interactive negative information is smaller than other classes, the improvement of accuracy is smaller. We can expect that much more interactive information achieve further improvement for the accuracy.

5 Conclusion

We proposed an approach to set expansion that uses interactive information for refining the topic model and showed that it can improve expansion accuracy. In our set expansion system, 2 stage discriminations are applied to discriminate coarse from fine grain in each stage. Since we also applied interactive Unigram Mixtures for treating interactive information, our set expansion system makes interaction highly effective.

The remaining problem is how to automatically determine the most appropriate threshold in set expansion. Also, we intend to compare the effectiveness of using manually detected negative examples (which were used in this paper) and automatically detected interactive negative examples.

References

David Andrzejewski, Xiaojin Zhu, and Mark Craven. 2009. Incorporating Domain Knowledge into Topic

Modeling via Dirichlet Forest Priors. In *Proceedings of the International Conference on Machine Learning.*, volume 382, pages 25–32.

Kedar Bellare, Partha P. Talukdar, Giridhar Kumaran, Fernando Pereira, Mark Liberman, Andrew McCallum, and Mark Dredze. 2006. Lightly-supervised attribute extraction. In *Proceedings of the Advances in Neural Information Processing Systems Workshop on Machine Learning for Web Search.*

David M. Blei, Andrew Y. Ng, and Michael I. Jordan. 2003. Latent dirichlet allocation. *The Journal of Machine Learning Research*, 3:993–1022.

Takeshi Fuchi and Shinichiro Takagi. 1998. Japanese Morphological Analyzer using Word Co-occurrence-JTAG. In *Proceedings of the 36th Annual Meeting of the Association for Computational Linguistics and 17th International Conference on Computational Linguistics*, pages 409–413.

Yuening Hu and Jordan Boyd-graber. 2011. Interactive Topic Modeling. In *Proceedings of the 49th Annual Meeting of the Association for Computational Linguistics: Human Language Technologies*, pages 248–257.

Thorsten Joachims. 1999. *Making large-Scale SVM Learning Practical. Advances in Kernel Methods - Support Vector Learning.* Software available at `http://svmlight.joachims.org/`.

Zhiyuan Liu, Yuzhou Zhang, Edward Y. Chang, and Maosong Sun. 2011. PLDA+: Parallel latent dirichlet allocation with data placement and pipeline processing. *ACM Transactions on Intelligent Systems and Technology, special issue on Large Scale Machine Learning.* Software available at `http://code.google.com/p/plda`.

Tara McIntosh and James R. Curran. 2009. Reducing semantic drift with bagging and distributional similarity. In *Proceedings of the Joint Conference of the 47th Annual Meeting of the Association for Computational Linguistics and the 4th International Joint Conference on Natural Language Processing of the Asian Federation of Natural Language Processing*, pages 396–404.

Tara McIntosh. 2010. Unsupervised discovery of negative categories in lexicon bootstrapping. In *Proceedings of the 2010 Conference on Empirical Methods in Natural Language Processing*, pages 356–365.

Kamal Nigam, Andrew K Mccallum, Sebastian Thrun, and Tom Mitchell. 2000. Text Classification from Labeled and Unlabeled Documents using EM. *Machine Learning*, 39(2):103–134.

Marius Paşca and Benjamin Van Durme. 2008. Weakly-supervised acquisition of open-domain classes and class attributes from web documents and query logs. In *Proceedings of the 46th Annual Meeting of the Association for Computational Linguistics*, pages 19–27.

Patrick Pantel and Marco Pennacchiotti. 2006. Espresso: Leveraging generic patterns for automatically harvesting semantic relations. In *Proceedings of the 21st International Conference on Computational Linguistics and the 44th annual meeting of the Association for Computational Linguistics*, pages 113–120.

Patrick Pantel, Eric Crestan, Arkady Borkovsky, Ana-Maria Popescu, and Vishnu Vyas. 2009. Web-scale distributional similarity and entity set expansion. In *Proceedings of the 2009 Conference on Empirical Methods in Natural Language Processing*, pages 938–947.

Alan Ritter and Oren Etzioni. 2010. A Latent Dirichlet Allocation method for Selectional Preferences. In *Proceedings of the 48th Annual Meeting of the Association for Computational Linguistics*, pages 424–434.

Kugatsu Sadamitsu, Kuniko Saito, Kenji Imamura, and Genichiro Kikui. 2011. Entity Set Expansion using Topic information. In *Proceedings of the 49th Annual Meeting of the Association for Computational Linguistics: Human Language Technologies*, pages 726–731.

Kugatsu Sadamitsu, Kuniko Saito, Kenji Imamura, and Yoshihiro Matsuo. 2012. Constructing a Class-Based Lexical Dictionary using Interactive Topic Models. In *Proceedings of the 8th International Language Resources and Evaluation*, pages 2590–2595.

Jun Suzuki, Erik McDermott, and Hideki Isozaki. 2006. Training Conditional Random Fields with Multivariate Evaluation Measures. In *Proceedings of the 21st International Conference on Computational Linguistics and the 44th annual meeting of the Association for Computational Linguistics*, pages 217–224.

Michael Thelen and Ellen Riloff. 2002. A bootstrapping method for learning semantic lexicons using extraction pattern contexts. In *Proceedings of the 2002 conference on Empirical methods in natural language processing*, pages 214–221.

Vishnu Vyas and Patrick Pantel. 2009. Semi-automatic entity set refinement. In *Proceedings of Human Language Technologies: The 2009 Annual Conference of the North American Chapter of the Association for Computational Linguistics*, pages 290–298.

Vishnu Vyas, Patrick Pantel, and Eric Crestan. 2009. Helping editors choose better seed sets for entity set expansion. In *Proceeding of the 18th ACM conference on Information and Knowledge Management*, pages 225–234.

Improving Chinese-to-Japanese Patent Translation Using English as Pivot Language

Xianhua Li Yao Meng Hao Yu
Fujitsu R&D Centre CO., LTD, Beijing, China
{lixianhua, mengyao, yu}@cn.fujitsu.com

Abstract

This paper implements and compares three different strategies to use English as pivot language for Chinese-Japanese patent translation: corpus enrichment, sentence pivot translation and phrase pivot translation. Our results show that both corpus enrichment and phrase pivot translation strategy outperform the baseline system, while the sentence pivot translation strategy failed to improve the system. We apply the strategies on large data set and figure out approaches to improve efficiency. Finally, we perform Minimum Bayes Risk system combination on the different results of direct translation system and pivot translation systems, which significantly outperforms the direct translation system by 4.25 BLEU scores.

1 Introduction

Statistical machine translation (SMT) has made rapid progress in recent years with the support of large quantities of parallel corpora. It's quite common that we use millions of bilingual parallel sentences to train a statistical machine translation system. Unfortunately, large parallel corpora are not always available for some language pairs, or for some specific domains. For example, there are few available bilingual corpora for Chinese-to-Japanese patent translation. Many research labs and companies face data bottleneck when they do research on scare-resourced language pairs or domains.

Much work has been done to overcome the data bottleneck problem. For example, Lu et al. (2009) exploited the existence of bilingual patent corpora and constructed a Chinese-English patent parallel corpus. Resnik and Smith (2003) took the web as a parallel corpus and mined parallel data from it. Munteanu and Marcu (2005) trained a maximum entropy classifier to extract parallel corpus from large non-parallel newspaper corpora. Our work differs in that we make use of the currently available bilingual corpora, without exploiting extra bilingual data to improve machine translation quality. In other words, we employ pivot translation strategies to improve the performance of SMT systems.

- How to apply pivot translation strategies to help scare-resourced language translation?
- How to take advantages of different pivot translation strategies to further improve machine translation quality?

In this paper, we introduce and implement three pivot translation strategies for SMT. The first is *corpus enrichment strategy*. It translates the pivot side of source-pivot corpus and pivot-target corpus into target and source language respectively to construct source-target language pairs. With these sentence pairs, it builds up a new SMT system so as to outperform the basic system. As the corpora we employ are quite large, we select sentence pairs according to their sentence value and do experiments on different size of parallel corpus. The second is *sentence pivot translation strategy*.

It builds two SMT systems on source-pivot and pivot-target corpus respectively. When translating a source sentence into target language, it first translates it into pivot language with the source-pivot system. Then the generated sentence is translated into target language with the pivot-target system. Here, we can keep N-best for each source sentence and see the influence of different N. The third is *phrase pivot translation strategy*. It trains two phrase tables on source-pivot corpus and pivot-target corpus respectively. Then, it uses the rules with the same pivot side to induce a new rule. To limit rule table size, we only keep top M best rules, so as to reduce computational cost.

Our main contributions are as follows. Firstly, we are the first to apply pivot translation strategies on Chinese-Japanese patent SMT translation. Though similar strategies have been implemented, most of them are applied on language pairs which are from the same nature. As far as we know, no one has applied pivot translation strategies on Chinese-Japanese patent translation. Secondly, we make use of three patent corpora which are independent of each other, due to the fact that multilingual corpora are usually not easy to exploit, while others usually use corpora in which the sentences are aligned to each other across all languages, such as Europarl (Koehn, 2005). Besides, as we use large Chinese-English and English-Japanese corpora to help Chinese-Japanese SMT translation, we figure out approaches to make these pivot translation strategies practicable on such big data set. Finally, we implement three pivot translation strategies and apply minimum bayes risk (MBR) system combination on the translation results to further improve translation quality, which achieves an absolute improvement of 4.25 BLEU4 (Papineni et al., 2002) points over baseline system.

The rest of this paper is organized as follows. We describe related work making use of pivot languages (Section 2), and introduce direct SMT system and three kinds of pivot translation strategies, as well as minimum bayes risk system combination (Section3). Then, we present our experimental data and pivot translation strategy results (Section 4). Discussion on our work is in Section 5. The last section draws our conclusion and future work.

2 Related work

Pivot languages have been used for different purposes. Gollins and Sanderson (2001) used multiple pivot languages to improve cross language information retrieval. Ramirez et al. (2008) makes use of existing English resources as a pivot language to create a trilingual Japanese-Spanish-English thesaurus. Wang et al. (2006) improved word alignment for scarce-resourced languages pairs using bilingual corpora of pivot languages. Zhao et al. (2008) extracted paraphrase patterns from bilingual parallel corpora with a pivot approach.

Concerning the contribution of pivot languages to SMT, researchers have done a lot of work on it. Al-Hunaity et al. (2010) used English as pivot language to enhance Danish-Arabic SMT. Babych et al. (2007) compared the direct translation method with pivot translation strategy and confirmed that better translation quality could be achieved with pivot translation strategy. Bertoldi et al. (2008) provided theoretical formulation of SMT with pivot languages and introduced new methods for training alignment models through pivot languages. Costa-jussa et al. (2011) implemented two pivot translation strategies (the cascade system and the pseudo corpus) and performed a combination of these strategies to outperform the direct translation system. Habash and Hu (2009) compared two pivot translation strategies and gave an error analysis on their best system to show improvement. Utiyama and Isahara (2007) implemented two pivot strategies (phrase translation and sentence translation) and did experiments on the Europarl corpus to evaluate system performance. Wu and Wang (2009) revisited three pivot translation strategies and employed a hybrid method to combine RBMT and SMT systems, which significantly improved translation quality. Paul and Sumita (2011) exploited eight factors that affect the quality of pivot language and investigated the impact of these factors on pivot translation performance.

To the best of our knowledge, we are the first to apply pivot translation strategies on Chinese-Japanese patent translation. We implement three pivot translation strategies and perform a sentence level system combination on different translation results to further improve translation quality.

3 Direct phrase-based SMT and pivot translation strategies

3.1 Direct phrase-based SMT

Moses [1] is a freely available statistical machine translation system, which is also the most popular open-source platform for researchers working on SMT. Currently, Moses offers two types of translation models: phrase-based translation model (Koehn et al., 2003) and tree-based translation model. We use phrase-based Moses to build up our direct phrase-based SMT system.

In phrase-based SMT model, there are mainly three kinds of translation resources: translation rule table, language model and reordering table. Both translation rule table and reordering table are learnt from segmented sentence aligned bilingual corpus. Language model is learnt from target monolingual corpus. We employ the phrase-based Moses which uses different feature functions, such as direct phrase translation probability, inverse phrase translation probability, direct lexical weighting, inverse lexical weighting, phrase penalty, language model, distance penalty, word penalty, distortion weights et al. Feature weights are tuned on development set by Minimum Error Rate Training (MERT) (Och, 2003), using BLEU as the objective function.

When translating a source sentence f into target sentence e, the source sentence f is firstly segmented into phrases. Each phrase can be translated into different target language phrases. Phrases can be reordered. The system chooses the output $\hat{e}$ which satisfies

$$\hat{e} = \arg\max_{e} \Pr(e \mid f) = \arg\max_{e} \sum_{m=1}^{N} \lambda_m h_m(e, f) \quad (1)$$

where λ_m denotes feature weights and $h_m(e, f)$ denotes feature functions used in phrase-based Moses.

3.2 Corpus enrichment strategy

A straightforward strategy to improve translation quality is to enrich the training corpus of the direct translation system. However, it is not always convenient for us to collect such bilingual parallel data. Instead, we can generate source-target corpus by either translating the pivot side of source-pivot corpus into target language, or translating the pivot side of pivot-target corpus into source language, given the translation systems built on already available source-pivot corpus and pivot-target corpus respectively. For corpus translation, we can also make use of publicly available statistical machine translation systems such as Google translator et al.

In this paper, we employ Google translator API to translate the pivot side of source-pivot corpus and pivot-target corpus. One problem is that the translation process may take a long time due to our corpus size and disturbance from Google translator. Meanwhile, too many sentence pairs constructed by machine translation are not always promising because of the not-that-good translation quality of SMT systems. We should take in a reasonable size of qualified corpus to keep a balance of efficiency and effect.

We can select an amount of sentences according to sentence value which distinguishes different sentences. After that, we translate the selected sentences and add the translated parallel corpus into original training data in direct translation system. Then, we train a new system with the enriched corpus.

The sentence value is measured by sentence similarity shown in Equation (2).

$$sentSimi(sent1, sent2) = ((\frac{count}{len(sent1)})^{-1} + (\frac{count}{len(sent2)})^{-1})^{-1} = \frac{count}{len(sent1) + len(sent2)} \quad (2)$$

where $count$ denotes the number of shared words in the two sentences, $len(sent1)$ and $len(sent2)$ denote the length of the two sentences respectively.

We can take in sentence pairs part by part to see the influence of corpus size on machine translation quality. We believe corpus enrichment strategy can improve SMT system performance as it makes use of more translation resources.

[1] http://www.statmt.org/moses/

3.3 Sentence pivot translation strategy

In sentence pivot translation strategy, there must be available source-pivot and pivot-target translation systems. A source sentence s is firstly translated into n pivot sentences $p_i (i=1,2...n)$. Then, all pivot sentences are translated into $n \times m$ target sentences $t_{ij} (i=1,2...n; j=1,2...m)$. We choose the best translation among the $n \times m$ candidates for source sentence by employing the method described in (Utiyama and Isahara, 2007). The process is shown in Figure 1.

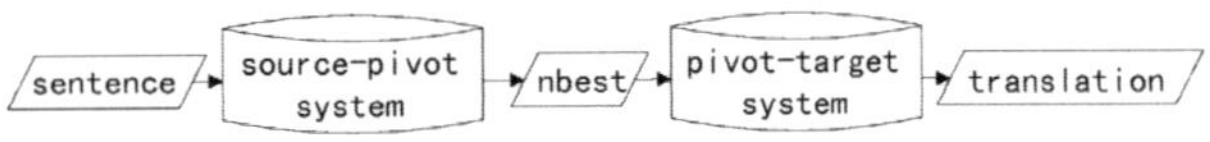

Figure 1. sentence pivot translation strategy

Suppose we use M and N features in source-pivot and pivot-target SMT systems which are $h_i^{sp} (i=1,2...M)$ and $h_j^{pt} (j=1,2..N)$ respectively, the score of target translation t_{ij} is defined as

$$S(t_{ij}) = \sum_{k=1}^{M} (\lambda_k^{sp} h_k^{sp}(s,p)) + \sum_{k=1}^{N} (\lambda_k^{pt} h_k^{pt}(p,t)) \quad (3)$$

where λ_k^{sp} and λ_k^{pt} are feature weights tuned on development set by MERT.

The best translation is that with the highest score

$$\hat{t} = \arg\max_t (S(t_{ij})) \quad (4)$$

3.4 Phrase pivot translation strategy

In phrase pivot translation strategy, a new phrase table T_{st} is generated from two existing phrase tables: one is source-to-pivot phrase table T_{sp} , the other is pivot-to-target phrase table T_{pt} . If the pivot side of two translation rules in these two tables are the same, these two rules can generate a new rule, in which the source side is the source side of the source-pivot rule and the target side is the target side of the pivot-target rule.

According to (Utiyama 2007), we estimate phrase and lexical translation probabilities for each rule as follows.

$$p(s|t) = \sum_{p \in T_{sp} \cap T_{pt}} p(s|p) p(p|t) \quad (5)$$

$$p(t|s) = \sum_{p \in T_{sp} \cap T_{pt}} p(t|p) p(p|s) \quad (6)$$

$$\phi(s|t) = \sum_{p \in T_{sp} \cap T_{pt}} \phi(s|p) \phi(p|t) \quad (7)$$

$$\phi(t|s) = \sum_{p \in T_{sp} \cap T_{pt}} \phi(t|p) \phi(p|s) \quad (8)$$

Here, $p(s|t)$ and $p(t|s)$ are phrase translation probabilities. $\phi(s|t)$ and $\phi(t|s)$ are lexical translation probabilities. $p \in T_{sp} \cap T_{pt}$ means pivot phrase p is included in T_{sp} as target side, and in T_{pt} as source side.

In phrase pivot translation strategy, the size of generated new rule table depends on the number of common phrases in target-side of T_{sp} and source-side of T_{pt} . If the number of phrase p in target side of T_{sp} is N, and in source side of T_{pt} is M, we may get $N*M$ rules maximally. The frequencies of the top 15 commonest rules in T_{sp} and T_{pt} are shown in table 1.

target-side of T_{sp}	frequency	source-side of T_{pt}	frequency
the	446189	the	848951
,	390232	,	471986
and	357239	a	309369
of	277004	of	251167
.	263823	and	250847
a	200072	to	231264
to	186682	is	191362
is	179179	in	179264
for	147076	.	145182
-	127692	, the	103469
in	123632	an	86151
with	90840	of the	82243
which	70257	by	82019
are	69505	-	77824
by	62827	, and	77554

Table 1: frequency of top 15 commonest rules in T_{sp} and T_{pt}

Corpus	Sentence pairs		Words	
			Source	Target
Chinese-Japanese (CJ)	Training set	105615	879953	1010620
	Tuning set	500	4674	5969
	Test set	1000	18552	18348/ 19122
Chinese-English (CE)	Training set	6174088	110116118	121837549
	Tuning set	1000	15963	17486
	Test set	1000	19465	17337/ 18456/ 17429
English-Japanese (EJ)	Training set	3159152	107601189	123917909
	Tuning set	1000	34171	40338
	Test set	1000	34342	38866

Table 2: Corpus details. For CJ, CE and EJ test set, we have two/three/one reference respectively

Here, we can limit the size of rule table by setting up a number limit K to filter low quality rules. We only keep the top K rules for the new rule table. The quality of the rules in the new rule table is measured by summarizing its translation and lexical probabilities.

$$Q(rule) = p(s \mid t) + p(t \mid s) + \phi(s \mid t) + \phi(t \mid s) \quad (9)$$

3.5 System combination

We use sentence level system combination to further improve the translation quality. Sentence level combination selects the best translation out from an N-best list and does not generate new translations.

With the 1-best translation results generated by direct translation system and different pivot systems, we can construct an N-best list for the source corpus. We employ MBR as a post-process to calculate the final translation.

$$E_{mbr} = \arg\min_{E'} \sum_{E} P(E \mid F) L(E, E') \quad (10)$$

where $P(E \mid F)$ is the posterior probability of candidate translation E, and $L(E \mid E')$ is the loss function. Here, we consider all the candidate translations equal, so $P(E \mid F)$ is a constant and can be omitted. We use $1 - BLEU$ as the loss function. Thus, Equation 10 can be rewritten as

$$E_{mbr} = \arg\min_{E'} \sum_{E} (1 - BLEU(E, E')) \quad (11)$$

$BLEU(E, E')$ is sentence level BLEU score.

4 Experiments

4.1 Datasets

We performed experiments on Chinese-Japanese (CJ), Chinese-English (CE), and English-Japanese (EJ) corpora. Corpus details are described in table 2. The training and tuning set of CJ corpus were collected from patent title and abstracts, so the sentences are quite short, while the 1000 sentence pairs of test data were extracted from patent contents, which are nearly twice as long as the ones in training and tuning set. For the CE corpus, training set consists of an in house corpus, and 1 million sentence pairs from NTCIR2011. We extracted the tuning set and test set from the training set. The EJ corpus is from NTCIR2011.

Beside these standard corpora, we also employed Google translator to translate the English side of the EJ corpus into Chinese, so as to construct a flawed CJ corpus. This flawed CJ corpus was used to enrich the original CJ corpus.

We used ICTCLAS (Zhang et al., 2003) to segment all Chinese corpora and standard Moses tokenizer to tokenize all English corpora. Mecab (Kudo 2006) was used to segment all Japanese corpora. We used GIZA++ to generate word alignment and training scripts in Moses to extract phrase pairs with maximum length 7. We employed Moses decoder to do translation with its default settings. We used Minimum Error Rate Training to tune the feature weights. SRILM (Stolcke, 2002) was employed to train a 5-gram language models with all Japanese corpus in CJ corpus and EJ corpus. Case insensitive BLEU4 was used to measure system quality.

4.2 Direct translation

We built a phrase-based Chinese-Japanese patent translation system on Chinese-Japanese corpus with Moses. As the training corpus only contained 105615 sentence pairs and most of them were rather short, the translation quality of the system was quite low, as shown in table 3.

	BLEU4
Direct translation	10.05

Table 3: BLEU of direct translation system

The direct translation system had a low quality because of the lack of training data, as well as the data quality problem as the training sentences were extracted from patent title and abstract, which were quite short and contained limited words, while the test data was from main context of patent documents.

We compared system performance with this baseline system in terms of BLEU4 scores. The percentages in later tables are relative to the BLEU4 score of this direct translation system.

4.3 Corpus enrichment

We used Google translator to translate the English side of the English-Japanese corpus into Chinese, so that to construct a Chinese-Japanese corpus, to enrich training data in 4.1. The reason why we translated English side in EJ corpus into Chinese, but not English side in CE corpus into Japanese was that we believed translation quality was much better for E-C translation than E-J translation, so the corpus we got by translating English into Chinese would be of better quality. After filtering the corpus, we got 2846799 sentence pairs.

We added the new corpus into training data in 4.1 and trained another translation system. The translation quality of this new system was measured by BLEU4 as follows.

	BLEU4	
Corpus Enrichment-All	9.22	-8.26%

Table 4: BLEU of corpus enrichment strategy

To our disappointment, adding the entire corpus into the original training corpus did not improve system performance. Contrarily, BLEU4 decreased by 0.83. Still, this result was acceptable after we looked into the new corpus. Due to SMT system limit, the new corpus introduced in more noise than knowledge.

We ranked the sentences according to sentence value and added corpus step by step into original training corpus. Then we retrained the Moses system. The results are shown in table 5.

Corpus size added	BLEU4	
+100K	10.17	+1.19%
+200K	10.24	+1.89%
+300K	10.36	+3.08%
+400K	11.11	+10.55%
+500K	**12.86**	**+27.96%**
+600K	9.91	-1.39%
+700K	9.09	-9.55%

Table 5: BLEU of corpus enrichment strategy

As we added in more data, BLEU score improved slowly until it reached a peak point where we added in 500K sentence pairs. Then BLEU score decreased. Since we had ranked the sentences according to sentence value, we didn't test the rest sentences. We took this as the best result for corpus enrichment strategy.

4.4 sentence pivot translation strategy

We built two SMT systems for Chinese-English and English-Japanese translation with CE and EJ corpus respectively. Translation quality of these two systems was measured in terms of BLEU4 as shown in table 6.

	BLEU4
Chinese-to-English	27.84
English-to-Japanese	31.85

Table 6: BLEU of CE and EJ SMT system

For Chinese-Japanese translation, we first used Chinese-English system to translate Chinese into English. Then we used English-Japanese system to translate English into Japanese. According to Utiyama and Isahara (2007), the improvement of sentence pivot translation strategy with n = 15 is not significant compared to that with n = 1, so we kept 1 best translation for each sentence. The results are shown in table 7.

BLEU4	
9.91	-1.39%

Table 7: BLEU of sentence pivot translation strategy

As we can see from table 7, due to error accumulation, translation quality decreased a lot from BLEU4 10.05 to BLEU4 9.91. So sentence pivot translation strategy failed to improve translation quality in our experiments.

4.5 phrase pivot translation strategy

We trained two rule tables respectively on CE and EJ corpus. For each CE rule, we found the rule with the same English side in EJ rule table, and generated a new rule with C side of CE rule and J side of EJ rule. Each probability of the CJ rule was computed by minus the corresponding probabilities in CE rule and EJ rule, assuming these probabilities are independent. We kept 20 Japanese candidates for each Chinese phrase at most, and obtained a CJ rule table with 433276 rules.

We added these rules into the original rule table in direct translation system and retuned the system. The results are shown in table 8.

	BLEU4	
phrase pivot	13.65	+35.82%

Table 8: BLEU of sentence pivot translation strategy

As we can see from table 8, introducing in more rules could obviously improve translation quality.

4.6 system combination

For each sentence in test set, we could get four different translation results from direct translation system and three pivot systems. We used sentence level system combination to get the final best translation. After system combination, the results are shown in table 9.

	BLEU4	
System combination	14.30	+42.29%

Table 9: BLEU of system combination

As we can see in table 9, system combination could improve translation quality significantly by 4.25 BLEU4 points compared to baseline 10.05. This is also the best result we could ever obtain.

5 Discussions and Analysis

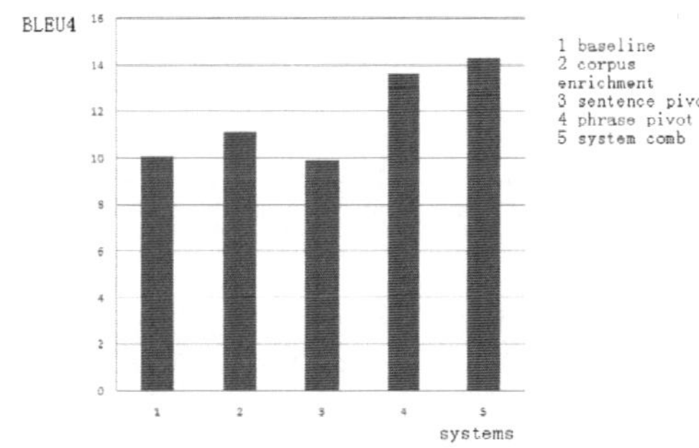

Figure 2. main results of different systems

Figure 2 shows the best machine translation performance of five different systems: baseline system, corpus enrichment system, sentence pivot translation system, phrase pivot translation system and a combined system. As we can see from Figure 2, baseline system performs better that sentence pivot translation system, while corpus enrichment system surpasses baseline system. Phrase pivot translation system obtained better BLEU score than corpus enrichment system. The combined system beat all other systems and achieved the best result. Thus, Figure 2 indicates that

$$\text{systemcomb} > \text{phrase pivot} > \text{corpus enrichment} > \text{baseline} > \text{sentence pivot}$$

where > means the system at the left hand side of it performs better that the one at the right hand side.

The reason why corpus enrichment system and phrase pivot translation system surpassed baseline system was mainly because they introduced in more translation resources into baseline system. As phrase pivot translation system introduced in selected translation rules from all pivot corpora, while corpus enrichment system only introduced in limited selected sentences, phrase pivot translation system achieved a better result. Sentence pivot translation system failed to improve translation quality, as it didn't make use of the original CJ training data, but translated the sentences only with the CE and EJ data. Its performance was also influenced by accumulative error during translation. System combination overtook all other systems as it selected the best translation from these systems for each sentence.

Source sentence	深水 区域 水底 筑堤 (坝) 施工 技术
English reference	Embankment (dam) construction technology at the bottom of deepwater area
Reference	深海 地域 の 水中 堤防 (ダム) 建設 技術
Baseline result	深い 水 で の エリア ( ) 施工 技術
System comb	深い 水 で の 地域 の 海底 堤防 (ダム) 施工 技術
Source sentence	画 三 条 斜线 处 为 透明 或 半透明 材料 。
English reference	Transparent or semitransparent materials are signed with three oblique lines.
Reference	斜線 を 描く ところ は 透明 あるいは 半 透明 材料 で ある 。
Baseline result	絵 の ために 三 条 で 透明 あるいは 半 透明 の 材料
System comb	画面 三 条 斜線 が 透明 あるいは 半 透明 の 材料 。
Source sentence	气 相 制备 芳 族 聚 异 氰酸 酯 化合物 的 方法
English reference	Preparation of aromatic polyisocyanate compounds in gaseous phase
Reference	ガス で 芳香 族 化合 物 を 作り出す 方法
Baseline result	気 相 調製 族 「 聚 へ エステル 化合 物 の 方法
System comb	気 相 調製 芳香 族 ポリイソシアネート 化合 物 の 方法
Source sentence	过滤 装置 由 合成树脂 制成 , 具有 重量 轻 和 机械 强度 高 的 特点 。
English reference	Filtration unit is made of synthetic resin, with the characteristics of light weight and high mechanical strength.
Reference	フィルタ は 合成 樹脂 から 作ら れ 、 軽量 と 高い 機械 強度 の 特徴 が ある 。
Baseline result	フィルタリング 装置 ルーティング 持つ で 作成 した 、 軽 重量 と 機械 強度 高 の
System comb	フィルタリング 装置 ルーティング する 合成 樹脂 と 、 は 重量 が 軽く と 機械 強度 高 の 正常 特性 。
Source sentence	本 发明 涉及 相当 纯 的 粉状 甘露 糖 醇 ， 其 在 试验 1 中 具有 适中 的 、 不 过分 的 脆性 ， 为 40-80 %
English reference	The invention relates to a very pure powder mannitol, with a modest brittleness of 40-80% in experiment 1
Reference	本 発明 は 純 の 粉 上 マンノース 糖 に 関し 、 実験 1 の 中 に ころあい の もろく 、 40-80% で ある 。
Baseline result	ブック の 純粋 な に かかわる 粉末 状 の アルコール その が 試験 1 の 中 で の 、 不 以上 持つ の 脆性 の ために
System comb	ブック の 発明 ほぼ 純粋 な 粉末 状 かかわる マンニトール その が 試験 1 の 中 、 適度 の の 、 不 以上 **40－80** の 脆性

Figure 3. Examples of Chinese-Japanese translation results. The differences between baseline result and our best result are highlighted in **bold.** English references are given to ease readability.

Figure 3 shows some translation examples of baseline system and system combination. As we can see from the examples, the results of system combination recognized more lexicons and achieved better translation quality.

6 Conclusions and Future Work

In this paper, we implemented three strategies (corpus enrichment, sentence pivot translation, phrase pivot translation) to make use of pivot languages to help statistical machine translation. We also introduced approaches to make these strategies practicable on large data set. MBR sentence level system combination was employed to further improve translation quality. We applied these strategies on Chinese to Japanese patent translation using English as a pivot language. The results showed that corpus enrichment and phrase pivot translation strategies both could improve SMT quality, while sentence pivot translation failed. After employing MBR sentence level system combination, we achieved significant improvement of SMT quality by 4.25 points in terms of BLEU. This is an absolute improvement over baseline.

Our future work would focus on exploiting pivot strategies on more advanced models (such as HPB model) to further improve Chinese-Japanese patent translation quality. Also, we would like to enhance our pivot strategies. We believe that phrase pivot translation strategy is quite promising and we would obtain more useful translation rules through phrase pivot strategy. Besides, we plan to collect more Chinese-Japanese patent corpus as the currently available corpus size is still too small. The corpus obtained would enrich the training data so as to help the learning process. We aim at high quality in Chinese-Japanese patent translation.

Acknowledgments

We would like to thank to Zhongguang Zheng, Naisheng Ge and Yiwen Fu for their helpful discussions. We also thank the anonymous reviewers for their insightful comments.

References

Mossab Al-Hunaity, Bente Maegaard, Dorte Hansen. 2010. Using English as a pivot language to enhance Danish-Arabic statistical machine translation. In Proc. of LREC 2010: Workshop on Language Resources and Human Language Technology for Semitic Languages, pages 108-113.

Bogdan Babych, Anthony Hartley, Serge Sharoff. 2007. Translating from under-resourced languages: comparing direct transfer against pivot translation. In Proc. of MT Summit XI, pages 29-35

Nicola Bertoldi, Madalina Barbaiani, Marcello Federico, Roldano Cattoni. 2008. Phrase-based statistical machine translation with pivot languages. In Proc. of IWSLT 2008: Proceedings of the International Workshop on Spoken Language Translation, pages 143-149

Mauro Cettolo, Nicola Bertoldi, Marcello Federico. 2011. Bootstrapping Arabic-Italian SMT through comparable texts and pivot translation. In Proc. of the 15th conference of the European Association for Machine Translation, pages 249-256.

Marta R. Costa-jussà, Carlos Henríquez, Rafael E.Banchs. 2011. Enhancing scarce-resource language translation through pivot combinations. In Proc. of the 5th International Joint Conference on Natural Language Processing, pages 1361-1365.

Tim Gollins, Mark Sanderson. 2001. Improving cross language retrieval with triangulated translation. In Proc. of the 24th annual international ACM SIGIR conference on Research and development in information retrieval, pages 90-95

Nizar Habash, Jun Hu. 2009. Improving Arabic-Chinese statistical machine translation using English as pivot language. In Proc. of the Fourth Workshop on Statistical Machine Translation, pages 173-181.

Philipp Koehn. 2005. Europarl: a parallel corpus for statistical machine translation. MT Summit X, pages 79-86.

Phillip Koehn, Franz Josef Och, Daniel Marcu. 2003. Statistical phrase-based translation. In Proc. of NAACL03.

Taku Kudo. 2006. Mecab: yet another part of speech and morphological analayzer. https://code.google.com/p/mecab/

Gregor Leusch, Aurélien Max, Josep Maria Crego, Hermann Ney. 2010. Multi-pivot translation by system combination. In Proc. of the 7th International Workshop on Spoken Language Translation, pages 299-306.

Wen Li, Lei Chen, Wudaba, Miao Li. 2010. Chained machine translation using morphemes as pivot language. In Proc. of the 8th Workshop on Asian Language Resources, pages 169-177.

Bin Lu, Benjamin K.Tsou, Jingbo Zhu, Tao Jiang, & Oi Yee Kwong. 2009. The construction of a Chinese-English patent parallel corpus. MT Summit XII: Third Workshop on Patent Translation, pages17-24

Dragos Stefan Munteanu, Daniel Marcu. 2005. Improving machine translation performance by exploiting non-parallel corpora. Computational Linguistics, 31(4), pages 477-504

Franz Josef Och. 2003. Minimum Error Rate Training for Statistical Machine Translation. In Proc. of the 41st Annual Meeting of the ACL, pages 160-167.

Franz Josef Och, Hermann Ney. 2003. A systematic comparison of various statistical alignment models. Computational Linguistics, 29(1).

Kishore Papineni, Salim Roukos, Todd Ward, Wei-Jing Zhu. 2002. Bleu: a Method for Automatic Evaluation of Machine Translation. In Proc. of the 40th Annual Meeting on Association for Computational Linguistics, pages 311-318.

Michael Paul, Andrew Finch, Paul R.Dixon, Eiichiro Sumita. 2011. Dialect translation: integrating Bayesian co-segmentation models with pivot-based SMT. In Proc. of DIALECTS2011: Proceedings of the First Workshop on Algorithms and Resources for Modeling of Dialects and Language Varieties, pages 1-9.

Michael Paul, Eiichiro Sumita. 2011. Translation quality indicators for pivot-based statistical MT. In Proc. of the 5th International Joint Conference on Natural Language Processing, pages 811-818.

Jessica Ramírez, Masayuki Asahara, Yuji Matsumoto. 2008. Japanese-Spanish thesaurus construction using English as a pivot. In Proc. of IJCNLP 2008: Third International Joint Conference on Natural Language Processing, pages 473-480.

Philip Resnik, Noah A. Smith. 2003. The web as a parallel corpus. Computational Linguistics, 29(3), pages 349-380

Andreas Stolcke. 2002. Srilm-an Extensible Language Modeling Toolkit. In Proc. of the International Conference on Spoken Language Processing, pages 901-904.

Rie Tanaka, Yohei Murakami, Toru Ishida. 2009. Context-based approach for pivot translation services. In Proc. of IJCAI-09: Twenty-first International Joint conference on Artificial Intelligence, pages 1555-1561.

Masao Utiyama, Hitoshi Isahara. 2007. A comparison of pivot methods for phrase-based statistical machine translation. In Proc. of Human Language Technology: the conference of the North American Chapter of the Association for Computational Linguistics, pages 484-491

Haifeng Wang, Hua Wu, Zhanyi Liu. 2006. Word alignment for languages with scarce resources using bilingual corpora of other language pairs. In Proc. of COLING/ACL on main conference poster sessions, pages 874-881

Hua Wu, Haifeng Wang. 2009. Revisiting pivot language approach for machine translation. In Proc. of the 47th Annual Meeting of the ACL and the 4th IJCNLP, pages 154-162.

Hua Wu, Haifeng Wang. 2007. Pivot language approach for phrase-based statistical machine translation. In Proc. of the 45th Annual Meeting of the Association for Computational Linguistics, pages 856-863

Huaping Zhang, Hongkui Yu, Deyi Xiong, Qun Liu. 2003. HHMM-based Chinese lexical analyzer ICTCLAS. In Proc. of the second SIGHAN workshop on Chinese language processing, pages 184-187.

Shiqi Zhao, Haifeng Wang, Ting Liu, Sheng Li. 2008. Pivot approach for extracting paraphrase patterns from bilingual corpora. In Proc. of HLT 46th Annual Meeting of the Association for Computational Linguistics: Human Language Technologies, pages780-788.

Combining Social Cognitive Theories with Linguistic Features for Multi-genre Sentiment Analysis

Hao Li[1], **Yu Chen**[2], **Heng Ji**[1], **Smaranda Muresan**[3], **Dequan Zheng**[2]
[1]Computer Science Department and Linguistics Department,
Queens College and Graduate Center, City University of New York, U.S.A
[2]School of Computer Science and Technology, Harbin Institute of Technology, China
[3]School of Communication and Information, Rutgers University, U.S.A
{haoli.qc,hengjicuny}@gmail.com
{chenyu,dqzheng}@mtlab.hit.edu.cn
smuresan@rci.rutgers.edu

Abstract

With the rapid development of social media and social networks, spontaneously user generated content like tweets and forum posts have become important materials for tracking people's opinions and sentiments online. In this paper we investigate the limitations of traditional linguistic-based approaches to sentiment analysis when applied to these informal genres. Inspired by various social cognitive theories, we combine local linguistic features and global social evidence in a propagation scheme to improve sentiment analysis results. Without using any additional labeled data, this new approach obtains significant improvement (up to 12% higher accuracy) for various genres in the domain of presidential election.

1 Introduction

Sentiment analysis is an important step for both Natural Language Processing (NLP) tasks such as opinion question answering (Yu and Hatzivassiloglou, 2003) and practical applications such as commercial product reputation mining (Morinaga et al., 2002), movie review mining (Pang et al., 2002) and political election prediction (Tumasjan et al., 2010).

With the prevalence of social media, spontaneously user generated content such as tweets or forum posts have become an invaluable source of people's sentiments and opinions. However, as with other NLP tasks, sentiment analysis on such informal genres presents several challenges: (1) informal text expressions; (2) lexical diversity (e.g., for example, in our training data only 10% of words in the discussion forums and tweets appear more than ten times, while in movie reviews over 20% of words appear more than ten times); (3) unpredictable shift in topics/issues. The prevalence of debate in both forum posts and tweets leads to the use of more complicated discourse structures involving multiple targets and sentiments, as well as the second-person voice. These difficulties are magnified in tweets due to necessarily compressed contexts (tweets are limited to 140 characters).

In this paper, we tackle these challenges from two perspectives. First, we approach the sentiment analysis task by identifying not only a specific "target" (e.g., presidential candidate) but also its associated "issues" (e.g., foreign policy) before detecting sentiment. This approach is similar to the idea of modeling "aspect" in product reviews (Titov and McDonald, 2008; Wang et al., 2011).

Second, a detailed error analysis has shown that currently available sentiment lexicons and various shallow linguistic features are not sufficient to advance simple bag-of-words baseline approaches due to the diverse ways in which sentiment can be expressed as well as the prevalence of debate in social media. Fortunately, documents in informal genres are often embedded in very rich social structures. Therefore, augmenting the context available for a target and an issue based on social structures is likely to provide a much richer context. We propose three hypotheses based on social cognitive theories and incorporate these hypotheses into a new framework of propagating consistent sentiments across documents. Without using any additional labeled data this new approach obtained significant improvement (up to 12% higher accuracy).

2 Related Work

Most sentiment analysis has been applied to movie/product reviews, blogs and tweets. Very little work has been conducted on discussion forums. Hassan et al. (2010) identified the attitudes of participants toward one another in an online discussion forum using a signed network representation of participant interaction. In contrast, we are interested in discovering the opinions of participants toward a public figure in light of their stance on various political issues.

Sentiment Analysis can be categorized into target-independent and target-dependent. The target-independent work mainly focused on exploring various local linguistic features and incorporating them into supervised learning based systems (Pang and Lee, 2004; Zhao et al., 2008; Narayanan et al., 2009) or unsupervised learning based systems (Joshi et al., 2011). Recent target-dependent work has focused on automatically extracting sentiment expressions for a given target (Godbole et al., 2007; Chen et al., 2012), or incorporating target-dependent features into sentiment analysis (Liu et al., 2005; Jiang et al., 2011). In this paper we focus on the task of jointly extracting sentiment, target and issue in order to provide richer and more concrete evidence to describe and predict the attitudes of online users. This bares similarity to the idea of modeling aspect rating in product reviews (Titov and McDonald, 2008; Wang et al., 2011).

When sentiment analysis is applied to social media, feature engineering is a crucial step (Agarwal et al., 2011; Kouloumpis et al., 2011). Most previous work based solely on lexical features suffers from data sparsity. For example, Saif et al. (2012) observed that 90% of words in tweets appear less than ten times. The semantic clustering approach they have proposed (e.g. grouping "Iphone" , "Ipad" and "Itouch" into "Apple Product") can alleviate the bottleneck, but it tends to ignore the fine-grained distinctions among semantic concepts. To address the lexical diversity problem, we take advantage of the information redundancy in rich social network structures. Unlike most previous work which only exploited user-user relations (Speriosui et al., 2011; Conover et al., 2011) or document-document relations (Tan et al., 2011; Jiang et al., 2011), we use user-document relations derived from social cognitive theories to design global features based on the interrelations among the users, targets and issues. Guerra et al. (2011) measured the bias of social media users on a topic, and then transferred such knowledge to improve sentiment classification. In this paper, we mine similar knowledge such as the bias of social media users on target-issue pairs and target-target pairs.

3 Experimental Setup

Our task focuses on classifying user contributed content (e.g., tweets and forum posts) as "Positive" or "Negative", for the domain of political elections. Tweet messages usually contain sentiments related to specific targets (e.g., presidential candidates), while forum posts often contain both specific targets and related issues (e.g., foreign policy) because participants often debate with each other and thus need to provide concrete evidence. Therefore, we define the sentiment analysis task as *target dependent* for tweets and *target-issue dependent* for forum posts. Consequently, we automatically extract targets and issues before conducting sentiment analysis. Table 1 presents some examples labeled as "Positive" or "Negative" for each genre.

3.1 Data

The tweet data set was automatically collected by retrieving positive instances with #Obama2012 or #GOP2012 hashtags[1], and negative instances with #Obamafail or #GOPfail hashtags. Similar to Gonzalez-Ibanez et al (2011), we then filtered all tweets where the hashtags of interest were not located at the very end of the message.

The discussion forum data set was adapted from the "Election & Campaigns" board of a political forum[2], where political candidates, campaigns and elections are actively discussed. We have collected the most recent posts from March 2011 to December 2011. About 97.3% posts contain either positive or

[1]"GOP" refers to the U.S. republican party which includes presidential candidates such as Ron Paul and Mitt Romney

[2]http://www.politicalforum.com/elections-campaigns

Genre	Sentiment	Target	Issue	Example
Review	Positive	N/A	N/A	The film provides some great insight into the neurotic mindset of all comics -- even those who have reached the absolute top of the game.
	Negative	N/A	N/A	Star trek was kind of terrific once, but now it is a copy of a copy of a copy.
Tweet	Positive	Ron Paul	Foreign Policy	Ron Pauls Foreign Policy Puts War Profiteers out of Business http://t.co/VGWfqcbs #ronpaul #tcot #tlot #gop2012 #FITN
	Negative	Mitt Romney	Economics	Mitt Romney said the "economy is getting better" fool!!! \#GOPFAIL
Forum	Positive	Ron Paul	Foreign Policy	I also find it interesting that so many people ridicule Ron Paul's foreign policy yet the people that are directly affected by it, our troops, support Ron Paul more than any other GOP candidate combined and more than Obama.
	Negative	Barack Obama	Economics	Obama screwed up by not fixing the economy first and leaving health care reform for a second term.

Table 1: Sentiment Examples of Different Genres

negative sentiments as opposed to neutral, therefore we only focus on the polarity classification problem.

We also used a more traditional set for sentiment analysis — the movie review polarity data set shared by (Pang et al., 2002) — to highlight the challenges of more informal texts.

Table 2 summarizes the statistics of data sets used for each genre. All experiments in this paper are based on three-fold cross-validation.

Genre	Positive	Negative
Review	5691	5691
Tweet	2323	2323
Forum	381	381

Table 2: Statistics of Data Sets

4 Linguistic-based Approach

In this section, we present our baseline approach using only linguistic features.

4.1 Pre-processing

We have applied the tool developed by Han and Baldwin (2011) together with the following additional steps to perform normalization for informal documents (tweets and forum posts).

- Replace URLs with "@URL".
- Replace @username with "@USERNAME".
- Replace negation words with "NOT" based on the list derived from the LIWCLexicon (Pennebaker et al., 2001).
- Normalize slang words (e.g. "LOL" to "laugh out loud") (Agarwal et al., 2011).
- Spelling correction using WordNet (Fellbaum, 2005) (e.g. "cooooool" to "cool")

In addition, each document has been tokenized and annotated with Part-of-speech tags (Toutanova et al., 2003).

4.2 Target and Issue Detection

After pre-processing, the first step is to detect documents which include popular targets and issues. A popular target is an entity that users frequently discuss, such as a product (e.g. "*Iphone4*"), a person (e.g. "*Ron Paul*") or an organization (e.g. "*Red Cross*"). A popular issue is a related aspect associated with a target, such as "*display function*" or "*economic issue*".

We have applied a state-of-the-art English entity extraction system (Li et al., 2012; Ji et al., 2005) that includes name tagging and coreference resolution to detect name variants from each document (e.g. "*Ron*", "*Paul*", "*Ron Paul*" and "*RP*" are all name variations for the presidential candidate Ron Paul). In order to detect issues, we mined common keywords from the U.S. presidential election web sites. The two most frequent issues are "*Economic*" which includes 647 key phrases such as "Debt", "Deficit", "Money", "Market", "Tax" and "unemployment", and "*Foreign Policy*" which includes 27 key phrases such as "military", "isolationism", "foreign policy", "Israel", "Iran" and "China". Sentiment analysis is applied on the documents that include at least one target and one issue.

We have evaluated the target and issue detection performance and the accuracy scores obtained 99.0% and 92.0%, respectively.

4.3 Sentiment Detection

We have developed a supervised learning model based on Support Vector Machines to classify sentiment labels for each document (a post, a tweet message or a movie review document), incorporating several features such as N-grams, POS, various lexicons, punctuation, capitalization (see Table 3).

Feature	Description
N-grams	All unique unigrams, bigrams and trigrams
Part-of-Speech	Part-Of-Speech tags generated by Stanford Parser (Toutanova et al., 2003)
Gazetteer	Lexical matching based on (Joshi et al., 2011), SentiWordNet (Baccianella et al., 2010), Subjectivity Lexicon (Wiebe et al., 2004), Inquirer (Stone et al., 1966), Taboada (Taboada and Grieve, 2004), UICLexicon (Hu and Liu, 2004), LIWCLexicon (Pennebaker et al., 2001)
Word Cluster	Use synset information provided by Wordnet to expand the entries of each gazettteer; Lexical matching based on the expanded gazetteers
Punctuation	Whether the document includes any exclamation mark or question mark
Capitalization	Unique words which include all capitalized letters

Table 3: Linguistic Features Used in the Baseline System

The classification results are normalized to probability based confidence values via a sigmoid kernel function (Wu et al., 2004).

4.4 Results and Analysis

Figure 1 presents the performance of the baseline system as we add each feature category. In general, N-gram based features provide a strong baseline, and thus it is difficult for local linguistic features (e.g., POS, gazetteers, punctuation) to make significant improvement. In addition, discussion forums prove to be the most challenging among these three genres. We provide a more detailed analysis for the impact of N-gram features as well as a discussion of the "long-tail" problem prevalent for informal genres.

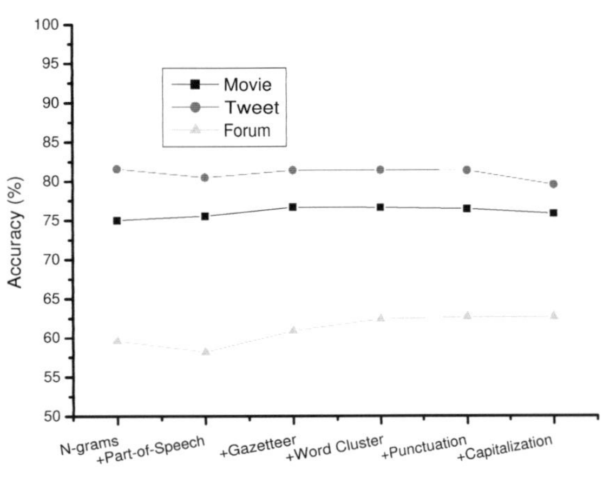

Figure 1: Baseline Performance

N-gram Features. Table 4 investigated various combinations of n-gram (n=1, 2 and 3) features. The unigram features were proven to be dominant for reviews and tweets, which is consistent with the observations by previous work on these two genres (Bermingham and Smeaton, 2010; Pak and Paroubek, 2010). However, bigram and trigram features significantly outperformed unigram features for the forum data, because forum posts tend to be longer and contain more complicated linguistic structures used to formulate arguments.

Features	Forum	Tweet	Review
Unigram	54.3%	81.6%	75.0%
Bigram	58.9%	79.3%	70.6%
Unigram+Bigram	58.2%	83.7%	**75.8%**
Unigram+Trigram	58.3%	**84.0%**	75.6%
Bigram+Trigram	**59.6%**	79.7%	69.7%

Table 4: Impact of N-gram Features on Accuracy

"Long-Tail" Problem. The limited gain (1%-2%) from gazetteer based features is due to long-tailed distribution of lexicon coverage. 53.3% of gazetteer entries do not cover any movie review documents, but about 87% of entries do not cover any forum posts or tweets, which clearly indicates that social media includes more diverse way to express sentiment. Similarly, 16% of entries cover 1 movie review document, but only about 6%-7% of entries cover 1 tweet message or 1 forum post; 6% of entries cover more than 10 movie review documents, but only about 0.8%-0.9% of entries cover more than 10 tweet messages or forum posts. All of the various gazetteers only cover 16.5% of movie documents, 12.4% of tweets and 17.6% of forum posts. The Word Cluster features (see Table 3) can cover more documents and achieved slight improvement (0.83% for forum posts and 0.40% for tweets) but it may require much deeper understanding and global knowledge to generalize to diverse lexical contexts.

5 Combining Linguistic Features with Global Social Evidence

The linguistic-based approach provided discouraging results. Fortunately, sentiment analysis is an inter-disciplinary task in that it attempts to capture people's social behavior. Sentiment differences within a group can result in social mitosis, leading to the emergence of two groups (Wang and Thorngate, 2003). In this section, we explore a different direction by applying social cognitive theories and propose three hypotheses that take user behavior into account in order to improve sentiment analysis.

5.1 Hypotheses based on Social Cognitive Theories

We formulate the following three hypotheses based on social cognitive theories, which we aim to prove for the domain of presidential election:

Hypothesis 1 (One sentiment per Indicative Target-Issue Pair). *The sentiment for a particular target is globally consistent across users because of the target's stance on some particular issue.*

The impression formation theory (Hamilton and Sherman, 1996) postulates a global coherence in perception, namely that users assume consistency in traits and behavior, such that observations about current behavior lead to causal attributions regarding past and future behaviors. Certain target-issue pairs are consistently associated with a particular sentiment across most users. For example, when a user is commenting on the target "*Ron Paul*" about his policy on "*Economy*" issue, the post usually indicates a positive sentiment. In contrast, the sentiments toward "*Barack Obama*"'s policy on "*Foreign Issue*" are usually negative.

Hypothesis 2 (One sentiment per Indicative Target-Target Pair). *The sentiment for a particular target is globally consistent when he or she is compared with another particular target.*

The social categorization process (Mason and Marcae, 2004) states that we mentally categorize people into different groups based on common characteristics. As a result, when commenting on an individual target, a user often compares the target with another target to express implicit sentiments or strengthen the opinions, which brings additional challenges for detecting the boundaries of sentiment words associated with specific targets. For example, the following sentence: "*NONE of the GOP candidates have a significant advantage on national polls against **Obama**.*" includes two different targets "*Obama*" and "*GOP*" and therefore a mixture of positive words (e.g. "significant" and "advantage") and negative words (e.g. "against" and "NONE"). However, some common pairs often retain consistent sentiments. For example, when compared to "*McCain*" or "*Nixon*", the sentiment towards "*Barack Obama*" is usually positive, while compared to "*Washington*", the sentiment is mostly negative.

In order to incorporate the above two hypotheses, we use a simple propagation approach. For each unique target-target pair or unique target-issue pair in the training data, we count the frequency of the sentiment labels in the training data, f_p for positive and f_n for negative. Then we adopt the following confidence metric to measure the degree of sentiment consistency for this pair:

$$c = max(f_p, f_n)/(f_p + f_n) \quad (1)$$

$Confidence$ value ranges from 0.5 to 1 and higher confidence value implies higher probability that the learned indicative pair is correct. If the $confidence$ value is larger than a threshold δ ($\delta = 0.8$ results in the best performance), we consider it as an indicative pair. Then we re-label all of the corresponding test instances which include this indicative pair with its most frequent sentiment.

Hypothesis 3 (One sentiment per User-Target-Issue during a short time). *One user's sentiment toward one target or his/her stance on one issue tends to be consistent during a short period of time.*

The social balance theory (Heider, 1946) aims to analyze the interpersonal network among social agents and see how a social group evolves to a possible balance state. Situngkir and Khanafiah (2004) extended Heider's theory to many agents. Example of possible balance states are given in Figure 2, where "+" means positive relations/sentiments among agents, while "-" means negative relations/sentiments among agents.

When applying social balance theory to our domain of presidential election, we consider the user as one agent and the two presidential candidates (tar-

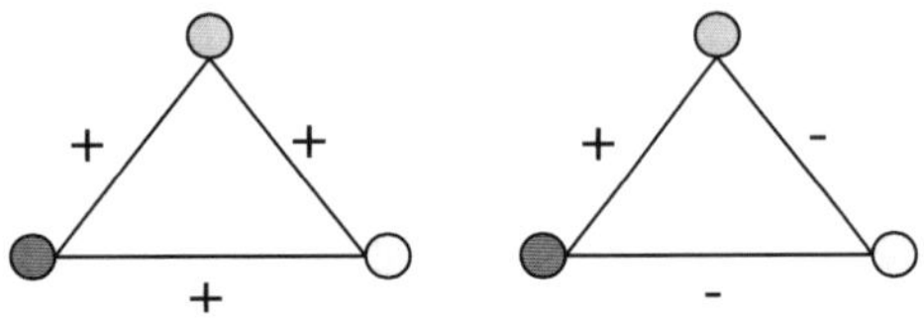

Figure 2: Social Balance Theory: Balanced States among Three People

gets) as the other two agents (see Figure 3). Since the two targets are competing in the election we assume the sentiment between them is negative; therefore, the only balanced state consists of two mutual negative and one mutual positive sentiment. In addition, a user often imposes sentiment upon a target because his or her stance on a particular political issue. The extended theory is presented in Figure 3.

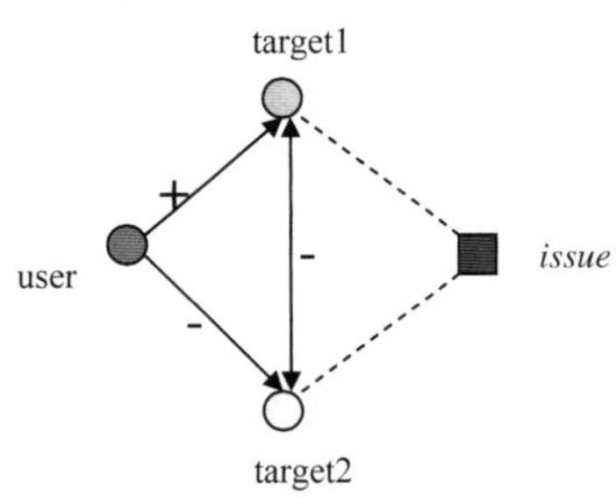

Figure 3: Balanced States for Presidential Election Domain

The Halo Effect or Halo Error theory (Thorndike, 1920) states that there exists a cognitive bias in which once we form a general impression of someone, we tend to assume that additional information will be consistent with that first impression. Abelson (1968) has proposed theories of cognitive consistency, which suggest that people will try to maintain consistency among their beliefs. Based on these social cognitive theories we have formulated Hypothesis 3. This hypothesis is valid for 90% of the training instances. The consistency of a user's sentiment regarding a target's stance on an issue is not a property of a single document, and it depends on the label for each document that mentions the target-issue pair in question. Therefore this property is not appropriately expressed as an SVM feature; instead, we incorporate Hypothesis 3 as follows: we cluster the documents authored by the same user and target (for tweets) or the same user, target, and issue (for forum posts) into one cluster. Then, within each cluster we apply one of three ways of correcting baseline results:

- **Most Confident Sentiment Propagation**: within each cluster, propagate the most confident sentiment through all instances.
- **Majority Voting**: within each cluster, re-label all the instances with the sentiment that appears most often.
- **Weighted Majority Voting**: the same as Majority Voting, but use the confidence values from the baseline system for possible sentiment labels during voting.

Approach	**Accuracy**
(1). Baseline	83.97%
(2). (1) + Propagating the Most Confident Sentiment	84.87%
(3). (1) + Majority Voting	84.87%
(4). (1) + Weighted Majority Voting	**85.35%**

Table 5: Impact of Hypothesis 3 on Tweets

5.2 Experiment Results

In the following we will present the performance of the enhanced approach on tweets and forum posts.

5.2.1 Impact on Tweets

The contexts of tweets are artificially compressed (each tweet message limited to 140 characters), so each single tweet message rarely includes a target-target pair or a pair target-issue pair. Therefore in this section we focus on evaluating the impact of Hypothesis 3 on tweets. The experimental results of applying Hypothesis 3 are presented in Table 5.

The results demonstrate that each voting method can provide consistent gains, with the majority voting method achieving significant gains at 99% confidence level over the baseline (using Wilcoxon Matched-Pairs Signed-Rank test). For example, the following three tweet messages about the target "*Obama*" were sent by the same user:

1. *#Obama rebuilding America using Chinese workers! http://t.co/Pk4HkvtL*
2. *But we had to rush #Obamacare thru? In the pipeline? Obama has it both ways on a controversial plan http://t.co/rb65LIx3*
3. *Small business owners confirm #Obamacare is a job killer: http://t.co/If7yNqVo*

Approach	Accuracy
Baseline	59.61%
+ Hypothesis 1	62.89%
+ Hypothesis 2	62.64%
+ Hypothesis 3	67.24%
+ Hypothesis 1+2	64.21%
+ Hypothesis 1+2+3	**71.97%**

Table 6: Impact of New Hypotheses on Forum Data

The baseline approach misclassified the first message as "Positive", but correctly classified the other two as "Negative" with high confidence. Therefore the voting approach successfully fixed the sentiment of the first message to "Negative".

5.2.2 Impact on Forum Posts

We conducted a systematic evaluation on the enhanced approach by gradually adding each hypothesis to improve sentiment analysis of the forum posts. As we have shown in Section 4, the baseline results for forum data are worse than for tweets. Applying the majority voting methods based on Hypothesis 3 to forum data would lead to compounding errors. Therefore, we only use the "most confident sentiment propagation" to incorporate Hypothesis 3. Table 6 presents the experimental results and shows that each hypothesis provides significant gain over the baseline. The overall new approach achieves up to 12.3% improvement in accuracy.

For the following post: "*If I threw you in a room with 400 corrupt politicians who each had mandates to expand government spending, I guarantee you that you could shout all you wanted for 20 years about cutting the deficit and they wouldn't hear you. Does that make Paul wrong? Does it make him a failure?*", the baseline system mistakenly labeled the sentiment for the target "*Ron Paul*" as "negative" because of the context words such as "shout", "wouldn't", "wrong" and "failure". However, based on Hypothesis 1, since in most cases the posts including the target "*Ron Paul*" and the issue "*Economics*" indicate a positive sentiment, we can correct the label successfully.

Similarly, Hypothesis 2 can correct instances when local linguistic features are misleading. For example, in the following post: "*Actually I see Newt as being more of an effective leader than Mitt with this speakership role and all, but Mitt has the business realm sealed tightly in his hip pocket, and jobs and economic progress are what we desperately need now.*", simply incorporating the context entity features from the first sub-sentence, this baseline system mistakenly labeled the sentiment on the target "*Mitt Romney*" as "negative". In addition, due to the lack of discourse features, the baseline system failed to recognize the scope of identification (the second sub-sentence). However more than 80% instances in the training data indicate that the sentiment on "*Mitt Romney*" is positive when he is compared to '*Newt*", therefore we can correct the sentiment of this post to "positive".

Hypothesis 3 can effectively exploit information redundancy and propagate the high-confidence results from posts with relatively simpler linguistic structures to those posts with more complicated structures. For example, it is difficult for the baseline system to determine the sentiment on the target "*Mitt Romney*" from the following post: "*Paul is the complete opposite of Romney. Romney has a political history that can be examined..and debated.. Paul has 22 years of voting No..but nothing else. Romney has 30 years of business experience. Paul was a doctor a long time ago.*" But the same user posted other messages that include simpler structures and therefore the baseline system can detect correct "positive" sentiment with high confidence: "*Romney saved failed business and political models. Paul merely participated.*". As a result, the sentiment analysis results of all the posts within the same cluster (posted by the same user, and including the same target and issue) can be corrected.

5.2.3 Parameter Tuning

Figure 4 shows the overall performance of our approaches when the indicative pairs are learned from training data with different thresholds set for confidence estimation given in 1. Figure 4 shows consistent performance improvement as the threshold is larger than 0.5. We also noticed that when the threshold is low (0.5), the overall approach performs a little worse than the baseline due to the propagation of erroneous results with low confidence values.

6 Remaining Challenges

Although the proposed approach based on social cognitive theories has significantly enhanced the

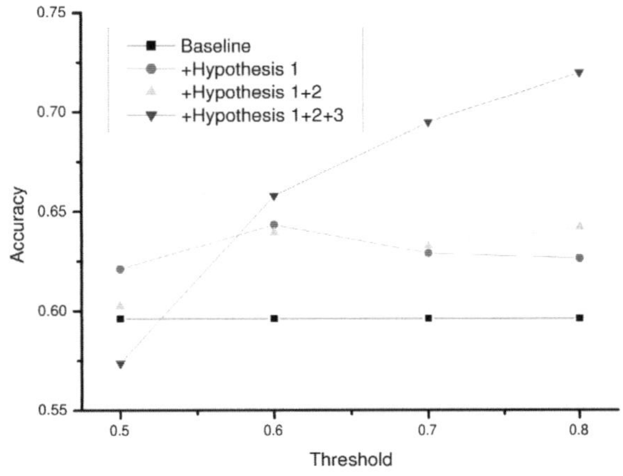

Figure 4: Impact of Parameters

performance of sentiment analysis, some challenges remain. We analyze the major sources of the remaining errors as follows.

Sarcasm Detection. For both tweets and forum posts, some remaining errors require accurate detection of sarcasm (Davidov et al., 2010; Gonzalez-Ibanez et al., 2011). For example, "*LOL..remember Obama chastising business's for going to Vegas. Vegas would have cost a third of what these locations costs. But hey, no big deal...* " contains sarcasm, which leads our system to misclassify this post.

Domain-specific Latent Sentiments. The same word or phrase might indicate completely different sentiments in various domains. For example, "*big*" usually indicates positive sentiment, but it indicates negative sentiment in the following sentence: "*tell me how the big government, big bank backing, war mongering Obama differs from Bush?*". Most of these domain-specific phrases do not exist in the currently available semantic resources and thus a system is required to conduct deep mining of such latent sentiments.

Thread Structure. A typical online forum discussion consists of a root post and the following posts which form a tree structure, or thread. Performing sentiment analysis at post level, without taking into account the thread context might lead to errors. For example, if a post disagree with another post, and the first post expresses "Positive" sentiment, we can infer that the second post should be "Negative". Identifying who replies to whom in a forum might not be straightforward (Wang et al., 2011). In addition, we would need to identify agreement/disagreement relations among posts.

Multiple Sentiments. Due to the prevalence of debate in discussion forums, the users tend to list multiple argument points to support their overall opinions. As a result, a single post often contains a mixture of sentiments. For example, the following post indicates "Positive" sentiment although it includes negative words such as "disagreement": "*....As a huge Ron Paul fan I have my disagreements with him........but even if you disagree with his foreign policy.......the guy is spot on with everything and anything else.....*". This requires a sentiment analyzer to go beyond lexical level analysis and conduct global logic inferences. This is not a challenge in social media genres that impose stringent length restrictions such as Twitter.

Figure 5 summarizes the distributions of the remaining errors for tweets and forum posts.

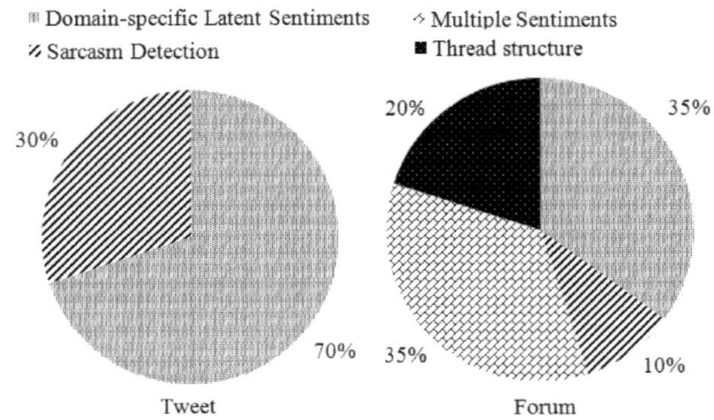

Figure 5: Remaining Challenges

7 Conclusion and Future Work

We have presented a novel approach to social cognitive theories to enhance sentiment analysis for user generated content in social media. We have investigated the limitations of approaches based solely on shallow linguistic features. We have introduced three hypotheses that incorporate global consistency within the rich social structures consisting of users, targets and associated issues, and have shown that using such social evidence improve the results of sentiment analysis on informal genres such as tweets and forum posts.

In the future, we aim to address the remaining challenges discussed in Section 6, especially to exploit the implicit global contexts by analyzing thread structures and discovering cross-post agreement/disagreement relations.

Acknowledgements

This work was supported by the U.S. ARL grant W911NF-09-2-0053, the U.S. NSF Grants IIS-0953149 and IIS-1144111 and the U.S. DARPA BOLT program. The views and conclusions contained in this document are those of the authors and should not be interpreted as representing the official policies, either expressed or implied, of the U.S. Government. The U.S. Government is authorized to reproduce and distribute reprints for Government purposes notwithstanding any copyright notation here on.

References

Robert Adelson. 1968. *Theories of Cognitive Consistency Theory*. Rand McNally.

Apoorv Agarwal, Boyi Xie, Ilia Vovsha, Owen Rambow, and Rebecca Passonneau. 2011. Sentiment analysis of twitter data. In *Proceedings of the 49th Annual Meeting of Association for Computational Linguistics Workshop on Languages in Social Media*.

Stefano Baccianella, Andrea Esuli, and Fabrizio Sebastiani. 2010. Sentiwordnet 3.0: An enhanced lexical resource for sentiment analysis and opinion mining. In *Proceedings of the 6th international conference on Language Resources and Evaluation*.

Adam Bermingham and Alan Smeaton. 2010. Classifying sentiment in microblogs: is brevity an advantage is brevity an advantage? In *Proceedings of the 19th ACM Conference on Information and Knowledge Management*.

Lu Chen, Wenbo Wang, Meenakshi Nagarajan, Shaojun Wang, and Amit P. Sheth. 2012. Extracting diverse sentiment expressions with target-dependent polarity from twitter. In *Proceedings of the 6th International Conference on Weblogs and Social Media*.

Michael Conover, Jacob Ratkiewicz, Matthew Francisco, Bruno Gonalves, Filippo Menczer, and Alessandro Flammini. 2011. Political polarization on twitter. In *Proceedings of the 5th International Conference on Weblogs and Social Media*. The AAAI Press.

Dmitry Davidov, Oren Tsur, and Ari Rappoport. 2010. Semi-supervised recognition of sarcastic sentences in twitter and amazon. In *Proceedings of the 48th Annual Meeting of the Association for Computational Linguistics*.

Christiane Fellbaum. 2005. Wordnet and wordnets. *Encyclopedia of Language and Linguistics*.

Namrata Godbole, Manjunath Srinivasaiah, and Steven Skiena. 2007. Large-scale sentiment analysis for news and blogs. In *Proceedings of the International Conference on Weblogs and Social Media*.

Roberto Gonzalez-Ibanez, Smaranda Muresan, and Nina Wacholder. 2011. Identifying sarcasm in twitter: A closer look. In *Proceedings of the 49th Annual Meeting of Association for Computational Linguistics*.

Pedro Henrique Calais Guerra, Adriano Veloso, Wagner Meira Jr., and Virgilio Almeida. 2011. From bias to opinion: a transfer-learning approach to real-time sentiment analysis. In *Proceedings of the 17th ACM SIGKDD International Conference on Knowledge Discovery and Data Mining*.

David L. Hamilton and Steven J. Sherman. 1996. Perceiving persons and groups. *Psychological Review*.

Bo Han and Timothy Baldwin. 2011. Lexical normalisation of short text messages: Makn sens a #twitter. In *Proceedings of the 49th Annual Meeting of Association for Computational Linguistics*.

Ahmed Hassan, Vahed Qazvinian, and Dragomir R. Radev. 2010. What's with the attitude? identifying sentences with attitude in online discussions. In *Proceedings of the 2010 Conference on Empirical Methods in Natural Language Processing*.

F. Heider. 1946. Attitudes and cognitive organization. *Journal of Psychology*, pages (21):107–112.

Minqing Hu and Bing Liu. 2004. Mining and summarizing customer reviews. In *Proceedings of the 10th ACM SIGKDD International Conference on Knowledge Discovery and Data Mining*.

Heng Ji, David Westbrook, and Ralph Grishman. 2005. Using semantic relations to refine coreference decisions. In *Proceedings of Human Language Technology Conference and Conference on Empirical Methods in Natural Language Processing*.

Long Jiang, Mo Yu, Ming Zhou, Xiaohua Liu, and Tiejun Zhao. 2011. Target-dependent twitter sentiment classification. In *Proceedings of the 49th Annual Meeting of Association for Computational Linguistics*.

Aditya Joshi, Balamurali A. R., Pushpak Bhattacharyya, and Rajat Kumar Mohanty. 2011. C-feel-it: A sentiment analyzer for micro-blogs. In *Proceedings of the 49th Annual Meeting of Association for Computational Linguistics (Demo)*.

E. Kouloumpis, T. Wilson, and J. Moore. 2011. Twitter sentiment analysis: The good the bad and the omg! In *Proceedings of the 5th International Conference on Weblogs and Social Media*.

Qi Li, Haibo Li, Heng Ji, Wen Wang, Jing Zheng, and Fei Huang. 2012. Joint bilingual name tagging for parallel corpora. In *Proceedings of the 21th ACM Conference on Information and Knowledge Management.*

Bing Liu, Minqing Hu, and Junsheng Cheng. 2005. Opinion observer: analyzing and comparing opinions on the web. In *Proceedings of the 14th international conference on World Wide Web.*

Malia F. Mason and C. Neil Marcae. 2004. Catagorizing and individuating others: The neural substrates of person perception. *Journal of Cognitive Neuroscience.*

Satoshi Morinaga, Kenji Yamanishi, Kenji Tateishi, and Toshikazu Fukushima. 2002. Mining product reputations on the web. In *Proceedings of the 8th ACM SIGKDD International Conference on Knowledge Discovery and Data Mining.*

R. Narayanan, B. Liu, and A. Choudhary. 2009. Sentiment analysis of conditional sentences. In *Proceedings of the 2009 Conference on Empirical Methods in Natural Language Processing.*

Alexander Pak and Patrick Paroubek. 2010. Twitter as a corpus for sentiment analysis and opinion mining. In *Proceedings of the 6th international conference on Language Resources and Evaluation.*

Bo Pang and Lillian Lee. 2004. A sentimental education: Sentiment analysis using subjectivity summarization based on minimum cuts. In *Proceedings of the 42th Annual Meeting of Association for Computational Linguistics.*

Bo Pang, Lillian Lee, and Shivakumar Vaithyanathan. 2002. Thumbs up? sentiment classification using machine learning techniques. In *CoRR*, volume cs.CL/0205070.

J.W. Pennebaker, M.E. Francis, and R.J. Booth. 2001. Linguistic inquiry and word count: Liwc2001. In *http://www.liwc.net/.*

Hassan Saif, Yulan He, and Harith Alani. 2012. Alleviating data sparsity for twitter sentiment analysis. In *The 2nd Workshop on Making Sense of Microposts.*

Hokky Situngkir and Deni Khanafiah. 2004. Social balance theory: Revisiting heider's balance theory for many agents. *Technical Report.*

Michael Speriosui, Nikita Sudan, Sid Upadhyay, and Jason Baldridge. 2011. Twitter polarity classification with label propagation over lexical links and the follower graph. In *Proceedings of the 2011 Conference on Empirical Methods in Natural Language Processing.*

Philip J. Stone, Dexter C. Dunphy, Marshall S. Smith, and Daniel M. Ogilvie. 1966. *The General Inquirer: A Computer Approach to Content Analysis.* MIT Press.

Maite Taboada and Jack Grieve. 2004. Analyzing appraisal automatically. In *Proceedings of the AAAI Spring Symposium on Exploring Attitude and Affect in Text: Theories and Applications.*

Chenhao Tan, Lillian Lee, Jie Tang, Long Jiang, Ming Zhou, and Ping Li. 2011. User-level sentiment analysis incorporating social networks. In *Proceedings of the 2011 Conference on Empirical Methods in Natural Language Processing.*

E. L. Thorndike. 1920. A constant error in psychological ratings. *Journal of Applied Psychology*, pages 4(1):25–29.

Ivan Titov and Ryan T. McDonald. 2008. A joint model of text and aspect ratings for sentiment summarization. In *Proceedings of the 46th Annual Meeting of the Association for Computational Linguistics.*

Kristina Toutanova, Dan Klein, Christopher Manning, and Yoram Singer. 2003. Feature-rich part-of-speech tagging with a cyclic dependency network. In *Proceedings of Human Language Technology Conference of the North American Chapter of the Association for Computational Linguistics.*

Andranik Tumasjan, Timm Oliver Sprenger, Philipp G. Sandner, and Isabell M. Welpe. 2010. Predicting elections with twitter: What 140 characters reveal about political sentiment. In *Proceedings of the 4th International Conference on Weblogs and Social Media.*

Zhigang Wang and Warrant Thorngate. 2003. Sentiment and social mitosis: Implications of heider's balance theory. *Journal of Artificial Societies and Social Simulation.*

Hongning Wang, Chi Wang, ChengXiang Zhai, and Jiawei Han. 2011. Learning online discussion structures by conditional random fields. In *Proceedings of the 34th International ACM SIGIR Conference on Research and Development in Information Retrieval.*

Janyce Wiebe, Theresa Wilson, Rebecca Bruce, Matthew Bell, and Melanie Martin. 2004. Learning subjective language. In *Computional Linguistics.*

Ting-Fan Wu, Chih-Jen Lin, and Ruby C. Weng. 2004. Probability estimates for multi-class classification by pairwise coupling. *Journal of Machine Learning Research.*

Hong Yu and Vasileios Hatzivassiloglou. 2003. Towards answering opinion questions: Separating facts from opinions and identifying the polarity of opinion sentences. In *Proceedings of the 2003 Conference on Empirical Methods in Natural Language Processing.*

J. Zhao, K. Liu, and G Wang. 2008. Adding redundant features for crfs-based sentence sentiment classification. In *Proceedings of the 2008 Conference on Empirical Methods in Natural Language Processing.*

Indonesian Dependency Treebank: Annotation and Parsing

Nathan Green[1], Septina Dian Larasati[1,2] and Zdeněk Žabokrtský[1]

[1]Charles University in Prague
Institute of Formal and Applied Linguistics
Faculty of Mathematics and Physics
Prague, Czech Republic

[2]SIA Tilde
Vienibas gatve 75a
LV-1004
Riga, Latvia

{green,larasati,zabokrtsky}@ufal.mff.cuni.cz

Abstract

We introduce and describe ongoing work in our Indonesian dependency treebank. We described characteristics of the source data as well as describe our annotation guidelines for creating the dependency structures. Reported within are the results from the start of the Indonesian dependency treebank.

We also show ensemble dependency parsing and self training approaches applicable to under-resourced languages using our manually annotated dependency structures. We show that for an under-resourced language, the use of tuning data for a meta classifier is more effective than using it as additional training data for individual parsers. This meta-classifier creates an ensemble dependency parser and increases the dependency accuracy by 4.92% on average and 1.99% over the best individual models on average. As the data sizes grow for the the under-resourced language a meta classifier can easily adapt. To the best of our knowledge this is the first full implementation of a dependency parser for Indonesian. Using self-training in combination with our Ensemble SVM Parser we show aditional improvement. Using this parsing model we plan on expanding the size of the corpus by using a semi-supervised approach by applying the parser and correcting the errors, reducing the amount of annotation time needed.

1 Introduction

Treebanks have been a major source for the advancement of many tools in the NLP pipeline from sentence alignment to dependency parsers to an end product, which is often machine translation. While useful for machine learning as well and linguistic analysis, these treebanks typically only exist for a handful of resource-rich languages. Treebanks tend to come in two linguistic forms, dependency based and constituency based each with their own pros and cons. Dependency treebanks have been made popular by treebanks such as the Prague dependency treebank (Hajic, 1998) and constituency treebanks by the Penn treebank (Marcus et al., 1993). While some linguistic phenomena are better represented in one form instead of another, the two forms are generally able to be transformed into one another.

While many of the world's 6,000+ languages could be considered under-resourced due to a limited number of native speakers and low overall population in their countries, Indonesia is the fourth most populous country in the world with over 23 million native and 215 million non-native Bahasa Indonesia speakers. The development of language resources, treebanks in particular, for Bahasa Indonesia will have an immediate effect for Indonesian NLP.

Further development of our Indonesian dependency treebank can affect part of speech taggers, named entity recognizers, and machine translation systems. All of these systems have technical benefits to the 238 million native and non-native Indonesian speakers ranging for spell checkers, improved information retrieval, to improved access to more of the Web due to better page translation.

Some other NLP resources exist for Bahasa Indonesia as described in Section 2. While these are a nice start to language resources for Indonesian, dependency relations can have a positive effect on word reordering, long range dependencies, as well as anaphora resolution. Dependency relations have also been shown to be integral to deep syntactic transfer machine translation systems (Žabokrtský et al., 2008).

2 Related Work

There was research done on developing a rule-base Indonesian constituency parser applying syntactic structure to Indonesian sentences. It uses a rule-based approach by defining the grammar using PC-PATR (Joice, 2002). There was also research that applied the above constituency parser to create a probabilistic parser (Gusmita and Manurung, 2008). To the best of our knowledge no dependency parser has been created and publicly released for Indonesian.

Semi-supervised annotation has been shown to be a useful means to to increase the amount of annotated data in dependency parsing (Koo et al., 2008), however typically for languages which already have plentiful annotated data such as Czech and English. Self-training was also shown to be useful in constituent parsing as means of seeing known tokens in new context (McClosky et al., 2008). Our work differs in the fact that we examine the use of ensemble collaborative models' effect on the self-training loop as well as starting with a very reduced training set of 100 sentences. The use of model agreement features for our SVM classifier is useful in its approach since under-resourced languages will not need any additional analysis tools to create the classifier.

Ensemble learning (Dietterich, 2000) has been used for a variety of machine learning tasks and recently has been applied to dependency parsing in various ways and with different levels of success. (Surdeanu and Manning, 2010; Haffari et al., 2011) showed a successful combination of parse trees through a linear combination of trees with various weighting formulations. Parser combination with dependency trees have been examined in terms of accuracy (Sagae and Lavie, 2006; Sagae and Tsujii, 2007; Zeman and Žabokrtský, 2005). POS tags were used in parser combination in (Hall et al., 2007) for combining a set of Malt Parser models with an SVM classifier with success, however we believe our work is novel in its use an SVM classifier solely on model agreements.

3 Data Description

The treebank that we use in this work is a collection of manually annotated Indonesian dependency trees. It consists of 100 Indonesian sentences with 2705 tokens and a vocabulary size of 1015 unique tokens. The sentences are taken from the IDENTIC corpus (Larasati, 2012). The raw version of the sentences originally were taken from the BPPT articles in economy from the PAN localization (PAN, 2010) project output. The treebank used Parts-Of-Speech tags (POS tags) provided by MorphInd (Larasati et al., 2011). Since the MorphInd output is ambiguous, the tags are also disambiguated and corrected manually, including the unknown POS tag. The distribution of the POS tags can be seen in Table 1.

The annotation is done using the visual tree editor, TreD (Pajas, 2000) and stored in CoNLL format (Buchholz and Marsi, 2006) for compatibility with several dependency parsers and other NLP tools.

4 Annotation Description

Currently the annotation provided in this treebank is the unlabeled relationship between the head and its dependents. We follow a general annotation guidelines as follows:

- The main head node of the sentence is attached to the *ROOT* node.
- Similarly as the main head node, the sentence separator punctuation is also attached to the *ROOT* node.
- The Subordinate Conjunction (with POS tag 'S–') nodes are attached to its subordinating clause head nodes. The subordinating clause head nodes are attached to its main clause head nodes.
- The Coordination Conjunctions (with POS tag 'H–') nodes, that connect between two phrases (using the conjunction or commas), are attached to the first phrase head node. The second phrase head nodes are attached to the conjunction node. It follows this manner when there are more than two phrases.

- The Coordination Conjunctions (with POS tag 'H–') nodes, that connect between two clauses (using the conjunction or commas), are attached to the first clause head node. The second clause head nodes are attached to the conjunction node. It follows this manner when there are more than two clauses.

- The prepositions nodes with the POS tag 'R–' are the head of Prepositional Phrases (PP).

- In Quantitative Numeral Phrases such as "3 thousand", 'thousand' node will be the head and '3' node attached to 'thousand' node.

In general, the trees have the verb of the main clause as the head of the sentence where the Subject and the Object are attached to it. In most cases, the most left noun tokens are the noun phrase head, since most of Indonesian noun phrases are constructed in Head-Modifier construction.

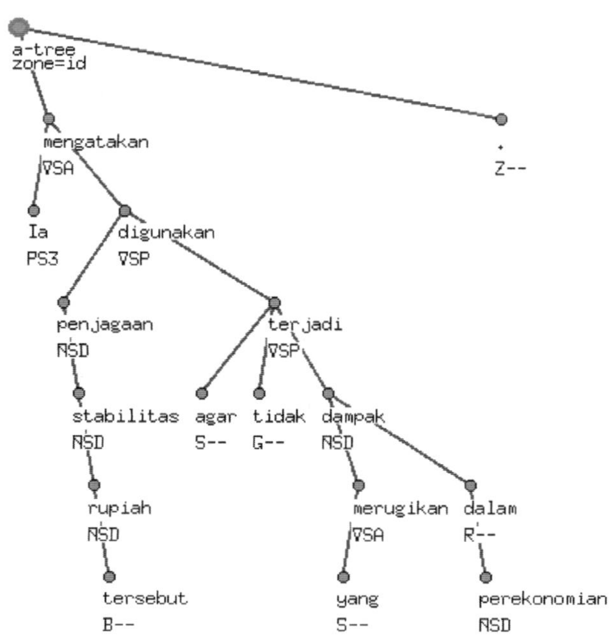

Figure 1: Dependency tree example for the sentence "He said that the rupiah stability protection is used so that there is no bad effect in economy."

POS tag	Description	Freq
NSD	Noun Singular	1037
Z–	Punctuation	278
VSA	Verb Singular Active	248
CC-	Cardinal Number	226
R–	Preposition	205
D–	Adverb	147
ASP	Adjective Singular Positive	127
S–	Subordinating Conjunction	104
VSP	Verb Singular Passiver	91
H–	Coordinating Conjunction	62
F–	Foreign Word	60
B–	Determiner	43
CO-	Ordinal Number	19
G–	Negation	17
PS3	Pronoun Singular 3rdPerson	12
W–	Question	7
O–	Copula	6
PP1	Pronoun Plural 1stPerson	6
ASS	Adjective Singular Superlative	4
PS1	Pronoun Singular 1stPerson	2
APP	Adjective Plural Positive	1
CD-	Colective Number	1
VPA	Verb Plural Active	1
VPP	Verb Plural Passive	1

Table 1: The distribution of the Part-Of-Speech tag occurrence.

5 Ensemble SVM Dependency Parsing

5.1 Methodology

5.1.1 Process Flow

When dealing with small data sizes it is often not enough to show a simple accuracy increase. This increase can be very reliant on the training/tuning/testing data splits as well as the sampling of those sets. For this reason our experiments are conducted over 18 training/tuning/testing data split configurations which enumerates possible configurations for testing sizes of 5%,10%,20% and 30%. For each configuration we randomly sample without replacement the training/tuning/testing data and rerun the experiment 100 times, each time sampling new sets for training,tuning, and testing. These 1800 runs, each on different samples, allow us to better show the overall effect on the accuracy metric as

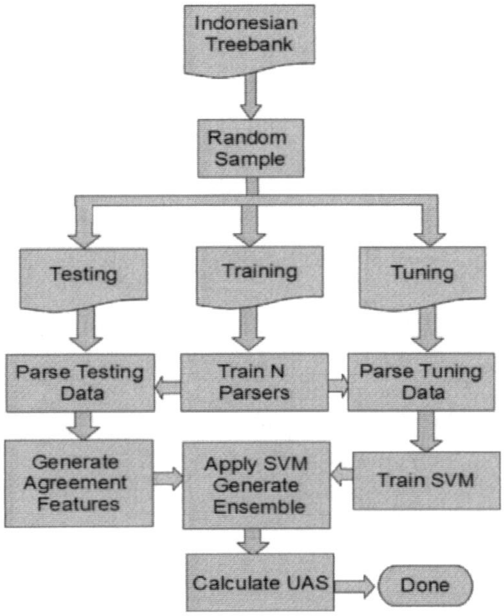

Figure 2: Process Flow for one run of our SVM Ensemble system. This Process in its entirety was run 100 times for each of the 18 data set splits.

well as the statistically significant changes as described in Section 5.1.5. Figure 2 shows this process flow for one run of this experiment.

5.1.2 Parsers

Dependency parsing systems are often optimized for English or other major languages. This optimization, along with morphological complexities, leads other languages toward lower accuracy scores in many cases. The goal here is to show that while the corpus is not the same in size as most CoNLL data, a successful dependency parser can still be trained from the annotated data and provide semi-supervised annotation to help increase the corpus size.

Transition-based parsing creates a dependency structure that is parameterized over the transitions used to create a dependency tree. This is closely related to shift-reduce constituency parsing algorithms. The benefit of transition-based parsing is the use of greedy algorithms which have a linear time complexity. However, due to the greedy algorithms, longer arc parses can cause error propagation across each transition (Kübler et al., 2009). We make use of Malt Parser (Nivre et al., 2007), which in the CoNLL shared tasks was often tied with the best performing systems.

For the experiments in this paper we only use Malt Parser, but we use different training parameters to create various parsing models. For Malt Parser we use a total of 7 model variations as shown in Table 2.

Training Parameter	Model Description
nivreeager	Nivre arc-eager
nivrestandard	Nivre arc-standard
stackproj	Stack projective
stackeager	Stack eager
stacklazy	Stack lazy
planar	Planar eager
2planar	2-Planar eager

Table 2: Table of the Malt Parser Parameters used during training. Each entry represents one of the parsing algorithms used in our experiments. For more information see http://www.maltparser.org/options.html

5.1.3 Ensemble SVM System

We train our SVM classifier using only model agreement features. Using our tuning set, for each correctly predicted dependency edge, we create $\binom{N}{2}$ features where N is the number of parsing models. We do this for each model which predicted the correct edge in the tuning data. So for $N = 3$ the first feature would be a 1 if model 1 and model 2 agreed, feature 2 would be a 1 if model 1 and model 3 agreed, and so on. This feature set is widely applicable to many languages since it does not use any additional linguistic tools.

For each edge in the ensemble graph, we use our classifier to predict which model should be correct, by first creating the model agreement feature set for the current edge of the unknown test data. The SVM predicts which model should be correct and this model then decides to which head the current node is attached. At the end of all the tokens in a sentence, the graph may not be connected and will likely have cycles. Using a Perl implementation of minimum spanning tree, in which each edge has a uniform weight, we obtain a minimum spanning forest, where each component is then connected and cycles are eliminated in order to achieve a well formed dependency structure. Figure 3 gives a graphical

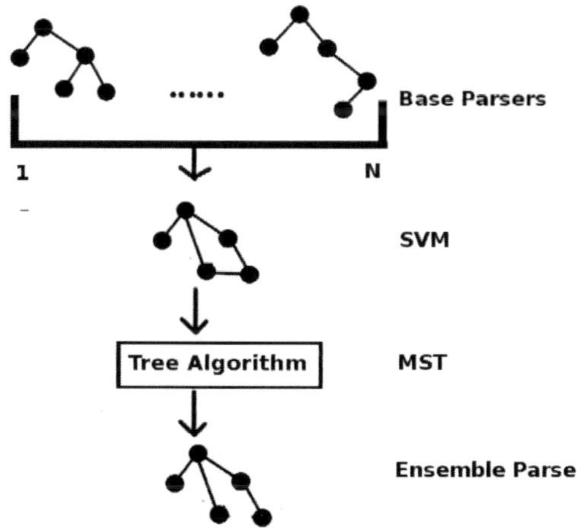

Figure 3: General flow to create an Ensemble parse tree

representation of how the SVM decision and MST algorithm create a final Ensemble parse tree which is similar to the construction used in (Hall et al., 2007; Green and Žabokrtský, 2012). Future iterations of this process could use a multi-label SVM or weighted edges based on the parser's accuracy on tuning data.

5.1.4 Data Set Split Configurations

Since this is a relatively small treebank and in order to confirm that our experiments are not heavily reliant on one particular sample of data we try a variety of data splits. To test the effects of the training, tuning, and testing data we try 18 different data split configurations, each one being sampled 100 times. The data splits in Section 5.2 use the format training-tuning-testing. So 70-20-10 means we used 70% of the Indonesian Treebank for training, 20% for tuning the SVM classifier, and 10% for evaluation.

5.1.5 Evaluation

Made a standard in the CoNLL shared tasks competition, two standard metrics for comparing dependency parsing systems are typically used. *L*abeled *a*ttachment *s*core (LAS) and *u*nlabeled *a*ttachment *s*core (UAS). UAS studies the structure of a dependency tree and assesses how often the output has the correct head and dependency arcs. In addition to the structure score in UAS, LAS also measures the accuracy of the dependency labels on each arc (Buchholz and Marsi, 2006). Since we are mainly concerned with the structure of the ensemble parse, we report only UAS scores in this paper.

To test statistical significance we use Wilcoxon paired signed-rank test. For each data split configuration we have 100 iterations of the experiment. Each model is compared against the same samples so a paired test is appropriate in this case. We report statistical significance values for $p < 0.01$.

5.2 Results and Discussion

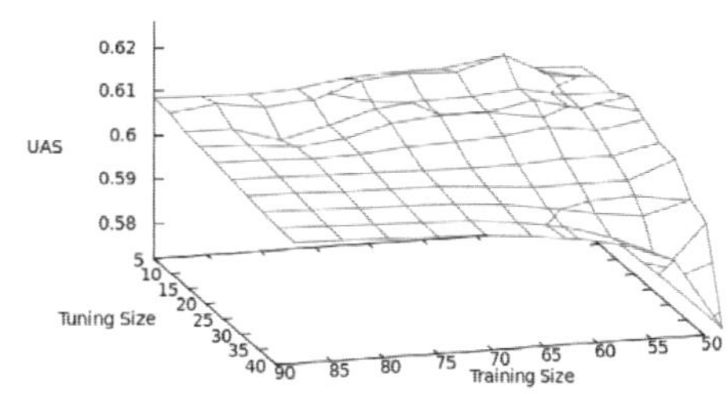

Figure 4: Surface plot of the UAS score for the tuning and training data split.

For each of the data splits, Table 3 shows the percent increase in our SVM system over both the average of the 7 individual models and over the best individual model. As the Table 3 shows, we obtain above average UAS scores in every data split. The increase is statistical significant in all data splits except one, the 90-5-5 split. This seems to be logical since this data split has the least difference in training data between systems, with only 5% tuning data. Our highest average UAS score was with the 70-20-10 split with a UAS of 62.48%. The use of 20% tuning data is of interest since it was significantly better than models with 10%-25% more training data as seen in Figure 4. This additional data spent for tuning appears to be worth the cost.

The selection of the test data seems to have caused a difference in our results. While all our ensemble SVM parsings system have better UAS scores, it is a lower increase when we only use 5% for testing. Which in our treebank means we are only using 5 sentences randomly selected per experiment. This does not seem to be enough to judge the improvement.

Data Split	Average SVM UAS	% Increase over Average	% Increase over Best	Statistical Significant
50-40-10	60.01%	10.65%	4.34%	Y
60-30-10	60.28%	10.35%	4.41%	Y
70-20-10	62.25%	10.10 %	3.70%	Y
80-10-10	60.88%	8.42%	1.94%	Y
50-30-20	61.37%	9.73%	4.58%	Y
60-20-20	62.39%	9.62%	3.55%	Y
70-10-20	62.48%	7.50%	1.90%	Y
50-20-30	61.71%	9.48%	4.22%	Y
60-10-30	62.57%	7.89%	2.47%	Y
90-5-5	60.85%	0.56%	0.56%	N
85-10-5	61.15%	0.56%	0.56%	Y
80-15-5	59.23%	0.54%	0.54%	Y
75-20-5	60.32%	0.54%	0.54%	Y
70-25-5	59.54%	0.54%	0.54%	Y
65-30-5	59.76%	0.54%	0.54%	Y
60-35-5	59.31%	0.53%	0.53%	Y
55-40-5	57.27%	0.50%	0.50%	Y
50-45-5	57.72%	0.51%	0.51%	Y

Table 3: Average increases and decreases in UAS score for different Training-Tuning-Test samples. The average was calculated over all 7 models while the best was selected for each data split. Each experiment was sampled 100 times and Wilcoxon Statistical Significance was calculated for our SVM model's increase/decrease over each individual model. $Y = p < 0.01$ and $N = p \geq 0.01$ for all models in the data split

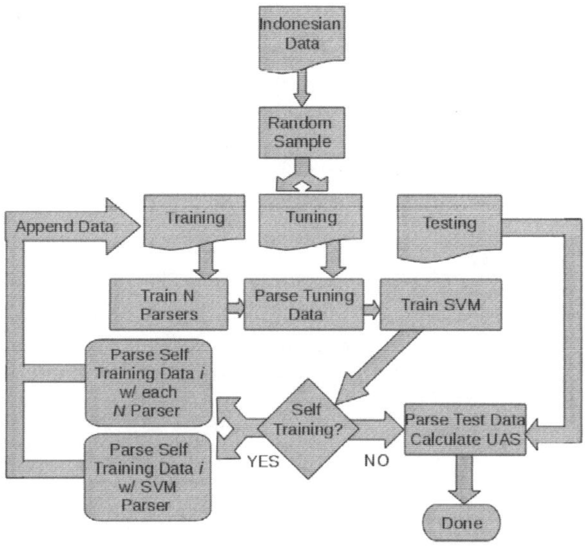

Figure 5: Process Flow for one run of our self-training system. There is one alternative scenario in which the system either does self-training with each N parser or with the ensemble SVM parser. These constitute two different experiments. For all experiments i=10 and N=7

6 Self-training

6.1 Methodology

The following methodology was run 12 independent times. Each time new testing/tuning/and training datasets were randomly selected without replacement. In each iteration the SVM classifier and dependency models were retrained using self-training. Also for each of the 12 experiments, new random self-training datasets were selected from the larger corpus. The results in the next section are averaged amongst these 12 independent runs. Figure 5 shows this process flow for one run of this experiment.

The data for self-training is also taken from IDENTIC and it consists of 45,000 sentences. The data does not have any dependency relation information but it is enriched with POS tags. It is processed with the same morphology tools as the training data described in section 3 but without the manual disambiguation and correction. This data and its annotation information are available on the IDENTIC homepage[1].

For self-training we present two scenarios. First, all parsing models are retrained with their own predicted output. Second, all parsing models are retrained with the output of our SVM ensemble parser. Self-training in both cases is done of 10 iterations of 20 sentences. Sentences are chosen at random from unannotated data. This allows us to examine self-training to a training data size of twice the original set.

The next section examines the differences between these two approaches and the effect on the overall parse.

6.2 Results of Self-training

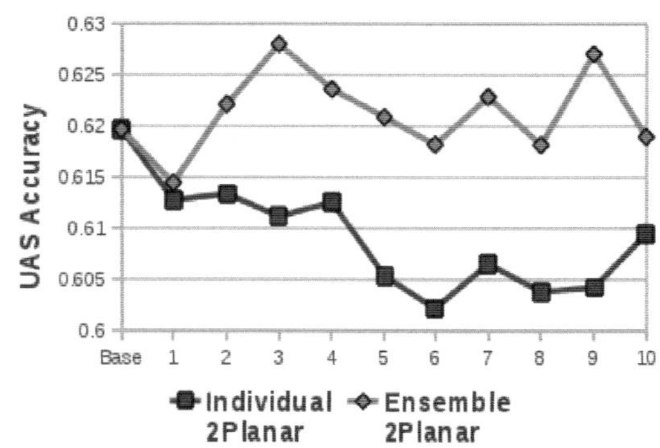

Figure 6: We can see that the self-trained Malt Parser 2Planar model that is trained with the ensemble output consistently outperforms the self-trained model that uses its own output. Results are graphed over the 10 self-training iterations

As can be seen in Figure 6, the base models did better when trained with additional data that was parsed by our SVM ensemble system. The higher UAS accuracy seems to of had a better effect then receiving dependency structures of a similar nature to the current model. We show the 2Planar model in Figure 6 but this was the case for each of the 7 individual models. On an interesting note, the SVM system had least improvement, 0.60%, when the component base models were trained on its own output. This seems warranted as other parser combination papers have shown that ensemble systems prefer models which differ more so that a clearer decision can be made (Hall et al., 2007; Green and Žabokrtský, 2012). The improvements when self-training on our SVM output over the individual parsers' output can be seen in Table 3. Again these are averages over 12 runs of the system, each run containing 10 self-training loops of 20 additional

[1] http://ufal.mff.cuni.cz/ larasati/identic/

sentences.

Model	% Improvement %
2planar	1.10%
nivreeager	0.40%
nivrestandard	1.62%
planar	0.87%
stackeager	2.28%
stacklazy	2.20%
stackproj	1.95%
svm	0.60%

Table 4: The % Improvement of all our parsing models including our ensemble svm algorithm over 12 complete iterations of the experiment.

7 Conclusion

We have shown a successful implementation of self-training for dependency parsing on an under-resourced language. Self-training in order to improve our parsing accuracy can be used to help semi-supervised annotation of additional data. We show this for an initial data set of 100 sentences and an additional self-trained data set of 200 sentences.

We introduce and show a collaborative SVM classifier that creates an ensemble parse tree from the predicted annotations and improves individual accuracy on average of 4.92%. This additional accuracy can release some of the burden on annotators for under-resourced language annotation who would use a dependency parser as a pre-annotation tool. Using these semi-supervised annotation techniques should be applicable to many languages since the SVM classifier is essentially blind to the language and only considers the models' agreement.

The treebank is the first of its kind for the Indonesian language. Additionally all sentences and annotations are being made available publicly online. We have described the beginnings of the Indonesian dependency treebank. Characteristics of the sentences and dependency structure have been described.

8 Acknowledgments

The research leading to these results has received funding from the European Commission's 7th Framework Program under grant agreement n° 238405 (CLARA), by the grant LC536 Centrum Komputační Lingvistiky of the Czech Ministry of Education, and this work uses language resources developed and/or stored and/or distributed by the LINDAT-Clarin project of the Ministry of Education of the Czech Republic (project LM2010013).

References

Sabine Buchholz and Erwin Marsi. 2006. CoNLL-X shared task on multilingual dependency parsing. In *Proceedings of the Tenth Conference on Computational Natural Language Learning*, CoNLL-X '06, pages 149–164, Stroudsburg, PA, USA. Association for Computational Linguistics.

Thomas G. Dietterich. 2000. Ensemble methods in machine learning. In *Proceedings of the First International Workshop on Multiple Classifier Systems*, MCS '00, pages 1–15, London, UK. Springer-Verlag.

Nathan Green and Zdeněk Žabokrtský. 2012. Hybrid Combination of Constituency and Dependency Trees into an Ensemble Dependency Parser. In *Proceedings of the Workshop on Innovative Hybrid Approaches to the Processing of Textual Data*, pages 19–26, Avignon, France, April. Association for Computational Linguistics.

R.H. Gusmita and R. Manurung. 2008. Some initial experiments with indonesian probabilistic parsing. In *Proceedings of the 2nd International MALINDO Workshop*.

Gholamreza Haffari, Marzieh Razavi, and Anoop Sarkar. 2011. An ensemble model that combines syntactic and semantic clustering for discriminative dependency parsing. In *Proceedings of the 49th Annual Meeting of the Association for Computational Linguistics: Human Language Technologies*, pages 710–714, Portland, Oregon, USA, June. Association for Computational Linguistics.

Jan Hajic. 1998. Building a syntactically annotated corpus: The prague dependency treebank. *Issues of valency and meaning*, pages 106–132.

Johan Hall, Jens Nilsson, Joakim Nivre, Gülsen Eryigit, Beáta Megyesi, Mattias Nilsson, and Markus Saers. 2007. Single Malt or Blended? A Study in Multilingual Parser Optimization. In *Proceedings of the CoNLL Shared Task Session of EMNLP-CoNLL 2007*, pages 933–939.

Joice. 2002. Pengembangan lanjut pengurai struktur kalimat bahasa indonesia yang menggunakan constraint-based formalism. undergraduate thesis. Master's thesis, Faculty of Computer Science, University of Indonesia.

Terry Koo, Xavier Carreras, and Michael Collins. 2008. Simple semi-supervised dependency parsing. In *Proceedings of ACL-08: HLT*, pages 595–603, Columbus, Ohio, June. Association for Computational Linguistics.

Sandra Kübler, Ryan McDonald, and Joakim Nivre. 2009. *Dependency parsing*. Synthesis lectures on human language technologies. Morgan & Claypool, US.

Septina Dian Larasati, Vladislav Kuboň, and Dan Zeman. 2011. Indonesian morphology tool (morphind): Towards an indonesian corpus. *Systems and Frameworks for Computational Morphology*, pages 119–129.

Septina Dian Larasati. 2012. Identic corpus:morphologically enriched indonesian-english parallel corpus.

Mitchell P. Marcus, Mary Ann Marcinkiewicz, and Beatrice Santorini. 1993. Building a large annotated corpus of english: the Penn Treebank. *Comput. Linguist.*, 19:313–330, June.

David McClosky, Eugene Charniak, and Mark Johnson. 2008. When is self-training effective for parsing? In *Proceedings of the 22nd International Conference on Computational Linguistics (Coling 2008)*, pages 561–568, Manchester, UK, August. Coling 2008 Organizing Committee.

Joakim Nivre, Johan Hall, Jens Nilsson, Atanas Chanev, Gulsen Eryigit, Sandra Kübler, Svetoslav Marinov, and Erwin Marsi. 2007. MaltParser: A language-independent system for data-driven dependency parsing. *Natural Language Engineering*, 13(2):95–135.

Petr Pajas. 2000. Tree editor tred, prague dependency treebank, charles university, prague. *See URL http://ufal. mff. cuni. cz/~ pajas/tred.*

Localization Project PAN. 2010. Pan localization project.

Kenji Sagae and Alon Lavie. 2006. Parser combination by reparsing. In *Proceedings of the Human Language Technology Conference of the NAACL, Companion Volume: Short Papers*, pages 129–132, New York City, USA, June. Association for Computational Linguistics.

Kenji Sagae and Jun'ichi Tsujii. 2007. Dependency parsing and domain adaptation with LR models and parser ensembles. In *Proceedings of the CoNLL Shared Task Session of EMNLP-CoNLL 2007*, pages 1044–1050, Prague, Czech Republic, June. Association for Computational Linguistics.

Mihai Surdeanu and Christopher D. Manning. 2010. Ensemble models for dependency parsing: cheap and good? In *Human Language Technologies: The 2010 Annual Conference of the North American Chapter of the Association for Computational Linguistics*, HLT '10, pages 649–652, Stroudsburg, PA, USA. Association for Computational Linguistics.

Zdeněk Žabokrtský, Jan Ptáček, and Petr Pajas. 2008. TectoMT: Highly Modular MT System with Tectogrammatics Used as Transfer Layer. In *Proceedings of the 3rd Workshop on Statistical Machine Translation, ACL*, pages 167–170.

Daniel Zeman and Zdeněk Žabokrtský. 2005. Improving parsing accuracy by combining diverse dependency parsers. In *In: Proceedings of the 9th International Workshop on Parsing Technologies.*

Handling Indonesian Clitics: A Dataset Comparison for an Indonesian-English Statistical Machine Translation System

Septina Dian Larasati
Charles University in Prague, Faculty of Mathematics and Physics
Institute of Formal and Applied Linguistics
Prague, Czech Republic
SIA TILDE
Riga, Latvia
larasati@ufal.mff.cuni.cz, septina@tilde.lv

Abstract

In this paper, we study the effect of incorporating morphological information on an Indonesian (id) to English (en) Statistical Machine Translation (SMT) system as part of a preprocessing module. The linguistic phenomenon that is being addressed here is Indonesian cliticized words. The approach is to transform the text by separating the correct clitics from a cliticized word to simplify the word alignment. We also study the effect of applying the preprocessing on different SMT systems trained on different kinds of text, such as spoken language text. The system is built using the state-of-the-art SMT tool, MOSES. The Indonesian morphological information is provided by MorphInd. Overall the preprocessing improves the translation quality, especially for the Indonesian spoken language text, where it gains 1.78 BLEU score points of increase.

1 Introduction

Incorporating linguistic information into statistical Natural Language Processing (NLP) applications usually helps to improve a particular NLP. Simplifying the problem beforehand, for languages with complex language constructions, is one of the approaches that is usually applied, especially when the constructions cannot be represented by a statistical model.

Incorporating morphological information as part of a preprocessing module in the SMT pipeline has been long studied, for instance in rich morphology languages such as Arabic (Habash and Sadat, 2006) or agglutinative languages such as Turkish (Bisazza and Federico, 2009) (Yeniterzi and Oflazer, 2010), and many more. This paper shows an example on how to use Indonesian morphological information on an Indonesian-English SMT system by preprocessing to gain better translation quality.

Indonesian has a complex morphology system, including affixation, reduplication, and cliticization. Here we address the problem of cliticized phrase constructions in Indonesian that occur more frequent in spoken language and social media text than in the formal written text. Having more cliticized phrases in a text makes a spoken dialogue text difficult to translate. Here we also evaluate the effect of the preprocessing on other different types of text.

2 Related Work

Indonesian or *Bahasa Indonesia* ("language of Indonesia"), is the official language of the country. Indonesian is the fourth most spoken language in the world with approximately 230 million speakers including its 30 million native speakers. In spite of that fact, Indonesian is an under-resourced language within the Austronesian language family. There is still a lot of work that is needed to be done to collect language resources or to build language tools for this language. Given the lack of language resources, the research on Indonesian Machine Translation (MT) is not so prolific, although MT is one of the major research topics in NLP.

Related MT research is mostly done for Malay, a mutually intelligible language to Indonesian, which has richer parallel language resources. Although Indonesian and Malay share a similar morphological mechanism, they mostly differ in vocabulary and in having several false friends.

There was a work done by (Nakov and Ng, 2009) for translating a resource-poor language, Indonesian, to English by using Malay, the related resource-rich language, as a pivot. There was another related work on incorporating morphological information for Malay-English SMT (Nakov and Ng, 2011), that focused on the pairwise relationship between morphologically related words for potential paraphrasing candidates. Unlike their previous research that focused on word inflection and concatenation, here they focused on derivational morphology. They used Malay Lemmatizer (Baldwin, 2006) and an in-house re-implementation of Indonesian Stemmer (Adriani et al., 2007) to get the paraphrasing candidates.

3 Indonesian Clitic

"A clitic is a morpheme that has syntactic characteristics of a word, but shows evidence of being phonologically bound to another word."[1]. In this paper, we focus on the Pronoun and Determiner clitics which are mainly bound to Indonesian Verbs and Nouns. Figure 1 shows examples on how these clitics are bounded.

(1)	*kumengirimkanmu*		
	ku+	*mengirimkan*	*+mu*
	I	send	you
	"I send you"		

(2a)	*bukunya*		(2b)	*bukunya*	
	buku	*+nya*		*buku*	*+nya*
	book	his/her		book	the
	"his/her book"			"the book"	

Figure 1: Indonesian cliticized phrase examples. The suffix '*-nya*' is ambiguously translated to English, which can be either a Possessive Pronoun or a Determiner depending on the context (2a and 2b).

A clitic can occur before its main words (proclitic) or after (enclitic). Figure 2 shows some of the patterns on how the clitics (proclitics and enclitics) are usually bounded to Verbs and Nouns as their main word.

[1] http://www.sil.org/linguistics/GlossaryOfLinguisticTerms /WhatIsACliticGrammar.htm

(1)	(I) *ku+*		*+ku* (I)
	(you) *kau+*	[Verbs]	*+mu* (you))
			+nya (him/her/it)
			+-nya (him/her/it)
(2)			*+ku* (my)
		[Nouns]	*+mu* (your)
			+nya (his/her/the/a)
			+-nya (his/her/the/a)

Figure 2: Examples of Indonesian clitic patterns on Verbs (1) and Nouns (2).

Clitics can also be bound to other Parts-of-Speech (PoS) as well, such as Adjectives, in a more complex Verb Phrase or Noun Phrase constructions.

4 Data

We want to observe the different kinds text that gain the most benefit, in terms of translation quality, from applying a preprocessing on Indonesian clitics. In order to do that, first we split the data into several different datasets that contain different kinds of text.

4.1 Data Source

The corpus we use in this work is the IDENTIC (Larasati, 2012) Indonesian-English parallel corpus. We chose this corpus because it consists of various types of text. We categorized the text in two categories by how it was produced, i.e. *en-to-id translated* text and *id-to-en translated* text. This corpus consists of ±45K sentences or ±1M words. In those categories, we also found different types or genres of text that we exploit. Given below are the two text categories, by how they were produced, and the types of text they consist of.

- **en-to-id translated text**: the text that was produced by translating English text to Indonesian and it consists of
  - **(p)** the Indonesian text that was translated from PENN Treebank sentences (Marcus et al., 1993)
  - **(a)** a small portion of comparable Indonesian-English international articles taken from the web
  - **(s)** English movie subtitles in which the texts are mainly in a spoken dialogue style

- **id-to-en translated text**: the text that was produced by translating Indonesian text to English and it consists of articles in Science (**c**), Sport (**o**), International (**t**), and Economy (**e**) genres.

The statistic of the text based on the sources are given in Table 1.

source	#sentences	id#token	en#token
p	17626	404540	424974
a	164	3208	3566
s	3161	24274	28544
c	6355	111065	123205
o	4465	112451	114155
t	6641	167839	177164
e	6532	168611	182795
Total	44944	991988	1054403

Table 1: Text source statistics in terms of number of sentences and number of tokens on Indonesian and English side.

4.2 Dataset

For our dataset comparison, we divide the text into five different datasets (F,H,S,E,I) to be compared in section 6. The division of the text for the datasets is shown in Figure 3.

- **F**: a dataset with proportional mixed texts for training, tuning, and testing data
- **H**: a dataset with proportional mixed texts for training, tuning, and testing data, but with a smaller training data compared to **F**
- **S**: a dataset with proportional mixed texts for training data (excluding the subtitles) and subtitles text as the tuning and the testing data
- **E**: a dataset with *en-to-id translated* text as the training data, and *id-to-en translated* text as the tuning and the testing data
- **I**: a dataset with *id-to-en translated* text as the training data, and *en-to-id translated* text as the tuning and the testing data

For each datasets, the sentences are chosen randomly without replacement, but keeping them in the same proportion as to the original text source. We keep the tuning and the testing data size similar (1K sentences), while the training data varies depending on the rest of the text available. We make the same tuning data for **F** and **H** dataset and for their testing data as well.

distribution		**training**	**tuning**	**testing**
		pas-cote	pas-cote	pas-cote
F		●●●-●●●●	●●●-●●●●	●●●-●●●●
H	*	●●●-●●●●	●●●-●●●●	●●●-●●●●
S		●●○-●●●●	○○●-○○○○	○○●-○○○○
E	*	●●●-○○○○	○○○-●●●●	○○○-●●●●
I	*	○○○-●●●●	●●●-○○○○	●●●-○○○○

● : *included in the dataset*
○ : *excluded from the dataset*

size		**training**	**tuning**	**testing**
F		42944	1000	1000
H	*	20951	1000	1000
S		41783	1000	1000
E	*	20951	1000	1000
I	*	23993	1000	1000

Figure 3: Division of the text for the datasets. Datasets marked with * are dataset with much smaller training data (±21-24K sentences) compare to the full size ones (±41-43K sentences). **p**,**a**,**s** text type are *en-to-id translated* text, while **c**,**o**,**t**,**e** are *id-to-en translated* text.

5 Experiment

For the SMT experiment, we built five *baseline* SMT systems each trained using different datasets (**F**,**H**,**S**,**E**, and **I**) and compare each of them against another system (*unclitic*) trained using its preprocessed dataset version.

5.1 *baseline* system

The *baseline* SMT system is in lowercased-to-lowercased Indonesian-to-English translation direction. We use the state-of-the-art phrase-based SMT system MOSES (Koehn et al., 2007) and GIZA++ tool (Och and Ney, 2003) for the word alignment.

We build our Language Models (LMs) from the seven English monolingual LM data provided by the Seventh Workshop on Statistical Machine Translation (WMT 2012) translation task[2]. Those monolin-

[2]http://www.statmt.org/wmt12/translation-task.html

input	*kumengirimkanmu*			*bukuku*	
	ku+	*mengirimkan*	*+mu*	*buku*	*+ku*
analysis	`aku<p>_PS1+`	`meN+kirim<v>+kan_VSA`	`+kamu_PS2`	`buku<n>_NSD`	`+aku<p>_PS1`
gloss	I	send	you	book	I
english	I send you			my book	
output	*ku*	*mengirimkan*	*mu*	*buku*	*ku*
input	*buku kecilku*			*buku-bukunya*	
	buku	*kecil*	*+ku*	*REDP.buku*	*+nya*
analysis	`buku<n>_NSD`	`kecil<a>_ASP`	`+aku_PS1`	`buku<n>_NPD`	`+dia<p>_PS3`
gloss	book	small	I	books	he/she/the
english	my small book			his/her/the books	
output	*buku*	*kecil*	*ku*	*buku-buku*	*nya*
input	*buku resepku*			*kukirim*	
	buku	*resep*	*+ku*	*ku+*	*kirim*
analysis	`buku<n>_NSD`	`resep<n>_NSP`	`+aku_PS1`	`aku<p>_PS1+`	`kirim<v>_VSA`
gloss	book	recipe	I	I	send
english	my recipe book			I send	
output	*buku*	*resep*	*ku*	*ku*	*kirim*

Figure 4: MorphInd analysis examples for Indonesian phrases that contain cliticized word and the preprocessing output after separating the clitic(s). The Verb Phrase's clitics are the Subject or Object of the Verb, while the enclitic on the Noun Phrase is a Possessive Pronoun of the Noun.

gual data are:

- Europarl Corpus
- News Commentary Corpus
- News Crawl Corpus (2007-2011)

We treat them as seven separate LMs, which correspond to seven LM features in MOSES configuration file. We use SRILM (Stolcke, 2002) to build the LMs. The quality of the translation result is measured using the BLEU score metric (Papineni et al., 2002).

5.2 *unclitic* system

As we have seen in Figure 2, Indonesian clitics have a fairly simple pattern and each is aligned to a different individual word in English. We use a finite state Indonesian morphological analyzer tool, MorphInd (Larasati et al., 2011) to find the correct clitics instead of just using a simple pattern matching with regular expression. This is to make sure that we do not cut the word in a wrong morpheme segmentation.

We preprocess the text by separating the clitics given the Indonesian clitics schema and MorphInd correct clitics detection, to make the alignment model simpler. Figure 4 shows several MorphInd analysis examples. The *input* shows the original words in Indonesian and the *output* shows the new text after we apply the preprocessing.

The preprocessing is applied on the training, the tuning, and the testing data. Then we build another SMT system (*unclitic*) with the same setting as the *baseline* system but using the new preprocessed data.

6 Result and Discussion

For this study, we make three combinations of dataset comparison (F-H, E-I-H, and F-S) to see how is the translation quality differs by using different datasets. Then we also observe the gain or loss caused by the preprocessing on the Indonesian clitics. The translation evaluation as a whole can be seen in Figure 5.

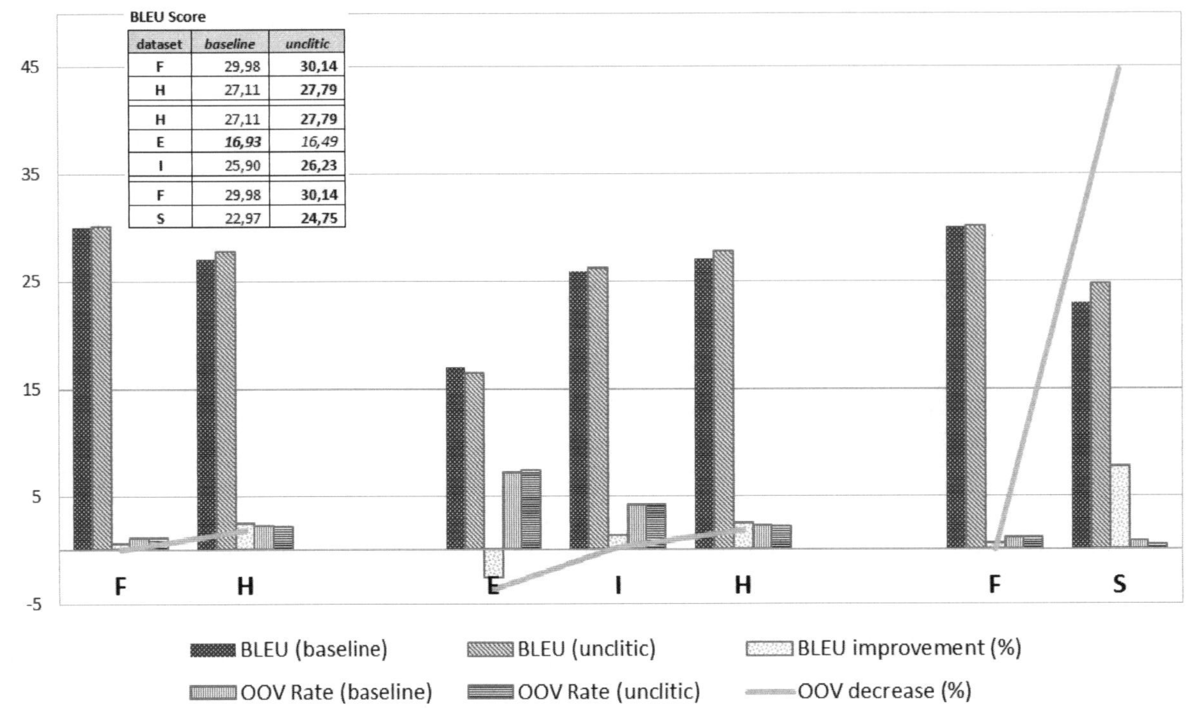

Figure 5: The *baseline* and *unclitic* SMT systems translation quality in terms of BLEU Score and their corresponding OOV Rate (%) on different datasets (F-H-S-E-I).

6.1 Working with Smaller Training Data (F-H)

The Indonesian-English parallel data is relatively small to begin with (±45K sentences or ±1M words). Here we try to push it even further to train an SMT system with only half of the training data that we have and observe the effect of applying the preprocessing on the clitics.

In this experiment, we compare the systems that are trained on **F** and **H** datasets, where the training data is in the same type but differ in size. Considering the small number of the training data that **H** has, having more data at this stage still helps to get a better translation quality. Here we also see that the smaller system gain more improvement by applying the preprocessing.

6.2 Different Text Categories (E-I-H)

Here we compare three different systems trained on three different smaller training data (21K-24K sentences), i.e. **E**,**I**, and **H** datasets. Here we see that the **E** dataset has a very high Out-of-Vocabulary (OOV) rate, which makes a poor translation result, and even the clitic preprocessing cannot help to improve the translation. In spite of that, the system trained on **H** and **I** datasets gain a better translation quality by applying the preprocessing.

6.3 Translating Spoken Indonesian (F-S)

Indonesian speakers tend to use more clitics in Indonesian spoken language, than in a formal written text. Here we put the focus on the spoken language by comparing system trained on **S** dataset (subtitles as the tuning and testing data) and compared it with system trained on **F** dataset (the mixed types text).

The BLEU score for the *baseline* **S** is far below the *baseline* **F**, although their training data sizes only differ slightly (±43K (F) and ±42K (S) sentences). This happens because Indonesian spoken dialogue is more difficult to translate.

In spite of the score difference, here we see that translating the subtitle text gains the most improvement by applying the clitic preprocessing.

7 Conclusion

We showed one linguistically motivated example on how to incorporate morphological information into an NLP application for Indonesian. We used the state-of-the art SMT tool, MOSES, and utilized the information provided from an Indonesian morphological analyzer, MorphInd.

We compared five different SMT systems in three different combinations, where we also applied a preprocessing on the datasets. We saw that the preprocessing overall improves the translation quality, except on the E dataset (with *en-to-id translated* text as the training data) where its OOV rate is too high. The S (subtitle text) dataset benefited the most from the preprocessing.

8 Future Work

There are still other straightforward Indonesian language constructions that can be exploited to improve Indonesian-English SMT system translation quality as part of a preprocessing.

Moving a step further from morphology, incorporating additional syntactical information will be an interesting approach to do. For example, since Indonesian and English have an opposite dependency for the Noun Phrase head-modifier construction, preordering Indonesian words in a Noun Phrase before the translation takes place will be a good approach to improve the translation quality.

Having more Indonesian-English parallel sentences for the training will hopefully improve the translation quality, since currently the parallel data is still very small. This will also increase the interest to do research in this language pair.

Acknowledgments

The research leading to these results has received funding from the European Commission's 7th Framework Program under grant agreement n° 238405 (CLARA), by the grant LC536 Centrum Komputační Lingvistiky of the Czech Ministry of Education, and this work has been using language resources developed and/or stored and/or distributed by the LINDAT-Clarin project of the Ministry of Education of the Czech Republic (project LM2010013).

References

M. Adriani, J. Asian, B. Nazief, SMM Tahaghoghi, and H.E. Williams. 2007. Stemming indonesian: A confix-stripping approach. *ACM Transactions on Asian Language Information Processing (TALIP)*, 6(4):1–33.

T. Baldwin. 2006. Open source corpus analysis tools for malay. In *In Proc. of the 5th International Conference on Language Resources and Evaluation*. Citeseer.

A. Bisazza and M. Federico. 2009. Morphological preprocessing for turkish to english statistical machine translation. In *Proc. of the International Workshop on Spoken Language Translation*, pages 129–135.

BPPT. 2009. Final report on Statistical Machine Translation for Bahasa Indonesia - English and English - Bahasa Indonesia. Technical report, Badan Pengkajian dan Penerapan Teknologi.

Nizar Habash and Fatiha Sadat. 2006. Arabic preprocessing schemes for statistical machine translation. In *Proceedings of the Human Language Technology Conference of the NAACL, Companion Volume: Short Papers*, pages 49–52, New York City, USA, June. Association for Computational Linguistics.

P. Koehn, F.J. Och, and D. Marcu. 2003. Statistical phrase-based translation. In *Proceedings of the 2003 Conference of the North American Chapter of the Association for Computational Linguistics on Human Language Technology-Volume 1*, pages 48–54. Association for Computational Linguistics.

Philipp Koehn, Hieu Hoang, Alexandra Birch, Chris Callison-Burch, Marcello Federico, Nicola Bertoldi, Brooke Cowan, Wade Shen, Christine Moran, Richard Zens, Chris Dyer, Ondrej Bojar, Alexandra Constantin, and Evan Herbst. 2007. Moses: Open source toolkit for statistical machine translation. In *Proceedings of the 45th Annual Meeting of the Association for Computational Linguistics Companion Volume Proceedings of the Demo and Poster Sessions*, pages 177–180, Prague, Czech Republic, June. Association for Computational Linguistics.

Septina Dian Larasati, Vladislav Kuboň, and Dan Zeman. 2011. Indonesian morphology tool (MorphInd): Towards an indonesian corpus. *Systems and Frameworks for Computational Morphology*, pages 119–129, august.

Septina Dian Larasati. 2012. IDENTIC corpus: Morphologically enriched indonesian-english parallel corpus. In *Proceedings of the Eighth conference on International Language Resources and Evaluation (LREC'12)*, Istanbul, Turkey, may. European Language Resources Association (ELRA).

M.P. Marcus, M.A. Marcinkiewicz, and B. Santorini. 1993. Building a large annotated corpus of english: The penn treebank. *Computational linguistics*, 19(2):313–330.

Preslav Nakov and Hwee Tou Ng. 2009. Improved statistical machine translation for resource-poor languages using related resource-rich languages. In *Proceedings of the 2009 Conference on Empirical Methods in Natural Language Processing*, pages 1358–1367, Singapore, August. Association for Computational Linguistics.

P. Nakov and H.T. Ng. 2011. Translating from morphologically complex languages: a paraphrase-based approach. In *Proceedings of the Meeting of the Association for Computational Linguistics (ACL2011), Portland, Oregon, USA*.

F.J. Och and H. Ney. 2003. A systematic comparison of various statistical alignment models. *Computational linguistics*, 29(1):19–51.

K. Papineni, S. Roukos, T. Ward, and W.J. Zhu. 2002. Bleu: a method for automatic evaluation of machine translation. In *Proceedings of the 40th annual meeting on association for computational linguistics*, pages 311–318. Association for Computational Linguistics.

James Neil Sneddon. 1996. *Indonesian Reference Grammar*. Allen & Unwin.

A. Stolcke. 2002. SRILM - an extensible language modeling toolkit. In *Seventh International Conference on Spoken Language Processing*.

Reyyan Yeniterzi and Kemal Oflazer. 2010. Syntax-to-morphology mapping in factored phrase-based statistical machine translation from english to turkish. In *Proceedings of the 48th Annual Meeting of the Association for Computational Linguistics*, pages 454–464, Uppsala, Sweden, July. Association for Computational Linguistics.

Two Types of Nominalization in Japanese as an Outcome of Semantic Tree Growth

Tohru Seraku
St. Catherine's College, University of Oxford
Manor Road, Oxford, UK.
OX1 3UJ
tohru.seraku@stcatz.ox.ac.uk

Abstract

The particle *no* in Japanese exhibits two types of nominalization: "participant" and "situation" nominalization. Despite several motivations for a uniform account, only a few attempts have been made to address *no*-nominalization uniformly. In this paper, I shall develop a unified account within the formalism Dynamic Syntax, and show that a number of properties of the phenomenon follow from the analysis.

1 Introduction

The particle *no* in Japanese displays two types of nominalization: "participant" nominalization (1) and "situation" nominalization (2).

(1) [*Akai* *no*]-*o* *Tom-ga* *nagu-tta.*
[red NO]-ACC Tom-NOM hit-PAST
'Tom hit a/the red one.'

(2) [*Mary-ga* *kireina* *no*]-*o* *Tom-ga* *shi-tteiru.*
[Mary-NOM beautiful NO]-ACC Tom-NOM know-PRES
'Tom knows that Mary is beautiful.'

In participant nominalization, the particle *no* turns a preceding clause into a nominal that denotes an object or a person. In situation nominalization, the particle *no* turns a preceding clause into a nominal that denotes an event or a proposition. A case of ambiguity is presented in (3).

(3) [*Nai-ta* *no*]-*o* *Tom-ga* *mi-ta.*
[cry-PAST NO]-ACC Tom-NOM see-PAST
a. 'Tom saw someone who cried.'
b. 'Tom saw the event of someone's having cried.'

Participant nominalization is exemplified by (3a), and situation nominalization by (3b).[1]

One issue that immediately arises is whether *no* in (1, 2, 3) should be treated uniformly. In other words, does *no* in (1, 2, 3) form a single item or are there two *no*s one of which appears in (1, 3a) and the other of which appears in (2, 3b)? Seraku (in press) defends a uniform analysis based on several motivations (e.g. methodological, cross-linguistic, functional, diachronic). Despite these motivations, a unified analysis of *no* has been largely untouched (e.g. Kitagawa, 2005; Kitagawa and Ross, 1982; Murasugi, 1991; Shibatani, 2009; Tonoike, 1990).

Against this background, the aim of the present paper is twofold as follows. First, I shall articulate a unified analysis of *no*-nominalization within the grammar formalism Dynamic Syntax (Cann et al., 2005; Kempson et al., 2001). Second, I shall show

[1] Seraku (in press) summarizes diachronic data that give credence to the exclusion of such data as (i) from the analysis to be developed in this paper.

(i) *Tom-no*
Tom-NO
'Tom's'

that the analysis captures a range of characteristics of the phenomenon.

2 Dynamic Syntax

Dynamic Syntax (DS) is a formalism that models "knowledge of language", which is conceived as a set of constraints on language use (Cann et al., 2005; Kempson et al, 2001). Language use consists of production and comprehension. DS is shown to model production (Cann et al., 2007; Purver et al., 2006), but this paper focuses on comprehension. DS is then said to provide a set of constraints on how a parser builds up an interpretation gradually as it processes a string word-by-word online.

DS models gradual growth of an interpretation as successive updating of a semantic tree. A string of words is directly mapped onto a semantic tree; in this view, a separate level of syntactic structures is not postulated. The initial state of semantic tree growth is specified by the AXIOM, which sets out an initial node to be subsequently developed.

(4) AXIOM

?t, ◇

?t is a requirement that this node be of type-t. That is, DS tree growth is goal-driven, the goal being to construct a type-t formula. This requirement must be satisfied before tree transitions come to an end. The pointer ◇ indicates a node under development. Once the initial node in (4) is set out, it is gradually updated by a combination of general, lexical, and pragmatic actions.

For illustration, consider the string (5).

(5) *Gakusee-ga* *nai-ta.*
student-NOM cry-PAST
'A/the student cried.'

The initial state (4) is updated into (6) by the parse of *gakusee-ga* (= 'student-NOM'). First, the general action LOCAL *ADJUNCTION introduces an unfixed node, and the lexical actions encoded in *gakusee* decorate the node with semantic content and type. This unfixed node is fixed as a subject node by the lexical actions of the nominative case particle *ga*. ("Unfixed nodes" is a central DS mechanism, but it is not directly relevant to the present paper.)

(6) Parsing *Gakusee-ga*

?t

(ε , x, *gakusee*'(x)) : e, ◇

The content of *gakusee* is (ε , x, *gakusee*'(x)), a type-e term expressed in the Epsilon Calculus.

In the Epsilon Calculus, every quantified noun is mapped onto a type-e term defined as a triple: an operator, a variable, and a restrictor. Syntactically, these type-e terms correspond to arbitrary names in natural-deduction proofs in predicate logic. So, the quantified noun *gakusee* (= 'a student')[2] is mapped onto the epsilon term (7), a type-e term consisting of the existential operator ε , the variable x, and the restrictor *gakusee*'(x).

(7) (ε , x, *gakusee*'(x))

If the term (7) is combined with the predicate *gakusee*', as in (8), the equivalence relation holds for (8) and the predicate-logic formula (9).

(8) *gakusee*'(ε , x, *gakusee*'(x))

(9) $\exists$x.*gakusee*'(x)

Semantically, the term (7) stands for an arbitrary witness of the predicate logic formula (9).

The next item to be parsed is *nai* (= 'cry'). As Japanese is fully pro-drop (i.e. arguments do not have to be explicitly uttered), a predicate builds up a template for a propositional structure. In the case of *nai*, it builds up an open propositional structure, where a subject node is decorated with a place-holding variable. Moreover, à la Davidson (1967), it is claimed that all predicates take a type-e event term as an argument (Gregoromichelaki, 2011). So, the predicate *nai* constructs an open propositional structure with the argument slots for a subject term and an event term, as in (10). The subject node is decorated with the place-holding variable V, and the event node with the place-holding variable U. In order to distinguish event terms from non-event terms, the type for event terms is notated as e_S, where "s" stands for a "situation".

[2] Japanese lacks determiners, and the quantificational force of a bare noun is contextually inferred (cf. §4.2).

(10)

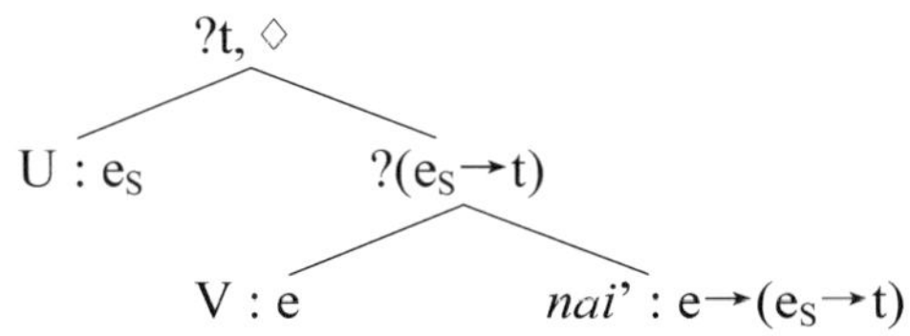

Notice that a subject node has already been created in (6). Thus, the subject node in (6) and that in (10) collapse. The content at the subject node in (10) is the place-holding variable V, and it is weaker than the content at the subject node in (6). Therefore, the collapse of the two subject nodes is harmless. At this stage, the tree (6) is updated into (11).

(11) Parsing *Gakusee-ga nai*

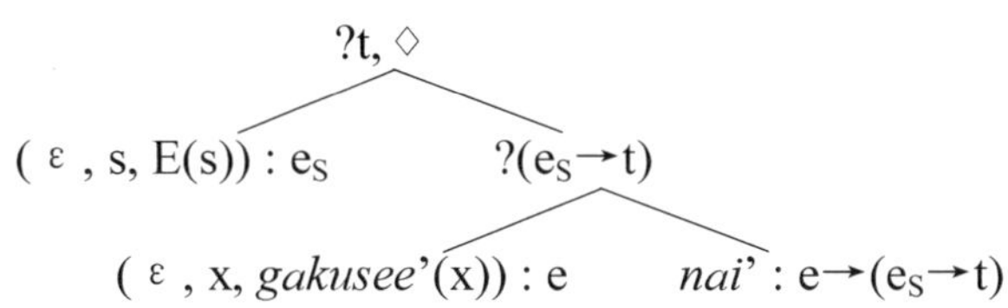

U is now replaced with the event term (ε , s, E(s)), where E is an event predicate. For discussion of event predicates, see Cann (2011).

As two daughter nodes are specified for content and type, functional application and type-deduction may occur. These processes are formalized as the general action ELIMINATION. Thus, the tree (11) is updated into (12) after ELIMINATION is run twice.

(12) ELIMINATION

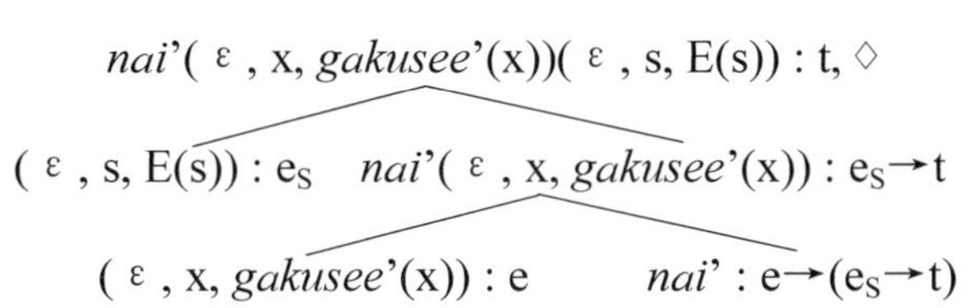

Notice that the requirement ?t has been deleted at the root node in (12) since the type-t formula has appeared at this node.

Finally, the parse of the past tense suffix *ta* adds tense information to the tree. Tense is represented as a restrictor within an event term (Cann, 2011), but this issue is disregarded in this paper. Thus, for the sake of simplicity, I take it that (12) is the final state of the tree transitions for the string (5).

The proposition in (12) contains two terms, and their scope relation needs to be explicated.[3] In a fully articulated tree, a top node of a propositional structure is decorated with a "scope statement", which is incrementally constructed as a string is parsed. The detail is not pertinent; what is at stake is that once tree transitions come to a final state, a proposition at the root node and a complete scope statement are subject to QUANTIFIER EVALUATION (Q-EVALUATION). Through this process, each term in the proposition is enriched so as to explicate the scope dependencies in the whole proposition. For illustration, consider the schematic formula (13).

(13) $\phi(\varepsilon, x, \psi(x))$

Firstly, the predicates ϕ and ψ, with the term "a" whose content is worked out below, are connected. The type of a connective is determined by the type of an operator; for the existential operator ε , the connective & is employed.

(14) $\phi(a) \& \psi(a)$

Secondly, "a" is constructed so that it reflects the predicates in the whole proposition.

(15) $\phi(a) \& \psi(a)$

$a = (\varepsilon, x, \phi(x) \& \psi(x))$

Now, let us return to the proposition in (12), which is repeated here as (16).

(16) *nai*'(ε , x, *gakusee*'(x))(ε , s, E(s))

Suppose that the scope statement declares that the event term out-scopes the non-event term. In this case, a parser first evaluates the non-event term.

(17) Evaluating the non-event term

gakusee'(a)&*nai*'(a)(ε , s, E(s))

a = (ε , x, *gakusee*'(x)&*nai*'(x)(ε , s, E(s)))

[3] In (12), different scope relations do not affect the truth-conditional content, because only existential quantifications are involved. But the issue is not trivial when different types of quantifications are involved.

Next, the event term in (17) is evaluated.

(18) Evaluating the event term

$$E(b)\&[\textit{gakusee}'(a_b)\&\textit{nai}'(a_b)(b)]$$

$b = (\varepsilon, s, E(s)\&[\textit{gakusee}'(a_s)\&\textit{nai}'(a_s)(s)])$
$a_b = (\varepsilon, x, \textit{gakusee}'(x)\&\textit{nai}'(x)(b))$
$a_s = (\varepsilon, x, \textit{gakusee}'(x)\&\textit{nai}'(x)(s))$

The technical detail is not germane; what should be noted is that the event term "b" and the non-event term "a_b" explicate the scope dependencies in the whole formula. ("a_s" is not a full-blown term since the variable "s" is not bound in the term; "a_s" is just part of "b".) The formula (18) represents the indefinite reading of (5): 'A student cried.'

To sum up, DS models the incremental nature of language use; a parser progressively constructs an interpretation in context on the basis of word-by-word parsing. This exegesis has not mentioned the mechanism of LINK, a core machinery of DS. This is illustrated in the next section since it is essential for the analysis of the particle *no*.

3 A Uniform Analysis

3.1 Proposal

A novel feature of DS tree transitions is a pair of structures that are connected by a LINK relation. A LINKed structure is an adjunct structure to a main structure, and their relation is guaranteed by the presence of a shared element.

Cann et al. (2005: p.285) analyze the particle *no* as a LINK-inducing device.

(19) <u>Lexical entry of *no*</u>

IF	t	
THEN	IF	Φ[a]
	THEN	make(L^{-1}); go(L^{-1}); put(a : e)
	ELSE	abort
ELSE	abort	

In general, every lexical item encodes a constraint on tree growth. The IF-line specifies a condition; if the condition is met, a parser looks at the THEN-line; otherwise the ELSE-line. In (19), "abort" is an action that quits tree transitions, in which case a string is said to be ungrammatical. "make(L)" is an action that introduces a LINK relation, "go(L)" is an action that moves the pointer ◇ to a LINKed node, and "put(a : e)" is an action that decorates a node with "a : e". In plain English, the entry of *no* amounts to the constraint (20); the corresponding tree-update is shown in (21).

(20) If a current node is decorated with a type-t proposition, a parser copies a type-e term in the evaluated proposition and pastes it at a type-e node across a LINK relation.

(21)

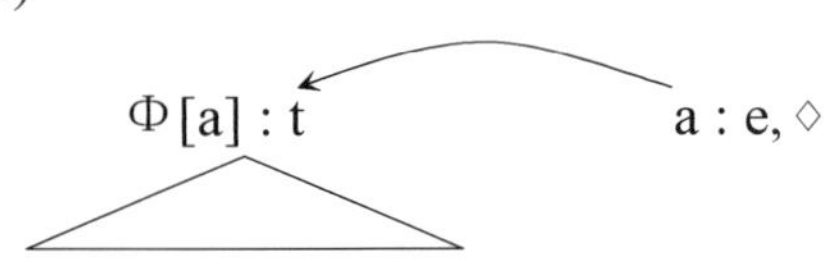

In (21), a parser copies the type-e term "a" in the evaluated version of the proposition Φ and pastes it at a type-e node across a LINK relation. The LINK relation is shown by the curved arrow.

Given the entry of *no* in (19), my proposals are formulated as (22).

(22) The two types of *no*-nominalization can be reduced to a parser's choice of what type-e term it copies in processing *no*.

a. Copying of a non-event term gives rise to participant nominalization.

b. Copying of an event term gives rise to situation nominalization.

3.2 Participant Nominalization

Let us start with the participant nominalization (1), reproduced here as (23).

(23) [*Akai* *no*]-*o* *Tom-ga* *nagu-tta.*
[red NO]-ACC Tom-NOM hit-PAST
'Tom hit a/the red one.'

The initial state is determined by the AXIOM:

(24) AXIOM

?t, ◇

The predicate *akai* (= 'red') in (23) constructs a propositional template with subject and event slots.

The event node is decorated with (ε , s, E(s)), and the subject node is decorated with (ε , x, P(x)), where P is an abstract restrictor (Kempson and Kurosawa, 2009: p.65). Then, the general action ELIMINATION is conducted twice, and the tree (24) is updated into (25).

(25) Parsing *Akai*

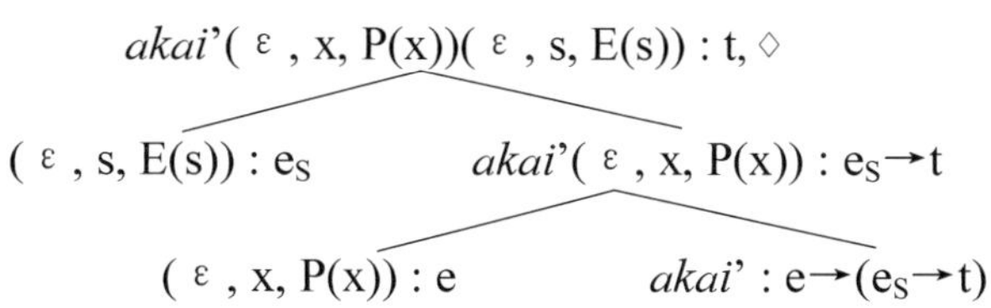

Once a proposition emerges, it is subject to Q-EVALUATION. As the proposition in (25), repeated here as (26), involves two terms, Q-EVALUATION is conducted twice.

(26) *akai*'(ε , x, P(x))(ε , s, E(s))

Let us suppose that the scope statement declares that the non-event term out-scopes the event term; in this case, the event term is evaluated first.

(27) Evaluating the event term (ε , s, E(s))

E(a)&*akai*'(ε , x, P(x))(a)

a = (ε , s, E(s)&*akai*'(ε , x, P(x))(s))

The formula (27) still contains a type-e term. This term is evaluated as follows:

(28) Evaluating the non-event term (ε , x, P(x))

P(b)&[E(a_b)&*akai*'(b)(a_b)]

b = (ε , x, P(x)&[E(a_x)&*akai*'(x)(a_x)])
a_b = (ε , s, E(s)&*akai*'(b)(s))
a_x = (ε , s, E(s)&*akai*'(x)(s))

The formula (28) is the final representation for the interpretation of the pre-*no* clause *akai*.

Now, it is time to parse *no*; a parser copies a type-e term and pastes it at a type-e node across a LINK relation. In (29), what is copied is the non-event term "b" in the evaluated proposition.[4]

(29) Parsing *Akai no*

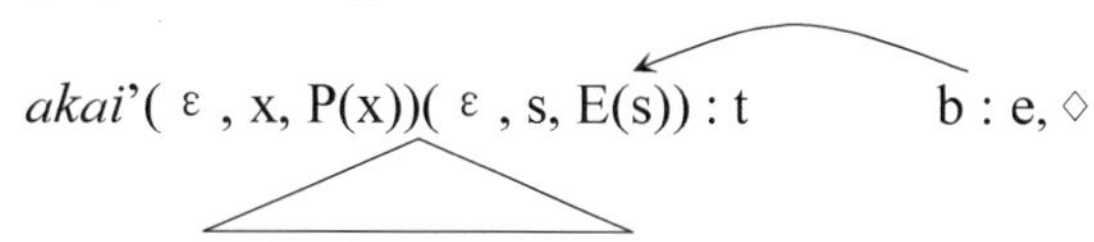

b = (ε , x, P(x)&[E(a_x)&*akai*'(x)(a_x)])
a_x = (ε , s, E(s)&*akai*'(x)(s))

The node decorated with "b" becomes an object node by the lexical actions of the accusative case particle *o*. Then, the matrix predicate *nagu* (= 'hit') constructs a propositional template; in (30), the event node is decorated with (ε , t, F(t)), the subject node is decorated with *Tom*', and the object node is decorated with "b". (As for the object node, the node decorated with "b" in (29) collapses with the object node introduced by *nagu*.)

(30) Parsing [*Akai no*]-*o Tom-ga nagu*

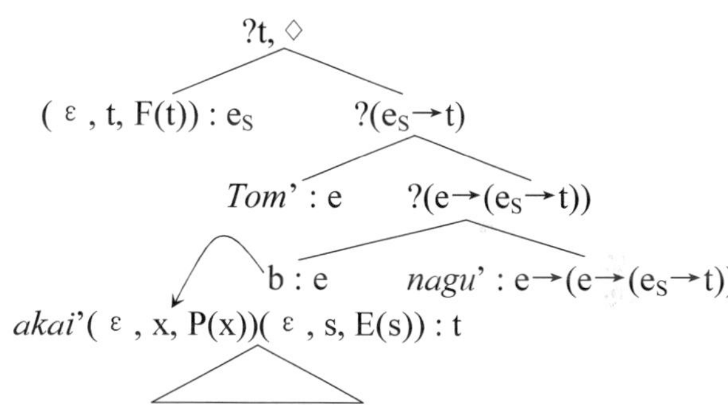

b = (ε , x, P(x)&[E(a_x)&*akai*'(x)(a_x)])
a_x = (ε , s, E(s)&*akai*'(x)(s))

Finally, the general action ELIMINATION is run three times. The past tense marker *tta* being set aside, the tree (31) is the final state, and the top node represents the indefinite reading of the string (23): 'Tom hit a red one.' (For the definite reading of (23), see Section 4.2.)

[4] A parser could copy the event term "a_b" but it leads to tree transition crash, since the matrix predicate *nagu* (= 'hit') cannot take an event term as an argument. As for "a_x", a parser cannot copy it, since it is not a full-blown term in that the variable "x" is not bound within the term; "a_x" is part of the evaluated non-event term "b".

(31) ELIMINATION

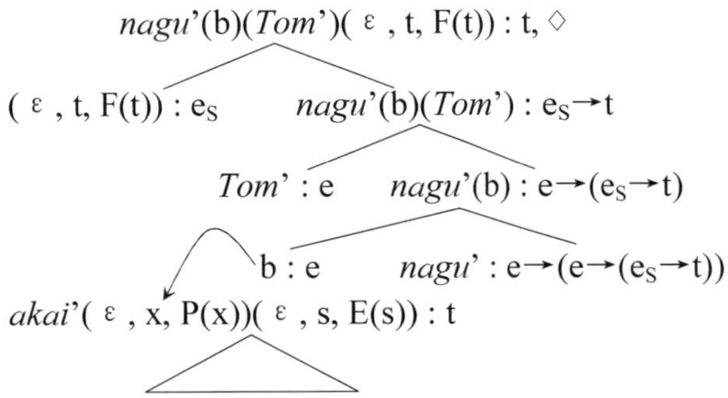

$b = (\varepsilon, x, P(x)\&[E(a_x)\&akai'(x)(a_x)])$
$a_x = (\varepsilon, s, E(s)\&akai'(x)(s))$

3.3 Situation Nominalization

Let us move on to situation nominalization. The example (2) is repeated here as (32).

(32) [*Mary-ga* *kireina* *no*]-*o*
[Mary-NOM beautiful NO]-ACC
Tom-ga *shi-tteiru.*
Tom-NOM know-PRES
'Tom knows that Mary is beautiful.'

As always, the initial state of tree transitions is set out by the AXIOM. Given the tree transitions in the last sub-section, the parse of (32) prior to *no* yields the tree (33).

(33) Parsing *Mary-ga kireina*

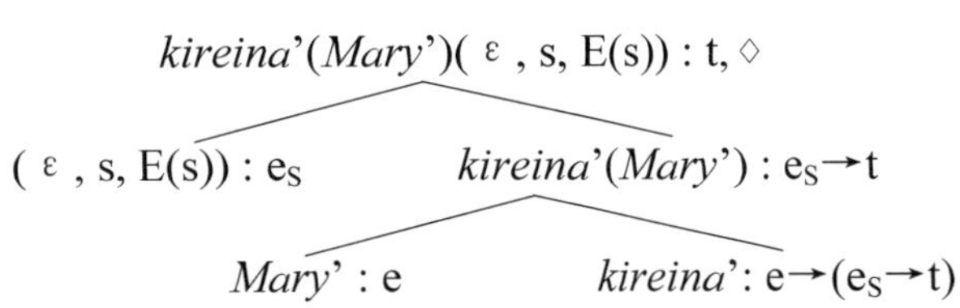

The lexical actions of *kireina* (= 'beautiful') builds up a propositional structure with two slots. The event slot is filled by the event term (ε, s, E(s)), and the subject slot collapses with the node that has been created by the parse of *Mary-ga*.

The top node in the tree (33) is decorated with the proposition, which is re-cited here as (34). This proposition is subject to Q-EVALUATION, and the proposition (35) is engendered.

(34) *kireina*'(*Mary*')(ε, s, E(s))

(35) Evaluating the event term (ε, s, E(s))

E(a)&*kireina*'(*Mary*')(a)

a = (ε, s, E(s)&*kireina*'(*Mary*')(s))

Next, *no* copies the evaluated event term "a" and pastes it at a node across a LINK relation.[5]

(36) Parsing *Mary-ga kireina no*

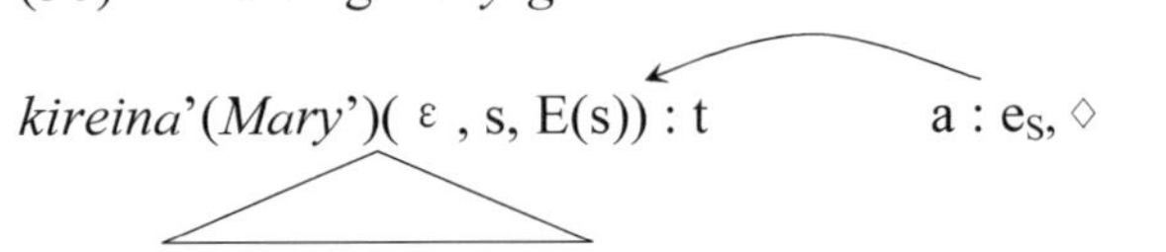

a = (ε, s, E(s)&*kireina*'(*Mary*')(s))

The current node in (36) is fixed as an object node by the accusative case particle *o*, and the parse of *Tom-ga* creates a subject node. These two nodes collapse with the nodes introduced by the predicate *shi* (= 'know'). After ELIMINATION is run three times, the tree (36) is updated into (37).

(37) Parsing [*Mary-ga kireina no*]-*o Tom-ga shi-tteitu*

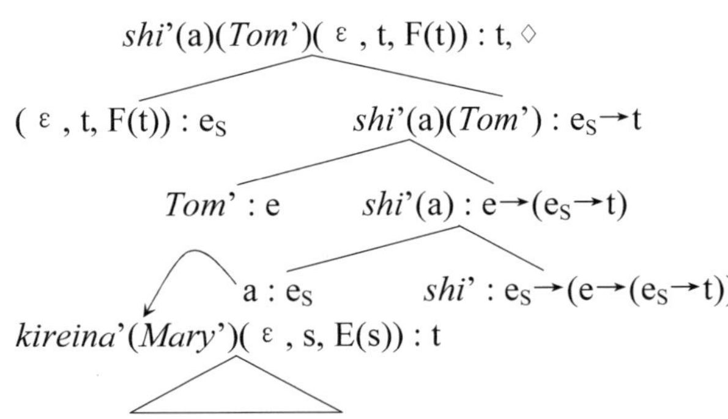

a = (ε, s, E(s)&*kireina*'(*Mary*')(s))

This is a final state of the tree transitions, and the root node represents the interpretation of the string (32): 'Tom knows that Mary is beautiful.'

---

[5] A parser could copy another type-e term: the evaluated term for *Mary*. (For this purpose, *Mary* is mapped onto an iota term.) In fact, copying of this term leads to Cann et al.'s (2005) analysis of head-internal relatives. However, the string in question cannot be so interpreted due to the Relevancy Condition (Kuroda, 1992: p.147).

4 Consequences

4.1 *No* as a Dependent Item

Makino (1968: p.51) observes that *no* cannot stand on its own. Compare (38) with (1)/(23).

(38)	**No-o*	*Tom-ga*	*nagu-tta.*
	NO-ACC	Tom-NOM	hit-PAST

Makino considers only participant nominalization, but it is also true of situation nominalization. (39) should be compared with (2)/(32).

(39)	**No-o*	*Tom-ga*	*shi-tteiru.*
	NO-ACC	Tom-NOM	know-PRES

These data are amenable to my analysis. The entry of *no* requires that a proposition should have been constructed before the parse of *no*. Formally, this requirement is expressed in the two IF-clauses in the entry of *no* in (19). In (38, 39), however, no items precede *no* in the strings, and a parser cannot build up a proposition before processing *no*.

4.2 Indeterminacy of Denotation

Denotation of the *no*-headed part is indeterminate in two respects. Firstly, as shown in (1), repeated here as (40), it is indeterminate with regard to the definiteness of the denotation.

(40)	[*Akai*	*no*]*-o*	*Tom-ga*	*nagu-tta.*
	[red	NO]-ACC	Tom-NOM	hit-PAST

'Tom hit a/the red one.'

In Section 3.2, it was argued that the parse of *Akai no* yields the epsilon term (41).

(41) $(\epsilon, x, P(x)\&akai'(x))$

Since DS is not encapsulated in Fodor's (1983) sense, pragmatics comes in during DS tree growth. For the model of pragmatics, I assume Relevance Theory (Sperber and Wilson, 1995). Thus, if it is inferable that the speaker has in mind a definite entity, a parser may strengthen the epsilon operator ϵ in (41) as the iota operator ι, as in (42).

(42) $(\iota, x, P(x)\&akai'(x))$

This models the definite reading of the string (40) à la Russellian treatment of definite descriptions (Russell, 1905).

Secondly, the content of the *no*-headed part is indeterminate. So, when it is pragmatically inferred that a speaker has in mind a specific entity, say, a red person, the term (41) may be enriched as (43), where *hito'* is the content of *hito* (= 'person').

(43) $(\epsilon, x, P(x)\&[akai'(x)\&hito'(x)])$

These two types of indeterminacies are captured in my analysis, since pragmatic inference interacts with DS structure building.

4.3 Expressivity

It is well known that if the *no*-headed part denotes a human in participant nominalization, derogatory expressivity is observed (Kitagawa, 2005: p.1259). Consider (1, 2, 3), repeated here as (44, 45, 46); expressivity is found in participant nominalization (44, 46a), but not in situation nominalization (45, 46b).

(44)	[*Akai*	*no*]*-o*	*Tom-ga*	*nagu-tta.*
	[red	NO]-ACC	Tom-NOM	hit-PAST

'Tom hit a/the red one.'

(45)	[*Mary-ga*	*kireina*	*no*]*-o*
	[Mary-NOM	beautiful	NO]-ACC
	Tom-ga	*shi-tteiru.*	
	Tom-NOM	know-PRES	

'Tom knows that Mary is beautiful.'

(46)	[*Nai-ta*	*no*]*-o*	*Tom-ga*	*mi-ta.*
	[cry-PAST	NO]-ACC	Tom-NOM	see-PAST

a. 'Tom saw someone who cried.'
b. 'Tom saw the event of someone's having cried.

What has not been reported in the literature is that expressivity is not always derogatory. To take (44) as an example, if the denoted person's face turns red after a pint of beer and the speaker hits the person in jest, expressivity may be "affectionate familiarity with the denoted person". Any adequate account of *no* must model this context-dependency of expressivity (Yuji Nishiyama, p.c.).

To account for the above data, I shall posit the constraint that the denotation of the *no*-headed part should be an object (rather than a human), the idea being that if the *no*-headed part denotes a human, expressivity emerges through pragmatic inference.[6]

First, in (44), given the predicate *nagu* (= 'hit'), a parser expects that *akai no* denotes a human, and constructs, say, the term (47), which denotes a red person (cf. §4.2).

(47) (ε , x, P(x)&[*akai*'(x)&*hito*'(x)])

That the term (47) denotes a human indicates that the speaker treats a denoted person as if s/he were a thing, which has a pragmatic implication that the speaker does not treat the person respectfully. This pragmatic inference yields derogatory expressivity.

This pragmatic analysis naturally accounts for the context-dependence of expressivity. Consider the context where the speaker is a good friend of the denoted person. In this context, that the term (47) denotes a human indicates that the speaker frankly describes a person, which has a pragmatic implication that the speaker shows a sign of close friendship. In this case, the type of expressivity is affectionate familiarity with the denoted person. This pragmatic analysis is extendable to (46a).

It is predicted that if the *no*-headed part denotes a non-human, expressivity should be absent:

(48) [*Akai* *no*]-*o* *Tom-ga* *tabe-ta.*
[red NO]-ACC Tom-NOM eat-PAST
'Tom ate a/the red one.'

In (48), due to the predicate *tabe* (= 'eat'), the term copied by *no* denotes a non-human (e.g. apple). So, the pragmatic inference mentioned above is not triggered, and expressivity is not engendered.

Next, how about the absence of expressivity in (45, 46b)? In these cases, *no* copies an event term (cf. §3.3). Since an event is not a human, the pragmatic inference mentioned above does not take place, and expressivity does not emerge.

The present account has some implications for a cross-linguistic study of nominalization. Consider (49), the Korean counterpart of (46).

(49) [*Wu-nun* *kes*]-*ul*
[cry-MOD KES]-ACC
Tom-i *pwa-ss-ta.*
Tom-NOM see-PAST-DECL
a. *'Tom saw someone who cried.'
b. 'Tom saw the event of someone's having cried.

While (49b) is acceptable, (49a) is not[7]. Of note is that, unlike *no*, the nominalizer *kes* derived from the noun *kes* meaning 'thing', and that this lexical meaning somehow persists in the nominalizer *kes* (Horie, 2008: p.178). So, the restriction that the denoted entity be an object is stronger in *kes* than in *no*; this is why the reading (46a) in Japanese is possible but the reading (49a) in Korean is not.

In closing, let me examine some previous works that are relevant to the present discussion. Firstly, McGloin (1985) also suggests, albeit very briefly, a pragmatic analysis of expressivity. However, in her analysis, neither situation nominalization nor the context-dependency of expressivity is treated.

Second, from the perspective of the Principles-and-Parameters Theory, Kitagawa (2005) suggests that expressivity emerges only if the external-head pro has an indefinite referent. However, suppose that (50) is uttered with a pointing gesture; further, the demonstrative *sono* (= 'that') is used in order to ensure that the small pro has a definite referent.

(50) *Sono* [*akai* *no*]-*o*
that [red NO]-ACC
Tom-ga *nagu-tta.*
Tom-NOM hit-PAST
'Tom hit that red one.'

In (50), expressivity is still observed, contrary to what Kitagawa (2005) would predict. My analysis

[6] This constraint may be modeled along the lines with Cann and Wu's (2011) analysis of the *bei* construction in Chinese. They argue that *bei* marks the pre-*bei* item as the locus of affect; *bei* projects a propositional structure where the Locus-of-Affect (LoA) predicate takes as an internal argument the content of the pre-*bei* item, and as an external argument the content of the rest of the string. In their analysis, the LoA predicate is underspecified for the type of affect, and thus it fits well with the context-dependency of *no*-expressivity. I shall assume that the entry of *no* has a constraint that if a term to be copied does not denote an object, it projects a structure involving the LoA predicate. This ramification of the entry of *no* is not attempted in this paper.

[7] The degraded status of (49a) does not mean that *kes* lacks participant nominalization. In fact, if *wu-nun* in (49) is replaced with *kkayeci-nun* (= break-MOD), the string exhibits the participant-nominalization reading: 'Tom saw something (e.g. machine) that was being broken.'

postulates neither a null element nor an external-head position; the presence of expressivity in (50) is expected as a result of pragmatic inference.

4.4 Nature of Denotation

In Kamio (1983) and McGloin (1985), it is stated that *no* in participant nominalization cannot refer to abstract entities. Consider the contrast between (51) and (52) (Kamio, 1983: p.82).

(51) [[*katai shinnen*]-*o* *motta*] *hito*
[[solid belief]-ACC have] person
'a person who has a solid belief'

(52) *[[*katai no*]-*o* *motta*] *hito*
[[solid NO]-ACC have] person
Int. 'a person who has a solid belief'

The string (52) is acceptable if the *no*-headed part is meant to denote some non-abstract entity, such as a stone.

It seems, however, that the above generalization is suspicious. In (52), the use of the predicate *katai* (= 'solid') is metaphorical; it drives the interpreter to look for a physical object to which the predicate *katai* normally applies (e.g. stone). This is why it is hard to get the intended interpretation in (52). If a predicate that is congruous with an abstract object is used, such as *settokutekina* (= 'convincing'), the *no*-headed part may denote an abstract entity:

(53) [*gakkai-de* [*settokutekina no*]-*o*
[conference-at [convincing NO]-ACC
teijishita] *hito*
presented] person
'a person who presented a convincing one (e.g. argument) at a conference'

Given my unitary analysis of *no*, it is expected that if the *no*-headed part may denote an abstract entity in participant nominalization, it should also hold of situation nominalization. This expectation is confirmed. First, consider (54).

(54) *Tom-wa* [[*ni tasu ni*]-*ga*
Tom-TOP [[2 plus 2]-NOM
yon dearu no]-*o* *shitteiru*
4 COPULA NO]-ACC know
'Tom knows that 2 plus 2 equals 4.'

In this example, the *no*-headed part denotes the abstract proposition that 2 plus 2 equals 4. Second, as pointed out by an anonymous reviewer, modal statements, which seem to denote propositions, can be nominalized by *no*. This is illustrated in (55).

(55) [*Mary-ga* *kuru* *kamoshirenai*
[Mary-NOM come might
no]-*o* *omoidashita.*
NO]-ACC remembered
'I remembered that Mary might come.'

But there is some indication that *no* in situation nominalization tends to denote a perceptible event. Kuno (1973: p.222) notes that in (56), if *no* is used, it denotes Tom's death as a tangible event, whereas if the situation nominalizer *koto* is employed, it denotes Tom's death as a less tangible event. (See also Watanabe (2008).)

(56) [*John-ga* *shinda no/koto*]-*wa*
[John-NOM died NO/KOTO]-TOP
tashika desu.
certain COPULA
'It is certain that John has died.'

I contend that this difference between *no* and *koto* reflects the origins of these two items. As noted in Horie (2008: p.174), there are no confirmed lexical origins for *no*, but *koto* is a diachronically bleached development of the noun *koto*, meaning 'matter' or 'event'. It may then be assumed that *koto* retains the property of denoting an event as a matter, and that this lexical residue is encoded as a constraint in the nominalizer *koto* (but not in the nominalizer *no*). Then, the difference in (56) can be analyzed as the difference in the encoded constraints of *koto* and *no*. But this reasoning raises another problem: as shown below, *koto* does not exhibit participant nominalization; compare (57) with (44).

(57) *[*Akai koto*]-*o* *Tom-ga* *nagu-tta.*
[red KOTO]-ACC Tom-NOM hit-PAST

As stated above, the nominalizer *kes* in Korean, which also derived from the noun meaning 'thing', allows not only situation but also participant nominalization. This functional difference between *koto* and *kes* is a remaining issue.

5 Conclusion

This article has proposed an integrated analysis of *no*-nominalization within Dynamic Syntax, and has accounted for a number of characteristics of the phenomenon. The particle *no* is assigned a single lexical entry, and the participant/situation divide boils down to an outcome of semantic tree growth, more specifically, a parser's choice of what type-e term it copies. In this account, incrementality is a key notion, as the participant/situation distinction arises at the timing of processing *no*.

Acknowledgments

I would like to thank Ronnie Cann, David Cram, Stephen Horn, Ruth Kempson, Jieun Kiaer, Yuji Nishiyama, and the anonymous PACLIC reviewers for helpful suggestions. I am grateful to Aimi Kuya and Eun Hyuk Chang for discussion of Korean examples. Any remaining inadequacies are solely my own.

References

Cann, Ronnie. 2011. Towards an Account of the Auxiliary System in English. In Kempson, R. et al. (eds.) The Dynamics of Lexical Interfaces. CSLI, Stanford.

Cann, Ronnie, Kempson, Ruth, and Marten, Lutz. 2005. The Dynamics of Language. Elsevier, Oxford.

Cann, Ronnie, Kempson, Ruth, and Purver, Matthew. 2007. Context-dependent Well-formedness. Research on Language and Computation, 5: 333-358.

Cann, R. and Wu, Y. 2011. The *Bei* Construction in Chinese. In Kempson, R. et al. (eds.) The Dynamics of Lexical Interfaces. CSLI, Stanford.

Davidson, Donald. 1967. The Logical Form of Action Sentences. In Rescher, N. (ed.) The Logic of Decision and Action. University of Pittsburgh Press, Pittsburgh.

Fodor, Jerry. 1983. The Modularity of Mind. The MIT Press, Cambridge, MA.

Gregoromichelaki, Eleni. 2011. Conditionals in Dynamic Syntax. In Kempson, R. et al. (eds.) The Dynamics of Lexical Interfaces. CSLI, Stanford.

Horie, K. 2008. The Grammaticalization of Nominalizers in Japanese and Korean. In López-Couso, M. J. and Seoane, E. (eds.) Rethinking Grammaticalization. John Benjamins, Amsterdam.

Kamio, Akio. 1983. Meeshiku no Koozoo. (Structure of Noun Phrases) In Inoue, K. (ed.) Nihongo no Koozoo. (Structure of Japanese) Sanseido, Tokyo.

Kempson, Ruth and Kurosawa, Akiko. 2009. At the Syntax-Pragmatics Interface. In Hoshi, H. (ed.) The Dynamics of Language Faculty. Kuroshio, Tokyo.

Kempson, Ruth, Meyer-Viol, Wilfried, and Gabby, Dov. 2001. Dynamic Syntax. Blackwell, Oxford.

Kitagawa, Chisato. 2005. Typological Variants of Head-internal Relatives in Japanese. Lingua, 115: 1243-1276.

Kitagawa, Chisato and Ross, Claudia. 1982. Prenominal Modification in Chinese and Japanese. Linguistic Analysis, 9: 19-53.

Kuno, Susumu. 1973. The Structure of the Japanese Language. The MIT Press, Cambridge, MA.

Kuroda, Shigeyuki. 1992. Japanese Syntax and Semantics. Kluwer, Dordrecht.

Makino, Seiichi. 1968. Some Aspects of Japanese Nominalization. Tokai University Press, Kanagawa, Japan.

McGloin, Naomi. 1985. *No*-pronominalization in Japanese. Papers in Japanese Linguistics, 10: 1-15.

Murasugi, Keiko. 1991. Noun Phrases in Japanese and English. Ph.D. Dissertation, UConn.

Purver, Matthew, Cann, Ronnie, and Kempson, Ruth. 2006. Grammars as Parsers. Research on Language and Computation, 4: 289-326.

Russell, Bertrand. 1905. On Denoting. Mind, 14: 479-493.

Seraku, Tohru. in press. An Incremental Semantics Account of the Particle *No* in Japanese. Proceedings of the Western Conference on Linguistics 2011.

Shibatani, Masayoshi. 2009. Elements of Complex Structures, where Recursion Isn't. In Givon, T. and Shibatani, M. (eds.) Syntactic Complexity. John Benjamins, Amsterdam.

Sperber, Dan and Wilson, Deirdre. 1995. Relevance, 2nd edn. Blackwell, Oxford.

Tonoike, Shigeo. 1990. *No* no Ronrikeeshiki. (LF Representation of *No*) Meijigakuin Ronsou, 467: 69-99.

Watanabe, Yukari. 2008. Bunhogohyooshiki "Koto" "No" no Imitekisooi nikansuru Kenkyuu. (Study of Semantic Differences between Complementizer "Koto" and "No") Keisuisya, Hiroshima, Japan.

Semantic Distributions of the Color Terms, *Black* and *White* in Taiwanese Languages

Huei-ling Lai
National Chengchi University /
64, Sec.2, Zhinan Rd., Wenshan District,
Taipei 11605, Taiwan
hllai@nccu.edu.tw

Shu-chen Lu
National Chengchi University /
64, Sec.2, Zhinan Rd., Wenshan District,
Taipei 11605, Taiwan
96555006@nccu.edu.tw

Abstract

This study, based on a variety of data sources, investigates the linguistic and cultural characteristics associated with the *black* and *white* expressions among Taiwanese Mandarin, Taiwanese Hakka, and Taiwanese Southern Min. The meaning distributions of the data profile four types: prototypical meanings, metonymic extensions, metaphorical extensions and idiosyncratic examples; and the associated cultural factors are examined. Some meaning extensions are widespread across the three languages, whereas some are language-specific because of cultural roots. Among the three languages, Taiwanese Mndarin develops the most prolific usages and this may be ascribed to the prosperity of cultural, economic or technological developments of the language.

1 Introduction

Studies of color terms can be found in fields like linguistics, psychology, neurophysiology or anthropology. The earlier representative work from a linguistic perspective can be attributed to Berlin and Kay's (1969) investigation of 98 languages, in which all languages are claimed to share similarity regarding the foci of basic color terms and to have similar evolutionary stages regarding color terms. Some studies (e.g. Derrig, 1978) propose cross-cultural generality in the extensional meanings of basic color terms and other studies (e.g. Wierzbicka, 1996) probe into human understanding of color terms based on conceptual prototypes.

Black and white are universally perceptible to all mankind and are the only two colors at stage one in Berlin and Kay's (1969) sequence of color evolution. Speakers of Taiwanese Mandarin (TM), Taiwanese Hakka (TH) and Taiwanese Southern Min (TSM) also share some similarities in the usages of the color terms *black* and *white*. However, while the three languages are so contiguous geographically in Taiwan, variations exist among usages of color terms, some of which are due to cultural factors. Hence, investigating the usages of the color terms *black* and *white* in TM, TH and TSM, we aim to uncover the similarities and variations in the meaning extensions of *black* and *white*, and further to find the cultural factors behind them.

1.2 The Data

The TM data are collected from *MOE Revised Mandarin Chinese Dictionary*, *Academia Sinica Balanced Corpus of Mandarin Chinese* and *The NCCU Corpus of Spoken Chinese*, and are transcribed into 漢語拼音 Hàn-yŭ Pīn-yīn 'Mandarin spelling' Phonetic Symbols. Taiwan Google Research Engine is also used to double check whether the data from the Chinese dictionary belong to Taiwanese Mandarin. Proper names are excluded. In total, 209 tokens of 黑 *hēi* 'black' color terms and 362 tokens of 白 *bái* 'white' color terms are found.

The TH data are gathered from *MOE Taiwanese Hakka Dictionary of Common Words*, *The NCCU Corpus of Spoken Taiwanese Hakka*,

Min and Hakka Language Archives, *Taiwanese Hakka Proverbial Expressions Dictionary*, *Hakka Dictionary of Taiwan*, *Sìxiàn Hakka Dictionary*, *A Chinese-English Dictionary Hakka-Dialect*, *Taiwanese Hakka Origins of Lexicon, Legend, Proverbs Anthology*, *Hakka Proverbs the Second Hundred—the Latest One Hundred Hakka Proverbs* and *Interesting 1500 Hakka Proverbs*, and are transcribed based on Taiwanese Hakka Pīnyīn Program designated by National Language Committee in 2009. The tone diacritics of 四縣 Sì-xiàn dialect are rendered for the data. In total, 68 items of 烏 *vu* 'black' color terms and 91 items of 白 *pag* 'white' color terms are found.

The TSM data are gathered from *MOE Taiwanese Southern Min Dictionary of Common Words*, *Taiwanese Concordancer*, *Taiwanese Southern Min Lexicon Dictionary*, *Tōngyòng Taiwanese Southern Min Dictionary*, *Min and Hakka Language Archives*, *Táoyuán Taiwanese Southern Min Proverbs and Riddles (1)*, *Táinán Taiwanese Southern Min Proverbs Collection*, *Taiwanese Southern Min Proverbs Dictionary*, *Origin of Taiwanese Southern Min Expressions*, *Learning Taiwanese Southern Min Together*, *The Wisdom of Taiwanese Southern Min* and *Taiwanese Southern Min Proverbs*, and are transcribed with tone diacritics based on Taiwanese Southern Min Rome Pīnyīn Program issued by National Language Committee in 2008. In total, 119 tokens of 烏 *oo* 'black' color terms and 99 tokens of 白 *pe̍h* 'white' color terms are found.

2 Previous Studies on Color Terms

The doctrine of the Sapir-Whorf hypothesis emphasizes the relativity of semantic structures instead of the role of linguistic universals. Nevertheless, studies of color terms (Berlin and Kay, 1969; McDaniel, 1974) hold that "all languages share a universal system of basic color categorization" and that "these universals are inherent in the human perception of color" (Kay and McDaniel, 1978: 610). Berlin and Kay (1969) investigate 98 languages, and contend that "the referents for the basic color terms of all languages appear to be drawn from a set of eleven universal perceptual categories, and these categories become encoded in the history of a given language in a partially fixed order"(4). They delineate seven evolutionary stages of basic color terms and black and white are the only two colors at stage one.

Some studies propose that languages share cross-cultural generality in the connotative meanings of basic color terms. Kay and McDaniel (1978) present the existence of biologically based semantic universals about color terms. Wierzbicka (1996) and Goddard (1998) maintain that visual and environmental things should be referred to as common reference points for color meanings. Take black and white for example. The most obvious distinction in all colors is the light vs. dark distinction. The most significant environmental prototypes of this distinction are the night and day because "the cycle of day and night is a recurrent and universal (or near-universal) human experience" Goddard (1998: 126). In sum, the representative colors for day and night are white and black, respectively.

Berlin and Kay (1969) point out that Chinese reaches stage five and its basic color terms are 黑 *hēi* 'black', 白 *bái* 'white', 紅 *hóng* 'red', 綠 *lǜ* 'green', 藍 *lán* 'blue' and 黃 *huáng* 'yellow'. Cheng (1991, 2002) identifies five basic color terms for TH and TSM: for TH, 烏 *vu* 'black', 白 *pag* 'white', 紅 *fung* 'red', 黃 *vong* 'yellow' and 青 *qiang* 'grue category of blue and green', and for TSM 烏 *oo* 'black', 白 *pe̍h* 'white', 紅 *âng* 'red', 黃 *ňg* 'yellow' and 青 *tshenn* 'grue category of blue and green'. In addition, Zeng (2002) examines color terms from traditional 陰陽五行 Yīn-Yáng-Wǔ-Xíng 'Yin Yang Five Elements'. He claims that since the color black in Chinese is situated in the north and belongs to winter, during which the world is in a recession period, *hēi* has always been regarded as inauspicious, disastrous, evil and negative in the Chinese community. The color white on the other hand is located in the north-east which is the position of death in Chinese 風水 Fēng-Shuǐ. Consequently *bái* has been connected with Chinese funerals and the funeral clothes are white.

While color universals seem to be pervasive among the three languages, language-specific usages exist. Uncovering color terms of different languages or dialects may open a window to the different facets of their lives (Cheng, 2002; Huang, 2003; Liang, 2005; He and Zeng, 2006; Zeng, 2002 and Xie, 2011). A comparison of color terms in TM, TH and TSM so as to observe their linguistic and cultural characteristics is worthwhile. Furthermore, preliminary analysis of the data shows that metonymic or metaphorical extension for color words happen only when they collocate with their modified components. We surmise that only two types of meanings are associated with the color terms. One refers to the meaning of the physiologically visual color, and the other refers to the extended meanings of the gestalt chunk. More in-depth investigation of the data will profile a more systematic distribution, as will be shown by the study.

3 Metaphor and Metonymy

The contemporary theory of metaphor (e.g., Lakoff and Johnson 1980; Lakoff 1993) considers metaphor to be a conceptual and inherent part of human thoughts and languages. Conceptual metaphor can be understood as a mapping from a source domain to a target domain. For example, in the conceptual metaphor LOVE IS A JOURNEY, the source domain is JOURNEY and is mapped onto the target domain, LOVE. The mapping is strictly structured and there are ontological correspondences. The English expressions of this conceptual metaphor can be illustrated by these sentences: Look *how far we've come*. We'll just have to *go our separate ways*. Ungerer and Schmid (2006) emphasize that another key element in metaphor is the mapping scope, "a set of constraints regulating which correspondences are eligible for mapping from a source concept onto a chosen target concept" (119). Most importantly, the mapping scope is culturally constrained and deeply entrenched in speakers' minds in a certain culture.

Kövecses and Radden (1998) define metonymy as "a cognitive process in which one conceptual entity, the vehicle, provides mental access to another conceptual entity, the target, within the same domain, or ICM" (39). ICMs (Idealized Cognitive Models) refer to a network of entities within one ontological realm and these entities are related to each other by specific conceptual relationships. They categorize metonymy-producing relationships into two major types: Whole ICM and its parts and Parts of an ICM.

4 Analysis

The data of the color term *black* or *white* in TM, TH, and TSM are categorized according to the meaning distributions based on different cognitive mechanisms. The prototypical meaning of *black* and *white* indicates their physiologically visual color. Metonymic extensions represent conceptual entities which derive from the source domain of the visual color black or white within the same ICM. Metaphoric extensions undergo a conceptual mapping from a source domain of the visual color to a different target domain. The metaphor ABSTRACT QUALITY IS PHYSICAL QUALITY (Goatly, 2011) is generalized to cover all the data. Idiosyncratic examples cover proverbial expressions or arbitrary usage of *black* and *white*. The overall distribution of the data across the three languages is reported in Table 1.

4.1 Meaning Distributions of *Black*

The prototypical meanings of *black* account for a significant proportion in all categories across the three languages. Examples such as 黑髮 hēi-fǎ 'black hair' in TM, 烏雲 vuˊ-iunˇ 'dark clouds' in TH or 烏豆 oo-tāu 'black beans' in TSM can illustrate.

Through mappings within ICMs, *black* expressions in the three languages have various metonymic extensions. For example, 黑手 hēi-shǒu 'a mechanic' in TM is a case of the metonymy PART FOR WHOLE. Mechanics' hands are constantly stained and therefore their distinguishing black hands are used (PART) to stand for their occupation (WHOLE). In addition, 烏人 vuˊ-nginˇ 'the black race' in TH illustrates a case of the metonymy DEFINING PROPERTY FOR CATEGORY. The skin color of Negro is black and is thus used (DEFINING PROPERTY) to refer to the black race (CATEGORY). 烏鬚到白鬚 oo-tshiu-kàu-pe̍h-tshiu 'from youth to old age' in TSM is a substantiation of the metonymy APPEARANCE FOR THE STATE THAT CAUSED IT. Youngsters' beards are black whereas the elder's beards are white. Beards of different colors represent different age periods and thus oo-tshiu-kàu-pe̍h-tshiu is from youth to old age.

Metaphorical extensions in the three languages are robust and diverse because numerous abstract attributes of the target domain can be conceptualized through the association of the color black. Some cases of metaphorical extensions are prevalent across the three languages. To begin with, when something is hidden and unseen in darkness, it is regarded as secret and mysterious. 黑箱作業 hēi-xiāng-zuò-yè 'an unknown operation' in TM, 烏面賊 vu ˊ -mien-ced 'objects from unknown resources' in TH and 烏批 oo-phue 'an anonymous letter' in TSM carry such an implication. Furthermore, the attribute of mystery which is usually considered negative extends to the notion of viciousness regarding people's inner temperaments and the notion of illegality concerning people's outer conducts. 黑心 hēi-xīn in TM, 烏心腸 vu ˊ -xim ˊ -cong ˇ in TH and 烏漉肚 oo-lok-tōo in TSM all refer to people's evil heart and vicious mind. 黑道 hēi-dào 'gangsters' in TM, 烏店 vu ˊ -diam 'a store extorting an extra large sum of money from customers' in TH and 烏市 oo-tshī 'a black market' in TSM are related to illegal and underground behavior and activities. In addition, reputations being blackened can be manifested through the *black* expressions such as 抹黑 mǒ-hēi 'smear people's reputation' in TM and 烏名單 oo-miâ-tuann 'a black list' in TSM.

On the other hand, some metaphorical extensions exclusively exist in one language. Some of these language-specific usages originate from cultural heritages or historical roots. For example, the TSM term 烏狗 oo-káu, whose origin manifests rich Taiwanese culture, contains the extensional meaning 'fashionable and handsome'. The notion of keeping a low profile is revealed by the expression 知白守黑 zhī-bái-shǒu-hēi, a line of classical drama in TM. The case 走黑運 zǒu-hēi-yùn in TM, which derives from terminologies of magical calculations in Chinese culture, implies inauspiciousness and unluckiness. The case 股市開黑盤 gǔ-shì-kāi-hēi-pán in TM particularly describes the sluggish phenomenon in the stock market via the conceptualization of the color black. In addition, other language-unique metaphorical expressions emerge because they have become entrenched frozen chunks in the language; cases such as 烏白來 oo-pėh-lâi 'reckless, capricious' and 烏有 oo-iú 'disappearing, nothing' in TSM can illustrate. Still other exclusive metaphorical extensions are influenced by English; cases such as 黑馬 hēi-mǎ 'a black horse' and 黑色幽默 hēi-sè-yōu-mò 'black humor' in TM can illustrate. The distribution of metaphorical extensions of *black* across the three languages is reported in Table 2.

Finally, there are some idiosyncratic examples, whereby *black* is arbitrarily used; cases such as 黑甜鄉 hēi-tián-xiāng 'dreamland' in TM or 烏紗 oo-se 'bribery' in TSM can illustrate. Also, proverbial expressions invariably carry some moral lessons or exhortation functions (Lakoff and Turner, 1989); cases such as 近朱者赤，近墨者黑 Jìn-zhū-zhě-chì, Jìn-mò-zhě-hēi. 'People are easily influenced by the environment' in TM or 烏矸仔貯豆油，無得看 Oo-kan-á té tāu-iû, bô-tit-khàn. 'Don't judge a person by his appearance.' in TSM can illustrate.

Metaphorical extensions can carry either positive or negative connotations. Regarding *black*, negative meanings account for a dominant proportion (79%) across the three languages. Such a tendency is natural since human conceptual universal about the color term *black* (Wierzbicka, 1996; Goddard, 1998) is the dark night, which somehow conveys the implications of mystery and ominousness. This tendency also corresponds to the traditional viewpoints of the color black in the Chinese community (Huang, 2003; Liang, 2005; Zeng, 2002). According to *Yin Yang Five Elements*, the color black belongs to winter when things in the natural world are during a recession period, hence plausibly accounting for the fact that the color term *black* develops so many negative metaphorical extensions.

4.2 Meaning Distributions of *White*

The prototypical meaning of *white*, which represents the physiological color white, can be seen across the three languages. Examples such as 白雪 bái-xuě 'white snow' in TM, 白米 pag-mi ˋ 'white rice' in TH and 白紙 pėh-tsuá 'white paper' in TSM can illustrate. Since white is the representative color of human conceptual universal about daytime, it can schematize the condition of brightness and light such as 白天 bái-tiān 'daytime' in TM, 白晝 pag-zu 'daytime' in TH or 當頭白日 tng-thâu-pėh-jit 'bright daytime' in TSM.

Metonymic extensions are diverse across the three languages. For instance, in TM 白眼 bái-yǎn 'showing the white eyeball' referring to a cold stare or a disdainful look realizes the PHYSIOLOGICAL EFFECTS FOR EMOTION metonymy. When a person looks at others with white eyeballs, he shows an indifferent and contemptuous attitude toward them. In TH, the case 采白 cai`-pag 'things that are used in a wedding, or a funeral' is the substantiation of the metonymy APPEARANCE OF THE OBJECT. In Hakka culture, 采 cai` means different colors or auspicious signs and usually stands for objects in a wedding. 白 pag symbolizes the white garments worn in a traditional funeral. In TSM, the case 白賊七仔 pe̍h-tsha̍t-tshit-á 'a person who likes to tell lies and play tricks on others' originates from a well-known TSM folk story. Through the metonymy CATEGORY FOR DEFINING PROPERTY, 白賊 pe̍h-tsha̍t stands for lies as can be seen in another TSM case 講白賊 kóng-pe̍h-tsha̍t 'telling lies'.

Some metaphorical extensions are widespread across the three languages. The concept of brightness can further delineate clear and transparent meanings; cases such as 明白 míng-bái 'clear' in TM or 打白講 da`-pag-gong` 'frankly speaking' in TH can illustrate. In addition, the white color which is without any hues can represent the idea of plain flavor as 白滾水 pe̍h-kún-tsuí 'plain boiled water' in TSM illustrates. The meanings of clarity and transparency can further extend to represent human's morality and innocence as implicated through 清白 qīng-bái in TM and its equivalent counterparts in TH and TSM.

Moreover, from another perspective, the color white which lacks hues can metaphorically imply emptiness or nothing as exemplified by cases like 平白無故 ping-bái-wú-gù 'without any reason or cause' in TM, 白手捉魚 pag-su`-zog`-ngˇ 'building up fortune from scratch' in TH or 白手成家 pik-siú-sîng-ka 'building up fortune from scratch' in TSM. Such extensions can further represent the concept of doing something in vain and being futile. Cases such as 白費力氣 bái-fèi-lì-qì 'all efforts have been in vain' in TM, 打白行 da`-pag-hangˇ 'come without achieving purpose' in TH and 白講 pe̍h-kóng 'speaking in vain' in TSM carry such implications. Another extension is gaining something without paying as manifested by 白吃白喝 bái-chī-bái-hē in TM, 白食 pag-siid in TH or 白吃白喝 pe̍h-tsia̍h-pe̍h-lim in TSM, all denoting having food or drink for free. Furthermore, the notion of nothingness can depict a situation in which people are so helpless that they cannot do anything in the face of an event. This extension is realized via the chunks 白白 bái-bái in TM and 白白 pe̍h-pe̍h in TSM as used in the TM sentence, 難道<u>白白</u>地看他們被欺負? Nán-dào <u>báibái</u> dì kàn tā-men bèi-qī- fù? 'We cannot do anything but watch them being bullied?'

While many metaphorical extensions regarding *white* are prevalent in the three languages, some language-specific extensions still exist. For example, in TM, the white color can be associated with an abstract concept of legality, as in the case 白道 bái-dào 'legal organization'. In addition, the white color indicates blankness on a piece of paper as in the case 繳白卷 jiǎo-bái-juàn 'submitting a blank answer sheet in an exam'. Another usage 不拿白不拿 bù-ná-bái-bù-ná 'It is wasteful if you don't take it.' indicating a pity or a wasteful matter in TM is often used colloquially. Such a usage occurs in a fixed chunk: 不 bù-verb-白 bái-不 bù-verb, with the same verb repeated twice. The distribution of metaphorical extensions of *white* across three languages is reported in Table 3.

Finally, idiosyncratic cases where *white* is arbitrarily used can also be seen across the three languages. Cases such as 白目眉 pag-mug´-miˇ 'brazen-faced and shameless people' in TH or 青磅白磅 tshenn-pōng-pe̍h-pōng 'out of sudden' in TSM can illustrate. Proverbial expressions containing *white* possess a wide variety of implications; cases such as 白紙黑字 Bái-zhǐ-hēi-zì 'substantial and convincing evidence' in TM or 白白的布染到烏 Pag-pag-did´-bu- ngiam-do-vu´ 'Innocent people are slandered and accused falsely.' in TH can illustrate.

Regarding meaning connotations of the *white* expressions, non-negative meanings take up a significant proportion (78%) in all three languages. Such a tendency is natural because the human conceptual universal about the color *white*

(Wierzbicka, 1996; Goddard, 1998) is the day, which carries the notion of brightness and hopes. This tendency may have something to do with people's observation of sunlight, which is white at the brightest moment (Xie, 2011), hence plausibly accounting for the dominant developments of non-negative meanings of the color term *white*.

4.3 Cultural Factors in Color Terms

One type of cross-cultural variation that Kövecses (2005) stipulates is alternative metaphor. Among the three types of alternative metaphor, the scope of the source is relevant for the discussion of color terms. The scope of source refers to the set of target domains that a particular source domain can correspond to. In terms of the source domain of the color black or white, TM has the most corresponding target domains (10 for black, 9 for white), TH has the least (4 for black, 5 for white) and TSM lies in between (7 for black, 6 for white). This indicates that TM has the widest scope of source, TH has the narrowest and TSM is in between. In brief, TM has the most versatile metaphorical extensions for both *black* and *white*.

Berlin and Kay (1969) once address the relationship between color lexicons and cultural and technological development as follows: "Color lexicons with few terms tend to occur in association with relatively simple cultures and simple technologies, while color lexicons with many terms tend to occur in association with complex cultures and complex technologies" (104). In other words, the number of color lexicons proportionally indicates the complexity of cultural and technological developments. From our data analysis, TM has the widest distributions of *black* and *white*, TSM lies in the second and TH has the least. Therefore, we presume that the complexity of TM color terms is closely related to the vivacity of cultural, economic or technological developments in TM.

Some usages also reflect intra-cultural variations, including the style dimension and the subculture dimension. The style dimension refers to linguistic variation along with levels of formality. For example, proverbial expressions of color terms invariably carry some moral lessons as illustrated by 近朱者赤，近墨者黑 Jìn-zhū-zhě-chì, Jìn-mò-zhě-hēi 'People are easily influenced by the environment.' in TM. In addition, versatile usages are developed colloquially; cases such as 黑掉 hēi-diào in TM as in the sentence 他在商業界黑掉了 Tā zài shāng-yè-jiè hēi-diào le 'His reputation is damaged in the field of commerce.' can illustrate. Also, some slang usages such as 白賊七仔 pe̍h-tsha̍t-tshit-á 'a great liar' in TSM are found.

The distinction of subcultures would lead to unique metaphorical conceptualization of important concepts. For example, the extended meaning 'illegal, underground' is relevant to the subculture of judicial organizations, law officers and governmental bureau. In TM, related usages such as 黑官 hēi-guān 'illegitimate government employees' or 掃黑 sǎo-hēi 'cracking down on crimes' are found. The metaphorical extension 'low, sluggish, not prosperous' in TM also displays another subculture dimension. Cases such as 開黑盤 kāi-hēi-pán and 長黑 cháng-hēi can only be seen in the stock market. Therefore, there are expressions like 股市開黑盤 gǔ-shì kāi-hēi-pán 'The stock market is sluggish.' and 股市長黑 gǔ-shì cháng-hēi 'The stock price is tumbling'. Moreover, some usages refer to certain types of people. In TM, 白丁 bái-dīng or 白民 bái-mín refers to commoners or illiterate people. The equivalent terms 白身 pag-siin´ in TH and 白丁 pe̍h-ting in TSM also reveals this subculture dimension.

5. Concluding Remarks

This study explores the semantic similarities and differences regarding *black* and *white* expressions among TM, TH and TSM. Black and white are the two most fundamental colors in the natural world as designated at stage one in Berlin and Kay's (1969) evolutionary sequence. The meaning distributions of the data profile four types: prototypical meanings, metonymic extensions, metaphorical extensions and idiosyncratic examples; and the associated cultural factors are examined. Some metaphorical extensions are widespread across the three languages; some are language-specific because of cultural roots, or entrenched frozen chunks. Among the three Taiwanese languages, TM develops the most prolific usages and this may be ascribed to the prosperity of cultural, economic or technological developments of the language.

The *black* and *white* expressions also distinctively contrast with each other concerning positive and negative connotations in TM, TH and TSM. Negative extensions associated with *black* expressions take up a significant proportion whereas non-negative extensions associated with *white* expressions account for a dominant proportion. Such a tendency may have something to do with human conceptual universals about black and white, connecting with the dark night and the bright day, respectively. The dark night implies mystery and ominousness while the bright day conveys hopes and brightness. This tendency also corresponds to the traditional viewpoint of *Yin Yang Five Elements* about black and white, with the former indicating a sign of recession and dormancy, and the latter indicating people's observation of sunlight. In addition, *black* and *white* expressions reveal evident contrasts of metaphorical extensions such as mystery and clarity, viciousness and innocence and illegality and legality.

References

Berlin, B., & Kay, P. (1969). *Basic color terms.* Berkeley: University of California Press.

Cheng, Y. (1991). *Basic color terms in Chinese dialects: structure and change.* Master's thesis, National Tsing Hua University, Taipei, Taiwan.

Cheng, Y. (2002). The semantic transfer of color terms. In Y. E. Hsiao (Ed.), *Proceedings of the first cognitive linguistics conference language and cognition* (pp. 321-343). Taipei: Graduate Institute of Linguistics National Chengchi University.

Derrig, S. (1978). Metaphor in the color lexicon. In D. Farkas, W. Jacobsen, and K. Todrys (Eds.), *Papers from the parasession on the lexicon* (pp. 85-96). Chicago Linguistic Society.

Goatly, A. (2011). *The Language of Metaphors.* USA: Routledge.

Goddard, C. (1998). *Semantic Analysis: A Practical Introduction.* New York: Oxford University Press.

Huang, J.-W. (2003). *Taiwan Dongshi keyu biaoxingzhuangci de yuyi fenxi [Semantic analysis of terms in Taiwan Dongshi Hakka].* Master's thesis, National Hsinchu University of Education, Hsinchu, Taiwan.

Jiaoyubu chongbian guoyu cidian xiudingben. [MOE revised Mandarin Chinese dictionary]. Retrieved from http://dict.revised.moe.edu.tw/

Jiaoyubu minnanyu changyongci cidian. [MOE Taiwanese Southern Min dictionary of common words]. Retrieved from http://twblg.dict.edu.tw/holodict_new/index.ht m

Jiaoyubu Taiwan kejiayu changyongci cidian. [MOE Taiwanese Hakka dictionary of common words]. Retrieved from http://twblg.dict.edu.tw/holodict_new/index.ht m

Kay, P. (1975). Synchronic variability and diachronic change in basic color terms. *Language in Society, 4*, 257-270.

Kay, P., & McDaniel, C. K. 1978. The linguistic significance of the meanings of basic color terms. *Language, (54)*3, 610-646.

Kövecses, Z., & Radden, G. (1998). Metonymy: developing a cognitive linguistic view. *Cognitive Linguistics, 9*(1), 37-77.

Kövecses, Z. (2005). *Metaphor in Culture: Universality and Variation.* Cambridge: Cambridge University Press.

Kövecses, Z. (2005). *Metaphor: A Practical Introduction.* New York: Oxford University Press.

Lakoff, G., & Johnson, M. (1980). *Metaphors we live by.* Chicago: University of Chicago Press.

Lakoff, G. (1987). *Women, Fire, and Dangerous Things: What Categories Reveal About the Mind.* Chicago: University of Chicago Press.

Lakoff, G., & Turner, M. (1989). *More than cool reason: a field guide to poetic metaphor.* Chicago: University of Chicago Press.

Lakoff, G. (1993). The contemporary theory of metaphor. In Andrew, Ortony (Ed.), *Metaphor and thought* (pp. 202-251). Cambridge: Cambridge University Press.

Liu, Y.-P. (2001). *A cognitive approach to the understanding of the six basic color words in Mandarin Chinese.* Master's thesis, National Taiwan Normal University, Taipei, Taiwan.

Ungerer, F., & Schmid, H.-J. (2006). *An introduction to cognitive linguistics.* UK: Pearson Education Limited.

Wierzbicka, Anna. (1996). *Semantics: Primes and Universals.* Oxford: Oxford University Press.

Williams, J. E., Morland, J. K., and Underwood, W. L.(1970). Connotations of color names in The United States, Europe, and Asia. *The Journal of Social Psychology, 82*, 3-14.

Zeng, C.-H. (2002). To analyze the literal meaning of five fundamental color as well as its relation with Ying Yang Five Elements. *Journal of Science and Technology, 11*(2), 121-135.

Zhongyanyuan pingheng yuliaoku. [Academia sinica balanced corpus of Mandarin Chinese]. Retrieved from http://dbo.sinica.edu.tw/SinicaCorpus/

Zhongyanyuan minkeyu diancang. [Min and Hakka language archives]. Retrieved from http://minhakka.ling.sinica.edu.tw/bkg/index.php

Table 1: Category Distributions of *Black* and *White* in TM, TH, and TSM

Category	TM		TH		TSM	
	black	*white*	*black*	*white*	*black*	*white*
Prototypical Meaning	46.14% (97)	30.47% (110)	56.18% (50)	39.47% (45)	51.19% (86)	47.69% (62)
Metonymic Extensions	11.96% (25)	14.68% (53)	2.24% (2)	12.28% (14)	10.12% (17)	15.38% (20)
Metaphorical Extensions	30.62% (64)	27.70% (100)	24.72% (22)	32.45% (37)	20.83% (35)	25.39% (33)
Idiosyncratic Examples	11.01% (23)	24.38% (88)	16.85% (15)	15.79% (18)	17.86% (30)	11.54% (15)
Total	100% (209)	100% (361)	100% (89)	100% (114)	100% (168)	100% (130)

Note: The number in the parentheses indicates the number of tokens.

Table 2: Distributions of Metaphorical Extensions of *Black* in TM, TH, and TSM

Category	TM	TH	TSM
Secret, Mysterious	17.19% (11)	28.57% (2)	8.57% (3)
Evil, Vicious	26.56% (17)	28.57% (2)	20% (7)
Illegal, Underground	25% (16)	28.57% (2)	28.57% (10)
Disgraceful, Dishonorable	7.81% (5)		2.86% (1)
Depressed, Frustrated	7.81% (5)		
Keeping a low profile	1.56% (1)		
Unexpectedly excellent	1.56% (1)		
Sarcastic, Biting	3.13% (2)		
Inauspicious, Unfortunate	6.25% (4)		
Low, Sluggish	3.13% (2)		
Fooling around		14.29% (1)	
Fashionable			11.43% (4)
Reckless, Capricious			25.71% (9)
Becoming nothing, Empty			2.86% (1)
Total	100% (64)	100% (7)	100% (35)

Table 3: Distributions of Metaphorical Extensions of *White* in TM, TH, and TSM

Category	TM	TH	TSM
Clear, Transparent	18.18% (20)	18.52% (5)	15.15% (5)
Moral, Unimpeachable	5.45% (6)	3.70% (1)	6.06% (2)
Legal	10.00% (11)		3.03% (1)
Plain, Ordinary	15.46% (17)	18.52% (5)	30.30% (10)
Empty, With nothing	13.64% (15)	25.93% (7)	9.10% (3)
In vain, Be futile	28.18% (31)	14.81% (4)	21.21% (7)
For Free	5.45% (6)	18.52% (5)	12.12% (4)
Powerless, Helpless	1.82% (2)		3.03% (1)
Wasteful	1.82% (2)		
Total	100% (110)	100% (27)	100% (33)

Language Independent Sentence-Level Subjectivity Analysis with Feature Selection

Aditya Mogadala
Search and Information Extraction Lab
IIIT-H
Hyderabad
India
aditya.m@research.iiit.ac.in

Vasudeva Varma
Search and Information Extraction Lab
IIIT-H
Hyderabad
India
vv@iiit.ac.in

Abstract

Identifying and extracting subjective information from News, Blogs and other user generated content has lot of applications. Most of the earlier work concentrated on English data. But, recently subjectivity related research at sentence-level in other languages has increased. In this paper, we achieve sentence-level subjectivity classification using language independent feature weighing and selection methods which are consistent across languages. Experiments performed on 5 different languages including English and South Asian language Hindi show that Entropy based category coverage difference criterion (ECCD) feature selection method with language independent feature weighing methods outperforms other approaches for subjective classification.

1 Introduction

Subjective text expresses opinions, emotions, sentiment and beliefs, while objective text generally report facts. So the task of distinguishing subjective from objective text is useful for many natural language processing applications like mining opinions from product reviews (M. Hu and B. Liu, 2004), summarizing different opinions(K. Ganesan.et.al, 2010), question answering (A. Balahur.et.al, 2009) etc.

But research work performed earlier on subjectivity analysis has been applied only on English and mostly at document-level and word-level. Some methods (Wiebe and Riloff, 2005) which concentrated at sentence-level to learn subjective and objective expressions are boot-strapping algorithms which lacks scalability. But, recently focus shifted to multilingual space (R. Mihalcea.et.al, 2007). Banea (C. Banea.et.al, 2008) worked on sentence-level subjectivity analysis using machine translation approaches by leveraging resources and tools available for English . Another approach (C. Banea.et.al, 2010) used multilingual space and meta classifiers to build high precision classifiers for subjectivity classification.

However, aforementioned work (C. Banea.et.al, 2008) concentrated more on language specific attributes due to variation in expression of subjectivity in different languages. This create a problem of portability of methods to different languages. Other approach (C. Banea.et.al, 2010) which tried achieving language independence created large feature vectors for subjectivity classification. Different languages parallel sentences are taken into consideration to build high-precision classifier for each language. This approach not only increases the complexity and time for classification but also completely dependent on parallel corpus to get good accuracies. A weakly supervised method (C. Lin.et.al, 2011) for sentence-level subjectivity detection using subjLDA tried to reduce training data is available only for English. There are some experiments conducted for Japanese (H. Kanayama.et.al, 2006), Chinese (T. Zagibalov.et.al, 2008), Romanian (C. Banea.et.al, 2008; R. Mihalcea.et.al, 2007) languages data. But these approaches are performed at document level and not language independent.

In this paper, we try to address three major problems highlighted from earlier approaches. First, can language portability problem be eliminated by selecting language independent features. Second, can language specific tools like POS taggers, Named Entity recognizers dependency can be minimized as they vary with language. Third, can accuracy of subjective classification is maintained after feature reduction using feature selection methods which are consistent across languages.

Remainder of this paper is organized into following sections. Related work is mentioned in the Section 2. Next Section 3 discuss about our approach for feature weighing and selection methods. While the experimental setup Section 4 describes collection and evaluation metrics used to analyze the accuracy of approach. Experimental Section 5 explains experiments performed on different languages, while results and performance between SVM and NBM is analyzed in Section 6 and Section 7 respectively. Conclusion and future work is discussed in Section 8.

2 Related Work

We divide the subjective and objective classification task into unsupervised, multilingual and supervised methods.

2.1 Unsupervised

Sentiment classification and opinion analysis can be considered as a hierarchical task of subjectivity detection. Improvement of precision in subjectivity detection can benefit the later. Therefore, lot of work is done for subjective sentence detection to achieve later. (G. Murray.et.al, 2009) proposed to learn subjective expression patterns from both labeled and unlabeled data using n-gram word sequences. Their approach for learning subjective expression patterns is similar to (T. Wilson.et.al, 2008) which relies on n-grams, but goes beyond fixed sequences of words by varying levels of lexical instantiation.

2.2 Multilingual

In the multilingual space good amount of work is done in Asian and European languages. Several participants in the Chinese and Japanese Opinion Extraction tasks of NTCIR-6 (Y. Wu.et.al, 2007) performed subjectivity and sentiment analysis in languages other than English. (C. Banea.et.al, 2008; R. Mihalcea.et.al, 2007) performed subjectivity analysis in Romanian. While, (C. Banea.et.al, 2010) performed subjectivity analysis in French, Spanish, Arabic, German, Romanian languages.

2.3 Supervised

Furthermore, tools developed for English were used to determine sentiment or subjectivity labeling for a given target language by transferring the text to English and applying an English classifier on the resulting data. The labels were then transfered back into the target language (M. Bautin.et.al, 2008). These experiments are carried out in Arabic, Chinese, English, French, German, Italian, Japanese, Korean, Spanish, and Romanian. (X. Wan, 2009) who constructs a polarity co-training system by using the multi-lingual views obtained through the automatic translation of product-reviews into Chinese and English.

3 Approach

Subjective sentence classification is treated as a text classification task. (C. Banea.et.al, 2008) used unigrams at word level as features to classify the subjective and objective sentences in different languages. But, unigrams can occur in different categories (subjective and objective) with equal probability. This hampers the classification accuracy. Also, selecting all possible words in the sentences can create a large index size when considered as entire training set increasing the dimensionality of the feature vector for each sentence.

Feature selection can be applied to efficiently categorize the sentences. It is an important process which is followed for many text categorization tasks. Now to achieve our major objective of language independent subjective classification. We use feature extraction, weighing and selection methods that are language independent.

3.1 Feature Extraction and Weighing

Features are categorized into syntactic, semantic, link-based, and stylistic features (G. Forman, 2003) from the previous subjective and sentiment studies. Here, we concentrate more on feature weighing methods based on syntactic and stylistic properties of the text to maintain language independence. Unigrams and Bigrams extracted as features are weighed as given below.

Syntactic Feature Weighing
Syntactic features used in earlier works (M. Gamon, 2004) where word n-grams and part-of-speech (POS) tags. But, POS tagging create dependency on language specific tools. In order to eliminate the language specific dependencies we will use only word n-grams.

Sentence Representation with Unigram (UF.ISF)
This feature extraction is inspired from vector space model (G. Salton, 1975) used for flat documents. **UF** represents the unigram frequency at word level in a sentence. While **ISF** represent the inverse sentence frequency of the unigram. For a given collection S of subjective and objective sentences, an Index $I = \{u_1, u_2, ..., u_{|I|}\}$, where $|I|$ denotes the cardinal of I, gives the list of unigrams u encountered in the sentences S.

A sentence s_i of S is then represented by a vector $\vec{s_i} = (w_{i,1}, w_{i,2}, ..., w_{i,I})$ followed by the subjective or objective label. Here, $w_{i,j}$ represents the weight of unigram u_j in the sentence s_i. Now to calculate the weight $w_{i,j}$ we use the formula similar to TF.IDF.

$$w_{i,j} = \frac{c_{i,j}}{\Sigma_l c_{i,l}} * log\frac{|S|}{|\{s_i : u_j \in s_i\}|} \quad (1)$$

where $c_{i,j}$ is the number of occurrences of u_j in the sentence s_i normalized by the number of occurrences of other unigrams in sentence s_i, $|S|$ is total number of sentences in the training set and $|\{s_i : u_j \varepsilon s_i\}|$ is number of sentences in which the unigram u_j occurs at-least once.

Sentence Representation with Bigram (BF.ISF)
This feature extraction is similar to UF.ISF mentioned in the earlier section, but we extract co-occurring words. **BF** represents the Bigrams frequency at word level in a sentence. While **ISF** represent the inverse sentence frequency of the Bigram. For a given collection S of subjective and objective sentences, an Bigram Index $BI = \{b_1, b_2, ..., b_{|BI|}\}$, where $|BI|$ denotes the cardinal of BI, gives the list of bigrams b encountered in the sentences S.

A sentence s_i of S is then represented by a vector $\vec{s_i} = (wb_{i,1}, wb_{i,2}, ..., wb_{i,BI})$ followed by the subjective or objective label. Here, $wb_{i,j}$ represents the weight of bigram b_j in the sentence s_i. Now to calculate the weight $wb_{i,j}$ we use the formula similar to UF.ISF.

$$wb_{i,j} = \frac{c_{i,j}}{\Sigma_l c_{i,l}} * log\frac{|S|}{|\{s_i : b_j \in s_i\}|} \quad (2)$$

where $c_{i,j}$ is the number of occurrences of b_j in the sentence s_i normalized by the number of occurrences of other bigrams in sentence s_i, $|S|$ is total number of sentences in the training set and $|\{s_i : b_j \varepsilon s_i\}|$ is number of sentences in which the bigram b_j occurs at least once.

Stylistic Feature Weighing
Structural and lexical style markers can be considered as stylistic features which has shown good results in Web discourse (A. Abbasi.et.al, 2008). However, style markers have seen limited usage in sentiment analysis research. Some (M. Gamon, 2004) tried in this direction.

Sentence representation with Normalized Unigram Word Length (NUWL)
This feature extraction considers length of unique unigram words in the sentence. Length of unigram is calculated by the number of characters present in the word. For a given collection S of subjective and objective sentences, an Word Index $WI = \{uw_1, uw_2, ..., uw_{|WI|}\}$, where $|WI|$ denotes the cardinal of WI, gives the list of unigram words uw encountered in the sentences S.

A sentence s_i of S is then represented by a vector $\vec{s_i} = (lw_{i,1}, lw_{i,2}, ..., lw_{i,I})$ followed by the subjective or objective label. Here, $lw_{i,j}$ represents the weight of unigram word uw_j in the sentence s_i. Now to calculate the weight $lw_{i,j}$.

$$lw_{i,j} = \frac{L_{i,j}}{\Sigma_n L_{i,n}} * log\frac{|S|}{|\{s_i : uw_j \in s_i\}|} \quad (3)$$

where $L_{i,j}$ is the character count in the uw_j in the sentence s_i normalized by length of all the unigram words in sentence s_i. $|S|$ is total number of sentences in the training set and $|\{s_i : uw_j \varepsilon s_i\}|$ is number of sentences in which the unigram uw_j occurs atleast once.

3.2 Feature Selection

Feature selection methods help in removing the features which may not be useful for categorization. To achieve it, feature selection techniques select subset of total features. But, it is important to reduce features without compromising on the accuracy of a classifier. Most methods like Information Gain(IG) (C. Lee.et.al, 2006), Correlation Feature Selection(CFS) (M.A. Hall, 1999), Chi-Squared (χ^2) (J. Bakus.et.al, 2006), Odds ratio (OR) (G. Forman, 2003) does not consider the frequency of the text or term between the categories which leads in reduction of accuracy of a classifier.

In-order to overcome this problem, we used Entropy based category coverage difference (ECCD) (C. Largeron.et.al, 2011) feature selection method which uses the entropy of the text or term. f_j is used to represent the text feature extracted (unigram or bigram), c_k for category of the class and c_k^- for the complement of the class. Where j represent number of features and k represents two classes either subjective or objective.

Entropy based category coverage Difference(ECCD)
This feature selection method (C. Largeron.et.al, 2011) was proposed to mine INEX XML documents. We use this approach for improving the subjective and objective sentence classification. Let T_j^k be number of occurrences of text feature f_j in the category c_k sentence and, fq_j^k is the frequency of f_j in that category c_k given by Equation 4.

$$fq_j^k = \frac{T_j^k}{\sum_k T_j^k} \tag{4}$$

So Entropy $Ent(f_j)$ of text feature f_j is given by Equation 5

$$Ent(f_j) = \sum_{k=1}^{r} (fq_j^k) * log_2(fq_j^k) \tag{5}$$

Entropy equals 0, if the text feature f_j appears only in one category. It means that feature has good discrimination ability to classify the sentences. Similarly, entropy of the text feature will be high if the feature is represented in two classes. If Ent_m represent the maximum entropy of the feature f_j, ECCD(f_j, c_k) is given by following equation 6.

$$ECCD(f_j, c_k) = P(f_j|c_k) - P(f_j|c_k^-) * \frac{Ent_m - Ent(f_j)}{Ent_m} \tag{6}$$

Where $P(f_j|c_k)$ and $P(f_j|c_k^-)$ are probability of observing the text feature f_j in a sentence belonging to category c_k and c_k^- respectively.

The advantage of ECCD is that higher the number of sentences of category c_k containing feature f_j and lower the number of sentences in other category containing f_j, we get higher value for equation 6. It means f_j becomes the characteristic feature of that category c_k which helps in better feature selection. Feature selection method which is similar to ECCD is mentioned below.

Categorical Proportional Difference (CPD)
CPD (M. Simeon.et.al, 2008) is a measure of the degree to which a text feature contributes to differentiating a particular category from other categories in a text corpus. We calculate the CPD for a text feature f_j by taking a ratio that considers the number of sentences in subjective category c_k in which the text feature occurs and the number of sentences in objective category c_k^- in which the text f_j also occurs. Equation 7 shows the details. Certain threshold of CPD score is kept to reduce the number of features.

$$CPD(f_j, c_k) = \frac{P(f_j, c_k) - P(f_j, c_k^-)}{P(f_j, c_k) + P(f_j, c_k^-)} \tag{7}$$

3.3 Contingency Table Representation of features

Feature selection methods mentioned in earlier section is estimated using a contingency table. Let A, be the number of sentences in the subjective category containing feature f_j. B, be the number of sentences in the objective category containing f_j. C, be the number of sentences of subjective category which do not contain feature f_j given by f_j^- and D, be the number of sentences in objective category c_k^- which do not contain f_j. Let ($M = A + B + C + D$) be the total possibilities. Table 1 represents the above mentioned details. Using the Table 1 each of the feature selection methods can be estimated. Table 2 show the details.

	Subjective	Objective
f_j	A	B
f_j^-	C	D

Table 1: Contingency Table

FS	Representation
$IG(f_j, c_k)$	$-\frac{A+C}{M}log(\frac{A+C}{M})+ \frac{A}{M}log(\frac{A}{A+B}) + \frac{C}{M}log(\frac{C}{C+D})$
$\chi^2(f_j, c_k)$	$\frac{M(A*D-B*C)^2}{(A+B)*(A+C)*(B+D)*(C+D)}$
$OR(f_j, c_k)$	$\frac{D*A}{C*B}$
$CPD(f_j, c_k)$	$\frac{A-B}{A+B}$
$ECCD(f_j, c_k)$	$\frac{(A*D-B*C)*Ent_m-Ent(f_j)}{(A+C)*(B+D)*Ent_m}$

Table 2: Estimation Table

4 Experimental Setup

In-order to achieve subjective and objective classification at sentence level for different languages. We performed our experiments using different datasets.

4.1 Datasets

Translated MPQA corpus provided in (C. Banea.et.al, 2010) containing subjective and objective sentences[1] of French, Arabic, and Romanian languages were used for experiments. For English, MPQA corpus[2] containing subjective and objective sentences used for translation of above mentioned corpus is used. Hindi experiments were performed using sentences from the news corpus (A. Mogadala.et.al, 2012) tagged with positive, negative and objective sentences. Positive and negative sentences are further clubbed into subjective sentences to do subjectivity analysis.

4.2 Evaluation

To evaluate various feature selection methods, we use F-measure scores which combines precision and recall. Precision (P_s) measures the percentage of sentences correctly assigned to subjective category, and recall (R_s) measures the percentage of sentences that should have been assigned to subjective category but actually assigned to subjective category. Using P_s and R_s subjective F-measure F_s is calculated. Similarly, Objective F-measure F_o is calculated using P_o and R_o. After F-measure is determined for both subjective and objective class, the macro-average F-measure $F_{macro-avg}$ is determined by the following Equation 8.

$$F_{macro-avg} = \frac{\Sigma_{i=o,s} F_i}{2} \quad (8)$$

[1]http://lit.csci.unt.edu/index.php/Downloads

[2]http://www.cs.pitt.edu/mpqa

5 Experiments

Initially, 1500 subjective and 1500 objective sentences of English, Romanian, French and Arabic languages are used to perform the experiments. While for Hindi, entire corpus constituting 786 subjective and 519 objective sentences was used. Different feature weighing and selection methods are evaluated with 2 different classifiers to obtain best combination for each language. Table 8 to Table 12 show the Macro-Average ($F_{macro-avg}$) scores obtained after 10 cross-validation using sequential minimal optimization algorithm (J. Platt, 1998) for training a support vector machine(SVM) using polynomial kernel and Naive Bayes Multinomial(NBM) classifiers. Feature space obtained after application of feature selection methods for each language are mentioned in Tables 3, 4, 5, 6, 7.

Once the best combination is obtained for each language. It is compared with multilingual space classifier proposed in (C. Banea.et.al, 2010)[3] along with the baseline constituting simple Naive Bayes classifier with unigram features. Multilingual space constitutes words as features from all languages used for experiments except Hindi.

Scalability of feature selection methods is an issue. In-order to understand the performance of ECCD feature selection method with classifiers. In every iteration 500 sentences are added to each class of initial 1500 subjective and objective sentences limiting to maximum of 3500 to get average scores. Table 13 show the comparison of average scores obtained for each language. Figures 1, 2, 3, 4 show precision and recall for subjective sentences obtained using different methods for English, Romanian, French and Arabic respectively using different number of sentences.

[3]Note that paper used the entire dataset which had unequal subjective and objective sentences. We used equal number of subjective and objective sentences taken each time from dataset. So, experiments using this method are again performed on our dataset.

[SVM]

Feature Selection	UF.ISF	BF.ISF	NUWL
None	0.705	0.660	0.705
CFS	0.710	0.670	0.705
IG,OR,χ^2	0.680	0.665	0.685
CPD	**0.840**	0.805	0.835
ECCD	0.830	0.805	0.830

[NBM]

Feature Selection	UF.ISF	BF.ISF	NUWL
None	0.745	0.690	0.740
CFS	0.730	0.685	0.725
IG,OR,χ^2	0.735	0.690	0.730
CPD	0.855	**0.925**	0.890
ECCD	0.850	**0.925**	0.875

Table 8: $F_{macro-avg}$ - English

[SVM]

Feature Selection	UF.ISF	BF.ISF	NUWL
None	0.685	0.665	0.680
CFS	0.715	0.675	0.695
IG,OR,χ^2	0.695	0.635	0.690
CPD	0.845	0.815	**0.850**
ECCD	0.845	0.815	0.845

[NBM]

Feature Selection	UF.ISF	BF.ISF	NUWL
None	0.740	0.685	0.730
CFS	0.735	0.690	0.740
IG,OR,χ^2	0.745	0.685	0.725
CPD	0.865	0.935	0.890
ECCD	0.865	**0.940**	0.885

Table 9: $F_{macro-avg}$ - Romanian

[SVM]

Feature Selection	UF.ISF	BF.ISF	NUWL
None	0.695	0.685	0.685
CFS	0.710	0.695	0.685
IG,OR,χ^2	0.690	0.685	0.685
CPD	**0.855**	0.825	0.850
ECCD	0.845	0.820	0.835

[NBM]

Feature Selection	UF.ISF	BF.ISF	NUWL
None	0.730	0.705	0.725
CFS	0.730	0.710	0.725
IG,OR,χ^2	0.725	0.690	0.710
CPD	0.860	0.940	0.900
ECCD	0.845	**0.950**	0.885

Table 10: $F_{macro-avg}$ - French

[SVM]

Feature Selection	UF.ISF	BF.ISF	NUWL
None	0.670	0.660	0.675
CFS	0.710	0.665	0.680
IG,OR,χ^2	0.665	0.645	0.660
CPD	0.855	0.825	0.850
ECCD	0.850	0.830	**0.860**

[NBM]

Feature Selection	UF.ISF	BF.ISF	NUWL
None	0.720	0.690	0.710
CFS	0.730	0.695	0.725
IG,OR,χ^2	0.720	0.690	0.710
CPD	0.910	**0.915**	0.910
ECCD	**0.915**	**0.915**	**0.915**

Table 11: $F_{macro-avg}$ - Arabic

[SVM]

Feature Selection	UF.ISF	BF.ISF	NUWL
None	0.665	0.655	0.650
CFS	0.635	0.655	0.600
IG,OR,χ^2	0.665	0.660	0.650
CPD	0.760	**0.845**	0.755
ECCD	0.735	**0.845**	0.735

[NBM]

Feature Selection	UF.ISF	BF.ISF	NUWL
None	0.615	0.655	0.635
CFS	0.460	0.440	0.460
IG,OR,χ^2	0.580	0.655	0.605
CPD	0.590	0.845	0.660
ECCD	0.555	**0.850**	0.655

Table 12: $F_{macro-avg}$ - Hindi

6 Result Analysis

It is observed from the Table 8 to Table 12 that ECCD feature selection and BF.ISF feature weighing method with NBM classifier performs consistently across languages. This behavior is observed due to capability of ECCD in efficiently discrimi-

Language	(Method)	P_s	R_s	F_s	P_o	R_o	F_o	$P_{macro-avg}$	$R_{macro-avg}$	$F_{macro-avg}$
English	Baseline	0.720	0.830	0.770	0.800	0.676	0.733	0.760	0.753	0.751
	NBM + BF.ISF + ECCD	**1.000**	0.865	**0.925**	**0.875**	**1.000**	**0.935**	**0.937**	**0.932**	**0.930**
	NB + MultiLingual Space (Banea,2010)	0.497	**0.927**	0.644	0.350	0.057	0.087	0.423	0.491	0.365
	Wiebe & Riloff (Wiebe and Riloff, 2005)	0.904	0.342	0.466	0.824	0.307	0.447	0.867	0.326	0.474
	Chenghua Lin (C. Lin.et.al, 2011)	0.710	0.809	0.756	0.716	0.597	0.651	0.713	0.703	0.703
Romanian	Baseline	0.713	0.830	0.766	0.796	0.663	0.723	0.755	0.746	0.745
	NBM + BF.ISF + ECCD	**1.000**	0.880	**0.940**	**0.890**	**1.000**	**0.940**	**0.945**	**0.940**	**0.940**
	NB + MultiLingual Space (Banea, 2010)	0.497	**0.913**	0.640	0.383	0.063	0.096	0.440	0.488	0.368
French	Baseline	0.703	0.826	0.760	0.790	0.643	0.713	0.746	0.736	0.736
	NBM + BF.ISF + ECCD	**1.000**	0.905	**0.950**	**0.915**	**1.000**	**0.955**	**0.957**	**0.952**	**0.952**
	NB + MultiLingual Space (Banea,2010)	0.490	**0.913**	0.636	0.370	0.056	0.096	0.430	0.485	0.366
Arabic	Baseline	0.703	0.800	0.750	0.770	0.666	0.713	0.736	0.733	0.731
	NBM + BF.ISF + ECCD	**1.000**	0.845	**0.915**	**0.865**	**1.000**	**0.925**	**0.932**	**0.922**	**0.920**
	NB + MultiLingual Space (Banea,2010)	0.497	**0.983**	0.656	0.293	0.006	0.016	0.353	0.495	0.336
Hindi	Baseline	0.680	0.900	0.770	0.690	0.350	0.460	0.685	0.625	0.615
	NBM + BF.ISF + ECCD	**0.810**	**1.000**	**0.900**	**1.000**	**0.650**	**0.790**	**0.905**	**0.825**	**0.850**

Table 13: Comparison of Average scores between proposed and other approaches

Feature Selection	Unigrams (UF.ISF,NUWL)	Bigrams (BF.ISF)
None	100.0	100.0
CFS	1.8	8.4
IG,OR,χ^2	60.0	60.0
CPD	66.2	90.0
ECCD	65.7	90.0

Table 3: Feature Space Used(%) - English

Feature Selection	Unigrams (UF.ISF,NUWL)	Bigrams (BF.ISF)
None	100.0	100.0
CFS	1.7	7.2
IG,OR,χ^2	60.0	60.0
CPD	65.5	90.1
ECCD	65.0	90.0

Table 4: Feature Space Used(%) - Romanian

Feature Selection	Unigrams (UF.ISF,NUWL)	Bigrams (BF.ISF)
None	100.0	100.0
CFS	1.4	5.7
IG,OR,χ^2	60.0	60.0
CPD	68.5	88.6
ECCD	68.0	88.5

Table 5: Feature Space Used(%) - French

Feature Selection	Unigrams (UF.ISF,NUWL)	Bigrams (BF.ISF)
None	100.0	100.0
CFS	1.2	3.9
IG,OR,χ^2	60.0	60.0
CPD	71.8	92.3
ECCD	71.4	92.2

Table 6: Feature Space Used(%) - Arabic

Feature Selection	Unigrams (UF.ISF,NUWL)	Bigrams (BF.ISF)
None	100.0	100.0
CFS	2.3	0.7
IG,OR,χ^2	60.0	60.0
CPD	58.1	81.1
ECCD	57.4	80.9

Table 7: Feature Space Used(%) - Hindi

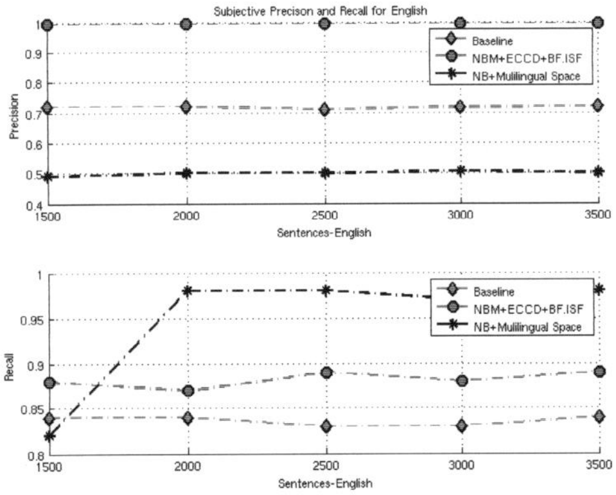

Figure 1: Subjective Precision and Recall (English)

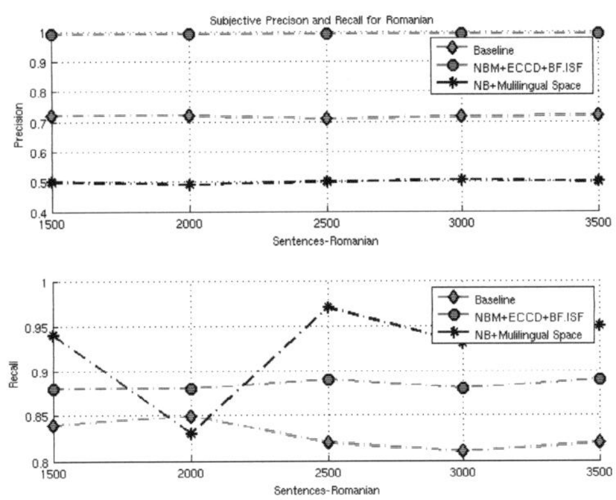

Figure 2: Subjective Precision and Recall (Romanian)

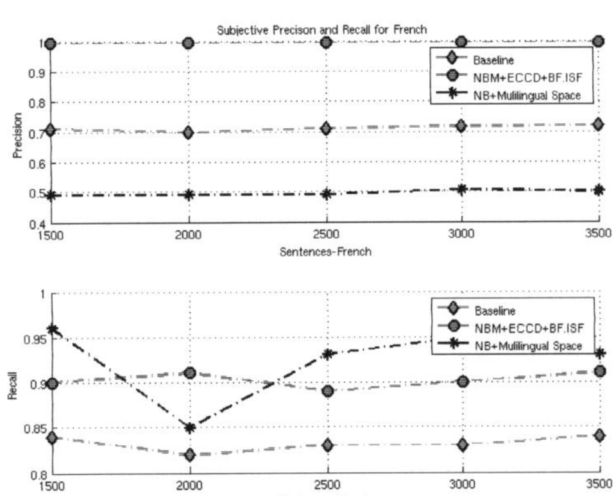

Figure 3: Subjective Precision and Recall (French)

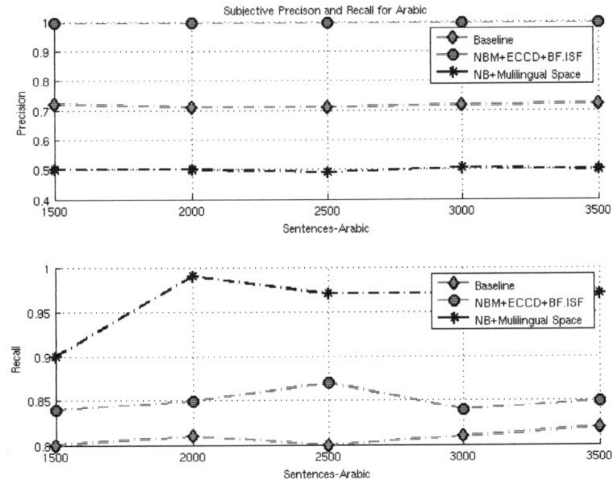

Figure 4: Subjective Precision and Recall (Arabic)

nating the features belonging to a particular class. Although, UF.ISF and NUWL with ECCD and CPD using SVM classifier has more scores than BF.ISF, it is not significantly contrasting with the results of NBM classifier. So, NBM classifier with ECCD feature selection and BF.ISF feature weighing method which obtained high $F_{macro-avg}$ scores is selected for comparison with other approaches in Table 13. The proposed method not only outperforms on $F_{macro-avg}$ compared to other approaches but also on $P_{macro-avg}$ and $R_{macro-avg}$ in all languages.

For English, proposed methods gains 23.8% over baseline in $F_{macro-avg}$ and 8.0% on $P_{macro-avg}$ on (Wiebe and Riloff, 2005). Similarly, from Table 13 it can be deducted that proposed method for Romanian attains 26.1% more $F_{macro-avg}$ than baseline and 155.4% more compared to Multilingual space classifier (C. Banea.et.al, 2010). Similar observations can be made for other languages. Even though (C. Banea.et.al, 2010) attains high recall for every language. It fails to attain high precision due to presence of large number of frivolous word features which are common for both classes. This being major drawback, ECCD feature selection method eliminates features which attains zero entropy. This reduces the randomness of features and leave only those features which are more eligible for discriminating the classes. Combining ECCD with BF.ISF, a language independent weighing method for Bi-gram features extracted from the sentences. We are able to attain a best classification accuracies which are consistent across languages.

Figures 1, 2, 3, 4 also show that increase in number of sentences does not effect the precision of the proposed method, as it still outperforms other methods. But, scalability problem persists for ECCD with BF.ISF for larger datasets, as it may not eliminate less random features due to noise and other constraints. Also, feature selection methods ensure the performance of classifiers is maintained by reducing number of features. But, it does not ensure reduction in fixed percentage of features. As observed our best performing feature selection method ECCD reduces feature size by 10% only.

7 Performance Analysis between SVM and NBM

From the Table 8 to 12 it is observed that SVM with some feature selection and weighing methods performs equivalent to the NBM. However, as the number of documents increases the performance of SVM may degrade. It can be derived that, as the training data size increases, it is rare to see SVM performing better than NBM.

7.1 Training Time behavior

SVM is in a clear disadvantage compared to NBM when processing time is considered. The training time of the SVM is particularly high, especially for larger feature spaces. It is probably attributed to the time taken in finding the proper separating hyperplane.

7.2 Features behavior

Large feature spaces do not necessarily lead to best performance. So feature selection methods are used to create small feature spaces to build SVM and NBM classifiers. Sometimes, small feature space sizes make SVM perform equivalent to NBM as observed in Table 12. Thus, this would explain why SVM is outperformed for small training set sizes and for small feature spaces with large training sets.

8 Conclusion and Future Work

In this paper, subjective classification is achieved using combination of feature selection and weighing methods which are consistent across languages. We found that our proposed method which combines ECCD feature selection and BF.ISF feature weighing method used along with NBM classifier perform across languages. It not only outperforms other feature selection methods but also achieve better scores compared to other approaches. In future, we want to apply this approach on bigger datasets and also extend it to multiple class problems.

References

M. Hu and B. Liu. 2004. *Mining opinion features in customer reviews.* Proceedings of the National Conference on Artificial Intelligence, 755–760.

K. Ganesan, C.X. Zhai and J. Han. 2010. *Opinosis: a graph-based approach to abstractive summarization of highly redundant opinions.* Proceedings of the 23rd International Conference on Computational Linguistics, 340–348.

A. Balahur and E. Boldrini and A. Montoyo and P. Martínez-Barco. 2009. *Opinion and Generic Question Answering systems: a performance analysis.* Proceedings of the ACL-IJCNLP 2009 Conference Short Papers, 157–160.

J. Wiebe and E. Riloff. 2005. *Creating subjective and objective sentence classifiers from unannotated texts.* Computational Linguistics and Intelligent Text Processing, 486–497, Springer.

R. Mihalcea, C. Banea and J. Wiebe. 2007. *Learning multilingual subjective language via cross-lingual projections.* ANNUAL MEETING-ASSOCIATION FOR COMPUTATIONAL LINGUISTICS , Volume 45, 976.

C. Banea, R. Mihalcea, J. Wiebe and S. Hassan. 2008. *Multilingual subjectivity analysis using machine translation.* Proceedings of the Conference on Empirical Methods in Natural Language Processing, 127–135, ACL.

C. Banea, R. Mihalcea and J. Wiebe. 2010. *Multilingual subjectivity: are more languages better.* Proceedings of the 23rd International Conference on Computational Linguistics, 28–36, ACL.

G. Murray and G. Carenini. 2009. *Predicting subjectivity in multimodal conversations.* Proceedings of Empirical Methods in Natural Language Processing: Volume 3, 1348–1357, ACL.

T. Wilson and S. Raaijmakers. 2008. *Comparing word, character, and phoneme n-grams for subjective utterance recognition.* Ninth Annual Conference of the International Speech Communication Association.

C. Lin, Y. He and R. Everson. 2011. *Sentence subjectivity detection with weakly-supervised learning.* Proceedings of International Joint Conference on Natural Language Processing (IJCNLP), Volume 2, 2.

H. Kanayama and T. Nasukawa. 2006. *Fully automatic lexicon expansion for domain-oriented sentiment analysis.* Proceedings of the 2006 Conference on Empirical Methods in Natural Language Processing, 355–363, ACL.

T. Zagibalov and J. Carroll. 2008. *Unsupervised classification of sentiment and objectivity in Chinese text.* IJCNLP, 304–311.

Y. Wu and D.W. Oard. 2007. *NTCIR-6 at Maryland: Chinese opinion analysis pilot task.* Proceedings of the 6th NTCIR Workshop on Evaluation of Information Access Technologies.

M. Bautin, L. Vijayarenu and S. Skiena. 2008. *International sentiment analysis for news and blogs.* Proceedings of the International Conference on Weblogs and Social Media (ICWSM).

X. Wan. 2009. *Co-training for cross-lingual sentiment classification.* Proceedings of the Joint Conference of the 47th Annual Meeting of the ACL and the 4th International Joint Conference on Natural Language Processing of the AFNLP: Volume 1-Volume 1, 235–243, ACL.

G. Forman. 2003. *An extensive empirical study of feature selection metrics for text classification.* The Journal of Machine Learning Research, Volume 3, 1289–1305.

M. Gamon. 2004. *Sentiment classification on customer feedback data: noisy data, large feature vectors, and the role of linguistic analysis.* Proceedings of the 20th international conference on Computational Linguistics, 841, ACL.

G. Salton, A. Wong and C.S. Yang. 1975. *A vector space model for automatic indexing.* Communications of the ACM, Volume 18, 613–620.

A. Abbasi, H. Chen and A. Salem. 2008. *Sentiment analysis in multiple languages: Feature selection for opinion classification in Web forums.* ACM Transactions on Information Systems (TOIS), Volume 26, 12, ACM.

C. Largeron, C. Moulin and M. Géry. 2011. *Entropy based feature selection for text categorization.* Proceedings of ACM Symposium on Applied Computing, 924–928, ACM.

M.A. Hall. 1999. *Correlation-based feature selection for machine learning.* Phd Thesis, The University of Waikato.

C. Lee and G.G. Lee. 2006. *Information gain and divergence-based feature selection for machine learning-based text categorization.* Information processing & management, Volume 42, 155–165, Elsevier.

J. Bakus and M.S. Kamel. 2006. *Higher order feature selection for text classification.* Knowledge and Information Systems, Volume 9, 468–491, Springer.

M. Simeon and R. Hilderman. 2008. *Categorical proportional difference: A feature selection method for text categorization.* Proceedings of the Seventh Australasian Data Mining Conference (AusDM), Volume 87, 201–208.

A. Mogadala and V. Varma. 2012. *Retrieval approach to extract opinions about people from resource scarce language News articles.* Proceedings of the First International Workshop on Issues of Sentiment Discovery and Opinion Mining (WISDOM), ACM KDD.

J. Platt. 1998. *Fast Training of Support Vector Machines using Sequential Minimal Optimization. Advances in Kernel Methods - Support Vector Learning.* B. Schoelkopf, C. Burges, and A. Smola, eds., MIT Press.

Annotation Scheme for Constructing Sentiment Corpus in Korean

Hyopil Shin, Munhyong Kim, Yu-Mi Jo, Hayeon Jang, and Andrew Cattle

[a]Department of Linguistics, Seoul National University
1 Gwanak-no Gwanak-gu, Seoul 151-741
{hpshin, likerainsun, jmocy84, hyan05, acattle}@snu.ac.kr

Abstract

This paper describes the first year of work constructing the Korean Sentiment Corpus, focusing on the theoretical background such as the annotation scheme. Our aim is to provide a solid theoretical background for the corpus which reflects the characteristics of the Korean language and includes approximately 8,050 sentences taken from news articles. The corpus annotation scheme, based on the MPQA, is described along with the results of inter-annotator agreement tests with a view to improving the annotation scheme.

1 Introduction

There has been much research on the automatic identification and extraction of sentiments and opinions in text. Researchers have been working on these issues by focusing mainly on subjectivity and sentiment classification either at the document or sentence level. Classifying editorials or movie reviews as positive or negative are examples of a document classification tasks while classifying individual sentences as subjective or objective would be an example of a sentence-level task (Wiebe et al., 2005).

Along with these lines of research, a need for corpora annotated with rich information about opinions and emotions has also emerged. This would allow for the development of statistical and machine learning approaches for various practical NLP applications. As such a resource, the Multiperspective Question Answering (MPQA) Opinion Corpus, developed by Wiebe (2002), Wiebe et al. (2005), and Wilson et al. (2008), plays an important role in sentiment and opinion analysis. It contains the manual annotation of a 10,000 sentence-corpus of articles from the world press. Since this corpus provides a fine-grained annotation scheme, it is widely used as a source for training data in machine learning approaches and serves as the gold standard in sentiment classification tests.

We started constructing a cross-language sentiment corpus, called the Korean Sentiment Corpus. We received two years of support in this project by the Korean Research Foundation (KRF) for two years. We aim to provide both a solid theoretical background for the Corpus, reflecting the characteristics of the Korean language, as well as fine-grained annotations for the 8,050 sentence-corpus of news articles. The total number of annotated sentences is less than that of the MPQA, but since our annotation is morpheme-based due to the agglutinative nature of Korean, the number of annotation units is much greater. We have also adopted the basic annotation scheme of the MPQA for comparative research purposes.

This paper describes the first year of work constructing the Korean Sentiment Corpus, focusing on the theoretical background such as the annotation scheme. Inter-annotator agreement tests were performed to improve annotation quality. The remainder of this paper is organized as follows. Section 2 gives a brief overview of the MPQA corpus as a starting point. Section 3 elaborates on the annotation scheme for the Korean sentiment corpus, providing examples of annotations with attributes. Section 4 shows observations on the inter-annotator agreements. Section 5 presents future work and conclusions.

2 The MPQA Corpus

As a fundamental resource for sentiment corpus construction in Korean, this work takes advantage of the Multiperspective Question Answering (MPQA) Opinion Corpus which began with the conceptual structure for private states in Wiebe (2002) and developed manual annotation instructions. The MPQA Corpus version 1.0 was released in 2003, and now version 2.0 is available with more detailed attitude annotations. In this section we briefly review the annotation scheme and structures of the corpus with a view to providing a theoretical background.

2.1 Private States

According to Quirk et al. (1985), a private state refers to mental and emotional states such as the opinions, beliefs, and intentions of a writer. Wiebe et al. (2005) focused on identifying private state expressions in contexts and presented numerous examples annotated with schemes that cover a broad range of linguistic expressions and phenomena.

Private states and speech events are the core of the MPQA corpus. Private states cover *opinions*, *beliefs*, *thoughts*, *feelings*, *emotions*, *goals evaluations*, and *judgments* (Wiebe et al. 2005). Private state frames cover expressive subjective element frames, which are used to represent expressive subjective elements, as well as direct subjective element frames, which are used to represent subjective speech events. In order to distinguish opinion-oriented material from fact, objective speech event frames are also defined in terms of speech events. Private state frames have the following attributes directly excerpted from Wiebe et al. (2005)

Direct subjective frame:

- text anchor: a pointer to the span of text that represents the speech event or explicit mention of a private state
- source: the person or entity that is expressing the private state, possibly the writer
- target: what the speech event or private state is about
- properties
  - intensity: the intensity of the private state (low, medium, high, or extreme)
  - expression intensity: the contribution of the speech event or private state expression itself to the overall intensity of the private state (neutral, low, medium, high, or extreme)
  - insubstantial: true, if the private state is not substantial in the discourse
  - attitude type: represents the polarity of the private state. The possible values are positive, negative, other, or none

Expressive subjective element frame:

- text anchor
- source
- properties
  - intensity
  - attitude type

2.2 Objective Speech Event

Objective speech event in the MPQA is used to distinguish opinion-oriented material from material presented as factual and has the following frames.

Objective speech event frame:

- text anchor
- source
- target

Unlike the MPQA, we do not distinguish direct subjective frames from expressive subjective elements. Rather, those two frames are merged into SEED subjective expressions in our approach.

2.3 Nested Sources

In sentiment analysis, it is very useful to recognize the person whose opinion or emotion is being expressed. Thus source is introduced in the MPQA. The source of a speech event is implicitly the speaker or the writer while the source of a private state is the experiencer. However, there are situations where speech events and private states are assessed by more than one source. In this case, an additional explicit source was introduced. This source generally corresponded to the subject of the embedded predicate. This is a so-called nested source, as adopted by Wiebe et al. (2005), Wilson (2008), and Sauri (2008). Nested sources include other people's speech events and private states as well as speaker's. Please look the following examples adopted from Wiebe et al. (2005: 9):

(1) a. Sue said, "The election was fair."
b. Sue thinks that the election was fair.
c. Sue is afraid to go outside.

In the above sentences, Sue is the source of speech event (1a) and of private states (1b, 1c). However, we do not know what Sue says, thinks, or feels directly. We only know Sue's speech event according to the writer. In the MPQA Corpus, such a nested source would be represented as *<writer, Sue>*. Private states can be directed toward the private states of others. Consider Wiebe et al. (2005)'s example:

(2) "The U.S. fears a spill-over," said Xirao-Nima.

In (2), it is not *the U.S.* that directly states its fear. Rather, according to the writer, the *Xirao-Nima* states that the U.S. fears a spill-over. Thus the nested source of the fear can be expressed as *<writer, Xirao-Nima, U.S>*.

3 Outline of Annotation Scheme for Korean Sentiment Corpus

Our work essentially follows the idea of the MPQA, but we have also modified the existing MPQA attributes as well as introduced new attributes to address the characteristics of Korean.

The annotation scheme starts with distinguishing a SEED from a whole sentence in terms of subjectivity. In a SEED, each individual unit expresses a private state. By contrast, the subjectivity of the whole sentence is about whether we feel the sentence is objectively true or not in terms of the speech event. Even though a sentence bears many subjective expressions in it, the sentence can carry objective facts. Thus our annotation principle separates basic subjective expressions from subjectivity of a whole sentence. That is, unlike the MPQA, we explicitly annotate subjectivity or objectivity of the sentence. This principle can be illustrated as follows.

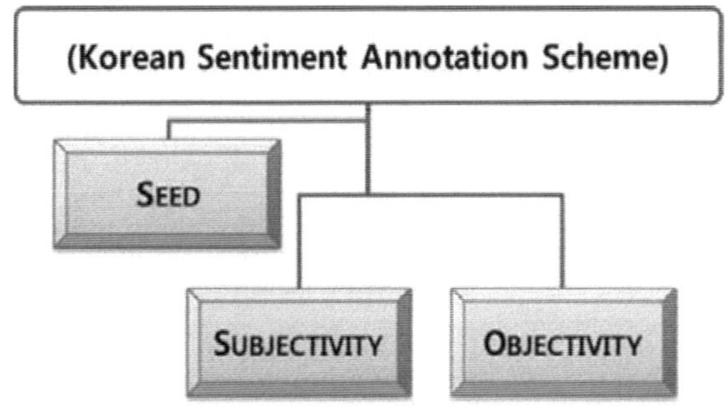

Figure 1. Korean Sentiment Annotation Scheme

As a basic annotation unit, we chose a morpheme rather than a word. Korean is an agglutinative language and many meaning-bearing particles and sentence endings can carry private states, therefore we need to be able to pinpoint these precise segments as a basic unit. Although such morpheme-based annotation helps to produce a fine-grained corpus, the trade-off is that it also requires a great deal of time and effort spent on annotating.

3.1 SEED

The elements of SEED are as follows:

- anchor: morpheme id(s)
- id: tag id
- expressive type: direct-explicit, direct-speech, direct-action, indirect, writing-device
- subjectivity type: emotion-pos, emotion-neg, emotion-neutral, emotion-complex, judgment-pos, judgment-neg, judgment-neutral, agreement-pos, agreement-neg, agreement-neutral, argument-pos, argument-neg, argument-neutral, intention-pos, intention-neg, speculation-pos, speculation-neg, others
- nested-source: w-sources
- target: target id(s)
- polarity: positive, negative, neutral, complex
- intensity: low, medium, high
- insubstantial: TRUE, FALSE

According to Wiebe et al. (2005: 4) private states are states of *experiencers* holding *attitudes*, optionally toward *targets*. For example, in the sentence *John hates Mary*, the experiencer is *John*, the attitude is *hate*, and the target is *Mary*. Thus, in order to annotate subjective expressions, all three attributes of the private state should be properly represented. In the MPQA, the following three main types of private states expressions were included: explicit mentions of private states, speech events expressing private states, and expressive subjective elements. Expressive subjective elements, speech events, and attitudes of a private state in the MPQA, roughly correspond to SEED, expressive type, and subjectivity type in our scheme.

3.1.1 Expressive Types

Express types specify either speech events (acts) that express private states (or other subjective elements) or non-speech events. These fit into five subtypes: *direct-explicit*, *direct-speech*, *direct-action*, *indirect*, and *writing-device*. While the former three types are related to speech events and usually originate from subject-predicate relations, *indirect* and *writing-device* are used for a writer to show his/her own subjectivity through non-predicate expressions. These include using a nominal as an argument, adverbials, conjunctive endings, or some particles in Korean. *Indirect* and *writing device* are common in that subjectivity is not carried through speech event. In the case of *indirect*, the source of the expression is not clear compared to *direct* or *writing device*. The following is some examples of each expression type.

- explicit: cikyepta 'boring' inkita 'be popular'
- direct speech: cwucanghata 'insist,' pinanhata 'blame,'
- direct action: elkwulsayki pyenhata 'turn pale,' hwanhohata, 'acclaim'
- indirect: isanghan salam 'strange people,' huylluynghi 'greatly'
- writing-device: -man 'only,' isanghakeyto 'strangely'

3.1.2 Subjectivity Types

The attribute subjectivity type is used to classify subjective expressions according to their sources' attitudes; lexically determined as the core meaning of subjective expression. It consists of the following subtypes: *emotion, judgment, agreement, argument, intention*, and *speculation*. These types can be further combined with other polarity attributes such as *positive, negative, neutral* and *complex* according to their semantic orientations which may lead to complex attributes such as *emotion-positive*, *emotion-negative*, and so on. Generally, a *complex* attribute is due to a combination of positive and negative words, such as in the Chinese character expression '幸不幸,' 'happiness and unhappiness'. The MPQA does not provide this kind of detailed classification. Considering our previous sentiment research, we think that classifying subjectivity into more refined types provides the benefits not just when determining whether a document is subjective but also when determining what kind of attitude the document contains. The subjectivity types are exemplified as follows:

Type	Values	Examples
emotion	emotion-positive	*kipputa* 'glad,' *misolul cista* 'make a smile'
	emotion-negative	*mwusepta* 'afraid,' *kothongsulepta* 'feel pain'
	emotion-neutral	*kamtong-i epsta* 'not touching'
	emotion-complex	*hayngpwulhayng* 'happiness and unhappiness'
judgment	judgment-positive	*yongkamhata* 'be brave,' *cangcem* 'merit'
	judgment-negative	*napputa* 'bad,' *kepcayngi* 'a coward'
	judgment-neutral	*aymayhata* 'vague,' *cal molukessta* 'don't know well'
agreement	agreement-positive	*tonguyhata* 'agree,' *yongnaphata* 'accept'
	agreement-negative	*pantayhata* 'do not agree,' *kikak* 'rejection'
	agreement-neutral	*kikwenhata* 'give up,' *cwunglip* 'be in the middle'
argument	argument-positive	*cungmyenghata* 'verify,' *seltukhata* 'persuade'
	argument-negative	*panpakhata* 'refute,' *kecisita* 'not true'
	argument-neutral	*cham kecis-ul kwupwunhal swu epsta* 'can't know if it is true or not

Intention	intention-positive	*uytohata* 'intend,' *kyelsimhata* 'make one's mind'
	intention-negative	*~hal maum-i epsta* '~not willing to,' *wuyenhi* 'accidentally'
speculation	speculation-positive	*chwuchukhata* 'speculate,' *somang* 'wish'
	speculation-negative	*epsta* 'there is not'

Table 1. Subjectivity types

3.1.3 Targets

Attribute targets are used to specify objects or themes to which the subjective expressions are directed. In many cases targets can be clearly specified but in some cases pinpointing source and target is not that simple. The following is a complicated example of target which requires an embedded clause as target.

(3) Mary-nun ku-wa hamkkey issnun
Mary-subj he-with together be-adnom
kes-i koylowessta
that-sub feel uncomfortable-past
"That he was with Mary made her feel uncomfortable

The target of *koylowessta* 'be hard' is not *ku* 'he' but an embedded clause which has a meaning of 'the fact that he was with Mary'. Next, due to the possibility of double subjects in Korean, some expressions can have more than two targets.

(4) Sakwa-ka pwumcil-i cohta.
apple-subj quality-subj good
"The apple has a good quality"

3.1.4 Nested Sources

Since source information is crucial to sentiment analysis, the MPQA elaborates on sources and nested sources in annotations. As described in 2.3, nested sources include other people's speech events or private states as well as those of the speaker or writer. Table 2 shows some examples of nested sources. Here, underlining means a subjective expression and bold face means a nested source.

Following the MPQA, we specify nested sources from left to right. That is, *<w-Tom-Mary>* means that writer states Mary's speech event through Tom's eye. *<w,>* and *<w-implicit>* represent generic sources and implicitly specified sources, respectively. In (f), we can guess the source of 'be popular' from the context. Meanwhile, general population is the source of the belief 'good' in (e).

3.1.5 Polarity, Intensity, and Insubstantial

The attribute polarity describes whether the (nested) source has an positive or negative subjectivity toward the target. An example of a positive value would be *coh-(ta)* 'good/well' while an example of a negative value would be *nappu-(ta)* 'bad'. In addition, there are two more values: neutral and complex. The value of attribute intensity depends on how intensely subjectivity is expressed. For example, (*i chayk-un*) ***kucekuleh**-ta* '(this book is) so-so' shows a neutral intensity while (*i chayk-un*) ***ssuleki**-ta* '(this book is) trash' shows a highly intense negative subjectivity. Similarly, intensity modifiers, e.g. *maywu* 'very,' *sangtanghi* 'considerably,' or *nemwu* 'too (bad),' can also affect the intensity of an expression. The attribute insubstantial specifies whether a subjective expressions carry actual or imaginary events such that a value of TRUE denotes that the event actually happened while FALSE denotes an intended event. The following illustrates a SEED annotation:

Manh$_0$-un$_1$ sayongca$_2$-tul$_3$-i$_4$ i$_5$ ceypwum$_6$-ul$_7$ cohaha$_8$-ko$_9$ iss$_{10}$-ta$_{11\cdot 12}$
Many$_0$-ADNOMINAL$_1$ user$_2$-PLURAL$_3$-NOM$_4$ this$_5$ product$_6$-ACC$_7$ like$_8$-DURATIVE$_{9,10}$-DECL$_{11\cdot 12}$
'Many users like this product'
<SEED> anchor= "8" id= "u1" type= "direct-explicit" subjectivity-type= "emotion-pos" nested-source= "w-manhun sayongcatul" target= "5-6" polarity= "positive" intensity= "medium" insubstantial= "FALSE" </SEED>

Types	Example	Values
a. Source = writer	Kwail-un sakwa-ka ceilita 'fruit'-topic apple-subj best-be As for fruit, apple is best	W
b. Source=writer According to = subject Subject=writer	**Na**-to sakwa-lul cohahanta I –too apple-obj like I like an apple too.	w w-I
c. Source=writer According to=subject	**Tom**-un sakwa-lul cohahanta Tom-subj apple-obj like Tom likes an apple	w-Tom
d. Source=writer According to= A According to=B	**Tom**-un **Mary**-ka sakwa-lul cohahanta-ko malhayssta Tom-subj Mary-subj apple-obj like-comp say-past Tom said that Mary likes an apple	w-Tom-Mary
e. Source = unclear, or general population	Cohun kamera-nun pissata 'good' camera-sub expensive Good cameras are expensive	w-general
f. Source=not explicitly specified source in a sentence	Yocum inkki- iss-nun kamera-nun gf-1 ita Now popular-be-adnom camera-subj gf-1 be Now popular camera is gf-1	w-implicit

Table 2 Example of Nested Sources

3.2 Sentence Level Subjectivity

Unlike MPQA, we explicitly specify the whole sentence's subjectivity. Although each sentence consists of various numbers of subjective expressions, we feel that a sentence may be an objective fact rather than subjective. Thus we mark the subjectivity of a whole sentence on the basis of the speech event, i.e. from the writer's perspective. We believe that this can help researchers to extract relevant features for subjectivity from those sentences and to train the corpus to see what makes the sentences subjective or objective. Information on the sentence level subjectivity or objectivity differs from SEED tags as they have relatively simple structures, as follows.

- The BNF of SUBJECTIVITY
  anchor: Morpheme id(s)
  id: s1
  polarity: positive, negative, neutral, complex
  intensity: low, medium, high

The OBJECTIVITY tag consists of only the attributes *anchor* and *id*.

- The BNF of OBJECTIVITY
  anchor: Morpheme id(s)
  id: o1

Examples of SUBJECTIVITY and OBJECTIVITY tags are listed in (5). The subjectivity of objectivity of a sentence can be influenced by SEED tags, but it is not completely dependent on them. In a case of a SEED tag affecting the subjectivity of the whole sentence, usually the original source of the subjectivity indicated by the SEED tag is the writer of sentence. That is, there is no nested-source except the writer: nested-source="w". In (5c), 'was reported as a regrettable event that Yumi bought a house,' the value of nested-source "w-general" represents general population.

(5)
a. Yumi$_0$-ka$_1$ cip$_2$-ey$_3$ ka$_4$-n$_5$ il$_6$-un$_7$ chamulo$_8$ yukamsulep$_9$-ta$_{10\text{-}11}$
Yumi$_0$-NOM$_1$ home$_2$-AT$_3$ go$_4$-ADNOMINAL$_5$ event$_6$-TOP$_7$ truly$_8$ regrettable$_9$-DECL$_{10\text{-}11}$
'It is truly regrettable that Yumi went home'

<SUBJECTIVITY> anchor="0-11" id="s1" polarity="negative" intensity="high" **</SUBJECTIVITY>**
<SEED> anchor="8-9" id="u1" type="direct-explicit" subjectivity-type="judgment-neg" nested-source="w" target="0-6" polarity="negative" intensity="high" insubstantial="FALSE" **</SEED>**

Measure	Recall (A1‖A2)	Recall (A2‖A1)	F-measure	Recall (A2‖A3)	Recall (A3‖A2)	F-measure	Recall (A3‖A1)	Recall (A‖A3)	F-measure
Agreement	0.9	0.29	0.595	0.78	0.83	0.80	0.43	0.92	0.675

Table3. SEED Tag Anchor Agreement

b. Yumi$_{12}$-nun$_{13}$ kkoley$_{14}$ cip$_{15}$-ul$_{16}$ sa$_{17}$-ss$_{18}$-ta$_{19\cdot 20}$
Yumi$_{12}$-TOP$_{13}$ in.a.pathetic.state$_{14}$ home$_{15}$-ACC$_{16}$ buy$_{17}$-PAST$_{18}$-DECL$_{19\cdot 20}$
'Yumi was pathetic but she bought a house'

<SUBJECTIVITY> anchor="12-19" id="s2" polarity="negative" intensity="high" **</SUBJECTIVITY>**
<SEED> anchor="14" id="u1" type="writing-device" subjectivity-type="judgment-neg" nested-source="w" target="12" polarity="negative" intensity="high" insubstantial="FALSE" **</SEED>**

c. Yumi$_{21}$-ka$_{22}$ cip$_{23}$-ul$_{24}$ sa$_{25}$-n$_{26}$ il$_{27}$-un$_{28}$ yukamsulewu$_{29}$-n$_{30}$ saken$_{31}$-ulo$_{32}$ pokotoy$_{33}$-ess$_{34}$-ta$_{35\cdot 36}$
Yumi$_{21}$-NOM$_{22}$ home$_{23}$-ACC$_{24}$ buy$_{25}$-ADNOMINAL$_{26}$ event$_{27}$-TOP$_{28}$ regrettable$_{29}$-ADNOMINAL$_{30}$ event$_{31}$-as$_{32}$ be.reported$_{33}$-PAST$_{34}$-DECL$_{35\cdot 36}$
'It was reported as a regrettable event that Yumi bought a house'

<OBJECTIVITY> anchor="21-36" id="o1" **</OBJECTIVITY>**
<SEED> anchor="29" id="u1" type="indirect" subjectivity-type="judgment-neg" nested-source="w," target="31" polarity="negative" intensity="medium" insubstantial="FALSE" **</SEED>**

4 Inter-Annotator Agreement Tests

4.1 The First Agreement Test

Once we set up our preliminary annotation schemes for the Korean Sentiment Corpus, we had three different annotators (A1, A2, and A3) created sample annotations and then checked the degree of agreement amongst their annotations. After careful investigation of these pilot annotations, we continued changing and developing these schemes.

Let's briefly look at the procedure. The first agreement test focused on three main issues. The first issue was whether annotators would recognize the same subjective expressions as SEED tags. The second and the third issues were whether annotators assigned the same values to the express types and subjectivity-type attributes respectively.

Cohen's Kappa (*k*) is not appropriate for measuring the inter-annotator agreement for SEED tags because it is only applicable to annotators annotating the same set of expressions. Instead, our annotators annotated different expressions, thus, following Wilson (2008), we used F-measure. F-measure is a harmonic mean of recalls from annotation results. When A and B are the set of anchors annotated by annotator *a* and *b*, the recall of *a* with respect to *b* (recall (a||b)) is as below

$$\text{Recall}\,(a||b) = \frac{|A\ matching\ B|}{|A|}$$

The F-measure in turn is the mean of recall (A1||A2) and recall (A2||A1). The SEED tag agreement result is shown in table 3. The result shows that there is a noticeable asymmetry in the recalls between (A1||A2) and (A2||A1). This is because the annotator *A2* created a much larger number of SEED tags compared to *A1*. The overall F-measure was not sufficient to settle on this annotation scheme. This SEED tag agreement could not be improved much since it was a measure of what people recognize as subjective expressions. Annotators are likely to depend on their intuition about subjective expressions.

The agreements between sentence level OBJECTIVITY and SUBJECTVITY values were even worse than the previous SEED tag agreement. There was no consensus amongst annotators on when to give what values for each attribute. For these measures, we used Krippendorff's Alpha [1] (Krippendorff, 1998; 2004)

krippendorff's alpha	A1-A2	A1-A3	A2-A3
Agreement	0.408	0.730	0.132

Table 4. Expressive Type Agreement

[1] $\alpha = 1$ indicates perfect reliability. $\alpha = 0$ indicates the absence of reliability. $\alpha < 0$ indicates disagreements are systematic and exceed what can be expected by chance.

krippendorff's alpha	A1-A2	A1-A3	A2-A3
Agreement	-0.343	-0.397	0.214

Table 5. Subjectivity Type Agreement

As seen in Table 4 and 5, the inter-annotator agreements for SUBJECTIVITY type were significantly different from each other. This indicated not only that all the annotators needed more training on the annotation guidelines, but also that some modification of the attributes and values was necessary.

After the first agreement test, we divided the *sentiment* value of the subjectivity type attribute into *emotion* and *judgment*, as we found the *sentiment* value category was too broad and vague to define all those expressions. Also, a *writing-device* category was added to expressive types Even though the *expressive* category seems to include many different types of subjective expressions, it was hard to make a clear boundary between expressions. Thus, we chose to mark them all as expressive, as we had previously done, except those of *writing-device* type. Beyond these two changes, many vague categories were more precisely defined and thoroughly discussed.

4.2 The Second Agreement Test

Another one-hundred sentences were annotated by the same annotators as the first agreement test. The agreement test results are stated in Table 6.

Despite some degree of disagreement for all types of tags, the overall agreement between annotators showed a marked improvement across all types except SEED tags. As mentioned, we expected that the SEED tag agreement would not increase during this second agreement test. Note how the SEED tag agreement between annotators A1 and A2 did show an increase but that this was canceled out by a decrease in agreement between the other two pairs.

On the other hand, the expressive type and subjectivity type agreements improved significantly. Despite this, we still needed to further refinement for our annotation guidelines. Due to experience gained during these evaluations, detailed instructions about how to annotate *writing-device* type expressions were created Additionally, 'say' type expressions, which were one of the most frequently confusing cases, were discussed in more detail. Furthermore, we were able to reach a consensus on the way SEED tags and targets should be annotated.

5 Future Work and Conclusions

We have begun this project building the Korean Sentiment Corpus. The goal of this first year was to investigate theoretical foundations and to make tools for manual annotations. Regarding theoretical background, we followed the annotation scheme and the framework proposed by the MPQA corpus. The framework of the MPQA is similar to that of Appraisal Theory by Martin (2000) and White (2002). The Appraisal framework is composed of concepts including *Affect, Judgment, Appreciation, Engagement*, and *Amplification*. *Affect, Judgment*, and *Appreciation* represent different types of positive and negative attitudes. According to Wiebe et al. (2005) the similarity between these approaches is that they are both concerned with systematically identifying expressions of opinions and emotions in context.

Nonetheless, the MPQA corpus does not distinguish different types of private states, such as *Affect* and *Judgment*, which can provide useful information in sentiment analysis. On the other hand, the MPQA corpus distinguished different ways that private states may be expressed, i.e. *directly* or *indirectly*.

Our annotation scheme, however, not only covers many types of attitudes as in Appraisal theory but also several expressive types as in the MPQA corpus. Subjectivity types correspond to *Attitude* in Appraisal theory and Expressive types correspond to *direct subjective* or *expressive subjective elements* in the MPQA. We believe that a corpus founded on a comprehensive annotation scheme could be used by researchers as a gold standard for training and testing

Measure	Recall (A1‖A2)	Recall (A2‖A1)	F-measure	Recall (A2‖A3)	Recall (A3‖A2)	F-measure	Recall (A3‖A1)	Recall (A‖A3)	F-measure
Agreement	0.89	0.39	0.64	0.27	0.7	0.46	0.6	0.55	0.58

Table 6. SEED Tag Agreement in the Second Test

krippendorff's alpha	A1-A2	A1-A3	A2-A3
Agreement	0.62	0.50	0.37

Table 7. Expressive Type Agreement

krippendorff's alpha	A1-A2	A1-A3	A2-A3
Agreement	0.57	0.62	0.54

Table 8. Subjectivity Type Agreement

Another important aspect of our work is that, following the MPQA corpus, information on nested sources is incorporated into the annotation scheme. Specifying nested sources can help allow annotated expressions to denote their context below the sentence-level (Wiebe et al. 2005). Furthermore, analyzing nested sources along with speaker's attitudes toward subjectivity allows for a new modality or pragmatics-based methodology for further Sentiment Analysis. We will pursue this approach further after our initial annotation task has been completed.

Along with the elaboration of annotation scheme for the Korean Sentiment Corpus, we also developed annotation tools to aid manual tagging. We created a Graphical User Interface (GUI) which allowed annotators to easily search our corpus of Korean news stories by individual morphemes, by words or by article. Annotators could then select entire sentences or individual morphemes along with specify the desired annotation attributes and automatically generate the appropriate annotation.

This tool utilized the wxPython library to create the GUI while a Python core communicated with a database. This database in turn stored the corpus text, already parsed and separated into morphemes, as well as any annotations an annotator created. This allowed annotators to review and modify previously created tags.

The main goal of the annotation scheme presented in this paper was to support the development of the Korean Sentiment Corpus. We plan to complete the annotation of about 8,750 Korean sentences by April, 2013 after which the corpus will be opened to public for research purposes. We believe that researchers will be able to extract useful information from the corpus and use the data for training and testing in sentiment and opinion analysis.

References

Dan Gusfield. 1997. Algorithms on Strings, Trees and Sequences. Cambridge University Press, Cambridge, UK.

Edward Finergan. 1995. Subjectivity and Subjectification: an Introduction. In D. Stein & S. Wright (Eds.), Subjectivity and Subjectification: Linguistic Perspectives:1-15. Cambridge University Press, Cambridge.

Ellen Riloff, Janyce Wiebe, and William Phillips. 2005. Exploiting Subjectivity Classification to Improve Information Extraction. In Proceedings of the 20th National Conference on Artificial Intelligence (AAAI-2005): 1106-1111.

James Pustejovsky, Patrick Hanks, Roser Sauri, Andrew See, Robert Gaizauskas, Andrea Setzer, Beth Sundheim, Lisa Ferro, Marcia Lazo, Inderjeet Mani, and Dragomir Radev. 2003. The TimeBank corpus. In Proceedings of Corpus Linguistics *2003*: 647-656.

Janyce Wiebe. 2002. Instructions for Annotating Opinions in Newspaper Articles. Department of Computer Science Technical Report TR-02-101, University of Pittsburgh.

Janyce Wiebe, Theresa Wilson, and Claire Cardie. 2005. Annotating Expressions of Opinions and Emotions in Language. Language Resources and Evaluations, 39(2):165-210.

Janyce Wiebe and Ellen Riloff. 2005. Creating Subjective and Objective Sentence Classifiers from Unannotated Texts. In Proceedings of the 6th International Conference on Intelligent Text Processing and Computational Linguistics (CICLing-2005): 486-497.

Krippendorff, Klaus. 1978. Reliability of Binary Attribute Data. *Biometrics*, 34 (1), 142-144.

Krippendorff, Klaus. 2004. Content Analysis: An Introduction to Its Methodology. Thousand Oaks, CA: Sage.

Lauri Karttunen. 1971. Some observations on Factivity. *Papers in Linguistics*, 47:340-358.

MPQA. 2005. Multi-Perspective Question Answering. University of Pittsburgh. http://www.cs.pitt.edu /mpqa/.

Ronald Langacker. 1985. Observations and speculations in subjectivity. In J. Haiman (Ed.*),* Iconicity in Syntax. Typological Studies in Language 6. John Benjamins, Amsterdam/Philadelphia.

Randolf Quirk, Sidney Greenbaum, Geoffry Leech, and Jan Svartvik. 1985. A Comprehensive Grammar of the English Language. New York.

Roger Sauri. 2008. A Factuality Profiler for Eventualities in Text. Ph.D Dissertation, Brandeis University.

Theresa Ann Wilson. 2008. Fine-Grained Subjectivity and Sentiment Analysis: Recognizing the Intensity, Polarity, and Attitudes of Private States. Ph.D Dissertation, University of Pittsburgh.

Wiebe, Janyce, Theresa Wilson, and Claire Cardie. 2005. Annotating Expressions of Opinions and Emotions in Language. Language Resources and Evaluation (formerly Computers and the Humanities), 39(2/3):164–210.

Wiebe, J. 2002. Instructions for annotating opinions in newspaper articles. Department of Computer Science Technical Report TR-02-101, University of Pittsburgh.

Lexical Gaps and Lexicalization: Implications for Word Segmentation Systems for Chinese NLP

Chan-Chia Hsu
Graduate Institute of Linguistics, National Taiwan University
No. 1, Sec. 4, Roosevelt Road, Taipei, 10617 Taiwan
chanchiah@gmail.com

Abstract

This paper is motivated by the observation that not all adjectives in Chinese have a canonical antonym. For example, most Chinese speakers choose to translate the English word *dishonest* into a word string *bu chengshi* 'not honest' instead of any antonym candidates of *chengshi* suggested in antonym dictionaries. Our discourse evidence from corpus data suggests that *bu chengshi* is evolving into a word in discourse at a faster pace than some other '*bu* + adjective' strings, and this may result from the lexical gap for a canonical antonym of *chengshi* and the communicative need for such a word. As a consequence, it is proposed that if the lexicalization process of *bu chengshi* continues in the future, the string may need to be considered a single word in a segmentation system (i.e., *buchengshi* 'dishonest'). For a segmentation system to distinguish between words and phrases, discourse factors should be taken into consideration.

1 Introduction

The issue of antonym canonicity has been empirically investigated in English and other languages (Paradis et al., 2009; Willners and Paradis, 2010). This paper is motivated by the observation that not all adjectives in Chinese have a generally accepted antonym. For example, although the antonym of *chengshi* 'honest', according to antonym dictionaries (e.g., Han and Song, 2001; Xu, 2000), can be *xuwei* 'hypocritical', *xujia* 'unreal', and *jiaohua* 'cunning', none of them are canonical for most native speakers. Intriguingly, in translating *dishonest* into Chinese, most Chinese speakers also choose to translate the English word into a word string *bu chengshi* 'not honest' instead of any antonym candidates of *chengshi*. The aim of this paper is thus to address the question: Will the lexical gap for a canonical antonym of *chengshi* enable the string *bu chengshi* to evolve into a word?

To answer the question, we adopt a corpus-based approach and see how *bu chengshi* behaves in discourse. The results will have implications for word segmentation systems for Chinese NLP in that if *bu chengshi* functions like a word both linguistically and conceptually, then the string may not need to be further segmented into '*bu* + *chengshi*' in a segmentation system. This line of study can shed light on the segmentation task from a discourse perspective.

This paper is organized as follows. Section 2 reviews different views of what a word is. Section 3 introduces the data examined in the present study, and Section 4 presents the results. Section 5 discusses the implications of the results for Chinese wordhood and the segmentation task in Chinese. Section 6 offers the conclusion and some suggestions for future research.

2 What Is a Word?

Generally, a word is defined as "a unit which has universal intuitive recognition by native-speakers, in both spoken and written language" (Crystal, 2008:521). Though most native speakers intuitively know what a word is, there exists no definition of the concept 'word' that is universally applicable. (Crystal, 1991; Dai, 1998; Packard, 2000). This has complicated the segmentation task in natural language processing.

Packard (2000) provides a comprehensive review of what a word is, and Packard's review suggests that a word can be defined from various perspectives. A common, straightforward way to define words is based on writing conventions, i.e., orthographic words. In many languages, words are separated by spaces. However, words in Mandarin cannot be discerned orthographically since they are not physically separated. Sociologically, words are forms intermediate between phonemes and sentences, forms the general public are conscious of and find relevant in many ways (Chao, 1968:136-138). Most speakers may regard Chinese characters as sociological words. Semantically, a word is seen as a form with a semantic value. Words can be combined to form complex expressions, but they may not be further decomposed into smaller units (e.g., Baxter and Sagart, 1997; Dowty et al., 1981).

Dai (1998), also reviewed in Packard (2000), argues that words can function in different domains and that words, as a consequence, can be defined in phonological, morphological, and syntactic terms (Dai, 1998:104-105):

> A syntactic word is a minimal constituent to which syntactic rules may refer; a phonological word is a certain prosodic domain in which internal phonological rules may apply (as opposed to external or phrasal sandhi rules); and a morphological word is a maximal domain in which morphological rules may apply.

Dai's conception of the word works in Chinese, as in many other languages.

Di Sciullo and Williams (1987) define words from a cognitive view. They suggest that words are *psychologically real* in our language use. Words are listed units in the lexicon and have idiosyncratic properties which are not governed by rules but must be memorized by speakers. Packard (2000) critically pinpoints the weaknesses of the previous approaches and also offers new insights into the cognitive nature of Chinese words (e.g., Chinese X-bar morphology).

However, while there have been various theories about how to define a word, few have taken discourse factors into account. This motivates us to examine corpus data and see how words emerge and function in our actual communication (cf. Sun, 2006).

3 Methodology

The database for the present study is the Academia Sinica Balanced Corpus of Modern Chinese.[1] In the Sinica Corpus, every text is segmented, and every word is tagged with its part-of-speech. There are 489,2324 words in total.[2] The Chinese Gigaword Corpus (the second edition), which is much larger than the Sinica Corpus, is an alternative, yet it only collects newswire texts. The present study prefers not to consider genre factors, so the data in the Chinese Gigaword Corpus were not used.

When the data were collected, it was specified that *bu* should occur within five words to the left of the target.[3] In addition to *bu chengshi*, *bu zhijie* 'not direct' and *bu hefa* 'not legal' were also examined for comparison. In Chinese, the canonical antonym of *zhijie* is *jianjie*, and that of *hefa* is *feifa*. Therefore, it was predicted that *bu chengshi*, which lacks a lexical counterpart against *chengshi*, would behave more like a word than *bu zhijie* and *bu hefa*.

Here are the criteria for selecting *bu zhijie* and *bu hefa* for analysis in the present study. First, gradable antonyms such as *kuaile*/*beishang* 'happy/sad' were not considered, for the negation of a gradable antonym does not entail its counterpart (i.e., *bu kuaile* 'not happy' does not necessarily mean *beishang* 'sad'). Thus, the present study selected complementary antonyms, which are mutually exclusive (Cruse, 1986); the negation of one can be regarded as near-synonymous with the other. Next, Jones' (2002) list is adopted as a point of departure. The list includes 56 antonym pairs in English, which are considered to be an effort to approximate a

[1] It is open to the public at http://db1x.sinica.edu.tw/kiwi/mkiwi/.

[2] For more information about the Sinica Corpus, refer to http://db1x.sinica.edu.tw/kiwi/mkiwi/98-04.pdf.

[3] The collocation span usually ranges from three words to five words (Sinclair, 1991), and the present study follows the tradition.

representative set for a study of antonymy. The scope of the present study was limited to adjectives, and the complementary pairs were singled out and then translated into Chinese. There are two problems, though. First, it can be impossible to find a Chinese equivalent for some antonyms in Jones' (2002) list. Second, after translated into Chinese, the negation of an antonym may sound inappropriate or be semantically different from the counterpart of that antonym (e.g., *si/?bu huo* 'dead/not alive'). With these problems, the present study finally selected two strings only, i.e., *bu zhijie* 'not direct' and *bu hefa* 'not legal', for a comparison with *bu chengshi*.[4]

In our analysis, accidental co-occurrences were excluded. The following is an example:

(1) 工作上遭遇**不**平等的待遇，**直接**與上司溝通多次仍屬無效。
Gongzuo shang zaoyu **bu** pingdeng de daiyu, **zhijie** yu shangshi goutong duo ci reng shu wuxiao.
'(Someone) was not fairly treated in the workplace, and it was useless to communicate with the supervisor many times.'

In (1), *bu* works with *pingdeng* 'equal' rather than *zhijie*. Therefore, the sentence in (1) was excluded.

The following table summarizes the numbers of the tokens analyzed in the present study.

Strings	Tokens
bu zhijie	9 (56.3%)
bu…zhijie	**7 (43.7%)**
bu hefa	**9 (100%)**
bu…hefa	0 (0%)
bu chengshi	**7 (87.5%)**
bu…chengshi	1 (12.5%)

Table 1: The numbers of the tokens analyzed in the present study

The analysis of how the tokens are used in Chinese will be presented in the following section.

4 Results

As Table 1 shows, the '*bu* X' strings do not occur frequently in the corpus. However, when the expected value was calculated, it was found that the token numbers were larger than expected by chance.

The formula for the expected value of the surface co-occurrence is as follows (cf. Event, 2008):[5]

(2) $f_1 \times f_2 / N$
(f_1: the token number of *bu*; f_2: the token number of the adjective; N: the token number of the corpus)

The trouble was that the online version of the Sinica Corpus does not provide the token number if a word occurs more than 5,000 times in the corpus. The negative marker *bu* is such a frequently-occurring word. We could estimate the token number of *bu* by referring to Xiao and McEnery (2008). On average, *bu* occurs approximately 800 times per 100,000 words (Xiao and McEnery, 2008:290). Based on their calculation, we estimated that *bu* occurs approximately 39,000 times in the Sinica Corpus.[6] Based on the formula in (2), Table 2 presents the expected values and the observed values of *bu zhijie*, *bu hefa*, and *bu chengshi*.[7]

Strings	Values
bu zhijie (ex.)	8.68
bu zhijie (ob.)	9
bu hefa (ex.)	1.32
bu hefa (ob.)	9
bu chengshi (ex.)	0.84
bu chengshi (ob.)	7

Table 2: The expected values and the observed values of *bu zhijie*, *bu hefa*, and *bu chengshi*

[4] The behavior of *jianjie* and that of *bu zhijie* were compared, and the same analysis was done for *hefa* and *bu hefa*. However, the analyses are beyond the scope of the present study, and the results will not presented here.

[5] The present study adopted the most common approach and calculated surface co-occurrences (Event, 2008) rather than textual co-occurrences and syntactic co-occurrences.

[6] There are 489,2324 words in the Sinica Corpus.

[7] In the Sinica Corpus, there are 1,089 tokens of *zhijie*, 166 tokens of *feifa*, and 106 tokens of *chengshi*.

As Table 2 shows, the observed values of *bu zhijie*, *bu hefa*, and *bu chengshi* are higher than their expected values. This justifies the analyses in the following, for the co-occurrences of *bu* and *zhijie*, *hefa*, and *chengshi* are not haphazard.

To address the issue of how close *bu* and its following adjective are, the present study analyzed how often *bu* and the adjective are interrupted and how often a modifier is used to modify *bu* rather than the whole construction '*bu* + adjective'. The first question has been answered in Table 1.

As shown in Table 1, *bu* and *zhijie* is interrupted by a modifier more often than the other two. Here is an example:

(3) 活動之間的關係錯綜複雜，並**不那麼直接**而明顯。
Huodong zhijian de guanxi cuozongfuza, **bing bu name zhijie** er mingxian.
'The relationships between activities are complex, not very direct and obvious.'

In (3), *name* 'so' is inserted between *bu* and *zhijie*. There are some other patterns, including *bu shi zhijie* 'not be direct', *bu hen zhijie* 'not very direct', and *bu shi name zhijie* 'not be that direct'.

As for the modifiers of *bu*, the following are two examples:

(4) 使用者**並不直接**指定所要的字。
Shiyongzhe **bing bu zhijie** zhiding suo yao de zi.
'The user does not directly specify words they want.'

(5) 儀式**根本不合法**。
Yishi **genben bu hefa**.
'The ceremony is not legal at all.'

In (4), *bing*, which serves as an intensifier, cannot modify *zhijie* if *bu* is not present. Therefore, *bing* is analyzed as modifying *bu* rather than *bu zhijie*. With a modifier attached to *bu*, the relationship between *bu* and *zhijie* seems to become weaker. The same analysis is true of the sentence in (5). Table 3 summarizes the modifying patterns:

Strings	Tokens
zero + *bu zhijie*	6 (66.7%)
modifier + *bu zhijie* (Attested pattern: *bing bu zhijie* 'entirely not direct')	3 (33.3%)
zero + *bu hefa*	6 (66.7%)
modifier + *bu hefa* (Attested patterns: *bing bu hefa* 'entirely not legal', *jibenbu hefa* 'basically not legal', *genben bu hefa* 'fundamentally not legal')	3 (33.3%)

Table 3: Modifiers of '*bu*'

As Table 3 shows, *bu* in *bu zhijie* and *bu hefa* can be modified. However, in the Sinica Corpus, *bu* in *bu chengshi* is not found to be modified.

It has been found that canonical antonyms co-occur far more frequently than expected by chance (e.g., Charles and Miller, 1989; Fellbaum, 1995; Jones, 2002, 2006, 2007; Jones and Murphy, 2005; Justeson and Katz, 1991). In the Sinica Corpus, *zhijie* and *jianjie* are found to co-occur twenty times, which confirms the previous observations.[8] Since *jianjie* is near-synonymous to *bu zhijie*, *zhijie* and *bu zhijie* may co-occur in the corpus. When the window size was specified as within four words, *zhijie* and *bu zhijie* were not found to co-occur in the Sinica Corpus. The same search was conducted for *hefa*/*bu hefa* and *chengshi*/*bu chengshi*, and no co-occurrences were attested when the span was specified as within four words. However, when the span was extended, *chengshi* and *bu chengshi* were found to co-occur. Of the seven tokens of *bu chengshi* in the Sinica Corpus, three (42.9%) co-occur with *chengshi* and serve some discourse functions. Here is an example:

(6) 你誠實，我就喜歡跟你交朋友。你**不誠實**，我就不喜歡跟你交朋友。
Ni **chengshi**, wo jiu xihuan gen ni jiao pengyou. Ni **bu chengshi**, wo jiu bu xihuan gen ni jiao pengyou.

[8] In the Sinica Corpus, there are 1089 tokens of *zhijie* and 134 tokens of *jianjie*. Based on the formula in (2), the two words are expected to co-occur fewer than once!

'If you are honest, I like to make friends with you. If you are not honest, I do not like to make friends with you.'

In (6), *chengshi* and *bu chengshi* co-occur in an ancillary manner (cf. Jones, 2002, 2006; Jones and Murphy, 2005). That is, the co-occurrence of *chengshi* and *bu chengshi* helps to signal another contrast in the context, i.e., whether the speaker wants to make friends with someone. Such a co-occurrence is not accidental, but helpful in organizing the discourse. Unlike *chengshi*/*bu chengshi*, *zhijie*/*bu zhijie* and *hefa*/*bu hefa* were not found to co-occur and serve discourse functions even though the span was extended.

5 Discussion

This study examined the behavior of *bu chengshi*, *bu zhijie* and *bu hefa* to deal with Chinese wordhood from a discourse perspective. Though *bu zhijie*, *bu hefa*, and *bu chengshi* have not been regarded as words by native speakers, they may be on the way of lexicalization at different paces. Table 4 demonstrates their distributional differences observed in the corpus (cf. Table 1, Table 2, Table 3).

Strings	Distributional differences
bu chengshi	1. **O/E: 8.33** 2. *bu…chengshi*: 1 (12.5%) 3. **modifier + *bu*: 0 (0.0%)** 4. **co-occurs with *chengshi* when the span is extended**
bu hefa	1. O/E: 6.82 2. *bu…hefa*: 0 (0.0%) 3. modifier + *bu*: 3 (33.3%) 4. never co-occurs with *hefa*
bu zhijie	1. O/E:[9] 1.04 2. *bu…zhijie*: 7 (43.7%) 3. modifier + *bu*: 3 (33.3%) 4. never co-occurs with *zhijie*

Table 4: Evidence for the lexicalization of *bu zhijie*, *bu hefa*, and *bu chengshi*

As shown in Table 4, the O/E ratio of *bu chengshi* is the highest of the three, which suggests that the combination of *bu* and *chengshi* is far from accidental. Second, *bu* and *chengshi* is interrupted only once in the Sinica Corpus, and *bu* in *bu chengshi* is never modified in the corpus. The two facts may indicate that the boundary between *bu* and *chengshi* may be breaking down. Third, only *bu chengshi* is found to be used as a whole contrastively with *chengshi*. The discourse evidence in Table 4 supports that *bu chengshi* is being lexicalized at a faster pace than the other two.

The strings *bu zhijie*, *bu hefa*, and *bu chengshi* share an identical structure, i.e., '*bu* + adjective', but they are functionally different from a

[9] In Table 4, O/E stands for the ratio between the observed value between the expected value. See Section 4 for more details.

communicative perspective. As mentioned earlier, the antonym of *chengshi* can be *xuwei*, *xujia*, and *jiaohua*, but such pairs are regarded as non-canonical by most native speakers. The three words are much more pejorative than *bu chengshi*, and they represent different ways of being dishonest. Therefore, a word is needed in Chinese to neutrally represent the concept of being dishonest. Moreover, such a word can serve as a canonical antonym for *chengshi*. These communicative needs may contribute to the relatively high O/E ratio of *bu chengshi* and help it to fulfill its potential to evolve into a single word (cf. Kjellmer, 2003, 2005). On the other hand, the semantic difference between *bu hefa* and *feifa* is not so substantial as that between *bu chengshi* and *xuwei/xujia/jiaohua*, and neither is that between *bu zhijie* and *jianjie*. In other words, *bu chengshi* is more useful than *bu zhijie* and *bu hefa* in communicative terms. This results in different lexicalization processes, and the functional differences have been formally reflected. By analyzing discourse data from the corpus, we can advance our understanding of Chinese wordhood.

However, in distinguishing between words and phrases, few studies have considered discourse data (Packard, 2000:15). This is reflected in most segmentation systems for Chinese. Since *bu zhijie*, *bu hefa*, and *bu chengshi* share an identical structure, the algorithm segments the three strings in a similar manner. The following results come from the segmentation system of Academia Sinica:[10]

(7) 不(D) 誠實(VH)
bu chengshi
'dishonest'

(8) 不(D) 直接(VH)
bu zhijie
'indirect'

(9) 不(D) 合法(VH)
bu hefa
'illegal'

In the present study, it is suggested that the string *bu chengshi* is more likely to further develop into a word than *bu zhijie* and *bu hefa* even though they share the same structure. If the evolution of *bu chengshi* continues, the string may need to be considered to be a single word in a segmentation system in the future (i.e., *buchengshi* 'dishonest'). Our results can serve as a reference for segmentation systems. With ample evidence from discourse data, strings with a similar, or even identical, structure can be segmented differently.

Then, how can we compromise with the conflict that after all, *buchengshi* is inarguably formed from the concatenation of the negation marker *bu* and an adjective? The speaker's communicative need may have helped *bu* + *chengshi* to achieve a relatively high frequency (in terms of its O/E value), and frequent repetitions may enable the whole string to gain an independent representation in the lexicon (cf. Bybee, 2000, 2006). Consequently, from a cognitive perspective, *buchengshi* may be processed as a whole rather than in a compositional manner. As manifested in discourse data, the boundary between *bu* and *chengshi* is less clear than that between *bu* and *zhijie* and that between *bu* and *hefa*. That is, *buchengshi* may become psychologically real if its lexicalization process continues, and it may eventually become a listed unit memorized by speakers in their lexicon (Di Sciullo and Williams, 1987; Hoosain, 1992). It appears that morphological rules alone cannot explain why strings with the same structure can have different representations in the grammar of Mandarin. The morphological boundary is fluid (Hoosain, 1992:118-120), and communicative needs and discourse factors should be taken into account in a theory about Chinese wordhood.

6 Conclusion

By analyzing corpus data, this study suggests that *bu zhijie*, *bu hefa*, and *bu chengshi* may be on the way of lexicalization at different paces. Of the three, *bu chengshi* is the most useful in communicative terms and is evolving the fastest in discourse. The boundary between *bu* and *chengshi* may gradually become blurred. In fact, words and phrases in Chinese are so closely connected that "one must investigate and study the links between speech sounds, syntax, semantics, and discourse

---

[10] The segmentation system of Academia Sinica is available at http://ckipsvr.iis.sinica.edu.tw/.

factors in forming Chinese words in actual communication" (Sun, 2006:75).

The findings of this study can have computational, lexicographical, and pedagogical applications. First, the results provide some feedback for segmentation programs for Chinese. In designing a segmentation system or a computer algorithm to parse texts, computational linguists need to take discourse factors into consideration. Second, if *bu chengshi* eventually evolves into a single word and gains a representation in the speaker's lexicon, a lexicographer may need to consider listing the word in the dictionary. Third, teaching materials may need to be revised according to corpus data so that language learners can learn to speak and write natural-sounding Chinese. For example, students should be taught to distinguish between *bu chengshi* and *xuwei* though both can serve as antonyms of *chengshi*.

Further studies are still needed to explore Chinese wordhood from a usage-based perspective. First, the present study decides to ignore genre factors at the cost of the sample size (cf. Section 3), yet more quantitative data are needed to make the calculations more reliable. Second, the present study focuses on three adjectival strings, yet more need to be analyzed. For example, the scope can extend to verbal ones (e.g., *fandui/bu tongyi* 'disagree/not agree') so that the generalizations made in the present study will be more valuable. Third, psycholinguistic experiments (e.g., self-paced reading tasks) can de conducted to investigate how the speaker processes the morphological boundary online. To develop a fuller understanding of Chinese grammar and provide more feedback on the performance of a segmentation system, converging evidence from different fields is encouraged.

References

徐安崇 [Anchong Xu]. 2000. 反義詞應用辭典 [Antonym Application Dictionary]. Language and Culture Press, Beijing.

Anna-Maria Di Sciullo and Edwin Williams. 1987. On the Definition of Word. MIT Press, Cambridge.

Carita Paradis, Caroline Willners, and Steven Jones. 2009. Good and bad opposites: using textual and experimental techniques to measure antonym canonicity. The Mental Lexicon 4:380-429.

Caroline Willners and Carita Paradis. 2010. Swedish opposites: A multi-method approach to 'goodness of antonymy'. In Petra Storjohann (ed.), Lexical-Semantic Relations: Theoretical and practical perspectives (pp. 15-48). John Benjamins, Amsterdam.

Chaofen Sun. 2006. Chinese: A Linguistic Introduction. Cambridge University Press, Leiden.

Christiane Fellbaum. 1995. Co-occurrence and antonymy. International Journal of Lexicography 8:281-303.

David Crystal. 2008. A Dictionary of Linguistics and Phonetics (6th edition). Blackwell, Oxford.

David R. Dowty, Robert E. Wall, and Stanley Peters. 1981. Introduction to Montague Semantics. D. Reidel, Dordrecht.

Göran Kjellmer. 2003. Lexical gaps. In Sylviane Granger and Stephanie Petch-Tyson (eds.), Extending the Scope of Corpus-based Research (pp. 149-158). Rodopi, Amsterdam.

Göran Kjellmer. 2005. Negated adjectives in modern English. Studia Neophilologica 77:156-170.

Jerome L. Packard. 2000. The Morphology of Chinese: A Linguistic and Cognitive Approach. Cambridge University Press, Cambridge.

韓敬體, 宋惠德 [Jingti Han and Dehui Song]. 2001. 反義詞辭典 [Antonym Dictionary]. Sichuan People's Publishing House, Chengdu.

Joan L. Bybee. 2000. The phonology of the lexicon: Evidence from lexical diffusion. In Michael Barlow and Suzanne Kemmer (eds.), Usage-based Models of Language (pp. 65-85). CSLI Publications, Center for the Study of Language and Information, Stanford.

Joan L. Bybee. 2006. From usage to grammar: The mind's response to repetition. Language 82:711-733.

John S. Justeson and Slava M. Katz. 1991. Co-occurrence of antonymous adjectives and their contexts. Computational Linguistics 17:1-19.

John Sinclair. 1991. Corpus, Concordance, Collocation. Oxford University Press, Oxford.

John Xiang-Ling Dai. 1998. Syntactic, phonological, morphological words in Chinese. In Jerome L. Packard (ed.), New Approaches to Chinese Word Formation: Morphology, Phonology and the Lexicon in Modern and Ancient Chinese (pp. 103-134). Mouton de Gruyter, Berlin.

Richard Xiao and Tony McEnery. 2008. Negation in Chinese: A corpus-based study. Journal of Chinese Linguistics 36:274-330.

Rumjahn Hoosain. 1992. Psychological reality of the word in Chinese. In Hsuan-Chih Chen and Ovid J. L. Tzeng (eds.), Language Processing in Chinese (pp. 111-130). North-Holland and Elsevier, Amsterdam.

Stefan Evert. 2008. Corpora and collocations. In Anke Lüdeling and Merja Kytö (eds.), Corpus Linguistics: An International Handbook (pp. 1212-1248). Mouton de Gruyter, Berlin.

Steven Jones and M. Lynne Murphy. 2005. Using corpora to investigate antonym acquisition. International Journal of Corpus Linguistics 10:401-422.

Steven Jones. 2002. Antonymy: A Corpus-based Perspective. Routledge, New York.

Steven Jones. 2006. A lexico-syntactic analysis of antonym co-occurrence in spoken English. Text & Talk 26:191-216.

Steven Jones. 2007. 'Opposites' in discourse: A comparison of antonym use across four domains. Journal of Pragmatics 39:1105-1119.

Walter G. Charles and George A. Miller. 1989. Contexts of antonymous adjectives. Applied Psycholinguistics 10:357-375.

William H. Baxter and Laurent Sagart. 1997. Word formation in Old Chinese. In Jerome L. Packard (ed.), New Approaches to Chinese Word Formation: Morphology, Phonology and the Lexicon in Modern and Ancient Chinese (pp. 103-134). Mouton de Gruyter, Berlin.

Yuen Ren Chao. 1968. A Grammar of Spoken Chinese. University of California Press, Berkeley.

Extracting Keywords from Multi-party Live Chats

Su Nam Kim
School of Information Technology
Monash University
Clayton, VIC, Australia
su.kim@monash.edu.au

Timothy Baldwin
Dept. of Computing and Information Systems
The University of Melbourne
VIC, Australia
tb@ldwin.net

Abstract

Live chats have become a popular form of communication, connecting people all over the globe. We believe that one of the simplest approaches for providing topic information to users joining a chat is keywords. In this paper, we present a method to automatically extract contextually relevant keywords for multi-party live chats. In our work, we identify keywords that are associated with specific dialogue acts as well as the occurrences of keywords across the entire conversation. In this way, we are able to identify distinguishing features of the chat based on structural information derived from live chats and predicted dialogue acts. In evaluation, we find that using structural information and predicted dialogue acts performs well, and that conventional methods do not work well over live chats.

1 Introduction

Keywords or **keyphrases**[1] are an effective way of representing the core topic of a document, and can effectively summarize and/or help index documents. They are usually found in the form of either simplex nouns (e.g. *library*) or noun phrases (e.g. *social issue*). They have been studied in the past to provide topic-related information for many applications such as text summarizers, search engines and indexers. For example, Barzilay and Elhadad (1997) used keywords as semantic meta-information for summarizers. DÁvanzo and Magnini (2005) used them to organize documents for search engines. Dredze et al. (2008) used keywords as summaries of email in order to better manage and prioritize emails. Hammouda et al. (2005) used keywords extracted from multiple documents in order to discover the topics of documents for clustering. Gutwin et al. (1999) used automatically extracted keywords to refine the queries to improve precision of search in an online library browser.

There has been much research on automatic keyword extraction (Frank et al., 1999; Turney, 1999; Hulth, 2003, inter alia). The majority of work has been done over specific domains such as scientific articles and newspapers, including the recent SemEval-2010 shared task on keyword extraction (Kim et al., 2010b). A small minority of researchers have used different sources of data such as email (Dredze et al., 2008) and HTML documents (Mori et al., 2004), as outlined in Section 2. However, existing approaches tend not to work well when applied to different target sources, and are often susceptible to domain-specific features of the target documents (e.g. structure).

In this paper, our aim is to automatically extract keywords for multi-party live chats. Live chats are essentially text-based dialogues, with less disfluencies than spoken dialogues but greater scope for overlapping utterances and out-of-sequence subthreading (Ivanovic, 2008). Researchers have variously proposed to use *dialogue acts* (or *DAs*) to analyze the structure of discourses. In this paper, we are primarily interested in extracting keywords, but hypothesise that keywords not only serve as summaries of live chats, but they can also track the top-

[1] In this work, we use the term *keywords* for consistency, while noting that it can be used to refer to multiword terms.

ics of the conversation. Furthermore, keywords provided at different points of a chat can benefit participants who are absent from the chat for a period of time. This would be especially beneficial to multiparty conversations which pose great challenges due to tangled and asynchronous nature of the interaction. One may easily imagine that keywords could provide contextualizing information for a conversation, helping a new participant to join a conversation mid-stream. Hence, the ability to extract keywords at any given time during the conversation has the potential to enhance the user-friendliness of live chat systems.

In this research, we target multi-party written dialogues for keyword extraction due to their popularity on the web, the ability for participants to readily join and leave chats, and the novel semi-asynchronous nature of interactions. However, we believe that the proposed methodology could be adapted to spoken dialogues, noting the challenges of automatic speech recognition, and the import of acoustic and prosodic features in keyword extraction.

In analyzing chat data, we observed that keywords vary over time due to topic changes as the conversation progresses. Also, we found that keywords are highly associated with specific dialogue acts. As such, we explored the structural information and dialogue acts predicted by our dialogue act classification system to accommodate the characteristics of live chats. During evaluation, we compared our proposed methods with the well-known `KEA` keyword extraction system. For our work, we collected data from live chat forums from the US Library of Congress (see Section 3 for details). Unlike casual chats (e.g. NPS live chats), the conversations are based on specific issues, and are thus similar to task-oriented settings such as meetings.

2 Related Work

Keyword (or keyphrase) extraction has been studied over the years, with the primary aim of deducing the topic of a document. The task involves selecting keyword candidates, ranking candidates in terms of the relatedness to the document topic(s), and evaluating the system and/or looking for suitable learning methods. A major portion of prior research work has focused on the ranking problem and has mostly used statistical approaches with various sets of features from symbolic resources and linguistically-motivated heuristics and machine learners (Frank et al., 1999; Turney, 1999; Hulth, 2003; Nguyen and Kan, 2007; Kim et al., 2010b). Since our effort focuses on feature engineering for live chats, we detail the previous efforts on feature engineering and variety of datasets keyword extraction has been applied to.

`KEA` (Frank et al., 1999) was one of the earliest keyword extraction systems, and was based on TF·IDF and the location of first appearance of each term in the document. Hereafter, we will refer to this term as *first appearance*. The `GenEx` system (Turney, 1999) employed nine heuristic features based exclusively on morphosyntax, such as word length and phrase frequency. Hulth (2003) used TF·IDF, first appearance and keyphraseness[2] as the basis of his method, and added POS tags assigned to candidate terms based on the observation that POS patterns such as (NN NN) and (JJ NN) are more frequent among keywords. Nguyen and Kan (2007) extracted keywords using structural information such as the document title and section headings derived from scientific articles. Wan and Xiao (2008) used a document clustering method to extract salient words, then utilized those to rank the candidates. Liu et al. (2009) developed an unsupervised method using TF·IDF and variants thereof. The main approach is to cluster the terms with respect to the sub-topics, rank candidates in each cluster, then select top-ranked candidates as keywords. Li et al. (2010) proposed a method based on semantic similarity among n-ary phrases, based on Wikipedia entities and links, and used the weighted Girvan-Newman algorithm for candidate ranking. More recently, Kim et al. (2010b) proposed a keyword extraction shared task over scientific articles. Participants used a broad range of features based on document structure, semantic similarity and various document and term heuristics.

Keyword extraction has also been carried out on various types of documents. Scientific articles and news articles are often the target of keyword extraction (Hulth, 2003; Nguyen and Kan,

[2]The intuition is that what is a good keyword in one context is likely to be a good keyword in similar contexts.

2007; Medelyan, 2009; Kim et al., 2010b). Hulth (2003) extracted 2,000 abstracts of journal articles from Inspec that contained controlled and uncontrolled terms assigned by professional indexers. Nguyen and Kan (2007) collected a dataset containing 120 computer science articles and labeled them with both author- and reader-assigned keywords. Medelyan (2009) collected 180 full-text publications from CiteULike using user tags. More recently, the SemEval-2010 keyword extraction task used 100 and 144 scientific articles with author and reader-assigned keywords for testing and training, respectively. In the biomedical domain, Schutz (2008) obtained 1,323 files with gold-standard answers and predictions from PubMed. Wan and Xiao (2008) developed a set of 308 documents with up to 10 manually-assigned keywords using newswire documents from DUC 2001. Dredze et al. (2008) used keywords as summaries of email in order to better manage and prioritize emails.

3 Dialogue Acts for Multi-party Live Chats

While developing keyword data for live chats, we observed a strong correlation between dialogue acts and keywords. As such, we chose to first annotate chat data with dialogue acts. We collected multi-party live chat data from forums from the US Library of Congress. The live chats contain 33 online discussions that the Library's Educational Outreach team hosted for teachers between 2002 and 2006.

To define dialogue acts that suit this data, we investigated existing sets of dialogue acts from both spoken dialogues and live chats. Many can be found in both spoken and written dialogues based on the Dialogue Act Markup in Several Layers (DAMSL) scheme (Allen and Core, 1997). For live chats, Wu et al. (2002) and Forsyth (2007) defined 15 dialogue acts for casual online conversations based on previous sets (Samuel et al., 1998; Shriberg et al., 1998; Jurafsky et al., 1998; Stolcke et al., 2000). Ivanovic (2008) proposed 12 dialogue acts applying DAMSL for customer service chats.

Given the fact that our live chat forum data is closer to customer service chats in terms of the nature of the data (e.g. question, request, gratitude etc.), we decided to adopt the set from Ivanovic (2008) and added two more dialogue acts – BACKGROUND and OTHER. The list of dialogue acts and examples can be found in Table 1.

We selected 15 forums containing at least 200 utterances. The data was first segmented into discourse units, and sentence tokenized. Then, we cleaned the data by tokenizing emoticons/expletives (e.g. *: −)*, *wow*), email addresses (e.g. *learningpage@loc.gov*), URLs (e.g. *http://memory.loc.gov*), locations (e.g. *Texas*), and institutes (e.g. *University of Houston*) into *EMOTION, EMAIL, URL, LOCATION, INSTITUTE*, respectively. We also replaced user names with *USER_ID* to anonymize the data. Our final dataset contains 5,276 utterances from 15 live chat forums, after removing system log data.[3] The proportion of instances corresponding to each dialogue act is shown in Table 1.

We annotated the dialogue acts in order to analyze the distribution of keywords over different dialogue acts, and further, to use dialogue acts as features for the keyword extractor. To manually assign dialogue acts, we used two annotators including the first author. The annotators have past experience in conducting annotations for similar tasks. Before the actual annotation task, we also did a pilot test using live chat forums which were not selected for our final dataset. The initial agreement was 81.4% and kappa value was 0.74, indicating a well-defined annotation task. Note that we employed an automatic dialogue act classifier based on previous work (Forsyth, 2007; Kim et al., 2010a) to pre-assign and post-edit dialogue acts for the keyword extraction task. Using the system significantly reduced annotation effort, and yet was found to not bias the annotation process, based on small-scale experimentation with and without the DA predictions. Details of the DA prediction model are provided in Section 4.

4 Dialogue Act Prediction

In this section, we present our attempt to automatically extract dialogue acts in order to use them for our main task: keyword extraction. It is important to note that we employ previously-proposed features without modification. Our goal in using these meth-

[3]System logs indicate the status of participants, such as a participant joining or departing

Dialog Act	Example	Percent	Dialog Act	Example	Percent
OPENING	Hi, Greeting!	3.03	RESPONSE-ACK	yes, great, i agree,..	11.73
CLOSING	bye, good night,..	1.55	WH-QUESTION	What is this?	3.26
BACKGROUND	i am user2, i teach 4th grad	4.76	YN-QUESTION	is there a website for .. ?	5.84
THANKING	thanks, thank you for ..	6.54	YES-ANSWER	yes, sure,	1.67
EXPRESSION	: −), wow, oh!	7.71	NO-ANSWER	no, nope	0.28
STATEMENT	we have a website for photo gallery.	47.76	DOWNPLAY	no problem, you're welcome!	0.49
REQUEST	click this, go to..	4.97	OTHER	or, but	0.40

Table 1: Dialogue act tagset: definitions and examples

ods is to avoid manual annotation on dialogue acts, and thus we do not detail the effectiveness of previous methods nor evaluate our system against previous methods.

We explored various features from recent work (Forsyth, 2007; Kim et al., 2010a) to automatically predict dialogue acts. Our features are based on high-frequency terms with respect to dialogue acts from Forsyth (2007), and contextual, structural, and dialogue act interaction from Kim et al. (2010a). Note that in Forsyth (2007), the author used the term *keyword*. Keywords in Forsyth (2007) are defined as terms which are frequently associated with specific dialogue acts, and thus differ from our definition of keywords in this work. We thus refer to Forsyth's "keywords" as high-frequency terms. Finally, we developed a linear-chain conditional random field-based dialogue act classification system using Mallet (McCallum, 2002),[4] based on Kim et al. (2010a). We used 15 fold-cross validation (i.e. one dialogue for test and remainings for training), as our data contains 15 live chats.

After experimenting with various features, we found that contextual and high-frequency terms w.r.t. dialogue act features generally performed well, while structural and dialogue act interaction features did not achieve high accuracy, despite claims to the contrary in other studies. We hypothesise that since our data contains large numbers of users (unlike the two-party chat data of Ivanovic (2008), e.g.), the resulting entanglement of sub-threads confuses the dialogue act tagger. To elaborate, stemming tended to reduce errors caused by ill-formed words (e.g. *noooooo* as *no*). *High-frequency terms* also performed well since they are highly associated with specific dialogue acts (e.g. *hi, hello* for OPENING, *ok, great* for RESPONSE-ACK). However, it takes intensive manual intervention to extract such words associated with particular dialogue acts. Also, *user information* from structural features improves performance. We observed that user names mentioned in the dialogues resolve the entanglement to some degree, and thus perform well for dialogue act classification (e.g. *you're right, USER25!!*). The features used to automatically predict dialogue acts are listed below:

- *Stemmed Bag-of-Words*
- *Highly frequent terms* per dialogue act
- *User/Participant information*

To summarize, our best dialogue act classifier achieved an accuracy of 82.79%. We postulate that the lower accuracy compared to that reported in previous work (e.g. Forsyth (2007; Kim et al. (2010a)) was mainly due to the different nature of the chats as well as the higher number of participants. However, we found this was sufficient to semi-automate the annotation process.

5 Feature Engineering

To build the baseline system, we first used three features from KEA: (1) *TF·IDF*, one of most frequently used features, measures the relateness between the document topic(s) and candidate terms; (2) *first appearance* is a heuristic that indicates the locality of the keywords; that is, keywords often appear at the

[4] http://mallet.cs.umass.edu

beginning or end as well as specific parts of a document (e.g. Frank et al. (1999; Nguyen and Kan (2007)); and (3) *keyphraseness*, based on the observation that keywords tend to share across documents with the same or similar topics.

For our system, we developed new features based on observation, and structural information. First, we observed that keywords occur across chats since the discussed topics change across time, unlike the globally-relevant keywords typically found in documents such as scientific articles and news articles. Ideally, a topic shift detection method could identify boundaries of topic change. However, automatic topic detection would introduce errors and manual topic detection would involve high cost and time. Thus, we leave this issue for our future work. Finally, we decided to equally split each live chat into 10 smaller documents and to treat each as a single smaller document to compute IDF. To compensate for the erroneous topic boundaries due to the equal split, we used a variant of the sliding window approach. That is, we also include the last 10% of dialogues from the previous split document, resulting in each document partition containing approximately 11% of the whole document.

Secondly, we found that some dialogue acts (e.g. STATEMENT, REQUEST) tend to contain most of the keywords. Also, utterances made by host users tend to have more keywords than those by non-host users. Based on these, we introduced two features: (1) TF of keywords in utterances tagged with selected dialogue acts; and (2) TF of keywords in utterances made by host users. Statistical analysis of these observations is provided in Section 6.

Thirdly, we used the distribution of candidate keywords over the 10 sub-documents. Ideally, when documents are well split by sub-topics, keywords would appear in only a few sub-documents and not the whole document.

We summarize our tested features below:

- Baseline Features from `KEA`

  F1: TF·IDF$_{all}$ IDF over all documents

  F2: First Appearance

  F3: Keyphraseness

- Structural and Dialogue Features

  F4: TF·IDF$_{split}$ IDF over $\frac{1}{10}$ splits of the document

  F5: TF over utterances tagged with selected dialogue acts The association between keywords and utterances tagged with selected dialogue acts, in the form of raw, local proportion, and global proportion

  F6: TF over Host Utterances The association between keywords and utterances made by host users, in the form of raw, local proportion, and global proportion

  F7: TF over 10 Sub-documents Distribution of TF over each 10% of the original document, in the form of the raw count, local proportion, and global proportion. The distribution of TF is represented in 10 vectors, each representing 10% of the original document.

For features F5, F6 and F7, we tested three different ways of calculating the feature values. *Raw* is the raw term count. *Local* is computed using the proportion of term counts in selected utterances against that in all utterances; the motivation behind this is that instead of using raw counts, we check if the term occurrence in selected utterances has an impact. Finally, *global proportion* is computed using the term frequency in selected vs. all utterances, and is a combination of raw and local proportion values.

1. *raw*: TF in utterances tagged with selected dialogue acts only (*selU*); cf. TF in all utterances is marked as *allU*.

2. *local proportion*: $\frac{\text{TF}\in\text{selU}}{\text{TF}\in\text{allU}}$

3. *global proportion*: $\frac{\frac{\text{TF}\in\text{selU}}{|selU|}}{\frac{\text{TF}\in\text{allU}}{|allU|}}$

6 Data

To evaluate our proposed keyword extraction method, we collected keywords from 15 live chat forums. To simplify the task, we only allowed the annotators to extract simplex nouns as keywords.[5] One annotator manually extracted keywords, then

[5]During the pilot annotation test, we observed that the vast majority of keywords are simplex nouns.

the second (and more experienced for this task) annotator reviewed the extracted keywords. For disagreed keywords, two annotators met to finalize the keywords.

In total, 148 keywords were assigned to the 15 live chats. We checked the occurrence of keywords over 14 dialogue acts in manually-labeled dialogues and found that all keywords were found in one of four dialogue acts — STATEMENT, REQUEST, YN-QUESTION, WH-QUESTION — which make up 61.73% of utterances in our data. Table 2 shows the distribution of keywords over the 14 dialogue acts.

We also observed that 140 keywords are found in utterances made by host users (94.59% coverage), which make up 52.50% of utterances in the data. As candidates, we used lemmatized nouns with frequency ≥ 2 after removing stop words, and the EMOTION, URL, EMAIL, INSTITUTE and LOCATION tokens. After selecting the keyword candidates, we checked the coverage of keywords in the candidates. Across all utterances, we extracted 1,717 token candidates including 144 keyword types. On the other hand, in utterances tagged with one of the 4 selected dialogue acts, we got 1,494 token candidates, making up 142 keyword types. It shows that using only the 4 selected dialogue acts reduced the token candidate set by 12.99% but missed only 2 keyword types. This underlines the strong association between keywords and the selected dialogue acts.

7 Evaluation

7.1 Experimental Setup

In the preprocessing step, we performed POS tagging with `Lingua::EN::Tagger`, lemmatization with `morph` (Minnen et al., 2001) and stemming with `English Porter stemmer`.[6]

To build the automatic keyword extractor, we used naive Bayes to rank the keyword candidates with various features, following Kim et al. (2010b).[7] Likewise, to run the system, we used 15 fold-cross validation since we have 15 live chats. Note that when computing the counts of term frequencies for features F5, F6, and F7, we used the training data to avoid overfitting. For evaluation, we used the evaluation metric used in Kim et al. (2010b) but changed the top-N selection to use the top-5, 7 and 10 ranked candidates, since the average number of keywords per document is 9.9.

7.2 Results

Tables 3 and 4 show the performance (micro-averaged precision, $\mathcal{P}_\mu$, recall, $\mathcal{R}_\mu$ and F-score, $\mathcal{F}_\mu$) over 3 different settings of top-N candidates. We also present the performance using all utterances (marked as **allU**) vs. only those utterances corresponding to one of the four dialogue acts which our dialogue act classifier automatically labeled (marked as **selU**). In addition, we used two different sets of documents — original documents vs. split documents — in order to compute TF·IDF. As a result, we have four sets of experiments for baseline features — (Original Documents vs. Split Documents for IDF) $\times$ (All Utterances vs. Selected Utterances)

For features F5 $\sim$ F7, since we already observed better performance with F4 (TF·IDF over split documents), we test these features with F4 only.

While the dialogue act tagger was used to semi-automate the DA annotation, it is important to note that the dialogue act labels used in this experiment are those taken directly from the automatic DA tagger. Our baseline system, `KEA`, was also tested over all utterances as well as selected utterances only.

Overall, the systems performed better when using TF·IDF over split documents for both all utterances and selected utterances. In our description of the occurrence of keywords in dialogues, we observed that using smaller document chunks would contain keywords, as the conversation has a specific topic to discuss in each time frame. Even with the original `KEA` using all three features (i.e. F1–F3), using TF·IDF alone performed much better. We observed that the first-occurrence heuristic (which indicates term locality) does not effectively identify keywords in live chat data, since the documents themselves have sequential structure and likewise, keywords occur all across the documents. This shows that keywords in dialogues are more associated with time than document structure, as is the case with scientific and/or news articles. As for the reappearance of keywords

[6]Using the Perl implementation available at `http://tartarus.org/~martin/PorterStemmer/`

[7]We also experimented with a maximum entropy learner, but found the results to be near-identical, and omit them from this paper.

DA	keyword	DA	keyword	DA	keyword
STATEMENT	1127	WH-QUESTION	62	THANKING	17
REQUEST	119	RESPONSE-ACK	37	OPENING	13
YN-QUESTION	99	BACKGROUND	31	CLOSING	1

Table 2: Distribution of keywords over dialogue acts

	Top 5			Top 7			Top 10		
Feature	$\mathcal{P}_\mu$	$\mathcal{R}_\mu$	$\mathcal{F}_\mu$	$\mathcal{P}_\mu$	$\mathcal{R}_\mu$	$\mathcal{F}_\mu$	$\mathcal{P}_\mu$	$\mathcal{R}_\mu$	$\mathcal{F}_\mu$
Baseline Features using Original Documents (KEA)									
F1	42.67	21.62	28.70	39.05	27.70	32.41	24.67	25.00	24.83
F1+F2	16.00	8.11	10.76	18.10	12.84	15.02	9.33	9.46	9.39
F1+F3	32.00	16.22	21.53	31.43	22.30	26.09	18.00	18.24	18.12
F1+F2+F3†	16.00	8.11	10.76	18.10	12.84	*15.02*	9.33	9.46	9.39
Baseline Features using Split Documents									
F4	53.33	27.03	35.88	57.14	40.54	**47.43**	33.33	33.78	33.55
F4+F2	16.00	8.11	10.76	20.00	14.19	16.60	10.00	10.14	10.07
F4+F3	8.00	4.05	5.38	18.10	12.84	15.02	4.67	4.73	4.70
F4+F2+F3	16.00	8.11	10.76	20.00	14.19	16.60	10.00	10.14	10.07
Dialogue Features using Split Documents									
F4+F5$_{raw}$	48.00	24.32	32.28	54.29	38.51	45.06	30.00	30.41	30.20
F4+F5$_{tf}$	1.33	0.68	0.90	3.81	2.70	3.16	2.00	2.03	2.01
F4+F5$_{percent}$	1.33	0.68	0.90	3.81	2.70	3.16	2.00	2.03	2.01
F4+F6$_{raw}$	49.33	25.00	33.18	54.29	38.51	45.06	30.00	30.41	30.20
F4+F6$_{tf}$	5.33	2.70	3.58	7.62	5.41	6.33	4.00	4.05	4.02
F4+F6$_{percent}$	5.33	2.70	3.58	7.62	5.41	6.33	4.00	4.05	4.02
F4+F7$_{raw}$	48.00	24.32	32.28	55.24	39.19	45.85	29.33	29.73	29.53
F4+F7$_{tf}$	12.00	6.08	8.07	10.48	7.43	8.70	6.00	6.08	6.04
F4+F7$_{percent}$	12.00	6.08	8.07	11.43	8.11	9.49	6.00	6.08	6.04

Table 3: Effectiveness of keyword extraction over **All Utterances (allU)** (the baseline [KEA] is marked with †, and its performance is in italics; the best performance is bold-faced). **Original Documents** means IDF computed as is, while **Split Documents** means IDF calculated over $\frac{1}{10}$ splits of the document.

(i.e. seen keyword heuristics), it did not work well since we have only 15 chats and many keywords occurred in most of the chats (whether as keywords or not).

Comparing all utterances vs. selected utterances, the performance was very similar. However, in some cases, using selected utterances performed better (e.g. with $F4 + F6$, 45.06% and 51.38% for allU and selU, respectively). We estimate that since the discarded utterances are relatively short and often contain general terms, even if we include these utterances, the effect of these discarded utterances is insignificant. However, given the best performance over the two different utterance sets, we can argue that using selected utterances achieves higher performance with much fewer candidates.

Among Top-5, 7, and 10, surprisingly, we found that the performance with the top-7 rated candidates consistently exceeded that with the top-10 rated candidates. To analyze this, we checked $\mathcal{P}_\mu$, $\mathcal{R}_\mu$ and $\mathcal{F}_\mu$, and found that precision tends to drop as we add more candidates.

Finally, we observed that our novel features based on dialogue structure and dialogue acts (F5–F7) contributed to correctly extract keywords, especially over the top-5 candidates. We found that the utterance author information (F6) is particularly effective at identifying keywords with high accuracy. Simi-

Feature	Top 5 $\mathcal{P}_\mu$	Top 5 $\mathcal{R}_\mu$	Top 5 $\mathcal{F}_\mu$	Top 7 $\mathcal{P}_\mu$	Top 7 $\mathcal{R}_\mu$	Top 7 $\mathcal{F}_\mu$	Top 10 $\mathcal{P}_\mu$	Top 10 $\mathcal{R}_\mu$	Top 10 $\mathcal{F}_\mu$
Baseline Features using Original Documents (KEA)									
F1	41.33	20.95	27.81	40.95	29.05	33.99	24.67	25.00	24.83
F1+F2	18.67	9.46	12.56	23.81	16.89	19.76	12.00	12.16	12.08
F1+F3	32.00	16.22	21.53	31.43	22.30	26.09	17.33	17.57	17.45
F1+F2+F3†	18.67	9.46	12.56	23.81	16.89	*19.76*	12.00	12.16	12.08
Baseline Features using Split Documents									
F4	53.33	27.03	35.88	58.10	41.22	48.23	33.33	33.78	33.55
F4+F2	20.00	10.14	13.46	24.76	17.57	20.55	12.67	12.84	12.75
F4+F3	5.33	2.70	3.58	16.19	11.49	13.44	5.33	5.41	5.37
F4+F2+F3	20.00	10.14	13.46	24.76	17.57	20.55	12.67	12.84	12.75
Dialogue Features using Split Documents									
$F4+F5_{raw}$	48.00	24.32	32.28	51.43	36.49	42.69	30.00	30.41	30.20
$F4+F5_{tf}$	1.33	0.68	0.90	2.86	2.03	2.37	0.67	0.68	0.67
$F4+F5_{percent}$	1.33	0.68	0.90	2.86	2.03	2.37	0.67	0.68	0.67
$F4+F6_{raw}$	53.33	27.03	35.88	61.90	43.92	**51.38**	32.67	33.11	32.89
$F4+F6_{tf}$	6.67	3.38	4.49	9.52	6.76	7.91	4.67	4.73	4.70
$F4+F6_{percent}$	6.67	3.38	4.49	9.52	6.76	7.91	4.67	4.73	4.70
$F4+F7_{raw}$	42.67	21.62	28.70	53.33	37.84	44.27	26.00	26.35	26.17
$F4+F7_{tf}$	13.33	6.76	8.97	14.29	10.14	11.86	8.00	8.11	8.05
$F4+F7_{percent}$	12.00	6.08	8.07	11.43	8.11	9.49	6.67	6.76	6.71

Table 4: Effectiveness of keyword extraction over **Selected Utterances (selU)** (the baseline [KEA] is marked with †, and its performance is in italics; the best performance is bold-faced). bold-faced). **Original Documents** means IDF computed as is, while **Split Documents** means IDF calculated over $\frac{1}{10}$ splits of the document.

larly, since keywords tend to appear in selected dialogue acts, term frequency over the utterances labeled with these dialogue acts only produced good results compared to term frequency over all utterances. Likewise, the distribution of keywords over the 10 sub-documents (F7) contributed to higher performance compared to the baseline system. Among the three different values we tested, we found that using raw counts performed the best. We speculate that due to the small size of the data, the normalised values did not work well.

8 Conclusion

In this paper, we proposed the task of automatic keyword extraction problem over multi-party live chats in order to provide in situ topic information. Based on our observations, we developed a system using structural information and automatically predicted dialogue acts, and achieved preliminary results applying an existing dialogue act classification method to live chats. Unlike previous research (e.g. Forsyth (2007; Kim et al. (2010a)), features based on structure and interaction did not perform well since multi-party live chats impose problems due to the tangled and asynchronous nature of chats. Finally, we showed that our method achieved higher performance than KEA, which implies that conventional methods (KEA in this paper) do not work well over structured data like live chats and web forums.

In this research, we found structural features to be one of the most important features in correctly identifying keywords. To date, none of topic detection methods appear to work. On the other hand, detecting topic boundaries with higher accuracy would improve the performance of the keyword extractor. As such, we leave this for future work.

References

James Allen and Mark Core. 1997. Draft of damsl: Dialog act markup in several layers.

Regina Barzilay and Michael Elhadad. 1997. Using lexical chains for text summarization. In *Proceedings of the ACL/EACL 1997 Workshop on Intelligent Scalable Text Summarization*, pages 10–17.

Ernesto DÁvanzo and Bernado Magnini. 2005. A keyphrase-based approach to summarization:the lake system. In *Proceedings of Document Understanding Conferences*, pages 6–8.

Mark Dredze, Hanna M. Wallach, Danny Puller, and Fernando Pereira. 2008. Generating summary keywords for emails using topics. In *Proceedings of the 13th international conference on Intelligent user interfaces*, pages 199–206.

Eric N. Forsyth. 2007. Improving automated lexical and discourse analysis of online chat dialog. Master's thesis, Naval Postgraduate School.

Eibe Frank, Gordon W. Paynter, Ian H. Witten, Carl Gutwin, and Craig G. Nevill-manning. 1999. Domain specific keyphrase extraction. In *Proceedings of the 16th International Joint Conference on AI*, pages 668–673.

Carl Gutwin, Gordon Paynter, Ian Witten, Craig Nevill-Manning, and Eibe Frank. 1999. Improving browsing in digital libraries with keyphrase indexes. *Journal of Decision Support Systems*, 27:81–104.

Khaled M. Hammouda, Diego N. Matute, and Mohamed S. Kamel. 2005. Corephrase: keyphrase extraction for document clustering. In *Proceedings of MLDM*, pages 265–274.

Annette Hulth. 2003. Improved automatic keyword extraction given more linguistic knowledge. In *Proceedings of the 2003 conference on Empirical methods in natural language processing*, pages 216–223.

Edward Ivanovic. 2008. Automatic instant messaging dialogue using statistical models and dialogue acts. Master's thesis, the University of Melbourne.

Daniel Jurafsky, Elizabeth Shriberg, Barbara Fox, and Traci Curl. 1998. Lexical, prosodic, and syntactic cues for dialog acts. In *Proceedings of ACL/COLING-98 Workshop on Discourse Relations and Discourse Markers*, pages 114–120.

Su Nam Kim, Lawrence Cavedon, and Timothy Baldwin. 2010a. Classifying dialogue acts in 1-to-1 live chats. In *Conference on Empirical Methods in Natural Language Processing (EMNLP)*, pages 862–871.

Su Nam Kim, Olena Medelyan, Min-Yen Kan, and Timothy Baldwin. 2010b. SemEval-2010 task 5: Automatic keyphrase extraction from scientific articles. In *Proceedings of the 5th International Workshop on Semantic Evaluation*, pages 21–26, Uppsala, Sweden.

Decong Li, Sujian Li, and Wenjie Li. 2010. A semi-supervised key phrase extraction approach: learning from title phrases through a document semantic network. In *Proceedings of the 48th Annual Meeting of the Association for Computational Linguistics*, pages 296–300.

Feifan Liu, Deana Pennell, Fei Liu, and Yang Liu. 2009. Unsupervised approaches for automatic keyword extraction using meeting transcripts. In *Proceedings of Human Language Technologies: The 2009 Annual Conference of the North American Chapter of the Association for Computational Linguistics*, pages 620–628.

A. K. McCallum. 2002. Mallet: A machine learning for language toolkit.

Olena Medelyan. 2009. *Human-competitive automatic topic indexing*. Ph.D. thesis, University of Waikato.

Guido Minnen, John Carroll, and Darren Pearce. 2001. Applied morphological processing of English. *Natural Language Engineering*, 7(3):207–223.

Junichiro Mori, Yutaka Matsuo, Mitsuru Ishizuka, and Boi Faltings. 2004. Keyword extraction from the web for personal metadata annotation. In *4th International Workshop on Knowledge Markup and Semantic Annotation*, pages 51–60.

Thuy Dung Nguyen and Min-Yen Kan. 2007. Key phrase extraction in scientific publications. In *Proceeding of International Conference on Asian Digital Libraries*, pages 317–326.

Ken Samuel, Carbeery Sandra Carberry, and K. Vijay-Shanker. 1998. Dialogue act tagging with transformation-based learning. In *Proceedings of COLING/ACL 1998*, pages 1150–1156.

Alexander Thorsten Schutz. 2008. Keyphrase extraction from single documents in the open domain exploiting linguistic and statistical methods. Master's thesis, National University of Ireland.

Elizabeth Shriberg, Rebecca Bates, Paul Taylor, Andreas Stolcke, Daniel Jurafsky, Klaus Ries, Noah Coccaro, Rachel Martin, Marie Meteer, and Carol Van Ess-Dykema. 1998. Can prosody aid the automatic classification of dialog acts in conversational speech? *Language and Speech*, 41(3-4):439–487.

Andreas Stolcke, Klaus Ries, Noah Coccaro, Elizabeth Shriberg, Rebecca Bates, Daniel Jurafsky, Paul Taylor, Rachel Martin, Carol Van Ess-Dykema, and Marie Meteer. 2000. Dialogue act modeling for automatic tagging and recognition of conversational speech. *Computational Linguistics*, 26(3):339–373.

Peter Turney. 1999. Learning to extract keyphrases from text.

Xiaojun Wan and Jianguo Xiao. 2008. Collabrank: Towards a collaborative approach to single-document keyphrase extraction. In *Proceedings of 22nd International Conference on Computational Linguistics*, pages 969–976, Manchester, UK.

Tianhao Wu, Faisal M. Khan, Todd A. Fisher, Lori A. Shuler, and William M. Pottenger. 2002. Posting act tagging using transformation-based learning. In *Proceedings of the Workshop on Foundations of Data Mining and Discovery, IEEE International Conference on Data Mining*.

Extracting Networks of People and Places from Literary Texts

John Lee and Chak Yan Yeung
Halliday Centre for Intelligent Applications of Language Studies
Department of Chinese, Translation and Linguistics
City University of Hong Kong
{jsylee,chayeung}@cityu.edu.hk

Abstract

We describe a method to automatically extract social networks from literary texts. Similar to those in prior research, nodes represent characters found in the texts; edges connect them to other characters with whom they interact, and also display sentences describing their interactions. Furthermore, other nodes encode places and are connected to characters who were active there. Thus, these networks present an overview of the "who", "what", and "where" in large text corpora, visualizing associations between people and places.

1 Introduction

To fully understand a matter, one must be able to answer, as it were, the "Five W" questions: *who*, *what*, *where*, *when*, and *why*. In Humanities research, scholars comb texts to answer similar questions --- who the principal figures were, with whom they interacted, what they did, where and when they lived, and why they made an impact. The vast amount of texts available in digital libraries has, on the one hand, enlarged the breadth on which scholars can perform textual research (Crane, 2006); on the other hand, the sheer volume overwhelms an individual's ability to read the texts in depth to answer these questions.

Overviews — information abstracted from a collection of texts — can help a reader rapidly grasp the scope and nature of the collection in question (Greene et al., 2000), thereby supporting "distant reading" of large text corpora (Moretti, 1999). Ideally, they should also serve as gateways to the primary source by helping the reader locate points of interest for closer reading.

Manually written overviews tend to be centered on one of the W's. For example, biographies summarize the "who" in a text; a plot précis explains the "what" of a novel; and a gazetteer gives a list of locations. Most approaches in computational linguistics also focused on each of the W's in isolation. Named entity recognition systems retrieve lists of personal entities, organizations, geographical names, and the like (Chinchor et al., 1999); temporal resolution systems detect temporal expressions (Mani and Wilson, 2000); discourse parsers can help answer *why* questions (Marcu, 1998).

In more recent work, there has been much effort to synthesize two or more of the W's, for example, detecting co-occurrences of dates and place names (Smith, 2002); linking time to events (Pustejovsky et al., 2005); connecting people to the events in which they interact with others (Doddington et al., 2004; Agarwal et al., 2010); as well as "nexus points" of groups of people at particular locations (Bingenheimer et al., 2009). This paper contributes another step in this direction, reporting the first attempt to automatically construct social networks from literary texts integrating *who*, *what*, and *where*.

The rest of the paper is organized as follows. The next section reviews previous work in the automatic generation of social networks. Section 3 defines the research question. Section 4 describes the baseline and our generation algorithm. Sections 5 and 6 outline our data and evaluation results. The paper concludes with future work in the last section.

2 Previous Work

2.1 Conversational networks

Most research in automatic generation of social networks has concentrated on extracting the "who" and the "what" from a corpus. More precisely speaking, these networks should be termed "*conversational networks*." Typically, they consist of nodes representing people, and directed edges encoding the nature of their communication. The earliest attempts are concerned with structured corpora, where the senders and receivers of such communications are clearly defined, such as in internet relay chat (Mutton, 2004) and e-mail messages (Diesner et al., 2005). The edges contain analyses of the content of the messages, such as the topics and the words used.

Likewise, when applied on literary texts, automatic generation of social networks has also focused on dialogues between characters. For example, in networks constructed from Shakespearean plays, two characters are considered connected if one is speaking and the other is also on stage (Stiller et al., 2003). The edge can also characterize the speech, for example the distribution of verb tense and person in networks of Classical Greek tragedies (Rydberg-Cox, 2011). For novels, dialogues between characters are not explicitly stated, and must be identified using techniques in quoted speech attribution. A conversational network can then be similarly built; the edges can characterize, for example, the length of dialogues between the two characters (Elson et al., 2010).

2.2 Social Networks

Relations between people, however, are not described only, or even primarily, by conversations, in most other genres. The Automated Content Extraction (ACE) task, which focuses on newswire text, aims to infer all entities mentioned in a text, the relations among them, and the events in which they participate (Doddington et al., 2004). Also using newswire corpora, Agarwal and Rambow (2010) extract social events using features from syntactic parse trees. Emphasizing the cognitive states of the participants, they classify the events into "interactions" or "observations". In the extraction of social networks from biographies, personal relationships are classified as "positive" or "negative" (van de Camp and van den Bosch, 2011).

Our goal is to produce overviews of large corpora of literary texts, and is thus most similar to that of (Elson et al., 2010). Our networks are not, however, limited to conversations, so that quoted speech needs not be assumed to be the main vehicle of encoding interpersonal relations; in this sense, our scope is closer to (Agarwal and Rambow, 2010). Besides people and their associated events, our networks also integrate locations. Whereas past research have focused on toponym resolution, i.e. linking place names to geographical coordinates (Smith and Crane, 2001; Speriosu et al., 2010), we attempt to link them to events in the text. In summary, this paper is the first attempt to extract beyond conversational networks from literary texts, and encompass not only *who*, but also *what* and *where*.

3 Research Question

For texts that are rich in dialogue interactions, such as novels and serials, social interactions can be well represented by conversational networks (Elson et al., 2010). Such networks are less suitable for texts in most other genres, where evidence concerning the characters' social relationships is found largely outside of dialogue interactions. For example, in the book of *Genesis*, the tense relationship between Sarai, Abram's wife, and Hagar, Sarai's servant, is mentioned frequently, but the two of them are never involved in any dialogue interactions in the book. In fact, there are 330 distinct personal names in *Genesis*, but only 53 are involved in any dialogue interactions, so the above method would only be able to capture the social relationships of one-sixth of the total characters.

An alternative method, therefore, is needed to extract social networks from texts that lack dialogue interactions. We now define the structure (Section 3.1) and meaning (Section 3.2) of the networks to be generated, then describe our proposed method (Section 4).

3.1 Network definition

Our network graphs contain two types of nodes, one encoding people ("who"), and the other encoding locations ("where"). Each personal name is presented as a node (a 'person-node'). Two person-nodes are connected by an edge (a 'person-person edge') if there is textual evidence, i.e. a set of sentences in the corpus attesting that the two people are kin or have at least one instance of social interaction, as defined in Section 3.2.

Since some social relationships do not occur in any geographical context, and some span over multiple locations, we decided to treat the geographical names as another type of nodes ('location-nodes'), rather than attaching them to the person-person edges. A person-node and a location-node are connected by an edge (a 'person-location edge') if the person has been to that location physically.

In both person-person and person-location edges, we encode the source text that supports the claim ("what"). This design allows the readers to see the relationships of each person and the activities in each location easily. Figure 1 shows an example social network graph.

3.2 Network Construction

Person-Person Edges: As pointed out by Agarwal and Rambow (2010), a text may describe social relations between two people *explicitly* or *implicitly*.

Explicit descriptions typically state the relationship, e.g., kinship, between two people. Consider the sentence "[Noah] had three sons: [Shem], [Ham], and [Japheth]." The father and son relationships (Noah - Shem, Noah - Ham and Noah - Japheth) are explicitly mentioned, but the sibling relationships (Shem - Ham, Shem - Japheth and Ham - Japheth) can also be inferred. Our practice is to annotate the former, but not the latter type of relationships.

Implicit descriptions, in contrast, "create or perpetuate a social relationship" between two people through an event. In our annotations, events can be verbal or non-verbal interactions.

Verbal interactions. Two people are said to have a verbal interaction when one or both of them speaks, and both are aware of the communication. This type of interaction may be either quoted speech[1], or communications that are implied but not presented in the text as actual dialogues[2].

Non-verbal interactions. Two people are said to have a non-verbal interaction when they interact non-verbally and are mutually aware of the interaction. This type of interaction may involve direct physical contact between the people[3], non-physical contact[4], and others which are ambiguous due to lack of detail[5].

For each relation, the words in the sentence that indicate that relation are also annotated. For implicit descriptions, the majority of these are verbs. For example, the word 'treated' in the sentence 'Sarai treated Hagar harshly' was extracted. For explicit descriptions, these are mostly nouns, e.g., 'son'.

Person-Location Edges: An edge is placed between a person-node and a location-node if it can be inferred from the text that the person has physically been to that location. For example, based on the sentence "[Esau] went to [Ishmael] and married [Mahalath]", both Esau and Mahalath are connected to the place Ishmael.

4 Proposed Approach

We first describe our baseline (Section 4.1); then our proposed algorithm, incorporating coreference (Section 4.2), syntactic and semantic information (Section 4.3); and finally a second baseline using a machine learning approach (Section 4.4).

4.1 Baseline

It is assumed that the input text already has its personal and geographical names marked up, either manually or with a named entity recognizer. For social relationships stated outside of dialogue interactions, the named entities may be expected to be in relatively close proximity to each other. Our baseline is therefore co-occurrence: any two personal names that co-occur in a sentence are connected in the graph. Likewise, any personal name and geographical name that co-occurred were also connected.

---

[1] E.g., "[Esau] said, "I have plenty, my brother. Keep what belongs to you." "No, please take them," [Jacob] said."
[2] E.g., "[Isaac] spoke to his son [Esau]."
[3] E.g., "While they were in the field, [Cain] attacked his brother [Abel]"
[4] E.g., "[Enoch] walked with [God] for 300 years."
[5] E.g., "[Sarai] treated [Hagar] harshly."

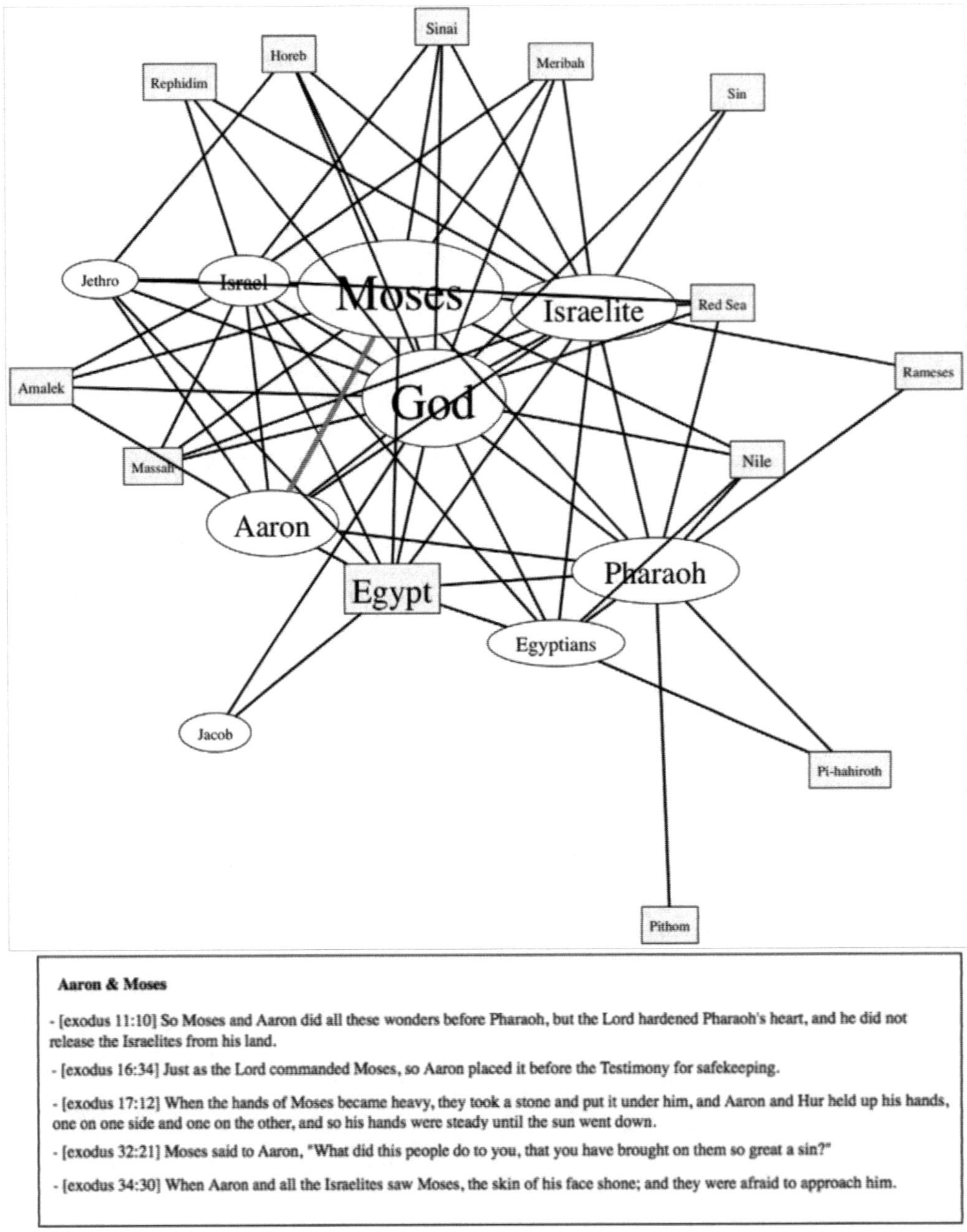

Figure 1: A portion of social network drawn automatically from *Exodus*, the second book in our test set. Person-nodes are circular in shape and location-nodes are rectangular in shape. Some of the sentences associated with the selected edge are displayed at the bottom. The more frequently a name is mentioned in the text, the larger its node is.

4.2 Coreference Resolution

A sentence needs not explicitly mention the names of the two people when describing their interaction; the most common alternative is the use of pronouns. Consider the sequences of sentences 'Joseph had been brought down to Egypt ... An Egyptian named Potiphar purchased him.' The 'him' clearly refers to Joseph. Whereas the baseline (Section 4.1) misses this relation between 'Joseph' and 'Potiphar', coreference information would enable a link to be established between the two.

With coreference information, recall is expected to improve. However, the accuracy of coreference resolution systems tend to deteriorate as the distance between the pronoun and the mention increases. We therefore only take into account those pronouns within *n* sentences of the mention, where *n* is to be tuned on development data.

4.3 Syntactic and Semantic Information

Even when two names co-occur in a sentence, they do not necessarily signal an interaction. Consider the sentence 'Hamor went to speak with Jacob about Dinah'. The proximity of the names 'Hamor' and 'Dinah' does not imply that the two of them were involved in any interaction. Likewise, despite the co-occurrence of 'Hadad' and 'Masrekah' in the sentence 'When Hadad died, Samlah from Masrekah succeeded him as king', it does not follow that Hadad had been to that location.

This section describes our use of a variety of syntactic and semantic information to address this problem. We leverage part-of-speech and dependency information from a state-of-the-art tagger (Toutanova et al., 2003) and dependency parser (De Marneffe et al., 2006), as well as semantic information from FrameNet (Ruppenhofer et al., 2010).

Person-Person Edges: We derived rules from our development data to filter out invalid edges obtained from the baseline.

Implicit descriptions. As described in Section 3.2, these descriptions involve social interactions, typically actions (e.g., 'kiss') performed by one or both of the people concerned (e.g., 'Jacob kissed Rachel and began to weep'). Therefore, to determine whether the two people are involved in a social interaction, we first check whether the two named entities were marked in the dependency tree either as a subject-object pair of a verb, or as a pair connected by a coordinating conjunction (e.g., 'and'), serving as a subject or object.

Furthermore, the verb must belong to a frame in FrameNet that is deemed to indicate social interactions. To be included in this set of frames, the frame must contain at least one word that is annotated as indicating an interaction in the development data (see Section 3.2). There are 316 selected frames, such as `request` and `cause harm`. During evaluation, the verb must belong to one of these frames in order to be counted towards a person-person edge. This procedure excludes frames such as `perception experience`, thereby successfully blocking such verbs as 'overhear' and 'see', which do not require participation from both parties, and thus do not contribute to a person-person edge.

Explicit descriptions. Personal relationships are usually explicitly realized (e.g., 'son'). They could be stated directly, like in the sentence 'The *sons* of Midian were Ephah, Epher, Hanoch, Abida, and Eldaah.' They could also be mentioned in passing, as in the sentence 'But Jacob did not send Joseph's *brother* Benjamin with his brothers.' In both cases, the relationship word and the relevant personal names are related in predictable dependency structure patterns.

To detect these explicit descriptions, we obtained the list of words that fall under the frames `kinship` or `personal relationship` in FrameNet. If the dependency tree of the sentence contains two or more personal names, both linked to one of these words, then an edge was drawn between the two corresponding person-nodes in the social network.

Limitations. We do not yet handle personal mentions that require compositional analysis. For example, in the sentence 'Sarah noticed the son of Hagar mocking', it was the son of Hagar, instead of Hagar herself, who was being referred to. In general, a noun phrase of the form "X of Y", where Y is a personal name and X is a noun belonging to the `kinship` or `personal relationship` frame, usually refers not to Y but to someone else. Such personal names are therefore ignored. The same policy applies to geographical names requiring compositional analysis, such as 'south of <location>'.

Person-Location Edges: A geographical name indicates the location at which a scene takes place. Once the scene is established, the location may not appear again in the text. For example, the sentence 'Joseph had been brought down to Egypt' is followed by the sentence 'An Egyptian named Potiphar purchased him.' It is clear that both Joseph and Potiphar were physically at Egypt. Whenever a geographical name does not appear with the relevant personal names in the same sentence, the baseline would fail to infer the person-location edges.

In order to improve the recall of these edges, whenever a geographical name is detected in a sentence, it is set as the 'current-location'. Any person mentioned in subsequent sentences is assumed to be present at that location, and an edge is drawn between the current location and that person. This continues until the next geographical name is detected, and the current-location updated.

A naive application of this strategy would, however, result in spurious associations between locations and personal names, since some locations are mentioned only in passing. For example, the location 'Egypt' in the sentence 'They finished eating the grain they had brought from Egypt' is only used to describe a property of the grain, rather than indicating a change of scene. The constituent in which the geographical name is located can help flag these cases; in particular, prepositions and relative clauses are good indicators.

Prepositions. If a geographical name is preceded by the preposition 'from', the location is often used for describing the origin of a person or an object, rather than a change of scene. Such geographical names, therefore, were not set as current locations but were only matched with the personal names that appeared in the same sentence.

Relative clauses. Relative clauses can also be used to determine whether the geographical name should be set as the current location. Geographical names within relative clauses are mainly used to describe a person or the position of another location, and should not be considered as a change of scene[6].

There is one exception. If the head of the relative clause is linked to a personal name, then any geographical names found within the clause are matched to that person[7].

Motion verbs. There is a third phenomenon, where the 'current-location' becomes unknown. Motion verbs, such as 'go out' and 'travel', suggest a change of scene, but the destination is not always specified. When a motion verb is not accompanied with a new geographical name (e.g., 'he left'), the current location is reset and becomes 'unknown'; subsequent sentences are not associated with a scene until the next current-location is found. All verbs in the `motion` frame in FrameNet are considered to have this property.

4.4 Baseline using Machine Learning

As a second baseline, we cast the problem of network extraction as a classification task. Two maximum-entropy classifiers (Bird et al., 2009) were trained. One determines whether to connect two person-nodes in the network; the other decides whether to connect a person to a location. As shown in Table 1, most of their features replicate those in the proposed algorithm (Section 4.3), with an additional feature for POS information that further improved performance.

Person-Person Edges	Person-Location Edges
Verbs connected to both names in tree	Prepositions heading the names
Presence of words in FrameNet indicating a personal relationship	Whether the name is designated as the current location
Dependency between name and its head	Whether the names are found within relative clauses
Distance between names in sentence	POS of names and surrounding words
POS of names and surrounding words	

Table 1: Features of the classifier for person-person edges and those for person-location edges.

5 Data

The first five books in the Hebrew Bible, or Old Testament, were used for evaluation. We used an

[6] To isolate such clauses, we made use of the dependency tree, which used the label `rcmod` to link the head of a relative clause to the main sentence.

[7] E.g., 'Hadad' should be linked to 'Moab' in the sentence "[Hadad] … who defeated the Midianites in [Moab], reigned in his place."

online, open-source English translation known as the New English Translation (NET, 2006). This corpus was chosen for two reasons. First, these five books, also known as the Pentateuch, contain a variety of writing style, from the mostly first-person account in Deuteronomy, and the commands and imperatives in Leviticus, to the narratives in the rest. It is a challenging corpus that can reveal the extent to which our algorithm can generalize. Second, as a well-read corpus, there are a lot of existing resources to enrich our evaluations. For example, we made use of previous published biographies (see Section 6.3).

In the proposed approach, the first book in the Pentateuch, *Genesis*, was used as development set, and the four remaining books, *Exodus*, *Leviticus*, *Numbers* and *Deuteronomy*, as test set. In the machine learning approach, for each book in the test set, a classifier is trained on the rest of the Pentateuch. The network graphs of all five books were drawn manually by annotating sentences according to the criteria set out in Section 3.2. Statistics of the test data are presented in Table 2.

	Exod.	Lev.	Num.	Deut.
# words	31257	23876	30465	25610
# sentences	1371	866	1452	1022
# P-nodes	9	7	27	14
# P-P edges	13	4	32	18
# L-nodes	30	7	116	76
# P-L edges	46	2	114	67

Table 2: Size of our test data. Statistics on the social network graphs include only those characters used in our evaluation, i.e. those mentioned ten times or more. 'P' stands for 'person', and 'L' for 'location'.

6 Evaluation

This section describes some data processing steps (Section 6.1), then reports experimental results (Section 6.2), and ends with an evaluation from a different perspective, using biographies written by humans (Section 6.3).

6.1 Data Preparation

We extracted named entities from our corpus using the Stanford NER tagger (Finkel et al., 2005). On the test set, for identifying the person-nodes, the tagger yielded 82.1% precision and 71.1% recall; for identifying the location nodes, it yielded only 37.8% precision and 56.7% recall. As for coreference resolution, we made use of the Stanford Deterministic Coreference Resolution System (Lee et al., 2011; Raghunathan et al., 2010).

Since it is common for characters to be referred to with multiple names, we employed the name clustering method in Elson et al. (2010), matching the named entities with their variations.

6.2 Results

We first analyze the results for person-person edges and person-location edges, using named entities extracted manually (gold named entities). We then report the effects of using automatic named entity recognition. In all evaluations, we considered only the major characters, defined as those mentioned at least ten times in the corpus.

Algorithm	Exod.	Lev.	Num.	Deut
Baseline	P: 0.43	0.40	0.35	0.53
	R: 1.00	1.00	0.97	0.89
	F: 0.60	**0.57**	**0.51**	**0.67**
Classifier	P: 0.65	0.50	0.69	0.64
	R: 0.85	1.00	0.69	0.50
	F: 0.73	**0.67**	**0.69**	**0.56**
Proposed	P: 0.59	0.67	0.64	0.58
	R: 1.00	1.00	0.78	0.61
	F: 0.74	**0.80**	**0.70**	**0.59**

Table 3: Precision (P), recall (R), and F-measure (F) of person-person edges in the automatically generated networks. Gold named entities are used.

Person-Person Edges: Experimental results are shown in Table 3. Overall, the proposed approach yielded an average F-measure of 0.71, an improvement [8] over both the baseline and the classifier. Whereas the baseline favors recall, and the classifier favors precision, the proposed approach strikes a balance between the two. It has the added benefit of requiring less training data than the classifier.

In all books except Deuteronomy, gains over the baseline came from improvement in the precision. In particular, the dependency

[8] The improvement is statistically significant for the first three books against both the baseline ($p<0.0001$ by McNemar's test) and the classifier ($p<0.02$).

information was able to discount name pairs that simply happen to be in the same sentence but do not concern one another. Furthermore, the filtering steps using FrameNet detected those that, despite being closely related grammatically (e.g., subject-object), do not involve interactions. Deuteronomy, which consists of mostly first-person, direct speech, proved to be more challenging.

Most mistakes in other books were caused by inaccuracy in coreference resolution, especially plural pronouns. As a typical case, the word 'they' in a sentence[9] refers to two characters, Nadab and Abihu, mentioned earlier as Aaron's sons. The coreference resolution unfortunately linked the word to Aaron himself, resulting in an extra edge and two missed edges.

Another source of error was inaccuracy in dependency parsing, particularly for explicit descriptions in sentences with multiple names. For example, in the sentence 'Now these are the names of the men who are to help you: from Reuben, Elizur son of Shedeur', the word 'son' was wrongly linked to Reuben, instead of Elizur.

Despite the improvement in precision, our proposed algorithm still extracted some extra edges because of ambiguity in meaning. Consider the sentence 'Then Miriam and Aaron spoke against Moses because of the Cushite woman he had married'. Since the verb 'speak' suggests an interaction, our algorithm reckoned this as a social relation. According to our definition, however, a social relationship is recorded only if both parties are aware of the interaction, and so this edge was not marked by the annotator.

Algorithm	Exod.	Lev.	Num.	Deut.
Baseline	P: 0.48	0.15	0.37	0.22
	R: 0.54	1.00	0.55	0.39
	F: 0.51	**0.27**	**0.44**	**0.28**
Classifier	P: 0.50	0.50	0.40	0.38
	R: 0.46	1.00	0.24	0.30
	F: 0.48	**0.67**	**0.30**	**0.33**
Proposed	P: 0.50	0.29	0.46	0.31
	R: 0.61	1.00	0.46	0.39
	F: 0.55	**0.44**	**0.46**	**0.34**

Table 4: Precision (P), recall (R) and F-measure (F) of person-location edges in the automatically generated networks. Gold named entities are used.

[9] In 'So fire went out from the presence of the Lord and consumed them so that they died before the Lord'.

Person-Location Edges: Experimental results for person-location edges are shown in Table 4. Our proposed algorithm improved[10] the average F-measure over both the baseline and the classifier. Similar to person-person edges, most gains were due to improved precision, contributed by the filtering performed with prepositions and relative clauses (Section 4.3).

Mistakes in the coreference resolution system, again, were responsible for many missed relations. For example, the sentence 'They were the men who were speaking to Pharaoh king of Egypt' was preceded by a list of more names, all of which should be linked to 'Egypt'. Also, in a number of cases, the personal names appeared before the location. Our strategy of maintaining the current-location failed to connect these names to the location.

Automatic named entity recognition: If named entities in the corpus are automatically extracted, mistakes in NER would trickle down to the social network. Unsurprisingly, both precision and recall deteriorated in most books, resulting in an average precision of 0.55, an average recall of 0.32 and an average F-measure of 0.40 for person-person edges, an average precision of 0.07, an average recall of 0.20 and an average F-measure of 0.09 for person-location edges.

6.3 Comparison with Biographies

For many well-known works of literature, including our evaluation corpus, there already exist human analyses of the characters and their inter-relationships, in the form of biographies. To provide a different angle of evaluation, we measure how these biographies differ from the kind of social networks constructed by our algorithm, using the book *Who's Who in the Old Testament* (Comay, 2001), which provides sketches of the lives of a number of major characters.

Out of these biographies, we constructed social networks by first inserting a node for each character that appears in the Pentateuch. We then scanned for personal and geographical names in the biography, and added edges between that node

[10] The improvement is statistically significant against the baseline for the book of Exodus ($p < 0.01$ by McNemar's test), and against the classifier for Deuteronomy ($p < 0.002$).

and the corresponding nodes representing those names.

The social networks constructed from these biographies are compared to our manually annotated ones. They yielded an average precision of 0.19, an average recall of 0.75 and an average F-measure of 0.29 for person-person edges; an average precision of 0.10, an average recall of 0.30 and an average F-measure of 0.14 for person-location edges. Both the precision and recall are substantially lower than the proposed algorithm.

These results must be qualified in two respects. First, although only the biographies for those characters that appear in the particular book under evaluation were considered, they still contain information on events that occurred outside of the book. Further, the biography-based networks were constructed with expert knowledge, and may include, therefore, social relations that are implied but without textual evidence. These mismatches with the gold networks contributed to a lower precision.

Second, certain social interactions may be deemed by the author as insignificant and therefore omitted; in contrast, no such judgment was made in our annotations. This led to a lower recall.

7 Conclusion and Future Work

We have described and evaluated an algorithm that automatically infers social networks from literary texts. The algorithm outperforms a co-occurrence baseline as well as a statistical classifier. A significant novelty of these networks is that they encode not only people and their relations, but also the locations at which they are active, and the sentences that attest to these claims. Readers can browse a higher-level view of the relationships among characters, and easily refer to the relevant sentences.

We plan to build on this work in several directions. First, we would like to improve the precision and recall of the automatically generated networks, by borrowing more techniques from relevant fields in natural language processing. Second, we intend to generalize our algorithm to other languages, so as to generate networks for international literary works. Third, it would be useful to further characterize the nature of the edges, such as whether two people are "friends" or "foes" (van de Camp and van den Bosch, 2010), and the kind of activities that a person is engaged at a location.

Acknowledgments

This research project was partially supported by a CityU Start-up Grant for New Staff.

References

Apoorv Agarwal and Owen Rambow. 2010. Automatic detection and classification of social events. *Proc. EMNLP*.

Apoorv Agarwal, Owen Rambow, and Rebecca J. Passonneau. 2010. Annotation Scheme for Social Network Extraction from Text. *Proc. ACL.*

Apoorv Agarwal, Owen Rambow, and Rebecca J. Passonneau. 2010. Annotation scheme for social network extraction from text. *Proc. Fourth Linguistic Annotation Workshop*.

NET 2006. *The Net Bible*. Biblical Studies Press.

Marcus Bingenheimer, Jen-Jou Hung, and Simon Wiles. 2009. Markup meets GIS – Visualizing the 'Biographies of Eminent Buddhist Monks'. *Proc. 13th International Conference on Information Visualisation*.

Steven Bird, Edward Loper and Ewan Klein. 2009. *Natural Language Processing with Python*. O'Reilly Media Inc.

Nancy Chinchor, Erica Brown, Lisa Ferro, and Patty Robinson. 1999. *Named Entity Recognition Task Definition*. Technical Report, MITRE Corporation and SAIC.

Joan Comay. 2001. Who's Who in the Old Testament (Who's Who (Routledge)). Routledge.

Jana Diesner, Terrill Frantz, and Kathleen Carley. 2005. Communication Networks from the Enron Email Corpus: It's Always about the People, Enron is no Different. *Computational and Mathematical Organization Theory* 11(3).

George Doddington, Alexis Mitchell, Mark Przybocki, Lance Ramshaw, Stephanie Strassel, and Ralph Weischedel. 2004. The Automatic Content Extraction (ACE) Program: Tasks, Data, and Evaluation. *Proc. LREC.*

Gregory Crane. 2006. What Do You Do with a Million Books? *D-Lib Magazine* 12(3).

Marie-Catherine de Marneffe, Bill MacCartney, and Christopher D. Manning. 2006. Generating typed dependency parses from phrase structure parses. *Proc. LREC.*

David K. Elson, Nicholas Dames, and Kathleen R. McKeown. 2010. Extracting social networks from literary fiction. *Proc. ACL.*

Jenny R. Finkel, Trond Grenager, and Christopher Manning. 2005. Incorporating non-local information into information extraction systems by gibbs sampling. *Proc. ACL.*

Stephan Greene, Gary Marchionini, Catherine Plaisant, and Ben Shneiderman. 2000. Previews and Oerviews in Digital Libraries: Designing Surrogates to Support Visual Information Seeking. *Journal of the American Society for Information Science* 51(4):380—393.

Heeyoung Lee, Yves Peirsman, Angel Chang, Nathanael Chambers, Mihai Surdeanu, and Dan Jurafsky. 2011. Stanford's Multi-Pass Sieve Coreference Resolution System at the CoNLL-2011 Shared Task. *Proc. CoNLL.*

Inderjeet Mani and George Wilson. 2000. Robust Temporal Processing of News. *Proc. ACL.*

Daniel Marcu. 1998. The Rhetorical Parsing of Natural Language Texts. *Proc. ACL.*

Franco Moretti. 1999. *Atlas of the European Novel 1800-1900.* Verso.

Paul Mutton. 2004. Inferring and Visualizing Social Networks on Internet Relay Chat. *Proc. 8th International Conference on Information Visualization.*

NET 2006. *The Net Bible.* Biblical Studies Press.

James Pustejovsky, Robert Knippen, Jessica Littman, and Roser Saurí. 2005. Temporal and Event Information in Natural Language Text. Language Resources and Evaluation 39:123---164.

Josef Ruppenhofer, Michael Ellsworth, Miriam Petruck, Christopher Johnson, and Jan Scheffczyk. 2010. *FrameNet II: Extended Theory and Practice.* http://framenet.icsi.berkeley.edu

Jeff Rydberg-Cox. 2011. Social Networks and the Language of Greek Tragedy. *Journal of the Chicago Colloquium on Digital Humanities and Computer Science* 1(3).

David A. Smith. 2002. Detecting and Browsing Events in Unstructured Text. *Proc. SIGIR.*

David A. Smith and Gregory Crane. 2001. Disambiguating Geographical Names in a Historical Digital Library. *Proc. ECDL.*

Michael Speriosu, Travis Brown, Taaesun Moon, Jason Baldridge, and Katrin Erk. 2010. Connecting Language and Geography with Region-Topic Models. *Proc. Workshop on Computational Models of Spatial Language Interpretation (COSLI).*

James Stiller, Daniel Nettle, and Robin I. M. Dunbar. 2003. The Small World of Shakespeare's Plays. *Human Nature* 14(4):397---408.

Kristina Toutanova, Dan Klein, Christopher D. Manning, and Yoram Singer. 2003. Feature-rich part-of-speech tagging with a cyclic dependency network. *Proc. NAACL-HLT.*

Matje van de Camp and Antal van den Bosch. 2011. A Link to the Past: Constructing Historical Social Networks. *Proc. Workshop on Computational Approaches to Subjectivity and Sentiment Analysis.*

Pre- vs. Post-verbal Asymmetries and the Syntax of Korean RDC

Daeho Chung
Hanyang University
cdaeho@hanyang.ac.kr

Abstract

Among various important issues pertaining to the so-called right dislocated construction (RDC) in Korean are the basic word order and the grammatical relation the right dislocated (RDed) element assumes to the rest of the structure. In his series of papers, J.-S. Lee (2007a,b, 2008a, 2009a,b, 2010, 2011, 2012) proposes a mono-clausal analysis of Korean RDC, according to which the RDed element is a direct dependent of the preceding predicate and Korean conforms to Kayne's (1994) universal SVO word order hypothesis due to the very existence of the RDC. In contrast, Chung (2008a, 2009b, 2010, 2011) advocates a non-mono-clausal approach, as in Tanaka (2001) and Kato (2007) for Japanese RDC, according to which the RDed element is taken as a fragment of a continuing sentence to which massive ellipsis has applied, while the head-finality is preserved. The current work tries to show that RDed elements cannot be viewed as direct dependents of the preceding predicate due to various asymmetries observed between pre- vs. post-verbal positions, favoring a non-mono-clausal analysis of Korean RDC.

1. Introduction

Predicates in Korean are generally fixed at the clause final position, although the dependents are freely ordered, as in (1). It is observed in Nam and Ko (1986: 250-251) and Huh (1988: 263) among others, however, that Korean allows the so-called right dislocated construction (RDC), in which some apparent part of the sentence may show up at the post-predicate position, as in (2).

(1) a. Cheli-ka Yuni-lul manna-ess-ta (SOV)
Ch.-Nom Y.-Acc meet-Pst-DE
'Cheli saw Yuni.'
b. Yuni-lul Cheli-ka manna-ess-ta (OSV)

(2) a. Cheli-ka manna-ess-ta Yuni-lul (SVO)
b. Yuni-lul manna-ess-ta Cheli-ka (OVS)
c. manna-ess-ta Cheli-ka Yuni-lul (VSO)
d. manna-ess-e Yuni-lul Cheli-ka (VOS)

The RDC in Korean has recently received a great deal of attention as to the architecture of the structure. (See J.-S. Lee 2007a,b, 2008a, 2009a,b, 2010, 2011, 2012, Chung 2008a, 2009b, 2010, 2011, Lee and Yoon 2009, C.-H. Lee 2009, 2011, among others.)

Among various issues around the RDC are the basic word order in Koran and the grammatical relation the RDed element in the post-verbal position assumes with the rest of the construction. Lee (2007a,b, 2008a, 2009a,b, 2010, 2011, 2012) proposes a mono-clausal structure based on Kayne's (1994) universal SVO hypothesis and treats the RDed element as a direct dependent of the preceding predicate. According to this analysis, (2a) is taken as the base word order and all other structures in (1) and (2) are derived from (2a), In contrast, Chung (2008a, 2009b. 2010, 2011), basically following Tanaka's (2001) analysis of Japanese RDC, advocates a non-mono-clausal analysis, according to which the RDC is derived as follows:[1]

[1] See also Kuno (1978), Whitman (2000), and Kato (2007), among others, for non-mono-clausal approaches. Chung (2008a, 2009b, 2010) postulates a null conjunction that conjoins two root clauses: $[_{\text{Root}} \ldots e_i \ldots]$ & $[_{\text{Root}}\ XP_i$ ~~[… t_i …]~~]. This paper does not opt for any particular version of non-mono-clausal analysis since the discussions may go through as far as the RDed element is taken as a fragmental expression.

(3) a. Parataxis of Clausal Copies, S1 and S2

$[_{S1} \ldots e_i \ldots$ Pred], $[_{S2} \ldots XP_i \ldots$ Pred]

b. Fronting in S2

$[_{S1} \ldots e_i \ldots$ Pred], $[_{S2}\ XP_i\ [_{S2} \ldots t_i \ldots$ Pred]]

c. Ellipsis in S2

$[_{S1} \ldots e_i \ldots$Pred], $[_{S2}\ XP_i$ ~~$[_{S2} \ldots t_i \ldots$Pred]~~]

First, two clauses/sentences, S1 and S2, are put together in an asyndetic form, as schematically represented in (3a). [2] Then, the RDed element undergoes fronting in S2, as in (3b). Finally, S2 undergoes a massive ellipsis, deleting all its content except for the fronted element, as in (3c), along the similar lines of Merchant's (2004) analysis of sentence fragments.

A crucial difference between the mono- vs. non-mono-clausal approaches lies in the treatment of the RDed element. A mono-clausal analysis as in J.-S. Lee (2007a,b, 2008a, 2009a,b, 2010, 2011, 2012) views it as a direct dependent of a predicate that precedes it. In contrast, a non-mono-clausal analysis as in Chung (2008a, 2009b. 2010, 2011) treats it as a fragmental element of a continuing sentence/clause.[3] Thus, under the latter approach, an RDed element has no direct thematic or modifying relation to the preceding predicate. They are only indirectly related due to the semantic identity of the two conjuncts of a paratactic coordinate structure.

It is expected under the former approach that the RDed element in a post-verbal position behaves like a pre-verbal counterpart except for the positional difference, i.e., the existence vs. lack of an EPP or edge feature in a certain functional category. This paper will show, however, that this expectation is not borne out. It will be illustrated that there are various asymmetric behaviors displayed between an RDed element in a post-verbal position and its pre-verbal counterpart. These asymmetric behaviors will be shown to indicate that the RDed element (the post-verbal expression) is best analyzed as a fragmental element of a continuing sentence, not as a direct dependent of the overtly realized predicate.

2. Asymmetry in the Locus of RDed Elements

An interesting restriction the RDC in Korean displays is that RD is only to the right of a matrix predicate, i.e., only to the right of a matrix mood. For example, RD is banned in an embedded context. Consider the following examples.

(4) a. na-nun [Cheli-ka Yuni-lul manna-ess-ta-ko]
I-Top Ch.-Nom Y.-Acc see-Pst-DE-C
sayngkakha-n-ta
think-Pres-DE
(Intended) 'I think that Cheli saw Yuni.'

b.*na-nun [Cheli-ka e_i manna-ess-ta-ko
I-Top Ch.-Nom see-Pst-DE-C
Yuni-lul$_i$] sayngkakha-n-ta
Y.-Acc think-Pres-DE
(Intended) 'I think that Cheli saw Yuni.'

c. na-nun [Cheli-ka e_i manna-ess-ta-ko]
I-Top Ch.-Nom see-Pst-DE-C
sayngkakha-n-ta Yuni-lul$_i$[4]
think-Pres-DE Y.-Acc
(Intended) 'I think that Cheli saw Yuni.'

(4a) is a normal word order under the traditional SOV word order hypothesis. (4b) results from placing the embedded object *Yuni-lul* at the right edge of the embedded clause. In (4c), RD placed the embedded object to the right of the matrix predicate. Sentences like (4b) are ungrammatical, while those like (4c) are grammatical.

The right edge restriction on the RDC is self-explanatory under a non-mono-clausal analysis. As schematically represented in (3), the RDed element is analyzed as being positioned at the left periphery of a continuing sentence/clause, the second conjunct of a paratactic structure. The RDed

[2] The RDed part can be overtly realized in the preceding clausal expression: $[_{S1} \ldots XP_i \ldots$ Pred], $[_{S2}\ XP_i$ ~~$[_{S2} \ldots t_i \ldots$ Pred]~~]. I will ignore the issue how XP_i in S1 becomes a null element in the RDC. Pronominalization or NP deletion may be responsible. Yoon and Lee (2009) claim that there exists no null element at all in syntax.

One may be curious about the *raison d'être* for the clausal copy, especially in relation to the interpretation of the event doubling due to the clausal copy. I do not have any definite answer for this question, but I would like to point out the fact that natural languages do allow reduplication of expressions including a clausal element.

[3] The architecture proposed in Yoon and Lee (2009) also implies no direct grammatical relation between the RDed element and the predicate. See also C.-H. Lee (2009, 2011), who claims that an intonation break may intervene between the predicate and the post-verbal element.

[4] To the best of my knowledge, Choe (1987) first observed that an element can be RDed out of an embedded clause in Korean.

element is uniquely pronounced at the second sentence/clause to which massive ellipsis has applied, suppressing all other elements. In short, being a fragmental element, an RDed element cannot be embedded, which accounts for the contrast in grammaticality between (4b) and (4c).

J.-S. Lee's (2007a,b, 2008a, 2009a,b, 2010, 2011, 2012) mono-clausal analysis under the SVO word order hypothesis makes a special assumption to account for the right edge restriction on the RDC. To rule out the sentences like (4b), Lee (2010: 113, 2012:101) makes the following suggestion:[5]

(5) ... the Comp *-ko* signaling embeddedness selects its whole TP complement to be in its domain, so the TP has to be pied-pied to Spec CP.

He attributes the obligatory TP movement to the Principle of Locality of Selection proposed by Sportiche (1998), which states that selection must be satisfied in a strictly local relation, whether head-complement or head-specifier. In short, the TP movement instantiates a case of specifier selection, triggered by the EPP or Edge Feature in C (Chomsky 2000).

The suggestion made in (5), however, faces some non-trivial empirical and theoretical problems. First, there exist empirical challenges. As observed in Choe (1987: 41), RD can be multiply applied. As expected, RD may apply to an element of a previously RDed embedded clause, as shown in the following example:

(6) na-nun e_j mit-nun-ta [Cheli-ka e_i
I-Top believe-Pres-DE Ch.-Nom
cohaha-n-ta-ko]$_j$ Yuni-lul$_i$.
love-Pres-DE-C Y.-Acc
'I believe Cheli loves Yuni.'

RD out of a post-verbal embedded clause is also possible in sentence fragments. Consider the following examples:

(7) A: ne cikum mwe-la-ko malha-ess-ni?
you now what-be-C say-Pst-QE
'What did you say a moment ago?'
B: [e_i Yuni-lul cohaha-n-ta-ko] [Cheli-ka]$_i$
Y.-Acc love-Pres-DE-C Ch.-Nom
'That Cheli loves Yuni.'

The surface order in (6) and (7B) does not conform to Lee's suggestion in (5), according to which the whole MP has to be located in the specifier position of a complementizer.

One might try to derive these sentences by locating the two RDed elements at specifier positions of two different functional categories and raising the predicate to the head of a third functional category. For example, (6) might be said to have undergone the following derivation, after the embedded clause has been built up and the object has scrambled:[6]

(8) a. [Cheli-lul$_i$ [Yuni-ka t_i coha-n-ta-ko]]
⇒ Merge V-v
b. [sayngkakha [Cheli-lul$_i$ [Yuni-ka t_i coha-n-ta-ko]]] ⇒Move CP
c. [Yuni-ka t_i coha-n-ta-ko]$_j$ [sayngkakha [Cheli-lul$_i$ t_j]] ⇒ Merge T(ense) *-n* and Move V-v to T
d. sayngkakhak-n [Yuni-ka t_i coha-n-ta-ko]$_j$ [t_k [Cheli-lul$_i$ t_j]] ⇒Merge Subject and M(ood) and Move T to M
e. [sayngkakhak-n]$_l$-ta na-nun t_l [Yuni-ka t_i coha-n-ta-ko]$_j$ [t_k [Cheli-lul$_i$ t_j]] ⇒Subject Raising
f. na-nun$_f$ [sayngkakhak-n]$_l$-ta t_f t_l [Yuni-ka t_i coha-n-ta-ko]$_j$ [t_k [Cheli-lul$_i$ t_j]]

Thus, it seems that sentences like (6) can be derived by Lee's SVO word order hypothesis.

Sentence fragments like (7B), however, may not be legitimate if ellipsis applies to a syntactic constituent only. Notice that *na-nun$_f$* and *[sayngkakhak-n]$_l$-ta* in (8f) do not form a

[5] Lee (2012: 98) follows Koopman (2005) in assuming the following order of verbal affixes: C(omp)-T(ense)-v-M(ood)-Asp-V. This work, however, adopts a more conservative view, i.e., the V-v-T-M-C order. TP in (5) equals MP in the majority of literature.

[6] Lee (2008: 224, fn 6) treats the verbal complex, for instance, *cohaha-n-ta* 'like-Pres-DE', as being introduced from the lexicon separately from C *-ko*.' Lee (2012: 99, his (42)), however, follows a projectionist view on all verbal endings (T and M as well as C). I abstract away from this issue, as the discussions remain unaffected.

constituent, as they are positioned in two different specifiers. Thus sentence fragments like (7B) would not be produced, contrary to fact. Furthermore, it will be shown below that introduction of a clausal excorporation process as in (8c) leads to a serious problem with respect to the asymmetric availability of such a process out of a pre- vs. post-verbal position. (See Section 4.)

The suggestion in (5) also faces theoretical difficulties. By the SVO order, Lee (2010, 2012) intends to mean the Spec-Head-Complement (SHC) order across all the categories, not just the 'subject-verb-object' word order. Thus, it is expected that every category is to have the SHC order in the base structure. It is evident, however, that the RDed element appears only to the right of the matrix clause, more precisely, to the right of a matrix mood. RD never applies to all other categories to the left of a (mood-inflected) matrix predicate. No other heads allow their dependents to appear to the right. For example, heads like N and P cannot precede their dependents, whether complement or specifier:

(9) a. {mikwuk-uy ilakh-uy kongkyek/*mikwuk-
U.S.-Gen Iraq-Gen attack/U.S.
uy kongkyek ilakh-uy/*ilakh-uy kongkyek
-Gen attack Iraq-Gen/Iraq-Gen attack
mikwuk-uy}-i impakha-ess-ta
U.S.-Gen -Nom impend-Pres-DE
'U.S.'s attack on Iraq is impending.'
b. Cheli-ka {na poko/*poko na} ku il-ul
Ch.-Nom I to to I that work-Acc
ha-ela-ko malha-ess-ta.[7]
do-Imp-C say-Pst-DE
'Cheli told me to do the work.'

To maintain Lee's (2010, 2012) SHC word order hypothesis, it is required to assume that every head except for the mood in the matrix clause always selects its whole complement to its specifier position. This is theoretically burdensome at least for the following two reasons. First, it has to assume a SHC order as a basic word order even if this order never surfaces for the categories in a pre-verbal position. Second, no principled reason seems to be provided for the difference between the matrix vs. embedded mood, other than the stipulation in (5), i.e., that *-ko* (or Cs in general) takes its whole complement (=MP) in its specifier position due to the EPP (or Edge) feature in C. According to him, an MP with an RDed element cannot precede a C, due to the morphological requirement that C is to follow a verbal element. It will be observed in Section 3, however, that no embedded RDC is allowed even when an embedded predicate has the same inflectional endings as a matrix one, i.e., even if there is no overt C, contrary to the expectation. Notice that there should be no asymmetry with respect to the availability of an RDC, as far as the morphological compositions are identical.

3. Asymmetry despite the Morphological Identity

There are cases in Korean in which an embedded clause ending is not different from the matrix one. Some question endings are cases in point. Consider the following sentences.

(10) a. Cheli-ka onul ttena-ess-na?
Ch.-Nom today leave-Pst-QE
'Did Cheli leave today?'
b. na-nun [Cheli-ka onul ttena-ess-na]
I-Top Ch.-Nom today leave-Pst-QE
kungkumha-ta.
wondrous-DE
'I wonder whether Cheli left today.'
(11) a. Chwungmukong-i etise censaha-ess-nunko?
Ch.-Nom where die;in;battle-Pst-QE_{wh}
'Where was Chwungmukong (Admiral Lee) killed in battle?'
b. ne-nun [Chwungmukong-i etise
you-Top Ch.-Nom where
censaha- ess-nunko] hwakinha-ess-na?[8]
die;in;battle-Pst-QE_{wh} confirm-Pst-$QE_{yes/no}$
'Did you confirm where Chwungmukong was killed in action?'

The embedded clauses in (10b) and (11b) are identical to the structures in (10a) and (11a), respectively. Such embedded interrogative clauses do not take any additional (declarative or

[7] I intentionally chose *poko* 'to', a non-affixal particle, to avoid a morphological problem that may otherwise arise.

[8] The examples in (11) are from Kyungnam Province Dialect. Suh (1987, Section 2.4.) reports that *-nunko* functions as a [+WH] QE in the embedded clause as well as in the matrix clause, although there is some subject person restriction in the matrix clause. (11b) is cited from Lee (1998: 131, his (120)).

interrogative) C. There being no overt marker signaling embeddeness, the suggestion made in (5) is irrelevant to such sentences. It is then expected in Lee's system that the embedded clauses in (10b) and (11b) should behave like (10a) and (11a) as to the availability of the RDC. This expectation is not borne out: RD is allowed in (10a) and (11a), but not in the embedded clauses in (10b) and (11b):

(10)' a. Cheli-ka ttena-ess-na? onul
Ch.-Nom leave-Pst-QE today
'Did Cheli leave today?'
b. *na-nun [[Cheli-ka ttena-ess-na] onul]
I-Top Ch.-Nom leave-Pst-QE today
kungkumha-ta.
wondrous-DE
'I wonder whether Cheli left today.'

(11)' a. etise censaha-ess-nunko? Chwungmukong-i
where die;in;action-Pst-QE_{wh} Ch.-Nom
'Where was Chwungmukong killed in battle?'
b. *ne-nun [[etise censaha-ess-nunko]
you-Top where die;in;action-Pst-QE_{wh}
Chwungmukong-i] hwakinha-ess-na?
Ch.-Nom confirm-Pst-$QE_{yes/no}$
'Did you confirm where Chwungmukong was killed in action?'

Lee's system, which attributes the lack of the embedded RD to a lexical property of C, does not expect the non-availability of the RDC in (10)' and (11)'. Since the selectional restriction is lexically represented on C, the identical question endings are supposed to behave alike, contra fact.[9]

4. Asymmetry in Clausal Excorporation

RDC cannot be embedded, but RD out of an embedded clause is possible in Korean, as far as the RDed element appears at the right edge of the whole sentence, as in (4c), repeated as (12) below:

(12) na-nun [Cheli-ka e_i manna-ess-ta-ko]
I-Top Ch.-Nom see-Pst-DE-C
sayngkakha-n-ta Yuni-lul_i
think-Pres-DE Y.-Acc
(Intended) 'I think that Cheli saw Yuni.'

Lee (2012, 103, fn 25, his (i)) tries to derive such a structure as follows. After an embedded clause is built up, the embedded object scrambles to the front as in (13a). The rest of derivation is illustrated in (13b) through (13d):

(13) a. [Yuni-lul_i [Cheli-ka t_i manna-ess-ta-ko]]
=> Merge V-v
b. [sayngkakha-n-ta [Yuni-lul_i [Cheli-ka t_i manna-ess-ta-ko]]] =>Move CP
c. [Cheli-ka t_i manna-ess-ta-$ko]_j$ [sayngkakha-n-ta [Yuni-lul_i t_j]] => Merge Subject
d. na-nun [Cheli-ka t_i manna-ess-ta-$ko]_j$ [sayngkakha-n-ta [Yuni-lul_i t_j]]

One crucial property of the derivation in (13) is that excorporation of an embedded clause is allowed after its object has scrambled. Notice that in (13a), the embedded object has scrambled within the embedded clause and in (13c) the whole embedded clause except for the object has been raised to the SPEC of the matrix V-v.

Such an excorporation device, however, comes across an immediate problem, when it is tried out of a pre-verbal embedded clause. Notice that Korean allows the following structure, in which the whole embedded CP including the scrambled embedded object appears between the matrix subject and matrix predicate:

(14) na-nun [Yuni-lul_i[Cheli-ka t_i manna-ess-ta-ko]]
I-Top Y.-Acc Ch.-Nom see-Pres-DE-C
sayngkakha-n-ta
think-Pres-DE
'I think that Cheli saw Yuni.'

Given the clausal excorporation as in (13c), it is expected under the SHC word order hypothesis that the embedded CP in (14) should be able to move to a higher position, leaving the scrambled object behind.[10] The expectation is not borne out, as shown below.

(15) *[[Cheli-ka t_i manna-ess-ta-$ko]_j$ [na-nun [Yuni-lul_i e_j] sayngkakha-n-ta]]]

A non-mono-clausal analysis of Korean RDC does

[9] Even if there existed a null C in such an embedded interrogative clause, the embedded RDC should be accepted since a null C does not have to satisfy the morphological condition on an overt C: C must follow a verbal element.

[10] It is noteworthy that extraction out of a specifier is permitted in Lee's system, or required if the so-called third factor principle in Lee (2012) is to be established.

not face any problem accounting for the grammatical status of sentences like (12) and ungrammatical status of sentences like (15). Sentences like (15) violate the so-called Proper Binding Condition (Fiengo 1977), or any principle that is responsible for the PBC effects, whatever it may be,[11] since t$_i$ in (15), a trace, remains unbound. In contrast, sentences like (12) do not violate the condition since the RDed element does not belong to the preceding clause and e$_i$ is not a trace.

5. Asymmetry in Leftward Extraction out of a CP

According to the system Lee adopts, the OV order is derived from VO order. With this in mind, observe that there is an asymmetry between the pre- vs. post-verbal positions, with respect to extraction. Extraction is allowed out of an embedded CP in a pre-verbal position, but not out of a post-verbal (RDed) position, as shown in the following examples:

(16) [Cheli-lul]$_i$ na-nun [Yuni-ka e$_i$ coha-n-ta-ko]
Ch.-Acc I-Top Y.-Nom like-Pres-DE-C
sayngkakha-n-ta
think-Pres-DE
'I think Yuni likes Cheli.'

(17) *[Cheli-lul]$_i$ na-nun sayngkakha-n-ta
Ch.-Acc I-Top think-Pres-DE
[Yuni-ka e$_i$ coha-n-ta-ko]
Y.-Nom like-Pres-DE-C
'I think Yuni likes Cheli.'[12]

This contrast is unexpected under the SVO word order hypothesis. There seems to be no reason to block the sentence in (17).[13] It should be derived, when the embedded object scrambles to the clause initial position, subsequently to the SPEC of the matrix V-v, and then to the sentence initial position.

Under a non-mono-clausal analysis, however, the ungrammaticality of the RDC in (17) naturally follows. Notice that the RDC consists of two (or more) clausal elements and the post-verbal elements belong to the second clause. Thus, the RDC will be illegitimate if the RDC minus the post-verbal element is illegitimate. This is exactly the case for (17), as shown below.

(18) *[Cheli-lul] na-nun saygkakha-n-ta

(18) is ungrammatical with the intended reading.

There could be various attempts to derive (17) but they all seem to fail under a non-mono-clausal approach to the RDC. First, the fronted nominal cannot be thought of as the direct complement of the verb *sayngkakha* 'to think' since the verb selects a clausal complement. (This will also violate the so-called parallelism requirement on coordination, given that RDC takes a coordinate structure. Notice that the RDed element is a CP, not an NP.) Second, one might think of a derivation in which *Cheli-lul* is extracted out of a CP in a pre-verbal position, while the rest of the clause undergoes ellipsis, as follows:

(19) *[Cheli-lul]$_i$ na-nun ~~[$_{CP}$ ... e$_i$ ...]~~
saygkakha-n-ta // [Yuni-ka e$_i$ coha-n-ta-ko]

This derivation is not permitted, given some restriction on the locus of [+E], the ellipsis triggering feature. According to Merchant (2004) and Ahn and Cho (2009a,b), ellipsis cannot apply to a complement of a lexical category since the feature resides only at a functional category.[14] Third, one might try to derive it by moving the embedded CP first and then deleting all other elements except for the object, as follows:

(20) [$_{CP}$ ~~Yuni-ka~~ [Cheli-lul] ~~coha-n-ta-ko~~]$_i$ na-nun
e$_i$ saygkakha-n-ta // [Yuni-ka e$_i$ coha-n-ta-ko]

[11] Kim (2012) resorts to Fox and Pesetsky's (2005) Principle of Order Preservation.

[12] One of the reviewers finds (17) acceptable. I suspect that, if it is acceptable at all, the fronted element is extracted from the matrix clause, out of the so-called major object position, not from the embedded clause. A clearer contrast emerges when the fronted element is a dative NP, which hardly functions as a major object:

(i) a. [Cheli-eykey]$_i$ na-nun [Yuni-ka e$_i$ cenhwaha-ess-ta-ko]
Ch.-Dat I-Top Y.-Nom call-Past-DE-C
saygkakha-n-ta
think-Pres-DE
'I think Yuni called Cheli.'
b. *[Cheli-eykey]$_i$ na-nun saygkakha-n-ta
Ch.-Dat I-Top think-Pres-DE
[Yuni-ka e$_i$ cenhwaha-ess-ta-ko]
Y.-Nom call-Past-DE-C
'I think Yuni called Cheli.'

[13] Extraction should be more readily available out of a complement clause than out of a specifier clause, due to the CED effects.

[14] See Park (2009) for a different solution.

As pointed out in Chung (2011), this is not legitimate, either, because ellipsis has applied to a non-constituent expression.

Therefore, there seems to be no way to derive the structure in (17) under a non-mono-clausal analysis of the RDC. Thus, the restriction on the extraction out of a post-verbal, i.e., RDed, embedded clause, naturally follows without making any stipulation.

6. Asymmetry in Permissible Expressions

It is interesting to observe that some expressions are acceptable only in a post-verbal position, and some others only in a pre-verbal position. (See Section 6.1. and 6.2., respectively.) This would be unexpected under a mono-clausal analysis, since there is no reason to distinguish a post- vs. pre-verbal position, except for the word order variation due to the presence or lack of the EPP feature.

6.1. Expressions Only in a Post-verbal Position

Some expressions are acceptable only in a post-verbal position. As shown below, possessives and relative clauses cannot appear in a pre-verbal position unless they are accompanied by their head noun. However, they can show up at the right edge of a sentence, with or without the head noun.[15]

(21) A: Cheli-nun Yuni-uy phal-ul cap-ess-ta.
Ch.-Top Y.-Gen arm-Acc grab-Pst-DE
'Cheli grabbed Yuni in the arm.'
B: Byeli-to Swunhi-uy *(phal-ul) cap-ess-ta.
B.-also S.-Gen (arm-Acc) grab-Pst-DE
'Byeli also grabbed Yuni in the arm.'

(22) A: Cheli-nun U.S.-eyse o-n phyenci-lul
Ch.-Top U.S.-from come-Rel letter-Acc
path-ess-ta.
receive-Pst-DE
'Cheli received a letter from the U.S.'
B: Yuni-to [U.K.-eyse o-n] *(phyenci-lul)
Y.-also U.K.-from come-Rel (letter-Acc)
path-ess-ta
receive-Pst-DE
'Yuni also received a letter from the U.K.'

(21)' A: Cheli-nun Yuni-uy phal-ul cap-ess-ta.
Ch.-Top Y.-Gen arm-Acc grab-Pst-DE
'Cheli grabbed Yuni in the arm.'
B: Byeli-to cap-ess-ta Swunhi-uy (phal-ul)
B.-also grab-Pst-DE S.-Gen (arm-Acc)
'Byeli also grabbed Yuni in the arm.'

(22)' A: Cheli-nun U.S.-eyse o-n phyenci-lul
Ch.-Top U.S.-from come-Rel letter-Acc
path-ess-ta.
receive-Pst-DE
'Cheli received a letter from the U.S.'
B: Yuni-to path-ess-ta
Y.-also receive-Pst-DE
U.K.-eyse o-n] (phyenci-lul)
U.K.-from come-Rel (letter-Acc)
'Yuni also received a letter from the U.K.'

(21B)' and (22B)' do not sound perfect without the head nouns within the parentheses but they are qualitatively better than (21B) and (22B).

This contrast in the acceptability of the pre-nominal expressions (possessives and relative clauses) between the pre- vs. post-verbal position can hardly be accounted for by Lee's theory based on the SVO word order hypothesis. There seems to be no principled reason why an expression is acceptable in a post-verbal position but it becomes unacceptable in a pre-verbal position.

With a non-mono clausal analysis there is some room for explaining the contrast. As the RDed element is treated as a fragment of a continuing sentence/clause, sentences in (21B)' and (22B)' even without their head nouns are expected to be acceptable. Notice that possessives and relative clauses may show up as fragments in Korean.

(23) A: Cheli-ka nwukwu-uy phal-ul cap-ess-ni?
Ch.-Nom who-Gen arm-Acc grab-Pst-QE
'Who did Cheli grab in the arm?
B; Yuni(-uy).
Y.-(Gen)
'Yuni's'

(24) A: Cheli-ka eti-se o-n phyenci-lul
Ch.-Nom where-from come-Rel letter-Acc
path-ess-ni?
receive-Pst-QE
'A letter from where did Cheli receive?'
B: U.S.-eyse o-n (phyenci)
U.S.-from come-Rel (letter)
'(A letter) from the U.S.'

No matter what theory is responsible for the formal restriction on fragments in Korean, the same story can be carried over to the salvation effects of the

[15] Park (2012: 220ff) also observes that Korean allows 'left branch extraction under fragmenting'.

RDC in (21B)' and (22B)'.

Similarly, the contrast in the following pair of sentences points in favor of a non-mono-clausal analysis rather than a mono-clausal analysis based on the SVO word order hypothesis.[16]

(25) a. na-eykey-to anay-ka philyoha-e,
I-to-also wife-Nom need-DE
[yeppu-ko ton-to cal pel-nun].
pretty-and money-also well make-Rel
'I also need a wife who is pretty and makes a lot of money as well.'

b. *na-eykey-to anay-ka [yeppu-ko
I-to-also wife-Nom pretty-and
ton-to cal pel-nun] philyoha-e
money-also well make-Rel need-DE
'I also need a wife who is pretty and makes a lot of money as well.'

A mono-clausal analysis based on the universal SHC word order hypothesis would have to derive (25a) by extracting the head noun from the post-verbal relative construction, leaving the relative clause behind. An analogous extraction of a head noun out of a relative construction in a pre-verbal position, however, leads to ungrammaticality. It is not clear under this analysis what prevents (25b) from being derived from (26) by extracting the head noun.[17]

(26) na-eykey-to [[yeppu-ko ton-to cal
I-to-also pretty-and money-aslo well
pel-nun] anay]-ka philyoha-e.
make-Rel wife-Nom need-DE
'I also need a wife who is pretty and makes a lot of money as well.'

Under a non-mono-clausal analysis, the RDed element in (25a) is simply a fragmental expression of a continuing clause. Thus, the salvation effects can be attributed to a property of sentence fragments, however it may be explained.

[16] (25a) is cited from Yoon and Lee (2009).

[17] A reviewer points out to me that the ungrammatical status of (25b) may be merely an instance of CED effects since the head noun is extracted out of a relative construction that has previously moved to a SPEC position in Lee's system. If, however, CED works at all in his system, grammatical sentences like (16) are to be incorrectly excluded as well. See footnote 10 also.

6.2. Expressions Only in a Pre-verbal Position

Let us now turn to a case where a post-verbal position tolerates a narrower range of expressions than a pre-verbal position. Choe (1987) observes that a wh-phrase cannot be RDed, as shown in the following example, (adapted from Choe 1987: 42, her (11)):

(27) a. Cheli-ka mwues-ul po-ess-upnikka
Ch.-Nom what-Acc see-Pst-QE
'What did Cheli see?'

b. *Cheli-ka po-ess-upnikka, mwues-ul
Ch.-Nom see-Pst-QE what-Acc

If the VO vs. OV order difference simply follows from the presence or absence of the EPP feature at a functional category, there should not be such an order restriction on RDed wh-phrases.

Being aware of this restriction, Lee (2009: 150, his (46)) resorts to the following condition:

(28) The Q marker [DC: e.g., *-upnikka* in (27)] must follow an overt wh-phrase for the proper formation of phonological deaccenting.

According to him, phonological deaccenting is formed with a falling intonation. In other words, (27b) is ruled out due to the fact that the QE cannot have a falling intonation because of the lack of a wh-phrase to its left.

Notice, however, that RD is not allowed even out of an embedded wh-question whose QE has little to do with an intonation contour.[18]

(29) a. na-nun [Cheli-ka etise o-ess-nunci]
I-Top Ch.-Nom where come-Pst-QE
kwungkumha-ta
wondrous-DE
'I wonder where Cheli comes from.'

[18] Jung (2012) reports that embedded wh-interrogatives in Busan Dialect do show a falling contour. However, in order for Lee's (2009) theory to be right about the restriction of wh-phrases in the RDC, it is yet to be confirmed whether the falling contour is unique to the embedded wh-interrogatives or its presence is due to the edge of a prosodic unit. Furthermore, it has to be checked whether phonological deaccenting (pitch lowering or compression) is solely induced by a wh-phrase or not. It is also noteworthy that deaccenting itself does not license a [+WH] C. As pointed out by Hee-Don Ahn (p.c.), sentences like (27b) and (29b) are ungrammatical even when deaccenting is forcefully imposed on the relevant [+WH] C.

b. *na-nun [Cheli-ka e_i o-ess-nunci]
I-Top Ch.-Nom come-Pst-QE
kwungkumha-ta, $etise_i$
wondrous-DE where
'I wonder where Cheli comes from.'

The SVO word order hypothesis expects sentences like (29b) to be legitimately derived, along the similar lines of derivation of (8) in Section 2, since the RDed wh-phrase has undergone scrambling in the embedded clause and then the embedded clause has moved to the SPEC of the matrix verb, leaving the wh-phrase behind.

A non-mono clausal analysis of the RDC may account for the contrast under the condition that a QE must have an overt wh-phrase in its domain. (See Chung 2008b for detail.) Notice that the QE remains unlicensed, since no overt wh-phrase is available at all in the domain of the QE. Note that, under a non-mono-sentential analysis of Korean RDC, the wh-phrase in (29b) belongs to a separate sentence/clause to which a massive size of ellipsis has applied.

7. Conclusion

This work has observed various asymmetric behaviors between pre- vs. post-verbal positions in the so-called right dislocated construction (RDC) in Korean. The existence of such asymmetries has shown to be readily accommodated when the RDed element is viewed as a fragmental element rather than as a direct dependent of the preceding predicate, favoring a non-mono-clausal approach to the construction. Thus, the RDC in Korean does not necessarily constitute evidence for the claim that the Korean language conforms to the universal SHC word order hypothesis, pace Lee (2007a,b, 2008a, 2009a,b, 2010, 2011, 2012), although there is no need to posit a rightward movement, lending only partial support to Kayne's (1994) LCA.

Acknowledgements

An earlier version of this work was presented at the spring conference of the Korea Generative Grammar Circle on May 26, 2012 at Sungshin Women's University. I would like to thank all the audience at the conference, especially Yeun-Jin Jung and Sang-Geun Lee for their valuable comments. I also would like to thank Hee-Don Ahn and Chungmin Lee and the three PACLIC 26 reviewers for their constructive comments and questions. All remaining errors are solely mine.

References

Ahn, Hee-Don and Seungun Cho. 2009a. On CP Ellipsis: A Reply to Chung (2009). *Proceedings of 2009 Spring Joint Conference of the Linguistic Association of Korea, Modern Grammar Circle, and Korean Generative Grammar Circle*, 142-150.

Ahn, Hee-Don and Seungun Cho. 2009b. On the Absence of CP Ellipsis in English and Korean. *Korean Journal of Linguistics*, 34.2: 267-281.

Ahn, Hee-Don and Seungun Cho. 2010. More on the Absence of CP Ellipsis: A Reply to Park (2009). *Studies in Generative Grammar*, 20: 549-576.

Choe, Hyon Sook. 1987. Successive-cyclic rightward movement in Korean. S. Kuno *et als* (eds.), *Harvard Studies in Korean Linguistics II*, 40-56.

Choi, Hyon-Pai. 1989. *Wulimalpon* 'Grammar of Our Language'. Seoul, Korea: Cengumunhwasa. (15th edition. The first edition was published in 1937.)

Chomsky, Noam. 2000. Minimalist Inquiries: The Framework. R. Marin, D. Michaels, and J. Uriagereka (eds.), *Step by Step: Essays on Minimalist Syntax*, 89-155. Cambridge, Mass.: MIT Press.

Chomsky, Noam. 2005. Three Factors in Language Design. *Linguistic Inquiry*, 36: 1-22.

Chung, Daeho. 2008a. On the Syntax of Non-final Predicate Constructions in Korean. *Proceedings of the 2008 Joint Conference of the Discourse and Cognitive Linguistics Society of Korea, the Linguistics Society of Korea, the Korean Generative Grammar Circle, and the Chungang University Humanities Institute*, 6-16.

Chung, Daeho. 2008b. Agree but Not Necessarily at the Same Time. *Studies in Generative Grammar*, 18: 509-524.

Chung, Daeho. 2009a. Do not Target a Predicate: It is not a Constituent. Paper Presented at the 6th WAFL, Nagoya, Japan.

Chung, Daeho. 2009b. An Elliptical Coordination Analysis of the Right Dislocated Construction in Korean. *The Linguistic Association of Korea Journal*, 17(4): 1-23.

Chung, Daeho. 2010. Replies to Lee (2009): In Defense of a Double Clause Approach to the Right Dislocated Construction in Korean. *Studies in Modern Grammar*. 61: 167-196.

Chung, Daeho. 2011. A Constituency-based

Explanation of Syntactic Restrictions on Korean Predicates. *Linguistic Research,* 28(1): 393-407.

Fiengo, Robert. 1977. On Trace Theory. *Linguistic Inquiry,* 8: 35-61.

Fox, Danny and David Pesetsky. 2005. Cyclic Linearization of Syntactic Structure. *Theoretical Linguistics,* 31: 1-45.

Huh, Woong. 1988. *Kwukehak* 'Korean Grammar'. Seoul, Korea: Saymmunhwasa.

Jung, Yeun-Jin. 2012. On the Nature of Wh-Prosody and its Syntactic Dependency. *Korean Journal of Linguistics,* 37(2): 417-444.

Kato, Takaomi. 2007. On the Nature of the Left Branch Condition: Syntactic or Phonological? Paper presented at the 9th Seoul International Conference on Generative Grammar.

Kayne, Richard. 1994. *The Anti-Symmetry of Syntax*. Cambridge: MIT Press.

Kim, Rhanghyeyun. 2012. Order Preservation Justifies Remnant Movement. Paper presented at the 1st World Congress of Scholars of English Linguistics. June 26-30, 2012, Hanyang University.

Koopman, Hilda. 2005. Korean (and Japanese) Morphology from a Syntactic Perspective. *Linguistic Inquiry* 36: 601-635.

Kuno, Susumu. 1978. *Danwa-no Bunpoo* 'Grammar of Dicourse'. Tokyo: Taishukan Shoten.

Lee, Chung-hoon. 2009. Hankwuke Hwupochwung Kwumwunuy Kwuco 'The Structure of Korean Afterthought Constructions', *Emwunyenkwu,* 142: 31-54.

Lee, Chung-Hoon. 2011. The Structure, Ω Head and Gap in Korean Afterthought Constructions. *Studies in Modern Grammar,* 64: 95-116.

Lee, Jeong-Shik. 2007a. Deriving SOV from SVO in Korean. *The Linguistic Association of Korea Journal,* 15: 1-20.

Lee, Jeong-Shik. 2007b. LCA, Linearization, and Phasehood. *Proceedings of the 2007 Fall Joint Conference of the Linguistic Association of Korea, the Korean Association for the Studies of English Language and Linguistics, and the Society of Modern Grammar,* 102-119.

Lee, Jeong-Shik. 2008. Minimizing Spell-out Material in the Phase. *Studies in Modern Grammar,* 52: 213-240.

Lee, Joeng-Shik. 2009a. Right Dislocated Constructions: A Single Clause Analysis. Proceedings of 2009 Spring Joint Conference of the Linguistic Association of Korea, Modern Grammar Circle, and Korean Generative Grammar Circle, 249-257.

Lee, Jeong-Shik. 2009b. A Verb-initial Single Clause Analysis of Right-dislocated Constructions in Korean. *Studies in Modern Grammar,* 57: 127-157.

Lee, Jeong-Shik. 2010. On the Absence of Embedded Predicate Ellipsis in Korean. *The Linguistic Association of Korea Journal,* 18: 125-145.

Lee, Jeong-Shik. 2011. Some Loopholes of the Double Clause Approach to the Right Dislocated Construction in Korean. *Studies in Modern Grammar,* 63: 113-146.

Lee, Jeong-Shik. 2012. Speculations on Typological Variation from a Third Factor Perspective. *Studies in Generative Grammar,* 22(1): 77-112.

Lee, Youngmin. 1998. *Kwuke Uymunmunuy Thongsalon* 'The Syntax of Korean Interrogatives'. Seoul, Korea: Pokosa

Merchant, Jason. 2004. Fragments and Ellipsis. *Linguistics and Philosophy,* 27: 661-738.

Nam, Ki-Shim and Yong-Keun Ko. 1986. *Phyocwun Kwuke Munpeplon* 'Standard Korean Grammar'. Seoul, Korea: Thap Press.

Park, Myung-Kwan. 2009. An (Impossible) Excursion into Matrix [Spec, vP] out of an Elided Complement Clause in Korean. *Korean Journal of Linguistics,* 34(4): 895-917.

Park, Myung-Kwan. 2002. Left Branch Extraction in Fragment and Truncated Cleft Constructions of Korean. *Studies in Generative Grammar,* 22(1): 219-233.

Sportiche, Dominique. 1998. *Atoms and Partitions of Clause Structure*. London: Routledge.

Suh, Chung-Mok. 1987. *Kwuke Uymwunmwun Yenkwu* 'A Study on the Interrogative Sentences in Korean', Thap Press, Seoul, Korea.

Tanaka, Hedekazu. 2001. Right Dislocation in English and Japanese. *Journal of Linguistics,* 37: 551-579.

Yoon, J. Hye-Suk and Wooseung Lee. 2009. The Architecture of Right Dislocation in Korean and Japanese. ms. University of Illinois, Urbana-Champaign.

Whitman, John. 2000. Right Dislocation in English and Japanese. Ken-ichi Takami, Ako Kamio, and John Whitman (eds)., *Syntactic and functional explorations: In honor of Susumu Kuno*, 445-470. Tokyo: Jurosio Publishers.

Pattern Matching Refinements to Dictionary-Based Code-Switching Point Detection

Nathaniel Oco
De La Salle University
2401 Taft Avenue Malate, Manila City
1004 Metro Manila, Philippines
nathan.oco@delasalle.ph

Rachel Edita Roxas
De La Salle University
2401 Taft Avenue Malate, Manila City
1004 Metro Manila, Philippines
rachel.roxas@delasalle.ph

Abstract

This study presents the development and evaluation of pattern matching refinements (PMRs) to automatic code switching point (CSP) detection. With all PMRs, evaluation showed an accuracy of 94.51%. This is an improvement to reported accuracy rates of dictionary-based approaches, which are in the range of 75.22%-76.26% (Yeong and Tan, 2010). In our experiments, a 100-sentence Tagalog-English corpus was used as test bed. Analyses showed that the dictionary-based approach using part-of-speech checking yielded an accuracy of 79.76% only, and two notable linguistic phenomena, (1) intra-word code-switching and (2) common words, were shown to have caused the low accuracy. The devised PMRs, namely: (1) common word exclusion, (2) common word identification, and (3) common n-gram pruning address this and showed improved accuracy. The work can be extended using audio files and machine learning with larger language resources.

1 Introduction

Code-switching (CS) is "the use of two or more linguistic varieties in the same interaction or conversation" (Myers-Scotton and Ury, 1977). It is often prevalent in communities where there is language contact. According to linguistic studies (Bautista, 1991; Bautista, 2004; Borlongan, 2009), code-switching reasons are mainly driven by proficiency or deficiency in the languages involved. Proficiency-driven code-switching takes place when a person is competent with the two languages and can easily switch from one to the other "for maximum efficiency or effect". On the other hand, deficiency-driven code-switching takes place when people are forced to code-switch to one language because they are "not competent in the use of the other language". Oral communication in both languages can be enhanced by the detection of code-switching points (CSPs). To detect CSPs, we developed a dictionary-based approach using a rule-based engine (Naber, 2003), and we also developed pattern matching refinements (PMRs) to improve accuracy.

As testbed, this study focuses on Tagalog-English code-switching, which can be classified into (1) intra-sentential and (2) intra-word code-switching. Intra-sentential CS is the switching between Tagalog and English words and clauses, while intra-word CS is the use of English root words with Tagalog affixes and morphological rules. An example of intra-sentential CS is "Unless let us say ***may*** *mga bisita siya*" (translated as: Unless let us say he/she has visitors) and an example of intra-word CS is "*nagdadrive*" (incompeleted aspect of the English verb "drive"). The system developed can effectively be used to detect intra-sentential (Tagalog to English and English to Tagalog) and intra-word CSPs.

This paper is organized as follows: related works in section 2, CSP detection in section 3, pattern matching refinements in section 4, testing and discussion in section 5, and conclusion in section 6.

2 Related Works

In the field of computing, several studies have been done to automatically detect CSPs. The areas that are commonly involved are machine learning, audio signal processing, and natural language processing (NLP). In machine learning, patterns are derived from large data sets such as in the CSP studies of Spanish-English (Solorio and Liu, 2008) and Chinese-English (Burgmer, 2009), which used the transcription of forty minutes and four hours of audio recordings, respectively. In audio signal processing, analyses of speech corpora (e.g. the Cantonese CUSENT and the English TIMIT) using acoustic models (White et al., 2008) are studied. Analyses of trained phone models (Chan et al., 2004) are also studied.

In NLP, a related study (Yeong and Tan, 2010) explored n-gram-based approaches and also presented dictionary-based approaches. N-gram-based approaches such as alphabet bigram, grapheme bigram, and syllable structure use similarity measures and language models extracted from a corpus. On the other hand, dictionary-based approaches such as language vocabulary list and affixation information match the word against a dictionary. Table 1 shows a performance comparison of different NLP approaches (Yeong and Tan, 2010). The table shows that dictionary-based approaches yield lower accuracy rates than model-based approaches and are known to have lower performance ratings.

Approach		Accuracy
Dictionary -based	Affixation Information	76.26%
	Vocabulary List	75.22%
N-gram-based	Alphabet Bigram	91.29%
	Grapheme Bigram	91.82%
	Syllable Structure	93.73%

Table 1: Performance comparison of different NLP approaches (Yeong and Tan, 2010)

3 CSP Detection

The system has been plugged into OpenOffice and it highlights CSPs in an OpenOffice document. Figure 1 shows a sample screenshot of the system detecting CSP in the sentence "And then ***kinuha*** *niya*" (translated as: And then he/she took it).

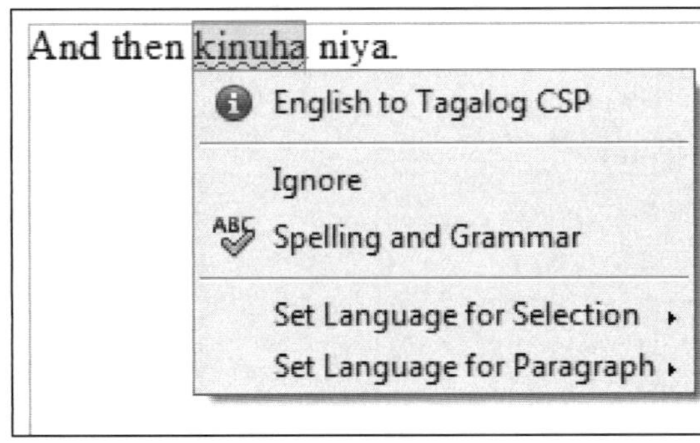

Figure 1: Sample screenshot of the system showing English to Tagalog CSP

After studying the Philippine component of the International Corpus of English (Bautista et al., 2004), we experimented on a dictionary-based approach to detect CSPs using LanguageTool (Naber, 2003) – a rule-based style and grammar checker engine that can run as an OpenOffice extension. Figure 2 shows the architecture of the developed system. LanguageTool requires two language resources to run: (1) the tagger dictionary and (2) the rule file. For the tagger dictionary, we utilized and edited word declarations from the English (ENG TD) and Tagalog (TAG TD) supports. For the rule file (RF), we developed pattern matching rules.

CSP detection works as follows: (1) an input text document is separated into sentences and each sentence is separated into tokens; (2) each token is given their tag – English, Tagalog, Proper Noun, Punctuation, or UNKNOWN – using the tagger dictionary declarations; (3) the tokens together with their tags are matched against the rule file, which contains code-switching patterns that we declared; (4) if a pattern matches, the user is notified. In a related work (Oco and Borra, 2011), LanguageTool was used in Tagalog grammar checking. Thus, this study is the first attempt to use LanguageTool in another language processing task.

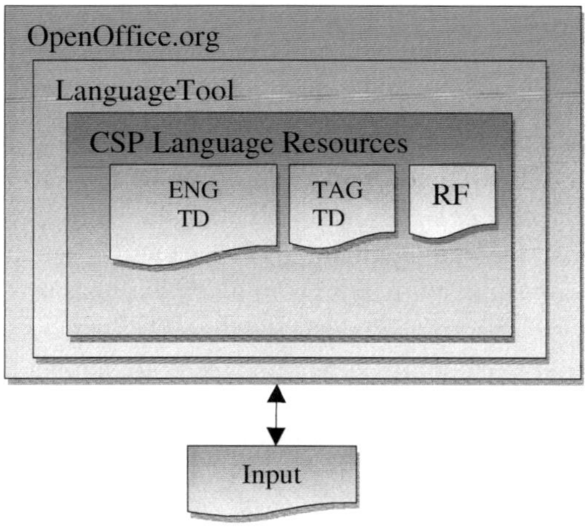

Figure 2: Architecture of the system

3.1 Tagger Dictionary

The CSP tagger dictionary contains approximately 298,498 words from the English language support, 7,441 words from Tagalog, 35 punctuation marks, 54,157 proper nouns and 1000 new word declarations, for a total of 361,131 words. File size was almost 10MB. We reduced it to 1MB by encoding[1] it to a smaller file, making it easier to load. Figure 3 shows sample word declarations. To distinguish between Tagalog and English words, a header tag was assigned to Tagalog words and a different one to English words. The words in the tagger dictionary are classified into four header tags: Tagalog words ("TAG"), English words ("ENG"), proper nouns ("NPRO"), and punctuations ("PSNS").

kasimputi	kasimputi	TAG ADCO S
#	#	PSNS
$	$	PSNS
nonsecluded	nonsecluded	ENG JJ
nonsecludedness	nonsecludedness	ENG NN
nonsecludedly	nonsecludedly	ENG RB
Abbottson	Abbottson	NPRO
Abboud	Abboud	NPRO
Abby	Abby	NPRO

Figure 3: Sample word declarations

LanguageTool supports different languages. As comparison, Table 2 shows the word count in six language supports. The numbers highlight that Tagalog is a poorly-resourced language.

Language Support	Word Count
German	4,158,968
Polish	3,662,366
French	550,814
English	354,744
Asturian	157,747
Tagalog	7,484

Table 2: Number of word declarations in six language supports

3.2 Rule File

The rule file, like any xml file, is composed of elements and attributes. Figure 4 shows a sample rule file. The three main elements are: (1) pattern, (2) message, and (3) example. Pattern refers to the token or sequence of tokens and/or part-of-speech (POS) to be matched; message refers to the feedback, which will be shown to the user if the pattern matches the input; and example refers to the sentences used for testing. If a pattern matches, CSPs are marked and message is shown to the user.

```
<rule id="ENGLISH-TAGALOG" name="Code
Switch to Tagalog">
<pattern case_sensitive="no" mark_from="1">
<token postag="ENG.*" postag_regexp="yes"/>
<token postag="TAG.*" postag_regexp="yes"/>
</pattern>
<message>English to Tagalog CSP</message>
<example type="incorrect">I want to be
<marker>sundalo</marker>.</example>
<example type="correct">They are
soldiers.</example>
</rule>
```

Figure 4: An English to Tagalog CSP rule using POS checking

Pattern matching in CSP detection works by checking if a word is English or Tagalog, i.e. has a header tag "ENG" or "TAG". This would result in false positives if it is a common word – a word that appears in both the English and Tagalog tagger dictionaries – as this would have both header tags. An example of a common word is "may" (e.g.

[1]Morfologik was used to convert text files to FSA-encoded .dict files. Morfologik is available at: http://sourceforge.net/projects/morfologik/files/

"may ENG..." and "may TAG..."), which could be an English Verb or a Tagalog existential marker. Another example is "raw", which could be an English adjective or a Tagalog enclitic.

Using POS checking, one true positive and one false positive are detected in the sentence "Unless let us say ***may*** *mga bisita siya*" (translated as: Unless let us say he/she has visitors). Both "*may*" and "*mga*" are detected as English to Tagalog CSP. We developed pattern matching refinements to improve accuracy.

4 Pattern Matching Refinements

Pattern matching refinements (PMRs) work by separating pattern matching for sentences involving common words and words with unknown POS. Figure 5 shows the diagram of the different word types. Words (W) are generally classified into four: unique English words (UEW), unique Tagalog words (UTW), common words (CW), and unknown words ($W-(UEW \cup UTW)$). Unique English words are words with "ENG" header tags only. The same applies for Tagalog words ("TAG"). Since the English tagger dictionary is well-resourced, unknown POS indicate either intra-word code-switching or undeclared Tagalog words.

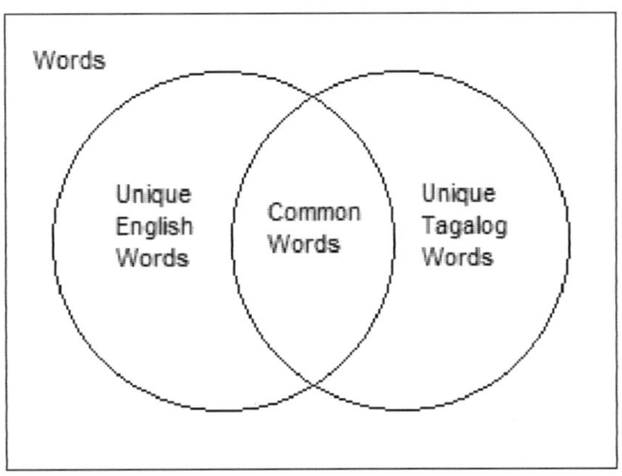

Figure 5: The set of words showing the intersection of UEW and UTW as common words

4.1 Common Word Exclusion

We developed common word exclusion to reduce the detection of false positives in sentences involving common words. The uniqueness of a word in a tagger dictionary is taken into consideration (i.e. a word does not have multiple declarations with different header tags) and common words are excluded from the pattern. If a unique English word is followed by a unique Tagalog word, then the second word is a CSP. The same applies if a unique Tagalog word is followed by a unique English word. Figure 6 shows a pattern without common word exclusion and Figure 7 shows a pattern with common word exclusion. The list of common words was generated by getting the intersection of word declarations with header tag "ENG" and those with header tag "TAG". For scalability, a new tag "CW" was created and common words were added in the tagger dictionary with this tag. This PMR is similar to common word pruning (Dimalen and Roxas, 2007), which was used as a language model improvement to increase the accuracy rate of language identification involving closely-related languages. The difference is common words are completely discarded in common word pruning while in this PMR, common words are excluded from the pattern and declared only as exceptions.

```
<token postag="ENG.*"
postag_regexp="yes"></token>
<token postag="TAG.*"
postag_regexp="yes"></token>
```

Figure 6: Pattern matching without common word exclusion

```
<token postag="ENG.*" postag_regexp="yes">
<exception postag="CW.*"
postag_regexp="yes">
</exception></token>
<token postag="TAG.*" postag_regexp="yes">
<exception postag="CW.*"
postag_regexp="yes">
</exception></token>
```

Figure 7: Pattern matching with common word exclusion

Using common word exclusion, no true positive nor false positive is detected in the sentence "Unless let us say ***may*** *mga bisita siya*" (translated as: Unless let us say he/she has visitors).

4.2 Common Word Identification

Since common words are excluded from pattern matching, common words that are also code-switching points are also not detected. We developed common word identification to identify the language of the word. This approach works by identifying which tokens or POS of tokens normally precede or succeed common words. Word window is one-previous and one-next. To determine word sequences, a word bigram model of English Wikipedia articles[2] was generated and bigrams involving common words were manually analyzed. POS sequences were derived and declared in the rule file. For example, if a common word has a verb tag and is preceded by an English verb, the common word is a CSP.

Using common word exclusion and common word identification, one true positive, "*may*", is detected in the sentence "Unless let us say ***may*** *mga bisita siya*" (translated as: Unless let us say he/she has visitors).

4.3 Common n-gram Pruning

The previous refinements do not detect words that are not declared in the tagger dictionary, i.e. words with UNKNOWN POS tag. We developed common n-gram pruning for this purpose. An n-gram is defined as an "n-character slice of a longer string" (Dimalen and Roxas, 2007). N-grams that are unique to a particular language are used and declared in the rule file. For example, if a word has an unknown POS tag and it contains n-gram sequences that are unique to English, then it is intra-word code-switching. To get the unique n-grams, n-gram profiles of the languages were generated using Apache Nutch[3]. A sampling of the English Wikipedia and the entire Tagalog Wikipedia[4] – containing approximately 10 million and 3 million words, respectively – were used as training data. Each generated n-gram profile contains approximately 500 bigrams, 3,000 trigrams, and 3,000 four-grams. Less than 50 unique n-grams were taken per language and regular expression was used for scalability. This PMR is similar to n-gram-based approaches (Yeong and Tan, 2010). However, in this study, no similarity measure was used, the number of characters varies in length, and all character sequences are unique to the language model. In a similar study, common word pruning (Dimalen and Roxas, 2007) was introduced to get the unique words. In this study, unique character sequences were instead generated.

5 Testing and Discussion

Approximately one hour of audio recording of actual conversations was transcribed for the study. It contains more than 500 sentences and approximately 80% of these sentences contain CSPs. The first 100 sentences with CSPs were taken from the transcription and used to test the system. Audio recordings of actual conversations were used because they show the natural usage of the languages. The test corpus contains 820 words, 243 of which are CSPs and verified by an expert. Five separate tests were conducted: (T1) an initial test with POS checking only; (T2) with common word exclusion only; (T3) with both common word exclusion and identification; (T4) with common n-gram pruning only; (T5) with all pattern matching refinements – common word exclusion, common word identification, and common n-gram pruning. Table 3 shows the results. The number of true positives (TP), false positives (FP), true negatives (TN), and false negatives (FN) are indicated in third, fourth, fifth, and sixth column, respectively.

Test Type	PMR	Results			
		TP	FP	TN	FN
T1	None – POS checking only	166	89	488	77
T2	With common word exclusion only	158	6	571	85
T3	With common word exclusion and CWID	193	6	571	50

[2] The English wiki articles are available in XML file format at this website: http://dumps.wikimedia.org/enwiki/

[3] http://nutch.apache.org/

[4] Tagalog wiki: http://dumps.wikimedia.org/tlwiki/

T4	With common n-gram pruning only	12	0	577	231
T5	With all PMRs	205	6	571	38

Table 3: Test results using 100 sentences containing 243 CSPs

With POS checking only, the system properly detected 166 CSPs but it also detected 89 instances of false positives. On the other hand, common word exclusion reduced the number of false negatives from 89 instances to 6. However, it does not detect common words that are also code-switching points, which is why the number of true positives is lower. When used with common word identification, the number of true positives increased to 193 instances. Meanwhile, common n-gram pruning detected 12 instances of intra-word CS that were not previously detected. Table 4 shows a list of properly detected verbs with intra-word CS. Syllable reduplication in contemplated and incompleted verb aspects was observed (e.g. *mag-aapprove*, *nagfoforum*). The number of true positives is low because common n-gram pruning detects only intra-word CS and words with unknown POS. A combination of all PMRs brings the total number of true positives to 205.

Token	Root Word	Aspect
idefault	default	Neutral
ikiclick	click	Contemplated
ipaupload	upload	Contemplated
mag-aapprove	approve	Contemplated
magmemorize	memorize	Neutral
mag-upload	upload	Neutral
nagclick	click	Completed
nagfoforum	forum	Incompleted

Table 4: Sample list of verbs with detected intra-word CS

Table 5 shows the accuracy, which increases as more PMRs are used. CSP detection using no pattern matching refinements yielded 79.76% accuracy. A comparison between our results and the results of a related work (Yeong and Tan, 2010) shows that basic dictionary-based approaches are not highly effective. Analyses of our results show that two phenomena cause false positives and false negatives. These are (1) intra-word CS and (2) common words – especially those with different semantic information. Consider the sentence "Unless let us say ***may*** *mga bisita siya*" (translated as: Unless let us say he/she has visitors). The word "*may*" is a common word. If a basic dictionary-based approach is applied, both "*may*" and "*mga*" are detected as CSPs. Table 6 shows a list of identified common words with different semantic information. Difference in the POS was observed.

Test Type	PMR used	Accuracy
T1	None – POS checking only	79.76%
T2	With common word exclusion only	88.90%
T3	With common word exclusion and CWID	93.05%
T4	With common n-gram pruning only	71.83%
T5	With all PMRs	94.51%

Table 5: Accuracy rate of the different tests conducted

Token	English POS	Tagalog POS
akin	Adjective	Pronoun
along	Preposition	Noun
at	Preposition	Conjunction
ate	Verb	Noun
away	Adverb	Verb
dating	Verb	Adjective
gusto	Noun	Verb
halos	Noun	Adjective
hanging	Verb	Noun
ho	Interjection	Polite Marker
kilos	Noun	Verb
may	Auxiliary Verb	Existential Marker
naming	Verb	Pronoun

Token	English POS	Tagalog POS
noon	Noun	Pronoun
paring	Verb	Noun
piling	Verb	Noun
raw	Adjective	Enclitic
ring	Noun	Enclitic
sawing	Verb	Adjective
tinging	Verb	Adjective

Table 6: Sample list of common words with different semantic information

A combination of all pattern matching refinements yielded the highest accuracy with 94.51%. This can be attributed to the detection of common words and intra-word CS.

A close analysis of the false negatives reveals that some intra-word CS was not detected. Table 7 shows a sample list. The n-gram sequence of these words is not unique and is found in the Tagalog n-gram profile. Intra-word CS with n-gram sequence similar to Tagalog words is not properly detected by the system.

Token	Root Word	Aspect
naghahang	hang	Incompleted
ilogin	login	Neutral
magregister	register	Neutral
inedit	edit	Completed
dinisable	disable	Completed
malilink	link	Contemplative
inonote	note	Contemplative
linalog	log	Incompleted
magreport	report	Neutral

Table 7: Sample list of verbs with intra-word CS that were not detected

6 Conclusion and Recommendation

This paper has shown that the application of PMRs significantly increased accuracy. The tests show that with all PMRs, the system was able to achieve 94.51% accuracy. The result is higher than no improvements used. The results are also higher than the results yielded by dictionary-based approaches in a related study (Yeong and Tan, 2010).

As future work, other forms of multilingualism can be considered. There are instances where more than two languages are involved in code-switching and these are rarely documented. Also, code-switching involving dialectal variations may be considered and since Tagalog is a poorly-resourced language, bootstrapping can be applied. Additional resources may also be added and machine learning be used, such as in (Solorio and Liu, 2008) and (Burgmer, 2009). Also, the work can be extended to cover audio files, such as in (White et al., 2008) and (Chan et al., 2004).

Acknowledgments

This work has been funded by the Department of Science and Technology - Philippine Council for Industry, Energy and Emerging Technology Research and Development (DOST-PCIEERD) through the "Inter-Disciplinary Signal Processing for Pinoys (ISIP): ICT for Education" Program and also supported by the University Research Coordination Office of De La Salle University (No. 20FU211).

We thank Prof. Dr. Ma. Lourdes S. Bautista, Dr. Ariane Borlongan, and Ms. Mary Anne Conde for being instrumental to the completion of this study. We also thank reviewers for their comments.

References

Ariane M. Borlongan. 2009. Tagalog-English Code-Switching in English Classes in the Philippines: Frequency and Forms. TESOL Journal, 1: 28-42.

Carol Myers-Scotton and William Ury. 1977. Bilingual Strategies: The Social Functions of Code-Switching. International Journal of the Sociology of Language, 13: 5-20.

Christoph Burgmer. 2009. Detecting Code-Switch Events based on Textual Features. Diploma Thesis. Karlsruhe Institute of Technology, Karlsruhe.

Christopher M. White, Sanjeev Khudanpur, James K. Baker. 2008. An Investigation of Acoustic Models for Multilingual Code-Switching. In Proceedings of the 9th Annual Conference of the International Speech Communication Association. Brisbane, Australia: International Speech Communication Association.

Daniel Naber. 2003. A Rule-based Style and Grammar Checker. Diploma Thesis. Bielefeld University, Bielefeld.

Davis Muhajereen D. Dimalen and Rachel Edita O. Roxas. 2007. AutoCor: A Query Based Automatic Acquisition of Corpora of Closely-related Languages. In Proceedings of the 21st Pacific Asia Conference on Language, Information, and Computation. Seoul, Korea: Korean Society for Language Information.

Joyce Y.C. Chan, P.S. Ching, Tan Lee, and Helen M. Meng. 2004. Detection of Language Boundary in Code-Switching Utterances using Bi-Phone Probabilities. In Proceedings of the 4th International Symposium on Chinese Spoken Language Processing. Hong Kong, China: Chinese University of Hong Kong.

Ma. Lourdes S. Bautista. 1991. Code-Switching Studies in the Philippines. International Journal of the Sociology of Language, 88: 19-32.

Ma. Lourdes S. Bautista. 2004. Tagalog-English Code-Switching as a Mode of Discourse. Asia Pacific Educational Review, 5 (2): 226-233.

Ma. Lourdes S. Bautista, Loy V. Lising, and Danilo T. Dayag. 2004. ICE-Philippines Lexical Corpus - CD-ROM. London: International Corpus of English.

Nathaniel A. Oco and Allan B. Borra. 2011. A Grammar Checker for Tagalog using LanguageTool. In Proceedings of the 9th Workshop on Asian Language Resources Collocated with IJCNLP 2011. Chiang Mai, Thailand: Asian Federation of Natural Language Processing.

Thamar Solorio and Yang Liu. 2008. Learning to Predict Code-Switching Points. In Proceedings of the 2010 Conference on Empirical Methods in Natural Language Processing. Honolulu, HI: Association for Computational Linguistics.

Yin-Lai Yeong and Tien-Ping Tan. 2010. Language Identification of Code-Switching Malay-English Words Using Syllable Structure Information. In Proceedings of the 2nd Workshop on Spoken Languages Technologies for Under-Resourced Languages. Penang, Malaysia: Universiti Sains Malaysia.

An Adaptive Method for Organization Name Disambiguation with Feature Reinforcing

Shu Zhang[1], **Jianwei Wu**[2], **Dequan Zheng**[2], **Yao Meng**[1] **and Hao Yu**[1]
[1] Fujitsu Research and Development Center
Dong Si Huan Zhong Rd, Chaoyang District, Beijing and 0086, China
{zhangshu, mengyao, yu}@cn.fujitsu.com
School of Computer Science and Technology, Harbin Institute of Technology
No.92, Xidazhi Street, Harbin 150001, China
{jwwu, dqzheng}@mtlab.hit.edu.cn

Abstract

Twitter is an online social networking, which has become an important source of information for marketing strategies and online reputation management. In this paper, we probe the problem of organization name disambiguation on twitter messages. This task is challenging due to the fact of lacking sufficient information both from organization and the tweets. We mine organization information from web sources to train a general classifier. Further, we mine tweets information. We train an adaptive classifier for a given organization name with more features derived from twitter messages labeled by the general classifier. The experiments on WePS-3 show mining web sources to enrich organization are effective. The adaptive classifier trained for a given organization is promising.

1 Introduction

Twitter is an online social networking and microblogging service, which rapidly gained worldwide popularity, with 140 million active users as of 2012[1], generating over 340 million tweets and handling over 1.6 billion search queries per day[2]. People share their opinions on almost anything on Twitter, such as news, governmental policies, products and companies. Therefore, Twitter becomes an important information resource for the purpose of marketing strategies and online reputation management. How to retrieval, analyze and monitor Twitter information has been receiving a lot of attention in natural language processing and information retrieval research community (Kwak, *et al.*, 2010; Boyd, *et al.*,2010; Tsagkias, *et al.*, 2011). One of the essential things of these researches is first to get the information which is related to the studied entity, such as product, company, or certain event. This work is caused by the ambiguity of entities. For example, the name of company "*Apple*" has a separate meaning referring to one kind of fruit. The word "*Amazon*" could be used to refer river or company. Therefore, when the entity name is ambiguous, filtering spurious name matches is important to accurate detection and analysis of contents that people say about the given entity.

This paper focuses on finding related tweets to a given organization. Assuming that tweets are retrieved by the query of organization name, such as "*apple*", the task is to identify whether a tweet is relevant to the target organization ("*Apple Inc.*") or not. Yerva *et al.* (2010) adopt support vector machines (SVM) classifier to classify tweets with external resources. Yoshida *et al.* (2010) classify

[1] http://blog.twitter.com/2012/03/twitter-turns-six.html

[2] http://engineering.twitter.com/2011/05/engineering-behind-twitters-new-search.html

organization names into "organization-like names" or "general-word-like names" categories, classify tweets by rules. Kalmar (2010) adopts bootstrapping method to classify the tweets.

This task is challenging owing to the fact of lacking sufficient information. A tweet contains less than 140 characters and is often freely written. Therefore the tweet is short and informal. It does not provide sufficient word occurrence or context shared information for effective similarity measure (Phan *et al.*, 2008). Furthermore, the representation of each organization is also an obstacle. Different from conventional word disambiguation, there is no authoritative source which lists all possible interpretations of an organization name. The information gotten from the homepage of organization is limited. It is difficult to cover the word occurring in tweets which are related to the given organization.

Aim to process any organization names but not one or some given organization names, the organization names in training data are different from those in test data. This leads that we could not train a classifier to a certain organization. It also makes the task more difficult than conventional classifying task.

In this paper, we propose an adaptive method for organization name disambiguation. We build a general classifier with the training data. Then we use the general classifier to label unlabeled twitter messages of a given organization. With more features derived from these twitter messages, we train an adaptive classifier to a given organization. The major contributions of our approach are as follows:

- Try to mine organization information from web sources, such as Wikipedia, linked pages and related pages. This is a way to solve the problem of insufficient information.
- Train an adaptive classifier for a given organization name with more features derived from twitter messages labeled by general classifier. This is a way to let the classifier more suitable for a given organization.

The remainder of the paper is organized as follows: Section 2 describes the related work on name disambiguation. Section 3 gives problem description and an overview of our approach. Section 4 presents supervised methods to classify tweets based on information from web sources. Section 5 introduces adaptive method to classify the tweets based on derived features. Section 6 gives the experiments and results. Finally section 7 summarizes this paper.

2 Related Work

Online social networks such as Twitter have attracted much interest from the research community. With little information contained in each tweets, it is a challenge for monitoring and analyzing them. There are some relevant works studied recent years.

Meij *et al.* (2012) add semantics to tweets by automatically mapping tweets to Wikipedia articles to facilitate social media mining on a semantic level. Liu *et al.* (2011) focus on NER on tweets and use a semi-supervised learning framework to identify four types of entities. Sriram *et al.* (2011) focus on classifying twitter messages to a predefined set of generic classes such as News, Events, Opinions, Deals, and Private Messages.

WePS-3 Online Reputation Management[3] held in 2010, aimed to identify tweets which are related to a given company. It provides standard training and test dataset that enable researchers to carry out and evaluate their methods (Amigó *et al.*, 2010).

In WePS-3, the research of (Yerva *et al.*, 2010) shows the best performance in the evaluation campaign. They adopt support vector machines (SVM) classifier with external resources, including Wordnet, metadata profile, category profile, Google set, and user feedback. To overcome the problem of tweets containing little context information, they create several profiles with external resources as a model for each company. The research of (García-Cumbreras *et al.*, 2010) shows the named entities in tweets are appropriate for certain company names.

There are some similar works. Perez-Tellez *et al.* (2011) adopt clustering technique to solve the problem of organization name disambiguation. Focus on identifying relevant tweets for social TV, Dan *et al.* (2011) propose a bootstrapping algorithm utilizing a small manually labeled dataset, and a large dataset of unlabeled messages.

General classifier of our work is similar to the research of (Yerva *et al.*, 2010) in the manner of constructing profiles for each organization and

[3] http://nlp.uned.es/weps/

forming general features. Different from theirs, we try to introduce different kinds of web pages to fully represent the organization as far as possible.

3 Overview

3.1 Problem Statement

Given a set of tweets and an organization name, the goal is to decide if each tweet in the set talks about this organization.

The input information per tweet contains: the tweet identifier, the entity name, the query used to retrieve the tweet, the author identifier and the tweet content. For each organization in the dataset, it gives the organization name and its homepage URL.

The output per tweet is True or False tag corresponding to related or non-related with the given organization. Table 1 shows the examples of tweet disambiguation for the company "Cadillac".

	Tweet content	Tag
1	On Sale: 2004 Hotwheels Crank Itz 3/5 Cadillac Escalade	TRUE
2	Update: Cadillac CTS-V vs BMW M5 Performance Testing......	TRUE
3	#nowwatching cadillac records while I' m finishing my paper	FALSE
4	......founded in 1701 by the Frenchman Antoine de la Mothe Cadillac	FALSE

Table 1: Examples of tweet ambiguity for the company name "Cadillac"

3.2 Our Method

Overcome the challenges of this task, we import web resources to enrich more information about the organization, such as homepage, Wikipedia page, related webpage, and unrelated webpage. With the general features extracted from these resources and training data, we train a general classifier.

Given an organization name in test data, we label the tweets by general classifier first. More features are derived from these tweets. The adaptive classifier for a given organization is trained with both the general features and derived features. Figure 1 gives an overview of our method.

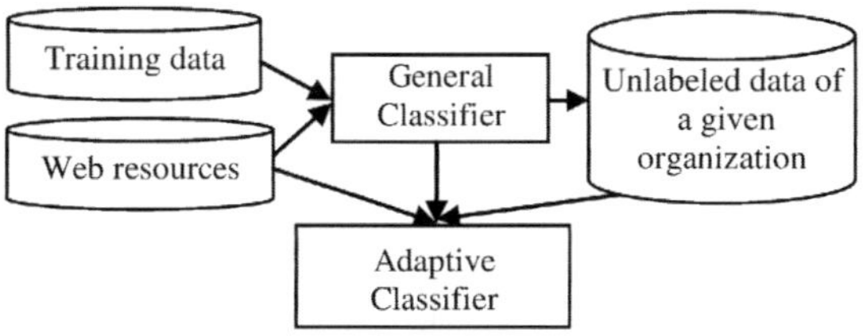

Figure 1. Overview of our method

4 General Classifier

From the input information, we may get the information related to the given organization from homepage URL. The information from homepage is important. However its coverage is limited. The tweet and organization homepage alone contain very little sharing information for effective similarity measure. Therefore, we try to mine web sources to enlarge the coverage of information related to the organization.

There is another problem. In this task, we have a training set corresponding to a few organization names. However, the organization names in test set do not appear in training set. This scenario can be seen as in-between supervised and unsupervised learning. The conventional lexical level features are not effective for classifying different organization names, because these organizations may belong to different domains. Therefore, we try to generate more general features from the web sources, train a classifier on training data, and classify the tweets corresponding to the unseen organization names in test set. We adopt Maximum Entropy, Support Vector Machine, and Naive Bayes methods to train the classifier.

4.1 Mine Organization Information from Web Sources

Here, we aim to mine the following web sources to get the information about the given organization.

Homepage

It is natural to regard that the organization's web site is indicative to represent the organization. We crawl through web pages from the homepage in maximum depth of 2.

However, some homepages are edited by javascripts or even flash, from which no valuable text could be extracted. At present, we discard these homepages.

Wikipedia related webpage

As a well organized and freely available knowledge, Wikipedia provide high quality information for some entity. Because lexical ambiguity exists, we utilize Wikipedia disambiguation page [4], which provides some candidates for a given entity name. If the wiki-webpage of an entity candidate contains the organization's homepage URL, we believe that this webpage is related to the organization. However, we can't find the related wiki-webpage for all of the organizations, because of the limited coverage of wikipedia or homepage URL mismatch.

Wikipedia unrelated webpage

Once finding Wikipedia related page, the remaining candidates of the disambiguation page are selected as Wikipedia unrelated pages. These web pages may contain the information that indicates the other meaning of organization name.

Figure 2 shows an example of Wikipedia disambiguation page of "http://en.wikipedia.org/wiki/Apple_(disambiguation) ". In this webpape, Apple Inc is the company we cared as Wikipedia related webpage, the others are treated as unrelated webpages.

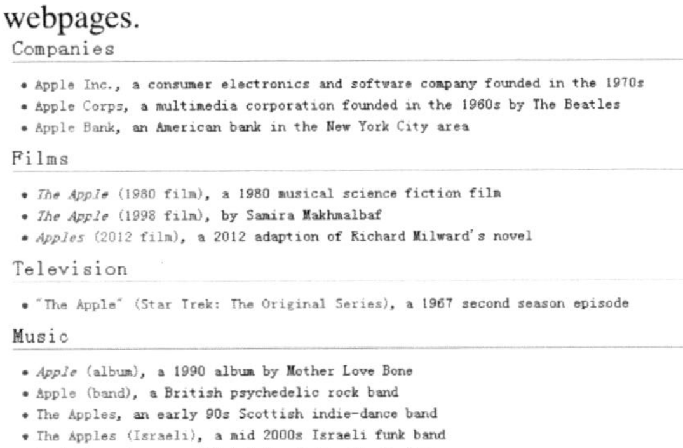
Companies

- Apple Inc., a consumer electronics and software company founded in the 1970s
- Apple Corps, a multimedia corporation founded in the 1960s by The Beatles
- Apple Bank, an American bank in the New York City area

Films

- *The Apple* (1980 film), a 1980 musical science fiction film
- *The Apple* (1998 film), by Samira Makhmalbaf
- *Apples* (2012 film), a 2012 adaption of Richard Milward's novel

Television

- "The Apple" (Star Trek: The Original Series), a 1967 second season episode

Music

- *Apple* (album), a 1990 album by Mother Love Bone
- Apple (band), a British psychedelic rock band
- The Apples, an early 90s Scottish indie-dance band
- The Apples (Israeli), a mid 2000s Israeli funk band
- Apple Records, record label founded by The Beatles

Figure 2. An example of Wikipedia disambiguation webpage

Related webpage

Google provides the search key word "related", which is used to find related or similar web page for a given URL. For example, input a query "related: http://www.apple.com", Google would return many web sites of other electronic companies, such as HP, DELL, and SONY as shown in Figure 3. These web pages contain the category information related to the given organization, which enlarge the coverage of organization information in some extent. Here, we collect top-100 retrieval result as related web pages.

Dell Official Site - The Power To Do More | Dell
www.dell.com/
2010年9月27日
Dell provides technology solutions, services and support. Visit Dell.com for Laptops, Netbooks, Tablet PCs ...

HP - United States | Laptop Computers, Desktops, Printers, Servers ...
www.hp.com/ - 翻译此页
Research or buy HP printers, desktops, laptops, servers, storage, enterprise solutions and more at the Official Hewlett-Packard Website.

AppleInsider | Apple news and rumors since 1997
www.appleinsider.com/ - 网页快照 - 翻译此页
Home · Reviews · Forums · Price Guides · Current-Gen Macs · Previous-Gen Macs · Apple Wireless Devices · iPads, iPhones & iPods · Used Apple Products ...

Microsoft Corporation: Software, Smartphones, Online, Games ...
www.microsoft.com/ - 网页快照 - 翻译此页
Get product information, support, news from Microsoft.

Figure 3. An example of related webpage

Link webpage

Similar with related web pages, Google provides another search key word "link", which is used to find web pages linked to a specified URL. For example, input a query "link: http://www.apple.com", we access to a wider variety of results which contain a URL of "http://www.apple.com", as shown in Figure 4. We think the web pages linked to given URL are information extension of organization, may have some relationship with the organization. Top-100 retrieval results are collected as link web pages.

Texthelp Systems Support - Order Tracking
www.texthelp.com/north-america/.../order-trackin... - 网页快照 - 翻译此页
When you ordered your product, you should have received notification via email with an order number. Please enter the order number below, and click the ...

Metadata Working Group: Member Companies
www.metadataworkinggroup.org/members/ - 网页快照 - 翻译此页
Member Companies. The Metadata Working Group currently is comprised of a variety of vendors representing a broad cross-section of the workflow of digital ...

Configuring Mac OS X for Stanford DSL | Information Technology ...
itservices.stanford.edu/service/ess/mac/docs/dsl - 网页快照 - 翻译此页
25 Feb 2010 – About Stanford DSL. A DSL connection effectively provides the same type of Ethernet connection as an on-campus SUNet connection (using ...

Figure 4. An example of link webpage

4.2 General Features and Representation

Once we have collected the above five kinds of web pages, the crawled web pages are preprocessed, including removing HTML tags, filtering stop words, and stemming. Finally, all unigrams and bigrams are chose to represent the

[4] http://en.wikipedia.org/wiki/xxx_(disambiguation)

organization. We extract the following four types of information to construct profiles, in fact each profile can be treated as a set of key words.

Unigram profile: $P_u = set\{uigram\}$

Bigram profile: $P_b = set\{bigram\}$

Metadata profile: $P_m = set\{word\}$

URL profile: $P_{url} = set\{host\_name\}$

We construct 22 binary general features as follows.

$$F(T_i, Org) = \{\underbrace{F_u^h, F_b^h, F_m^h, F_{url}^h}_{home\_page}, \underbrace{F_u^w, \ldots, F_{url}^w}_{wiki\_page}, \underbrace{F_u^{nw}, \ldots, F_{url}^{nw}}_{neg\_wiki\_page}, \underbrace{F_u^l, \ldots, F_{url}^l}_{link\_page}, \underbrace{F_u^r, \ldots, F_{url}^r}_{related\_page}, \underbrace{H_1, H_2}_{heuristics}\}$$

$$T_i = set\{key\}$$

$$F_j = \begin{cases} 1, if\ T_i \cap P_j \neq NULL \\ 0, else \end{cases}$$

Where T_i represents the i-th tweet, Org is the given organization, and P_j is a profile. F_j is the weight of the corresponding feature. T_i use the unigram, bigram and URL as the key to represent tweet corresponding to different profiles of organization.

For different organization names, the given organizations are needed to have their own profiles from the five given web sources. We use the similarity between the tweet and organization profiles as the general features. These features are stable for different organizations. However, the classifier built with conventional lexical features is highly dependent on organizations, because it has different weights of lexical features for different organizations. In this task, the set of organization names in training and test data set are different. Therefore, general features are more suitable than lexical features for building a classifier with training data.

From these general features, we measure the similarities between a tweet and a given organization on a level of different web sources, but not lexical level.

In addition, we also utilize the following two heuristic rules:

H1: if an organization name have multiple words, we set value as 1, else set as 0;

H2: if a tweet contains the full organization name, we set value as 1, else set as 0;

We think organization name with multiple words may contain more information. For example, "Yale University" contains more semantic information to distinguish it from other entity.

So far, we have formed general features, which are not organization specific. Each tweet is represented by this kind of features would have the same distribution between training and test set. So, traditional supervised classifiers could be applied and have good generalization performance on unseen data.

4.3 Supervised Classifiers

Here, we train three classical supervised classifiers with the general features gotten from the web sources, with the aim to get general classifiers to classify the tweets.

Maximum Entropy Classifier

The classifier is to classify tweets as True or False with the given feature vector. We aim to train a Maximum Entropy Classifier for this task. The principle of Maximum Entropy Model is that the model should maximize entropy, or "uncertainty" with satisfying all the constraints. This is a straightforward idea that just model what is known, and just keep uniform what is unknown. Here, we utilize all features described above in this classification task. NLTK [5] tool is used to implement Maximum Entropy Classifier.

Support Vector Machine

Support Vector Machine (SVM) is a popular machine learning approach. Based on the structural risk minimization of statistical learning theory, SVM finds an maximum-margin hyperplane to separate the training examples into two classes. Due to maximum-margin preventing over-fitting in high-dimensional data, SVM usually achieves good performance on a range of tasks.

We use SVMLight [6] toolkit to achieve the classification result. RBF kernel function is used and all the other parameters are set to their default values.

Naive Bayes Classifier

The Naive Bayes Classifieris based on Bayesian theorem. Though it is simplicial, Naive Bayes Classifier has been proved very effective for text

[5] http://www.nltk.org/

[6] http://svmlight.joachims.org/

categorization. We use the Naive Bayes Classifier provided by the NLTK toolkit.

5 Adaptive Classifier

In this task, organization names in training data are different from those in test data. In Section 4, we train supervised classifier with general features on training data. In this section, we aim to get an adaptive classifier to a certain organization in test data. The adaptive classifier is trained with more features gotten from the tweets in the test set for a given organization.

5.1 Adaptive Process

The adaptive process includes three parts: (1) get labeled data, (2) derive more features, and (3) train classifier. The detail is given in the following algorithm.

Algorithm: Adaptive process

Input: general classifier(GC) and Tweet set(TS) of a given organization

Output: adaptive classifier

Algorithm:

(1) Label TS using GC, and get result(GR) ;

(2) Derive features from GR, choose feature type and extract feature using feature selection method ;

(3) Train adaptive classifier (AC) to a certain organization, using both general features and derived features with GR.

Here, we try two ways to get the tweet set of a given organization. One is to use the data in test set directly, the other is to crawl tweets from twitter with organization name as query. To different organization name, the scale of the retrieved tweets from twitter is more than 2,000, which is larger than the test data with about 400 tweets for a given organization name.

We use general classifier to label the tweets of a given organization. From the results, we could derive more features and train an adaptive classifier.

For training the adaptive classifier, we use both general features and derived features, with the aim of utilizing both the information from web sources and data set of a given organization.

5.2 Derived Features

Lexical level features are important for classification task. We do not use lexical features for general classifier because they are changing for different organizations. The weights of lexical features are quite different for different organizations. However when the organization is given, lexical features could distinguish related or unrelated tweets effectively.

Feature type

We adopt two types of features: one is the unigram word unit, the other is 4-gram character unit.

The tweet is short and informal. There are little information contain in one tweet. One keyword missing may lead the change of the tweet's classification result. Therefore, we adopt character unit as feature to allow the mistake of spelling in some extent.

Feature selection

The features derived from the labeled tweets are large scale and contain much noise. We need adopt feature selection method to get more effective features.

Here, we first select the features which have more than five times occurrences in tweet set of a given organization. Then we adopt Information Gain (IG) method to select top N features with high value of IG. IG is one of the classical feature selection methods. We set N as 2,000.

6 Experiments and Results

6.1 Corpus and Evaluation Metric

We have conducted experiments on the WePS-3 task 2 data. The training data contain about 50 organizations with about 400 tweets for each organization. The test data also contain about 50 organizations. There is no intersection between training and test data.

The task is to classify the tweets related or non-related to the given organization, it belongs to classification task. In details, there are four categories for the tweets in evaluation phase: true positive(TP), false positive(FP), true negative(TN), false negative(FN). Therefore, we measure the performance by accuracy, precision, recall and F-measure.

$$Accuracy = \frac{TP + TN}{TP + FP + TN + FN}$$

$$Precision^{+} = \frac{TP}{TP + FP} \qquad \text{Recall}^{+} = \frac{\text{TP}}{\text{TP} + \text{FN}}$$

$$Precision^{-} = \frac{TN}{TN + FN} \qquad \text{Recall}^{-} = \frac{\text{TN}}{\text{TN} + \text{FP}}$$

$$F - Measure^{+} = \frac{2 * Precision^{+} * \text{Re}call^{+}}{Precision^{+} + \text{Re}call^{+}}$$

$$F - Measure^{-} = \frac{2 * Precision^{-} * \text{Re}call^{-}}{Precision^{-} + \text{Re}call^{-}}$$

6.2 Results and Analysis

We testify our proposed methods from the following aspects:

- The effectiveness of general classifier built with training data and information from web sources
- The influence of information gotten from different web sources for the performance of general classifier
- The effectiveness of adaptive classifier with derived features and unlabeled tweets of a given organization

Performance of general classifier

First, we testify the performance of supervised classifiers built with training data and information from web sources.

Table 2 shows their performance and also lists the performance of the state of art methods. Top_1, Top_2 and Top_3 are the 3 best system results in Weps-3 task 2 evaluation. BASELINE_{R}, BASELINE_{NR} are the baselines with arbitrary prediction that tag all tweets just related or non-related respectively.

	ACC	F +	F -
NB	**0.7508**	**0.5823**	0.6444
ME	**0.7510**	0.5375	0.6755
SVM	0.7383	0.5153	0.6506
Top_1	**0.8267**	0.6264	0.5606
Top_2	0.7491	0.4935	0.5651
Top_3	0.7312	0.5062	0.4683
BASELINE_{NR}	0.5652	0.0000	0.6563
BASELINE_{R}	0.4348	0.5274	0.0000

Table 2: Performance of supervised methods and other methods

In Table 2, the accuracy of BASELINE_{NR} is higher than that of BASELINE_{R}, which shows that there are more unrelated tweets in the whole test data. The performances of Naive Bayes (NB), Maximum Entropy (ME) and Support Vector Machines (SVM) have similar values of accuracy. They are much higher than those of BASELINE_{NR} and BASELINE_{R}. It proves that adopting some methods to disambiguate tweets is necessary.

Our proposed methods have the similar accuracy values with Top_2 and Top_3. It proves that proposed supervised classifiers, built with training data and information from web sources, are effective for this task.

The accuracy value of our methods is lower than that of Top_1. Its accuracy value is nearly 0.83, Top_1 method adopts manually constructed user feedback profile. With only homepage as features, its accuracy is about 0.66, which is similar with performance of our methods shown in Figure 5. Different from theirs, our methods are all automatically.

Compare with ME and SVM classifiers, NB classifier has better performance in F+ values. F+ value is important to measure the ability of finding the related tweets to a given organization.

Influence of different web sources for performance of general classifier

We select NB classifier to find the influence of information gotten from different web sources. Figure 5 lists the performance of NB classifier built with information gotten from only one of five different web sources.

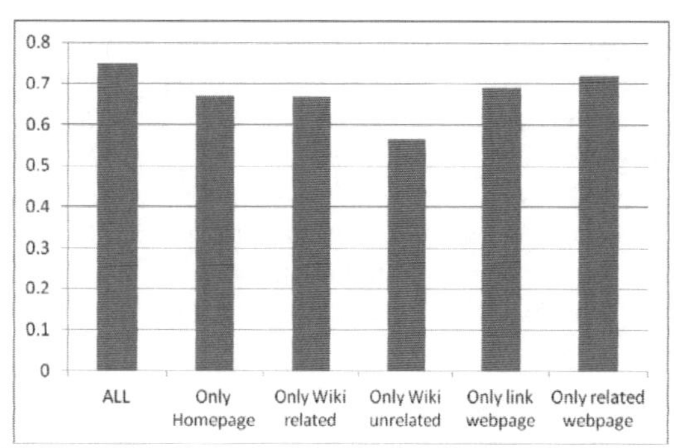

Figure 5. Accuracy of supervised methods (NB classifier) with different web sources

From Figure 5, we can see that the accuracy of classifier combining these five web sources is highest, which means the combination of five web sources is effective and feasible. This also shows that mining web sources is an effective way to enhance the performance of disambiguation.

Among the five classifiers built with features gotten from only one of web source, the accuracy of classifier built with information from related webpage is much higher than that of others. That means the related webpage containing the category information related to the given organization is much useful, which enlarge the coverage of organization information in some extent.

The accuracy of classifier built with only link webpage is also higher than that of homepage or wiki unrelated webpage. This shows link webpage and related webpage give more information about the given organization, our proposed web sources is effective for this task.

However, the performance of classifier built with the features gotten only from homepage is not as good as expectation. This may be caused by the information limitation, which could not cover the information of tweets. The focus of tweets may be different from that of homepage.

The accuracy of classifier built with information from Wiki unrelated webpage is the lowest. Our purpose of importing Wiki unrelated webpage is to mine the negative information about a given organization. Therefore, it should not be used by only itself. It is better to combine wiki unrelated webpage with other web sources.

Performance of adaptive classifier

We select NB classifier as the general classifier to label the tweets of a given organization name. Then we utilize them to train an adaptive classifier for this given organization. As described in Section 5.1, we adopt two ways to get the tweets of a given organization. One is to use test data, which is tagged as Adaptive-T. The other is to retrieve tweets from Twitter, which is tagged as Adaptive-U. The scale of unlabeled data is shown in Table 3. The performances are shown in Table 4.

	Number of tweets
Tweets of test data	~400
Tweets from Twitter	2,500-8,000

Table 3: Number of unlabeled tweets of one given organization

	ACC	**F+**	**F-**
NB	0.7508	0.5823	0.6444
Adaptive-T	0.7629	0.5676	0.6334
Adaptive-U	**0.7697**	0.5982	0.6618

Table 4: Performance of adaptive classifier

Table 3 shows that the scale of tweets from Twitter is much larger than that of test data. The size of tweets from Twitter is ranged from 2,500 to 8,000. This is dependent on whether the organization is hot point or not.

From Table 4, we can see that the accuracies of both adaptive classifiers are higher than that of NB classifier, which show that the proposed adaptive process is effective. With unlabeled data, derived more lexical features in adaptive process is one way to improve the performance of disambiguation.

The scale of tweets retrieved from Twitter is much larger than that of test data. Therefore, the coverage of lexical features of adaptive-U is larger than that of adaptive-T, the performance of adaptive-U is better than that of adaptive-T.

Besides accuracy, F+ and F- of adaptive-U are also higher those of NB classifier. This shows that mining large scale of unlabeled tweets is an effective way to get more information about a given organization.

7 Conclusion

In this paper, we probe the problem of organization name disambiguation on twitter information. We propose an adaptive method for organization name disambiguation. We build a general classifier with the training data and different web sources. Then we use the general classifier to label unlabeled twitter messages of a given organization. With more features derived from these messages, we train an adaptive classifier to a given organization. The experiments on WePS-3 show that the general classifier is effective for this task. The adaptive classifier improves the performance of general classifier, especially with a large scale of tweets gotten from Twitter.

In the future, we will try to select more features in the adaptive process, and find their influences for the performance of adaptive classifier. Furthermore, we will try to propose some methods to reduce the noise from both tweets and organization information.

References

Bharath Sriram, Dave Fuhry, Engin Demir, Hakan Ferhatosmanoglu, Murat Demirbas. 2011. Short Text Classification in Twitter to Improve Information Filtering. Proceedings of the 33rd International ACM SIGIR Conference on Research and Development in Information Retrieval, 841-842.

Danah Boyd, Scott Golder, Gilad Lotan. 2010. Tweet, Tweet, Retweet: Conversational Aspects of Retweeting on Twitter. In Hawaii International Conference on System Sciences, 1-10.

Edgar Meij, Wouter Weerkamp, Maarten D. Rijke. 2012. Adding Semantic to Microblog Posts. Proceedings of the 4th ACM Web Search and Data Mining, 563-572.

Enrique Amigó, Javier Artiles, Julio Gonzalo, Damiano Spina, Bing Liu, Adolfo Corujo. 2010. WePS-3 Evaluation Campaign: Overview of the Online Reputation Management Task. Proceedings of the 3rd Web People Search Evaluation Workshop

Fernando Perez-Tellez, David Pinto, John Cardiff, Paolo Rosso. 2011. On the Difficulty of Clustering Microblog Texts for Online Reputation Management. Proceedings of the 2nd Workshop on Computational Approaches to Subjectivity and Sentiment Analysis, 146-152.

Haewoon Kwak, ChanghyunLee, Hosung Park, Sue Moon.2010. What is Twitter, a Social Network or a news Media? Proceedings of the 19th International Conference on World Wide Web, 591-600.

Manos Tsagkias, Maarten D. Rijke, Wouter Weerkamp. 2011. Linking Online News and Social Media. Proceedings of the 4th ACM Web Search and Data Mining, 565-574.

Miguel García-Cumbreras, Manuel García-Vega, Fernando Martínez-Santiago, José M. Peréa-Ortega. 2010. SINAI at WePS-3: Online Reputation Management. Proceedings of the 3rd Web People Search Evaluation Workshop

Minoru Yoshida, Shin Matsushima, Shingo Ono, Issei Sato, Hiroshi Nakagawa. 2010. ITC-UT: Tweet Categorization by Query Categorization for On-line Reputation Management. Proceedings of the 3rd Web People Search Evaluation Workshop

Ovidiu Dan, Junlan Feng, Brian D. Davision. 2011. A Bootstrapping Approach to Identifying Relevant Tweets for Social TV. Proceedings of the 5th International AAAI Conference Weblogs and Social Media

Paul Kalmar. 2010. Bootstrapping Websites for Classification of Organization Names on Twitter. Proceedings of the 3rd Web People Search Evaluation Workshop

Surender R. Yerva, Zoltán Miklós, Karl Aberer. 2010. It was Easy, when Apples and Blackberries were only Fruits. Proceedings of the 3rd Web People Search Evaluation Workshop

Xiaohua Liu, Shaodian Zhang, Furu Wei, Ming Zhou. 2011. Recognizing Named Entities in Tweets. Proceedings of the 49th Annual Meeting of the Association for Computational Linguistics, 359-367.

Xuan-Hieu Phan, Le-Minh Nguyen, Susumu Horiguchi. 2008. Learning to classify short and sparse text & web with hidden topics from large-scale data collections. Proceedings of the 17th International Conference on World Wide Web, 91-100.

Predicting Answer Location Using Shallow Semantic Analogical Reasoning in a Factoid Question Answering System

Hapnes Toba, Mirna Adriani, and Ruli Manurung
Faculty of Computer Science
Universitas Indonesia
Depok 16424, Indonesia
hapnes.toba@ui.ac.id, {mirna, maruli}@cs.ui.ac.id

Abstract

In this paper we report our work on a factoid question answering task that avoids named-entity recognition tool in the answer selection process. We use semantic analogical reasoning to find the location of the final answer from a textual passage.We demonstrate that without employing any linguistic tools during the answer selection process, our approach achieves a better accuracy than a typical factoid question answering architecture.

1 Introduction

The task of a question answering system (QAS) is to provide a single answer for a given natural language question. In a factoid QAS, the system tries to give the best answer of an open-domain fact-based question. For example, the question "*Where was an Oviraptor fossil sitting on a nest discovered?*". A QAS should return '*Mongolia's Gobi Desert*' as the final answer.

A typical pipeline architecture in a fact-based QAS consists of four main processes, i.e.: question analysis, query formulation, information retrieval and answer selection. The main source of complexity in a QAS lies in the question analysis and answer selection process rather than in the information retrieval (IR) phase, which is usually achieved by utilizing third-party modules such as Lucene, Indri, or a web search engine.

The question analysis process seeks to determine the type of a given question, which in turn provides the expected answer type (EAT) of that question as a specific fact type, such as person, organization or location. The EAT will be used to select the best answer during the answer selection process, usually by utilizing a named-entity recognizer (NER) tool in a factoid QAS (Schlaefer et al., 2006). Different approaches have been used in order to improve the performance of the answer selection component. Ko et al. (2010) employed probabilistic models for answer ranking of NER-based answer selection by utilizing external semantic resources such as WordNet. More advanced techniques utilizing linguistic tools have been proposed in Sun et al. (2005), which uses syntactic relation analysis to extract the final answer, and Moreda et al. (2010), which employs semantic roles to improve NER-based answer selection. Recent work by Moschitti and Quarteroni (2011) proposed classification of paired texts that learn to select answers by applying syntactic tree kernels to pairs of questions and answers.

In our current work, we try to reduce the dependency of the answer selection process on linguistic tools such as NER systems. Our main concern is that in reality we do not always have a complete NER tool for every fact type. In our example mentioned above, the answer has a fact type which is neither an exact location, person nor an organization, i.e.: '*Mongolia's Gobi Desert*'. In such case, a NER-based system might fail to extract the answer. Further, if we have a complete NER-tool, it is still a complex problem to predict the location of the exact answer in a retrieval result.

We propose an approach which we call semantic analogical reasoning (SAR). Our approach tries to predict the location of the final answer in a textual passage by employing the analogical reasoning

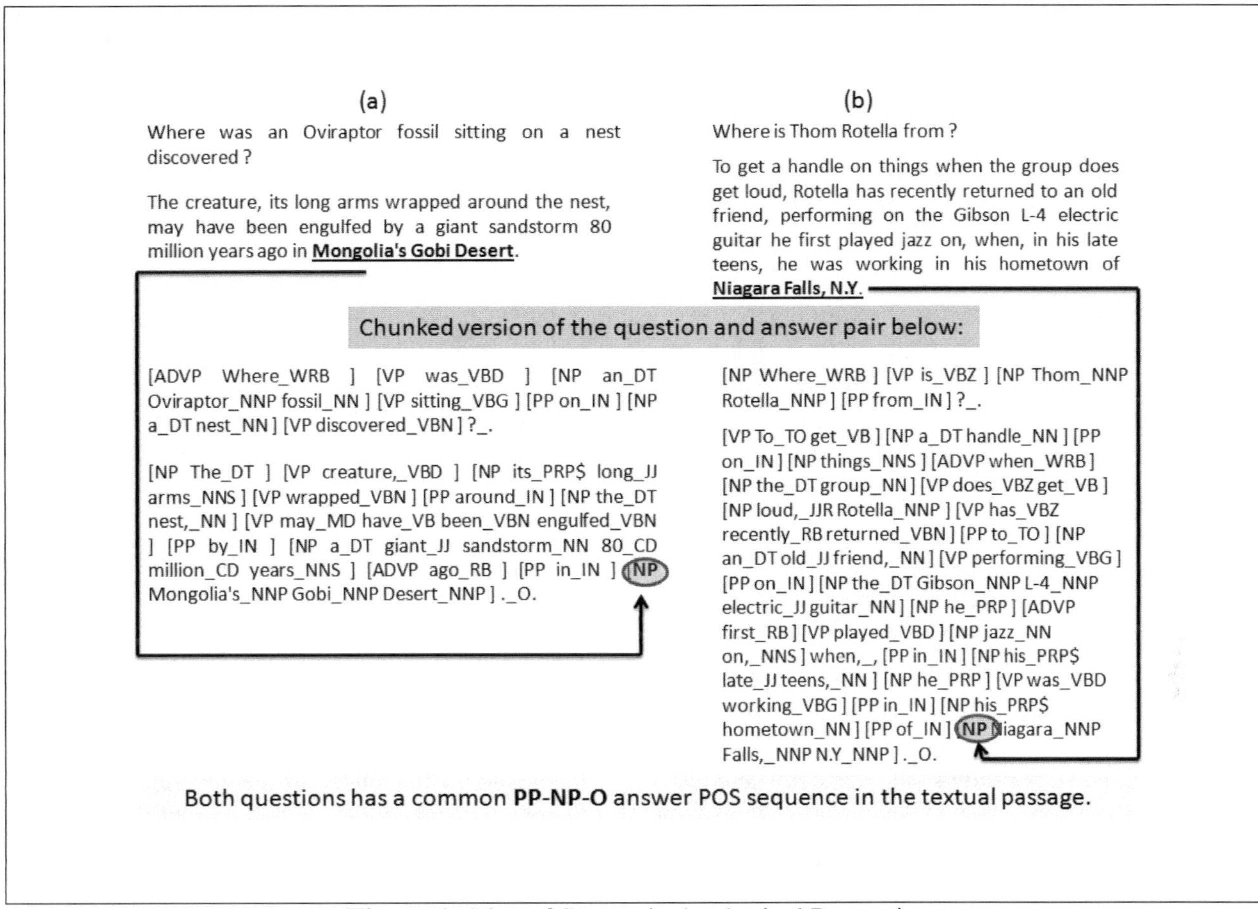

Figure 1: Idea of Semantic Analogical Reasoning

framework from Silva et al. (2010). We hypothesize that similar questions give similar answers. Based on the retrieved similar questions, our approach tries to provide the best example of question-answer pairs and use the influence level (weights) of the semantic features to predict the location of the final answer.

In the remainder of this paper, our basic idea and related works of semantic analogical reasoning will be presented in Section 2. The system architecture, procedures, experiments, and performance evaluation will be presented in Sections 3 and 4. Finally, our conclusions and future work will be drawn in Section 5.

2 Semantic Analogical Reasoning

The basic idea of semantic analogical reasoning is to find a portion of text in a passage which is considered useful during the answer selection process. Consider the two pairs of question and answer in Figure 1. Both questions need a fact type as the final answer, i.e. *Mongolia's Gobi Desert* (a) and *Niagara Falls, N.Y.* (b). We postulate that both questions have a high probability to share common answer features that will be useful to find the location of the final answer.

If we investigate the structure of the answer passage of question (a), we can see that the final answer is a noun phrase (NP), which is surrounded by a preposition (PP) and a stop sign (O). In question (b), we also found that the final answer is located in a sequence of PP-NP-O. Thus, if we can learn these kinds of related structures between question answer pairs for any EAT, we will have useful information to predict the location of the final answer in a textual passage. In this sense, we focus our work in learning the relational feature similarity between question answer pairs.

Silva et al. (2007; 2010) has investigated a statistical-based analogical reasoning (AR) framework. It is a method for ranking relations based on the Bayesian similarity criterion. The underlying idea of AR is to learn model parameters and priors from related objects (question and answer pairs in our case), and update the priors during the retrieval process of a query. The objective of the AR framework is to obtain a marginal probability that relates a new object pair (query) with a set of objects that have been learnt.

Most methods of classification or similarity measures focus on the similarity between the features of objects in a candidate pair and the features of objects in a query pair. AR focuses instead on the similarity between functions that map pairs to links. To some extent, this is the main reason that AR is appropriate for our idea.

Wang et al. (2009) has shown that AR is effective in retrieving similar question-answer pairs in a community-based QAS. They use statistical features such as term frequency, common *n*-gram length, and question answer length ratio. In contrast to our approach which tries to validate the location of a final answer; their work is limited to the retrieval of similar question.

The SAR approach, that we develop in this research is an extension of our previous work (Toba et al., 2011), which showed that AR can be used to construct EAT patterns. In our previous research, we used named-entity occurrences as features to relate the question and answer pairs. This time, instead of using named-entities as features, we use semantic information - which is based on syntactic features - to predict the corresponding named-entities.

Moschitti and Quarteroni (2011) use predicate argument structures, syntactic and shallow semantic tree kernel features to train question and answer pairs on SVM rank. Two consequences of using complex linguistic features is high computational cost and the requirement to have access to adequate linguistic resources and tools. For these reasons, we propose to use a simpler feature set, i.e. the trigram sequences of syntactic chunk. Unlike the research in Moschitti and Quarteroni (2011) that uses the whole syntactic tree, in this research we only keep the order of the root of any partial tree segment in trigrams of part-of-speech (POS) sequences.

In short, we develop a set of procedures to determine the best similar question-answer pair and predict the final answer location of a given factoid question. Our SAR approach extends the above mentioned related works in the following aspects:

1. We extend the AR framework from Silva, et al. (2007; 2010) to re-rank the AR retrieval process according to the most influential semantic features.

2. We extend the question-answer retrieval process of Wang, et al. (2009) and Moschitti and Quarteroni (2011) to find the most possible final answer location in a textual passage by utilizing POS sequences as semantic features.

Question Features	**Answer Features**
Question word (W5H) of a question and its syntactic chunk. Example: *[NP which_WDT]*	POS-tagger and syntactic chunk of the final answer. Example: *NP-NNP*
Trigram of syntactic chunk sequence which appears in the question. Example: *PP-NP-PP*, *VP-NP-VP*	Trigram of the final answer, [left - answer - right chunk] (during training). Example: *PP-NP-VP*. Trigram chunk sequences of the whole answer passage (during testing)

Table 1: Question Answer Semantic Features used in the Analogical Reasoning

3 System Architecture

Our architecture is depicted in Figure 2. There are two main process flows in the architecture. The first one is the training process (noted by the dashed lines), and the second one is the question answering process (noted by the solid lines).

3.1 Question Answering Framework

During the training process, the semantic features as described in Table 1 will be extracted and used in the AR training module. The training process will produce an AR model. Another important step in the training process is the evaluation of the features importance level. We need to know which semantic feature has the most influence in the model. This information will be important to select the best question answer pair later in the re-ranking process.

In the question answering step, the shallow semantic features of the question and the related answer passages - which have been retrieved during

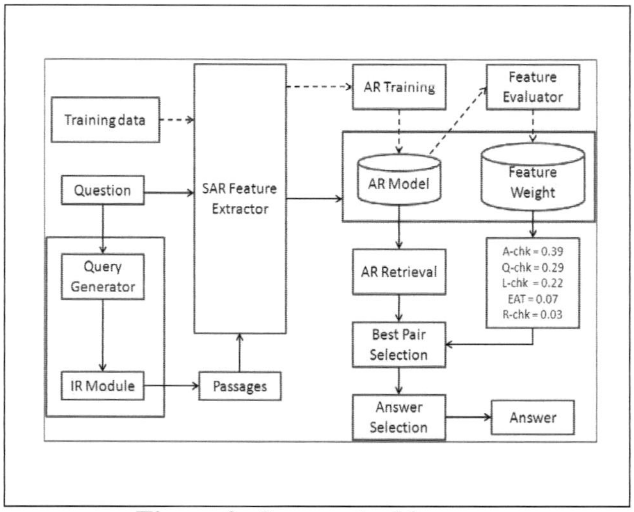

Figure 2: System Architecture

the IR process - are extracted. In this step, we will have a collection of ranked similar question answer pairs from the learnt AR model. Each similar pair needs to be evaluated (re-ranked), to make sure that we will have the best similar pair. In the final step, based on the best similar question answer pair, we search for the location of the answer from the textual passage by matching the sequence of the answer chunk to produce the final answer.

3.2 Analogical Reasoning, Re-rank Process and Final Answer Selection

In this part we summarize first the AR framework as introduced by Silva et al. (2007; 2010). The framework consists of two phases, i.e. the training and retrieval process. Consider a collection of related objects with some unseen labels L_{ij}'s, where $L_{ij} \in \{0, 1\}$ is an expected indicator of the existence of a relation between two related objects *i* and *j*. Consider then that we also have *K*-dimensional vectors, each consisting of features which relates the objects *i* and *j* : $\Theta = [\Theta_1 \ldots \Theta_k]^T$. In general, this vector will represent the presence or absence of relation between two particular objects.

Given the vectors of features Θ , the strength of the relation between two objects *i* and *j* is computed by performing logistic regression estimation as follows:

$$P(L^{ij}|x^{ij}, \Theta) = logistic(\Theta^T X^{ij}) \quad (1)$$

where $logistic(x)$ is defined as:

$$\frac{1}{1 + e^{-x}} \quad (2)$$

During AR training phase, the framework learns the weight (prior) for each feature by performing the following equation:

$$P(\Theta) = N(\tilde{\Theta}, (c\tilde{T})^{-1}) \quad (3)$$

where $\tilde{\Theta}$ is the logistic estimator of Θ, and $N(m, v)$ is a normal of mean *m* and variance *v*. Matrix $\tilde{T}$ is the empirical second moment's matrix of the link object features, and *c* is a smoothing parameter which is set by the user.

During the AR retrieval phase, a final score that indicates the rank of predicted relations between two new objects *i* and *j* (query) and the related objects that have been learnt in a given set *S* is compute as follows:

$$score(Q^i, A^j) = log\frac{P(L^{ij}|X^{ij}, S, L^S = 1)}{P(L^{ij} = 1|X^{ij})} \quad (4)$$

Silva et al. (2010) use the variational logistic regression approach to compute the scoring function in equation 4. This score gives the rank of similarity of how "analogous" a new query is to other related objects in a given learnt set *S*.

A drawback of AR as mentioned in Silva et al. (2010) is that by conditioning on the link indicators, the similarity score (eq. 4) between two objects *i:j*, and other objects *x:y*, is always a function of pairs *(i,j)* and *(x,y)* that is not in general decomposable as similarities between *i* and *x*, and *j* and *y*. Due to this limitation, we propose to evaluate the importance level (weight) of each feature which is used to relate the objects, and use the weights to re-rank the similarity score.

We empirically calculate the weighting factors for each feature set in Table 1, with respect to the expected answer-type, by performing chi-square (x^2) evaluation ((Manning et al., 2008), pp. 255-256) of overlapped features. The chi-square evaluation of the weighting factors are computed from the AR-retrieval results of the training data. To calculate the importance of each feature, we performed a top-10 retrieval for each question during the training phase on several parameter settings.

No.	Feature Set	Weight
1.	Answer Chunk	0.39
2.	Question Word + Chunk	0.29
3.	Left of Answer Chunk	0.22
4.	Expected Answer Type	0.07
5.	Right of Answer Chunk	0.03

Table 2: Weighting Factors of the Feature Sets. *'Expected Answer Type'* is not part of the extracted and learnt feature set in the AR model. The information about EAT during the experiments is provided by the gold standard.

As suggested in Silva et al. (2010), the value of the smoothing parameter is set as the *'number of positive links'* in the training data. We took variations of this smoothing parameter by multiplying the *'number of positive links'* by a factor of: 0.1, 0.5, 2, 4, 8, 10 and 16 during the chi-square evaluation. Finally, we compute an average value to form the final weighting factor of each feature, as can be seen in Table 2.

The final answer selection strategy is started by selecting the best question-answer analogous pair. To select the best pair we performed first a top-10 AR retrieval, re-ranked them by using the feature weighting factors, and finally took the best score pair. This pair is considered as the best pair which has the most overlapped features to the new question. To select the final answer in a passage, we performed a feature matching process of the answer features, i.e.: the overlap of trigram POS chunks sequences *'[left chunk - answer chunk - right chunk]'*.

4 Experiments and Evaluation

The main objectives of our experiments are twofold: on one hand, we try to find the importance level of the feature set that we use. On the other hand, we evaluate the potential of our approach to locate factoid answers in snippets and document retrieval scenarios without using any NER-tool. For the second objective we run two kinds of experiments. The first one is by using the gold standard snippets and the second one is by performing a document retrieval process.

In our experiments we use the question answer pairs from CLEF [1] English monolingual of the year 2006, 2007 and 2008. For the training data we use the 2007 and 2008 collections. In total it consists of 321 factoid question answer pairs. For the testing data we use the 2006 collection, consisting of 75 factoid questions (Magnini et al., 2006).

In our empirical experiments, by performing chi-square statistics, we find that the answer chunk is the most important feature. The right-chunk of an answer is the least significant feature. The complete weighting factors of the feature set can be seen in Table 2. In our experiments, we also add the EAT parameter as one of the factors which will be important in the re-ranking process.

We use the accuracy metric during evaluation (Schlaefer et al., 2006) (Peñas et al., 2010), which covers the proportion the number of questions correctly answered in the test set. We choose this kind of evaluation because we are interested in the potential of our approach to predict the location of an answer in a given snippet / document.

4.1 Gold Standard Snippets

In this first experiment we assume that the IR process performed perfectly and returns the best snippet which covers the final answer. We choose Open Ephyra (Schlaefer et al., 2006) as our competing pipeline. This decision is based on the fact that Open Ephyra employs two types of NER integrated in it. The first type is the model-based NER which consists of OpenNLP [2] and Stanford NER [3]. The second type is a dictionary-based NER that was specially design for TREC-QA competition.To maintain the fairness of the evaluation, we decided to only use the first type (model-based NER) and build a special trained answer-type classifier for CLEF datasets as described in Toba et al. (2010). In short, we hold the QA components of our approach and those of Open Ephyra all the same, except for the final answer selection.

The result of this experiment can be seen in Table 3. Our approach outperforms the overall result of Open Ephyra. The best accuracy of our approach is achieved in the OTHER and LOCATION answer-type, both 0.83, whereas the worst accuracy is for the TIME-typed questions, 0.45. In particular, our

[1] Question Answering at Cross Language Evaluation Forum (http://celct.fbk.eu/ResPubliQA/index.php)

[2] http://opennlp.apache.org

[3] http://nlp.stanford.edu/ner/index.html

Q.Type	#.Quest.	SAR	OE-NER
measure	14	0.57	0.64
person	13	0.77	0.69
other	12	0.83	0.25
location	12	0.83	0.92
organization	13	0.62	0.54
time	11	0.45	0.73
all	75	0.68	0.63

Table 3: Gold Standard Experiment Accuracy

approach performs exceptionally well in the 'OTHER' type. We believe this is due to the fact that our strategy finds the location of an expected answer without depending on the performance of an NER-tool. An example of 'OTHER-typed' questions is (CLEF 2006 #8): *"What is the Bavarian National Anthem?"*. The expected answer for this question is: *"God be with you, land of Bavarians"*. The answer chunk constituent in the gold standard snippet is a sequence of "VP-NP-O", which comes from the following snippet: *"They ended their demonstration by singing the Bavarian Anthem "God be with you, land of Bavarians". Then many of them moved on to support another Bavarian tradition – Oktoberfest."*.

If we look deeper into the feature set which is used in the AR training in Table 1, our trigram chunk features actually consist of two bigrams: *(left+answer)*-chunk and *(answer+right)*-chunk. During the final answer selection we consider these left and right chunk-bigrams as part of the selection process, not only the trigram sequence. This strategy is to ensure that the answer could be covered in one of the possibilities: a chunk trigram, a chunk left-bigram, or a chunk right-bigram.

In this first experiment, the most difficult questions to be answered are the TIME and MEASURE question-types. The answer of the TIME answer-type can be in the form of: dd/mm/yy, dd-mmm-yy, a single year number, or in the form of hh:mm a.m./p.m. These variations give rise to problems during the feature extraction process, because sometimes the chunker recognizes variations as numbers or as nouns. This problem also occurred in the MEASURE-typed questions. A measurement can be written as numbers (for example: "40") or as text ("forty"), and the chunker recognizes them differently, even though they express the same thing.

Figure 3(a) gives the number of expected "AR trigram sequences" in each answer-type which needs to be found in the snippets. We can see that for a factoid question answering task, the expected answers are mostly in the form of an NP (noun phrase).

4.2 Indri Document Retrieval

In our second experimental setting, we try to simulate our approach in a more realistic question answering system. In the real situation, we will not have any information about the semantic chunk of the final answer. We assume that the best pair (i.e. the top-*1* pair after the re-ranking process) of the AR answer features will supply us with that information. We performed IR process by using Indri Search Engine to retrieve the top-5 documents and pass them on to Open Ephyra and our system.

In this experiment, we use the same AR feature set as in the first experiment during the training phase. However, unlike the first experiment, during the top-*10* AR retrieval process, we only use the question feature set, i.e.: the question word and its chunk, and the question trigram of the semantic chunks. Due to the lack of the answer features, we need to adjust the way of the re-ranking process. We use a scoring function (*sf*) which takes the AR and Indri retrieval results into consideration. We use the formula in equation 5. We adjust the weight of the parameters to fit the question features during the re-ranking process of the AR retrieval results.

$$sf = \{\alpha OV(a_i, a_j) + \beta OV(b_i, b_j)\} * log(AR) * IR * \frac{1}{100} \quad (5)$$

where:

a	=	question chunk
b	=	expected answer type
α	=	weight of overlap question word and chunk (0.92)
β	=	weight of overlap expected answer type (0.08)
AR	=	score of the AR retrieval (see eq. 4)
IR	=	the weight of the Indri top-*5* retrieval rank (5 to 1)
OV(x,y)=		1, if there is overlap between x and y in a question *i* and its analogy pair *j*, otherwise 0

The result of this second experiment can be seen in Table 4. Both the SAR approach and Open E-

(a)

Patterns 3-g	Meas	Pers	Oth	Loc	Org	Time
ADVP-NP-NP	1	0	0	0	0	0
NP-NP-O	0	0	0	0	0	1
NP-NP-VP	0	1	1	0	0	0
O-NP-O	2	0	0	0	0	1
O-NP-PP	0	3	0	1	1	0
O-NP-VP	2	3	1	0	2	0
PP-NP-PP	1	0	0	0	0	1
PP-NP-VP	0	0	2	4	1	3
PP-NP-ADJP	1	0	0	0	0	0
PP-NP-ADVP	0	0	0	2	0	1
PP-NP-NP	0	0	1	2	1	0
PP-NP-O	1	3	1	3	5	1
PP-NP-PP	1	1	1	0	0	0
VP-NP-ADVP	0	1	0	0	1	0
VP-NP-NP	0	0	1	0	0	0
VP-NP-O	2	0	2	0	2	0
VP-NP-PP	2	1	2	0	0	3
VP-NP-VP	1	0	0	0	0	0
# Questions	14	13	12	12	13	11
# of Patterns	10	7	9	5	7	7

(b)

Patterns 3-g	Meas	Pers	Oth	Loc	Org	Time
ADVP-NP-O	1	0	0	0	0	0
NP-NP-NP	0	1	0	0	0	0
NP-NP-PP	2	0	0	0	0	0
NP-NP-VP	1	0	0	0	0	0
O-NP-NP	0	2	0	1	0	0
O-NP-O	0	1	2	2	2	0
O-NP-PP	0	1	1	0	1	0
O-NP-VP	1	0	1	0	2	0
PP-NP-NP	0	0	0	1	0	0
PP-NP-O	2	5	3	5	5	8
PP-NP-PP	2	1	0	1	0	2
PP-NP-VP	1	1	0	0	1	0
VP-NP-O	2	1	3	2	0	0
VP-NP-PP	0	0	2	0	2	1
VP-NP-VP	2	0	0	0	0	0
# Questions	14	13	12	12	13	11
# of Patterns	9	8	6	6	6	3

ADVP = Adverb phrase
NP = Noun phrase
PP = Prepositional phrase
O = Begin/End of a sentence;
or a coordinating conjunction

Figure 3: Number of Chunk Trigram Sequences in each EAT: (a) Snippet Experiment (b) Indri Retrieval Experiment

phyra have a lower accuracy compared to the first experiment. Once again, our approach achieves a higher accuracy. In the NER-based system, the errors are mainly caused by the model in the NER tools which cannot find the appropriate answer. For example for a person name "Carl Lewis", the NER tools can only recognize it either as Carl or Lewis, but not the whole name.

Q.Type	#.Quest.	SAR	OE-NER
measure	14	0.57	0.36
person	13	0.62	0.08
other	12	0.17	0.08
location	12	0.17	0.42
organization	13	0.23	0.15
time	11	0.27	0.27
all	75	0.33	0.23

Table 4: Indri Retrieval Experiment Accuracy

We classify the error types of our approach in three groups, i.e.: (1) not covered by Indri retrieval, (2) decreasing rank of relevant document because of the AR re-ranking score function, and (3) irrelevant example from the best AR pair. The frequency of these error groups can be seen in Table 5.

Error Class	Fre
AR Re-ranking (decreasing rank of relevant documents)	19
Irrelevant AR Example	17
Indri Retrieval	14
Total not found answers	50

Table 5: Frequency of Error Classification of SAR Approach

In our opinion, the main drawback of our approach is that it suffers from the variations of sentence structures - those of the snippets in the training set and those of the retrieved documents. These variations influence the AR re-ranking and matching process of chunk sequences. For instance, if the AR best pair suggests that the answer should be located at the end of a sentence, while that chunk could not be found in the retrieved document, then we will have a negative result. An example of such case can be seen in Table 6. The complete occurrences of the expected trigram sequences in this second experiment can be found in Figure 3(b).

Question and Answer	**SAR (found in relevant document)**	**Expected (AR retrieval)**
Q: Who is head of Bank of Tokyo? (CLEF 2006 #52) **A**: Tasuku Takagaki	Sequence: PP-NP-VP Bank_B-NP of_**B-PP** Tokyo_**B-NP** president_I-NP Tasuku_I-NP Takagaki_I-NP said_**B-VP**	Sequence: VP-NP-O said_**B-VP** series_**B-NP** creator_I-NP Sherwood_I-NP Schwartz_I-NP ._O

Table 6: Influence of Sentence Structures

5 Conclusion and Future Work

In this paper we have shown that by learning analogical linkages of question-answer pairs we can predict the location of factoid answers of a given snippet or document. Our approach achieves a very good accuracy in the OTHER answer-type (cf. Section 4.1). It shows the potential of our approach for dealing with an answer-type with no available corresponding NER tool.

Another finding in our experiments is that there is no trigram answer chunk sequence that really dominates in each answer-type. This suggests that each question depends on the sentence structure of a given snippet, and has a different way to be answered. This fact also suggests that our approach could suffer from the variations of the sentence structures.In our opinion, this is one of the reasons why the accuracy drops when the AR retrieval does not guarantee the occurrence of an answer (cf. Section 4.2). However, our approach has achieved a higher accuracy than a pure NER-based question answering system.

For our future work, we plan to develop a hybrid method of our approach with NER-based methods on larger and different datasets with more answer-type variations. We also plan to conduct another research in which we consider the trained question answer pairs as a kind of rule set. In this sense we look forward to combining the statistical approach, i.e. the analogical framework, and the semantic approach, i.e. the knowledge (rule) acquisition from the trained question answer pairs.

References

Alessandro Moschitti and Silvia Quarteroni. 2011. Linguistic Kernels for Answer Re-ranking in Question Answering Systems. *Information Processing and Management*, 47:825–842.

Anselmo Peñas, Pamela Forner, Alvaro Rodrigo, Richard Sutcliffe, Corina Forascu, and Christina Mota. 2010. Overview of ResPubliQA 2010: Question Answering Evaluation over European Legislation. *CLEF Notebook Papers.*

Bernardo Magnini, Danilo Giampiccolo, Pamela Forner, Christelle Ayache, Valentin Jijkoun, Petya Osenova, Anselmo Peñas, Paulo Rocha, Bogdan Sacaleanu, and Richard Sutcliffe. 2006. Overview of the CLEF 2006 Multilingual Question Answering Track. *CLEF Question Answering Working Notes.*

Christopher D. Manning, Prabhakar Raghavan, and Hinrich Schtze. 2008. *Introduction to Information Retrieval.* Cambridge University Press, New York, USA.

Hapnes Toba, Mirna Adriani, Ruli Manurung. 2010. Contextual Approach for Paragraph Selection in Question Answering Task. *CLEF Notebook Papers.*

Hapnes Toba, Mirna Adriani, Ruli Manurung. 2011. Expected Answer Type Construction using Analogical Reasoning in a Question Answering Task. *Proc. of ICACSIS.*

Jeongwoo Ko, Luo Si, Eric Nyberg, and Teruko Mitamura. 2010. Probabilistic Models for Answer-Ranking in Multilingual Question-Answering. *ACM Trans. on Information Systems*, 28(3) article 16: 1–35.

N. Schlaefer, P. Gieselmann, T. Schaaf, and A. Waibel. 2006. A Pattern Learning Approach to Question Answering within the Ephyra Framework. *LNAI*, 4188: 687-694. Springer, Heidelberg.

P. Moreda, H. Llorens, E. Saquete, and M. Palomar. 2010. Combining Semantic Information in Question Answering System. *Information Processing and Management*, doi: 10.1016/j.ipm.2010.03.008.

Ricardo Silva, Katherine Heller, and Zoubin Ghahramani. 2007. Analogical Reasoning with Relational Bayesian-sets. *Proc. of AISTATS.*

Ricardo Silva, Katherine Heller, Zoubin Ghahramani, and Eduardo M. Airoldi. 2010. Ranking Relations Using Analogies in Biological and Information Networks. *The Annals of Applied Statistics*, 4(2):615–644.

Renxu Sun, Hang Cui, Keya Li, Min-Yen Kan, and Tat-Seng Chua. 2005. Dependency Relation Matching for Answer Selection. *Proc. of SIGIR.*

X-J. Wang, X. Tu, D. Feng, and L. Zhang. 2009. Ranking Community Answers by Modeling Question-Answer Relationship via Analogical Reasoning. *Proc. of SIGIR.*

On the Alleged Condition on the Base Verb of the Indirect Passive in Japanese

Tomokazu Takehisa
Niigata University of Pharmacy and Applied Life Sciences
265-1 Higashijima, Akiha-ku, Niigata 956-8603, Japan
takehisa@nupals.ac.jp

Abstract

This paper argues against the view that Japanese indirect passives are restricted with respect to the base verb that they take. Specifically, it argues that, despite its initial plausibility, the oft-proposed generalization that unaccusatives cannot appear in indirect passives is too strong and the alleged distribution is a tendency at most, albeit a strong one. After closely examining the restriction along with the counterevidence discussed in the literature, this paper presents novel empirical evidence against the restriction. Moreover, it also argues that no stipulations specific to indirect passives need to be introduced in accounting for the purported evidence for the unaccusative restriction: pragmatic inferences play a crucial role in deriving the observed aversion to unaccusative-based indirect passives.

1 Introduction

Japanese passives have attracted much attention and have been a topic of intense debate due to their peculiar characteristics which present challenges to contemporary linguistic theories. One such characteristic is the existence of two types of passive: direct and indirect passives. Direct passives are passives with the active counterparts, where the passive subject corresponds to an object in the active, as in (1), whereas indirect passives have no such counterparts, as shown in (2).[1]

(1) Boku-wa sensei-ni home-rare-ta
1SG-TOP teacher-DAT praise-PASS-PST
'I was praised by the teacher.'
cf. Sensei-ga boku-o home-ta
teacher-NOM 1SG-ACC praise-PST
'The teacher praised me.'

(2) Boku-wa kodomo-ni nak-are-ta
1SG-TOP child-DAT cry-PASS-PST
'The child cried on me.'
cf. Kodomo-ga (*boku-o/-ni) nai-ta
child-NOM 1SG-ACC/-DAT cry-PST
'The child cried (*me).'

Of the many issues brought up by these two types of passive, it is sometimes proposed that indirect passives are restricted with respect to the base verb they take. Specifically, researchers such as Dubinsky (1985, 1997), Kageyama (1993, 1996) and Washio (1989-90) argue for what we refer to as the unaccusative restriction, which bans unaccusatives from appearing as the base verb of the indirect passive. For instance, Kageyama (1996) presents the following examples in (3) and

[1] The following abbreviations are used: 1 = first person, 2 = second person, ACC = accusative, CAUS = causative, COM = comitative, COMP = complementizer, COND = conditional, CONJ = conjunction, DAT = dative, DV = dummy verb, GEN = genitive, IMP = imperative, INCH = inchoative, INST = instrumental, LOC = locative, NEG = negative, NPST = nonpast, PASS = passive, PL = plural, POT = potential, pro = null pronoun, PST = past, SG = singular, STV = stativizer, TOP = topic.

(4), whose base verbs are unergatives and unaccusatives, respectively.

(3) a. Torakku-ni soba-o hasir-are-ta
truck-DAT side-ACC run-PASS-PST
'The truck ran by my side on me.'

b. Titioya-ni sofaa-de ner-are-ta
father-DAT couch-LOC sleep-PASS-PST
'I was adversely affected by my father sleeping on the couch.'

(4) a. *Seiseki-ni ot-i-rare-ta
grade-DAT fall-INCH-PASS-PST
'My grades slipped on me.'

b. *Syatyoo-ni sikyo-s-are-ta
president-DAT death-DV-PASS-PST
'The president died on us.'

(Kageyama, 1996 with minor changes)

This paper attempts to shed some light on Japanese indirect passives by placing special focus on the unaccusative restriction. Specifically, I will make the following two claims: first, the restriction is empirically too strong and it is at most a tendency, not a solid descriptive generalization; second, pragmatic inferences derive the purported cases for the unaccusative restriction, which in turn proves to be illusionary and superfluous.

The paper is organized as follows: Section 2 discusses the nature of the unaccusative restriction and issues concerning split intransitivity. Section 2.1 examines the counterevidence pointed out in the literature, and then Section 2.2 presents novel empirical evidence from two-place unaccusatives. Section 3 considers the purported cases for the unaccusative restriction and argues that pragmatic inferences play a crucial role in accounting for them, thereby showing that the unaccusative restriction can be dispensed with entirely. Section 4 concludes the paper.

Before going into discussion, I would like to mention three things that should be kept in mind. First, I assume without argument that, aside from the customary distinction between direct and indirect passives, the distinction between *ni*-passives and *niyotte*-passives is real (Kuroda, 1979 inter alia) and that *ni*-passives involve the introduction of an affected argument by one type of *-rare*, an unaccusative applicative predicate, as in (5)a (cf. Dubinsky, 1985, 1997; Pylkkänen, 2002), while *niyotte*-passives involve the suppression of the external argument of the base verb by another type of *-rare*, the passive voice head (Kratzer, 1996), as in (5)b.

(5) a. as an applicative predicate ($Appl_{Malefactive}$)[2]
[[-rare]] = λx.λe. Affectee(e,x)

b. as the passive voice head ($Voice_{Passive}$)
[[-rare]] = λe.∃x[Agent(e,x)]

Thus, I assume two homophonous morphemes which function completely differently. Though I consider that the homophony is not accidental and should receive a principled explanation along with other uses of *-rare*, I keep to the naïve assumption for the purposes of this paper.

Second, my aim in this paper is rather modest: it is to show that no stipulations, syntactic or otherwise, need to be introduced in accounting for the strong aversion to unaccusative-based indirect passives because it can be derived by what we already know about pragmatics, and it is not to choose between inferential pragmatic theories like Grice (1975), Horn (1984), Levinson (1987, 2000), and Sperber and Wilson (1995), although I couch my analysis in neo-Gricean terms. To this end, I simply follow the common view on the divide between grammar and pragmatics, with the former defined as a set of codes and the latter as inference.

Finally, there is great variability in acceptability judgments, especially when unaccusative-based indirect passives are involved. Thus, when I cite examples from the previous literature, I cite their reported judgments as well, with minor changes made to the examples when necessary. While the divide appears to be wide between 'conservative' and 'liberal' speakers, it is also true that an example once judged as unacceptable can become acceptable if a proper context of utterance is carefully constructed and provided, suggesting that the divide results partly from inadequate control of the context of utterance. With this in mind, I will spell out contextual and conceptual settings as much as possible when I present my analysis.

2 The Unaccusative Restriction

As noted above, the unaccusative restriction prohibits unaccusative verbs from appearing as the base verbs in indirect passives. In addition to (4), I give several more examples in (6):

[2] The benefactive counterpart ($Appl_{Benefactive}$) is as follows:
[[-te moraw-]] = λx.λe. Benefactive (e,x)

(6) a. *Nooka-no hito-tati-wa kaze-de
farmer-GEN person-PL-TOP wind-INST
ringo-ni ot-i-rare-ta
apple-DAT fall-INCH-PASS-PST
'The farmers were adversely affected by the apples' falling because of the wind.'
b. *Taroo-wa anata-no nimotu-ni
Taro-TOP 2SG-GEN belongings-DAT
konna tokoro-ni ar-are-ta
this place-LOC be-PASS-PST
'Taro was adversely affected by your belongings being in this place.'
c. *Taroo-wa situon-ni ag-ar-are-ta
T.-TOP rm.temp.-DAT rise-INCH-PASS-PST
'Taro was adversely affected by the room temperature's rising.'
((6)a,b: Kuno and Takami, 2002 w/minor changes)
((6)c: Dubinsky, 1997 with minor changes)

Moreover, the contrast in (8) below between the causative and inchoative forms may also help elucidate what the restriction is intended to capture: as (7) shows, while both the causative and inchoative alternants are fine in the active, they show a stark contrast when indirect passives are formed from them. Specifically, unlike indirect passives based on causatives, as in (8)a, those based on inchoatives are quite awkward and marked in acceptability, as shown in (8)b.

(7) a. Kodomo-ga mado-o wat-Ø-ta
child-NOM window-ACC break-CAUS-PST
'A child broke the window.'
b. Mado-ga war-e-ta
window-NOM break-INCH-PST
'The window broke.'
(8) a. Kodomo-ni mado-o
child-DAT window-ACC
war-Ø-are-ta
break-CAUS-PASS-PST
'A child broke the window on me.'
b. *mado-ni war-e-rare-ta
window-DAT break-INCH-PASS-PST
'The window broke on me.'
((8)b: Washio, 1989-90 with minor changes)

The restriction has sometimes received an explanation in terms of the 1-Advancement Exclusiveness Law (henceforth, 1AEX). 1AEX is originally a law proposed in the framework of Relational Grammar (Perlmutter and Postal, 1984), which states, in informal terms, that raising to subject occurs at most once in a single clause. Thus, it precludes cases such as double passives and passives based on unaccusatives, both of which require raising to subject to occur more than once. A contemporary explanation of this law takes the suppression of an external argument, as in (5)b, as the key component: the process can apply to predicates with an external argument like transitives and unergatives, but not to those without like unaccusatives and passives, given that vacuous application is impossible.

2.1 Evidence against the Restriction

Although the unaccusative restriction can be clearly stated, the situation is not as clear when we consider the relevant data because there are two complications pertaining to split intransitivity. First, it is not always the case that one verb is fixed with only one verb class—unergative or unaccusative—and some verbs display variable behavior with respect to the class membership, as shown in (9):[3]

(9) a. Unergative *slide*
i. Ted slid into the closet.
ii. The closet was slid into by Ted.
b. Unaccusative *slide*
i. The soap slid into the desk.
ii. *The desk was slid into by the soap.
(Perlmutter and Postal, 1984)

Second, these verbs are variable in syntactic behavior, depending on the syntactic context where they appear. That is, they show unergative behavior in some syntactic contexts and unaccusative behavior in others, but not both at the same time. Given this, if one wants to argue that a variable behavior verb is unaccusative in some syntactic context *C*, it only makes sense to show its unaccusative status in *C*, and it may be irrelevant to the argument to do so in other contexts.

With these in mind, let us turn to the following three types of counterevidence to the unaccusative restriction pointed out in the literature.

First, consider cases where the same verb appears to display different behavior. Kuno and Takami (2002) take the contrast in (10) as counter to the unaccusative restriction on the assumption that the base verb is invariable as unaccusative.

[3] See Borer (2005) for more on variable behavior verbs.

(10) a. *Dentyuu-ni tao-re-rare-ta
utility.pole-DAT fall-INCH-PASS-PST
'The utility pole fell down on me.'
b. Dooryoo-ni tao-re-rare-ta
coworker-DAT fall-INCH-PASS-PST
'The coworker got ill on me.'
(Kuno and Takami, 2002 with changes)

However, the restriction can still be defended if the verb is variable in such a way that it is unaccusative in (10)a but unergative in (10)b, as in (9). Thus, for (10)b to be true counterevidence, it must be demonstrated that the verb is unaccusative in its behavior in the syntactic context of (10)b.

It is well known that floated numeral quantifiers (henceforth, (F)NQ) in Japanese can be used as a test for unaccusativity (Miyagawa, 1989a): unaccusative subjects can be associated with floated numeral quantifiers, as in (11)a, while unergative subjects cannot, as in (11)b.

(11) a. Gakusei-ga ofisu-ni huta-ri ki-ta
student-NOM office-to two-CL come-PST
'Two students came to the office.'
b. *Gakusei-ga zibun-no kane-de
student-NOM self-GEN money-INST
huta-ri denwa-si-ta
two-CL telephone-DV-PST
'Two students called at their own expense.'

Applying this test to (10)b gives the following result:[4]

(12) Dooryoo-ni ofisu-de batabata-to
coworker-DAT office-LOC by.turns-COM
go-nin ?(-mo) tao-re-rare-ta
5-CL-even fall-INCH-PASS-PST
'We had as many as five of coworkers fall down in the office one after another on us.'

In (12), the locative phrase and the comitative-marked manner adverbial are added to ensure that the NQ is inside the VP, which is a prerequisite for the test. The scalar focus particle *-mo* 'even' is also added to the NQ and, as indicated, the lack of it slightly degrades the acceptability for some reason or other. Hence, it is still possible to assume that the verb in (10) is uniformly unaccusative, thus taking (10)b to be a true counterexample, but this holds with the proviso that more research is needed to clarify whatever effects the focus particle has on the FNQ test.

The next case, also discussed by Kuno and Takami (2002), involves another unaccusative diagnostic in Japanese, accusative case marking with Sino-Japanese roots (Miyagawa, 1989b): it is possible with unergative or transitive roots, as in (13), but not with unaccusative roots, as in (14).

(13) a. Taroo-wa iede(-o) si-ta
Taro-TOP house.out-ACC do-PST
'Taro ran away from home.'
b. John-wa murabito-ni ookami-ga
John-TOP villagers-DAT wolf-NOM
ku-ru-to keikoku(-o) si-ta
come-NPST-COMP warning-ACC do-PST
'John gave the villagers the warning that a wolf is coming.'
(Grimshaw and Mester, 1988 with minor changes)

(14) a. Taroo-wa sono kekka-o kii-te
Taro-TOP that result-ACC hear-CONJ
zetuboo(??-o) si-ta
despair-ACC DV-PST
'Hearing the result, Taro despaired.'
b. Taroo-ga kaidan-de tentoo(*-o) si-ta
T.-NOM stairs-LOC fall-ACC DV-PST
'Taro fell down in the stairs.'
(Kageyama, 1993 with minor changes)

Thus, while restricted in its scope, accusative case marking can be used as a test for unaccusativity, and, as shown in (15), unaccusatives can indeed appear in indirect passives.

(15) a. Sonna koto-de kimi-ni zetuboo(*-o)
that thing-INST 2SG-DAT despair-ACC
s-are-tara komar-u
DV-PASS-COND get.annoyed-NPST
'It bothers me if you despair of that.'
b. Titi-ni tentoo(*-o) s-are-ta
father-DAT fall-ACC DV-PASS-PST
'My father fell in the stairs on me.'
(Kuno and Takami, 2002 with minor changes)

Finally, consider non-alternating unaccusatives, like *sin(-u)* 'die' and *hur(-u)* 'fall', which can appear in indirect passives, as shown in (16).

[4] Kuno and Takami (2002) also employ this test, but they do not apply it in the relevant context.

(16) a. Titioya-ni sin-are-ta
father-DAT die-PASS-PST
'My father died on me.'
b. Ame-ni hur-are-ta
rain-DAT fall-PASS-PST
'It rained on me' (Lit.: 'Rain fell on me.')

These verbs are unaccusative when they appear in indirect passives, as shown by the FNQ test in (17).

(17) a. Sensee-wa osiego-ni sensoo-tyuu
teacher-TOP student-DAT war-during
nampoo-de zyuu-nin-mo sin-are-ta
south-LOC 10-CL-even die-PASS-PST
'The teacher had as many as ten students die in the south during the war.'
b. Sansei-u-ni ip-pun-kan-ni
acid-rain-DAT one-min.-period-LOC
zyuu-miri-mo hur-are-ta
10-millimeter-even fall-PASS-PST
'Acid rain fell as much as 10mm for 1 min. on us.'

While Washio (1989-90) treats these verbs as unaccusatives immune to 1AEX, Kageyama (1993, 1996) classifies them as unergatives, assuming that only unergatives can form imperatives. See (18):

(18) a. Hayaku sin-e
soon die-IMP
"Die soon."
b. Ame, ame, hur-e, hur-e
rain rain fall-IMP fall-IMP
"Rain, fall!"
(Kageyama, 1993)

However, as Matsumoto (2000) correctly points out, unaccusative imperatives can be used to represent a wish of the speaker, and it is exactly the case with (18). Hence, unaccusatives as well as unergatives can form imperatives after all.

Taking the preceding two arguments together, we can conclude that non-alternating unaccusatives are neither unergatives nor variable behavior verbs functioning as such in indirect passives. Therefore, they also falsify the unaccusative restriction.

In sum, we have examined the counterevidence in the literature carefully, keeping in mind the caveat against confusing the different uses of variable behavior verbs, and demonstrated that the unaccusative restriction is too strong, as it would wrongly exclude cases like (10)b, (15) and (17).

2.2 New Evidence from Two-place Verbs

We have so far considered the counterevidence to the unaccusative restriction in the literature. The counterevidence examined involved only one-place verbs. In this subsection, I will present new evidence against the restriction involving two-place unaccusative verbs. Consider (19) below:

(19) Pittyaa-ga {kare-no/zibun-no/Ø}
pitcher-NOM he-GEN/self-GEN/pro
ude-o ot-Ø-ta
arm-ACC break-CAUS-PST
'The pitcher broke his arm.'

The subject in (19) can be construed in two ways, as an agent, who did the breaking, or as an affectee, whose arm underwent the breaking.

The fact that the ambiguity is not illusionary can be shown by the following example, where the agentive interpretation is negated and the affectee interpretation survives.

(20) Pittyaa$_1$-ga {kare$_1$-no/zibun$_1$-no/Ø$_1$}
pitcher-NOM he-GEN/self-GEN/pro
ude-o ot-Ø-ta kedo,
arm-ACC break-CAUS-PST but
zibun$_1$-de-wa or-Ø-anak-at-ta
self-INST-TOP break-CAUS-NEG-DV-PST
'The pitcher broke his arm, but he didn't break it himself.'

To obtain this kind of ambiguity, there are two conditions to be met (Inoue 1976): (i) a verb must be such that it does not necessarily select an agent (e.g., causative/inchoative verbs); (ii) there must be a "proximate" relation (e.g., inalienable possession relation) between the subject and the object. Thus, the ambiguity cannot be obtained with non-alternating verbs like *nagur(-u)* 'punch' in (21)a. This can be demonstrated by the conjunction test, as given in (21)b, where the sentence results in a contradiction due to the unambiguous subject.

(21) a. Pittyaa$_1$-ga {kare$_1$-no/zibun$_1$-no/Ø$_1$}
pitcher-NOM he-GEN/self-GEN/pro
ude-o nagut-ta
ude-ACC punch-PST
'The pitcher punched his arm.'

b. *Pittyaa$_1$-ga {kare$_1$-no/zibun$_1$-no/Ø$_1$}
pitcher-NOM he-GEN/self-GEN/pro
ude-o nagut-ta kedo,
ude-ACC punch-PST but
zibun$_1$-de-wa nagur-anak-at-ta
self-INST-TOP punch-NEG-DV-PST
'*The pitcher punched his arm, but he didn't punch it himself.'

The lack of a "proximate" relation also makes the ambiguity unavailable, as shown in (22).

(22) a. Pittyaa$_1$-ga {kare$_1$-no/zibun$_1$-no/Ø$_1$}
pitcher-NOM he-GEN/self-GEN/pro
batto-o ot-Ø-ta
baseball.bat-ACC break-CAUS-PST
'The pitcher broke his baseball bat.'

b. *Pittyaa$_1$-ga {kare$_1$-no/zibun$_1$-no/Ø$_1$}
pitcher-NOM he-GEN/self-GEN/pro
batto-o ot-Ø-ta kedo,
baseball.bat-ACC break-CAUS-PST but
zibun$_1$-de-wa or-Ø-anak-at-ta
self-INST-TOP break-CAUS-NEG-DV-PST
'*The pitcher broke his baseball bat, but he didn't break it himself.'

Moreover, the ambiguity becomes unavailable even when the two conditions are met, if the sentence undergoes *niyotte*-passive formation, which serves to eliminate the affectee reading, as shown in (23).

(23) *Pittyaa$_1$-no ude-ga kare$_1$-niyotte
pitcher-GEN arm-NOM he-by
or-Ø-are-ta kedo,
break-CAUS-PASS-PST but
kare.zisin$_1$-wa or-Ø-anak-at-ta
he.self-TOP break-CAUS-NEG-DV-PST
'*The pitcher's arm was broken by him, but he didn't break it himself.'

Furthermore, the affectee subject passes the FNQ test, as in (24).

(24) Gakusei-ga ziko-de san-nin
student-NOM accident-LOC three-CL
ude-o ot-Ø-ta kedo minna
arm-ACC break-CAUS-PST but all
zibun-de-wa or-Ø-anak-at-ta
self-INST-TOP break-CAUS-NEG-DV-PST
'Three (of the) students broke their arm in the accident, but they all didn't break it themselves."

The facts that only the agentive interpretation survives in *niyotte*-passives and that the affectee subject passes the FNQ test strongly suggest that the verb is unaccusative with the affectee subject.

If unaccusatives can appear in indirect passives, it is predicted that sentences with the affectee subject can be embedded under indirect passives. This prediction is borne out, with the affectee argument marked dative in this case, as shown in (25): the sentence can be construed in such a way that the pitcher didn't cause, but his arm underwent, the breaking.

(25) Kantoku-ga pittyaa$_1$-ni ziko-de
coach-NOM pitcher-DAT accident-LOC
Ø$_1$ ude-o or-Ø-are-ta
pro arm-ACC break-CAUS-PASS-PST
'The coach had the pitcher break his arm in an accident on him.'

All in all, substantial evidence points to the unaccusative restriction being too strong. Therefore, the alleged generalization is a tendency at most, and unaccusatives, monadic or dyadic, can appear as the base verb in indirect passives.

3 Deriving the Unaccusative Restriction Effects

We have seen that the unaccusative restriction is not valid as a descriptive generalization and what it is intended to capture is a tendency at most. However, the observed tendency is so strong that it is quite unlikely that an array of facts arises from accidents. Thus, there still remains something that demands an explanation.

In this section, I attempt to give an account of the observed tendency with an eye to dispensing with stipulations specific to indirect passives as much as possible. The basic line of thought I would like to pursue is that the aversion to unaccusative-based indirect passives comes from the preference for other alternatives, which arises as a result of pragmatic inferences. In a nutshell, if an unaccusative-based indirect passive is unacceptable, it is infelicitous because there is a better alternative: its causative-based counterpart or active counterpart. Moreover, if it is still unacceptable with no better alternative, this results from the failure in the access to the relevant conceptual setting.

In the following, I will present an analysis in three steps, with the help of neo-Gricean principles.

3.1 The Q-Principle at Work: The Preference for Causatives over Inchoatives

If you consider again the unacceptable examples of unaccusative-based indirect passive that we saw in Sections 1 and 2, you will notice that the observed tendency is in large part supported by those with the inchoative alternants of causative-inchoative verbs. Moreover, replacing the inchoative verb with its causative counterpart renders the sentence acceptable, as shown by the contrast in (8), repeated here as (26) below.

(26) a. Kodomo-ni mado-o
child-DAT window-ACC
war-Ø-are-ta
break-CAUS-PASS-PST
'A child broke the window on me.'
b. *mado-ni war-e-rare-ta
window-DAT break-INCH-PASS-PST
'The window broke on me.'

I argue that part of the tendency can be restated in such a way that the causative alternant is preferred over its inchoative counterpart as the base verb in indirect passives, and moreover that this preference can be reduced to the classic observation on the use of the two alternants in general (Fillmore, 1981; McCawley, 1978, 1989): "you must expressly indicate an agent's involvement in an event [with the causative alternant -TT] as soon as you know of the agent's involvement in it" (McCawley, 1989: 315).

This observation can be reduced further to the following principle of neo-Gricean pragmatics:[5]

(27) The Q-Principle
a. Horn (1984)
Say as much as you can [given I]. (p.13)
b. Levinson (1987)
Do not provide a statement that is informationally weaker than your knowledge of the world allows, unless providing a stronger statement would contravene the I-principle (p.401)

In light of the Q-Principle, causative-based indirect passives like (26)a are more informative than, and thus are preferred over, those based on the inchoative alternants like (26)b, in the context where there is a salient agent in the embedded event. The use of the inchoative implies otherwise, thereby resulting in infelicity.

As it only partially explains the contrast in (26), the Q-Principle does not explain why (26)b is infelicitous when there is no contextually salient agent in the embedded event. We will turn to this in the next subsection.

3.2 The I-Principle at Work: The Preference for Actives over Indirect Passives

As the Q-Principle is operative, the I-Principle, given in (28), is also at work, being responsible for the preference for actives over their corresponding indirect passives:

(28) The I-Principle
a. Horn (1984)
Say no more than you must [given Q]. (p.13)
b. Levinson (1987)
Say as little as necessary, i.e. produce the minimal linguistic information sufficient to achieve your communicational ends (bearing the Q-principle in mind) (p.402)

When we compare an indirect passive and its active counterpart with respect to informativeness, it is always the case that the former is more informative than, i.e. asymmetrically entails, the latter, with the difference being that the former expresses a relation in which the individual introduced by the indirect passive morpheme is adversely affected by the embedded event. Thus, if it is unclear to the hearer how the adverse relation is established between the individual and the embedded event, then the use of an indirect passive makes the utterance irrelevant and unnecessary, and that of its corresponding active form suffices.

For brevity's sake, I assume that indirect passives based on causatives (or, transitives for that matter) trivially satisfy the I-Principle because there is no observed aversion to them and it is fairly easy to come up with contexts where the adverse relation is properly established.

[5] The I-Principle corresponds to Horn's (1984) R-Principle.

This said, consider the following examples:

(29) a. *Kigi-ni seityoo-s-are-te
tree.tree-DAT growth-DV-PASS-CONJ
uti-ni hi-ga atar-anai (<-anak-Ø)
home-DAT sun-NOM hit-NEG-NPST
'I am adversely affected by the trees growing, which blocks out the sunlight on my house.'

a'. Kigi-ga seityoo-si-te [...]
tree.tree-NOM growth-DV-CONJ

b. *Okane-ni naku-nar-are-te
money-DAT lost-INCH-PASS-CONJ
kaimono-ga deki-nak-at-ta
shopping-NOM do.POT-NEG-DV-PST
'My money disappeared on me and I could not do the shopping.'

b'. Okane-ga naku-nat-te [...]
money-NOM lost-INCH- CONJ

(29)a involves a non-alternating unaccusative, and (29)b the inchoative alternant. Moreover, for (29)b, suppose the context where there is no salient agent in the embedded event. In both the examples, though some unfavorable consequence is explicitly stated in the second conjunct to facilitate the judgments, the active form is preferred over the indirect passive counterpart. This is because, in normal situations, it is nonsense to attribute responsibility to inanimate objects, such as trees or money, which have no control over what happened. Therefore, since it makes no sense unless some special context is given, the use of an indirect passive is irrelevant and unnecessary, and thus, that of its active counterpart is more preferable.

In accounting for (29), I mention the dative subject of the embedded event being responsible for it, following the spirit of Kuno and Takami (2002), who invoke the notion of animacy and propose the hierarchy expressing preference for the dative subject (i.e., human > animate > natural force > inanimate).

I take a step forward by arguing that Kuno and Takami's hierarchy can be captured in terms of Dowty's (1991) proto-agent properties in (30), with the hierarchy effects dissolved into the number of proto-agent properties that the dative subject has. Moreover, for an indirect passive to be felicitous with an inanimate, insentient being as the embedded dative subject, it should be understood as having at least (30)c and hence some degree of controllability over the event in which it is a participant; otherwise, the use of the indirect passive would be infelicitous, as shown in (29).[6]

(30) Contributing properties for Proto-agent
a. volitional involvement in the event or state
b. sentience (and/or perception)
c. causing an event or change of state in another participant
d. movement (relative to the position of another participant)
(e. exists independently of the event named by the verb)

(Dowty, 1991: 572)

It should be emphasized that in Dowty's original system, proto-role properties are lexical entailments coded by the predicate. Here I assume that they are also properties that are inferred for the satisfaction of the I-Principle. In other words, they can contribute to pragmatic meaning as well as lexical semantic meaning. Thus, it is possible that, even when a predicate does not entail the sentience of an argument that it takes, the argument should be understood as sentient as imposed by the I-Principle and allowed by the context.

Returning to indirect passives based on the inchoative alternants of causative/inchoative verbs like (26)b and (29)b, it is now clear that they end up violating either the Q- or the I-Principle, irrespective of the presence of a salient agent in the embedded event. Likewise, indirect passives based on non-alternating unaccusatives violate the I-Principle. This way, we effectively derive the aversion to unaccusative-based indirect passives, without making recourse to stipulations such as the unaccusative restriction. Note, however, that this only holds when normal contexts are involved, and, in what follows, we will see cases where unaccusative-based indirect passives are allowed.

To sum up, the aversion to unaccusative-based indirect passives is in fact the preference for such alternatives as causative-based indirect passives or unaccusative actives, which can be explained in terms of the general neo-Gricean principles. Therefore, pragmatic inferences play a crucial role in deriving the unaccusative restriction effects.

[6] Natural phenomena such as rain seem irrelevant to (30), but the required adverse relation can be easily established for them, thereby satisfying the I-Principle.

3.3 When Unaccusative-based Indirect Passives are Felicitous

If the present approach is on the right track, it is predicted that unaccusative-based indirect passives are felicitous when they best satisfy both the Q- and the I-Principles. Specifically, they should be possible if the following two conditions are met: (i) there should be no contextually salient agent in the embedded event; (ii) the individual introduced by the indirect passive morpheme must be adversely affected by the embedded event for which its dative subject argument is responsible. In the following, I will show two cases which satisfy both.

First, consider again the examples with an animate being as the embedded dative subject, as in (10)b, (15), and (16)a. They are felicitous because they can be construed as utterances in the contexts which trivially satisfy both (i) and (ii): the dative subject is sentient and with some degree of controllability, and thus it can be held responsible for what happened. Thus, the prediction is clearly borne out, and as far as I can see, this much is uncontroversial.

The other case which satisfies both (i) and (ii) involves inanimate beings as the dative subject, and most examples of this kind fall under the M-Principle of Levinson (2000), given in (31), and they vary greatly in acceptability judgments.[7]

(31) The M-Principle (Levinson 2000: 136)
Indicate an abnormal, non-stereotypical situation by using expressions that contrast with those you would use to describe the corresponding normal, stereotypical situation.

Simply put, according to the M-Principle, the use of a marked expression will implicate a marked message or situation. Such a message or situation often requires the hearer to stretch the imagination so as to comprehend the relevant conceptual setting, and thus, the acceptability of the marked expression depends on whether or not that relevant conceptual setting can be successfully accessed or not. The successful access renders the marked expression acceptable and felicitous, while the failure in the access renders it unacceptable and unnecessary, eventually the expression resulting in a violation of the I-Principle.

With this consideration in mind, let us quickly go over the following two examples, one involving a marked situation and the other a marked message. I do not discuss their acceptability status, only explicating their marked contexts of utterance.[8]

Suppose the following marked situation: Taro had an artificial tooth for one of his upper front teeth, but he was annoyed because it frequently came out despite all his efforts to the contrary. It just came out by itself again and again. What was worse, his tooth came out at one of the most inappropriate occasions, when he was on a lunch date. Later, in response to the question of how the date went, Taro described the incident as follows:

(32) Mata ha-ni nuk-e-rare-ta
again tooth-DAT come.out-INCH-PASS-PST
'My tooth came out on me again.'

Next, suppose the following context: due to a sharp decline in BMR in his mid-thirties combined with a fattening diet, Taro gained 10 kg in one month. Since he did not want to accept the rightful responsibility for the result of his action, he said the following in an attempt to impute his overweight to something else:[9]

(33) Ikinari taizyuu-ni
abruptly weight-DAT
hu-e-rare-ta (<huy-e-rare-ta)
increase-INCH-PASS-PST
'Weight gain happened abruptly on me.'

These examples will lend further support to the present approach, provided that they are acceptable.

In this subsection, we have seen that unaccusative-based indirect passives are acceptable when the pragmatic principles are satisfied. Moreover, in case they are still unacceptable, the unacceptability results from the failure in the access to the relevant conceptual setting.

4 Concluding Remarks

We started with the validity of the unaccusative restriction and rejected it in the presence of a variety of counterevidence. Instead, we provided an alternative pragmatic account, couched in neo-

[7] We are not concerned with the question of whether the M-Principle is an epiphenomenon.

[8] Even for the 'conservative' speakers, who detest them, anthropomorphosis, or personification, works as a wildcard.

[9] This falls under the case of flouting the Q-Principle.

Gricean terms, for the unaccusative restriction effects, i.e. the aversion to unaccusative-based indirect passives. The current approach derives the effects without stipulations specific to indirect passives, while leaving room for exceptional instances to the restriction, which I take to be an advantage over the rigid syntactic approach.

Since this paper is quite restricted in its scope, there are many questions that are left out. One question particularly relevant to the present account is how to define the alternatives. In this paper, I simply take it for granted that causative-based indirect passives and active unaccusatives are among the alternatives to consider in the process of pragmatic inferencing. Needless to say, a complete account should give an analysis of what mechanism makes such competition possible.

Acknowledgments

I would like to thank three anonymous reviewers and Chigusa Morita for comments on an earlier version of this paper. The usual disclaimers apply.

References

Borer, H. 2005. *Structuring Sense, Vol. II: The Normal Course of Events*. Oxford University Press, Oxford.

Dowty, D. 1991. Thematic Proto-roles and Argument Selection. *Language*, 67(3): 547-619.

Dubinsky, S. 1985. Japanese Union Constructions: A Unified Analysis of *-Sase* and *-Rare*. Ph.D. Thesis. Cornell University.

Dubinsky, S. 1997. Predicate Union and the Syntax of Japanese Passives. *Journal of Linguistics*, 33(1): 1-37.

Fillmore, C. J. 1981. Pragmatics and the Description of Discourse. In P. Cole ed. *Radical Pragmatics*, pp.143-66. Academic Press, New York.

Grice, P. H. 1975. Logic and Conversation. In P. Cole and J. L. Morgan, eds., *Syntax and Semantics 3: Speech Acts*, pp. 41-58. Academic Press, New York.

Grimshaw, J. and A. Mester. 1988. Light Verbs and Theta-marking. *Linguistic Inquiry* 19(2): 205-232.

Inoue, K. 1976. *Henkei-Bumpoo to Nihongo [Transformational Grammar and Japanese]*, volume 2. Taishuukan, Tokyo.

Kageyama, T. 1993. *Bumpoo to Gokeisei [Grammar and Word Formation]*. Hituzi Syobo, Tokyo.

Kageyama, T. 1996. *Doosi-Imiron [Verb Semantics]*. Kurosio Publishers, Tokyo.

Kratzer, A. 1996. Severing the External Argument from its Verb. In J. Orrick and L. Zaring, eds., *Phrase Structure and the Lexicon*, pp. 109-137. Kluwer Academic Publishers, Dordrecht.

Kuno, S. and K. Takami. 2002. *Nichi-Eigo no Zidoosi-Koobun [Intransitive Constructions in Japanese and English]*. Kenkyusha, Tokyo.

Kuroda, S.-Y. 1979. On Japanese Passives. In G. Bedell, E. Kobayashi, and M. Muraki eds., *Exploration in Linguistics: Papers in Honor of Kazuko Inoue*, 305-347. Kenkyusha, Tokyo.

Horn, L. 1984. Toward a New Taxonomy for Pragmatic Inference: Q-based and R-based Implicature. In D. Schiffrin ed., *Meaning, Form, and Use in Context: Linguistic Applications*, pp.11-42. Georgetown University Press, Washington, DC.

Levinson, S. C. 1987. Pragmatics and the Grammar of Anaphora: A Partial Pragmatic Reduction of Binding and Control Phenomena. *Journal of Linguistics* 23(2): 379-434.

Levinson, S. C. 2000. *Presumptive Meaning: The Theory of Generalized Conversational Implicature*. MIT Press, Cambridge, MA.

Matsumoto, Y. 2000. Causative Alternation in English and Japanese: A Closer Look. *English Linguistics*, 17(1):160-192.

McCawley, J. D. 1978. Conversational Implicature and the lexicon. In P. Cole ed., *Syntax and Semantics 9: Pragmatics*, pp.245-259. Academic Press, San Diego.

McCawley, J. D. 1989. *Everything You Always Wanted to Know About Logic* (*But Were Ashamed to Ask)*, 2nd edition. Chicago University Press, Chicago.

Miyagawa, S. 1989a. *Syntax and Semantics 22: Structure and Case-marking in Japanese*. Academic Press, San Diego.

Miyagawa, S. 1989b. Light Verb and the Ergative Hypothesis. *Linguistic Inquiry* 20(4): 659-668.

Perlmutter, D. M. and P. Postal. 1984. The 1 Advancement Exclusiveness Law, In D. M. Perlmutter and C. A. Rosen eds., *Relational Grammar 2*, pp.81-125. Chicago University Press, Chicago.

Pylkkänen, L. 2002. Introducing Arguments. Ph.D. Thesis. MIT.

Sperber, D. and D. Wilson. 1995. *Relevance: Communication and Cognition*, 2nd edition. Blackwell, Oxford.

Washio, R. 1989-90. The Japanese Passive. *The Linguistic Review*, 6(3): 227-263.

Comparing Classifier use in Chinese and Japanese

Yue Hui Ting and **Francis Bond**
Division of Linguistics and Multilingual Studies
Nanyang Technological University
{htyue1@e.ntu.edu.sg, bond@ieee.org}

Abstract

Numeral classifiers present a challenge to successful machine translation. We investigate two numeral classifier languages: Mandarin Chinese and Japanese. This paper presents a quantitative analysis of classifier translations between these two languages to better understand differences in classifier usage.

Keywords – numeral classifier, sortal, translation, Mandarin Chinese, Japanese, contrastive linguistics

1 Introduction

Mandarin Chinese (CMN) and Japanese (JPN) are numeral classifier languages. Numeral classifier languages express the quantity of referents by modifying a noun phrase (NP) with an obligatory numeral-classifier construction where the classifier denotes inherent referent attributes (Bond and Paik, 2000; Downing, 1996). Hence, for a numeral-classifier construction that is assigned to a noun, the numeral denotes the numerical quantity of the noun referent while the numeral classifier denotes the quality of the noun referent.

Bond and Paik (2000) identified five main types of classifiers. **Event** classifiers classify events (Japanese: *-kai* 回 'time'; Mandarin Chinese: *-cì* 次'time'). **Mensural** classifiers are employed for the measurement of physical properties (Japanese: *-sun* 寸 'inches'; Mandarin Chinese: -*cùn* 寸 'inches'). **Group** classifiers classify groupings of referents (Japanese: *-kumi* 組 'pair, set'; Mandarin Chinese: *-shuāng* 双 'pair'). **Taxonomic** classifiers effect a generic interpretation of the noun phrase (Japanese: *-shu* 種 'kind, type'; Mandarin Chinese: *-zhǒng* 种 'kind, type'). Finally, when quantifying the noun, **Sortal** classifiers classify the type of referent that is being counted, as in (1) and (2)*.

(1)	JPN:	*pen*	*2-hon*
		pen	2-CL (long, cylindrical)
		"2 pens"	
(2)	CMN:	*6- zhāng*	*piào*
		6-CL(flat, broad)	tickets
		"6 tickets"	

The numeral classifier system is organized differently for different languages. Mok et al.'s (2012) parallel studies focusing on generating sortal classifiers found that there are differences in classifier usage for the same semantic hierarchy of noun classes, suggesting differing conceptual organization between Mandarin Chinese and Japanese.

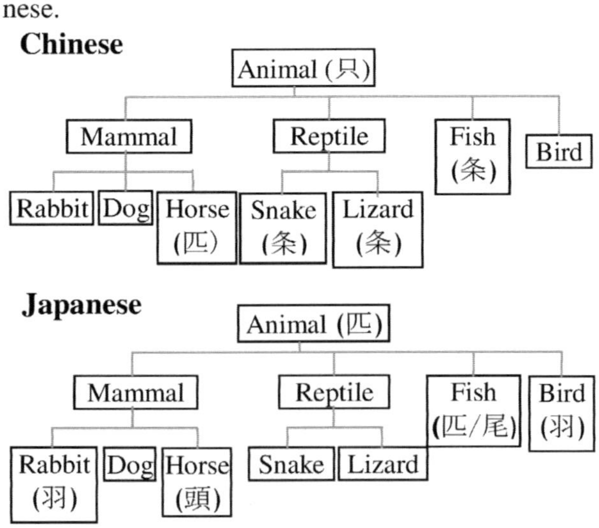

Figure 1. Semantic Hierarchies in Chinese and Japanese

For example, the semantic hierarchies in Fig.1 show that there is not always one-to-one correspondence between the classifier characters of

* Abbr. used are CL for classifier, PTCL for particle, DET for determiner, num for numeral or numerative

these two languages. For example, although the same character 匹 exists in both classifier systems, it is used differently, as a general animal classifier in Japanese and as a specific classifier for horses in Mandarin Chinese. Japanese and Mandarin Chinese are an interesting pair of languages to compare for classifiers because they share to a limited extent the same Chinese character system and occasionally there are one-to-one correspondences for classifiers (e.g. 件 'case').

Because the classifier organization in both semantic hierarchies is different, the context in which a certain classifier is used may differ. Hence in Mandarin Chinese and Japanese, it is not the case that the same character for a classifier may be used as an equivalent translation in the same context. Classifiers have proven notoriously tricky to translate automatically with precision in various contexts.

Japanese and Mandarin Chinese classifiers also differ in terms of syntax (Ueda, 2009). Our approach to studying classifier use is to observe classifier phrases between hand-translated parallel sentences to search for predictable patterns in translation. There may also be lexical differences between the two numeral classifier systems. Understanding these differences offer us an insight into how the need for a classifier in certain semantic, grammatical, lexical or pragmatic contexts is negotiated within each language. Knowledge of classifier usage between Mandarin Chinese and Japanese will also be useful when considering crucial classifier features of each language to be addressed for classifier generation.

This paper will focus on sortal classifiers only and taps on the source data from Mok et al.'s (2012) parallel studies on Mandarin Chinese and Japanese classifiers.

The structure of the paper is as follows. In Section 2, we introduce the aims of our study. Section 3 presents a review of literature relevant to the grammar of both languages as well as their numeral classifier systems. In Section 4 we present our methodology and data for the pairwise comparison of sentences and our observations will be collated in Section 5 where we count and describe notable translations of categorized patterns. Section 6 discusses the implications of our findings and how they relate to existing literature. Finally we offer ideas for further research in our conclusion in Section 7.

2 Aims

This paper carries out pairwise comparison of parallel sentences to investigate the differences in sortal classifier usage between the two languages; Mandarin Chinese and Japanese. Based on our findings, we aim to come up with a better description of the use of classifiers in both Mandarin Chinese and Japanese.

3 Literature Review

In a numeral classifier phrase (consisting of the numeral, classifier, noun and the occasional particle), the numeral always occurs next to the classifier (Yamamoto, 2005, p. 5). The tighter constituent is hence composed of the classifier and numeral, as the noun constituent may occasionally occur distantly in cases of anaphora. Mok et al. (2012) listed classifier phrase combinations found from newspaper data. Combinations for Japanese include **num-CL-no-N** (where *no* 'of' is the adnomial particle), **N-PTCL-num-CL** (where PTCL can be case particles such as *ga, wo,* and *mo* which also appear in classifier phrases), and **N-num-CL**. For Mandarin Chinese, possible combinations are **DET-num-CL-N**, **DET-CL-N**, and **num-CL-N**.

There are several differences as to when classifiers can be omitted in Mandarin Chinese and Japanese.

One of these differences is the dropped or omitted numeral construction and non-numeral construction in Mandarin Chinese. The latter is an example of using a numeral classifier without a numeral in the classifier phrase. When a determiner precedes the classifier phrase, it gives rise to a *DET-CL* construction (Yamamoto, 2005, p. 6), (3).

(3) CMN: *na zhang zhi*
that CL paper
"that piece of paper"

A dropped numeral construction occurs when the noun in question may be quantified as a single item, in which some cases the numeral *one* is dropped (Yamamoto, 2005, p. 23) from the usual indefinite use construction *1-CL-N*. This construction functions almost like an indefinite determiner when a verb precedes the numeral and classifier combination instead (4). It is not certain if the dropping of the numeral *one* follows certain syntactic rules or if it simply serves as a shortening of the complete indefinite phrase.

(4) CMN: *zhao zhang zhaopian*
snap CL photo
"snap(or take) a photo"

Li and Thompson (1989) also describe numeral omission in Mandarin Chinese in determiner and numerative containing classifier constructions (Li and Thompson, 1989, p. 104).

Another difference between the numeral classifier systems of these two languages is the number of types of classifiers that exist in the system. To illustrate this, there is a phenomenon of "semantic split" (Hansen and Chen, 2001, p. 89) in classifier categories for Japanese where a group of nouns classified by a single classifier may be divided into smaller groups which are each classified by a different classifier in Mandarin Chinese, suggesting that nouns are classified in Japanese by a smaller number of classifiers.

Yin et al. (2006) came up with rules to translate classifiers from Mandarin Chinese to Japanese. These rules addressed the indefinite determiner and numerative classifier phrase in addition to the usual numeral-classifier phrase. However they did not seem to have addressed dropped numeral or demonstrative constructions.

4 Methodology

4.1 Data

The data for pairwise comparison were annotated sentences and classifiers done by Mok et al. (2012). These sentences were taken from the NICT Multilingual Corpus which is a Japanese-Chinese-English parallel corpus based on the Mainichi Newspaper (Zhang et al., 2005). 38,000 Japanese sentences from the Mainichi Shinbun (1984) have been translated into both Chinese and English by professional translators. Only 500 sentences were considered for analysis for this paper. The newspaper domain is a formal domain and the more formal the style of writing, the more variation and occurrence of classifiers the writing style exhibits, providing a rich pool of classifiers to work with (Craig, 1986, p. 8). Parallel sentences were compared with the help of equivalent English translations and the differences in classifier use in the sentences were analyzed.

A preliminary run-through of the data was done by hand on the first 100 parallel sentences to identify interesting and recurring observations and to classify them with a name (or tag). This would serve to make classification of observed patterns easier later. A program generated the sentence id and extracted parallel sentences, the English equivalent, as well as classifier information. For example, in a sentence without a classifier, *(N)* is generated to indicate that there was no classifier. Where there was a classifier, the character for the classifier was generated, such as *(回)*.

In the preliminary study, we noticed a few problems with the automatic tagging. Occasionally we had target NP mismatches where the classifier phrase in a sentence did not match any target NP phrase recognized by the program. Also, where one sentence had 2 classifier NPs and the other had only one, if the first classifier NP pair that was a correct match was not sortal, the next classifier was selected as a parallel match for the classifier in the sentence with only one classifier. This sometimes resulted in blatant errors. Additionally, we realized from our initial counts that the program did not consider the Japanese つ and Mandarin Chinese 人 classifiers in its tagging and hence missed out on those. These errors were later corrected.

Where both sentences have an equivalent classifier, they were considered aligned. In many cases, a classifier was present in only one language. We expected that the classifier would be more frequently absent from the Japanese sentence. The rationale for this expectation is Mandarin Chinese has more types of classifiers in its classifier system than Japanese (as addressed in Section 3). Also, Mandarin Chinese uses classifiers in one common construction that Japanese does not; the DET-CL-N combination. The preliminary observations identified a few categories (explained below); *non-classifier equivalents, omission of classifier, demonstrative, indefinite use,* and *aligned.*

We did not attempt to identify differences in classifier usage due to translator choice or judgment as the decisions of the translators are sometimes ambiguous and hence beyond the scope of what we can hope to discuss extensively and satisfactorily.

4.2 Hand-annotation of sentence pairs

For the actual data analysis, a set of 243 sentence pairs was used. These were sentences in the original set of 500 that had a part-of-speech tagged numeral classifier in at least one sentence. (This means that there were no sentence pairs in which both sentences had no classifiers.) The parallel sentences were run through a program which generated the sentence id, the Japanese sentence, the parallel Chinese sentence, the English translation as well as additional information about the classifiers, (5).

(5)
* 95010108001 *
お正月 が 来る と 、 思い出す こと が ある 。
每逢 新年 来临 ， 我 就 会 想起 一 件_9 事 。
When a New Year comes, I remember one thing.
95010108001 N:-1 件:9 (N:sortal)

This program detects the presence of a classifier or classifiers and annotates to indicate the absence of a classifier or if otherwise, the classifier itself, as well as the word id which is the numerical position of the classifier in the sentence. Also annotated is the type of classifier in each sentence, whether it is *sortal*, *mensural,* or simply a non-classifier function; tagged as *not*. To compensate for any mistakes that might have been made in the automatic process as well as to enrich the information with the earlier identified tags, these 243 sentence pairs were hand-annotated to correct where needed, the automatically identified classifiers as well as the type of classifiers. In addition, the tags were added onto (5) to indicate if classifiers aligned or if it was a specific phenomenon if the classifier was found in one sentence only.

The tags used for the subsequent hand-annotation in the actual data analysis are as follows: *aligned, non-classifier equivalents* (jpn only), *indefinite use* (cmn only)*, indefinite use no numeral* (cmn only)*, demonstrative* (cmn only), and *omission* (jpn only).

(a) Classifier present in one language only

Non-classifier equivalents:
e.g. JPN: ある (N)
a certain
CMN: 一位 (位)
1-CL
Non-classifier equivalents in JPN do not employ the use of classifiers. In other words, these fixed, expressions convey roughly the same meaning without needing a classifier.

Omission of classifier:
e.g. JPN: 十五 の 訓練所 (N)
15 PTCL training centre
CMN: 十五 个 训练所 (个)
15 CL training centre
Omission of classifier in JPN, with presence of の.
JPN: 二 億 缶 (N)
2 hundred million can
CMN: 2 亿多 个 (个)
2 hundred million CL
Omission of classifier in JPN due to a large, round number.

Demonstrative:
e.g. JPN: その 珊瑚 (N)
that coral
CMN: 那 串 珊瑚 (串)
That CL coral
A demonstrative (this/that) alone suffices for reference in Japanese while in Mandarin Chinese a classifier is needed.

Indefinite use:
e.g. JPN: 「X」という 項目 (N)
such a question
CMN: “X” 一项 提问 (项)
1 CL question
(Where *X* represents a question.) The indefinite use of a classifier phrase includes the equivalent of the English ‘a’ used in Mandarin Chinese to introduce indefinite NPs.

Indefinite use no numeral:
e.g. JPN: 野蛮 人 に 見えた (N)
wild person PTCL seen to be
CMN: 像 个 野 人 (个)
Like CL wild-person

A variant of the above mentioned indefinite use where the numeral in the *1-CL* construction is dropped.

(b) Classifier present in both CMN and JPN

Aligned:

e.g. JPN: 到着客 約 百五十人 (人)
passengers approx. 150 CL
CMN: 大约 一百五十 名 抵达旅客(名)
approx 150 CL passengers

Equivalent classifiers exist in both languages.

The above list of tags was refined in consideration of observations during the annotation process. The annotation was also revised where it was deemed needed due to revelations in the annotation process.

5 Results

Table 1. Automatic Classification (non-sortal included)

Scenario	No. of instances*
Classifier in JPN & CMN	101
Classifier in CMN only	177
Classifier in JPN only	29
Total	307

*Counts represent classifier comparisons, not sentences.

Based on the counts in Table 1 above, we have found that numeral classifiers appear much more frequently in Mandarin Chinese only than in Japanese only. Looking at counts in Table 2 in the next column, most of these cases come from the use of demonstratives and indefinite use in Mandarin Chinese.

The discrepancy between the 101 count for classifier in both languages in Table 1 and the 51 count for align in Table 2 is mostly due to alignment of non-sortal classifiers, most of which involve ordinal expressions (6) which formed an overwhelming proportion, and classifier characters not functioning as classifiers.

(6) JPN: 第 四百 回 定期 (回)
ORD 400 CL season
"the 400th season"
CMN: 第 四百 场 定期 (场)
ORD 400 CL season
"the 400th season"

Table 2. Manual Classification

Tag	No. of instances*	
Aligned	(CMN & JPN)	**51**
Non-classifier equivalents	(CMN & JPN)	**17**
Indefinite use	(CMN only)	**37**
Numeral present		30
Numeral absent		7
Demonstrative	(CMN only)	**17**
Numeral present		4
Numeral absent		13
Omission	(CMN only)	**22**
Other (*non-sortal* and *not*)	(CMN & JPN)	**156**
Total		**300**

*Counts represent classifier comparisons, not sentences.

5.1 Aligned (51)

Cases of alignment were the most frequent. The bulk of the classifier alignment cases were for specific classifiers. Another sizeable portion were for sentences that involved the person classifier *hito* (人) in Japanese, which was translated to one of three person classifiers in Mandarin Chinese: *rén* (人), *míng* (名) and *wèi* (位), which differ in terms of formality and pragmatic importance of the status of the people in question. The Mandarin Chinese general classifier *gè* (个) was used in translation for the Japanese classifier *tsu* (つ) (general inanimacy classifier), and some specific classifiers. In addition, *tsu* was on occasion translated to more specific classifiers in Mandarin Chinese.

5.2 Non-classifier equivalents (17)

In most cases of non-classifier equivalents, the Japanese sentence employed an expression that did not contain a classifier but whose translated equivalent required a classifier. Consistent observations were in the counting of months and countries where the Japanese expressions following a number are *ka-getsu* (ヶ月) and *ka-kkoku* (各国) respectively and these may be known as fused classifier nouns. Hence, these count nouns are directly modified by the numeral. More interesting expressions were *ikutsuka no* 'a few of', where the classifier *tsu* is included in the lexical item *ikutsu,* 'a few' and *to iu*, which is an expression concluding a description that corresponds to an indefinite determiner classifier phrase when translated to

Mandarin Chinese, as well as noun and verb non-classifier equivalents.

e.g. **Noun non-classifier expression**
JPN: 片手 (N)
katate
"single-hand"
CMN: 一 只 手 (只)
1 CL shǒu
"one hand"
Verb non-classifier expression
JPN: ボーッとして (N)
boottoshite
"to be in a daze"
CMN: 一 片 空白 (片)
1 CL kòngbái
"a sheet of blankness"

5.3 Indefinite Use (37)

Indefinite use of classifier phrases in Mandarin Chinese was common; *1-CL-N*, where no determiners precede the *1-CL-N* construction and where no expression that renders definiteness on the noun precedes the construction as well (e.g. *zuì hòu* (最后) 'final/last'). The equivalent Japanese sentences did not employ the use of classifiers or numerals. The English translations involved indefinite expressions, such as involving "a" or "an". The preceding environment of such Mandarin Chinese phrases were mostly verbs (with *shì* (是) 'is/be' coming up repeatedly), and some few cases were the spatial preposition *nèi* (内) 'within'. Dropped numerals were observed in this category under *indefinite use no numeral* where the preceding environment is a verb but the construction is simply *V-CL* where there is no numeral. *CL-N* classifier phrases with no preceding determiner were always judged to have a singular interpretation; that the numeral is *one* and can be omitted.

There was one exception where the sortal *1-CL-N* classifier construction as defined in this sub-section was translated in English to a definite expression involving the determiner "one".

e.g. JPN: 思い出す こと が ある (N)
Recall matter PTCL exist
CMN: 想起 一 件 事 (件)
Recall 1 CL matter
ENG: I remember one thing

This was the only relevant example that involved the sortal use of classifiers and where the English translation was faithful to the CMN expression. An example of a 'non-faithful' translation was where the CMN expression was *V-1-CL-N* (*there was-1-CL-television*) but was translated as *possessive-N* (*their television).*

5.4 Demonstrative (17)

Not all demonstrative classifier constructions omit numerals. The construction *DET-num-CL-N* was present for both the numeral *one* (*DET-1-CL-N*) and *two* (*DET-2-CL-N*) and was unlikely to be limited to just those numbers. The majority of the demonstrative classifier constructions (13 out of 17) omitted the numeral and the nouns in these expressions were interpreted as singular. The use of determiners *zhè* (这) 'this', *nà* (那) 'that', *cǐ* (此) 'this', and *gāi* (该) 'this, that' before the classifiers, as well as the lack of numerals seem to point to an interpretation of singularity.

5.5 Omission (22)

Straightforward cases of classifier omission occurred in Japanese where it seemed possible for a classifier to be present but it was not. The Mandarin Chinese translation however still required a classifier. In this case the numeral directly modifies a count noun. Some of these cases occurred when the Japanese numeral was a large, round number such as *800* or *50*. However in most cases the numeral was under ten.

e.g. JPN: 四 都市 (N)
4 toshi
"four cities"
CMN: 四 个 城市 (个)
4 CL chéngshì
"four cities"

5.6 Other (156)

These are made up of non-sortal classifiers such as *event, mensural, group,* and ordinal expression classifiers (7) with or without aligned classifiers, as well as classifier characters appearing in non-classifier uses (7) and hence not analyzed.

(7) JPN: 七 番 勝負 (番)
7 CL match
"seven-game match"
CMN: 七盘 比赛 (盘)
7 CL match
"seven-game match"

6 Discussion and Future Work

In cases of classifier alignment, the earlier mentioned phenomenon of "semantic split" (Greenberg, 1990, p. 89) observed in primary research with speakers is observed here. This is manifested when a classifier character that appears twice in the same Japanese sentence is translated to different classifier characters in Mandarin Chinese (8), suggesting the existence of more specific classifier categories in Mandarin Chinese.

(8)

JPN: はがき 約 二千 通… (通)
Postcards approx. 2000 CL
…郵便物の 約 千 通 (通)
Mail PTCL approx 1000 CL

CMN: 两千 枚 贺年片… (枚)
2000 CL new year postcards
…一千 封 普通 邮件 (封)
1000 CL mail

Also, it seems that there are plenty of Japanese non-classifier noun and verb equivalents corresponding to classifier-including expressions in Mandarin Chinese, doing away with the need for a classifier phrase, further reducing the frequency of classifiers appearing in Japanese.

With regards to omission, the newspaper is a formal and impersonal domain and the omission of classifiers in Japanese seems to reflect this as it seems characteristic to drop classifiers in impersonal presentations of quantity, resulting in the construction *num-N*. This however does not occur in our Mandarin Chinese data. Also, if the characteristic of the hand-translation process is that translators tend to translate into a less rigid form of language, it might explain why there are many cases of *num-N* in Japanese being translated to a longer and more natural expression in Mandarin Chinese. If however, both the newspaper domain and translator behaviour are not the reasons for such an observation, it is possible that Japanese is moving towards allowing counting with no classifiers (compare Align 51 and Omission 22) and is getting a small class of fully countable nouns such as *shou* 勝 'victory' and *hai* 敗 'loss' which can be counted simply by having a numeral precede it, 三勝 and 三敗 (*san* 三 '3').

For demonstrative classifier constructions in Mandarin Chinese, if the numeral is a number other than *one*, it logically cannot be omitted. It is also possible that wherever a noun is referred to, its classifier must come up as well though not performing a numeral classifier function but simply a noun classifier function instead.

For indefinite use in Mandarin Chinese however, it is unclear from our findings if there are rules governing the dropping of the numeral *one*. In most cases it is not dropped. Pragmatic choices or phonological reduction may solely be at play here (Chen, 2003, p. 1171).

Based on our findings for demonstratives and indefinite use, where the numeral is omitted, it seems that Mandarin Chinese uses classifiers in phrases that appear to function like determiners, basically showing information structure by indicating whether a piece of information is old (by using a demonstrative) or whether it is new (by indefinite use with a classifier). Chen (2003) offers an interesting discussion on the indefinite use of classifiers in Mandarin Chinese and mentions a "presentative use" of the indefinite article in the *yi 'one'-CL-N* construction that may be used for new and stressed information (Chen, 2003, p. 1171) but also talks about a tendency towards non-referential use when the numeral *yi* is omitted. It is also possible to divide the indefinite use respectively into (i) numeral use and (ii) the English equivalent 'a' according to whether *yi* is stressed or unstressed (Rullmann and You, 2006), giving rise to implications for presenting new and old information. Two further questions we would like to answer by comparing the Japanese and Chinese to English are: (i) Are the indefinite uses always translated with an indefinite article? And (ii) Are the demonstratives always translated as demonstratives or also with the definite article?

Greenberg (1990, p. 253) proposes that the demonstrative is the most common starting point of the development of a definite article (known as

Stage I). Further development then sees it offering both definite and indefinite uses (Stage II). Our findings on how demonstratives and indefinite use in classifier phrases act as determiners seem to suggest that Mandarin Chinese is in the process of evolving articles.

Finally, for future research, translation comparison for less impersonal domains (e.g. editorials) might shed light on whether certain classifier usage differences may be due to pragmatic factors. With regards to cross-linguistic interests, the NTU multilingual Corpus (Tan and Bond, 2011) contains more corpora linked to other classifier languages such as Thai, Vietnamese, Indonesian and Korean. These resources may be exploited in future studies to observe classifier usage patterns and a comparison may be done later between the studied languages to determine if similar (or dissimilar) phenomena and patterns exist.

7 Conclusion

In this paper, we identified categories of classifier translations from Japanese to Mandarin Chinese and looked at notable translations that have implications for understanding lexical, syntactic and pragmatic differences. The analysis of classifier translations reveals that it will be tricky to translate non-classifier expressions from Japanese to classifier-including expressions in Mandarin Chinese, posing this as a noteworthy problem to overcome.

References

Bond, F., & Paik, K. (2000). Re-using an ontology to generate numeral classifiers. *Proceeding s of the 19th International Conference on Computational Linguistics: COLING-2000:* Saarbrucken.

Chen, P. (2003). Indefinite determiner introducing definite referent: a special use of '*yi* 'one' + classifier' in Chinese. *Lingua, 113,* 1169-1184.

Craig, C.G. (1986). *Noun Classes and Categorization.* Philadelphia: John Benjamins.

Downing, P. (1996). *Numeral classifier systems: The case of Japanese.* Philadelphia: John Benjamins.

Greenberg, H. (1990). How Does a Language Acquire Gender Markers? In K. Denning and S. Kemmer (Eds.) *On Language: Selected Writings of Joseph H. Greenberg*, pp. 241-270. Stanford: Stanford University Press

Hansen, L., & Chen, Y.L. (2001). What counts in the acquisition and attrition of numeral classifiers? *JALT Journal, 23*(1), 83-100.

Li, C.N., & Thompson, S.A. (1989). *Mandarin Chinese: A Functional References Grammar.* London, England: University of California Press.

Mok, H.S.W., Gao, H.N.E., & Bond, F. (2012) Using WordNet to predict numeral classifiers in Chinese and Japanese. In *Proceedings of the 6th Global WordNet Conference (GWC 2012)*:Matsue.

Rullmann, H., & You, A.L. (2006). General Number and the Semantics and Pragmatics of Indefinite Bare Nouns in Mandarin Chinese. In K. von Heusinger and K. P. Turner (Eds.) *Where Semantics Meets Pragmatics*, pp. 175-196. Amsterdam: Elsevier.

Tan, L., & Bond, F. (2011). Building and annotating the linguistically diverse NTU-MC (NTU-multilingual corpus). In *Proceedings of the 25th Pacific Asia Conference on Language, Information and Computation (PACLIC 25),* pp. 367–376. Singapore.

Ueda, Y. (2009). Number in Japanese and Chinese. *Nanzan Linguistics, 5*, 105-130.

Yamamoto, K. (2005). The Acquisition of Numeral Classifiers: The Case of Japanese Children. In P. Jordens (Ed.), *Studies on Language Acquisition* (Vol. 27). Berlin, Germany: Walter de Gruyter.

Yin, D.P., Shao, M., Jiang, P.L., Ren, F., & Kuroiwa, S. (2006). Proceedings from ICCOMP-2006: *Rule-based translation of quantifiers for Chinese-Japanese machine translation*, pp. 558-563. Athens, Greece.

Zhang, Y., Uchimoto, K., Ma, Q., & Isahara, H. (2005). Proceedings from MTS-2010: *Building an Annotated Japanese-Chinese Parallel Corpus – A Part of NICT Multilingual Corpora*, pp. 71-78. Phuket.

Nominative-marked Phrases in Japanese Tough Constructions

Akira Ohtani
Faculty of Informatics,
Osaka Gakuin University
2-36-1 Kishibe-minami, Suita-shi,
Osaka, 564-8511, Japan
ohtani@ogu.ac.jp

Maria del Pilar Valverde Ibañez
Faculty of Foreign Language,
Aichi Prefectural University
1522-3 Ibaragabasama, Nagakute-shi,
Aichi, 480-1198, Japan
valverde@for.aichi-pu.ac.jp

Abstract

In this paper we conduct a detailed examination of the tough construction in Japanese with the main focus on some types of nominative case particles *ga*. They are correlated with the difference not only in the nominative-genitive case alternation but also in the semantic or pragmatic interpretation. Based on these data, we discuss the categories of the nominative case particles and derivations for tough predicates within the framework of Combinatory Categorial Grammar.

1 Introduction

In English, it is well known that infinitival clauses can be used after certain adjectives that express *easiness* as (1), *difficulty* as (2) and so on.

(1) a. It is easy to please John.

b. John is easy to please.

(2) a. It is hard for the students to read this paper.

b. This paper is hard for the students to read.

Sentences (1a) and (1b) convey the same meaning: *John* is interpreted as an EXPERIENCER or a recipient of the action of pleasing, regardless of whether it is the object of the verb *please* in the complement clause as (1a), or it is the subject of the matrix clause with the object of *please* missing as (1b). From the beginning of transformational grammar, much attention has been paid to the so-called *tough construction* (1b) and (2b) (Postal, 1971; Chomsky, 1973; among others).

In Japanese, it has often been noted in the literature on transformational generative grammar that sentence (3)[1] below shares syntactic properties with the tough sentences listed in (1b) and (2b).

(3) Gakusei-ni-wa kono zisyo-ga
student-for-TOP this dictionary-NOM
tukai-yasui.
use-easy
'This dictionary is easy for students to use.'
(Inoue, 2004:76)

Different from English, phrase(s) other than the direct object of the main predicate can be marked with nominative case *ga* in Japanese tough sentences, as we will see below. To account for such a difference, we will argue that there are two types of nominative case marking in Japanese.

The organization of this paper will be as follows: In section 2 and 3, we will observe several types and properties of Japanese tough construction. In section 4 and 5, we will show that there are two types of the nominative case particle *ga* and their formal analysis. Section 6 will conclude our paper.

2 Tough Construction in Japanese

The tough construction in Japanese is a sentence that involves a main predicate with adjectives such as *yasui* 'easy' or *nikui* 'hard', 'difficult', or 'tough'. According to Inoue (1978; 2004), there are four types of tough constructions in Japanese:

[1] Examples cited from other papers are slightly modified because of lack of space. In (3), for example, *tukai-yasui* (use-easy) is originally glossed on as *tukai-yasu-i* (use-easy-PRES) and the PRES(ENT) tense is not relevant to our discussion.

(4) a. Type I (=(3))

b. Type II
Saikin watasi-wa kooon-de
recently I-TOP high-pitched notes-in
utai-nikui.
sing-hard
'To sing high-pitched notes has recently been hard for me.' (Inoue, 2004:76)

c. Type III
Senzai-wa yu-ni toke-yasui.
detergent-TOP warm water-in dissolve-easy
(lit.)*'Detergent is easy to dissolve in warm water.' (ibid.:82)

d. Type IV
Awatemono-wa ziko-o
hasty people-TOP accident-ACC
okosi-yasui.
cause-tend to
'Hasty people tend to cause accidents.' (ibid.:85)

In Type I, the direct object of the main predicate is marked with nominative case. In Type II, in contrast, the direct object of the main predicate cannot be marked with nominative. In Type III, it expresses the speaker's judgment towards the easiness and difficulties of an action/event. In Type IV, in contrast, it expresses the speaker's judgment toward the tendencies of an action/event. For the detailed discussion of these characteristics, see Inoue (1978; 2004).

Kuroda (1987), admits only Type I as the genuine tough sentence. Type I, and not other types, may contain an EXPERIENCER argument, which can be marked by the morphologically complex postposition *nitotte* 'for'. See the examples (5) and (6):

(5) Masao-nitotte-wa Nihon-de-wa eigo-ga
Masao-for-TOP Japan-in-TOP English-NOM
hanasi-nikui.
speak-hard
'English is hard for Masao to speak in Japan.' (Kuroda, 1987:234)

(6) Masao-nitotte sono yuubinkyoku-kara-ga
Masao-for that post office-from-NOM
kozutumi-o okuri-yasui.
package-ACC send-easy
'It is easy for Masao to send packages from that post office.' (ibid.:235)

Following Kuroda's (1987) analysis, we assume that there are two types of tough constructions in Japanese: Type I on the one hand, and Type II, III, and IV, on the other, and throughout this paper we focus on only Type I tough construction.

3 Distribution of the Nominative-marked Phrase(s)

3.1 Nominative-marked Phrase Requirement

As noted by Inoue (1978), a phrase other than the subject in the embedded clause may have the nominative case particle. See the examples (7) and (8).

(7) a.*Kodomo-ni-wa suwari-nikui.
child-for-TOP sit-hard
(lit.)*'For a child is hard to sit.'

b. Kodomo-ni-wa ano isu-ga
child-for-TOP that chair-NOM
suwari-nikui.
sit-hard
'That chair is hard for a child to sit on.' (Inoue, 2004:78)

(8) a.*Sensyu-ni-wa tobi-nikui.
athlete-for-TOP jump-hard
(lit.)*'For athletes are hard to jump.'

b. Sensyu-ni-wa kono
athlete-for-TOP this
dai-kara-ga tobi-nikui.
spring board-from-NOM jump-hard
'This springboard is hard for athletes to jump from.' (ibid.:78)

In (7) and (8), the main predicate is an intransitive verb, and without the phrase with the nominative case particle *ga*, the sentence is unacceptable.

In order to account for the contrast shown above, Inoue (1978) made a generalization as cited in (9):

(9) If the complement predicate is not transitive, the complement sentence has at least one more NP or PP besides the subject. (Inoue, 1978:123)

Put in a different way, the requirement for Type I tough construction is that the phrase other than the subject must bear the nominative case particle *ga*.

3.2 A Nominative-marked Adjunct NP

Takezawa (1987) notes that in Type I tough construction, a phrase other than the argument of the main predicate can bear the nominative case particle. See the examples (10) and (11).

(10) Kooitta ziko-ga (higaisya-nitotte)
this kind of accident-NOM injured party-for
bakudaina amount of songaibaisyoo-o
enormous compensation-ACC
seikyuusi-yasui.
claim-easy
(lit.)'This kind of accident is easy (for the injured party) to claim an enormous amount of compensation.' (Takezawa 1987:210)

(11) Kotosi (gakusei-nitotte-wa) gengogaku-ga
this year students-for-TOP linguistics-NOM
ii sigoto-o mituke-nikui rasii.
good job-ACC find-difficult seem
(lit.)'It seems that this year, linguistics is difficult (for students) to find a good job.' (ibid.)

In (10), for example, *kooitta ziko* 'this kind of accident' is not an argument of the main predicate *seikyuusuru* 'claim'. It is worth noting that *kooitta ziko* is marked with the nominative case particle only and does not bear any postpositions.

3.3 Multiple Nominative-marked Phrases

Kuroda (1987) notes that in Type I tough construction, more than one nominative case-marked phrase can cooccur in the sentence, as shown in (12) below:

(12) a. Kodomotati-nitotte-wa
children-for-TOP
kono kaizyoo-de-wa baiorin-de
this hall-in-TOP violin-on
sonata-ga hiki-yasui.
sonata-NOM play-easy

b. Kodomotati-nitotte-wa
children-for-TOP
kono kaizyoo-de baiorin-de
this hall-in violin-on
sonata-ga hiki-yasui.
sonata-NOM play-easy

c. Kodomotati-nitotte-wa
children-for-TOP
kono kaizyoo-de-wa baiorin-(de)-ga
this hall-in-TOP violin-on-NOM
sonata-ga hiki-yasui.
sonata-NOM play-easy

d. Kodomotati-nitotte-wa
children-for-TOP
kono kaizyoo-(de)-ga baiorin-de
this hall-in-NOM violin-on
sonata-ga hiki-yasui.
sonata-NOM play-easy

e. Kodomotati-nitotte-wa
children-for-TOP
kono kaizyoo-(de)-ga baiorin-(de)-ga
this hall-in-NOM violin-on-NOM
sonata-ga hiki-yasui.
sonata-NOM play-easy
'It is easy for children to play sonatas on violins in this hall.' (Kuroda 1987:248)

In (12), there are three phrases, *kono kaizyoo-(de-wa)* 'in this hall', *baiorin-(de)* 'on violin' and *sonata* 'sonata', that can bear the nominative case particle. Only *sonata* is a direct object of the main predicate *hiku* 'play', and the other two phrases *kaizyoo-(de-wa)* and *baiorin-de* are considered as adjuncts.

3.4 Summary

In this section, we have observed that in addition to the direct object of the main predicate, other adjuncts of the Type I tough construction can bear the nominative case particle whether they bear any postpositions or not.

4 Two Types of Nominative Case Particle

In section 3, we have observed that in addition to the direct object of the main predicate, other phrases, such as PPs, can bear the nominative case particle in the Type I tough construction.

The question that arises here is whether the nominative case particle in sentence (3) (repeated as (13a)), which the direct object of the main predicate bears is identical to the particle in sentence (6) (repeated as (13b)), which is assigned to PP.

(13) a. Gakusei-ni-wa kono zisyo-ga
student-for-TOP this dictionary-NOM
tukai-yasui.
use-easy
'This dictionary is easy for students to use.'

b. Masao-nitotte sono yuubinkyoku-kara-ga
Masao-for that post office-from-NOM
kozutumi-o okuri-yasui.
package-ACC send-easy
'It is easy for Masao to send packages from that post office.'

To answer the question, we will carry out the diagnostics, which is whether the nominative case particle undergoes the case alternation.

4.1 Nominative-Genitive Conversion

One of the prominent case alternations in Japanese is nominative-genitive conversion (heneafter NGC), which is also often called *ga-no* conversion. Such a grammatical process allows optional conversion between the two case particles *ga* and *no*, typically in relative clauses and noun-complement construction (Harada (1971; 1976): See also Miyagawa (1993); Hiraiwa (2001) for more recent discussion.)

Putting technical details aside, the type of evidence we give involves a complex NP with a head noun such as *riyuu* 'reason' as exemplified in (14).

(14) a. Ken-ga/*no kuru.
Ken-NOM/GEN come
'Ken comes.'

b. Ken-ga/no kuru riyuu
Ken-NOM/GEN come reason
'the reason why Ken comes'

In embedded clause (14b), but not in main clause (14a), the nominative case particle *ga* is variably substituted for the genitive case particle *no*.

It is worth noting that the NGC does not change any grammatical nor thematic relations.[2] Thus, *Ken-ga* 'Ken-NOM' in (14a) and *Ken-no* 'Ken-GEN' in (14b) are the subject of each clause.

[2]Miyagawa (1993) points out that there is a scope difference in the application of NGA. In gapless clauses the nominative-marked subject cannot take scope over the head noun, but the genitive-marked subject can take scope over the head noun. For the detailed discussion of this matter, see Miyagawa (1993).

4.2 Availability of the NGC

With the diagnostics setting above, let us firstly consider the following sentences (15) in order to see how the NGC works in sentences (13).

(15) a. Gakusei-nitotte kono
student-for this
zisyo-ga/no tukai-yasui riyuu
dictionary-NOM/GEN use-easy reason
'the reason why this dictionary is easy for students to use.'

b. Masao-nitotte sono
Masao-for that
yuubinkyoku-kara-ga/*no kozutumi-o
post office-fro-NOM/GEN package-ACC
okuri-yasui riyuu
send-easy reason
'the reason why that post office is easy for Masao to send packages from.'

As illustrated in (15) above, the nominative case-marked NP *kono zisyo* 'this dictionary' in (15a) is the direct object of the main predicate, and the NGC is possible. However, the nominative case particle with the PP *sono yuubinkyoku-kara* 'from that post office' in (15b) cannot convert to the genitive case particle. The contrast in (15a) and (15b) shows that there are two kinds of nominative case particles in Japanese in which the NGC is possible in some cases.

With this in mind, let us then consider whether postpositions are sensitive to NGC. In (10a), for example, *kooitta ziko-ga* 'this kind of accident' is not an argument of the main predicate *seikyuusuru* 'claim', and it also does not bear any postpositions.

One might predict that the nominative case particle in the sentences (10a) and (10b) can be substituted for the genitive case particle via the NGC. However, this prediction is not correct:

(16) a. Kooitta ziko-ga/*no
this kind of accident-NOM/GEN
(higaisya-nitotte) bakudaina
injured party-for enormous
songaibaisyoo-o
amount of compensation-ACC
seikyuusi-yasui riyuu
claim-easy reason

(lit.)'the reason why this kind of accident is easy (for the injured party) to claim an enormous amount of compensation.'

b. Kotosi (gakusei-nitotte-wa)
this year students-for-TOP
gengogaku-ga/*no ii sigoto-o
linguistics-NOM/*GEN good job-ACC
mituke-nikui rasii. riyuu
find-difficult seem reason
(lit.)'the reason why this year, linguistics is difficult (for students) to find a good job.'

The unacceptable sentences (16) above suggest that not only the nominative case particle with adjunct PP, but also the nominative case particle with adjunct NP cannot undergo the NGC.

Finally consider how the multiple nominative-marked phrases in sentences like (12) above interact with the NGC.

(17) a.*Kodomotati-nitotte
children-for
kono kaizyoo-(de)-no baiorin-(de)-ga
this hall-in-GEN violin-on-NOM
sonata-ga hiki-yasui riyuu
sonata-NOM play-easy reason

b.*Kodomotati-nitotte
children-for
kono kaizyoo-(de)-no baiorin-(de)-no
this hall-in-GEN violin-on-GEN
sonata-ga hiki-yasui riyuu
sonata-NOM play-easy reason

c.*Kodomotati-nitotte
children-for
kono kaizyoo-(de)-no baiorin-(de)-ga
this hall-in-GEN violin-on-NOM
sonata-no hiki-yasui riyuu
sonata-GEN play-easy reason

d?*Kodomotati-nitotte
children-for
kono kaizyoo-(de)-no baiorin-(de)-no
this hall-in-GEN violin-on-GEN
sonata-no hiki-yasui riyuu
sonata-GEN play-easy reason

e.*Kodomotati-nitotte
children-for
kono kaizyoo-(de)-ga baiorin-(de)-no
this hall-in-NOM violin-on-GEN
sonata-no hiki-yasui riyuu
sonata-GEN play-easy reason

f.*Kodomotati-nitotte
children-for
kono kaizyoo-(de)-ga baiorin-(de)-no
this hall-in-NOM violin-on-GEN
sonata-ga hiki-yasui riyuu
sonata-GEN play-easy reason

g. Kodomotati-nitotte
children-for
kono kaizyoo-(de)-ga baiorin-(de)-ga
this hall-in-NOM violin-on-NOM
sonata-no hiki-yasui riyuu
sonata-GEN play-easy reason
(lit.)'the reason why sonata is easy for children to play on violin in this hall'

In the acceptable sentence (17g), the NGC is only applied to the direct object of the main predicate. All the unacceptable sentences in (17a-f) show that the PP adjuncts fail to undergo the NGC.

4.3 Summary

We have examined how the NGC can be applied to the Type I tough constructions, and shown that there are two kinds of the nominative case particle in Japanese: the particle with the direct object of the main predicate undergoes the NGC but the particle with the NP/PP adjunct does not.

5 A Formal Analysis

5.1 Combinatory Categorial Grammar

In this section we will seek the answer to two questions within the framework of Combinatory Categorial Grammar (CCG) (Steedman, 1996; 2000) :

(i) how can we account for the different behaviors of the two types of nominative case particles?

(ii) how can be the tough constructions dealt with?

In CCG, information about word order and valency is encoded in syntactic categories which are assigned to words. These categories specify the number of arguments a word can take, as well as the relative position of arguments with respect to the head. They are also paired with a semantic interpretation. For instance, the category of the transitive verb *hiku* 'play' is as follows:

(18) hiku := $(S\backslash NP_n)\backslash NP_n : \lambda x \lambda y\ play'xy$

In addition to standard function application (19a,b) below, CCG allows constituents to combine via a set of combinatory rules, which are stated as schemata over categories (backward composition (19c) and forward type-raising (19d) in the following):

(19) a. $X/Y: f \quad Y: a \;\Rightarrow\; X: fa$ (>)

b. $Y: a \quad X\backslash Y: f \;\Rightarrow\; X: fa$ (<)

c. $Y\backslash Z: g \quad X\backslash Y: f \;\Rightarrow\; X\backslash Z: \lambda x.f(gx)$ (<**B**)

d. $X: a \;\Rightarrow\; T/(T\backslash X): \lambda f.f[a]$ (>**T**)

The normal-form derivation of ordinary sentences such as (20) mainly requires function application (19a,b). See (21) below.

(20) Ken-ga baiorin-de sonata-o hiku.
Ken-NOM violin-on sonata-ACC play
'Ken plays sonata (on violin).'

In (21), *Ken* 'Ken' and *sonata* 'sonata' are type-raised. Type-raising turns argument categories such as NP into functions over the functions that take them as arguments, such as the verbs, into the results of such functions. This operation can be strictly limited to argument categories NP, AP, PP, VP and S. One way to do this is to specify it in the morpho-lexicon, in the categories for proper names, determiners, and the like. Therefore it resembles the traditional operation of *case*.

PP *baiolin-de* 'on violin' is not an adjunct. Following Steedman (1996), we assume that adjuncts are also subcategorized for by verbs in some sense and that they are the most oblique (and optional) arguments of verbs.

It is worth noting that the category of the verb encodes the missing argument, i.e., PP as a feature, which is passed up through the derivation. Such a feature can be linked with another category by some semantic or pragmatic rules although it is not realized as a PP.

5.2 Tough Predicate

Let us now consider the following example (22) in which the direct object of the main predicate bears the nominative case particle:

(22) (Ken-nitotte-wa) . . . sonata-ga hiki-yasui.
Ken-for-TOP sonata-NOM play-easy
'Sonata is easy (for Ken) to play.'

The following is the relevant part of the syntactic category (23) and the derivation the construction (24) with a tough adjective *yasui* 'easy':

(23) yasui := $(S\backslash NP_n)\backslash((S\backslash NP_n)\backslash NP_o)$
$: \lambda p \lambda x.easily'(px.one')$

Tough constructions involve syntactic complementation. Namely, the tough adjective *yasui* exemplified in (23) functions as a word with its own lexical contents, where the constant one' represents an arbitrary EXPERIENCER. Thus, the specification of the category is the same as English tough adjectives, except the word order information.

In (24), functional composition allows the complement verb to be an unboundedly large fragment, accounting for the unbounded character of the dependency involved. Different from English, the subject, or more precisely the nominative-marked phrase of the construction, is merged with the predicate by a semantic or pragmatic relation which we represent as *about(ness)*.

The specification of the particle is given below.

(25) -ga := $(S/(S\backslash NP_n))\backslash N$
$: \lambda p \lambda q \exists x.px \wedge about'(x, qx)$

This analysis accounts for the nominative-marked phrase requirement in Section 3.1 from the semantic or pragmatic viewpoint. The relevant data (7) is repeated with some modifications:

(26) a.*[$_\theta$ Kodomo-ni-wa] [$_\rho$] suwari-nikui.
child-for-TOP sit-hard
(lit.)*'For a child is hard to sit.'

b. [$_\theta$ Kodomo-ni-wa] [$_\rho$ ano isu-ga]
child-for-TOP that chair-NOM
suwari-nikui.
sit-hard
'That chair is hard for a child to sit on.'

(21) Ken – ga | baiolin | –de | sonata – o | hiku

$$\begin{array}{lllll}
\text{Ken}-\text{ga} & \text{baiolin} & -\text{de} & \text{sonata}-\text{o} & \text{hiku}\\
\overline{(S/(S\backslash NP_n))}^{>\mathbf{T}} & \overline{NP} & \overline{PP_{on}\backslash NP} & \overline{((S\backslash NP_n)\backslash PP_{on})/(((S\backslash NP_n)\backslash PP_{on})\backslash NP_a)}^{>\mathbf{T}} & \overline{((S\backslash NP_n)\backslash PP_{on})\backslash NP_a}\\
:\lambda p.p\ ken' & : violin' & :\lambda x.on'x & :\lambda p.p\ sonata' & :\lambda x\lambda y\lambda z.play'xyz
\end{array}$$

$$PP : on'violin' \quad (<)$$

$$(S\backslash NP_n)\backslash PP_{on} : \lambda y\lambda z.play'sonata'yz \quad (>)$$

$$S\backslash NP_n : \lambda z.play'sonata'(on'violin')z \quad (<)$$

$$S : play'sonata'(on'violin')ken' \quad (>)$$

(24)

$$\begin{array}{llll}
\text{sonata} & -\text{ga} & \text{hiki} & -\text{yasui}\\
\overline{N} & \overline{(S/(S\backslash NP_n))\backslash N} & \overline{(S\backslash NP_n)\backslash NP_a} & \overline{(S\backslash NP_n)\backslash((S\backslash NP_n)\backslash NP_o)}\\
:\lambda x.sonata'x & :\lambda p\lambda q\exists x.px \wedge about'(x,qx) & :\lambda x\lambda y.play'xy & :\lambda p\lambda x.easily'(px\ one')
\end{array}$$

$$S/(S\backslash NP_n) : \lambda q\exists x.sonata'x \wedge about'(x,qx) \quad (<) \qquad S\backslash NP_n : \lambda x\ easily'(play'x\ one') \quad (<\mathbf{B})$$

$$S : \exists x.sonata'x \wedge about'(x, easily(play'x\ one')) \quad (>)$$

(29)

$$\begin{array}{llll}
\text{baiorin} & -\text{ga} & \text{sonata}-\text{ga} & \text{hiki}-\text{yasui}\\
\overline{N} & \overline{(S/S)\backslash N} & \overline{S/(S\backslash NP_n)}^{<} & \overline{S\backslash NP_n}^{<\mathbf{B}}\\
:\lambda y.violin'y & :\lambda p\lambda q\exists y.px \wedge about'(y,q) & :\lambda q\exists x.sonata'x \wedge about'(x,qx) & :\lambda x\ easily'(play'x\ one')
\end{array}$$

$$S/S : \lambda q\exists y.violin'y \wedge about'(y,q) \quad (<) \qquad S : \exists x.sonata'x \wedge about'(x, easily(play'x\ one')) \quad (>)$$

$$S : \exists y.violin'y\ \wedge about'(y, \exists x.sonata'x \wedge about'(x, easily(play'x\ one'))) \quad (>)$$

The information conveyed by a sentence is split into new information *rheme* (ρ, *focus*) and information already present in the discourse *theme* (θ, *topic*). The sentence-initial *ga*-marked phrase is obligatorily marked with focus if the predicate of a sentence presents a state or a habitual/generic action (Kuno, 1973). (26a) lacks such a phrase of a sentence describing a state, and becomes unacceptable.

5.3 Multiple Nominative Construction

In Section 5.2, we discussed the semantics or pragmatics of focus using examples (22) and (26). (22) is a part of the multiple *ga*-marked phrase sentence (12), repeated as (27) with some modifications, which we referred as one of the characters of Type I tough construction in Section 3.3.

(27) Kono kaizyoo-(de)-ga baiorin-(de)-ga
this hall-in-NOM violin-on-NOM
sonata-ga hiki-yasui.
sonata-NOM play-easy
(lit.)'It is this hall that violin is easy to play sonata.'

Another character of the construction shown in Section 3.2 is adjunction. An element other than the argument of the main predicate can bear the case particle, as shown in (10), repeated as (28) with some modifications.

(28) Kooitta ziko-ga
this kind of accident-NOM
songaibaisyoo-ga/o seikyuusi-yasui.
compensationNOM/ACC claim-easy
(lit.)'It is this kind of accident that compensation is easy to claim.'

Japanese has several types of multiple nominative construction that generates more than one *ga*-marked phrase (Tateishi, 1991). We claim that sentences (27) and (28) above are the instances of such a construction.[3]

The following (29) and (30) are the relevant part of the derivation of sentence (27) and the feature specification of another type of case particle, respectively.

(30) -ga := $(S/S)\backslash N$
$: \lambda p\lambda q\exists x.px \wedge about'(x, q)$

[3](28) is the *adjunct multiple nominative construction*. For the detailed discussion of the classification of multiple nominative constructions, see Tateishi (1991).

Different from the particle (25), (30) introduces an element which is not the argument of the predicate. Successive layers of *ga*-marked NPs, namely, multiple nominative constructions are derived recursively with the predication function encoded in (30).

6 Concluding Remarks

In this paper, we have proposed two types of nominative case particles in Japanese. They are correlated with the difference not only in the GNC but also in the semantic or pragmatic interpretation. Based on those data, we have shown the specification of the nominative case particles and the derivations for tough predicates within the CCG framework.

This analysis is related to the issue of the licensing of the nominative case particle in Japanese. Saito (1982) argues that the Japanese nominative case is an inherent Case. Takezawa (1987) offers an analysis that the nominative case is assigned by INFL within the GB framework, and extending Takezawa's analysis, Ura (1996) argues that nominative case is licensed by T under the minimalist assumptions. They all imply that there is only one nominative case licensing condition in Japanese.

Since the NGC behaves in a different way in tough sentences, we claim that there are two (or more) kinds of the nominative case licensing, which constitutes evidence against the former analyses.

In this paper, we only utilized the NGC as the diagnostics of such a case distinction and did not show any formal mechanisms of alternation. The condition of the case alternations, nominative-genitive (*ga-no*), accusative-nominative (*o-ga*) and dative-nominative (*ni-ga*), in Japanese are one of the most intriguing issues in Japanese syntax. We will leave the analyses of the issue for future work.

Acknowledgments

We are indebted to three anonymous PACLIC reviewers, Mark Steedman and Robert Logie for their invaluable comments on an earlier version of this paper. All remaining inadequacies are our own. This research is partially supported by the Grant-in-Aid for Scientific Research (C), 24500189 of the Japan Society for the Promotion of Science (JSPS).

References

Noam Chomsky. 1973. Conditions on Transformation. Stephen R. Anderson and Paul Kiparsky (eds). *A Festschrift for Morris Halle*, 232–286. Holt, Rinehart, and Winston, New York.

Shin-Ichi Harada. 1971. Ga-No Conversion and Idiolectal Variations in Japanese. *Gengo Kenkyu*, 60:25–38.

Shin-Ichi Harada. 1976. Ga-No Conversion Revisited – A Reply to Shibatani. *Gengo Kenkyu*, 70:23–38.

Ken Hiraiwa. 2001. *On Nominative-Genitive Conversion*. Elena Guerzoni and Ora Matushansky (eds). *A few from building E39: Papers in Syntax, Semantics and Their Interface, MIT Working Papers in Linguistics*, 39:66–125.

Kazuko Inoue. 1978. Tough Sentences in Japanese. John Hinds and Irwin Howard (eds). *Problems in Japanese Syntax*, 122–154. Kaitakusha, Tokyo.

Kazuko Inoue. 2004. Japanese 'Tough' Sentences Revisited. John Hinds and Irwin Howard (eds). *Scientific Approaches to language*, 3:75–112. Kanda University of International Studies, Tokyo.

Susumu Kuno. 1973. *The Structure of the Japanese Language*. The MIT Press, Cambridge, MA.

Shige-Yuki Kuroda. 1987. Movement of Noun Phrases in Japanese. Takashi Imai and Mamoru Saito (eds). *Issues in Japanese Linguistics*, 229–271. Foris, Dordrecht.

Shigeru Miyagawa. 1993. LF Case-checking and Minimal Link Condition. Colin Phillips (ed). *Papers on Case and Agreement II, MIT Working Papers in Linguistics*, 19:213–254.

Paul M. Postal. 1971. *Cross-over Phenomena*. Holt, Rinehart, and Winston, New York.

Mamoru Saito. 1982. Case Marking in Japanese: A Preliminary Study. Ms. Massachusetts Institute of Technology, Cambridge, MA.

Mark Steedman. 1996. *Surface Structure and Interpretation*. The MIT Press, Cambridge, MA.

Mark Steedman. 2000. *The Syntactic Process*. The MIT Press, Cambridge, MA.

Koichi Takezawa. 1987. *A Configurational Approach to Case-marking in Japanese*. Ph. D. dissertation, University of Washington, Seattle.

Koichi Tateishi. 1991. *The Syntax of 'Subjects'*. Ph. D. dissertation, University of Massachusetts, Amherst.

Hiroyuki Ura. 1996. *Multiple Feature-Checking: A theory of Grammatical Function Splitting*. Ph. D. dissertation, Massachusetts Institute of Technology, Cambridge, MA.

Emotional Tendency Identification for Micro-blog Topics Based on Multiple Characteristics

Quanchao Liu **Chong Feng** **Heyan Huang**
Department of Computer Science and Technology
Beijing Institute of Technology
Beijing, China
{liuquanchao, fengchong, hhy63} @bit.edu.cn

Abstract

Public opinion analysis for micro-blog post is a new trend, and wherein emotional tendency analysis on micro-blog topic is a hot spot in the sentiment analysis. According to the characteristics of contents and the various relations of Chinese micro-blog post, we construct the dictionaries of sentiment words, internet slang and emoticons respectively, and then implement the sentiment analysis algorithms based on phrase path and the multiple characteristics for emotional tendency of micro-blog topics. Using micro-blogs' forwarding, commentaries, sharing and so on, We take a future step to optimize the algorithm based on the multiple characteristics. According to the experimental results, our approach greatly improves the performance of emotional tendency identification on micro-blog topic.

1 Introduction

As the fast development of New media, the internet gradually advocates open architecture philosophy that users participate in actively, and has been developed from a simple "reading webpage" to "writing webpage", "building webpage together" for users. So a huge user generated content (UGC) has been developed, especially the emergence of micro-blog post. According to the reports[1], users applying micro-blog have exceeded 300,000,000. As a result of releasing diversely and writing randomly, micro-blog post is more and more popular in China, and it has brought a tremendous effect on network opinions and human society.

Micro-blog contents formed on internet express people's various emotion and sentiment, such as joy, anger, grief, praise, criticism and so on. More and more people like to use micro-blog post to share their views or experience, which makes people's opinion information expanded rapidly. So it is very difficult to rely on the artificial method to deal with the micro-blog information's collection and processing, there is an urgent need to help user analyse the massive information using computer.

Chinese micro-blog post has multiple characteristics as following:

1) Due to the short text message, micro-blog post has terms' sparsity. Feature extraction based on terms is not suitable for micro-blog post.
2) There exist many homophonic words, abbreviated words, internet slang in micro-blog post, such as "杯具" standing for "悲剧", "亲" standing for "亲爱的", "3Q" standing for "谢谢", or using emoticons to express emotion and so on.
3) Many popular new words made by network events would appear in micro-blog post. Taking "皮鞋很忙" for example, it appeared because the news report that the materials for producing shoes are processed into edible gelatin.
4) There are a variety of relations between micro-blogs. It is very convenient to forward, comment and share micro-blog post.

[1] The Eleventh China Network Media Forum

According to the above characteristics of micro-blog post, we analyse emotional tendency on micro-blog topic, and obtain a set of feasible and effective emotional tendency identification algorithm on micro-blog topic.

The remainder of this paper is structured as follows. In section 2, we briefly summarize related work. Section 3 gives an overview of data construction, including emotional symbol library, emotional dictionary and network slang dictionary. In order to improve the rate of target coverage, the target extended algorithm is described in section 4. We design the different emotional tendency identification algorithms on micro-blog topic in sections 5 and 6 respectively. In section 7, sentiment optimization algorithm is described. Experimental results are reported in section 8 and section 9 concludes our work.

2 Related Work

In the research domain of sentiment analysis, emotional tendency for twitter has been concerned for some time, such as Tweetfeel[1], Twendz[2], Twitter Sentiment[3]. In previous related work, (Go et al., 2009) use distant learning to acquire sentiment data. They use tweets ending in positive emoticons like":)" as positive and negative emoticons like":(" as negative. They build models using Naives Bayes(NB), MaxEnt(ME) and Support Vector Machines(SVM), and they report SVM outperforms other classifiers. In terms of feature space, they try a Unigram, Bigram model in conjunction with parts-of-speech (POS) features. They note that the unigram model outperforms all other models. However, the unigram model isn't suitable for Chinese micro-blog post, and we make full use of new emoticons which appear frequently in Chinese micro-blog post.

Another significant effort for sentiment classification on Twitter data is by (Barbosa and Feng, 2010). They use polarity predictions from three websites as noisy labels to train a model. They propose the use of syntax features of tweets like retweet, hashtags, link, punctuation and exclamation marks in conjunction with features like prior polarity of words and POS of words. In order to improve target-dependent Twitter sentiment classification, (Long et al., 2011) incorporate target-dependent features and take the relations between twitters into consideration, such as retweet, reply and the twitters published by the same person. We extend their approach by adding a variety of Chinese dictionaries of sentiment, internet slang and emoticons, and then by using syntactic parser[4] and LIBSVM[5] respectively to achieve the sentiment analysis algorithms based on phrase path and the multiple characteristics for emotional tendency of micro-blog topic. Using micro-blogs' forwarding, commentaries and sharing, we take a future step to optimize the algorithm based on the multiple characteristics.

The problem we address in this paper is to determine emotional orientation for micro-blog topic. So the input of our task is a collection of micro-blogs containing the topic and the output is labels assigned to each of the micro-blogs.

3 Data Description

Micro-blog post is a social networking that allows users to post real time messages, and its content is restricted to 140 Chinese characters. Our data set comes from Sina[6] and Tencent[7] micro-blog, and micro-blogs are commonly displayed on the Web as shown in figure 1. "# #" identifies the micro-blog topic, "//" labels user's forwarding relation, "@" specified the user who we speak to, and "V" labeling on the user shows the user's information is identified by the Sina or Tencent.

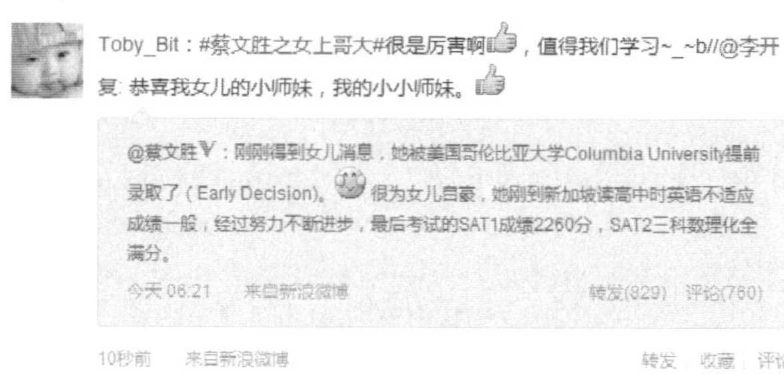

Fig.1 Micro-blog post example

People usually use sentiment words, internet slang and emoticons to express their opinions and sentiment in micro-blog post. In order to obtain

[1] http://www.tweetfeel.com/
[2] http://twendz.waggeneredstrom.com/
[3] http://teittersentiment.appspot.com/
[4] http://nlp.stanford.edu/downloads/lex-parser.shtml
[5] http://www.csie.ntu.edu.tw/~cjlin/libsvm
[6] http://s.weibo.com/
[7] http://t.qq.com/

emotional orientation on micro-blog topic, we construct some dictionaries described as follows.

3.1 The Dictionaries of Sentiment Words and Internet Slang

According to (Du et al., 2009), the sentiment word is one of the best emotional features representations of text, and the rich sentiment words can be conductive to improving emotional tendency identification algorithm. Internet slang that more and more people use in social network is also important factor for emotional orientation. The constructions of them are not only a significant foundation, but also a time-consuming, labor-intensive work.

3.1.1 The Dictionary of Sentiment Words

In order to obtain more abundant sentiment words, we regard these sentiment words provided by HowNet[1] and National Taiwan University Sentiment Dictionary (NTUSD)[2] as the foundation, and then use lexical fusion strategy to enrich the dictionary of sentiment words. HowNet is commonsense knowledge base that describes the concepts and reveals the relation between concepts, including the relation between the attributes of concept. Since October 2007, HowNet has released "emotional words collection for sentiment analysis", containing a total of about 17,887 words, of which about 8,942 Chinese words. NTUSD has been summed up by National Taiwan University, including simplified Chinese version and traditional Chinese version, and each version contains 2,812 positive emotion words as well as 8,276 negative emotion words.

(Turney and Littman, 2003; Wang et al., 2011) use lexical fusion strategy to compute the degree of correlation between test word and seed words that have more obvious emotional orientation, and then obtain emotional orientation of test word. We respectively take 20 words with obvious emotional orientation as seed words in this paper, as shown in Tables 1 and 2.

Table 1 Seed words with positive emotion

辉煌	美妙	漂亮	俱佳	动听
体面	淳美	良好	出色	完美
美丽	精英	优秀	高手	先进
快乐	最佳	优质	幸福	积极

Table 2 Seed words with negative emotion

罪恶	诅咒	责备	丑陋	丑恶
藐小	累赘	错误	失败	麻烦
不良	恶意	色情	暴力	讨厌
魔鬼	野蛮	腐败	流氓	残酷

So emotional orientation of the test word is computed as follows:

$$SO(word) = \sum_{pword \in Pset} PMI(word, pword) - \sum_{nword \in Nset} PMI(word, nword) \quad (1)$$

Where *pword* and *nword* are positive seed word and negative seed word, *Pset* and *Nset* are positive seed words collection and negative seed words collection respectively. $PMI(word_1, word_2)$ is described in formula (2), $P(word_1\&word_2)$, $P(word_1)$ and $P(word_2)$ are probabilities of $word_1$ and $word_2$ co-occurring, $word_1$ appearing, and $word_2$ appearing in a micro-blog post respectively. When $SO(word)$ is greater than zero, sentiment orientation of word is positive. Otherwise it is negative.

$$PMI(word_1, word_2) = \log(\frac{P(word_1 \,\&\, word_2)}{P(word_1)P(word_2)}) \quad (2)$$

3.1.2 The Dictionary of Internet Slang

People usually use homophonic words, abbreviated words and network slang to express their sentiment in social network, and (Agarwal et al., 2011) has analysed the sentiment of twitter data. Sometimes new words, produced by important events or news reports, are used to express their opinions. So we construct the dictionary of internet slang to support emotional tendency identification algorithm on micro-blog topic, containing homophonic words, abbreviated words, network slang and many new words.

National Language Resource Monitoring & Research Center (Network Media)[3] has some internet slang, two persons from our lab manually collect more network language through social network, and then integrate these resources together. Finally we achieve this dictionary, containing 861 words with emotional orientation. Table 3 shows part of the dictionary.

[1] http://www.keenage.com/html/c_index.html

[2] http://nlg18.csie.ntu.edu.tw:8080/opinion/index.html

[3] http://www.clr.org.cn/

Table 3 Part of the dictionary of internet slang

Internet slang	Meaning	Polarity
达人	高人	Positive
狂顶	强烈支持	Positive
萝莉	16 岁以下的可爱小女孩	Positive
灰常桑心	非常伤心	Negative
菜鸟	网上低手	Negative

3.2 The dictionary of emoticons

We construct the dictionary of emoticons by combining emotional symbol library in micro-blog post with other statistical methods. The former is used to select obvious emotion symbols in micro-blog post, such as Sina, Tencent micro-blog et al. The latter choose emoticons used in other social network, containing user-generated emoticons.

Firstly, two laboratory personnel obtain emotional symbol library, and keep the emoticons with the same emotional orientation after their analysis, and then get rid of emotional symbols with ambiguous orientation, the result is described in Table 4.

Table 4 Part of the dictionary of emoticons

Emoticons	Meaning	Polarity
	good	Positive
	给力	Positive
	鄙视	Negative
	怒骂	Negative

Secondly, in order to enrich the dictionary of emoticons, especially user-generated emoticons in social network, two laboratory personnel collect and analyse emotional orientation, and finally obtain the result shown in Table 5.

Table 5 Part of the dictionary of user-generated emoticons

Emoticons	Meaning	Polarity
:o)	大笑	Positive
:)	微笑	Positive
:(	伤心	Negative
T_T	哭泣	Negative

In order to deal with the content conveniently, we pre-process all the micro-blogs and replace all the emoticons with a their sentiment polarity by looking up the dictionary of emoticons.

4 Extended Topics

People usually express their sentiment about object by commenting not on the object itself but on some related things of the object. (Yao et al., 2006) expresses the sentiment about automobile by commenting on the attributes or functionalities of the automobile. As shown in the micro-blog post below, user expresses a positive sentiment about Nokia 5800 by expressing a positive sentiment directly about its screen, keyboard et al.

"#诺基亚 5800#屏幕很好，键盘操作也很方便，质量不错哦~亲:)"

It is assumed that user can clearly infer the sentiment about the topic based on those sentiments about the related things. We define those related things as Extended Topics. In order to obtain more micro-blogs' emotional orientation on the topic, we design topic's expansion algorithm, and expand the extended topic set with formula (2). Formula (2) describes the correlation between two words, the greater *PMI* value, the stronger the correlation. So we identify the top 10 nouns and noun phrases which have the strongest association with the topic in micro-blog set, and then take them as the original topic's extended set.

5 Sentiment Analysis Based on Phrase Path for Micro-blog Topic

Chinese syntactic analysis has been considered to be an important technique in the process of Chinese information processing. It can be divided into two methods: one is the phrase structure parsing described in (Zhou and Zhao, 2007), namely splits the sentence into phrases, and analyses hierarchical relations among phrases. The other is dependency structure analysis described in (Cheng et al., 2005), namely parse the dependency relations between words. In terms of social network, because the content is brief, and the meaning of the expression is centered relatively, the distance between the sentiment words and evaluation objectives usually is short, and we can use the phrase structure tree to evaluate objectives' emotional orientation.

Take the micro-blog post in section 4 for example, its phrase structure tree is described in figure 2, and its original topic is "诺基亚 5800", we obtain the topic's extended set {屏幕, 键盘, 操作, 质量} using topic expansion algorithm. So we can confirm the emotional orientation of "诺基亚 5800" by analyzing the sentiment of the element of extended set. At first, starting from evaluation objectives, we find out the shortest phrase path between topic (extended topics) and sentiment word. Phrase path defined in (Zhao et al., 2011) is to link any two phrase nodes in the phrase structure tree. Such as "诺基亚 5800—CD—QP—NP—IP—VP—VP—VA—好", "屏幕—NN—NP—NP—IP—VP—VP—VA—好" et al. Secondly, according to the dictionary of sentiment words, we confirm emotional orientation of the last word in the shortest phrase path. Phrase structure tree is divided into several sub tree by the punctuations, starting from each sub tree, we find out the shortest phrase path, and determine emotional orientation of the topic.

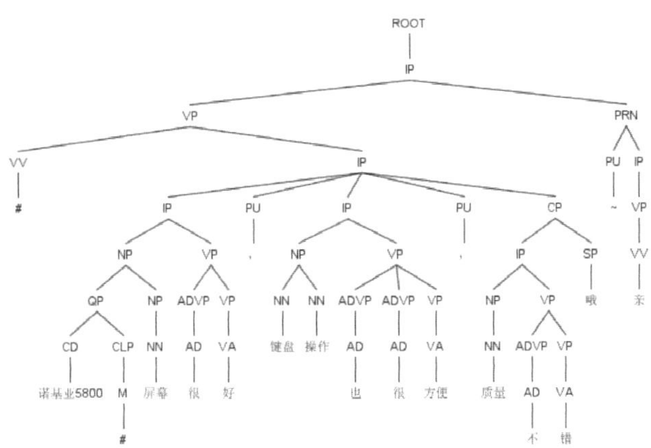

Fig.2 Phrase structure tree of micro-blog example

However, the negative word makes the internal sentiment words tend to shift. Such as "整个店面的装修不是很漂亮", "表演极不自信" et al. "漂亮" and "自信" originally are commendatory terms, but after adding "不是" and "不", the whole sentence semantic changes as a pejorative. In this paper, we adopt matching negative rules method, sentiment words matched by the rules adopt opposite emotional orientation to properly reflect the sentiment. At first, we select negative sentences 6,639 from 20,000 micro-blogs which come from the lab[1], and then accomplish the rule set containing high frequency negative rules 227. Secondly, the rule set is used to match the test sentence, and if sentiment words are the focus of negation, we take the opposite emotional orientation.

The negative words used in this algorithm are acquired through HowNet. We select the concepts containing negative sememe, such as {neg|否}, {impossible|不会}, {OwnNot|无}, {inferior|不如} et al, and obtain 21 negative words after filtering.

6 Multiple Characteristics-based Sentiment Classification for Micro-blog Topics

Based on supervised classification is our another method to determine emotional orientation on micro-blog topic. According to previous related studies (Go et al., 2009; Bermingham and Smeaton, 2010; Agrawal et al., 2003; Pang et al., 2002), NB, ME and SVM are mainly classifiers for text classification, (Go and Barbosa et al.) have ever performed sentiment classification of twitter data, and summarize that SVM is more suitable for short text sentiment classification than other classification models.

We use LIBSVM to achieve sentiment classification based on multiple characteristics for micro-blog topic. LIBSVM is an integrated software for support vector classification, and makes everything automatic—from data scaling to parameter selection. We propose the following procedure:

1) Transform data to the format of an SVM package;
2) Conduct simple scaling on the data;
3) Consider the RBF kernel $K(x,y)=e^{-\gamma\|x-y\|^2}$;
4) Use cross-validation to find the best parameter C and γ;
5) Use the best parameter C and γ to train the whole training set;
6) Test the whole corpus.

SVM needs categorical features, so we take the features of the Chinese micro-blog post into account. At first, take the data features described in section 3 as some categorical features. According to the polarity of sentiment words, internet slang and emoticons, we compute emotion values and then take these values as some attribute values of SVM. Secondly, take the syntax features of micro-blog content as other categorical features. These syntax features are described as following:

[1] www.nlpir.org

1) Verb-Object structure. Sentiment words are verbs and the topic is their object.
2) Adjective-Center structure, namely a combination of adjective and noun. Sentiment words are adjectives and the topic is their attributive center.
3) Adverb-Center structure, namely an adverb phrase. Sentiment words are adverbs and the topic is their adverbial center.
4) Comparative structure. It is suitable for "A than B + sentiment word" construction. When A is the topic, its emotional orientation is consistent with the polarity of sentiment word; otherwise B is the topic, we adopt the opposite polarity of sentiment word.
5) Emotional orientation shifting. When the emotional orientation shifting is taken place in 1), 2), 3) and 4), we adopt matching negative rules method described in section 5.

According to the polarity of sentiment words, we compute emotion values and then take these values as other attribute values of SVM.

7 Sentiment Optimization Based on Relation Features

To some extent, it is limited that only depends on data and syntax features for sentiment analysis of micro-blog topic. In order to improve the accuracy of sentiment analysis, we take relation features between micro-blogs into consideration and then take a future step to optimize sentiment classification based on multiple characteristics.

Micro-blog post is propagated through their forwarding, commentaries, sharing. The forwarding, commentaries and sharing usually means the user agrees with the original user, and they have the same sentiment on the topic. At the same time, micro-blogs published by the same person within a short timeframe[1] should have a consistent sentiment about the same topic. Based on these four kinds of relation features, we can construct a graph using the input micro-blog collection of a given topic. As illustrated in Figure 3, each node in the graph indicates a micro-blog post. The four kinds of edges indicate forwarding (solid line), commentaries (long dash line), sharing relations (dash line) and being published by the same person (round dotted line) respectively. The isolated nodes have not any relations with other micro-blogs.

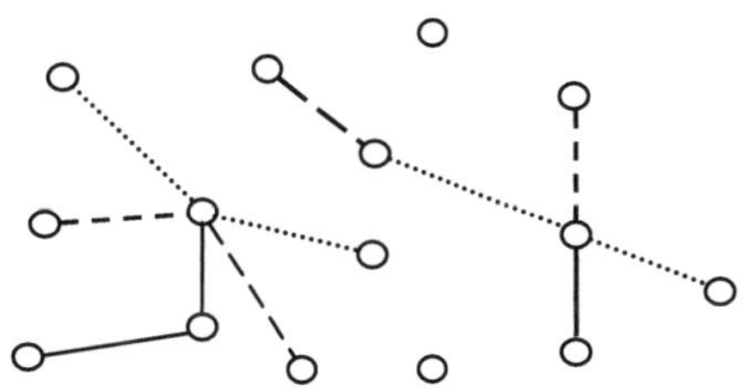

Fig.3 Relationship graph of micro-blogs about a given topic

We consider that the sentiment of a micro-blog post only depends on its content and immediate neighbors, and then compute the sentiment of the current node with the following formula:

$$\Phi_{c,d} = p(\lambda(d)=c \mid \tau(d)) \sum_{\lambda(N(d))} p(\lambda(d)=c \mid \lambda(N(d)))p(\lambda(N(d))) \quad (3)$$

Where $\lambda(d)$ is the sentiment label of node d and value $c \in \{positive, negative, neutral\}$, $\tau(d)$ is the content of node d, $N(d)$ is all immediate neighbors of node d. The sentiment label of the micro-blog post only depending on its content is represented by $\pi_{c,d} = p(\lambda(d) = c \mid \tau(d))$. According to relaxation labeling algorithm described in (Angelova and Weikum, 2006), we can simplify the formula (3) into (4), and use formula (4) to iteratively estimate the sentiment for all micro-blogs in the graph.

$$\Phi_{c,d}^{(r)} = \pi_{c,d} \cdot \sum_{\lambda(N(d))} \Big(\prod_{d' \in N(d)} p(\lambda(d) = c \wedge \lambda(d') = c') \Big)^{(r-1)}, \quad r > 1 \quad (4)$$

Where r is iterative superscript. With the short-hand notation $\phi_{c,c'} = p(\lambda(d) = c \wedge \lambda(d') = c')$ we can rewrite this into:

$$\Phi_{c,d}^{(r)} = \pi_{c,d} \cdot \sum_{\lambda(N(d))} \Big(\prod_{d' \in N(d)} \phi_{c,c'} \Big)^{(r-1)} \quad (5)$$

The original sentiment label of each node in Fig.3 is computed by the algorithm described in section 6. After the iteration ends, for any micro-blog in Fig.3, the sentiment label that has the maximum $\Phi_{c,d}$ is considered the final label.

[1] Taking one week (7 days) as the unit in our experiment

8 Experiments and Results

8.1 Resources and Pre-processing of data

Because there is no annotated micro-blog post corpus publicly available for evaluation of micro-blog topic sentiment classification, we design topic-focused web crawler and respectively crawl 1,000 micro-blogs on three hot topics {iphone5, 袁隆平, 北京爱情故事}. After removing duplicate micro-blogs, we obtain 983 "iphone5", 993 "袁隆平", and 998 "北京爱情故事". Two persons from our lab manually classify each micro-blog post as positive, negative or neutral towards the topics. Among the micro-blogs, 83 of them are neutral-subjective disagreement. In order to manually determine the sentiment for the next step, we assume that these micro-blogs are neutral. 103 of them are positive-negative disagreement, we adopt three people ballot to determine emotional orientation, and finally obtain 1,526 positive, 685 negative and 763 neutral micro-blogs. Take each 500 of them as the training corpus and the other 1,474 as the test set.

8.2 The Evaluation of Micro-blog Topic Sentiment Analysis

Sentiment analysis on micro-blog topic is evaluated by Precision, Recall, F-measure and Coverage. The coverage is used to measure integrity and adequacy for the test, and help us understand the test coverage scope.

$$Precision = \frac{\#system\_correct}{\#system\_proposed} \quad (6)$$

$$Recall = \frac{\#system\_correct}{\#person\_correct} \quad (7)$$

$$F-measure = \frac{2 \times Precision \times Recall}{Precision + Recall} \quad (8)$$

$$Coverage = \frac{\#weibo\_topic}{\#weibo\_total} \quad (9)$$

Where *#system_correct* is the correct result from system, *#system_proposed* is the whole number of micro-blogs from system, *#person_correct* is the number of micro-blogs that has been annotated correctly by people, *#weibo_topic* is the number of micro-blogs containing topic words, *#weibo_total* is the whole number of micro-blogs in the collection.

8.3 Results

According to the evaluation in section 8.2, we respectively adopt the algorithms in sections 5, 6 and 7 to determine the emotional orientation for the topics {iphone5, 袁隆平, 北京爱情故事}. As shown in Table 6, we conclude that extending topic is a vital factor, especially it has an obvious effect on sentiment analysis based on phrase path. The mainly reason is that the distance between topic word and sentiment word influences emotional judgment. Extending topic largely shortens the distance and improves the topic coverage, and promotes sentiment analysis performance.

In order to conveniently analyse the results and comparisons, the precision in Tables 7 and 9 is the proportionality of correct micro-blogs identified, containing positive, negative and neutral micro-blogs.

Using sentiment words to determine emotional orientation plays an important role for sentiment analysis. However, as for micro-blog post, the effects of internet slang and emoticons are more significant, the result is described in Table 7. This is because internet slang is simple and flexible to write and expresses rich meanings, emoticons are easy to use and have obvious emotional orientation, they have been used pervasively in social network and welcomed by many Chinese internet users.

Table 7 The influence of internet slang and emoticons for emotional orientation

Characteristics	Precision（%）
Content characteristics	**83.9**
- Sentiment words	81.7
- Internet slang	75.3
- Emoticons	**71.3**

However, in order to improve the performance of the evaluation, we take relation features between micro-blogs as an important factor. As seen in Figure 3, there are several micro-blogs which are not connected with any other micro-blogs. For these micro-blogs, our sentiment optimization will have no effect. The following table 8 shows the percentages of the micro-blogs in the collection which have at least one related micro-blog post according to various relation types.

Table 6 The comparisons of algorithms

Extending topic	Sentiment analysis	Precision（%）			Recall（%）			F-measure（%）			Coverage（%）
		Positive	Negative	Neutral	Positive	Negative	Neutral	Positive	Negative	Neutral	
Before extending	Based on phrase path	80.5	53.2	23.9	**43.9**	**31.3**	**73.4**	56.8	39.4	36.1	68.7
	Multiple characteristics-based	87.4	62.5	54.7	80.9	70.3	65.8	84.0	66.2	59.7	
	Based on relation features	**90.8**	59.1	73.0	86.7	70.3	76.0	88.7	64.2	74.5	
After extending	Based on phrase path	81.8	55.0	43.9	**68.5**	**58.9**	**69.6**	74.6	56.9	53.8	82.6
	Multiple characteristics-based	92.9	69.0	69.2	83.3	78.4	90.5	87.8	73.4	78.4	
	Based on relation features	**93.6**	60.9	82.9	91.1	75.7	77.2	92.3	67.5	79.9	

Table 8 The proportion of micro-blogs having at least one related micro-blog in the collection

Relations features	Proportion（%）
Forwarding	39.8
Commentaries	32.7
Sharing	22.3
Published by the same person	25.9
All	**80.3**

According to Table 8, for 80.3% of the tweets concerning the topics, we can use optimization algorithm to determine their emotional orientation. That means our sentiment optimization based on relation features is potentially useful for most of the micro-blogs. The results reported in Table 9 show that every kind of relation influences on the precision of emotional orientation.

Table 9 Comparison of contributions made by every kind of relations

Relation features	Precision（%）
Forwarding	67.3
Commentaries	61.5
Sharing	78.8
Published by the same person	70.9
All	**86.7**
（Long Jiang et al., 2011）	**83.9**

As shown in Table 9, compared to 85.6% in (Long Jiang et al., 2011), the precision of our optimization algorithm is increased by more than one percentage points. This mainly attributed to three aspects: firstly, taking internet slang and emoticons as Micro-blog's characteristics is greatly suitable for Micro-blog's sentiment analysis. Secondly, the relations between micro-blogs also play an import role to determine emotional orientation, especially the sharing relation. Thirdly, to some extent the different data set can also influence the precision. We also apply the same data set into (Long Jiang et al., 2011), and the precision is 83.9% which is still lower than our algorithm.

What's more, as a result of micro-blog content published with time characteristic, we can use time characteristic to analyse and forecast micro-blog topic's emotion tendency. We do experiment for the topic "北京爱情故事" published within one week, as shown in Figure 4, the horizontal axis represents time characteristic, and the vertical axis represents the numbers of micro-blogs having emotional orientation.

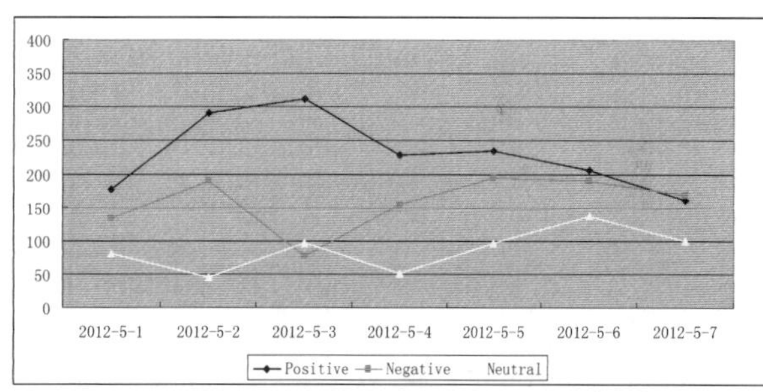

Fig.4 Emotion tendency of the topic "北京爱情故事"

9 Conclusions and Future Work

With the emergence of new media, sentiment analysis for new media is becoming more and more important. In this paper, we make full use of multiple characteristics on micro-blog post, and design two kinds of algorithms to achieve micro-blog topic's sentiment analysis. In future the work will focus on the following two aspects:

1) Micro-blog topic's expansion algorithm.
2) The effect produced by the attention relation between users as well as the numbers of fans for micro-blog topic sentiment analysis.

The relations between micro-blog users have equal importance with the multiple characteristics came from micro-blog post itself, they also play a positive effect for micro-blog's sentiment analysis.

Acknowledgments

This paper is financially supported by National Natural Science Foundation of China (No. 61132009) and National Key Technology R&D Program (No. 2012BAH14F06). We would like to thank the anonymous reviewers for many valuable comments and helpful suggestions.

References

Apoorv Agarwal, Xie Boyi, Ilia Vovsha, et al. Sentiment Analysis of Twitter Data [C]. Proceedings of the Workshop on Language in Social Media (LSM 2011). Portland, Oregon, 2011: 30-38

Rakesh Agrawal, Sridhar Rajagopalan, Ramakrishnan Srikant, et al. Mining Newsgroups Using Networks Arising From Social Behavior [C]. Proceedings of the 12th international conference on World Wide Web. Budapest, Hungary: WWW'03, 2003: 529-535

Ralitsa Angelova, Gerhard Weikum. Graph-based Text Classification: Learn from Your Neighbors [C]. Proceedings of the 29th annual international ACM SIGIR conference on Research and development in information retrieval. Seattle, Washington, USA: SIGIR'06, 2006: 485-492

Luciano Barbosa and Feng Junlan. Robust Sentiment Detection on Twitter from Biased and Noisy Data. Proceedings of COLING 2010. Beijing, China, 2010: 36-44

Adam Bermingham, Alan Smeaton. Classifying Sentiment in Microblogs: Is Brevity an Advantage? [C]. Proceedings of the 19th ACM international conference on Information and knowledge management. Toronto, Ontario, Canada: CIKM'10, 2010: 1833-1836

Cheng Yuchang, Masayuki ASAHARA, Yuji MATSUMOTOY. Machine Learning-based Dependency Analyzer for Chinese [C]. Proceedings of the International Conference on Chinese Computing 2005. Singapore: COLIPS Publication, 2005: 66-73

Du Weifu, Tan Songbo, Yun Xiaochun, et al. A New Method to Compute Semantic Orientation [J]. Journal of Computer Research and Development, 2009, 46(10): 1713-1720

Alec Go, Richa Bhayani, Huang Lei. Twitter Sentiment Classification using Distant Supervision. CS224N Project Report, Stanford, 2009

Jiang Long, Yu Mo, Zhou Ming, et al. Target-dependent Twitter Sentiment Classification [C]. Proceedings of the 49th Annual Meeting of the Association for Computational Linguistics. Portland, Oregon, 2011: 151-160

Pang B, Lee L, Vaithyanathan S. Thumbs up? Sentiment Classification using Machine Learning Techniques [C]. Proceedings of the Conference on Empirical Methods in Natural Language Processing (EMNLP). Philadelphia, PA: Association for Computational Linguistics, 2002: 79-86

Turney P D, Littman M L. Measuring praise and criticism: inference of semantic orientation from association [J]. ACM Trans on Information Systems, 2003, 21(4): 315-346

Wang Suge, Li Deyu, Wei Yingjie. A Method of Text Sentiment Classification Based on Weighted Rough Membership [J]. Journal of Computer Research and Development, 2011, 48(5): 855-861

Yao Tianfang, Nie Qingyang, Li Jianchao, et al. An opinion mining system for Chinese automobile reviews. In: Cao Youqi, Sun Maosong, eds. Proceedings of the Frontiers of Chinese Information Processing. Beijing: Tsinghua University Press, 2006: 260-281 (in Chinese with English abstract)

Zhou Qiang, Zhao Yingze. Automatic Parsing of Chinese Functional Chunks [J]. Journal of Chinese Information Processing. 2007, 21(5): 18-24

Zhao Yanyan, Qin Bing, Che Wanxiang, et al. Appraisal Expression Recognition Based on Syntactic Path [J]. Journal of Software. 2011, 22(5): 887-898

Zhao Yanyan, Qin Bing, Liu Ting. Sentiment Analysis [J]. Journal of Software. 2010, 21(8): 1834-1848

Product Name Classification for Product Instance Distinction

Hye-Jin Min
CS Department, KAIST
Daejeon, Republic of Korea
hjmin@nlp.kaist.ac.kr

Jong C. Park
CS Department, KAIST
Daejeon, Republic of Korea
park@cs.kaist.ac.kr

Abstract

Product names with a temporal cue in a product review often refer to several product instances purchased at different times. Previous approaches to product entity recognition and temporal information analysis do not take into account such temporal cues and thus fail to distinguish different product instances. We propose to formulate the resolution of such product names as a classification problem by utilizing time expressions, event features and other temporal cues for a classifier in two stages, detecting the existence of such temporal cues and identifying the purchase time. The empirical results show that term-based features and existing event-based features together enhance the performance of product instance distinction.

1 Introduction

Traditional work on product entity recognition has been conducted on competing products for comparative opinion mining from forum data (Jindal and Liu, 2006; Ding et al., 2009; Li et al., 2010), but not on the same type of products purchased at different times, thus failing to distinguish products at the instance level. The use of temporal information would help to make such distinction, but previous studies of temporal information have been made only for the detection and determination of temporal relations between time expressions and events, through the relevant shared tasks, or TempEval-1 and TempEval-2 tasks (Pustejovsky et al., 2003; Verhagen et al., 2009; Verhagen et al., 2010), but not for the distinction of products.

There is evidence that temporal relations between product instances of the same type are found quite often in product reviews, to give rise to important differences in the respective opinion of the reviewer. Consider Examples (1) and (2)[1] below, with two product names *other Levis 501s* and *these new ones* that refer to the product instances that the customer bought. While the former refers to the past purchase, the latter refers to the recent purchase.

(1) My husband has [*other Levis 501s*]$_a$ and [*these new ones*]$_b$ are different in the weight of fabric (light), (…) We are not happy with *these jeans*.

(2) a. I don't wear boots and I wear *these jeans* when I ride my bike.
b. *Jeans* were exactly like one purchased from Khols or Sears.
c. I'm done with buying *jeans* online.

Resolving such different product instances properly is found crucial to identifying long-term customers, among others, whose opinions count at least as important as those of human annotators for influential reviews (Min and Park, 2012). Moreover, it is also crucial to identifying such long-term customer's sentiment change over several purchases of the same product (cf. Min and Park, 2012).

First, we note that sortal anaphoric expressions such as *these jeans* in (1) indicate the presence of a temporal cue but may also refer to the whole product as shown in (2a). We also note that the product name without a demonstrative or definite article as shown in (2b) may refer to the purchased

[1] The examples are taken from the reviews at Amazon.com.

product instance, unlike the one without temporal cue in (2c) that refers to a generic object.

We thus argue that, for the proper resolution of such product names, it is important to see if the given product name bears temporal information and to identify the temporal order among the product instances. We propose to formulate the resolution of such product names as a classification problem, by utilizing time expressions, event features and other temporal cues as relevant features for a classifier. We construct the classifier in two stages, first detecting the existence of such temporal cues and then detecting the recency of the purchase time. The proposed features are utilized in conjunction with the event-based temporal features in the TempEval task and the experience mining task.

We employ a support vector machine (SVM) classifier with cost-sensitive learning by taking minor classes into consideration. The empirical results show that the term-based features and existing event-based features can be made to work in different combinations to enhance the overall performance for product instance distinction.

We also apply our results of product name classification to two applications. One is to classify product reviews with respect to a customers' sentiment change (cf. Min and Park, 2012). The other is to automatically rate product reviews based on the detected sentiment in the given review. Our results show that the results of the product name classification are important for distinguishing the sentiment towards the recent purchase from the sentiments towards other purchases in the past.

The rest of the paper is organized as follows. Section 2 reviews the related work. Section 3 examines product names with temporal information. Section 4 compares event and time expression features with term-based temporal features. Section 5 shows the classification results and Section 6 discusses classification errors. Section 7 shows the applications and Section 8 concludes the paper with further work.

2 Related Work

Product entity recognition has been conducted to identify comparative opinions between competing products. Jindal and Liu (2006) proposed label sequential rules to detect comparable entities based on association rule mining. Ding and colleagues (2009) added the process of filtering with pruning patterns about brand and model names for product names of comparable entities. Li and colleagues (2010) used weakly-supervised bootstrapping to detect comparable entities with sequential seeds derived from typical comparative questions. Our work is slightly different from the previous work in that each instance purchased at a time is regarded as an independent 'entity'. Thus, the temporal information about each candidate target works as an essential clue as compared to the previous work. We will discuss why we did not apply the approach in the previous work in Section 5.

Systems were developed for TempEval tasks by utilizing features from time expressions and events. For tasks C and E, TRIOS (UzZaman and Allen, 2010) achieved the best performance on English news data. The system employed a Markov Logic Network-based classifier with feature-based first-order logic formulae. The utilized features are event-related, timex-related, and TLINK event-time signal. The system JU_CSE_TEMP that showed the second best performance (Kolaya et al., 2010) also utilized a similar time expression and event features for a CRF-based classifier. As events in the news reports are mostly in the form of a verb phrase, they focused on verb-related clues for event features.

Researches to mining experiences in user-generated web documents addressed the issue of distinguishing 'experience sentences' from others. Park and colleagues (2010) proposed a discrimination method based on the linguistic properties of the mentioned events in such sentences, including verb class, tense, aspect, mood, modality and experiencer. Since we focus on classification at the term level, we utilize not only time expression and event-based features but also term-based temporal features.

3 Product Names

3.1 Temporal Class vs. Atemporal Class

We use temporal class to include product names whose instances are purchased and used by the customer of a given review (Ex. (3) ~ (8)). We also use atemporal class to include product names that refer to generic objects or those with unknown purchase time (Ex. (9) ~ (13)). One might think the product name in (3) should be classified as the atemporal class because it refers to the brand and the model name of the given product. However, we perceive that it also implies that the customer has been wearing the product for such a long time if we look at the time expression 'for 22 years' and 'since I was 16'. Since the purpose of the classification in this paper is to identify long-term customers who have purchased the product several times, we classify such name as the temporal class. On the contrary, the product name with 'no article' such as (10) or (12) should be classified as the atemporal class as it is just used in order to describe a generic object not an product instance.

Temporal Class

(3) I have been wearing *Levis 501* since I was 16 - which means that for 22 years I keep returning to the classic, and it always fits just right.

(4) In the past (at least up until 2 or 3 years ago) my husband would have about *4 pairs of jeans*.

(5) This is [*the second pair of levis*]$_a$ I ordered through amazon. It was identical to [*the first pair*]$_b$ except the first was made in Lesotho the second in Egypt.

(6) Now, I'm doomed for eternity to constantly checking the back of *my other two pairs of jeans* every time I wear them to make sure there isn't another big rip in them.

(7) Currently I have over *10 pairs* that have never been worn because there is no quality control at Levi Strauss.

(8) *My oldest pair*, which is holding up well, is over 10 years old.

Atemporal Class

(9) No matter how tall or short you are, these are *the best jeans* you can buy.

(10) *Real 501s* are made of 14 oz canvas-like material.

(11) Of course this is simply a matter of personal preference on how you want *your jeans* to fit.

(12) I will not buy *501s* again unless they are from trusted chain retail store.

(13) [*These good old 501s*]$_a$ with their slightly-inconvenient button-fly are [*the best-looking jeans*]$_b$ on a middle-aged body I've found.

3.2 Recent Purchase vs. Past Purchase

Unlike relatively formal documents such as news reports, most of the temporal information mentioned in a product review is somewhat vague, as in 'a few months ago'. It thus makes sense to consider simply two sub-temporal classes, or 'recent purchase' and 'past purchase' subclasses, in order to tell apart whether or not the customer has experiences in the product over an extended period of time. Some names refer to both the recent purchases and past purchases, requiring compound class as well.

Recent Purchase (P_r): includes product names that refer to the product instances that are most recently purchased (Ex. (1b), (5a)).

Past Purchase (P_p): includes product names that refer to the product instances purchased prior to the most recent purchase (Ex. (1a), (4), (5b), (6), (8)).

Recent&Past Purchase ($P_{r\&p}$): includes (3), (7).

3.3 Annotation

In order to establish the proof-of-concept, we crawled 382 product reviews of men's jeans from Amazon.com. Note that there is no annotated corpus yet for product names that bear temporal information. Two annotators performed the task of annotating the text span for product names and the class for each name. The inter-annotator agreement score (kappa statistic) for the classification is substantially high (0.72). The disagreements resulted mostly from names with no articles, which made it ambiguous to determine whether they have temporal information or not. After setting-up more fine-grained guidelines for such cases, the annotators adjusted them together. Table 1 shows the distribution of the annotated product names.[2]

Temporal			Atemporal
P_r	P_p	$P_{r\&p}$	
326	63	51	390
440			
830			

Table 1: Distribution of product names

4 Linguistic Features for Classification

4.1 Temporal Features in the Literature

Time Expressions:
past duration/simple past/present

Following the previous work on the TempEval-2 task C (UzZaman and Allen, 2010; Kolaya et al., 2010), we utilized types and values of time

[2] The annotated data is available at http://nlp.kaist.ac.kr/resources/.

expression as the basic features. For example, the 'duration' type of expression such as 'for 22 years' as in (3) can work as an important clue for the 'recent & past purchase' subclass. For the present purpose, we only need to know each expression's type and its symbolic value (e.g., past duration instead of 'DURATION' and 'P22Y' for 'for 22 years'). Hence, we used the 'duration' relation for product use and the 'before' relation between several purchases among the relations defined in the Timebank Corpus (Pustejovsky et al., 2003). We re-classified them into three types as shown in Table 2, based on TYPE/VALUE information in the <TIMEX> tag, and set each type as the feature with the value either true or false.

TIMEX2/TIMEX3		POS	Type	Examples
TYPE	VALUE	IN/RB		
DURATION	PNY	for, until	Past duration	for 22 years
DATE	PRESENT_REF;	-	Present	Currently, now
	PND, PNW	in/ago		A few days ago
	PAST_REF;	-	Simple past	before
	PNM, PNY	in/ago		2 years ago

Table 2: Types of time expression

Event Features: We adopted the event features for the TempEval-2 C and such as event class, tense, aspect, and polarity. We also adopted several verb-related features including verb class, tense, aspect, mood, modality and experiencer in order to determine whether the given sentence is experience-revealing or not (Park et al., 2010), because the first stage of the classification into temporal and atemporal classes in the present work is similar to their work in that the temporal aspect of events is considered as important for detecting mentions about the actual experiences.

In addition to the features adopted from the previous work, we considered syntactic and semantic types of verbs, because the whole phrase including the verb and the name can be a generic object as shown in (2c), or because copular verbs are frequently used to express opinions, which characterize the products as shown in (9). Since we focus on classification at the term level, unlike at the sentence level in their work, we utilize three types of verbs: 1) the verb type taking the given name as an argument (v1, 'have' in (7)); 2) the verb type which functions in a relative clause modifying the name (v2, 'worn' in (7)); and 3) the matrix verb to which the name belongs (v3, 'have' in (7)).

1) Tense & Aspect:
present/past/future/present perfect/past perfect/ present progressive/past progressive/ present perfect progressive/past perfect progressive

Tense and aspect information of a verb can also be an important clue because instances already purchased would be mentioned in the sentence with the past tense and the perfect aspect. For example, the tense and aspect of the v1 type verbs as shown in (3) and (4) and those of the v2 type verb as shown in (5) indicate that the product names are classified into the temporal class. By contrast, future and present tenses are more likely to suggest that the relevant names refer to generic objects, as shown in (10) and (12).

2) Syntactic type: gerund/to-inf/general verb

We set the indication of whether the v1 type verb is the main verb or not as another feature because the whole phrase including the verb and the term can be a generic object as shown in (2c).

3) Semantic type:
purchase/possess/purchasing process/ copular verbs/emotional expressions

While verbs such as 'purchase', 'possess' or emotional expressions are most likely used in the sentence that contains product names in the temporal class as shown in (4), copular verbs are frequently used to express opinions, which describe the product instances as shown in (9).

4) Event class:
OCCURRENCE/I_ACTION/I_STATE/STATE/ REPORTING/PERCEPTION/ASPECTUAL

The event class of a verb may also affect the classification of the given product name into the temporal or atemporal class. For example, events such as 'know' or 'want' (I_STATE) as shown in (11) are related to the atemporal class. On the other hand, events such as 'buy', 'have', or 'wear' (OCCURRENCE) as shown in (3) and (4) are related to the temporal class. We semi-automatically annotated the event class of each verb in our corpus by following the event annotation guidelines of the TempEval-2 task.[3]

[3] http://www.timeml.org/tempeval2/tempeval2-trial/guidelines/EventGuidelines-050409.pdf

5) Event polarity: positive/negative

Negation often reveals the product name to be classified into the atemporal class such as a generic object *original Levis* in the sentence "all they sell are Levis Signature jeans, and not *original Levis*." We set either the positive or negative value depending on the presence of negation about the verb.

Experiencer:
I or we/you/3rd person/product/ETC

We adopted the experiencer feature from Park and others (2010) but we further distinguished 1st person subject from 2nd person subject and 3rd person subject with the intuition that the sentence with 2nd person or 3rd person is likely to contain a suggestion for potential customers as shown in (11).

If clause: true/false

The clause with the *if* or *unless* marker mostly expresses condition or supposition, and hence, the product name in such a clause may refer to the atemporal type as shown in (12). We set either true or false depending on the existence of the *if* or *unless* clause in the sentence.

4.2 Term-based Temporal Features

We also consider term-based features. Customers may use specific cue words (e.g., *these new ones*) and/or ordinal words (e.g., *the second pair I bought)* in order to distinguish a product instance from others that are purchased at different times. We also add clues for identifying the coreference relations between the product names (Soon et al., 2001).

Temporal cue words: recent purchase-related cue /past purchase-related cue

Adjectives within a product name or adverbs modifying the verb that takes the name as an argument furnish the given product name's temporal information (e.g., *new* for *these new ones* as in (1b), *currently* for *10 pairs* as in (7), and *oldest* for *my oldest pair* in (8)). In order to avoid counting the word with a different sense in the given context such as *these good old 501s* as in (13a), we filter out such cases from a bi-gram model for our corpus. For each type of cue, its value is set to either true or false.

Quantity-based cue words:
(one, two, several)/(first, second, nth)

Cardinal or ordinal numbers in the given product name (e.g., (4) and (5), respectively) may also work as good clues for the membership in the temporal class. In particular, ordinal numbers may also suggest temporal orders among several product names as shown in Example (5). The name *the second pair* refers to a more recently purchased instance as compared to the name *the first pair*, which obviously refers to the past purchase. After detecting cardinal or ordinal number words in the given product name, we set the categorical value of the cardinal and ordinal number features.

Determiner/JJ: this/the/a(n)/(any)other/another

The product names containing 'this'/'these' may refer to the recent purchase(s) (e.g., (1b)), and the product names containing an indefinite article 'a'/'an' or the definite article 'the' may also be used to indicate an instance of a given product (e.g., (5)). The determiner 'another' or the adjective 'other' is often used for separating one instance from others, and hence, the instances mentioned in the same review with different temporal information can be disambiguated (e.g., *other Levis 501s* in (1a) and (6)). For each determiner or adjective, its value is set to either true or false.

Possessive pronouns: my/your/his/her/their

The possessive pronoun 'my' indicates that the given product name is more likely to refer to the instance that the customer possesses currently (e.g., *my other two pairs of jeans* in (6) and *my oldest pair* in (8)). On the other hand, the possessive pronoun 'your' indicates that it is more likely to refer either to a generic object or to the instance with an unknown purchase time (e.g., *your jeans* in (11)). For each pronoun type, its value is set to either true or false.

Keywords for an instance or an entire product: instance/class/brand/model

While keywords such as 'pair' or 'item' (e.g., (4)) are somewhat likely to indicate temporal information of the given product name, keywords such as 'product' or the product category 'jeans' or 'pants' are less likely to indicate such temporal information (e.g., (11)). In addition, the brand name and the model name, for example, 'Levis' and '501', respectively, in the name *Levis 501*, can be utilized as keywords for an entire product or an instance. We set four feature values of instance, class (an entire product), brand name and model name to either true or false.

Argument type:
(object, subject, complement, object of preposition)

Our intuition is that opinion sentences are mostly expressed with either adjectives or descriptive product names so that copular verbs are frequently used, whereas experience sentences are mostly expressed with general verbs. This suggests that some types of argument of verbs such as complement or subject serve to describe a particular instance or generic object (e.g., (9), (10)). On the other hand, the object term of a verb (e.g., 'wear', 'purchase' or 'possess') denotes or refers to the instance with temporal information (e.g., (3), (7)). We use one of the categories as the feature value for the argument type.

Table 3 summarizes the term-based temporal features discussed in this section.

Type	Sub types: values	Examples
Temporal cue words (cue)	recent purchase-cue/past purchase cue: {true, false}	new (1b), currently (7), oldest (8)
Quantity-based cue words (quant)	cardinal: {one, two, several}/ordinal: {first, second, nth}	4 (4), second (5a)
DET/JJ (co-refer)	this/the/a(n)/other/another: {true, false}	other (1a), these (1b)
PRP$ (co-refer)	my/your/his/her/their: {true, false}	my (8); your (11)
Instance/ Product (co-refer)	instance/class/brand/model: {true, false}	pair, (4), jeans (11)
Argument type (arg)	argument type: {object, subject, complement, object of preposition}	compl (9), subj (10), obj (4)

Table 3: Product name-based Temporal Features

To detect the syntactic features discussed above, such as tense, aspect, polarity, argument types of product names and syntactic types of verb, we utilized the dependency parse tree from the Stanford parser (Klein and Manning, 2003). For time expressions, we employed the rule-based time expression tagger[4] which covers time expressions according to the TIMEX2 2001 guidelines. For the semantic types of verb, we manually collected frequent verbs related to purchase and emotional expressions.

[4] http://fofoca.mitre.org/taggers/timex2_taggers.html

5 Experiment

5.1 Experimental Setup

We used annotated product names for the classification experiment since our main focus is on classifying the product names into suitable temporal classes. For comparison, we conducted an experiment on product name extraction based on a parser with a regular grammar (RegexpParser in the NLTK; Bird and Loper, 2004). For the experiment, we also utilized predefined product name patterns for pruning unrelated candidates from the NP chunks. We achieved the F1 score of 88.1%. We believe that the performance can be improved further by bootstrapping the patterns, but this process is left as future work.

We employed the LIBSVM toolkit with RBF kernel for both stages of product name classification (Chang and Lin, 2011). We used annotated product names for the experiment. As Table 1 shows, the distribution of the product names in the temporal class is skewed. To improve the performance with such a skewed class distribution, we incorporated cost-sensitive learning for the second stage of the classification (McCarthy et al., 2005). We empirically varied the penalty cost factors for minor classes (P_p and $P_{r\&p}$).

We used the prediction accuracy, precision, recall and F1 scores for each class by 10-fold cross validation for the first stage. For the second stage, we used the geometric mean (G-mean), which is known as a good indicator for the performance as it is independent of the data distribution between classes (Kubat and Matwin, 1997). The G-mean score can be calculated as follows.

Actual \ Predicted	Positive	Negative
Positive	TP	FN
Negative	FP	TN

$$ACC^{+} = \frac{TP}{TP+FN} \qquad ACC^{-} = \frac{TN}{FP+TN}$$

$$G\text{-}mean = \sqrt{\left(ACC^{+} \cdot ACC^{-}\right)}$$

For the comparison with the previous work on product entity recognition, we carefully implemented a class sequential pattern mining (CSR) method (Ding et al., 2009). We considered the adjectives as cue words such as 'new', 'previous' and the nouns for the product (e.g., pants) and the instance (e.g., pair). The length of the sequence is 11. The mined patterns cut by the threshold 0.01, 0.005, 0.001, 0.0005, 0.0001 are 5, 10, 35, 52, and 23 respectively from the overall 895 patterns. The example pattern are 'DT ENT/NNS' (threshold: 0.01; e.g., the jeans) and 'DT ENT/NNS IN NN NNS' (threshold: 0.001; e.g., these jeans in size 34x30). However, such patterns are not so promising for our purpose because of the following reasons. First, the high-score patterns are very short (the length is less than 3) and simple, so newly discovered names must be short as well. In fact, the pattern 'DT ENT/NNS IN NN NNS' is more helpful than 'DT ENT/NNS' in spite of its lower support score. One of the reasons why shorter patterns get high score is the CSR depends on frequency when generating a new pattern from the current pattern. Second, for our purpose we split the keyword sets into two sub sets for each subclass (P_r and P_p). However, due to the small amount of sequence data sets for the P_p, the minded patterns are not effective. Thus, we argue that the mined patterns by CSR are not that effective for product name distinction.

Instead, we employed the CRF++ toolkit[5] for a CRF-based classifier that has been popular for the named entity recognition (NER) task. The CRF-based classifier was also compared with Ding and colleagues' work (2009). We regarded the co-refer features in Table 3 as the term-based baseline feature sets.

5.2 Classification Results

Table 5 shows the first stage of the classification result. The system achieved the best averaged accuracy 79.0% (ANOVA, $F(6,63) = 6.03$; $p = .000$). The best F1 scores for the temporal class and the atemporal class are 80.2% (ANOVA, $F(6,63) = 7.14$; $p = .000$) and 77.4% (ANOVA, $F(6,63) = 5.43$; $p = .000$), respectively. As for the second stage of the classification, the best G-mean scores for the P_r and P_p subclasses, and the P_r and $P_{r\&p}$ subclasses are 0.74 (ANOVA, $F(7,72) = 4.17$; $p = .001$) and 0.82 (ANOVA, $F(6,63) = 2.43$; $p = .035$) when the costs are set to 4 and 5, respectively, as shown in Figure 1. The best combination of features for classifying into the P_p subclass is different from that for classifying into the $P_{r\&p}$ subclass. This suggests that while the contribution of time expressions and event features is critical to distinguishing product names in the P_r subclass from those in the $P_{r\&p}$ subclass, time expressions and term-based features are critical to distinguishing product names in the P_r subclass from those in the P_p subclass. Overall, combining time expressions, event-based features and term-based features is found to enhance the performance of temporal cue identification and temporal instance distinction.

Table 4 shows the classification results by the CRF-based classifier. The scores for the P_p subclass or $P_{r\&p}$ class are quite low. These results imply that the temporal information-based features are crucial to such subclasses. This also happens to the SVM-based classifier with the same feature sets (Term-based Base) as shown in Table 5 and Figure 1.

Class\Score	P	R	F1
P_r	60.9	59.4	60.1
P_p	27.8	9.6	14.0
$P_{r\&p}$	35.7	13.4	19.4
Atemporal	61.8	48.8	54.4
Overall	59.9	48.2	53.4

Table 4: The classification results by the CRF-based classifier.

6 Error Analysis and Discussion

We analyzed errors from each stage of classification and listed major errors related to temporal features as follows.

Misclassified by dominant temporal features: The dominant temporal features may trigger misclassification into atemporal class as shown in (14) and (15).

(14) Levis have been around forever and will continue to be because it is a great product.

(15) Starting almost a year ago it is an absolute fact that *these jeans* no longer hold up for years the way they used to.

Although present perfect tense and simple past time expression were detected, the names do not refer to the particular product instance that the customer of the review purchased. In this case, either the argument or the syntactic type of a verb should be taken into account with more weight.

[5] http://crfpp.googlecode.com/

Feature set	Temporal class			Atemporal class			Acc.
	P	R	F1	P	R	F1	
Base (timex + event features: v1, v2)	72.3	65.6	68.6	65.1	71.5	68.0	68.4
Base + cue	74.9	66.8	70.4	66.6	74.3	70.1	70.3
Base + cue + quant	74.6	67.9	70.9	67.2	73.6	70.0	70.6
Base + cue + quant + arg	71.1	75.4.	73.0	70.5	65.1	67.4	70.6
Base + cue + quant + arg + co-refer	**80.5**	**80.6**	**80.2**	**78.3**	**77.1**	**77.4**	**79.0**
Term-based base (co-refer)	68.3	76.1	71.8	69.4	59.7	63.7	68.4
Timex + term-based (co-refer + cue + quant)	74.3	76.3	75.2	72.2	69.7	70.8	73.2

Table 5: The classification results for temporal cue identification

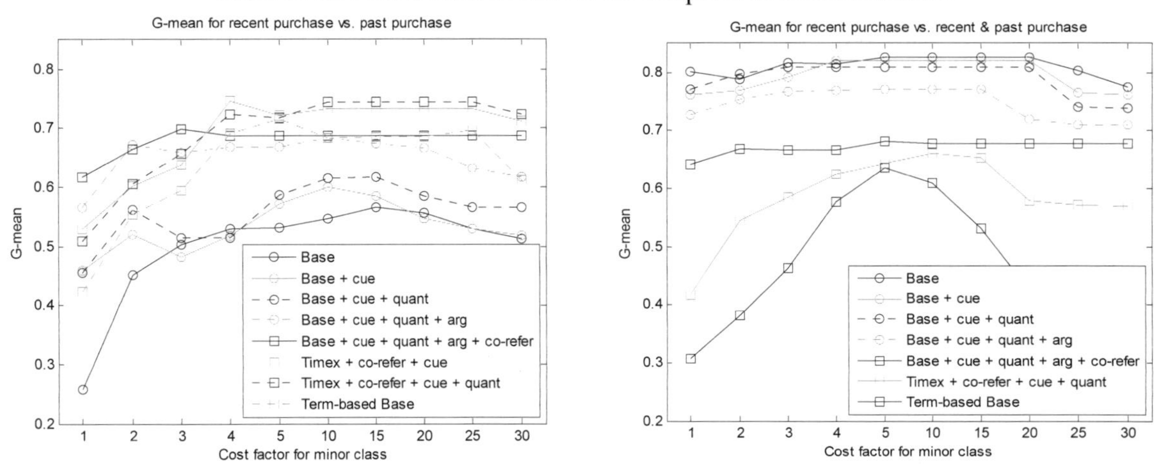

Figure 1: The classification results for temporal instance distinction (G-mean)

Contrastive relation between past purchase and recent purchase in the same sentence: The present work used the feature values extracted for each product name only for the given product name. However, the following case of errors as shown in (16) would be handled properly if the feature values for one product name are shared with its adjacent product name. Contrastive words (e.g., 'new' vs. 'worn out') and the syntactic structure of the sentence (e.g., 'infinitive') indicate that two given names may refer to different instances.

(16) To sum it up, these were *some **new** pants* to replace *some **worn out** ones*.

Chained coreference relation: We did not consider the coreference relation between adjacent product names due to the rarity of such cases. However, if the first mentioned product name has a coreference relation with all the following product names as shown in (17), the classification for each name may not be meaningful.

(17) Until this week, I had been wearing *levis* all my life and in recent years was only wearing *501s* for all occasions. Currently I have over *10 pairs* that have never been worn (…) The labels all match in size however *some of the jeans* are at least a full size smaller at the waist and *some of the pairs* have the correct waist but very narrow legs.

In order to deal with contrastive relations and coreference relations properly, we may have to incorporate the pair or cluster-based term classification model that shares features among mentioned expressions, determining the degree of which is left as future work.

7 Applications

7.1 Sentiment Change over Time

An old customer with long-term experiences sometimes expresses her sentiment change over product reviews as shown in Example (18). While customer A in (18a) expresses her sentiment change on the given product, customer B in (18b) reports that his sentiment on the product has been positive.

(18) a. My husband has *other Levis 501*s and *these new ones* are different in the weight of fabric (light), fit (tighter in the leg and crotch) and color of stitching (white). (…) They are made in Mexico, *his older ones* are made in

Colombia (…) We are not happy with *these pants* but have already washed and used them.
b. I have been wearing *501s* since I can remember. These are just as good as *my original ones*. (…) hey they are 501s hard to go wrong with these.

In (18a), we see that the sentiment towards the past purchase (e.g., *other Levis 501s*, *his older ones*) is positive but that the one towards the recent purchase (e.g., *these new ones*, *these pants*) is negative. Based on this difference in sentiment with respect to product instance, we can identify such sentiment change expressed in a product review by simple heuristic rules. For example, if the major polarity towards P_r is 'Negative' and the major polarity towards P_p is 'Positive' in a given review we classify it as the review with a sentiment change 'positive to negative'.

In order to apply some heuristic rules to sentiment change identification, we performed product-wise sentiment detection (cf. Min and Park, 2012). As for target detection, we utilized our results of product name classification. As for polarity classification, we utilized the 'compositionality-based polarity propagation' method (Moilanen and Pulman, 2007; Min and Park, 2011). As for target-sentiment association, in order to determine whether each candidate target is associated with the detected sentiment, we applied the association rules in order to prevent a generic object from being associated with the sentiment (cf. Min and Park, 2012).

Table 6 shows the classification results in the same data sets as used in product name classification. We believe that these results can be utilized to cluster customer reviews in a novel way to help customers make their decision more wisely on re-purchase as well as on their first purchase.

Sentiment Change	P	R	F
PtoN	0.69	0.48	0.56
PtoP	0.37	0.91	0.53
No change	0.96	0.89	0.92

Table 6: The classification results of sentiment change[6]

After analyzing the major errors, we observed that sentiment detection regarding target product names at the instance level is crucial to the class PtoN. However, we also realized that detecting the existence of the product names in the $P_{r\&p}$ subclass is also significant for the class of PtoP, (i.e., 28% of the instances require the detection of such clues for correct classification).

7.2 Review Rating with Enhanced Credibility

Based on the results of identifying the sentiment change, we implemented an automatic review rating system. The system assigns +1 to the clause/sentence in the 'Positive' class and -1 to the clause/sentence in the 'Negative' class with respect to a product instance. It then calculates the total score for the rating by applying positive weights to the 'Positive' class if the sentiment is maintained (i.e., PtoP) and negative weights to the 'Negative' class if the sentiment is changed (i.e., PtoN). We compared the performance of our system with that of the baseline system. The baseline system calculates the rating based on the detected sentiment in each clause without utilizing the results of the product instance distinction or the sentiment change identification. We showed two ratings calculated by both systems to 6 evaluators and asked them to choose the more credible rating. We tested 140 reviews of 7 products (20 reviews of each product; we randomly selected 20 reviews from the reviews of each product except the review cases where the two ratings are even.). The ratings calculated by our system are chosen more often than the ratings by the baseline system. Overall, the ratings by our system were preferred (statistically significant at the level 0.001). We believe that our rating system is considered more credible because of product instance distinction and sentiment change identification.

8 Conclusion

In this paper, we proposed linguistically meaningful novel features for classifying product names at the instance level in customer reviews about a particular product with respect to the

[6] We annotated a sentiment change with the code '$S(P_p)toS(P_r)$', where $S(P_p)$ is the sentiment toward the past purchase, $S(P_r)$ the sentiment towards the recent purchase, and P denotes positive, and N negative. The inter-annotator agreement is 0.734 (Kappa; p<.001). The reason why 'NtoP' and 'NtoN' categories are missing is that we found only one or two examples classified as in these categories from the sample reviews. We think that the customers with such experiences tend to express their opinions in the forum sites rather than in online shopping web sites. We leave this issue as future work.

instance's temporal information. We formulated the problem as a classification problem with respect to the existence of temporal cues and the recency of the purchase time. The results show that combining time expressions, event-based features and term-based features does enhance the performance of product name classification with a statistical significance. Two applications, 'sentiment change identification' and 'automatic review rating', also show that the results of product instance classification are useful. For future work, we will impose further constraints against penalizing minority. We will also look into effective clues for handling more complex cases such as contrastive and coreference relations.

Acknowledgements

This work was supported in part by the National Research Foundation of Korea (NRF) grant funded by the Korea government (MEST) (No.2011-0018262), and in part by the Intelligent Robotics Development Program, one of the 21st Century Frontier R&D Programs funded by the Ministry of Knowledge Economy of Korea. We thank the three anonymous reviewers for helpful comments and insightful suggestions.

References

Steven Bird, and Edward Loper. 2004. NLTK: The Natural Language Toolkit, In *Proceedings of the ACL demonstration session.* pages 214-217.

Chih-Chung Chang and Chih-Jen Lin. 2011. LIBSVM: A library for support vector machines. *ACM Transactions on Intelligent Systems and Technology*, 2(3): 1-27, http://www.csie.ntu.edu.tw/~cjlin/libsvm.

Xiaowen Ding, Bing Liu, and Lei Zang. 2009. Entity discovery and assignment for opinion mining applications, In *Proceeding of KDD'09,* Paris, France.

Nithin Jindal and Bing Liu. 2006. Mining Comparative Sentences and Relations, In *Proceedings of AAAI*, pages 1331-1336.

Dan Klein and Christopher D. Manning. 2003. Accurate Unlexicalized Parsing. In *Proceedings of the 41th ACL*, pages 423-430.

Anup Kumar Kolya, Asif Ekbal, and Sivaji Bandyopadhyay. 2010. JU_CSE_TEMP: A First Step towards Evaluating Events, Time Expressions and Temporal Relations, In *Proceedings of SemEval-2010,* pages 345-350, Uppsala, Sweden.

Miroslav Kubat and Stan Matwin. 1997. Addressing the curse of imbalanced data sets: One-sided sampling. In *Proceedings of the 14th ICML*, pages 179-186.

Shasha Li, Chin-Yew Lin, Young-In Song, and Zhoujun Li. 2010. Comparable Entity Mining from Comparative Questions, In *Proceedings of the 48th ACL*, pages 650–658, Uppsala, Sweden.

Kate McCarthy, Bibi Zabar, and Gary Weiss. 2005. Does Cost-Sensitive Learning Beat Sampling for Classifying Rare Classes?, In *Proceedings of UBDM'05*, pages 69-77, Chicago, Illinois, USA.

Hye-Jin Min and Jong C. Park. 2011. Detecting and Blocking False Sentiment Propagation, In *Proceedings of IJCNLP*, pages 354–362.

Hye-Jin Min and Jong C. Park. 2012. Identifying Helpful Reviews Based on Customer's Mentions about Experiences, *Expert Systems With Applications*, 39(15): 11830-11838, Elsevier.

Hye-Jin Min and Jong C. Park. 2012. Product-wise Sentiment Detection for Sentiment Change Identification (draft).

Karo Moilanen and Stephen Pulman. 2007. Sentiment Composition, In *Proceedings of RANLP*, pages 378-382, Borovets, Bulgaria.

Keun Chan Park, Yoonjae Jeong, and Sung Hyoon Myaeng. 2010. Detecting Experience from Weblogs, In *Proceedings of the 48th ACL*, pages 1464-1472.

James Pustejovsky, Jose Castano, Robert, Ingria, Roser Sauri, Robert Gaizauskas, Andrea Setzer, and Graham Katz. 2003. TimeML: Robust Specification of Event and Temporal Expressions in Text, *the 5th International Workshop on Computational Semantics*.

Wee Meng Soon, Hwee Tou Ng, and Daniel Chung Yong Lim. 2001. A machine learning approach to coreference resolution of noun phrases. *Computational Linguistics*, 27(4): 521–544.

Naushad UzZaman and James F. Allen. 2010. TRIPS and TRIOS System for TempEval-2: Extracting Temporal Information from Text, *In Proceedings of SemEval-2010*, pages 276-283, Uppsala, Sweden.

Marc Verhagen, Robert Gaizauskas, Frank Schilder, Mark Hepple, Jessica Moszkowicz, and James Pustejovsky. 2009. The tempeval challenge: identifying temporal relations in text. *Language Resources and Evaluation*, 43(2): 161-179.

Marc Verhagen, Roser Saurí, Tommaso Caselli, and James Pustejovsky. 2010. SemEval-2010 Task 13: TempEval-2, In Proceedings of the 5th SemEval-2010, pages 57-52, Uppsala, Sweden.

Automatic Detection of Gender and Number Agreement Errors in Spanish Texts Written by Japanese Learners

Maria del Pilar Valverde Ibañez
Faculty of Foreign Languages
Aichi Prefectural University
1522-3 Ibaragasama, Nagakute-shi
Aichi, 480-1198, Japan
`valverde@for.aichi-pu.ac.jp`

Akira Ohtani
Faculty of Informatics
Osaka Gakuin University
2-36-1 Kishibe-minami, Suita-shi
Osaka, 564-8511, Japan
`ohtani@ogu.ac.jp`

Abstract

This paper describes the creation of a grammar to automatically detect agreement errors (gender and number) in Spanish texts written by Japanese learners. The grammar has been written using the Constraint Grammar formalism (Karlsson et al., 1995), and uses as input the morphosyntactic analysis provided by the Spanish parser HISPAL (Bick, 2006). For developing and testing the grammar, a learner corpus of 25,000 words has been manually annotated with agreement error tags. Both the grammar and the data from the corpus serve us to draw some conclusions about the characteristics of agreement errors in Japanese learners' Spanish.

1 Introduction

In this paper we describe the creation of a grammar to automatically detect agreement errors -in gender and number- in Spanish texts written by Japanese learners.

Automatic detection of grammatical learner errors can be used for the automatic annotation of learner corpora and for the creation of intelligent computer-assisted language learning systems (Heift and Schulze, 2007). Such tools can benefit both teachers -who will be able to study learner errors and the language acquisition process more systematically- and learners -who can foster their language learning with the help of automatic tools and improved traditional language materials-.

There are two reasons why we focus on agreement errors. First, for Japanese students, agreement is a problematic aspect for learning Spanish and indeed agreement errors are significantly more frequent among Japanese learners than among speakers of other languages (Fernández, 1997). Second, agreement errors in texts can be identified and corrected straightforwardly by a native speaker, unlike other type of errors like article and preposition usage, for example, where annotator agreement may be problematic.

While there is a substantial research on detecting grammatical errors in Learners' English, Spanish has received little attention, probably because of the lack of freely available large learner corpora (Lozano, 2009). For the construction of the grammar, we have manually annotated with agreement error tags a fragment of 25,000 words from the CORANE learner corpus (Mancera et al., 2001) and to control false positives of the grammar, we have also used native corpora: 22,000 words for development amd 12,000 words for test.

The paper is organized as follows. Section 2 deals with the characteristics of gender and number agreement in Spanish and the coverage of the grammar, section 3 deals with the development phase (the corpus, grammar formalism and design principles), section 4 gives the results and analysis of the evaluation, section 5 studies the data in the learner corpus and section 6 presents the conclusions.

2 Gender and number agreement in Spanish

Agreement, defined as the condition of having the same number or gender, serves to relate and identify lexically and syntactically the agreeing words.[1] In Spanish, for a structure to be grammatically correct, the inflecting words involved in a head-dependent syntactic relation must agree in gender and number.

Nouns can be classified into two categories, masculine and feminine, and the gender of the noun determines the gender of its dependendents. Here follow some examples of agreement between a noun and an adjective (1 to 4).

(1) Coche pequeño.
car.MASC small.MASC.SING
'small car'

(2) Coches pequeños.
cars.MASC small.MASC.PLUR
'small cars'

(3) Bicicleta pequeña.
bicycle.FEM small.FEM.SING
'small bicycle'

(4) Bicicletas pequeñas.
bicycles.FEM small.FEM.PLUR
'small bicycles'

(5) chiisai kuruma.
small car
'small car'.

(6) chiisai jitensha.
small bicycle
'small bicycle'.

Examples 1 and 2 show gender and number agreement with a masculine noun, while 2 and 3 show agreement with a feminine noun. Since Japanese does not have number agreement, 1 and 2 correspond to 5 in Japanese, and 3 and 4 correspond to 6. As for gender agreement, the Spanish adjective "pequeño" ('small') changes its ending to agree with a masculine noun in 1 and 2 and a feminine noun in 3 and 4, while in Japanese the noun nor the adjective have gender (the adjective "chiisai" is the same in 5 and 6).

Our grammar contains rules to detect gender and/or number errors. With regard to gender, in Spanish the following word classes have gender: determiners, nouns, pronouns, adjectives and participle verbs. Our grammar checks the following gender agreement cases:

1. Agreement within the noun phrase: between the head (noun or pronoun) and its dependents (the determiner, the adjective and the past participle).

2. Agreement within the clause:

   (a) Between the subject and the subject complement (adjective or past participle) in attributive clauses.

   (b) Between the subject and the past participle verb in passive clauses.

As for number, the previous word classes in addition to the verb have number. Our grammar checks the following number agreement cases:

1. Agreement within the noun phrase: between the head (noun or pronoun) and its dependents (the determiner, the adjective and the past participle).

2. Agreement within the clause:

   (a) Between the subject and the verb.

   (b) Between the subject and the subject complement (adjective or participle) in attributive clauses.

   (c) Between the verb and the subject complement (adjective or participle) in attributive clauses.

   (d) Between the subject and the past participle verb in passive clauses.

   (e) Between the indirect object (prepositional phrase) and the dative pronoun.

3 Development

3.1 The learner corpus

Given the lack of annotated learner corpus, for the development and test of the grammar we have created a manually annotated 25,000 words corpus, extracted from the CORANE learner corpus (Mancera et al., 2001). Our corpus contains 133 Spanish

[1] This relation could be achieved by other linguistic means, specially by the fixed order of words. For example, in Spanish the systematic anteposition and contiguity of the article with the noun in the noun phrase makes agreement between them redundant.

texts written by 47 Japanese native speakers studying Spanish, and it has been divided into two parts, as shown in table 1: 15,000 words for development, corresponding to learners with a level A2 to B1;[2] and 10,000 words for testing, corresponding to learners with a level B2 to C1.

Language level	Learners	Texts	Words
Development			
A2	2	7	1,105
B1	19	90	13,947
Total	21	97	15,052
Test			
B2	9	18	4,758
C1	17	18	5,321
Total	26	36	10,079
Corpus	47	133	25,131

Table 1: Learner corpus: development and test. Language level, number of learners, texts and words.

The annotation/evaluation process has been carried out by one native speaker. Although it would have been desirable to involve more than one annotator in order to report inter-annotator agreement, we believe that the error type treated here shows very high reliability (inter-annotator disagreement may be limited to lapses in concentration), unlike other type of errors like article or preposition usage, which are likely to be much less reliable (Tetreault and Chodorow, 2008).

The error tag appended to the word not only identifies the error but also provides a straightforward correction; since gender and number have only two possible values, there is no possibility of confusion -a masculine token with a gender error tag should be feminine, a singular token with a number error tag should be plural, and so on-.

To control false positives of the grammar, in addition to learner corpora we have also used native corpora: 22,000 words for development and 12,000 words for test, extracted from the Spanish section of the Europarl Parallel Corpus (Koehn, 2005).

[2]A level = basic user, B = independent user and C = Proficient user, according to the Common European Framework of Reference for Languages

3.2 Grammar formalism

Different techniques have been used in the literature to detect different error types (made by learners of English) (Leacock et al., 2010): for errors that require large amounts of contextual information, like preposition and article errors, statistical approaches seem particularly advantageous, while for more local errors, like over-regularized inflection, a rule-based approach seems to work quite well. Error detection systems for learners of languages other than English are scarce, as in the case of learner corpora.

To write our grammar we have use the Constraint Grammar (CG) formalism (Karlsson et al., 1995), which has already been used to detect grammatical errors in other languages: Swedish (Arppe, 2000; Birnn, 2000), Norwegian (Johannessen et al., 2002) Catalan (Badia et al., 2004) and Basque (Uria et al., 2009).

To be able to detect agreement errors, a variable amount of linguistic information is needed: since agreement can occur both at the clause-level and at the phrase-level (as seen in section 2), more syntactic information is needed to resolve the former than the latter. Our grammar uses as input the morphosyntactic analysis provided by the Spanish parser HISPAL (Bick, 2006), which provides us with a full syntactic analysis of sentences (in constituents and syntactic functions) and is error-tolerant, that is, it is capable of parsing (correctly or not) sentences containing grammatical errors.

CG is basically a disambiguation and information mapping methodology designed to operate on token-based grammatical tags that can be added, removed or changed in an incremental and context-sensitive fashion. In a CG rule, a context condition (in parenthesis) contains an obligatory position marker, consisting of a number indicating relative distance in tokens. The default (positive number) is a right context, while a negative number indicates a left context. For example, the following rule adds a plural tag (%agr-p) to a singular noun (NP-HEAD-S) if it is immediately preceded (-1) by a definite determiner (DET-DEF), which is immediately preceded by preposition "de" (PRP-DE), which is immediately preceded by the word "uno").

```
ADD (%agr-p) TARGET NP-HEAD-S
(-1 DET-DEF LINK -1 PRP-DE LINK -1 ("uno"));
```

This rule will assign the tag "%agr-p" (plural agreement) to the noun "hombre" (man) in the following fragment that contains an agreement error:

(7) Uno de los hombre
One of the man
'One of the men'

3.3 Design principles

In the design of our grammar our main aim is to achieve a high precision, keeping false positives to a minimum, even at a noticeable loss of recall, following the common practice in grammatical error detection applications.

Even though we can use the full syntactic analysis provided by the HISPAL parser as input, we have written our rules using as low-level information as possible, that is, morphological information, instead of higher-level information like syntactic function, whenever possible. The reason for this is an interesting problem found during the construction of rules: on the one hand, it is necessary to have as much grammatical information as possible about the text we are going to analyse; on the other hand, it is difficult to have such information because even though the parser always provides a syntactic analysis, it is hard to parse a text with grammatical errors correctly, and the errors of the parser may cause our grammar to fail -even for a native speaker it can be hard to parse and understand some fragments of learner language-.

Another decision that has to be made, both during the manual annotation of the corpus and the design of the grammar is, given two (or more) words syntactically related, which word determines the correct gender and number. That is, if we find for example a masculine determiner followed by a feminine noun (or a singular determiner followed by a plural noun), we know that there is a disagreement but we also want to know which is the correct gender (or number) from the native point of view.

For gender, we consider that the syntactic head determines the gender of the dependents (whether the gender of the head is correct or not).[3] Therefore, within the noun phrase, the noun or pronoun determines the gender of the other words. Within the clause, the subject determines the gender of the subject complement.

For number, in most cases the head of the syntactic dependency determines the number of the dependent. However, this is not as straightforward as with gender. In the following cases, the right number is not given by the head of the syntactic dependency, instead:

1. The subject "gives" the number to the verb.

2. In copulative sentences, the subject gives the number to the verb and to the subject complement. (When there is no subject, the verb determines the number of the subject complement.)

3. Inherently plural determiners (e.g. numerals) give the number to the noun.

4. The indirect object gives the number to the dative clitic.

3.4 Construction of the rules

For the manual construction and refinement of the rules we have looked at example sentences with errors from the annotated learner corpus (a fragment of 15,000 words, corresponding to texts written by learners with a level A1 or B1, as seen in table 1). In addition to that, to control false positives we have also used a 22,000 words native corpus, extracted from the Spanish section of the Europarl Parallel Corpus (**?**). Finally, our grammar contains 31 rules to detect gender agreement errors and 50 rules to detect number agreement errors.

4 Evaluation

We have evaluated the performance of the grammar with a fragment of 10,000 words from the learner corpus (approximately 5,000 words from level B2 and 5,000 words from level C1, as seen in table 1). The results are shown in tables 2 for gender (64.52% precision and 71.43% recall) and 3 for number (58.62% precision and 31.48% recall).[4]

[3]We do not treat here the wrong assignment of gender to words but only the wrong agreement. If the learner makes a mistake choosing the gender of the noun but its complements agree with it, there is no agreement error.

[4]Precision is calculated by dividing the number of true positives (tp) by the number of (true (tp) or false (fp)) positives (Precision = tp / (tp + fn).

Level	tp	fp	fn	Precision	Recall
B2	25	14	13	64.10%	65.79%
C1	15	8	3	65.22%	83.33%
Total	40	22	16	64.52%	71.43%

Table 2: Gender agreement. Grammar results in the test part of the learner corpus.

Level	tp	fp	fn	Precision	Recall
B2	10	9	13	52.63%	43.48%
C1	7	3	24	70.00%	22.58%
Total	17	12	37	58.62%	31.48%

Table 3: Number agreement. Grammar results in the test part of the learner corpus.

To analyse false alarms (that is, false positives and false negatives) with more detail, following (Uria et al., 2009), we have classified them into 4 types:

1. Spelling errors: the text contains a spelling error (which may cause the parser to provide an erroneous input to our grammar).

2. Structural errors: the words in the text are correctly written but the structure contains some error –different from an agreement error-.

3. Parser errors: the words and structure do not contain a learner error -different from an agreement error- but the parser provides a wrong analysis (usually wrong word class).

4. "Real" errors: None of the above, the grammar fails detecting or non detecting an agreement error.

4.1 Gender

The main source of false alarms in detecting gender disagreement are parser errors: because of the fact that the words do not agree in gender, or simply because of the limitations of the parser, sometimes the words do not receive the correct morphosyntactic interpretation, which makes the grammar fail.

Table 4 shows the frequency of the causes that make the grammar fail, and its precision and recall taking into account only "real" false alarms.

Recall is calculated by dividing the number of true positives (tp) by the number of true positives (tp) plus false negatives (fn) (Recall = tp / (tp+fn).

False positive	B2	C1	Total
Spelling	0	6	6
Structure	2	0	2
Parser	6	2	8
Real	6	0	6
Total	14	8	22
False negative			
Spelling	1	0	1
Structure	0	0	0
Parser	9	2	11
Real	3	1	4
Total	13	3	16
"Real" precision	80.65%	100.00%	86.96%
"Real" recall	89.29%	93.75%	90.91%

Table 4: Gender agreement. Grammar results in the test part of the learner corpus taking into account only "real" false alarms.

4.1.1 Recall: false negatives

As for false negatives, the parser provides a wrong analysis of the word in 11 cases. In 7 of them, an article -followed by a noun with different gender values- is analysed instead as a pronoun by the parser.

False negatives also inform us about some phenomena that were not treated by our grammar, and should be addressed in the future:

1. Agreement between the subject and the subject complement -in attributive clauses- when the subject complement is a noun.

2. Agreement between the subject and the subject complement in non-attributive clauses.

3. Agreement between the object and object complement.

4. Agreement between the accusative clitic and the object.

5. Agreement between the relative pronoun and its antecedent.

6. Agreement between the noun and its coordinated dependents (when the noun is comple-

mented by two coordinated adjectives, such adjectives should both agree in gender with the noun.)

7. Agreement across the prepositional phrase boundaries (which requires solving pp-attachment): when a noun is complemented by a prepositional phrase and an adjective, we need to know which noun the adjective depends on (the noun inside the prepositional phrase or the head noun) to determine its correct gender.

4.1.2 Precision: false positives

As for tagger errors, for example, in B2 texts the complex word "carne=picada" ("minced meat") appears 4 times analysed as a masculine noun instead of a feminine noun, and thus our grammar detects a (false) disagreement with the article.

With regard to the behaviour of the grammar in the 12,000 words native corpus, our grammar has flagged only 10 false positives (and no true positive).

4.2 Number

The main source of false alarms in the detection of number agreement errors are not learner or parser errors but the design of the grammar itself. Table 5 shows the frequency of the causes that make the grammar fail, and its precision and recall taking into account only "real" false alarms. As we can see, recall is still considerably low, so our grammar needs to be improved to detect more disagreement contexts.

4.2.1 Recall: false negatives

As we see in table 5, there is a clear difference in the performance of the grammar depending on the language level: in C1 level texts, recall is specially low. This is due to the fact that the higher the language level, the more syntactically elaborated the learner errors, and thus the more difficult for our grammar to detect them safely. As we can see in table 6,[5] the percentage of errors that occur at the clause-level (as opposed to the phrase-level) increases with the language level.

[5]Level A2 texts are excluded because of their low frequency (they contain only 9 errors, 6 at the clause-level and 3 at the phrase-level).

False Positive	B2	C1	Total
Spelling	3	0	3
Structure	1	0	1
Parser	2	2	4
Real	3	1	4
Total	9	3	12
False negative			
Spelling	0	0	0
Structure	0	0	0
Parser	4	0	4
Real	9	24	33
Total	13	24	37
Precision	76.92%	87.50%	80.95%
Recall	52.63%	22.58%	34.00%

Table 5: Number agreement. Grammar results in the test part of the learner corpus taking into account only "real" false alarms.

Phrase-level errors are those in which the head and the dependent are within the same constituent (the determiner and the noun in the noun phrase, the noun and the adjective in the noun phrase, and so on.), while clause-level errors are those in which the head and the dependent are in different constituents (the subject and the verb, the subject and the subject complement, the object and the object complement, and so on.). Phrase-level errors are easier to detect automatically than clause-level errors, because the latter require a full syntactic analysis or even more to be detected.

	B1	B2	C1
Phrase-level	45.65%	45.45%	32.26%
Clause-level	54.35%	54.55%	67.74%

Table 6: Number agreement. Percentage (and frequency) of phrase-level and clause-level errors by language level.

Therefore, among false negatives, there is still room for improvement for our grammar. Table 7 shows the frequency of some syntactic phenomena in the test part of the corpus where false negatives occurred.

Number 3, 4, 5 and 6 type of agreement have in common the fact that there is a distance between the words involved in the agreement; to identify such agreement errors we need a full sentential analysis with syntactic function information (4, 5) or even the reference of pronouns within or between sentences (3, 6), which is difficult due to the fact that agreement is one of the clues used to identify such relationships. We consider these kind of number agreement errors are specially difficult to detect.

Number 1, 2, 7 , 8 and 9 type of agreement have in common the fact that in those structures, the subject is confused with the direct object by the learner (because the subject occupies a non canonical position or works like a direct object from the semantic point of view) and because of that it is a assigned the wrong number feature. To detect these kind of errors, we need to solve the ambiguity between the subject and the object. Considering that in Spanish the subject can be (usually is) ellided, detecting such errors would require identifying the explicit subject or the referent of the ellided subject safely, which is considerably difficult to achieve, too.

To sum up, even though number agreement errors have a low recall, it is rather difficult to improve recall significantly because to detect such errors we would need a safe full sentential analysis, identifying the referent of the pronouns or the reference of the ellided subject.

Constituents that agree in number	B2	C1
1) Subject-Unaccusative verb	1	3
2) Impersonal verb-*Direct object	1	2
3) Relative Subject-Verb (not 3)	0	3
4) Subject/Verb-Subject complement	1	0
5) Object-Object complement	1	0
6) Indirect object – Clitic	1	0
7) Postposed subject - Verb (not 3.)	0	1
8) Subject-Verb in a clause with “se”	0	1
9) Subject-Verb with “gustar”-like verbs	0	1
Total	5	11

Table 7: Number agreement. Analysis of false negatives.

4.2.2 Precision: false positives

Out of the 29 flagged errors by the grammar, there have been 12 false positives. However, 3 of them were due to misspellings in the learner corpus, 1 to syntactic errors, 4 to parser errors, and 4 of them are "real" false alarms due to the grammar.

In the 12,000 words native corpus, our grammar has flagged 15 agreement errors, from which 1 is a true positive, and the rest are false positives. Although agreement errors are typical in learner corpora, native corpora also contains such kind of errors because being an inflecting language, the last letters of the word reveal its gender or number value, so a spelling or typing mistake can easily lead to an "agreement" error.[6]

5 Data from the learner corpus

We can use the data in the annotated corpus not only to develop and evaluate the grammar but also to draw some conclusions about gender and number agreement among Japanese learners.

The 25,000 words fragment contains 154 number agreement errors and 171 gender agreement errors, distributed by language level as table 8 shows. We can see that the frequency of gender errors per word decreases as language level increases, while the frequency of number errors does not show a clear pattern.

Tag	A2	B1	B2	C1	Total
Sing	1	20	4	8	33
Plur	8	72	18	23	121
Total	9	92	22	31	154
% word	0.81	0.66	0.46	0.65	0.61
Masc	5	35	20	9	69
Fem	11	67	17	7	102
Total	16	102	37	16	171
% word	1.45	0.73	0.78	0.34	0.68

Table 8: Learner corpus: frequency of error tags by language level. Number: Singular (Sing) or Plural (Plur). Gender: Masculine (Masc) or Feminine (Fem).

With the evaluation of the grammar and this data, it is clear that number errors need more attention. When dealing with agreement, teachers of Spanish as a foreign language and students usually focus on

[6]In (Bustamante and León, 1996)'s native Spanish 70,000 words error annotated corpus (errors including spelling, structural and non structural errors) 18.5% of errors consist on agreement errors in gender, number or person.

gender, considered the most difficult type of agreement to learn, probably because from the beginning, it requires much effort for the learner to know which is the inherent gender value of every noun than to choose the right number value depending on the context (although there are some morphological hints, gender is arbitrary and must be memorized). However, among Japanese learners, gender errors tend to decrease as the language level increases, while number agreement errors are considerably frequent even among advanced students. In the evaluation of the grammar and in the corpus we have confirmed that number agreement requires a higher level of syntactic analysis than gender agreement: while gender errors occur mainly within the noun phrase, number errors move from the phrase-level to the clause-level as students proficiency increases, affecting distant constituents of the clause or requiring the distinction between syntactic and semantic object.

6 Conclusions and future work

In this paper we have presented a grammar for the detection of agreement errors in Spanish learners texts. Gender error has a precision of 64.52% and recall of 71.43%, and number errors have a precision of 58.62% and recall of 31.48%.

The comparison with other work in the area is particularly difficult, since unlike other NLP areas, grammatical error detection systems do not have a shared corpus or task upon which to evaluate. Although work on different languages is hardly comparable, we can refer to other rule-based systems like (Fliedner, 2002) who detects noun phrase agreement errors in German with precision and recall scores of 67%, and (Gill and Lehal, 2008) error detection system for Punjabi with recall at 76.8% for modifier and noun agreement errors and 87.1% on subject-verb agreement errors.

During the construction of the rules we have tried to find a balance between the necessity of using an input text with as much syntactic information as possible and the fact that parser errors in learner texts are more frequent, which will make the error grammar fail. By writing safe rules we have given priority to precision over recall.

In the gender part of the grammar the main source of false alarms are parser errors, usually a wrong word class tag. If we only take into account the false alarms attributed to our grammar the precision would be 86.96% and recall 90.91%.

In the number part of the grammar the main source of false alarms is the design of the grammar itself, and not learners' or parser errors. Number errors can happen at the phrase level and at the clause level, but as the learners' proficiency progresses, they are more common at the clause level, and thus more difficult for the grammar to detect them because a full syntactic analysis (with information about syntactic functions, the pronoun referent, or the referent of the elided subject, for example) would be required. Therefore, although the grammar's recall is rather low, we consider it is very difficult to improve it without lowering its precision.

By examining the manually annotated learner corpus we have used for the development and test of the grammar, we have confirmed that teachers and learners should pay more attention to number errors: gender errors are more frequent in the beginning but, as students' proficiency increases, gender errors decrease and number errors increase. The type of number errors also change, from phrase-level errors to clause-level errors in the most advanced language group.

The automatic detection of learner errors can contribute to language teaching and learning in several ways: the automatic annotation of corpora with error information, automatic detection of errors in intelligent computer assisted language learning systems and the design of improved learning materials based on corpus data, among others.

The construction of the grammar has served us to confirm the validity of our approach and to gain expertise in the writing of the rules for error detection. As future lines of research, we would like to treat a more challenging error type like article usage, specially prevalent among Japanese students. That will require a more elaborated annotation of corpus and the use of more categories for the evaluation of the system.

Finally, after the evaluation of our grammar, we would like to evaluate the usefulness of the system for language learners in a real language learning context.

Acknowledgments

This work was supported by *kakenhi* (22820047), Grant-in-Aid for Scientific Research (Start-up) from the Japan Society for the Promotion of Science.

References

A. Arppe. 2000. Developing a grammar checker for swedish. In *Proceedings of the 12th Nordic Conference in Computational Linguistics*, pages 13–27.

T. Badia, A. Gil, M. Quixal, and O. Valentín. 2004. Nlp-enhanced error checking for catalan unrestricted text. In *Proceedings of the fourth international conference on Language Resources and Evaluation*, pages 1919–1922.

E. Bick. 2006. A constraint grammar-based parser for spanish. In *Proceedings of TIL 2006 - 4th Workshop on Information and Human Language Technology*, Ribeirão, Preto.

J. Birnn. 2000. Detecting grammar errors with lingsoft's swedish grammar checker. In *Proceedings of the 12th Nordic Conference in Computational Linguistics*, pages 28–40, Norway.

F. R. Bustamante and F. S. León. 1996. Gramcheck: A grammar and style checker. In *The proceedings of the 16th International Conference on Computational Linguistics*, pages 175–181.

S. Fernández. 1997. *Interlengua y análisis de errores en el aprendizaje del español como lengua extranjera*. Edelsa.

G. Fliedner. 2002. A system for checking np agreement in german texts. In *Proceedings of the Student Research Workshop at the 40th Annual Meeting of the Association for Computational Linguistics (ACL)*, pages 12–17, Philadelphia.

M. S. Gill and G. S. Lehal. 2008. A grammar checking system for punjabi. In *Proceeding of the 22nd International Conference on Computational Linguistics (COLING)*, pages 149–152.

T. Heift and M. Schulze. 2007. *Errors and Intelligence in Computer-Assisted Language Learning: Parsers and Pedagogues*. Routledge Studies in Computer Assisted Language Learning.

J. B. Johannessen, K. Hagen, and P. Lane. 2002. The performance of a grammar checker with deviant language input. In Association for Computational Linguistics, editor, *Proceedings of the 19th international conference on Computational Linguistics*, pages 1–8.

F. Karlsson, A. Voutilainen, J. Heikkilä, and A. Anttila. 1995. *Constraint grammar. A language-independent system for parsing unrestricted text*. Mouton de Gruyter, Berlin/New York.

P. Koehn. 2005. Europarl: A parallel corpus for statistical machine translation. In *MT Summit 200*.

C. Leacock, M. Chodorow, M. Gamon, and J. Tetreault. 2010. Different approaches for different errors. In *Automated Grammatical Error Detection for Language Learners*. Morgan & Claypool.

C. Lozano. 2009. Cedel2: Corpus escrito del español l2. In *Applied Linguistics Now: Understanding Language and Mind*, pages 197–212.

A.M. Cestero Mancera, I. Penadés Martínez, A. Blanco Canales, L. Camargo Fernández, and J.F. Simón Granda. 2001. Corpus para el análisis de errores de aprendices de E/LE (CORANE). In Ana Gimeno Sanz, editor, *Actas del XII Congreso Internacional de ASELE: tecnologías de la información y de las comunicaciones en la enseñanza de la E/LE*, pages 527–534. Asociación para la Enseñanza del Español como Lengua Extranjera. Congreso Internacional.

J. Tetreault and M. Chodorow. 2008. Native judgments of non-native usage: Experiments in preposition error detection. In *Proceedings of the Workshop on Human Judgments in Computational Linguistics at the 22nd International Conference on Computational Linguistics (COLING)*, pages 24–32.

L. Uria, B. Arrieta, A. Díaz de Ilarraza, M. Maritxalar, and M. Oronoz. 2009. Determiner errors in basque: Analysis and automatic detection. *Procesamiento del Lenguaje Natural*, (43):41–48.

A Reranking Approach for Dependency Parsing with Variable-sized Subtree Features

Mo Shen, Daisuke Kawahara, and Sadao Kurohashi
Graduate School of Informatics
Kyoto University
Yoshida-honmachi, Sakyo-ku,
Kyoto, 606-8501, Japan
shen@nlp.ist.i.kyoto-u.ac.jp {dk,kuro}@i.kyoto-u.ac.jp

Abstract

Employing higher-order subtree structures in graph-based dependency parsing has shown substantial improvement over the accuracy, however suffers from the inefficiency increasing with the order of subtrees. We present a new reranking approach for dependency parsing that can utilize complex subtree representation by applying efficient subtree selection heuristics. We demonstrate the effectiveness of the approach in experiments conducted on the Penn Treebank and the Chinese Treebank. Our system improves the baseline accuracy from 91.88% to 93.37% for English, and in the case of Chinese from 87.39% to 89.16%.

1. Introduction

In dependency parsing, graph-based models are prevalent for their state-of-the-art accuracy and efficiency, which are gained from their ability to combine exact inference and discriminative learning methods. The ability to perform efficient exact inference lies on the so-called factorization technique which breaks down a parse tree into smaller substructures to perform an efficient dynamic programming search. This treatment however restricts the representation of features to in a local context which can be, for example, single edges or adjacent edges. Such restriction prohibits the model from exploring large or complex structures for linguistic evidence, which can be considered as the major drawback of the graph-based approach.

Attempts have been made in developing more complex factorization techniques and corresponding decoding methods. Higher-order models that use grand-child, grand-sibling or tri-sibling factorization were proposed in (Koo and Collins, 2010) to explore more expressive features and have proven significant improvement on parsing accuracy. However, the power of higher-order models comes with the cost of expensive computation and sometimes it requires aggressive pruning in the pre-processing.

Another line of research that explores complex feature representations is parse reranking. In its general framework, a K-best list of parse tree candidates is first produced from the base parser; a reranker is then applied to pick up the best parse among these candidates. For constituent parsing, successful results has been reported in (Collins, 2000; Charniak and Johnson, 2005; Huang, 2008). For dependency parsing, the efficient algorithms for produce K-best list for graph-based parsers have been proposed in (Huang and Chiang, 2005) for projective parsing and in (Hall, 2007) for non-projective parsing; Improvements on dependency accuracy has been achieved in (Hall, 2007; Hayashi et al., 2011). However, the feature sets in these studies explored a relatively small context, either by emulating the feature set in the constituent parse reranking, or by factorizing the search space. A desirable approach for the K-best list reranking is to encode features on subtrees extracted from the candidate parse with arbitrary orders and structures, as long as the extraction process is tractable. It is an open question how to design this subtree extraction process that is able to selects a set of subtrees which provides reliable and concrete linguistic evidence. Another related challenge is to design a proper back-off strategy for any structures extracted, since large subtree instances are always sparse in the training data.

In this paper, we explore a feature set that makes fully use of dependency grammar, can capture global information with less restriction in the structure and the size of the subtrees, and can be encoded efficiently. It exhaustively explores a candidate parse tree for features from the most simple to the most expressive while maintaining the efficiency in the sense that it does not add additional complexities over the K-best parsing.

We choose the K-best list reranking framework rather than the forest reranking in (Huang, 2008) because an explicit representation of parse trees is needed in order to compute the features for reranking. We implemented an edge-factored parser and a second-order sibling-factored parser which emulate models in the MSTParser described in (McDonald et al., 2005; McDonald and Pereira, 2006) as our base parsers.

In the rest part of this paper, we first give a brief description of the dependency parsing, then we describe the feature set for reranking, which is the major contribution of this paper. Finally, we present a set of experiment for the evaluation of our method.

2. Dependency Parsing

The task of dependency parsing is to find a tree structure for a sentence in which edges represent the head-modifier relationship between words: each word is linked to a unique "head" such that the link forms a semantic dependency while the main predicate of the sentence is linked to a dummy "root". An example of dependency parsing is illustrated in Figure 1. A dependency tree is called projective if the links can be drawn on the linearly ordered words without any crossover. We will focus on projective trees throughout this paper.

We formally define the dependency parsing task. Give a sentence x, the best parse tree is obtained by searching for the tree with highest score:

$$\tilde{y} = \mathrm{argmax}_{y \in \mathcal{Y}(x)} Score(y, x) , \quad (1)$$

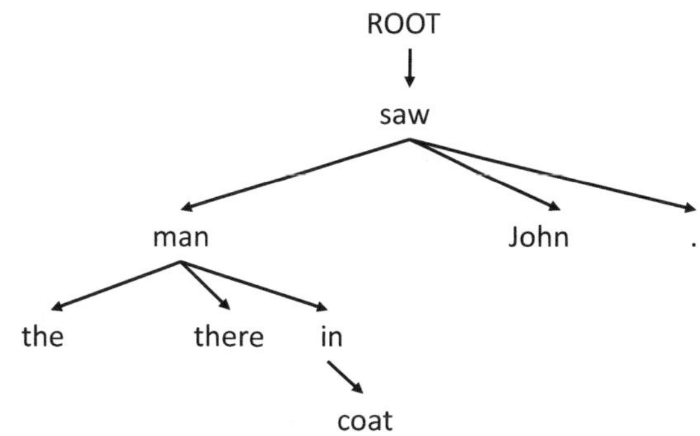

Figure 1. A dependency parse tree of the sentence "the man there in coat saw John."

where $\mathcal{Y}(x)$ is the search space of possible parse trees for x, and y is a parse tree in $\mathcal{Y}(x)$. A problem in solving equation (1) is that the number of candidates in the search space grows exponentially with the length of the sentence which makes the searching infeasible. A common remedy for this problem is to factorize a parse tree into small subtrees, called factors, which are scored independently. The score of parse tree under a factorization is the summation of scores of factors:

$$Score(y, x) = \textstyle\sum_{t \in y} Score(t, x) , \quad (2)$$

where t is a factor of y. The search space can be therefore encoded in a compact form which allows dynamic programming algorithms to perform efficient exact inference. The score function for each factor is assigned as an inner product of a feature vector and a weight vector w:

$$Score(t, x) = w \cdot f(t, x) . \quad (3)$$

The feature vector is defined on the factor t which means it is only able to capture tree-structure information from a small context. This can be seen as the off-set for performing exact inference. The goal of training a parser is to learn a weight vector that assigns scores to effectively discriminate good parses from bad parses.

We use the edge factorization and the sibling factorization models described in (McDonald et al., 2005; McDonald and Pereira, 2006) to construct our base parsers. We learn the weight vector by applying the averaged perceptron algorithm (Collins, 2002) for its efficiency and stable performance. An illustration for generic perceptron algorithm is shown in Pseudocode 1.

Pseudocode 1: Generic perceptron learning

for training data $(x_i, y_i), \mathrm{i} = 1..\mathrm{N}$
  for iteration $\mathrm{t} = 1..\mathrm{T}$
    $\tilde{y} = \mathrm{argmax}_{y \in \mathcal{Y}(x)} w \cdot f(y, x_i)$
    if $\tilde{y} \neq y_i$
      $w \leftarrow w + f(y_i, x_i) - f(\tilde{y}, x_i)$
  end
End

3. Parse Reranking

In this section, we describe our reranking approach and introduce the feature set consists of three different types.

3.1 Overview of Parse Reranking

The task of reranking is similar with that of parsing instead of that the searching of parse tree is performed on a K-best list with selected parse candidates rather than the entire search space:

$$\tilde{y} = \mathrm{argmax}_{y \in Kbest(x)} Score'(y, x) \quad (4)$$

The scoring function is defined as:

$$Score'(y, x) = L(y, x) + w \cdot f(y, x) \quad (5)$$

Where $L(y, x)$ is the score of y output by the base parser. We define the oracle parse y^+ to be the parse in the K-best list with highest accuracy compared with the gold-standard parse. The goal of reranking is to learn the weight vector so that the reranker can pick up the oracle parse as many times as possible. Note that in the reranking framework, the feature is defined on the entire parse tree which enables the encoding of global information. We learn the weight vector of the reranker also by the averaged perceptron algorithm shown in Pseudocode 1 with slight modification that only substitute the search space $\mathcal{Y}(x)$ with the K-best output Kbest(x), and gold parse y_i with oracle parse y_i^+.

3.2 Feature Sets for Reranking

Benefit from the K-best list obtained in the parsing stage, we are able to perform discriminative learning in order to select a good parse among candidates in a shrunk search space, which allows utilization of global features. We define three types of features below.

Trimmed subtree: For each node in a given parse tree, we check its dominated subtrees to see whether they are likely to appear in a good parse tree or not. To efficiently obtain these subtrees, we set a local window that bound a node from its left side, right side and bottom. We then extract the maximum subtree inside this window, means that we cut off those nodes that are too distant in sequential order or too deep in a tree.

The above subtree extraction often results in very large instances which are extremely sparse in the training data, therefore it is necessary to keep smaller subtrees as back-offs. In most cases, however, it is prohibitively expensive to enumerate all the smaller subtrees. Instead of enumeration, we design a back-off strategy that select subtrees by attempting to leave out nodes that are far away from the subtree's root and keeps those that are nearby. Precisely, after extracted the first subtree of a node, we vary the three boundaries (the left, the right and the bottom boundary respectively) from their original positions to positions that are closer to the root of the subtree, such that it tightens up the local window. For each possible combination of the variable boundaries, we extract the largest subtree from the new local window and add it to the set of the so called "trimmed subtrees" set of the node. This back-off strategy comes from our observation that nodes that are close to the root may provide more reliable information than those that are distant. As it is infeasible to enumerate all small subtrees as back-offs, throwing away the redundant nodes from the outer part of a large subtree is a reasonable choice.

Figure 2 illustrates the construction of the "trimmed subtrees" set of the node "saw", for the sentence in Figure 1. The initial boundary parameters are set large enough so the local window contains the entire parse tree[1]. #LEFT, #RIGHT and #BOTTOM represents the three boundary variables, which range from -6 to -1, from 3 to 1 and from 3 to 0 respectively. Context

[1] In practice we use smaller local window with fixed size.

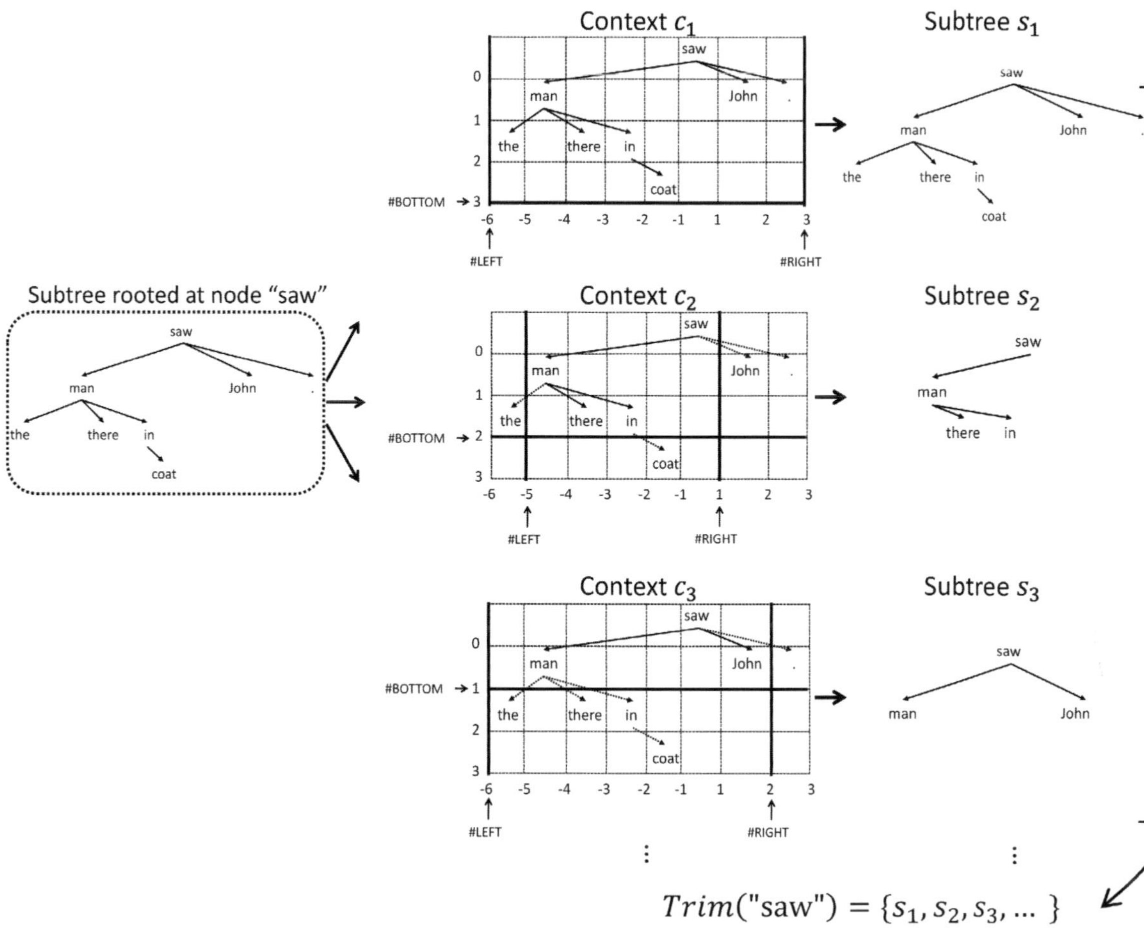

Figure 2. Extraction of trimmed subtrees from the node "saw". "#LEFT", "#RIGHT" and "#BOTTOM" represents the three boundaries that can vary along possible positions on the corresponding axis. Contexts c_1, c_2 and c_3 represnt three instances of possible combinations of boundary positions. s_1, s_2 and s_3 are resulted subtrees that are elements in the trimmed subtrees set of the node "saw".

c_1, c_2 and c_3 represent three different combinations of boundary positions. Subtree s_1, s_2 and s_3 are the extracted subtrees in the correspond context. They and other similarly extracted subtrees together consist in the set $Trim(\text{"saw"})$, the trimmed subtrees set of the node "saw". We use this set in two ways. First, for each element in this set, we encode a series of features. Second, this set is kept for reuse in another type of feature, which we describe latter. We repeat this extraction process for all nodes in a parse tree and keep their trimmed subtrees set.

In Figure 3 we show some of the extracted subtrees in the set $Trim(\text{"saw"})$, among which the subtree (c) can be regard as a grand sibling factor and the subtree (d) is similar with a tri-sibling factor in (Koo and Collins, 2010), but the siblings are located in both sides of the head node. The subtree (a) and subtree (b) are subtrees we extracted that cannot be represented in common factorization methods, which confirmed the ability of this feature set to capture a large variety of structures.

It should be noted that, while in a direct calculation there are 72 (6-by-3-by-4) possible combinations for boundary positions in the example in Figure 2, this number can almost always be reduced in practice. In this example, when #LEFT reached the position at index -4, the entire left branch of the root node is in fact cut so no further movement for #LEFT is allowed. Moreover, after #BOTTOM moved to the position

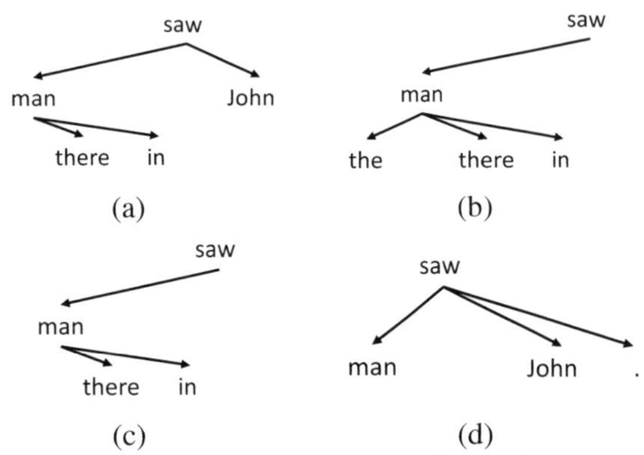

Figure 3. Some of the extracted trimmed subtrees by the process described in Figure 2. (c) is identical with a grand-sibling factor in a third-order parsing model and (d) is similar to a tri-sibling factor but siblings are on both sides of the head.

at index 1, the sequential order distance between "man" and "saw" is updated and reduced to 1, which restricts #LEFT to only two possible positions, either to the left or to the right of the word "man". Therefore one can verify that the true number of combinations of boundary positions is actually 25. Briefly, for a node we are focusing on, we decompose the extracted subtree from the initial local window into three parts: the node itself, the sequence of its left descendants and the sequence of its right descendants. The two sequences of descendants are in a preordering of depth-first search, during which we mark "anchor" nodes as the next-possible cut-in positions for the left/right boundary variables. Furthermore, the list of anchor nodes will keep updating whenever the bottom boundary variable moved to a new position. As a result, we are able to minimize the number of boundary combinations to speed up the subtrees extraction.

For each extracted subtree, we encode features as follow. A trimmed subtree feature is represented as an n-tuple: $\langle a_1, \dots, a_n \rangle$ where a_1 is the root of the subtree, and $a_i, i > 1$ are nodes in the subtree in preordering through a depth-first search from a_1. For a_1 we encode its word form, Part-of-Speech tag, and the combination of them. For any non-root node, we encode its Part-of-Speech tag, a binary value indicating the branch direction from its head, and its depth from a_1. We also encode features that omit the Part-of-Speech tags of the sequence $a_2, \dots, a_n$, so that only the structural preference of the subtree's root is retained. An example is shown below which illustrates a feature for the subtree in Figure 3(a):

$$\langle (\text{saw}, \text{V}), (\text{N}, \text{LEFT}, \text{depth} = 1), \\ (\text{N}, \text{RIGHT}, \text{depth} = 2), (\text{P}, \text{RIGHT}, \text{depth} = 2), \\ (\text{N}, \text{RIGHT}, \text{depth} = 1) \rangle,$$

where V, N and P are Part-of-Speech tags of corresponding nodes; we use simplified tags for illustration purpose. The preordering of nodes together with their branch direction and depth information guarantees that the mapping from a given subtree structure to its corresponding feature string is injective. Another example below shows a feature that omits all the Part-of-Speech tags except on the root of the subtree:

$$\langle (\text{saw}, \text{V}), (-, \text{LEFT}, \text{depth} = 1), \\ (-, \text{RIGHT}, \text{depth} = 2), (-, \text{RIGHT}, \text{depth} = 2), \\ (-, \text{RIGHT}, \text{depth} = 1) \rangle$$

Finally, we associate the list of features encoded for a subtree rooted on a node a with the corresponding element in the set $Trim(a)$. We make use of this set in the next type of features to avoid repeated computation.

Sibling subtree: The trimmed subtree features consider the preference of a node toward its dominated subtree—whether the subtree is likely to appear in a good parse. In the reranking framework, however, as we do not factorize a parse tree, we may suffer from a problem that the information we got among candidates are unbalanced. Typically, when computing the trimmed subtree features, a candidate parse with most nodes being leaves will provide little information except on the root node, while on another parse that has fewer leaves and more depth we can have a bunch of features that give more information. This defect makes the comparison between candidates be "unfair" and thus less reliable. Therefore, it is natural to raise the question the other way round—whether a node is a good head for a subtree. To answer this question, we consider a dynamic programming structure called *complete span* introduced in (Eisner, 1996).

A complete span consists of a head node and all its descendants on one side, which can also be

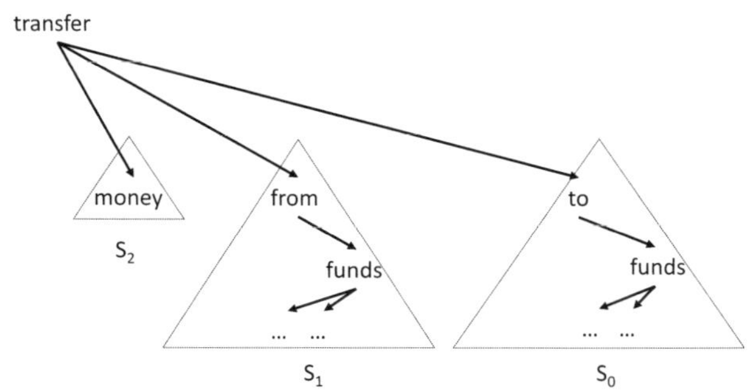

Figure 4. A complete span for the clause "transfer money from the new funds to other investment funds" where we omitted some of the details. This structure functions as a relatively independent and complete component in the entire parse tree. Features are encoded over the tuples: <transfer, -,s_2>, <transfer, s_2,s_1>, <transfer, s_1,s_0>, <transfer, s_0,->.

considered as a head node and sibling subtrees shown in Figure 4. In our observation, a complete span functions as a relatively independent and complete semantic structure in the parse tree, we thus believe that it can provide sufficient information to decide the head of a subtree without looking at any larger context.

Specifically, for each node m in a candidate parse, its sibling subtree features is the collection of all 3-tuples:

$$\langle h, \mathrm{f}(s, p_1, i_1), \mathrm{f}(m, p_2, i_2)\rangle$$

where h represents the word form, the Part-of-Speech tag, or the combination of the word form and the Part-of-Speech tag of the head node of m; s is the nearest sibling node of m in-between h and m; and the expression $\mathrm{f}(a, p, i)$ represents the i_{th} feature encoded on a trimmed subtree in the set $Trim(a)$, such that the trimmed subtree is the one extracted within the local window p. Here an important point is that we make use of trimmed subtrees extracted in the previous phase. As mentioned before, since we keep the history of trimmed subtree extraction, it eliminates the need to re-compute any subtree structures on the sibling nodes and hence is efficient to encode.

The way we define our sibling subtree features for reranking can also be seen as the natural extension of the sibling factorization in (McDonald and Pereira, 2006) from the word-based case to the subtree-based case, while the original sibling factor can be represented as a 3-tuple $\langle h, s, m\rangle$ using the same notation.

Chain: A chain type feature encodes information for a subtree that each node has exactly one incoming edge and one outgoing edge, except on the two ends (hence a "chain"). We extract all these kind of subtrees from a parse tree in the candidates list with a parameter set to limit the number of edges in the subtree. This type of features emulates the common grandparent-grandchildren structure in dependency parsing, while we loosen the restriction on the order of the subtree. It functions as a complementary for other types of features.

From the parse tree of the sentence in Figure 1, we extract all chains whose order is larger than 2, since otherwise features defined on edges have already been utilized in our base parsers which are edge-factored and sibling factored. We show these chain type subtrees in Figure 5. For a consideration of efficiency, a proper value of the order limit should be set no larger than 5 according to our experience.

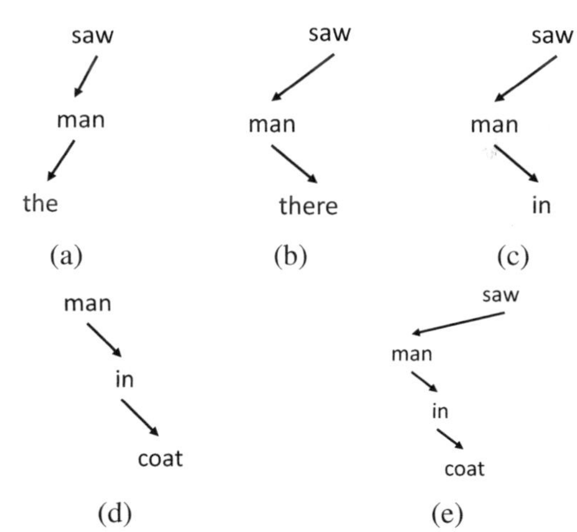

Figure 5. All chain type subtrees extracted from the gold-standard parse tree of the sentence "the man there in coat saw John."

The information encoded from extracted subtrees includes word form, Part-of-Speech tag and relative position in the subtree for each node. When dealing with long subtrees, however, encoding lexical information suffers from data sparsity. We therefore encode lexical information only on one of the two ends of the subtree in each time, while for all nodes we encode their grammatical and positional information. Thus for the subtree (e) in Figure 5, a feature can appear as:

$$\langle (\mathrm{V}, \mathrm{saw}, -), (\mathrm{N}, -, \mathrm{left}), (\mathrm{P}, -, \mathrm{right}), (\mathrm{N}, -, \mathrm{right}) \rangle$$

A binary value, here we denote as "left" and "right", is used to indicate the direction of branch of a node from its head.

4. Evaluation

We present our experimental results on two languages, English and Chinese. For English experiment, we use the Penn Treebank WSJ part. We convert the constituent structure in the Treebank into dependency structure with the tool Penn2Malt and the head-extraction rule identical with that in (Yamada and Matsumoto, 2003). To align with previous work, we use the standard data division: section 02-21 for training, section 24 for development, and section 23 for testing. As our system assumes Part-of-Speech tags as input, we use MXPOST, a MaxEnt tagger (Ratnaparkhi, 1996) to automatically tag the test data. The tagger is trained on the same training data.

For Chinese, we use the Chinese Treebank 5.0 with the following data division: files 1-270 and files 400-931 for training, files 271-300 for testing, and files 301-325 for development. We use Penn2Malt to convert the Treebank into dependency structure and the set of head-extraction rules for Chinese is identical with the one in (Zhang and Clark, 2008). Moreover, for Chinese we use the gold standard Part-of-Speech tags in evaluation.

We apply unlabeled attachment score (UAS) to measure the effectiveness of our method, which is the percentage of words that correctly identified their heads. For all experiments conducted, we use the parameters tuned in the development set.

We train two base parsers which are the re-implementation of the first-order and second-order parsers in the MSTParser (McDonald et al., 2005; McDonald and Pereira, 2006) with 10 iterations on English and Chinese training dataset. We use 30-way cross-validation on the identical training dataset to provide training data for the rerankers. We use the following parameter setting for the feature sets throughout the experiments: for chain-type features, the maximum order of chains is set to 5; the left, right and bottom boundary for the trimmed subtree features are 10, 10 and 5 respectively. For the main experiments we use K=50, the capacity of the list of parse tree candidates, in the training of the rerankers. Moreover, as it is not necessary to use identical value of K in the training and the test, we also conduct an experiment using miss-matching K values on Chinese dataset.

System	**English UAS**
McDonald05	90.9
McDonald06	91.5
Zhang11	92.9
Koo10	93.04
Martins10	93.26
Order 1	90.91
Order 2	91.88
Order 1 reranked	92.50
Order 2 reranked	**93.37**
Koo08^{+}	93.16
Chen09^{+}	93.16
Suzuki09^{+}	93.79

Table 1. English UAS of previous work, our base parsers, and reranked results. "$^{+}$": semi-supervised parsers.

4.1 Experimental Results

We show the experimental results for English in Table 1. Each row in this table shows the UAS of the corresponding system. "McDonald05" and "McDonald06" stand for the first-order and second-order models in the MSTParser (McDonald et al., 2005; McDonald and Pereira, 2006). "Zhang11" stands for the transition-based parser proposed in (Zhang and Nivre, 2011). "Koo10" stands for the Model 1 in (Koo and Collins, 2010) which is a third-order model. "Martins10" stands for the turbo parser proposed in (Martins et al., 2010). "Order 1" and "Order 2" are our re-implementation of MSTParser and are used as the base parsers for our reranking experiments. "Order 1 reranked" and "Order 2 reranked" are rerankers pipelined on the two base parsers. "Koo08", "Chen09" and "Suzuki09" are parsers using semi-supervised methods (Koo et al., 2008; Chen et al., 2009; Suzuki et al., 2009). In Table 2 we show the results for Chinese. "Duan07" and "Yu08" stands for the two probabilistic parsers in (Duan et al., 2007; Yu et al., 2008). "Chen09" stands for the same system in Table 1.

System	Chinese UAS
Duan07	84.36
Yu08	87.26
Order 1	85.44
Order 2	87.39
Order 1 reranked	87.63
Order 2 reranked	**89.16**
Chen09+	89.91

Table 2. Chinese UAS of previous work, our baseline parsers, and reranked results. "+": semi-supervised parsers.

As we can see from the results, for English, the accuracy increased from 90.91% ("Order 1") to 92.50% ("Order 1 reranked") for the first-order parse reranker and from 91.88%("Order 2") to 93.37%("Order 2 reranked") for the second-order parse reranker. For Chinese, the accuracy increased from 85.44% to 87.63% for the first-order parse reranker, and for the second order case it increased from 87.39% to 89.16%. It shows that our reranking systems obtain the highest accuracy among supervised systems. For English, the reranker "Order 2 reranked" even slightly outperforms "Martins10", the turbo parser which to the best of our knowledge achieved the highest accuracy in Penn Treebank. Although our rerankers are beaten by the semi-supervised systems "Suzuki09" and "Chen09", but as our method is orthogonal with semi-supervising methods, it is possible to further improve the accuracy by combing these techniques.

We investigate the effects of the three feature types we proposed in this paper. We in turn activate each feature type and their combinations in the evaluation, while during the training we keep all types of feature due to the limitation of time. We conduct this experiment based on the system "Order 2 reranked" for English. The result is shown in Table 3. The first row represents the system with all feature types activated; others are systems with corresponding feature sets activated in the evaluation phase. Here "Ch" stands for the chain-type feature set, "Trim" stands for the trimmed subtree feature set, and "Sib" stands for the sibling subtree feature set.

System	UAS
$\text{Reranker}_{\text{Ch+Trim+Sib}}$	93.37
$\text{Reranker}_{\text{Ch}}$	92.41
$\text{Reranker}_{\text{Trim}}$	92.77
$\text{Reranker}_{\text{Ch+Trim}}$	93.03
$\text{Reranker}_{\text{Trim+Sib}}$	93.10

Table 3. Influence of activated feature types on English test data. "Ch": chain-type features activated; "Trim": trimmed subtree features activated; "Sib": sibling subtree features activated.

In Table 4 we investigate the influence of miss-matched K values for the training and the evaluation. We traine a separate system for the Chinese dataset using "Order 1" with K=10 in the reranker's training and variant K values in the evaluation. The row "Rerank" shows that even for a small K used in the training, a better accuracy can be achieved with relatively larger K: the highest accuracy for this system is achieved when K=20 in the evaluation. We also show the oracle accuracies among the top-K candidates in the last row.

K	1	10	20	30	50
Rerank	85.44	86.81	87.49	87.45	87.33
Oracle	85.44	89.66	90.70	91.17	91.65

Table 4. Reranking experiment for Chinese with miss-matched K values.

In Table 5 we show the oracle accuracies among top-K candidates using the "Order 2" parser. The oracle accuracies can increase as much as absolutely 5.14% for English and absolutely 5.15% for Chinese compared with the 1-best accuracies.

K	1	10	20	30	50
English	91.88	95.61	96.30	96.65	97.02
Chinese	87.39	90.43	91.28	92.02	92.54

Table 5. Oracle accuracies of top-K candidates.

4.2 Efficiency

We show the training time and the parsing time of the base parser "Order 2" and the pipelined reranking system "Order 2 reranked" in Table 6.

	Training	Parsing
Order 2	1642 min	0.24 sec/sent
Order 2 reranked	3552 min	11.54 sec/sent

Table 6. Training time and parsing speed comparison for English.

Both systems run on a Xeon 2.4GHz CPU. We calculated the parsing time by running the systems on the first 100 sentences on the development data of the two languages. The reranking system takes twice the time than the base parser in the training. It is much slower than the base parser in parsing new sentences, which is mainly due to the time required for outputting the 50-best candidates list; this can be seen as an unavoidable trade-off to obtain high accuracy in the reranking framework.

5. Related Work

McDonald (2005, 2006) proposed an edge-factored parser and a second-order parser that both trained by discriminative online learning methods. Huang (2005) proposed the efficient algorithm for produce K-best list for graph-based parsers, which add a factor of $K \log K$ to the parsing complexity of the base parser. Sangati (2009) has shown that a discriminative parser is very effective at filtering out bad parses from a factorized search space which agreed with the conclusion in (Hall, 2007) that an edge-factored model can reach good oracle performance when generating relatively small K-best list. Successful results have been reported for constituent parse reranking in (Collins, 2000; Charniak and Johnson, 2005; Huang, 2008), in which feature sets defined on constituent parses have been proposed that are able to capture rich non-local information. These feature sets, however, cannot be directly applied to parse tree under dependency grammar. Attempts have been made to use similar feature sets in dependency parse reranking, which include the work in (Hall, 2007) that defined a feature set similar with the one in (Charniak and Johnson, 2005). Hayashi in (Hayashi et al., 2011) presented a forest reranking model which applied third-order factorizations emulating Model 1 and Model 2 in (Koo and Collins, 2010) on the search space of the reranker.

6. Conclusion

We have proposed a novel feature set for dependency parse reranking that successfully extracts complex structures for collecting linguistic evidence, and efficient feature back-off strategy is proposed to relieve data sparsity. Through experiment we confirmed the effectiveness and efficiency of our method, and observed significant improvement over the base system as well as other known systems.

To further improve the proposed method, we mention several possibilities for our future work. An advantage of the reranking framework we used is that it has no overlap with many of the semi-supervised parsing methods, such as word clustering (Koo et al., 2008) and subtree features integration using auto-parsed data (Chen et al., 2009). We are interested in the performance of our system when combining with these methods. Another interesting approach is to incorporate information from large-scale structured data, such as case frame (Kawahara and Kurohashi, 2006), which provides lexical predicate-argument selection preference and is an effective way to help to overcome data sparse problem in discriminative learning. While the relatively complex data structure in the case frame prohibits its incorporation in any existing factorization methods, it can be well utilized in the reranking framework with the proposed feature set.

References

E. Charniak and M. Johnson. 2005. Coarse-to-fine N-best Parsing and MaxEnt Discriminative Reranking. In Proceedings of the 43rd ACL.

M. Collins. 2000. Discriminative Reranking for Natural Language Parsing. In Proceedings of the ICML.

M. Collins. 2002. Discriminative Training Methods for Hidden Markov Models: Theory and Experiments with Perceptron Algorithms. In Proceedings of the 7th EMNLP, pages 1–8.

W. Chen, J. Kazama, K. Uchimoto and K. Torisawa. 2009. Improving Dependency Parsing with Subtrees from Auto-Parsed Data, In Proceedings of EMNLP2009, pages 570-579.

X. Duan, J. Zhao, and B. Xu. 2007. Probabilistic Models for Action-based Chinese Dependency Parsing. In Proceedings of ECML/ECPPKDD.

J. Eisner. 1996. Three New Probabilistic Models for Dependency Parsing: An Exploration. In Proceedings of the 16th COLING, pages 340–345.

K. Hall. 2007. K-best Spanning Tree Parsing. In Proceedings of ACL 2007.

K. Hayashi, T. Watanabe, M. Asahara and Y. Matsumoto. 2011. Third-order Variational Reranking on Packed-Shared Dependency Forests. In Proceedings of EMNLP 2011, pages 1479-1488.

L. Huang and D. Chiang. 2005. Better K-best Parsing. In Proceedings of the IWPT, pages 53–64.

L. Huang. 2008. Forest reranking: Discriminative Parsing with Non-local Features. In Proceedings of the 46th ACL, pages 586–594.

D. Kawahara and S. Kurohashi. 2006. Case Frame Compilation from the Web Using High performance Computing. In Proceedings of the 5th International Conference on Language Resources and Evaluation.

T. Koo, X. Carreras, and M. Collins. 2008. Simple Semi-supervised Dependency Parsing. In Proceedings of the 46th ACL, pages 595–603.

T. Koo and M. Collins. 2010. Efficient Third-order Dependency Parsers. In Proceedings of the 48th ACL, pages 1–11.

A. F. T. Martins, N. A. Smith, and E. P. Xing. 2010. Turbo Parsers: Dependency Parsing by Approximate Variational Inference. In Proceedings of EMNLP 2010, pages 34–44.

R. McDonald, K. Crammer, and F. Pereira. 2005. Online Large-Margin Training of Dependency Parsers. In Proceedings of the 43rd ACL, pages 91–98.

R. McDonald and F. Pereira. 2006. Online Learning of Approximate Dependency Parsing Algorithms. In Proceedings of the 11th EACL, pages 81–88.

A. Ratnaparkhi. 1996. A Maximum Entropy Model for Part-Of-Speech Tagging. In Proceedings of the 1st EMNLP, pages 133–142.

F. Sangati, W. Zuidema, and R. Bod. 2009. A Generative Re-ranking Model for Dependency Parsing. In Proceedings of the 11th IWPT, pages 238–241.

J. Suzuki, H. Isozaki, X. Carreras, and M. Collins. 2009. An Empirical Study of Semi-supervised Structured Conditional Models for Dependency Parsing. In Proceedings of EMNLP 2009, pages 551–560.

H. Yamada and Y. Matsumoto. 2003. Statistical Dependency Analysis with Support Vector Machines. In Proceedings of the IWPT 2003, pages 195–206.

K. Yu, D. Kawahara, and S. Kurohashi. 2008. Chinese Dependency Parsing with Large Scale Automatically Constructed Case Structures. In Proceedings of Coling 2008, pages 1049–1056.

Y. Zhang and S. Clark. 2008. A Tale of Two Parsers: Investigating and Combining Graph-based and Transition-based Dependency Parsing. In Proceedings of EMNLP 2008, pages 562–571.

Y. Zhang and J. Nivre. 2011. Transition-based Dependency Parsing with Rich Non-local Features. In Proceedings of ACL 2011, page 188-193.

Applying Statistical Post-Editing to English-to-Korean Rule-based Machine Translation System

Ki-Young Lee and Young-Gil Kim

Natural Language Processing Team,
Electronics and Telecommunications Research Institute,
138 Gajeongno, Yuseong-gu, Daejeon, Korea
{leeky, kimyk}@etri.re.kr

Abstract

Conventional rule-based machine translation system suffers from its weakness of fluency in the view of target language generation. In particular, when translating English spoken language to Korean, the fluency of translation result is as important as adequacy in the aspect of readability and understanding. This problem is more severe in language pairs such as English-Korean. It's because English and Korean belong to different language family. So they have distinct characteristics. And this issue is very important factor which effects translation quality. This paper describes a statistical post-editing for improving the fluency of rule-based machine translation system. Through various experiments, we examined the effect of statistical post-editing for FromTo-EK[1] system which is a kind of rule-based machine translation system, for spoken language. The experiments showed promising results for translating diverse English spoken language sentences.

[1] FromTo-EK is an English-to-Korean rule-based machine translation system for some various domains (patent, paper, email and messenger).

1 Introduction

There have been many improvements in machine translation from rule-based machine translation (RBMT) to the latest statistical machine translation (SMT). Approaches for machine translation can be typically classified into conventional rule-based approach and statistical approach (Jin et al., 2008). RBMT translates a source sentence to a target sentence through analysis process, transfer process and generation process using analysis rules, dictionaries and transfer rules as its main translation knowledge. On the other hand, SMT system accomplishes translation using translation model and language model obtained from training large parallel corpus composed of source sentences and the corresponding target sentences (Koehn et al. 2003). Comparing two approaches, they have opposite features. That is, rule-based approach is better than statistical approach in the aspect of translation accuracy. However, fluency is contrary to each other. The language pairs that linguistic differences are huge such as English-Korean show these kinds of features apparently.

We aim to improve the translation fluency of RBMT system by introducing SPE. The proposed method is similar to SMT. Difference is the composition of parallel corpus used to build statistical models. To build model for post-editing, parallel corpus should be ready, which is composed of the pairs of the sentence translated by RBMT and the corresponding correct sentence translated by human translators. Using this parallel corpus, we can build statistical model to post-edit RBMT results. Also, we explain some points to consider when applying SPE to English-to-Korean translation by various experiments.

Our method consists of the following steps:

- Constructing parallel corpus composed of translation results by English-to-Korean RBMT system and translation results by human translator of English source sentences.
- Building translation model and language model for applying SPE (at this phase, SMT toolkits are used).
- Applying decoder for SPE to the output of RBMT system.

The section 2 of this paper presents weakness of conventional rule-based machine translation system. And the overview of our method will be described in the section 3. The section 4 describes experimental parameter, experimental results. In the section 5 and the section 6 we sum up the discussion and show the future research direction.

2 Weakness of RBMT system

Figure 1 shows the configuration of our rule-based machine translation system, FromTo-EK. The flow of machine translation as follows. First, roots of words in an input sentence is restored and part-of-speech (POS) tagging is carried out by morphological analysis and tagging module. Second, syntactic structure is found out by syntactic analysis module (parser). FromTo-EK engine employs full parsing strategy to analyze English source sentences. Third, input sentence structure (parse tree) is transferred to adequate target language structure using transfer patterns. At this step, lexical transfer based on context is conducted using dictionaries and word sense disambiguation knowledge (Yang et al., 2010). Fourth, Korean generator generates final Korean translation sentence.

The advantage of RBMT engine is that it can catch the exact dependency relation between the words in input sentence. It is very helpful to achieve high translation accuracy. In particular, in the case of language pairs which are very similar in the sense of linguistics (for example, Korean-Japanese), rule-based approach has showed good translation performance.

However, the problem of RBMT system is its poor fluency compared to SMT system. In particular, in translating spoken language sentences, such features are outstanding. Actually, when translating English spoken language sentences, it is found that unnatural, rigid and dried expressions are frequently used. It results from stereotyped language transfer phase, translation knowledge and the limit of translation methodology. We cannot achieve the fluency like human translation by assembling translation knowledge pieces. This is why we propose SPE for RBMT system.

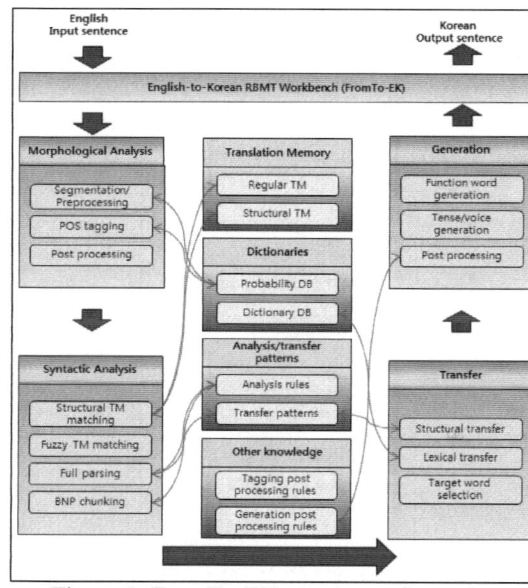

Figure 1. FromTo-EK system configuration

3 Statistical Post-Editing

3.1 Target of post-editing

First of all, to find out the target of applying SPE, we manually evaluated FromTo-EK (English-to-Korean RBMT system) using test set composed of 200 English spoken language sentences.

The measure for human evaluation is showed in Table 1 (Doyon et al., 1998). The score of one sentence in test set is the average of scores assigned by three human translators.

Score	Evaluation categories
4	All meaning expressed in the source fragment appears in the translation fragment
3	Most of the source fragment meaning is expressed in the translation fragment
2	Much of the source fragment meaning is expressed in the translation fragment
1	Little of the source fragment meaning is expressed in the translation fragment
0	None of the meaning expressed in the source fragment is expressed in the translation fragment

Table 1: Accuracy test of machine translation system

Score	Error category	# sent	# errors	Error rate
Score over 2.5	Morphological analysis or POS tagging errors	179	4	2.2%
	Parsing errors		9	5.0%
	Transfer or generation errors		15	**8.4%**
	Knowledge error		6	3.4%
Score under 2.5	Morphological analysis or POS tagging errors	21	3	**14.3 %**
	Parsing errors		6	**28.6 %**
	Transfer or generation errors		3	14.3 %
	Knowledge errors		4	19.0 %

Table 2: FromTo-EK evaluation analysis

As is shown in Table 2, analysis of the result of human evaluation shows that the sentences under average 2.5 have errors caused by analysis failure (including POS tagging errors and parsing errors). In this case, input to a transfer module (output from analysis module) is parse tree which already includes incorrect dependency relations. Because of syntactic (or morphological) analysis errors, these kinds of translation results have difficulty conveying the meaning of the original sentences. So, the sentences under 2.5 have little improvements by SPE. Meanwhile, in the case of the translation results scored over 2.5, it is not difficult to understand the overall meaning of source sentences except one or two words. Sentences over 2.5 have very little of errors from analysis phases. So, misunderstanding brought by analyzing source sentences incorrectly is rarely found. However, the sentences over 2.5 have some other problems. It may be summarized as Table 3.

As we know by Table 3, the problem with the sentences over 2.5 can be divided into two categories. The first is intrinsic to English-to-Korean transfer module and Korean generation module. These are because of the limit of RBMT paradigm and the lack of translation knowledge. The second, on the other hand, is some different in that source sentence was well translated to target sentence without the loss of meaning. That is, the only problem is that in the aspect of the command of Korean, RBMT result is not so natural. At the same time, to improve the fluency of RBMT is the target of this paper.

factors	comment
Wrong position of adverb	In Korean, the wrong position of adverb can change the object of modification.
Awkward expression	The lack of ambiguity resolution knowledge generates target words not matched in context.
Stereotyped target word	In most RBMT system, there is perfect strategy to select more natural target word depending on context in the aspect of target language.

Table 3: Factors which cause fluency problems in FromTo-EK

The fluency problem with RBMT system is that translation process has a mechanism with an emphasis on source sentence analysis. In RBMT approach, after input sentence analysis phase, transfer is based on just analysis result and translation knowledge such as dictionaries and transfer patterns. During source-to-target transfer and target sentence generation, the fluency of translation output sentence is not considered. In this paper, we demonstrate the impact of SPE for

RBMT and explain improvements by SPE in the concrete.

3.2 Statistical Post-Editing Architecture

SPE is based on SMT. SPE and SMT differ from the composition of training corpus. For building translation model, SMT uses large parallel corpus composed of the pairs of source sentence and corresponding target sentence. The parallel corpus for SPE training is the pairs of translation sentence by RBMT system and the corresponding correct translation sentence by human translator.

Table 4 shows parallel corpus composed of translation by RBMT and Human respectively. In Table 4, first column is English sentence, second column is Korean translation sentence by RBMT and third column is Korean translation sentence by human translator. In the meaning point, translations by RBMT (second column) have not bad accuracy. However their fluency is not natural. In the other words, the sentences at second column convey right meaning, but are not fluent sentences. We aim to align translation by RBMT into translation by human for getting knowledge for SPE. Through this learning process, the useful data for improving erroneous expressions to correct expressions can be acquired.

Source sentence	Translation by RBMT	Translation by Human
What time does it leave?	Geugeoseun myeotsie chulbalhamnikka[2] ? (그것은 몇 시에 출발합니까)	Myeot sie chulbalhajyo? (몇 시에 출발하죠)
Do you have any other colors?	Dangsineun dareun saegi itsseumnikka? (당신은 다른 색이 있습니까)	Dareun saekkal jom boyeo jusigetsseoyo? (다른 색깔 좀 보여 주시겠어요)
It's too flashy for me.	Geugeoseun nareul wihae neomu yahamnida. (그것은 나를 위해 너무 야합니다)	Jeohanteneun neomu hwaryeohandeyo (저한테는 너무 화려한데요)
I'm looking for something for my friend.	Je chingureul wihan eotteon geoseul chatkko itsseoyo (제 친구를 위한 어떤 것을 찾고 있습니다)	Je chinguege julmanhan geoseul chatkko itsseoyo (제 친구에게 줄 만한 것을 찾고 있어요)
Do you have bags made of softer leather?	Dangsineun gabangeul deo budeureoun gajugeuro mandeureojigeha mnikka (당신은 가방을 더 부드러운 가죽으로 만들어지게 합니까)	Deo budeureoun gaguk gabang itnayo (더 부드러운 가죽 가방 있나요)
Please show me some ladies' watches.	Naege yakkanui eoseongui sigereul boyeojuseyo (나에게 약간의 여성의 시계를 보여주세요)	Eoseongyong sige jom boyeojuseyo (여성용 시계 좀 보여 주세요)

Table 4: Parallel corpus for SPE

[2] We follow the Romanization system of Korean, hereafter.

We can build translation model and language model for SPE using this corpus composed of Korean (by RBMT) - Korean (by human). For building models for SPE, the tools for SMT are used at the same way. These models are used to post-edit RBMT results.

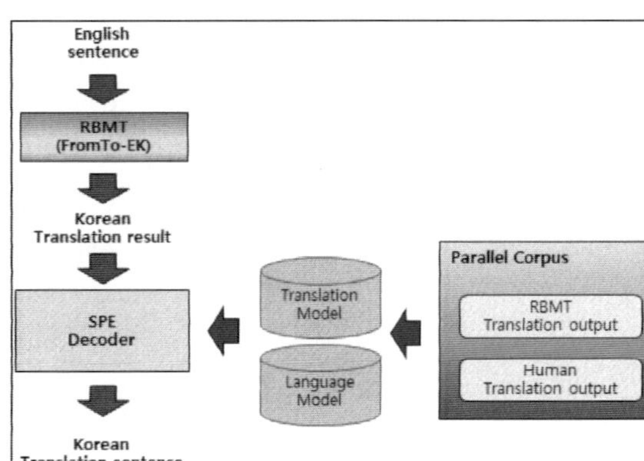

Figure 2. Statistical post-editing architecture

Figure 2 shows the configuration of SPE. We thought that by training based on alignment between incorrect machine translation result and correct human translation result, knowledge to improve the fluency of RBMT can be obtained. In applying SPE to RBMT system, SPE module is located at last place which take the translation result by RBMT as input. In figure 3, translation model and language model means statistical post-editing models which are thought in the concept of statistical machine translation. We use the same tools as SMT for getting SPE models.

4 Experiments

4.1 Setup

Table 5 explains 2 types of training corpora, tuning corpus and test set. The domain for our experiments is tour/travel. For considering the property of Korean, we prepared 2 training corpora. The training_corpus_s is built from Korean surface forms of words in sentences. The training_corpus_m is obtained from Korean morpheme through POS tagging. We tested on translating spoken language test set belonging to tour domain from English to Korean.

Corpus	# Sentences
Training_Corpus_s	1,082 K
Training_Corpus_m	1,082 K
Tuning Set	1 K
Test Set	200

Table 5: Training corpus for evaluation

Table 6 shows the baseline system for building statistical model for post-editing.

Moses[3] (Koehn, 2007)	Revision = "4383" as the baseline system for training and decoding
GIZA++[4] (Och and Ney, 2003)	Version 1.0.5 for alignment between translation result by FromTo-EK and human translation result.
SRI LM[5] (Stolcke, 2002)	version 1.5.12 for building a 3-gram language model

Table 6: Baseline system for evaluation

[3] http://www.statmt.org/moses/

[4] http://giza-pp.googlecode.com/files/giza-pp-v1.0.5.tar.gz

[5] http://www.speech.sri.com/projects/srilm/

4.2 Evaluation results

We tested the coverage of SPE using two different training corpora. Table 7 describes the impact of SPE to the translation result of FromTo-EK engine. Regardless of training corpus, many sentences were changed by applying SPE.

	# sent changed	Change rate
Training_Corpus_s	154	77%
Training_Corpus_m	144	72%

Table 7: The number of sentences changed by SPE

Table 8 shows the analysis of the result of applying SPE to the result of FromTo-EK. In table 8, # sent, # imp and # deg means the number of sentences belonging to corresponding score, the number of sentences improved and degraded respectively. Table 8 presents something interesting. First, the characteristic of translation target language should be considered for better SPE performance. In this paper we focused English-to-Korean translation. Korean belonging to agglutinative language has distinct features that function words are well developed and these function words are closely related to fluency. So, when using parallel corpus composed of surface forms of words for training, SPE doesn't work well. Second, the target of SPE should be defined clearly. Because SPE doesn't consider source sentence in training phase, translation results under 2.5, including already analysis errors, don't have the advantage of SPE. This means that it is difficult for SPE to fix errors occurred at analysis phase. Third, translation results over 3.5 are apt to be degraded by SPE, contrary to expectation. This is related to reordering. We explain this with Table 9.

Target sent	# sent	Training _Corpus_s		Training _Corpus_m	
		# imp	# deg	# imp	# deg
over 3.5	96	9	36	7	10
Over 2.5 and under 3.5	83	13	24	**29**	21
Under 2.5	21	0	0	5	0
Total	200	22	**60**	**41**	31

Table 8: The improvement by SPE

Based on experiment with training_corpus_m, we categorized the operation of SPE and had a look at the effect of each operation. Table 9 provides detail figures of SPE for sentences over score 2.5.

Category		# imp	# deg	# imp / # deg
Word change	Function word	**9**	4	2.25
	Noun	12	11	1.09
	Verb	18	9	2.0
	Adjective	2	0	
	Adverb	1	1	1.0
	Compound word	8	2	4.0
Reordering		2	**13**	0.15
Subject omission		9	0	

Table 9: The effect of SPE operations for sentences over 2.5

In table 9, "word change" includes insertion, change and deletion. In FromTo-EK engine, function word is generated using just dictionaries and transfer patterns without consideration for rich context. This leads FromTo-EK into its own fluency problems, so does word of other part-of-speech. However, we can know that these kinds of problems can be improved by SPE. In Korean spoken language, "subject omission" is frequent and SPE reflects it well.

However, reordering raises serious side effects. Reordering frequently makes correct dependency relation incorrect. How to minimize the side effects of reordering is also important issue.

There are some examples of the result of applying SPE in Table 10. By SPE, we can see that word change including word insertion and word deletion occurred and fluency is improved. Final translation result by SPE is very good. The literary style expressions appeared in RBMT results are changed to colloquial style by SPE. And many abbreviation forms which are used in spoken language are introduced by SPE. Conventional RBMT cannot get such fluent sentences just using analysis rules, transfer patterns so on.

5 Discussion

We surveyed the effect of statistical post-editing method applied to English-to-Korean rule-based machine translation system. There still remain some problems to be solved necessarily:

- How to select the sentences and words which could be improved by post-editing? It is needed to devise method to select the target to apply post-editing with minimizing degradation of translation quality. We are considering some language models for resolving these problems.
- Is there a method to apply post-editing for the part of sentence partially? If it is, how to find the phrase or clause to apply post-editing? This problem is similar to first problem to discuss. Up to now, table 9 shows word change category is best target of SPE. However, it is necessary to extend the boundaries of post-editing.
- To improve performance, how to use other information such as source language information? Proposed method considers the alignment data only in target language aspects. If source language clues are used in combination with target language alignment data, the accuracy of post-editing will be improved.
- How to implement RBMT system with SPE module? It is the same as the structure which employs two translation engines sequentially. So its feasibility in application domains should be considered.

6 Conclusion

We proposed how to make use of SPE to improve the fluency of RBMT system. We could see that to maximize the effect of SPE, the consideration on target language has to be preceded. We categorized the factors which can increase the quality of RBMT by SPE. In the case of FromTo-EK system, a kind of RBMT, we knew that SPE works effectively for the sentences in which morphological or syntactic analysis errors did not occur. So, our next research topic is how to decide the target sentences/phrases/words of SPE. And, utilizing the source sentence and its related information (source word, its POS and its syntactic role) is also important research topic to effect SPE performance.

English sentence	FromTo-EK result	score	SPE result	score
What do I have to wrap it with?	Mueoseuro geugeoseul ssayahamnikka? (무엇으로 그것을 싸야 합니까?)	3.83	Mworo pojanghalkkayo? (뭐로 포장할까요?)	4.0
It closes at 11 o'clock at night.	Geugeoseun bame dacheo itsseumnida. (그것은 밤에 11시에 닫혀 있습니다.)	3.33	Bam 11sie kkeunnamnida. (밤 11시에 끝납니다.)	4.0
They depend on the freshness.	Geudeureun sinseonmie uijonhanda. (그들은 신선미 에 의존한다.)	3.0	Geudeureun sinseonmie ddara dareuda. (그들은 신선미 에 따라 다르다.)	3.5
The restroom door on the first floor is locked.	1cheung wiui hwajangsil muneun jamgyeojimnida. (1층 위의 화장실 문은 잠겨집니다.)	2.83	1cheunge itneun hwajangsil muni jamgyeotseumnida. (1층에 있는 화장실 문이 잠겼습니다.	4.0

Table 10: Example of SPE result

References

Yun Jin et al. 2008. The Trends of Machine Translation Technology and Case Study. Electronics and Telecommunications Trends, vol. 23, no. 1, pp.89-98.

Philipp Koehn et al. 2003. Statistical Phrase Based Translation. In Proc. of the HLT/NAACL.

Seong Il Yang, Young Ae Seo, Young Kil Kim, and Dongyul Ra. 2010. Noun Sense Identification of Korean Nominal Compounds Based on Sentential Form Recovery, ETRI Journal, vol.32, no.5, pp.740-749.

J. Doyon, K. Taylor and J. White. 1998. The DARPA machine translation evaluation methodology. Proc. of AMTA-98.

Philipp Koehn, Hieu Hoang, Alexandra Birch, Chris, Callison-Burch, Marcello Federico, Nicola Bertoldi, Brooke Cowan, Wade Shen, Christine Moran, Richard Zens, Chris Dyer, Ond ˇ rej Bojar, Alexandra Constantin, and Evan Herbst. 2007. Moses: Open source toolkit for statistical machine translation. the ACL '07 Demo-Poster, pp.177 - 180.

Franz Josef Och and Hermann Ney. 2003. A systematic comparison of various statistical alignment models. Computational Linguistics, 2003, pp.19 - 51.

Andreas Stolcke. 2002. Srilm - an extensible language modeling toolkit. Proc. of ICSLP, pp.901 - 904.

A Model of Vietnamese Person Named Entity Question Answering System

Mai-Vu Tran, Duc-Trong Le
KTLab, University of Engineering and Technology – Vietnam National University, Hanoi
{vutm, trongld}@vnu.edu.vn

Xuan- Tu Tran, Tien-Tung Nguyen
KTLab - University of Engineering and Technology – Vietnam National University, Hanoi
{tutx_52, tungnt_5}@vnu.edu.vn

Abstract

In this paper, we proposed a Vietnamese named entity question answering (QA) model. This model applies an analytical question method using CRF machine learning algorithm combined with two automatic answering strategies: indexed sentences database-based and Google search engine-based. We gathered a Vietnamese question dataset containing about 2000 popular "Who, Whom, Whose" questions to evaluate our question chunking method and QA model. According to experiments, question chunking phase acquired the average F1 score of 92.99%. Equally significant, in our QA evaluation, experimental results illustrated that our approaches were completely reasonable and realistic with 74.63% precision and 87.9% ability to give the answers.

Keywords: Vietnamese question, QA, VPQA, question analysis, answer extraction, question parser

1 Introduction

Numerous researches about Question Answering (QA) systems have been discussed in recent years. Initially, they only answered simple questions; however, currently researches have been focused on methods for more complex questions. Those methods analyze and parse complex questions to various simple questions before using existed techniques to respond. [1]

Automatic question answering – the ability of computers to answer simple or complex questions, posed in ordinary human language – is the most exciting. Building the question answering system is a difficult issue in terms of natural language processing tasks. Presently, automatic question answering systems are revolutionizing the processing of textual information. By coordinating complex natural language processing techniques, sophisticated linguistic representations and advanced machine learning methods, automatic question answering systems can detect exact responses from a wide variety of natural language questions in unstructured texts.

Recent researches demonstrated that the increasing in performance of systems is dependent on the number of probable answers in documents. The exact answer detection is one of the most significant problems in QA systems. For this purpose, our model utilized CRF [5] machine learning algorithm to parse natural questions and some IR strategies to extract answers. The model works on closed domain by extracting human names based on knowledge warehouse and search engines. If answers are not found in database, the question will push into Google search engine. The QA system just supports questions (such as "Who?", "Whom?", "Whose?") in factoid form or one sentence.

The aim of this paper is to design and implement a new classification model, reformulation and answer validation in a QA system. The methodology in our system is to discover correct answer in person domain with NLP techniques, CRF model to parse question, and some strategies to extract answer: knowledge-based, search engine-based and hybrid method. The primary reason of an answer validation component in the system concerns the difficulty of picking up from a document the "exact answer".

Our approach relies on investigating a statistical machine learning method to parse natural question and extract answer candidates by mining the documents or a domain text corpus for their co-occurrence tendency [2]. In the initial phase, questions are parsed by using CRF model. Subsequently, query patterns based on their types are clarified before the search engine detect candidate answer documents and send them to answer processing module to extract correct answers. The system filters candidate answers collection based on their similarities with question and assigns a priority number to the candidate answers. Finally, the system ranks the answers and sends to user for final validation in order to extract the exact answer. Our system modeled in person domain however it could be expanded to open domains in QA systems.

2 Related work

Question answering researches wereclassified by diverse competitive evaluations which are conducted by the question answering track of the Text Retrieval Conference[1], an annual event sponsored by the U.S. National Institute of Standards and Technology (NIST). Starting in 1999, the TREC question answering evaluation initially focused on factoid (or fact-recall) questions, which could be answered by extracting phrase length passages. Some of the TREC systems achieved a remarkable accuracy: the best factoid QA systems can now answer over 70% of arbitrary, open domain factoid questions.

In Webclopedia [6], with each question type, the system provides a set of pattern questions and answers. The system has to determine the type of question based on the similarities between the input question and each of the question patterns. Then the corresponding pattern will be used to find passages containing the answer. Finally, the answer is extracted from the found passages.

The True Knowledge Answer Engine[2] attempts to comprehend a given question by disambiguation from all possible meanings of the words in the question to find the most likely one.It discoverson its database of knowledge of discrete facts. As these facts are stored in a form that a computer can understand, the answering engine attempts to produce an answer according to its comprehended meaning of the input question [8].

Wolfram Alpha[3]is an answering engine developed by Wolfram Research. It is an online service that answers factual questions directly by computing the answer from structured data, rather than providing a list of documents or web pages that might contain the answer as a search engine does, Knowledge Base [9].

In Vietnamese text experiments, Vu M.T, et al [7] proposed a model of question answering system which is based on semantic relation extraction. It is a combination of two methods: snowball of Agichtein, Gravano and the search engine of Ravichandran, Hovy to extract semantic relation patterns from the Vietnamese texts. The experimental system achieves positive results on the domain of tourism and also shows the correctness of the model. However, the statistic relation impacts on the system precision and executed time is depended on network speed.

Nguyen Q.D, et al proposed an ontology-based Vietnamese question answering system that allows users to express their questions in natural language [4]. It includes two components: a natural language question analysis engine and an answer retrieval module. They built a set of relations in the ontology which includes only two person relations. According the system's experimental results are relatively high, the cost for building the database is high, and sometimes the extracted relations cannot cover the data domain.

From these systems, this paper introducesa model of person named entity question answering system in Vietnamese domain with machine learning CRF-based method in question analysis phase; sentences data collection-based and search engine-based strategies in answer extraction phase.

3 System architecture

VPQA model consist of three fundamental modules. The first module (1) focuses on Vietnamese natural language question analysis by CRF. The result set of tagged component in the 3rd step is used in the recommendation sub-module (2). It offers user answers and question patterns by Lucene searching from QA Log Database. Additionally, it is also utilized for the question expansion step and expands queries which are the output for next module.

[1]http://www.trec.nist.gov

[2]http://www.trueknowledge.com

[3]http//www.woframalpha.com/

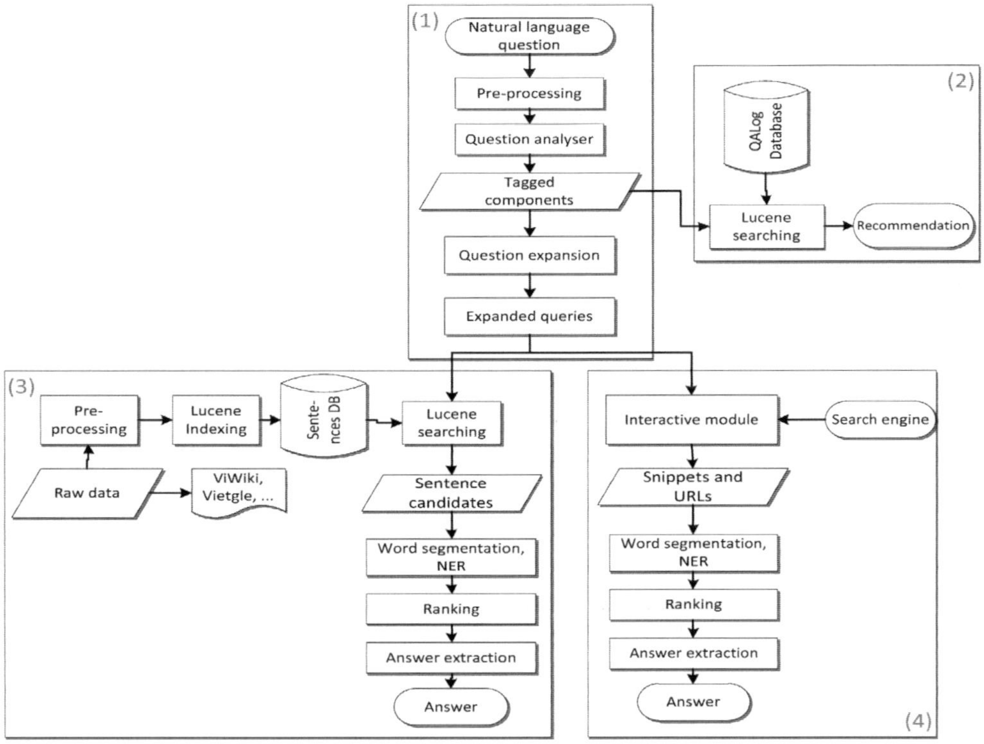

Figure 1: VPQA Model

According to those results, the second module (3) looks its candidates in Lucene[1] indexed sentences' database before determining answer for user by conducting some steps such as: Word Segmentation, NER, Ranking and Answer extraction. Instead of looking in Lucene Database, the last module extracts the set of candidates from snippets returned from Google. The next steps are similar with the 2nd module.

3.1 Question analysis module

3.1.1 "Who, Whom, Whose" question in Vietnamese

Vietnamese linguists have classified Vietnamese sentences by alternative criteria or syntax structure. By Vietnamese "Who, Whom, Whose" questions properties and their mean, they are classified in some forms with four types of component such as: Subject/agent, Verb/action, Object/theme, and Indirect_Ojbect/Co_themyge[6].Commonly, a simple question relate to two forms: two classes of object and three classes of object. Example:

- Relating two classes of objects:
  - ✓ Subject/agent + Verb/action + Object/theme
  - ✓ Object/Theme + Subject/agent + Verb/action
  - ✓ Object/Theme + Verb/action + Subject/agent

Example 1: The question "Who was the Harry Potter book written by?" is same as the Vietnamese question "Cuốn sách Harry Potter được viết bởi ai?"

Above examples have two classes: Tácgiả/Author and Sách/Book

- Relating three classes of objects:
  - ✓ Object/Theme: Indirect_Object/Co_theme+ Verb/action + Subject/agent

Example 2: The Vietnamese question "Ai là tác giả của cuốn Harry Potter xuất bản năm 2004?" is same meaning with "Who is author of the Harry Potter book published in 2004?" include 3 classes: Tác giả/Author, Sách/Book, Năm/Year

[1]http://lucene.apache.org

Label	Meaning	Type of component
WH	Question type	
D_Attr	Feature of job, position	Subject/Agent
D_Time	Feature of time	Idirect_Object/Co_theme
D_Loc	Feature of location	
A_W	Adjective phrase	Verb/Action
V_W	Verb phrase	
N_W	Noun phrase	
Obj	Object	Object/Theme
O	Others	

Table 1: Proposed features and labels

Feature	Meaning	Sign	Example
Lexicon	The existence in Vietnamese dictionary	meaning:0, meaning:±1, meaning:±2	**meaning:**-1:là **meaning:0**:tác+giả
POS tag	Part of speech	pos:N, pos:V, pos:adj, etc.	**meaning:0:**tác+giả **pos:N**
Letter character	Length, capital letter	char:length:n, cap:k:i, cap:k:a	**char:length:11 cap:0:i**
Prefix	The existence of previous word in prefix dictionary	per:prefix	**per:prefix:-2**
Dictionary	Name, location, organization, job dictionary	Per:job, org:i:, etc	**org:0:FPT per:job:-2**

Table 2: Features used in VPQA system

3.1.2 The proposed method

The primary purpose in this module is to determine the feature components of the initial question: Object, Adjective, Verb, Adverb, etc. before making queries for the next modules. This is an automatic chunking problem for natural language question. Its solution is similar with the solution of the POS-tagging problem in information extraction. Using machine learning method CRF (Condition Random Fields) is one of the best solutions in Vietnamese. In many Vietnamese problems, it conduces to satisfactory results, for instances: Word segmentation (93%), POS-tagging (89.69%), Name entity recognition (92.31%), chunking (79.58%), etc.

Through the investigation of data and Vietnamese question features, the model proposed 9 labels and their features respectively. These labels represent four types of component as above in the table 1.

Example 3: Ai là người tìm ra châu Mỹ ? (Who discovered the American?) Ai là (Who)/WH người/O tìm ra (discovered)/V_W châu Mỹ(the America)/Object

In example 3, the set of keywords after implementing the module contain: tìm ra (Discovered)/V_W, châu Mỹ (the American)/Object.

3.1.3 Module processing

The feature selection is the most important step in CRF method. It impacts on the quality of NER and chunking systems. The more careful selection is, the more accurate system is. At a position i of observed data sequence include two parts. The former is data features, the other is respective label. The information of data features helps us determine the information of respective label at an observed data position. It means that labels can be automatically extracted model when has data features. From this point of view, the features used in our system are shown in Table2. From the features in Table 2, the using CRF method for about 2000 tagged questions (Training dataset).

Atthe result, a model which is base for analyzing user question components later is built.

3.2 Answer processing module

Answer extraction module proposes two primary answering strategies: sentences data collection-based and search engine-based. We will address in greater detail each strategy in the following sections.

3.2.1 Sentences data collection-based strategy

First, documents are retrieved and extracted using freely available Wikipedia dumps[1] of Vietnamese editions in XML format in which document contain fields: title, URL, content of article in Wikipedia respectively. Finally, question answering will be conducted follow three steps:

Step 1: Building data collection

The obtained documents are conducted noise reduction and sentence tokenization using JVnTextPro[2] toolkit. After that, we index this new data with some specific fields such as: title, URL, sentences of document using Lucence.

Step 2: Candidate Answer Extraction

Underlying each component of our question answering system is keyword-based document retrieval using Lucene. The system explored two modifications to extract answer: baseline method (Baseline) using word tokenization and CRF method in the question analysis phase (KLB). These strategies are described in greater detail below, and summarized in table4

- Baseline: this is a basic approach to compare with our proposed method which it only uses keywords taken from question to make query for Lucence. To illustrate our method clearer let us observe the example which will use in this paper:
  - ✓ With a question: "Ai là người tìm ra Châu Mỹ?" ("Who discovered theAmerican?")
  - ✓ Keywords: "tìm ra", "Châu Mỹ" ("discovered", "the American")
  - ✓ Query in lucence: +"tìm ra" +"Châu Mỹ" (+"discovered"+"the American")
- KLB: In this section, the system proposed an algorithm to extract answers. Firstly, components of a question have been sent by the question processing phase. These components consist of parts with tag of question, for instance: "Ai là - WH", "người - O", "tìm ra – V_W", "Châu Mỹ - Obj" ("Who - WH", "discovered – V_W", "the American - Obj"). Subsequently, the system chooses potential words to make Lucene query contains labels: "V_W", "A_W", "N_W", "Obj" and other words such as: "D_Time", "D_Loc", "D_Attr" to acquire exact answer by filtering retrieved results from Lucene. Finally, to get more exact answer, the system supplements a query expansion procedure by using a Vietnamese synonym dictionary.

Step 3: Answer selection

Candidate answers collection which has been sent by answer extraction feed in a filteringcomponent. These candidates are ranked by using score formula of Lucene (1). Sentence ranking is based on precision- and recall-like measures. Each question term is assigned by a weight based on its idf. Words that are synonymous according to our lexicons are pooled and their weights summed. The weights of words in the final sentence, and of some other useful terms, are boosted. Synonymous terms from the question are included in the Lucene query as well, each with the pooled weight. We note each document's Lucene DocScore. Finally, answer sentence candidates are recognized person entity answer by using Java open source library VSW[3] and ranked by a formula (2).

In there: $rank_{entity/d}$: rank of answer entity; scored: score of sentence candidate which contain entity; $freq_{entity}$: Frequency of entity in N candidates; N: Number of sentences candidates, δ Threshold

$$score_d = \sum_{tinq} (tf(tind) \times idf(t)^2 \times boost(t.fieldind) \times lengthNorm(t.fieldind) \times coord(q,d) \times queryNorm(q) \quad (1)$$

$$rank_{entity\ /N} = \delta \times score_d \times freq_{entity} + \frac{1-\delta}{N} \quad (2)$$

[1]http://dumps.wikimedia.org/viwiki/20101031/
[2]http://jvntextpro.sourceforge.net/

[2]http://code.google.com/p/vsw/

3.2.2 Search engine-based

In previous section, our system proposed a strategy based on collected data (SEB). The capability of answering in this strategy depends on amount of data warehouse. Therefore, to improve this as well as increase accuracy of answer, we observed other method based on obtained results of search engine. These strategies are described in greater detail follow two step:

Step 1: Snippet Retrieval

Same to previous strategy, after achieve keywords from question processing phase, these keywords will be made Google query by adding wildcard "*" or "**" into keywords. By this way, the system achieve some Google queries form: "*k1 k2...*" "*k1 * k2...*", "*k1 ** k2...*" (k_i: is ith keyword).

Example: "tìm ra * Châu Mỹ" ("discovered * the American"); "tìm ra" "Châu Mỹ" ("discovered", "the American")

Next, queries will be pushed to Google search engine and obtain candidate snippets by using JSOAP API.

Step 2: Answer extraction

Candidate snippets collection which has been sent by step 1 are recognized person entity answer by using Java open source library VSW and ranked by using frequency of each entity.

4 Experiment and Discussion

In this section, the paper present some achieved results which illustrate that the proposed model as well as our approach is completely reasonable and highly applicable. Our model conducted two main experiments to evaluate system: one to appraise question analysis phase and another one to appraise entire system.

In question analysis phase, initially, we built a question dataset containingabout 2000 popular"Who, Whom, Whose" questions. This dataset was majorly drawn from Yahoo! Answer and some Vietnamese e-newspaper websites with some following requirements: the question must be less ambiguous and meaningful in natural language. After that, we standardized these questions into suitable syntax as well as Vietnamese context and conducted labeling to obtain a standard training dataset. Next, we used 10 fold cross validation in which were dividedthe training data randomly by 9:1 ratio. Then we carried out test and exposed the validated measures: precision, recall and F1 measure as show in table 3.

In Table 3, we presented a chart to compare the measures of 10 folds. The figure shown that the precision of using CRF in question analysis is quite high with F1 measure approximate 93%. This result illustrated that our approach is completely reasonable. However, the chart shown some unexpected results in several sample tests but these will be made well by supplement some specific dictionary as well as strengthen the training data much more.

	Precision	Recall	F1
Fold 1	89.7	90.2	89.95
Fold 2	94.1	95.05	94.57
Fold 3	96.4	96.83	96.61
Fold 4	93.07	94.23	93.64
Fold 5	94.58	96.11	95.33
Fold 6	92.43	93.45	92.93
Fold 7	91.3	92.67	91.98
Fold 8	88.35	89.45	88.89
Fold 9	91.5	92.11	91.80
Fold 10	93.32	95.01	94.15
Average	**92.475**	**93.51**	**92.99**

Table 3: Table of experiment results: 10 foldscross-validation

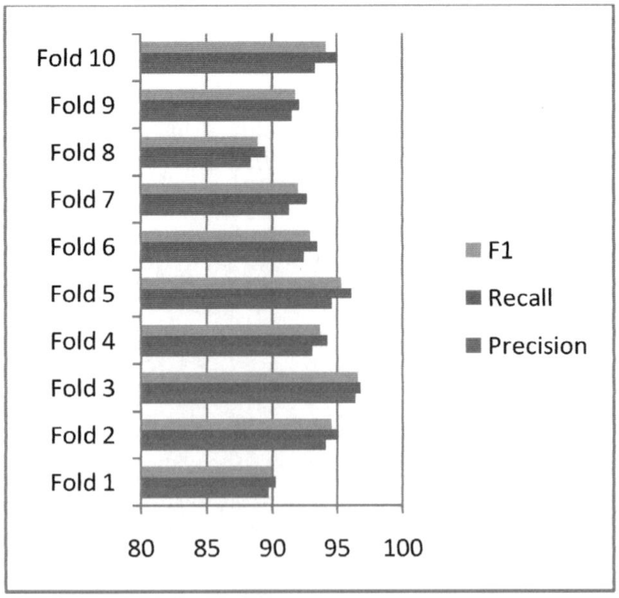

Figure 2: 10-folds cross-validation results chart

	Top 1			Top 3			Top 5		
	ρ	C	*T*	ρ	C	T	ρ	C	*T*
Baseline	41.07	54.3	46	42.23	54.7	49	42.29	55.1	52
KLB	79.68	55.6	58	89.39	60.3	59	90.03	60.2	61
SEB	71.44	90	28059	72.18	91.3	29820	73.17	91.7	30123
KLB+SEB	74.63	87.9	11630	79.62	89.3	12657	80.02	91.1	12799

Table 4: The comparisons of KLB, SEB, (KLB+SEB), and Baseline with 3 measures: precision (ρ), capability of answering (C), responded time (*T*)

In the next phase, we evaluated precision and responding time of entire system in which we proposed a method for question analysis as basic system to compare with our system. Here, we used 1000 questions taken from training data. After that we compared obtained result from 3 strategies of answering: knowledge-based (KLB), search engine-based (SEB) and hybrid method of these two strategies (KLB+SEB). Especially, with knowledge-basedstrategy, we carried out one more experiment named Baseline, instead of using CRF we only analyze questions at morphological layer to illustrate the effectiveness of CRF.The result is divided into 3 levels: Top one, three, and five per question, respectively. These obtained results are presented in Table 4.

In this experiment, we used 3 main measures to evaluate. The first one is capability of answering which is defined by $C = \frac{q}{Q}$ (q is amount of questions which system get answers; Q is amount of tested questions). The second one is precision of answers which is defined by $\rho = \frac{q_x}{q}$ (q_x is amount of questions which system get exact answers). And the last one is system performance which is time that system obtains an answer with each question. To evaluate this measure we run system with 1000 loops to answer one question before computing total running time and divided by total of loops. Particularly, it is defined by $\frac{t}{1000}$ (t is total running time 1000 times).

Table 4 presents a chart to compare obtained result per strategy. The chart shows that accuracy of answers and system performance is satisfactory. Top three levels generates the best results, however capability of answering is not really good because of its dependence on covered knowledge warehouse as well as ranking algorithms for returned answer did not achieve highly effectiveresults. Whilst the strategy using search engine has capability of answering as well as its accuracy of answer is acceptable but the running time is too slow. This is not efficient to build a real system, thus we proposed building a two layer system (combine both of above strategy) and achieved result which illustrates that hybrid system is completely reasonable. Additionally, we observed that the result of baseline method and compared it to CRF- based method. Using CRF create results which are much higher than baseline. These shown that the approach based on machine learning algorithms achieved results quite highly as well as illustrated that our proposed system is reasonable and realistic.

5 Conclusion and Future works

In this paper, we proposed and built a model of automatic system to answer questions about name of person in Vietnamese data domain. The achieved results illustrated that our approaches were completely reasonable and realistic. Furthermore, we also built an open framework for building an automatic question answering system. However, the system still remains some limitations due to the lack of amount of training question dataset as well as pessimistic rank algorithms for returned answers.We recommend the knowledge-based method to acquire the most remarkable performance and F1 score. Our future works will focus on building a huge training question dataset, boost a more optimal rank algorithm as well as improve system performance to deploy a real application. Additionally, we'll also extend knowledge warehouse and question domain to build an automatic open domain question answering system.

References

1. Demner-Fushman, Dina, *"Complex Question Answering Based on Semantic Domain Model of Clinical Medicine",* OCLC's Experimental Thesis Catalog, College Park, Md.: University of Maryland (United States), 2006.
2. Magnini, B., Negri, M., Prevete, R., Tanev, H.: *"Comparing Statisticaland Content-Based Techniques for Answer Validation on the Web"*, Proceedings of the VIII Convegno AI*IA, Siena, Italy, 2002.
3. Boris Katz,*Annotating the World Wide Web using Natural Language*, In Proceedings of the 5th RAIO conference on Computer Assisted information searching on the internet (RIAO'97) 1997.
4. Dai Quoc Nguyen, Dat Quoc Nguyen, Son Bao Pham, *A Vietnamese Question Answering System*, KSE, pp.26-32, 2009 International Conference on Knowledge and Systems Engineering, 2009
5. John D. Lafferty, Andrew McCallum, Fernando C. N. Pereira: *Conditional Random Fields: Probabilistic Models for Segmenting and Labeling Sequence Data*. ICML 2001: 282-289
6. TuoiT.Phan, ThanhC.Nguyen, ThuyN.T.Huynh. *Question Semantic Analysis in Vietnamese QA System*. The Advances in Intelligent Information and Database Systems book, Serie of Studies in Computational Intelligence, Volume 283, pp.29-40, (2010)
7. Vu Mai Tran, Vinh Duc Nguyen, Oanh Thi Tran, Uyen Thu Thi Pham, Thuy Quang Ha. *An Experimental Study of Vietnamese Question Answering System*. In Proceedings of IALP'2009. pp.152~155
8. Catalin David, Christoph Lange, Florian Rabe: *Interactive Documents as Interfaces to Computer AlgebraSystems: JOBAD and Wolfram|Alpha*; Centre d'Étude et de Recherche en Informatique du CNAM (Cédric) 2010
9. http://corporate.trueknowledge.com/architecture/

A Machine Translation Approach for Chinese Whole-Sentence Pinyin-to-Character Conversion*

Shaohua Yang and **Hai Zhao**† and **Bao-liang Lu**
MOE-Microsoft Key Laboratory for Intelligent Computing and Intelligent Systems,
Center for Brain-Like Computing and Machine Intelligence
Department of Computer Science and Engineering, Shanghai Jiao Tong University
800 Dongchuan Road, Shanghai 200240, China
shyang.ok@gmail.com, zhaohai@cs.sjtu.edu.cn, blu@cs.sjtu.edu.cn

Abstract

This paper introduces a new approach to solve the Chinese Pinyin-to-character (PTC) conversion problem. The conversion from Chinese Pinyin to Chinese character can be regarded as a transformation between two different languages (from the Latin writing system of Chinese Pinyin to the character form of Chinese,Hanzi), which can be naturally solved by machine translation framework. PTC problem is usually regarded as a sequence labeling problem, however, it is more difficult than any other general sequence labeling problems, since it requires a large label set of all Chinese characters for the labeling task. The essential difficulty of the task lies in the high degree of ambiguities of Chinese characters corresponding to Pinyins. Our approach is novel in that it effectively combines the features of continuous source sequence and target sequence. The experimental results show that the proposed approach is much faster, besides, we got a better result and outperformed the existing sequence labeling approaches.

1 Introduction

There are more than twenty thousand different Chinese characters adopted by Chinese language so that it is a difficult task to type the Chinese character directly from a Latin-style keyboard. Chinese Pinyin is such an encoding scheme that can map the Chinese character to a group of Latin letters so that each character usually has an unique Pinyin representation[1]. Pinyin is originally designed as the phonetic symbol of a Chinese character. For example, Pinyin for the Chinese character **"我"**(I,me) is **"wo"**. As one of the most important topic in Chinese natural language process, Pinyin-to-character(PTC) problem refers to the automatic transformation from Chinese Pinyin sequence to Chinese character sequence. It plays an important or even key role in areas such as speech recognition, Chinese keyboard input method and etc.

There are five different tones for Chinese pronunciation. In Chinese Pinyin system, tone is represented as an accent symbol over Latin letters, which is not convenient to input and thus usually ignored in most Chinese keyboard input methods.

The Chinese PTC problem can be very challenging for the following reasons: there are about 410 Pinyins(without considering five different tones), however, there are ten thousands Chinese characters, even the most popular accounts for about 5,000. So it is quite common to see the phenomenon that different Chinese characters have the same Pinyin. On the average, there are about ten or more Chinese characters which are corresponding to one Pinyin.

When longer Pinyin sequence is given, number of the corresponding legal character sequences will be heavily reduced. Thus, to alleviate the ambiguity

*This work was partially supported by the National Natural Science Foundation of China (Grant No. 60903119 and Grant No. 61170114), the National Research Foundation for the Doctoral Program of Higher Education of China under Grant No. 20110073120022, the National Basic Research Program of China (Grant No. 2009CB320901) and the European Union Seventh Framework Programme (Grant No. 247619).

†Corresponding author

[1] A few Chinese characters are pronounced in several different ways, so they may have multiple Pinyin representation.

zi	ran	yu	yan	chu	li
字	**然**	与	严	出	**理**
子	染	**语**	眼	除	离
自	燃	于	烟	**处**	力
紫	冉	鱼	**言**	初	李
资	髯	雨	演	触	利

Table 1: One Pinyin can be mapped to multiple Chinese character (the bolded characters are the correct choices corresponding to the Pinyin sequence.

and speedup the process, in a typical Chinese (Latin) keyboard input method, one always try to type as long Pinyin sequence as possible.

In this paper, we consider such a typical PTC task when a whole sentence of Pinyin sequence is given, and we attempt to recover its original character sequence. In detail, the object of the PTC is to find correct character sequence $C = c_1, c_2, ..., c_n$ given a Pinyin sequence $S = s_1, s_2, ..., s_n$ of which s_i refers to the Pinyin character and c_i refers to the Chinese character. For example, Table 1 illustrates the Pinyin sequence "zi ran yu yan chu li" (自然语言处理, natural language processing) and its corresponding Chinese character sequence. From this table we can observe that one Pinyin can be aligned to too many Chinese characters, though only the underlined bolded Chinese characters are the sequence that we actually intent to get. For example, the Pinyin "zi" can be mapped to Chinese characters include "字","子" and etc. Even in this simple example, we can also see that there are 5^6 possible Chinese sequences which can be generated. It is easy to show that the number of the possible sequence is exponential to the length of source or target sequence.

Formulated as a sequence labeling task, PTC will require a much larger label set to work on than any other traditional sequence labeling tasks such as named entity recognition (NER) or part-of-speech (POS) tagging. In machine learning, sequence labeling is a type of pattern recognition task that involves the algorithmic assignment of a categorical label to each member of a sequence of observed values. Sequence labeling can be treated as a set of independent classification tasks,one per element of the sequence. Typically, the latter have dozens of labels, while the former will have thousands of ones. A too large label set makes the sequence labeling inefficient and low-performance.

In this paper, we propose a new approach by formulating the PTC problem as a machine translation task. Considering the obvious constraint that the target Chinese sequence's order keeps the same as the source Pinyins' order, there exists no reordering step in the translation procedure. It greatly alleviates the difficulty of training such a machine translation system. In this sense, this approach is similar to a monotone SMT, which means that we can decode the source sentence from left to right without any reordering. At the same time, we can also make a full use of the phrase-based features in the machine translation framework and effective parameter estimation method. The motivation for our works lie in the phenomenon that the whole sentence pinyin input method is far more mature and even for the typical input method, there are also many conversion errors which need people to correct manually, this way heavily reduces the efficiency of people's work efficiency.

The rest of the paper is organized as follows: Section 2 describes previous relevant works about PTC problem. Section 3 introduces the proposed approach. Experimental results are given in Section 4. Then a discussion about the experiment result are given in Section 5. We reach our conclusion in Section 6.

2 Related Work

Similar with the task of PTC, the grapheme-to-phoneme or phoneme-to-grapheme conversion problem has also developed many different approaches. For example, (Chen, 2003) introduces several models for grapheme-to-phoneme conversion, including a joint conditional maximum entropy model, a joint maximum n-gram model and a joint maximum n-gram model with syllabification.

To effectively solve the PTC problem, many natural language processing techniques have been applied. By and large, these methods can be separated into two main categories: rule-based methods and statistical methods. the rule-based methods can make use of concrete linguistic information to understand language meanwhile plentiful features and automatic learning and prediction can be integrate to the statistical one effectively.

Wang et al. (2004) put forward a rough set approach to extract a number of rules from the corpus. (Zhang et al., 2006) presented an error correction post-processing approach based on grammatical and semantic rules. However, natural languages are so sophisticated that the rule-base methods can not effectively tackle all the situations. Recently, most works turn to statistical learning methods.

One of the earliest attempts to address this problem is to make use of language models. Now, many Chinese Pinyin input methods are still based on this model. (chen and Lee, 2000) successfully applied language models to the Chinese Pinyin input method. (Lee, 2003) extended language models further to disambiguate the Chinese homophone.

(Liu and Wang, 2002) built a machine learning approach to solve Chinese Pinyin-to-character for small memory application. Their approach lied on iterative new word identification and word frequency increasing that results in more accurate segmentation of Chinese character gradually. Their work can be applied to many small-memory platform such as Personal Digital Assistant(PDA) and etc.

(Zhao. and Sun, 1998) presented a word-self-made Chinese Phonetic-Character Conversion(CPCC) algorithm based on the Chinese Character Bigram which combined the advantages of CPCC based on Chinese character N-gram and advantages of CPCC based on Chinese word N-gram.

The paper (Zhang, 2007) presented a way to transform Chinese Pinyins to Chinese characters based on hybrid word lattice and study the related problems with hybrid language model and algorithms to solve the word lattice.

In the work of (Zhou et al., 2007), they utilized a segment-based hidden Markov model for Pinyin-to-Chinese conversion compared with the character based hidden Markov model.

(Lin and Zhang, 2008) presented a novel Chinese language model and studies their application in Chinese Pinyin-to-character conversion. Their model associate a word with supporting context including the frequent sets of the word's nearby phrases and the distances of phrases to the word.

Support vector machine(SVM) can also be used to deal with PTC problem as PTC can also be regarded as classifying the Pinyin to one of the Chinese characters. SVM replaces minimizing empirical risk in the traditional machine learning methods with minimizing the structure risk principle and shows a satisfied performance. (Jiang et al., 2007) put forward a PTC framework based on the SVM model. It effectively overcomes the drawback that language models cannot conveniently integrate rich features, and achieves a state-of-the-art accuracy of 92.94%.

As one of the most frequent tools to the classification and sequence labeling problem, Maximum Entropy(ME) model were also adopted to settle the PTC issue as in (Wang et al., 2006). A Class-based MEMM model is proposed to address the PTC conversion problem through exploitation of the pinyin constraints.

(Li et al., 2009) applied the conditional random field(CRF) model to the PTC problem in order to alleviate the label bias problem that usually occurs in the ME model (Andrew et al., 2001). (Li et al., 2009) made use of the constraint that one Pinyin can only map to limited number of Chinese characters thus greatly reducing the computation cost. However, their results show that CRF model does not outperform ME model(Li et al., 2009) and the CRF training will cost about approximately 200 days.

Artificial Immune Network based model is proposed to deal with the task of PTC conversion(Jiang and Pang, 2009). They propose an online learning approach the problems of sparse data and independent identical distribution.

The PTC problem can also be seen as one kind of machine transliteration which aims to generate a string in target language given a character string in source language. (Li et al., 2004) proposed a joint source-channel model to allow direct orthographical mapping between two different languages.

(Hatori and Suzuki, 2011) applied the phrase-based SMT model to predict Japanese Pronunciation, however, the differences between our work and theirs lie in a visual aspects. Both Japanese and Chinese adopt Chinese characters in their writing system, the work of (Hatori and Suzuki, 2011) was approximately a task to predict the pronunciation of a Chinese character, and ours is to predict a Chinese character sequence from a Pinyin(pronunciation) sequence. The task defined in this paper as discussed in the above is a much more difficult disambiguation task than the one in (Hatori and Suzuki, 2011). That is, a Chinese character seldom has multiple pronunciations, but the same pronunciation may refer to quite a lot of Chinese characters, usually, dozens of characters.

3 PTC Conversion Model

In this section, we apply a monotone phrasal SMT-based approach to solve the PTC problem. The whole framework is illustrated in Figure 1. Firstly, we should prepare a sentence aligned corpus, then do the word alignment process. After this, we need to extract a translation table from the aligned corpus. Then we will use all of the features to train a translation model. The last process is decoding the source sentence.

3.1 Translation Model

Our SMT model is based on the discriminative learning framework which contains different real-valued features. In this model, F is a given foreign sentence F=$f_1, f_2, ..., f_J$, and needs to be translated into another sentence E=$e_1, e_2, ..., e_I$. The real-valued features are defined over F and E as $h_i(E, F)$. The score can be given by a log-linear formulation(Och and Ney, 2004) with respect to a series of weight parameters λ_1,...,λ_n. For a given source language sentence f, we can obtain the target language sentence e according to the following equation:

$$\begin{aligned} e_1^I &= \arg\max_{e_1^I} p_{\lambda_1^m}(e_1^I|f_1^J) \\ &= \arg\max_{e_1^I} \frac{exp[\sum_{m=1}^{M} \lambda_m h_m(e_1^I, f_1^J)]}{\sum_{\bar{e}_1^I} exp[\sum_{m=1}^{M} \lambda_m h_m(\bar{e}_1^I, f_1^J)]}, \end{aligned} \tag{1}$$

where h_m is the m-th feature function and λ_m is the m-th feature weight. The most common features used in modern phrased-based machine translation include phrase translation feature, language model feature, reordering model feature and word penalty feature.

As usual, to train the SMT model parameters, we adopt the minimum error rate training(MERT)(Och, 2003), which obtained the model towards getting the highest score corresponding to the concrete evaluation metric. For the sequence decoding, we use a stack decoder(Germann et al., 2001).

3.2 Features

The following real-valued features are adopted for learning, the bidirectional phrase translation probabilities, $p(\hat{e}|\hat{f})$ and $p(\hat{f}|\hat{e})$, the bidirectional lexical weighting $lex(\hat{e}|\hat{f})$ and $lex(\hat{f}|\hat{e})$, the target Chinese character n-gram probability, $p(\hat{e})$ and the phrase penalty. The estimation of these features requires a training corpus with source and target alignment at the character or word level.

The bidirectional conditional phrase translation probability contain much richer information than the one directional phrase translation probability. When translating the source phrase $\hat{f}$ into the target phrase $\hat{e}$, we take both $p(\hat{e}|\hat{f})$: the target phrase's probability given the source phrase, and $p(\hat{f}|\hat{e})$: the source phrase's probability given the target phrase. The bidirectional conditional phrase translation probabilities can be estimated by the relative frequency of the phrases extracted from the aligned corpus. Note that the phrase used is not a meaningful word combination any more, it just refers to a series of consequent characters. In practice, a model using both translation directions, with the proper weight setting, often outperforms a model that uses only one direction.

The lexical weighting feature is such a measurement that can be effectively used to estimate whether a phrase pair is reliable or not. Empirically, the lexical weighting(Berger et al., 1994; Brown et al., 1993; Brown et al., 1990) is defined as follows:

$$lex(e|f, a) = \prod_{i=1}^{length(e)} \frac{1}{|\{j|(i,j) \in a\}|} \sum_{\forall(i,j)\in a} w(e_i|f_j)$$

Here a is an alignment function defining each Chinese character with its corresponding Pinyin and w refers to the lexical conditional probability. The above equation shows that for the phrase pair(f,e), the translation probability can be interpreted as the product of the aligned lexical pairs (f_j,e_i). For the PTC conversion problem, the lexical pair refers to the pinyin-character pair. Based on the alignment we can estimate the possibility of the transformation of phrase pairs from the lexical translation aspect.

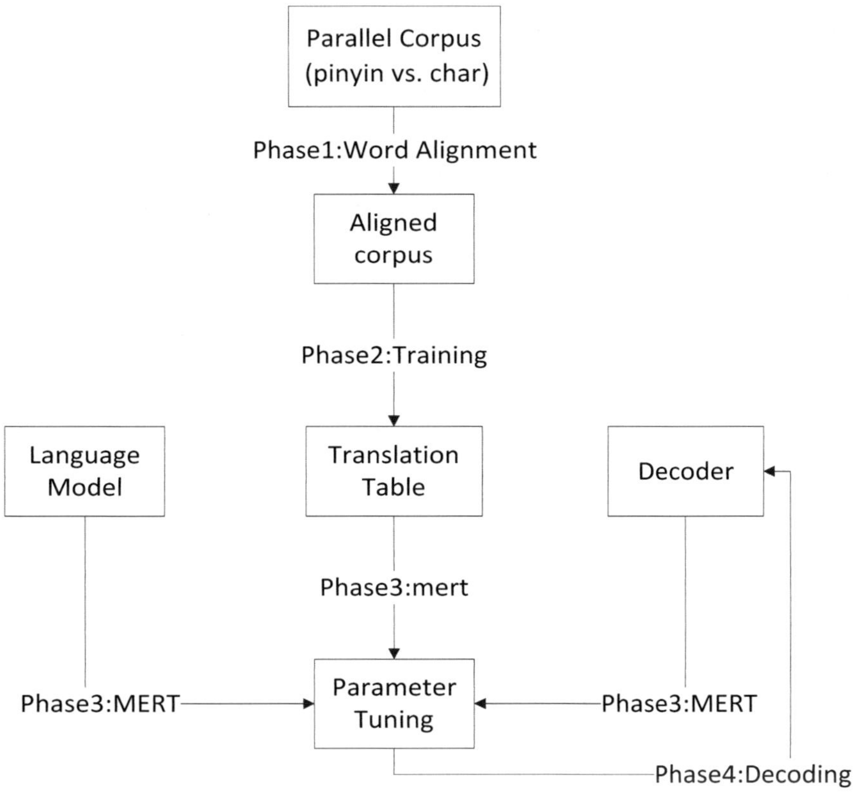

Figure 1: An overview of machine translation system which consists of several phases.

	Training			Development	Test
#sentence	10K	100K	1M	2K	100K
#character	452056	4371102	43679593	83765	4123184

Table 2: The size of different datasets

qi_ n _ zhou_ ian _ dao_ 17_ 7 she_
hi_ du_ ._

features	samples
pin n	hou
suffix	hou,ou,u
prefix	z,zh,zho
previous pin n	
previous character	也
pre-pre pin n	n

Figure 2: The sample training sentence and its ME features.

The phrase penalty is used to estimate the preference towards a sentence which has more segmented phrases or less segmented phrases. Practically, a factor is introduced for each phrase translation. If the factor is less than 1 we would prefer a longer phrase and otherwise shorter phrase is preferred.

4 Experiment

It is natural to formulize PTC as a sequence labeling task, which usually adopt maximum entropy Markov model(Berger et al., 1996) as the standard tool in most existing literatures[2]. Thus we conducted a group of experiments to evaluate the proposed SMT approach with the ME model as the baseline system. The features we use are the most frequent used ones in related works(Wang et al., 2006; Li et al., 2009).

4.1 Experiment settings

Firstly, we realize a way to get large Pinyin and Chinese character sentence pairs because to our best knowledge there is no such open dataset available. Given a Chinese character sequence, it is much easier to convert it to a Pinyin sequence because when a Chinese character is put in a context, it usually has an unique Pinyin counterpart. Based on this observation, we label the Chinese text with Pinyins through the forward maximal matching algorithm (kwong Wong and Chan, 1996) incorporated with a word-Pinyin dictionary from Sogou [3]. The data from the People's Daily of 1998 year is used as the training set and the development and test data are token from 1997 year's. The size of datasets is in table 2, the data of 10K and 100K are extracted from the data of 1M. Then we check the auto-labeled data and correct few mistakes.

The sample sentence "qi_气 wei_温 ye_也 zhou_骤 jiang_降 dao_到 ling_零 xia_下 17_1 7 she_摄 shi_氏 du_度 ._。(The temperature also dropped abruptly to seventeen below zero centidegrees.)" is shown in figure2, where the Pinyin and the Chinese character is separated by "_".

4.2 Maximum Entropy model

The implementation of ME model is from the OpenNLP tools[4].

4.2.1 Feature template

We assume the current Pinyin sequence is $p_1, ..., p_n$ and the corresponding Chinese character sequence is $c_1, ..., c_n$. The current Pinyin is p_k. As usually being regarded as an sequence labeling task, we design the feature set for the ME model as follows:

- the current Pinyin itself p_k;
- the suffixes of the Pinyin. For a given Pinyin s which is made of $s_1, ..., s_n$, the suffix of s refers to the substrings $s_i, ..., s_n (i \geq 2)$;
- the prefixes of the Pinyin. For a given Pinyin s which is made of $s_1, ..., s_n$, the suffix of s refers to the substrings $s_1, ..., s_i (i < 2)$;
- the previous Pinyin p_{k-1};
- the Chinese character c_{k-1} with respect to the previous Pinyin p_{k-1}(Markov feature);
- the Pinyin before previous Pinyin p_{k-2};
- the Pinyin before previous Pinyin and the previous Pinyin $p_{k-2}p_{k-1}$;
- the next Pinyin p_{k+1};

[2]Though conditional random field has shown more effective than ME model to solve sequence labeling problem, it is not a practical tool for PTC due to too many labels that PTC requires causing too high computational cost.

[3]The resource includes 4,083,906 Chinese word and Pinyin pairs, and it can be download from http://code.google.com/p/hslinuxextra/downloads/list.

[4]The tool can be downloaded from http://incubator.apache.org/opennlp/index.html

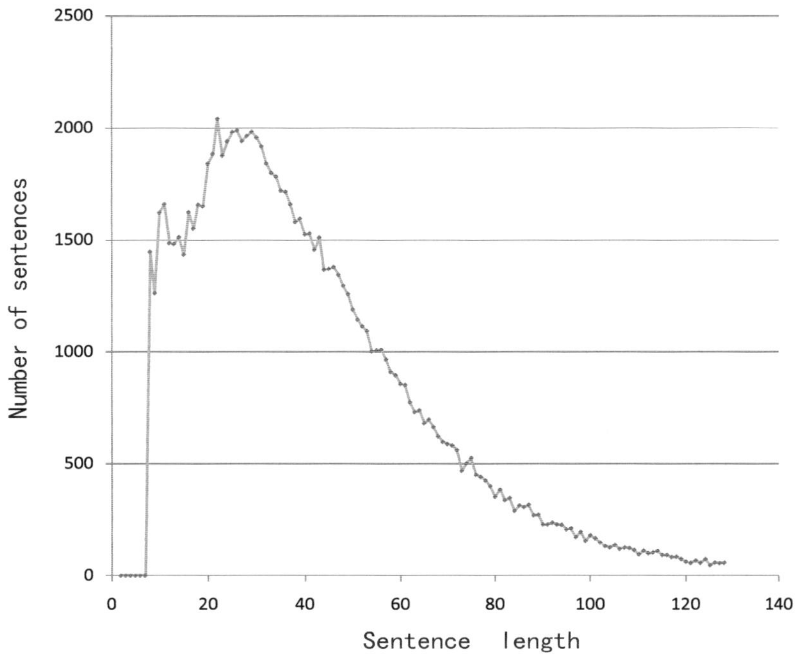

Figure 3: The sentences' length distribution.

Model \ Dataset	10K	100K	1M
ME	0.829	0.891	0.933
SMT	0.947	0.952	0.955

Table 3: The accuracy for ME model and SMT model on different datasets in terms of words.

- the Pinyin after the next one p_{k+2};

Figure 2 illustrates a full feature set sample, for the given sample sentence at the upper part of the figure, all related features for Pinyin-character pair, "zhou_骤(abruptly)", can be shown in the bottom table of the Figure.

Finally, the converted Chinese character sequences are compared to the golden data, the accuracy results can be seen in Table 3.

4.3 Machine Translation Framework

In this experiment, we conduct the process based on Stanford's phrasal(Cer et al., 2010) which is an open source phrase-based machine translation system. For the traditional phrase-based machine translation method, the processing steps are often stated as following:

- train an alignment model from the parallel corpus(not needed for our experiments.)
- extract phrases based on the former alignment model
- minimum error rate training
- decoding

As we have known that it must be an one-to-one alignment for PTC, it is unnecessary to train the alignment model and the phrases can be directly extracted based on the one-to-one alignment of character and Pinyin. Our experiment is based on 3-gram language model and our maximum phrase length is set to 7.

The results given by the SMT approach are in Table 3. We get the results based on three different training sets.

5 Discussion

In this section, we make a detailed experimental analysis to distinguish the result of the SMT model from that of the ME model on the whole sentence accuracy and time cost.

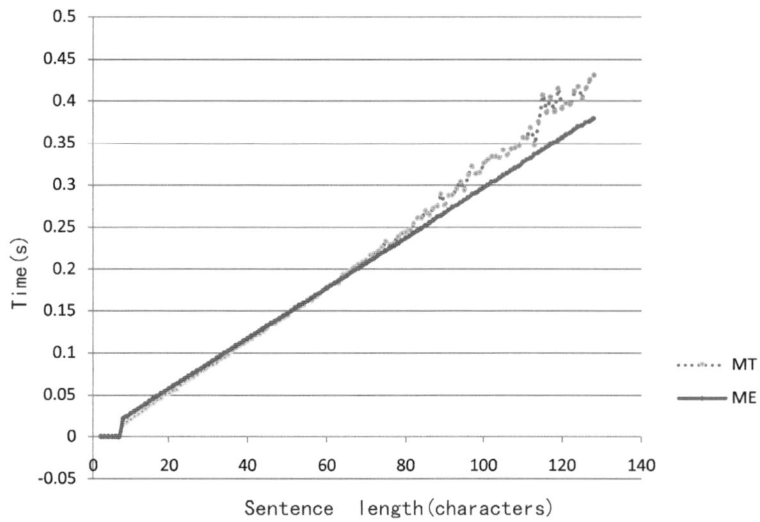

Figure 4: The comparison of decoding time of SMT model and ME model.

5.1 Main Result

Table 3 shows the main results of our experiments. Here the accuracy means the percentage of the correct labels in our decoding results. On all of three training data sets, the results of SMT are much better than ME.

To illustrate this point concretely, we can see the different result produced by the two models on the sample sentence

- Pinyin Sequence: *zhe yi cheng ji zai quan guo wu da tie lu ju zhong ming lie bang shou*
- Character sequence: *这一成绩在全国五大铁路局中名列榜首(This result ranks the best among the five biggest railway bureaus all over the country)*

ME model outputs "这一成绩在全国五大铁路局中名列帮手" while the result of SMT model is "这一成绩在全国五大铁路局中名列榜首". The ME model makes an error as it translate 'bang shou' into '帮手'(helper) and the SMT model outputs are the completely equal to the golden sentence, and 'bang shou' has been correctly translated into '榜首'(the best on the list).

By comparing outputs of these two sentence we can see that the SMT model is much more representative than the ME model. As the features we defined are based on the phrase pairs, the model can deduce that the score of target sentence which is composed of phrase pair(ming lie bang shou,名列榜首(who is best on the list)) is greater than the score of sentence which is compose with phrase pair(ming lie,名列(who is)) and phrase pair(bang shou, 帮手(helper)). This result also verifies the effectiveness of the SMT features to capture the local property of the source sentence and the target sentence and can combine longer dependencies.

To show how the proposed SMT approach outperforms the ME model, we give a comparison on another metric, the whole sentence accuracy which represents the ratio how many sentences are completely correctly decoded by the system. This metric could be very useful to evaluate a practical Chinese input method. As even one incorrect decoded character may ask human users to pay too many keyboard hits to correct, which user has to backspace the cursor one by one and re-choose the right character candidate one by one, the whole sentence accuracy could be more effective to evaluate user experience of a Chinese input method. Besides, the whole sentence's accuracy also reflects the model's efficiency in another view.

The distribution of sentence length is shown in Figure 3, from which we can see that most sentences are of length between 20 Chinese characters and 40 Chinese characters. The whole sentence's accuracy for both these two models can be shown in Table 4. From this table we can see that the results of SMT model is much better than the ME model, which in-

Model \ Dataset	10K	100K	1M
ME	0.075	0.169	0.302
SMT	0.402	0.429	0.454

Table 4: The whole sentence accuracy on test dataset.

dicates that a SMT decoder for PTC could bring out much better user experience.

5.2 Time Cost

For the training time of these two models, we make a comparison on the biggest training dataset, which has 1M training sentences. It took about a week or so to train a ME model while the training time of our approach cost about within one day which is much faster than the that of ME model. From the description in (Li et al., 2009) we know that the training of CRF would cost much more than ME and the result of CRF is not better than ME.

Being a core component of Chinese input method, PTC is sensitive to the computational cost. Thus time cost of decoding for the two models is reported as follows.

To make the differences more exactly, the decoding time of the two models is compared on sentences with the same length. The results are shown in Figure 4. We can see that the decoding time increases when the sentence length becomes larger. However, even when the sentence length is larger than 120 characters, the decoding time is still less than 0.45s. From this graph, it is apparent that the ME model decoding is slightly faster than the SMT model as the sentence is quite long. However, for most sentences with 20 to 40 characters, the SMT model does not decodes slower than the ME model.

6 Conclusion

We present a novel approach to the problem of Pinyin-to-character conversion(PTC). Motivated by the similarities between machine translation and PTC, we re-formulize the latter as a simplified machine translation problem. In the new formulization, the most computational expensive part of machine translation, alignment learning, could be conveniently ignored by considering that PTC could build one-to-one mapping pairs in the whole text. Meanwhile, the SMT model for PTC maintains the merit that it integrates more effectively helpful features to outperform the baseline system, ME model, which is a standard sequence labeling tool for traditional PTC task. A group of experiments are carried out to verify the effective of the proposed MT model. The results show that MT model outperforms the previous ME model and provides satisfactory performance.

References

McCallum Andrew, Pereira Fernando, and Lafferty John. 2001. Conditional random fields: probabilistic models for segmenting and labeling sequence data. In *Proceedings of the Eighteenth International Conference on Machine Learning (ICML)*, pages 282–289, Williamstown, MA.

Adam L. Berger, Peter F. Brown, Stephen A. Della Pietra, Vincent J. Della Pietra, John R. GiUet, John D. Lafferty, Robert L. Mercer, Harry Printz, and Luboš Ureš. 1994. The candide system for machine translation. In *Proceedings of the workshop on Human Language Technology*, pages 157–162. Association for Computational Linguistics.

Adam L. Berger, Vincent J. Della Pietra, and Stephen A. Della Pietra. 1996. A maximum entropy approach to natural language processing. *Computational linguistics*, 22(1):39–71.

Peter F. Brown, John Cocke, Stephen A. Della Pietra, Vincent J. Della Pietra, Fredrick Jelinek, John D. Lafferty, Robert L. Mercer, and Paul S. Roossin. 1990. A statistical approach to machine translation. *Computational linguistics*, 16(2):79–85.

Peter F. Brown, Vincent J. Della Pietra, Stephen A. Della Pietra, and Robert L. Mercer. 1993. The mathematics of statistical machine translation: Parameter estimation. *Computational linguistics*, 19(2):263–311.

Daniel Cer, Michel Galley, Daniel Jurafsky, and Christopher D.Manning. 2010. Phrasal: A statistical machine translation toolkit for exploring new model features. In *Proceedings of the NAACL HLT 2010 Demonstration Session*, pages 9–12, Los Angeles, California, June. Association for Computational Linguistics.

Zheng Chen and Kai-Fu Lee. 2000. A new statistical approach to chinese pinyin input. In *Proceedings of the 38th Annual Meeting on Association for Computational Linguistics*, pages 241–247, Hong Kong. Association for Computational Linguistics.

Stanley F. Chen. 2003. Conditional and joint models for grapheme-to-phoneme conversion. In *Eighth European Conference on Speech Communication and Technology*.

Ulrich Germann, Michael Jahr, Kevin Knight, Daniel marcu, and Kenji Yamada. 2001. Fast decoding and optimal decoding for machine translation. In *Proceedings of the 39th Annual Meeting on Association for Computational Linguistics*, pages 228–235. Association for Computational Linguistics.

Jun Hatori and Hisami Suzuki. 2011. Japanese pronunciation prediction as phrasal statistical machine translation. In *Proceedings of 5th International Joint Conference on Natural Language Processing*, pages 120–128. Asian Federation of Natural Language Processing.

Wei Jiang and Xiuli Pang. 2009. An artificial immune network approach for pinyin-to-character conversion. In *Virtual Environments, Human-Computer Interfaces and Measurements Systems, 2009. VECIMS'09. IEEE International Conference on*, pages 27–32. IEEE.

Wei Jiang, Yi Guan, Xiaolong Wang, and BingQuan Liu. 2007. Pinyin-to-character conversion model based on support vector machines. *Journal of Chinese information processing*, 21(2):100–105.

Pak kwong Wong and Chorkin Chan. 1996. Chinese word segmentation based on maximum matching and word binding force. In *Proceedings of the 16th conference on Computational linguistics-Volume 1*, pages 200–203. Association for Computational Linguistics.

Yue-Shi Lee. 2003. Task adaptation in stochastic language model for chinese homophone disambiguation. *ACM Transactions on Asian Language Information Processing (TALIP)*, 2(1):49–62.

Haizhou Li, Min Zhang, and Jian Su. 2004. A joint source-channel model for machine transliteration. In *Proceedings of the 42nd Annual Meeting on Association for Computational Linguistics*, pages 159–166. Association for Computational Linguistics.

Lu Li, Xuan Wang, Xiaolong Wang, and Yanbing Yu. 2009. A conditional random fields approach to chinese pinyin-to-character conversion. *Journal of Communication and Computer*, 6(4):25–31.

Bo Lin and Jun Zhang. 2008. A novel statistical chinese language model and its application in pinyin-to-character conversion. In *Proceeding of the 17th ACM conference on Information and knowledge management*, pages 1433–1434. ACM.

Bingquan Liu and Xaiolong Wang. 2002. An approach to machine learning of chinese pinyin-to-character conversion for small-memory application. In *Machine Learning and Cybernetics, 2002. Proceedings. 2002 International Conference on*, volume 3, pages 1287–1291. IEEE.

Franz Josef Och and Hermann Ney. 2004. The alignment template approach to statistical machine translation. *Computational Linguistics*, 30(4):417–449.

Franz Josef Och. 2003. Minimum error rate training in statistical machine translation. In *Proceedings of the 41st Annual Meeting on Association for Computational Linguistics-Volume 1*, pages 160–167. Association for Computational Linguistics.

Xiaolong Wang, Qingcai Chen, and Daniel So Yeung. 2004. Mining pinyin-to-character conversion rules from large-scale corpus: a rough set approach. *Systems, Man, and Cybernetics, Part B: Cybernetics, IEEE Transactions on*, 34(2):834–844.

Xuan Wang, Lu Li, Lin Yao, and Waqas Wanwar. 2006. A maximum entropy approach to chinese pin yin-to-character conversion. In *IEEE International Conference on Systems, Man and Cybernetics*, volume 4, pages 2956–2959. IEEE.

Yan Zhang, Bo Xu, and Chengqing Zong. 2006. Rule-based post-processing of pinyin to chinese characters conversion system. In *International Symposium on Chinese Spoken Language Processing*.

Sen Zhang. 2007. Solving the pinyin-to-chinese-character conversion problem based on hybrid word lattice. *CHINESE JOURNAL OF COMPUTERS-CHINESE EDITION-*, 30(7):1145–1153.

Yibao Zhao. and Shenghe Sun. 1998. A word-self-made chinese phonetic-character conversion algorithm based on chinese character bigram [j]. *ACTA ELECTRONICA SINICA*, 10.

Xiaohua Zhou, Xiaohua Hu, Xiaodan Zhang, and Xiajiong Shen. 2007. A segment-based hidden markov model for real-setting pinyin-to-chinese conversion. In *Proceedings of the sixteenth ACM conference on Conference on information and knowledge management*, pages 1027–1030. ACM.

Emotion Estimation from Sentence Using Relation between Japanese Slangs and Emotion Expressions

Kazuyuki Matsumoto **Kenji Kita** **Fuji Ren**

The University of Tokushima
Minami-josanjima, Tokushima, 770-8506, Japan
{matumoto;kita;ren}@is.tokushima-u.ac.jp

Abstract

Most of Japanese slang words such as Wakamono Kotoba are analyzed as "unknown word" or segmented wrongly by the morphological analysis system. These problems are causing negative effect on sentiment analysis in text. These words generally have many varieties of notations and conjugations, and they lack versatility. As a result, many of them are not registered in the dictionaries, making morphological analysis more difficult. In this paper, we aimed to decrease such negative effects of Wakamono Kotoba for the accuracy of emotion estimation from sentence and proposed a method to increase the accuracy by using a classification method based on machine learning. In this method we used emotional expressions which had high relevance with Wakamono Kotoba as feature. As a result, the proposed method obtained 20% higher accuracy than the method only using morpheme N-gram as feature.

Emotion Corpus, Japanese Slang, Out of Vocabulary

1 Introduction

The words that are not registered in the dictionaries are called unknown words. In the field of Natural Language Processing unknown words have been traditionally studied. However, many of these studies focused on proper noun, onomatopoeia or emoticon, while a few research targeted slang such as Wakamono Kotoba. One of the reasons might be that Wakamono Kotoba has been usually treated as "improper expression" or "bad word"(Noguchi , 2004). However, considering that these words are getting more and more frequently used on WWW, it is inevitable to treat Wakamono Kotoba even though they are improper expressions.

In Japan, many of the Internet users are people from teens to people in their fourties[1]. One of the characteristics of Wakamono Kotoba is that they are specialized in expressing how people especially in their younger age feel. By dealing with such Wakamono Kotoba, we will be able to use effectively the huge amount of documents on WWW as precious resources for language processing.

This paper aims to estimate emotion from utterances including Wakamono Kotoba. Most of the existing emotion estimation studies from text did not treat the problem of slang such as Wakamono Kotoba. One of the reasons was that there were few text corpora including Wakamono Kotoba. Currently Weblog became very popular and many documents on WWW are written in spoken language. These texts are available as huge corpus. As the result, recently there are active research on new words or unknown words (Murawaki , 2010),(Jiean *et al.*, 2011) and there are also research on emotion estimation based on their findings (Matsumoto *et al.*, 2011),(Matsumoto and Ren, 2011). For example, in (Matsumoto *et al.*, 2011), they used the conventional statistic method to estimate emotion of the sentence including Wakamono Kotoba, then compared the estimation accuracy when Wakamono Kotoba was included in the sentence and it was not included in the sentence. In (Matsumoto and Ren, 2011), they tried to estimate emotion of Wakamono Kotoba by using

[1] http://www2.ttcn.ne.jp/honkawa/6210.html

features of character.

In this paper, we focused on Wakamono Kotoba, which was traditionally not intended for research on Natural Language Processing, and proposed an emotion estimation method which was robust for utterance including Wakamono Kotoba. Because the notation of Wakamono Kotoba is various, many Wakamono Kotoba are generally low-frequency words in the corpus. Therefore, we attempted to improve the estimation accuracy by using the emotion expressions with strong relation with Wakamono Kotoba as feature instead of using Wakamono Kotoba as feature.

2 Wakamono Kotoba Emotion Corpus

In this section, we collected example sentences including Wakamono Kotoba. Firstly, we chose the Wakamono Kotoba to be the target of analysis, and then collected the example sentences including these target words automatically. Finally, the example sentences were manually annotated emotion tags to construct a corpus.

2.1 Definition of Wakamono Kotoba

The definition of Wakamono Kotoba we treated in this paper was presented. It is difficult to clearly judge whether the word is Wakamono Kotoba or not. In this paper, we regarded the Japanese slangs fulfilling the following two conditions as Wakamono Kotoba.

- The meanings of the words are defined in the glossaries on WWW.
- The words are introduced in the literature on new words or slangs such as "Afureru shingo"(Kitahara, 2009), (Yonekawa , 1998), (Yamaguchi , 2007) and "Japanese Slang Dictionary[2]."

2.2 Construction of Corpus

Wakamono Kotoba has various forms of expressions. It sometimes takes a form of phrase and sometimes takes a form of sentence final expressions. Although our final aim is to propose an emotion estimation method that can be applied to all expressive forms, this paper focused on Wakamono Kotoba taking a form of single word following the definition described in the previous section.

The example sentences were collected in the following steps. The basic Wakamono Kotoba (a set of seed words) were selected from the dictionaries or books that were open to the public(Yonekawa , 1998),(Kitahara, 2009). Using these words as search query we automatically collected the sentences on Web. We used Yahoo! blog search[3] as WWW search engines.

We thought that many Wakamono Kotoba used in the Web texts were likely to be unknown Wakamono Kotoba which were not seed word. First, the small corpus was constructed based on the seed words list. Then we looked for unknown words which were not seed word from the corpus manually. Using the obtained unknown words as new target for collection, the corpus was extended. We regarded these target unknown words as Wakamono Kotoba following the definition described in section2.1.

The features were manually annotated to the collected sentences.

- Wakamono Kotoba in the sentence and its representative notation
- Emoticons included in the sentence
- Emotion tags (emotion of writer or speaker): Joy, Anger, Sorrow, Surprise and Neutral

Plural emotion tags were allowed to be annotated per a sentence. The kind of emotion tags was selected based on Fischer's emotion systematic tree(Fischer, 1989) which was made according to the word classification. The highest classification categories in this systematic tree are "Love and Joy," "Surprise," "Anger" and "Sorrow and Fear." We defined four kinds of emotion tags: "Surprise," "Anger," "Joy" and "Sorrow." [4]

Although we considered and selected emotions from the lowest categories in the Fischer's emotion systematic tree at the time of annotation, we referred to and actually annotated emotions in the four highest categories. When the speaker of the sentence

[2]http://zokugo-dict.com/

[3]http://blog.search.yahoo.co.jp/

[4]We regarded the category of "Love and Joy" as "Joy" and the category of "Sorrow and Fear" as "Sorrow."

did not express any emotion, we annotated the tag of "Neutral." We named this corpus as "Wakamono Kotoba Emotion Corpus"(WKEC).

The outline of the corpus is shown in Table1. MeCab ver.0.98 was used as morphological analysis tool and UniDic 1.3.12[5] was used as morphological analysis dictionary. The number of the annotated emotion tags is shown in Table2. A part of the example sentences included in the corpus is shown in Table3.

Total number of morphemes	401,678
Unique number of morphemes	16,998
Total number of sentences	20,500
Total number of emoticons	2,846
Unique number of emoticons	908
Total number of Wakamono Kotoba	23,644
Unique number of Wakamono Kotoba	2,231
Total number of emotion tags	21,514

Table 1: Outline of the Wakamono Kotoba Emotion Corpus(WKEC).

Joy	Anger	Neutral	Sorrow	Surprise
7,242	5,475	4,620	3,385	792

Table 2: Number of the annotated emotion tags.

3 Relation Analysis between Wakamono Kotoba and Emotion

3.1 Relation between Emotion Expression and Emotion of the Sentence

Matsumoto et al.(Matsumoto *et al.*, 2011) studied about the relation between Wakamono Kotoba and emotion. Their research took the probabilistic classification approach for emotion estimation from sentences and improved the estimation accuracy by using Wakamono Kotoba as feature. This result suggested that special expressions such as Wakamono Kotoba should have some potential to contribute to express emotion.

However, if we use Wakamono Kotoba as feature for probabilistic classification approach, Wakamono Kotoba might result in decreasing the estimation accuracy because the frequency of Wakamono Kotoba is low. We thought that we should also consider emotional expressions such as "delightful" and "dislike" as features besides Wakamono Kotoba. The "Emotional Expression Dictionary"(Nakamura , 1993) is a dictionary listing up the keywords to express emotion. In the Wakamono Kotoba Emotion Corpus, the total number of the emotional expressions included in this dictionary was 3,171.

5 categories(WKEC)	10 categories (EED)
Joy	Joy, Like
Anger	Anger, Hate
Sorrow	Sorrow, Fear, Shame
Surprise	Surprise, Excitement
Neutral	Relief

Table 4: Correspondence of the 10 kinds of emotions and the 5 kinds of emotions.

The words included in the Emotion Expression Dictionary(EED) were classified into ten kinds of emotions. We further classified these ten kinds of emotions into the five kinds of emotions which we used in the Wakamono Kotoba Emotion Corpus. This correspondence table is shown in Table 4. We excluded the emotion expressions classified into "Relief" in the following analysis because we did not target the emotion of "Neutral" for analysis in this paper.

The match rate between the emotion of the emotional expression appeared in WKEC and the emotion of the sentence was calculated by equation 1. $|S|$ indicates the number of the sentences including emotional expressions in WKEC[6]. Table 5 shows the match rate of each emotion category.

$$\text{Match Rate} = \frac{\sum_{i=1}^{|S|} M_{ij}}{N_E} \quad (1)$$

Emotion	Joy	Anger	Sorrow	Surprise
Match Rate	0.77	0.86	0.04	0.0

Table 5: Match rate of each emotion category.

[5] http://www.tokuteicorpus.jp/dist/

[6] excluding the sentences annotated "Neutral"

Sentence	Wakamono Kotoba	Emotion
Shikashi, yappari mukatsukuze–!!! (But I am pissed off after all!!!)	*Mukatsuku*	Anger
Riaju-ppoi kanjino charao ya uzakimo kappuru toka hotondo inakattanode, sonnani kutsuu deha nakatakann w (Because there were only few play boys having fulfilling lives or annoying and disgusting couples, it was not such torture for me.)	*Riaju, Charao, Uzakimo*	Joy
Asu no asa yarou... Shibou Flag kanaa (I will do it tomorrow morning... Postponing might end in failure though.)	*Shibou Flag*	Sorrow

Table 3: Example of corpus.

M_{ij} indicates the number of the emotions matched between s_i and $e_j \in s_i$. N_E indicates the total number of emotion expressions in the corpus.

From this result, it was found that the emotion of the emotional expression and the sentence emotion highly matched when the emotions were "Joy" and "Anger." They rarely matched when the emotions were "Sorrow" and "Surprise."

This reason might be that most of the emotional expressions classified into "Sorrow" and "Surprise" are not commonly used in case of spoken language. Actually, we do not often use the expressions such as "*Hiai*" meaning "woe" to express "Sorrow" in spoken language. If only emotion expressions are used as features, the accuracy of emotion estimation in the categories of "Sorrow" or "Surprise" is expected to become low.

3.2 Relevance between Wakamono Kotoba and Emotional Expressions

In the preceding section, the relevance between emotional expressions and emotion of the sentence was investigated and the high relevance was found in the specific emotions of "Joy" and "Anger." If highly related emotional expressions are used as features instead of Wakamono Kotoba when the Wakamono Kotoba is unknown word in training data, we thought that we would realize robust emotion estimation from the sentences including unknown expressions.

This section analyzed the relation of co-occurrence between emotional expressions and Wakamono Kotoba to acquire "emotional expressions highly related to Wakamono Kotoba."

To calculate co-occurrence relation it is necessary to have a huge corpus including both of Wakamono Kotoba and emotional expressions. We used a corpus randomly collected from weblog articles which is called "Wakamono Kotoba Raw Corpus"(WKRC). The sentences included in the corpus are not annotated emotion tags but Wakamono Kotoba are annotated automatically.

The details of the WKRC is shown in Table 6. Because annotation was automatically made in WKRC, there were some example sentences whose substrings matched Wakamono Kotoba. However, instead of manual correction, we automatically removed HTML tags and too short or too long sentences[7].

# of Sentences	128,394
# of Morphemes	2,129,931
# of Uniq. Morphemes	32,144

Table 6: Details of raw corpus including Wakamono Kotoba.

As a criterion to indicate how strong the co-occurrence is between each word, pointwise mutual information (MI-score) and t-score are often used. LogLog score(Kilgarriff *et al.*, 2001) is a criterion which lays weight on co-occurrence frequency. The co-occurrence scores between Wakamono Kotoba yw_i and emotional expression ew_j were calculated by equation 2 (MI), equation 3 (t-score) and equation 4 (LogLog score).

[7]We registered the sentences consisting of 10 to 75 characters in double-byte.

$$MI_{ij} = log_2 \frac{f_{ij} \times f_{all}}{f_i \times f_j} \quad (2)$$

$$t\text{-score}_{ij} = \left(f_{ij} - \frac{f_i \times f_j}{f_{all}} \right) \times \frac{1}{\sqrt{f_{ij}}} \quad (3)$$

$$LogLog_{ij} = MI_{ij} * log_2 f_{ij} \quad (4)$$

f_i, f_j indicates frequency of Wakamono Kotoba yw_i and emotional expression ew_j, f_{ij} indicates co-occurrence frequency of yw_i and ew_j. f_{all} shows the total number of Wakamono Kotoba and emotional expressions in the corpus. These scores were not calculated in the combinations which did not appear together in the corpus. These scores can become high when Wakamono Kotoba co-occur a few times with the frequently appeared emotional expressions even if the Wakamono Kotoba do not express any emotion. In this paper, we proposed a score to keep down the value by multiplying the log value of the appearance frequency of the emotional expression by the co-occurrence frequency. This co-occurrence score was defined as e-score and calculated with equation 5. df_i is a weight to decrease the value more when the co-occurrence frequency with other emotional expression becomes higher [8]. f_{y_u} indicates the unique number of Wakamono Kotoba in the corpus.

$$e\text{-score} = f_{ij} \times log_2 \left(\frac{f_{y_u}}{df_i} \right) \times log_2 \left(\frac{1}{f_j + 1} \right) \quad (5)$$

We judged which co-occurrence score was effective to calculate the relevance between Wakamono Kotoba and emotional expressions. We investigated how often the emotion of the emotional expression co-occurred with each Wakamono Kotoba and the positive / negative evaluation of Wakamono Kotoba matched[9].

We calculated the average of the match rates for the top 1 to 10 co-occurred emotional expressions. Fig. 1 shows the result. The vertical scale indicates the average of the match rate (%), and the horizontal scale indicates the threshold of the rank.

[8] df_i indicates the number of the kinds of emotional expressions that co-occurred with yw_i

[9] The positive / negative evaluation of Wakamono Kotoba was annotated manually

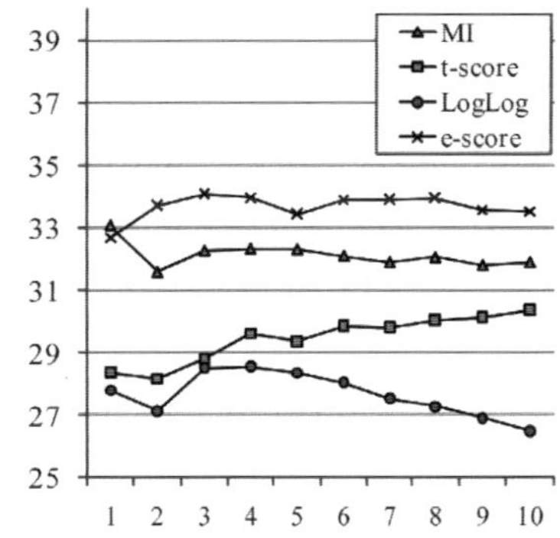

Figure 1: Comparison of the match rates for the co-occurrence score in higher rank.

The e-score showed a little higher match rate than other co-occurrence scores. The LogLog score is likely to become 0 value when the appearance frequency of the emotional expression is low. Therefore, when the threshold of the score's rank increases, the emotional expressions whose emotions do not match the emotions of Wakamono Kotoba are more included. As the result, the match rate tended to become lower. From this result, we thought that it would be able to extract emotional expressions with strong relevance with Wakamono Kotoba by using e-score.

However, because this emotional match rate did not exceed 33% to 34%, if this method is used to add feature, many emotional expressions whose emotions do not match the emotions of Wakamono Kotoba would be included and consequently the accuracy of emotion estimation would decrease. To solve this problem, it would be necessary to filter the additional emotional expressions as for the Wakamono Kotoba included in the training data.

4 Emotion Estimation Method Using Emotional Expression Related to Wakamono Kotoba

Fig. 2 shows the distribution of the appearance frequency of Wakamono Kotoba in WKEC. The vertical scale indicates the log value of the number of kinds of Wakamono Kotoba which appeared k times, and the horizontal scale indicates the appearance frequency k in the corpus. This distribution of the appearance frequency was limited because the corpus size was small. It would be possible to acquire the web appearance frequency by using search engines such as Google. However, because the purpose of this paper was to estimate emotion using small corpus, we did not investigate that possibility.

Fig. 2 shows that many of Wakamono Kotoba appeared 1 to 40 times, and 1,265 kinds of Wakamono Kotoba appeared once in the corpus, which was approximately 57%. For example, even commonly used Wakamono Kotoba such as "*Dekikon*" meaning shotgun marriage and "*Doyagao*" meaning smug look appeared only once in the corpus in the exact notations.

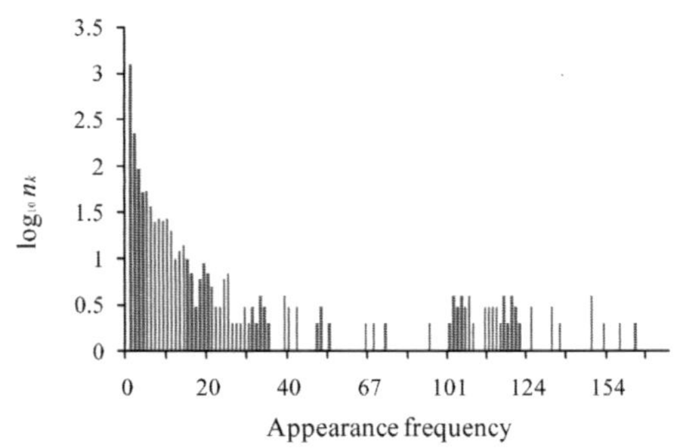

Figure 2: Distribution of the appearance frequency of Wakamono Kotoba.

One of the possible solution for such problem of the difference of notations would be to replace Wakamono Kotoba to other existing words having the same or similar meanings. However, we thought that for the purpose of emotion estimation, semantic equality was not necessarily required if only the emotions matched each other.

In our proposed method the Wakamono Kotoba with low appearance frequency were converted into the co-occurring emotional expressions extracted from huge corpus. This method enables to use effectively Wakamono Kotoba with low appearance frequency.

4.1 Experiment of Emotion Estimation Using Co-occurring Emotional Expressions

The co-occurrence score between Wakamono Kotoba and emotional expressions was calculated with the equations described in the section 3.2. Then the emotional expressions whose co-occurrence score with Wakamono Kotoba was high were added. We also weighted the features based on the following conditions:

1. Add high weight when the emotion of the emotional expression matches the negative / positive evaluation of Wakamono Kotoba

2. Add high weight when the emotion of the emotional expression and the emotion of the sentence match in the training data.

Of course, the WKRC includes the sentences that do not express any emotion. Therefore, the emotional expressions whose emotions are different from the emotions of the Wakamono Kotoba are sometimes extracted.

Feature should not be always added only because it has the same emotions with Wakamono Kotoba. We focused on the emotional expressions with high co-occurrence rate and having the same emotions with Wakamono Kotoba, and treated them as features. The training data was created combining multiple features and the evaluation experiment was conducted with 10-fold cross validation. The target emotions were "Joy," "Anger," "Sorrow" and "Surprise." The 792 sentences were randomly selected from WKEC for each emotional category. We used Naive Bayes classifier (multinomial model) for emotion estimation which was probabilistic classifier. The multinomial model is a model to consider the appearance frequency of the feature in the sentences.

The equation 6 is to classify sentence s into $\hat{e}$. $\hat{e}$ is the emotion that maximizes the probability $P(e)(s|e)$ when a set of the features included in s is defined as $w \in V$. E is a set of the emotional categories. $|E|$ indicates the number of the categories. $n_{w,s}$ indicates the appearance frequency of w in s. $q_{w,e}$ indicates the probability of the feature w being selected when the emotion is e.

We also had to solve the zero frequency problem in which the probability became zero if the inputted sentence included unknown features. For this problem, we used MAP estimation for parameters.

The equation 7 calculates appearance probability of word w and emotion e based on MAP estimation. $n_{w,e}$ indicates the appearance frequency of the word$w$ included in the sentences whose emotions are e. n_e indicates the number of the sentences whose emotion are e. In this paper we set $\alpha = 2$. In this case the calculation results become the same with those when 1 is added to the appearance frequency in the training data, and it is generally called Laplace smoothing.

$$\begin{aligned} \hat{e} &= \arg\max_{e \in E} P(e)P(s|e) \\ &= \arg\max_{e \in E} \ p_e \prod_{w \in V} q_{w,e}^{n_{w,s}} \end{aligned} \quad (6)$$

$$\begin{aligned} q_{w,e} &= \frac{n_{w,e} + (\alpha - 1)}{\sum_w n_{w,e} + |W|(\alpha - 1)} \\ p_e &= \frac{n_e + (\alpha - 1)}{\sum_e n_e + |E|(\alpha - 1)} \end{aligned} \quad (7)$$

The training data added feature and the estimation accuracy for each training data are shown in Table 7. FY indicates using Wakamono Kotoba as feature, FE indicates using emotional expression as feature, FF indicates using emoticon as feature, and N_1 indicates using morpheme 1-gram as feature.

T_4 and T_5 are training data where the Wakamono Kotoba in the sentence were converted into the emotional expressions with high co-occurrence scores[10] FE_{mi}, FE_e are features which were converted Wakanomo Kotoba into the emotional expressions by using MI and e-score respectively.

We added weight on each feature. In the table, 'w' means the value that changes according to the emotion of the feature. As described in section 3.1, due to low matching rate of the emotions in between emotional expression and sentence, we thought that estimation accuracy would decrease. Therefore, the feature weight was changed in T_4, T_5 depending on whether both emotions matched or not. T_4', T_5' are the changed feature weight. Concretely, if the emotions of the emotional expression and the sentence matched, the weight was set as 10, and if they did not match, the weight was set as 1. The weights of other features, i.e. morpheme n-gram or emoticons, were set as 0.5 because their effect on emotion was not clear.

Then, when the positive / negative evaluation of Wakamono Kotoba and the emotion of the emotional expression matched, the feature weight was set as 1.0, otherwise, set as 0.1. Finally, the emotional expressions whose co-occurrence scores with Wakamono Kotoba were lower than half of the maximum co-occurrence score were excluded from features.

[10]We used the emotional expressions having the 10 highest co-occurrence scores.

	Feature Combinations (Weight)	**Accuracy(%)**
T_0	$N_1(1)$	62.2
T_1	$N_1(1) + FY(1)$	66.1
T_2	$N_1(1) + FY(1) + FE(1)$	66.4
T_3	$N_1(1) + FY(1) + FE(1) + FF(1)$	66.5
T_4	$N_1(1) + FE(1) + FF(1) + FE_{mi}(1)$	63.2
T_5	$N_1(1) + FE(1) + FF(1) + FE_e(1)$	62.9
T_4'	$N_1(0.5) + FE(\text{w}) + FF(0.5) + FE_{mi}(\text{w})$	**83.8**
T_5'	$N_1(0.5) + FE(\text{w}) + FF(0.5) + FE_e(\text{w})$	**76.6**

Table 7: Comparison of estimation accuracy feature combinations.

4.2 Discussion

The experimental result showed that only adding emotional expressions that had high relevance with Wakamono Kotoba could not increase the accuracy of emotion estimation. In fact, it might decrease the accuracy. However, by changing the feature weight, the accuracy was improved to 83.8% at T_4'. Because Wakamono Kotoba tend to appear less frequently due to their varieties of notations even though they are expressing emotions. Therefore, they were difficult to be used as a trigger for emotion estimation. However, it was effective to replace these Wakamono Kotoba into the emotional expressions that have strong co-occurrence with the Wakamono Kotoba.

5 Conclusion

This paper proposed the emotion estimation method from the sentence including Wakamono Kotoba. Wakamono Kotoba were not always effective as feature for emotion estimation because they generally tended to have low appearance frequency, therefore, we proposed to convert the features based on the co-occurrence frequency between the Wakamono Kotoba and the emotional expressions. The conversion did not largely improve the estimation accuracy, however, by adjusting the weight of feature the accuracy was improved approximately 17.7% than when Wakamono Kotoba and word 1-gram were used as feature.

The proposed method only targeted the sentence including known Wakamono Kotoba. However, whether Wakamono Kotoba are included in the corpus or not, by extracting unknown and low-frequency words and by adding the emotional expressions having high relevance to them to the learning feature at the time of expanding the training data, more effective emotion estimation was thought to become possible.

In future, we would like to confirm the efficiency of the proposed method to the sentences including the unknown Wakamono Kotoba which were extracted automatically. Then, without limiting in the unknown words of Wakamono Kotoba, we would like to evaluate our method in the sentences including new words related to emotion.

Acknowledgement

This research has been partially supported by the Ministry of Education, Science, Sports and Culture, Grant-in-Aid for Scientific Research(A), 22240021, (B), 21300036, and Grant-in-Aid for Young Scientists (B), 23700252.

References

Keiko Noguchi. 2004. *Kanari kigakari na nihongo* (in Japanese). Shueisha.

Yugo Murawaki and Sadao Kurohashi. 2010. Online Acquisition of Japanese Unknown Morphemes using Morphological Constraints. *Journal of Natural Language Processing*, 17(1):55–75.

Jian Qu, Le Minh and Akira Shimazu. 2011. Web based English-Chinese OOV term translation using adaptive rules and recursive feature selection. *25th Pacific Asia Conference on Language, Information and Computation*, 1–10.

Kazuyuki Matsumoto, Hidemichi Sayama, Yusuke Konishi and Fuji Ren. 2011. Analysis of Wakamono Kotoba Emotion Corpus and Its Application in Emotion Estimation. *International Journal of Advanced Intelligence*, 3(1):1–24.

Kazuyuki Matsumoto and Fuji Ren. 2011. Construction of Wakamono Kotoba Emotion Dictionary and Its Application, *Computational Linguistics and Intelligent Text Processing*, LNCS6608:405–416.

Akihiko Yonekawa. 1998. *Wakamonogo wo kagakusuru* (in Japanese). Meiji shoin.

Nakami Yamaguchi. 2007. *Wakamono kotoba ni mimi wo sumaseba* (in Japanese). Kohdansha.

Yasuo Kitahara. 2009. Afureru shingo (in Japanese), *Taishukan shoten*.

Kurt W. Fischer, Phillip R. Shaver and Peter Carnochan. 1989. A Skill Approach to Emotional Development: From Basic-to Subordinate-category Emotions. *Child Development to Day and Tomorrow*, Jossay-Bass.

Akira Nakamura. 1993. *Emotional Expression Dictionary* (in Japanese). Tokyodo shuppan.

Adam Kilgarriff and David Tugwell. 2001. WASP-Bench: an MT Lexicographers' Workstation Supporting State-of-the-art Lexical Disambiguation. *Proceedings of MT Summit VIII*, 187–190.

Can Word Segmentation be Considered Harmful for Statistical Machine Translation Tasks between Japanese and Chinese?

Jing Sun and Yves Lepage
NLP Laboratory / Hibikino 2-7, Wakamatsu-ku
Graduate School of IPS / Kitakyushu-shi, Fukuoka-ken
Waseda University / Japan 808-0135
{cecily.sun@akane., yves.lepage@}waseda.jp

Abstract

Unlike most Western languages, there are no typographic boundaries between words in written Japanese and Chinese. Word segmentation is thus normally adopted as an initial step in most natural language processing tasks for these Asian languages. Although word segmentation techniques have improved greatly both theoretically and practically, there still remains some problems to be tackled. In this paper, we present an effective approach in extracting Chinese and Japanese phrases without conducting word segmentation beforehand, using a sampling-based multilingual alignment method. According to our experiments, it is also feasible to train a statistical machine translation system on a small Japanese-Chinese training corpus without performing word segmentation beforehand.

1 Introduction

Unlike most European languages, there are no explicit typographic boundaries like white spaces between words in many written Asian languages such as Chinese, Japanese, Korean, Thai, Lao and Vietnamese. Therefore, word segmentation for such languages is usually the first important step in most Natural Language Processing (NLP) applications especially in statistical machine translation. Although word segmentation techniques have improved greatly in recent years, there are still some difficulties that remain to be addressed.

Word segmentation schemes are not system-independent, application-independent nor language-independent. Different Chinese Word Segmentation (CWS) tools applied to the same Chinese sentence may lead to different results depending on their segmentation. For instance, 学生会 (pinyin: xué shēng huì) in Chinese may be interpreted as 学生_会 'student(s) can (do)' or 学生会 'Students' Union' respectively.

Figure 1 gives an example of pre-segmented text and unsegmented text in both Chinese and Japanese. We applied four CWS tools: Urheen (Wang et al., 2010), ICTCLAS (Zhang et al., 2003) and Standford Chinese word segmenter (Tseng et al., 2005) trained on CTB and PKU. This example clearly shows that word segmentation tools may do harm to cross-lingual tasks, because:

(i) there may be inconsistencies of segmentation results across languages such as different sizes of granularity in Japanese and Chinese;

(ii) for the same language, different word segmentation tools may produce different results;

(iii) the same word segmentation tool trained on different corpora may produce different results.

Such inconsistencies lead to increased error rates in Statistical Machine Translation.

Significant improvements in Chinese word segmentation techniques have been obtained recently and reported accuracy rates (compared to those of human *Golden Standard*) have reached 98%. However, for cross-lingual NLP tasks, such as phrasal extraction or Machine Translation, Zhang et al. (2008) showed that even the most accurate word segmentation may not produce the best translation out-

Original Chinese sentence:	没**事先**约好，白跑了回**津屋崎。**
Translation in Japanese:	事前予約をしなかったので、むだに津屋崎に行きました。
Meaning in English:	I went to Tsuyazaki in vain without prior appointment.
JWS (JUMAN):	事前_予約_を_し_なかった_ので_、_むだに_津屋崎_に_行き_ました_。
CWS Reference:	没_**事先**_约好_，_白_跑了回_**津屋崎**_。
CWS (ICTCLAS):	没_**事先**_约_好_，_白_跑_了_回_**津_屋_崎**_。
CWS (STANDFORD-CTB):	没**事_先**_约_好_，_白_跑_了_回**津屋崎**_。
CWS (STANDFORD-PKU):	没_**事先**_约好_，_白_跑_了_回_**津_屋崎**_。
CWS (URHEEN):	没_**事先**_约_好_，_白_跑_了_回**津_屋崎**_。

Figure 1: An example of inconsistency in Chinese word segmentation. All segmentation in Chinese by the four different systems are different. In addition, across Japanese and Chinese, although 津屋崎 (Tsuyazaki) is one word in Japanese, it was decomposed into different units in segmented Chinese.

puts. To solve the problem, it has been proposed to drive word segmentation using predefined bilingual knowledge, such as bilingual dictionaries or bilingual lexica extracted from parallel corpora. Instead of relying on an existing bilingual lexicon, Sun et al. (1998) automatically learned rules from a corpus and group unsegmented Chinese segments into words according to their mutual information. Xu et al. (2004) developed a system which extracts a lexicon from the trained alignment corpus. They showed that it is possible to work without performing Chinese word segmentation beforehand with only a minor loss in translation quality.

Bilingual resources are unavailable for many language pairs that do not involve English, like Japanese-Chinese or Japanese-Vietnamese. Although many researchers and several institutions have been working on constructing bilingual resources between Asian languages, rarely are these resources made freely available.

In this paper, we show how to use a small Japanese-Chinese bilingual corpus to perform phrase table extraction so as to build a statistical machine translation system and conduct translation experiments between Chinese and Japanese without conducting word segmentation on either the Japanese nor Chinese sides beforehand. The purpose of this paper is to determine:

- Whether it is possible to produce phrase tables and extract sub-sentential alignments from unsegmented texts in Chinese and Japanese.
- Whether it is possible to perform statistical machine translation with reasonable quality without conducting word segmentation beforehand.

Section 2 introduces our proposed method which consists in using the sampling-based sub-sentential aligner, Anymalign, to extract Japanese-Chinese sub-sentential fragments (phrase translation tables) from an unsegmented bi-corpus. Section 3 describes the machine translation experiment that uses the phrase tables produced by our method and gives an evaluation of the translation quality when translating using the character as the basic unit. Section 4 discusses the experiment results and Section 5 gives the conclusion.

2 Producing Phrase Tables from Unsegmented Japanese and Chinese Corpus

2.1 Text Corpus Used

We start with an in-house corpus of 9,500 aligned Japanese-Chinese sentence pairs collected from the Internet as training data. They include bilingual Web-blogs, movie subtitles, fable stories and conversations.

To compare the performance of phrasal extraction from both the pre-segmented corpus and the unsegmented corpus, we also conduct word segmentation on the same data set. Juman (Masuoka and Kabuto,

1989; Knuth, 2012) and Urheen (Wang et al., 2010) are used to perform Japanese and Chinese word segmentation.

The average length for the unsegmented Japanese sentences are 17 (std. dev. ±9.95) characters and 11 (std. dev. ±7.40) for Chinese. For pre-segmented text corpus, the average length is 10 (std. dev. ±5.93) words for Japanese and 8 (std. dev. ±4.99) for Chinese.

Sentence length distributions in both pre-segmented and unsegmented corpora are shown in Figure 2 and Figure 3 respectively,

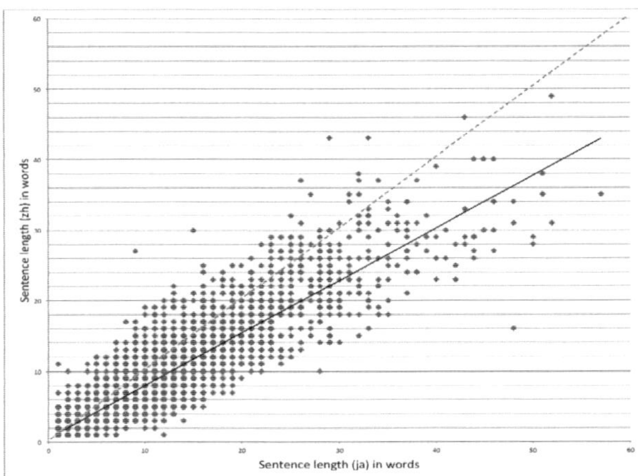

Figure 2: Sentence length distribution in our **pre-segmented** corpus. The dashed line shows the average, the solid line is linear regression.

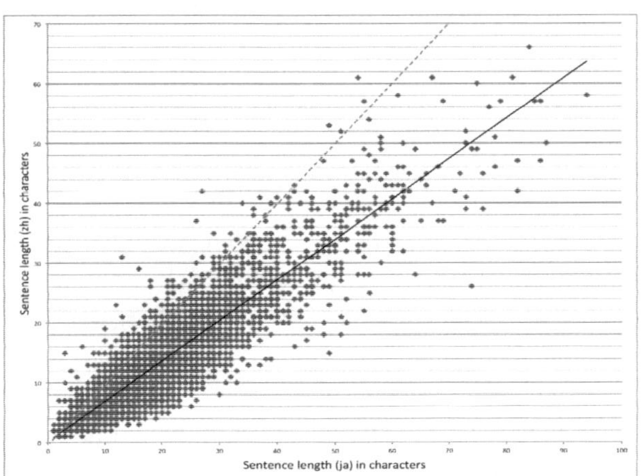

Figure 3: Sentence length distribution in our **unsegmented** corpus. The dashed line shows the average, the solid line is linear regression.

2.2 Aligners and Configurations Used

In our experiments, we use the open source implementation of the sampling-based approach, Anymalign (Lardilleux and Lepage, 2009)[1], to perform sub-sentential extraction from the above-described bi-corpus. Anymalign was run for three hours in its basic version (Anym b.) and with the option *-i* (Anym *-i*), where parameter *i* ranged from 1 to 10. The use of this option allows to extract longer phrases by enforcing n-grams to be considered as tokens. For pre-segmented texts, option *-i* allows to group words into phrases more easily. For unsegmented texts, as a token is a single character, the use of option *-i* allows to group characters into words, and then, into phrases, more easily.

In order to compare the performance of our phrase extraction method and statistical machine translation with unsegmented text corpus, we also applied GIZA++ (Och and Ney, 2003), the most commonly used tool for word and phrase alignment.

2.3 Numbers of Phrase Pairs Produced

Different values of parameter *i* lead to different numbers of phrase pairs entries in the phrase translation tables produced (see Table 1). The highest number of entries is obtained for *i* equal to 2, i.e., when each two connect characters in a sentence are possibly considered as one unit.

Index *i*	Output Entries
1	782,465
2	967,173
3	852,932
4	782,585
5	715,182
6	668,134
7	599,316
8	586,992
9	581,131
10	577,040
i-merged	1,628,241

Table 1: Numbers of entries in phrase translation tables obtained with Anymalign option *-i*.

[1] Anymalign: `http://perso.limsi.fr/Individu/alardill/anymalign/`

Aligner	Segmentation	Phrase-Table Entries	Intersection	Avg. P_{EDR}	Avg. P_{table}	Score
GIZA++	Pre-seg	36,888	1,086	0.6237	0.8269	1,575.323
	Unseg	56,002	**1,954**	0.6128	0.7804	**2,709.9344**
Anym b.	Pre-seg	326,748	2,190	0.5872	0.5841	2,565.0188
	Unseg	784,004	**3,294**	0.5141	0.2975	**2,673.4151**
i-merge	Pre-seg	553,156	2,265	0.5863	0.5850	2,652.968
	Unseg	1,628,241	**3,643**	0.5122	0.3909	**3,290.2923**

Table 2: Size of the intersection of phrase translation tables with the EDR Chinese-Japanese lexicon.

Figure 4 shows that when *i* reaches 7, the decrease in the number of entries in the phrase translation table reaches its asymptote. We also merged the 10 phrase translation tables for each value of parameter *i* into one phrase translation table that we name *i*-merge.

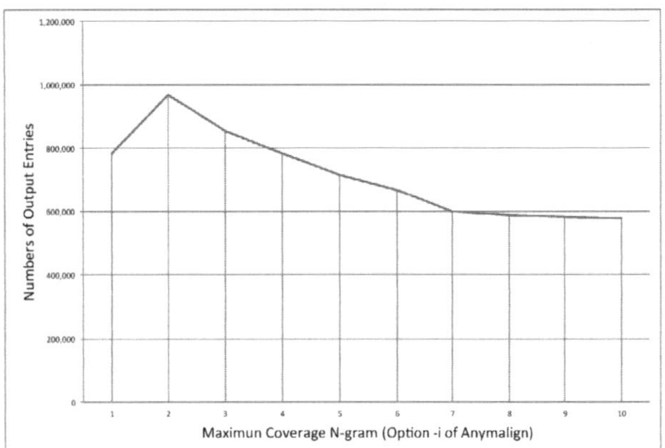

Figure 4: Number of entries in phrase translation tables for different values of parameter *i* between 1 and 10. This graph plots the figures given in Table 1.

Table 2 (See: Column 3 for *Phrase-Tables Entries*), shows that the use of an unsegmented corpus leads to larger phrase translation tables than the use of a pre-segmented corpus: twice the size for the basic version of Anymalign and 5 times for the merge of the all results of Anymalign run with option *-i*.

2.4 N-Grams × M-Grams Distribution

We investigated the $N \times M$-gram distribution in the phrase translation tables generated from both unsegmented and pre-segmented text corpora with Anymalign and GIZA++.

As presented in Appendix, Table 7 and 8 show the distribution for the pre-segmented corpus, where Tables 9, 10 and 11 are for the unsegmented corpus. Figures 5 - 9 provide a visualization of $N \times M$-Grams distributions in these phrase tables (see also Appendix.). They show that the phrase translation tables generated by GIZA++ exhibit a smoother decrease against the length of phrases, i.e. when N and M increase. Phrase translation tables output by Anymalign have significantly more entries when N and M are equal to or smaller than 2.

2.5 Comparison with an Existing Japanese-Chinese Bilingual Lexicon: EDR

The number of entries in the phrase translation tables does not give clues on the linguistic correctness of the entries. We thus compare the phrase translation tables against an existing Japanese-Chinese bilingual lexicon to check the correct word coverage rate.

The EDR Japanese-Chinese Bilingual Dictionary[2] contains 323,871 unique entries with an average length of words of 3.56 characters for Japanese and 3.46 for Chinese. Phrase translation tables generated with our method are not limited to words, but also contain phrases, fragments and short sentences that may not be included in the EDR bilingual lexicon. Therefore, we filtered the EDR lexicon to produce a filtered lexicon that contains only those entries which can actually be extracted from the training corpus. Using our corpus, the EDR lexicon has been filtered to 13,062 entries (96% reduced).

We then inspect the intersections between the filtered EDR lexicon and the phrase translation tables generated from both unsegmented and pre-segmented corpora output by Anymalign, basic version or *i*-merge, and GIZA++.

[2]The EDR Electronic Dictionary: National Institute of Information and Communication Technology (NiCT). URL: `http://www2.nict.go.jp/out-promotion/techtransfer/EDR/index.html`

As shown in Table 2, the phrase translation table extracted from the unsegmented corpus with Anymalign i-merge has 3,643 entries in common with the filtered EDR lexicon.

We would also like to take the translation probabilities $P(t|s)$ in the generated phrase translation tables into consideration in our comparison. When there are m common entries of two phrase tables tt_1 and tt_2, we can compute the Intersection Score using metrics where $P(t|s)$ stands for the translation probability appearing in phrase translation tables.

$$\text{Score}(tt_1, tt_2) = \frac{\sum_{k=1}^{m} P_{tt_1}(t|s) + \sum_{k=1}^{m} P_{tt_2}(t|s)}{2}$$

The intersection scores obtained are reported in the last column in Table 2. These results show that the phrase translation table extracted from unsegmented corpus with Anymalign i-merge has the highest overlap with the filtered EDR lexicon.

2.6 Monolingual Recall

In order to know how effective the method can correctly extract phrases, we inspected the coverage rate of phrases by comparing with existing Japanese and Chinese word lists respectively.

We merged the Chinese resources listed below to build a Chinese word list (numbers are in unique entries):

- LDC Wordlist[3] (Chinese part): 128,341
- Baidu Baike[4]: 823,333
- Sogou Chinese Word List[5]: 35,650
- EDR (Chinese part): 151,651

For Japanese, the resources are listed below.

- LDC Wordlist (Japanese part): 187,267
- CTS Japanese Frequency List[6]: 15,000
- EDR (Japanese part): 229,392

[3]http://projects.ldc.upenn.edu/Chinese/
[4]http://baike.baidu.com/
[5]http://www.sogou.com/
[6]http://corpus.leeds.ac.uk/list.html

In total, we obtained a Chinese monolingual word list of 1,032,919 unique entries and a Japanese monolingual word list of 330,610 unique entries. We then filtered the two monolingual word lists to restrict them to the items found in our training corpora. This resulted in two filtered monolingual word lists of 19,037 entries in Chinese and 14,166 in Japanese. Table 3 shows the Recall Rate of monolingual phrases extracted in the phrase translation tables against the filtered monolingual Japanese and Chinese word lists.

Monolingual Recall for Japanese

	Pre-seg		Unseg	
Aligner	Retrieved	Recall	Retrieved	Recall
GIZA++	3,358	23.70%	5,228	**36.91%**
Anym b.	6,953	49.08%	9,479	**66.91%**
Anym -i	7,110	50.19%	10,520	**74.26%**

Monolingual Recall for Chinese

	Pre-seg		Unseg	
Aligner	Retrieved	Recall	Retrieved	Recall
GIZA++	4,909	25.79%	7,450	**39.13%**
Anym b.	9,666	50.77%	14,186	**74.52%**
Anym -i	9,967	52.36%	15,031	**78.96%**

Table 3: Monolingual Recall in phrase tables for Japanese and Chinese

3 Machine Translation Experiment

In this section, we use the phrase translation tables extracted in the previous sections in statistical machine translation experiments.

3.1 Data

We keep using our in-house Japanese-Chinese bilingual parallel corpus to test the feasibility of utilizing a training corpus of such a limited size. Table 4 shows the statistics of the training, tuning and testing corpora in their sizes and average lengths of sentences (numbers of characters or words per sentence) in their unsegmented corpus and pre-segmented forms.

3.2 Evaluation Metrics and Results

We use the state-of-the-art phrase-based machine translation system Moses (Koehn et al., 2007) to

		Japanese	Chinese
Train	Sentences	9,500	9,500
	Avg. len(w)	10 (±5.93)	8 (±4.99)
	Avg. len(c)	17 (±9.95)	11(±7.40)
Tune	Sentences	500	500
	Avg. len(w)	10 (±5.96)	8 (±5.10)
	Avg. len(c)	17 (±9.98)	11(±7.55)
Test	Sentences	500	500
	Avg. len(w)	10 (±5.88)	8 (±5.19)
	Avg. len(c)	17 (±9.85)	11(±7.94)

Table 4: Statistics of the training, tuning and testing corpora. Avg. len(w) stands for the average number of words in each sentence. Avg. len(c) stands for the average number of characters in each sentence.

Eval.	Anymalign *i*-merge	
Metric	Pre-seg	Unseg
$BLEU_{c4}$	0.1586	**0.1900**
$BLEU_{c5}$	0.1162	**0.1436**
$BLEU_{c6}$	0.0868	**0.1099**
$BLEU_{c7}$	0.0660	**0.0850**
$BLEU_{c8}$	0.0509	**0.0673**
WER	0.7595	**0.7121**
NIST	4.6215	**5.2904**
TER	0.7744	**0.7144**

Table 5: Evaluation of Chinese translation output. Aligner used: **Anymalign *i*-merge.**

Eval.	GIZA++	
Metric	Pre-seg	Unseg
$BLEU_{c4}$	0.1472	**0.1938**
$BLEU_{c5}$	0.1117	**0.1517**
$BLEU_{c6}$	0.0873	**0.1210**
$BLEU_{c7}$	0.0696	**0.0979**
$BLEU_{c8}$	0.0565	**0.0806**
WER	0.8373	**0.7214**
NIST	4.2198	**5.1438**
TER	0.8337	**0.7290**

Table 6: Evaluation of Chinese translation output. Aligner used: **GIZA++**

perform our machine translation experiments. As for the evaluation, we use the standard metrics WER (Nießen et al., 2000), BLEU (Papineni et al., 2002), NIST (Doddington et al., 2000) and TER (Snover et al., 2006).

Being a fast, automated and open source tool, the BLEU metric has been adopted as the main measure of fluency and adequacy (Akiba et al., 2004) in the domain of machine translation. It basically evaluates the precision of N-grams according to a reference translation.

However, word-level BLEU metric has been challenged in recent years. Denoual and Lepage (2005) studied the equivalence of applying BLEU metrics in characters and suggested that the use of BLEU at the character level could eliminate the word segmentation problem. Li et al.,(2011) stated that character-level metrics correlate better with human assessment. Chinese word segmentation is not needed for auto-evaluation. Besides, the campaigns like IWSLT '08 and NIST '08 both adopted character-level evaluation metrics.

Table 5 shows the evaluation results obtained when using Anymalign *i*-merge and Table 6 when using GIZA++. $BLEU_{cN}$ stands for the measure in characters for a given order N.

In both tables, so as to ensure consistency, the quality of Chinese translation outputs has been measured in characters. The results show that the phrase translation table generated from the unsegmented corpus outperfoms the phrase translation tables generated from the pre-segmented corpus. From this, it can be concluded that word segmentation is not a necessary step for statistical machine translation experiments between Japanese and Chinese language.

4 Discussion

The results of the experiments we conducted with an unsegmented corpus outperformed the results of the same experiments conducted with the same pre-segmented corpus. This applies for both phrasal extraction and statistical machine translation between Chinese and Japanese. We explain below the reasons that may explain this fact.

Firstly, the unsegmented corpus gives more chances to match with correct alignment in Chinese and Japanese corpus. For example, 学生会(Students' Union) can be segmented into either 学生_会 or 学生会. Its translation in Japanese is 学友会 which is segmented into 学友_会 by Juman. As such, the chance for Chinese 学生会 to match with Japanese 学友会 in the pre-segmented corpus is either zero or fifty percent. By opposition, for character-based text, their match rate is 66.67%. This shows that Chinese and Japanese word segmentation may vary in terms of refinement. Word segmentation performed on the output text and the reference text in the same language may not be consistent either.

Many Chinese Hanzi and Japanese Kanji are common to both languages. When applying phrase extraction, such linguistic feature may become very helpful in phrasal extraction and statistical machine translation. Goh et al. (2005) studied the accuracy of possible conversion between Chinese Hanzi and Japanese Kanji. Their study shows that around two thirds of the nouns and verbal nouns in Japanese are Kanji words and more than one third of them can be transposed into Chinese directly.

5 Conclusion

In this paper, we used a small-size Japanese-Chinese parallel corpus to conduct experiments in phrasal extraction and statistical machine translation. Our corpus was used under two forms: in a pre-segmented form obtained using Japanese and Chinese word segmentation tools, and in an unsegmented form, i.e., under this form, the processing unit was the character. Our experiment results show that the unsegmented form lead to better results than the pre-segmented form in both tasks. We believe that unsegmented forms of Chinese and Japanese corpora have the potential of improving translations between Japanese and Chinese. In summary, our experiments have shown that word segmentation may not be necessary for some NLP tasks between Japanese and Chinese.

Acknowledgments

This research has been supported in part by the Kitakyushu Foundation for the Advancement of Industry, Science and Technology (FAIS) with Foreign Joint Project funds.

References

Yusuhiro Akiba, Marcello Federico, Noriko Kando, Hiromi Nakaiwa, Michael Paul, and Jun'ichi Tsujii. 2004. Overview of the IWSLT'04 evaluation campaign. In *Proceedings of the International Workshop on Spoken Language Translation*, pages 1–12, Kyoto, Japan.

Etienne Denoual and Yves Lepage. 2005. BLEU in characters: Towards automatic MT evaluation in languages without word delimiters. In *IJCNLP-05: Second International Joint Conference on Natural Language Processing*, pages 79–84, Jeju Island, Republic of Kore, October.

George R. Doddington, Mark A. Przybocki, Alvin F. Martin, and Douglas A. Reynolds. 2000. The NIST speaker recognition evaluation - overview, methodology, systems, results, perspective. *Speech Communication*, 31(2-3):225–254.

Chooi-Ling Goh, Masayuki Asahara, and Yuji Matsumoto. 2005. Building a Japanese-Chinese Dictionary Using Kanji/Hanzi Conversion. In LNAI 3651, editor, *R. Dale et al. (Eds.): IJCNLP*, pages 670–681.

Donald E. Knuth. 2012. Satisfiability and the art of computer programming. In *SAT*, page 15.

Philipp Koehn, Hieu Hoang, Alexandra Birch, Chris Callison-Burch, Marcello Federico, Nicola Bertoldi, Brooke Cowan, Wade Shen, Christine Moran, Richard Zens, Chris Dyer, Ondrej Bojar, Alexandra Constantin, and Evan Herbst. 2007. Moses: Open source toolkit for statistical machine translation. In *Proceedings of the 45th Annual Meeting of the Association for Computational Linguistics (ACL'07)*, pages 177–180, Prague, Czech Republic.

Adrien Lardilleux and Yves Lepage. 2009. Sampling-based multilingual alignment. In *International Conference on Recent Advances in Natural Language Processing (RANLP'09)*, pages 214–218, Borovets, Bulgaria.

Maoxi Li, Chengqing Zong, and Hwee Tou Ng. 2011. Automatic evaluation of chinese translation output: Word-level or character-level? In *Proceedings of the 49the Annual Meeting of the Association for Computational Linguistics: shortpapers*, pages 159–164, Portland, Oregon.

Sun Maosong, Shen Dayang, and Benjamin K Tsou. 1998. Chinese word segmentation without using lexicon and hand-crafted training data. In *Proceedings of the 36th Annual Meeting of ACL and 17th International Conference on Computational Linguistics (COLING-ACL 98)*, pages 1265–1271, Montreal, Quebec, Canada, August.

Takashi Masuoka and Yukinori Kabuto. 1989. *Basic Japanese Grammar*. Kuroshi Publishers.

Sonja Nießen, Franz Josef Och, Gregor Leusch, and Hermann Ney. 2000. An evaluation tool for machine translation: Fast evaluation for machine translation research. In *Proceedings of the Second International Conference on Language Resources and Evaluation (LREC)*, pages 39–45, Athens.

Franz Josef Och and Hermann Ney. 2003. A Systematic Comparison of Various Statistical Alignment Models. In *Computational Linguistics*, volume 29(1), pages 19–51.

Kishore Papineni, Salim Roukos, Todd Ward, and Wei-Jing Zhu. 2002. BLEU: a method for automatic evaluation of machine translation. In *Proceedings of the 40th Annual Meeting of the Association for Computational Linguistics (ACL 2002)*, pages 311–318, Philadelphia.

Matthew Snover, Bonnie Dorr, Richard Schwartz, Linnea Micciulla, and John Makhoul. 2006. A study of translation edit rate with targeted human annotation. In *Proceedings of Association for Machine Translation in the Americas (AMTA 2006)*, pages 223–231, Cambridge, Massachusetts.

Huihsin Tseng, Pichuan Chang, Galen Andrew, Daniel Jurafsky, and Christopher Manning. 2005. A conditional random field word segmenter for sighan bakeoff 2005. In *Proceedings of the Fourth SIGHAN Workshop on Chinese Language Processing*, pages 168–171, Jeju Island, Korea.

Kun Wang, Chengqing Zong, and Keh-Yih Su. 2010. A character-based joint model for Chinese word segmentation. In *Proceedings of the 23rd International Conference on Computational Linguistics (COLING)*, pages 1173–1181, August.

Jia Xu, Richard Zens, and Hermann Ney. 2004. Do we need Chinese word segmentation for Statistical Machine Translation? In *Proceedings of the ACL SIGHAN Workshop 2004*, pages 122–128, Barcelna, Spain.

Huaping Zhang, Qun Liu, Xueqi Cheng, Hao Zhang, and Hongkui Yu. 2003. Chinese lexical analysis using hierarchical hidden markov model. In *Proceedings of the Second SIGHAN Workshop on Chinese Language Processing*, pages 63–70, sapporo, Japan.

Ruiqiang Zhang, Keiji Yasuda, and Eiichiro Sumita. 2008. Chinese word segmentation and statistical machine translation. *ACM Transactions on Speech and Language Processing*, 5(2):1–19.

Appendix: $N \times M$-Grams Distribution in Phrase Tables for Pre-segmented and Unsegmented Corpus with Different Aligners and Their Visualisation Graphs.

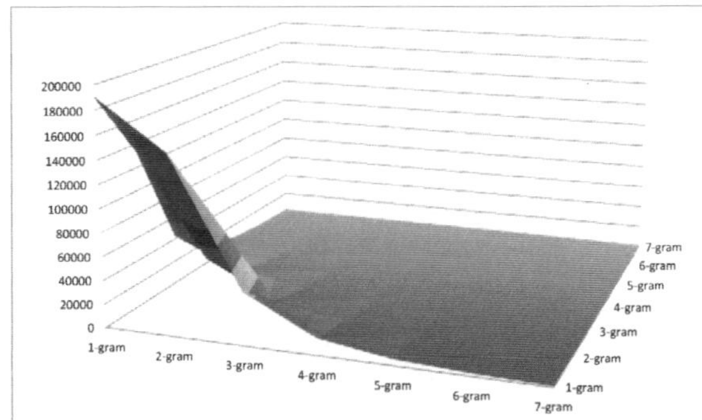

Figure 5: A visualization of N x M-grams distribution in phrase translation tables obtained from the **unsegmented** corpus using the basic version of Anymalign.

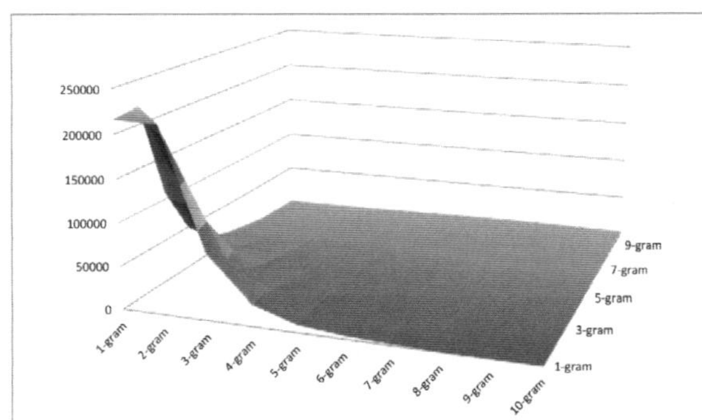

Figure 6: A visualization of N x M-grams distribution in phrase translation tables obtained from the **unsegmented** corpus using Anymalign *i*-merge.

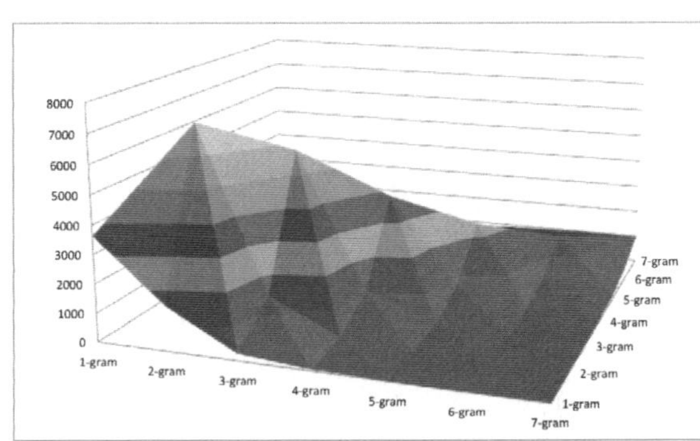

Figure 7: A visualization of N x M-grams distribution in phrase translation tables obtained from the **unsegmented** corpus using GIZA++.

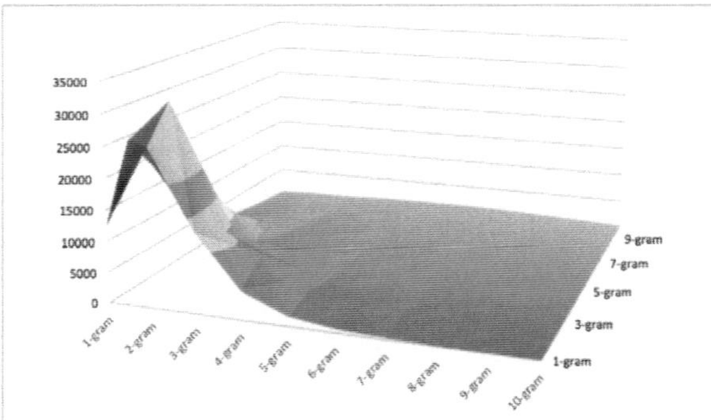

Figure 8: A visualization of N x M-grams distribution in phrase translation tables obtained from **pre-segmented** corpus using the basic version of Anymalign.

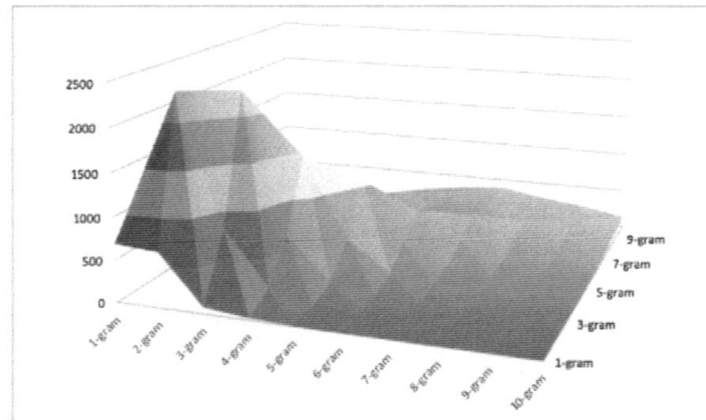

Figure 9: A visualization of N x M grams distribution in phrase translation tables obtained from the **pre-segmented** corpus using GIZA++.

		Target											
		1-char	2-char	3-char	4-char	5-char	6-char	7-char	8-char	9-char	10-char	···	total
Source	1-char	12,501	25,559	12,876	4,612	1,569	604	264	102	53	19	···	58,163
	2-char	24,272	**31,111**	11,640	8,216	2,830	1,857	762	356	167	54	···	81,307
	3-char	18,375	18,554	7,550	4,875	2,025	1,135	497	235	113	34	···	53,420
	4-char	10,958	11,264	4,950	4,063	1,855	1,319	577	321	149	71	···	35,577
	5-char	6,008	6,576	3,378	2,894	1,759	1,115	611	280	142	45	···	22,838
	6-char	3,479	4,282	2,562	2,481	1,622	1,184	635	375	175	58	···	16,898
	7-char	1,956	2,642	1,883	1,960	1,635	1,228	821	439	249	77	···	12,937
	8-char	1,266	1,810	1,484	1,690	1,521	1,320	959	571	320	138	···	11,154
	9-char	736	1,118	1,047	1,286	1,322	1,260	1,080	714	439	224	···	9,354
	10-char	455	727	727	1,028	1,135	1,143	1,066	802	553	267	···	8,083
	···	···	···	···	···	···	···	···	···	···	···	···	···
	total	80,576	104,654	492,008	34,555	19,164	14,462	9,677	6,459	4,195	2,160	···	**326,748**

Table 7: $N \times M$-grams (characters) distribution in the phrase translation table obtained from the **pre-segmented** corpus using the basic version of Anymalign.

		Target											
		1-char	2-char	3-char	4-char	5-char	6-char	7-char	8-char	9-char	10-char	···	total
Source	1-char	681	650	77	24	6	1	4	1	0	0	···	1,444
	2-char	741	**2,341**	816	189	42	17	14	1	1	0	···	4,162
	3-char	478	1,707	2,285	649	136	48	32	11	5	2	···	5,353
	4-char	220	887	1,326	1,438	489	133	48	22	10	9	···	4,583
	5-char	92	549	786	980	1,057	340	110	46	17	8	···	3,986
	6-char	38	338	560	786	766	604	263	85	36	17	···	3,499
	7-char	14	167	329	549	591	493	450	173	75	18	···	2,876
	8-char	10	84	194	380	502	442	390	269	134	53	···	2,483
	9-char	3	63	110	231	369	428	386	291	199	86	···	2,212
	10-char	0	14	66	164	264	341	382	296	230	140	···	1,976
	···	···	···	···	···	···	···	···	···	···	···	···	···
	total	2,281	6,828	6,629	5,579	4,611	3,433	2,838	1,954	1,331	808	···	**36,888**

Table 8: $N \times M$-grams (characters) distribution in the phrase translation table obtained from the **pre-segmented** corpus using GIZA++

		Target							
		1-char	2-char	3-char	4-char	5-char	6-char	7-char	total
	1-char	3,625	1,549	242	50	5	4	1	5,476
	2-char	2,683	**7,046**	1,384	248	51	12	6	11,430
	3-char	995	3,731	5,788	1,008	208	37	18	11,785
Source	4-char	462	1,539	2,928	3,806	794	173	34	9,736
	5-char	199	849	1,401	2,106	2,352	555	123	7,585
	6-char	79	434	749	1,185	1,450	1,449	426	5,772
	7-char	44	173	423	700	917	984	977	4,218
	total	8,087	15,321	12,915	9,103	5,777	3,214	1,585	**56,002**

Table 9: $N \times M$-grams (characters) distribution in the phrase translation table obtained from the **unsegmented** corpus using GIZA++.

		Target							
		1-char	2-char	3-char	4-char	5-char	6-char	7-char	total
	1-char	**190,967**	150,445	44,562	14,522	5,436	2,438	959	409,329
	2-char	132,744	46,374	17,632	7,671	3,403	1,650	743	210,217
	3-char	42,967	16,959	8,012	4,246	2,126	1,125	491	75,926
Source	4-char	16,673	8,244	5,185	3,401	2,000	1,121	561	37,185
	5-char	7,350	4,612	3,590	2,819	1,934	1,177	639	22,121
	6-char	3,974	2,919	2,765	2,489	1,939	1,285	780	16,151
	7-char	2,362	1,922	2,074	2,210	1,988	1,491	1,028	13,075
	total	397,037	231,475	83,820	37,358	18,826	10,287	5,201	**784,004**

Table 10: $N \times M$-grams (characters) distribution in the phrase translation table obtained from the **unsegmented** corpus using the basic version of Anymalign.

		Target										
		1-char	2-char	3-char	4-char	5-char	6-char	7-char	8-char	9-char	10-char	total
	1-char	215,840	214,475	76,268	24,808	8,818	3,806	1,545	158	54	12	545,784
	2-char	**220,226**	121,635	47,728	24,868	13,562	9,403	6,250	2,207	1,154	462	447,495
	3-char	107,143	55,351	25,963	15,659	9,596	6,978	4,787	1,785	910	369	228,541
	4-char	50,381	31,074	17,561	12,999	9,215	7,311	5,279	2,049	1,125	463	137,457
	5-char	23,597	16,812	11,495	9,932	8,053	6,725	5,126	2,067	1,140	457	85,404
Source	6-char	12,372	10,233	8,304	8,232	7,475	6,762	5,483	2,468	1,499	673	63,501
	7-char	7,040	6,509	6,111	6,886	6,780	6,662	5,696	2,799	1,804	857	51,144
	8-char	1,946	1,992	2,424	3,302	3,898	4,304	3,918	3,059	2,192	1,140	28,175
	9-char	974	1,014	1,431	2,257	3,065	3,768	3,690	3,100	2,566	1,462	23,327
	10-char	401	440	678	1,291	1952	2,745	2,975	2,785	2,354	1,792	17,413
	total	639,920	459,535	197,963	110,234	72,414	58,464	44,749	22,477	14,798	7,687	**1,628,241**

Table 11: $N \times M$-grams (characters) distribution in the phrase translation table obtained from the **unsegmented** corpus using Anymalign *i*-merge.

Introduction of a Probabilistic Language Model to Non-Factoid Question-Answering Using Example Q&A Pairs

Kyosuke Yoshida, Taro Ueda, Madoka Ishioroshi, Hideyuki Shibuki, and Tatsunori Mori
Graduate School of Environment and Information Sciences, Yokohama National University
79-7 Tokiwadai, Hodogaya-ku,Yokohama 240-8501, Japan
{kyoshida, kks, ishioroshi, shib, mori}@forest.eis.ynu.ac.jp

Abstract

In this paper, we propose a method which utilizes a probabilistic language model in non-factoid type question-answering system in order to improve its accuracy. The model is a mixture probabilistic language model of part-of-speech and surface expressions. We introduced the model into two sub-processes which calculate similarity of texts in terms of writing style. The first process collects example questions similar to a submitted question. The second one measures similarity between an answer candidate and example answers paired with the collected example questions. Experimental results showed that the accuracy of the system was improved by introducing the proposed method.

1 Introduction

In recent years, the amount of data available on the Web is increasing by growing computer performance and network traffic. Therefore, technologies that give us access to neccessary information in the large amount of data are required. One of such technologies is question-answering (QA), which is to extract an answer for a question written in natural language from source documents. In general, QA systems are categorized into the following two types: factoid and non-factoid(Fukumoto, 2007). We focus on the non-factoid type QA in this paper. Table 1 shows some typical types of non-factoid questions. The appropriateness of the answer candidates is often estimated on the basis of following two measures (Han *et al.*, 2006).

Measure 1 : Relevance to the topic of the question, how relevant is the candidate to the topic of the question?

Measure 2 : Appropriateness of writing style, how well does the candidate satisfy the writing style that is appropriate for answers of the class of the given question?

Here, by the term "writing style", we refer to the style of expressions peculiar to a class of questions and their answers, as shown in Table 1. Although these two measures depend on each other to some extent, we assume that they are independent in this study.

Non-factoid type QA systems are categorized into the following two types according to how to handle Measure 2. The first type classifies submitted questions into several predefined question types such as definition-type, why-type, how-type, and so on, in order to separately handle each type of questions by different methodologies. Han *et al.* (2006) calculated the above-mentioned two measures for definition-type questions based on probabilistic models built from corpora. The model for Measure 1 is calculated from retrieved documents. The model for Measure 2 is calculated from a corpus of definitions. However, this type of systems has some difficulties as follows. Since the classes of non-factoid questions are not well defined, it is difficult to distinguish and define all classes comprehensively. Moreover, the accuracy of a question classifier affects the overall accuracy of question-answering, because misclassified questions are incorrectly routed to an answering module for different classes.

The second type of systems handles submitted questions based on a unified framework without question classification. Mizuno *et al.* (2009) proposed a method that is able to calculate Measure 2 without classification of questions. Using example Q&A pairs from a Q&A community site, it learns a binary classifier that judges whether or not the class

Table 1: Typical types of non-factoid questions

Type of question	Examples of typical writing style	
	Question	Answer
Definition-type	∼ *tte-nani* (What is ∼)	∼ *towa* ⋯ *dearu*(∼ is ⋯)
Why-type	*Naze* ∼ (Why ∼)	⋯ *tame*(Because ⋯)
How-type	∼ *suru-niwa dou-shitara ii* (How can I do ∼)	∼ *suru-niwa mazu* ⋯ (In order to do ∼, ⋯)
Other types	*X-to Y-no chigai wa nani* (What is the difference between X and Y)	*X-wa* ∼ *-daga, Y-wa* ⋯ (While X is ∼, Y is ⋯)

of a given answer candidate is consistent with the class of a submitted question. By using this classifier, Measure 2 is realized without question classification. Soricut et al. (2006) also proposed a system without question classification. They introduced a statistical translation model between questions and the corresponding answers in order to bridge the lexical gap between the questions and the answers. A set of example Q&A pairs from FAQ sites on the Web is used for the estimation of the model.

In these methods, the length of answers should be predetermined. The length of answers cannot be changed dynamically and is necessary to be estimate from the length of the question.

Therefore, Mori *et al.* (2008) proposed a method of the second type approach that is able to adaptively determine the length of an answer candidate according to a submitted question. They use example Q&A pairs on a Q&A community site in order to find appropriate writing styles to answers for submitted questions. They utilize simple n-gram model as features to retrieve example questions similar to a submitted question in terms of writing style and to find appropriate writing styles to answer. However, the simple n-gram model is not appropriate to model dependency among words that appear in the distant positions because it only captures linguistic phenomena that appear within the n-words window. Therefore, sometimes the selection of example questions is not carried out correctly. There exist some incorrectly retrieved example questions that are not similar to the whole submitted question in terms of writing style, while those n-grams happen to be very similar to the n-grams of the question. Their method of scoring answer candidate is based on a naive frequency model of word 2-grams as feature expressions. Therefore, ungrammatical sentences, which often appear in Web documents and are not suitable to answer candidates, happen to have high scores when they have the feature expressions. It decrease the accuracy of the system.

In this paper, we employ the method of Mori *et al.* (2008) as a baseline method. We introduce a probabilistic language model to the baseline method in order to solve the above problems and improve the method in terms of accuracy.

Our method has the following three feature parts. Firstly, a probabilistic language model is used to retrieve examples similar to an submitted question. Secondly, another probabilistic language model is constructed from the retrieved example answers, which is used to measure the appropriateness of answer candidates for submitted questions. Finally, the answer candidates are clustered into several groups, and the candidates that have unsuitable writing styles as answers for the submitted question are removed.

The rest of this paper is organized as follows. In Section 2, we explain the related works. In Section 3, we explain the outline of the baseline method. In Section 4, we discuss the problems of the baseline method. In Section 5, we describe the detail of the proposed method. In Section 6, we conduct examinations of our QA system, and discuss the results. In Section 7, we provide our conclusion.

2 Related Works

The methods which utilize probabilistic language model have been developed including followings.

Takahashi *et al.* (2010) combine several types of language models in order to retrieve questions similar to users' queries from a Q&A archive of a Q&A community site. In order to examine the mixture ratio of the language models, they investigated the following two cases: 1) the ratio is fixed for all Q&A pairs, and 2) the ratio adaptively varies according to Q&A pairs. They showed that the performance is improved in both of the cases. The purpose of this study is different from ours because we retrieve example questions similar to submitted question in terms of writing styles while they retrieve questions similar to submitted questions in terms of content.

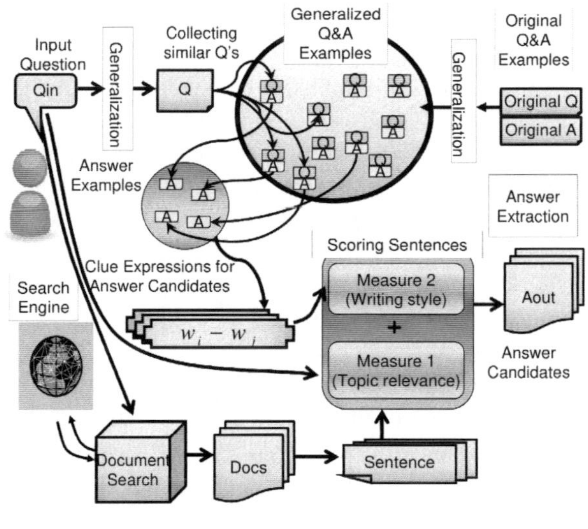

Figure 1: Outline of the baseline system

Heie *et al.* (2012) proposed a method to obtain answers by calculating the relation between the submitted question Q and an answer candidate A in terms of probability. They supposed that the probability of having the answer A depends on two sets of feateures, W and X, as $P(A|Q) = P(A|W, X)$. The set of feateures W $(= w_1, \ldots, w_{|W|})$ denotes feature expressions that indicate "type of question" , e.g. "when", "why", "how". 2,522 words are obtained from TREC question set as the candidate of W. X $(= x_1, \ldots, x_{|X|})$ denotes a set of features comprising the "information-bearing" words of submitted quesions, e.g. what the question is actually about and what it refers to. They used $P(A|X)$ as a retrieval model and $P(W|A)$ as a filter model.

Although two above-mentioned studies do not explicitly handle the questions in a question-type-by-question-type manner, they explicitly use surface expressions. On the other hand, our method take account of not only surface expressions but also their part-of-speech tags as their abstractions. In order to take account of writing styles, we utilize a mixture probabilistic language model in terms of part-of-speech tags and surface expressions.

3 Baseline Method

In this section, we describe the baseline method according to Mori *et al.* (2008). Figure 1 shows the outline of the baseline QA system.

3.1 Extracting Keywords from a Question and Obtaining Their Related Words

From a question submitted by a user(a submitted question, hereafter), content words are extracted as keywords. Let K, K_n, and K_p be the set of all keywords, the set of keywords of simple nouns (one-morpheme words), and the set of keywords except nouns, respectively. Since sequences of simple nouns may form compound nouns, let K_c be the set of all compound nouns and other remaining simple nouns. A question usually contains only a few keywords and these may not be enough to estimate Measure 1. Therefore, the following keyword expansion and weighting are performed by using Web documents.

1. Create all subsets that contain three words from K_c.
2. Form boolean "AND" query q_i from each subset and submit it to a Web search engine to obtain a set of snippets. Let n_i be the number of the obtained snippets.
3. The weight value $T(w_j)$ defined as the following equation is calculated for each word w_j in snippets:

$$T(w_j) = \max_i \frac{freq(w_j, i)}{n_i} \tag{1}$$

where $freq(w_j, i)$ is the frequency of the snippets that contain the word w_j for the query q_i.

In order to give each keyword $k \in K$ a weight value that is not less than those of the expanded words, the weight value is defined as the following equation:

$$T(k) = \max_j T(w_j) \tag{2}$$

3.2 Retrieving Example Questions Similar to the Submitted Question

In order to obtain clue expressions peculiar to answer candidates for the question submitted by a user, in this stage, the baseline method retrieves example Q&A pairs whose questions are similar to the submitted question from the viewpoint of writing style. Mori *et al.* (2008) adopted the word 7-gram whose center word is an interrogative as the core part of a given question, because it represents enough context to determin the class of question. Thorefore, they defined the similarity between two questions as the similarity between the word 7-grams extracted from the questions. According to the similarity, N-best example Q&A pairs are obtained by using an ordinary information retrieval technique.

3.3 Extracting Clue Expressions from Example Answers

In this stage, clue expressions are extracted from the answers in the example Q&A pairs obtained in the stage described in Section 3.2. A 2-gram was adopted as a clue expression unit because it is the smallest unit that can represent relations between words. It is assumed that the effectiveness of each 2-gram as a clue expression can be estimated by the degree of correlation between the 2-gram and the answers from the retrieved Q&A pairs.

As the measurement of the correlation, Mori *et al.* (2008) adopted the χ^2 value shown in Equation (3) for the following two kinds of events for the answers from the entire set of example Q&A pairs:

event α Being an example answer that corresponds to one of the retrieved example questions, which are similar to the submitted question. The set of example answers for the event is denoted by A.

event $\beta(b)$ Being an example answer that contains a certain 2-gram b. The set of example answers for the event is denoted by $B(b)$.

$$\chi^2(b) = \frac{n}{|A| \cdot |\bar{A}| \cdot |B(b)| \cdot |\bar{B(b)}|} \cdot (|A \cap B(b)| \cdot |\bar{A} \cap \bar{B(b)}| - |\bar{A} \cap B(b)| \cdot |A \cap \bar{B(b)}|)^2 \quad (3)$$

where n is the total number of example Q&A pairs. The more correlated two events are, the larger the value of $\chi^2(b)$ is. According to the value of $\chi^2(b)$, the M-best 2-grams are selected as clue expressions of the answers for the submitted question.

3.4 Extracting Answer Candidates

In this stage, by using the method in Section 3.3, it extracts a set of 2-grams as clue expressions from the example answers of the example Q&A pairs retrieved by the method in Section 3.2 and calculates the corresponding $\chi^2(b)$ value for each 2-gram b. The score of each sentence is calculated by using the following equation:

$$\mathrm{Score}(S_i) = \frac{1}{\log(1 + |S_i|)} \cdot \left\{ \sum_{j=1}^{l} T(w_{ij}) \right\}^{\gamma} \cdot \left\{ \sum_{k=1}^{m} \sqrt{\chi^2(b_{ik})} \right\}^{1-\gamma} \quad (4)$$

where l is the number of different words in the sentence S_i, m is the numer of different 2-grams in S_i, w_{ij} is the j-th word in sentence S_i, and b_{ik} is the k-th 2-gram in S_i. Since the terms $\sum_{j=1}^{l} T(w_{ij})$ and $\sum_{k=1}^{m} \sqrt{\chi^2(b_{ik})}$ in Equation (4) correspond to Measure 1 and Measure 2, respectively, the parametar γ is used to determine the mixture ratio of Measure 1 and Measure 2. The normalization term $\frac{1}{\log(1+|S_i|)}$ is inroduced to calculate the density of content words related to the question (i.e. keywords and their related words) and clue expressions (i.e. 2-grams that correlated with example answers). In order to reward longer sentences, the logarithm of sentence length is adopted.

4 Problems of Baseline Method

In the baseline method, the $\chi^2(b)$ value of a word 2-gram mentioned in Section 3.3 is used in order to extract clue expressions from example answers. This method uses only the frequency of word 2-grams for the purpose of calculation based on the $\chi^2(b)$ value. As a result, the word order and the contexts of clue expressions are ignored. In this method, example questions are retrieved according to the similarity between submitted question and example questions in terms of the 7-gram whose center word is an interrogative. However, the selection of example questions occasionally fails because some retrieved example questions are not similar to the submitted question in terms of the writing style of whole sentence in spite of high degree of similarity in terms of the 7-gram. The following is a submitted question and a wrongly-retrieved example Q&A pair which is not similar to the submitted question in terms of the writing sytle of whole sentence. The system handles Japanese texts. In the following example, the sentences written in italics are Japanese.

> **Question (submitted)** : *BSE ga hito ni kansen suru to dou nari masu ka.*
> (What happens for people when they are infected with BSE?)

> **Question (example)** : *"Yuri no hana saku basho de" wo eigo ni suru to dou nari masu ka.*
> (How do you say *"Yuri no hana saku basho de"* in English?)
> **Answer (example)** : *"At the place where lilies bloom" desu.*
> ("At the place where lilies bloom" in English.)

In this example, the 7-grams are "kansen suru to dou nari masu ka" and "eigo ni suru to dou nari masu ka", and they are very similar to each other. However, they are very different from each other in terms of the writing style of the first half of sentences because the former is "noun (kansen) _ verb (suru) _ postposition (to)" and the latter is "noun (eigo)

_ postposition (ni) verb (suru) _ postposition (to)". They are also different from each other in terms of the topic of question because the former is "what the symptom is" and the latter is "translation in English of Japanese words". For these reasons, this example Q&A pair does not have a suitable writing style for the answer of the submitted question. The following is a retrieved example Q&A pair whose question part is similar to the submitted question, but whose answer part is not suitable as an answer to the submitted question in terms of writing style.

Question (submitted) : *Beikoku ga kyoutogiteisho wo hijun shi nai riyuu wa nan desu ka.*
(Why the U.S. government doesn't ratify Kyoto protocol?)

Question (example) : *Camping car wo katta riyuu wa nan desu ka.*
(Why did you purchase a camper?)
Answer (example) : *Trailer wo katte 7 nen ni nari masu. Katte yokatta desu.*
(It has been seven years since I purchased the camper. I'm glad I bought it.)

In this example, both questions ask a reason of an action, and the writing style of the example question is similar to one of the submitted question. However, the example answer is not an appropriate answer to the example question because it does not describe any reasons. Questions and answers in example QA pairs are not always consistent with each other, while the example answers correspondig to the example questions are the best answers in a QA community site. In this study, by resolving the above problems, we improve the baseline method in order for it to correctly retrieve the following question examples.

Question (submitted) : *Fog lamp wa nan no tame ni aru no desu ka.*
(What is a fog lamp for?)

Question (example) : *Mayuge wa nan no tame ni aru no desu ka.*
(What are eyebrows for?)
Answer (example) : *Ame ya ase ga me ni hairu no wo fusegu tame desu.*
(Because they prevent rains and sweat entering the eyes.)

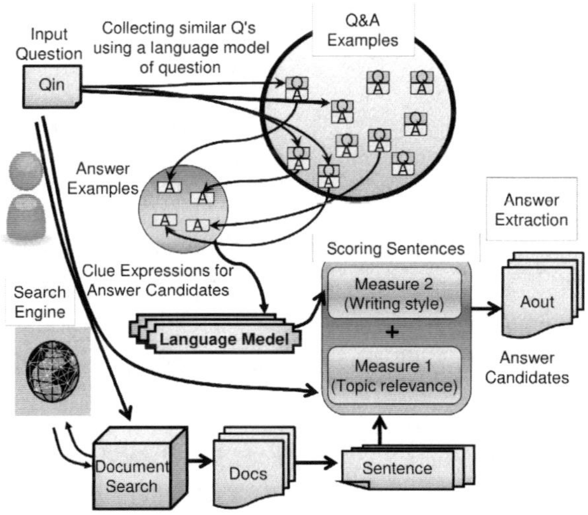

Figure 2: Outline of the proposed system

5 Proposed Method

In this study, we introduce probabilistic language models to following two processing steps. The first one is retrieving example questions similar to the submitted question mentioned in Section 3.2. The second one is extracting answer candidates mentioned in Section 3.3 and 3.4. In other words, we calculate Measure 2 by using the probabilistic language models instead of the original naive method. Our approach is expected to have the following three advantages.

- In the step of retrieving example questions, we can retrieve example questions that are more similar to the submitted question by using an appropriate probabilistic language model of question than example questions by using the baseline method because the probabilistic language model can take into account the effect of writing style in longer context, i.e., whole sentences.
- We can remove texts that include ungrammatical expressions and meaningless symbols from answer candidates by using an appropriate probabilistic language model of answer examples to extract answer candidates.
- We can remove example answers which have unsuitable writing style for the submitted question from example answers by using the language model of answer examples because we perform a clustering of example Q&A pairs by using skip 2-grams obtained from not only example questions but also example answers.

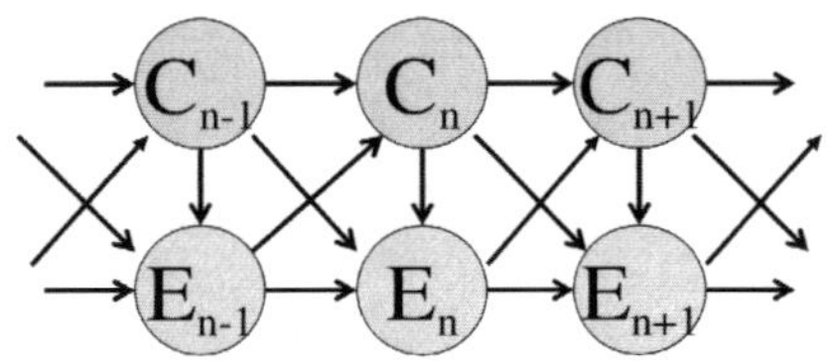

Figure 3: A mixture probabilistic language model in terms of part-of-speech tags and surface expressions

Figure 2 shows the outline of QA system we proposed.

5.1 Mixture Probabilistic Language Model in Terms of Part-of-Speech Tags and Surface Expressions

5.1.1 Outline

In the baseline method, 2-grams, which are used to extract clue expressions from example answers, are treated as the following two ways: 1) the following surface expressions are used as they are: the functional words (e.g. interrogatives particles and auxiliary verbs) and some predetermined content words that tend to express the focus of questions, 2) the other words are replaced with their part-of-speech tags in order to generalize them. However, it is unpredictable what words express the focuses of questions in the process of extracting clue expressions. Moreover, the words expressing focuses may vary according to question types and it is difficult to prepare a universal word list for any question type. In order to adaptively capture the adequate level of generalization of each word, i.e. adopting its surface expression as it is or its part-of-speech tags as generalization, we use a mixture probabilistic language model of part-of-speech tags and surface expressions. The model is shown in Figure 3. $P(E_1, E_2, \ldots, E_n)$, which is the probability of generating a sequence of surface expressions $E_1, E_2, \ldots, E_n$ as a sentence, may be estimated by using the mixture model as Equation (5).

$$\begin{aligned} P(E_1\,E_2 ... E_n) &\approx P(E_n|C_n E_{n-1} C_{n-1}) \\ &\quad \cdot P(C_n|E_{n-1}C_{n-1}) \cdot P(E_1 E_2 ... E_{n-1}) \\ &= \prod_{i=1}^{n} \{P(E_i|C_i E_{i-1} C_{i-1}) \cdot P(C_i|E_{i-1}C_{i-1})\} \end{aligned} \quad (5)$$

where C_i is the part-of-speech tag of E_i.

In order to adaptively determine the mixture ratio of surface expressions and their part-of-speech tags, we approximately estimate $P(E_1, E_2, \ldots, E_n)$ by a 2-gram model of words and their part-of-speech tags , which is obtained by a smoothing based on the deleted interpolation method.

5.1.2 Derivation of Generation Probability of a Given Sentence

We perform morphological analysis on a given sentence, divide the result of morphological analysis into a sequence of 2-grams and estimate a generation probability $P(E_1, E_2, \ldots, E_n)$ for the sequence by Equation (5).

5.2 Retrieving Example Questions Similar to the Submitted Question Using a Probabilistic Language Model

In this study, in order to retrieve example questions (along with their paired example answers) similar to the submitted question in terms of writing style, we obtain an optimal subset of example questions adaptively as follows: 1) generate subsets of example questions, 2) generate a language model from each subset, 3) calculate the generation probability of the submitted question for each language model, and 4) select the optimal subset, whose language model gives the highest probability to the submitted question. In other words, we retrieve subset of example questions which construct the best language model for the submitted question.

Ideally, the method can be implemented as the enumeration of all subsets in the above step 1), and the subsequent steps 2),3), and 4). Since, however, the corpus used in this study includes about 0.9 million Q&A pairs, the number of subsets explodes. Obviously it is not realistic to implement the method as above mentioned. Therefore, in order to shorten the processing time, we introduce an approximation based on the clustering according to the following procedure.

1. Determine the number of example questions which is retrieved finally. Let the number called "*target number*". In our experiments, we set it 500.

2. Retrive example questions (along with their paired answer examples) from a given Q&A corpus in descending order of similarity based on 7-gram mentioned in Section 3.2. In the baseline method, top-most example questions are simply employed as many as *target number* at this step. On the other hand, in the proposed method, we only utilize the 7-gram similarity as the first approximating to reduce the number of example questions. Let the number of exam-

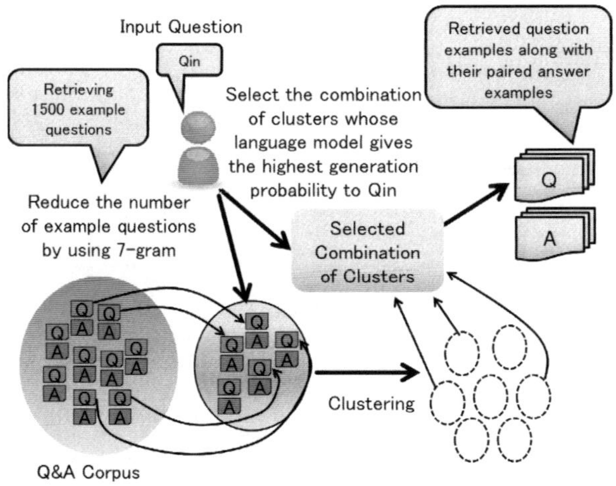

Figure 4: Retrieving question examples (along with answer examples) similar to an submitted question in terms of writing style

ple questions retrieved in this step three times of *target number*, in our experiment.

3. Apply a clustering algorithm to example questions extracted in the above step 2, and obtain several clusters.

4. Obtain combinations of clusters created in Step 3. Generate a probabilistic language model from the example questions in each combination of clusters. Calculate the generation probability of the submitted question for each model. Obtain the combination of clusters whose language model gives the highest probability to the submitted question.

The reason why we divide examples into some clusters is to shorten the processing time compared to calculating for all sebsets of example questions. The outline of this processing is shown in Figure 4.

5.2.1 Clustering Example Q&A Pairs

As described later in Section 5.3, we finally need to obtain example answers paired with the example questions that are similar to the submitted question. The clustering process described above is for not only example questions but also example answers, namely, for example Q&A pairs. In order to calculate similarity between sentences for clustering by taking account of word co-occurrence in distance positions of a sentence, we use word skip 2-grams as sentence features for clustering. A skip 2-gram is any pair of words in their sentence order. It may have some gaps between two words. Both question examples and answer examples are generalized for clustering (not for obtaining probabilistic language models) as follows: 1) the following surface expressions are used as they are: the functional words (e.g. interrogatives particles and auxiliary verbs) and some predetermined content words described below, 2) the other words are replaced with their part-of-speech tags. The predetermined context words includes a) words that tend to express the focus of question (e.g. "riyuu (reason)", "houhou (method)", "imi (meaning)", "chigai (difference)"), and b) verbs and adjectives that frequently appear in corpus. As the words expressing the focuses of questions, we collect nouns X that frequently appear in the following contexts of corpus: "...X-wa nan-desuka (What is X of ...)", "... X-wo oshiete (Tell me X of ...)", and so on.

There are, at least, following three choices for similarity calculation when we cluster example questions and answers into some clusters.

Similarity 1
Similarity between Q&A pairs in terms of skip 2-grams. We take account of both the question part and the answer part of a Q&A pair simultaneously.

Similarity 2
Similarity between example questions only in terms of skip 2-grams.

Similarity 3
Similarity between example answers only in terms of skip 2-grams.

In the calculation of Similarity 1, we calculate the similarity of the question parts and that of the answer parts separately, then mix the values into one similarity, because the feature expressions from the answer parts should be treated independent of those of the question parts, and vice versa. As the clustering algorithm, we employed the k-means method.

5.2.2 Obtain the Optimal Combinations of Clusters

We employed a simple hill climbing method to retrieve the optimal combination of clusters whose language model of question parts gives the maximal generation probability to the submitted question. We use Equation (5) to calculate the generation probability and the combination is greedily searched through the following steps.

1. Let the cluster set CL be the given cluster set, and let the candidate set CA be an empty set.

2. In CL, find the cluster whose language model of question parts gives the maximum probability

Table 2: Case of use of Similarity 1 (using both question part and answer part) in clustering examples Q&A pairs

	Proposed method ($\gamma = 0.7$)		Proposed method ($\gamma = 0.8$)		Proposed method ($\gamma = 0.9$)		Baseline ($\gamma = 0.5$)	
Type of Question	MRR	Number of Correct Response	MRR	Number of Correct Response	MRR	Number of Correct Response	MRR	Number of Correct Response
Definition	0.433	5/10	0.475	6/10	**0.570**	**7/10**	0.425	6/10
Why	0.377	9/17	0.345	9/17	**0.435**	**10/17**	0.240	6/17
How	0.222	2/3	0.261	**3/3**	0.317	**3/3**	0.111	1/3
Other	0.350	9/20	0.374	13/20	0.502	**14/20**	0.412	**14/20**
All	0.372	25/50	0.378	31/50	0.482	**34/50**	0.338	27/50

Table 3: Case of use of Similarity 2 (using question part only) in clustering examples Q&A pairs

	Proposed method ($\gamma = 0.7$)		Proposed method ($\gamma = 0.8$)		Proposed method ($\gamma = 0.9$)		Baseline ($\gamma = 0.5$)	
Type of Question	MRR	Number of Correct Response	MRR	Number of Correct Response	MRR	Number of Correct Response	MRR	Number of Correct Response
Definition	0.458	6/10	0.475	6/10	0.550	6/10	0.425	6/10
Why	0.325	8/17	0.355	8/17	0.422	9/17	0.240	6/17
How	0.511	**3/3**	0.178	2/3	0.4	2/3	0.111	1/3
Other	0.329	10/20	0.385	11/20	0.514	**14/20**	0.412	**14/20**
All	0.365	27/50	0.380	27/50	**0.483**	31/50	0.338	27/50

to the submitted question, move it from CL to CA.

3. For each cluster C in CL, calculate the generation probability of the submitted question on the model of question parts of $CA \cup \{C\}$, then find the cluster Cm that gives the maximum probability and move it from CL to CA.

4. Repeat the step 3 until the number of example questions in CA exceeds *target number*.

5.3 Extracting Answer Candidate of the Submitted Question Using the Probabilistic Language Model of Retrieved Example Answers

In this stage, we construct a langeuage model of example answers paired with example questions retrieved in Section 5.2. By Equation (5) in Section 5.1, according to the mixture probabilistic language model of part-of-speech tags and surface expressions, each sentence in answer candidates, which are retrieved by the same way as the baseline method in Section 3, are evaluated in terms of the appropriateness of writing style for the answers to the submitted question.

However, because of the nature of probability, the estimation of the appropriateness based on the probability unreasonably gives higher values to shorter sentences. Therefore, in order to resolve the problem, we normalized the Equation (5) as follows.

$$\bar{P}(E_1 E_2 ... E_n) = \frac{1}{n} \log\{P(E_1 E_2 ... E_n)\} \quad (6)$$

After the normalization, we calculate a score of the sentence S_i with Equation (7). We replace the last term in Equation (4) with Equation (6). Since the terms $\sum_{j=1}^{n} T(w_{ij})$ and $\bar{P}(E_1 E_2 ... E_m)$ in Equation (7) correspond to Measure 1 and Measure 2, respectively, the parametar γ is used to determine the mixture ratio of Measure 1 and Measure 2.

$$\text{New Score}(S_i) = \frac{\left\{\sum_{j=1}^{n} T(w_{ij})\right\}^{\gamma}}{\log(1 + |S_i|)} \cdot \left\{\bar{P}(E_1 E_2 ... E_m)\right\}^{1-\gamma} \quad (7)$$

6 Experiments

We conducted some experiments to examine the effectiveness of the proposed method. In order to do it, we compared the system based on the proposed method with the system based on the baseline method described in Section 3. In the experiments, we especially investigated the dependence of the accuracy on the following two settings: 1) the value of parameter γ, which represents the mixture ratio

Table 4: Case of use of Similarity 3 (using answer part only) in clustering examples Q&A pairs

	Proposed method ($\gamma = 0.7$)		Proposed method ($\gamma = 0.8$)		Proposed method ($\gamma = 0.9$)		Baseline ($\gamma = 0.5$)	
Type of Question	MRR	Number of Correct Response	MRR	Number of Correct Response	MRR	Number of Correct Response	MRR	Number of Correct Response
Definition	0.458	6/10	0.483	6/10	0.500	6/10	0.425	6/10
Why	0.332	9/17	0.345	8/17	0.345	9/17	0.240	6/17
How	0.400	**3/3**	**0.611**	**3/3**	0.511	**3/3**	0.111	1/3
Other	0.527	13/20	**0.543**	14/20	0.502	**14/20**	0.412	**14/20**
All	0.439	31/50	0.464	31/50	0.437	32/50	0.338	27/50

of Measure 1 and Measure 2 in Equation (7) and 2) the similarity calculation methods in the clustering described in Section 5.2.

6.1 Experimental Settings

As the question set, we use the latter half of Japanese question set of NTCIR-6 QAC formal run test set (Fukumoto *et al.*, 2007).

As a Web search engine for information source of QA, we adopted Yahoo! Japan API[1]. With regard to Q&A examples, we used a corpus of 0.9 million Q&A pairs that comes from "Yahoo! Chiebukuro," which is a Q&A community site and the Japanese version of "Yahoo! answers." Let the parameter *target number* described in Section 5.2 be 500. The systems output five answers for each submitted question in the descending order of score. Judgment whether an answer candidate is correct or not is performed by one assessor. The assessor judged an output answer candidate correct, when the candidate includes correct answer for the question as its part. We use Mean Reciprocal Rank (MRR[2]) as the evaluation metrics. In addition to MRR, we also investigate the number of the questions for which the system can return, at least, one correct answer in the top five answer candidates (number of correct responses, hereafter).

6.2 Experimental Results

Experimental results are shown in the Table 2,3, and 4.

With regard to the baseline method, we employed 0.5 for the parameter γ, because it gives the best performance in terms of MRR. On the other hand, as for the proposed method, the results are shown for the three settings, γ =0.7,0.8,and 0.9, which give the better performance than other settings.

[1]http://developer.yahoo.co.jp/

[2]Reciprocal Rank (RR) is the inverse of the rank of the first correct answer candidate. MRR is the average of RRs over the question set.

Although the proposed method and the baseline method do not perform any question classification, the results are shown on a type-by-type basis in order to investigate the effectiveness of the method for each typical question type described in Table 1.

6.3 Discussion

All of Table 2, 3, and 4 show that the proposed method outperforms the baseline method.

With regard to the number of correct responses, the proposed method gives more correct responses than the baseline method except for the case of use of Similarity 1 (using both question part and answer part) and $\gamma = 0.7$.

With regard to MRR, the proposed method gives better performance than the baseline method for not only the average of all questions but also the average of each type of question. One of the reasons for the good performance may be the fact that the propose method can appropriately filter out ungrammatical expressions in answer candidates, while the baseline method sometimes employ them as answer response. It means that the introduced probabilistic language model contribute to removing ungrammatical text from answer candidates. Another one of the reasons for the good performance may be the fact that the proposed method can reduce the number of example Q&A pairs which include unsuitable expressions for answers of the submitted question when the system retrieves example Q&A pairs. It means that more example answers suitable to the submitted question can be retrieved by introducing the clustering and the probabilistic estimation to the process of retrieving example questions, and as a result, by refining the language model of answers. The following shows an example for which the baseline method cannot give correct answer, but the proposed method can.

Question (submitted)
What is required to effectuate the Kyoto Protocol? (Originally in Japanese)

Answer (Baseline)
After deposit of instrument of ratification of Kyoto protocol by the Russian goverment, a condition for ratification is satisfied, it is effectuated on February 16, 2005. (Originally in Japanese)

Answer (Proposed method)
In order to effectuate the Kyoto Protocol, the ratification by more than 50 signatory countries and contries whose carbon-dioxide emission is more than 55% of advanced industrial countries' are needed. (Originally in Japanese)

With regard to the methods of similarity calculation in clustering example Q&A pairs, Similarity 1 (using both question part and answer part) generally gives better performance than other similarity calculation methods in terms of both the number of correct response and MRR. The following reason may be supposed.

- The features from question parts of retrieved Q&A examples seem not to be suitable for clustering the Q&A examples because the writing styles of question parts are very similar to each other on account of the method for retrieving Q&A examples. In order to retrieve example questions similar to the submitted question, we use the 7-gram in each question part whose center word is an interrogative.
- Since answer parts have longer text than question parts in Q&A examples and are consequently described in various writing styles, it may be possible to find subgroups of answer parts according to the variations of writing styles.

For these reasons, the use of answer parts of Q&A examples is more efficient for clustering the examples. Although there is no significant difference between Similarity 1 and Similarity 3 (using answer part only) as shown in Table 2 and 4, the system with Similarity 1 (γ=0.9) stably outperforms the system with Similarity 3 in terms of the number of correct response. Moreover, MRR of the system with Similarity 1, 0.482, is almost the same as the best performance, 0.483, among all settings.

7 Conclusion

In this study, we poposed a method to introduce a probabilistic language model into non-factoid question answering in order to improve the accuracy ot the system proposed by Mori *et al.* (2008)

We introduced the model into two sub-processes which calculate similarity in terms of writing style. The first process collects example questions similar to an submitted question. The second one measures similarity between an answer candidate and example answers paired with the collected example questions. The experimental results showed that the system with the propose method outperforms the baseline system.

References

Fukumoto, J. 2007. Question Answering System for Non-factoid Type Questions and Automatic Evaluation based on BE Method. *Proceedings of the Sixth NTCIR Workshop Meeting*, Tokyo, Japan,441–447.

Fukumoto, J., T. Kato, F. Masui and T. Mori. 2007. An Overview of the 4th Question Answering Challenge (QAC-4) at NTCIR Workshop 6. *Proceedings of the Sixth NTCIR Workshop Meeting*, 433–440.

Han, K.-S., Y.-I. Song and H.-C. Rim. 2006. Probabilistic model for definitional question answering. *Proceedings of the 29th annual international ACM SIGIR conference on Research and development in information retrieval*, SIGIR '06, New York, 212–219.

Heie, M.H., E.W.D. Whittaker and S. Furui. 2012. Question answering using statistical language modelling. *Computer Speech and Language 26*, 193–209.

Mizuno, J., T. Akiba, A. Fujii and K. Itou. 2009. Non-factoid Question Answering Experiments at NTCIR-6:Towards Answer Type Detection for Realworld Questions. *Proceedings of the Sixth NTCIR Workshop*, 487–492.

Mori, T., M. Sato and M. Ishioroshi. 2008. Answering any class of Japanese non-factoid question by using the Web and example Q&A pairs from a social Q&A website. *Proceedings of the 2008 IEEE/WIC/ACM International Conference on Web Intelligence and Intelligent Agent Technology*, 59–65.

Soricut, R., T. Akiba and E. Brill. 2006. Automatic Question Answering Using the Web: Beyond the Factoid. *Journal of Information Retrieval - Special Issue on Web Information Retrieval*, vol.9, 191–206.

Takahashi, A., A. Takatsu and J. Adachi. 2010. Language Model Combination for Community-based Q&A Retrieval. *Proceedings of the 2010 22nd IEEE International Conference on Tools with Artificial Intelligence*, 241–248.

Answering Questions Requiring Cross-passage Evidence

Kisuh Ahn
Dept. of Linguistics
Hankuk University of Foreign Studies
San 89 Wangsan-li, Mohyeon-myeon
Yongin-si, Gyeongi-do, Korea
kisuhahn@gmail.com

Hee-Rahk Chae
Dept. of Linguistics
Hankuk University of Foreign Studies
San 89 Wangsan-li, Mohyeon-myeon
Yongin-si, Gyeongi-do, Korea
hrchae@hufs.ac.kr

Abstract

This paper presents methods for answering, what we call, Cross-passage Evidence Questions. These questions require multiply scattered passages all bearing different and partial evidence for the answers. This poses special challenges to the textual QA systems that employ information retrieval in the "conventional" way because the ensuing Answer Extraction operation assumes that one of the passages retrieved would, by itself, contain sufficient evidence to recognize and extract the answer. One method that may overcome this problem is factoring a Cross-passage Evidence Question into constituent sub-questions and joining the respective answers. The first goal of this paper is to develop and put this method into test to see how indeed effective this method could be. Then, we introduce another method, Direct Answer Retrieval, which rely on extensive pre-processing to collect different evidence for a possible answer off-line. We conclude that the latter method is superior both in the correctness of the answers and the overall efficiency in dealing with Cross-passage Evidence Questions.

1 Distinguishing Questions Based on Evidence Locality

Textual factoid Question Answering depends on the existence of at least one passage or text span in the corpus that can serve as sufficient evidence for the question. A single piece of evidence may suffice to answer a question, or more than a single piece may be needed. By "a piece of evidence", we mean a snippet of continuous text, or passage, that supports or justifies an answer to the question posed. More practically, in factoid QA, a piece of evidence is a text span with two properties: (1) An Information Retrieval (IR) procedure can recognise it as relevant to the question and (2) an automated Answer Extraction (AE) procedure can extract from it an answer-bearing expression (aka an *answer candidate*).

With respect to a given corpus, we call questions with the following property *Single Passage Evidence Questions* or SEQs:

> A question Q is a SEQ if evidence E sufficient to select A as an answer to Q can be found in the same text snippet as A.

In contrast, we call a question that requires multiple different pieces of evidence (in multiple text spans with respect to a corpus) a *Cross-passage Evidence Question* or CEQ:

> A question Q is a CEQ if the set of evidence $E1$, ..., En needed to justify A as an answer to Q cannot be found in a single text snippet containing A, but only in a set of such snippets.

For example, consider the following question:

> Which Sub-Saharan country had hosted the World Cup?

If the evidence for the country being located south of Sahara dessert and the evidence for this same country having hosted the World Cup is not contained in the same passage/sentence, but are found in two distinct passages, the question would be a Cross-passage Evidence Question. This distinction between SEQs and CEQs lies only in the locality of evidence within a corpus. It does not imply that the corpus contains only one piece of text sufficient for a SEQ: Often there are multiple text snippets, each with sufficient evidence for the answer. Such redundancy is exploited by many question answering systems to rank the confidence of an answer candidate (e.g. including (Brill et al., 2002)) but the evidence is redundant rather than qualitatively different.

Now, as opposed to Single-passage Evidence Questions, which had been the usual TREC type questions (White and Sutcliffe, 2004), Cross-passage Evidence Question poses special challenges to the textual QA systems that employ information retrieval in the "conventional" way. Most textual QA system uses Information Retrieval as document/passage pre-fetch. The ensuing Answer Extraction operation assumes that one of the passages retrieved would, by itself, contain sufficient evidence to recognize and extract the answer. Thus the reliance on a particular passage to answer a question renders the task of question answering essentially a *local* operation with respect to the corpus as a whole. Whatever else is expressed in the corpus about an entity being questioned is ignored, or used (in the case of repeated evidence instances of the same answer candidate) only to increase confidence in particular answer candidates. This means that *factoid questions whose correct answer depends jointly on textual evidence located in different places in the corpus cannot be answered.* We call this *the locality constraint* of factoid QA. Thus special methods are needed to overcome this locality constraint in order to successfully handle CEQs. In the following sections, we explore two methods for answering CEQs, first, based on Question Factoring for conventional IR based QA systems, and second, based on what we call Direct Answer Retrieval method in place of conventional IR.

2 Solving CEQs by Question Factoring

While whether a question is a CEQ or not depends entirely on the corpus, it can be guessed that the more syntactically complex a question, the more likely that it is a CEQ, given that a complex question will have more terms and relations that need to be satisfied. For example, the above question is of the form "What/Which <NBAR> <VP>?" such as *Which* [NBAR *Sub-Saharan country*] [VP *had hosted the World Cup?*], and has at least two predicates/constraints that must be established, the one or more conveyed by the NBAR, and the one or more conveyed by the VP. These multiple restrictions might call for different pieces of evidence depending on the particular corpus from which the answer is to be found.

In database QA, CEQs correspond to queries that involve joins (usually along with selection and projection operations). The database equivalent of the afore-mentioned question about the certain World Cup hosting country might involve joining one relation linking country names with the requisite location, and another linking the names of countries with World Cup hosting history. Note that this involves breaking up the original query into a set of sub-queries, each answerable through a single relation. Answering a CEQ through sub-queries therefore involve the fusion of answers to different questions.

Analogously, we apply this method of joining sub-queries for database to the task of textual QA to deal with the CEQs. The solution we explore here can be adopted by any existing system with the conventional Information (Passage) Retrieval and Answer Extraction (IR+AE) pipeline architecture. It involves:

1. Dividing a CEQ into sub-questions SQ_1, ..., SQ_n, each of which is a simple question about the same question variable.[1]
2. Finding the answer candidate(s) for each sub-question,
3. Selecting the best overall answer from the answer candidates for the sub-questions.

2.1 Dividing a CEQ into sub-questions

Decomposing a CEQ into simpler sub-questions about the question variable involves:

[1]We have only considered sub-questions that are *naturally joined* on the question variable. Extending to the equivalent of joins on several variables would require an even more complex strategy for handling the answer candidate sets than the one we describe in Section 2.2.

- Resolving all co-referring expressions within the question;
- If the WH-phrase of the question is a complex phrase, making a sub-question asking the identity of its head noun phrase (e.g. "Which northern country is ..." → "What is a northern country?");
- Breaking up the question at clause boundaries (including relative clauses);
- Within a single clause, if there is a conjoined set of restrictors (e.g. " ... German physician, theologian, missionary, musician and philosopher .."), copying the clause as many times as the number of restrictors, so that each clause now contains only one restrictor;
- Finally, reformulating all the individual clauses into questions.

Some examples of CEQs which have been factored into sub-questions are as follows[2].:

- Which French-American prolific writer was a prisoner and survivor of the infamous Auschwitz German concentration camp, Chairman of the U.S. President's Commission on the Holocaust, a powerful advocate for human rights and a recipient of the Nobel Peace Prize?
    1. Who was a French-American prolific writer?
    2. Who was a prisoner and survivor of the infamous Auschwitz German concentration camp?
    3. Who was a Chairman of the U.S. President's Commission on the Holocaust?
    4. Who was a powerful advocate for human rights?
    5. Who was a recipient of the Nobel Peace Prize?

It should be clear that factoring a CEQ into a set of sub-questions is often tricky but doable. The intra-sentential anaphora resolution can be less than straight-forward. So often, it is a matter of choice as to how to break a question into how many sub-questions and at what boundaries. In the evaluation reported in Section 2.3, the CEQs were manually broken into sub-questions, based on the procedure outlined above, since our focus was on evaluating the viability of the overall method rather than individual components. Our results may thus serve as an upper-bound to what a fully automated procedure would produce. (For work related to the automatic decomposition of a complex question in order to deal with temporal questions, see (Saquete et al., 2004).)

[2]All the evaluation questions are from a pub-quiz site http://www.funtrivia.com

2.2 Selecting an Answer to the CEQ from Sub-question Answer Candidates

From the answer candidates to the sub-questions, an answer must be derived for the CEQ as a whole. The most obvious way would be to pick the answer candidate that is the answer to the largest number of sub-questions. So if a CEQ had three sub-questions, in the ideal case there would be one answer candidate that would be the answer to all of these sub-questions at the same time and thus be the most likely answer to the CEQ. This is like a simple voting scheme, where each sub-question votes for an answer candidate, and the candidate with the most votes win.

Complications from this ideal situation arise in two ways: First, a sub-question can be very general because it results from separating away other restrictions from the question. Hence, the answer to a sub-question must be regarded instead as a set of answers as in list questions, several of which may be correct rather than being one correct answer to that subquestion. In other words, a sub-question can vote for multiple candidates rather than just one.

Second, simply maximising overlap (i.e. the number of sub-questions to which an answer candidate is the answer, which we call simply *votes* from now on) ignores the possibility that multiple answers can tie for the same maximum votes, especially if this number is small compared to the number of sub-questions. Thus, there is the need for a method to rank the answers with the same number of votes.

In summary, a sub-question can vote for multiple candidates and more than one candidates can receive the same largest number of votes from the sub-questions. This means we need an additional way to break the ties among the candidates by ranking the candidates according to some other criteria. The answer selection method we have chosen is described below.

Let's assume that a question has been factored into N sub-questions, and each sub-question is answered with a (possibly empty) set of answer candidates. So for the set of N sub-questions for the original question, there are N answer candidate sets. The most likely answer would be the answer candidate shared by all the N sub-questions (i.e. the answer candidate present in all the N sets of answer candidates.). To see if there is such a common answer candidate, these N sets of answer candidates are first intersected (via generalized intersection).

If the intersection of these N sets is empty (i.e., there is no one answer candidate that all the sub-questions share.), then it must be investigated whether there is a common answer candidate for N-1 sets of answer candidates (i.e. an answer shared by N-1 sub-questions.). There will be N cases to consider since there will be N cases of N-1 sub-question sets to intersect. If all these are empty, then all subsets of size N-2 are considered, and so on, until a non-empty intersection is obtained. This means considering the *power set* of the original set of answer candidate sets.

This process may result in one answer candidate or several with the same maximum number of votes. If there is only one, this is chosen as the answer. Otherwise, there is a need for a further way to rank these answer candidates to produce the most likely as the answer. Specifically, if there is more than one non-empty intersection with the same maximum votes, we do the expected thing of taking into account the original ranking of answer to the sub-questions (in most QA systems, the answer candidates are ranked according to their plausibility). If an answer is found to be the second ranked answer to one sub-question and the sixth ranked answer to another, its overall rank is taken to be the simple mean of the ranks. So in this case, the answer would have the rank four overall. This algorithm can be more formally stated as follows[3].

- Step 1: Let S be the set of the sets of answers, $A1, .. , An$, to the sub-questions, $Q1 .. Qn$ respectively.
- Step 2: Produce the power-set of S, i.e. $P = POW(S)$.
- Step 3: Produce a set of ordered pairs, V, such that $V = \{\langle o, R\rangle \mid R \subset P \wedge \forall x \in R.\ |x| = o$ for every distinct $o = |y|$ of every $y \in P\}$
- Step 4: Pick the ordered pair, L such that $L = \langle o, R\rangle \in V$ with the largest o among the members of V, and do:
    1. Produce T from R such that $T = \bigcup\{x \mid x = \bigcap t$ for every $t \in R\}$. (Note that t is a set.)
    2. If R' is an empty set, repeat this step 4 for the ordered pair with the next largest o.
    3. Else if T has a unique member, then pick that unique member as the answer and terminate.
    4. Otherwise, go to the next step.
- Step 5: For each member, $x \in T$, get the ranks, $r_1, .. , r_n$ in the sub-questions, $Q_1 .. Q_n$ and compute the mean M of the ranks.
- Step 6: Pick the member of T with the lowest M score as the answer.

To illustrate the steps described above, consider a CEQ M that can be split into three sub-questions Q1, Q2 and Q3. Then:

- Step 1: Assume that the sets A1, A2, A3 are the answer candidate sets for sub-questions Q1, Q2 and Q3 respectively:

  A1 = {CLINTON, BUSH, REAGAN}
  A2 = {MAJOR, REAGAN, THATCHER}
  A3 = {FORD, THATCHER, NIXON}

  Let S = {A1,A2,A3}
- Step 2: P = POW(S) = {{A1,A2,A3},{A1,A2},{A2,A3},{A1,A3},{A1}, {A2},{A3},{}}
- Step 3:
  $V = \{\langle 3, \{\{A1, A2, A3\}\}\rangle,$
  $\langle 2, \{\{A1, A2\}, \{A2, A3\}, \{A1, A3\}\}\rangle,$
  $\langle 1, \{\{A1\}, \{A2\}, \{A3\}\}\rangle, \langle 0, \{\{\}\}\rangle\}$

[3]This will be easier to understand if considered together with the example that follows.

- Step 4:

  First pick $L = \langle o, R \rangle = \langle 3, \{\{A1, A2, A3\}\} \rangle$ based on the largest o in consideration (i.e. 3).

  Then, get T such that $T = \bigcup\{x \mid x = \bigcap t$ for every $t \in R\} = \bigcup\{A1 \cap A2 \cap A3 = \{\}\}$

  Since T is an empty set, no answer can be picked. So repeat this step for the ordered pair with the next largest votes.

- So again Step 4:

  The second pick $L = \langle o, R \rangle = \langle 2, \{\{A1, A2\}, \{A2, A3\}, \{A1, A3\}\} \rangle$

  Now get T by $T = (A1 \cap A2) \cup (A2 \cap A3) \cup (A1 \cap A3) = \{\text{REAGAN}, \text{THATCHER}\}$

  Since R' is non-empty, which at the same time does not have a unique member, go to the next step.

- Step 5:

  REAGAN: 4th candidate for Q1 and 10th in Q2 – average rank 7

  THATCHER: 1st candidate for Q2 and 5th in Q3 – average rank 3

- Step 6:

  Take the candidate with the highest average rank as the answer – here, THATCHER.

2.3 Evaluation of the Sub-question Method

The evaluation has two purposes. The first is to see how well the sub-question method works with respect to CEQs. The second is to provide a baseline results for the performance of the Direct Answer Retrieval method introduced in the next section.

For the evaluation of this strategy, we chose 41 "quiz" questions (i.e. ones designed to challenge and amuse people rather than to meet some real information need, like the IBM Watson system doing Jeopardy questions (David Ferrucci, 2012)) as likely Cross-passage Evidence Questions (CEQs) with respect to the knowledge base corpus, AQUAINT corpus in this evaluation. They were filtered based on the following criteria:

- Did the question contain multiple restrictions of the entity in question?
- Did the answer appear in the AQUAINT corpus?
- Was the answer a proper name?
- Was it a difficult question? (Questions from the original site have been manually marked for difficulty.)

The questions, varying in length from 20 to 80 words[4], include:

> *What was the name of the German physician, theologian, missionary, musician and philosopher who was awarded the Nobel Peace Prize in 1952?*
>
> *Which French-American prolific writer was a prisoner and survivor of the infamous Auschwitz German concentration camp, Chairman of the U.S. President's Commission on the Holocaust, a powerful advocate for human rights and a recipient of the Nobel Peace Prize?*
>
> *He was born in 1950 in California. He dropped out of the University of California at Berkeley and quit his job with Hewlett-Packard to co-found a company. He once built a "Blue Box" phone attachment that allowed him to make long-distance phone calls for free. Who is he?*

The QA system we have used to test this method was developed previously and had shown good performance for TREQ QA questions (Ahn et al., 2005). In order to accomodate this method, a question factoring module must be added. But as we have previously mentioned, question factoring has been done manually offline as we have not implemented a fully automatic module for that as of yet. The joining of answers to sub-questions are done automatically, however, using a specially added post-processing module. Thus, this QA system is a simulation of a fully-automatic CEQ handling QA system.

The evaluation procedure ran as follows. First, a CEQ was factored into a set of sub-questions manually. Then each sub-question was fed into the QA

[4]This is long compared to TREC questions, whose mean length is less than 10 words.

QID	SQ	MaxV	ACI	Rank
1	2	1	0	0
3	4	1	0	0
6	3	1	0	0
7	4	1	0	0
8	3	1	0	0
9	5	2	6	3
10	4	1	0	0
12	3	1	0	0
13	2	2	2	1
16	3	1	0	0
17	2	2	1	1
18	4	1	0	0
20	2	2	4	1
21	3	2	7	1
22	2	1	0	0
23	3	3	1	1
24	2	1	0	0
25	3	3	1	1
26	5	3	1	1
27	2	2	23	1
28	2	1	0	0
29	2	2	86	1
30	3	3	3	1
31	2	2	9	5
32	2	2	1	1
36	9	1	0	0
37	2	1	0	0
38	8	1	0	0
40	9	3	1	1

Table 1: Questions with answer candidates identified for $\geq$1 sub-questions.

engine to produce a set of 100 answer candidates. The resulting sets of answers were assessed by an Answer Selection/Ranking module that uses the algorithm described in Section 2.2 to produce a final set of ranked answer candidates.

2.4 Results and Observations

Among the 41 questions, 12 questions are found to have no correct answer candidates by the QA engine, and so these questions are ignored in the rest of the analysis. For the remaining 29 questions, Table 1 shows the value of ranking (i.e., Step 5 above) when more than one answer candidate shares the same number of largest votes. Such answer candidates need to be ranked in order to pick the best answer. Here, **QID** indicates the question ID which did have at least one sub-question with answers, where **SQ** more specifically tells how many sub-questions each question was factored into.

A@N	SQ-Combined
1	0.317:13
2	0.317:13
3	0.341:14
4	0.366:15
5	0.366:15
6	0.366:15
7	0.366:15
8	0.366:15
9	0.366:15
10	0.366:15
15	0.366:15
20	0.366:15
ACC	0.317
MRR	0.341
ARC	1.333

Table 2: Results for Sub-question Method

In Table 1, column **MaxV** indicates the largest number of votes received by an answer candidate across the set of sub-questions. Column **ACI** indicates the number of answer candidates with this number of Votes. For example, CEQ 9 has 5 sub-questions. Its **MaxV** of 2 indicates that only the intersection of the answer candidate sets for two sub-questions (out of maximum 5) produced a non-empty set (of 6 members according to **ACI**). These 6 members are the final answer candidates that will be ranked.

The column labelled **Rank** indicates the ranking of final answer candidates by mean ranking with respect to the sub-questions they answer and identifies where the correct answer lies within that ranking. So for Question 9, the correct answer was third in the final ranking. Fifteen questions had no answer candidates common to any set of sub-questions (i.e., **ACI**=0). Of the 14 remaining questions, six had only a single answer candidate, so ranking was not relevant. (That answer was correct in all 6 cases.) Of the final eight questions with $\geq$1 final answer candidates, Table 1 shows that ranking them according to the mean of their original rankings led to the correct answer being ranked first in six of them. In the most extreme case, starting with 86 ties between answers for two sub-questions (all of which have a set of 100 answers), ranking reduces this to the correct answer being ranked first. Table 1 also shows the importance of the proportion of sub-questions that contain the correct overall answer. For CEQs with 2 sub-questions, in every case, both sub-questions needed to have contained the correct overall answer in order for that CEQ to have been answered correctly. (If only one sub-question contains the correct overall answer, our algorithm has not selected the correct overall answer.) For CEQs with 3 sub-questions, at least two of the 3 sub-questions need to have contained the correct overall answers in order for the CEQ to be answered correctly by this strategy. This seems to be less the case as the number of sub-questions increases. However, the strategy does seem to require at least two sub-questions to agree on a correct overall answer in order for a CEQ to be correctly answered. It is possible that another sub-question ranking strategy could do better.

In sum, starting with 41 questions, the "sub-question method found 14 with at least one "intersective" answer candidate. Of those 14, the top-ranked candidate (or, in 6 cases, the only "intersective" candidate) was the correct answer in 12 cases. Hence the "sub-question" method has succeeded in 12 of 41 cases that would be totally lost without this method. Table 2 shows the final scores with respect to A@N, accuracy, MRR and ARC.

2.5 Discussion

The evaluation shows that the method based on sub-question decomposition and ranking can be used for answering Cross-passage Evidence Questions, but we also need to consider the cost of adopting this method as a practical method for doing real time Question Answering; clearly multiplying the number of questions to be answered by decomposing a question into sub-questions can make the overall task even more resource-intensive than it is already. Pre-caching answers to simple, frequent questions, as in (Chu-Carroll et al., 2002), which reduces them to database look-up, may help in some cases. Another compatible strategy would be to weigh the sub-questions, so as to place more emphasis on more *important* ones or to first consider ones that can be answered more quickly (as in database *query optimisation*). This would avoid, or at least postpone, very general sub-questions such as "Who was born in 1950?", which are like list questions, with a large number of candidate answers and thus expensive to process. The QA system would well process more specific sub-questions first by learning the appropriate weight as in (Chali and Joty, 2008) The second issue is for the need of a method that can reliably factor a CEQ into simple sub-questions automatically, which would not be trivial to develop. Direct Answer Retrieval for QA offers another alternative that does not require the factoring of a question in the first place, which is the subject of the next section.

3 Direct Answer Retrieval for QA

The answers to many factoid questions are named entities. For example, "Who is the president of France?" has as its answer a name referring to a certain individual. The basic idea of Direct Answer Retrieval for Question Answering is to extract these kinds of expressions off-line from a textual corpus as potential answers and process them in such a way that they can be directly retrieved as answers to questions. Thus, the primary goal of Direct Answer Retrieval is to turn factoid Question Answering into fine-grained Information Retrieval, where answer candidates are directly retrieved instead of documents/passages. For simple named entity answers, we have previously shown that this can make for fast and accurate retrieval (Ahn and Webber, 2007).

In addition, as the process gathers and collates all the relevant textual evidence for a possible answer from all over the corpus, it becomes possible to answer a question based on *all* the evidence available in the corpus regardless of its locality. Whether this is indeed so is what we are going to put to test here.

3.1 The Off-line Processing

The supporting information for a potential answer (named-entity), for the present research, is the set of all text snippets (sentences) that mentions it. With the set of all sentences that mention a particular potential answer put into one file, this can literally be regarded as a document on its own with the answer name as its title. The collection of such documents could be regarded as the index of answers and the retrieval of documents as answer retrieval (Hence the name *Direct Answer Retrieval*).

The processes of generating the collection of answer documents for all the potential answers run as follows. First, the whole base corpus is run through POS tagging, chunking and named-entity recognition. Then, each sentence in each document is examined as to whether it contains at least one named-entity. If so, then whether this named-entity represents an already identified answer candidate and stored in the repository is examined. If so, then this sentence is appended to the corresponding answer document in the collection. If not, then a new answer entity is instantiated and added to the repository and a new corresponding answer document is created with this sentence. If more than answer candidate is identified in a sentence, then the same process is applied to every one of them.

In order to facilitate the retrieval of answer documents, this answer document collection is itself indexed using standard document indexing technique. At the same time, for each answer entity, its corresponding named entity type is stored in a separate answer repository database(using external resources such as YAGO (Suchanek et al., 2007), it is possible to look up very fine-grained entity type information, which we did in our evaluation system). Answer Index together with this repository database make up the knowledge base for Direct Answer Retrieval QA system.

3.2 The On-line Processing

With the knowledge base built off-line, the actual on-line QA processes run through several steps. The first operation is the answer type identification. For this, in our evaluation system, the question is parsed and a simple rule based algorithm is used that looks at the WH-word (e.g. "Where" means location), the head noun of a WH-phrase with "Which" or "What" (e.g. "Which president" means the answer type is of president), and if the main verb is a copula, the head of the post-copula noun phrase (e.g. for "Who is the president ..", here again "president" is the answer type. The identified answer type is resolved to one the base named entity type (PERSON, LOCATION, ORGANIZATION and OTHER) using ontology database such as the WordNet if the named entity type is derived from the head noun of WH-word or the noun after the copula, which do not have the corresponding entity type in the answer repository. The next operation is the retrieval of answers as answer candidates for a given question. This involves formulating a query, retrieving answer documents as answer candidates. If the index has been partitioned into sub-indices based on the NER type, as we have done, an appropriate index can be chosen based on the answer type identified, and thereby make the search more effiecient.

In the actual retrieval operation, there can be different ways to score an answer candidate with respect to a query depending on the model of retrieval used. The model of retrieval implemented for the evaluation system is an adaptation of the document inference network model for information retrieval (Turtle, 1991). For a more thorough description of the answer retrieval model, please refer to our previous work (Ahn and Webber, 2008).

When the search is performed and a ranked list of answers is retrieved, this ranked list is then run through the following procedures:

1. Filter the retrieved list of answers to remove any named-entity that was mentioned in the question itself if any.

2. Re-rank with respect to answer type, preferring the answer that match the answer type precisely.

3. Pick the highest ranking answer as the answer to the question.

The first procedure is heuristically necessary because, for example, "Germany" in "Which country has a common border with Germany", can pop up as an answer candidate from the retrieval. From the remaining items in the list, each item is looked up with respect to its answer type using the answer-type table in the answer repository. The re-ranking is performed according to the following rules:

- Answers whose type precisely matches the answer type are ranked higher than any other answers whose types do not precisely match the answer type.

- Answers whose type do not precisely match the answer type but still matches the base type traced from the answer type are ranked higher than any other answers whose types do not match the answer type at all.

Now using these rules, the answer which is ranked the highest is picked as the number one answer candidate.

This method, by itself, looks more like an answer candidate retrieval system rather than a full-fledged QA system with sophisticated answer extraction algorithm as found in most QA systems. However, the structured retrieval algorithm that we employ makes up for this answer extraction operation. Again for a full exposition of this structural retrieval operation, refer to our previous work.

3.3 Answering CEQs by Direct Answer Retrieval Method

Direct Answer Retrieval enables a direct approach to Cross-passage Evidence Questions: There is no need for any special method for question factoring. With respect to an answer document, a possible answer is already associated with all the distributed pieces of evidence about it in the corpus: In other words, CEQs are exactly the same as SEQs.

Here, for example, to the question, "Which US senator is a former astronaut?" the conventional approach requires different set of textual evidence (passages) to be assembled based on the decomposition of the question as we have presented in the previous section, whereas in the Direct Answer Retrieval approach, only one answer document needs to be located.

Thus there are three advantages for using Direct Answer Retrieval method over the conventional IR with the special sub-question method:

- No multiplication of questions.
- No need for question factoring.
- No need to combine the answers of the sub-questions.

Whether, despite these advantages, the performance would hold good, is evaluated next.

3.4 Evaluation and Comparison to IR+AE

The purpose of the evaluation is to see how well this method can deal with CEQs, particularly as compared to simulated IR+AE system with a sub-question method as presented in the previous section.

The implemented QA system had been previously evaluated with respect to the more simple TREC QA questions and found to have good performance. The particular configuration that we used for our test here utilizes naturally the same questions and the same textual corpus as the source data as in the sub-question method.

For each question, the system simply retrieves answer candidates and the top 20 answers are taken for the score assessment.

A@N	Sub-QA	Answering
1	0.317:13	0.317:13
2	0.317:13	0.512:21
3	0.341:14	0.585:24
4	0.366:15	0.634:26
5	0.366:15	0.659:27
6	0.366:15	0.659:27
7	0.366:15	0.659:27
8	0.366:15	0.659:27
9	0.366:15	0.659:27
10	0.366:15	0.659:27
15	0.366:15	0.659:27
20	0.366:15	0.659:27
ACC	0.317	0.317
MRR	0.341	0.456
ARC	1.333	1.889

Table 3: Comparison of the Scores

Table 3 summarises the results of the evaluation for the Direct Answer Retrieval system (**Ans-Ret**) compared to the Sub-question method based system (**Sub-QA**).

The Ans-Ret system has returned more correct answers than the **Sub-QA** system (in all cut-off points except having tied in number 1 rank). Also all the correct answers that were found by the **Sub-QA** system were also found by the **Ans-Ret** system irrespective of the ranks. Twelve correct answers that were found by **Ans-Ret** (at **A@5**) were missed by the **Sub-QA** system. Among those answers that were found by both systems, **Sub-QA** produced better rank in 5 cases whereas in only one case the **Ans-Ret** produced a better rank. However, Table 3 shows that **Ans-Ret** in general found more correct answers (27 vs 15) in total, and more answers in higher rank (e.g. top 2) than **Sub-QA** system.

In order to verify the performance difference, we used a statistical test, *Wilcoxon Matched Signed Rank Test* (Wilcoxon, 1945), which is used for small samples and assumes no underlying distribution. According to this test, the difference is statistically significant (W+ = 17.50, w- = 172.50, N = 19, p = 0.0007896). Hence, it is possible to conclude that Direct Answer Retrieval method is superior to the simulated IR+AE method with special sub-question method for this type of questions. The fact that Direct Answer Retrieval Method has superior performance is no surprise considering that the more the evidence from the question for an answer, more information is available for the method in matching the relevant answer document of a candidate answer to the question. This is in contrast to the IR+AE based systems, which, without a special strategy such as the sub-question method discussed here, require that whatever evidence exist in a question must be found within one sentence in the corpus due to the locality constraint.

4 Conclusion

Cross-passage Evidence Questions are the kind of questions for which the locality constraint bear out its constraining effect. A special method is devised in order to overcome this constraint with the conventional QA with IR+AE architecture. This involves partitioning a question into a set of simpler questions. The results show that the strategy is successful to a degree in that some questions are indeed correctly answered but it also comes with a cost of multiplying the number of questions. On the other hand, Direct Answer Retrieval method is process-wise more efficient, has a better performance in terms of accuracy, and does not require tricky question factoring regarding this type of questions. Direct Answer Retrieval method, thus, clearly shows a clear advantage for CEQs.

References

Ahn, K., Bos, J., Clark, S., Curran, J., Kor, D., Nissim, M., and Webber, B. (2005). Question answering with qed at trec-2005. In *Proceedings of TREC'05*.

Ahn, K. and Webber, B. (2007). Nexus: A real time qa system. In *SIGIR '07: Proceedings of the 30th annual international ACM SIGIR conference*.

Ahn, K. and Webber, B. (2008). Topic indexing and retrieval for qa. In *COLING '08: Proceedings of the Coling 2008 IR4QA Workshop*.

Brill, E., Dumais, S., and Banko, M. (2002). Analysis of the askmsr question-answering system. In *Proceedings of the Conference on Empirical Methods in Natural Language Processing (EMNLP-2002)*, pages 257–264, Philadelphia PA.

Chali, Y. and Joty, S. R. (2008). Selecting sentences for answering complex questions. In *Proceedings of the 2008 Conference on Empirical Methods in Natural Language Processing*, pages 304–313.

Chu-Carroll, J., Prager, J., Welty, C., Czuba, K., and Ferrucci, D. (2002). A multi-strategy and multi-source approach to question answering. In *Proceedings of the 11th Text Retrieval Conference (TREC 10)*, National Institute of Standards and Technology.

David Ferrucci, Eric Brown, e. a. (2012). Building watson: An overview of the deepqa project. *AI Magazine, Volume 31, No 3*, 31(1).

Saquete, E., Martínez-Barco, P., Muñoz, R., and González, J. L. V. (2004). Splitting complex temporal questions for question answering systems. In *ACL*, pages 566–573.

Suchanek, F. M., Kasneci, G., and Weikum, G. (2007). Yago: A core of semantic knowledge - unifying WordNet and Wikipedia. In Williamson, C. L., Zurko, M. E., and Patel-Schneider, Peter F. Shenoy, P. J., editors, *16th International World Wide Web Conference (WWW 2007)*, pages 697–706, Banff, Canada. ACM.

Turtle, H. R. (1991). *Inference Networks for Document Retrieval*. PhD thesis, University of Massachusetts.

White, K. and Sutcliffe, R. F. E. (2004). Seeking an upper bound to sentence level retrieval in question answering. In *Proceedings of the 23rd Annual International ACM SIGIR Workshop on Question Answering (SIGIR 2004)*.

Wilcoxon, F. (1945). Individual comparisons by ranking methods. *Biometrics*, (1):80–83.

Thai Sentence Paraphrasing from the Lexical Resource

Krittaporn Phucharasupa and Ponrudee Netisopakul
Faculty of Information Technology
King Mongkut's Institute of Technology Ladkrabang
Bangkok, Thailand
phucharasupa@hotmail.com, ponrudee@it.kmitl.ac.th

Abstract

Paraphrase generation in any language has gained much attention and importance in the study of Natural Language Processing. Therefore, the focus of this paper is on Thai language paraphrase generation for the sentence level. Six sentence paraphrasing techniques for Thai are proposed and illustratively explained. In addition, the *Thai–sentence Paraphrase Generation (TPG) system* is designed using a lexical resource based system subsequently entitled the *Thai Lexical Conceptual Structure with Thai Lexicalized Tree Adjoining Grammar (TLCS–TLTAG) Resource.*

1 Introduction

For any language, putting the same content in different ways can indicate the richness of the language culture. Since the language is one of the major communication tools in every society, the ability to paraphrase what we want to say or write can also imply the society's civilization.

Paraphrasing techniques for the sentence level and others in several languages have been examined and suggested during the past several years (Stede, 1996; Dras, 1999; Barzilay and Lee, 2003; Pang et al., 2003; Qiu et al., 2006; Ellsworth and Janin, 2007; Zhao et al., 2009; Madnani and Dorr, 2010). These paraphrasing techniques were enormously used in several areas of Natural Language Processing such as Question Answering (Duboue and Carroll, 2006), Machine Translation (Shimohata, 2004; Barreiro, 2008), Summary Evaluation (Zhou et al., 2006) and Textual Entailment Recognition (Marsi et al., 2007; Malakasiotis, 2011).

In Thai language, its writing structure contains no space between words and no full stops between sentences. This could be potential problems in doing research pertaining to Thai computational paraphrasing. Nevertheless, the construction and patterns of Thai sentences have been partially investigated by a number of renown Thai linguists (Vongsantivanit, 1983; Kanchanacheeva, 1996; Thonglor, 2007; Songsilp, 2008; Settanyakan, 2011). Some researchers classified Thai verbs, identified their arguments, as well as recognized their corresponding thematic roles (Wongsiri, 1981; Sungkhavon, 1984; Panthumetha, 2010).

To be able to work on Thai sentence paraphrasing, previous research regarding constructing and paraphrasing sentences in other languages was essential and therefore surveyed (Shimohata, 2004; Barreiro, 2008; Dorr, 1994; Kozlowski et al., 2003; Fujita, 2005). It was subsequently adjusted by (Phucharasupa and Netisopakul, 2011) to fit Thai language more appropriately. Thai sentence paraphrase patterns were categorized into fourteen groups, some of which will be explained and used as examples in this research.

To achieve the goal of automatic paraphrase generation, two critical considerations must be addressed. One is that an appropriate semantic structure of the original sentence must be designed so that it facilitates the automatic system to easily generate paraphrases. The other is that the algorithm must be able to generate syntactically correct paraphrases of the original sentence and these paraphrases must faithfully preserve its original meaning.

The focal method for semantic representation of this research is the *Lexical Conceptual Structure (LCS)* associated with each lexical item (Fujita, 2005; Jackendoff, 1990; Dorr and Palmer, 1995) whereas the method of interest for syntactic structure representation is the *Lexicalized Tree Adjoining Grammar (LTAG)* (Joshi, 1999; Palmer and Rosenzweig, 1999) that captures the realization of the lexical item. In addition, the LTAG operations, namely, substitution and adjoining, ensure that the resulting sentence is well-formed. The above two representations, i.e., LTAG and LCS have been utilized to facilitate multilingual generation (Dorr and Palmer, 1995; Netisopakul, 1997).

In this paper, six paraphrasing techniques for generating Thai sentence paraphrases are proposed based collaboratively on LCS and LTAG. This paper is organized as follows. In the next section, the process of *the Thai–sentence Paraphrase Generation (TPG) system* is described in details. In Section 3, how each of the six paraphrasing techniques works is illustratively explained. Then, in Section 4, combinations of the proposed Thai sentence paraphrasing techniques used in some of the fourteen Thai sentence paraphrase patterns are identified along with one particular combination explicitly illustrated in details. In the last section, a conclusion and suggestions of this research are provided.

2 Processes of TPG System

Thai sentence paraphrase generation in the designed TPG system is driven by the semantic input or the *Composed LCS (CLCS)*, that is, the meaning of complex phrases composed from several *Root LCSs (RLCSs)* corresponding to individual words (Dorr, 2001). This TPG system contains three primary processes, namely, the *CLCS Decomposition*, the *Thai LTAG (TLTAG) Selection*, and the *Surface Realization* as illustrated in Figure 1.

In the very first process of the TPG system or the *CLCS Decomposition* process, one CLCS is semantically broken into many elementary LCSs corresponding to each individual word. Each elementary LCS is then normalized into its semantic base form according to the *Thai Lexical Conceptual Structure with Thai Lexicalized Tree Adjoining Grammar (TLCS–TLTAG) Resource*.

In the second process called the *TLTAG Selection*, each semantic base formed LCS is mapped with TLCS part in the TLCS–TLTAG Resource so as to pull out the corresponding TLTAG tree which defines the syntactic structure of the elementary word.

The last process entitled the *Surface Realization* combines all TLTAG trees using the LTAG operations. This process produces syntactically well-formed sentences, each of which can be read off of the leaf nodes of a combined TLTAG tree.

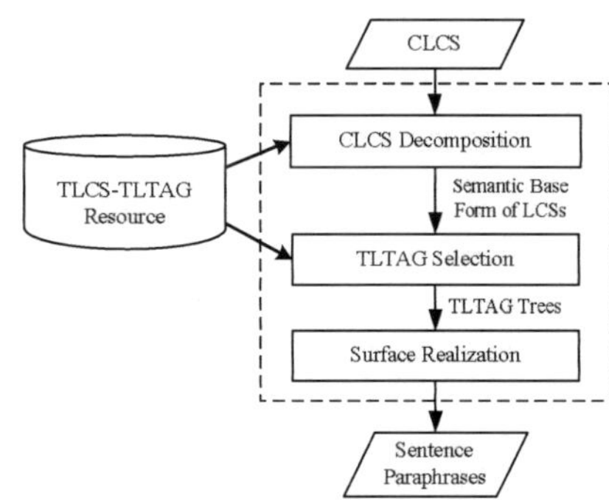

Figure 1: The Architecture of TPG System

The TLCS–TLTAG Resource is designed to assist the TPG system in generating the paraphrases because it encapsulates information necessary for the paraphrase generation process. The information in the TLCS–TLTAG Resource contains the following:

- General information of each Thai word such as the part of speech, the word sub-category, the synonyms, the antonyms, and the definition. For example, the word "เปล่งประกาย/*shine*" has "intransitive verb" as its part-of-speech, "Immotion Action" (Sungkhavon, 1984) as its sub-category, "ส่องประกาย/*glitter*" as its synonym, "หมอง/*cloud*" as its antonym, and "สะท้อนแสง/*reflect light*" as its definition.
- *Thai LCS* or TLCS semantics corresponding to individual words useful for the *CLCS Decomposition* process and the *TLTAG Selection* process.
- Syntactic structures in the TLTAG portion projected from Thai lexicon items based on the LTAG theory (Joshi, 1999).

The *Surface Realization* of TLCSs can be processed by mapping semantic arguments to the substitution nodes in TLTAGs. Considering an example drawn from the TLCS–TLTAG Resource shown in Figure 2, a TLCS consists of a category *event*, a predicate *ACT* and its arguments *agent-agt, factitive-fac,* and *cause-cau* of the verb "ทำ/*do*". Each argument is mapped to each corresponding substitution node in the TLTAG of the verb "ทำ/*do*" as illustrated in Figure 2(a) for an affirmative sentence and in Figure 2(b) for a productive causative sentence.

(a) An Affirmative Sentence

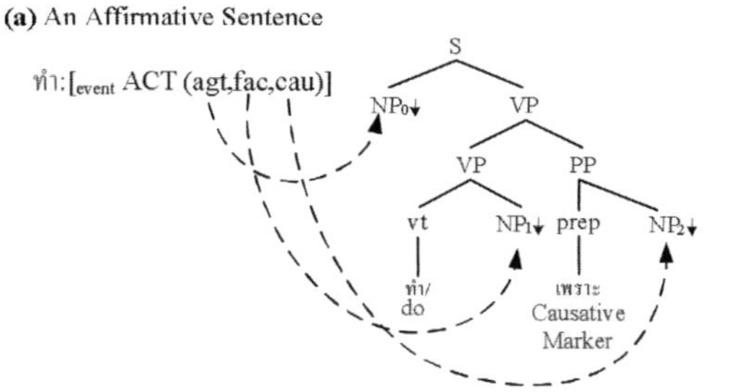

Ex. (a) นักเรียน/*students* ทำ/*do* การบ้าน/*homework* เพราะ/*because of-CausativeMarker* ครู/*teacher*

Students do their homework because of the teacher.

(b) A Productive Causative Sentence

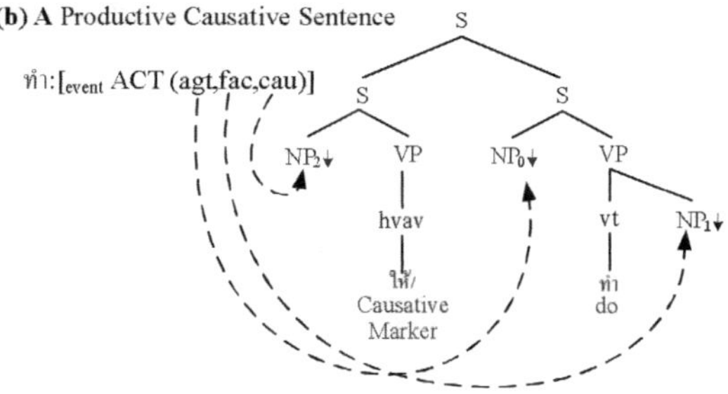

Ex. (b) ครู/*teacher* ให้/*order-CausativeMarker* นักเรียน/*students* ทำ/*do* การบ้าน/*homework*

The teacher orders the students to do their homework.

Figure 2: A Semantic (TLCS) of "ทำ/*do* something activated by a cause" Represented in Different Constructions (TLTAGs)

During the automatic paraphrasing, an initial sentence represented by a CLCS is decomposed into many TLCSs in the *CLCS Decomposition* process. Next, each decomposed TLCS is looked up in the TCLS–TLTAG Resource during the *TLTAG Selection* process to find a mapped TLCS in order to obtain its associated TLTAG. Note that the number of the obtained TLTAGs can be more than one depending on the numbers of the mapped TLCSs. The *TLTAG Selection* process may therefore result in several surface structures indicated by each TLTAG paired with the mapped TLCS as shown in Figure 2(a) and Figure 2(b). The *Surface Realization* process links the TLCS arguments to the TLTAG empty substitution nodes according to the hierarchical order of the arguments in the thematic roles.

The *TLTAG Selection* and the *Surface Realization* processes are performed based on the fourteen Thai sentence paraphrase patterns previously suggested by (Phucharasupa and Netisopakul, 2011) using the six Thai sentence paraphrasing techniques proposed in this paper and described elaborately in the following sections.

3 Thai Sentence Paraphrasing Techniques

In Phucharasupa and Netisopakul (2011), besides exploring Thai sentence paraphrase patterns from Thai linguistic phenomena, previous research related to the analysis of language constructions and paraphrases was also reviewed. The paraphrase patterns were classified based on Thai verb classes proposed by Sungkhavon (1984). During the classification, it was noticed that one paraphrasing technique was used in several paraphrase patterns and in turn, several paraphrasing techniques could be used in one Thai paraphrase pattern.

Hence, this analysis of paraphrase patterns and techniques gives a total of six Thai sentence paraphrasing techniques to be proposed here. Later in this section, these techniques along with their operating procedures and examples will be described. Out of these six, three techniques including the *Replacement Technique*, the *Movement Technique*, and the *Left-Out/Insert Technique* involve changing individual words or phrases, all by itself. The second group of the proposed paraphrasing techniques includes the *Switching Technique* and the *Promotion/Demotion Technique*. These techniques involve making a change of the words, phrases, or clauses *in pairs*. Finally, the remaining paraphrasing technique called the *Nominalization Technique* changes the structure of the original sentence or phrase.

Throughout this section and the next, the initial sentence to be paraphrased for demonstration purposes of the six paraphrasing techniques is given in the following S_i.

(S_i) เขา/*he-Agent* และ/*and-ParallelMarker* เธอ/*she-Dative* ท่องเที่ยว/*travel-MotionAction* อย่าง/*AdverbMarker* สนุกสนาน/*joyfully-Quality* ใน/*in-PositionMarker* กรุงเทพฯ/*Krung Thep-Locative*

He and she travel joyfully in Krung Thep.

In addition, the meaning of S_i is represented in the CLCS form shown in Figure 3 to be used as an input for starting the paraphrase generation processes.

CLCS Input

ท่องเที่ยว : [$_{event}$ ACT ([$_{thing}$ CO_and ([$_{living\text{-}thing}$ เขา+],[$_{living\text{-}thing}$ เธอ+])])
,[$_{event}$ HOW ([$_{mien}$ สนุกสนาน+])]
,[$_{path}$ IN ([$_{place}$ กรุงเทพฯ+])]
]

Figure 3: The CLCS Form for S_i

CLCS Decomposition

1) Decomposition		2) Generalization	
ท่องเที่ยว:		ท่องเที่ยว:	
[$_{event}$ ACT ([$_{thing}$ CO_and ([$_{living\text{-}thing}$ เขา+],[$_{living\text{-}thing}$ เธอ+])])]	→	[$_{event}$ ACT (agt)]	TLCSs (Semantic Base Form)
[$_{thing}$ CO_and ([$_{living\text{-}thing}$ เขา+],[$_{living\text{-}thing}$ เธอ+])]	→	[$_{thing}$ CO_and (agt,par)]	
[$_{living\text{-}thing}$ เขา+]	→	[$_{living\text{-}thing}$ เขา+]	
[$_{living\text{-}thing}$ เธอ+]	→	[$_{living\text{-}thing}$ เธอ+]	
[$_{event}$ HOW ([$_{mien}$ สนุกสนาน+])]	→	[$_{event}$ HOW (man)]	
[$_{mien}$ สนุกสนาน+]	→	[$_{mien}$ สนุกสนาน+]	
[$_{path}$ IN ([$_{place}$ กรุงเทพฯ+])]	→	[$_{path}$ IN (loc)]	
[$_{place}$ กรุงเทพฯ+]	→	[$_{place}$ กรุงเทพฯ+]	

Figure 4: The Decomposition of the CLCS for S_i

When the TPG system is triggered, the CLCS input is decomposed into many TLCSs in the *CLCS Decomposition* process. Then TLCSs are normalized into semantic base forms, which will be hereafter called the "TLCSs input", as illustrated in Figure 4. Afterwards, the *TLTAG Selection* and the *Surface Realization* processes will be activated on the TLCSs input for all fourteen Thai sentence paraphrase patterns under the restriction of each pattern using the following six Thai sentence paraphrasing techniques to be described in more details now.

3.1 The Replacement Technique

This *Replacement Technique* makes use of the variety of words having similar meanings. One existing word or phrase in a sentence can then be *replaced* by a new word or phrase with the similar meaning in the same syntactic category without changing its position and its thematic role. Figure 5 also show two types of elementary TLTAG trees, according to the LTAG theory (Joshi, 1999), which correspond to TLCSs of the initial sentence S_i.

An example of using this *Replacement Technique* will be illustrated in the context of one paraphrase patterns, namely, the *Lexical Replacement by Its Synonym* pattern. Typically, the *TLTAG Selection* process selects all elementary TLTAG trees from the TLCS–TLTAG Resource in which their TLCSs precisely agree with the TLCS input. However, in this case, the *Lexical Replacement* pattern forces the process to specifically choose the trees not just only whose TLCSs are identical to the TLCS input but also whose syntactic structures are the same as that of the TLCS input tree.

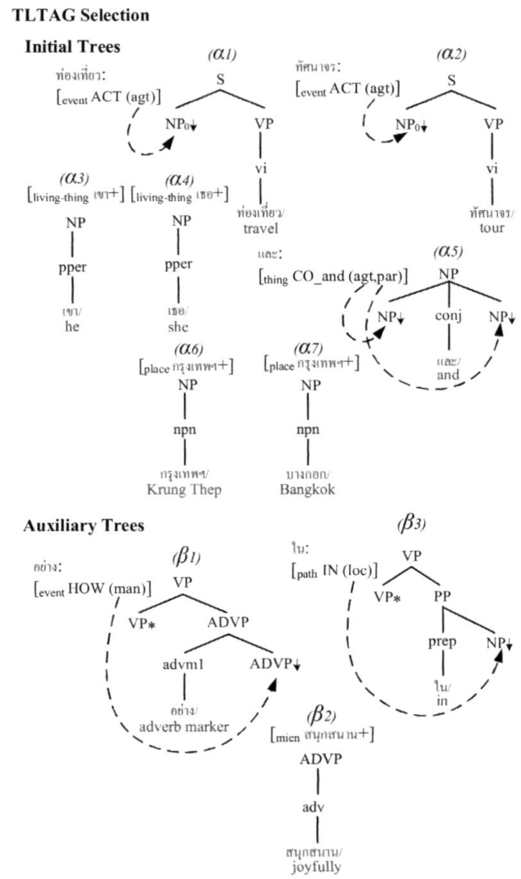

Figure 5: The Elementary TLTAG Trees Corresponding to TLCSs for S_i

Let *α1* in Figure 5 be TLCS and TLTAG of an original decomposed word "ท่องเที่ยว/*travel*" retrieved from the TLCS–TLTAG Resource and let *α2* in Figure 5 be TLCS and TLTAG of another word "ทัศนาจร/*tour*" retrieved again from the TLCS–TLTAG Resource. Since *α2* has both the same TLCS and TLTAG as *α1*, *α2* is thus selected as *a synonym* of $\alpha 1$. Similar process can be applied to another original decomposed word "กรุงเทพฯ/*Krung Thep*" and results in the TLCS and TLTAG $\alpha 6$ whereas $\alpha 7$ is TLCS and TLTAG for the synonym "บางกอก/*Bangkok*" of this decomposed word.

In the next step, these elementary trees are realized into well-formed surfaces by LTAG's operations shown in Figure 6.

Surface Realization

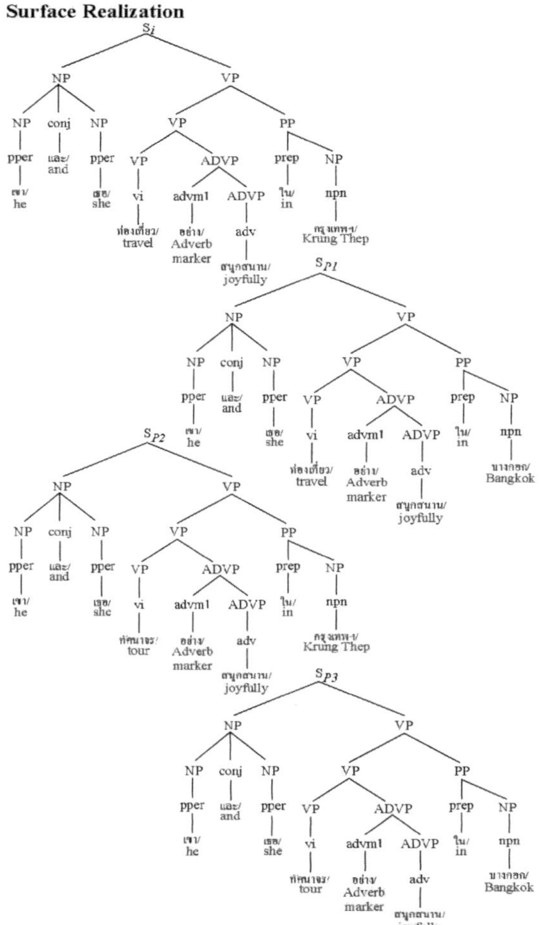

Figure 6: The TLTAG Derived Trees for Both S_i and Its Paraphrases (S_{p1}-S_{p3}) Obtained from the Replacement Technique

Each sentence paraphrase can be read off of the leaf nodes of its associated TLTAG derived tree as follows.

(S_{p1}) เขา/*he-Agent* และ/*and-ParallelMarker* เธอ/*she-Dative* ท่องเที่ยว/*travel-MotionAction* อย่าง/*AdverbMarker* สนุกสนาน/*joyfully-Quality* ใน/*in-PositionMarker* **บางกอก**/*Bangkok-Locative*

He and she travel joyfully in Bangkok.

(S_{p2}) เขา/*he-Agent* และ/*and-ParallelMarker* เธอ/*she-Dative* **ทัศนาจร**/*tour-MotionAction* อย่าง/*AdverbMarker* สนุกสนาน/*joyfully-Quality* ใน/*in-PositionMarker* กรุงเทพฯ/*Krung Thep-Locative*

He and she travel joyfully in Krung Thep.

(S_{p3}) เขา/*he-Agent* และ/*and-ParallelMarker* เธอ/*she-Dative* **ทัศนาจร**/*tour-MotionAction* อย่าง/*AdverbMarker* สนุกสนาน/*joyfully-Quality* ใน/*in-PositionMarker* **บางกอก**/*Bangkok-Locative*

He and she travel joyfully in Bangkok.

3.2 The Movement Technique

In a Thai sentence, the *Movement Technique* is usually used for emphasizing on one constituent over the rest by moving the emphasized constituent to the front of the sentence. Its syntactic category and thematic role remain unchanged (Thonglor, 2007; Songsilp, 2008). For example, this *Movement Technique* is used in the *Direct Object Promotion* pattern of the fourteen Thai sentence paraphrase patterns by moving the direct object to the front of the sentence.

In another example, moving around the negative marker in a sentence can reduce or sometimes increase the negative sense of the sentence and thus make it more or sometimes less polite than the initial sentence as demonstrated in the *Moving Negation Separated from Adjective/Adverb* pattern.

The *Movement Technique* in the *Preposition Phrase Promotion* pattern will be explained here. For the given initial sentence S_i, the *TLTAG Selection* process selects TLTAG elementary trees corresponding to TLCS inputs. These elementary trees are realized into surface strings which contain the preposition modifier of the main verb. Subsequently, the *Moving Technique* will move the entire preposition branch around these three locations, namely, the front of the sentence, right after the main verb, or the back of the sentence, depending on its *promotion/demotion* switch.

In Figure 7, each sentence paraphrase can be read off of the leaf nodes of its associated TLTAG derived tree as follows.

(S_{p4}) **ใน**/*in-PositionMarker* **กรุงเทพฯ**/*Krung Thep-Locative* เขา/*he-Agent* และ/*and-ParallelMarker* เธอ/*you-Dative* ท่องเที่ยว/*travel-MotionAction* อย่าง/*AdverbMarker* สนุกสนาน/*joyfully-Quality*

In Krung Thep, he and she are joyfully traveled.

(S_{p5}) เขา/*he-Agent* และ/*and-ParallelMarker* เธอ/*you-Dative* ท่องเที่ยว/*travel-MotionAction* **ใน**/*in-PositionMarker* **กรุงเทพฯ**/*Krung Thep-Locative* อย่าง/*AdverbMarker* สนุกสนาน/*joyfully-Quality*

He and she travel in Krung Thep that they are joyfully.

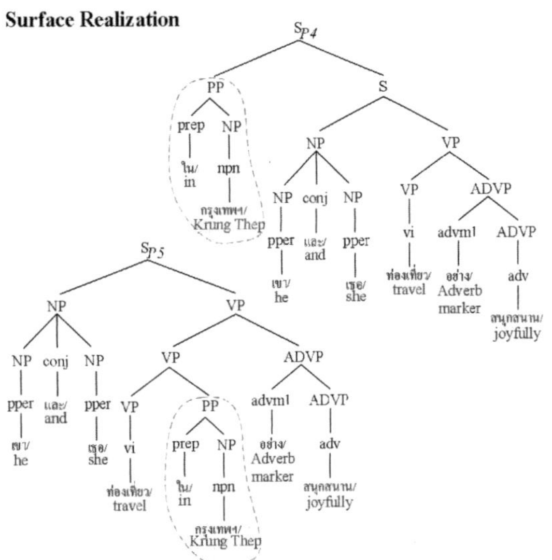

Figure 7: The TLTAG Derived Trees for Both S_{p4} and S_{p5} Obtained from the Movement Technique

3.3 The Removal/Insertion Technique

This technique comprises of two independent operations. One involves removing a word from the sentence in order to make it more compact and probably more appealing. The other operation of this technique involves inserting a word into the sentence in order to make it clearer or more sophisticated. These operations are both in fact employed in the *Quantifier Removal/Insertion* pattern but only the insertion operation will be explicitly demonstrated here.

The *Insertion Technique* first investigates the TLCS input. For the case that the initial sentence has more than one agent doing the same action such as "เขา/*he* and เธอ/*she*" of S_i taking the same action "ท่องเที่ยว/*travel*", the quantifier "ล้วน/*all*" can be inserted after the agents and before the action/modifier to emphasize that *every* single component really performs the same action or share the same property at the same time. By inserting this type of word, the meaning of the sentence is stressed more strongly. Caused by the *Insertion Technique*, an additional tree for the quantifier "ล้วน/*all*" is selected by the *TLTAG Selection* process and then realized as part of the sentence paraphrase during the *Surface Realization* process as shown in Figure 8.

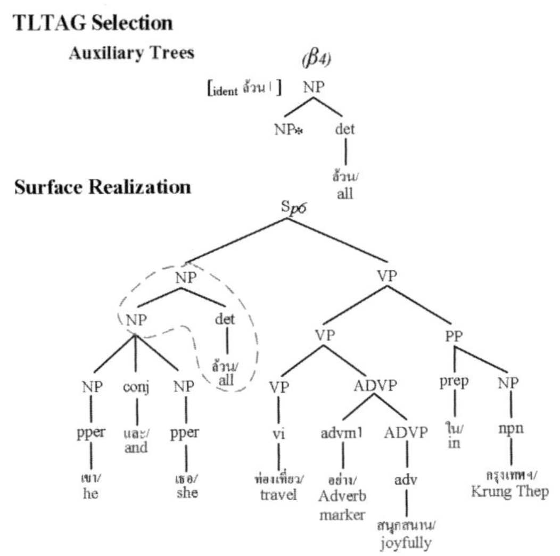

Figure 8: The Elementary Tree for "ล้วน/*all*" and the TLTAG Derived Tree for S_{p6} Obtained from the Insertion Technique

The sentence paraphrase is read off of the leaf nodes of the S_{p6} tree, as follows.

(S_{p6}) เขา/*he-Agent* และ/*and-ParallelMarker* เธอ/*she-Dative* **ล้วน**/*all-Amount* ท่องเที่ยว/*travel-MotionAction* อย่าง/*AdverbMarker* สนุกสนาน/*joyfully-Quality* ใน/*in-PositionMarker* กรุงเทพฯ/*Krung Thep-Locative*

All he and she are joyfully traveled in Krung Thep.

As for the next three paraphrasing techniques, the ideas behind each technique along with its operating procedure will be briefly discussed in this section. However, the examples of these techniques will be collaboratively demonstrated in Section 4 to show how these techniques can be used in combination to generate more complex sentence paraphrases.

3.4 The Switching Technique

This technique switches the thematic roles of the agent and the participant in the *Reciprocity* verb class (Sungkhavon, 1984). The verbs in this class must be followed by the preposition "กับ/*with-ParticipantMarker*" to indicate the togetherness of its subject and object. Every word in the Reciprocity Action verb class such as "เผชิญหน้า/*confront*", "ต่อสู้/*fight*", "สัญญา/*engage*", and "หมั้น/*engage*" etc. can switch its arguments, i.e., its thematic roles. This *Switching Technique* is exercised in the *Arguments Switching in the Reciprocity Action* paraphrase pattern as follows:

(ex_{i1}) สมศรี/*Somsri-Agent* **หมั้น**/*engages-ReciprocityAction* **กับ**/*with-ParallelMarker* สมชาย/*Somchai-Participant*

Somsri engages (with) Somchai.

(ex_{p1}) สมชาย/*Somchai-Agent* **หมั้น**/*engages-ReciprocityAction* **กับ**/*with-ParallelMarker* สมศรี/*Somsri-Participant*

Somchai engages (with) Somsri.

The switching technique can also apply to other paraphrase patterns, such as *Verb/Adverb Position Switching*, which will be demonstrated in Section 4, and *Switching Clauses in Multi-Clause sentence* as explained in the following example.

(ex_{i2}) ขโมย/*a thief-Agent* หนีไป/*flee-MotionAction* **ก่อน**/*before-TimeMarker* ตำรวจ/*a policeman-Agent* มาถึง/*arrive-MotionAction*

A thief had fled before a policeman arrived.

(ex_{p2}) ตำรวจ/*a policeman-Agent* มาถึง/*arrive-MotionAction* **หลัง**/*after-TimeMarker* ขโมย/*a thief-Agent* หนีไป/*flee-MotionAction* แล้ว/*ago-PastTense*

A policeman arrived after a thief had fled.

3.5 The Promotion/Demotion Technique

The *Promotion* mechanism usually occurs at the same time with the *Demotion* mechanism. The idea behind this technique is that as one word/phrase is promoted, another grammatically related word/ phrase must be demoted. Since this technique is often used in conjunction with other techniques in generating paraphrases, the generation procedure will then be explained in Section 4.

3.6 The Nominalization Technique

The last technique to be presented changes the structure of a simple sentence/phrase but still preserves the original meaning of its initial sentence.

In Thai language, there are two prefixes for transforming a verb into an abstract noun (Thonglor, 2007). The first prefix is "การ-/*karn-*" comparable to the suffix "*-ing*" in English, to put in front of an *action* verb, e.g., "กิน/*eat*" to make a noun, e.g., "การกิน/*eating*". The second prefix is "ความ-/*kwam-*" comparable to the suffix "*-ness*" to put in front of a *mental* verb, e.g., "เสียใจ/*sad*" to make a noun, e.g., "ความเสียใจ/*sadness*". Notice that in this case, to and maintain its similar forms in both Thai and English, the Thai mental verb becomes an adjective in English.

This process can be extended to nominalize a simple sentence into a noun phrase for use in combination with the previous paraphrasing techniques for obtaining a new sentence paraphrase.

Given a simple sentence, the first step of this *Nominalization Technique* inserts the prefix "การ-/*karn-*" or "ความ-/*kwam-*" in front of the verb phrase. Then, the subject is moved to the end of the sentence and connected to the just-constructed noun phrase using the preposition marker such as "ของ/*of*" or "โดย/*by*". The new noun phrase is often used as a subject phrase or an object phrase or a modifier phrase in generating a new and more complex paraphrase as shown in the following example.

(ex_{i3}) นิวตัน/*Newton-Agent* **ค้นพบ**/*discover-TargetAction* แรงโน้มถ่วง/*gravity-Target*

Newton discovers gravity.

(ex_{p3}) [**การ**-*prefix/karn* ค้นพบ/*discover-TargetAction* แรงโน้มถ่วง/*gravity-Target*]/*AbstractNoun* **ของ**/*of-PossessorMarker* นิวตัน/*Newton-Agent*

Gravity discovering of Newton.

4 Combinations of the Proposed Thai Sentence Paraphrasing Techniques

To generate a new and probably more complex Thai sentence paraphrase, a combination of the paraphrasing techniques in Section 3 will be employed. All possible combinations for use in the Thai sentence paraphrase patterns are depicted in Table 1. For illustration purposes, the paraphrase generation process of a combination of these particular three techniques, namely, the *Switching*, the *Promotion/Demotion* and the *Nominalization Techniques* will be applied to the *Verb/Adverb Position Switching* pattern and also fully explained now as follows.

In Thai grammar, an adverb usually acts as a modifier or sometimes an intransitive verb. This is where the *Switching Technique* comes in. However, since the syntactic functions of the verb and the adverb should also be interchanged, the adverb is grammatically promoted to a new verb while the current verb is demoted to a modifier of the new verb. Consequently, the *Promotion/ Demotion Technique* is therefore used. Last but not least, during the Demotion mechanism, the *Nominalization Technique* is also needed in transforming the current verb into an abstract noun in order to make the modifier complete.

Figure 9 illustrates an example of the above process in generating a paraphrase of the initial sentence S_i using the combination of the three mentioned techniques.

After the *TLTAG Selection* and *Surface Realization* processes yield the TLTAG Derived Trees for S_i, the *Verb/Adverb Position Switching* pattern guides the process to look for the main verb and the adverb of the sentence. The obtained main verb "ท่องเที่ยว-*vi*/*travel*" and its adverb "สนุกสนาน-*adv*/*joyfully*" are switched constituting the *Switching Technique*. Then, the adverb is promoted to a new verb "สนุกสนาน-*vi*/*enjoy*" while the old verb is demoted to a modifier for the new verb constituting the *Promotion/Demotion Technique*. During the demotion mechanism, a new elementary tree "กับ-*perp*/*with*" is acquired. This step then forces the *Nominalization Technique* to activate and form a newly transformed abstract noun "การ-*prefix*/*karn* ท่องเที่ยว-*vi*/*travel*" into a new branch of the S_{p7} TLTAG Derived Tree so that the new resulting paraphrase will be grammatically correct. Finally, the obtained sentence paraphrase can be read off of the leaf nodes of the S_{p7} tree as follows.

(S_{p7}) เขา/*he-Agent* และ/*and-ParallelMarker* เธอ/*she-Dative* **สนุกสนาน**/*enjoy-AdditionAction* **กับ**/*with-GoalMarker* [การ-*prefix*/*karn* **ท่องเที่ยว**/*travel-MotionAction*]/*AbstractNoun-Complementary* ใน/*in-PositionMarker* กรุงเทพฯ/*Krung Thep-Locative*

He and she enjoy (with) traveling in Krung Thep.

In addition, other Thai sentence paraphrase patterns may use different combinations of the proposed six paraphrasing techniques to generate more complex paraphrases. For example, the *Replacement* and the *Movement Techniques* are both used in the *Negation of the Opposite Quantifier* pattern while the *Switching* and the *Promotion/Demotion Techniques* are employed in the *Preposition with Instrument-Verb Phrase Switching* pattern. Other combinations of the paraphrasing techniques used in the Thai sentence paraphrase patterns are identified and explicitly shown in Table 1.

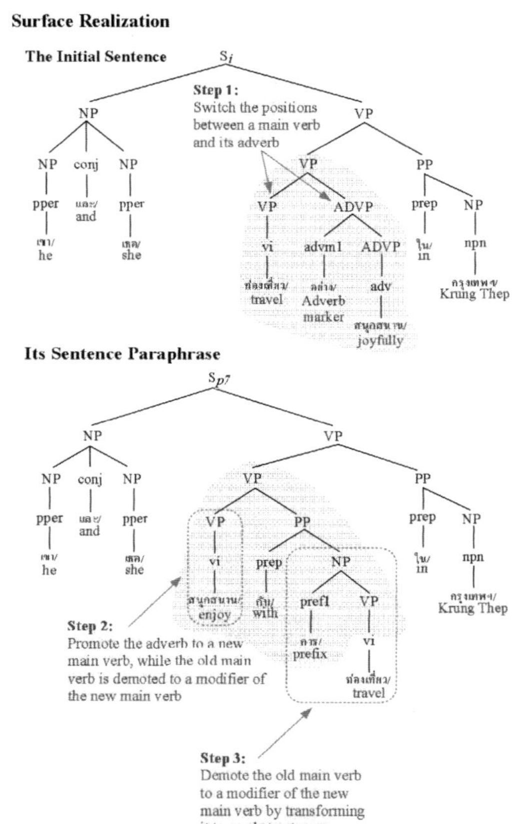

Figure 9: The TLTAG Derived Trees for Both S_i and Its Paraphrase Obtained from a Combination of the Switching, the Promotion/Demotion and the Nominalization Techniques

Thai sentence paraphrase patterns	Replacement	Movement	Removal/ Insertion	Switching	Promotion/ Demotion	Nominalization
1. Lexical Replacement						
1.1) Lexical Replacement by Its Synonym	✓					
1.2) Noun Replacement by Its Abbreviation	✓					
1.3) Common Noun Replacement by Its Definition	✓					
1.4) Grouping of Many Singular Pronouns into a Plural Pronoun	✓					
2. Preposition with Instrument-Verb Phrase Switching				✓	✓	
3. Simple Active-Passive Voices		✓		✓	✓	
4. Preposition Removal			✓			
5. Constituent Promotion/Demotion						
5.1) Direct Object Promotion/Demotion		✓				
5.2) Preposition Phrase Promotion		✓				
6. Paraphrasing in Dative Verbs						
6.1) Preposition Removal in Dative Verbs			✓			
6.2) Direct Object Promotion in Dative Verbs		✓				
6.3) Indirect Object Promotion				✓		
6.4) Passive Voice of Dative Verbs		✓			✓	
7. Arguments Switching in Reciprocity Action				✓		
8. Verb Phrase-Noun Phrase Transformation						✓
9. Verb/Adverb Position Switching				✓	✓	✓
10. Words Removal/Insertion						
10.1) Omissible Words Removal/Insertion						✓
10.2) Quantifier Removal/Insertion			✓			
11. Negation Movement						
11.1) Moving Negation Separated from Adjective/Adverb		✓				
11.2) Negation of the Opposite Quantifier	✓	✓				
12. In-Comparison Sentence Paraphrasing						
12.1) Paraphrasing in Positive Degree				✓		
12.2) Paraphrasing in Comparative Degree				✓		
12.3) Paraphrasing in Superlative Degree	✓			✓		
13. Mood Change						
13.1) Requesting ←→ Imperative Sentence	✓					
13.2) Question → Requesting or Imperative Sentence			✓			✓
14. Paraphrasing in Multi-Clause Sentences						
14.1) Switching Clauses in Multi-Clause Sentence				✓		
14.2) Collapsing A Complex Sentence into A Simple Sentence		✓	✓		✓	

Table 1: Thai Sentence Paraphrasing Techniques Identified in Thai Sentence Paraphrase Patterns

5 Conclusion

Sentence paraphrasing techniques for Thai language are discovered and proposed in this paper based mainly on the fourteen Thai sentence paraphrase patterns classified in (Phucharasupa and Netisopakul, 2011). Among these paraphrasing techniques are the *Replacement*, the *Movement*, the *Removal/Insertion*, the *Switching*, the *Promotion/ Demotion* and the *Nominalization Techniques*. Some techniques involve changing only individual words or phrases and some involve changing words, phrases, or clauses in pairs. Some others may even involve changing the structure of the original sentence or phrase.

The design of *the Thai–sentence Paraphrase Generation (TPG) system* incorporating those six techniques for computationally generating paraphrases has been illustratively explained. This TPG system is based on a proposed lexical resource called the *Thai Lexical Conceptual Structure with Thai Lexicalized Tree Adjoining Grammar (TLCS–TLTAG) Resource*. This resource keeping tracks of the syntactic and the semantic structures of a lexicon simplifies Thai paraphrase generation process. The construction of this semi-automatic system is an on-going process.

References

Anabela M. Barreiro. 2008. Make It Simple with Paraphrases: Automated Paraphrasing for Authoring Aids and Machine Translation. Ph.D. Dissertation, Faculdade de Letras da Universidade do Porto, Porto, Portugal.

Aravind K. Joshi. 1999. Explorations of a Domain of Locality: Lexicalized Tree-Adjoining Grammar (LTAG). University of Utrecht (CLIN meeting).

Atsushi Fujita. 2005. Automatic Generation of Syntactically Well-formed and Semantically Appropriate Paraphrases. Ph.D. Dissertation, Nara Institute of Science and Technology, Ikoma, Nara.

Bo Pang, Kevin Knight, and Daniel Marcu. 2003. Syntax-Based Alignment of Multiple Translations: Extracting Paraphrases and Generating New Sentences. in Proceedings of HLT-NAACL, vol. 1, pp. 102–109.

Bonnie J. Dorr. 1994. Machine Translation Divergences: A Formal Description and Proposed Solution. Computational Linguistics, 20(4): 597–633.

Bonnie J. Dorr and Martha S. Palmer. 1995. Building a LCS-Based Lexicon in TAGs*. AAAI Technical Report SS-95-01, pp. 33–38.

Bonnie J. Dorr. 2001. LCS Documentation. Retrieved March 7, 2012, from University of Maryland Institute for Advanced Computer Studies, Bonnie Dorr page website: http://www.umiacs.umd.edu/~bonnie/ LCS_Database_Documentation.html

Chotikaa. Settanyakan. 2011. Translation Strategies of Focus Clausal Constructions in Academic Texts. Journal of Humanities Narasuan University, 8(1):31–54.

Erwin Marsi, Emiel Krahmer, and Wauter Bosma. 2007. Dependency-based Paraphrasing for Recognizing Textual Entailment. Proceedings of the Workshop on Textual Entailment and Paraphrasing, pp. 83–88.

Kamchai Thonglor. 2007. Principles of Thai Language. Ruamsarn (1977) Press, Bangkok, Thailand.

Krittaporn Phucharasupa and Ponrudee Netisopakul. 2011. Classification of Thai Sentence Paraphrase. International Symposium on Natural Language Processing and the Agriculture Ontology Service (SNLP-AOS 2011), pp. 197–203.

Liang Zhou, Chin-Yew Lin, Dragos S. Munteanu, and Eduard Hovy. 2006. ParaEval: Using Paraphrases to Evaluate Summaries Automatically. in Proceedings of HLT-NAACL, pp. 447–454.

Long Qiu, Min-Yen. Kan, and Tat Seng. Chua. 2006. Paraphrase Recognition via Dissimilarity Significance Classification. 2006. in Proceedings of the 2006 Conference on Empirical Methods in Natural Language Processing (EMNLP 2006), pp. 18–26.

Manfred Stede. 1996. Lexical Paraphrases in Multilingual Sentence Generation, Machine Translation, vol. 11. Kluwer Academic Publishers, Netherlands, pp. 75–107.

Mark Dras. 1999. Tree Adjoining Grammar and the Reluctant Paraphrasing of Text. Ph.D. Dissertation, Department of Information and Communication Sciences, Macquarie University, Australia.

Martha Palmer and Joseph Rosenzweig. 1999. Capturing Motion Verb Generalizations in Synchronous Tree Adjoining Grammars. Kluwer Press, pp. 76–85.

Michael Ellsworth and Adam Janin. 2007. Mutaphrase: Paraphrasing with FrameNet. in Proceedings of the Workshop on Textual Entailment and Paraphrasing, pp. 143–150.

Mitsuo Shimohata. 2004. Acquiring Paraphrases from Corpora and Its Application to Machine Translation. Ph.D. Dissertation, Department of Information Processing, Graduate School of Information Science, Nara Institute of Science and Technology, Japan.

Nawawan Panthumetha. 2010. Thai Grammar, vol. 5. Faculty of Arts, Chulalongkorn University, Thailand.

Nim Kanchanacheeva. 1996. Principles of Thai Language. Thai Watana Panich Press, Bangkok, Thailand.

Nitin Madnani and Bonnie J. Dorr. 2010. Generating Phraseal and Sentential Paraphrases: A Survey of Data-Driven Methods. Computational Linguistics, 36(3):341–387.

Pablo A. Duboue and Jennifer Chu-Carroll. 2006. Answering the Question YouWish They Had Asked: The Impact of Paraphrasing for Question Answering. in Proceedings of HLT-NAACL, pp. 33–36.

Penkhae Wongsiri. 1981. Thai Intransitive Verbs: A Study and Classification in Case Grammar. M. Arts Thesis, Department of Linguistics, Graduate School, Chulalongkorn University, Thailand.

Phanu Sungkhavon. 1984. Semantic Relationships between Nous and Verb in Thai Sentences. M. Arts Thesis, Department of Thai, Graduate School, Chulalongkorn University, Thailand.

Ponrudee Netisopakul. 1997. Alternative Solution to Language Divergences: Separation of Lexical Syntax from Lexical Semantics. 9th European Summer School in Logic, Language and Information (ESSLLI'97), PhD Workshop on Natural Language Generation.

Prayoon Songsilp. 2008. Principles and Using Thai Language, vol. 1. Dhonburi Rajabhat University, Bangkok, Thailand.

Prodromos Malakasiotis. 2011. Paraphrase and Textual Entailment Recognition and Generation. Ph.D. Dissertation, Department of Informatics, Athens University of Economics and Business, Greece.

Ray S. Jackendoff. 1990. Semantic Structures. MIT Press, Cambridge, Mass.

Regina Barzilay and Lillian Lee. 2003. Learning to Paraphrase: An Unsupervised Approach Using Multiple-Sequence Alignment. in Proceedings of HLT-NAACL 2003, vol. 1, pp. 16–23.

Raymond Kozlowski, Kathleen F. McCoy, and K. Vijay-Shanker. 2003. Generation of Single-Sentence Paraphrases from Predicate/Argument Structure Using Lexico-Grammatical Resources. PARAPHRASE '03 Proceedings of the Second International Workshop on Paraphrasing, vol. 16.

Shiqi Zhao, Xiang Lan, Ting Liu, and Sheng Li. 2009. Application-Driven Statistical Paraphrase Generation. in Proceedings of the 47th AnnualMeeting of the Association for Computational Linguistics (ACL) – the 4th International Joint Conference on Natural Language Processing of the Asian Federation of Natural Language Processing (IJCNLP), pp. 834–842.

Vipa Vongsantivanit. 1983. Causative Verbs in Thai. M. Arts Thesis, Department of Linguistics, Graduate School, Chulalongkorn University, Thailand.

Anaphora Annotation in Hindi Dependency TreeBank

Praveen Dakwale
LTRC, IIIT-H, India
dakwale.praveen@gmail.com

Himanshu Sharma
LTRC, IIIT-H, India
himanshu_s@students.iiit.ac.in

Dipti M Sharma
LTRC, IIIT-H, India
diptims@gmail.com

Abstract

In this paper, we propose a scheme for anaphora annotation in Hindi Dependency Treebank. The goal is to identify and handle the challenges that arise in the annotation of reference relations in Hindi. We identify some of the issues related to anaphora annotation specific to Hindi such as distribution of markable span, sequential annotation, representation format, annotation of multiple referents etc. The scheme hence incorporates some characteristics specific to these issues in order to achieve a consistent annotation. Most significant among these characteristics is the head-modifier separation in referent selection. The modifier-modified dependency relations inside a markable is utilized for this head-modifier distinction. A part of the Hindi Dependency Treebank, of around 2500 sentences has been annotated with anaphoric relations and an inter-annotator study was carried out which shows a significant agreement over selection of the head referent using the proposed scheme as compared to MUC annotation format. The current annotation is done for a limited set of pronominal categories.

1 Introduction

In this paper we present a scheme for annotating anaphoric relations in the Hindi Dependency TreeBank. Anaphora Resolution is one of the important problems in Natural Language Processing, and is used by various applications such as Text Summarization, Question answering etc. An anaphora annotated corpus along with other features (like POS, morph, Parse structure etc.) is required in both statistical as well as rule based anaphora resolution systems. Various corpus based studies of anaphoric variation also make use of such a corpus. While a significant number of corpora with anaphora annotation for English and other languages like Spanish, Czech etc. are available, for Indian languages, such corpora are scarce.

With a view of developing an Anaphora Resolution system in Hindi, our project aims at extending the dependency annotated (Hindi Dependency TreeBank) corpus with anaphoric relations. Hence we propose an anaphora annotation scheme in accordance with the representation format (SSF)(Bharati et al., 2007) of the Treebank, that uses attribute-value pairs to represent linguistic information. In this scheme, we attempt to address some of the issues that are commonly faced while annotating anaphora and require efficient handling. Although the scheme is developed while keeping in view the structure of the Dependency Tree-Bank, it is convertible to other formats of annotation as well.

In recent years, due to increasing interest in development of statistical systems for anaphora resolution, there have been significant attempts for creation of anaphora annotated corpora and annotation schemes. The most well known among these are MUC-7 annotation scheme (Hirschman and Chinchor, 1997) and other MUC based schemes, which are used for co-reference annotation via markup tags. The MATE/GNOME project has another important scheme suitable for different types of dialogue annotations (Poesio and Artstein, 2008). Kucova and Hajicova (2005) is also a notable work to-

wards annotating co-reference relations in a dependency TreeBank (Czech, PragueDT). Some other proposed schemes are, in Spanish and Catalan (Recasens et al., 2007; Navarro et al., 2004) and in Basque (Aduriz et al., 2004) for 3LB corpus. A known attempt for Hindi is, for demonstrative pronouns in EMILLE corpus (Sinha, 2002).The above mentioned schemes are used for anaphora annotation in English and various other languages.
The motivation behind proposing a new scheme is that some of the challenges like annotation of distributed referent span, annotation of multiple constituents, and identification of head and modifiers are difficult to handle in above mentioned schemes. Such challenges, though faced in various languages, are more frequent in Hindi. In this paper these issues are discussed in detail and an annotation scheme is proposed in order to handle them consistently.

2 Anaphora in Hindi

A significant amount of discussion about anaphora in Hindi is available in literature. However, in this section, we discuss the categorization of anaphoric relation and pronouns in Hindi that are considered while taking decisions regarding the annotation in this project.
First, we consider classification based on pronominal forms which includes personal pronouns and reflexives as two major classes. Personal pronouns in Hindi are a separate lexical category, with the exception of first person singular and plural forms. The third person forms are also the forms of demonstrative determiners. The pronoun forms reflect the categories of person, number and respect. They include मैं(I), हम(we), तुम(you sg), आप(you resp), वह(he/she/it distal), यह(it proxml). Determiner pronouns form a major category in Hindi which include demonstratives, relatives (जो which), indefinites and interrogatives(Davison, 2003). Pronoun forms are inflected for case according to the case marking system in Hindi. It should be noted here that in Hindi gender is not directly encoded in the pronoun, however it can be accessed from verb agreement in case of nominative usage. Reflexive pronouns, which form a major pronoun category in Hindi, are not marked for gender, number or person. They include अपने-आप, स्वयं, खुद representing 'self' for different persons.
Second, we consider classification based on reference type which includes abstract and concrete reference(Dipper and Zinsmeister, 2010). Abstract reference includes the cases where an anaphor refers to an event, proposition or clause, while in concrete reference an anaphor refers to a concrete(individual) entity like noun phrase(person,place etc), quantifiers etc. It is important to note here that in Hindi same pronoun can refer to both concrete as well as abstract anaphora. For the first phase of the annotation, we consider anaphoric relations to be annotated based on the ease of identification of the referent. Thus only concrete reference type is annotated because it is easier to identify the referent in this case as compared to that in abstract anaphora. Also, we do not consider demonstratives, null pronouns, gap, ellipsis because identification of referent in these cases is relatively difficult. Reference relations can also be classified on the basis of directionality i.e. anaphora as backward reference and cataphora as forward reference. In current annotation, while anaphoric references are annotated within and across sentences, only those cataphoric pronouns are annotated which have referent in the same sentence.

3 Hindi Dependency TreeBank

The 'Hindi/Urdu Dependency Treebank' is being developed as a part of the Multi-Representational and Multi-Layered Treebank for Hindi/Urdu (Bhatt et al., 2009). It is a rich corpus with various linguistic information like POS-tag, dependency relation,morphological features in the Treebank. In order to further enrich the corpus with anaphoric reference information, we intend to annotate anaphora relations as a layer on top of the dependency layer. In the representation format of the Treebank(SSF)(Bharati et al., 2007), the information on the node is of attribute-value type, where the features are represented as values of some pre-defined attributes (e.g. name, morph, dependency relation etc.). Since Dependency relations are inherently modifier-modified type, this property can be exploited to divide the markable into head and modifiers.

4 Annotation scheme

The design of the scheme is inspired by some of the issues involved with the format of the treebank data and problems faced while using other annotation schemes. In section 4.1 we discuss some of the problems that are faced while annotating anaphora using MUC scheme, we subsequently propose the solutions to these problems that we implemented in our scheme in Section 4.2. Section 4.3 describes some additional specifications that extend the basic annotation scheme.

4.1 Design Issues

4.1.1 Markable Identification

In most of the existing schemes, the markable identification is the first step in annotation(van Deemter and Kibble, 2000). Markables are the lexical expressions, acting as potential candidates which are either referred by another referring expression or can be part of a reference chain. Without consistent specification, higher disagreement can arise among the annotators about what could constitute a markable. For instance consider example(1), in which MUC scheme would allow a markable to consist of any continuous span with arbitrary length. Thus inconsistency could arise among annotators if there is disagreement on inclusion of even a single lexical element.

(1) मैंने मोहन के भाई की किताब
I.ERG mohan.GEN brother.POSS book
ली है । मै आज उसे पढ़ूंगा
have taken I.NOM today it.ACC will read

'I have taken Mohan's brother's book. I will read it today.'

In the above example possible markables for pronoun उसे(it) are : मोहन के भाई की किताब(Mohan's brother's book) , भाई की किताब(brother's book) and किताब(book). MUC handles this problem by considering all the above candidate markables as distinct referents, while they share common constituents. Thus there is a need to introduce an option in the scheme to represent this commonality.

4.1.2 Referent span identification

One of the most difficult problem faced while annotating anaphora is that of identifying the actual span of the referent for larger noun-phrases and named entities. This could also lead to increased disagreement in annotation because the length and content of the annotated span could differ depending on the comprehension by different annotators.

(2) राम के टूटे हुए हाथ का इलाज
ram.POSS broken hand.GEN treatment
अस्पताल में हो रहा है। उस पर
hospital.LOC be.PRS.CONT It.LOC
सोमवार तक पट्टी बंधी रहेगी।
monday till cast.NOM tie.FUT

Ram's broken hand is being treated in hospital. Cast will be tied over it till monday.

In example 2, There are 3 candidate referents of the pronoun उस पर(it) are : राम के टूटे हुए हाथ का(Ram's broken hand's) , टूटे हुए हाथ का(broken hand's) , हाथ का(hand's).

Using the MUC scheme different annotators could mark different candidates as the actual referent, thus leading to the disagreement.

However, it is much easier to identify the head of the possible referent with sufficient agreement. Also, most of the features required for anaphora resolution can be computed from the features of the head of the possible referent. For Example, in all the 3 candidates above, हाथ का (hand) is the head of the markable, and is most essential for identifying the correct referent entity.

4.1.3 Multiple Non-continuous Referents

Due to the relatively free word order of Hindi and frequent instances of gap, ellipsis, NP-coordination; cases have been observed in which there are multiple referents for a pronoun separated by intervening text-span.

(3) राम कल शाम मोहन के
Ram.NOM yesterday evening mohan.GEN
घर गया था। वे कई दिनों बाद
home went They many days after
एक दूसरे से मिले।
with each other met.

'Ram went to mohan's home yesterday evening. They met each other after many days.'

In example 3,the referent of pronoun: वे (They) includes both राम (Ram) and मोहन (Mohan).

To be able to mark the above mentioned constituents, the scheme must support annotation of multiple referents for an anaphora. However, such cases can not be handled by schemes like MUC that use simple co-indexing and marking of continuous spans.

4.1.4 Distributed referent span

In Hindi many instances are observed where the referent span is not continuous, instead, it is distributed over large distances. Such referent instances are difficult to annotate with MUC's co-indexing scheme, in which a continuous span is annotated as markable.

(4) बडा भाई कल आ रहा है मेरा ।
elder-brother tomorrow is coming my.
वह शनिवार को दिल्ली जायेगा ।
He saturday.TEMP delhi go.FUTURE .

'My elder brother is coming tomorrow. He will go to Delhi on Saturday'

In above example the referent of वह(He) is मेरा बडा भाई(my elder brother), but it is not possible to annotate it as one continuous span as used in MUC scheme.

(5) भारत की गिरती हुई अर्थव्यवस्था के लिए
India's falling economy.PURPOSE
केंद्र सरकार जिम्मेदार है । हालांकि
union-government responsible is. Though
पिछले दशक में यह काफी अच्छी स्थिति
in-last-decade it much better condition
में थी ।
in was.

'Union government is responsible for India's falling economy. Though in last decade it was in much better condition.'

Similarly, in example(5), the referent of pronoun यह(It) is भारत की अर्थव्यवस्था(India's economy) and this discontinuous referent span cannot be annotated here due to the occurrence of गिरती हुई(falling) in between.

4.1.5 Sequential annotation

Anaphors in discourse usually form chains that refer to a single entity. This evokes the issue of selection of a particular entry from the multiple previous occurrences of a single entity. The linguistic aspect of this problem addresses the issue of marking a referent that is bound to the anaphora(GB Theory). e.g. In case of reflexive, if a referent-anaphora pair occurs in a construction that inherently binds the anaphora to a particular occurrence of an entity, then it is suitable to select that occurrence as the referent. However, from a computational point of view, it is more efficient to select the nearest preceding occurrence of the entity as the referent of the anaphora because it reduces number of possible candidates for the referent of an anaphora in the previous discourse. This in turn adds to computational efficiency in anaphora resolution.

(6) जयसिंह मेवार के राजा थे ।
Jayasingh mewar.GEN king was.
वे एक महान शासक थे ।
He.NOM.HON a-great-ruler was.
उन्होंने जयपुर शहर की स्थापना की ।
He.NOM jayapur city founded.

'Jayasingh was king of mewar. He was a great ruler. He founded Jaipur city.'

In above example the referent of pronoun वे(He) in second sentence is जयसिंह(Jayasingh) in first sentence. Similarly उन्होंने(He.HON) refers to the same reference category. However, it is computationally efficient to annotate the referent of उन्होंने(He.HON) as वे(He) rather than जयसिंह(Jayasingh) since it is more nearer to उन्होंने(He.NOM), hence reducing the search space.

On the other hand consider example 7

(7) राम ने कहा कि अपनी गाडी चलाना
ram.ACC told that his car to drive
उसे पसंद है ।
he.ACC likes.

'Ram told that he likes to drive his car.'

Considering sequential annotation in example 7, राम(Ram) would be selected as the referent of अपनी(his). However, reflexive pronoun अपनी(his) is bound to उसे(he.ACC), thus it would be linguistically justified to select उसे(he.ACC) as the referent.

4.1.6 Representation

Hindi Dependency TreeBank comprises of feature structures that are associated with lexical and chunk nodes. In feature structures, information(POS, morph, dependency relation etc.) is represented in the form of attribute-value pairs. Thus, to keep the scheme consistent with the existing format, information about anaphoric relations should also be represented in the same format.

4.2 Basic Scheme Specification

4.2.1 Markable Identification

As a solution to Design Issue(Markable Identification)(Section 4.1.1), we consider chunk(Abney and Abney, 1991) to be the minimal unit of annotation. Firstly because , in Hindi dependency Treebank dependency structure has chunks[1] at node level and secondly, the features of the head element in a chunk projects its properties upto the chunk level. Chunks are already annotated with unique ids. Hence, for annotating markables, we opt to represent the markable span as a set of chunks instead of marking a continuous span. A referent span can minimally be a chunk, thus increasing the agreement by not allowing the span to be partial chunks. These chunks can later be grouped together using multiple value property. For instance, example(1) from section 4.1.1 can be chunked as follows :

(8) [$_{NP1}$ मैंने] [$_{NP2}$ मोहन के] [$_{NP3}$ भाई की]
I.ERG mohan.GEN brother.POSS
[$_{NP4}$ किताब] [$_{VGF1}$ ली है] ।[$_{NP5}$ मै]
book have taken I.NOM
[$_{NP6}$ आज] [$_{NP7}$ उसे] [$_{VGF1}$ पढ़ूंगा ।]
today it.ACC will read

'I have taken Mohan's brother's book. I will read it today.'

In above example, one of the possible markable is मोहन के भाई की किताब(Mohan's brother's book). This can be represented as a group of 3 chunks (NP2 + NP3 + NP4).

4.2.2 Reference Attributes

As discussed above in Section 4.1.2, it is easy to identify the head of the referent span as compared to the complete span. In our scheme we propose to separately annotate the easily identifiable head part (called head-referent) of the referent span and annotate the modifiers of the head-referent as a secondary information (called referent-modifiers). This could lead to a higher agreement for head-identification. For each possible anaphora, we annotate the reference information as attribute-value pairs in the feature structure of the anaphora. Two attributes have been introduced in the feature structure namely, *'ref'* to represent the head-referent and *'refmod'* to represent the referent-modifiers. The value of these attributes specifies the unique address(es) of the above elements respectively. The addressing in current annotation is via the global address of the chunk in the document. Thus re-considering example(2) annotated with chunk information as follows :

(9) [$_{NP1}$ राम के] [$_{VGNF1}$ टूटे हुए] [$_{NP2}$ हाथ का]
ram.POSS broken hand.GEN
[$_{NP3}$ इलाज] [$_{NP4}$ अस्पताल में] [$_{VGF1}$ हो
treatment hospital.LOC be
रहा है ।] [$_{NP5}$ उस पर] [$_{NP6}$ सोमवार तक]
PRS.CONT It.LOC monday till
[$_{NP7}$ पट्टी] [$_{VGF2}$ बंधी रहेगी ।]
Caste.NOM tie.FUT

Ram's broken hand is being treated in hospital. Caste will be tied over it till monday.

The modifiers of the head of the span can be identified by looking at the dependency structure of the referent span. The dependency structure for the span राम के टूटे हुए हाथ (Ram's broken hand) would be as follows :

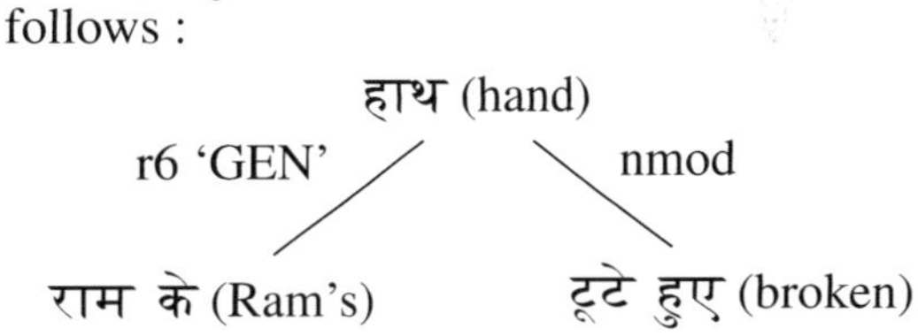

With the proposed scheme, if the pronoun (NP5) उस पर (It) has the referent राम के हाथ का, then it will be annotated as follows, since in this span हाथ का (NP2) is the head and राम के is the modifier :

उस पर <fs name='NP5' ref='NP2' refmod='NP1'>

Similarly if the pronoun (NP5) उस पर (It) has the referent टूटे हुए हाथ का (broken hand), than it will be annotated as follows :

उस पर <fs name='NP5' ref='NP2' refmod='VGNF1'>

[1]Hindi dependency treebank uses the definition of chunk as "A minimal (non recursive) phrase(partial structure) consisting of correlated,inseparable words/entities, such that the intra-chunk dependencies are not distorted"(Bharati et al., 2006)

Thus, we can see that even if different annotators identify different span for the referent, a significant agreement over the head could be achieved by separating head from the modifier.

The selection criteria for the modifiers can vary depending upon the extent of information marked and the type of problem being solved. A scheme may choose to mark only those referent-modifiers that are required to uniquely identify a referent, or it may choose to mark those referent-modifiers that help in establishing co-reference relations via lexical similarity.

4.2.3 Multiple Referents

As described in the design issues 4.1.3(Multiple Value Entries), an anaphor can have multiple head-referents. Multiple instances have been found where a part of the referent can be moved via scrambling, movement or where elements can be inserted in between. Thus it is natural to mark the referent in a way that enables maximum retrieval of information about the referent.

Chunks retain the head element feature structure and have a fixed word order internally, as is already established. Hence, by considering chunk as the minimal unit for anaphora referent annotation, it can be assured that multiple referents and their respective dependencies can be handled without any information loss. In order to annotate multiple referents, in the proposed scheme the chunk address/id of these multiple referents is specified in the '*ref*' attribute separated by a delimiter(comma). Thus reconsidering the chunked example 3 as follows :

(10) [$_{NP1}$ राम] [$_{NP2}$ कल शाम]
Ram.NOM yesterday evening
[$_{NP3}$ मोहन के] [$_{NP4}$ घर] [$_{VGF1}$ गया था।]
mohan.GEN home went
[$_{NP5}$ वे] [$_{NP6}$ कई दिनों बाद]
They many days after
[$_{NP7}$ एक दूसरे से] [$_{VGF2}$ मिले] ।
with each other met.

'Ram went to mohan's home yesterday evening. They met each other after many days.'

Thus, in above example, the feature structure of pronoun NP5(वे)(They) would be as follows:

वे <fs name='NP5' ref='NP1,NP3' refmod=''>

<ref='NP1,NP3'>implies that the pronoun has 2 head-referents, NP1 and NP3.

4.2.4 Multiple Referent-Modifiers

As discussed in section 4.1.4 (Distributed referent span), if a referent span is distributed discontiguously then it poses a problem in marking the exact span of the referent. Our scheme attempts to resolve this problem via marking the head with multiple modifiers. These modifiers are required for the correct interpretation of the pronoun; address values of all such modifier chunks are assigned in the 'refmod' attribute separated by a delimiter(/). Thus reconsidering example(4) as follows :

(11) [$_{NP1}$ बडा भाई] [$_{NP2}$ कल] [$_{VGF1}$ आ रहा है]
elder-brother tomorrow is
[$_{NP3}$ मेरा ।] [$_{NP4}$ वह] [$_{NP5}$ शनिवार को]
coming my.He Saturday.TEMP
[$_{NP6}$ दिल्ली] [$_{VGF2}$ जायेगा ।]
Delhi go.FUTURE .

'My elder brother is coming tomorrow. He will go to Delhi on Saturday'

In above example the referent of वह(He) is मेरा बडा भाई(my elder brother), where बडा भाई (brother)is the head and मेरा is the modifier. Hence it will be annotated as follows :

वह <fs name='NP4' ref='NP1' refmod='NP3' >

Similarly reconsidering example(5) as follows :

(12) [$_{NP1}$ भारत की] [$_{VGNF1}$ गिरती हुई]
India's falling
[$_{NP2}$ अर्थव्यवस्था के लिए] [$_{NP3}$ केंद्र सरकार]
economy.PURPOSE union-government
[$_{VGF1}$ जिम्मेदार है ।] [$_{NP4}$ हालांकि]
is responsible. Though
[$_{NP5}$ पिछले दशक में] [$_{NP6}$ यह]
in-last-decade it
[$_{NP7}$ काफी अच्छी स्थिति में] [$_{VGF2}$ थी ।]
in-much-better-condition was.

'Union government is responsible for India's falling economy. Though in last decade it was in much better condition.'

The referent of the pronoun NP6 (यह)(It) is (भारत की अर्थव्यवस्था)(India's economy). Head of the span NP2 (अर्थव्यवस्था)(economy) has two modifiers NP1 (भारत की) (India's) and VGNF1 (गिरती हुई)(falling) as shown in the diagram below :

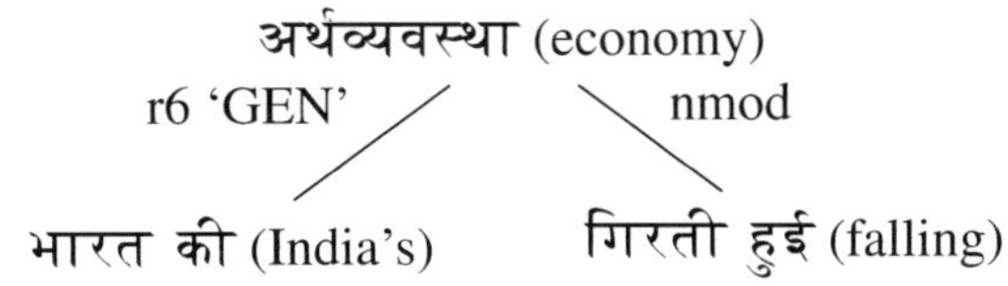

However, only NP1 is required as a modifier of NP2 for the correct interpretation of the pronoun. With the proposed scheme, we can annotate only those pronoun which are required in the referent span as shown below :

यह <fs name='NP6' ref='NP2' refmod='NP1' >

If in some case, both the modifiers are required for the interpretation of the pronoun than both the modifiers can be included in 'refmod' attribute as follows :

यह <fs name='NP6' ref='NP2'
refmod='NP1/VGNF1' >

4.2.5 Sequential annotation

In view of the computational efficiency, as discussed in section 4.1(Sequential annotation), we adopt chain marking for anaphora annotation in this scheme. That is, if an entity is referred by more than one pronouns or has repeated mentions in a discourse, then for each pronoun, we annotate the last mention of the corresponding referent-entity as the antecedent.
However, in cases where marking the nearest occurrence of the entity as referent, is not linguistically justified; the scheme allows to annotate the bound entity as the referent. Thus consider example(6) can be reconsidered as follows :

(13) [$_{NP1}$ जयसिंह] [$_{NP2}$ मेवार के] [$_{NP3}$ राजा]
Jayasinh mewar.GEN king
[$_{VGF1}$ थे ।] [$_{NP4}$ वे] [$_{NP5}$ एक महान शासक]
was. He a-great-ruler
[$_{VGF2}$ थे ।] [$_{NP6}$ उन्होंने] [$_{NP7}$ जयपुर]
was. He.NOM jayapur
[$_{NP8}$ शहर की] [$_{VGF3}$ स्थापना की ।]
city founded.

'Jayasingh was king of mewar. He was a great ruler. He founded Jaipur city.'

The referent of pronoun NP4 (वे)(He)in second sentence is NP1 (जयसिंह)(Jayasingh) in first sentence. Similarly NP6 (उन्होंने)(He) refers to the same reference category. However, it is computationally efficient to annotate the referent of NP6 as NP4 rather than NP1 since it is more nearer to NP6, hence reducing the search space. Considering sequential annotation, we annotate the pronouns NP4 and NP6 as follows

वे <fs name='NP4' ref='NP1' refmod='' >
उन्होंने <fs name='NP6' ref='NP4' refmod='' >

On the other hand consider example 7 :

(14) [$_{NP1}$ राम ने] कहा कि [$_{NP2}$ अपनी] गाडी
ram.ACC told that his car
चलाना [$_{NP3}$ उसे] पसंद है ।
to drive he.ACC likes.

'Ram told that he likes to drive his car.'

Considering sequential annotation in above example, NP1(राम ने)(Ram) would be selected as the referent of NP2(अपनी)(his). However, reflexive pronoun NP2(अपनी)(his) is bound to NP3(उसे)(he.ACC), thus it would be linguistically justified to select NP3(उसे)(he.ACC) as the referent.

Hence in this example the referent of NP2(अपनी)(his) will be NP3(उसे)(he.ACC) and the referent of NP3(उसे)(he.ACC) will be NP1(राम)(Ram), with the feature structure as follows :

अपनी <fs name='NP2' ref='NP3' refmod='' >
उसे <fs name='NP3' ref='NP1' refmod='' >

4.3 Extended Scheme Specification

In this section we further describe the extended specification of the scheme that can be used to handle cases of abstract anaphora, co-reference and can be used to add additional information tags like type of anaphora, reference type, direction etc.

4.3.1 Handling Abstract Anaphora

For cases in which the referent is an event or a proposition, the main verb is marked as the referent (*'ref'*). The *'refmod'* takes the participants (modifiers) of the verb as it's values. It can either take all the participants of the event as it's values, or it can choose to take only those that are required for the correct interpretation of the referent of the abstract anaphora.

(15) [$_{NP1}$ राम ने] [$_{NP2}$ मोहन को] [$_{NP3}$ पुरानी
Ram.ERG Mohan.DAT old
गाडी] [$_{NP4}$ ऊंचे दाम में] [$_{VGF1}$ बेची ।]
car high price-in sold
[$_{NP5}$ इससे] [$_{NP6}$ उसे] [$_{NP7}$ 5 लाख रुपए का]
Due-to-this he.DAT 5-lakh-Rs.GEN
[$_{NP8}$ लाभ] [$_{VGF2}$ हुआ ।]
profit be.PST

'Ram sold an old car to Mohan at a high price. Due to this he made a profit of 5 Lakh Rs.'

In example 6, the complete referent span is NP3+NP4+VGF1 (पुरानी गाडी ऊंचे दाम में बेची), but the head-referent is the verb VGF1 (बेची) and NP3(पुरानी गाडी), NP4(ऊंचे दाम में) are the referent-modifiers. The feature structure for pronoun NP5(इससे) is as follows :

इससे <fs name='NP5' ref='VGF1' refmod='NP3\NP4'>

Note that only NP3 and NP4 are considered in the *'refmod'* attribute, because only these modifiers are required for the correct interpretation of the anaphoric relation.

4.3.2 Handling Co-reference

With the above scheme, the co-reference relations can also be annotated. In the case of co-reference, the value of the ref attribute would take the address/id(s) of the lexical items it co-refers with. However, including the addresses of all the lexical items (which may be large in number) can make the value field very lengthy. To avoid this, span marking is introduced. In span marking, the value contains the address of the starting and the ending lexical item joined by a delimiter(semicolon).

4.3.3 Additional Tags

Along with the reference attributes, additional tags could be incorporated in the feature structure which provide information about the anaphoric relation. Some of the important tags are :

- Pronoun Type : Personal, Reflexive, Relative, Co-relative, Indefinite.
- Referent Type : Concrete, Abstract.
- Direction : Cataphora, Anaphora.

5 Corpus Annotation and Applications

5.1 Annotation Work

In the first part of this project, 162 news items from the Treebank were considered for annotation. They contain 2477 sentences with 2122 instances of pronouns, out of which 1408 pronouns have been annotated till date. The remaining 714 pronouns were identified, but have not been annotated for the first part of annotation.

5.2 Inter-Annotator Study

We conducted Inter-Annotation studies in order to verify a higher consistency of the proposed scheme, as compared to the MUC-7 annotation framework which is commonly used for Co-reference and anaphora annotation. We divide the study in two parts as follows :

5.2.1 Experiment 1

As stated in Section 2, only Concrete reference types were annotated in the first phase of the annotation. However, in Hindi same lexical pronoun can refer to Concrete as well as Abstract reference entity and many a times it becomes difficult to identify this distinction. We first establish this by conducting an experiment which involves annotating the category of a reference type as 'Concrete','Abstract',or 'Other'(including the exo-phoric and indefinite reference types). Fleiss's Kappa (Fleiss, 1971) is used to calculate the agreement, which is a commonly used measure for calculating agreement over multiple annotators. Table 1 shows the method to interpret kappa values
The Fleiss's kappa is calculated as :

$$\kappa = \frac{Pr(a) - Pr(e)}{1 - Pr(e)} \quad (1)$$

The factor 1 - Pr(e) gives the degree of agreement that is attainable above chance, and, Pr(a) - Pr(e) gives the degree of agreement actually achieved above chance.

We conducted the experiment over 29 news items from the Treebank containing 446 identified pronouns across annotations by 3 raters. Annotators were asked to assign one of the three categories, as

Kappa Statistic	Strength of agreement
<0.00	Poor
0.0-0.20	Slight
0.21-0.40	Fair
0.41-0.60	Moderate
0.61-0.80	Substantial
0.81-1.00	Almost perfect

Table 1: Coefficients for the agreement-rate based on (Landis and Koch, 1977).

No. of Annotations	Agreement	Pr(a)	Pr(e)	Kappa
446	353	0.856	0.435	0.746

Table 2: Kappa statistics for Category experiment

stated above, according to the type of entity it refers to. Table 2 summarizes the experiment's results.

The non-perfect agreement for this experiment establishes that the type of the referent of a pronoun is ambiguous and hard to determine in many cases. Hence, to avoid inconsistencies in the distinction of Concrete, Abstract and Other types of reference; we separate out the concrete references in the above used data for the comparative study of the proposed scheme with MUC. We consider agreement over those pronouns in Experiment 2, for which all the annotators have a perfect agreement in concrete category.

5.2.2 Experiment 2

In the second experiment the inter-annotator analysis is conducted for the concrete pronouns separated in Experiment 1. Krippendorff's alpha (Krippendorff, 2004) was then used as a statistical measure to obtain the inter-annotator agreement. As suggested in (Passonneau, 2004) and (Poesio and Artstein, 2005) Krippendorff's alpha is a better metrics for calculating agreement for co-reference/anaphora annotation as compared to other metrics because it considers degrees of disagreement and in anaphora it is difficult to define discrete categories. Similar to (Passonneau, 2004) we consider co-reference chain as discrete categories. Experiment (2) also invloved the same data and the same raters who carries out annotation in experiment (1). Krippendorff's alpha is defined as follows :

Statistics	MUC-7	Proposed Scheme
No. of Annotations	239	239
alpha	0.825	0.880

Table 3: Krippendorff alpha agreements

$$\alpha = 1 - \frac{Do}{De} \tag{2}$$

$$Do = \frac{1}{i * c(c-1)} \sum_{i \in I} \sum_{k \in K} \sum_{k' \in K'} \mathbf{n}_{ik} \mathbf{n}_{ik'} \mathbf{d}_{kk'} \tag{3}$$

$$De = \frac{1}{i * c((i * c) - 1)} \sum_{k \in K} \sum_{k' \in K'} \mathbf{n}_k \mathbf{n}_{k'} \mathbf{d}_{kk'} \tag{4}$$

where **I** = set of all items of annotation, **K** = set of categories, $\mathbf{n}_{ik}$ = number of times item i is given the value k, $\mathbf{n}_k$ = any number of times any item is given the value k, **i** = no. of items to be annotated, **c** = no. of annotators

The distance measure $d_{kk'}$ is defined as

$$d_{kk'} = \begin{cases} 0 & \text{if k and k' are exactly same chains} \\ 0.33 & \text{if k is a subset of k' or vice versa} \\ 0.66 & \text{if there is at least one element common between k and k'} \\ 1 & \text{if intersection of k and k' is empty} \end{cases}$$

Table 3 shows the statistics obtained for the MUC annotation and with the proposed scheme.

As shown in table 3, there is a significant increase in the Krippendorff's alpha agreement over the proposed annotation scheme, as compared to the MUC annotation scheme. This indicates that the proposed scheme with the separation of head and modifiers in the referent span helps in achieving a consistent agreement than the continuous span annotation scheme used in MUC.

5.3 Applications

The annotated data is convertible to other formats like MUC, CONLL etc. The dataset was also used for ICON-2011 Anaphora Resolution Tool Contest in Indian Languages after conversion to the required format. A hybrid anaphora resolution system reported an average F1-score of 52.20 (ranked 1st for Hindi) using the annotated corpus for Hindi.

6 Conclusion and Future Work

In this paper we described a scheme for annotating anaphora information as a layer in Hindi Dependency Treebank. The main contribution of this paper is to discuss language specific issues that occur in anaphora annotation and outline a scheme that handles them efficiently. The identified issues relate to representation format, referent span identification etc. Decisions like sequential annotation and subtree inheritance help in reducing the computational complexity in resolution systems. The comparative inter-annotator analysis of the proposed scheme verifies that the separation of the referent span, and other features help to achieve a consistent annotation by increasing the inter-annotator agreement. The scheme can be extended for co-reference and the annotated data is convertible to other annotation formats like MUC etc.

For the purpose of this paper we have annotated concrete anaphora as described in section(2). As a further step in the project we aim to annotate abstract anaphora and co-reference relations. Also, anaphoric instances of gaps, ellipsis and demonstratives are to be included in the next phase of annotation. While the experimental results shows that proposed scheme performs well as compared to MUC format, in the future we plan to suggest improvement over MUC shceme to handle the issues discussed in this paper.

References

Steven Abney and Steven P. Abney. 1991. Parsing by chunks. In *Principle-Based Parsing*, pages 257–278. Kluwer Academic Publishers.

Itziar Aduriz, Klara Ceberio, Euskal Herriko Unibertsitatea, and Daz de Ilarraza. 2004. Pronominal anaphora in basque: annotation of a real corpus. *Procesamiento del lenguaje natural*, pages 99–104.

Akshar Bharati, Dipti Misra Sharma, Lakshmi Bai, and Rajeev Sangal. 2006. Anncorra : Annotating corpora guidelines for pos and chunk annotation for indian languages. Technical report, LTRC, IIIT-Hyderabad.

Akshar Bharati, Rajeev Sangal, and Dipti M Sharma, 2007. *SSF: Shakti Standard Format Guide*. LTRC, IIIT-Hyderabad, India.

Rajesh Bhatt, Owen Rambow, Bhuvana Narasimhan, Dipti Misra Sharma, Martha Palmer, and Fei Xia. 2009. A multi-representational and multi-layered treebank for hindi/urdu. In *Proceedings of the Third Linguistic Annotation Workshop, ACL-IJCNLP*.

Alice Davison. 2003. Lexical anaphors and pronouns in hindi. In *Lexical Anaphors and Pronouns in Selected South Asian Languages: A Principled Typology*.

S. Dipper and H Zinsmeister. 2010. Towards a standard for annotating abstract anaphora. In *LREC 2010 Workshop on Language Resources and Language Technology Standards*, pages 54–59, Valletta, Malta.

J.L. Fleiss. 1971. Measuring nominal scale agreement among many raters. *Psychological bulletin*, 76(5):378.

Lynette Hirschman and Nancy Chinchor. 1997. Muc7 coreference task definition. In *Message Understanding Conference*.

K. Krippendorff. 2004. *Content analysis: An introduction to its methodology*. Sage Publications, Inc.

Lucie Kucova and Eva Hajicova. 2005. Coreferential relations in the prague dependency treebank. In *Proceedings of the 5th International Conference on Discourse Anaphora and Anaphor Resolution*.

J.R. Landis and G.G. Koch. 1977. The measurement of observer agreement for categorical data. *Biometrics*, pages 159–174.

Borja Navarro, Ruben Izquierdo, and Maximiliano Saiz-Noeda. 2004. Exploiting semantic information for manual anaphoric annotation in cast3lb corpus. In *ACL 2004 Workshop on Discourse Annotation*.

R.J. Passonneau. 2004. Computing reliability for coreference annotation. In *Proceedings of LREC*, volume 4, pages 1503–1506.

M. Poesio and R. Artstein. 2005. Annotating (anaphoric) ambiguity. In *In Proc. of the Corpus Linguistics Conference*.

Massimo Poesio and Ron Artstein. 2008. Anaphoric annotation in the arrau corpus. In *LREC*.

Marta Recasens and Maria Antnia Mart. 2010. Ancora-co: Coreferentially annotated corpora for spanish and catalan. *Language Resources and Evaluation*, 44:315–345.

Marta Recasens, M. Antonia Marti, and Mariona Taule. 2007. Where anaphora and coreference meet. annotation in the spanish cess-ece corpus. *Proceedings of RANLP*.

Srija Sinha. 2002. A corpus-based account of anaphor resolution in hindi. Masters thesis, University of Lancaster, UK.

Kees van Deemter and Rodger Kibble. 2000. On coreferring: Coreference in muc and related annotation schemes. *Computational Linguistics*, 26:629–637.

Improving Statistical Machine Translation with Processing Shallow Parsing

Hoai-Thu Vuong, Vinh Van Nguyen
University of Engineering and Technology,
Vietnam National University
144, Xuan Thuy, Cau Giay , Hanoi
{thuvh, vinhnv}@vnu.edu.vn

Viet Hong Tran
Department of Information Technology
University Of Economic And Technical Industries
456 Minh Khai, Hai Ba Trung, Hanoi
thviet@uneti.edu.vn

Akira Shimazu
Japan Advanced Institute of Science and Technology
1-1, Asahidai, Nomi, Ishikawa, 923-1292, Japan
shimazu@jaist.ac.jp

Abstract

Reordering is of essential importance for phrase based statistical machine translation (SMT). In this paper, we would like to present a new method of reordering in phrase based SMT. We inspired from (Xia and McCord, 2004) using preprocessing reordering approaches. We used shallow parsing and transformation rules to reorder the source sentence. The experiment results from English-Vietnamese pair showed that our approach achieves significant improvements over MOSES which is the state-of-the art phrase based system.

1 Introduction

In SMT, the reordering problem (global reordering) is one of the major problems, since different languages have different word order requirements. The SMT task can be viewed as two subtasks: predicting the collection of words in a translation, and deciding the order of the predicted words (reordering problem). Currently, phrase-based statistical machine translation (Koehn et al., 2003; Och and Ney, 2004) is the state-of-the-art of SMT because of its power in modelling short reordering and local context.

However, with phrase based SMT, long distance reordering is still problematic. In order to tackle the long distance reordering problem, in recent years, huge research efforts have been conducted using syntactic information. There are some studies on integrating syntactic resources within SMT. Chiang (Chiang, 2005) shows significant improvement by keeping the strengths of phrases, while incorporating syntax into SMT. Some approaches have been applied at the word-level (Collins et al., 2005). They are particularly useful for language with rich morphology, for reducing data sparseness. Other kinds of syntax reordering methods require parser trees , such as the work in (Quirk et al., 2005; Collins et al., 2005; Huang and Mi, 2010). The parsed tree is more powerful in capturing the sentence structure. However, it is expensive to create tree structure, and building a good quality parser is also a hard task. All the above approaches require much decoding time, which is expensive.

The approach we are interested in here is to balance the quality of translation with decoding time. Reordering approaches as a preprocessing step (Xia and McCord, 2004; Xu et al., 2009; Talbot et al., 2011; Katz-Brown et al., 2011) is very effective (improvement significant over state of-the-art phrase-based and hierarchical machine translation systems and separately quality evaluation of reordering models).

Inspiring this preprocessing approach, we have proposed a combine approach which preserves the strength of phrase-based SMT in local reordering and decoding time as well as the strength of integrating syntax in reordering. Consequently, we use an intermediate syntax between POS tag and parse tree: shallow parsing. Firstly, we use shallow parsing for preprocessing with training and testing. Second, we apply a series of transformation rules which are learnt automatically from parallel corpus to the shallow tree. The experiment results from English-Vietnamese pair showed that our approach achieves significant improvements over MOSES which is the state-of-the art phrase based system.

The rest of this paper is structured as follows. Section 2 reviews the related works. Section 3 briefly introduces phrase-based SMT. Section 4 introduces how to apply transformation rules to the shallow tree. Section 5 describes and discusses the experimental results. And, conclusions are given in Section 6.

2 Related works

As mentioned in section 1, some approaches using syntactic information are applied to solve the reordering problem. One of approaches is syntactic parsing of source language and reordering rules as preprocessing steps. The main idea is transferring the source sentences to get very close target sentences in word order as possible, so EM training is much easier and word alignment quality becomes better. There are several studies to improve reordering problem such as (Xia and McCord, 2004; Collins et al., 2005; Nguyen and Shimazu, 2006; Wang et al., 2007; Habash, 2007; Xu et al., 2009).

They all performed reordering during preprocessing step based on the source tree parsing combining either automatic extracted syntactic rules (Xia and McCord, 2004; Nguyen and Shimazu, 2006; Habash, 2007) or handwritten rules (Collins et al., 2005; Wang et al., 2007; Xu et al., 2009).

(Xu et al., 2009) described method using dependency parse tree and a flexible rule to perform the reordering of subject, object, etc... These rules were written by hand, but (Xu et al., 2009) showed that an automatic rule learner can be used.

(Collins et al., 2005) developed a clause detection and used some handwritten rules to reorder words in the clause. Partly, (Xia and McCord, 2004; Habash, 2007) built an automatic extracted syntactic rules.

Compared with theses approaches, our work has a few differences. Firstly, we aim to develop the phrase-based translation model to translate from English to Vietnamese. Secondly, we build a shallow tree by chunking in recursively (chunk of chunk). Thirdly, we use not only the automatic rules, but also some handwritten rules, to transform the source sentence. As the same with (Xia and McCord, 2004; Habash, 2007), we also apply preprocessing in both training and decoding time.

The other approaches use syntactic parsing to provide multiple source sentence reordering options through word (phrase) lattices (Zhang et al., 2007; Nguyen et al., 2007). (Nguyen et al., 2007) applied some transformation rules, which is learnt automatically from bilingual corpus, to reorder some words in a chunk. A crucial difference between their methods and ours is that they do not perform reordering during training. While, our method can solve this problem by using a complicated structure, which is more efficient with a shallow tree (chunk of chunks).

3 Brief description of the baseline Phrase-based SMT

In this section, we will describe the phrase-based SMT system which was used for the experiments. Phrase-based SMT, as described by (Koehn et al., 2003) translates a source sentence into a target sentence by decomposing the source sentence into a sequence of source phrases, which can be any contiguous sequences of words (or tokens treated as words) in the source sentence. For each source phrase, a target phrase translation is selected, and the target phrases are arranged in some order to produce the target sentence. A set of possible translation candidates created in this way is scored according to a weighted linear combination of feature values, and the highest scoring translation candidate is selected as the translation of the source sentence. Symbolically,

$$\hat{t} = \arg\max_{t,a} \sum_{i=1}^{n} \lambda_i f_j(s,t,a) \qquad (1)$$

when s is the input sentence, t is a possible output sentence, and a is a phrasal alignment that specifies how t is constructed from s, and $\hat{t}$ is the selected output sentence. The weights λ_i associated with each feature f_i are tuned to maximize the quality of the translation hypothesis selected by the decoding procedure that computes the argmax. The log-linear model is a natural framework to integrate many features. The baseline system uses the following features:

- the probability of each source phrase in the hypothesis given the corresponding target phrase.

- the probability of each target phrase in the hypothesis given the corresponding source phrase.
- the lexical score for each target phrase given the corresponding source phrase.
- the lexical score for each source phrase given the corresponding target phrase.
- the target language model probability for the sequence of target phrase in the hypothesis.
- the word and phrase penalty score, which allow to ensure that the translation does not get too long or too short.
- the distortion model allows for reordering of the source sentence.

The probabilities of source phrase given target phrases, and target phrases given source phrases, are estimated from the bilingual corpus.

(Koehn et al., 2003) used the following distortion model (reordering model), which simply penalizes nonmonotonic phrase alignment based on the word distance of successively translated source phrases with an appropriate value for the parameter α:

$$d(a_i - b_{i-1}) = \alpha^{|a_i - b_{i-1} - 1|} \quad (2)$$

4 Shallow Syntactic Preprocessing for SMT

In this section, we describe the transformation rules and how applying it to shallow tree for reordering an English sentence.

4.1 Transformation Rule

Suppose that T_s is a given lexicalized tree of the source language (whose nodes are augmented to include a word and a POS label). T_s contains n applications of lexicalized CFG rules $LHS_i \rightarrow RHS_i$ ($i \in \overline{1,n}$). We want to transform T_s into the target language word order by applying transformational rules to the CFG rules. A transformational rule is represented as ($LHS \rightarrow RHS, RS$), which is a pair consisting of an unlexicalized CFG rule and a reordering sequence (RS). For example, the rule (NP $\rightarrow$ JJ NN, 1 0) implies that the CFG rule (NP$\rightarrow$ JJ NN) in the source language can be transformed into the rule (NP$\rightarrow$NN JJ) in the target language. Since the possible transformational rule for each CFG rule is not unique, there can be many transformed trees. The problem is how to choose the best one (we can see (Nguyen and Shimazu, 2006) for a description in more details). We use the method described in (Nguyen and Shimazu, 2006) to extract the transformation rules from the parallel corpus and induce the best sequence of transformation rules for a source tree. Besides, we also built a small set of transformation rules by hand (the handwritten rules).

4.2 Shallow Syntactic Processing

In this section, we describe a method to build a translation model for a pair English to Vietnamese. We aim to reorder an English sentence to get a new English, and some words in this sentence are arranged as Vietnamese words order.

tom	's	[two	blue	books]
tom	's	[two	books	blue]
[two	books	blue]	's	tom
hai	cuốn sách	màu xanh	của	tom

Figure 1: An Example of phrase before and after our preprocessing

Figure 1 gives examples of original and preprocessed phrase in English. The first line is the original English phrase with a chunk (two blue books), and the second line is the phrase with a modified chunk (two books blue). This chunk is arranged as the Vietnamese order. However, we aim to preprocess the words outside the chunk (the phrase "tom 's" in Figure 1), and the third line is the output of our method. Finally, the fourth line is the Vietnamese phrase. As you can see, the third and fourth line have the same word order.

After pre-processed, this new sentence is used in training process to get a phrased translation model, and in decoding process to get a target sentence (by using translation which is trained in training process). To preprocess, we follow these steps:

- building shallow syntactic

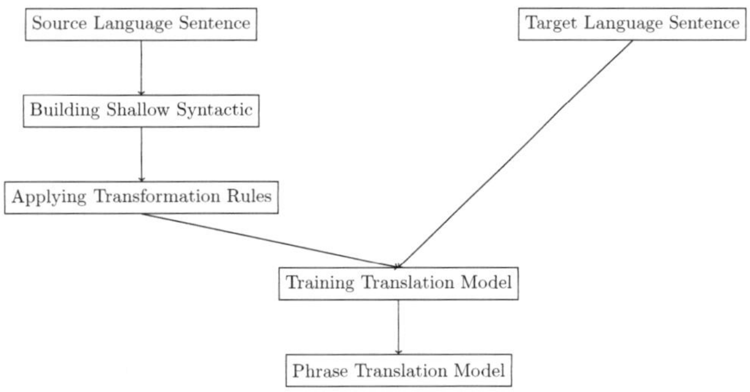

Figure 2: Our training process

- applying transformation rules

So as to build shallow syntactic, we use a method described in (Tsuruoka et al., 2009). Their approach introduced the method to parse an English sentence by using chunking (balance accuracy with speed time). Their method is high accuracy (accuracy with 88.4 F-score) and fast parsing time: using CRFTagger to chunk the sentence, and then setup a tree from the chunks and recursive until they cannot chunk the sentence. Their result showed that this method is outstanding in performance with high accuracy. As they did, we also receive a shallow syntactic when parse the source sentence in English. However, we stop chunking after two loop steps. So that, *the highest deep of node in syntactic tree is two*. By doing that, we will balance between accuracy and performance time. We can use the method of (Tsuruoka et al., 2009) to build full parse tree, but that will be leave it for future work.

After building the shallow syntactic, the transformation rules are applied. After finding the matching rule from the top of the shallow tree, we arrange the words in the English sentence, which is covered by the matching node, like Vietnamese words order. And then, we do the same for each children of this node. If any rule is applied, we use the order of original sentence. Not only rule is learnt automatically from bilingual corpora, we also try applying handwritten rules.

5 Experiment

5.1 Implementation

- We developed the shallow parsing by using the method from (Tsuruoka et al., 2009) to parse a source sentences (English sentences) including a shallow tree.

- The rules are learnt from English-Vietnamese parallel corpus and Penntree Bank Corpus. We used the CFG transformation rules (chunk levels) for extraction from (Nguyen and Shimazu, 2006)'s method to reorder shallow tree of a source sentences.

- We implemented preprocessing step during both training and decoding time.

- Using the SMT Moses decoder (Koehn et al., 2007) for decoding.

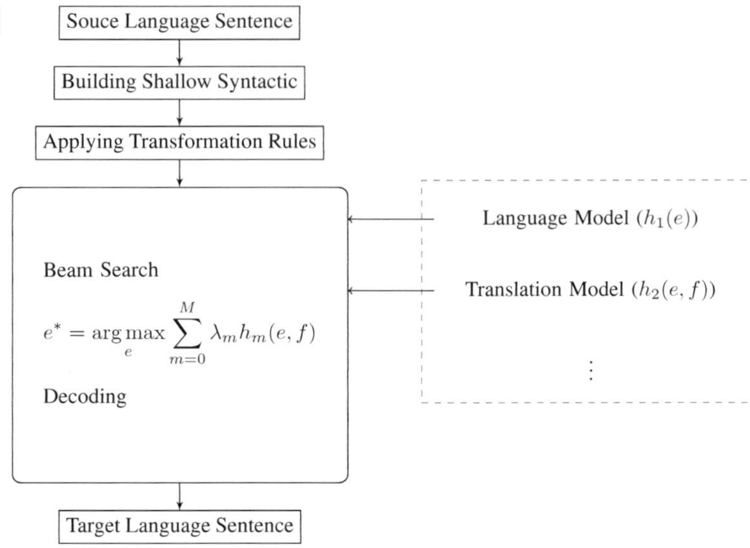

Figure 3: Our decoding process

5.2 Data set and Experimental Setup

For evaluation, we used an English-Vietnamese corpus (Nguyen et al., 2008), including about 54642 pairs for training, 500 pairs for testing and 200 pairs for development test set. Table 1 gives more statistical information about our corpora. We conducted some experiments with SMT Moses Decoder (Koehn et al., 2007) and SRILM (Stolcke, 2002). We trained a trigram language model using interpolate and kndiscount smoothing with 89M Vietnamese mono corpus. Before extracting phrase table, we use GIZA++ (Och and Ney, 2003) to build word alignment with grow-diag-final-and algorithm.

Corpus	Sentence pairs	Training Set	Development Set	Test Set
General	55341	54642	200	499

		English	Vietnamese
Training	Sentences	54620	
	Average Length	11.2	10.6
	Word	614578	580754
	Vocabulary	23804	24097
Development	Sentences	200	
	Average Length	11.1	10.7
	Word	2221	2141
	Vocabulary	825	831
Test	Sentences	499	
	Average Length	11.2	10.5
	Word	5620	6240
	Vocabulary	1844	1851

Table 1: Corpus Statistical

Besides using preprocessing, we also used default reordering model in Moses Decoder: using word-based extraction (wbe), splitting type of reodering orientation to three class (monotone, swap and discontinuous – msd), combining backward and forward direction (bidirectional) and modeling base on both source and target language (fe) (Koehn et al., 2007). First system in 2 is our baseline system. The second and the third system are the baseline system which is applied the transformation rules (include the automatic and handwritten rules). In these experiments, we only use the chunking level. The fifth experiment is the result of our works: applied automatic transformation rules into shallow syntactic. By doing these experiments, we can show the effective of our method. In addition, we also did the fourth and sixth experiment with a specific parameter for the MOSES Decoder (monotone). By using this flag, we will discard the distortion model, so that, the decoder only do monotone decode.

5.3 BLEU score

The result of our experiments in table 3 showed our applying transformation rule to process the source sentences. Thanks to this method, we can find out various phrases in the translation model. So that, they enable us to have more options for decoder to generate the best translation.

Table 4 describes the BLEU score (Papineni et al., 2002) of our experiments. As we can see, by applying preprocess in both training and decoding, the BLEU score of our best system increase by 0.82 point "Baseline + AR (shallow syntactic)" system) over "Baseline system". Improvement over 0.82 BLEU point is valuable because baseline system is the strong phrase based SMT (integrating lexicalized reordering models). The improvement of "Baseline + AR (shallow syntactic)" system is statistically significant at $p < 0.01$.

System	BLEU (%)
Baseline	36.84
Baseline + MR	37.33
Baseline + AR	37.24
Baseline + AR (monotone)	35.80
Baseline + AR (shallow syntactic)	**37.66**
Baseline + AR (shallow syntactic + monotone)	37.43

Table 4: Translation performance for the English-Vietnamese task

We also carried out the experiments with handwritten rules. Using some handwritten rules help the phrased translation model generate some best translation more than the automatic rules. Besides, the result proved that the effect of applying transformation rule on the shallow syntactic when the BLEU score is highest. Because, the cover of handwritten rules is larger than the automatic rules.

Furthermore, handwritten rule is made by human, and focus on popular cases. So that, we get some

Name	Description
Baseline	Phrase-based system
Baseline + MR	Phrase-based system with corpus which is preprocessed using handwritten rules
Baseline + AR	Phrase-based system with corpus which is preprocessed using automatic learning rules
Baseline + AR (monotone)	Phrase-based system with corpus which is preprocessed using automatic learning rules and decoded by monotone decoder
Baseline + AR(shallow syntactic)	Phrase-based system with corpus which is shallow syntactic analyze and applied automatic transformation rules
Baseline + AR(shallow syntactic+monotone)	Phrase-based system with corpus which is shallow syntactic analyze and applied automatic transformation rules

Table 2: Details of our experimental, AR is named as using automatic rules, MR is named as using handwritten rules

Name	Size of phrase-table
Baseline	1237568
Baseline + MR	1251623
Baseline + AR	1243699
Baseline + AR (monotone)	1243699
Baseline + AR (shallow syntactic)	**1279344**
Baseline + AR (shallow syntactic + monotone)	1279344

Table 3: Size of phrase tables

pair of sentences with the best alignment, and then, we can extract more and better phrase tables. Finally, the BLEU score of using monotone decoder decrease by 1% when we use preprocessing in only base chunk level, and our shallow syntactic decreased a bit. As, the default reordering model in baseline system is better than in this experiment[1].

6 Conclusion

In this paper, we would like to present a new method for reordering in phrase based SMT. We inspired from (Xia and McCord, 2004) using preprocessing reordering approaches. We used shallow parsing and transformation rules for reordering the source sentence. Meanwhile, we limit the height of syntactic tree to balance the accuracy with performance of system. The experiment results with English-Vietnamese pair showed that our approach achieves significant improvements over MOSES which is the state-of-the art phrase based system. In the future, we would like to evaluate our method with tree with higher and deeper syntactic structure and larger size of corpus.

[1]The reordering model in the monotone decoder is distance based, introduced in (Koehn et al., 2003). This model is a default reordering model in Moses Decoder (Koehn et al., 2007)

Acknowledgment

This work described in this paper has been partially funded by Hanoi National University (QG.12.49 project) and the Vietnam National Foundation for Science and Technology Development (Nafosted).

References

David Chiang. 2005. A hierarchical phrase-based model for statistical machine translation. In *Proceedings of the 43rd Annual Meeting of the Association for Computational Linguistics (ACL'05)*, pages 263–270, Ann Arbor, Michigan, June.

M. Collins, P. Koehn, and I. Kucerová. 2005. Clause restructuring for statistical machine translation. In *Proc. ACL 2005*, pages 531–540. Ann Arbor, USA.

N. Habash. 2007. Syntactic preprocessing for statistical machine translation. *Proceedings of the 11th MT Summit.*

Liang Huang and Haitao Mi. 2010. Efficient incremental decoding for tree-to-string translation. In *Proceedings* of the 2010 Conference on Empirical Methods in Natural Language Processing, pages 273–283, Cambridge, MA, October. Association for Computational Linguistics.

Jason Katz-Brown, Slav Petrov, Ryan McDonald, Franz Och, David Talbot, Hiroshi Ichikawa, Masakazu Seno, and Hideto Kazawa. 2011. Training a parser for machine translation reordering. In *Proceedings of the 2011 Conference on Empirical Methods in Natural Language Processing*, pages 183–192, Edinburgh, Scotland, UK., July. Association for Computational Linguistics.

Philipp Koehn, Franz Josef Och, and Daniel Marcu. 2003. Statistical phrase-based translation. In *Proceedings of HLT-NAACL 2003*, pages 127–133. Edmonton, Canada.

Philipp Koehn, Hieu Hoang, Alexandra Birch, Chris Callison-Burch, Marcello Federico, Nicola Bertoldi, Brooke Cowan, Wade Shen, Christine Moran, Richard Zens, Chris Dyer, Ondrej Bojar, Alexandra Constantin, and Evan Herbst. 2007. Moses: Open source toolkit for statistical machine translation. In *Proceedings of ACL, Demonstration Session.*

Thai Phuong Nguyen and Akira Shimazu. 2006. Improving phrase-based smt with morpho-syntactic analysis and transformation. In *Proceedings AMTA 2006.*

Phuong Thai Nguyen, Akira Shimazu, Le-Minh Nguyen, and Van-Vinh Nguyen. 2007. A syntactic transformation model for statistical machine translation. *International Journal of Computer Processing of Oriental Languages (IJCPOL)*, 20(2):1–20.

Thai Phuong Nguyen, Akira Shimazu, Tu Bao Ho, Minh Le Nguyen, and Vinh Van Nguyen. 2008. A tree-to-string phrase-based model for statistical machine translation. In *Proceedings of the Twelfth Conference on Computational Natural Language Learning (CoNLL 2008)*, pages 143–150, Manchester, England, August. Coling 2008 Organizing Committee.

Franz J. Och and Hermann Ney. 2003. A systematic comparison of various statistical alignment models. *Computational Linguistics*, 29(1):19–51.

Franz J. Och and Hermann Ney. 2004. The alignment template approach to statistical machine translation. *Computational Linguistics*, 30(4):417–449.

K. Papineni, S. Roukos, T. Ward, and W. J. Zhu. 2002. 2002. Bleu: a method for automatic evaluation of machine translation. In *Proc. of the 40th Annual Meeting of the Association for Computational Linguistics (ACL)*, pages 311–318. Philadelphia, PA, July.

Chris Quirk, Arul Menezes, and Colin Cherry. 2005. Dependency treelet translation: Syntactically informed phrasal smt. In *Proceedings of ACL 2005*, pages 271–279. Ann Arbor, Michigan, USA.

Andreas Stolcke. 2002. Srilm - an extensible language modeling toolkit. In *Proceedings of International Conference on Spoken Language Processing*, volume 29, pages 901–904.

David Talbot, Hideto Kazawa, Hiroshi Ichikawa, Jason Katz-Brown, Masakazu Seno, and Franz Och. 2011. A lightweight evaluation framework for machine translation reordering. In *Proceedings of the Sixth Workshop on Statistical Machine Translation*, pages 12–21, Edinburgh, Scotland, July. Association for Computational Linguistics.

Yoshimasa Tsuruoka, Jun'ichi Tsujii, and Sophia Ananiadou. 2009. Fast full parsing by linear-chain conditional random fields. In *Proceedings of the 12th Conference of the European Chapter of the Association for Computational Linguistics*, EACL '09, pages 790–798, Stroudsburg, PA, USA. Association for Computational Linguistics.

Chao Wang, Michael Collins, and Philipp Koehn. 2007. Chinese syntactic reordering for statistical machine translation. In *Proceedings of the 2007 Joint Conference on Empirical Methods in Natural Language Processing and Computational Natural Language Learning (EMNLP-CoNLL)*, pages 737–745, Prague, Czech Republic, June. Association for Computational Linguistics.

Fei Xia and Michael McCord. 2004. Improving a statistical mt system with automatically learned rewrite patterns. In *Proceedings of Coling 2004*, pages 508–514, Geneva, Switzerland, Aug 23–Aug 27. COLING.

Peng Xu, Jaeho Kang, Michael Ringgaard, and Franz Och. 2009. Using a dependency parser to improve smt for subject-object-verb languages. In *Proceedings of Human Language Technologies: The 2009 Annual Conference of the North American Chapter of the Association for Computational Linguistics*, pages 245–253, Boulder, Colorado, June. Association for Computational Linguistics.

Yuqi Zhang, Richard Zens, and Hermann Ney. 2007. Chunk-level reordering of source language sentences with automatically learned rules for statistical machine translation. In *Proceedings of SSST, NAACL-HLT 2007 / AMTA Workshop on Syntax and Structure in Statistical Translation*, pages 1–8.

Psycholinguistics, Lexicography, and Word Sense Disambiguation

Oi Yee Kwong
Department of Chinese, Translation and Linguistics
City University of Hong Kong
Tat Chee Avenue, Kowloon, Hong Kong
Olivia.Kwong@cityu.edu.hk

Abstract

Mainstream word sense disambiguation systems have relied mostly on supervised approaches. Complex interactions have been observed between learning algorithms and knowledge sources, but the factors underlying such phenomena are under-explored. This calls for more qualitative analysis of disambiguation results, possibly from an inter-disciplinary perspective. The current study thus preliminarily explores the relation between sense concreteness and the linguistic means for sense distinction with reference to the context availability model proposed in psycholinguistics and common practice in corpus-based lexicography. It will be shown that to a certain extent the varied usefulness of individual knowledge sources for target words, nouns in particular, may be related to the concreteness of the meanings concerned, which predicts how the sense is distinguished from other senses of the word in the first place. A better understanding of this relation is expected to inform the design of disambiguation systems which could then combine algorithms and knowledge sources in a genuine lexically sensitive way.

1 Introduction

Word sense ambiguities tend to escape people's awareness in everyday communication, except in deliberately biased artificial examples or when context is severely limited, since otherwise we almost effortlessly resolve them using a variety of linguistic and extra-linguistic knowledge. This wide range of information is often rendered as various knowledge sources in automatic word sense disambiguation (WSD) systems, partially modelled with different feature sets.

As exemplified in recent SENSEVAL and SEMEVAL evaluation exercises (e.g. Kilgarriff and Rosenzweig, 1999; Edmonds and Cotton, 2001; Mihalcea et al., 2004), state-of-the-art WSD systems are mostly based on supervised approaches. Machine learning algorithms are trained on sense-tagged examples, using a wide range of features extracted from the text approximating a variety of knowledge sources deemed useful for the purpose. Ensembles of different types of classifiers based on different feature sets with some voting scheme often report better performance than individual classifiers alone, though the advantage may just be marginal. While complex interactions between learning algorithms and knowledge sources have been observed (e.g. Mihalcea, 2002; Yarowsky and Florian, 2002), and although factors like sense granularity, availability of training data, part-of-speech (POS), etc. are found to relate to such interactions in one way or another, the nature underlying such interactions, which points to the lexical sensitivity issue of WSD, is still somehow under-explored. In particular, more qualitative analysis is needed for disambiguation results, possibly from an inter-disciplinary perspective, for a better understanding of the issue.

In the current study, we make a preliminary effort in this regard, and attempt to analyse disambiguation results with respect to the relation between sense concreteness and the means for sense distinction in the first place. To this end, we refer to the context availability model proposed in psycholinguistics and common practice in modern corpus-based lexicography.

In Section 2, we will first briefly review related work with particular focus on the complex interaction between learning algorithms and knowledge sources in WSD revealed in recent evaluation exercises and various comparative studies, and present the Context Availability Model and discuss how it accounts for the concreteness effect in psycholinguistics. Section 3 reports on our qualitative analysis of the results from a simple WSD experiment on the noun samples in the SENSEVAL-3 English lexical sample task, for which we also made use of the Sketch Engine, a corpus query system popularly used in lexicography, as a tool for comparing the linguistic context availability among word senses. The paper will be concluded with future directions in Section 4.

2 Related Work

2.1 WSD: State of the Art

Two critical factors have been identified for the success of supervised WSD systems: learning algorithms and knowledge sources.

Individual learning algorithms are found to vary in their disambiguation performance. For instance, Màrquez et al. (2006) compared five machine learning algorithms widely used in previous studies, namely Naïve Bayes (NB), k-Nearest-Neighbor (kNN), Decision Lists (DL), AdaBoost (AB), and Support Vector Machines (SVM). They were trained on the same set of data and tested on examples selected from the DSO corpus. Knowledge sources were in the form of 15 local feature patterns (with words and POS) and topical context as bag of words (content words in the sentence). The most-frequent-sense classifier was used as baseline. It was found that all algorithms outperformed the baseline (46.55%), with SVM (67.07%) and AB performing significantly better than kNN, which in turn performed significantly better than NB and DL (61.34%).

Multiple knowledge sources are indispensable in WSD systems, and they contribute in different ways to disambiguation. Agirre and Stevenson (2006) summarised from many WSD studies the different knowledge sources available or extracted from various lexical resources and corpora, and their realisation as different features in individual systems. They generalised that all knowledge sources seem to provide useful disambiguation clues. Each POS profits from different knowledge sources, e.g. domain knowledge and topical word association are most useful for disambiguating nouns while local context benefits verbs and adjectives. The combination of all knowledge sources consistently gets the best results across POS categories. In addition, some learning algorithms are better suited to certain knowledge sources, and different grammatical categories may benefit from different learning algorithms.

Such a complex interaction between learning algorithms and knowledge sources was also exemplified in other comparative studies (e.g. Mihalcea, 2002; Yarowsky and Florian, 2002). The comprehensive study by Yarowsky and Florian (2002), for instance, compares the relative system performance across different training and data conditions with SENSEVAL-2 data on four languages. The results clearly show the interaction among feature sets, training sizes, and learning algorithms. They concluded that "there is no one-size-fits-all algorithm that excels at each of the diverse challenges in sense disambiguation". For example, discriminative and aggregative algorithm classes often have complementary regions of effectiveness across numerous parameters, the former such as decision trees tend to perform well with local collocations or syntactic features, whereas the latter like Naïve Bayes tend to perform well with bag-of-word features. Some algorithms are more tolerant than others of sparse data, high degree of polysemy and noise in the training data.

2.2 The Lexical Sensitivity Issue

Despite such findings on the complex relationship between learning algorithms and knowledge sources, which possibly lead to the use of ensembles of classifiers with diverse knowledge sources in state-of-the-art systems, there are nevertheless some questions regarding their differential effectiveness left unanswered. One of the most important questions is how we could account for the intra-POS variation of the effectiveness of individual knowledge sources. Hence, while we find that target words of different

POS categories favour different knowledge sources for disambiguation, e.g. although local contexts are found to benefit verbs and adjectives more, they do contribute to the disambiguation of some nouns. What properties do such nouns possess? Can we predict the information susceptibility of individual words to optimize the use of different knowledge sources during disambiguation, and to consider the outcome given by different knowledge sources with different levels of confidence?

As Resnik and Yarowsky (1999) remarked, WSD is a highly lexically sensitive task which in effect requires specialized disambiguators for each polysemous word. But in what way precisely is the combination of algorithms and knowledge sources sensitive to individual (groups of) lexical items? Factors like the number of senses and how closely they are related will have an impact on the difficulty of disambiguation, and the varied difficulty may be reflected from the system performance (Chugur et al., 2002; Pedersen, 2002), but there is still more to learn, especially from an inter-disciplinary perspective. For instance, Krahmer (2010) encouraged mutual learning between computational linguists and psychologists, using as an example the possible influence of the general distinction between concrete and abstract language on perception shown in psychology studies, while such effects are somehow largely ignored in computational linguistics. We have also raised similar concerns for research on automatic word sense disambiguation (Kwong, 2012). In this study, we refer to the Context Availability Model in psycholinguistics (Schwanenflugel, 1991), which is used to explain human comprehension processes in general and more specifically to account for the concreteness effect in human word processing, to analyse WSD system performance on individual target words.

2.3 Context Availability Model

Polysemy, familiarity and concreteness have been considered important semantic characteristics which influence human lexical processing (e.g. Taft, 1991). While polysemy (in terms of sense number and granularity) and familiarity (in terms of frequency or prior probability) have also been addressed by computational linguists to account for differential system performance, the concreteness effect is somehow seldom discussed in the WSD literature. A few examples include: Jorgensen (1990) suggested that concreteness of a word may increase agreement between judges for sorting word usages and concrete words are easier to define; Kwong (2008) studied the relation between concreteness and system performance in SENSEVAL-2, though the findings were not particularly conclusive, partly because of the confusion from discussing concreteness at both the sense and word level; Yuret and Yatbaz (2010) mentioned that the abstract classes were responsible for most of the errors in their supersense tagging with unsupervised method. Given the significance of the concreteness effect in human lexical processing (e.g. Paivio et al., 1968; Kroll and Merves, 1986; Bleasdale, 1987; Schwanenflugel, 1991), more in-depth analysis of the concreteness effect is definitely needed especially for mainstream supervised WSD.

Psychologists have put forth various plausible explanations to account for the concreteness effect observed in human lexical processing, one of which is the context availability model. It suggests that the advantage of concrete words comes from their stronger and denser association to contextual knowledge than abstract words (Schwanenflugel 1991). The availability of contextual information enables a person to draw the relations between concepts that are needed for comprehension. Such contextual information may come from a person's prior knowledge or from the stimulus environment. According to this model, lexical decisions tend to take longer for abstract words because related contextual information that is used in deciding that an item is a word is less available for abstract words. Schwanenflugel et al. (1988) thus pointed out that the lexical decision times for abstract words are not necessarily longer than those for concrete words, especially when abstract concepts are also presented in relevant contexts. In addition, they found that rated context availability makes a better predictor for lexical decision time than imageability, familiarity, and age-of-acquisition. Thus the concreteness effects are rather attributable to the ease of retrieving related contextual information from prior knowledge for individual words, that is, context availability matters.

Such emphasis on the contextually based character of word meanings is obviously in line with current mainstream practice in WSD. The following comment particularly highlights the relevance and potential applicability of the model in our investigation of lexical sensitivity in WSD: "... It is possible that words rated low in context availability largely possess context-dependent knowledge which is relatively inaccessible when the words are presented in isolation. However, when such words are presented in supportive contexts, this context-dependent information becomes highly available for deriving meaning, eliminating potential differences in comprehension between abstract and concrete words." (Schwanenflugel, 1991: p.246)

Hence in the current study, we try to apply the context availability model in our investigation of the relationship between the effectiveness of various knowledge sources (in terms of the disambiguation performance) and the availability of characteristic linguistic context distinguishing one sense from the others for a particular target word. However, we will have to introduce a variation to the model. We have to distinguish between lexical and sense concreteness, the confusion of which is also a major inadequacy in psycholinguistic studies of the concreteness effect. On the one hand, the existence of polysemy means that a word can have multiple senses, but when psycholinguists attempt to norm the concreteness ratings from human subjects, there has been no control on how the subjects actually come up with a rating for the word as a whole. On the other hand, especially in view of the phenomena of sense extensions and metaphorical usages, polysemous words may consist of a mix of both concrete and abstract meanings, and it would make better sense to discuss the concreteness effect at the sense level instead of, or at least in addition to, the word level. This is particularly critical when word sense disambiguation is concerned.

We thus hypothesise that the differential effectiveness of individual knowledge sources is a result of the varied availability of characteristic linguistic context which serves to distinguish one sense from the others for a particular target word in the first place. This difference thus leads to different information susceptibility of individual target words, which is in turn reflected in the disambiguation performance, indirectly as the difficulty of WSD, giving rise to the long standing issue of lexical sensitivity.

3 The Current Study

We first set up a simple WSD experiment, running a supervised learning algorithm based on Support Vector Machines, with various knowledge sources (including topical contexts, local collocations, and local syntactic contexts) and their combinations on the noun samples in the SENSEVAL-3 English lexical sample task. The most frequent sense was used as the baseline. The disambiguation results were analysed and compared across individual target words. The algorithms implemented in the WEKA package (Hall et al., 2009), with all default settings, were used. For tokenisation and tagging of the data, the tokeniser and tagger available with the Lund University dependency parser (Johansson and Nugues, 2008) were used, although we did not use the parser specifically for this study.

3.1 Dataset

The data available for target nouns tested in the SENSEVAL-3 English lexical sample task were used. According to Mihalcea et al. (2004), the examples were extracted from the British National Corpus and the sense annotation was done using the Open Mind Word Expert system (Chklovski and Mihalcea 2002), and the sense inventory used for the nouns was WordNet 1.7.1 (Miller, 1995). Table 1 shows the target nouns with the number of senses and the distribution of concrete and abstract senses, as well as the number of training and testing instances for each noun. There are 20 items, with 3 to 9 senses, averaging at 5.35 senses.[1] The number of training examples for each sense varies considerably. The concrete/abstract classification of the senses was based on the lexicographer files in WordNet. Senses are organised under 45 lexicographer files based on syntactic category and logical groupings, and 26 of them are relevant to noun senses. We considered 7 of them concrete classes and the remaining 19 abstract classes. The concrete classes thus include *animal*, *artifact*, *body*, *food*, *object*, *person*, and *plant*. The abstract classes are *act*, *attribute*, *cognition*, *communication*, *event*, *feeling*, *group*, *location*, *motive*, *phenomenon*, *possession*, *process*, *quantity*, *relation*, *shape*, *state*, *substance*, *time*, and *Tops* (the unique beginner for nouns).

[1] These only cover the senses with training examples, not all senses listed in the sense inventory, hence the slight difference from the figures stated in Mihalcea et al. (2004).

3.2 Knowledge Sources

In this study, we focus on three types of disambiguating information: topical contexts, local collocations, and shallow syntactic information. They are realised in the form of bag of words, single words and word combinations in surrounding context, and the POS n-grams of neighbouring words, respectively, as binary features for the learning algorithm.

Topical Contexts (TC)

Topical contexts capture the broad conceptually related words, which are expected to reflect the topic or domain in which a sense often occurs. For this study we collected from the training examples all the noun and verb lemmas within a window of ±50 words from the target as features. Then in each testing instance, if any of those lemmas are found in a window of ±50 words from the target, the corresponding feature will have value 1, otherwise 0.

Local Collocations (LC)

The collocation patterns were approximated by the lemma unigrams, bigrams and trigrams in the local context of the target word, within a window of ±3 words. From the training instances, unigrams w_{-3}, w_{-2}, w_{-1}, w_1, w_2, and w_3, bigrams $w_{-3}w_{-2}$, $w_{-2}w_{-1}$, w_1w_2, and w_2w_3, and trigrams $w_{-3}w_{-2}w_{-1}$, $w_{-1}w_0w_1$, and $w_1w_2w_3$, were extracted as features. The word form of the target word was also included.

Shallow Syntactic Information (SS)

For this knowledge source, we collected features from the POS n-grams of the neighbouring words and the target word itself in the training instances, namely p_{-3}, p_{-2}, p_{-1}, p_0, p_1, p_2, p_3, $p_{-3}p_{-2}$, $p_{-2}p_{-1}$, p_1p_2, p_2p_3, $p_{-3}p_{-2}p_{-1}$, $p_{-1}p_0p_1$, and $p_1p_2p_3$.

3.3 Procedures

WSD results were first obtained with individual classifiers using various combinations of the knowledge sources. The results were then subject to comparison and error analysis, with respect to the intra-POS variation for the effectiveness of different knowledge sources.

3.4 Results and Analysis

As seen from Table 1, the target words have considerably different number of training and testing instances. Moreover, most of them are abstract. Of the 20 items, 9 only have abstract senses, and the rest have a mix of concrete and abstract senses. None is entirely concrete. Among the 107 senses for all words, only 24 are concrete senses. So the data is in some way biased in their concreteness. Although running WSD experiments on SENSEVAL data allows better comparison with previous studies, ideally there should be better control over the concreteness distribution especially for the purpose of this investigation. For this study, we will just note this deficiency.

Target Word	Senses	Con	Abs	Train	Test
argument	5	0	5	221	111
arm	5	4	1	266	133
atmosphere	5	1	4	161	81
audience	4	0	4	200	100
bank	9	4	5	262	132
degree	7	0	7	256	128
difference	5	0	5	226	114
difficulty	4	0	4	46	23
disc	4	3	1	200	100
image	6	3	3	146	74
interest	7	0	7	185	93
judgment	7	0	7	62	32
organization	4	0	4	112	56
paper	7	1	6	232	117
party	5	1	4	230	116
performance	5	0	5	172	87
plan	3	1	2	166	84
shelter	4	2	2	196	98
sort	4	1	3	190	96
source	7	3	4	64	32

Table 1: Sense distribution and data size

Table 2 shows the results from the various classifiers with different knowledge sources (TC for Topical Contexts, LC for Local Collocations, SS for Shallow Syntactic Information, ALL for the combination of the above, and Base is the baseline from the most frequent sense). The figures refer to precision, which is the same as recall in this case since coverage is 100% for all target words.

Most results in Table 2 are above the baseline. However, contrary to what most previous studies might have observed, especially if we look at individual target words, combining all knowledge sources does not necessarily give the best result. Hence the overall scores may sometimes be misleading as to the effectiveness of various knowledge sources to individual target words. It can be seen that the accuracy varies across different target words. For instance, using all knowledge sources, the result ranges from 0.391 for "difficulty" to 0.881 for "plan". The number of training instances available may make a difference, but for contrasting cases like "performance" and "plan" in this study, something else must be responsible for the different levels of difficulty as is apparent in the disambiguation results.

Target Word	TC	LC	SS	ALL	Base
argument	0.486	0.532	0.486	0.505	0.514
arm	0.850	0.872	0.857	0.865	0.820
atmosphere	0.716	0.667	0.580	0.679	0.667
audience	0.750	0.820	0.710	0.800	0.670
bank	0.841	0.765	0.614	0.818	0.674
degree	0.734	0.797	0.648	0.773	0.609
difference	0.474	0.518	0.447	0.623	0.404
difficulty	0.348	0.478	0.261	0.391	0.174
disc	0.780	0.480	0.420	0.710	0.380
image	0.595	0.608	0.419	0.649	0.365
interest	0.570	0.667	0.656	0.731	0.419
judgment	0.563	0.344	0.313	0.531	0.281
organization	0.768	0.768	0.643	0.768	0.732
paper	0.504	0.513	0.462	0.632	0.256
party	0.759	0.664	0.552	0.741	0.621
performance	0.506	0.322	0.322	0.425	0.264
plan	0.845	0.833	0.774	0.881	0.821
shelter	0.551	0.653	0.582	0.643	0.449
sort	0.646	0.719	0.688	0.698	0.656
source	0.688	0.563	0.406	0.625	0.656
Overall	0.666	0.652	0.572	0.698	0.542

Table 2: Disambiguation results

Regarding the concreteness effect, Table 3 shows the overall results with all knowledge sources and the baselines with respect to the concreteness of the senses for the words. Although the SENSEVAL-3 data contain more words with only abstract senses, the results apparently suggest that words with only abstract senses are more difficult to disambiguate than those with a mix of concrete and abstract senses, as is evident from the lower scores for the former in general.

Considering the effectiveness of various knowledge sources on individual target words, words with entirely abstract senses are apparently more susceptible to local features in addition to topical features. For instance, LC alone already gives better results than TC for 5 of the 9 target nouns with only abstract senses, compared to 6 of 11 words with a mix of abstract and concrete senses showing the same trend, not to mention that many of the nouns in the latter group actually consist of more abstract senses than concrete senses. In addition, with the addition of local features, only 2 out of 9 nouns with only abstract senses suffered a drop in the final score, compared to 5 out of 11 nouns with a mix of concrete and abstract senses were adversely affected. Topical contexts have usually been found to work well for nouns, but obviously their advantage is not as apparent in this study in the presence of predominantly abstract senses for the target nouns.

Concreteness	Baseline	SVM (All)
Only abstract senses	0.489	0.645
Both abstract and concrete	0.579	0.734
Overall	0.542	0.698

Table 3: WSD results w.r.t. concreteness

As mentioned, we will attempt to explain for the disambiguation results on concrete and abstract senses from the perspective of context availability. To this end, we consider the sense distinctions from the lexicographers' perspective.

Lexicographers distinguish senses by many criteria, most notably including: syntactic patterns, collocation patterns, colligation patterns, and domain. If one considers senses the artifacts from lexicography (e.g. Kilgarriff, 2006), it makes sense to think about WSD from lexicographers' point of view, because whether they rely on sufficient characteristic contextual difference to distinguish the senses to start with will directly affect the difficulty of subsequent disambiguation and the usefulness of various knowledge sources for this purpose. Hence we try to assess context availability with the Sketch Engine, an important tool for computational lexicography.

The Sketch Engine is a corpus query system widely used in modern computational corpus-based lexicography. It takes as input a corpus of any language and a corresponding set of grammar patterns, and generates word sketches for the words of that language; whereas word sketches are one-page automatic, corpus-based summaries of a word's grammatical and collocational behaviour (Kilgarriff et al., 2004). Sketch difference is also one of the many functions available in the Sketch Engine. It provides useful summaries in how pairs of near-synonyms differ, allowing users to compare and contrast the grammatical and collocational patterns of two words with apparently similar meanings.

We take advantage of the sketch difference function for comparing and contrasting individual senses of a word, to identify important grammatical and collocational patterns within specific grammatical relations critical for their distinction. To do this, we created sense sub-corpora for the Sketch Engine. All examples were extracted from the training data and stored in different files according to individual senses. A corpus was created in Sketch Engine, treating each set of examples as a sub-corpus, and all other senses of the same word as another sub-corpus, to facilitate subsequent comparison of prominent contexts among senses. For each target noun, we obtained the sketch difference for each of its senses with the rest of its senses, and analysed for common patterns and unique patterns with respect to sense concreteness and difficulty of WSD. For the word sketch patterns, we used the default English Penn Treebank sketch grammar available from the Sketch Engine. Typical grammatical relations specified in the word sketch patterns relevant to nouns include object_of (indicating the verbs which usually take the noun as object), a_modifier (indicating the adjectival pre-modifier for the noun), pp_%s (indicating common prepositional phrases following the noun), etc.

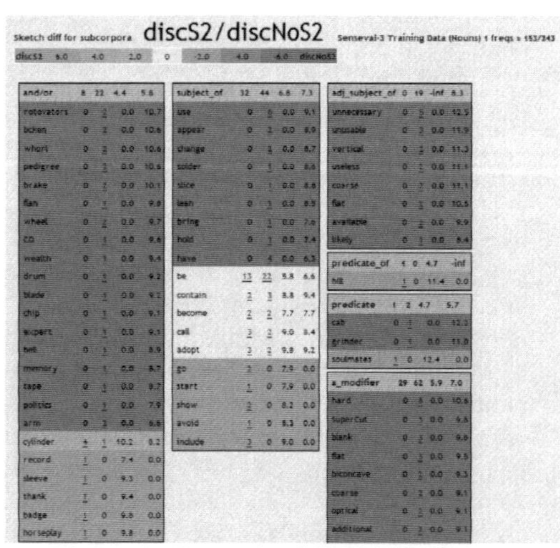

Figure 1: Example of Sketch Difference

Figure 1 shows an example of the sketch differences between the second sense of the target noun "disc" (phonograph record) and its other senses (circular plate / magnetic disk / saucer) displayed by the Sketch Engine.

Let us illustrate our analysis with two examples. For instance, all senses for "degree" are abstract, as shown below. Table 4 shows a partial confusion matrix when TC and LC are used respectively.

1: [Attribute] {degree, grade, level} – a position on a scale of intensity or amount or quality

2: [Attribute] {degree} – the seriousness of something

3: [Cognition] {degree} – the highest power of a term or variable

4: [Communication] {academic degree, degree} – an award conferred by a college or university signifying that the recipient has satisfactorily completed a course of study

5: [Quantity] {degree, arcdegree} – a measure for arcs and angles

6: [Quantity] {degree} – a unit of temperature on a specified scale

7: [State] {degree, level, stage, point} – a specific identifiable position in a continuum or series or especially in a process

Expected \ Predicted	1	4	7
1	TC: 76 LC: 74	TC: 2 LC: 4	--
4	TC: 13 LC: 2	TC: 16 LC: 27	--
7	TC: 10 LC: 11	TC: 1 LC: 0	--

Table 4: Partial confusion matrix for "degree"

For the "degree" example, only Sense 1, 4 and 7 could be considered to have a reasonable number of training examples. Looking at the performance with TC and LC respectively, obviously Sense 7 is the most difficult because neither knowledge source was able to get any of the Sense 7 test instances correct. The confusion between Sense 1 and Sense 4 is obvious, and it is apparent that the use of local collocations is very effective to tell apart Sense 4 from Sense 1. The sketch differences show that Sense 1 has a lot of common patterns with non-Sense 1 data. However, it is the most frequent sense and might therefore have an advantage. On the other hand, Sense 4 has few common patterns with other senses but has considerable distinct patterns of its own with regard to local collocation and syntactic relations. Sense 7, however, shares many common patterns with other senses, but only has a few distinct yet not so characteristic patterns. This probably explains the benefits of adding local features for reducing the errors for Sense 4, as well as its lack of effect on disambiguating for Sense 7.

Turning to an example of mixed-sense target word, local features are destructive for "disc". The senses for the word are listed below. Sense 1 to Sense 3 are concrete, and Sense 4 is abstract. Table 5 shows the confusion matrix when TC and LC are used respectively.

1: [Artifact] {disk, disc} – a thin flat circular plate

2: [Artifact] {phonograph record, phonograph recording, record, disk, disc, platter} – sound recording consisting of a disc with continuous grooves; formerly used to reproduce music by rotating while a phonograph needle tracked in the grooves

3: [Artifact] {magnetic disk, magnetic disc, disk, disc} – (computer science) a memory device consisting of a flat disk covered with a magnetic coating on which information is stored

4: [Shape] {disk, disc, saucer} – something with a round shape like a flat circular plate

For the "disc" example, the impact of availability of training instances can be considered insignificant, as all four senses have over 30 instances. From Table 5, obviously TC is a much more effective knowledge source, at least for distinguishing among Senses 1 to 3. The sketch differences show that Sense 1 shares relatively many common patterns with non-Sense 1 data, and so does Sense 4. Sense 2 and Sense 3, on the other hand, share fewer common patterns with others. This possibly predicts the confusability between Sense 1 and Sense 4. Moreover, the unique patterns for individual senses are still restricted to the collocation patterns within particular grammatical relations, instead of any sense enjoying a unique syntactic pattern not found in others. This could explain why features based on words and lemmas are more effective for disambiguating this word, while the addition of local syntactic information does not help at all.

Expected \ Predicted	1	2	3	4
1	TC: 24 LC: 11	TC: 1 LC: 13	TC: 2 LC: 3	--
2	TC: 1 LC: 3	TC: 37 LC: 32	TC: 0 LC: 2	TC: 0 LC: 1
3	TC: 9 LC: 7	TC: 0 LC: 12	TC: 15 LC: 5	--
4	TC: 6 LC: 6	TC: 3 LC: 4	TC: 0 LC: 1	TC: 2 LC: 0

Table 5: Confusion matrix for "disc"

3.5 Implications on Lexical Sensitivity

From the above analysis, we have observed the following: First, nouns with only abstract senses are relatively more difficult to disambiguate than those with a mix of abstract and concrete senses, as seen from the overall scores for the two kinds of words. Second, the addition of local collocation and syntactic information to topical contexts often improves the overall score, but the actual effect varies across individual target words. Some benefit more from the combined features while others may suffer a drop in the final scores. Third, local collocation and syntactic features seem to play a more significant role on the disambiguation of abstract senses than concrete senses.

Past studies have observed that in general adding topical or bag-of-word features is more beneficial for nouns whereas adding local and collocational features works better for verbs and adjectives, but as we have observed in this study, such advantages do not necessarily apply to all words (and their senses) in the whole syntactic category. This means that POS alone may not be adequate to account for the lexical sensitivity of WSD, especially in view of the intra-POS variation with respect to individual knowledge sources. The common property shared by instances which can be effectively disambiguated by a certain kind of knowledge source or contextual feature is, simply speaking, context availability and the linguistic properties used by lexicographers for their distinction in the sense inventory in the first place.

The POS effect observed in previous studies could thus be understood this way. There are typical syntactic contexts in which words of different POS are bound to occur. For instance, nouns are often used in the subject and object positions and thus whether we find a verb before or after the target noun or whether its previous word is a determiner may not be a very good contextual feature in general because the various senses of a given noun may all occur in such similar contexts. On the contrary, if one sense of the noun tends to appear in very specific constructions, such as in very unique prepositional phrases, then in such cases one can expect local collocations and n-gram combinations to be relatively useful for distinguishing this sense from the others. An illustrative example is the target word "audience", as one of its senses is based on the specific usage of "the rights of audience", which accounts for the particular effectiveness of LC and SS. Thus one problem with previous findings on the relation between knowledge sources and POS is that it may be too crude to look at lexical sensitivity in terms of POS alone and from the overall disambiguation scores, as the precise effect on individual words could vary considerably. For example, for the intra-POS variations among nouns, in this study we have observed the concreteness effect. The analysis suggested that concrete senses tend to rely more on topical information or they are more often used in distinctively different domains, while abstract senses are more likely to be characterised by their special local contexts such as the occurrence in particular PP or followed by particular PP, in addition to the topic or domain in which they are often used. The impact of sense concreteness, after all, is coupled with the actual context availability of individual senses, which affects the ease of disambiguation and the effectiveness of various knowledge sources. The model will thus predict that while sense dispersion or granularity will affect the difficulty of disambiguation, but if sufficient characteristic contexts can be associated with the senses and such contexts exist in the data, even closely related senses (such as an originally concrete sense and its abstract and metaphorical extension) could still be effectively disambiguated with the relevant knowledge sources.

4 Conclusion and Future Directions

While many previous studies have demonstrated the benefits or disadvantages of using certain knowledge sources for words of particular POS, in the current study we further address the intra-POS variations and discuss lexical sensitivity with respect to sense concreteness. As the context availability model in psycholinguistics predicts, although concrete words are more easily understood than abstract words, the concreteness effect will disappear if the stimuli were controlled for the ease to come up with an associative context.

Our analysis of WSD results on the noun samples in the SENSEVAL-3 English lexical sample task has allowed us to observe that words with only abstract senses tend to have lower disambiguation scores and are thus more difficult than those with a mix of abstract and concrete senses. Moreover, the benefit of adding local contextual information to topical contexts in disambiguation varies across target words, and it depends on the context availability of individual senses and the basis by which lexicographers distinguish and characterise them in the first place. These observations shed further light on the lexical sensitivity issue. In addition to factors like POS, sense granularity, number of senses, availability of training samples, etc., there is something about the intrinsic nature of individual words, such as concreteness, which may affect their susceptibility to different knowledge sources in disambiguation. It is therefore more appropriate to consider the lexical sensitivity in WSD in terms of information susceptibility, which depends on how the senses of the words were distinguished in the first place and whether their typical contexts are characteristic enough and available in most instances, resulting in the differential effectiveness of individual knowledge sources on different target words. To this end, WSD might be treated as the reverse engineering of lexicography, especially if one accepts that senses are the artifacts from lexicography. In this way, the selection of features and their combinations and weighting with specific learning algorithms could be made genuinely sensitive to individual lexical items.

For future work, we plan to deepen our investigation, making more systematic use of tools like the Sketch Engine to quantify context availability and to predict the usefulness of individual knowledge sources for WSD; and extend our testing and analysis to verbs and adjectives, to give a fuller picture of lexical sensitivity across different parts-of-speech.

Acknowledgments

The work described in this paper was supported by grants from the Department of Chinese, Translation and Linguistics of the City University of Hong Kong.

References

Agirre, E., & Stevenson, M. 2006. Knowledge sources for WSD. In E. Agirre, & P. Edmonds (Eds.), *Word Sense Disambiguation: Algorithms and Applications*. Dordrecht, The Netherlands: Springer.

Bleasdale, F.A. 1987. Concreteness dependent associative priming: Separate lexical organization for concrete and abstract words. *Journal of Experimental Psychology: Learning, Memory, and Cognition, 13*, 582-594.

Chklovski, T., & Mihalcea, R. 2002. Building a sense tagged corpus with Open Mind Word Expert. In *Proceedings of the Workshop on Word Sense Disambiguation: Recent Successes and Future Directions*, Philadelphia. pp.116-123.

Chugur, I., Gonzalo, J., & Verdejo, F. 2002. Polysemy and Sense Proximity in the Senseval-2 Test Suite. In *Proceedings of the Workshop on Word Sense Disambiguation: Recent Successes and Future Directions*, Philadelphia. pp.32-39.

Edmonds, P., & Cotton, S. 2001. SENSEVAL-2: Overview. In *Proceedings of the Second International Workshop on Evaluating Word Sense Disambiguation Systems (SENSEVAL-2)*, Toulouse, France. pp.1-6.

Hall, M., Frank, E., Holmes, G., Pfahringer, B., Reutemann, P., Witten, I.H. 2009. The WEKA Data Mining Software: An Update. *SIGKDD Explorations, Volume 11, Issue 1*.

Johansson, R., & Nugues, P. 2008. Dependency-based syntactic-semantic analysis with PropBank and NomBank. In *Proceedings of the 12th Conference on Computational Natural Language Learning (CoNLL 2008)*, Manchester. pp.183-187.

Jorgensen, J. 1990. The psychological reality of word senses. *Journal of Psycholinguistic Research, 19*, 167-190.

Kilgarriff, A. 2006. Word Senses. In E. Agirre, & P. Edmonds (Eds.), *Word Sense Disambiguation: Algorithms and Applications*. Dordrecht, The Netherlands: Springer.

Kilgarriff, A., & Rosenzweig, J. 1999. English SENSEVAL: Reports and results. In *Proceedings of the 5th Natural Language Processing Pacific Rim Symposium (NLPRS '99)*, Beijing, China.

Kilgarriff, A., Rychly, P., Smrz, P., and Tugwell, D. 2004. The Sketch Engine. In *Proceedings of EURALEX 2004*.

Krahmer, E. 2010. What Computational Linguists Can Learn from Psychologists (and Vice Versa). *Computational Linguistics, 36(2)*, 285-294.

Kroll, J.F., & Merves, J.S. 1986. Lexical access for concrete and abstract words. *Journal of Experimental Psychology: Learning, Memory, and Cognition, 12*, 92-107.

Kwong, O.Y. 2008. A preliminary study on the impact of lexical concreteness on word sense disambiguation. In *Proceedings of the 22nd Pacific Asia Conference on Language, Information and Computation (PACLIC 22)*, Cebu, Philippines. pp.235-244.

Kwong, O.Y. 2012. *New Perspectives on Computational and Cognitive Strategies for Word Sense Disambiguation*. Springer Briefs in Speech Technology. Springer.

Màrquez, L., Escudero, G., Martínez, D., & Rigau, G. 2006. Supervised corpus-based methods for WSD. In E. Agirre, & P. Edmonds (Eds.), *Word Sense Disambiguation: Algorithms and Applications*. Dordrecht, The Netherlands: Springer.

Mihalcea, R. 2002. Word sense disambiguation with pattern learning and automatic feature selection. *Natural Language Engineering, 8(4)*, 343-358.

Mihalcea, R., Chklovski, T., & Kilgarriff, A. 2004. The SENSEVAL-3 English Lexical Sample Task. In *Proceedings of the 3rd International Workshop on the Evaluation of Systems for the Semantic Analysis of Text (SENSEVAL-3)*, Barcelona, Spain. pp.25-28.

Miller, G. 1995. WordNet: A lexical database. *Communication of the ACM, 38(11)*, 39-41.

Paivio, A., Yuille, J.C., & Madigan, S.A. 1968. Concreteness, imagery, and meaningfulness values for 925 nouns. *Journal of Experiment Psychology, Monograph Supplement, 76(1, Pt.2)*, 1-25.

Pedersen, T. 2002. Assessing system agreement and instance difficulty in the lexical sample tasks of SENSEVAL-2. In *Proceedings of the Workshop on Word Sense Disambiguation: Recent Successes and Future Directions*, Philadelphia, PA, USA. pp.40-46.

Resnik, P., & Yarowsky, D. 1999. Distinguishing systems and distinguishing senses: new evaluation methods for word sense disambiguation. *Natural Language Engineering, 5(2)*, 113-133.

Schwanenflugel, P.J. 1991. Why are abstract concepts hard to understand? In P.J. Schwanenflugel (Ed.), *The Psychology of Word Meanings*. Hillsdale, NJ: Lawrence Erlbaum Associates, Inc.

Schwanenflugel, P.J., Harnishfeger, K.K., & Stowe, R.W. 1988. Context availability and lexical decisions for abstract and concrete words. *Journal of Memory and Language, 27*, 499-520.

Taft, M. 1991. *Reading and the Mental Lexicon*. Hove, East Sussex: Lawrence Erlbaum Associates.

Yarowsky, D., & Florian, R. 2002. Evaluating sense disambiguation across diverse parameter spaces. *Natural Language Engineering, 8(4)*, 293-310.

Yuret, D., & Yatbaz, M.A., 2010. The noisy channel model for unsupervised word sense disambiguation. *Computational Linguistics, 36(1)*, 111-127.

Thought *De se*, first person indexicals and Chinese reflexive *ziji*

Yingying Wang
Sun Yat-sen University
City University of Hong Kong
yingyingzsu@yahoo.com.cn

Haihua Pan*
City University of Hong Kong
Beijing Language and Culture University
Haihua.Pan@cityu.edu.hk

Abstract

In this paper, we make a distinction between the *de se* and non-*de se* interpretations of first person indexicals and Chinese reflexive *ziji*. Based on the distinction, we discuss the relationship between these expressions in Chinese, and point out the problems with Wechsler's (2010) *de se* theory of person indexicals as well as the inappropriateness of characterizing Chinese long-distance *ziji* as a logophor.

1. Background and motivation

According to Corazza (2004), the use of the first person pronoun has a special, privileged and primitive function among linguistic expressions: (i) its reference depends on the context of use. When you use the word *I*, it designates you; when I use the same word, it designates me; and (ii) this difference cannot be explained away or replaced by a co-referring term without destroying the cognitive impact the relevant use conveys, i.e., the so-called Irreducibility Thesis (Lewis 1979; Perry 1979).[1] We can use Perry's (1979) tale of the spilled sugar as an illustration:

(1) I once followed a trail of sugar on a supermarket floor, pushing my cart down the aisle on one side of a tall counter and back the aisle on the other, seeking the shopper with the torn sack to tell him that he was making a mess. With each trip around the counter, the trail became thicker. But I seemed unable to catch up. Finally it dawned on me. I was the shopper that I was trying to catch.

a. The shopper with the torn sack is making a mess.

b. John Perry is making a mess.

c. He [pointing to a reflection of himself in the mirror] is making a mess.

d. I am making a mess.

As Corazza explains, Perry may hold any one of the beliefs in (1a-1c) without realizing that he himself is making a mess, thus without adjusting his behavior and acting accordingly. Only when he comes to entertain the thought expressed in (1d) is he likely to straighten the sugar sack in his shopping cart. This special mode of presentation of an utterance containing a first-person indexical is called *self-ascription* or reference/thought *de se* in the philosophical literature.

Although in English the first person pronoun *I* is unique in terms of (i) and (ii) mentioned above, we find that this is not the case in Chinese, as, besides first person pronoun *wo*, reflexive pronoun *ziji* also possesses these two properties, when it is in its indexical use with its reference to the speaker of the utterance, even though one does not find its counterpart in English. For instance, in Perry's tale of the spilled sugar example, once Perry holds the

* Corresponding Author

[1] According to Corazza, the same story can be told about paradigmatic uses of 'now' and 'here'. In this paper, we shall concentrate on the first-person pronoun.

following belief (suppose that Perry understands Chinese), he will also fix the torn sugar sack in his shopping cart, just like what he will do when he holds the belief in (1d).

(2) ziji ba dongxi gaode yi-tuan zao.
Self BA things make one-CL mess
'Self is making a mess'.

In the literature, such a sentence-free use of *ziji* and its *de se* reading have been suggested by Pan (1997, 2001), Huang & Liu (2001), etc.

The questions that spring to mind are: (a) Are all the first/second person indexcials always interpreted *de se*? Can they be used as non-*de se* at all? (b) What is the relationship between first person *wo* and reflexive *ziji*? Is the *de se*/non-*de se* ambiguity involved in the latter?[2] In the following two sections, we will try to answer the qustions in (a) and (b) respectively, based on previous research as well as our new observations. In Section 4 we will discuss the empirical and theoretical impacts of our discussion on these issues. The paper will be concluded in Section 5.

2. The first person indexical and the *de se*/non-*de se* distinction

It is acknowledged that thought *de se* is usually expressed by 'I'-sentences. For instance, my utterance 'I am hungry' expresses a *de se* thought of mine, which means that I self-ascribes the property of *being hungry*, according to Lewis' (1979) semantics on *de se* beliefs. Wechsler (2010) offers a *de se* theory of person indexicals, wherein the first person pronoun, and also the second person pronoun, indicates reference *de se* (or self-ascription). More specifically, it is proposed that the person feature of a pronoun specifies the speech-act roles that must be played by the self-ascriber in question: a [spk] pronoun (e.g. *I*) designates the speaker in the context as the self-ascriber; a [addr] pronoun (e.g. *you*) designates the addressee in the context as the self-ascriber. Anyone who is not a designated self-ascriber for a given pronoun can only interpret it indirectly by inferring the self-ascriber's interpretation, a process requiring the theory of mind (Premack & Woodruff, 1978). So, for Wechsler, all pronominal reference to speech-act participants takes place via self-ascription, as suggested by the following:

(3) THE SELF-ASCRIPTION MONOPOLY: only as a consequence of grammatically specified self-ascription can a pronoun be knowingly used to refer to the speaker or addressee.

Therefore, no other person can use the first-person pronoun except for the speaker himself, and the same also applies to the addressee.

Following Crimmins (1992), Wechsler suggests to represent reference *de se* in the framework of DRT by the self-notion. Self-ascription is simply ascription via self-notion. For instance, in Perry's story, his pronoun *I* in (1d) is grammatically specified for referring via his self-notion $^{Perry}n_{self}$. In contrast, other co-referring expressions such as those in (1a)-(1c) do not necessarily involve the self-notion. Utterance (1b), for example, involves the notion of someone named Perry, i.e., $^{Perry}n_{named\text{-}perry}$. Therefore, the self-notion axiom, *Necessarily,* $\forall x[ContentOf(^{x}n_{self})=x]$, applies to the former, but not to the latter, and this explains why Perry is likely to fix the sugar sack when he holds the belief in (1d). Only if Perry knows his notion of $^{Perry}n_{named\text{-}perry}$ and his self-notion $^{Perry}n_{self}$ have the same content will he behave the same.

Although Wechsler's (2010) *de se* theory of person indexicals seems attractive, we do not think that the self-ascription monopoly, as shown in (3), is appropriate to interpret all

[2] Note that non-*de se* does not mean *de re*. In Section 3.3, we explain that Chinese long-distance reflexive *ziji* used in a speech report is not obligatorily *de se*, and in this situation, it can't be interpreted *de re*, either, for it is a long-distance bound anaphor, and its licensing condition needs speaker's empathy.

occurrences of person indexicals, especially the ones used in the embedded clauses of the first/second person belief reports. For us, the first/second person pronoun used in the embedded clause of a belief report may be interpreted *de se* or non-*de se* with respect to the matrix subject, and then get its reference to the speaker/hearer indirectly through the matrix subject, in addition to being interpreted *de se* with respect to the speaker/hearer in the context directly. Note that, the latter situation can be easily seen when the first person pronoun *I* is used in the embedded clause of the third person belief report 'John believes that I am smart'. And so is the case for the first person pronoun *I* used in the embedded clause of the first person belief report 'I believe that I am smart'. That is, in this case, both *I*'s can be understood as referring to the speaker in the context directly, and neither is dependent on the other.

To see the possible *de se* and non-*de se* interpretations of the first person pronoun with respect to the matrix subject, let's check Kaplan's mistaken self-identity scenario mentioned in Maier (2009):

(4) Scenario: Kaplan is thinking about the time he saw a guy on TV whose pants were on fire without him noticing it yet. A second later he realized he was watching himself through the surveillance camera system and it was his own pants that were on fire.
a. I thought that I was at a safe distance from the fire.
b. I thought that I was remarkably calm.

The embedded *I* used in (4a) can be interpreted *de se* with respect to the matrix subject, for what the agent thought at the time was 'I am at a safe distance from the fire', which is a first-person thought. However, in (4b), since its reported thought is 'That guy is remarkably calm', and *that guy* just happens to be Kaplan - the belief subject himself, the embedded *I* has to be interpreted non-*de se* with respect to the matrix subject (though it is still possible for it to be interpreted *de se* with respect to the speaker in the context directly). Note that, according to the scenario above, the two *I*s used in (4b) actually refer to the speaker at different times: the one in the matrix subject refers to the speaker when uttering 'that guy is remarkably calm' (t_1); the embedded one refers to the speaker at the speech time of (4b) (t_2). And the licensing of (4b) in such a situation needs the speaker's empathy, i.e., the speaker at t_2 empathizes with the speaker at t_1.[3] Since the speaker at t_2 knows that *that guy* in fact is he himself, though the speaker at t_1 does not know this, the former helps the latter do the self-reference. As can be seen from these two cases, the embedded *I* in (4b), but not in (4a), has two readings: (i) it is knowingly used to refer to the speaker at t_2 by the speaker t_2; and (ii) it is knowingly used by the speaker t_2 to refer to the matrix subject, without the awareness of the matrix subject, the speaker at t_1, that is, the embedded *I* is used by the speaker at t_2 to attribute the property 'being remarkably calm' to the matrix subject, the speaker at t_1, without his awareness, which is the non-*de se* interpretation of the embedded *I*, as mentioned above. The non-*de se* interpretation of the embedded *I* in (4b) thus shows that Wechsler's (2010) proposal that the reference of the first person pronoun to the speaker has to be obtained via the grammatically specified self-ascription is not really correct. If one insists on using Wechsler's theory to analyze the embedded *I*s used in the two sentences in (4), then their possible different interpretations as *de se* and non-*de se* (empathy) with respect to the matrix subject can't be explained.

So, the appropriate use of the first person pronoun in the embedded clause of the first person *de se*/non-*de se* belief reports indicates

[3] As to the notion of empathy, we adopt Kuno's (1987) definition that empathy is the speaker's identification, which may vary in degree, with a person/thing that participates in the event or state that he describes in a sentence.

that 'I'-sentences do not always involve the self-ascription of the speaker in the context. The fact is that the first person pronoun is possibly interpreted *de se*/non-*de se* with respect to the matrix subject, meaning that its reference to the speaker is not direct, and it is indirect via the matrix subject. Thus, Wechsler's (2010) self-ascription monopoly does not apply to all uses of the first and second person pronouns, and actually it only applies to all the first and second person pronouns that are interpreted directly to the speaker in the context, i.e., not via the matrix subject.

3. Chinese reflexive *ziji* and the *de se*/non-*de se* distinction

Chinese reflexive pronoun *ziji* basically has the following three uses: sentence-free *ziji*, locally bound *ziji*, and long-distance (LD) bound *ziji*. The first use was mentioned in Section 1, and the latter two can be illustrated by the sentence below:

(5) Zhangsan$_i$ renwei Lisi$_j$ hen ziji$_{i/j}$.
  Zhangsan think Lisi hate self
  'Zhangsan thinks that Lisi hates him/himself.'

As can be seen in (5), *ziji* has two readings: one referring to Lisi is locally bound and the other referring to Zhangsan is LD bound. Only *ziji* in the former case observes Chomsky's (1981) Binding Condition A.[4] In the following, we will discuss the *de se* and non-*de se* distinction of the interpretations of these three uses of *ziji*.

3.1 Sentence free *ziji*

As noted in Section 1, sentence free *ziji* expresses thought *de se* when it is used to refer to the speaker. In this situation, *ziji* can be replaced by first person pronoun *wo* without changing the meaning of the relevant sentence. As mentioned eariler, the *de se* interpretation of sentence free *ziji* is suggested by Pan (1997, 2001), Huang & Liu (2001), etc. Contrary to Huang and Liu's view that unbound *ziji* has to refer to the speaker, Pan claims that, besides the speaker, *ziji* can also refer to the addressee, or even a third party salient in the discourse. Below is a case in point, as provided in (Pan, 2001):

(6) Ziji weishenme bu qu ne?
  Self why   not go Q
  'Why didn't self (you) go?'

In such a question form, *ziji* is naturally read as referring to the addressee. Besides, we can give another example to illustrate that *ziji* is possible to refer to a third party salient in the discourse. Suppose that Zhangsan's mother wants him to bring the chair near him to her, but he is busy with his computer game and refuses to help her. In this situation, I can express my dissatisfaction with Zhangsan to my friend Lisi in the following way:

(7) Zhangsan zhen lan. Yizi jiu zai ziji de pangbian ne.
  Zhangsan very lazy Chair just is self DE near Ne
  'Zhangsan is very lazy. The chair is just near him!'

In (7), Zhangsan is salient in the discourse, and *ziji* can refer to him in the above scenario.

Note that *ziji* need not be treated as an adverb in (6), as suggested in Tsai (2002) who thinks sentence-free *ziji* is an adverb, not a reflexive pronoun.

(8) Zuotian, Zhangsan ziji qu le   Taibei.
  Yesterday, Zhangsan self go-PERF Taipei
  'Yesterday, Zhangsan went to Taipei by himself.'

One may think that it is possible that all the occurrences of sentence-free *ziji* are adverbs, and the subject is just deleted for short. For instance, (8) can be treated as a reduced form of (9):

[4] Note that Chinese reflexive *ziji* is not marked for person or number. It is compatible with first, second and third person antecedents, both in the singular and in the plural.

(9) Ni ziji weisheme bu qu ne?
You self why not go Q
'Why didn't self (you) go?'

However, this is not true, for the analysis of sentence free *ziji* as an adverb may be harmless for cases with *ziji* in the subject position, but not for cases with *ziji* in other positions. For example, in the following sentence, it is obvious that *ziji* as a complement to *chule* is not an adverb.

(10) Zhe-ge xiangfa, chule ziji, zhiyou san-ge ren zancheng.
This-CL idea, besides self only three-CL people agree
'As for this idea, besides myself, only three people agree.'

Besides, the adverb use of *ziji* should follow the negation marker *bu* when they co-occur in a sentence (see Pan (1997)), which means that the use of *ziji* in (9) has to be a subject reflexive, or the intensive pronoun like *you yourself* (Baker 1989). In this paper, we follow Pan's (1997, 2001) analysis of the sentence free *ziji* in sentences like (6) as a reflexive pronoun.

Therefore, given that Chinese first person pronoun *wo* behaves just like its English counterpart *I*, its difference from sentence free *ziji* lies in that it is impossible for the former to refer to the individual other than the speaker, though the latter can sometimes refer to the addressee or a third person salient in discourse. However, when sentence free *ziji* is used to refer to the speaker, it can be replaced by *wo* without losing the *de se* content of the relevant sentence.

3.2 Locally bound *ziji*

The *de se*/non-*de se* ambiguity is also detected in reflexive sentences where *ziji* is locally bound. A case exemplifying this type of ambiguity is given below:

(11) Zhangsan zai jingzi-li kan ziji.
Zhangsan at mirror-in see self
Zhangsan saw himself in the mirror.

We can utter this sentence in situations no matter whether Zhangsan recognizes himself or not. The following two sentences illustrate this point:

(12) Zhangsan zai jingzi-li kan ziji, bingqie yishi-dao ziji mei chuan yifu.
Zhangsan at mirror-in see self and realize self no wear clothes
Zhangsan saw himself in the mirror, and realized he himself was naked.

(13) Zhangsan zai jingzi-li kan ziji, dan mei renchu ziji.
Zhangsan at mirror-in see self but no recognize self
Zhangsan saw himself in the mirror without recognizing himself.

Clearly, (12) and (13) suggest that local bound *ziji* is susceptible of *de se* and non-*de se* interpretations, respectively. There is no doubt that reflexive *ziji* is not interpreted *de se* in (13) because the whole sentence would come out as contradictory if it were interpreted *de se*.

3.3 Long-distance (LD) bound *ziji*

Compared to sentence free *ziji* and locally bound *ziji*, the *de se*/non-*de se* distinction is discussed more often in the research in LD bound *ziji*. The *de se* interpretation of LD *ziji* is first proposed by Pan (1997). According to him, LD *ziji* corresponds to the quasi-indicator *he** (Castañeda, 1966) in English, and hence always gets a *de se* interpretation. This is to say, given the following two scenarios, the sentence in (14) can only be uttered in the first scenario, but not in the second:

(14) S1: Zhangsan says, "That thief stole my purse!"
S2: Zhangsan says, "That thief stole that purse!" (can't see that it was his purse).
Zhangsan renwei pashou tou-le ziji-de pibao.

Zhangsan think pickpocket steal-PERF self-DE purse

'Zhangsan thought that the pickpocket stole his purse.'

However, Pan's proposal has met with criticism in the literature. Consider the following example which is originally provided by Huang and Tang (1991):

(15) Diving Scenario: Zhangsan is watching the video of the dives with some aquaintances. He likes one diver the best, but notices some people in the back snickering at the diver's form. He leans over and tells his neighbor, "I don't like those people who criticized that diver." Unbeknownst to him, he himself is the diver.

$Zhangsan_i$ bu xihuan naxie piping $ziji_i$ de ren.

Zhangsan NEG like those criticize self DE person

'Zhangsan does not like those people who criticize him.'

As indicated above, this sentence is acceptable even if *Zhangsan* does not know that he is speaking about himself. This is contrary to Pan's (1997) claim that LD *ziji* is obligatorily interpreted *de se*. Pollard and Xue (2001) make a similar point by giving the following example:

(16) Scenario: Zhangsan is trapped in a burning building and faints. When he wakes up, he is safely outside. He thinks he was lucky, but in fact was saved by a passerby.

$Zhangsan_i$ zai meiyou jian-guo jiu-le $ziji_i$ ming de na-ge ren.

Zhangsan again not have see-PERF save-PERF self life DE that-CL person

'Zhangsan didn't see again the person who saved his life.'

Clearly, this sentence shows again that the antecedent of LD *ziji* need not be the holder of the relevant *de se* attitude.

Although these examples are not consistent with Pan's claim, Anand (2006) points out that there is no attitude predicate in the two sentences above, thus making issues of *de se* interpretation moot. According to Anand, Pan's generalization should be that LD *ziji* is definitely interpreted *de se* in intensional contexts, while not necessarily so in extensional contexts. This description apparently explains away the above two so-called counterexamples. However, we do not endorse Anand's (2006) claim on the *de se* and non-*de se* distinction of LD *ziji*, for we observe that LD *ziji* used in intensional contexts, especially in reported speech, is not obligatorily interpreted *de se*, either.[5]

Check the scenarios mentioned earlier in (14) (we repeat them as (17) below):

(17) S1: Zhangsan says, "That thief stole my purse!"

S2: Zhangsan says, "That thief stole that purse!" (can't see that it was his purse).

Zhangsan shuo pashou tou-le ziji-de pibao.

Zhangsan say pickpocket steal-PERF self-DE purse

'Zhangsan said that the pickpocket stole his purse.'

In (17), the speaker reports Zhangsan's utterance by using the speech predicate *shuo (say)*, instead of the epistemic predicate *renwei (think)* as in (14). Although it is generally held in the literature (e.g., Huang & Liu (2001), Anand (2006)) that the reported speech in (17) can only be uttered in the first scenario (if the scenario is the second one, the speaker has to replace *ziji* by the third person pronoun *he* with a *de re* interpretation), we do not think the obligatory *de se* reading of *ziji* in speech reports is definitely

[5] It is not difficult to see that reported speech provides intensional contexts rather than extensional ones. For instance, we can't infer 'John said that the morning star is the evening star' from "John said that the morning star is the morning star'. This means that the replacement of one expression by another with the same extension in a reported speech affects the truth value of the whole sentence, and therefore the context in a speech report is intensional.

required. According to our intuition, there is no problem for the speaker to utter the sentence in (17) in the second scenario if he/she knows that it is Zhangsan's purse that got lost, and then empathizes with Zhangsan, taking Zhangsan's point of view.

According to the literature, the empathic use of long-distance reflexives has already been detected in other languages such as Japanese (Kuno, 1987; Oshima, 2004, 2006). According to Oshima (2006), Japanese LD *zibun* basically has two uses: logophoric and empathic, and in attitude reports, although the logophoric use of *zibun* which requires obligatory *de se* reading is strongly preferred, the non-*de se* interpretation is not totally excluded. Just like Japanese *zibun*, we believe that Chinese *ziji* in attitude reports is not always a *de se* anaphor. So to speak, the empathic *ziji* with a non-*de se* interpretation is possible in indirect speech. Nevertheless, we find that these two languages differ in the hierarchy of attitude predicates in terms of their availability of the non-*de se* mode. According to Oshima (2006), the non-*de se* mode in Japanese is available for any type of the attitude predicate below: speech predicates, epistemic predicates, psychological predicates, and knowledge predicates, though with the following hierarchy:

(18) Speech Predicates < Epistemic Predicates /Psychological Predicates < Knowledge Predicates

Sentence (18) suggests that it is easier to use the non-*de se* mode in contexts with knowledge predicates, while it is harder to use the non-*de se* mode in contexts with speech predicates. According to Oshima, this conforms to the cross-linguistic generalization that, if in a given language (some) predicates in one class allows reports in the non-*de se* mode, so do (some) predicates in every class higher on the hierarchy. For instance, in Mapun, the non-*de se* mode can never be associated with *say*, though it is possible with other predicates. However, according to our judgment of the relevant Chinese data, we do not think this generalization holds in Chinese. According to our intuition, while speech predicates and psychological predicates allow the non-*de se* mode, this mode marginally occurs in contexts with epistemic predicates or knowledge predicates, as we have already pointed out the possible non-*de se* reading of LD *ziji* in reported speech by using the example in (17). To further support this point, as an illustration of the possible non-*de se* reading of LD *ziji* in contexts with psychological verbs, consider the following example:

(19) Scenario: In Zhangsan's class, Lisi won a prize for his painting. Zhangsan, as Lisi's teacher, was very happy to hear this news. However, Lisi actually is Zhangsan's son, though he does not know this, because his son was lost at the age of three years old, and then was adopted by another family that he has never met.

Ziji erzi dejiang de xiaoxi rang Zhangsan hen gaoxing.

Self son win-the-prize DE news make Zhangsan very happy

'That his son won the prize made Zhangsan very happy.'

In the scenario above, we think it is appropriate to utter the sentence in (19) if we empathize with Zhangsan, namely taking Zhangsan's point of view, as we know Lisi is actually Zhangsan's son, though he himself did not know this. But in the belief contexts, we see the opposite. For instance, the utterance of the sentence in (14) is very likely judged as false in the second scenario, and it is not getting better even if we change the epistemic predicate *renwei (think)* to the knowledge predicate *zhidao (know)*. For now, the explanation of the difference between the hierarchy concerning the availability of non-*de se* mode in Chinese and other language (e.g., Japanese) is still not very clear to us, and we thus leave it for future research.

To sum up, we observe that LD *ziji* is not an obligatory *de se* anaphor in either intensional or extensional contexts. In addition, we believe that the non-*de se* but empathic interpretation of LD *ziji* is more acceptable in contexts with speech predicates or psychological predicates than in contexts with epistemic predicates or knowledge predicates.

4. Discussion

Based on our observations above about the *de se* and non-*de se* distinction of the interpretation of the first person indexical and Chinese reflexive *ziji,* we discuss the empirical and theoretical impacts of our findings in this section.

First, the following implications can be put forward. (a) Neither the first person indexical nor the three uses of Chinese reflexive *ziji* is obligatorily interpreted *de se.* (b) Since the first person pronoun *wo* in Chinese does not have a shifted use in attitude reports, we need to use reflexive pronoun *ziji* (or third person pronouns, of course) in the embedded clause to refer to the believer or the speaker, if the relevant reports are third-person ones. (c) In the embedded clause of a first-person *de re* belief report in Chinese, the first person pronoun *wo,* rather than the reflexive *ziji,* is preferred to be used, due to the fact that the latter strongly favors a *de se* interpretation in belief reporting contexts.

Second, Wechsler's DRT framework for person indexicals is inadequate to characterize the belief reports involving the first/second person pronoun in the embedded clauses, though it works well for single-clause sentences. For instance, the single-clause sentence 'I am smart' uttered by Zhangsan can be characterized as follows:

(20) speaker: Conceives (Zhangsan, $\langle {}^{z}i_{smart}, {}^{z}n_{self} \rangle$, smart'(Zhangsan))

However, the belief report with an embedded clause 'Lisi believes that I am smart' uttered by Zhangsan apparently can't be analyzed in the same way. But Wechsler himself ignore such cases in his paper. Besides, as mentioned in Section 2, the first/second person pronoun may also be interpreted as *de se* or non-*de se* with respect to the matrix subject in the sentence, thus getting its reference to the speaker/hearer indirectly through the matrix subject, in addition to being interpreted as *de se* with respect to the speaker in the context directly. Although the latter situation can be still interpreted in Wechsler's way, how to deal with the former situation is still a problem for us to solve in the future. For now, in Wechsler's DRT framework one cannot distinguish the possible different readings (i.e., *de se* and non-*de se*) of the embedded *I* used in the *de se* and non-*de se* attitude reports. We believe Kamp's (2011) work on DRT analysis of complex thoughts may shed some light on this issue.

Third, given the *de se* and non-*de se* distinction of the interpretation of the Chinese reflexive *ziji,* we find that the prevailing analysis of Chinese LD *ziji* as a logophor (e.g., Huang & Liu, 2001; Anand, 2006) may be problematic. At first, according to Oshima (2004, 2006), Sells' (1987) notion of logophority which incorporates the notion of point of view/empathy is misleading. Actually, Japanese data show that logophoricity and empathy play distinct roles in binding. Therefore, it is also inappropriate to treat Chinese LD *ziji* as a logophor in Sells' sense. Second, following Oshima's split treatment of Japanese LD *zibun,* one may propose that Chinese LD *ziji* also has two uses: logophoric and empathic. However, we think the purely logophoric use of LD *ziji* is suspicious because LD *ziji* has different distributions from the logophoric use of LD *zibun.* First, LD *ziji* is always subject-oriented (see (21)); and second, LD *ziji* involves the blocking effect induced by the first and second person pronouns (see (22)).

(21) Bill_i cong John_j na tingshuo $\text{ziji}_{i/*j}$

ying-le.

Bill from John there hear-from self win-Perf

'Bill$_i$ heard from John$_j$ that he$_{i/*j}$ had won.'

(22) Zhangsan$_i$ juede wo/ni$_j$ zai piping ziji$_{*i/j}$.

Zhangsan think I/you at criticize self

'Zhangsan thinks that I/you am criticizing myself/yourself/*him.'

But, according to Oshima's (2004) analysis of the properties of the logophoric use of Japanese LD *zibun*, the above two properties are unexpected to be possessed by Chinese LD *ziji* if it has a purely logophoric use. Below we illustrate that Japanese logophoric *zibun* can be bound to a non-subject and can also co-occur with the first person pronoun.

(23) Bill-wa John$_i$-Kara zibun$_i$-ga Kat-ta koto-o kii-ta.

Bill-Top John-from self-Nom win-Past fact-Acc hear-Past

'Bill heard from John$_i$ that he$_i$ had won.'

(24) Taro$_i$-wa boku-ga zibun$_i$-o but-ta koto-o mada urande-i-ru.

Taro-Top I-Nom self-Acc hit-Past fact-Acc still resent-Asp-pres

'Taro$_i$ still resents that I hit him$_i$.'

For this reason, our conjecture is that Chinese LD *ziji* does not have a purely logophoric use, and instead, it is an anaphor with the empathy requirement, as its properties such as subject-orientation and the blocking effect are also required for an anaphor with the empathy requirement (e.g., the empathic use of LD *zibun* has these two properties, as in (25) and (26)).

(25) Taro$_i$-wa Hanako$_j$-ni zibun-ga sekkei-si-ta ie-de at-ta.

Taro-Top Hanako-Dat self-Nom design-Past house-Acc meet-Past

'Taro$_i$ met Hanako$_j$ in a house which he$_i$/*she$_j$ designed.'

(26) *Taro$_i$-wa boku-ga zibun$_i$-ni kasi-ta okane-o nakusite-simat-ta rasi-i.

Taro-Top I-Nom self-Dat lend-past money-Acc lose-end.up-Past seem-Pres

'It seems that Taro$_i$ lost the money I lent him$_i$.'

And its preferred (but not obligatory) *de se* interpretation can be accounted for through pragmatics.[6]

5. Conclusion

In this paper, by making the *de se* and non-*de se* distinction of the interpretation of the first person pronoun and Chinese reflexive *ziji*, we have the following empirical and theoretical observations. (a) Neither of the first person indexical nor the three uses of Chinese reflexive *ziji* is obligatorily interpreted *de se*. (b) Since the first person pronoun *wo* in Chinese does not have a shifted use in attitude reports, we need to use reflexive pronoun *ziji* (or third person pronouns, of course) in the embedded clause to refer to the believer or the speaker, if the relevant reports are third-person ones. (c) In first-person non-*de se* belief reports in Chinese, the first person pronoun *wo* (not *ziji*) is preferred to be used in the embedded clause to express the speaker's non-*de se* beliefs. (d) Wechsler's (2010) self-ascription monopoly does not apply to all the occurrences of the first and second person pronouns; his theory has troubles when turning to first/second person belief reports with embedded *I/you* used to express *de se* or non-*de se* with respect to the matrix subject. (e) The prevailing analysis of Chinese LD *ziji* as a logophor is not appealing. Given the special properties of Chinese LD *ziji*, our conjecture is that it is an anaphor with the empathy requirement, and its preferred *de se* interpretation can be accounted for through pragmatics.

[6] We have argued at length in another paper that Chinese LD *ziji* is not a logophor, but an anaphor with an empathy requirement.

Acknowledgments:

This paper is supported by the GRF grant CityU 148610, funded by Research Grants Council, Hong Kong. We also appreciate the suggestions and comments made by the anonymous reviewers of the PACLIC 26 conference.

References:

Anand, P. 2006. *De de se*. Ph.D. thesis, MIT Cambridge, MA.

Baker, C. L. 1995. Contrast, discourse prominence, and intensification, with special reference to locally free reflexives in British English. *Language* 71: 63-101.

Castañeda, H-N. 1966. "he": A study in the logic of self-consciousness. *Ratio* 8: 130-157.

Chomsky, N. 1981. *Lectures on Government and Binding*. Dordrecht: Foris.

Corazza, E. 2004. Essential indexicals and quasi-indicators. In *Journal of Semantics* 21: 341-374.

Crimmins, M. 1992. *Talk about beliefs*. Cambridge, MA: MIT Press.

Huang, J. & L. Liu. 2001. Logophoricity, Attitudes, and *ziji* at the interface, *Long Distance Reflexives*, P. Cole et al. (eds.), Syntax and Semantics 33, 141–195. Academic Press : New York.

Huang, J. & J. Tang. 1991. The local nature of the long distance reflexives in Chinese, In J. Koster and E. Reuland (eds.), *Long-distance Anaphor*. 263-282. Cambridge: Cambridge University Press.

Kamp, H. 2011. Representing *de se* thoughts and their reports, http://nasslli2012.com/files/kamp_2011.pdf

Kuno, S. 1987. *Functional Syntax: Anaphora, Discourse and Empathy*. Chicago: University of Chicago Press.

Lewis, D. 1979. Attitudes *de dicto* and *de se*. *The Philosophical Review* 88: 513-543.

Maier, E. 2009. Proper names and indexicals trigger rigid presuppositions. *Journal of Semantics*. 26, 253-315.

Oshima, D. 2004. On empathic and logophoric binding. Proceedings of Workshop on Semantic Approaches to Binding Theory, Nancy, France.

Oshima, D. 2006. *Perspectives in Reported Discourse*. Ph.D. Dissertation. Stanford University.

Pan Haihua. 1997. *Constraints on Reflexivization in Mandarin Chinese*. Garland Publishing, Inc., New York.

Pan Haihua. 2001. Why the blocking effect? *Syntax and Semantics* Vol. 33, *Long Distance Reflexives*, edited by Peter Cole, James Huang, and G. Hermon, New York: Academic Press, pp. 279-316.

Perry, J. 1979. The problem of the essential indexical. *Noûs* 12: 3-21.

Polland, C. & P. Xue. 2001. Syntactic and non-syntactic constraints on long-distance binding. *Syntax and Semantics* Vol. 33, *Long Distance Reflexives*, edited by Peter Cole, James Huang, and G. Hermon, New York: Academic Press, pp. 279-316.

Premack, D and G. Woodruff. 1978. Does the chimpanzee have a theory of mind? *The Behavioral and Brain Sciences* 1: 515-526.

Sells, P. 1987. Aspects of Logophoricity. *Linguistic Inquiry* 18: 445-479.

Tsai, W.-T. Dylan. 2002. Ziji, zixing yu ziran: tan hanyu zhong de fanshen zhuangyu (Self, selfhood, and nature - on reflexive adverbials in Chinese). *Zhongguoyuwen* 289: 357-362.

Wechsler, S. 2010. What 'you' and 'I' mean to each other: person indexicals, self-ascription, and theory of mind. *Language* 86(2): 332-365

The Headedness of Mandarin Chinese Serial Verb Constructions: A Corpus-Based Study

Jingxia Lin[1] Chu-Ren Huang[1] Huarui Zhang[1,2] Hongzhi Xu[1]
[1]The Hong Kong Polytechnic University; [2]Peking University
{ctjlin; churen.huang}@polyu.edu.hk; hrzhang@pku.edu.cn; hongz.xu@gmail.com

Abstract

Existing treebanks of Mandarin Chinese such as the Sinica Treebank, the Harbin Institute of Technology Treebank, and the Penn Chinese Treebank, parse Chinese serial verb constructions incorrectly or inconsistently in terms of headedness, i.e. which verb to be assigned with the label of syntactic and/or semantic "head". Aspectual markers in serial verb constructions can help determine the head of these constructions (Li, 1991; among others). However, the majority of Chinese serial verb constructions do not have overt aspectual markers. Based on large-scale corpus studies, this work investigates the distribution of aspectual markers in Chinese serial verb constructions in order to explore which verb in the serial verbs is more likely to function as the head, and thus provides a reference for parsing serial verb constructions without overt aspectual markers. We find that contrary to previous studies such as Collins (1997), Law and Veenstra (1992) and Sebba (1987) that treat the first verb in a serial verb construction as the head, Chinese serial verb constructions more often have the second verb as the head. The results of this work can not only serve as a reference for automatic parsing of Chinese data, but also shed light on theoretical studies of the structure of serial verb constructions in Chinese and other serial verb languages.

1 Introduction

This section first introduces the kind of serial verb constructions (SVCs) under discussion; then, it shows the difficulties in identifying the head verb of an SVC, both in terms of theoretical linguistics and automatic parsing.

1.1 The SVCs of this study

"Serial verb construction" is not a unified notion in previous studies (Sebba, 1987; Lord, 1993; Durie, 1997; Aikhenvald, 2006; Li and Thompson, 1981; Paul, 2008; among many others). This paper focuses on SVCs in Mandarin Chinese, in particular, the type of SVCs in a narrower scope and is usually treated as typical SVCs by previous studies. Such SVCs display the following properties (cf. Li and Thompson, 1981; Paul, 2008; Muller and Lipenkova, 2009; Zhang, 2010; among others):[1]

(i) An SVC consists of a sequence of VPs with no overt connective markers; these VPs express simultaneous or immediately consecutive actions that can be conceived as one event.

(ii) The VPs share the same grammatical subject. For instance, (1a) is an SVC, but (1b) is not because the object of the first verb (V1) is the subject of the second verb (V2).

(1) a. *chuqu kai-men*
exit open-door
'go out to open the door'

b. *qing ta he-cha*
invite him drink-tea
'invite him to drink the tea'

(iii) The VPs in an SVC can occur as the main VP in a clause. For instance, (2a) is an

[1] The majority of Chinese SVCs consist of two VPs. For convenience, this study only discusses SVCs of this type.

SVC, but (2b) is not, because *na* 'hold' and its object in (2a) can occur as the main VP in a clause, whereas *na* and its object in (2b) cannot occur alone and is treated as a PP.

(2) a. *ta na-le shu lai wo-jia*
she hold-ASP book come my.home
'She took books and came to my home.'

b. *ta na nage chouwen xiao ta*
she hold that scandal laugh him
'She laughed at him with the scandal.'

(iv) The relative order of the VPs in an SVC cannot be switched without a significant change of the meaning, e.g., *chuqu kai-men* 'go out to open the door' vs. *kai-men chuqu* 'open the door to go out'; this distinguishes SVCs from coordinate structure that describes two independent and parallel events, e.g., *changge tiaowu* 'sing songs and dance', *tiaowu changge* 'dance and sing songs'

1.2 The Problem of Identifying the Head Verb of Chinese SVCs

Identifying the head of an SVC in Chinese has been a difficult issue for linguists. Previous studies such as Collins (1997), Law & Veenstra (1992), Sebba (1987), Seuren (1991) argue that the first verb is usually the head of SVCs in serial verb languages. However, this is found not true for Chinese (Li, 1991; Law, 1996; Matthews, 2006; Paul, 2008; among others). For instance, Paul (2008) points out that either V1 or V2 can function as the head in a Chinese SVC. According to her, both V1 and V2 can be the head of the SVC in (3) depending on whether the SVC is understood as a purpose clause structure (3a) or an adjunct structure (3b), cf. Li and Thompson (1981).

(3) *ta gui xialai qiu wo*
he kneel down beg me
a. He knelt down in order to beg me.
b. He begged me kneeling down.
(Paul, 2008: 382, (41-42))

However, Paul's (2008) proposal does not help automatic parsing because the identification of the head heavily relies on larger context.

Muller and Lipenkova (2009), within the HPSG framework, analyze Chinese SVC as a structure with two parallel verbal daughters and do not mark any verb as the structural head, although they claim that the first verbal daughter is always a complete VP. Similarly, Yu et al. (2010) treat serial verbs as a type of coordinate structure and assign no head to any of the verbs. Such a representation, however, ignores the internal relationship between the (sub)events described by the serial VPs as well as the fact that the serial VPs in an SVC describe a single event. For instance, the SVC *kaiche lüyou* drive-car travel 'travel by driving a car' describes an event of travelling in a manner of driving a car, but treating the two VPs in a parallel way indicates that there are two independent events, i.e. an event of driving and an event of travelling.

Other studies such as Li (1991) and Law (1996) propose that in a Chinese SVC, the verb suffixed with aspect markers is the head because the non-head verbs are usually bare verbs, cf. Sebba (1987). For instance, Li (1991) points out that *qie* 'cut' in (4a) and *na* 'take' in (4b) are the heads respectively in the two SVCs because these two verbs are suffixed with the perfective aspectual marker *le*.

(4) a. *ta na dao qie-**le** rou*
he take knife cut-ASP meat
'He cut the meat with a knife.'
(Li, 1991:104 (11))

b. *ta na-**le** dao qie rou*
he take-ASP knife cut meat
'He took the knife to cut meat.'
(Li, 1991:112 (13a))

However, problems still exist because not all Chinese SVCs are overtly marked with aspectual markers. For instance, in the 436 SVCs that we collect from the Sinica Corpus, there are only 33 instances (7.5%) where the verb(s) is suffixed with aspectual markers.[2] Accordingly, the difficulty in

[2] The 436 SVCs are manually collected from 3,000 automatically extracted clauses with more than two verbs in the Sinica Corpus (Chen et al. 1996), which consists of about ten million POS-tagged words.

identifying the head causes troubles for automatic parsing of Chinese SVCs. The same SVC is sometimes found to be mistakenly or inconsistently analyzed by the Sinica Treebank[3], the Harbin Institute of Technology (HIT) treebank[4], and the Penn Chinese Treebank[5]. For example, the SVC in (5) describes an event of eating fruit by going to the kitchen (the perfective marker *le* is suffixed to V2 *chi* 'eat'). However, as illustrated in Figure (1a) and Figure (1b), both the Sinica Treebank and the HIT Treebank mark the first verb *qu* 'go' as the head and indicate that the SVC describes an event of going to the kitchen with a result of eating fruit, whereas the latter suggests that the SVC

(5) *qu chufang chi-**le** shuiguo*
go kitchen eat-LE fruit
'eat the fruit by going to the kitchen'

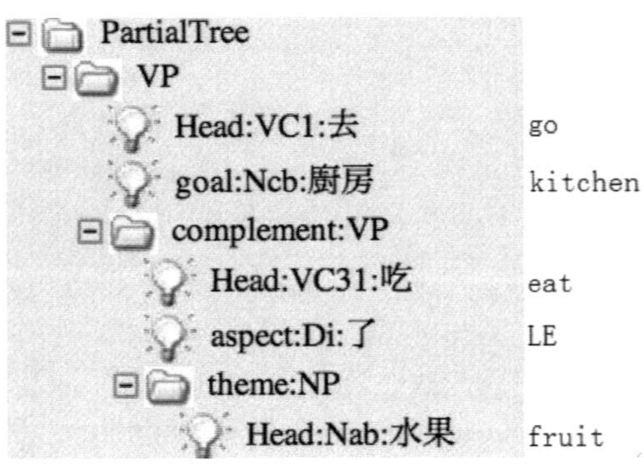

Figure 1(a). The parsing of (5) by the Sinica Treebank

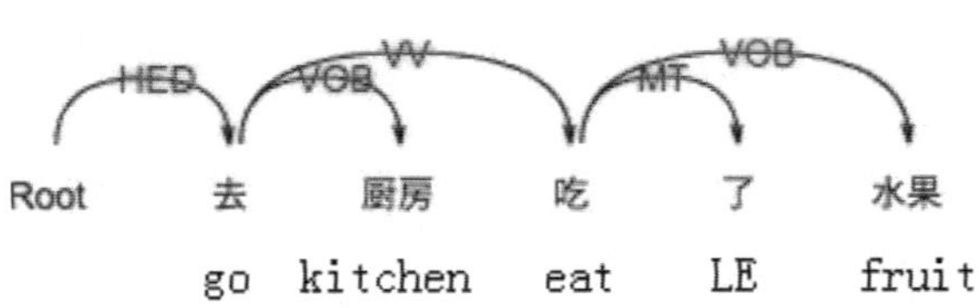

Figure 1(b). The parsing of (5) by the HIT Treebank

Also, the same SVC may be parsed differently by different treebanks. For instance, the SVC *mai-shu kan* buy-book read is treated as a headless coordinate structure by the Penn Chinese Treebank (Figure 2(a)), but a purpose clause with V1 as the head by the Sinica Treebank (Figure 2 (b)) and the HIT Treebank (Fiture 2(c)).

```
(IP (NP-PN-SBJ (NR 张三))          Zhangsan
    (VP (VP (VV 买)                buy
            (NP-1 (NN 书))         book
        (VP-PRP (VV 看)            read
                (NP (-NONE- *-1))))))
```

Figure 2(a) The parsing of *mai-shu kan* by the Penn Chinese Treebank (Xue and Xia, 2000: 114)

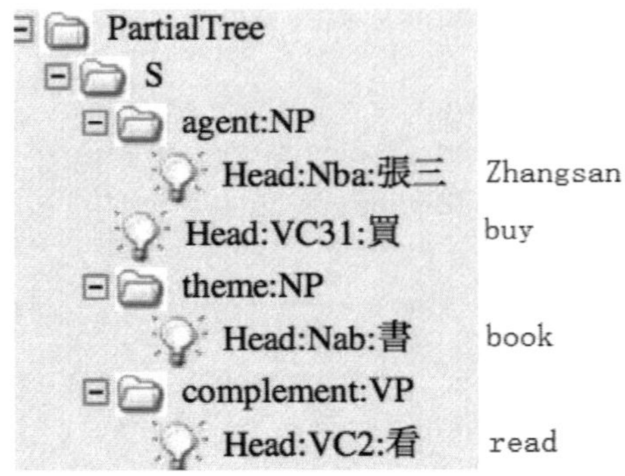

Figure 2(b) The parsing of *mai-shu kan* by the Sinica Treebank

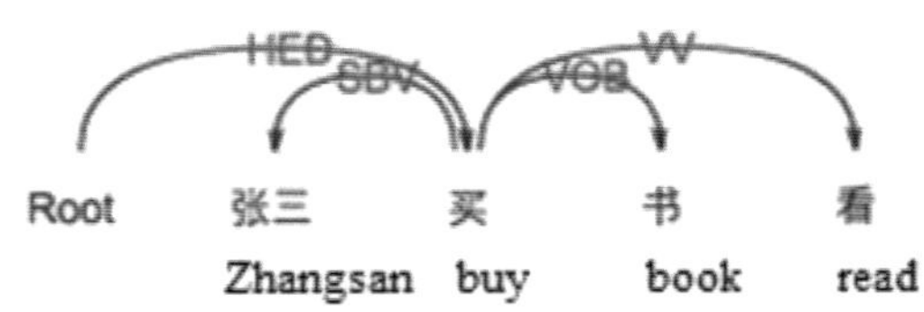

Figure 2(c) The parsing of *mai-shu kan* by the HIT Treebank

The incorrect or inconsistent parsing by these treebanks indicates that a better understanding of the headedness of Chinese SVCs is necessary. Based on the 10-million-word Sinica Corpus, this work investigates the distribution of aspectual markers in SVCs in order to find whether there is a systematic preference for either V1 or V2 to be marked as the head.[6] We find that in Chinese SVCs, V2 is much more often suffixed with aspectual markers that are indicators of head, whereas V1 is more often suffixed with aspectual markers that are indicators of non-head. In other words, the finding suggests that Chinese SVCs tend to have V2 as the head. Accordingly, for SVCs without overt aspectual markers, annotating V2 as the head will

[3] http://turing.iis.sinica.edu.tw/treesearch
[4] http://ir.hit.edu.cn/demo/ltp/#
[5] http://www.cis.upenn.edu/~chinese/

[6] Other linguistic hints such as negators can help identify the head of SVCs (Sebba, 1987; Lin, 2004). For instance, Sebba (1987) argues that non-head verbs are not directly negated. Due to the scope of this study, we only investigate the distribution of aspectual markers, and leave the others for future.

yield a higher accuracy rate than annotating V1 as the head (as by Sinica Treebank and HIT Treebank), or annotating V1 and V2 as coordinated verbs (as by Penn State Chinese Treebank).

In the following of this paper, we introduce our study in Section 2, and draw the conclusion in Section 3.

2 A Corpus-based Investigation of the Distribution of Aspectual Markers in Chinese SVCs

This section first introduces the possible distribution of Chinese aspectual markers in SVCs. Then, it introduces two corpus studies that examine the distribution of aspectual markers in SVCs of natural Chinese language; both studies show that it is V2 that is much more frequently marked as the head.

2.1 The Possible Distribution of Aspectual Markers in Chinese SVCs

In Modern Chinese, *le* 'perfective', *guo* 'experiential', and *zhe* 'durative' are among the most commonly used aspectual markers in Chinese. All three can be suffixed to V1, V2, or both verbs in an SVC. A few examples are given in (6)-(8), where the aspectual markers are suffixed to V1 in (a) sentences, V2 in (b) sentences, and both V1 and V2 in (c) sentences.

(6) a. *ta dao-**le** tushuguan kan na-ben shu*
he arrive-LE library read that book
'He went to the library to read the book.'
b. *ta dao tushuguan kan-**le** na-ben shu*
he arrive library read-LE that book
'He read the book by going to the library.'
c. *ta dao-**le** tushuguan kan-**le** na-ben shu*
he arrive-LE library read-LE that book
'He went to the library and read the book.'

(7) a. *ta qu-**guo** Xianggang lüyou*
he go-GUO Hong.Kong travel
'He had the experience of going to Hong Kong to travel.'
b. *ta qu Xianggang lüyou-**guo***
he go Hong.Kong travel-GUO
'He went to Hong Kong and had the experience of travelling there.'
c. *ta qu-**guo** Xianggang lüyou-**guo***
he go-GUO Hong.Kong travel-GUO
'He had the experience of going to Hong Kong and travelling there.'

(8) a. *ta pai-**zhe**-shou xiao*
he clap-ZHE-hand laugh
'He laughed, clapping his hands.'
b. *ta pai-shou xiao-**zhe***
he clap-hand laugh-ZHE
'He clapped his hands, laughing.'
c. *ta pai-**zhe**-shou xiao-**zhe***
he clap-ZHE-hand laugh-ZHE
'He is clapping his hands and laughing.'

The verb suffixed with the perfective marker *le* or the experiential marker *guo* is often treated as the head of a construction, both syntactically and semantically, as in (4) (Li, 1991). On the contrary, as for the verb that is suffixed with the durative marker *zhe* in an SVC, we argue that the VP containing the verb functions as an adverbial to modify the other VP (unless the verb in the other VP is also suffixed with *zhe*) (cf. Li, 1991). For instance, in *xiao-zhe guzhang* laugh-ZHE applaud 'applaud with laughing', *xiao-zhe* is understood as an adverbial describing an event of laughing that accompanies the event of applauding, i.e. the event described by the bare verb *guzhang* 'applaud'. According to Gao (2006), in Modern Chinese, examples are found in which the adverbial marker *de* is overtly used after the VP with the aspectual marker *zhe*, as in (9); this further shows that a verb suffixed with the durative marker *zhe* functions as an adverbial rather than a syntactic or semantic head.

(9) *wo hui weixiao-**zhe-de** gaosu ni*
I will smile-ZHE-MOD tell you
'I will tell you with a smile.' (Baidu example)

Therefore, as for SVCs with overt aspectual markers, their heads can be identified by looking at the distribution of the aspectual markers in the SVCs. For instance, in (6a) and (7a), the first verbs are the head because they are the only verbs that are suffixed with *le/guo*, whereas in (6b) and (7b), the second verbs are the head because they are suffixed with *le/guo*; on the contrary, although V2 in (8a) is not suffixed with any markers, it should be treated as the head because V1 is suffixed with *zhe*, and in (8b), V1 is the head since V2 is suffixed with *zhe*. In addition, for each (c) sentence in (6)-(8), both verbs are marked with the same aspectual markers, and thus there is no clear clue to identify the headedness. A comprehensive distribution of aspectual markers and the identification of headedness is presented in Table 1.

	Distribution of aspectual markers in SVCs
V1 = head	(a) V1-*le*/*guo* ... V2... (b) V1...V2-*zhe*... (c) V1-*le*/*guo*...V2-*zhe*...
V1/V2 parallel	(a) V1-*le*/*guo*...V2-*le*/*guo*... (b) V1-*zhe*...V2-*zhe*...
V2 = head	(a) V1...V2-*le*/*guo* (b) V1-*zhe*...V2 (c) V1-*zhe*...V2-*le*/*guo*...

Table 1. Identification of headedness in SVCs based on the distribution of aspectual markers.

The fact that both V1 and V2 are found with all three aspectual markers indicates that Chinese SVCs show both possibilities in terms of the position of their heads, in contrast to other languages such as Korean where all aspectual markers fall onto the final verb of a clause (Kim, 2010). However, we argue that despite the possibility of appearing in either V1 or V2 position of an SVC as in (6)-(8) and Table 1, Chinese aspectual markers do not have an even distribution in SVCs; but rather, *le* and *zhe*, which are indicators of headedness, are more frequently suffixed to V2, whereas the non-head marker *zhe* is more frequently found with V1. In other words, although Chinese SVCs can have either V1 or V2 as the head, it is more likely for V2 to be the head.

In the next section, we introduce two corpus studies to show that V2 is indeed much more frequently marked as the head in Chinese SVCs according to the distribution of aspectual markers.

2.2 A Corpus-based Investigation of Aspectual Markers in Chinese SVCs

We carried out two corpus studies to investigate the distribution of aspectual markers in Chinese SVCs; both studies support our claim that V2 is preferred to be the head. The data used is the Sinica Corpus (Chen et al.; 1996), which consists of about ten million segmented and POS-tagged words.

Corpus Study 1

In the first study, we searched in the whole Sinica Corpus for the distribution of aspectual markers ("ASP") in the following three sequences: "V1-ASP1 + N1 + V2 + N2", "V1-ASP1 + N1 + V2-ASP2 + N2", "V1 + N1 + V2-ASP2 + N2".[7,8] The retrieved data is then manually analyzed to exclude the sequences that are not SVCs.[9] The results are given in Table 2.

Table 2 shows that differences indeed exist for the suffixation of aspectual markers to the verbs in SVCs. The perfective marker *le* and the experiential marker *guo* tend to be suffixed to V2 in SVCs, whereas the durative marker *zhe* is more often suffixed to V1 position. Such distribution indicates that V2 much more frequently functions as the head: as summarized in Table 2, the frequency of V2 being the head (261 instances, 76.5%) is about four times higher than that of V1 being the head (66 instances, 16.2%), which thus is consistent with our claim.

[7] All SVCs examined in the first corpus study consist of verbs that are followed by nouns. The reason for choosing such sequences is that in Chinese, there are two kinds of *le*, one as an aspectual marker and the other as a sentence final particle, and if a verb (usually intransitive) is followed by *le* and occurs in a sentence final position, it is difficult to determine whether the *le* is an aspectual marker or a sentence final particle. It is beyond the scope of this study to manually check all instances of "V2+ *le*" in the sentence final position for all verbs, so this study only investigates the SVCs where V2 is followed by a noun in order to guarantee that all instances of *le* are aspectual markers. However, the second corpus study introduced in Section 2.2.2 analyzes all kinds of SVCs because the nature of the data is suitable for manual check.

[8] The Sinica Corpus tags adjectives, cause marker (e.g., *rang* and *shi*), and copular as verbs. In this study, we do not treat verbal sequences with these words as SVCs. More specifically, we only searched for verbs with the following tags: VA, VB, VC, VAC, VCL, VD, VE, VF, and VG. For more information of the tagging, readers are referred to the technical report at http://db1x.sinica.edu.tw/kiwi/mkiwi/98-04.pdf.

[9] The search results retrieved a total of 1,638 instances, but our manual examination of the results found that only 579 instances (as in Table 2) are the SVCs under discussion.

	V1=head	V1/V2 parallel	V2=head
V1-ASP1 + N1 + V2 + N2	(a) ASP1 = *le*: 54 (b) ASP1 = *guo*: 4	NA	(a) ASP1 = *zhe*: 281
V1-ASP1 + N1 + V2- ASP2 + N2	(a) ASP1 = le; ASP2 = *zhe*: 4	(a) ASP1= *le*; ASP2 = *le*: 22 (b) ASP1= *zhe*; ASP2 = *zhe*: 16 (c) ASP1 = *guo*, ASP2 = *guo*: 3 (d) ASP1 = *guo*, ASP2 = *le*: 1	(a) ASP1 = *zhe*; ASP2 = *le*: 16
V1 + N1 + V2-ASP2 + N2	ASP2 = *zhe*: 32	NA	(a) ASP2 = *le*: 130 (b) ASP2 = *guo*: 16
SUM	94 (16.2%)	42 (7.3%)	443 (76.5%)

Table 2. Distribution of aspectual markers in "V1 + N1 + V2 + N2" SVCs

Corpus Study 2

In this study, we first select nine verbs with high frequencies based on the 436 SVCs (see Footnote 2) found in the Sinica Corpus; then, we search for SVCs with these verbs and investigate the distribution of aspectual markers. The verbs are listed in (9).

(9) *dao* 'arrive', *dai* 'bring', *liyong* 'use', *shuo* 'say', *canjia* 'attend', *kan* 'see', *na* 'hold', *xiao* 'laugh', *mai* 'buy'

According to the 436 SVCs, these nine verbs tend to occur in different position of SVCs: *dao* 'arrive', *dai* 'bring', and *liyong* 'use' are more often found in V1 position, *shuo* 'say', *canjia* 'attend', and *kan* 'see' more often occur in V2 positions, whereas *na* 'hold', *xiao* 'laugh', *mai* 'buy' are found to occur in V1 and V2 positions with equivalent frequency.

Nonetheless, this study examines the distribution of aspectual markers in two kinds of sequences for each verb, one with the verb in V1 position, and the other with the verb in V2 position. For instance, for the verb *xiao* 'laugh', we analyze both the SVCs with the sequence "*xiao* + … + V2" and the sequence "V1 + … + *xiao*", where "…" stands for all kinds of elements that may appear in between the two verbs in an SVC. For each sequence, there are three possible distributions for the aspectual markers: for "*xiao* + … + V2", there are "*xiao*-ASP1 + … + V2", "*xiao* + … + V2-ASP2", and "*xiao*-ASP1 + … + V2-ASP2"; whereas for "V1 + … + *xiao*", there are "V1-ASP1 + … + *xiao*", "V1-ASP1 + … + *xiao*-ASP2", and "V1 + … + *xiao*-ASP2". The search results not only retrieve the frequency of each sequence, but also the whole clause where the sequence is found from the original texts, which thus enables manual check to exclude the instances that are not SVCs.[10]

Table 3 presents the frequency counts of headedness in SVCs of the nine verbs. It shows that among the nine verbs, only when the verb *mai* 'buy' occurs in V1 position and when the verb *dai* 'bring' occurs in V2 position do the SVCs have V1 more frequently marked as the head by the aspectual markers. On the contrary, the SVCs of all other verbs, be these verbs in V1 or V2 position, all have V2 functioning as the head.

Table 4 summarizes the distribution of aspectual markers in the SVCs found in this corpus study. The distribution is consistent with that in Corpus Study 1. For instance, *le* and *guo* that indicates headedness are much more often suffixed to V2 than to V1 (about five times). In addition, the table shows that there are only 1.7% of the SVCs where the serial verbs are marked in a parallel relation, i.e. the two verbs are suffixed with the same aspectual markers.

To summarize, both corpus studies provide quantitative support that Chinese SVCs tend to have V2 as the head, whereas the number of SVCs with V1 being the head, or V1 and V2 being of equal status is much smaller. Such a preference for V2 thus can serve as a reference for the parsing of headedness for SVCs without overt aspectual markers and yield a higher rate of accuracy than the current treebanks, i.e. the Sinica Treebank and

[10] The search results retrieved a total of 5,987 instances for the nine verbs. We then manually checked each instance and collected 2,154 instances that are the SVCs under the discussion of this paper (as in Table 3 and Table 4).

the HIT Treebank that often mark V1 as the head and the Penn Chinese Treebank that marks V1 and V2 as coordinated verbs.

3 Conclusion

This study pointed out the problem of identifying and parsing the head for Chinese SVCs. Based on corpus studies on the distribution of aspectual markers in Chinese SVCs, we found that it is V2 that is preferred to be the head in Chinese SVCs. The findings of this study are consistent with that of Huang and Lin (2012): their corpus study suggests that in Chinese SVCs, V1 does not tend to function as the head because the VP that occurs earlier in a linear sequence very often carries information such as location, manner/instrument, comitative, and condition, which is usually represented by adjuncts in a language.

We expect that this study can serve as a reference for automatic parsing of Chinese data with a higher accuracy rate, and shed light on theoretical studies of the structure of SVCs in Chinese as well as other serial verb languages.

	Searched verb = V1			Searched verb = V2			Sum-diff	Avrg-diff
	V1=head	V1/V2 parallel	V2=head	V1=head	V1/V2 parallel	V2=head		
xiao 'laugh'	3	0	203	1	4	23	222	0.959
dai 'bring'	46	9	505	11	2	2	450	0.782
shuo 'say'	0	0	12	62	3	476	426	0.770
canjia 'attend'	1	0	1	3	0	16	13	0.619
dao 'arrive'	37	5	97	25	1	115	150	0.536
na 'hold'	33	0	114	4	0	8	85	0.535
liyong 'use'	5	0	14	0	0	0	9	0.474
kan 'see'	12	0	29	74	10	128	71	0.281
mai 'buy'	30	0	3	8	4	15	-20	-0.333

*Sum-diff = Freq. (V2=head) – Freq. (V1=head)

Table 3. The distribution of aspectual markers in SVCs of nine Chinese verbs

	SVCs with ASP	Freq.	SUM
V1 = head	(a) V1-*le* ... V2...	241	355 (16.5%)
	(b) V1...V2-*zhe*...	102	
	(c) V1-*guo*...V2...	9	
	(d) V1-*le*...V2-*zhe*...	3	
V1/V2 Parallel	(a) V1-*zhe*...V2-*zhe*...	18	38 (1.7%)
	(b) V1-*le*...V2-*le*...	16	
	(c) V1-*guo* ...V2-*guo*...	4	
V2= head	(a) V1-*zhe*...V2...	1,499	1,761 (81.8%)
	(b) V1...V2-*le*...	192	
	(c) V1-*zhe*...V2-*le*...	52	
	(d) V1...V2-*guo*	18	
	(e) V1-*zhe*...V2-*guo*...	2	
SUM			2,154

Table 4. Distribution of aspectual markers in SVCs of the nine verbs

Acknowledgments

This work was supported by PolyU project 1-ZV8E.

References

Aikhenvald, Alexandra Y. 2006. Serial verb constructions in typological perspective. In A. Aikhenvald and R. M. W. Dixon (eds.), *Serial verb constructions - A cross-linguistic typology*, 1-68. Oxford: Oxford University Press.

Chen, Keh-Jiann, Chu-Ren Huang, Li-Ping Chang, and Hui-Li Hsu. 1996. Sinica corpus: Design methodology forbalanced corpora. *Proceedings of the 11th PacificAsian Conference on Language, Information and Computation*, 167–176.

Collins, Chris. 1997. Argument sharing in serial verb constructions. *Linguistic Inquiry*, 28: 461-497.

Durie, Mark. 1997. Grammatical structures in verb serialization. In A. Alsina, J. Bresnan, and P. Sells (eds.), *Complex Predicates*, 289–354. Stanford: CSLI Publications.

Gao, Zengxia. 2006. *Xiandai Hanyu Liandongshi de Yufahua Shijiao* [Serial Verb Constructions in Modern Chinese: A Perspective from Grammaticalization]. Beijing: Zhongguo Dang'an Chubanshe.
Kim, Jong-Bok. Argument composition in Korean Serial Verb Constructions. *Studies in Modern Grammar* 61, 1-24.
Law, Paul, and Tonjes Veenstra. 1992. On the structure of serial verb constructions. *Linguistic Analysis,* 22:185-217.
Law, Paul. 1996. A note on the serial verb construction in Chinese. *Cahiers de linguistique - Asie orientale*, 25(2), 199-233.
Huang, Churen and Jingxia Lin. 2012. The Order of Serial VPs in Mandarin Chinese SVCs: A Proto-VP Approach. *The 20th Annual Conference of the International Association of Chinese Linguistics (IACL-20)*. Hong Kong, August 29-31.
Li, Charles N. and Sandra A. Thompson. 1981. *Mandarin Chinese: A Functional Reference Grammar*. Berkeley: University of California Press.
Li, Yafei. 1991. On deriving serial verb constructions. In C. Lefebvre (ed.) *Serial Verbs: Grammatical, Comparative and Cognitive Approaches*, 103-35. Amsterdam: John Benjamins.
Lin, Huei-Ling. 2004. Serial verb constructions vs. secondary predication. *Concentric: Studies in Linguistics* 30.2, 93-122.
Lord, Carol. 1993. *Historical Change in Serial Verb Constructions*. Amsterdam: John Benjamins.
Matthews, Stephen. 2006. On serial verb constructions in Cantonese. In *Serial Verb Constructions. A Cross-Linguistic Typology*, A. Y. Aikhenvald and R. M.W. Dixon (eds.), 69-87. Oxford: Oxford University Press.
Müller, Stefan and Janna Lipenkova. 2009. Serial Verb Constructions in Chinese: An HPSG Account. *Proceedings of the HPSG-2009 Conference*, 234-254.
Paul, Waltraud. 2008. The 'serial verb construction' in Chinese: A tenacious myth and a Gordian knot. *The Linguistic Review* 25(3/4): 367-411.
Sebba, Mark. 1987. *The Syntax of Serial Verbs*. Amsterdam: John Benjamins.
Seuren, Pieter. 1991. The definition of serial verbs. In F. Byrne and T. Huebner (eds.), *Development and Structures of Creole Languages,* 193-205. Amsterdam: John Benjamins.
Xue, Nianwen and Fei Xia. 2000. The Bracketing Guidelines for the Penn Chinese Treebank (3.0). available at http://www.cis.upenn.edu/~chinese/parseguide.3rd.ch.pdf.
Yu, Kun, Yusuke Miyao, Xiangli Wang, Takuya Matsuzaki, Junichi Tsujii. 2010. Semi-automatically Developing Chinese HPSG Grammar from the Penn Chinese Treebank for Deep Parsing. *Coling 2010*, 1417-1425.
Zhang, Bin. 2010. *Xiandai Hanyu Miaoxie Yufa* [A descriptive grammar of Modern Chinese]. Beijing: Shangwu Chubanshe.

Japanese Pseudo-NPI *Dare-mo* as an "Unrestricted" Universal Quantifier

Katsuhiko Yabushita
Department of English
Naruto University of Education
Naruto, Tokushima 772-8502, Japan
yabuchan@naruto-u.ac.jp

Abstract

Japanese *dare-mo* has been widely acknowledged to be an NPI, furthermore, a "strict" NPI in the sense of Giannakidou (2011) as it seems to be licensed only in an "antiveridical" environment, specifically, with a clausemate negation. However, there is a type of positive sentences in which *dare-mo* can appear, i.e. non-episodic sentences, which indicates that *dare-mo* is in fact not an NPI and its NPI-like distribution is an epiphenomenon due to *dare-mo*'s lexical meaning and the resulting interpretational properties of *dare-mo* sentences. In the current work, based on novel data we will propose that *dare-mo* is an "unrestricted" universal quantifier and demonstrate that the proposed meaning of *dare-mo* and a reasonable assumption about episodic predicates predict that positive episodic *dare-mo* sentences will be contradictory while negative episodic ones and non-episodic ones, positive or negative will be contingent, nicely characterizing the grammaticality facts of *dare-mo* sentences.

1 Introduction of Japanese *Dare-mo* in Question ("NPI" *Dare-mo*) in Contrast to *Dáre-mo* ("Non-NPI" *Dare-mo*)

In this section the Japanese expression in question, *dare-mo* will be introduced in terms of its morphological, phonological, and preliminary semantic features.

1.1 Morphological Features

Dare-mo is morphologically composed of indefinite pronoun *dare* 'who' and particle *mo*, which has been sometimes glossed as 'also' and other times as 'even'.[1]

1.2 Phonological Features

As will be seen in the next subsection, there is another *dare-mo* distinct from *dare-mo* in question here syntactically and semantically. In correlation with the syntactic and semantic differences, there is a phonetic and phonological difference between them at least in Tokyo Japanese.

In Japanese, a pitch accent language, the placement of accent induces difference in meaning, as is illustrated in (1):

---

[1] In this paper the issue is not addressed whether *mo* in question is polysemous, there is a unique meaning, or there are two distinct *mo*'s, in which case, which one is relevant here. In any case, the compositional analysis of the meaning of *dare-mo* out of that of *dare* and that of *mo* will not be dealt with here; thus, throughout this paper, *mo* will be glossed rather ambiguously simply as 'MO'.

(1) (Adopted from Haraguchi 1995: (6))

Nouns	*Glosses*	*Placement of Accent*
a. káki (-ga) HL L	'oyster'+Nom	initial-accented
b. kakí (-ga) LH L	'fence'+Nom	final-accented
c. kaki (-ga) LH H	'persimmon'+Nom	unaccented

In Tokyo Japanese, the accent is placed on the mora before the pitch drop; in other words, the accent is on the H immediately before L. (Haraguchi 1999: 5)

As *dare-mo* in question has the same tone melody as (1c), as is shown in (2), it is considered to be an unaccented word.

(2) The tone melody of "NPI" *dare-mo*

dare-mo
L H H

On the other hand, the near-homonymous, "non-NPI" *dare-mo* has the tone melody as illustrated in (3), which is of the same pattern as in (2a). Thus, "non-NPI" *dare-mo* is regarded to be a word with the accent on *da(re)* 'who'.

(3) The tone melody of "Non-NPI" *dare-mo*

dáre-mo
H L L

In the above, we have reviewed the features differentiating the so-called "NPI" *dare-mo* and "non-NPI" *dare-mo* from each other. Henceforth, however, we will abandon the nomenclature, for it will be demonstrated that "NPI" *dare-mo* in fact is not an NP, rendering the current term misleading/a misnomer. Instead, we will designate/denote "NPI" *dare-mo* and "non-NPI" *dare-mo* as (plain) "*dare-mo*" and "*dáre-mo*", respectively, reflecting the accentual contrast between them.

1.3 Syntactic Distribution of *Dare-mo* and *Dáre-mo*

Having identified two "dare-mo"s, i.e. *dare-mo* and *dáre-mo*, let us consider some example sentences in which they do or do not occur:

(4) a. *Dare-mo paatii-ni ki-ta.
who-MO party-Dat come-Past

b. Dare-mo paatii-ni ko-nakat-ta.
who-MO party-Dat come-Neg-Past
'Nobody came to the party.'

(5) a. Dáre-mo-ga paatii-ni ki-ta.
who-MO-Nom party-Dat come-Past
'Everybody came to the party.'

b. Dáre-mo-ga paatii-ni ko-nakat-ta.
who-MO-Nom party-Dat come-Neg-Past
'Nobody came to the party.'

What is to be noted in the contrast between (4) and (5) is that first, *dáre-mo* is followed by a case marker, e.g. nominative marker *ga* in (5) while *dare-mo* is not, second, *dare-mo* seems to be licensed only in negative sentences while *dáre-mo* is not sensitive to polarity. Because of the second feature, *dare-mo* has been widely acknowledged to be an NPI. However, in the next section, we will see some evidence that *dare-mo* is not a genuine NPI.

2 *Dare-mo* IS a Pseudo-NPI

Data like (4) apparently suggest that *dare-mo* is an NPI, which has been widely accepted and prompted many analyses of *dare-mo* as such (e.g. Kato 1985, Kawashima 1994, Kishimoto 2008).

However, there is a type of sentences questioning the legitimacy of *dare-mo* as a genuine NPI. Consider the following examples:

(6)[2]

a. Hito-wa dare-mo itsukawa shinu.
human-Top who-MO someday die
'Everyone (Anyone) dies someday.'

b. Hito-wa dare-mo jibun-ni amai.
human-Top who-MO self-Dat lenient
'Everyone (Anyone) is lenient to herself.'

c. Hito-wa dare-mo yume yabure, furikaeru.
human-Top who-MO dream break reflect
'Everyone (Anyone) loses in her dream and reflect on herself.'

In terms of tone melody and co-occurrence with a case marker, *dare-mo* in (6) is to be identified with *dare-mo*, not *dáre-mo*, as it has LHH as its tone melody and the sentences resulting from (6a-c) by adding a (nominative-)case marker will be ungrammatical.

Contrary to what has been widely acknowledged about *dare-mo*; i.e., it is an NPI, specifically, *strict* NPI, which requires the accompaniment of negation for its being licensed, in terms of Giannakidou (2011), the data like (6) clearly show that *dare-mo* is not an strong NPI, not even a weak NPI, which is licensed in antiveridical contexts; in short, not an NPI at all.

Now that *dare-mo* has been shown not to be an NPI, has the "NPI"-ness of *dare-mo* been lessened accordingly? The answer is Yes and No. No because the fact remains that *dare-mo* cannot grammatically cooccur with a positive predicate in examples like (4a). Yes because the "NPI"-ness of *dare-mo* is now characterized not as a feature of *dare-mo* on its own, but an epiphenomenon mirroring its interaction with its environment whatever it is. Thus, *dare-mo* is now better termed as "Pseudo-NPI" and will be analyzed as such in the following.

[2] Someone suggested that *dare-mo* in (6) should be considered a phonetic variant of "free-choice anyone" *dare-demo* 'who-even', as is indeed the case that the resulting sentences from the examples in (6) with *dare-mo* being replaced by *dare-demo* would be basically synonymous with the original ones. Nonetheless, as *dare-demo* is not always replaced by *dare-mo*, as is illustrated in *dare-demo/*dare-mo sono kouenkai-ni sanka-suru koto ga dekiru* 'Anyone can participate in the lecture', the apparent replacability of *dare-mo* by *dare-demo* in (6) cannot justify the claim unless it is augmented with an principle predicting when the phonetic variation is possible.

3 *Dare-mo* as an "Unrestricted" Universal Quantifier

In this section we will argue that *dare-mo* denotes a universal quantifier as well as *dáre-mo*, but unlike the case of *dáre-mo*, the universal quantifier denoted by *dare-mo* is "unrestricted" in that it lacks the restrictor in terms of the *tripartite structure* of quantification (Kamp (1981), Heim (1982), Partee (1995)).

3.1 Analyses of *Dare-mo* as an Existential Quantifier á la Kadmon and Landman (1993)

Because of the apparent similarity of *dare-mo* to English *any* N′, specifically, *anyone* in this case in that they both are "NPI"s and mean 'no one' in the context of negation, it was widely assumed that a very influential analysis of *any* by Kadmon and Landman (1993) would/should be carried over to Japanese *dare-mo* with the basic assumption that *dare-mo* was an existential quantifier; furthermore, it needs to be under the scope of negation. Among the analyses proposed along the line are Kato (1985), Kawashima (1994) , and Kishimoto (2008).

However, given that *dare-mo* can occur in a non-negative sentence as in (6) and the resulting sentence is of a universal-quantificational force, *dare-mo* as a quantifier should be taken to be a universal one instead of an existential one; consequently, the logical structure of the "nobody"-interpretation associated with a negative *dare-mo* sentence should be construed as a universal quantifier over negation, $\forall\neg$ instead of negation over an existential quantifier, $\neg\exists$. This conclusion in fact has been independently reached by Shimoyama (2008, 2011) and Kataoka (2006, 2007), neither of whom, however, has an account for *dare-mo*'s "(pseudo-)NPI-ness".

3.2 Domain of Quantification for *Dare-mo*

In philosophical logic, the question has been hotly debated whether there is an absolute, unrestricted quantifier, while in linguistic semantics, it is a general understanding that there is no expression denoting an unrestricted quantifier in the absolute sense in natural languages.

Consider the following English sentence.

(7) Every student had a good time.

The universal quantifier involved in (7), (denoted by) *every* has its domain restricted to the set of students. Furthermore, as the sentence is about not all the students in the world, but some contextually determined group of students.

In general, quantifiers in natural languages are considered to have their domains of quantification restricted linguistically, e.g. common noun (phrases), relative clauses, and partitives for D(eterminer)-quantifiers, and *when/if*-clauses for A(dvervial)-quantifiers, and furthermore, contextually. The linguistic and contextual restriction of domain is illustrated by the following logical forms of (7) in some semantic frameworks, where variable C represents the contextual restriction.

(8)

a. $\forall x[\underline{[student(x) \wedge C(x)]} \rightarrow had\text{-}a\text{-}good\text{-}time(x)]$ (first-order logic)

b. $[\![every]\!]\ (\underline{[\![student]\!] \cap [\![C]\!]})([\![had\text{-}a\text{-}good\text{-}time]\!])$ (generalized quantifier theory) (von Fintel (1994))

c. $every_x\ [_{Restrictor}\ student(x) \wedge C(x)]\ [_{Nuclear\ Scope}\ had\text{-}a\text{-}good\text{-}time(x)]$ (tripartite structure of quantification: Kamp (1981), Heim (1982), Partee (1995))

3.3 *Dare-mo* as an "Unrestricted" Quantifier

Contrary to the widely acknowledged assumption about natural-language quantifiers, i.e., they are restricted quantifiers, we would like to propose that *dare-mo* is an "unrestricted" quantifier. Obviously, a word is in order here. In the above we have agreed that *dare-mo* basically means 'every person'; therefore, its domain is clearly restricted (at least) to the set of humans. That being correct, *dare-mo* cannot be an unqualified, unrestricted quantifier, which is why "unrestricted" has scare quotes around it. Then the question is in what sense the domain of quantification for *dare-mo* is "unrestricted".

We propose that the domain of quantification for *dare-mo* is indeed restricted to the set of humans, but that's it; that is, no further restricted linguistically or contextually. Admittedly that may sound counterintuitive given examples like the following.

(9) Yamada-sensei-no gakusei-wa
Yamada-professor-of student(s)-Top

dare-mo paatii-ni ko-nakat-ta
who-MO party-Dat come-Neg-Past
'None of Professor Yamada's students came to the party.'

As the gloss of the example suggests, it seems natural to take *Yamada-sensei's gakusei* 'Professor Yamada's students' as restricting the domain of quantification for *dare-mo*; however, we will argue and see some evidence that the nominal is to be interpreted as part of not the restrictor, but the nuclear scope in terms of the tripartite structure of quantification. In fact, we propose that the meaning of *dare-mo* should be something as follows:

(10) The proposed meaning of *dare-mo*

dare-mo: $\lambda Q \forall x^h[Q(x^h)]$, where x^h is a sortal variable for humans.

As the variable bound by $\forall$ is a sortal one for humans, the domain of the universal quantifier is naturally restricted to the set of humans; however, as the restrictor is lacking, there will be no more restriction on the domain. As a consequence, the content of the nominals construed with *dare-mo* will be entered into the nuclear scope. For instance, the logical form of (9) will be analyzed to be as in (11) instead of (12)

(11) $\forall x^h \neg[Prof.Y'sStudents(x^h) \wedge Came(x^h)]$

(12) $\forall x^h\ [Prof.Y'sStudents(x^h) \rightarrow \neg Came(x^h)]$

Some readers might be quick to point out that (11) and (12) are equivalent, which is true. But what we are concerned here is not just the right truth conditions, but also the correct logical form. Sure enough, later we will see some examples in which the interpretation of a nominal as part of the restrictor and that of the nuclear scope differ in the resulting truth conditions and the latter ones are correct.

3.4 Evidence against the Restrictivity of the Domain for *Dare-mo*

Incompatibility with Partitives: A Partitive occurring with a nominal quantifier is considered to restrict the domain of quantification, as in (13).

(13) All/Most/None of the students laughed.

In (13), *of the students* clearly functions as restricting the domain of the quantifier denoted by *all/most/none*. In Japanese as well, partitives serve as the restrictor of quantifiers as illustrated in the example corresponding to (13).

(14)

a. Gakusei-no zen-in ga ki-ta.
students-of all-Cl Nom come-Past
'All of the students came.'

b. Gakusei-no hotondo ga kit-ta.
students-of most Nom come-Past
'Most of the students laughed.'

Then, let us see the cases of *dare-mo* and *dáre-mo*; that is, whether they can be restricted with a partitive. Starting with *dáre-mo*, it can cooccur with a partitive grammatically with the latter restricting the domain of the former, as exemplified by (15).

(15) Gakusei-no dáre-mo ga ko-nakat-ta.
students-of who-MO Nom come-Neg-Past
'None of the students came.'

Next, consider the following example, (16), which is minimally different from (15) in that *dare-mo* appears in place of *dáre-mo* and (since *dare-mo* cannot cooccur with a case marker,) the nominative marker, *ga* is missing.

(16) ??Gakusei-no dáre-mo ko-nakat-ta.
students-of who-MO come-Neg-Past

As the "??" indicates, compared with (14) and (15), (16) is considerably less unacceptable if not downright ungrammatical.

In the above, it has been shown that a partitive as a domain restrictor sits well with *dáre-mo*, but not with *dare-mo*. This, we contend, strongly imply that unlike the "regular" quantifiers or *dáre-mo*, *dare-mo* does not have the restrictor in terms of the tripartite structure of quantification. In the following we will see additional evidence to the effect.

Incompatibility with Relative Clauses: In the same vein as with partitives, when occurring with a quantificational nominal, (restrictive) relative clauses are regarded as restricting the domain of the quantifier, as illustrated in the following example:

(17) Every one who came to the party had a good time.

In (17), the relative clause, *who came to the party* clearly restricts the domain from the set of (contextually-determined) people denoted by *one* further into that of people who came to the party.

In this regard, let us examine the compatibility of *dare-mo* with relative clauses. Consider, for instance, the following example.

(18) ??/*[Paatii-ni kita] dare-mo
party-Dat came who-MO

osake-o noma-nakat-ta.
alcohol-Acc drink-Neg-Past

As the "??/*" indicates, (18) is almost ungrammatical or simply ungrammatical, along with which the intended reading "nobody who came to the party drank alcoholic beverages" is not available, either. On the other hand, the *dáre-mo* counterpart, i.e. (19) is perfectly grammatical.

(19) [Paatii-ni kita] dáre-mo ga
party-Dat came who-MO Nom

osake-o noma-nakat-ta.
alcohol-Acc drink-Neg-Past
'Everybody who came to the party didn't drink alcoholic beverages/Nobody who came to the party drank alcoholic beverages.'

The incompatibility of *dare-mo* with relative clauses again implies the absence of the restrictor for *dare-mo*. The plausibility is further strengthened by the contrast with *dáre-mo*, which is perfectly compatible with relative clauses. In the above we have argued against the restrictivity of the domain of quantification for *dare-mo* by demonstrating its incompatibility with typical domain-restricting expressions, specifically, partitives and relative clauses. This time, we will argue for the same thesis by presenting (grammatical) examples such that if a nominal construed with *dare-mo* were interpreted as restricting the domain for *dare-mo*, that would result in the wrong readings.

Restricted Quantification Predicts Wrong Readings: Consider the following sentence, (20).

(20) [[Paatii-ni kita] gakusee]-wa
party-Dat came students-Top

dáre-mo ga i-nakat-ta
who-MO Nom be/exist-Neg-Past

The sentence has the reading in which the nominal in the topical phrase, i.e. *paatii ni kita gakusee* 'the students who came to the party' restricts the domain of the universal quantifier denoted by *dáre-mo*, i.e., that all students who came to the party were not/no students who came to the party weer at some place which is unspecified, but contextually understood place. For instance, you can imagine the classroom for a class on the following day of the party. The question is whether the sentence that is minimally different from (20) in that *dáre-mo* is replaced by *dare-mo* with nominative-marker *ga* deleted, i.e. (21) will have the same reading as (20). If the nominal in the topical phrase, i.e. *paatii ni kita gakusee* 'the students' restricted the domain of *dare-mo* as in the case of *dáre-mo*, (21) would be expected to have the same reading as (20).

(21) [[Paatii-ni kita] gakusee]-wa
party-Dat came students-Top

dare-mo i-nakat-ta
who-MO be/exist-Neg-Past

However, the matter of fact is that the reading of (21) is that no student came to the party, which is truth-conditionally distinct from that of (20). The reading in fact corresponds to the one expected of the meaning of *dare-mo* as in (10) and the content of the topical phrase being entered into the nuclear scope, which is represented in (22), where "St." and "C.T.P" are abbreviations of "Student" and "CameToTheParty", respectively.

(22) $\forall x^h \neg[\text{St.}(x^h) \wedge \text{C.T.T.P.}(x^h) \wedge \text{Existed}(x^h)]$

The interpretational difference we have observed between a *dáre-mo* sentence, (20) and the corresponding *dare-mo* one, (21), again points to the unrestrictiveness of *dare-mo*.

Nominals Construed with *Dare-mo* Are Interpreted Predicatively: Consider the following two example sentences.

(23) okyaku-ga dare-mo ko-nakat-ta.
customer(s)-Nom come-Neg-Past.
'There were no customers (who) came.'

(24) okyaku-wa dáre-mo-ga ko-naka-tta.
customer(s)-Top -Nom come-Neg-Past.
'None of the customers came.'

The two sentences are minimally different from each other with some necessary adjustments; *dare-mo* occurs in (23) while *dáre-mo* with the nominative case-marker, *ga* in (24), and *okyaku* 'customer(s)' can be marked only with the topic marker, *wa*, not the nominative marker in (24), which is presumed to be due to there being a nominative-case marked phrase, i.e. *dáre-mo-ga*.

There is a difference between (23) and (24) in interpretation, specifically, with respect to whether the speaker has some particular clientele in mind when uttering the sentences. (24) can be felicitously uttered only when the speaker has some preexisting set of people as the clientele, of whom she checked whether they came or not. On the other hand, (23) can be felicitously uttered without the speaker having any clientele in mind; the sentence can be interpreted that there were no events of visiting by people who would have been predicated of as customers if they had visited the (implicit) store.

We propose that the above interpretational difference between (23) and (24) is an reflection of the difference between *dare-mo* and *dáre-mo* with regards to the presence and absence of the restrictor. It has been generally acknowledged that for a given natural-language quantified sentence with the tripartite structure, it is presupposed that there exists an (at least one) instance satisfying the content of the restrictor. In terms of felicity conditions, this would be rendered that when one utters a quantified sentence, she has a particular set of individuals as satisfying the restrictor. Then, what is the function of the nuclear scope? Given a set of individuals that satisfy the restrictor as given, it is asserted that the content of the nuclear scope is or is not predicated of a certain quantity of the individuals.

With the understanding of the restrictor and the nuclear scope, it is proposed that the difference between (23) and (24) in interpretation corresponds to where the content of the nominal construed with the quantifier, *okyaku* 'customer' is entered, the nuclear scope or the restrictor. Specifically, it is proposed that *dare-mo* has the content of the nominal entered into the nuclear scope, which is necessitated by the absence of the restrictor while *dáre-mo*, into the restrictor. Thus, the logical form of (23) and that of (24) are as in (23)′ and (24)′, respectively.

(23)′ $\forall x^h \neg[\text{customer}(x^h) \wedge \text{came}(x^h)]$

(24)′ $\forall x^h[\text{customer}(x^h) \rightarrow \text{came}(x^h)]$

However, (23)′ and (24)′ are equivalent and do not properly represent the distinction between the nominal being used attributively/entered into the restrictor and being used predicatively/entered into the nuclear scope. Although we cannot go into detail because of lack of space, we amend (23)′ and (24)′ to (23)′′ and (24)′′, respectively.

(23)′′ $\forall x^h \neg \exists e[\text{customer}(e, x^h) \wedge \text{came}(e, x^h)]$

(24)′′ $\forall x^h[\text{customer}(x^h) \rightarrow \neg \exists e[\text{came}(e, x^h)]]$

In (23)′′ and (24)′′, "e" is an event variable and "customer(e, x^h)" reads "x^h manifests herself as a customer in e", which is in contrast with "customer(x^h)" where x^h is designated as a customer independently of a(n) (shopping) event. All in all, (23)′′ and (24)′′ are contended to represent the readings of (23) and (24), capturing the differences between (23) and (24) in interpretation. That is made possible by the hypothesis that *dare-mo* does not have the restrictor.

3.5 Truth Conditions of *Dare-mo* Sentence

In the current section we hypothesized that *dare-mo* is an "unrestricted" universal quantifier that lacks the restrictor part, with the proposed meaning in (10), which is reproduced here, and have seen some pieces of evidence for the thesis.

(10) The proposed meaning of *dare-mo*

dare-mo: $\lambda Q \forall x^h[Q(x^h)]$, where x^h is a sortal variable for humans.

We conclude this section with the truth conditions of a *dare-mo* sentence that are necessitated by the proposed meaning of *dare-mo*, i.e. (10). The logical form of a *dare-mo* sentence is now $\forall x^h[P(x^h)]$, where P is a possibly complex, one-place predicate. It is assumed that sortal, human variable x^h ranges over the entire set of humans at world w in model M, denoted $D_{h,w,M}$. From which, the truth conditions of a *dare-mo* sentence, $\forall x^h[P(x^h)]$ are determined as follows:

(25) Truth Conditions of *Dare-mo* Sentences $\forall x^h[P(x^h)]$

$[\![\forall x^h[P(x^h)]]\!]^{M,t,w} = 1$ if and only if the entire set of humans at world w in model M is a subset of the extension of P, i.e.,

$D_{h,w,M} \subseteq \{a : [\![P(x)]\!]^{M,g[x/a],t,w} = 1\}$.

4 Condition on the Extension of Episodic Predicates

Putting the meaning of *dare-mo* itself aside for now let us go back to a phenomenon surrounding *dare-me* we observed in sections 1 and 2, i.e., *dare-mo* cannot occur in some positive sentences as in (4a), which is why *dare-mo* was believed to be an NPI, but it can appear in other positive sentences, as in (6), which disqualifies *dare-mo* from being a genuine NPI. Although *dare-mo* has turned out to be a pseudo-NPI, it remains a fact that its distribution is somewhat restricted, which deserves to be explained. Since *dare-mo* does not always require negation for occurring grammatically in sentences, the necessary co-occurrence of negation for it in some sentences cannot be a direct consequence from a lexical feature or requirement of *dare-mo* alone. The phenomenon should rather be taken to be an epiphenomenon mirroring some interaction of the lexical semantics of *dare-mo* with its environment. The question is what aspect of the environment is relevant to the interaction. In the following we will propose that it is the (non-)episodicity of the predicate that is relevant and formulate a condition on the extension of episodic predicates.

4.1 Condition on the Extension of Episodic Predicates

The obvious differences between sentences in which *dare-mo* requires negation, e.g. (4) and those in which it doesn't, e.g. (6) is that the former is an episodic sentence while that in the latter is a non-episodic, or "tenseless" one.

As events or situations, which are referred to by episodic sentences, are spatio-temporally bounded, it is reasonable to suppose that the extensions of episodic predicates cannot contain the entire domain of individuals of any sort. For illustration, let us take episodic predicate "came to the party" as an example. Referring to a certain coming-to-the-party event at some time in the past, the predicate cannot contain the entire set of humans, for a spatio-temporally bounded event cannot have as its participants, humans who were dead or unborn at the time of the event. The property of episodic predicates can be formulated as the following condition on the extension of episodic predicates:

(26) Condition on the Extension of Episodic Predicates

Given model M, variable assignment g, point of time t, possible world w, sort s, the domain of sort s at world w in M, $D_{s, w, M}$, and episodic predicate P, the following condition holds:

$$D_{s, w, M} \not\subseteq \{a : [\![P(x)]\!]^{M, g[x/a], t, w} = 1\}.$$

5 An Account of *Dare-mo*'s NPI-like Distribution

With the meaning of *dare-mo* proposed and the condition on the extension of episodic predicate postulated, from which follows some consequence relevant to *dare-mo*'s NPI-like distribution. To see that, the truth conditions of a *dare-mo* sentence , (25) and the condition on the extension, strictly speaking, its special case where the sort is human, (26)′ are reproduced here:

(25) Truth Conditions of *Dare-mo* Sentences $\forall x^h[P(x^h)]$

$[\![\forall x^h[P(x^h)]]\!]^{M, t, w} = 1$ if and only if the entire set of humans at world w in model M is a subset of the extension of P, i.e.,

$$D_{h, w, M} \subseteq \{a : [\![P(x)]\!]^{M, g[x/a], t, w} = 1\}.$$

(26)′ Condition on the Extension of Episodic Predicates

Given model M, variable assignment g, point of time t, possible world w, human sort h, the domain of sort h at world w in M, $D_{s, w, M}$, and episodic predicate P, the following condition holds:

$$D_{h, w, M} \not\subseteq \{a : [\![P(x)]\!]^{M, g[x/a], t, w} = 1\}.$$

From (25) and (26)′, it immediately follows that positive episodic *dare-mo* sentences will never be true. Since (26) and (26)′ are considered to hold at any admissible models it follows that positive episodic *dare-mo* sentences will never be true at any admissible model; that is, they are contradictory.

On the other hand, negative *dare-mo* sentences will be a contingent proposition irrespective of the kind of the predicate, episodic or not, as can be seen in their truth conditions, (27).

(27) Truth Conditions of Negative *Dare-mo* Sentences $\forall x^h\neg[P(x^h)]$

$[\![\forall x^h\neg[P(x^h)]\ ]\!]^{M, g, w} = 1$ if and only if the entire set of humans in the model is outside the extension of P, i.e.,

$$D_{h, w, M} \cap \{a : [\![P(\ldots, x, \ldots)]\!]^{M, g[x/a], t, w} = 1\} = \varnothing.$$

Compared with the impossibility of conceiving an event in which absolutely every human being in the world, dead, alive, or to be born at the time of the event participates, it is easy to imagine a poor party or concert to which absolutely no one came or a property which cannot be applicable to any human being throughout history, e.g., being immortal.

How about positive non-episodic predicate *dare-mo* sentences? A non-episodic predicates is not subject to the condition of (32)′; thus, it can have a superset of the entire set of humans as its extension, which is the truth conditions for a *dare-mo* sentence as given in (25). For instance, let us take (6a) for an example. This example is not about any particular group of people at any time at any place, but expresses a timeless truth about humanity. Although human beings are normally assumed invariably to die sooner or later, it is easy to conceive worlds such that at least some people are immortal in them. That is why (6a) is contingent.

As is shown in (28), the logical properties of *dare-mo* sentences characterized by the current analysis, contradictory and contingent coincide with the grammaticality of the sentences, ungrammatical and grammatical, respectively. In the current analysis, the grammaticality facts of *dare-mo* sentences, or the NPI-like distributions of *dare-mo* are now reduced to the logicality, or the contingency/contradiction of *dare-mo* sentences. Giannakidou (2011) has strongly opposed to such a pragmatic approach to NPIs pursued in, e.g. Kadmon & Landman (1993), Krifka (1995) and Chierchia (2006), on the basis that pragmatic infelicity is too weak to characterize the categorical nature of the ungrammaticality judgments involving (strict) NPIs. Alternatively, she has argued that strict NPIs are lexicalized, or grammaticalized as such and their distributions are dealt with in syntax; for *dare-mo*, Giannakidou (2007, 2011) and Yoshimura (2007) argued that the characteristic rising tone on *dare-mo* is a marker of the lexicalization of its NPI-ness on a par with, e.g. the accent on Greek emphatic n-word KANENA. Now that there is evidence that *dare-mo* is not a strict NPI or a weak one for that matter, as is indicated by data like (2), the hard-wired, syntax-based account has lost its rationale, while the current pragmatic, semantics-based analysis is empirically better motivated to say the least.

(28) Logical Properties and Grammaticality of *Dare-mo* Sentences

Dare-mo sentences	Logical Property	Grammaticality
positive episodic predicate	contradictory	ungrammatical
negative episodic predicate	contingent	grammatical
non-episodic, or "tenseless" predicate	contingent	grammatical

6 Conclusion

We have seen that Japanese *dare-mo* is in fact a pseudo-NPI, being licensed in some type of positive sentences, which suggests that its NPI-like distribution should be attributed to other factors than the hard-wired requirement of negation in syntax. We have proposed that *dare-mo*'s NPI-like distribution is a reflection of some logicality property of a *dare-mo* sentence; that is, *dare-mo* is licensed in a contingent sentence while it is not licensed in a contradictory sentence. The above analysis is crucially dependent on the hypothesis that *dare-mo* is an "unrestricted" universal quantifier in contrast to *dáre-mo*, which is a restrictive quantifier.

References

Chierchia, Gennaro. (2006). "Broaden your views. Implicatures of domain widening and the "Logicality" of language". Linguistic Inquiry 37, 535–590.

von Fintel, Kai (1994) *Restrictions on Quantifier Domains*. Ph.D. Dissertation, University of Massachusetts, Amherst.

Giannakidou, Anastasia. (2007). "The Landscape of EVEN". *Natural Language and Linguistic Theory* 25: 39-81.

Giannakidou, Anastasia (2011) "Negative and positive polarity items". In K. von Heusinger, C. Maienborn and P. Portner (eds.) *SemanticsAn International Handbook of Natural Language Meaning* (HSK 33.2), de Gruyter. 1660–1712

Haraguchi, Shosuke. (1999) "Accent" In Natsuko Tsujimura (ed.), *The Handbook of Japanese Linguistics*. Blackwell Publishers. 1-32.

Kadmon, Nirit & Fred Landman. (1993), 'Any'. *Linguistics and Philosophy* 16:353–422.

Kataoka, Kiyoko (2006) "Neg-sensitive elements, neg-c-command, and scrambling in Japanese". In T.J. Vance and K. Jones (eds.), *Japanese/Korean Linguistics*. Vol. 14. CSLI Publications. Stanford, CA. 221–33.

Kataoka, Kiyoko (2007) "Neg-o c-toogyosuru huteigo+mo" [*Wh-mo* outside the Neg-c-command Domain]. *Gengo Kenkyu* 131: 77-114.

Kato, Yasuhiko. (1985), 'Negative sentences in Japanese'. In Sophia Linguistica Monograph 19. Sophia University. Tokyo.

Kawashima, Ruriko. (1994), The Structure of Noun Phrases and the Interpretation of Quantificational NPs in Japanese. Ph.D. thesis, Cornell University.

Kishimoto, Hideki. (2008), 'On the variability of negative scope in Japanese'. Journal of Linguistics 44:379–435.

Krifka, Manfred. (1995). "The semantics and pragmatics of polarity items in assertion". *Linguistic Analysis* 15, 209–257.

Partee, Barbara H. (1995) "Quantificational Structures and Compositionality" In Bach, E. et al. (eds.), *Quantification in Natural Languages*, 541-601. Kluwer Academic Publishers

Shimoyama, Junko (2008) "Indeterminate NPIs and scope". In Tova Friedman and Satoshi Ito, (eds.), *Proceedings of Semantics and Linguistic Theory XVIII* (SALT18), CLC Publications, Cornell University, Ithaca.

Automatic Tripartite Classification of Intransitive Verbs

Nitesh Surtani, Soma Paul
Language Technologies Research Centre
IIIT Hyderabad
Hyderabad, Andhra Pradesh-500032
nitesh.surtaniug08@students.iiit.ac.in, soma@iiit.ac.in

Abstract

In this paper, we introduce a tripartite scheme for the classification of intransitive verbs for Hindi and claim it to be a more suitable model of classification than the classical binary unaccusative/unergative classification. We develop a multi-class SVM classifier based model for automatic classification of intransitive verbs into proposed tripartite classes. We rank the unaccusative diagnostic tests for Hindi based on their authenticity in attesting an intransitive verb under unaccussative class. We show that the use of the ranking score in the feature of the classifier improves the efficiency of the classification model even with a small amount of data. The empirical result illustrates the fact that judicious use of linguistic knowledge builds a better classification model than the one that is purely statistical.

1 Introduction

An automatic classification of verbs that are distinct in terms of their syntactic behavior is a challenging NLP task. Some works have been done for automatic determination of argument structure of verbs (Merlo and Stevenson, 2001) as well as automatic classification of verbs (Lapata and Brew, 1999; Schulte, 2000; Schulte, 2006) following (Levin, 1993) proposal. However, automatic sub-classification of intransitive verbs has not been attempted majorly till now. Sub-classification of intransitive verbs has bearing on various NLP tasks such as machine translation, natural language generation, parsing etc. For example, we take here a case from English-Hindi MT system. English uses nominative subject for all kinds of intransitive verbs whereas Hindi uses ergative case marker *'ne'* on subject when the verb is unergative and in perfect tense whereas unaccusative doesn't as exemplified in (1a) and (1b) respectively.

(1) a. English: Ram ran a lot.

Hindi:	*raam-ne*	*khub*	*dauRaa.*
	Ram-erg	very much	run-3 pft

b. English: The glass broke.

Hindi:	*glaas*	*TuT-aa.*
	Glass	break-3 pft

Classifying intransitive verbs of (1a) and (1b) into subclasses can result in producing right case marking on the subject in the target language Hindi. In parsing, identifying the subclass of the intransitive verb helps in predicting the position of the subject in the Phrase structure tree. One effort of subclassification of intransitive verbs is described in Sorace (2000) where intransitive verbs are further automatically classified into unergative and unaccusative following Perlmutter's (1978) proposal of Unaccusativity Hypothesis. This paper follows the proposal of Surtani et al. (2011) where it has been argued that a a tripartite classification better classify Hindi intransitive verbs. This paper develops a multi-class SVM classifier based model for the automatic classification of intransitive verbs in the tripartite classification scheme. We propose in this paper two approaches for developing multi-class classifier: (a) a Language dependent Classifier and (b) a Language Independent Classifier.

The paper is organized into the following subsections. In Section 2, we present the related works. Section 3 discusses the issues involved in a bipartite classification of intransitive verbs. Section 4 talks about the Data preparation. In Section 5, we introduce the tripartite classification scheme and gives a mathematical formulation of how it captures the distribution better than the bipartite distribution. Section 6 discusses the ranking and scoring of the syntactic diagnostics proposed by Bhatt (2003). Section 7 presents the SVM-based classification model. Section 8 presents the results of the two classification models which are compared in Section 9. Section 10 concludes the paper and discusses the future directions.

2 Related Works

With Perlmutter's proposal of Unaccusativity Hypothesis, the unergative-unaccusative distinction of intransitive verbs has become cross-linguistically a widely recognized phenomenon and the distinction has been shown to exist in many languages including German, Dutch, Hindi etc. Unergative verbs entail a willed or volitional act while unaccusative verbs entail unwilled or non-volitional act. Various language specific tests have been proposed as diagnostics for the distinction of the verbs of these two classes. Bhatt (2003) proposes various diagnostic tests for Indian languages. We have examined the seven tests that Bhatt (2003) has proposed in his work.

(i) Ergative Subjects: Unergatives sometimes allow ergative subjects with an ergative case marker *'ne'* esp. when paired with the right adverbials and compound verbs (as in (2a)). On the other hand, Unaccusatives do not allow ergative subjects (as in (2b)).

(2) (a.) *raam-ne bahut naach-aa.*
3P.M.Sg-Erg a lot dance-Pfv
'Ram danced a lot.'

(b.) **raam-ne bahut ghabraaya.*
3P.M.Sg-Erg a lot panic-Pfv
'Ram panicked a lot.'

(ii) Cognate objects: These are simply the verbs noun form. Unergatives verbs sometime allow for Cognate objects (as in (3a)) whereas Unaccusatives do not allow for cognate objects.

(3) (a.) *raavan-ne bhayaanaka hasii has-ii.*
3P.M.Sg-Erg horrifying laugh laugh-Pfv
'Ravan laughed a horrifying laugh.'

(iii) Impersonal Passives: The impersonal passive deletes the subject of an intransitive verb and reduces its valency to zero. Unergatives allow for the impersonal passive (as in (4a)) whereas unaccusatives do not.

(4) (a.) *thodii der aur jhool-aa jaaye.*
Some time more swing-Pfv go-Sbjv
'Swing for some more time.'

(iv) Past Participial Relatives: Past participial relatives target the internal/theme argument of the verb, if there is one. The past participial relatives on Unaccusatives have an active syntax taking *'hua'* be-Pfv/ *'gaya'* go-Pfv (as in (5b)) whereas unergatives are ungrammatical with past participial relatives (as in (5a)).

(5) (a.) **kal dauR-aa huaa chhaatra*
yesterday run-Pfv be-Pfv student
'The student who ran yesterday'

(b.) *vahaan bandh-aa huaa ladkaa*
there tie-Pfv be-Pfv boy
'The boy who is tied there'

(v) Inabilitatives: Inabilitatives describe the inability of the agent towards an action which applies to the class of verbs that undergo the transitivity alternation. Unaccusatives enter the inabilitative with active syntax (as in (6b)) whereas Unergatives do not (as shown in (6a)).

(6) (a.) **raam-se ramaa nahii has-ii.*
3P.M.Sg-Instr 3P.F.Sg neg laugh-Pfv.f
'Ram couldn't make Rama laugh.'

(b.) *raam-se ghar nahii banaa.*
3P.M.Sg-Instr house neg build-Pfv
'Ram couldnt build the house.'

(vi) Compound Verb Selection: There seems to be a kind of selection between compound verbs and main verbs. The unaccusative compound verb *'jaa'* go appears most naturally with unaccusatives while Unergatives tend to take transitive compound verbs like *'le'* -take / *'de'*-give / *'daal'*-did and seem unhappy with *'jaa'* go (as in (7a)).

(7) (a.) *raam-ne pahaaR chaD liyaa.*
3P.M.Sg-Erg mountain climb take-Pfv
'Ram climbed the mountain.'

(vii) Unmarked Subjects for Non-Finite Clauses: Non-Finite clauses in Hindi do not permit overt unmarked subjects (as in (8a)). But inanimate subjects of the Unaccusative verbs can appear without an overt genitive.

(8) (a.) *[raam-ka/*raam tez bhaagna]*
*3P.M.Sg-Gen/*Nom fast run*
zaruurii hai.
necessary is
'It is necessary for Ram to run.'

3 Issues Involved in Binary Classification of Intransitive Verbs

In Hindi as well, syntactic behavior of intransitive verbs, in many cases, depends on which subclass the verb belongs to. However, the neat unergative-unaccusative classification breaks down in Hindi when an intransitive verb takes an animate subject whose volitionality is bleached off by the very semantics of the verb. The absence of a clear-cut distinction due to varied behavior of the verbs of same classes has led to abandoning of this strict two-way classification, as reported for various languages such as German (Sorace, 2000; Kaufmann, 1995), Dutch (Zaenen, 1998), Urdu (Ahmed, 2010) etc. Bhatt also supports the observation that the distinction is not clear-cut for the language. Surtani et al. (2011) argues that a clear-cut two way distinction does not work for Hindi. Let us consider the verb *marnaa* 'die'. The subject of this verb can be an animate volitional entity; however volitionality of the subject is suppressed because one apparently cannot exercise one's own will for 'dying'. The syntactic behavior of such verbs becomes unstable. For example, *marnaa* 'die' behaves like unaacusative verbs as it does not take ergative subject as in:

(9) *kal-ke bhUkamp me bahut log-ne* marA.*
Yesterday-Gen earthquake Loc many people-Erg die- 3 pfv
'Many people died in yesterday's earthquake.'

However, it takes cognate object like other unergative verbs as illustrated in the following example, where *'maut'* is the cognitive object variant of the verb *marnaa* 'die'

(10) *wo kutte ki maut marA.*
'He died like a dog.'

Another case is the verb *girnaa* 'fall'. This verb was originally being classified as an unaccusative verb because the subject of the verb is an undergoer undergoing some kind of change of state. When the subject is inanimate, the unaccusativity feature holds; the verb does not occur with adverb of volitionality as is true for other unaccustive verb. Therefore the following sentence is illegitimate:

(11 a.) **patta jaan-buujh-kar giraa.*
leaf deliberately fall-Pfv
'The leaf deliberately fell.'

However the situation changes when the verb takes an animate human subject. The construction licenses adverb of volitionality as illustrated below:

(11 b.) *raam jaan-buujh-kar giraa.*
ram.M.Sg deliberately fall-Pfv
'Ram deliberately fell.'

With an animate subject, the verb also allows impersonal passive like unergative verbs as shown below:

(11 c.) *calo, eksaath giraa jaaye.*
move, together fall dgo-Sbjv
'Come let us fall down together.'

These verbs taking animate non-volitional subjects [+Ani -Vol] show some properties of unergatives and some properties of unaccusatives. Due to their fuzzy behavior, it becomes hard to classify these verbs. We discuss in Section 5 why it becomes important to keep such verbs in a separate class.

4 Data Preparation

For the preparation of the data for training and testing the model, we have selected a set of 106 intransitive verbs of Hindi and have manually classified them into the proposed tripartite classification scheme. We have applied seven unaccusativity diagnostics (as discussed in Section 2) on each verb. But due to the polysemous nature of intransitive verbs, the total number of instances rises to 134.

4.1 Polysemous Nature of Intransitive Verbs

While working with intransitive verbs we observe that verbs are highly polysemous in nature. The same verb root might take different kind of subject as a result of which its semantic nuance changes. That affects its syntactic behavior as well. Let us illustrate the case with verb *uR* -'fly'. It can take an animate and also an inanimate subject as shown below:

(12) a. *pancchii uR raha hai.*
The bird is flying.

b. *patang uR gayi.*
The kite is flying.

The difference in animacy of subject determines that the verb in (a) can occur in inabilitative mood while that is not true for the second use of verb as illustrated below:

(13) a. *Pancchii se uRa nahin gaya.*
The bird was unable to fly.

b. **Patang se uRa nahin gaya.*
The kite was unable to fly.

Verb	Gloss	Ergative case?	Cognate object?	Impersonal Passives?	Past Participial?	Inabilitatives with active syntax?	Light verb selection	Overt genitive marker?	Class
uR	fly	Yes	Yes	Yes	No	No	Yes	Yes	1
uR	fly	No	No	No	Yes	Yes	No	No	3

Table 1: Polysemous nature of verb

Since animacy is an important factor for determining subclasses of intransitive verbs we will consider the polysemy of the kind instantiated above as different instances of verbs. Going by that, we have applied the diagnostics on 106 verbs but on a total number of 134 verb instances.

4.2 Training Data

Table 2 presents three instances of our training data. The results of the seven diagnostic tests applied to three intransitive verbs i.e. *jump, sink, get build* ,

Verb	English gloss	Ergative case?	Cognate object?	Impersonal Passives?	Past Participial?	Inabilitatives with active syntax?	Light verb selection	Overt genitive marker?	Class
kUDa	jump	Yes	Yes	Yes	No	No	Yes	Yes	1
DUba	sink	No	No	No	Yes	Yes	No	Yes	2
baNa	get build	No	No	No	Yes	Yes	No	No	3

Table 2: Diagnostic applied on Verbs

each belonging to a different class of the tripartite scheme are shown.

The corresponding feature values are obtained from the results of these diagnostic tests, maintaining the original unergativity/unaccusativity distinction. The feature corresponding to each diagnostic test is assigned a value 1 in case a instance shows unergative behavior for that diagnostic test and a feature value -1 in case the instance behaves as an unaccusative for that diagnotic test. As already discussed in Section 2, Unergatives take a Ergative case marker, occur in Cognate object, form impersonal passives, do not form part participial, their inabilitatives do not occur with active syntax, select *'le'* -take and *'de'*-give in compound verb formation and take a Overt genitive marker. So, considering the first instance i.e. 'jump' in Table 2, we find that it behaves as unergative for each diagnostic test, and correspondingly is assigned value 1 for each feature. Similarly, the third instance 'get build', behaves as unaccusative for all the diagnostic tests,is assigned value -1 for each feature. The second instance 'sink', belonging to class 2, behaves as unaccusative for first 6 diagnostic tests but as unergative for the last diagnostic test. Table 3 below shows the feature vectors of these 3 intransitive verbs.

Verb	English gloss	Feature Values							Class
kUDa	jump	1	1	1	1	1	1	1	1
DUba	sink	-1	-1	-1	-1	-1	-1	1	2
baNa	get build	-1	-1	-1	-1	-1	-1	-1	3

Table 3: Diagnostic applied on Verbs

The results of the diagnostic tests are used as features for training and testing the SVM model.

5 Triparite Classification

On applying the diagnostics on the intranstive verbs, we make the following observation:

(i) There is no single distinguishing criterion for sub-classifying Hindi intransitive verbs. Some diagnostic tests, however, perform better than the other giving more accurate results.

(ii) Although all the classes tend to show some inconsistency with the diagnostics, verbs taking animate non-volitional [+Ani -Vol] subjects perform most fuzzily. They are therefore most difficult to classify.

The primary purpose of any classification model is to cluster the elements showing similar behavior within same group so that one can predict the properties of the element once its class is known. The aforementioned observations motivate us for introducing a tripartite classification scheme, as a better classification model for classifying the intransitive verbs for Hindi. The major problem in the classification of the intransitive verb is because of the fuzzy behavior of the verbs that take [+Ani -Vol] subejcts. But the number of such verbs is fairly low (15.7%). The unaccusative class approximately covers all the verbs taking non-volitional i.e. [+Ani -Vol] and [-Ani -Vol] subjects and comprises of 67% of the total intransitive verbs. Thus, even after classifying the verb to the unaccusative class, one is not able to predict its properties as one does not know whether that verb belongs to the fuzzy group. The major drawback of the binary classification model is that the complete class of unaccusative suffers because of a fairly small number of fuzzy verbs. On the other hand, a tripartite scheme provides more confidence in predicting the behavior of the intransitive verbs than the binary classification as we are able to predict the behavior of large portion of verbs. We mathematically show that the tripartite model handles the distribution of the intransitive verbs better than the bipartite model for our data.

5.1 Tripartite Classification Scheme

The intransitive verbs are classified in the following manner under the tripartite classification scheme:

Class 1. Verbs that take animate subject and agree with adverb of volitionality.
Property: [+Vol +Ani]
Class 2. Verbs that take volitional animate subject but are not compatible with adverb of volitionality.
Property: [-Vol +Ani]
Class 3. Verbs that take non-volitional subject.
Property: [-Vol -Ani]

5.2 Does Tripartite Distribution Fits Our Data Well?

A distribution model with higher scatter among the classes and low scatter within the classes is considered to be a better distribution, as it ensures that all the classes are well separated and the instances within a class are close to each other. In order to show that the tripartite classification model handles the distribution better than the bipartite model, we use a mathematical formulation which maximizes the inter-class scatter and minimizes the intra-class scatter. The F-test in one-way ANOVA (ANalysis Of VAriance) technique is used for this. It compares the models by determining the scatter within the class and across the class, and the model that maximizes the F-score i.e. the one that has a higher scatter among the class and low scatter within the class, is identified as the model that best fits the population. The feature vectors corresponding to each verb, after the ranking of the diagnostic tests, as shown in Table 6 are used for calculating the F-score.

F-Score: It is the ratio of the measures of two spreads:

$$\mathbf{F} = \frac{MSTr}{MSE} = \frac{Between - sampleVariation}{Within - sampleVariation}$$

MSTr: MSTr (*mean square treatment*) provides a measure of the spread **among** the sample means $\bar{x_1}$, $\bar{x_2}$,.....,$\bar{x_k}$ **(between-sample variation)** by providing a weighted average of the squared differences between the sample means and the grand sample mean $\bar{\bar{x}}$.

$$MSTr = \frac{SSTr}{k-1}$$

where,

$$SSTr = n_1(\bar{x_1}-\bar{\bar{x}})^2+n_2(\bar{x_2}-\bar{\bar{x}})^2+\cdots+n_k(\bar{x_k}-\bar{\bar{x}})^2$$

$$= \sum_{i=1}^{k} n_i(\bar{x_i} - \bar{\bar{x}})^2$$

and n_1,n_2,....,n_k are the *k* samples, $\bar{x_1}$,$\bar{x_2}$,.....,$\bar{x_k}$ are the *k* sample means, and $\bar{\bar{x}}$ is the average of all the $n = n_1 + n_2 + \cdots\cdot + n_k$ observations.

MSE: MSE *(mean square error)* provides a measure of the spread **within** the *k* populations **(within-sample variation)** by providing a weighted average of the sample variances ${S_1}^2$,${S_2}^2$,.....,${S_k}^2$ **(within-samples variation)**:

$$MSE = \frac{SSE}{n-k}$$

where,

$$SSE = \sum_{j=1}^{n_1}(x_{1j} - \bar{x_1})^2 + \sum_{j=1}^{n_2}(x_{2j} - \bar{x_2})^2 + \cdots\cdot + \sum_{j=1}^{n_k}(x_{kj} - \bar{x_k})^2$$

$$= (n_1 - 1){S_1}^2 + (n_2 - 1){S_2}^2 + \cdots\cdot + (n_k - 1){S_k}^2$$

$$= \sum_{i=1}^{k}(n_i - 1){S_i}^2$$

where x_{ij} denotes the *j*th value from the *i*th sample.

The results of the F-test are shown below in Table 4.

	BIPARTITE DISTRIBUTION		TRIPARTITE DISTRIBUTION		
	Unaccusative	Unergative	Class1	Class2	Class3
No. of samples	90	44	52	21	61
Sb_i	0.374	0.183	0.415	0.080	0.404
Sw_i	27.407	9.407	10.851	1.208	15.611
SST	0.5569		0.8985		
MSTr	0.5569		0.4492		
SSE	0.8622		0.5333		
MSE	0.0065		0.0041		
F-Score	85.2645		110.3417		

Table 4: Binary Vs Tripartite model statistics

where

$$Sb_i = \sum_{i=1}^{n_k} n_i(\bar{x_i} - \bar{\bar{x}})^2$$

$$Sw_i = \sum_{j=1}^{n_i}(x_{ij} - \bar{x_i})^2$$

In the tripartite classification model, the within-class scatter for the class is low. Although Class2 has considerable intra-class variability, but the small percentage of verbs in that class doesn't affect the overall MSE value. On the other hand, the unaccusative class has high intra-class variability, and having a high number of intransitive verbs, it affects the MSE value significantly. As shown in Table 4, the higher value of inter-class scatter (MSTr) for the bipartite distribution is compensated by the large MSE value of its distribution. Thus F-score calculated by taking the ratios of MSTr and MSE is higher for the tripartite distribution showing that the tripartite model fits the data better than the bipartite model.

This paper applies a novel computational approach and develops a classification model by employing a Support Vector Machine (SVM) for the automatic classification of intransitive verbs in the triparite classification scheme. We implement two approaches (a) Language Dependent Classifier and (b) Language Independent Classifier for the classification. In order to build the language dependent classifier, i.e., approach (a), we rank the diagnostic tests that Bhatt (2003) has proposed for identifying unergative/unaccusative distinction. These diagnostic tests are in a way checking possibility of occurring of these verbs in various syntactic constructions. We observe that the performance of "Language dependent classifier" is better than the "Language independent classifier" for our data. The classification accomplished by the classifier confirms the fact that verbs of class 2 perform most inconsistently. Thus the paper argues that the model developed in this paper can be used for a better classification of intransitive verbs. The next section proposes a method for ranking the diagnostics proposed by Bhatt (2003).

6 Ranking and Scoring the Diagnostics

We have observed that some diagnostic tests (as discussed in Section 2) are more trustworthy than others in the sense that they can more accurately classify verbs in their respective class. One such test is "Impersonal passive". Most verbs that form impersonal passives are unergative. Such tests are assigned high score which are used as features in developing the classifier model of approach (a). We evaluate the direct correlation of the diagnostic test on the performance of the model in the following manner:

- If the performance of the learning model is largely affected on removal of a diagnostic test as a feature of the model, then that diagnostic is more important for the model. This entails that introduction of that diagnostic test in the feature vector of the model increases the models accuracy, and hence is more significant for the model.

Table 5 shows the results of the model on pruning the particular diagnostic as feature from the model. The accuracy of the model without the pruning of features is calculated to be 87.42% which is shown to reduce in every case in Table 5. This is because every diagnostic test is adding some useful information to the model. The overt genitive (Unmarked subjects for non-finite clauses) diagnostic seems to perform best for the model on pruning of which the baseline accuracy is reduced by 6.82%.

A diagnostic whose removal from the feature vector affects the model more is regarded to be the better diagnostic test for the model. The %effect on the performance of the model on removal of the diagnostic test is used to calculate the rank and score for the diagnostic. A diagnostic with a better rank is supposed to achieve a higher score. We calculate the score of the diagnostic using the formula:

$$Score = \frac{E_p}{E_b}$$

where
Ep=%Effect on accuracy on pruning the diagnostic
Eb= Accuracy of the model without removal of any diagnostic (87.42%).

Diagnostic	Model Performance On Pruning	%Effect on Accuracy	Rank	Score
Ergative Subjects	84.33	3.09	3	0.03534
Cognate Objects	86.57	0.85	5	0.00972
Impersonal Passives	82.09	5.33	2	0.06097
Past Participial Relatives	86.57	0.85	5	0.00972
Inabilitatives	85.82	1.60	4	0.01830
Compound Verb Selection	85.82	1.60	4	0.01830
Overt Genitive	80.60	6.82	1	0.07801

Table 5: Diagnostic Rank and score

These scores are used to design a new feature vector for the model of approach (a). The feature values corresponding to each diagnostic are multiplied with the corresponding diagnostic scores as shown in Table 6. This feature vector captures the relative significance of the diagnostic with a more relevant diagnostic having a higher ability in unergative/unaccusative distinction. The comparison between the two models: the one which incorporates the ranking score information and the other which do not has been discussed in Section 11.

Verb	Gloss	Feature Values							Class
kUDa	jump	0.035	0.01	0.061	0.01	0.018	0.018	0.078	1
DUba	sink	-0.035	-0.01	-0.061	-0.01	-0.018	-0.018	0.078	2
baNa	get build	-0.035	-0.01	-0.061	-0.01	-0.018	-0.018	-0.078	3

Table 6: Feature vector after Ranking

7 Classification Model

We employ a multiclass SVM as a computational model to analyse behavior of the intransitive verbs. In response to the observations, we use the model to show that Class2 samples are indeed hard to classify with maximum misclassification rate. On the other hand, Class1 and Class3 verbs are classified quite well with a low misclassification rate. We develop two models: (a) Language dependent Classifier which takes a feature vector that incorporates diagnostic scores (as shown in Table 6) and (b) Language Independent Classifier which takes feature vector with binary values as shown in Table 3. We then compare the two models, one without prior diagnostic rank information and the other incorporating the relative linguistic significance of the diagnostic by calculating the ranked diagnostic scores, and show that the ranked model outperforms the one without ranking information. This learned model can also be applied for the classification of new intransitive verbs.

7.1 Support Vector Machine

Support vector machines, (Vapnik, 1995), are computational models used for the classification task in a supervised learning framework. They are poular because of their good generalization ability, since they choose the optimal hyperplane i.e. the one with the maximum margin and reduces the structural error rather than empirical error. Kernel-SVMs, (Joachims, 1999), are much more powerful nonlinear classifiers which obtain a maximum-margin hyperplane in a transformed high (or infinite) dimensional feature space, non-linearly mapped to the input feature space. Although SVMs are originally designed for binary classification tasks, they are extended for building multi-class classification models. We use LIBSVM library (Chang and Lin, 2011) which implements the "one-against-one" approach for multi-class classication. The next section describes the implementation of the SVM model for classifying intransitive verbs of Hindi.

7.2 Pre-processing

Before performing the experiments, first the data is preprocessed by centering the mean for each feature. Mean centered data have a mean expression of zero, which is accomplished by subtracting the feature mean from each data entity.

$$X_M = X - \bar{X}$$

7.3 Training and Testing

Since the data is scarce, so for the better prediction of the error, we use the k-fold cross-validation. The data is first partitioned into k equally (or nearly equally) sized segments or folds. Subsequently *k* iterations of training are performed such that in each iteration, a different fold of the data is held-out for testing while the remaining *k*-1 folds are used for training. When *k* is equal to the number of samples, there is only one test sample in each experiment and the technique is referred to as *Leave-One-Out* (LOO). The advantage of k-fold cross-validation is that all the samples in the dataset are eventually used for both training and testing. So, the true-error, i.e. that error over the test data is estimated as average error rate.

$$E = \frac{1}{k}\sum_{i=1}^{k} E_i$$

We calculate the average true error, E, for different values of *k*. Table 7 shows the accuracy of the model for different values of *k*. Other model parameters are varied keeping the k constant. We find that the average accuracy of the model is maximum for $k = 15$, for which the true error, E is minimum. Optimal values of other parameters are discussed in Section 7.4. So, $k = 15$ is chosen as the best k value and is used in further calculations.

K	3	5	7	9	12	15	134
Accuracy	77.57	83.06	85.99	86.90	87.19	87.42	86.56

Table 7: Accuracy on different folds

For calculating the class accuracies, the set of 134 intransitive verbs is partitioned into $k = 15$ folds, and each fold is used once for testing while other folds are used for training the model. While testing the model in each iteration, the correctly classified and the misclassified samples of each class are identified. For this experiment, we have taken the optimal model parameters i.e. $C = 1$ and sigmoid kernel function, as discussed in Section 7.4. The numbers of misclassified and correctly classified samples for each class are presented below in Table 8.

7.4 Model Parameters

Two model design parameters i.e. C value and the kernel functions and their ranges after optimization are discussed below.

C Value: C value decides the weight for the rate of misclassification. The accuracy of the classifier at lower value of C is low but it increases drastically on increasing C upto a point and then drops down again on further increment. The value of C has been varied from 0.001 to 100000. It has been represented in log scale in Figure 1.

Kernel Function: Four kernel functions, namely, Linear, Polynomial, Radial Basis and Sigmoid are used in order to tune the model to the best performance for different C values, as shown in Figure 1. The results show that the Sigmoid kernel outperforms other kernel functions.

The optimal parameters of the model are achieved when the value C is set to 1 and kernel function used is sigmoid with a accuracy of 87.42%.

8 Results

Table 8 below represents the number of verbs of corresponding class classified into Class1, Class2 and Class3. So, the diagonal elements of the matrix represent the correctly classified samples and the rest of the samples are misclassified. Correspondingly, the class accuracies are calculated as the ratio of correctly classified verbs and the frequency of that class. The results confirm our motivation that Class2

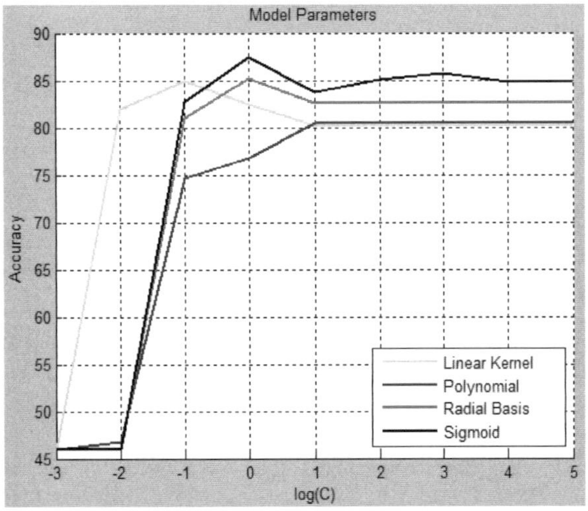

Figure 1: Parameters for Language Independent Model

	Class1	Class2	Class3	Total	Class Accuracy (in %)
Class1	48	4	0	52	92.3
Class2	3	14	4	21	66.67
Class3	1	8	52	61	85.24

Table 8: Results of the model

verbs perform most fuzzily with the highest misclassification rate. This fuzzy behavior of these verbs causes both the unergative and unaccusative classes suffer having low class accuracy in a bipartite classification. A tripartite approach for the classification of intransitive verbs handles this problem efficiently. In the tripartite classification scheme described in this paper, verbs that take [+Ani +Vol] and [-Ani -Vol] subjects are classified in Class1 and Class3 respectively with high class accuracies of 92.3% and 85.24%. The verbs taking [+Ani -Vol] subjects are handled separately in Class2, which has a class accuracy of only 66.67%. The verbs such as *ruk* 'stop', *bhool* 'forget' and *sarak* 'creep' which belong to Class1 are misclassified into Class2 whereas the verbs such as *bacch* 'saved' and *darr* 'scared' are misclassified from Class2 to Class1.

9 Comparison Of The Models

The two classifiers models, (a) Language dependent Classifier and (b) Language Independent Classifier are compared for their performance on the Hindi data. The accuracies of the two models at different values of k are shown in Figure 2. The findings show that the model constructed by approach (a), incorporating linguistic information in terms of relative diagnostic scores, outperforms the model designed using approach (b), the one that doesn't uses any prior linguistic information. Even for smaller values of k, the Language-Dependent model gives a considerably high accuracy showing that the model has good generalization ability and is able to learn a classifier that performs quite well even on small training data. As the number of folds increase, both models attain approximately equal accuracies. The Language Dependent model achieves a maximum accuracy of 87.69% for k=7 when C=100 and kernel function is sigmoid function whereas the Language-Independent model achieves a maximum accuracy of 87.42% for k=15 when C=1 and kernel function is sigmoid function.

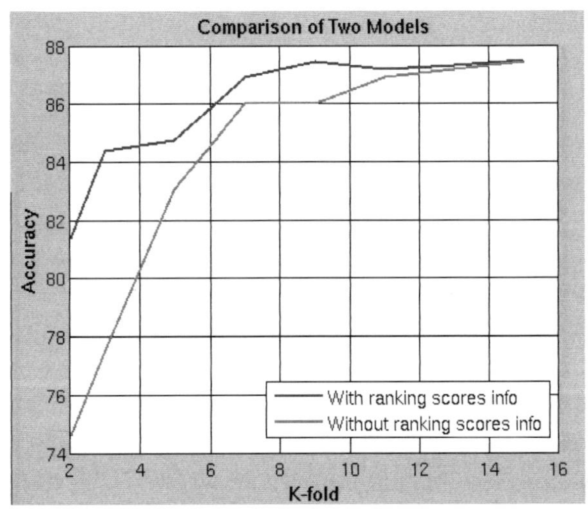

Figure 2: Performance of the two models

10 Conclusion

This paper presents a tripartite approach for the classification of intransitive verbs and the results reveal that it does handle the distribution of intransitive verbs better than the binary distribution. The intransitive verbs that take [+Ani -Vol] subjects are most incompatible with the Unaccusativity diagnostics, which are kept in Class2 in our classification scheme. The verbs of this class are most incompatible with the unaccusativity diagnostics and show fuzzy behavior causing a major problem in the unergativity/unaccusativity distinction. With this observation, we keep these verbs in a separate class so that the other two classes, which perform well over the diagnostic tests, are well separated. The results given by the model reveals that this observation is correct and Class2 verbs indeed show fuzzy behavior with a high misclassification rate. The other two classes have low misclassification rate and have shown to perform quite well. The ranking of the diagnostics with their corresponding scores gives the relative significance of the diagnostic for the unaccusative-unergative distinction of the intransitive verbs. The model incorporating this relative rank information in the form of diagnostic score has shown to outperform the model without that information. The training of the model will be improved by increasing the number of verbs used for training.

As part of the future work, we will explore the applications of the work in Machine Translation systems and Natural Language Generation.

References

Annie Zaenen 1998. *Unaccusatives in Dutch and the Syntax-Semantics Interface*. CSLI Report 123. Center for the Study of Language and Information, Stanford, CA.

Antonella Sorace 2000. *Gradients in auxiliary selection with intransitive verbs*. Language 76, 859890.

Beth Levin. 1993. *English Verb Classes and Alternations*. Chicago University Press, Chicago.

Beth Levin and Malka Rappaport Hovav. 1995. *Unaccusativity: At the Syntax-Semantics Interface*. Cambridge, MA: MIT Press.

Cengiz Acartrk and Deniz Zeyrek. 2010. *Unaccusative/Unergative Distinction in Turkish: A Connectionist Approach*. the 23rd International Conference on Computational Linguistics. Proceedings of the 8th Workshop on Asian Language Resources. Beijing, China, 2010. pp. 111-119.

Chih-Chung Chang and Chih-Jen Lin. 2011. *LIBSVM : a library for support vector machines*. ACM Transactions on Intelligent Systems and Technology, 2:27:1–27:27.

David M. Perlmutter. 1978. *Impersonal passives and the unaccusative hypothesis*. Proceedings of the 4th Berkeley Linguistics Society, 157-189.

Deniz Zeyrek. 2004. *The role of lexical semantics in unaccusative-unergative distinction in Turkish*. In Comrie, B. Soloveyv, V., Suihkonen, P (Eds), international Symposium on the Typology of Argument Structure and Grammatical Relations in Languages Spoken in Europe and North and Central Asia LENCA-2). pp 134-135. Kazan State University, Tatarstan Republic, Russia, 2004.

Ingrid Kaufmann 1995. *O- and D-Predicates: A Semantic Approach to the Unaccusative-Unergative Distinction*. Journal of Semantics 12, 377-427.

Maria Lapata and Chris Brew. 1999. *Using Subcategorization to Resolve Verb Class Ambiguity*. In Proceedings of the Joint SIGDAT Conference on Empirical Methods in Natural Language Processing and Very Large Corpora, 397-404. College Park, MD.

Nitesh Surtani, Khushboo Jha and Soma Paul. 2011. *Issues with the Unergative/Unaccusative Classification of the. Intransitive Verbs*. International Conference on Asian Language Processing (IALP), Penang, Malaysia.

Paola Merlo and Suzanne Stevenson. 2001. *Automatic verb classification based on statistical distributions of argument structure*. Computational Linguistics, 27(3):373408.

Rajesh Bhatt. 2003. *Causativization, Topics in the Syntax of the Modern Indo-Aryan Languages*. Handout.

Sabine Schulte im Walde. 2000. *Clustering verbs semantically according to their alternation behaviour*. In Proceedings of COLING, pages 747753, Saarbrucken, Germany.

Sabine Schulte im Walde. 2006. *Experiments on the automatic induction of german semantic verb classes*. Computational Linguistics, 32(2):159194.

Tasveer Ahmed 2010. *The Unaccusativity/Unergativity Distinction in Urdu*. Journal of South Asian Linguistics, North America.

Vladimir N. Vapnik 1995. *The Nature of Statistical Learning Theory*. Springer.

Thorsten Joachims 1999. *Making large-Scale SVM Learning Practical. Advances in Kernel Methods - Support Vector Learning*. B. Schlkopf and C. Burges and A. Smola (ed.). MIT Press.

The Transliteration from Alphabet Queries to Japanese Product Names

Rieko Tsuji[a], Yoshinori Nemoto[a], Wimvipa Luangpiensamut[a], Yuji Abe[a], Takeshi Kimura[a], Kanako Komiya[a], Koji Fujimoto[b], Yoshiyuki Kotani[a]

[a]Department of Computer and Information Science, Tokyo University of Agriculture and Technology / 2-24-16 Nakamachi Koganei-shi Tokyo JAPAN

[b]Tensor Consulting/ 2-10-1 Koujimachi Chiyoda-ku Tokyo JAPAN

{Riekon.m, wimvipa, kittykimura}@gmail.com, 50012646127@st.tuat.ac.jp,wizdomowl@yahoo.co.jp, koji.fujimoto@tensor.co.jp, {kkomiya, kotani}@cc.tuat.ac.jp

Abstract

There are some cases where the non-Japanese buyers are unable to find products they want through the Japanese shopping Web sites because they require Japanese queries. We propose to transliterate the inputs of the non-Japanese user, i.e., search queries written in English alphabets, into Japanese Katakana to solve this problem. In this research, the pairs of the non-Japanese search query which failed to get the right match obtained from a Japanese shopping website and its transcribed word given by volunteers were used for the training data. Since this corpus includes some noise for transliteration such as the free translation, we used two different filters to filter out the query pairs that are not transliterlated in order to improve the quality of the training data. In addition, we compared three methods, BIGRAM, HMM, and CRF, using these data to investigate which is the best for the query transliteration. The experiment revealed that the HMM was the best.

1 Introduction

In recent years, e-commerce is widely used throughout the world and it enables people to purchase products from foreign countries. However, sometimes it is not easy for foreign buyers to find the products they want because of the language difference. In our case, the alphabetic queries that are input by non-Japanese buyers should be translated into Japanese to show product pages which they want to find.

There are many cases that non-Japanese people get no or wrong result from their research queries and they are classified into three cases. The first is the case where the non-Japanese people write Japanese product names in alphabets and we expected that this case would be solved by transliteration. The second is the case where non-Japanese people write English product names and this would be solved by translation. The final is the others, for example, the proper nouns such as the names of the animation characters etc., and the misspellings. Among them, we expected that the first case is the most frequent because 53.7% of them could be fully transliterated in the corpus. Hence, we propose the transliteration from the alphabetic queries to Japanese product names cf., from lunchbox to "ランチボックス (translation into English: lunchbox, pronunciation in Japanese: ranchibokkusu)".

Also, many researches about transliteration have been accomplished for clean data, however, as far as we know, there have been no research about transliteration for noisy query data. Thus, we investigated which method is the best for query transliteration, using the parallel data of the alphabetic queries which did not provide any products when non-Japanese people searched (i.e., the Alphabet Queries) and the Japanese queries which are transcribed from them (i.e., the Correct Queries). We refer to this parallel data as the pair corpus and Table1 shows the examples of it. Here, the Alphabet Queries are the keywords which were actually used by non-Japanese user on a Japanese website and the Correct Queries were transcribed by volunteers. However, some pairs of them were not transliterated into Japanese phonogram, i.e., Katakana or Hiragana; they also have some free translations or Chinese characters. Instead of manually editing the raw data, we automatically filter out those word pairs using two filters: Chinese character filter (CF) and Chinese character and alphabet filter (CAF). The experiments revealed that the HMM worked the best which gave precision of 0.448 when the CF was used for the looser evaluation.

2 Related Works

Many works on transliteration have been accomplished so far including phonemic, orthographic, rule based approaches, and approaches which use machine learning. For example, Aramaki et al. (2009) presented the discriminative transliteration model using the CRF with the English-to-Japanese transliteration. In other language, Wang et al. (2011) worked on the English-Korean translation. They compared four methods: grapheme substring-based, phoneme substring-based, rule-based and mixture of them. Jing et al. (2011) developed the English-Chinese transliteration, which consists of many-to-many alignment and the CRF (conditional random fields) using accessor variety.

However, as far as we know, the transliteration using noisy query data has not been accomplished so far. Hence, we propose to transliterate the Alphabet Queries into the Correct Queries using the pair corpus and compared three transliteration methods to investigate which is the best for query transliteration.

It is also possible to use the dictionary-based approaches, however, the pair corpus includes many new words like the title of the comics and the names of the animation characters that are not listed in the dictionaries. Therefore, the dictionary based approach is not so powerful for transliteration comparing with that for translation. Thus, we employed the phonemic approach and the probabilistic method or the machine learning was used for the transliteration from phonemes to Japanese product names (i.e., the Correct Queries).

3 Transformation from the Alphabet Query to Phoneme

We employed the phonemic approach; the Alphabet Queries were transformed into phonemes and then are transliterated. The transliteration was carried out as follows:

1. Transform the Alphabet Queries into phonemes using a English-Phoneme dictionary (Section 3.1)
2. Filter the Correct Queries to clean the noisy data (Section 3.2)
3. Calculate the translation probabilities from phonemes to Japanese characters (Section 3.3)
4. Align the phonemes and Japanese characters (Section 3.4)
5. Transliterate the phoneme queries into Japanese words using the probabilistic method or machine learning (Section 3.5)

The remainder of this section describes these five steps. The steps from one to four were the generation phase of the training data and the step five was the transliteration phase.

3.1 Transform the Alphabet Queries

CMU Pronunciation Dictionary[1] (CMUdict) was used for the transformation from the Alphabet Queries to phonemes. Thus, we targeted only the alphabetic queries which include at least one phoneme in it. We obtained 2833 Alphabet Queries after this process.

3.2 Filter

Since the pair corpus is noisy, the training data were narrowed down and were refined using the following two different filters:

[1] http://www. speech.cs.cmu.edu/cgi-bin/cmudict

method	BASE	BIGRAM	HMM	CRF
system output	ファブーンク (fabuunku)	ファブリック (faburikku: the correct answer)	ファブリック (faburikku: the correct answer)	フブック (fubukku)
evaluation	1	3	3	2

Table 2: The system output when the input was "fabric" (Alphabet Query) and evaluation

1. Chinese character filter (CF)
2. Chinese character and alphabet filter (CAF)

These two filters were compared to adjust the quality and the amount of the training data. CF filtered out the pair which has Chinese character Correct Queries and CAF filtered out the pair which has Chinese character Correct Queries and alphabetic Correct Queries. In other word, the pair filtered by CFA has only Katakana and Hiragana Correct Query

Table 1 lists the example of the pair corpus and the characteristics of the Alphabet and Correct Queries. Here, we focused on the character type of the Correct Queries because of the characteristics of the pair corpus.

As shown in the table, although we want to use only the transliteration pairs as the training data, it is not easy to distinguish them. (The pair corpus consists of only the Alphabet and Correct Queries.) The first problem was that some Correct Queries are written not only in Japanese phonogram, i.e., Katakana or Hiragana, but also in ideograms, i.e., Chinese characters that have many ways to pronounce (cf. Tokyo-東京 (Tokyo,toukyou)).

Thus, we carried out the filtering by the character types to obtain as many transliteration pairs as possible. We expected that this process would improve the quality of the training data because in many cases, if the Correct Queries were in Katakana, they were transliterated. However, we have to keep in mind that the Correct Queries in Katakana could be free translation as shown in Table1 on the second line (cf. Miyazaki –ジブリ (translation into English: GHIBRI, pronunciation in Japanese: ziburi, meaning: a film studio name) .

Alphabet Query (type of query)	Correct Query (translation into English, pronunciation in Japanese)	transliteration (L) or translation(T)	Type of Characters of Correct Query
Doraemon (animation's character name)	ドラえもん (Doraemon, doraemon)	L	Katakana, Hiragana
Miyazaki (person's name)	ジブリ (GHIBRI, ziburi)	T	Katakana
AKB48 poster (pop group's name, poster)	AKB48 ポスター (AKB48 poster, eikeibii48 posutaa)	L	Katakana, Alphabet
Ufm rod (brand name, rod)	Ufm ロッド (Ufm rod, uefuemu roddo,)	L	Katakana, Alphabet
Tokyo adidas (place name, brand name)	東京 adidas (Tokyo adidas, toukyou adidasu)	L	Chinese character, Alphabet
Dress Tokyo (general noun, place name)	原宿 ドレス (Harajuku dress, Harajuku doresu)	L, T	Chinese character, Katakana

Table 1: The example of the pair corpus and the characteristics of the Alphabet and Correct Queries

Here, we filtered out the pair which has alphabetic or Chinese character Correct Queries to refine the pair corpus more (CAF: The shaded data with light gray and the shaded data with gray were removed). However, if we filter out too many query pairs to improve the quality of the training data, we may not be able to obtain enough training data for the probabilistic methods or machine learning. Therefore, we filtered out the pair corpus which has Chinese character Correct Queries (CF: The shaded data with gray were removed). Namely, we used two kinds of filters to find out which of those is the best for query transliteration.

We could use 78.5% and 25.2% of the pair corpus to calculate the translation probabilities by using the CF and the CAF, respectively.

3.3 Calculation of Translation Probabilities

The transliteration probabilities, from the phonemes of the Alphabet Queries which were transformed in Section 3.1 to the Correct Queries which were filtered in Section3.2, were calculated using the filtered pair corpus. We used the GIZA++[2] toolkit (Och and Ney, 2003) to calculate them. Here, we set phonemes as the source language and Japanese character as the target language.

3.4 Alignment

The alignment of phonemes and Japanese characters which is necessary before the transliteration was carried out for each query pair. The Dijkstra algorithm was used to make alignments. Fig.1 shows the alignment of the phonemes of document and its transcribed word ドキュメント (document, dokyumento). In Fig 1, the horizontal axis represents the phonemes of the Alphabet Queries and the vertical axis represents the Correct Queries. We used the negative logarithm of the translation probabilities (which are calculated in Section3.3) as costs of the alignment. Also, we set logarithm of 10-20 as the cost when no translation probabilities were obtained. (cf., the horizontal direction and vertical direction in Fig 1 are the cases).

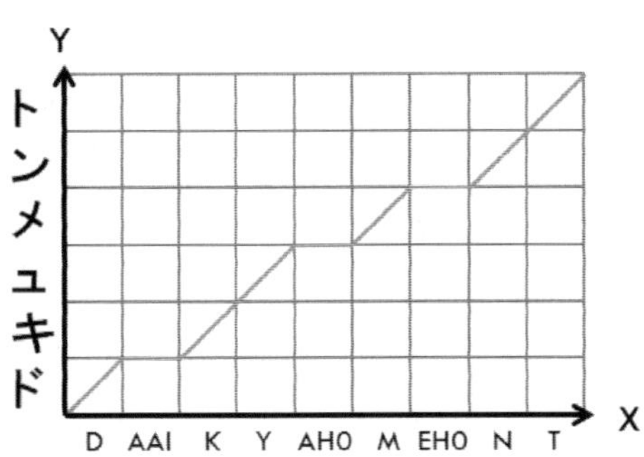

Figure 1: The alignment of the phonemes of *document* and its transcribed word ドキュメント (document, dokyumento)

Figure 2 shows the result of the alignment when the Alphabet Queries was *document* and the Correct Queries was ドキュメント (document, dokyumento). NULLJ and NULLP in Figure 2 represent the alignments in the horizontal and vertical directions respectively.

[D - ド(do)]
[AAI - NULLJ]
[K - キ(ki)]
[Y - ュ(yu)]
[AH0 - NULLJ]
[M - メ(me)]
[EH0 - NULLJ]
[N - ン(n)]
[T - ト(to)]

Figure 2: The result of the alignment of the phonemes of document and ドキュメント (document, dokyumento)

3.5 Transliteration

The transliteration was carried out using the probabilistic method or machine learning. We compared the following three different approaches were applied based on the alignments which were obtained in Section 3.4:

1. BIGRAM: The Bigram Model
2. HMM: The Hidden Marcov Model
3. CRF: The CRF model

We used NLTK[3] for BIGRAM and the HMM and adopted the CRF++[4] toolkit for the CRF. We trained the CRF models with the unigram, bigram, and trigram features. The features are shown in the following.

- Unigram: s-2, s-1, s0, s1, and s2
- Bigram: s-1s0 and s0s1
- Trigram: s−2s−1s0, s−1s0s1, and s0s1s2

We set parameters as f=50 and c=2. We set f=50 because the kinds of features were so variable.

[2] http://www.fjoch.com/GIZA++.html

[3] http://www.nltk.org/

[4] http://crfpp.googlecode.com/svn/trunk/doc/index.html

In addition, we used BASE method without machine leaning as baseline.

- BASE: The method where the most probable Japanese characters were selected for each phoneme from the translation probabilities.

4 Experiment and Evaluation

Five-fold cross validation was used in the experiments using the pair corpus. Note that we used 2833 Alphabet Queries which include at least one phoneme in the CMU dictionary. Here, only the training data were refined via two kinds of filter that are introduced in Section 3.1 because the system should not know the Correct Queries of the test data. Thus, the test data include some cases that cannot be transliterated, such as the case whose Correct Query is free translated from the Alphabet Query. One thousand five hundreds twenty one queries out of 2833 can be fully transliterated, which means a kind of upperbound of our system is 0. 537.

The system outputs were evaluated by twenty native Japanese speakers. We used human raters rather than the automatic evaluation such as the automatic method which uses the edit distance to evaluate this system because the Correct Queries is noisy and not always transliterated. The evaluations were graded on three scales (three is the highest and one is the lowest). Table2 presents the system outputs and evaluations when the input is "fabric". In this table, the evaluation score is three when we got the ideal output, i.e., "ファブリック" (fabric, faburikku). We defined "precision 3" and "precision 3 or 2" as follows:

$$\text{precision 3} = \frac{\left(\begin{array}{c}\textit{The total number of system outputs}\\ \textit{which are evaluated as 3}\end{array}\right)}{\textit{The total number of Query pairs}}$$

$$\text{precision 3 or 2} = \frac{\left(\begin{array}{c}\textit{The total number of system outputs}\\ \textit{which are evaluated as 3 or 2}\end{array}\right)}{\textit{The total number of Query pairs}}$$

Tables 3 and 4 summarize the precision of strict and looser evaluation respectively (i.e., the precision 3 and the precision 3 or 2). We also evaluated the system of BIGRAM and HMM without those filters and Table 5 show their precisions.

	CF	CAF
BASE	0.036	0.044
BIGRAM	0.029	0.071
HMM	0.062	**0.121**
CRF	0.064	0.046

Table 3: "The precision 3" of strict evaluation

	CF	CAF
BASE	0.323	0.209
BIGRAM	0.190	0.270
HMM	**0.448**	0.373
CRF	0.316	0.199

Table 4: "The precision 3 or 2" of looser evaluation.

	The precision 3	The precision 3 or 2
BIGRAM	0.032	0.151
HMM	0.043	0.273

Table 5: The precisions of BIGRAM and HMM without the filters.

5 Discussion

Although there were some reports that say the CRF model achieved high accuracy for transliteration when English to non-Japanese language was carried out (Shishtla et al 2009), the HMM was the best in this research according to Tables 3 and 4. We think this is because that we used trigram features for the CRF in this experiment. When the Alphabet Query is a compound word which contains two or more words, we could not find that those words are separated and they are treated as one word. For example, suppose that the Alphabet Query was "super mario", and their phonemes were" S UW1 P ER0 M AA1 R IY0 OW0". When the system considered the transliteration of M, it used the P in "S UW1 P ER0", which is two phonemes before M, as a feature. However, this "P" is unrelated with "M AA1 R IY0 OW0". These features sometimes caused some errors for the CRF in this manner.

In addition, according to these tables, the HMM and the CRF were always superior to BASE but BIGRAM was not the case. This indicates that BIGRAM should not be used for the query transliteration.

Next, according to Tables 3, 4, and 5, the precisions without the filters were completely lower than those with the CF and CAF. It indicates that the filters were useful for transliteration of the noisy data.

In addition, as mentioned in Section 3.2, the amount of training data after the CAF was used (714 records) is much less than those after CA was used (2223 records). Nevertheless, as shown in Table 3, the CAF had the better result for the strict evaluation. These results revealed that it is better to use the CAF if we could obtain much more data.

Moreover, according to Table 3, the precisions when the CAF was used are higher than when the CF was used except the case when the CRF was used. In contrast, the CAF filter outperformed the CAF filter except the case when BIGRAM was used for machine learning in Table 4. In other words, the CAF is superior to the CF in Table 3, i.e., the precision of the strict evaluation, but the CF was superior to the CAF in Table 4, i.e., the precision of the looser evaluation. We think that these results indicate that the CAF should be used to obtain transliteration whose quality is high and the CF should be used if we want loose but many transliterations. These results indicate that the filters should be selected depending on the amount of the training data and the purpose of the application.

Then, we counted frequencies of the Alphabet Queries whose score is three and found that many of them frequently occurred. For example, the word *figure* appeared 102 times in the Alphabet Queries. Here, Table 6 lists the number of the Alphabet Queries and their averaged scores according to their frequencies when the HMM and the CAF were used. For example, the Alphabet Queries which occurred once were 417 and their averaged score was 1.77. Figure 3 shows the relation between the frequencies of the Alphabet Queries in the training data and their averaged score when the HMM and the CAF were used.

These table and figure show that the Alphabet Queries which occur many times tend to be high quality. We think this indicates that the precision of the transliteration may improve if we can have more data.

Furthermore, the number of Japanese characters tended to be smaller than that of the phonemes of the Alphabet Queries. We think that this is because the tag NULLJ frequently occurred in the alignment step and the precision may improve if the cost of NULLJ was selected more carefully.

Finally, we think we can use the translation system using the other methods such as the dictionary-based approach in conjunction with our transliteration system to get the right match for many queries. We think we can also try the orthographic approach in the future.

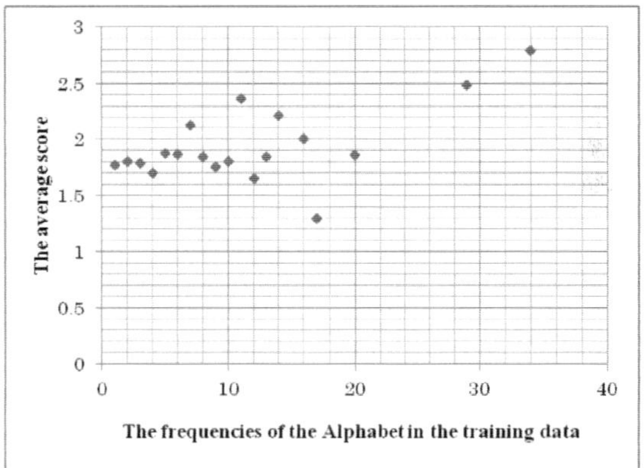

Figure 3: The relation between the frequencies of the Alphabet Queries in the training data and their averaged score when the HMM and the CAF were used.

Frequencies	The number of the Alphabet Queries	Averaged scores
1	417	1.77
2	124	1.78
3	57	1.79
4	21	1.67
5	14	1.87
6	13	1.87
7	4	2.13
8	4	1.84
9	3	1.75
10	5	1.81
11	2	2.36
12	3	1.65
13	1	1.85
14	1	2.21
16	1	2.00
17	1	1.29
20	2	1.86
29	1	2.48
34	1	2.79

Table 6: The number of the Alphabet Queries and their averaged scores according to their frequencies when the HMM and the CAF were used.

6 Conclusion

In this paper, we proposed to transliterate the inputs of the non-Japanese user i.e., search queries written in English alphabets, into Japanese Katakana using the pair corpus. Since this corpus includes some noise for transliteration such as the free translation, we carried out the filtering using the character types. Two kinds of filters, i.e., the CF and the CAF, were compared to adjust the quality and amount of the train data. The experiments revealed that the filters should be selected depending on the amount of the training data and the purpose of the application.

In addition, we compared three probabilistic or machine leaning methods, i.e., BIGRAM, the HMM, and the CRF using the pair corpus to investigate which is the best for query transliteration. The experiments show that the HMM methods worked the best. We think the HMM outperformed the CRF because we used trigram features for the CRF. Since the Correct Queries include many compound words, they caused some errors.

Finally, the experiments also indicate that the precision of the transliteration may improve if we can have more data or if the cost of NULLJ was selected more carefully in the alignment step.

Acknowledgement

We would like to thank jGrab (http://www.j-grab.com/) which provide us the parallel data of alphabet queries and Japanese product names.

References

Eiji ARAMAKI and Takeshi ABEKAWA. 2009. Fast decoding and Easy Implementation:Transliteration as Sequential Labeling, Proceedings of the 2009 Named Entities Workshop , ACL-IJNLP 2009, pages 65-68.

Steven Bird, Ewan Klein, and Edward Loper. 2009. Natural Language Processing with Python: Analyzing Text with The Natural Language Toolkit, O'Reilly.

Mike Tia-Jian Jiang, Chan-Hung Kuo, Wen-Lian Hsu. 2011. English-Chinese Machine Translitaration using accessor Variety Features of Source Graphemes. Proceedings of the 2011 Named Entities Workshop, IJCNLP 2011, pages 86-90.

Canasai Kruengkrai, Thatsanee Charoenporn, Virach Sornelertlamvanich 2011. Simple Discriminative Training for Machine Transliteration. Proceedings of the 2011 Named Entities Workshop, IJCNLP 2011, pages 28-31.

Franz Joseph Och, Hermann Ney 2003. A sys-tenmatic comparison of various statistical alighnment models. Association for Computational Linguistics, ACL 2003, 29(4):417-449.

Praneeth Shishtla, Surya Ganesh V, Sethuramalingam Subramaniam, and Vasudeva Varma. 2009. A Language-Independent transliteration Schema-Using Character Aligned Model At NEWS 2009, Proceedings of the 2009 Named Entities Workshop , IJNLP 2009, pages 40-43.

Yu-Chun Wang, Richard Tzong-Han Tsai. 2011. English-Korean Named Entity Transliteration Using Statistical Substring-based and Rule-based Approaches. Proceedings of the 2011 Named Entities Workshop, IJCNLP 2011, pages .32-35.

Min Zhang, Haizhou L, A Kumaran and Haizhou Li. 2011. Report of NEWS 2011 Machine Transliteration Shared Task. Proceedings of the 2011 Named Entities Workshop, IJCNLP 2011, pages 1–13.

Classifying Dialogue Acts in Multi-party Live Chats

Su Nam Kim
School of IT
Monash University
Clayton, VIC, Australia
su.kim@monash.edu.au

Lawrence Cavedon
School of CS and IT
RMIT University
Melbourne, VIC, Australia
lawrence.cavedon@rmit.edu.au

Timothy Baldwin
Dept. of Computing and
Information Systems
The University of Melbourne
VIC, Australia
tb@ldwin.net

Abstract

We consider the task of classifying chat contributions by dialogue act in a multi-party setting. This extends the problem significantly over the 1-1 chat scenario due to the semi-asynchronous and "entangled" nature of the contributions by chat participants. We experiment with a number of machine learning approaches, using different categories of features: lexical, contextual, structural, keyword and dialogue interaction information. For evaluation, we developed gold-standard data using online forums from the USA Library of Congress. We found that, for multi-party dialogues, features based on 1-gram and keywords produced best performance, while features exploiting structure and interaction did not perform as well as previously reported results over 1-to-1 chats.

1 Introduction

Dialogue Acts (or **DAs**) are discourse units (or utterances) that represent the semantics of contributions to a dialogue at the level of illocutionary force. Dialogue acts have been studied in various types of conversations — spoken/written dialogue contributions (Stolcke et al., 2000; Wu et al., 2002; Kim et al., 2010a), sentence-level (Lampert et al., 2008), paragraph-level (Cong et al., 2008), or complete messages consisting of several paragraphs (Cohen et al., 2004). Authors have argued that automatic dialogue act identification could help in a range of applications, such as meeting summarisation (Murray et al., 2006), email summarisation, conversational agents, speech recognition (Stolcke et al., 2000), or human social intention detection (Jurafsky et al., 2009). They can also be useful in information-sharing chats in online forums (Kim et al., 2010b; Wang et al., 2011).

Recently, **live chat** has received growing attention since chat services and similar applications have gained popularity as a communication method. However, the majority of previous work on dialogue act classification for dialogue has been carried out over *spoken* dialogue. Although spoken and written dialogue have similarities, they have distinct features which make it difficult to reuse existing methods for live chats. For example, spoken dialogue introduces difficulties due to errors inherent in speech recognition output, but allows acoustic and prosodic features to be leveraged (e.g. Stolcke et al. (2000)). Conversely, live chats introduce other types of complications, including ill-formed data and *entanglement* (especially for multi-party conversations) due to the semi-asynchronous nature of the interaction (e.g. (Werry, 1996)). As a result, studying live chats is a necessary step toward building accurate live chat systems.

To date, relatively little work has targeted dialogue act classification over live chat data. Wu et al. (2002) and Forsyth (2007) investigated multi-party casual chats, while Ivanovic (2008) and Kim et al. (2010a) focused on 1-on-1 chats in customer service centre settings. However, these previous approaches are not directly applicable to other types of live chats, such as forum-style chats that allow multiple participants. Additionally, many live chat applications, such as online forums and online meetings, presume an environment that allows multiple participants to discuss specific topics. While Forsyth (2007) investigates chat involving multiple participants, the conversations are casual and not topic-focused. The semantics and structure of dialogues depend on the nature and structure of the conversations, thus requiring different dialogue act categories and classification approaches.

In this paper, we target the classification of dialogue acts in multi-user forums carried out through live chats. 1-on-1 live chats are popular for consumer service support or individual meetings. However, this does not allow multiple users to participate in the chats. On the other hand, as more meetings are taking place via live chat, we believe that studying live chats in multi-user environments is a necessary step towards building such systems. In addition, we have developed a live chat dataset from library forum chats, involving multiple simultaneous users. The dataset contains live chats extracted from online forums conducted at the US Library of Congress.

To develop automatic methods for dialogue act classification in live chats, we explored four types of features: *context*, *structure*, *keyword*, and *dialogue interaction*. In addition, we compare the systems in terms of the number of participants as well as the types of chats (i.e., casual vs. forum chats). In evaluation, we investigate the utility of each feature category over different types of live chat over two multi-user datasets: (i) online forums from the US Library of Congress, and (ii) Forsyth's NPS (Naval Postgraduate School) casual chats, and.

2 Task Setup

We experiment with two different types of live chats: (i) forum chats involving specific discussion topics; and (ii) casual chats (i.e., (Forsyth, 2007)'s NPS casual chat data). Since there was no existing available data for the first type, we developed the data for evaluation ourselves. The remainder of this section describes the data and dialogue act categories in detail.

2.1 Dataset 1: Live Forum Chats

We collected online forum chats with multiple participants from the US Library of Congress. The live chats contain 33 online discussions that the Library's Educational Outreach team hosted for teachers between 2002 and 2006.

To define dialogue acts suitable for this data, we investigated existing sets of dialogue acts from both spoken dialogues and live chats. Many have been based on the Dialogue Act Markup in Several Layers (DAMSL) scheme (Allen and Core, 1997), initially applied to the TRAIN corpus of transcribed spoken task-oriented dialogues. In live chats, Wu et al. (2002) and Forsyth (2007) defined 15 dialogue acts for casual online conversations based on previous sets (Samuel et al., 1998; Jurafsky et al., 1998; Stolcke et al., 2000) and characteristics of conversations. Ivanovic (2008) proposed 12 dialogue acts applying DAMSL to customer service chats.

We found that forum chats are not dissimilar to customer service chats in terms of the nature of conversations (e.g. question, request, thanking, etc.), and so decided to adopt the DA set defined by Ivanovic (2008). To the 12 dialogue acts from Ivanovic (2008), we added two further dialogue acts — BACKGROUND and OTHER. BACKGROUND is designed to cover contributions containing information about the participants themselves, which often occurs before discussions. OTHER covers chat contributions that do not belong to any other dialogue acts. We also compared our defined set of DAs to that for NPS casual chats in Forsyth (2007). Although both datasets contain multiple participants, they differ in the nature of their content; thus, we found problems applying the DA set from Forsyth (2007) directly to the library chat forums. However, we observed that there is overlap between the two sets of dialogue acts (e.g. (OPENING vs. GREET), (EXPRESSION vs. EMOTION), YN/WH-QUESTION for both, etc.). The final list of dialogue acts we applied to the library dataset is shown in Table 1.

In preprocessing, we first removed system log messages.[1] Second, we replaced expressions such as emoticons and exclamations (e.g. *:-), wow*), email addresses (e.g. (learningpage@loc.gov), URLs (e.g. *http://memory.loc.gov*), locations (e.g. *Texas*), and institute names (e.g. *University of Houston*) with the tokens *EMOTION, EMAIL, URL, LOCATION, INSTITUTE*, respectively. We also replaced user

[1]System log messages indicate the status of participants, such as *join* and *depart*.

Dialog Act	Example	%	Dialog Act	Example	%
STATEMENT	we have a website for photo gallery.	47.76	WH-QUESTION	What is this?	3.26
RESPONSE-ACK	yes, great, i agree,..	11.73	OPENING	Hi, Greeting!	3.03
EXPRESSION	:-), wow, oh!	7.71	YES-ANSWER	yes, sure,	1.67
THANKING	thanks, thank you for ..	6.54	CLOSING	bye, good night,..	1.55
YN-QUESTION	is there a website for .. ?	5.84	DOWNPLAY	no problem, you're welcome!	0.49
REQUEST	click this, go to xx..	4.97	OTHER	or, but	0.40
BACKGROUND	i am user2, i teach 4th grad	4.76	NO-ANSWER	no, nope	0.28

Table 1: Dialogue Act Tagset for the USA Library of Congress forum Chats: definitions and examples

names with the unique token *USER_ID* for privacy. Third, we applied a sentence tokenizer in order to separate the data into tentative discourse units, then further manually segmented/confirmed the units. This culminated in 5,276 utterances over 15 library forum chats, each containing at least 200 discourse units (between 238 and 666 discourses per live chat). The proportion of utterances for each dialogue act type is listed in Table 1.

To develop a gold-standard, we hired two annotators (including one of the authors) both of whom have significant experience in annotating similar datasets. Before conducting the actual annotation task, we conducted a pilot task over library forum chats which were not selected in our final dataset, and confirmed the feasibility of the dialogue acts. The inter-annotator agreement was 81.4% with kappa value 0.74, indicating reliable agreement.

2.2 Dataset 2: Casual Live Chats

We used the NPS casual chats developed by Forsyth (2007) as our second dataset. Table 2 shows the dialogue act tags, examples, and the distribution of dialogue acts in the dataset. The dataset contains 10,567 utterances spanning 15 conversations. It also includes POS tags which are modified to make it more specific to the categories based on Penn Treebank tags. For privacy, the actual user names have been replaced with anonymous IDs. Forsythe reports that one person labeled and verified the gold-standard labels and automatically tagged POS tags; thus, Forsythe does not report any inter-annotator agreement statistics on the NPS dataset. It is also hard to re-annotate the NPS dataset to ascertain inter-annotator agreement statistics, due to a lack of published guidelines.

3 Features

3.1 Bag-of-words Features

Contextual information has been used for dialogue act classification with both spoken and written dialogues (e.g. (Samuel et al., 1998; Bangalore et al., 2006; Ivanovic, 2008)). For live chats, Ivanovic (2008) and Kim et al. (2010a) used unigrams and/or variations of n-grams as basic features. Kim et al. (2010a) suggest that higher-order n-grams (i.e., 2-grams and both 1,2-grams) do not perform significantly better than using unigrams only, and that using lemmas performs better than using raw words. Based on these previous results, we tested raw and lemmatized unigrams only, with TF·IDF and Boolean values as our base features. In addition, we noticed that despite the data appearing cleaner than that of Ivanovic (2008), there are still typos and out-of-vocabulary words in the data. To handle these, we tested word-stems as an attempt to reduce errors from those words. In sum, we tested 12 combinations, using (raw, lemmatized, stemmed 1-grams), (with and without POS), (with Boolean vs. TF·IDF values). Details of lemmatization and stemming are presented in Section 4.1.

3.2 Structural Information

Kim et al. (2010a) has demonstrated the effectiveness of structural information for classifying dialogue acts over 1-on-1 live chats. Most live chat sessions we used are significantly longer and contain multiple participants, thereby reducing the alignment of related dialogue-contributions. However, we observed that there is still some degree of structural regularity, e.g. GREETING at the beginning and ending, and the presence of BACKGROUND

Dialog Act	Example	%	Dialog Act	Example	%
STATEMENT	well i thought you and I will end up together :-(	30.14	EMPHASIS	I do believe he is right.	1.80
SYSTEM	JOIN	24.91	CONTINUER	an thought I'd share	1.59
GREET	hiya 10-19-40sUser43 hug	12.90	REJECT	u r not on meds	1.50
EMOTION	lol	10.47	YES ANSWER	why yes I do 10-19-40sUser24, lol	1.02
YES/NO Q.	cant we all just get along	5.20	NO ANSWER	no I had a roomate who did though	0.68
WH-QUESTION	11-08-20sUser70 why do you feel that way?	5.04	CLARIFY	i meant to write the word may	0.36
ACCEPT	yeah it does, they all do	2.20	OTHER	sdfjsdfjlf	0.33
BYE	night ya'all	1.85			

Table 2: Dialogue Act Tagset for the NPS Casual Chats: definitions and examples

after GREETING. Our second observation is that some dialogue acts are associated with shorter dialogues, e.g. *hi, bye* for GREETING, or *excellent* for EXPRESSION. Third, we observed that some users tend to ask questions while others tend to answer them. Similar to representatives at customer service centers, hosts of the forums tend to request actions or to pose questions. Based on our observations, we tested the following four features:

- *Distance*: The distance from the first utterance to the target utterance. We test both absolute distance ($Distance_{absolute}$) and percentage distance relative to the total conversation ($Distance_{relative}$);
- *TermCount*: The number of terms in the target utterance;
- *UserID*: User ID (1–180 for library forum chats, 1 –1,377 for NPS casual chats);
- *User=Host?*: If User of target utterance is the host (1) or not (0). Note that this feature is applied to library forum chats only.

Note that in online systems, we do not know the total length of conversations, and thus the feature $Distance_{relative}$ (relative position of the target utterance) is tested only for comparison purposes.

3.3 Keyword Information

Forsyth (2007) used manually-crafted keywords for classification and reported high accuracies even with this simple technique. Stolcke et al. (2000) also reported that lexical features were strong indicators of dialogue act in spoken dialogue. We similarly observed that some words are strongly associated with specific dialogue acts. However, since the nature and dialogue acts of different datasets are themselves different, specific keywords are needed for our library forum chats. As such, we first selected candidate terms for keywords by using the frequent terms per DA and manually extracted keywords which are associated with specific dialogue acts. In essence, keywords are not equivalent to the full set of n-grams, but rather a targeted subset of n-grams (of varying length) associated with specific dialogue acts. The following list shows examples of keywords for dialogue acts over library forum chats. Note that since STATEMENT includes unfocused chats, we do not propose keywords for this dialogue act.

- BACKGROUND: *I live, location, institute*
- OPENING: *hi, hello, greeting, welcome*
- CLOSING: *see you, bye, goodnight*
- THANKING: *thank you, thanks*
- DOWNPLAY: *no problem, you're welcome*
- EXPRESSION: *emotion*
- YES-ANSWER: *yes* with a question mark in the preceding 5 sentences
- NO-ANSWER: *no* (without *problem*)
- REQUEST: *please, click, let's*

- RESPONSE-ACK: *!, great, yes, ok* in Utterances of length ≤ 3

- WH-QUESTION: question mark with *how, what, when, where, who, why*

- YN-QUESTION: question mark without *how, what, when, where, who, why*

For the NPS casual chats, we used all keyword features (f0–f26) defined in Forsyth (2007). However, we observed that some of his features are not available at the time of the target utterance unless we have access to the completed conversation (e.g. *f3. Number of posts in the future that contained a Yes or No word*) — i.e., for online systems, these features are not usable. As a result, we tested two different sets of features: using all features; and using only those based on information available at the target utterance. It is also not clear how to extract the exact same keywords as used in Forsyth (2007), and as such, we expect our results to differ slightly from those in the original paper.

In addition, to overcome the data dependency of the keyword feature, we proposed new features using the distribution of terms over dialogue acts. That is, we computed the term frequency (TF) of each term over the 14 dialogue acts in the training data, and accumulated TF from all terms in the target utterance into a 14×1 vector to represent the feature for the target utterance. For example, suppose that for the target utterance *Welcome back*, *welcome* occurs 100 and 20 times with dialogue-acts OPENING and DOWNPLAY, respectively, and *back* occurs 10 and 5 times with OPENING and STATEMENT, respectively. Then the TF vectors for the terms are "100 0 0 0 0 0 0 0 0 0 0 0 20 0" and "10 0 0 0 0 5 0 0 0 0 0 0 0 0". By adding all TFs from both terms, we finally obtain "110 0 0 0 0 5 0 0 0 0 0 0 20 0" as the final feature for the target utterance. We also tested three different TF values listed below. Further, we tested two different options for choosing terms in an utterance: using <u>all</u> terms vs. using <u>selected</u> terms for which the majority label has TF of at least 50%. Returning to our example from above, for *back*, the proportion of TF with OPENING and STATEMENT is 0.333 and 0.677, respectively — thus, none of the labels have 50% total TF for *back*, and we would hence discard this term for the "selected terms" option.

- *InfoDistribution*$_{Raw/Raw.5}$: raw counts;

- *InfoDistribution*$_{Percent/Percent.5}$: percentage counts;

- *InfoDistribution*$_{Label/Label.5}$: a dialogue act with maximum TF.

3.4 Interaction among Utterances

Finally, we investigated the interaction between features proposed in Bangalore et al. (2006) and Kim et al. (2010a). Bangalore et al. (2006) used sentences to provide dialogue act information of previous utterances over spoken dialogues; Kim et al. (2010a) used predicted dialogue acts directly. A major point of difference for us is that our data contains multiple participants; thus, the interactions among utterances tend to be more indirect. Moreover, due to difficulties in utterance disentanglement similarily shown in Elsner and Charniak (2008)), we expect reduced effectiveness over our data of such information (although some degree of interaction exists). However, to partly help with disentanglement, we noticed that some users mentioned the user name(s) of the users they are responding to in their posts, which allows us to identify the utterances they link to. Based on these observations, we tested the five interaction features listed below:

- *Prev1, Prev2, Prev3*: dialogue act(s) or sentence(s) from $1 \sim 3$ previous utterances;

- *User*: a dialogue act or sentence from 1 previous utterance in which the user is the same as the author in the target utterance;

- *TextUser*: A dialogue act or sentence from 1 previous utterance which is authored by the user mentioned in the target utterance. For example, for *USER63, thanks for the information.*, we would identify *USER63* as the user and use his/her latest utterance as a feature.

4 Evaluation

4.1 Experimental Setup

To develop our system, we first performed POS tagging using Lingua::EN::Tagger, lemmatization using *morph* (Minnen et al., 2001), and stemming using the English Porter stemmer.[2]

For our learners, we used the Naïve Bayes (NB) implementation in the WEKA machine learning toolkit (Witten and Frank, 2005), a support vector machine (SVM),[3] and the CRF implementation in Mallet (McCallum, 2002).[4] We ran 15-fold cross validation, using our 15 dialogues. All results are reported in terms of micro-averaged F-score, unless otherwise noted. As a baseline, instead of using the majority vote (**47.76** and **24.91** for library forum chats and NPS casual chats, respectively), we used a system built using bag-of-words features only (see Table 3), one for each machine learner.

4.2 Result 1: Bag-of-Words

Table 3 shows the performances of our different dialogue act classification systems using variations of 1-grams. It shows that stemmed unigrams without POS tags performed best with BoW features over library forum chats, while stemmed unigrams with POS tags generally achieved the highest performance over NPS casual chats. Note that we only show performance using *Boolean* values, since those using TF·IDF were lower. We also tested 2-grams and mixed 1/2-grams, and found they each reduced performance. Overall, we found that stemming improved performance. We noticed that for library forum chats, due to ill-formed data, POS tagging did not perform well. On the other hand, POS tags in NPS casual chats were improved by the automatic method (see Forsyth (2007) for how to correctly perform POS tagging over casual chats). As a result, performance using POS tags is different over the two different sets. However, by considering the performance over NPS casual chats, we conclude that high-quality POS tags would help to improve classification performance. Between the three learners, the CRF performance is superior to the others; this aligns with previous research (e.g. (Kim et al., 2010a)) most likely because the conversations are structured, despite the entanglement issue.

[2] Available at http://tartarus.org/~martin/PorterStemmer/

[3] http://www.cs.cornell.edu/People/tj/svm_light/svm_hmm.html

[4] http://mallet.cs.umass.edu

4.3 Result 2: Structural Information

Table 4 shows the performance using structural features. As base systems, we used *stemmed unigrams* for library forum chats and *stemmed unigrams with POS tags* for NPS casual chats, since all three learners generally performed best using stemmed unigrams. Overall, we found that structural features did not work well in multi-party live chats, in contrast to the results of Kim et al. (2010a) over 1-on-1 live chats. We presume this is because the data contains multiple participants, blurring the structural information. The semi-asynchronous nature of the interaction also poses serious issues for disentanglement, thus adding more difficulty in identifying the association between dialogue acts and structural information. However, term counts and user ids improved the performance slightly over NPS casual chats. Also, the *User=Host?* feature worked best using the CRF for library forum chats. We hypothesize that this is because the hosts tend to have stronger association with specific dialogue acts (e.g. REQUEST) in this setting. A user's contribution to the conversation would also be associated with some specific dialogue acts (e.g. some tend to ask while others tend to answer). As discussed in Section 3.2, we compared absolute and relative distances and found no difference.

4.4 Result 3: Keyword Information

Table 5 shows the performance using keyword features. As above, the base systems use *stemmed unigrams* for library forum chats and *stemmed unigrams with POS tags* for NPS casual chats, since overall, structural information did not improve performance. With library forum chats, we found that adding keywords to contextual features improved performance over all three learners, since some terms occur only in specific dialogue acts. However, with the NPS casual chats, keyword features did not perform well, in contrast to the findings of Forsyth (2007). We hypothesis that the lower performance is due to the specific keywords used in this work, as compared to those used in Forsyth (2007). We also found that using selected features that are available at the time of the target utterance performed better. This suggests that classifying dialogue acts can be performed as an online task. Further, using the dis-

	Library Forum						NPS					
	without POS			with POS			without POS			with POS		
	NB	SVM	CRF	NB	SVM	CRF	NB	SVM	CRF	NB	SVM	CRF
Raw†	76.88	76.18	**79.38**	72.75	73.06	74.79	75.91	74.89	78.53	**72.97**	**73.54**	**75.46**
Lemma	**76.90**	74.68	79.25	**73.09**	58.03	**76.67**	76.02	73.82	78.58	**74.02**	68.22	**78.17**
Stem	**77.58**	**76.48**	79.26	**73.23**	59.51	**76.66**	76.59	75.17	78.13	**74.28**	68.61	**78.39**

Table 3: **Performance with BoWs**: performances exceeding the baseline are bold-faced. The baseline system is marked with †.

	Library Forum			NPS		
Feature	NB	SVM	CRF	NB	SVM	CRF
Baseline	77.58	76.48	79.26	74.28	68.61	78.39
+Distance$_{Relative}$	77.22	74.72	78.09	73.77	65.43	77.17
+Distance$_{Absolute}$	70.05	74.79	78.87	67.47	55.52	76.09
+TermCount	75.17	72.59	79.26	72.27	**71.06**	**78.93**
+UserID	68.18	48.01	79.11	64.47	**71.90**	**78.56**
+User=Host?†	77.12	75.11	**79.40**	–	–	–

Table 4: **F-score when adding Structural Features**: *Relative/Absolute* means the distance from the first utterance by relative or absolute position, *TermCount* indicates the number of words in an utterance. Features tested for Library Forum Chats only are marked with †. Results exceeding the baseline are bold-faced.

tribution of term frequencies over dialogue acts improved the performance over both datasets. From the results, we believe that term distribution information is a useful "data-independent" feature to use, compared to heuristically hand-crafted keywords.

4.5 Result 4: Interaction among Utterances

Table 6 shows the performance using utterance interactions. As baseline systems, we used *stemmed unigram* and *keywords* for library forum chats, while we used the same *stemmed unigram with POS tags* for NPS causal chats — this choice was made because keyword features improved the performance only over library forum chats. We found that this group of features did not help improve performance, in contrast to the findings of Bangalore et al. (2006) and Kim et al. (2010a). We expect this is due to similar reasons as above — i.e., although we found some degree of interaction among utterances, entanglement caused by having multiple participants meant that interactions between dialogue acts were not directly detected, even when using the CRF. Further, errors in predicted dialogue acts exacerbate the errors. However, we found that when using dialogue acts from the gold-standard data, the results for the CRF improved dramatically. Further, among the five individual features in this group, we saw that *TextUser* improved the performance slightly using CRF, since it resolves entanglement to some degree. From these observations, we conclude that utterance interaction features work well even in multi-party live chats when predicted dialogue acts are less noisy, and entanglement issues are resolved. Thus, we believe that disentanglement would be a necessary step to achieve higher performance on dialogue act classification in multi-party live chats.

5 Error Analysis

From the results above, we observed that the results over both datasets are similar. In particular, while analyzing the errors over library forum chats, we found that the majority of errors are from pairs of dialogue acts such as REQUEST → STATEMENT, STATEMENT → RESPONSE-ACK, REQUEST, RESPONSE-ACK → STATEMENT, and YES-ANSWER → RESPONSE-ACK. We noticed that REQUEST is similar to STATEMENT, except that the structure of the utterance is imperative. This could potentially be resolved by adding utterance-structure information. We also found that some terms often occur in multiple dialogue acts, e.g. *yes* in YES-ANSWER and RESPONSE-ACK. In addition, excessive use of markers such as ? and ! (even found in STATE-

Feature	Library Forum NB	Library Forum SVM	Library Forum CRF	NPS NB	NPS SVM	NPS CRF
Baseline	77.58	76.48	79.26	74.28	68.61	78.39
+Keywords$_{all}$†	**81.61**	**81.77**	**82.77**	51.27	61.35	74.77
+Keywords$_{part}$	–	–	–	**74.79**	65.28	78.00
+InfoDistribution$_{Raw}$	56.96	**80.29**	74.07	49.97	**79.39**	72.33
+InfoDistribution$_{Percent}$	**77.63**	72.73	**79.49**	**75.58**	**71.46**	**78.62**
+InfoDistribution$_{Label}$	75.09	71.47	**79.59**	67.64	51.24	78.32
+InfoDistribution$_{Raw.5}$	55.72	**80.52**	75.25	53.29	**77.52**	75.69
+InfoDistribution$_{Percent.5}$	**77.75**	73.94	**79.47**	**75.98**	**70.74**	**78.59**
+InfoDistribution$_{Label.5}$	75.27	72.21	**79.40**	68.10	59.56	78.38

Table 5: **F-score when adding Keyword Features**: *Raw/Percent* mean raw/relative term counts over the 15 labels, respectively. *Label* means the label which has the highest count. *Keywords$_{all}$* indicates the system using all keyword features described in Forsyth (2007), and *Keywords$_{part}$* is the system using only keywords available at the time of conversation. Results exceeding the baseline are bold-faced.

Data	Feature	Sentence NB	Sentence SVM	Sentence CRF	PredictLabel NB	PredictLabel SVM	PredictLabel CRF	GoldLabel NB	GoldLabel SVM	GoldLabel CRF
Library	Baseline	81.61	81.77	82.77	–	–	–	–	–	–
	Prev1	78.92	81.67	82.03	81.24	80.59	82.58	81.05	80.74	**97.80**
	Prev2	76.67	81.46	77.62	80.06	80.44	82.66	79.91	80.61	**94.98**
	Prev3	74.87	81.12	75.42	78.75	80.61	82.64	78.41	80.63	**90.85**
	User	78.81	81.41	79.17	80.82	80.67	82.37	80.72	80.88	**85.35**
	TextUser	79.74	81.80	81.94	80.02	81.65	**82.79**	79.89	81.65	**82.79**
NPS	Baseline	74.28	68.61	78.39	–	–	–	–	–	–
	Prev1	69.73	67.82	73.15	70.24	53.59	77.79	70.11	50.71	**99.03**
	Prev2	68.48	59.40	47.96	69.55	50.57	77.42	69.51	49.73	**96.64**
	Prev3	67.47	65.98	43.67	69.24	50.35	77.07	69.05	51.06	**92.66**
	User	70.16	59.03	61.99	72.04	55.43	77.52	72.13	60.58	77.58
	TextUser	72.47	51.04	73.13	68.68	60.75	78.10	68.70	59.81	78.18

Table 6: **F-score when adding Dialogue Interaction**: *User* means the label from the previous utterance by the same author, and *TextUser* means the label from immediate utterance by user mentioned in the target utterance. *Label.G* indicates using gold-standard labels. Results exceeding the baseline are bold-faced.

MENT) caused confusion.

Tables 7 and 8 show the the performance of each label produced by *stemmed unigram, keywords, TextUserL* features. We observed that some dialogue acts, such as EXPRESSION, OPENING, THANKING, are relatively easy to detect; others, such as NO-ANSWER, REQUEST, RESPONSE-ACK are hard to predict accurately. We also noticed that the lower recall produced the lower F-score for those dialogue acts which are hard to detect.

Finally, we conducted randomized estimation to calculate whether any performance differences between methods are statistically significant (Yeh, 2000). We found that the keyword features led to statistically significant improvements over the baseline system ($p < 0.05$).

6 Conclusion

We have investigated the task of classifying dialogue acts in multi-party chats, and proposed features to automatically classify dialogue acts based on context, structure, keyword, and interactions among utterances. We found that the system using contextual and keyword features performed the best. Further, we have shown that features from structure and interactions did not perform well, unlike their effectiveness over 1-on-1 live chats in Kim et al. (2010a). Our evaluation suggests that entanglement amongst utterances from different participants caused lower performance using structural and dialogue interaction features. We thus conclude that disentangle-

	Ope.	Clo.	Bac.	Tha.	Exp.	Sta.	Req.	Res.	WhQ	YNQ	Yes	No	Don.	Oth.
Precision	89.19	80.95	89.78	97.66	99.25	81.16	60.28	69.58	83.45	89.69	84.13	33.33	100	0.00
Recall	82.50	62.20	80.48	96.81	97.30	91.79	32.44	66.88	67.44	84.74	60.23	13.33	34.62	0.00
F-score	85.71	70.34	84.87	97.23	98.26	86.15	42.18	68.20	74.60	87.15	70.20	19.05	51.43	0.00

Table 7: Results over individual dialogue acts in the Library Forum Chats: The features used are *stemmed unigram+keyword+TextUserL*.

	Acc.	Bye	Cla.	Con.	Emo.	Emp.	Gre.	nAn.	Oth.	Rej.	Sta.	Sys.	whQ.	yAn.	ynQ.
Precision	33.78	84.73	0.00	12.00	70.47	57.95	91.15	46.15	100.0	30.91	68.51	97.38	77.32	40.38	68.86
Recall	21.46	56.92	0.00	3.57	85.90	26.84	90.68	16.67	14.29	10.69	82.26	96.12	63.98	19.44	55.09
F-score	26.25	68.10	0.00	5.50	77.42	36.69	90.92	24.49	25.00	15.89	74.76	96.75	70.02	26.25	61.21

Table 8: Results over individual dialogue act in NPS Casual Chats: features used are *stemmed unigram+keyword+TextUserL*.

ment of utterances is needed to improve the accuracy of dialogue act classification—we consider this task to be important future work.

References

James Allen and Mark Core. 1997. Draft of damsl: Dialog act markup in several layers. Technical report, University of Rochester, Rochester, USA. The Multiparty Discourse Group.

Srinivas Bangalore, Giuseppe Di Fabbrizio, and Amanda Stent. 2006. Learning the structure of task-driven human-human dialogs. In *Proceedings of the 21st International Conference on Computational Linguistics and 44th Annual Meeting of the Association for Computational Linguistics*, pages 201–208, Sydney, Australia.

William W. Cohen, Vitor R. Carvalho, and Tom M. Mitchell. 2004. Learning to classify email into speech acts. In *Proceedings of the 2004 Conference on Empirical Methods in Natural Language Processing (EMNLP 2004)*, pages 309–316, Barcelona, Spain.

Gao Cong, Long Wang, Chin-Yew Lin, Young-In Song, and Yueheng Sun. 2008. Finding question-answer pairs from online forums. In *Proceedings of 31st International ACM-SIGIR Conference on Research and Development in Information Retrieval (SIGIR08)*, pages 467–474, Singapore.

Micha Elsner and Eugene Charniak. 2008. You talking to me? a corpus and algorithm for conversation disentanglement. In *Proceedings of the 46th Annual Meeting of the ACL: HLT (ACL 2008)*, pages 834–842, Columbus, USA.

Eric N. Forsyth. 2007. Improving automated lexical and discourse analysis of online chat dialog. Master's thesis, Naval Postgraduate School.

Edward Ivanovic. 2008. Automatic instant messaging dialogue using statistical models and dialogue acts. Master's thesis, The University of Melbourne.

Daniel Jurafsky, Elizabeth Shriberg, Barbara Fox, and Traci Curl. 1998. Lexical, prosodic, and syntactic cues for dialog acts. In *Proceedings of ACL/COLING-98 Workshop on Discourse Relations and Discourse Markers*, pages 114–120, Montreal, Canada.

Dan Jurafsky, Rajesh Ranganath, and Dan McFarland. 2009. Extracting social meaning: identifying interactional style in spoken conversation. In *Proceedings of Human Language Technologies: The 2009 Annual Conference of the North American Chapter of the Association for Computational Linguistics (NAACL HLT 2009)*, pages 638–646, Boulder, USA.

Su Nam Kim, Lawrence Cavedon, and Timothy Baldwin. 2010a. Classifying dialogue acts in 1-to-1 live chats. In *Proceedings of the 2010 Conference on Empirical Methods in Natural Language Processing (EMNLP 2010)*, pages 862–871, Boston, USA.

Su Nam Kim, Li Wang, and Timothy Baldwin. 2010b. Tagging and linking web forum posts. In *Proceedings of the Fourteenth Conference on Computational Natural Language Learning*, pages 192–202, Uppsala, Sweden.

Andrew Lampert, Robert Dale, and Cecile Paris. 2008. The nature of requests and ecommitments in email messages. In *Proceedings of the AAAI 2008 Workshop on Enhanced Messaging*, pages 42–47, Chicago, USA.

Andrew Kachites McCallum. 2002. MALLET: A machine learning for language toolkit. `http://mallet.cs.umass.edu`.

Guido Minnen, John Carroll, and Darren Pearce. 2001. Applied morphological processing of English. *Natural Language Engineering*, 7(3):207–223.

Gabriel Murray, Steve Renals, Jean Carletta, and Johanna Moore. 2006. Incorporating speaker and discourse features into speech summarization. In *Proceedings of the Main Conference on Human Language Technology Conference of the North American Chapter of the Association of Computational Linguistics*, pages 367–374, New York, USA.

Ken Samuel, Sandra Carberry, and K. Vijay-Shanker. 1998. Dialogue act tagging with transformation-based learning. In *Proceedings of COLING/ACL 1998*, pages 1150–1156, Montreal, Canada.

Andreas Stolcke, Klaus Ries, Noah Coccaro, Elizabeth Shriberg, Rebecca Bates, Daniel Jurafsky, Paul Taylor, Rachel Martin, Carol Van Ess-Dykema, and Marie Meteer. 2000. Dialogue act modeling for automatic tagging and recognition of conversational speech. *Computational Linguistics*, 26(3):339–373.

Li Wang, Marco Lui, Su Nam Kim, Joakim Nivre, and Timothy Baldwin. 2011. Predicting thread discourse structure over technical web forums. In *Proceedings of the 2011 Conference on Empirical Methods in Natural Language Processing (EMNLP 2011)*, pages 13–25, Edinburgh, UK.

Christopher C. Werry. 1996. Linguistic and interactional features of internet relay chat. In Susan C. Herring, editor, *Computer-Mediated Communication*. John Benjamins, Amsterdam, the Netherlands.

Ian Witten and Eibe Frank. 2005. *Data Mining: Practical Machine Learning Tools and Techniques*. Morgan Kaufmann, San Francisco, USA.

Tianhao Wu, Faisal M. Khan, Todd A. Fisher, Lori A. Shuler, and William M. Pottenger. 2002. Posting act tagging using transformation-based learning. In *Proceedings of the Workshop on Foundations of Data Mining and Discovery, IEEE International Conference on Data Mining*, Maebashi City, Japan.

Alexander Yeh. 2000. More accurate tests for the statistical significance of result differences. In *Proceedings of the 18th International Conference on Computational Linguistics (COLING 2000)*, pages 947–953, Saarbrücken, Germany.

Syntax-semantics mapping of locative arguments

Seungho Nam
Seoul National University
599 Gwanak-ro, Gwanak-gu
Seoul, KOREA
nam@snu.ac.kr

Abstract

This paper proposes a syntax-semantics correspondence of locative expressions: This proposal is based on the syntactic hierarchy among three locative structures (PPs, VPs, and verbal affixes) and the semantic hierarchy among four locative arguments (Goal, Source, Symmetric Path, Stative Location). As for the syntactic hierarchy, the verbal affixes are closer to the head verb than the locative/path verbs are, and the locative/path verbs than the locative PPs. As for the semantic hierarchy, the following four arguments form a hierarchy due to their semantic closeness to the motion event: Goal > S-Path > Source > St-Location. (cf. Nam 1995, 2004) We argue for this correspondence claim by identifying some crucial typological implications holding between the syntactic/semantic hierarchies.

1 Introduction

Natural language uses various constructions to express spatial properties and relations. Languages like English and Russian employ prepositional phrases (PPs) to denote locations or trajectory of movement, but some languages like Kinyarwanda and Swahili use an applicative prefix or a separate locative verb. This paper, based on Nam's (1995) semantic typology of locatives, aims to characterize the formal (syntactic/morphological) structures of locative expressions in natural language, and identifies typological implications among the different types of locatives. Thus, for example, we show that locative PPs are relatively free to scramble (fronting/extraposing) but locative VPs are not; and that if goal arguments can be expressed in a PP in a language L, then source arguments can, too.

Nam (1995) proposes a semantic typology of locative expressions in English, where belong five classes of locatives as follows:

- Goal locatives: *John ran to the office*.
  – denote an ending place of a movement [PPs with *to, into, onto*]
- Source locatives: *John came from the office*.
  – denote a starting place of a movement [PPs with *from*]
- Symmetric Path locatives:[1] *John ran across the street*.
  – denote a symmetric relation between the start point and the end point [PPs with *across, over, through, past, around*]
- Directional locatives: *John ran towards the office*.
  – denote a direction of a movement [PPs with *towards, up, down*]
- Stative Locatives: *John ran on the street*.
  – denote a place where an event take place without location change [PPs with *at, on, in, in front of, above*]

The paper will show that the above semantic typology forms a coherent hierarchy among the different locative types, and further claims that the semantic hierarchy is closely linked to the syntactic hierarchy of the locatives. That is, the closer semantically is a locative to an event of a

[1] Nam (1995) calls them "symmetric" since the relation between source and goal is symmetric with respect to the reference object (landmark), thus symmetric locatives do not specify an inherent direction between the two regions.

motion verb, the closer syntactically is the locative to the motion verb. For example, a goal locative is essential to the semantic content of a VP whereas a source locative is not, so the goal locative is syntactically more united to the head verb than the source locative is.

The paper is organized as follows: Section 2 characterizes three types of formal structures of locative expressions – PPs, verbal affixes, and locative verbs – and identifies their semantic roles – goal, source, symmetric path, and stative locatives. Section 3 shows syntactic asymmetries among the three formal structures and four semantic types. Section 4 proposes the correspondence claim between syntax and semantics of locatives in terms of typological implications mapping the two levels.

2 Formal types of Locative expressions

Locative expressions take a variety of syntactic/morphological structures. Here, we group them into three formal types: (i) adpositional phrases – prepositional/postpositional phrases, (ii) verbal affixes – applicative/promotional affixes, and (iii) locative verbs specialized to denote a path. This section will illustrate representative examples in a few languages for each formal type, and discuss their general syntactic and semantic properties.

2.1 Adpositional Phrases

The following gives a short list of languages which take a prepositional phrase (PreP) or a postpositional phrase (PostP) to express locative arguments.

(1) a. Prepositional Phrases: English, German, Dutch (for source locatives), Russian, Malay, Kinyarwanda, Chichewa, Thai (for source), etc.
b. Postpositional Phrases: Korean, Japanese, Nepali, Kazakh, Turkish, Dutch (for goal), etc.

Some languages like Dutch use both a preposition or a postposition to denote spatial relations, thus goal arguments are realized as a PreP or PostP whereas source arguments take a form of PreP only. (2a, b) below have a source PreP, but the goal arguments in (3a, b) show up as a PreP and a PostP, respectively.

(2) a. zij zijn gelopen van Amsterdam.
they are walked from Amsterdam
'They walked from Amsterdam.'
b. dat dit book [van [onder het bed]] is gekomen.
that this book from under the bed is come
'that this book came from under the bed'

(3) a. Zij is meteen [in het water] gesprongen.
she is immediately in the water jumped
'She jumped into the water immediately.'
b. Zij is meteen [het water in] gesprongen.
she is immediately the water in jumped
'She jumped in the water immediately.'

The sentences in (3) derive a directional motion reading rather than a stative locative, so the PPs do not denote a stative location but a goal location of the events. This goal reading is also confirmed by the telic interpretation of the sentences with the auxiliary BE, i.e., *is* in (3). The PreP in (4a), however, is interpreted as denoting a stative location of a non-directional event, so the sentence refers to an atelic event. Thus the PreP cannot be substituted by a PostP as in (4b).

(4) a. Zij heeft [in het water] (op en neer) gesprongen.
she has in the water (up and down) jumped
'She jumped up and down in the water.'
b. *Zij heeft [het water in] (op en neer) gesprongen.
she has the water in (up and down) jumped
'She jumped in the water.'

The following data in (5) show us that the symmetric path locatives employ a PostP rather than a PreP. This tells us that the symmetric path locatives like 'through under the bridge' behave more like a goal locative than a source locative.[2]

(5) a. dat zij snel [$_{PathP}$ [$_{PlaceP}$ achter het konijn zijn] aan] gelopen.
that they quickly behind the rabbit be at walk
'that they chased the rabbit'
b. Het vliegtuig is [$_{PathP}$ [$_{PlaceP}$ vlak onder de brug] door] gevlogen.
The airplane is right under the bridge through flown
'The airplane flew right under the bridge'

[2] The sentences in (5) contain a complex PostP which consists of a preposition (*achter* 'behind' and *vlak unter* 'right under') and a postposition (*aan* 'at' and *door* 'through'). This is why such PostPs are called a "circumpositional phrase" in the literature.

Notice that the stative locatives are realized as a PreP in (5), so they have the same structure as the source locatives illustrated under (2).

Now let us see more typical locative PPs in other languages. Just like English, Russian and Malay use PrePs for locative expressions. Thus we have Russian in (6) and Malay in (7)

(6) a. ja pobežal k parku. (Russian)
I ran to park-Dat
'I ran to the park.'
b. on bežal ot parka.
He ran from park-Gen
'He was running from the park.'
c. John šël čerez park/uliču.
John went through park/street
'John went through/across the park/street.'

(7) a. Saya telah berlari ke taman itu. (Malay)
I Perf run to park the
'I ran to the park.'
b. Dia telah berlari dari taman itu.
He Perf run from park the
'He ran from the park.'

But, we will see shortly in 2.3 that Malay, unlike Russian, employs a separate locative verb to express symmetric path locatives like 'through/across the park.'

As mentioned in (1) at the beginning, many languages use a PostP to denote a spatial relation. Kazakh and Turkish data below illustrate goal and source locatives in a PostP.

(8) a.Men park-ka jügir-dim. (Kazakh)
I park-to ran
'I ran to the park.'
b. Ol park-ten jügir-di.
He park-from ran
'He ran from the park.'

(9) a.ben park-a kostum. (Turkish)
I park-to ran
'I ran to the park.'
b. o.adam park-tan kostu.
he park-from ran
'He ran from the park.'

Chinese also makes use of locative verbs as well as locative prepositions. Thus a source argument or a stative locative shows up as a PreP, whereas the goal argument accompanies a locative verb. In (10b), the locative verb *dao* 'arrive' is incorporated to the verb *pao* 'run' to get the reading of 'run to.' Such incorporation is not available for the source locatives as shown in (10c). Chinese also uses a PreP for a stative locatives as in (11) below.

(10) a. ta [cong gongyuan] pao le. (Chinese)
he from park run Asp
'He ran from the park.'
b. wo [cong shangdian] pao-dao-le bangongshi.
I from store run-arrive-Asp office
'I ran from the store to the office.'
c.*ta pao-cong-le gongyuan.
he run-from-Asp park
'He ran from the park.'

(11) a.ta zheng zou [zai jie shang].
he Prog walk on street top
'He is walking on the street.'
b. zhege nüren [zai tushuguan li] xuexi le.
this woman in library inside study Asp
'This woman studied in the library.'

2.2 verbal affix

Verbal affixes in many languages denote a goal or a source of a motion event. Let us consider some data from two groups of languages: (i) African languages like Chichewa and Kinyarwanda and (ii) some North American aboriginal languages like Chickasaw and Choctaw. The former uses a few applicative suffixes and the latter a wide variety of applicative prefixes. We have taken the Chichewa sentences in (12) from Baker (1988), and the Kinyarwanda in (13) from Kimenyi (1980). Notice that the preposition *kwa* 'to' in (12a) is incorporated into the verb *tumiz* 'send' as an (goal) applicative suffix *ir* in (12b).

(12) (Chichewa)
a. Ndi-na-tumiz-a chipanda cha mowa kwa mfumu.
1sS-PAST-send-Asp calabash of beer to chief
'I sent a calabash of beer to the chief.'
b. Ndi-na-tumiz-ir-a mfumu chipanda cha mowa.
1sS-PAST-send-Appl-Asp chief calabash of beer
'I sent the chief a calabash of beer.'

Baker (1988) dubbed this phenomenon "preposition incorporation," which extends the valency of the stem verb via an applicative affix (prefix or suffix). We note that the applicative suffixes are mostly used for goal and benefactive arguments, but not for source arguments. In (13b), we can find the applicative suffix *er* is used for the benefactive argument of the verb *som* 'read.'

(13) (Kinyarwanda)
a. Umukoobwa a-ra-som-a igitabo.
girl SP-PRES-read-ASP book
'The girl is reading the book.'
b. Umukoobwa a-ra-som-er-a umuhuungu igitabo.
girl SP-PRES-read-Appl-ASP boy book
'The girl is reading the book for the boy.'

Choctaw and Chickasaw use applicative prefixes for a source argument as well as a goal argument.[3] The following data in (14) and (15) are from Broadwell (2006) and Munro (2000).

(14) (Choctaw)
a. South Carolina miti-li-h
come-1SI-TNS
'I came to South Carolina.'
b. South Carolina aa-miti-li-h
Appl-come-1sI-TNS
'I came from South Carolina.'
c. Holissaapisa' aa-sa-fama-tok
school Appl-lsII-be.whipped-Past
'I was whipped at school.'

(15) (Chicasaw)
a. Nampanaa'-at kow-oshi' a-shiiyalhchi.
string-nom cat-small Appl-be.tied
'The string is tied onto the kitten.'
b. As-o-malli-tok.
lsII-Appl-jump-Past
'He jumped on me'
c. Ihoo-at bala'-a chipot in-chompa.
woman-Nom beans-Acc child DatAppl-buy
'The woman buys beans for the child.'

German also uses such prefixes for goal argument, so the sentence in (16b) has an incorporated prefix *be-* to denote a directional goal argument 'onto the fence.' Such incorporated prefixes are called "promotional prefixes" in the literature. (cf. Kracht 2002)

[3] Chickasaw and Choctaw are Western Muskogean languages of south-central Oklahoma. Munro (2000) claims that Chickasaw has no prepositions/postpositions and no oblique case markers, whereas Broadwell (2006: 248-256) reports that Choctaw has "postpositionlike" words denoting a location such as 'on top of, inside, behind, under, on the other side of, across from, etc.' Broadwell discusses some verbal/nominal properties of the words.

(16) a. Ein Mädchen sprang auf den Zaun.
A girl jumped on the fence
b. Ein Mädchen be-sprang den Zaun.
A girl BE-jumped the fence
'A girl jumped onto the fence.'

2.3 Locative verbs in a serial verb construction

Some languages employ special verbs in order to introduce source, goal, or symmetric path of a motion event. Let us first consider Swahili sentence of (17a), where the infinitival form of the verb *kw-enda* 'to go/come' is used to mark the goal location together with the place name *bustani* 'park.' We note here that the infinitival verb *kw-enda* 'to go/come' allows an extra goal argument for the manner verb *likimbia* 'ran.' Let us call the verb *kw-enda* a "locative (path) verb," since it does not denote a core event of the sentence but it only introduces an extra locative argument – goal in (17) – just like the applicative affixes in Chichewa and Kinyarwanda. (17b) illustrates another locative verb *ku-toka* 'to move from' which introduces a source argument.

(17) a.Joni a-likimbia kw-enda bustani-ni. (Swahili)
John he-ran Inf-go park-Loc
'John ran to the park.'
b. a-li-kimbia ku-toka bustani-ni.[4]
he-Past- run Inf-move.from park-Loc
'He ran from the park.'

Swahili makes extensive use of locative verbs to allow various locative arguments. The sentences in (18) below contain a locative verb *ku-pita* 'to pass' or *ku-zunguka* 'to cross' for a symmetric path argument.

(18) a.Joni a-li-tembea ku-pitia bustani-ni. (Swahili)
John he-Past-walk Inf-pass park-Loc
'John walked through the park.'

[4] Notice that both of the locative verbs in (17) are infinitival and follow the main verb. But we will see in section 3 that a locative verb for source can move to the front of the sentence whereas a locative verb for goal cannot. This contrast suggests that the source locative is less closely united to the main verb than the goal locative is. The following sentence also support this idea, for the same word *toka* '(away) from' is used as a preposition taking a source argument.
(i) a-me-kwenda toka nyumbani.
he-Past-go away.from house
'He went away from the house.'

b. Mvulana a-li-kimbia ku-zunguka mtaa.
boy he-Past-run Inf-cross street
'The boy ran across the street.'

Thai also uses locative verbs *bpai* 'to go' for goal, *phaan* 'to pass' for symmetric path, and *maa* 'to come' for source locatives. However, the source locative verb *maa* 'to come' is optional and should be followed by a preposition *jaag* 'from.' (19a, b, c) below illustrate the uses of locative verbs in Thai.

(19) a. chan wing bpai suansaataarana. (Thai)
I run go park
'I ran to the park.'
b. John deern phaan suansaathaarana.
John walk pass park
'John walked through the park.'
c. khao wing (maa) jaag suansaataarana.
he run come from park
'He ran from the park.'

In 2.1, we saw Malay uses PPs for goal and source locatives, but Malay also uses locative verbs for symmetric path locatives. Thus each of the sentences in (20) contains a locative verb in between *me-* and *-i*: (i) *lalu* 'to pass,' (ii) *lintas* 'to cross,' and (iii) *lampau* 'to pass over.'

(20) a.John telah berjalan me-lalu-i taman itu. (Malay)
John Past walk ME-pass-I park the
'John walked through the park.'
b. Budak.lelaki itu telah berlari me-lintas-i
Boy the Past run ME-cross-I
jalanraya itu.
street the.
'The boy ran across the street.'
c.Seorang budak.perempuan telah melompat
A girl Past jump
me-lampau-i pagar itu.
ME-pass.over-I fence the.
'A girl jumped over the fence.'

Chinese is another language which uses both prepositions and locative verbs, but Chinese locative verbs exhibit wider distribution than Malay ones. Thus, the following data of (21) show that goal arguments are expressed by a locative verb *dao* 'to arrive,' whereas the source argument uses a preposition *cong* 'from.' The symmetric path locatives are also expressed by a locative verb *guo* 'to pass' as shown in (21c).[5]

(21) a.wo pao-dao-le bangongshi. (Chinese)
I run-arrive-Asp office
'I ran to the office.
b. wo [cong shangdian] pao-dao-le bangongshi.
I from store run-arrive-Asp office
'I ran from the store to the office.
c. yuehan zou-guo-le gongyuan.
John walk- through-Asp park
'John walked through the park.'

Choctaw and Chickasaw are also reported to use locative verbs. Broadwell (2006) gives examples like the following in (22). Broadwell claims that the verbal element *hikii-t* is a reduced participial form of the locative verb *hikiiyah* 'to stand' which introduces a source argument. Notice that the goal argument in (22) shows up like a direct object. He also reports that Chickasaw uses locative verbs for symmetric paths listed under (23).

(22) Moore hikii-t Norman ona-li-tok. (Choctaw)
Moore stand-Part Norman arrive-1SI-PT
'I went from Moore ro Norman.'

(23) a.'across' – *abaanabli, lhop'li, lhopolli* 'to go across' (Chicasaw)
b. 'through' – *lhopolli, ootkochcha, ootlhopolli* 'to go through'
c. 'past' – *abaanapa, ímmayya'chi, lhopolli* 'to go/run over, to pass'

Korean is another language which use several locative verbs for symmetric path locatives. Thus we have the list of locative verbs in (24), and (25) illustrate some of their uses. The goal and source of motion events in Korean, however, are expressed by a postpositional phrase.

(24) a. *kenne-, nem-* 'to go over/across' (Korean)
b. *cina-* 'to pass'
c. *tol-* 'to go around'
d. *thongha-* 'to go through'

---

[5] In (21), the locative verbs *dao/guo* are incorporated into the main verb, and this verbal complex is more like Cheng and Huang's (1994) "resultative verb compound" illustrated below, where the resulting state of the subject is expressed by the verb *lei* 'to be tired' incorporated into the main verb *qi* 'to ride.'

(i) zhangsan qi-lei-le.
Zhangsan ride-tired-Asp
'Zhangsan rode himself tired.'

(25) a. Koni-ka ttwie-se kil-ul kenne
Koni-Nom run-Conn road-Acc go.across
ka-ass-ta.
go-Past-Decl
'Koni ran across the street.'
b. Koni-ka kakey-lul cinna kele-ka-ass-ta.
Koni-Nom store-Acc pass walk-go-Past-Decl
'Koni walked past the store.'

3 Syntactic asymmetries among locative arguments

Now we briefly show that the semantic types of locative expressions – goal, source, and symmetric locatives – induce syntactic asymmetries in various phenomena. Nam (2004) argues for this claim with evidence mainly from English and Dutch, and we find the similar asymmetries in a variety of languages.

Nam (2004) claims that goal PPs in English are generated as a VP internal complement as illustrated in (26b) below (under the lower VP2), and that source PPs are generated as an adjunct of a higher VP1 as shown in (27b). Thus his claim predicts that a goal argument is less free in scrambling out of the VP than a source argument is.

(26) a. John swam *to the boat*.
b. [$_{VP1}$ John [$_{V1'}$ swim [$_{VP2}$ [$_{V2'}$ V2 [$_{PP}$ to the boat]]]
(27) a. John swam to the boat *from the beach*.
b. [$_{VP1}$ John [$_{V1'}$ swim [$_{VP2}$ [$_{V2'}$ V2 [$_{PP}$ to the boat]]] [$_{PP}$ from the beach]]

Further, Nam claims that the source argument is interpreted as a modifier of the event denoted by the VP, and the goal argument is interpreted as a result state of the event. Thus, we have the following event structures (Nam 2004):

(28) John swam *to the boat*.

```
            E0:Transition
            /           \
    E1:Process          E2:State
        |                   |
   [john swim]    [john BE-AT the-boat]
```

(29) John swam to the boat *from the beach*.

```
               E0: Transition
               /              \
      E1:Process               E2:State
      /        \                  |
   MOD          E1       [john BE-AT the-boat]
    |           |
[from the beach] [john swim]
```

We will provide with various syntactic phenomena from different languages, which show (i) a goal phrase is more closely united to the lexical verb than a source is, (ii) the source phrase is relatively free to move/scramble, while the goal phrase is much restricted to, and (iii) the goal phrase can be an object of an applicative (PI) verbal complex. The data will include the following:

(30) (i) constraints on movement/scrambling of PPs and locative VPs:
- PPs are relatively free to move/scramble.
- Locative VPs in Chinese and Thai may not scramble.
- Source locatives and Stative locatives (in PPs rather than Verbal) are easy to move.
(ii) thematic hierarchy of (applicative) preposition incorporation
- PI is available for goal locatives, but not for sources or stative locatives.
(iii) prepositional (pseudo-) passives
(iv) degree of markedness of locative relations
- Many languages may delete goal prepositions/markers, but not source or symmetric path markers.

Let us just consider a little fragment of Chinese data, which expose subtle syntactic differences among the semantic types of locatives. First of all, as shown in (31), stative locatives are most free to move, so *zai jie shang* 'on the street' can show up before and after the verb, and freely move to the front of the sentence.

(31) a. ta zheng zou [zai jie shang].
he Prog walk on street top
'He is walking on the street.'
b. ta [zai jie shang] zheng zou.
he on street top Prog walk
c. [zai jie shang], ta zheng zou.
on street top, he Prog walk
'On the street, he is walking.'

The other types are not free in scrambling, so as shown in (32-33), the locative verbs like *dao* 'to arrive' and *guo* 'to pass' are not allowed to move out of the verbal compound, and the source PP with *cong* 'from' is not free but marginal in scrambling.

(32) a. yuehan zou-guo-le gongyuan.
John walk- through-Asp park
'John walked through the park.'
b. *[guo gongyuan] yuehan zou-le.
through park John walk-Asp
'Through the park, John walked.'

(33) a. wo [cong shangdian] pao-dao-le bangongshi.
I from store run-arrive-Asp office
'I ran from the store to the office.'
b. *[cong gongyuan], yuehan pao-le.
from park John run-Asp
'From the park, John ran.'
c. ?wo pao-dao-le bangongshi [cong shangdian].
I run-arrive-Asp office from store
'I ran to the office form the store.'

4 Typological implications and syntax-semantics correspondence

<Table 1> summarizes the discussions in section 2.

<table>
<tr><th>language groups</th><th>formal types
semantic types</th><th>PP</th><th>Locative VP</th><th>Verbal Affix + NP</th></tr>
<tr><td rowspan="4">English, Russian, Spanish, Nepali, (Turkish, Kazakh)</td><td>Goal</td><td rowspan="4">PreP/PostP[6]</td><td rowspan="4">*</td><td rowspan="4">*</td></tr>
<tr><td>Symmetric-Path</td></tr>
<tr><td>Source</td></tr>
<tr><td>Stative-Location</td></tr>
<tr><td rowspan="4">Chichewa, Kinyarwanda, German, Dutch</td><td>Goal</td><td rowspan="4">PreP or PostP</td><td rowspan="4">*</td><td rowspan="2">Promotional Pref/PI[7]</td></tr>
<tr><td>Symmetric-Path</td></tr>
<tr><td>Source</td><td rowspan="2">*</td></tr>
<tr><td>Stative-Location</td></tr>
<tr><td rowspan="4">Korean, Japanese, Malay, (Turkish, Kazakh)</td><td>Goal</td><td>PreP or PostP</td><td>*</td><td rowspan="4">*</td></tr>
<tr><td>Symmetric-Path</td><td>*</td><td>Locative VP</td></tr>
<tr><td>Source</td><td rowspan="2">PreP or PostP</td><td rowspan="2">*</td></tr>
<tr><td>Stative-Location</td></tr>
<tr><td rowspan="4">Chinese, Thai, Swahili</td><td>Goal</td><td rowspan="2">*</td><td rowspan="3">Locative VP[8]</td><td rowspan="4">*</td></tr>
<tr><td>Symmetric-Path</td></tr>
<tr><td>Source</td><td rowspan="2">PreP</td></tr>
<tr><td>Stative-Location</td><td>*</td></tr>
<tr><td rowspan="4">Chicasaw, Choctaw</td><td>Goal</td><td rowspan="4">*</td><td>*</td><td>Applicative Affix</td></tr>
<tr><td>Symmetric-Path</td><td rowspan="2">Locative VP[9]</td><td>*</td></tr>
<tr><td>Source</td><td>Applicative Affix</td></tr>
<tr><td>Stative-Location</td><td>*</td><td>Applicative Affix</td></tr>
</table>

Table 1. Correspondence between semantic and formal types of locative expressions

[6] Dutch postpositions are employed to express Goal and S-Path locatives.

[7] German and Dutch uses promotional prefixes and incorporated Postpositions, respectively.

[8] Chinese locative verbs, unlike Thai and Swahili ones, incorporate into the head verb to form a complex VP. Chinese does not employ a Source locative verb but a preposition *cong* 'from'.

[9] In Choctaw, a Source is indicated with the word *hikiit*, a reduced participle form of a locative verb *hikii yah* 'to stand.' (Broadwell 2006: 247)

We can see that PPs are most widely used for locative expressions, but some languages like Chickasaw and Choctaw do not employ PPs but verbal elements like applicative affixes and locative verbs. Nam (2009) claims that the three formal structures form a syntactic hierarchy in terms of the degree of constituency as follows: Verbal affixes > Locative PPs > PPs. That is, the higher one is more closely united to the main verb than the lower one is. Here we propose that the four types of locatives also form a semantic hierarchy depending on the degree of semantic unity between the locative and the VP. Thus we have the following correspondence between the two hierarchies:

(34) (i) [formal hierarchy]
Verbal Affix > Locative Verb > PP
(ii) [semantic hierarchy]
Goal > S-Path > Source > St-Location

We can identify their close correspondence from Table-1, so we get the following typological implications:

(35) (i) If Goal locatives can be expressed as a PP in L, then Source/Stative locatives can, too. That is, <Goal, PP> → <Source, PP> and <Stative-L, PP>
(ii) <Goal, Locative V> → <Source, Locative V> and <Sym-Path, Locative V>
(iii) <Stative-L, Applicative> → <Source, Applicative> → <Goal, pplicative>

The correspondence of (iii), for instance, states that the goal argument is easier to take an applicative structure than the stative or source argument, and further implies that the applicative affixes are more closely united to the head verb than a locative verb or a PP.

References

Baker, Mark. 1988. *Incorporation: A Theory of Grammatical Function Changing*. Chicago University Press.

Broadwell, George Aaron. 2006. *A Choctaw Reference Grammar*. University of Nebraska Press.

Chao, Yuen R. 1968. *A grammar of Spoken Chinese*. Berkeley, CA: University of California Press.

Cheng, Lisa Lai-Shen, and C-T. James Huang. 1994. On the argument structure of resultative compounds, in Matthew Y. Chen and Ovid J. L. Tzeng, eds., *In honor of William S-Y. Wang: Interdisciplinary studies on language and language change*, 187–221. Taipei: Pyramid Press.

Couper-Kuhlen, E. 1979. *The Prepositional Passive in English*. Tuebingen: Max Niemeyer.

Dowty, David. 1991. "Thematic Proto-roles and Argument Selection," *Language* 67, 547-619.

Fong, Vivienne. 1997. *The Order of Things: What Directional Locatives Denote*, PhD thesis, Stanford University.

Göksel, A. & C. Kerslake (2005) *Turkish: A Comprehensive Grammar*. Routledge. London & New York.

Hale, Kenneth and Samuel J. Keyser. 2002. *Prolegomenon to a Theory of Argument Structure*. Linguistic Inquiry Monograph series #39. Cambridge, MA: MIT Press.

Kimenyi, A. 1980. *A Relational Grammar of Kinyarwanda*. Berkeley: University of California Press.

Kracht, Marcus. 2002. On the Semantics of Locatives, *Linguistics and Philosophy* 25, 157-232.

Munro, Pamela. 2000. The Leaky Grammar of the Chickasaw Applicatives, in Arika Okrent and John P. Boyle, eds., *The Proceedings from the Main Session of the Chicago Linguistic Society's Thirty-sixth Meeting*. Volume 36-1, 285-310. Chicago: Chicago Linguistic Society.

Nam, Seungho. 1995. *Semantics of Locative Prepositional Phrases in English.* Ph.D. thesis, University of California, Los Angeles.

Nam, Seungho. 2004. Goal and Source: Their Syntactic and Semantic Asymmetry, *Proceedings of the 30th Annual Meeting of the Berkeley Linguistics Society*. Berkeley, CA: Berkeley Linguistics Society.

Deep Lexical Acquisition of Type Properties in Low-resource Languages: A Case Study in Wambaya

Jeremy Nicholson,[†‡] **Rachel Nordlinger**[‡] **and Timothy Baldwin**[†‡]
† NICTA Victoria Research Laboratories
‡ The University of Melbourne, VIC 3010, Australia
{nj,racheln,tbaldwin}@unimelb.edu.au

Abstract

We present a case study on applying common methods for the prediction of lexical properties to a low-resource language, namely Wambaya. Leveraging a small corpus leads to a typical high-precision, low-recall system; using the Web as a corpus has no utility for this language, but a machine learning approach seems to utilise the available resources most effectively. This motivates a semi-supervised approach to lexicon extension.

1 Introduction

Deep lexical acquisition (DLA) is the process of (semi-)automatically creating or extending linguistically-rich lexical resources (Baldwin, 2005a; Baldwin, 2005b; Baldwin, 2007). Conventionally, DLA has been applied to high-resourced languages such as English, German or Japanese to broaden the coverage of a medium-coverage resource, or enrich existing linguistic annotation in resources. However, it also has tremendous potential in accelerating the documentation of low-density languages, a fact that is often discussed but very rarely delivered on in the literature. This paper attempts to deliver on this promise, and asks the question: how well do standard approaches to DLA perform over low-density languages? For example, one of the standard approaches to DLA is to extract n-gram counts for patterns involving a target lexeme from the web, and use these as the basis for predicting the lexical class membership of the lexeme. While there is little expectation that we will find significant amounts of text for low-density languages on the web, we nevertheless run the experiment to test the general applicability of this style of approach.

In this work, we take Wambaya as a real-world chronically low-density language, and examine the task of predicting the grammatical gender of nominal lexical items. Wambaya is a nearly extinct language (Gordon, 2005) from the Mirndi group of Australian languages. Like many languages from the Australian family, its complicated syntax and rich morphology makes natural language processing of Wambaya difficult. Unlike many of its neighbours, however, it has been well documented in a descriptive grammar (Nordlinger, 1998) and a Head-driven Phrase Structure Grammar (Bender, 2008). While resources for Wambaya are of little intrinsic value as it is doubtful that new text will be generated in the language, developing these resources is still instructive for parallel development in comparable languages (Warlpiri, for example, has a notable speech community (Gordon, 2005)). Additionally, it provides an invaluable test bed for DLA research, to test the potential of methods over similarly low-density languages, and truly test the bounds of DLA for the purposes of language preservation.

Lexicon extension for Wambaya is a task comparable to the state of many resources: the available lexicon is small, of only about 1500 entries. About half of these are nominals, which is the focus of this research. Furthermore, the sum total of available data in the language on which to base our methods is minimal: fewer than 5000 words across about 1100 sentences. We identify instances of the nominals in the small corpus, and examine standard machine learning approaches based on evidence in terms of lexically-disambiguating surface cues, which are intended as a proxy for features which could easily be designed with minimal assistance from a lexicographer familiar with the language.

While using surface cues to observe lexical properties has seen broad study in a number of languages, Wambaya represents a relatively extreme case in terms of difficulty: since NPs are often discontiguous, a given modifier that carries the grammatical marking of a token can be outside any reasonable context window.

(1) ***Garngunya*** *gin-aji* *yabu*
many.II 3SG.M.A-HAB.PST have
garirda-rdarra *garndawugini-ni.*
wife.II-GROUP one.I-ERG
"One [man] used to have many wives"

In (1), the modifier *garngunya* "many" of the class II noun *garirda* "wife", appears initial to the sentence, and agrees in gender and grammatical number with its displaced head. The behaviour is somewhat similar to referential pronouns in English, but can occur with any modifier. Having this discontiguity makes identifying surface cues problematic; in addition, the rich morphology means that even identifying token instances of a given type is non-trivial, as a lemma typically has hundreds of inflected forms.

Our approach is to take a standard inventory of DLA techniques and apply them naively to Wambaya, to gauge their effectiveness over a truly low-density language, with the added complexity of non-configurationality and complex morphology.

We will demonstrate that a number of strategies that have been shown to be competitive in some languages (primarily English) unsurprisingly perform poorly for Wambaya. Machine learning, on the other hand, is remarkably effective, with minimal feature engineering.

2 Background

2.1 Wambaya

Wambaya is a critically endangered Australian language (Nordlinger, 1998), spoken by only a handful of people in the Northern Territory, Australia. The language is radically non-configurational, with very free word order apart from a verb clitic cluster in second position. It is a split ergative language, with nominative–accusative pronouns and ergative–absolutive nominals otherwise. There are about nine nominal cases,[1] as well as four adnominal cases that further inflect for grammatical gender; there are furthermore three grammatical numbers: a singular, a dual, and a plural. In this work, we examine the four grammatical genders: semantically, class I and class II loosely correspond to masculine and feminine animates, class III to non-flesh food items and some round body parts, and class IV to the semantic residue. Gender morphology in Wambaya is mostly regular, but this is less true in other Australian languages, often because of vowel harmony, so we focus primarily on morphosyntax.

Nordlinger's grammar has been implented in a Head-driven Phrase Structure Grammar (HPSG; Bender (2008)) as part of an analysis of the LinGO Grammar Matrix (Bender et al., 2002; Bender and Flickinger, 2005; Drellishak and Bender, 2005; Bender et al., 2010). We use the lexical items from the HPSG lexicon to construct a set of nominal types marked for gender. There are 786 class assignments for 724 distinct nominals; their distribution is shown in Table 1.

I	II	III	IV
233	199	51	303

Table 1: Distribution of classes for Wambaya nominals.

Most of the multi-class items are animates (humans and animals) that belong to both class I and class II (masculine and feminine). These pairs have the same stem, but different forms in the absolutive, which is the unmarked case from which the lemma is derived. For example, *alag-* "child" can be realised as the class I absolutive nominal *alaji* "boy" or the class II absolutive nominal *alanga* "girl."

For each item in the lexicon, we use Bender's implementation of the grammar to generate the (absolutive) lemma from the stem, as well as all of the inflected forms that are licensed by the grammar. Nominals were observed to have between about 400 and about 2200 distinct inflected forms. We construct surface cues based on demonstratives in the language: Nordlinger indentifies four singular absolutive proximal demonstratives (one for each gender class), and 62 demonstratives overall (24 for each of class I and II, and 7 for III and IV), for proximal and

[1]There is some disagreement as to the exact number.

distal demonstratives in nominal classes. 28 of these do not occur in the corpus (described below). The demonstratives we examined appeared to usually act as deictic determiners qualifying a nominal, but they also occured as pronouns; we chose not to examine comitative and possessive demonstratives, or indefinites or interrogatives, which appeared to function more often as pronouns.

Along with the grammar is a treebank of sentences and phrases that occur in Nordlinger's descriptive grammar, combining the inline linguistic examples and eight provided transcribed texts. These amount to 1131 unique sentences (many of the sentences from the text were also used as linguistic examples): about a third of these were from the texts. We used these sentences — without the syntactico-semantic annotation from the treebank — as a raw corpus of Wambaya.

2.2 Lexical properties

The analysis of lexical information is often done on individual tokens, often under the banner of "lexical disambiguation". Some examples are context-sensitive spelling correction (Banko and Brill, 2001), selecting between target candidates for machine translation (Grefenstette, 1998), and determining the semantic gender of nouns in context (Bergsma et al., 2009). All of these were based on English data. Lapata and Keller (2005) examine a range of English tasks whereby frequencies of events can be used as evidence for the disambiguation. They assert that using Web page counts as a *de facto* corpus is a model that is generally as good as, or better than, established results in the field.

Lapata and Keller also examine a type-level task: that of the countability of English nouns (Baldwin and Bond, 2003). In this type of task, the token context is not available, and context must instead be generated to observe evidence. They construct a set of surface cues — *much* and *many* to disambiguate mass and count nouns respectively — and extract evidence from these. The performance is good, but not as high as that which Baldwin and Bond observe by using more sophisticated tools such as chunkers. A similar experiment was performed by Nicholson and Baldwin (2009), for a set of about 50 count classifiers in Malay; again, the Web was observed to be a strong performer for observing useful evidence.

As for grammatical gender, research has tended to focus on Indo-European languages. Hajič and Hladká (1997) examine grammatical gender in Czech as part of the part-of-speech tagging process. In Czech, morphological surface cues on a noun token give a strong indication of gender; more so in a stream of tokens where modifier inflection can also be taken into account. This method would probably also be effective for Wambaya, due to its mostly regular gender morphology. Morphological surface cues were also motivated for lexical semantics of derivational morphology by Light (1996). Finally, Cucerzan and Yarowsky (2003) explore a minimally-supervised approach for the prediction of grammatical gender of a mixture of tokens and types by extracting contextual cues from a seed set of nouns and bootstrapping to morphological cues. Token-level performance is high for the five languages they examine.

3 Methodology

Based on standard DLA methodology, we examine three prediction methods for Wambaya nominals:

- co-occurrence frequencies with demonstratives from a Wambaya corpus;
- co-occurrence frequencies with demonstratives from Web page counts estimated using the Yahoo! API[2]; and
- machine learning using context windows around token instances identified from the corpus.

As stated in Section 1, the selection of methods at this level is not intended to reflect any keen insights into Wambaya so much as a standard inventory of DLA methods, which we apply to the task.

Note that these features attempt to leverage token–level observations into type–level information; if we were examining token predictions in a tagging framework, then the feature engineering approaches for POS tagging as performed by Hajič and Hladká (1997) or morphological analysis in Chrupała et al. (2008) could provide further sophistication.

[2] http://developer.yahoo.com/search/

3.1 Corpus Frequency

Corpus frequency-based methods involve identifying lexical cues in the given language, and using observation of the relative frequency of each cue to classify instances. The frequencies are based on a monolingual corpus of the language, in our case, the small set of 1131 unique sentences of Wambaya.

We use cues observed from the Wambaya corpus as evidence for the gender of a lexical item. This is based on the intuition that a given nominal will only co-occur with demonstratives that agree in gender.

(2) ***Ngangaba*** ***yana*** *gi-n*
fire.IV.ABS this.IV.SG.ABS 3SG.S.PR-PROG
najbi.
burn
"There's a fire burning [here]."

We consider instances like (2) as evidence that the nominal *ngangaba* is of class IV, because *yana* is a class IV demonstrative.

Wambaya has a rich inflectional morphology, so that a given token instance of a nominal within a corpus can display one of hundreds of surface forms. The surface cues also display rich inflectional paradigms. When collating our corpus counts for a given lexical item, we attempt three different strategies of dealing with this phenomenon.

The first, ABS, assumes we have access to the absolutive form of the lexeme. This is the least-marked form, and also the lemma. For inflectional agreement, the corresponding surface cue must also be in the absolutive form; here we use the singular proximal absolutive demonstrative for each of the four gender classes. A sentence where both the absolutive nominal and an absolutive demonstrative occur is considered to be a positive count for the corresponding gender class. Although an NP can be discontiguous, sentences where the demonstrative is in direct apposition to the nominal can provide stronger evidence — as such, we also consider a cue strategy for instances in direct apposition (either pre-modifying, post-modifying, or either). A short example is shown for the absolutive nominal *alaji* across Examples (3)–(6) in Table 2.

Alternatively, with access to a morphological analyser, we could generate all of the possible inflected surface forms for a given nominal (INFL). On average, this is about 700 different forms. Here, we do not attempt to enforce morphological agreement: if any form of the nominal co-occurs with any cue, we consider that to be positive evidence. There are 62 fully-inflected demonstratives given by Nordlinger, and the aggregated count for a class is the sum of all of the sentences where one of the corresponding surface cues occurred. We again contrast direct apposition with sentence co-occurence. Table 3 shows the counts for *alaji* in the given examples.

If no morphological analysis tools are available, we could simply search for the stem (STEM); since morphology in Wambaya is primarily suffixing, we allow any number of other characters to optionally follow the stem. In this case, we consider both of the above cue strategies: the four absolutive nominals, where the stem is a proxy for the absolutive form, or all sixty-two, where the stem is a proxy for the entire set of inflected forms. This method fails for the given examples below, because none of the inflected forms of *alaji* begin with the stem *alag-*. About 30% of the stems in the lexicon are homologous with the corresponding absolutive form; many are proper prefixes thereof.

Classification proceeds by choosing the most frequent aggregated count; in most cases, this is the only non-zero count. Because of the small corpus and the sparsity of the cue set, we also explored a classification routine where any non-zero count is treated as a positive classification: predictably, a small boost in recall is traded off with a small drop in precision. Across the Wambaya corpus, these differences are not statistically significant at the 0.05 level, and are not reported in detail.

3.2 Web-as-Corpus Frequency

The methodology for using the Web as a corpus is very similar to the corpus frequency approach, except that page count estimates returned by a search engine are used in place of actual observed instances. The assumption that these values are strongly correlated was found to be accurate by Keller and Lapata (2003) for a range of classification tasks.

At first glance, using the Web to estimate corpus counts for a language close to extinction is patently absurd, as there is no speech community generat-

(3)

Gulug-ardi	*ng-u*	***ini***	***alaji*.**
sleep-CAUS(NF)	1SG.A-FUT	this.I.SG.ABS	boy.I.ABS

"I'm going to put this boy to bed."

(4)

Garnguji	*nyi-n*	*yabu*	***alaji*.**
many.I.ABS	2SG.A.PR-PROG	have	boy.I.ABS

"You have a lot of kids."

(5)

Alangi-nka	*yana*	*jalyu.*
boy.I-DAT	this.IV.SG.ABS	bed.IV.ABS

"This is the boy's bed."

(6)

Jawaranya	*ng-u*	*yidanyi*	*ngaba*	*ng-u*	*yardi*	*yaniya*	*cool*	*drink*
billycan.II.ABS	1SG.A-FUT	get	then	1SG.A-FUT	put	that.IV.SG.ABS	cool	drink.IV

ninaka	*nanga*	***alangi-nka*.**
this.I.SG.DAT	3SG.M.OBL	boy.I-DAT

"I'm going to get the billycan and put that cool drink [in it] for the boy."

ABS	I (*ini*)	II (*nana*)	III (*mama*)	IV (*yana*)
Pre	1	0	0	0
Post	0	0	0	0
Pre/Post	1	0	0	0
No apposition	1	0	0	0

Table 2: Counts for examples (3)–(6) for the ABS paradigm of the class I nominal *alaji*

INFL	I	II	III	IV
Pre	1	0	0	0
Post	0	0	0	1
Pre/Post	1	0	0	1
No apposition	2	0	0	2

Table 3: Counts for examples (3)–(6) for the INFL paradigm of the class I nominal *alaji*

$t-4$	$t-3$	$t-2$	$t-1$	$t+1$	$t+2$	$t+3$	$t+4$
cool	*gulugardi*	*ngu*	*ini*	*yana*	*jalyu*		
	garnguji	*nyin*	*yabu*				
	drink	*ninaka*	*nanga*				

Table 4: Machine learning features based on the fully-inflected (INFL) forms of *alaji*, from examples (3)–(6)

$p1$	$p2$	$p3$	$p4$	$s1$	$s2$	$s3$	$s4$
a	*al*	*ala*	*alaj*	*i*	*ji*	*aji*	*laji*

Table 5: Machine learning features based on the prefixes and suffixes of the absolutive form of *alaji*

ing Web documents in that language. However, it may be the case that we actually observe documents which are linguistic descriptions of the target language, and not simply noise[3]. The ODIN project (Lewis and Xia, 2009) is an attempt to leverage such linguistic data into resources automatically. An additional reason for performing the experiment is that it is a standard DLA method which is used for higher-density languages, but there is no indication in the literature of how well to expect it to perform over low-density languages.

In our case, we experiment with the Yahoo! search engine API. Since the API rate-limits queries, we chose to only examine the ABS nominal set with the four proximal absolutive demonstratives, and the STEM set with the four demonstratives. We continued to contrast the surface cues in apposition, which were constructed as phrasal queries, with non-phrasal versions, i.e. that the demonstrative simply occurred in the same document as the nominal.

The frequencies that we observed from the Web were again sparse, but much less so than the corpus frequencies. Part of this was because of homology with wordforms in other languages; for example, the class I absolutive demonstrative is *ini*. Thresholding classification at zero frequency — that is, having a positive classification for any non-zero observation — becomes somewhat absurd over Web-scale data, particulary for the non-phrasal queries. Performance in these cases approaches that of the baseline classifier where every nominal is assigned to every class; the utility of this baseline is low.

3.3 Machine Learning

The third standard approach to DLA is machine learning, where a corpus provides not just frequency estimates of lexical patterns as for the corpus frequency approach, but the source of a potentially rich variety of features.

In applying the machine learning method to Wambaya, we relax the requirement for observing demonstratives. This is useful if a representative cue set is unknown or cannot be constructed. Instead, for each nominal in the data set, we identify corpus instances, and build feature vectors according to the tokens observed within a context window. We used a window size of up to four tokens, labelled for their distance from the target nominal; very little performance difference was observed when using different window sizes, possibly due to the fact that the average sentence length in the corpus was quite short. The feature values for all of the inflections of *alaji* for the given examples are shown in Table 4.

We then split the instances into training and test sets using 10-fold cross-validation. Our preferred machine learning model was the maximum entropy classifier.[4]; we do not expect substantial differences to result from using other types of machine learning models over this feature set. We also thresholded the classification so that if all classes were equally likely, no decision was made; otherwise, the class assigned with the greatest probability was chosen.

For contrast, we also built a model whose features were substrings of the nominal itself, rather than using contextual features. We considered prefixes of length 1 to 4 and suffixes of length 1 to 4, again varying this parameter was not observed to greatly affect performance. The feature vectors for the absolutive nominal *alaji* are shown in Table 5. This type of classification takes into account the regular morphological processes of Wambaya, and is consequently very effective, but would be less effective for many other Australian languages.

4 Results

For each methodology, we present the precision and recall, as well as the F-score. In fact, because of the low recall of most systems, the F-score is strongly correlated with recall, even though precision becomes the most interesting metric.

For the majority class baseline, that is, classifying every lexical item as class IV, the precision is 0.419 and the recall 0.385, for an F-score of 0.401. Most of the systems are well below this figure, due to low recall.

4.1 Corpus Frequency

The results of the corpus frequency assignment methods are shown in Tables 6 through 9, for Pre-modification frequencies, Post-modification fre-

[3]For example, of the top ten documents returned by Google for the query *ngabulu* "milk, breast", three are about Wambaya and another four are about Australian languages with a cognate.

[4]We used the OpenNLP implementation available at `http://www.sourceforge.net/projects/maxent/`.

quencies, the combination of those two, and frequencies where the demonstrative and nominal simply co-occur in a sentence.

The first notable fact is that recall is uniformly awful, where even the most generous system only classifies 49 instances correctly. On the other hand, precision is high, markedly higher than the baseline in almost all cases. Because there are so few instances being classified, it is difficult to draw significant comparisons between different systems; it seems though that there are fewer instances where the demonstrative post-modifies the noun, and that the methods that require apposition maintain higher precision and lower recall than the one that relaxes the requirement of contiguous NPs.

Context	Precision	Recall	$F_{\beta=1}$
Pre	0.944	0.022	0.043
Post	1.000	0.008	0.016
Pre/Post	0.950	0.024	0.047
No apposition	0.821	0.030	0.058

Table 6: Performance of corpus frequency assignment according to the four absolutive demonstratives over the set of absolutive nominals (ABS)

Context	Precision	Recall	$F_{\beta=1}$
Pre	0.824	0.018	0.035
Post	0.692	0.011	0.022
Pre/Post	0.783	0.023	0.045
No apposition	0.617	0.037	0.070

Table 7: Performance of corpus frequency assignment according to the four absolutive demonstratives over the set of nominal stems (STEM)

Context	Precision	Recall	$F_{\beta=1}$
Pre	0.794	0.034	0.065
Post	0.800	0.010	0.020
Pre/Post	0.784	0.037	0.071
No apposition	0.694	0.055	0.102

Table 8: Performance of corpus frequency assignment according to the full demonstrative set over the fully inflected nominal set (INFL)

4.2 Web-as-corpus Frequency

The results of the Web frequency assignment methods are shown in Tables 10 and 11, for the same ob-

Context	Precision	Recall	$F_{\beta=1}$
Pre	0.718	0.036	0.069
Post	0.545	0.015	0.029
Pre/Post	0.673	0.042	0.079
No apposition	0.620	0.062	0.113

Table 9: Performance of corpus frequency assignment according to the full demonstrative set over the set of nominal stems (STEM)

servation methods as the corpus frequency approach, except that non-phrasal queries are now at the document level instead of the sentence level.

Recall is generally not substantially higher than the corresponding approaches from the 1131 corpus sentences in Tables 6 and 7. As the precision is so much lower, significantly lower than the baseline in most cases, it appears that any classifications that this model makes correctly are completely accidental. If there is any useful evidence, it is swamped by extra-lingual or extra-linguistic material across the greater Web.

Context	Precision	Recall	$F_{\beta=1}$
Pre	0.304	0.031	0.056
Post	0.309	0.032	0.058
Pre/Post	0.315	0.037	0.066
Non-phrasal	0.238	0.086	0.121

Table 10: Performance of Web frequency assignment according to the four absolutive demonstratives over the set of absolutive nominals (ABS)

Context	Precision	Recall	$F_{\beta=1}$
Pre	0.216	0.031	0.054
Post	0.236	0.033	0.058
Pre/Post	0.244	0.041	0.070
Non-phrasal	0.177	0.074	0.104

Table 11: Performance of Web frequency assignment according to the four absolutive demonstratives over the set of nominal stems (STEM)

4.3 Machine Learning

The results of machine learning using the maximum entropy classifier are shown for the three nominal sets in Table 12. The performance differences between the three sets were primarily caused by the number of corpus instances (and consequently feature windows) that could be observed for nominals in each set: for ABS, only 16.5% of the nominals were observed at least once in the corpus, compared to 26.7% and 31.7% for INFL and STEM respectively.

Feature set	Precision	Recall	$F_{\beta=1}$
ABS	0.511	0.087	0.149
INFL	0.634	0.214	0.320
STEM	0.713	0.281	0.403
MORPH	0.914	0.903	0.908

Table 12: Performance of the maximum entropy classifier over the various nominal sets

The precision of the model for all three datasets was markedly higher than that of the baseline. The low performance over the ABS dataset was primarily caused by sparsity of features: even though each instance was accurate, there were at best one or two windows with which to make a classification.

On the other hand, the fact that we saw higher performance across the STEM data set than the INFL dataset was surprising, particularly for precision ($\chi^2 = 3.87, p < 0.05$), somewhat less so for recall ($\chi^2 = 7.46, p < 0.01$). Examining the features, it was clear that there were erroneous corpus instances identified for the stem set, including verbs and other nouns that happened to share the first few characters. This makes its significantly higher performance all the more puzzling.

One observation from the feature sets was that some of the stems were wrong, or at least infelicitous in their interaction with the morphological generation component of the grammar to produce licensed wordforms in Wambaya. This would be artificially lowering the recall of the INFL set slightly, and possibly reducing the amount of discriminatory data for the model. This could also be affecting the STEM set, but it seems that many of the stems were proper prefixes of the lemma anyway.

The likely cause of the difference in precision between the STEM and INFL sets was that the machine learning model was picking up on spurious regularity in the corpus. Most of the sentences in the corpus were derived from inline linguistic citations, where it is often valuable to have a pair of sentences with minimal changes to highlight a particular property or construction. (For example, *Ngajbi gina ganggu yarruwarda* "He saw grandfather walking" and *Ngajbi gina gangguliji yarruwarda* "He saw his grandfather walking" to illustrate use of the reflexive-possessive suffix *-liji*.) If there was a morphological bias in the stems where corpus instances were observed for STEM and the inflected forms were not observed, that morphological bias could make classification easier because morphology is an accurate predictor of gender in Wambaya. To examine this, we attempted to construct the model using only the transcribed free text and not the linguistic inline citations, but this removed two-thirds of the data — consequently, the model struggled to classify any instances. One other possibility would be to train the model using features based on the linguistic citations and test on the features from the free texts.

Finally, we show results of using the pseudo-morphological features (prefixes and suffixes of the nominal of length 1 to 4) under MORPH in Table 12. When features were constructed from the lemma, both precision and recall were close to gold-standard, because gender is morphologically marked on the absolutive suffix. In some respects, this is a circular problem, because the gender must be known to correctly generate the absolutive form from the stem. If the morphological features are constructed from the stem instead of the lemma, accuracy drops to 68.6%. This approach is effective for Wambaya, but would be less so for many neighbouring languages.

5 Discussion

We presented several modes of classification for grammatical gender of nominals in Wambaya. Most of these had prohibitively low recall, showing that it is generally difficult to make such classifications, partly due to the complexity of the language, and partly due to the paucity of data available to provide evidence for one gender over another.

In general, it appears that for the few instances where evidence can be evinced from the small number of sentences in the corpus, that evidence leads to a correct classification. Presumably, if one had access to more Wambaya text, one could make more correct classifications. This follows our intuition, and that of corpus-based computational linguistics over the past few decades.

However, the Web will not be the provider of that data. This may be because of the almost non-existent nature of the Wambaya speech community, but despite its gigantic size the value of the Web as a source of raw text for minority languages still remains to be demonstrated. Any Wambaya text that was returned by the search engine was swamped by other data, to the point where a Web frequency-based system was utterly hopeless — in contrast to other observations of such a system.

On the other hand, machine learning provided a promising approach in terms of having a high precision system that can actually make a non-trivial number of classifications, even from a small amount of data. The learner appears to be making best use of the data, without rigid constraints on co-occurrence with surface cues; this is possibly grounded in the distributional hypothesis. It is also possible that the model is overfitting to the regular structure of the linguistics-focussed corpus — this hypothesis is difficult to test, and, as little new text will be written for Wambaya, may remain unverified.

For the rich morphology in Wambaya, we contrasted identifying instances or cues based upon a simple set (the lemma, ABS, and the four proximal demonstratives), with a richly inflected set (INFL, and the full 62 demonstratives), and a resource-poor approach to morphology (STEM, where only the primarily-suffixing assumption is made). While performance between the systems was similar, it seems that having the full approach to morphology does indeed provide improvement in precision, at the cost of substantial development time. Simpler approaches, where assumptions about properties of the language can be quickly made and verified (using WALS Online[5] (Haspelmath et al., 2008), for example), seem like a reasonable trade-off.

All in all, the low-recall and moderate-to-high-precision results motivate a semi-automatic approach to lexicon extension: the model posits classifications, and the lexicographer examines these from high-confidence downward. As new entries are confirmed or corrected, the model can be re-run to suggest further classifications. This seems like a productive interaction for rapid lexicon extension.

While Wambaya probably presents the most extreme case of difficulty for the languages that have so far been analysed in deep lexical acquisition or lexical disambiguation, it also has its own idiosyncracies that make classification based on morphosyntax and contextual cues somewhat uninteresting. The very regular morphology may also be introducing biases in spite of its richness. As such, further analysis is required on other Australian languages — insofar as resources are available.

[5]http://wals.info

6 Conclusion

We have analysed a number of approaches to the prediction of grammatical gender of nominals in Wambaya, using Wambaya as a test case for a critically low-density language requiring documentation. While co-occurrence frequencies of gender-marking demonstratives give high precision in corpus frequency-based methods, recall is prohibitively low. Using the Web as a corpus does not allay this problem, as the Wambaya text available on the Web did not lead to useful frequency observations of the surface cues. Machine learning did appear to provide a more robust classification model, with some caveats for the nature of the data set; learning of morphological cues proved very effective, as these are distinctive in Wambaya. We envision these results as evidence for a semi-supervised approach to lexicon extension.

Acknowledgements

NICTA is funded by the Australian Government as represented by the Department of Broadband, Communications and the Digital Economy and the Australian Research Council through the ICT Centre of Excellence program.

References

Timothy Baldwin and Francis Bond. 2003. Learning the countability of English nouns from corpus data. In *Proc. of the 41st Annual Meeting of the ACL*, pages 463–470, Sapporo, Japan.

Timothy Baldwin. 2005a. Bootstrapping deep lexical resources: Resources for courses. In *Proc. of the ACL-SIGLEX 2005 Workshop on Deep Lexical Acquisition*, pages 67–76, Ann Arbor, USA.

Timothy Baldwin. 2005b. General-purpose lexical acquisition: Procedures, questions and results. In *Proc. of the 6th Meeting of the Pacific Association for Computational Linguistics (PACLING 2005)*, pages 23–32, Tokyo, Japan. (Invited Paper).

Timothy Baldwin. 2007. Scalable deep linguistic processing: Mind the lexical gap. In *Proc. of the 21st Pacific Asia Conference on Language, Information and Computation*, pages 3–12, Seoul, Korea.

Michele Banko and Eric Brill. 2001. Scaling to very very large corpora for natural language disambiguation. In *Proc. of the 39th Annual Meeting of the ACL and 10th Conference of the EACL (ACL-EACL 2001)*, pages 26–33, Toulouse, France.

Emily M. Bender and Dan Flickinger. 2005. Rapid prototyping of scalable grammars: Towards modularity in extensions to a language-independent core. In *Proc. of the Second International Joint Conference on Natural Language Processing*, pages 203–208, Jeju Island, Korea.

Emily M. Bender, Dan Flickinger, and Stephan Oepen. 2002. The grammar matrix: An open-source starter-kit for the rapid development of cross-linguistically consistent broad-coverage precision grammars. In *Proc. of the COLING 2002 Workshop on Grammar Engineering and Evaluation*, pages 8–14, Taipei, Taiwan.

Emily M. Bender, Scott Drellishak, Antske Fokkens, Laurie Poulson, and Safiyyah Saleem. 2010. Grammar customization. *Research on Language & Computation*, 8(1):23–72. 10.1007/s11168-010-9070-1.

Emily M. Bender. 2008. Evaluating a crosslinguistic grammar resource: A case study of Wambaya. In *Proc. of the 46th Annual Meeting of the Association for Computational Linguistics: Human Language Technologies*, pages 977–985, Columbus, USA.

Shane Bergsma, Dekang Lin, and Randy Goebel. 2009. Glen, Glenda or Glendale: Unsupervised and semi-supervised learning of English noun gender. In *Proc. of the Thirteenth Conference on Computational Natural Language Learning*, pages 120–128, Boulder, USA.

Grzegorz Chrupała, Georgiana Dina, and Josef can Genabith. 2008. Learning morphology with Morfette. In *Proc. of the 6th International Conference on Language Resources and Evaluation*, Marrakech, Morocco.

Silviu Cucerzan and David Yarowsky. 2003. Minimally supervised induction of grammatical gender. In *Proc. of the 3rd International Conference on Human Language Technology Research and 4th Annual Meeting of the NAACL (HLT-NAACL 2003)*, pages 40–47, Edmonton, Canada.

Scott Drellishak and Emily M. Bender. 2005. A coordination module for a crosslinguistic grammar resource. In *Proc. of the 12th International Conference on Head-Driven Phrase Structure Grammar*, pages 108–128, Stanford, USA.

Raymund G. Gordon, Jr, editor. 2005. *Ethnologue: Languages of the World, Fifteenth Edition*. SIL International.

Gregory Grefenstette. 1998. The World Wide Web as a resource for example-based machine translation tasks. In *Proc. of the ASLIB Conference on Translation and the Computer*, London, UK.

Jan Hajič and Barbora Hladká. 1997. Probabilistic and rule-based tagger of an inflective language - a comparison. In *Proc. of the Fifth Conference on Applied Natural Language Processing*, pages 111–118, Washington, USA.

Martin Haspelmath, Matthew S. Dryer, David Gil, and Bernard Comrie, editors. 2008. The world atlas of linguistic structures online.

Frank Keller and Mirella Lapata. 2003. Using the Web to obtain frequencies for unseen bigrams. *Computational Linguistics*, 29:459–484.

Mirella Lapata and Frank Keller. 2005. Web-based models for natural language processing. *ACM Transactions on Speech and Language Processing*, 2:1–30.

William Lewis and Fei Xia. 2009. Parsing, projecting & prototypes: Repurposing linguistic data on the web. In *Proc. of the 12th Conference of the European Chapter of the ACL*, pages 41–44, Athens, Greece.

Marc Light. 1996. Morphological cues for lexical semantics. In *Proc. of the 34th Annual Meeting of the Association for Computational Linguistics*, pages 25–31, Santa Cruz, USA.

Jeremy Nicholson and Timothy Baldwin. 2009. Web and corpus methods for Malay count classifier prediction. In *Proc. of Human Language Technologies: The 2009 Annual Conference of the North American Chapter of the Association for Computational Linguistics*, pages 69–72, Boulder, USA.

Rachel Nordlinger. 1998. *A Grammar of Wambaya, Northern Territory (Australia)*. Pacific Linguistics, Canberra, Australia.

Chinese Sentiments on the Clouds:

A Preliminary Experiment on Corpus Processing and Exploration on Cloud Service

Shu-Kai Hsieh, Yu-Yun Chang, Meng-Xian Shih
Graduate Institute of Linguistics, National Taiwan University
No. 1, Sec. 4, Roosevelt Road, Taipei, 10617 Taiwan
shukaihsieh@ntu.edu.tw, {june06029;simon.xian}@gmail.com

Abstract

This study aims to propose a novel pipeline architecture in building and analyzing large-scaled linguistic data on the cloud-based environment, an experimental survey on Chinese Polarity Lexicon will be taken as an example. In this experiment, data are evaluated and tagged by applying crowd sourcing approach using online Google Form. All the data processing and analyzing procedures are completed on-the-fly with free cloud services automatically and dynamically.The paper shows the advantages of using cloud-based environment in collecting and processing linguistic data which can be easily scaled up and efficiently computed. In addition, the proposed pipeline architecture also brings out the potentials of merging with mashups from the web for representing and exploring corpus data of various types.

1 Introduction

With the emergence of huge amount of web data available in recent years, corpus linguistics as well as other related empirical fields such as the collecting and processing of language resources, and their evaluation are facing with the greatest challenges ever. The spread of corpus and lexical resources in linguistics has been led to a great level of theoretical survey and enhanced the empirical foundation, not only with respect to sampling and annotation, but also with exploratory data analysis. However, more recently there have been long discussions about what the current state of art in corpus linguistics fails to do, which can be pinpointed at least in two respects: (1) the lack of socio-cultural (meta-) information reflected in the data, is incompetent for pragmatic usages and discourse analysis; (2) rather skewed with data in the public domain, heterogeneity of (individualized) language usages and development is not able to be traced.

With the advanced technological progress in data availability with storage and computing ability, the issues mentioned can be tackled to a great extent. We take it as the turning point for *corpus-based* linguistics to transform into a data-intensive and *cloud-based* linguistics. In light of that, we want to explore the transformation viability in this paper. As a first step, we present a novel pipeline architecture to build Chinese Polarity Lexicon on the cloud environment by taking the data from the web as resource. Polarity lexicon contains sentiment-bearing words and phrases, encoded with polarities to each word or phrase, usually either assigned as positive or negative. The study of polarity lexicon has attracted much attention in recent years for classifiers to train on the lexical dataset, and is becoming important for applications such as Sentiment Analysis and Opinion Mining.

For the purpose of constructing automatic identifying and classifying polarity lexicon systems, a lot of (semi-) unsupervised machine learning methods for recognizing polarities of words and phrases have been proposed. In terms of language resources, these approaches either consider the information provided from the synonyms or glosses of a thesaurus or WordNet (Hu and Liu, 2004; Kamps et al., 2004; Kim and Hovy, 2004; Esuli and Sebastiani, 2005), or based on the co-occurrence relationship messages derived from the corpus (Hatzivassiloglou and McKeown, 1997; Turney, 2002; Kanayama and Nasukawa, 2006) to assign and determine the word polarity.

Notwithstanding their significant success in achieving accuracy rate, in this paper, we will argue that current approaches to the problem might face with the *methodological* drawbacks due to the lack of **scalability** on the one hand, and indifference to the **individual sentimental varieties** on the other hand. First, referring to the lack of scalability, it is rather difficult to handle out-of-vocabulary (OOV) issue on the lexical and corpus resources, in particular, those OOV words and phrases (or called as neologisms) often carried with popular usage meanings generated from the social network, and given with explicit polarities; and secondly, regarding the individual sentimental varieties, which may correspond to the linguistic varieties, subjectivities and sentiments, are largely *ad-hoc*, that is with whom s/he chats and temporal, geographical, and communication situations, etc. will have influence on her/his sentiment. Those heterogeneous properties are not properly embodied in lexical and corpus resources.

2 Cloud-based vs Corpus-based Linguistics

To track the essentially emergent, ever-changing, and large-scaled lexicalized sentimental social web data, we argue that corpus statisticians and linguists will need to tap into the opportunities that cloud computing environment offers. In this paper, rather than corpus-based, we propose a novel *crowd-aided cloud-based* methodology for constructing Language Resource and its Evaluation (LRE), with an experiment on Chinese Polarity Lexicon as example. The advantages of connecting LRE with cloud computing environment are multi-fold:

1. [**Easy and multi-sourced online data collection, management, integration and collaboration**] Linguistic and sentimental data can be gathered online easily using Web as Corpus (WaC), and further powered by the increasing evaluating possibilities through crowdsourcing and the enlarging of cloud storage space for reserving large-scaled data.

2. [**Seamless data preprocessing and exploratory data analysis**] The collected WaC data in the cloud storage, can be processed seamlessly online (without downloading the data) for the preliminary data preprocessing (e.g., Chinese segmentation and POS tagging), and may further apply to early data introspection with online preprocessing statistical analysis and data visualization. These techniques could be accomplished by using various application programming language interfaces (e.g., APIs for R and Python). By hosting a web interface could even facilitates the scattered tasks that used to be.

3. [**Mashup for data and models**] Once the data is collected and processed, the owner can adapt the data and mashup with others (textual, pictures or videos) to make the resource even more creative and full of varieties, which is in line with emerging trend of 'web of data' ('linked data web') proposed by Tim Berners-Lee (Tim, 2009) recently. In addition, the data can be taken as seeds and fed up the prediction models processing on the clouds, which is so-called (dynamically) stream learning .

We believe the proposed architecture above will unlock the potentials and values of linguistic data instantiated by the web. In the following, we focus on the preliminary survey of Chinese Polarity Lexicon as an example adapting the *cloud-based* methodology.

3 Review of Polarity Lexicons

This session explores different paradigms for how to build and evaluate polarity lexicons.

Words had been discovered with three main factors, which were evaluative factor, potency factor and activity factor, as described by Osgood et al. (1957). Within the three factors, what many researchers generally mentioned is the evaluative factor. The evaluative factor, also known as **polarity** or **semantic orientation** called by Hatzivassiloglou and McKeown (1997), which can present the intensity and the positive or negative of a word. Some researchers have found that most antonyms can be assigned with relevant polarities (e.g. *happy* can be assigned as positive; and its antonym *sad* as negative).

Learning the polarity of words can be helpful for an amount of applications, in addition, the synonyms in the data could be further refined as well. Hatzivassiloglou and McKeown (1997) had taken the polarity of words into a system, and tried to investigate antonyms from the collected corpus and also to disambiguate the synonyms automatically. Also, Turney and Littman (2003) mentioned that an automated system containing polarity information, could be applied to text classification, analysis of survey response, filtering, tracking online opinions, and even generating chatbots.

There are a lot of ways for collecting and detecting word polarity from the text or corpora. For collecting data, Turney and Littman (2003), and Rao and Ravichandran (2009) had taken the General Inquirer lexicon (Stone et al., 1966) as their reference data, which the word polarity list was already constructed by manually tagged and evaluated via a group of people. In addition, other papers used different methods for collecting data, such as taking the 1987 Wall Street Journal with tagged data as corpus (Hatzivassiloglou and McKeown, 1997; Wiebe, 2000), WordNet (Rao and Ravichandran, 2009; Wiebe, 2000) and via crowd sourcing (Mohammad, 2011).

As for detecting polarity, Hatzivassiloglou and McKeown (1997) introduced using conjunctions of adjectives to train the model and then labeled an orientation to each adjective through clustering. Also, Rao and Ravichandran (2009) tried using three graph-based semi-supervised learning methods to detect the word polarity, which were Mincuts, Randomized Mincuts, and Label Propagation.

Most previous papers chose to use the existed large databases for their experimental usages, and followed with different training approaches to extract or detect word polarities. Since our goal in this paper does not focus on the machine learning performance in this experimental task, we would rather demonstrate the data collection *on the fly*, so we use a naive PMI method enriched with emoticon information to dynamically and semi-automatically detect Chinese word polarity based on Plurk API (Chen et al., 2010), [1] by which all the training and testing tasks are constructed and pipelined to Google Form.

4 Pipelining Cloud and Crowd Computing in Lexicon Resource Development

This session explains the proposed framework, generally speaking, the data retrieved from Plurk API and preprocessed (segmented and POS-tagged) by other Chinese NLP APIs, is sent to the collaborative platform of Google called Google Form for evaluation, once evaluated they are sent to Google Fusion Table for data exploration and visualization, and stored in Google Cloud Storage with Google BigQuery. For leaning purpose, the corpus is also sent to Google Prediction model with stream machine learning method. Detailed procedures are explained in the following.

4.1 General framework

Once the data are collected, many of the typical preprocessing tasks can be done in a pipeline, like the tools adapted from openNLP [2]. In this paper, we propose to pipeline the processing tasks in the cloud and crowd computing environment schematized as follows, taking the extracted Plurk data as example:

We used third-party APIs (e.g. Plurk API) to get the training data from the Mood classifier (Chen et al., 2010), and evaluated two types of resulting data given the testing data: automatically tagged by Mood classifier (Chen et al., 2010) against the crowd tagged data collected from Google Form[3] (Crowd sourcing). Only the data that have the same evaluated results from the two types are considered and sent to Google Fusion Table [4] for visualizing introspection, and once the coming data scaled up, it was sent to the backend of Google Cloud Storage[5] with

[1] Plurk, like Twitter, is the most popular social microblogging system in Taiwan, we focused on it because of the advantages of tracking attitudes by mining prevalent language usages, the thus constructed Plurk Corpus can be browsed at `lope.linguistics.ntu.edu.tw/plurk/`

[2] `opennlp.sourceforge.net`

[3] `http://www.google.com/google-d-s/forms/`

[4] `http://www.google.com/fusiontables/public/tour/index.html`

[5] `https://developers.google.com/storage/`

Figure 1: Proposed pipeline framework

Google BigQuery[6]. Then finally, it was sent forward to prediction model with stream machine learning.

4.2 Formulate seed-sets from emotion-tagged Plurk Corpus

We have collected a total of 13534 Chinese posts extracted from Plurk corpus. The data have been segmented and POS-tagged by importing yahoo! Chinese Segmentator and Tagger [7], for which the yahoo! segmentation system is powerful for its lexicon extension on new emerged words from the social web (e.g. trendy words and code-mixing words). From the previous research (Chen et al., 2010), a Mood classifier had built up by training the target text with the keywords generated from Anctconc using log-likelyhood feature selection method (Kilgarriff, 2001; Anthony, 2004). Also, a manually classified result was used to evaluate the accuracy of Mood classifier. In this paper, in order to construct the word polarity prediction model more specifically, the Plurk posts are collected and fed on only if the posts have identical resulting results from Mood classifier and manual evaluation.

After the chosen posts are selected and segmented, a list of 100 seed words (all seed words are content words, including nouns, adjectives and verbs) are chosen based on the following three criteria: the balance in corpus frequency distribution, opinion relevance, and wordnet POS representatives. The first criterion is used to create a corpus frequency word list, and the 100 seed words are extracted in balance according to the corpus frequency distribution. Then the last two criteria are applied to confirm whether each seed word has opinion expressions in meaning and an relevant description from wordnet. The above seed word selecting elements are integrated to ensure the seed words have apparent meaning descriptions before adapting to the prediction model.

An online survey is created by using Google Form, which we ask the participants to evaluate the 100 seed words with a finer granularity of 5 star rating (scaling from 1 (Extremely Positive) to 5 (Extremely Negative)). Instead of taking a readily prepared corpus as previous studies (which the word polarity corpora are manually tagged by a specific group of people), for example as using the General Inquirer corpus, we let the participants to decide the polarities of each seed word, and then assign different weights to each seed word based on the overall survey statistical results. Therefore, a list of seed words with polarities is created, which only the seed words given with positive weights are tagged with positive polarity, and reversely, assigned with negative polarity.

So far, we already have 100 people complete this evaluation survey. The advantages of using Google Form to construct this word polarity evaluation survey, are that the scale of the investigation can be easily expanded and its statistical results can be renewed automatically and rapidly online, whenever there are more participants join this task. Figure 2

[6]https://developers.google.com/bigquery/
[7]http://tw.developer.yahoo.com/cas/

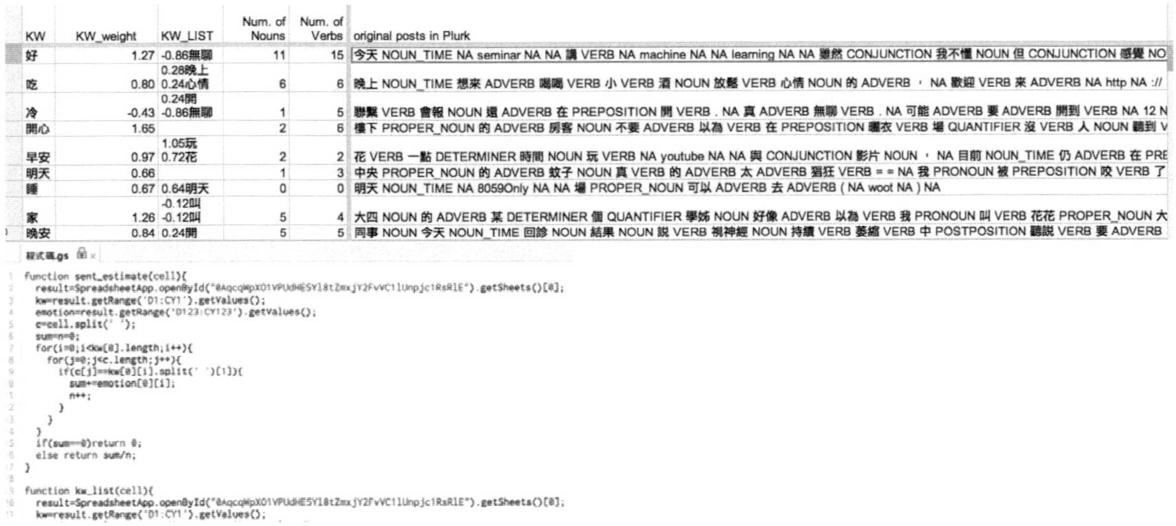

Figure 2: Score form with functions written online

shows a snapshot of this scored form.

4.3 Preprocessing and Exploratory Data Analysis

In order to compute the model training more efficiently, we use Google API to write our own functions and apply them to the data in Google Form. This is a convenient way for training and analyzing the data online without needing to run the whole programs on our own devices. To be even better, once the data is renewed, the programs will run the functions automatically in an instant and no need to execute the programs manually. Through this small experiment of this paper, we hope to provide a practical method for linguists to deal with data in a more skilled and dynamic way.

With the data imported into Google Fusion Table, it is convienient to use a variety of Visualize plots as shown in Figure 3. The Visualize function contains table, map, line, bar, pie and other plotting tools to help quickly analyze the data. In addition, it allows us to add some specific conditions while plotting. By applying the line chart, we can quickly find out which city has the greatest Plurk population. Visualize function has also implanted the Geocode (geography codes) which takes the location data to tag places on a map or colored up the related regions. Also, once clicking on the tagged places or colored regions, the related meta information will be presented. For investigating data distribution (for example gender, location, and age), the pie chart can be used which provides results calculated in percentages. On the other hand, for more detailed distribution analysis, bar chart is shown to be better presenting the statistic results between two variables, such as location and age.

4.4 Prediction Model

The prior polarity lexicons thus constructed are used as training data for cloud-based prediction model in extracting more polar words and determining the overall sentiment of Plurk texts. As the first attempt, we are using the Google-hosted prediction model as a black-box for primer experiment,[8] and a Predictive Model Markup Language (PMML)-based[9] *adaptive* prediction model is envisioned which combines Chinese wordnet-based sense/sentiment propagation approach (by assuming that sentiment and lexical relatedness are linked) with bootstrapped individualized parameters.

4.5 Limitations

With its versatility in processing and exploring corpus data, the limitations we encountered with this framework so far lie in two aspects: First, due to the free service provided by Google, the experiment is largely dependent on the services provided by the

[8] http://lope.linguistics.ntu.edu.tw/wordpola/iosubscribe.html

[9] http://dmg.org/pmml-v4-0-1.html

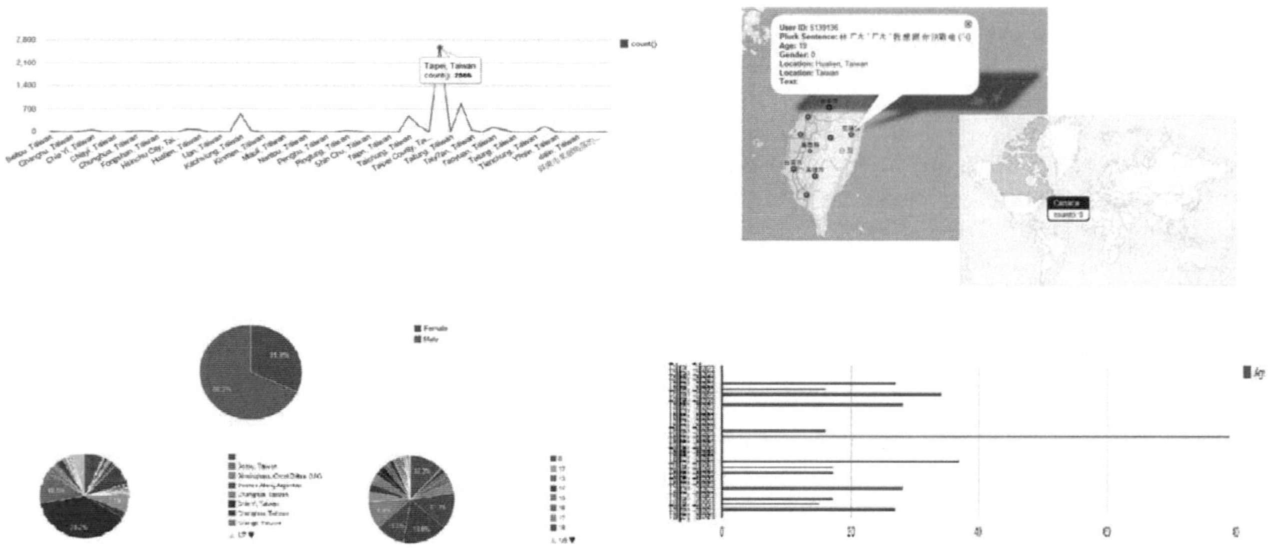

Figure 3: Corpus data exploratory analysis using Fusion Table APIs

commercial company, which could be a weak point in terms of stability in the future; and (2) what is also at stake here is indeed the embedded use of other tools and APIs can be a problem due to their compatibility with Google services. However, with the downside mentioned, we believe that much more can be improved with respect to the likelihood of future convergence for the open collaboration between academic and commercial fields.

5 Conclusion

In conclusion, we showed a novel architecture of language resource construction and evaluation on the cloud computing environment, and illustrated it with the experiment on Chinese Polarity Lexicon. We believe that this approach will open up many possibilities to be explored. This mixed scenario of folksonomy and cloud computing allow us to not only detect how different groups of people recognize prior polarities and their weights from the contextual clues, but also understand further which parameters should be modeled as patterns for polarity detection. The compiled lexicon can be served as a dynamic input for the cloud-based streaming prediction model(s) for the maximum performance.

In future work, we will apply the proposed architecture to augment the newly released Chinese Wordnet[10] by polarity classification of synsets instead of lemma, since the current way is not able to capture the fact that a word with various senses could have different polarities. In addition, although these methods can be applied on Chinese words, word sentiment is in fact a function of the composite characters and the way as how people process an ideogram while encountering a new word. In the future, we will consider running an experiment on Character Sentiment in parallel.

References

L. Anthony. 2004. AntConc: A Learner and Classroom Friendly, Multi-Platform Corpus Analysis Toolkit. In *Proceedings of IWLeL 2004: An Interactive Workshop on Language e-Learning*, pages 7–13.

M.-Y. Chen, H.-N. Lin, C.-A. Shih, Y.-C. Hsu, P.-Y. Hsu, and S.-K. Hsieh. 2010. Classifying Mood in Plurks. In *The 22th Conference on Computational Linguistics and Speech Processing*. Chi-Nan University, Taiwan.

A. Esuli and F. Sebastiani. 2005. Determining the semantic orientation of terms through gloss analysis. In *Proceedings of the 14th ACM International Conference on Information and Knowledge Management (CIKM05)*, pages 617–624. Bermen, DE.

[10] `http://lope.linguistics.ntu.edu.tw/cwn`

V. Hatzivassiloglou and K. R. McKeown. 1997. Predicting the semantic orientation of adjectives. In *Proceedings of the European Chapter of the Association for Computational Linguistics (EACL)*, pages 174–181.

M. Hu and B. Liu. 2004. Mining and summarizing customer reviews. In *Proceedings of the International Conference on Knowledge Discovery and Data Mining (KDD)*, pages 168–177. ACM.

J. Kamps, M. Marx, R. J. Mokken, and M. de Rijke. 2004. Using WordNet to measure semantic orientation of adjectives. In *Proceedings of LREC-04, 4th International Conference on Language Resources and Evaluation*, volume IV, pages 1115–1118. Lisbon, Portugal.

H. Kanayama and T. Nasukawa. 2006. Fully automatic lexicon expansion for domain-oriented sentiment analysis. In *Proceedings of the Conference on Empirical Methods in Natural Language Processing (EMNLP)*, pages 355–363.

A. Kilgarriff. 2001. Comparing corpora. *International Journal of Corpus Linguistics*, 6(1):97–133.

S.-M. Kim and E. Hovy. 2004. Determining the sentiment of opinions. In *Proceedings of the International Conference on Computational Linguistics (COLING)*. Geneva.

S. Mohammad. 2011. From once upon a time to happily ever after: Tracking emotions in novels and fairytales. In *Proceedings of the 5th ACL-HLT Workshop on Language Technology for Cultural Heritage, Social Sciences, and Humanities*, pages 105–114. Association for Computational Linguistics.

C. E. Osgood, G. J. Suci, and P. H. Tannenbaum. 1957. *The measurement of meaning*. Urbana, USA: University of Illinois Press.

D. Rao and D. Ravichandran. 2009. Semi-Supervised Polarity Lexicon Induction. In *The 12th Conference of the European Chapter of the Association for Computational Linguistics (EACL-09)*.

P. J. Stone, D. C. Dunphy, M. S. Smith, and D. M. Ogilvie. 1966. *The General Inquirer: A Computer Approach to Content Analysis*. MIT Press.

B.-L. Tim. 2009. Linked data. In *TED 2009 conference*. "The Great Unveiling" in Long Beach, CA, USA.

P. D. Turney and M. L. Littman. 2003. Measuring praise and criticism: inference of semantic orientation from association. *ACM Transactions on Information Systems*, 21:315–346.

P. Turney. 2002. Thumbs up or thumbs down? sentiment orientation applied to unsupervised classication of reviews. In *Proceedings of the Annual Conference of the Association for Computational Linguistics (ACL)*.

J. Wiebe. 2000. Learning subjective adjectives from corpora. In *Proceedings of the 17th National Conference on Artificial Intelligence (AAAI-2000)*.

Cross-Lingual Topic Alignment in Time Series Japanese / Chinese News

Shuo Hu Yusuke Takahashi Liyi Zheng Takehito Utsuro
Graduate School of Systems and Information Engineering, University of Tsukuba,
Tsukuba, 305-8573, JAPAN

Masaharu Yoshioka
Graduate School of Information Science and Technology,
Hokkaido University,
Sapporo, 060-0808, Japan

Noriko Kando
National Institute of Informatics,
Tokyo 101-8430, Japan

Tomohiro Fukuhara
National Institute of Advanced Industrial Science and Technology
Tsukuba, 305-8568 Japan

Hiroshi Nakagawa
Information Technology Center,
University of Tokyo, Tokyo 113-0033, Japan

Yoji Kiyota
NEXT Co., Ltd.,
Tokyo, 108-0075, Japan

Abstract

Among various types of recent information explosion, that in news stream is also a kind of serious problems. This paper studies issues regarding topic modeling of information flow in multilingual news streams. If someone wants to find differences in the topics of Japanese news and Chinese news, it is usually necessary for him/her to carefully watch every article in Japanese and Chinese news streams at every moment. In such a situation, topic models such as LDA (Latent Dirichlet Allocation) and DTM (dynamic topic model) are quite effective in estimating distribution of topics over a document collection such as articles in a news stream. Especially, as a topic model, this paper employs DTM, but not LDA, since it can consider correspondence between topics of consecutive dates. Based on the results of estimating distribution of topics in Japanese / Chinese news streams, this paper proposes how to analyze cross-lingual alignment of topics in time series Japanese / Chinese news streams.

1 Introduction

Among various types of recent information explosion, that in news stream is also a kind of serious problems. This paper studies issues regarding topic modeling of information flow in multilingual news streams. If someone wants to find differences in the topics of Japanese news and Chinese news, it is usually necessary for him/her to carefully watch every article in Japanese and Chinese news streams at every moment.

In such a situation, topic models such as LDA (Latent Dirichlet Allocation) (Blei et al., 2003) and DTM (dynamic topic model) (Blei and Lafferty, 2006) are quite effective in estimating distribution of topics over a document collection such as articles in a news stream. Especially, as a topic model, this paper employs DTM, but not LDA, since it can consider correspondence between topics of consecutive dates. In DTM, we suppose that the data is divided by time slice, for example by date. DTM models the documents (such as articles of news stream) of each slice with a K-component topic model, where the k-th topic at slice t smoothly evolves from the k-th topic at slice $t-1$.

Based on the results of estimating distribution of topics in Japanese / Chinese news streams, this paper proposes how to analyze cross-lingual alignment of topics in time series Japanese / Chinese news streams. The overall flow of the proposed framework is illustrated in Figure 1. In order to bridge the gaps between the two languages, namely, Japanese and Chinese, we use Japanese and Chinese term translation pairs extracted from Wikipedia utilizing interlanguage links. With those translation knowledge, we first cross-lingually align Japanese and Chinese news articles. Then, after collecting those cross-lingually aligned news article pairs, we then apply DTM to those collected news articles and estimate time series monolingual topic models for both Japanese and Chinese. Finally, those monolingual

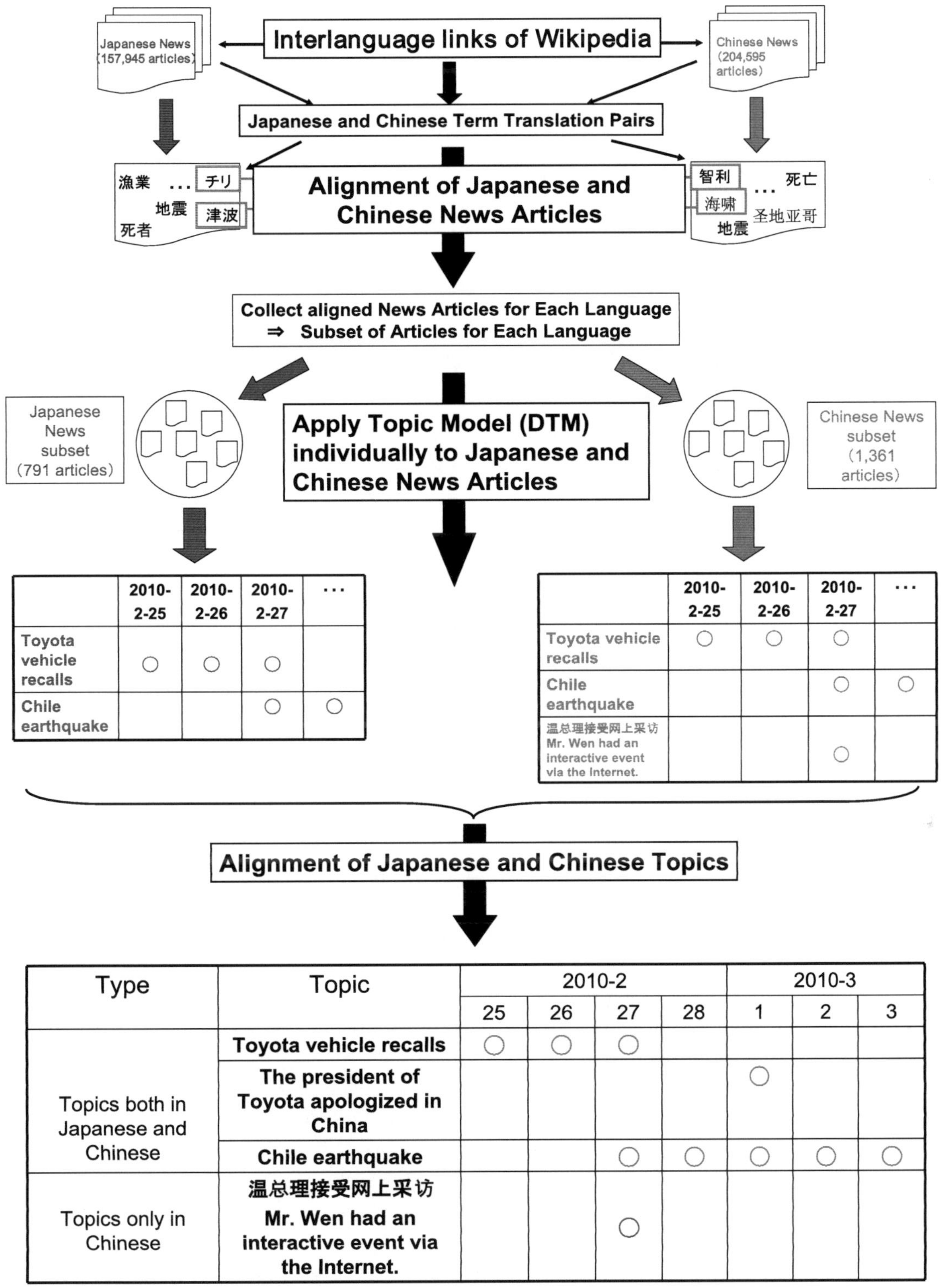

Figure 1: Overall Flow of Topic Alignment in Time Series Japanese / Chinese News

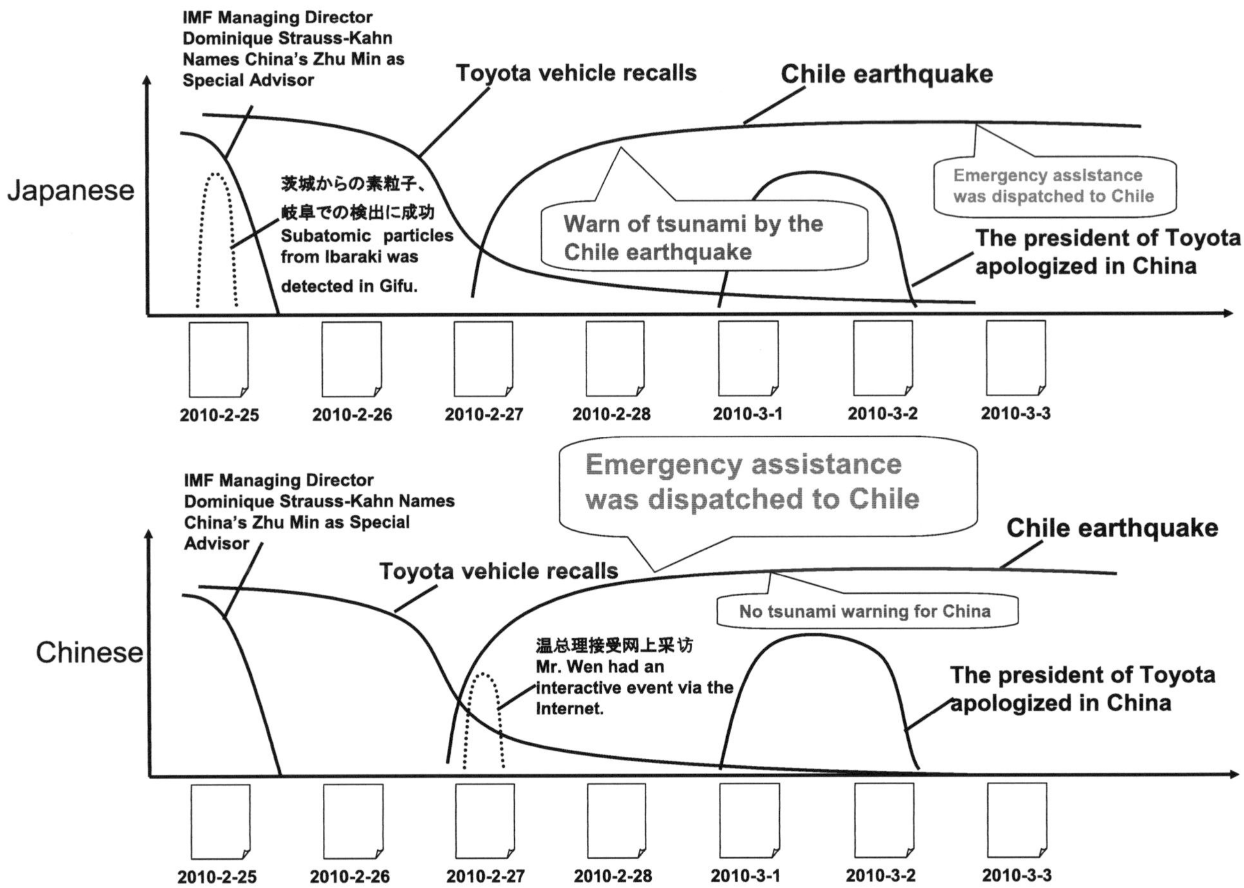

Figure 2: Topic Estimation in Time Series Japanese / Chinese News

topics are cross-lingually aligned considering cross-lingual alignment of Japanese and Chinese news articles.

Figure 2 shows an example of estimating time series topics monolingually for both Japanese and Chinese. The proposed method of cross-lingual topic alignment is successfully applied to those Japanese and Chinese time series news articles, where several topics such as "Toyota vehicle recalls" and "Chile earthquake" are cross-lingually aligned between Japanese and Chinese. Once we have such a cross-lingual topic alignment, it becomes quite easier for us to find certain differences in concerns. For example, in the case of the topic "Chile earthquake", in Japan, "warn of tsunami" is apparently one of the major concerns, while in Chinese, "emergency assistance was dispatched to Chile" is one of the major concerns.

2 Topic Model

As a time series topic model, this paper employs DTM (dynamic topic model) (Blei and Lafferty, 2006). Unlike LDA (Latent Dirichlet Allocation) (Blei et al., 2003), in DTM, we suppose that the data is divided by time slice, for example by date. DTM models the documents (such as articles of news stream) of each slice with a K-component topic model, where the k-th topic at slice t smoothly evolves from the k-th topic at slice $t-1$.

In this paper, in order to model time series news stream in terms of a time series topic model, we consider date as the time slice t. Given the number of topics K as well as time series sequence of batches each of which consists of documents represented by a sequence of words w, on each date t (i.e., time slice t), DTM estimated the distribution $p(w \mid z_n)$ ($w \in V$) of a word w given a topic z_n ($n = 1, \ldots, K$) as well as that $p(z_n \mid d)$ ($n = 1, \ldots, K$) of a topic

z_n given a document d, where V is the set of words appearing in the whole document set. In this paper, we estimate the distributions $p(w \mid z_n)$ $(w \in V)$ and $p(z_n \mid d)$ $(n = 1, \ldots, K)$ by a Blei's toolkit[1], where for the number of topics $K = 10$, as well as $\alpha = 0.01$.

3 Extracting Japanese-Chinese Term Translation utilizing Interlanguage Links in Wikipedia

In this paper, we use Japanese and Chinese term translation pairs extracted from Wikipedia utilizing interlanguage links. More specifically, since we collect Chinese news articles distributed within mainland China which are written in simplified Chinese characters, we extract translation pairs of Japanese terms and simplified Chinese character terms. Figure 3 describes the rough idea of how to extract translation pairs of Japanese terms and simplified Chinese character terms from interlanguage links of Wikipedia.

Let a Japanese Wikipedia entry e_J to be denoted as $e_J = \langle J_0, \{J_r^1, \ldots, J_r^l\}\rangle$, where J_0 is the title of the entry e_J, and $J_r^1, \ldots, J_r^l$ are redirects of the entry e_J. Let e_C be a Chinese Wikipedia entry for which at least one of a interlanguage link from e_J to e_C or that from e_C to e_J exists. In the Chinese version of Wikipedia, entries including entry titles are usually written in traditional Chinese characters and equivalent terms in simplified Chinese characters are listed as redirects of terms in traditional Chinese characters. Thus, e_C is denoted as $e_C = \langle T_0, \{S_r^1, \ldots, S_r^k, T_r^{k+1}, \ldots, T_r^h\}\rangle$, where T_0 is the title string of the entry e_C in traditional Chinese characters, $S_r^1, \ldots, S_r^k$ are redirects of the entry e_C in simplified Chinese characters, and $T_r^{k+1}, \ldots, T_r^h$ are redirects of the entry e_C in traditional Chinese characters.

Since it is not easy for us to automatically distinguish character codes for simplified Chinese and traditional Chinese, we utilize news articles of the collection of one year that are written in simplified Chinese characters, and employ the following procedure to extract translation pairs of Japanese terms and simplified Chinese character terms. First, suppose that we detect one of those redirects of the entry e_C in simplified Chinese characters, namely S_r^i, in a Chinese news article written in simplified Chinese characters. Then, following the interlanguage link between the entries e_C and e_J, we collect the term translation pairs below between Japanese and simplified Chinese characters into the set $JS(\langle e_J, e_C, S_r^i\rangle)$ of term translation pairs including S_r^i:

$$JS(\langle e_J, e_C, S_r^i\rangle) = \{\langle J_0, S_r^i\rangle, \langle J_r^1, S_r^i\rangle, \ldots, \langle J_r^l, S_r^i\rangle\}$$

Then, we collect the term translation pairs in the whole sets $JS(\langle e_J, e_C, S\rangle)$ into JS_W:

$$JS_W = \bigcup_{\langle e_J, e_C, S\rangle} JS(\langle e_J, e_C, S\rangle)$$

In the evaluation of this paper, we first collect Japanese and Chinese news stream text articles during the period from June 1st, 2009 to May 31st, 2010. In total, 157,945 Japanese news articles are collected from three newspaper companies Yomiuri[2], Nikkei[3], and Asahi[4], while 204,595 Chinese news articles are collected from People's Daily[5]. Then, from the collected news articles, 93,258 Japanese Wikipedia entry titles are collected, out of which 28,071 have interlanguage links to Chinese, while 94,164 Chinese terms in simplified Chinese characters are collected, out of which 28,127 have interlanguage links to Japanese. Finally, from them, 78,519 term translation pairs are collected between Japanese and simplified Chinese characters[6].

4 Cross-lingual Topic Alignment

This section proposes the whole framework of cross-lingual topic alignment, where its major steps are illustrated in the overall flow in Figure 1.

[1]`http://www.cs.princeton.edu/~blei/topicmodeling.html`

[2]`http://www.yomiuri.co.jp/`

[3]`http://www.nikkei.com/`

[4]`http://www.asahi.com/`

[5]`http://www.people.com.cn/`

[6]In addition to those term translation pairs extracted from Wikipedia, it is also helpful to incorporate an existing Japanese-Chinese bilingual lexicon as well as a certain machine translation service between Japanese and Chinese. Those issues are to be examined as a future work.

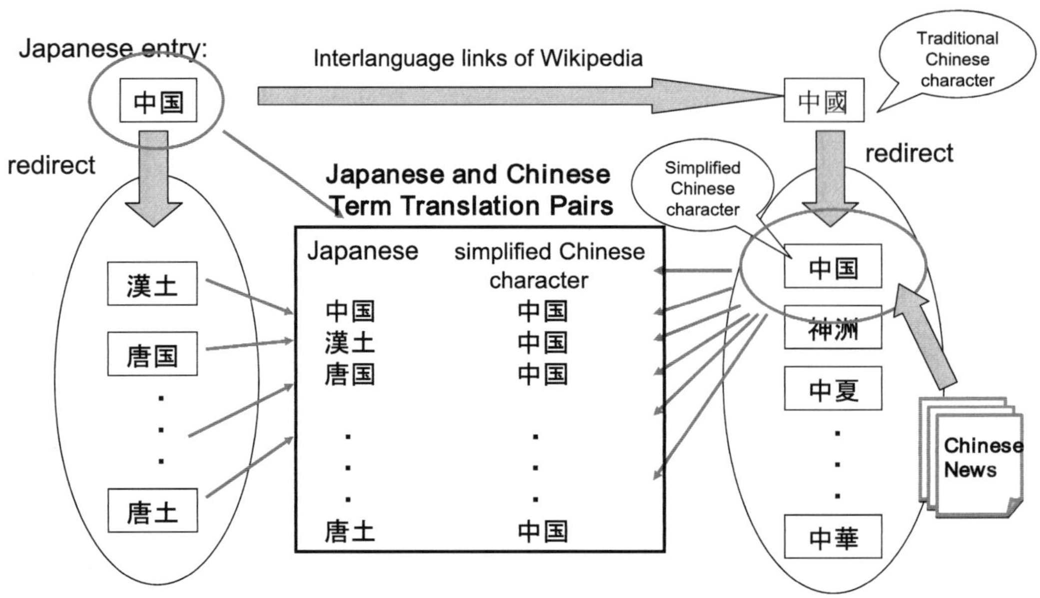

Figure 3: Extracting Japanese-Chinese Term Translation utilizing Interlanguage Links in Wikipedia

4.1 Cross-Lingual Alignment of News Articles

When cross-lingually aligning Japanese and Chinese news articles, we first count the number of Japanese and Chinese term translation pairs which are shared between the Japanese and Chinese news articles published on the same day. We then align the pair of a Japanese and a Chinese news articles for which the number of shared Japanese and Chinese term translation pairs is more than or equal to the lower bound θ_{JC} (in this paper, θ_{JC} is 10).

More specifically, given a pair of a Japanese news article d_J and a Chinese news article d_C published on the same day, let $N_{JC}(d_J, d_C)$ be the number of Japanese and Chinese term translation pairs included in JS_W, which are shared between d_J and d_C:

$$N_{JC}(d_J, d_C) = \Big|\{\langle J, S\rangle (\in JS_W) \mid J \text{ appears in } d_J.\ S \text{ appears in } d_C.\}\Big|$$

Then, for each date, the sets $DD_{JC}(\theta_{JC})$ and $DD_{CJ}(\theta_{JC})$ of pairs of Japanese and Chinese news articles for which the number of shared Japanese and Chinese term translation pairs is more than or equal to the lower bound θ_{JC} are defined as below:

$$DD_{JC}(\theta_{JC}) = \Big\{\langle d_J, d_C\rangle \mid N_{JC}(d_J, d_C) \geq \theta_{JC},\ d_C = \operatorname*{argmax}_{d'_C} N_{JC}(d_J, d'_C)\Big\}$$

$$DD_{CJ}(\theta_{JC}) = \Big\{\langle d_J, d_C\rangle \mid N_{JC}(d_J, d_C) \geq \theta_{JC},\ d_J = \operatorname*{argmax}_{d'_J} N_{JC}(d'_J, d_C)\Big\}$$

Here, $DD_{JC}(\theta_{JC})$ is created by collecting pairs $\langle d_J, d_C\rangle$, where, for each d_J, d_C is the one with the maximum number N_{JC}. In the similar way, $DD_{CJ}(\theta_{JC})$ is created by collecting pairs $\langle d_J, d_C\rangle$, where, for each d_C, d_J is the one with the maximum number N_{JC}.

4.2 Cross-Lingual Alignment of Topics

Next, this section proposes how to cross-lingually align topics estimated by a topic model.

First, for each date, all the Japanese news articles are collected from the sets $DD_{JC}(\theta_{JC})$ and $DD_{CJ}(\theta_{JC})$. Next, collected Japanese news articles are accumulated during the period of evaluation, and the DTM topic modeling toolkit is applied to the accumulated news articles and K topics are estimated for each date during the period of evaluation. Then, on the i-th day of the period of evaluation, we have the set TT^i_J of estimated Japanese topics.

In the similar way, all the Chinese news articles are collected from the sets $DD_{JC}(\theta_{JC})$ and $DD_{CJ}(\theta_{JC})$. Collected Chinese news articles are accumulated during the period of evaluation, and the DTM topic modeling toolkit is applied to the accumulated news articles and K topics are estimated for each date during the period of evaluation. Then, on the i-th day of the period of evaluation, we have the set TT_C^i of estimated Chinese topics.

Once we have the sets TT_J^i and TT_C^i on the i-th day, we align the Japanese and Chinese topics of TT_J^i and TT_C^i according to the following procedure. First, for each Japanese topic $t_J (\in TT_J^i)$, we collect news articles d_J which satisfy $P(t_J|d_J) \geq \theta_t$ (in this paper, θ_t is 0.6). In the similar way, for each Chinese topic $t_C (\in TT_C^i)$, we collect news articles d_C which satisfy $P(t_C|d_C) \geq \theta_t$. Then, out of the pairs of collected news articles $\langle d_J, d_C \rangle$, we count the number of those included in $DD_{JC}(\theta_{JC})$ or $DD_{CJ}(\theta_{JC})$, and define $M_{JC}(t_J, t_C, \theta_t, \theta_{JC})$ to be the count.

$$
\begin{aligned}
& M_{JC}(t_J, t_C, \theta_t, \theta_{JC}) = \\
& \quad \Big|\big\{ \langle d_J, d_C \rangle \;\big|\; \big(\langle d_J, d_C \rangle \in DD_{JC}(\theta_{JC}) \\
& \qquad \text{or } \langle d_J, d_C \rangle \in DD_{CJ}(\theta_{JC}) \big), \\
& \qquad P(t_J|d_J) \geq \theta_t, \; P(t_C|d_C) \geq \theta_t \big\}\Big|
\end{aligned}
$$

Finally, we align a Japanese topic t_J to a Chinese topic $t_C (\in TT_C^i)$ which maximizes the count $M_{JC}(t_J, t_C, \theta_t, \theta_{JC})$, only if the count is more than one. Also, we align a Chinese topic t_C to a Japanese topic $t_J (\in TT_J^i)$ which maximizes the count $M_{JC}(t_J, t_C, \theta_t, \theta_{JC})$, only if the count is more than one. For our convenience, we introduce the notations $TA_C(t_J, TT_C^i, \theta_t, \theta_{JC})$ and $TA_J(t_C, TT_J^i, \theta_t, \theta_{JC})$ below in order to denote the results of alignment judgements above:

$$
TA_C(t_J, TT_C^i, \theta_t, \theta_{JC}) =
\begin{cases}
\phi & \left(\max\limits_{t_C \in TT_C^i} M_{JC}(t_J, t_C, \theta_t, \theta_{JC}) = 1 \right) \\
\operatorname*{argmax}\limits_{t_C \in TT_C^i} M_{JC}(t_J, t_C, \theta_t, \theta_{JC}) & \left(\max\limits_{t_C \in TT_C^i} M_{JC}(t_J, t_C, \theta_t, \theta_{JC}) \geq 2 \right)
\end{cases}
$$

$$
TA_J(t_C, TT_J^i, \theta_t, \theta_{JC}) =
\begin{cases}
\phi & \left(\max\limits_{t_J \in TT_J^i} M_{JC}(t_J, t_C, \theta_t, \theta_{JC}) = 1 \right) \\
\operatorname*{argmax}\limits_{t_J \in TT_J^i} M_{JC}(t_J, t_C, \theta_t, \theta_{JC}) & \left(\max\limits_{t_J \in TT_J^i} M_{JC}(t_J, t_C, \theta_t, \theta_{JC}) \geq 2 \right)
\end{cases}
$$

4.3 Cross-Lingual Alignment of Time Series Topic Sequence

Suppose that the period of evaluation consists of n consecutive days, then the procedure of cross-lingual alignment of time series topic sequence is described as follows.

First, let $Q_J = TT_J^1, TT_J^2, \ldots, TT_J^n$ be the sequence of sets of Japanese topics, which are estimated through the DTM topic modeling toolkit, and each set TT_J^i of topics is for the news articles published on the i-th day of the evaluation period. Also, let $Q_C = TT_C^1, TT_C^2, \ldots, TT_J^n$ be the sequence of sets of Chinese topics, which are estimated through the DTM topic modeling toolkit. Then, for each of the n consecutive days, cross-lingual topic alignment is performed according to the following procedure:[7]

- On the i-th day, for each Japanese topic $t_J (\in TT_J^i)$, obtain the topic alignment judgement result $TA_C(t_J, TT_C^i, \theta_t, \theta_{JC})$.
- Similarly on the i-th day, for each Chinese topic $t_C (\in TT_C^i)$, obtain the topic alignment judgement result $TA_J(t_C, TT_J^i, \theta_t, \theta_{JC})$.

[7]In DTM, on the i-th day, it is possible to refer to topic models of neighboring days such as $i-1$-th and $i+1$-th days. Although in our cross-lingual topic alignment technique, we do not utilize such information, the evaluation results of cross-lingual topic alignment did not conflict with those of topics of neighboring days.

Table 1: Evaluation Results (Correct Rate): Alignment of Japanese / Chinese News Articles (%)

(a) *With* News Articles on Japanese / Chinese Domestic Economy

Date	Japanese to Chinese		Chinese to Japanese	
February 25, 2010	53.0	(26/49)	54.8	(40/73)
February 26, 2010	62.1	(18/29)	62.5	(15/24)
February 27, 2010	76.7	(23/30)	88.6	(31/35)
February 28, 2010	88.2	(30/34)	87.8	(36/41)
March 1, 2010	58.7	(27/46)	54.7	(35/64)
March 2, 2010	43.5	(10/23)	40.0	(12/30)
March 3, 2010	61.1	(22/36)	25.8	(25/97)
Total	63.2	(156/247)	53.3	(194/364)

(b) *Without* News Articles on Japanese / Chinese Domestic Economy

Date	Japanese to Chinese		Chinese to Japanese	
February 25, 2010	83.9	(26/31)	93.0	(40/43)
February 26, 2010	94.7	(18/19)	100	(15/15)
February 27, 2010	76.7	(23/30)	88.6	(31/35)
February 28, 2010	88.2	(30/34)	87.8	(36/41)
March 1, 2010	93.1	(27/29)	87.5	(35/40)
March 2, 2010	90.1	(10/11)	92.3	(12/13)
March 3, 2010	95.7	(22/23)	67.6	(25/37)
Total	88.1	(156/177)	86.6	(194/224)

5 Evaluation

5.1 News Articles for Evaluation

As we described in section 3, when extracting Japanese-Chinese term translation pairs from Wikipedia, we collected Japanese and Chinese news articles for the whole one year and extracted candidates of Japanese and Chinese Wikipedia entry titles from them. However, in the evaluation of cross-lingual topic alignment, we used Japanese and Chinese news articles for only one month. This is mainly due to time complexity of the DTM topic modeling toolkit. The DTM topic modeling toolkit performs fairly well even with news articles for only one week. Therefore, in this paper, we report evaluation results with news articles for one month, for which the DTM topic modeling toolkit performs quite well with moderate time complexity.

For the evaluation, we first collect Japanese and Chinese news stream text articles during the period from February 25th to March 23rd, 2010. In total, 12,288 Japanese news articles are collected from three newspaper companies Yomiuri, Nikkei, and Asahi, while 22,049 Chinese news articles are collected from People's Daily.

5.2 Cross-Lingual Alignment of News Articles

After we cross-lingually align Japanese and Chinese news articles by the method we presented in section 4.1, each of 791 Japanese articles is aligned to a Chinese news article, while each of 1,361 Chinese articles is aligned to a Japanese news article. Out of evaluation results for the whole one month, Table 1 shows the excerpts for that of one week (February 25th to March 3rd, 2010). Table 1 (a) shows the results without manually removing a certain subset of news articles, where correct rate of cross-lingual alignment of news articles is around 60% on the average. Relatively low correct rate is mainly due to Japanese and Chinese news articles on domestic

Table 2: Evaluation Results: Cross-Lingual Topic Alignment (*with* news articles on Japanese / Chinese domestic economy)

<table>
<tr><th rowspan="3">Type</th><th rowspan="3">Topic</th><th colspan="8">Dates</th></tr>
<tr><th colspan="4">February, 2010</th><th colspan="4">March, 2010</th></tr>
<tr><th>25</th><th>26</th><th>27</th><th>28</th><th>1</th><th>2</th><th>3</th><th>4 $\sim$ 23</th></tr>
<tr><td rowspan="4">topics both in Japanese and Chinese (correct alignment)</td><td>Toyota vehicle recalls</td><td colspan="3">correct topic alignment</td><td></td><td></td><td></td><td></td><td rowspan="5">topics are not cross-lingually aligned.</td></tr>
<tr><td>The president of Toyota apologized in China</td><td></td><td></td><td></td><td></td><td>correct topic alignment</td><td></td><td></td></tr>
<tr><td>Chile earthquake</td><td></td><td></td><td colspan="5">correct topic alignment</td></tr>
<tr><td>IMF Managing Director Dominique Strauss-Kahn Names China′s Zhu Min as Special Advisor</td><td>correct topic alignment</td><td></td><td></td><td></td><td></td><td></td><td></td></tr>
<tr><td>Topics only in Chinese</td><td>Mr. Wen had an interactive event via the Internet</td><td></td><td></td><td>alignment error</td><td></td><td></td><td></td><td></td></tr>
<tr><td>topics both in Japanese and Chinese (alignment error)</td><td>Domestic Economy News</td><td colspan="8">topics are aligned every day with error.</td></tr>
<tr><td colspan="10">Evaluation results (correct rate) : Japanese to Chinese 80.0% (4/5) Chinese to Japanese 66.7% (4/6)</td></tr>
</table>

economies. Both Japanese and Chinese news articles on domestic economies include numerical figures as well as technical terms on the economy domain, although their contents are not cross-lingually related to each other at all. It is also interesting to note that February 27th and 28th, 2010 were Saturday and Sunday. It is quite natural that, since much less news articles on domestic economies are published on holidays, correct rates on those dates are apparently higher than those on other dates.

Next, we manually remove those news articles on domestic economies, and measure the correct rates of cross-lingual alignment of news articles as we show in Table 1 (b). In this case, correct rates drastically go up to more than 85% on the average. One obvious future plan for automatically removing news articles on domestic economies for both languages is to simply apply a well studied techniques of burst detection such as the one proposed in Kleinberg (2002). Since, both in Japanese and in Chinese, news articles on domestic economies are constantly published on every week day, it is strongly estimated that they are not detected at all.

5.3 Cross-Lingual Alignment of Topics

Next, the DTM topic modeling toolkit is applied to the 791 Japanese articles as well as the 1,361 Chinese articles introduced in the previous section. Then, cross-lingual topic alignment procedure presented in section 4.2 is applied to them[8], whose evaluation results are shown in Table 2.

Out of the evaluation period of the whole one month, cross-lingually aligned topics are detected only for the first one week, except that the topics on domestic economies are cross-lingually aligned every day throughout the whole one month. Among the remaining five topic alignment results, only the one "Mr. Wen had an interactive event via the In-

[8]When applying the cross-lingual topic alignment procedure, we keep errors in the process of cross-lingual alignment of news articles, which means that only about 50$\sim$60% of the results of cross-lingual alignment of news articles are correct.

ternet" is alignment error. This topic is somehow concerned with a Chinese domestic issue and the topic itself is successfully estimated only in Chinese. About ten Chinese news articles are aligned to exactly the same Japanese article and this cross-lingual article alignment result causes the cross-lingual topic alignment error. Considering those evaluation results, if we count a sequence of cross-lingual topic alignment on consecutive days as one if aligned topics on those consecutive days are exactly the same, the correct rate of Japanese to Chinese topic alignment is 80.0%, while that of Chinese to Japanese direction is 66.7%.

In this evaluation result, one erroneous topic alignment from Japanese to Chinese and one of the two erroneous topic alignments from Chinese to Japanese are the ones about domestic economies. Thus, if we remove those erroneous alignment results of topics on domestic economies, we have the correct rate of Japanese to Chinese topic alignment as 100% (=5/5) and that of Chinese to Japanese direction as 80.0% (=4/5).

6 Related Works

Wang et al. (2007) studied how to detect correlated bursty topic patterns across multiple text streams such as multilingual news streams, where their method concentrated on detecting correlated bursty topic patterns based on the similarity of temporal distribution of tokens. Unlike the method of Wang et al. (2007), in this paper, we do not utilize burst detection techniques, but employ a time series topic model and cross-lingually align time series topics utilizing translation knowledge automatically extracted from Wikipedia.

Boyd-Graber and Blei (2009), De Smet and Moens (2009), Zhang et al. (2010), and Jagarlamudi and Daumé III (2010) concentrated on applying variants of topic models which have certain functions of bridging cross-lingual gaps by exploiting clues such as translation knowledge from bilingual lexicon or distribution of named entities. Compared with those previous works, the approach we take in this paper is different in that we focus on a time series topic model and align time series topics across two languages. It is one of our future works to introduce those other models and compare them with our proposed framework in terms of effectiveness of aligning time series topics across two languages.

7 Concluding Remarks

This paper studies issues regarding topic modeling of information flow in multilingual news streams. Based on the results of estimating distribution of topics in Japanese / Chinese news streams, this paper proposed how to analyze cross-lingual alignment of topics in time series Japanese / Chinese news streams. Evaluation results show that the proposed method is quite effective in discovering cross-lingual topic alignment between Japanese and Chinese news streams.

Future works include precise evaluation of recall, where we annotate topic alignment information to certain random samples of Japanese and Chinese time series news stream, and then, examine whether they are actually detected by the proposed method. Also, we plan to incorporate our recently invented technique (Takahashi et al., 2012) which is capable of detecting bursty topics within a time series text stream, and then cross-lingually align Japanese and Chinese bursty topics.

References

D. M. Blei and J. D. Lafferty. 2006. Dynamic topic models. In *Proc. 23rd ICML*, pages 113–120.

D. M. Blei, A. Y. Ng, and M. I. Jordan. 2003. Latent Dirichlet allocation. *Journal of Machine Learning Research*, 3:993–1022.

J. Boyd-Graber and D. M. Blei. 2009. Multilingual topic models for unaligned text. In *Proc. 25th UAI*, pages 75–82.

W. De Smet and M.-F. Moens. 2009. Cross-language linking of news stories on the Web using interlingual topic modelling. In *Proc. 2nd SWSM*, pages 57–64.

J. Jagarlamudi and H. Daumé III. 2010. Extracting multilingual topics from unaligned comparable corpora. In *Proc. 32nd ECIR*, pages 444–456.

J. Kleinberg. 2002. Bursty and hierarchical structure in streams. In *Proc. 8th SIGKDD*, pages 91–101.

Y. Takahashi, T. Utsuro, M. Yoshioka, N. Kando, T. Fukuhara, H. Nakagawa, and Y. Kiyota. 2012. Applying a burst model to detect bursty topics in a topic model. In H. Isahara and K. Kanzaki, editors, *JapTAL 2012*, volume 7614 of *LNAI*, pages 239–249. Springer.

X. Wang, CX. Zhai, and R. Sproat X. Hu. 2007. Mining correlated bursty topic patterns from coordinated text streams. In *Proc. 13th SIGKDD*, pages 784–793.

D. Zhang, Q. Mei, and C.-X. Zhai. 2010. Cross-lingual latent topic extraction. In *Proc. 48th ACL*, pages 1128–1137.

A CRF Sequence Labeling Approach to Chinese Punctuation Prediction

Yanqing Zhao, Chaoyue Wang, Guohong Fu
School of Computer Science and Technology, Heilongjiang University
Harbin 150080, China
yanqing_zhao@live.cn, chariey_nlp@yahoo.cn, ghfu@hlju.edu.cn

Abstract

This paper presents a conditional random fields based labeling approach to Chinese punctuation prediction. To this end, we first reformulate Chinese punctuation prediction as a multiple-pass labeling task on a sequence of words, and then explore various features from three linguistic levels, namely words, phrase and functional chunks for punctuation prediction under the framework of conditional random fields. Our experimental results on the Tsinghua Chinese Treebank show that using multiple deeper linguistic features and multiple-pass labeling consistently improves performance.

1 Introduction

Punctuation prediction, also referred to as punctuation restoration, aims at inserting proper punctuation marks at right position of an unpunctuated text (Gravano et al., 2009; Guo et al., 2010). Punctuation is obviously an essential indicator for sentence construction. For Chinese, adding proper punctuation marks can not only enhance the readability of text, but also can provide additional information for further language analysis, such as word segmentation, phrasing and syntactic analysis (Guo et al., 2010; Chen and Huang, 2011; Xue and Yang, 2011). As such, punctuation prediction plays a critical role in many natural language processing applications such as automatic speech recognition (ASR), machine translation, automatic summarization, and information extraction (Matusov et al., 2006; Lu and Ng, 2010).

Over the past years, numerous studies have been performed on the insertion of punctuations in speech transcripts using supervised techniques. However, it is actually very difficult or even impossible to develop a large high-quality corpus to achieve reliable models for predicting punctuations in speech transcripts or ASR outputs (Takeuchi et al., 2007). Furthermore, most previous research on punctuation prediction exploited very shallow linguistic features such as lexical features or prosodic cues (viz. pitch and pause duration) (Lu and Ng, 2010), few studies have been done on the exploration of deeper linguistic features like syntactic structural information for punctuation prediction, particularly in Chinese (Guo et al., 2010).

In this paper we draw our motivation from speech transcripts to written texts. On the one hand, a number of large annotated corpora of written texts are available to date. On the other hand, we intend to examine the role of different linguistic features on Chinese punctuation prediction. To this end, we reformulate Chinese punctuation prediction as a multiple-pass labeling task on word sequences, and then explore multiple features at three linguistic levels, namely words, phrases and functional chunks, for punctuation labeling under the framework of conditional random fields (CRFs). Furthermore, we have also performed evaluation on the Tsinghua Chinese Treebank (Zhou, 2004).

The rest of the paper is organized as follows: In Section 2, we will provide a brief review of the related work on punctuation prediction. In Section

3, we will describe in detail a labeling method to Chinese punctuation prediction. Section 4 will summarize the experimental results. Finally in Section 6, we will give our conclusion and some possible directions for future work.

2 Related Work

Punctuation prediction has been well studied in the communities of ASR, and a variety of techniques have been attempted, including n-grams (Takeuchi et al., 2007; Gravano et al., 2009), maximum entropy models (MEMs) (Huang and Zweig, 2002; Guo et al., 2010), and CRFs (Liu et al., 2005; Tomanek et al., 2007; Lu and Ng, 2010).

Current research focuses on seeking informative features for punctuation prediction. Huang and Zweig (2002) attempted to explore POS features and prosodic features for inserting punctuations in automatically recognized speech texts using MEMs. Takeuchi et al. (2007) exploited silence information from ASR systems and head or tail phrases within sentences. They showed that using head and tail phrases could result in improvement of performance in sentence boundary detection. Gravano et al. (2009) examined the effect of different orders of n-grams on performance in punctuation prediction. More recently, Huang and Chen (2011) used CRFs to combine different features for labeling pause and stop in Chinese texts, including the beginning and end features of voice fragments, character features, word features, POS features, syntactic features and topic features.

In addition to speech transcripts or ASR outputs, recently a number of researchers start to study punctuation prediction via written texts. Tomanek et al (2007) employed CRFs to phrase a biological article, and then inserted punctuation to sentences during sentence segmentation. Xue and Yang (2011) used MEMs to explore contextual words, POS features and syntax trees for inserting commas in Chinese texts. Laboreiro and Sarmento (2010) applied support vector machines to exploit multiple cues, including such as characters, character types, symbols and punctuations, for sentence segmentation and punctuation correction in micro-blog texts.

From these studies, it is clear that systems with more and deeper features outperform systems only using simple features. However, most previous studies only used lexical cues for punctuation prediction. This might be that a well-annotated corpus of speech texts is not available to date. As such, in the present study we address the problem of Chinese punctuation prediction from the perspective of written texts. Specially, we attempt to exploit multiple levels of features under the framework of CRF-based sequence labeling and thus examine the role of for Chinese punctuation

3 Approach

This section details the CRFs-based multiple pass labeling method to Chinese punctuation prediction.

3.1 Task Formulation

Chinese punctuation prediction is a process of inserting proper punctuation marks into a raw Chinese text without punctuation marks. In the present study, we reformulate Chinese punctuation prediction as a multiple-pass labeling task on an unpunctuated word string with the help of word pattern tags defined in Table 1. Furthermore, we consider eleven main punctuation marks as shown in Table 2.

Tag	Definition
B	The preceding word of the current punctuation.
A	The following word of the current punctuation.
O	Words not adjacent to the current punctuation.
BOT	The head word of a text.
EOT	The tail word of a text.

Table 1: Patterns of words in punctuation labeling

No.	Name	Punctuation	Tag
1	Comma	，	COM
2	full stop	。	FUL
3	exclamation mark	！	EXC
4	Colon	：	COL
5	Bracket	（）{}[]	BRA
6	question mark	？	QUE
7	Semicolon	；	SEM
8	enumeration comma	、	ENU
9	book title mark	《》 〈〉	BOO
10	quotation mark	“” ‘’	QUO
11	Ellipsis	……	ELL

Table 2: Types of Chinese punctuation marks

In order to reduce the interference between different types of punctuation marks and to simplify the problem of punctuation prediction as well, we take the following order to perform punctuation labelling: sentence-final delimiters (viz. period, question mark and exclamation mark) → sentence-internal delimiters (viz. comma, semicolon, colon, and enumeration comma) → indicators (viz. bracket, book title mark, quotation mark, and ellipsis).

After punctuation labeling, each word within the unpunctuated text will receive a hybrid punctuation tag of the form t_1-t_2, if it is adjacent to a punctuation mark, or is at the beginning or end of a text. Otherwise, it will only receive a tag *O*. Here, t_1 denotes the pattern of the current word in punctuation labeling (as shown in Table 1), and t_2 stands for the type of the punctuation mark (as defined in Table 2) that precedes or follows the current word if applicable.

(a) **Punctuated text:** 执法部门是反腐败斗争 、搞好廉政建设的重点部门之一。

(b) **Unpunctuated word string:** 执法/部门/是/反/腐败/斗争/搞好/廉政/建设/的/重点/部门/之一/

(c) **POS:** 执法/vN 部门/n 是/vC 反/v 腐败/a 斗争/vN 搞好/v 廉政/vN 建设/vN 的/uJDE 重点/n 部门/n 之一/rN

(d) **Phrases:** [np-ZX 执法/vN 部门/n] [vp-SG 是/vC] [np-ZX 反/v 腐败/a 斗争/vN] [vp-SG 搞好/v] [np-ZX 廉政/vN 建设/vN] 的/uJDE [np-ZX 重点/n 部门/n] [np-SG 之一/rN]

(e) **Functional chunks:** [S 执法/vN 部门/n] [P 是/vC] [P 反/v 腐败/a 斗争/vN] [P 搞好/v] [O 廉政/vN 建设/vN] 的/uJDE [H 重点/n 部门/n] [H 之一/rN]

(f) **Punctuation labeling:** 执法/BOT-O 部门/O 是/O 反/O 腐败/O 斗争/B-ENU 搞好/A-ENU 廉政/O 建设/O 的/O 重点/O 部门/O 之一/EOT-FUL

Figure 1: Representation of punctuation labeling

To further illustrate the problem of punctuation labeling, consider the following exemplar text "执法部门是反腐败斗争 、搞好廉政建设的重点部门之一。" (Law enforcement agencies are one of the priority sectors for the fight against corruption and the construction of a clean government.), along with its unpunctuated word string, three levels of linguistic annotations and the corresponding punctuation labeling representation.

It is worth noting the major motivation of this study is to investigate the effects of different levels of linguistic cues on Chinese punctuation prediction. To achieve this, we take the following three steps: First, we remove all punctuation marks within a given original punctuated text like line (a) in Figure 1 and reduce it to an unpunctuated text (viz. line (b)) before punctuation labeling. Then, we explore three levels of linguistic information to restore the removed punctuation marks using the CRF-based multiple-pass labeling strategy. Finally, we evaluate punctuation prediction performance by comparing the automatically restored punctuation marks with the corresponding original ones.

Considering the availability of linguistic information, we perform punctuation prediction on the Tsinghua Chinese Treebank (Zhou, 2004), a corpus of written Chinese with a variety of linguistic annotation information, including word segmentation, POS, phrases and functional chunks. Also, the relevant annotation scheme is used throughout our present study.

3.2 CRFs for Punctuation Labeling

We choose CRFs as the basic framework for punctuation labeling in that CRFs have proven to be one of the most effective techniques for sequence labeling tasks (Lafferty et al., 2001). Compared with other methods, CRFs allow us to exploit numerous observation features as well as state sequence based features or other features to punctuation labeling.

Let $X=(x_1,x_2,\cdots,x_T)$ be an input sequence of Chinese words, $Y=(y_1,y_2,\cdots,y_T)$ be a sequences of punctuation tags as defined in Section 3.1. From a statistical point of view, the goal of punctuation labeling is to find the most likely sequence of punctuation tags $\hat{Y}$ for a given sequence of words X that maximizes the conditional probability $p(Y\mid X)$. CRFs modeling uses Markov random fields to decompose the conditional probability $p(Y\mid X)$ of a tag sequence as a product of probabilities below

$$p(y\mid x)=\frac{1}{Z(x)}\exp(\sum_{i=1}^{T}\sum_{j}\lambda_j f_j(y,x,i)) \quad (1)$$

Where $f_j(y,x,i)$ is the jth feature function at position i, associated with a weight λ_j, and $Z(x)$ is a moralization factor that guarantees that the summation of the probability of all sequences of punctuation tags is one, which can be further calculated by

$$Z(x) = \sum_y \exp(\sum_{i=1}^{T} \sum_j \lambda_j f_j(y,x,i)) \qquad (2)$$

3.3 Features

We explore cues for punctuation prediction from three linguistic levels, namely words, phrases and functional chunks.

At word level, we exploit word forms and their POS tags in a window of three words, including the current word w_i, the preceding word w_{i-1} and the following word w_{i+1}, and their respective POS tags t_i, t_{i-1}, and t_{i+1}. Table 3 details the feature template at word level.

No.	Feature	Definition
L1	$w_{i-1}w_i$	The current word and the preceding word.
L2	$w_{i-1}w_{i+1}$	The current word and the following word.
L3	$w_{i-1}t_i$	The preceding word and the current word's POS tag
L4	t_iw_{i+1}	The current word's POS tag and the following word
L5	$t_{i-1}w_i$	The preceding word's POS tag and the current word
L6	w_it_{i+1}	The current word and the following word's POS tag
L7	w_i	The current word

Table 3: Word-level features

At phrase level or functional chunk level, we consider some possible combinations of the current word, the preceding word, the following word and their relevant phrase tags or functional chunk tags as features for punctuation prediction. The templates for phrase-level and functional chunk-level features are given in detail in Table 4 and Table 5, respectively. Where, p_i, p_{i-1} and p_{i+1} denote the category tags of the phrases containing words w_i, w_{i-1} and w_{i+1}, respectively, while p_i, p_{i-1} and p_{i+1} stands for the corresponding functional chunk tags.

No.	Feature	Definition
P1	$w_{i-1}p_{i-1}w_i p_i$	The preceding word and its phrase tag, the current word and its phrase tag.
P2	$w_ip_iw_{i+1} p_{i+1}$	The current word and its phrase tag, the following word and its phrase tag
P3	$w_{i-1}\ p_{i-1}t_i p_i$	The preceding word and its phrase tag, the current word's POS and phrase tag
P4	$t_ip_iw_{i+1} p_{i+1}$	The current word's POS and phrase tag, the following word and its phrase tag
P5	$t_{i-1}\ p_{i-1}w_i p_i$	The preceding word's POS and phrase tag, the current word and its phrase tag
P6	$w_ip_it_{i+1} p_{i+1}$	The current word and its phrase tag, the following word's POS and phrase tag
P7	$p_{i-1}w_ip_i$	The preceding word's phrase tag, the current word and its phrase tag
P8	$w_i\ p_ip_{i+1}$	The current word and its phrase tag, the following word's phrase tag
P9	$p_{i-1}t_ip_i$	The preceding word's phrase tag, the current word's POS and phrase tag
P10	$t_i\ p_ip_{i+1}$	The current word's POS and phrase tag, the following word's phrase tag

Table 4: Phrase-level features

No.	Feature	Definition
F1	$w_{i-1}f_{i-1}w_i f_i$	The preceding word and its functional chunk tag, the current word and its functional chunk tag
F2	$w_if_iw_{i+1}f_{i+1}$	The current word and its functional chunk tag, the following word and its functional chunk tag
F3	$w_{i-1} f_{i-1}t_i f_i$	The preceding word and its functional chunk tag, the current word's POS and its functional chunk tag
F4	$t_if_iw_{i+1} f_{i+1}$	The current word's POS and its functional chunk tag, the following word and its functional chunk tag
F5	$t_{i-1} f_{i-1}w_i f_i$	The preceding word's POS and functional chunk tag, the current word and its functional chunk tag
F6	$w_if_it_{i+1} f_{i+1}$	The current word and its functional chunk tag, the following word's POS and functional chunk tag
F7	$f_{i-1}w_if_i$	The preceding word's functional chunk tag, the current word and its functional chunk tag
F8	$w_i f_if_{i+1}$	The current word and its functional chunk tag, the following word's functional chunk tag
F9	$f_{i-1}t_if_i$	The preceding word's functional chunk tag, the current word's POS and its functional chunk tag
F10	$t_i f_if_{i+1}$	The current word's POS and its functional chunk tag, the following word's functional chunk tag

Table 5: Functional chunk-level features

4 Experimental Results and Discussions

To assess the effectiveness of our approach, we have conducted several experiments on the Tsinghua University Chinese Treebank (Zhou, 2004). This section will present the relevant results.

4.1 Experiment Setup

In our experiment, we divide the Tsinghua University treebank (Zhou, 2004) into two parts: One for training and the other for testing. Table 6 shows the distribution of different punctuation marks in these datasets.

Punctuation	Training dataset		Test dataset	
	Number	Rate	Number	Rate
comma	25918	44.79	5924	43.83
period	12670	21.90	3350	24.79
enumeration comma	7769	13.43	1896	14.03
quotation mark	5484	9.48	920	6.81
title mark	1656	2.86	360	2.66
bracket	1394	2.41	388	2.87
semicolon	1048	1.81	330	2.44
colon	1009	1.74	223	1.65
dash	260	0.45	44	0.33
question mark	243	0.42	42	0.31
exclamation mark	215	0.37	22	0.16
connective mark	199	0.34	16	0.12
Total	57865	100	13515	100

Table 6: Distribution of different punctuation marks in the experimental datasets

Sentence length	Total	Rate	Average number of punctuation per sentence
< 10	2307	16.19	1.04
10~19	4543	31.89	2.66
20~29	3598	25.25	4.19
30~39	1986	13.94	5.75
40~49	936	6.57	7.51
50~59	430	3.02	9.44
60~69	222	1.56	10.80
≥ 70	226	1.59	15.80
Total	14248	100	4.06

Table 7: Average number of punctuation within sentences of different length in training dataset

Table 7 and Table 8 present the average numbers of punctuations within sentences of different length in the training dataset and the test dataset, respectively. From these two tables, we can see that the number of words in most Chinese sentence is less than 40, and the average number of punctuation marks per sentence in Chinese is about 4.

Sentence length	Total	Rate	Average number of punctuation per sentence
< 10	666	17.76	0.94
10~19	1381	36.82	2.56
20~29	937	24.98	4.05
30~39	447	11.92	5.72
40~49	164	4.37	7.19
50~59	79	2.11	8.75
60~69	27	0.72	11.26
≥ 70	50	1.33	16.94
Total	3751	100	3.60

Table 8: Average number of punctuation marks within sentences of different length in test dataset

In addition, we employ three metrics to score punctuation prediction performance, namely the precision (denoted by P), the recall (denoted by R) and the F-score.

4.2 Effects of Features at Different Levels

Our first experiment intends to examine the effects of different features at different linguistic levels on Chinese punctuation prediction. This experiment is conducted with a single-pass strategy, which performs punctuation labeling in one pass. The results are presented in Tables 9, 10 and 11.

Feature	P	R	F
L1, L2, L7	0.699	0.444	0.543
L4, L5	0.625	0.493	0.551
L4, L5, L7	0.597	0.536	0.565
L1-L5	0.677	0.478	0.560
L1-L6	0.667	0.492	0.566
L1-L7	0.644	0.515	0.572

Table 9: Results for different word-level features under single-pass sequence labeling

As can be seen in these three tables, combining a variety of contextual features can improve the performance of Chinese punctuation prediction. Take the evaluation of word-level features in Table

9 as an example: the F-score is 0.543 when using word unigrams and bigrams only. But when integrating contextual words with their corresponding POS, the F-score can be increased by nearly 3 percents. Furthermore, we can also observe that among the three levels of linguistic cues, using functional chunk cues yields the best performance under the strategy of single-pass sequence labeling.

Feature	P	R	F
P1-P6	0.713	0.464	0.563
P1-P8	0.698	0.489	0.575
P1-P10	0.649	0.640	0.645

Table 10: Results for different phrase-level features under single-pass sequence labeling

Feature	P	R	F
F1-F6	0.788	0.462	0.583
F1-F8	0.782	0.505	0.613
F1-F10	0.738	0.637	0.684

Table 11: Results for different functional chunk-level features under single-pass sequence labeling

4.3 Using Multiple-Pass Sequence Labeling

As we have mentioned above, we employ a multiple-pass sequence labeling strategy to predict different types of punctuation marks in Chinese text. Therefore, our second experiment is designed to examine the effect of using multiple-pass sequence labeling in Chinese punctuation prediction. This experiment is conducted by comparing the outputs of the two labeling strategies, namely multiple-pass sequence labeling and single-pass sequence labeling. The results are given in Table 12.

Feature	Single-pass sequence labeling			Multiple-pass sequence labeling		
	P	R	F	P	R	F
L1-L7	0.644	0.515	0.572	0.785	0.467	0.585
P1-P10	0.649	0.640	0.645	0.773	0.586	0.666
F1-F10	0.738	0.637	0.684	0.817	0.611	0.699

Table 12: Comparing multiple-pass sequence labeling with single-pass sequence labeling

We can observe from Table 12 that compared with single-pass sequence labeling, multiple-pass sequence labeling results in a substantial improvement of precision and F-score, while the recall slightly declines. The reason might be that multiple-pass strategy treats different types of punctuation marks separately and thus can handle their individual characteristics.

4.4 Combining Phrase-Level and Functional Chunk-Level Features

Intuitively, functional chunk features are more informative in short sentence segmentation while phrase-level features are more helpful in tokenization within short sentences. At this point, phrase-level features and functional features might be complementary each other during punctuation prediction. As such, we believe that combining different levels of features would result in further improvement of performance. To prove this, we finally conducted an experiment by comparing the output before and after the combination of phrase-level and functional chunk-level features. The results are presented in Table 13.

Punctuation	P	R	F
comma	0.753	0.743	0.748
period	0.945	0.984	0.964
exclamation mark	0.667	0.09	0.160
colon	0.603	0.184	0.282
bracket	0.829	0.088	0.159
question mark	0.889	0.381	0.533
semicolon	0.529	0.027	0.052
enumeration comma	0.820	0.497	0.619
title mark	0.895	0.047	0.090
quotation mark	0.409	0.03	0.056
Overall	0.820	0.649	0.725

Table 13: Results for combining phrase-level features and functional chunk-level features under multiple-pass sequence labeling

From Table 13 we can see that incorporating functional chunk-level features with phrase-level features can obtain the best overall F-score of 0.725, 2.6 percents higher than that of only using functional chunk-level features (shown in Table 12). This confirms in a sense our intuition.

5 Conclusions

In this paper, we proposed a CRFs-based multiple-pass labeling approach to Chinese punctuation prediction. In particular, we have explored features for punctuation prediction at three levels, namely words, phrases and functional chunks, and thus examined their respective effects on Chinese punctuation prediction through experiments on the Tsinghua Treebank. We show that using multiple deeper features under multiple-pass labeling strategy can result in performance improvement.

Although the proposed method yields good results for periods and commas, the prediction of brackets, quotations and title identifier is still not satisfactory. This might be due to the data sparseness caused by the small number of these punctuations. Another possible reason is that the features in use are not effective or informative for these punctuation marks. Therefore, in the future research we plan to improve our current system by expanding the scale of the training corpus and seeking more informative features for Chinese punctuation prediction.

Acknowledgments

This study was supported by National Natural Science Foundation of China under Grant No.60973081 and No.61170148, the Returned Scholar Foundation of Educational Department of Heilongjiang Province under Grant No.1154hz26, and Harbin Innovative Foundation for Returnees under Grant No.2009RFLXG007, respectively.

References

Agusting Gravano, Martin Jansche, and Michiel Bacchiani. 2009. Restoring punctuation and capitalization in transcribed speech. In Proceedings of ICASSP'09, pp.4741-4744.

Evgeny Matusov, Arne Mauser, and Hermann Ney. 2006. Automatic sentence segmentation and punctuation prediction for spoken language translation. In Proceedings of IWSLT'06, pp.158-165.

Gustavo Laboreiro, and Luís Sarmento. 2010. Tokenizing micro-blogging messages using a text classification approach. In Proceedings of AND'10, pp.81-87.

Hen-Hsen Huang, and Hsin-Hsi Chen. 2011. Pause and stop labeling for Chinese sentence boundary detection. In Proceedings of Recent Advances in Natural Language Processing, pp.146-153.

Hironori Takeuchi, L. Venkata Subramaniam, Shourya Roy, Diwakar Punjani, and Tetsuya Nasukawa. 2007. Sentence boundary detection in conversational speech transcripts using noisily labeled examples. International Journal of Document Analysis and Recognition, 10(3):147-155.

Jing Huang, and Geoffrey Zweig. 2002. Maximum entropy model for punctuation annotation from speech. In Proceedings of ICSLP'02, pp. 917-920.

John Lafferty, Andrew McCallum, and Fernando Pereira. 2001. Conditional random fields: Probabilistic models for segmenting and labeling sequence data. In Proceedings of ICML'01, pp.282-289.

K. Tomanek, J. Wermter, and U. Hahn. 2007. Sentence and token splitting based on conditional random fields. In Proceedings of PACLING'07, pp.49-57.

Nianwen Xue, and Yaqin Yang. 2011. Chinese sentence segmentation as comma classification. Proceedings of ACL '11, pp. 631-635.

Qiang Zhou. 2004. The annotation scheme for Chinese Treebank. Journal of Chinese information processing, 18(4): 1-8.

Wei Lu, and Hwee Tou Ng. 2010. Better punctuation prediction with dynamic conditional random fields. In Proceedings of EMNLP '10, pp.177-186.

Yang Liu, A. Stolcke, E. Shriberg, and M. Harper. 2005. Using conditional random fields for sentence boundary detection in speech. In Proceedings of ACL '05, pp.451-458.

Yuqing Guo, Haifeng Wang, and J. V. Genabith. 2010. A linguistically inspired statistical model for Chinese punctuation generation. ACM Transactions on Asian Language Information Processing, 9(2): Article 6.

Analysis of Social and Expressive Factors of Requests by Methods of Text Mining

Daša Munková[1], Michal Munk[1], Zuzana Fráterová[2] and Beáta Ďuračková[1]
[1]Constantine the Philosopher University / Tr. A. Hlinku 1, 94974 Nitra, Slovakia
[2]University of Economics / Dolnozemská cesta 1, 85235 Bratislava, Slovakia
{dmunkova,mmunk}@ukf.sk, {zfraterova,bdurackova}@gmail.com

Abstract

In our paper we focus on analysing textual information usage (selected politeness factors of speech act) in mother tongue and in foreign language to identify phenomena of a language consciousness transfer from the mother tongue into a foreign language communication – transference phenomena – and their impact on textual structures of politeness in chosen languages. Our aim was to make an analysis of request texts written in English, Spanish and Slovak language, where we examined the occurrence of keywords, in our case the factors of politeness in mother tongue (Slovak) and in foreign languages (English and Spanish). We examined the formulation of requests made by two different groups, requests formulated by linguists - Slovak students studying English as their major subject - on one side, and the requests formulated by non-linguists - Slovak students studying Economy, with the knowledge of Spanish, - on the other side. We used cross-tabulation analysis and association rule analysis as our research methods. The findings are interesting mainly in terms of differences in the use of politeness factors in English and Slovak language, and also the concordance in the use of politeness factors in Slovak and Spanish texts of requests.

1 Introduction

One of the most important tasks of foreign language learning is to learn how to communicate with native speakers properly and fluently not only in routine but also in less common situations, so that the foreign language communication sounds natural, that the students learn how to fulfil their communicative goals or are able to integrate into the life of a different culture.

This requires the development of awareness of the nature of language and its impact on the world (Svalberg, 2007).

Trompenaars (1998) called the culture as a common network of meanings. Different "cultural" meanings through the semantic codes are anchored in language and are created by the communication structures according to different principles and laws. One of these principles is politeness, which is examined by Pragmalinguistics. In pragmalinguistic language study, politeness communication represents one of the basic topics of successful implementation of language functionality and development of communicative competence (Hymes, 1996; Canale and Swain, 1980).

The politeness theory we used when examining production of speech acts of the requesters is the Brown and Levinson model (1987) that is, in various elaborated forms, still applicable today and forms the basis for newer models and definitions of politeness (Scollon and Scollon, 1995; Lim, 1994; Yabuuchi, 2006). Today, authors studying politeness rather focus on cultural relativity of politeness (Watts, Ide and Ehlich, 1992; Blum-Kulka, House and Kasper 1989; Wierzbicka, 1985) and on transition from examining static aspects of politeness to the dynamic ones. Older forms of static examining of politeness typically focused on speaker's activity, speaker and listener's image, and on rules applied in production of politeness speech acts.

Learning to communicate in an additional language involves developing an awareness of the ways in which culture interrelates with language whenever it is used (Liddicoat, Papademetre, Scarino and Kohler, 2003; Hašková and Malá, 2008).

Each interlocutor creates his/her own unique speech acts (Cohen, 1996; Searle, 1979) and within them he/she uses the factors of politeness in various combinations and meanings. Since the level of foreign language acquisition is not on intermediate level (B1 or B2), the speaker (sender) usually simplifies his/her utterance in foreign language, applies utterances from his/her mother tongue or sometimes translates them (word by word) into foreign language, hence he/she cannot be aware of differences in meanings, which one and the same element can acquire in the other language.

We therefore believe that it is important to examine the rules of production of politeness speech acts, which the interlocutors use in the production of their spoken and written utterances in mother tongue as well as in foreign language.

Politeness communication involves various types of speech acts: a request, an apology, a complaint, an acknowledgement etc. A request is a communicative act whose aim is to achieve, through proper communicative tools, that the interlocutor fulfils a particular requirement. A request can take various forms depending on the relation between the interlocutors (if social power is present, a request can take the form of a command etc.). Usually, the interlocutor recognizes that the fulfilment of the request on his/her side is voluntary and its fulfilment is negotiated according to the way the request was formulated and what politeness factors were used. Consensually, the interlocutor, especially in situations when social power and social distance are present, tries to use common formulas and features (politeness patterns) to ensure "commonly" used requests, not to raise his/her partner's doubts about his/her credibility by using a certain unusual communicative feature.

The graphic form of a politeness communication is a written text, mostly unstructured, providing various kinds of information exchanged between the sender and the receiver. It provides a large amount of information, suitable mainly for a particular research or text mining. Text mining includes several research areas. Similarly to KDD (Knowledge Discovery in Databases) statistical methods and methods of machine learning are tools for data analysis in text mining (Hearst, 1999; Sullivan 2001). On the other hand, text mining builds mainly on theoretical and computational linguistics by data pre-processing (Neuendorf, 2002; Titscher et al, 2002; Hajičová, Panevová and Sgall, 2003; Weiss et al., 2005). The gist of text mining is processing of unstructured (textual) information, extraction of meaningful variables (turning words into numbers - meaningful indexes) from a text document, so that the information from the text can be used (made accessible) for various statistical methods and methods of machine learning. It allows us, for instance, to analyse the words or clusters of words used in a given text, their association or order, or to analyse whole texts in terms of determining similarities among them, relations among variables, or how the occurrence of one variable depends on others and so on. We can find some methods and applications in various research works (Maa, Sakagamia and Muratab, 2011), (Blache and Rauzy, 2011) and (Das and Bandyopadhyay, 2010; Stastny and Skorpil, 2007; Balogh, Magdin, Turcani and Burianova, 2011).

The order, association and variability of the factors of politeness are different in every language and culture, because they are based on different association rules in the given culture – based on a general but also an individual level.

The interlocutor has many features at his disposal to formulate a request, which are usually classified according to a specific structure (culturally given). According to Trosborg (1995), a request consists of internal and external features, thus its inner and basic part is its gist, a so called minimal unit, which can serve as the specific speech act. Its components are speaker's or listener's perspective, modality (a wish), direct vs. indirect request formulation, sentence and syntactical modifiers etc. Components that are added to the request gist (with different intensity according to the used features) and make its effect stronger are considered to be external features. Some of the external features are e.g. conversation opening sequences - greetings, appeals, attention getters (sorry, excuse me etc.); features that soften the request impact on decision making (image/field) of the listener – external sequences such as commands, minimizers, explanations, asking for speaker's agreement, pre-sequences, compliments, mitigating devices, politeness features, reducers, promises etc. (examples of which we introduce in the next chapter).

In our paper we focus on the analysis of the structure of collected unstructured texts of requests through a description of association rules found, which the Slovak students of English and Spanish language use in formulating requests. Within the structure of requests, we will try to find similarities and differences in the use of chosen social and expressive factors of politeness in the mother tongue (Slovak) and a foreign language (English and Spanish). The collected texts were formulated by intermediate students of English language, studying philological study programmes of English (teacher training or interpreting and translation studies), and intermediate students of Spanish language, non-philological study programme - Economy (level B1 or B2). This research sample was chosen to allow us to examine the transference phenomena in foreign language and to compare their characteristics (properties) in case of advanced and intermediate students in foreign language.

The rest of the paper is structured as follow. The next chapter deals with the methods of data pre-processing. We describe a particular corpora - text acquisition and information extraction from a text. The third chapter focuses on specific linguistic data analysis. At the end, we discuss the obtained results from the cross-tabulation analysis and association rules.

2 Methods

2.1 Corpora - Texts Acquisition

To obtain suitable information from text documents it is important, indeed essential to prepare and process data well. Tools like categorization, clustering and information extraction are used for data preparation (Feldman and Sanger, 2007). For instance, by proper categorization of documents, we can make the whole process of obtaining information easier (Paralič and Koštiaľ, 2003).

If we want to do data mining, it is inevitable that the text has undergone several of following steps of pre-processing (Paralič et al., 2010):

1. Text conversion into an electronic form.
2. Cleaning of non-textual information, so-called conversion on plain text. To remove the non-textual information boards of tools in Java platform can be used.
3. Tokenization and segmentation. They belong to basic steps of text processing. Tokenization (Koehn, 2010) splits up the plain text into elementary units - tokens. By tokenization, we try to reduce text into sequence of tokens.
4. Lemmatisation and tagging. Porter's algorithm is one of the most used algorithms for stemming of English words. For Slovak language this algorithm is not so much effective, since Slovak belongs to synthetic languages with a rich morphology. The best known algorithm, using the list of prefixes and suffixes which are separated from the token to obtain the stem in basic form, is minimal machine for stemming (Páleš, 1994), but it is complicated and computationally more demanding. For non-English languages, SnowballStemmer supporting also Spanish is very common. The next step of linguistic data pre-processing is tagging, which lies in assignment of grammatical tags.
5. Removing redundant, insignificant words, so-called stop words. These are words containing no significant information in texts.

By data pre-processing, it is important to take into account the following linguistic features:

Homonyms – words voiced or spelled in the same way, but having different meanings (*bat - animal; bat - baseball equipment; which/witch*). For the quality of text preparation, homonyms should be divided according to context into different terms, thereby their diversity will be ensured.

Synonyms – different words with the same or similar meaning (*beautiful, pretty, attractive*). For synonyms, it is advisable to integrate them under the same term, thereby the uniformity of meaning will be ensured.

Compounds – indicate one object, are made when two or more words are joined to form a new word. By separating, individual terms carrying different meaning are formed (*passport, grandmother, sister-in-law etc.*). For this reason, compounds should be included under one term.

In our case, we applied the above mentioned steps of data preparation from linguistic documents on texts of requests. These requests were obtained from students studying Linguistics (linguists) and students studying Economy at university (non-linguists) with a B2 level of knowledge of foreign language, whether in electronic or handwritten form, as in their mother tongue (Slovak) so in a foreign language (English, Spanish). We classified the texts of requests into individual categories according to Díaz-Pérez (2003) and Trosborg (1995), who summarized the scenarios of speech acts.

2.2 Information Extraction from the Texts

Text sources in natural language offer lots of information, but not all of them are suitable for computational analysis. Though by using software for linguistic data preparation, large amounts of sources can be sorted out and useful information from the individual words, phrases or sentences can be extracted. Therefore the gist of information extraction is the identification of specific information, such as in our case, expressive and social factors.

Methods based on rules and statistical methods are used to identify specific information. The statistical methods are used by data of lower quality (e.g. information extraction from blogs etc.). The methods based on rules, which we also used in our case, are based on fixed characteristics under which they are generated (e.g. association or sequence rules). We chose them because they are appropriate for specific tasks such as extraction of social and expressive factors. If we want to extract them, we must have a defined list of social and expressive factors. In our case, we used classification of politeness factors in line with Trosborg (1995) and Díaz-Pérez (2003) and we defined the following 9 factors:

F1 Attention getter: combination of salutations, a form to express a social role: e.g. *addressing people (title, first name, last name, friendly appeal markers) and politeness factors.*

F2 Speaker's perspective: *could I, may I etc.*

F3 Listener's perspective: *can you, would you etc.*

F4 Politeness features: e.g. *thank you, please* immediately before or after the request core.

F5 Pre-sequences: elements before a request core.

F6 Post-sequences: features after the expressed request, usually it is explanation.

F7 Mitigating devices: features expressing an apology for disturbing.

F8 Minimizers: features minimising the impact of request.

F9 Compliments: features intensifying the likelihood of request fulfilment.

The first three represent social factors and the rest are expressive factors.

3 Linguistic Data Analysis

3.1 Cross-tabulation Analysis

In our case, a cross-tabulation analysis consists of two analyses. The first is an analysis of texts of requests formulated in mother tongue (Slovak) and in foreign language (English). These texts of requests were written by Slovak students studying Linguistics, whether within their teacher training or translation and interpreting studies. The second analysis includes texts of requests formulated in Slovak (mother tongue) and Spanish (foreign language). Texts of requests were obtained from students, non-linguists, who had learnt one foreign language during their own university studies and who had passed a basic language state exam (a level B2 of the Common European Framework of Reference for Languages).

With the help of the cross-tabulation analysis we investigated whether there is a difference in the use of various factors in Slovak and foreign language (English or Spanish).

	Chi-square	df	p
Pearson	114.9155	8	0.0000
Cont. coeff. C	0.2434		
Cramér's V	0.2509		

	Chi-square	df	p
Pearson	4.2681	8	0.8322
Cont. coeff. C	0.0412		
Cramér's V	0.0412		

Table 1. Results of cross-tabulation analysis a) Slovak vs. English b) Slovak vs. Spanish.

The only requirement (a validity assumption) of the use of chi-square test is a large amount of expected frequencies. The requirement is not violated, the expected frequencies $e_{ij} = r_i s_j / n$ are large enough (i.e. they are positive and not more than 20% of e_{ij} are less than 5, e_{ij} >34.36). The contingency coefficient represents the degree of dependency between two nominal variables. The value of coefficient (see Table 1a) is approximately 0.25, where 1 means perfect dependency and 0 means independency. There is a medium dependency between the occurrence of individual factors of politeness and the language in case of Slovak vs. English, the contingency coefficient is statistically significant. The zero hypotheses (see Table 1a) are rejected, which means that the occurrence (use) of individual factors of politeness depends on the language (Slovak or English).

In the second case (Slovak vs. Spanish), the contingency coefficient (see Table 1b) is approximately 0.04. Therefore, there is no dependency between the occurrence of individual factors of politeness and the language, the contingency coefficient is statistically insignificant. The zero hypotheses (see Table 1b) are not rejected, which means that the use of individual factors of politeness does not depend on language in case of Slovak vs. Spanish.

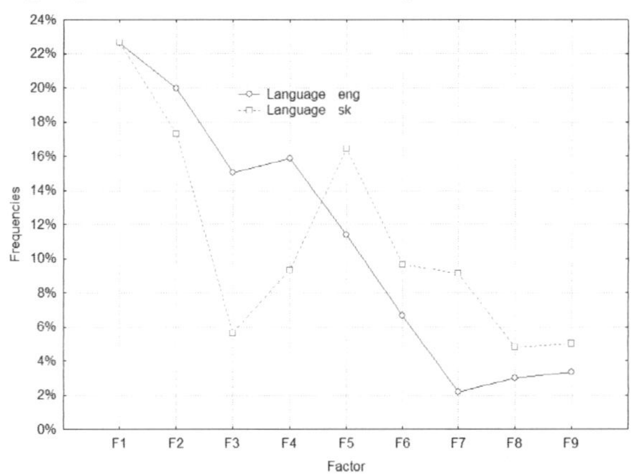

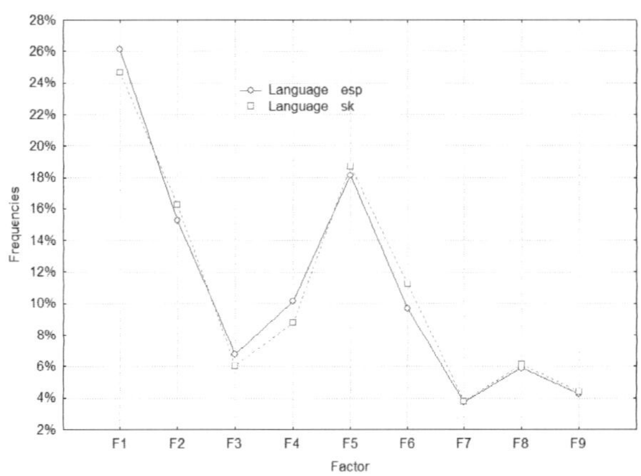

Figure 1. Interaction Plot - Language x Factor a) Slovak vs. English b) Slovak vs. Spanish.

The graph (Fig. 1a) shows the interaction frequencies *Language x Factor*. The graph presents a categorized polygon, where the factors of politeness are on the *x* axis and the observed frequencies of their usage (the occurrence) are on the *y* axis; while for each level of the variable *Language* one polygon is depicted. If the curves copy each other – they show the same course, the use of individual factors of politeness does not depend on the selected language. And vice versa, if there is any defined degree of dependency, the curves would not copy each other – which has been confirmed by the results of the analysis. We can observe different course for English and a different for Slovak. As we can see on the graph (Fig. 1a), the differences are mainly in factors F3, F4, F5 and F7. The factors F3 and F4 are considerably less used in Slovak than in English. Factor F3 (lis. perspective) represents a more direct and shorter utterance of a request. In terms of frequency, factor F2 (spe. Perspective) is much more preferred in the decision of perspective in mother tongue and also in foreign language. It means that an indirect utterance of a request and an attempt to avoid a direct addressing of requestee is more preferred. Factor F2 reduces the impact of a request, a requester, through the formulations (*May I borrow, copy ...*), takes over a part of "the effort" needed to fulfil the request upon him/herself, assuming, that the potential "alleviation" increases the likelihood of request fulfilment. The factor F4 is considerably less used in Slovak, that shows the requester's knowledge of politeness structures in English requests with factor F4 (with words such as *please or thank you*) in comparison to Slovak. On the contrary, the factors F5 and F7 are much more often used in English. These are expressive factors. When the requester uses factor F5, he/she assumes that explaining the reasons to the requestee and requestee's potential understanding of reasons of request may increase the likelihood of the fulfilment of a request. Consequently, the requester appeals to the empathy and imagination of the requestee, since he/she considers their influence as an effective strategy. Factor F7 (mitigating devices) reduces the impact of a request on the requestee, in terms of whether the requester does not interfere or over-interfere with his/her request in the requestee's time, space or decision making.

The previous graph (Fig. 1b) visualises the interaction frequencies *Language x Factor* for Slovak and Spanish. In this case, the curves copy each other, they have the same course – the occurrence of individual factors of politeness does not depend on selected language, which is a confirmation of our analysis results. We can observe a similar course for Slovak as well for Spanish.

3.2 Association Rule Analysis

Similarly to cross-tabulation analysis, an association rule analysis is divided into two analyses - the analysis of requests written by linguists and the analysis of requests written by non-linguists.

The association rule analysis represents a non-sequential approach to the data being analysed. We will not analyze the sequences but transactions, so we will not include the order of factors used into the analysis. In our case, a transaction represents the set of factors observed in the texts of requests separately for English or Spanish and for Slovak.

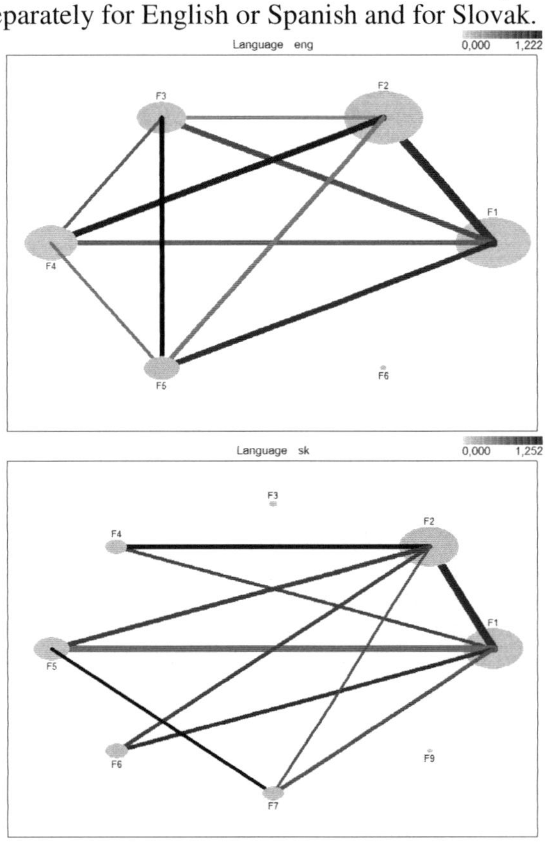

Figure 2. Web graph – a visualization of the discovered rules a) English b) Slovak.

The web graph (Fig.2a) depicts the discovered association rules for English requests, specifically the size of node represents the support of occurrence of the politeness factor, the thickness of the line represents the support of rule – pairs of factors (probability of occurrence in the pair) and the darkness of the line colour indicates a lift of the rule – the probability of a pair occurrence in transaction separately. We can see from the graph (Fig. 2a) that the factors of politeness F2, F1, F4 and F3 (support>51%) belong to the most frequently used factors. Similarly, like the combination of these factor pairs F1, F2; F2, F4, and F1, F3 (support>39%), the factors F5=>F3, F5=>F1, F2=>F4 and F1=>F3 occur in sets of factors of politeness more often together than as separate units (lift>1.11). In these cases the highest degree of interestingness was achieved – the lift, which defines how many times the selected factors of politeness occur more often together as if they were statistically independent. In case, that the lift is more than 1, the selected pairs occur more often jointly than separately in the set of used factors of politeness. It is necessary to take into account that in characterising the degree of interestingness – the lift, the orientation of the rule does not matter.

We found different association rules for Slovak requests than for English. The web graph (Fig. 2b) illustrates the discovered association rules. The most frequently used factors of politeness are F1, F2 and F5 (support>49%), as well as their pairs F1, F2 and F1, F5 (support>43%). The factors F7=>F5, F5=>F1, F4=>F2, F1=>F7 and F6=>F1 occur more often together in transactions of used factors of politeness than separately (lift>1.02).

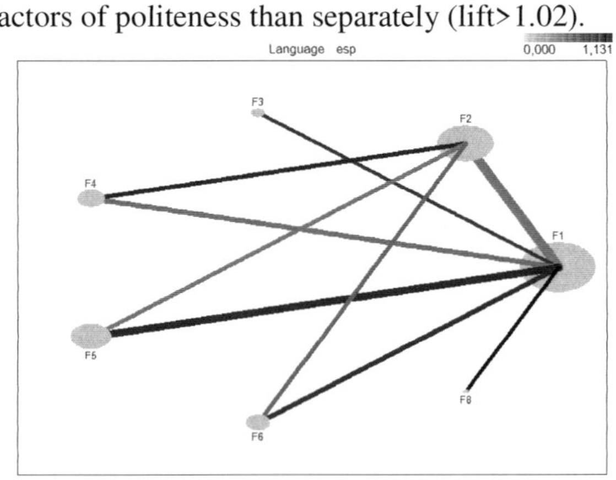

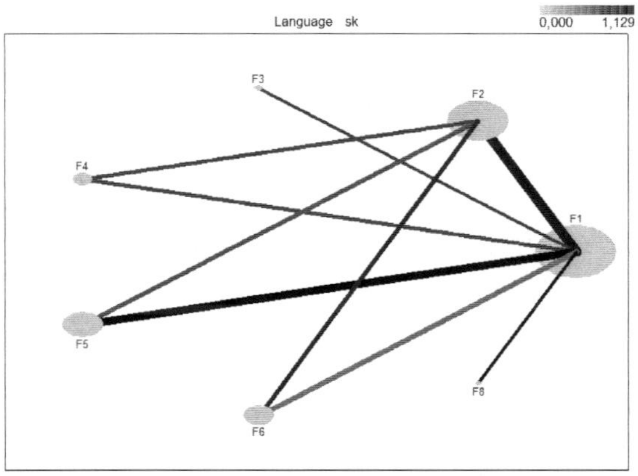

Figure 3. Web graph – a visualization of the discovered rules a) Spanish b) Slovak.

The web graph (Fig. 3a) visualizes the discovered association rules for requests written in Spanish. The graph (Fig. 3a) shows, that the factors of politeness F1, F2 and F5 (support>51%) belong to the most frequently used, similarly as the combinations of these couples of factors F1,F2 and F1,F5 (support>47%). The factors F1=>F8, F5=>F1, F4=>F2 and F1=>F3 occur in sets of used factors of politeness more often jointly than separately (lift>1.02).

We discovered almost identical association rules for texts of requests written in Slovak as those for Spanish. The previous graph (Fig. 3b) depicts the discovered association rules. The factors of politeness F1, F2 and F5 (support>51%) belong to the most frequently used, similarly as the combinations of these couples of factors F1, F2 and F1, F5 (support>48%). The factors F5=>F1, F2=>F4, F1=>F8 and F2=>F1 occur in transactions of used factors of politeness more frequently together than separately (lift>1.02).

The analysis results refer to the functioning of language consciousness of the requesters and the creation of politeness structure of utterance through the choice of factors. The politeness structure of Slovak has so far been investigated very peripherally. Therefore, in terms of comparison with Germanic and Romance languages this investigation is unique, and based on its results we can speculate not only about the decrease of transference regularities, but also about the politeness in Slovak language as such.

From our point of view, there are interesting pairs of expressive and social factors of politeness, i.e. mitigating device combined with pre-sequences but also with att. getter in a reverse order. It means that, when a requester used an att. getter (a specific greeting etc.), it is more likely that he/she used an expressive factor, which raised the indirectness of the utterance and decreased its possible negative effect. Similarly, if he/she used indirect expression of perspective – F2 then he/she combined it with politeness features, so the most frequently observed association rules were those indicating the preference of indirect expression in Slovak.

4 Discussion and Conclusion

If we look at the results from the point of view of language used, in Slovak requests formulated by linguists the factors F1 (22.64%), F2 (17.30%) and F5 (16.46%) occurred most and the factors F8 (4.82%) and F9 (5.03%) the least frequently. In English requests, the factors F1 (22.62%), F2 (19.98%) and F4 (15.84%) occurred most frequently and factors F7 (2.18%), F8 (2.99%) and F9 (3.33%) least frequently.

The results of cross-tabulation analysis showed, that there is a difference between the language (Slovak or English) and the use of selected factors of politeness. This means that the occurrence of individual factors of politeness depends on the language used in the text of request.

We consider these findings interesting, because we examined the same requests but in different languages. Here, different patterns of request formulations are being created depending on the language used.

We presume that the level of English language acquisition influences in our case the use of politeness factors in requests and the concept, that the structure of politeness is different in target language than it is in mother tongue in case of factors F3, F4, F5 and F7. The requesters are aware of the differences, which weakens the possible transference of utterance and reduces the likelihood of errors in appropriateness of the utterance. Their utterance is simplified and more direct in the texts of requests in written English. We think, this is in order to ensure the understandability of their requests and is based on a well-known structure of politeness, which they know very well, so there is less risk of failure. In case of factors F1, F2, F8 and F9, they assume similar or the same usage in both languages and consciously do not think about (in)appropriateness of their frequency in foreign language, thus they intensify the possible occurrence of errors caused by transference of consciousness of mother tongue into the foreign language.

The results of association rule analysis for texts of requests written in English showed, that the factors F2, F1, F4 and F3 (support: 71.24%; 68.58%; 53.98%; 51.77%) occurred most frequently among all factors of politeness in examined texts of requests.

The English requests are more direct with a politeness feature, which is a paradox. Linguists used much more often the lis. perspective (F3 for Slovak is 5.66% and for English 15.04%), and similarly also the politeness feature (F4 for Slovak is 9.33% and for English 15.84%), and considerably less pre-sequences (F5 for Slovak is 16.46% and for English 11.34%) and mitigating devices (F7 for Slovak is 9.12% and for English 2.18%), which are typical features of politeness in Slovak. The requester uses them to "ensure" the request fulfilment, which seems to be a successful strategy to approach the requestee and his/her understanding of the request. In English, their occurrence is less frequent.

In terms of factor combination, the following factors were combined the most: att. getter with spe. perspective, spe. perspective with politeness factor and att. getter with lis. perspective (support: 48.67%; 42.92%; 39.38%). From the point of view of pair occurrence F5=>F3, F5=>F1, F2=>F4 and F1=>F3 occurred more frequently jointly in transactions of used factors of politeness than as separate factors (lift: 1.22; 1.22; 1.12; 1.11).

In case of the couple pre-sequences => lis. perspective, the association of direct factors of politeness is shown. This means that when the requester used a pre-sequence, he/she also used the lis. perspective (to mitigate the directness of a request and its impact and effect on the listener). Pre-sequence and lis. perspective were associated with salutations and greetings (F5 with F1) or (F3 with F1) by requesters. They reinforce the request with them, i.e. they express the respect to the introductory - opening communication structures in the specific language and will not risk the failure of supposed communicated expectations of the partner – a native speaker. The next pair was spe. perspective and politeness feature (F2 with F4). In case when the author of English request used more direct utterance through factor F3, he/she mitigated this directness with expressive factor F4 (politeness feature). When he/she decided to express him/herself in a more indirect way, he/she used a combination with politeness feature (F2 with F4) reinforcing the likelihood of request fulfilment, which is confirmed by the last couple of factors.

The analysis results for Slovak requests were partially different. The most frequent factors used were: F1, F2 and F5 (support: 73.21%; 73.21%; 49.55%), contrary to English. As we mentioned before, Slovak language prefers indirect expressions with social factors of politeness that express the politeness model of requests in Slovak. Slovak expresses politeness through a more indirect utterance, explanation or compliments, and avoids interrupting the image of the communication partner, contrary to Spanish, which prefers a direct expression of request, considerably in the use of different expressive and language factors in request (as its politeness structure showed, the expressions of confidence – openness, directness are more preferred). The most frequent factor combinations are: att. getter with spe. perspective and att. getter with pre-sequences (support: 52.68%; 43.30%); and F7=>F5, F5=>F1, F4=>F2, F1=>F7 and F6=>F1 occur in transactions of used factors more frequently together than separately (lift: 1.25; 1.19; 1.16; 1.11; 1.02).

In Spanish requests written by students, whose major subject is not language, the following factors F1 (26.12%), F5 (18.14%) and F2 (15.27%) occurred most and factors F7 (3.72%), F9 (4.26%) and F8 (5.89%) least frequently. In requests formulated in Slovak, factors F1 (24.65%), F5 (18.69%) and F2 (16.24%) occurred most frequently and factors F7 (3.76%), F9 (4.41%) and F3 (6.04%) the least.

As we mentioned in chapter 3, no statistically significant difference between the used language (Slovak or Spanish) and chosen factors (contingency coefficient is 0.41) were proven. So it does not matter whether the requests are formulated in Slovak or Spanish, the requesters, students studying a non-philological subject, used the same factors of politeness.

Based on the differences in politeness structure of Spanish and Slovak language, we assumed that there would be differences in the use of factor F1 – considering other types of salutations and att. getter in both languages, differences in the use of factors F2 and F3 - considering more direct expressions of requests in Spanish, and considerably lower factors F4, F7 and F9 used in Spanish language. Our assumption was not proven; in Spanish all factors of politeness have been fully applied in concordance with Slovak (general) but also with individual structure of politeness.

The results of the analysis showed for Spanish requests that factors F1, F2 and F5 (support: 82.00%; 65.00%; 51.33%) occurred among all the factors of politeness most frequently. In terms of factor pairs, att. getter with spe. perspective and att. getter with pre-sequences are used together most frequently (support: 53.00%; 47.00%). If we look at the factors in terms of couple occurrence, F1=>F8, F5=>F1, F4=>F2 and F1=>F3 occurred more often together in transactions of used factors of politeness than separately (lift: 1.13; 1.12; 1.06; 1.03; 1.02).

There is no point in discussing results for Slovak in detail because the results of association rule analysis were similar to those for Spanish language. Only one difference was shown in pair occurrence of post-sequences/explanation => spe. perspective and att. getter => lis. perspective occurred more frequently together than separately in Spanish and not in Slovak and vice versa, the couple lis. perspective => att. getter in Slovak and not in Spanish language.

We can say, that the requests in Slovak (the same in Spanish - considering the strong transference structure of these utterances) are less direct, using more mitigating devices (F7 - apologies for interference), such as I hope you don't mind me asking but could you read my outline and give some bibliographical references, please?; minimizers (F8), such as Please, can I borrow a book from the university library? I'll photocopy it and give it back to library next day, and compliments (F9) such as Excuse me, I know that you are a specialist on this and I asked myself if you could read my outline and if you could give me some bibliographical references., etc.

Partial differences between the use of factors of politeness of linguists and non-linguists are interesting. The linguists prefer factors F1, F2 and F5 in their mother tongue, combining them in varying degree and then complementing them with other expressive factors such as mitigating devices and post-sequences. Non-linguists add these three factors (although in a lower degree) to mitigating devices, post-sequences and compliments. With their help non-linguists "ensure", to a higher degree, the request fulfilment by requestee.

The findings are interesting mainly in terms of differences in the use of politeness factors in English and Slovak, and also the concordance in the use of politeness factors in Slovak and Spanish requests formulations. Here we can see the impact of transference - a transfer of language awareness of native speaker in an utterance of foreign language mainly in case of students non-linguists, whose Spanish competency is at a lower level and they copy the usage of politeness factors without any knowledge and consideration of (in)appropriateness of their application in a given situation. The level of English competency of the linguists is higher and in case of factors F3, F4, F5 and F7, they choose different association rules, as well as the frequency of the use of individual factors. We assumed that some more complicated expressive factors (F5, F7, F8 and F9) would occur more frequently in foreign language, too. Students rather avoided them and they expressed themselves more directly in English or copied the Slovak politeness structure and "translated" their requests into another language without the awareness of its different politeness structure in Spanish. We assume that this could have been caused by uncertainty in foreign language use, mainly in English, but that is a focus of another research.

Acknowledgment

This work was supported by the Slovak Research and Development Agency under the contract No.APVV-0451-10.

References

Agneta M-L. Svalberg. 2007. Language awareness and language learning. Language Teaching, 40:287-308.

Alena Hašková and Eva Malá. 2008. Cudzí jazyk ako súčasť informačnej gramotnosti v zjednotenej Európe. In: Informatika v škole 33/34, 2008, s. 36 – 39. ISSN 1335-616X.

Andrew D. Cohen. 1996. Speech acts. In Sociolinguistics and Language Teaching, Cambridge University Press, Cambridge.

Anna Trosborg. 1995. Interlanguage pragmatics: Requests, complaints, and apologies. Mouton de Gruyter, Berlin.

Anna Wierzbicka. 1985. Different cultures, different languages, different speech acts. Journal of Pragmatics, 9:145-178.

Anthony J. Liddicoat et al. 2003. Report on intercultural language learning. Report to the Australian Government Department for Education Science and Training.

A. Yabuuchi. 2006. Hierarchy politeness: What Brown and Levinson refused to see. Intercultural Pragmatics, 3(3):323-351.

Dan Sullivan. 2001. Document Warehousing and Text Mining: Techniques for Improving Business Operations, Marketing and Sales. John Willey & Sons.

Dell H. Hymes. 1996. On communicative competence. In The Communicative Approach to Language Teaching, Oxford Univesity Press.

Dipankar Das and Sivaji Bandyopadhyay. 2010. Identifying Emotional Expressions, Intensities and Sentence level Emotion Tags using a Supervised Framework. In PACLIC 24, 95-104.

Emil Páleš. 1994. SAPFO – Parafrázovač slovenčiny. VEDA, Bratislava.

Eva Hajičová, Jarmila Panevová and Petr Sgall. 2003. Úvod do teoretické a počítačové lingvistiky. Karolinum, Praha.

Fons Trompenaars. 1998. Riding the Waves of Culture. Nicolas Brealey, London.

Francisco J. Diaz Pérez. 2003. La cortesía verbal en inglés y en español. Actos de habla y pragmática intercultural. Universidad de Jaén, Jaén.

Ján Paralič and Ivan Koštiaľ. 2003. A Document Retrieval Method Based on Ontology Associations. Journal of Information and Organizational Sciences, 27:93-99.

Ján Paralič et al. 2010. Dolovanie znalostí z textov. Equilibria, Košice.

Jiri Stastny and Vladislav Skorpil. 2007. Genetic Algorithm and Neural Network. In Proceedings of the 7th WSEAS International Conference on Applied Informatics and Communications, 347-351.

John R. Searle. 1979. Expression and meaning: Studies in the theory of speech acts. Cambridge University Press, Cambridge.

Kimberly A. Neuendorf. 2002. The Content Analysis Guidebook. Sage, London.

Marti A. Hearst. 1999. Untangling text data mining. In ACL '99 Proceedings of the 37th annual meeting of the Association for Computational Linguistics on Computational Linguistics, 3-10.

Michael Canale and Merrill Swain. 1980. Theoretical bases of communicative approaches to second language teaching and testing. Applied Linguistics, 1:1-47.

Penelope Brown and Stephen C. Levinson. 1987. Politeness: Some universals in language usage. Cambridge University Press, New York.

Philipp Koehn. 2010. Statistical Machine Translation. Cambridge University Press.

Philippe Blache and Stéphane Rauzy. 2011. Predicting Linguistic Difficulty by Means of a Morpho-Syntactic Probabilistic Model. In PACLIC 25, 160-167.

Richard J. Watts, Sachiko Ide and Konrad Ehlich. 1992. Politeness in Language: Studies in its History, Theory, and Practice. Mouton de Gruyter, Berlin/New York.

Ron Scollon and Suzanne Wong Scollon. 1995. Intercultural Communication: A Discourse Approach. Blackwell, Oxford.

Ronen Feldman and James Sanger. 2007. The Text Mining Handbook: Advanced Approaches in Analyzing Unstructured Data. Cambridge University Press.

Sholom M. Weiss et al. 2005. Text Mining: Predictive Methods for Analyzing Unstructured Information. Springer.

Shoshana Blum-Kulka, Juliane House and Gabriele Kasper. 1989. Cross-cultural pragmatics: requests and apologies. Ablex, Norwood.

Stefan Titscher et al. 2002. Methods of Text and Discourse Analysis. Sage, London.

Tae-Seop Lim. 1994. Facework and interpersonal relationships. In The Challenge of Facework: Cross-Cultural and Interpersonal Issues, 209-229.

Qing Maa, Shinya Sakagamia and Masaki Muratab. 2011. Extraction of Broad-Scale, High-Precision Japanese-English Parallel Translation Expressions Using Lexical Information and Rules. In PACLIC 25, 577-586.

Zoltan Balogh et al. 2011. Interactivity elements implementation analysis in e-learning courses of professional informatics subjects. In 8th International Conference on Efficiency and Responsibility in Education, 5-14.

Set Expansion using Sibling Relations between Semantic Categories

Sho Takase **Naoaki Okazaki** **Kentaro Inui**
Graduate School of Information Sciences
Tohoku University, Japan
{takase, okazaki, inui}@ecei.tohoku.ac.jp

Abstract

Most set expansion algorithms assume to acquire new instances of different semantic categories independently even when we have seed instances of multiple semantic categories. However, in the setting of set expansion with multiple semantic categories, we might leverage other types of prior knowledge about semantic categories. In this paper, we present a method of set expansion when ontological information related to target semantic categories is available. More specifically, the proposed method makes use of sibling relations between semantic categories as an additional type of prior knowledge. We demonstrate the effectiveness of sibling relations in set expansion on the dataset in which instances and sibling relations are extracted from Wikipedia in a semi-automatic manner.

1 Introduction

Set expansion is the task of expanding a list of named entities from a few named entities (seed instances). For example, given a few instances of car vehicles "Prius", "Lexus" and "Insight", the task outputs new car instances such as "Corolla", "Civic", and "Fit". Set expansion has many applications in NLP including named entity recognition (Collins and Singer, 1999), word sense disambiguation (Pantel and Lin, 2002), document categorization (Pantel et al., 2009), and query suggestion (Cao et al., 2008).

Set expansion is often implemented as bootstrapping algorithms (Hearst, 1992; Yarowsky, 1995; Abney, 2004; Pantel and Ravichandran, 2004; Pantel and Pennacchiotti, 2006). A bootstrapping algorithm iteratively acquires new instances of the target category using seed instances. First, a bootstrapping algorithm mines phrasal patterns that co-occur frequently with seed instances in a corpus. Given the words "Prius" and "Lexus" as seed instances of the car category, the algorithm finds patterns such as "Toyota produce X" and "X is a hybrid car" (X is a variable filled with a noun phrase). Next, the bootstrapping algorithm acquires instances that co-occur with patterns, i.e., noun phrases that appear frequently in the variable slots in the patterns. For example, the pattern "Toyota produce X" might retrieve vehicles manufactured by Toyota. Bootstrapping algorithms repeat these steps, expanding patterns using newly acquired instances.

However, bootstrapping algorithms often suffer from patterns that retrieve instances not only of the target category but also of other categories. For example, given the seed instances "Prius" and "Lexus", a bootstrapping algorithm might choose the pattern "new type of X", which might extract unrelated instances such as "iPhone" and "ThinkPad". The *semantic drift* problem (Curran et al., 2007), the phenomenon by which a bootstrapping algorithm deviates from the target category, has persisted as the major impediment of bootstrapping algorithms.

Bootstrapping algorithms assume prior knowledge about a semantic category in the form of seed instances. Recently, researchers have been more interested in self-supervised learning of every semantic category in the world from massive text corpora, as exemplified by the *Machine Reading* project (Oren et al., 2006). In the setting of set expansion with multiple semantic categories, we might leverage prior knowledge of other types that were unexplored in previous studies. For example, a person cannot belong to both actor and actress categories simultaneously. Additionally, we know that two distinct categories of car and motorcycle products share similar properties (e.g., vehicle, gasoline-powered, overland), but have some crucial differences (e.g., with two or four wheels, with or without windows).

In this paper, we present a method of set expansion when ontological information related to target semantic categories is available. More specifically, the proposed method makes use of sibling relations between semantic categories as an additional type of prior knowledge. We demonstrate the effectiveness of sibling relations on the dataset (seed and test instances) extracted from Wikipedia.

This paper is organized as follows. Section 2 reviews the Espresso algorithm as the baseline algorithm of this study. The section also describes the problem of semantic drift and previous approaches to the problem. Section 3 presents the proposed method, which uses sibling relations of semantic categories as an additional source of prior knowledge. Section 4 demonstrates the effectiveness of the proposed method and discusses the experimental results. In section 5, we conclude this paper.

2 Related Work

2.1 Espresso algorithm

Pantel and Pennacchiotti (2006) proposed the Espresso algorithm, which fundamentally iterates two steps: candidate extraction and ranking. In candidate extraction, the algorithm collects patterns that are co-occurring with seed instances and instances acquired in the previous iteration. The algorithm also finds candidates of new instances using patterns extracted in the previous iteration.

In the ranking step, the algorithm finds the top N candidates of patterns and instances based on their scores. The espresso algorithm defines score $r_\pi(p)$ for candidate pattern p and score $r_\iota(i)$ for the candidate instance i as

$$r_\pi(p) = \frac{1}{|I|} \sum_{i \in I} \frac{\mathrm{pmi}(i,p)}{\max \mathrm{pmi}} r_\iota(i), \quad (1)$$

$$r_\iota(i) = \frac{1}{|P|} \sum_{p \in P} \frac{\mathrm{pmi}(i,p)}{\max \mathrm{pmi}} r_\pi(p), \quad (2)$$

$$\mathrm{pmi}(i,p) = \log_2 \frac{|i,p|}{|i,*||*,p|}. \quad (3)$$

In these equations, P and I are sets of patterns and instances of each category. $|P|$ and $|I|$ are the numbers of patterns and instances in the sets. $|i,*|$ and $|*,p|$ are the frequencies of instance i and pattern p in a given corpus. $|i,p|$ presents the frequency by which instance i co-occurs with pattern p. Also, max pmi is the maximum of pmi values in all instances and patterns.

First, the Espresso algorithm extracts patterns that co-occur with seed instances. Next, the algorithm ranks the patterns based on their score calculated using equation (1) and acquires the top N patterns. The more a pattern co-occurs with reliable instances, the higher the score the pattern obtains. In this way, the algorithm acquires patterns that correspond to the target semantic category.

2.2 Semantic Drift

The major obstacle of bootstrapping algorithms is semantic drift (Curran et al., 2007). Semantic drift is the phenomenon by which a bootstrapping algorithm deviates from the target categories. For example, one can consider the car category, which includes "Prius" and "Lexus" as seed instances. The Espresso algorithm might extract patterns that co-occur with many categories such as "new type of X" and "performance of X" after some iterations. These generic patterns might gather unrelated instances such as "iPhone" and "ThinkPad". These instances obscure the characteristics of the target semantic category. Therefore, the patterns extracted in the next iteration might not represent at the semantic category of the seed instances.

Semantic drift is also caused by polysemous words. For example, to expand the set of motor vehicle manufacturers using seed instances "Saturn" and "Subaru", a bootstrapping algorithm might find instances representing the star category (e.g., "Jupiter" and "Uranus"). This is because "Saturn" and "Subaru" are polysemous words, belonging not only to motor vehicle manufacture but also to astronomical objects: planets and stars.

2.3 Approaches to semantic drift

Many researchers have presented various approaches to reduce the effects of semantic drift. The approaches range from refinement of the seed set (Vyas et al., 2009), applying classifier (Bellare et al., 2007; Sadamitsu et al., 2011; Pennacchiotti and Pantel, 2011), using human judges (Vyas and Pantel, 2009), to using relationships between semantic categories (Curran et al., 2007; Carlson et al., 2010).

Vyas et al. (2009) investigated the influence of seed instances on bootstrapping algorithms. They reported that seed instances selected by human who are not specialists sometimes yield worse results than those selected randomly. They proposed a method that refines seed sets generated by humans to improve the set expansion performance.

Bellare et al. (2007) proposed a method using a classifier instead of scoring functions in the ranking step of bootstrapping algorithms. The classifier approach can use multiple features to select instances. Sadamitsu et al. (2011) extended the method of Bellare et al. (2007) to use topic information estimated using Latent Dirichlet Allocation (LDA). They use not only contexts but also topic information as features of the classifier. Pennacchiotti and Pantel (2011) proposed a method for the automatic construction of training data for the classification approach. However, these researchers did not target set expansion for multiple semantic categories.

Vyas and Pantel (2009) proposed an algorithm that finds and removes the causes of semantic drift. The algorithm employs a human judge to prevent semantic drift in the iterative process of a bootstrapping algorithm. When a human judge detects an incorrect instance, the algorithm removes the patterns that acquired the incorrect instance. The algorithm also removes instances having a similar context vector to that of the incorrect instance to avoid a similar error. Although they used human judges, they ignored ontological information such as relations between categories.

Curran et al. (2007) proposed Mutual Exclusion Bootstrapping, which incorporates exclusiveness constraint between categories into the bootstrapping algorithm. Mutual Exclusion Bootstrapping uses the restriction that an instance and a pattern must belong to only one category. Instances or patterns appearing in multiple categories are ambiguous. Therefore, they are likely to cause semantic drift. By removing ambiguous instances and patterns, Curran et al. (2007) achieved high precision.

Carlson et al. (2010) proposed the Coupled Pattern Learner (CPL) algorithm which also uses mutual exclusiveness. The CPL algorithm acquires entity instances (e.g., instances of the car category) and relation instances (e.g., *CEO-of-Company (Larry Page, Google)* and *Company-acquired-Company (Google, Youtube)*) simultaneously. To acquire those instances, the algorithm requires knowledge about exclusiveness constraint between categories and links between categories (e.g., an instance of the CEO category must be CEO of some instance of the company category). However the algorithm uses only the exclusiveness constraint as prior knowledge related to multiple semantic categories.

Curran et al. (2007) and Carlson et al. (2010) use not only seed instances but also exclusiveness constraint between semantic categories as a prior knowledge. However, we have more prior knowledge about semantic categories at hand. For example, we can obtain ontological information between semantic categories easily from existing resources such as Wikipedia. Ontological information provides sibling relations between semantic categories, i.e., categories that should have common properties. In this study, we explore the usefulness of sibling relations between semantic categories in set expansion.

At last, we mention the relationship between this study and ontology learning. Ontology learning (Maedche and Staab, 2001; Navigli et al., 2003) is the task of constructing hierarchical structure of ontology by extracting terms and ontological relations between terms. In contrast, this study utilizes an existing resource as a hierarchical structure of ontology, and expands the list of instances of semantic categories on the hierarchical structure.

3 Proposed method

3.1 Filtering with patterns of sibling categories

In this section, we present the method using sibling relations between semantic categories as a prior knowledge. We gather categories that are siblings as a *sibling group*. For example, car and motorcycle categories belong to the same sibling group. We ex-

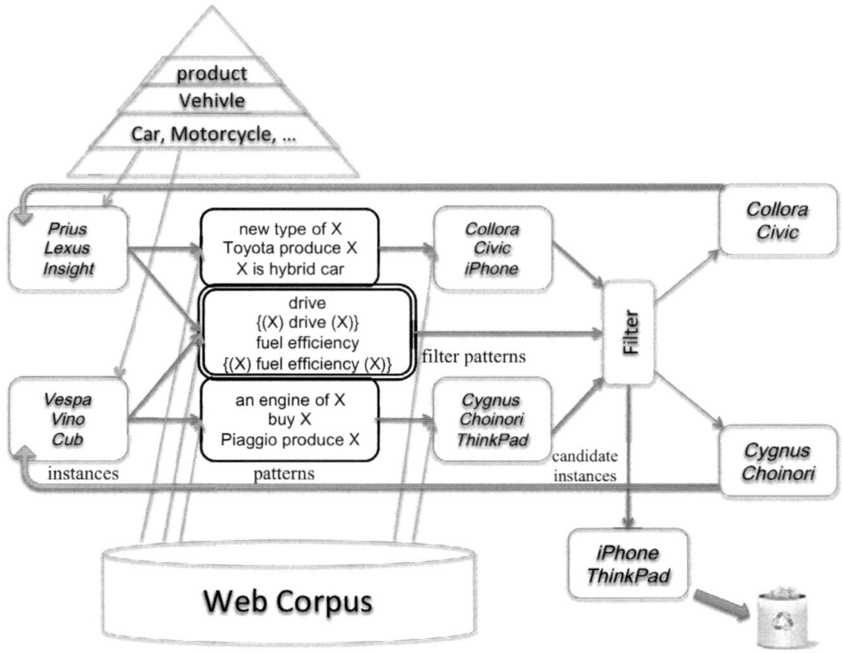

Figure 2: Set expansion using sibling relations.

Algorithm 1 The proposed method.

Input: C: a set of categories, $S_1, S_2, ..., S_T$: sibling groups (subset of C), I_c: seed instances of each $c \in C$, L: the number of iterations

Output: I_c: instances for each $c \in C$

for $j = 1, 2, ..., T$ **do**
  $F_{S_j} \leftarrow$ pattern-extraction(S_j)
end for
for $l = 1, 2, 3..., L$ **do**
  for $j = 1, 2, ..., T$ **do**
    I = []
    for all $c \in S_j$ **do**
      $R \leftarrow$ ESPRESSO(I_c)
      $R' \leftarrow$ FILTER(R, F_{S_j})
      I += R'
    end for
    for (i, c, s) in I in descending order of score **do**
      if $|I_c| \leq N * l$ and $i \notin I_{c'}$ for all $c' \in S \setminus c$ **then**
        insert i into I_c
      end if
    end for
  end for
end for
function FILTER(R, F)
  R' = []
  for (i, c, s) in R **do**
    if i co-occur with $\forall f \in F$ **then**
      insert (i, c, s) into R'
    end if
  end for
  return R'
end function

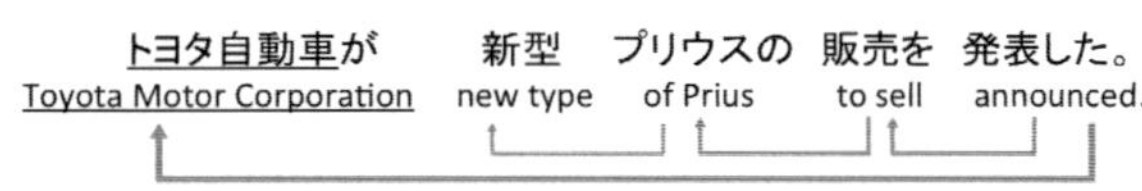

Figure 1: Example of syntactic dependencies.

pect that instances including the same sibling group hold common properties. We assume the common property to be represented by patterns of the sibling group. These patterns, which can check the common property of the sibling group, are denoted as *filter patterns*. Our proposed method obtains filter patterns using the sibling group and ascertains whether an instance co-occurs with the filter patterns.

Figure 2 presents examples of car and motorcycle categories included in the same sibling group. The method detects "drive" and "fuel efficiency" as filter patterns. Note that filter patterns are unconstrained by the difference of parent–child in the dependency tree. In the previous studies on bootstrapping, if the method obtains "new type of X" as the pattern of car category, then the method does not have a mechanism to reject incorrect instances such as "iPhone". In contrast, the proposed method ascertains whether each candidate instance co-occurs with the filter patterns before the final decision of acquiring instances. The method approves instances that co-occur with the filter patterns (e.g., "Corolla").

The detail of the method is described in Algorithm 1. The method is given a set of target categories C, sibling groups $(S_1, S_2, ..., S_T)$, seed instances I_c of each category $c \in C$ and the number of iterations L. Each sibling group is a subset of C, and disjoint from each other. The method chooses filter patterns F_{S_j} of each sibling group S_j from lines 1 to 3. In line 8, the method extracts instances of each category c of the sibling group S_j using the function ESPRESSO. ESPRESSO requires an instance set I_c of category c. ESPRESSO returns R, the list of the tuples each of which consists of instance i, category c and score s (i.e., (i, c, s)), using the Espresso algorithm described in Section 2.1.

In the experiments, using a Japanese large-scale corpus, we employ a phrase-like unit ($bunsetsu$) having dependency with an instance as a pattern. Figure 1 shows an example of Japanese sentence and its English translation[1]. Consider the instance "Toyota Motor Corporation" in the sentence shown in Figure 1. The algorithm extracts the pattern:

- X⟵ 発表した (X⟵announced)

In line 9, the method checks whether each candidate instance i in R has a common property of a sibling group using FILTER function (lines 19 to 27). FILTER examines that each i in R co-occurs with a filter pattern f in F. The function returns the list of instances and their scores which co-occur with the filter patterns. In short, this function filters out an instance which lacks the common property of the sibling group captured by the filter patterns F.

The method uses the exclusiveness constraint between categories of the sibling group to prevent drift within the group. If a pattern or an instance appears in multiple categories of the sibling group, then the method decides a single category that suits the best to the pattern or the instance. The method makes this decision based on a ranking. For example, consider a pattern "muffler of X", in which a pattern appeared in car and motorcycle categories. If the pattern is ranked 13th in the car category and fourth in the motorcycle category, then the pattern belongs only to the motorcycle category. In algorithm 1, function Espresso incorporates an exclusiveness constraint for patterns. The exclusiveness constraint for instances is implemented from lines 12 to 16.

The method acquires top N instances in order of score s while applying the exclusiveness constraint from lines 12 to 16. After the method secures new instances of each category, the method proceeds to the next iteration.

[1]The words in the English sentence are ordered as they appear in the Japanese sentence. For this reason, the word order and dependency edges in the English sentence look strange, but these are correct in the Japanese original sentence.

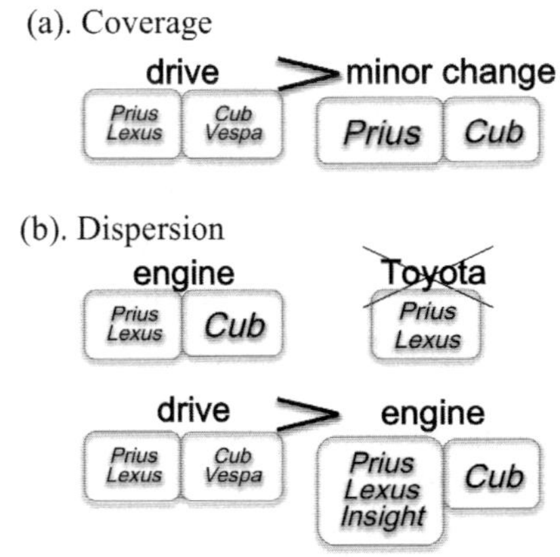

Figure 3: Two desirable properties for filter patterns.

3.2 Acquisition of filter patterns

As described above, using filter patterns, our proposed method checks whether an instance has a common property of the sibling group. We describe how to extract and score the filter patterns.

Acquisition of filter patterns has two phases: candidate extraction and ranking. In candidate extraction, our method collects patterns that co-occur with seed instances of the sibling group. For example, given a sibling group consisting of car and motorcycle categories, the method finds patterns co-occurring with seed instances of car or motorcycle categories.

Filter patterns do not acquire instances of one sibling group but examine whether the instances have a common property of the sibling group. It is therefore unnecessary that filter patterns are of strict form to locate entities. For filter patterns, we disregard the difference of parent–child in the dependency tree.Please refer to *filter patterns (top 3)* column of Table 2 as an example of filter patterns.

After extracting candidates, the method selects the most suitable filter patterns in the candidates. The method selects filter patterns based on the two factors: *Coverage* and *Dispersion*. *Coverage* is the number of instances with which a filter pattern co-occurs. *Dispersion* is the degree of scattering categories in which the pattern appears. Figure 3 shows example of suitable filter patterns based on these factors. In Figure 3, a caption in bold font presents a filter pattern, and a caption in italic font presents an instance supported by the corresponding filter pattern.

The filter pattern is expected to cover all correct instances of the sibling group. Therefore, a pattern co-occurring with many seed instances is desirable. For example, in Figure 3 (a), the pattern "drive" is more suitable than "minor change" because "drive" supports more correct instances. This factor, *Coverage*, is modeled by recall. Recall of the pattern f of the sibling group S_j is calculated using equation (4).

$$Recall(S_j, f) = \frac{\sum_{c \in S_j} \sum_{i \in I_c} cooccur(f, i)}{\sum_{c \in S_j} |I_c|} \quad (4)$$

$$cooccur(f, i) = \begin{cases} 1 & \text{if } i \text{ co-occurs with } f \\ 0 & \text{otherwise} \end{cases} \quad (5)$$

I_c is the set of seed instances of category c. $|I_c|$ is the number of seed instances of category c. $cooccur(f, i)$ indicates whether the seed instance i co-occurs with the pattern f. $\sum_{i \in I_c} cooccur(f, i)$ is the number of seed instances co-occurring with pattern f.

A filter pattern co-occurring with specific instances of the sibling group is inappropriate because filter patterns must ascertain whether candidate instances have a common property among categories. Therefore the method applies the restriction that the patterns must appear in two or more categories of the sibling group [2]. In Figure 3 (b), the pattern "engine" co-occurs with seed instances of both car and motorcycle categories but "Toyota" appears only in the car category. The method removes the latter in this example. Furthermore, we should respect a pattern which co-occurs with seed instances in each category in a sibling group equally. For example, Figure 3 (b) shows that the filter pattern "drive" is more suitable than "engine" because "drive" co-occurs with seed instances of car and motorcycle categories equally. This factor, *Dispersion*, is modeled by entropy. Entropy of the pattern f of the sibling group S_j is calculated using equation (6).

$$Entropy(S_j, f) = -\sum_{c \in S_j} P_c(f) \log_{|C|} P_c(f) \quad (6)$$

$$P_c(f) = \frac{\sum_{i \in I_c} cooccur(f, i)}{\sum_{c \in S_j} \sum_{i \in I_c} cooccur(f, i)} \quad (7)$$

$|C|$ is the number of categories in which the pattern f appears. If the pattern f co-occurs with seed instances of each category equally, then $Entropy(S_j, f)$ obtains the highest score.

To prioritize patterns with consideration of *Coverage* and *Dispersion*, we score the pattern f:

$$Score(S_j, f) = Entropy(S_j, f) * Recall(S_j, f) \quad (8)$$

Calculating $Score(S_j, f)$ for candidate pattern f of each sibling group S_j, the method acquires the top 15 patterns of each sibling group. We presume that a sibling group is exclusive to the other sibling groups. Therefore if a pattern is considered as candidates in multiple sibling groups, then the method decides that the pattern belongs to only the sibling group in which the pattern appears most frequently.

4 Experiments

4.1 Experimental setting

We evaluated the effect of sibling relations as a prior knowledge for set expansion. We compare the Espresso algorithm (Pantel and Pennacchiotti, 2006), the Espresso algorithm with exclusiveness constraint between categories (Espresso + exclusiveness constraint), and the Espresso algorithm with exclusiveness constraint and sibling relations (the proposed method). Each method was configured to extract 15 patterns and instances at every iteration. Because set expansion is the task to obtain unknown

[2] We found that the number of candidate patterns was too small when we adopted the restriction that filter patterns must appear in all categories of the sibling group. Therefore, we introduced the restriction that filter patterns must appear in two or more categories of the sibling group. Furthermore, we measure *Coverage* to obtain filter patterns that appear many categories of the sibling group.

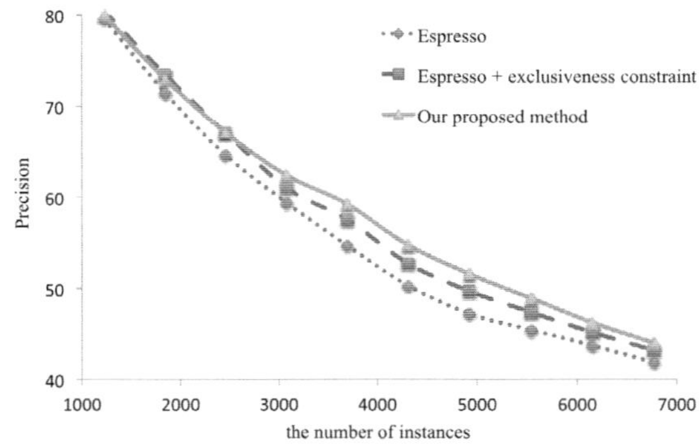

Figure 4: Precision of each method in accordance with the number of acquired instances.

instances, it is difficult to measure recall. Therefore, we compare the precision of each method when each method acquires fixed quantities of instances. We asked three human annotators to judge the correctness of acquired instances. We conducted the experiments in Japanese. The results described herein have been translated into English for presentation.

Table 2 reports all categories used for the experiments. Each category belongs to only one sibling group. Each sibling group consists of two or more categories. We prepared sibling groups by manually based on Wikipedia. Each category starts with 15 seed instances extracted from Wikipedia in a semi-automatic manner (Sumida et al., 2008). Because the automatic method yields incorrect seed instances, we removed errors manually.

We used 110 million Japanese web pages from which patterns and instances are extracted. We parsed sentences in the web pages using KNP, a Japanese dependency parser (Kurohashi et al., 1994). To reduce the computational time for the Espresso algorithm, we removed patterns and instances occurring fewer than three times.

4.2 Results

Figure 4 shows the precision of each method in accordance with the number of acquired instances. The dotted line depicts the precision curve of the Espresso algorithm. Espresso + exclusiveness constraint (depicted in dash line) improved the precision of extracted instances by 2.4 percents (with 4305 instances) and 1.3 percents (with 6765 instances). The proposed method (in solid line) with exclusive and sibling relations outperformed other baselines. In particular, the proposed method improved the precision from Espresso by 4.4 percents (with 4305 instances) and 2.1 percents (with 6765 instances). This result demonstrates that prior knowledge about sibling relations improves the performance of set expansion.

Table 1 shows the top 15 instances with high scores of Shinto shrine and temple categories, which belong to the same sibling group, acquired by each method in the 5th iteration. In Table 1, we divided instances into correct or incorrect ones. In Table 1, Espresso and Espresso + exclusiveness constraint obtained many incorrect instances, but each method acquired different instances. In Espresso, some instances (e.g., "Hachiman Shrine" and "Dazaifu Tenman-gu") were identified as instances of both Shinto shrine and temple categories. In contrast, Espresso + exclusiveness constraint prohibits an instance from belonging to multiple categories and tries to choose the best category for the instance. This example suggests that mutual exclusivity mitigates semantic drift. However, in the temple category, Espresso + exclusiveness constraint obtains many unrelated instances such as "Fukuroya Soy Sauce Shop" and "Adashinomayu Village". The proposed method removed these incorrect instances with knowledge about commonality of the sibling group. These results suggest that sibling relations are useful additional knowledge for set expansion.

Table 2 describes the precision of acquired instances of each category when each method has finished the 5th iteration. Table 2 also describes the improvement ratio of precision of the proposed method against Espresso. In Table 2, each line divides categories into a sibling group. Additionally, Table 2 exhibits the top three filter patterns used in each sibling group, along with their scores. Table 2 shows that the proposed method and Espresso + exclusiveness constraint improved the precision from Espresso in many categories. This fact indicates that sibling relation and exclusivity between categories improve the set expansion accuracy. However, in some categories, knowledge about sibling relations is ineffectual. We classify the possible causes of these failures into two types.

Table 1: Top 15 instances of the Shinto shrine and temple categories obtained by each method.

		Top 15 instances of each method		
category	correct/incorrect	Espresso	Espresso + exclusiveness constraint	The proposed method
Shinto shrine	correct	Hachiman Shrine, Dazaifu Tenman-gu, Meiji Shrine, Tenman-gu, Tsurugaoka Hachiman-gu, Ise Grand Shrine, Yasaka Shrine, Kasuga Shrine, Izummo Shrine, Yasukuni Shrine, Kanda Shrine, Shinto Shrine	Dazaifu Tenman-gu, Meiji Shrine, Hachiman Shrine, Ise Grand Shrine, Tenman-gu, Izumo Shrine, Tsurugaoka Hachiman-gu, Kasuga Shrine, Yasaka Shrine, Yasukuni Shrine, Kanda Shrine, Atago Shrine, Shinto Shrine	Meiji Shrine, Ise Grand Shrine, Dazaifu Tenman-gu, Hachiman-gu, Tsurugaoka Hachiman-gu, Izumo Shrine, Yasaka Shrine, Kasuga Shrine, Tenman-gu, Yasukuni Shrine, Itsukushima Shrine, Kanda Shrine, Atago Shrine, Shinto Shrine
	incorrect	Senso-ji, Narita Mountain, Temple	Narita Mountain, Senso-ji	Narita Mountain
temple	correct	Senso-ji, Zenko-ji, Narita Mountain, Temple	Jio-ji, Tokurin-an	Nanzen-ji, Daitoku-ji, Chion-in, Myoshin-ji, Rokuharamitsu-ji, Shokoku-ji, Jojako-ji, Sekizanzen-in, Raige-in, Konzo-ji, Temple, Temple
	incorrect	Shinto Shrine, Hachiman Shrine, Dazaifu Tenman-gu, Tenman-gu, Tsurugaoka Hachiman-gu, Meiji shrine, Yasaka Shrine, Kasuga Shrine, Ise Grand Shrine, Izumo Shrine, Yasukuni Shrine	Konoshimanimasu Amaterumitama Shrine, Kohata Shrine, Kyoto Prefectural Insho-Domoto Museum of Fine Arts, Adashinomayu Village, Uji-Kanbayashi Musium, Fukuroya Soy Sauce Shop, Kyoto Orthodox Church, Konjyakunishimura, Ichiharaheibei Shop, Kungyokudo, Catholic Miyazu Parish, Ise Bay Tour Boat, Lake Biwa Canal Memorial	Shimogamo Shrine, Imamiya Shrine, Hirano Shrine

1. Low score of filter patterns
2. High precision in the baseline

In cause 1, precision drops in categories (e.g., motor vehicle manufacture, medical supplies manufacture, art museum, and theater categories) of some sibling groups. For example, in motor vehicle manufacture and medical supplies manufacture categories, improvement ratios are -14.44 percent and -2.22 percent, respectively. In this sibling group, the highest score of filter patterns is as low as 0.1837. Recall that scores of filter patterns are computed for a small number of seed instances in a sibling group. Low scores of filter patterns imply that the proposed method could not find patterns with of *Coverage* and *Dispersion*. We suspect that the lack of commonality of categories in the sibling group (e.g., motor vehicle manufacture and medical supplies manufacture) does not fit well to the assumption of using filter patterns. Therefore, investigating the impact of choosing sibling groups would be an interesting future direction of this research.

The film director and the comedian categories are affected by cause 2. In cause 2, although semantic drift does not occur in Espresso, the proposed method filtered out some positive instances. In other words, the proposed method removed correct instances more than incorrect ones. The proposed method forces instances to co-occur with filter patterns but the constraint may be too strong. Moreover, because filter patterns are determined only by seed instances, filter patterns may not cover the common property of newly-acquired instances as the method iterates the bootstrapping process. In order to remedy this effect, it might be necessary to update filter patterns in the middle of iterations.

5 Conclusion

In this paper, we demonstrated that sibling relations between semantic categories provide useful knowledge for set expansion. We proposed the method that uses sibling relations as prior knowledge. In the experiments, we reported that the proposed method gained 4.4 percent improvements (with 4305 instances) from the baseline Espresso algorithm.

However, as explained in Section 4.2, the proposed method suffers from some side effects. We suspect that the causes of the side effects derive from the design of sibling groups and the constant use of filter patterns. Addressing these issues is left for future work. We also plan to extend this approach for extracting relation instances where each relation has semantic constraints on arguments (entity instances) and where pairwise relations (e.g., *is-president-of* and *is-citizen-of*) also have hierarchy (e.g., entailment and causality relations).

Table 2: Precision for each category and each method after five iterations.

category	Espresso (%)	Espresso + exclusiveness constraint(%)	The proposed method(%)	improvement ratio(%)	filter patterns (top 3)	pattern score
Shinto shrine	72.22	73.33	75.56	3.33	precicnct plum *hatsumode*	0.9658 0.5946 0.5266
temple	14.44	37.78	63.33	48.89		
Japanese city	97.78	97.78	100.00	2.22	live go leave	1.0000 1.0000 0.9319
American city	28.89	34.44	36.67	7.78		
Chinese city	37.78	58.89	60.00	22.22		
infection	26.67	47.78	47.78	21.11	illness treatment symptom	1.0000 0.9658 0.9658
mental illness	34.44	46.67	46.67	12.22		
film director	97.78	97.78	74.44	-23.33	original work masterpiece best work	0.6235 0.5832 0.3167
cartoonist	87.78	86.67	91.11	3.33		
novelist	95.56	93.33	94.44	-1.11		
car	95.56	95.56	95.56	0.00	drive own car you	0.7572 0.5510 0.5409
motorcycle	83.33	83.33	93.33	10.00		
board game	24.44	23.33	22.22	-2.22	play game enjoy	0.9092 0.8651 0.4434
computer game	98.89	98.89	98.89	0.00		
card game	63.33	61.11	61.11	-2.22		
motor vehicle manufacture	62.22	62.22	47.78	-14.44	stock quote Takeda Pharmaceutical meeting	0.1837 0.1333 0.1333
medical supplies manufacture	5.56	5.56	3.33	-2.22		
Asian country	34.44	33.33	33.33	-1.11	Japan nation speak	1.0000 1.0000 1.0000
African country	44.44	45.56	45.56	1.11		
European country	44.44	48.89	48.89	4.44		
art museum	35.56	37.78	17.78	-17.78	outward appearance front yard close	0.1618 0.1203 0.1082
theater	50.00	50.00	24.44	-25.56		
island	66.67	66.67	61.11	-5.56	flow fish sea	0.5757 0.4412 0.3749
mountain	96.67	96.67	92.22	-4.44		
river	95.56	95.56	95.56	0.00		
radio station	20.00	61.11	61.11	41.11	program broadcasting announcer	0.9658 0.8630 0.8630
TV station	68.89	67.78	67.78	-1.11		
station	98.89	100.00	100.00	1.11	get off near Haneda Airpoat	0.6989 0.6042 0.5090
airport	37.78	37.78	44.44	6.67		
chemical element	20.00	20.00	20.00	0.00	contain quantity component	1.0000 0.9299 0.8518
chemical combination	41.11	41.11	41.11	0.00		
lake	31.11	21.11	21.11	-10.00	beside command cape	0.8518 0.7146 0.6618
pool	2.22	0.00	0.00	-2.22		
actor	95.56	94.44	94.44	-1.11	picture movie perform	0.8920 0.8518 0.8324
comedian	98.89	98.89	97.78	-1.11		
bacterium	37.78	45.56	40.00	2.22	bacterium bacillus microbe	0.4585 0.4460 0.4183
virus	32.22	28.89	14.44	-17.78		
news paper	48.89	48.89	53.33	4.44	publish article print	0.8920 0.7635 0.5698
magazine	44.44	44.44	96.67	52.22		
publisher	32.22	23.33	97.78	65.56	publisher familiar manufacture	0.6473 0.2014 0.1656
record company	38.89	47.78	48.89	10.00		

Acknowledgments

This research was partly supported by JST, PRESTO. This research was partly supported by JSPS KAKENHI Grant Numbers 23240018 and 23700159.

References

Steven Abney. 2004. Understanding the yarowsky algorithm. *Comput. Linguist.*, 30(3):365–395.

Kedar Bellare, Partha Pratim Talukdar, Giridhar Kumaran, O Pereira, Mark Liberman, Andrew Mccallum, and Mark Dredze. 2007. Lightlysupervised attribute extraction for web search. In *Proceedings of Machine Learning for Web Search Workshop, NIPS 2007*.

Huanhuan Cao, Daxin Jiang, Jian Pei, Qi He, Zhen Liao, Enhong Chen, and Hang Li. 2008. Context-aware query suggestion by mining click-through and session data. In *Proceedings of the 14th ACM SIGKDD international conference on Knowledge discovery and data mining*, pages 875–883.

Andrew Carlson, Justin Betteridge, Richard C. Wang, Estevam R. Hruschka Jr., and Tom M. Mitchell. 2010. Coupled semi-supervised learning for information extraction. In *Proceedings of the Third ACM International Conference on Web Search and Data Mining*.

Michael Collins and Yoram Singer. 1999. Unsupervised models for named entity classification. In *In Proceedings of the Joint SIGDAT Conference on Empirical Methods in Natural Language Processing and Very Large Corpora*, pages 100–110.

James R. Curran, Tara Murphy, and Bernhard Scholz. 2007. Minimising semantic drift with mutual exclusion bootstrapping. In *Pacific Association for Computational Linguistics*, pages 172–180.

Marti A. Hearst. 1992. Automatic acquisition of hyponyms from large text corpora. In *Proceedings of the 14th conference on Computational linguistics*, pages 539–545.

Sadao Kurohashi, Sadao Kurohashi, and Makoto Nagao. 1994. Kn parser : Japanese dependency/case structure analyzer. In *In Proceedings of the Workshop on Sharable Natural Language Resources*, pages 48–55.

Alexander Maedche and Steffen Staab. 2001. Ontology learning for the semantic web. *IEEE Intelligent Systems*, 16(2):72–79.

Roberto Navigli, Paola Velardi, Universit Roma, and La Sapienza. 2003. Ontology learning and its application to automated terminology translation. *IEEE Intelligent Systems*, 18(1):22–31.

Etzioni Oren, Banko Michele, and Cafarella Michael J. 2006. Machine reading. In *Proceedings of The Twenty-First National Conference on Artificial Intelligence and the Eighteenth Innovative Applications of Artificial Intelligence Conference*.

Patrick Pantel and Dekang Lin. 2002. Discovering word senses from text. In *Proceedings of the eighth ACM SIGKDD international conference on Knowledge discovery and data mining*, pages 613–619.

Patrick Pantel and Marco Pennacchiotti. 2006. Espresso: Leveraging generic patterns for automatically harvesting semantic relations. In *Proceedings of the 21st International Conference on Computational Linguistics and 44th Annual Meeting of the Association for Computational Linguistics*, pages 113–120.

Patrick Pantel and Deepak Ravichandran. 2004. Automatically labeling semantic classes. In *Proceedings of Human Language Technology/North American chapter of the Association for Computational Linguistics*, pages 321–328.

Patrick Pantel, Eric Crestan, Arkady Borkovsky, Ana-Maria Popescu, and Vishnu Vyas. 2009. Web-scale distributional similarity and entity set expansion. In *Proceedings of the 2009 Conference on Empirical Methods in Natural Language Processing*, pages 938–947.

Marco Pennacchiotti and Patrick Pantel. 2011. Automatically building training examples for entity extraction. In *Proceedings of the Fifteenth Conference on Computational Natural Language Learning*, pages 163–171.

Kugatsu Sadamitsu, Kuniko Saito, Kenji Imamura, and Genichiro Kikui. 2011. Entity set expansion using topic information. In *Proceedings of the 49th Annual Meeting of the Association for Computational Linguistics: Human Language Technologies: short papers*, pages 726–731.

Asuka Sumida, Naoki Yoshinaga, and Kentaro Torisawa. 2008. Boosting precision and recall of hyponymy relation acquisition from hierarchical layouts in wikipedia. In *Proceedings of the Sixth International Conference on Language Resources and Evaluation*.

Vishnu Vyas and Patrick Pantel. 2009. Semi-automatic entity set refinement. In *Proceedings of Human Language Technologies: The 2009 Annual Conference of the North American Chapter of the Association for Computational Linguistics*, pages 290–298.

Vishnu Vyas, Patrick Pantel, and Eric Crestan. 2009. Helping editors choose better seed sets for entity set expansion. In *Proceedings of the 18th ACM conference on Information and knowledge management*, pages 225–234.

David Yarowsky. 1995. Unsupervised word sense disambiguation rivaling supervised methods. In *In Proceedings of the 33rd Annual Meeting of the Association for Computational Linguistics*, pages 189–196.

Building a Diverse Document Leads Corpus Annotated with Semantic Relations

Masatsugu Hangyo **Daisuke Kawahara** **Sadao Kurohashi**
Graduate School of Informatics, Kyoto University
Yoshida-honmachi, Sakyo-ku
Kyoto, 606-8501, Japan
{hangyo,dk,kuro}@nlp.ist.i.kyoto-u.ac.jp

Abstract

In these days, semantic analysis has been actively studied in natural language processing. For the study of semantic analysis, corpora with semantic annotations are essential. Although there are such corpora annotated on newspaper articles, there are various genres and styles, including linguistic expressions that are not found in newspaper articles. In this paper, we build a diverse document leads corpus annotated with semantic relations. To reduce the workload of annotators and annotate as many various documents as possible, we restrict the annotation target of each document to only the first three sentences. We have completed building a corpus of 1,000 documents and report the statistics of this corpus.

1 Introduction

In recent years, semantic analysis including predicate-argument structure analysis and anaphora resolution, has been studied as a subsequent task of syntactic parsing. Most existing studies of semantic analysis have used newspaper corpora with manual annotation. However, there are sources other than newspapers, such as encyclopedias, diaries and novels each with diverse styles in each genre. There are linguistic phenomena that rarely appear in newspapers such as requests and honorific expressions. To deal with texts that include the above phenomena, it is essential to build an annotated corpus that includes diverse-domain documents. Web pages include various genres and text styles such as news articles, encyclopedia articles, blog and business pages. Using web pages as the target documents of annotation, we build a Japanese annotated corpus that consists of various genres.

We annotate predicate-argument structures and anaphoric relations as semantic relations. We illustrate these relations and annotations in Example (1)[1]. "A←*rel*:B" represents annotating B to A with relation *rel*. In the following examples, we sometimes omit annotations that are not related to the discussion.

(1) a. 太郎は　時計を　買った。
Taro-TOP *watch*-ACC *bought.*
'Taro bought a watch.'
(買った ← GA:太郎, WO:時計)

b. 弟に　それを あげた。
Little brother-DAT *it*-ACC *gave*
'He gave it to his little brother.'
(弟 ←NO:太郎
それ ←=:時計
あげた ←GA:太郎, NI:それ, WO:弟)

Predicate-argument structures express the relations between a predicate and its arguments. In Example (1a), the GA (nominative) case of 買った (bought) is 太郎 (Taro) and the WO (accusative) case of 買った is 時計 (watch). In this example, there is a topic marker (は) which hides the case relation between 太郎 and 買った. Since the hidden actual case relation is GA, we annotate which the GA case of 買った is 太郎. Such disappearances

[1]In this paper, we use the following abbreviations: NOM (nominative), ABL(ablative), ACC (accusative), DAT (dative), ALL (allative), GEN (genitive), CMI (comitative), CNJ (conjunction), INS(instrumental) and TOP (topic marker).

of case markers occur also when a topic marker も (too) is used and when an argument is modified by the predicate.

Anaphora is a phenomenon that an expression in text (anaphor) refers to other expressions (referent). In Example (1b), それ (it) refers to 時計 (watch) in the first sentence. In Japanese, ellipses of arguments of a predicate frequently occur. They are called zero anaphora because it is considered that there exist unseen pronouns, which are called zero pronoun, in the place where the ellipsis occurs. By annotating 太郎 with the GA case of あげた (gave), we can express that there is a zero pronoun in the GA case and the referent of the zero pronoun is 太郎. Additionally, we deal with exophoric relations, whose referents do not appear in the document.

There are bridging references among the anaphoric relations. In bridging references, anaphors do not refer to referents directly but some attributes of anaphors refer to antecedents. In Example (1), we can consider that 弟 (little brother) has an attribute "big brother" that refers to 太郎. Various attributes such as hypernym-hyponym, part-whole and contrast relations refer to the referent in bridging references.

We annotate can morphological and syntactic information independently of each sentence and thus the labor of annotators increases linearly with document length. In contrast, since annotating semantic relations deals with inter-sentence relations, elements that annotators should consider increase combinationally. Therefore, if we attempt to annotate whole documents, the annotation processing time of each document becomes longer and few documents could be annotated. Since our target is building a corpus that consists of various documents, we confine the annotation target to the first several sentences. Semantic analysis systems usually use the results of previously analyzed sentences and analysis errors propagate to the following analyses. By building a corpus that consists of document leads, we expect to raise the accuracy of the analysis of both document leads and the document as a whole.

In this paper, we describe related work in Section 2. We describe the documents that the corpus consists of in Section 3 and the annotation criteria in Section 4. In Section 5 we discuss the statistics and properties of the corpus and conclude in Section 6.

2 Related Work

Existing corpora that are annotated with predicate-argument structures and anaphoric relations include the Kyoto University Text Corpus (Kawahara et al., 2002) and the Naist Text Corpus (Iida et al., 2007). These corpora are based on Mainich Newspaper articles from 1995 and annotated with predicate-argument structures and anaphoric relations. Since there are only reports and editorial articles in the newspaper, the writing styles are consistent, making it difficult to adapt a semantic analysis system based on this corpus to texts other than newspaper articles.

Corpora that consist of documents from various genres include the Balanced Corpus of Contemporary Written Japanese (BCCWJ)[2]. BCCWJ includes publications such as books and magazines and text from the Internet. BCCWJ has publications form various genres but the Internet text in BCCWJ is restricted to blogs and forums. For this reason, although company pages and other pages exist on the Internet, they are not included.

Ohara annotated predicate-argument structures defined in FrameNet to the predicates in BCCWJ (Ohara, 2011). Although the predicate-argument structures of FrameNet include the existence of zero pronoun, referents are not annotated if the referents do not exist in the same sentence. Furthermore, since anaphoric relations are not annotated, they do not annotate the inter-sentence semantic relations.

In other languages, corpora dealing with multiple genres include Z-corpus (Rello and Ilisei, 2009) and LMC (Live Memories Corpus) (Rodríguez et al., 2010). Z-corpus consists of Spanish law books, textbooks and encyclopedia articles, and they are annotated with zero anaphoric relations. They only treat zero anaphora and do not treat other anaphora and predicate-argument structures. This is because the zero anaphoric relations can be annotated independently of predicate-argument structures since the pronoun-dropping only occurs in subject in Spanish.

LMC consists of Italian wikipedia and blogs and are annotated with anaphoric relations. They deal with zero anaphora as a part of anaphora, but do not deal with predicate-argument structures. Since pronoun-dropping only occurs in subject also in Italian, they regard the predicates that contain pronoun-

[2] http://www.tokuteicorpus.jp/

Headline : *2008. 07. 10 Thursday*

(1) 気が　つけば 梅雨も
Mood-NOM *stick* *rainy season*-NOM

明けてました。
have ended.

'I think that the rainy season has ended.'

(2) 毎日　暑い 日が　続きますね。
Everyday hot *day*-NOM *continue.*

'It's hot every day.'

(3) 父の　手術も　終わり
Father-GEN *surgery*-NOM *finish*

少しだけ ほっとしています。
short *feel easy.*

'I'm feeling a little better because my father's surgery is over.'
(The rest is omitted.)

Figure 1: Example of a document whose headline does not appear in the body

dropping as anaphors.

3 Annotation Target Document

Most existing corpora annotated with semantic relations consist of newspaper articles. However, there are linguistic phenomena that rarely occur in newspaper articles, and thus we need to target various documents in order to study these phenomena. Using the web without limiting by domain, we collect various documents. To build the annotated corpus consisting of various documents, we need to reduce the workload of each document. We limit the annotating targets to the first three sentences of the document leads. The target number of documents in this corpus is 1,000 documents.

There are many inadequate documents that should not be included in the corpus in the web documents. Checking and filtering them all manually is time-consuming. The number of documents in the web is much more than the target number of documents. Therefore, we first filter out inadequate documents automatically by simple rules. Then, the remaining documents are checked manually and we only annotate the adequate documents.

Headline : 売布神社 'Mefu shrine'

(1) どもども、 森田です。
Hi, *be Morita.*

'Hi, I'm Morita.'

(2) さてさて、 前回
Now, *previous time*

中山寺に　行きましたが、 その
Nakayama temple-LOC *went but,* *that*

続きです。
continuation

'Now, this is the continuation of my previous article when I went to Nakayama temple.'
(Three sentences are ommited)

(6) この 池の　左上あたりに
This *pond*-GEN *upper-left*-LOC

歩いていくと、 売布神社 に
walk to *Mefu shrine*-LOC

着きます。
reach

'Walking around the upper-left of the pond, I had reached Mefu shrine.'
(The rest is omitted.)

Figure 3: Example of a document that cannot be understood without its headline

3.1 Inadequate Documents for Semantic Annotation

Language is used based on a shared situation between a speaker/writer and an audience/reader. The topic of the speech and the document has some sort of relevance to the situation.

When annotating the morphological and syntactic information, there is no need to consider this shared situation because of dealing with each sentence independently. However, in a semantic relation corpus, the shared situation must be considered. Since we deal with only text as our annotation target, documents retering to figures, tables and hyperlinks are inadequate for this corpus.

Some documents have headlines and they often have a key role to interpret the documents. However, we remove the headlines from the annotation target

Headline : 地震被害 264 億円に 県まとめ 'The damage caused by the earthquake reached 26.4 billion yen according to Prefectural survey

(1) 岩手・宮城内陸地震の 被害は 22 日現在、
Iwate-Miyagi inland earthquake-GEN *damage*-TOP *as of 22nd,*

県災害対策本部の まとめで 264 億円に 膨らんだ。
disaster countermeasures office of prefecture-GEN *survey*-INS *26.4 billion*-ACC *swelled.*

'According to a survey by The Disaster Countermeasures Prefectural Office, the damage to Iwate-Miyagi inland earthquake swelled to 26.4 billion as of the 22nd.'

(2) 依然として 農村、土木関係を 中心に 被害が 拡大している。
Still *farming village and construction*-ACC *focus on damage*-NOM *is increasing.*

'The damage is still increasing with focus on farming villages and construction.'
(The rest is omitted.)

Figure 2: Example of a document that the elements of its headline appear in the first three sentences

because some of the headlines are ungrammatical sentences such as series of noun phrases. In newspaper articles, there are sentences in the leads that are abstract of the whole document and most of such documents can be understood without headlines. In web pages, some documents do not have sentences acting as an abstract and some documents cannot be understood without headlines. On the other hand, if the headlines are the date of the blog articles, the documents can be understood without headlines. We discard documents that cannot be understood without their headlines.

We automatically determine if a document has a headline. Web pages have structure information such as HTML tag, but the headlines are sometimes described by tags other than the <h> tag, which renders headlines, and there is non-headline text which are marked up with <h> tags. Therefore, we determine the headline by the content of the text. If the first sentence does not end with punctuation or ends with a noun phrase, we determine that the first sentence is the headline, otherwise we determine that the document does not have a headline. If the first sentence is the headline, we extract the following three sentences. If the first sentence is not a headline, we extract the first three sentences. We deal with these extracted sentences as our annotation target. If the document cannot be understood with only these sentences, the document is not included in the corpus. Before manual filtering, the documents which seem that they cannot be understood without the headline are removed automatically. The understandable documents are determined by the following criteria.

If no words in the headline appear in the body of the document, it is assumed that removing the headline has little influence to understand the semantic relations. For example, in Figure 1 since the headline is the date, removing the headline have no effect on understanding the document. In case of that all the words in the headline appear in the first three sentences, it would be apparent that the semantic relations can be understood without the headline. In Figure 2, the first sentence has a role as the abstract and the all content words in the title appear in the first three sentences. In this case, the document can be understood without the headline. On the other hand, if the words in the headline are only mentioned after the first three sentences, it is hard to understand the document because it is impossible to reconstruct the information in the headline from the first three sentences. In Figure 3, 売布神社 (Mefu shrine) appears in the 6th sentence. However, 売布神社 does not appear in the first three sentences, so that it is difficult to understand the context that the author was going to Mefu shrine. Therefore, if the word in the headline only appears after the first three sentences, we determine that removing the headline makes the semantic relation difficult to be understood and we remove the document from the corpus automatically.

3.2 Determination of Inadequate Document

The documents collected form the web include many unsuitable documents for annotation. We determine that the following documents are difficult to annotate and are not included in the corpus.

Need technical knowledge to understand It is difficult to annotate documents that require technical knowledge because the annotator cannot understand these documents correctly.

Discontinuous sentences Collected documents possibly contain continuous sentences that are erroneously extracted from originally separated areas in the layout. Such documents are not suitable for inter-sentential semantic annotation.

Using too much slang It is difficult to annotate text that contains too much slang.

We automatically remove the documents that have the following sentences.

- End with a noun phrase: most of such sentences are rhetorical sentences or the part of a list.
- Not end with a Japanese period: these sentences are likely to be ungrammatical such as an error of the text extraction
- More than 10 phrases: the results are often caused by morphological analysis errors.
- Contain Roman characters: these are frequently used in technical terms, acronyms or slang in Japanese, and thus they indicate that the document is domain-specific or unnatural Japanese.
- Include stop phrases shown in Table 1: these phrases are defined to eliminate input forms and automatically generated pages.

Additionally, in order to remove duplicate pages, we remove documents whose edit distance is less than 50 to another document.

ボタンを押してください
(please push the button)
自動的に移動します
(should automatically go to another page)
検索できます
(can search)

Table 1: Examples of stop phrases

4 Annotation Criteria

4.1 Types of Annotation

We annotate many types of information: morpheme, phrase, dependency, named entity, predicate-argument structure and anaphoric relation. The predicate-argument structure and anaphoric relation correspond to semantic relations. The annotations of morpheme, phrase and dependency are necessary to annotate these semantic relations in order to define the annotation unit. A named entity is not needed to annotate the semantic relations, but we annotate named entities, as they provide good clues for semantic analysis.

We annotate morpheme, phrase and dependency by the criteria of the Kyoto University Text Corpus.

We define a basic phrase, which is composed of one independent word and preceeding and following attached words, as the annotation unit for the predicate-argument structure and the anaphoric relation. We show an example of the partitions by basic phrases in Example (2). We annotate the predicate-argument structure and the anaphoric relation to each basic phrase and the arguments and the referents are selected from basic phrases. If the referent is a compound noun, we consider the head basic phrase of the compound noun as the argument and the referent. In Example (2), the referent of 党 (party) is 国民新党 (People's New Party) and thus we annotate 新党 (new party), which is the head of 国民新党, as the referent.

(2) 7月17日 国民 新党 災害
July 17th People new party disaster
対策 事務 局長と して、
countermeasures office cheaf-ABL *do*
党を 代表して 現地へ
party-ACC *represent field*-ALL
向かいました。
went
(党 ←=:新党)

We annotate the predicate-argument structure in the same way as the Kyoto University Text Corpus. The arguments are sorted into three types. One is the argument which has dependency relation with

Author
Reader
Unspecified-Person
Unspecified-Matter
Unspecified-Situation

Table 2: Candidate referents of zero exophora

ORGNIZATION
PERSON
LOCATION
ARTIFACT
DATE
TIME
MONEY
PERCENT

Table 3: The types of Named entity

predicate, another is the argument omitted in zero anaphora and the other is the argument omitted in zero exophora. In zero anaphora and zero exophora annotation, we annotate whether zero pronoun exists and also the referent of the zero pronoun as information of the argument. We show the candidate referents of zero exophora in Table 2.

In the Kyoto University Text Corpus, GA2 case is defined for double-subject construction and they are annotated as the following example.

(3) 彼は　ビールが　飲みたい。
He-TOP *beer*-NOM *want to drink.*
'He wants to drink beer.'
(飲みたい ←GA2:彼, GA:ビール)

In Example (4), since "象が長い" (The elephant is long) is a contrived expression, 象 is not handled as the argument of GA2 case under the basis of the Kyoto University Text Corpus. In contrast, we deal with words that express a topic as the argument of GA2 case and thus annotated "GA2:象, GA:鼻" to 長い.

(4) 象は　鼻が　長い。
Elephant-TOP *trunk*-NOM *long.*
'The elephant's trunk is long'
(長い ←GA2:象, GA:鼻)

The anaphoric relations are annotated according to the criteria of the Kyoto University Text Corpus. In the Kyoto University Text Corpus, the anaphoric relations are categorized into three types. The first of these is the anaphoric relation that has a coreference relation and we annotate this relation by using "=" tag. In Example (5), 自分 (himself) and ティーンエージャー (teenager) are coreferential and we annotate "=:ティーンエージャー" to 自分.

(5) ティーンエージャーが、 懸命に
Teenager-NOM *intently*
ライトセーバーを 振り回している
Lightsaber-ACC *be swinging*
自分の　姿を　密かに
himself-GEN *figure*-ACC *secretly*
ビデオに 収めた。
video-DAT *took.*
'A teenager secretly took a video of himself intently swinging a Lightsaber.'
(自分 ←=:ティーンエージャー)

The second anaphoric relations is the bridging reference that can be expressed in the form "A の B" (B of A), and we annotate "NO:A" to B. In 相手 (opposition) of Example (6), it is possible to express "ラズナーの相手" (the opposition of Rasner) and so we annotate "NO:ラズナー" to 相手.

(6) アタマの　先発は　ラズナー、
First-GEN *starter*-TOP *Rasner,*
相手は　陽と
opposition-TOP *You*-ABL
なっています。
is
'First starter is Rasner and the opposition is You.'
(相手 ←NO:ラズナー)

The third anaphoric relations is anaphoric relations that do not have a coreference relation and the bridging reference cannot be expressed in the form, "A の B" (B of A). We annotate these with "≃." In Example (7), the hyponym of 語学 (language study) refers to 英語 (English) in the first sentence and is a bridging reference and it is impossible to express "英語の語学" (language study of English). Therefore, we annotate "≃:英語" to 語学.

(7) 英語　力を　付けたい
English power-ACC *want to acquire*
読者の　ために 毎月　様々な
reader-GEN *for* *every month varied*
学習法を　特集します。
learning method-ACC *feature.*
'We feature varied learning methods for readers who want to acquire English-language ability every month.'

語学は　モチベーションが
Language study-TOP motivation-NOM
大事。
important.

'Motivation is important for language study.'
(語学 ←≃:英語)

In the Kyoto University Text Corpus, the referents of anaphoric relations are confined to the expressions that are mentioned in the document itself, but we additionally annotate exophora that refer to the author and the reader. The details of this are described in Section 4.2.

We annotate named entities according to the basis of IREX[3]. Named entities are expressed by their scope and type. The types of Named entity are 8 types shown in Table 3. In Example (8), ラズナー (Rasner) is annotated with "PERSON" and ホークス (Hawks) is annotated with "ORGANIZATION."

(8) そこで ラズナー と ホークス の
And so *Rasner*-COM *Hawks*-GEN
今季　対戦　成績を
this season match-up result-ACC
掲載します。
post.
(ラズナー ←PERSON
ホークス ←ORGNIZATION)

In the actual annotation, we first automatically annotated by the Japanese morphological analyzer JUMAN[4] and the Japanese predicate-argument structure analyzer KNP[5], and then manually modified the annotation by using the GUI tool.

4.2 Mentions of Author and Reader

The author and the reader of the document are important in discourse. Since there are phenomena that are influenced by the author/reader and the author/reader tend to be omitted, the author/reader behave differently from other discourse elements. Because of this, it is important to detect which elements are the author/reader in the document.

Because the author/reader rarely appear in context of the newspaper corpus, the author/reader have not been treated properly in existing research. However, the author/reader often appear in context of the documents other than the newspaper articles. In case of the author/reader appearing in the document, the author/reader sometimes are not mentioned explicitly. In Figure 1, the author appears in the discourse but there is no mention of the author. On the other hand, the author/reader are mentioned in the documents by various expressions other than personal pronouns. Sometimes the mentions of the author/reader are proper names or position names. In Example (9), the author is mentioned by such as こま, (Koma) which is a proper name, 主婦 (housewife) and 母 (mother), which are the position name.

(9) 東京都に　住む 「お気楽
Tokyo-metropolis-LOC *live "easygoing*
主婦」　こま です。
housewife" be Koma.
'I am Koma, an easygoing housewife living in Tokyo metropolis.'
(主婦 ←=:Author
こま ←=:主婦)

0才と　6才の
0 years old-COM *6 years old*-GEN
男の子の　母を　しています。
boys-GEN *mother*-ACC *doing*

'I am the mother of two boys who a baby and 6 years old.'
(母 ←=:主婦)

Additionally, since personal pronouns are little-used in Japanese, it is difficult to identify which element is the author/reader[6]. Therefore, identifying which elements are the author/reader requires to annotate the mentions of the author/reader expricitly.

To annotate the mentions of the author/reader in discourse, we annotate "=:Author" and "=:Reader" to the mentions of the author/reader as exophora. Assuming that the author and the reader are only one element in each document, we annotate respectively "=:Author" and "=:Reader" up to one expres-

[3]http://nlp.cs.nyu.edu/irex/NE/df990214.txt
[4]http://nlp.ist.i.kyoto-u.ac.jp/EN/index.php?JUMAN
[5]http://nlp.ist.i.kyoto-u.ac.jp/EN/index.php?KNP

[6]In English, it can be assumed that the expression which have a coreference relation with "I" is the author.

No. of documents	1000
No. of sentences	3000
No. of morphemes	59644
No. of phrases	18905
No. of basic phrases	23938
No. of annotated basic phrases	14865

Table 4: Statistics of the corpus

	Explicit	Implicit	No appearance
Author	258	364	378
Reader	105	290	605

Table 5: Author/reader appearance in documents

sion. If the author/reader is mentioned in some expressions, which are coreferential, we annotate it to one of them. In Example (9), the three underlined parts are the author mentions and thus we annotate "=:Author" to 主婦.

In the web site of an organization such as a company, the site administrator often writes the document on behalf of the organization. In such case, we annotate the organization as the author. In Example (10), it is thought that the site administrator wrote the document to represent 神戸徳州会病院 (Kobe Tokusukai Hospital), and so 病院, which is the head of 神戸徳州会病院, is annotated with "=:Author."

(10) 神戸 徳州会 病院では 地域の
Kobe Tokusukai hospital-TOP *area*-GEN
医療 機関との 連携を
medical agency-COM *coordination*-ACC
大切にしています。
value
'Kobe Tokusukai Hospital values coordination with community medical agency.'
(病院 ←=:Author)

5 Statistics of the Corpus and Discussion

1,000 documents have been annotated by three annotators. The statistics of the annotated corpus is listed in Table 4. More than half of the basic-phrases are annotated with some relations. The corpus includes various documents such as personal web sites, news articles, publicity pages of local governments, billing pages and recipe pages. There are some documents that cannot be categorized uniquely such as publicity blog articles from companies.

The number of the documents with respect to types of the author/reader annotations are shown in Table 5. "Explicit" means that an author or a reader is mentioned explicitly and annotated. "Implicit" means that an author or a reader is not mentioned explicitly but is referred from zero pronouns as zero exophora. The remaining documents fall into "No appearance." As a result, the author appeared in the discourse on about 63% of documents and the reader appreared on about 39%. The author/reader are sometimes not mentioned explicitly though the author/reader appear in the discourse.

Word	Frequency
私 (I)	63
弊社 (our company)	12
店 (shop)	10
会 (society)	10
当社 (our company)	9
自分 (self)	8
管理人 (moderator)	5
病院 (hospital)	3
主婦 (housewife)	2
カーブス (Curves)	1
こま (Koma)	1

Table 6: Example of the mentions of authors

Word	Frequency
皆様 (you all)	28
客 (customer)	24
あなた (you)	23
方 (gentleman/lady)	9
自分 (self)	8
人 (person)	7
自身 (self)	3
読者 (reader)	1
生徒 (student)	1
贈り主 (giver)	1
市民 (citizen)	1

Table 7: Examples of the mentions of readers

The author appeared in documents 356 times and the reader appeared 134 times. The examples and their frequency are shown in Table 6 and Table 7. Among words that mention the author, 私 (I) is the most frequent expression, which appeared 63 times, but there are various words such as the position names (管理人 (moderator), and 主婦 (housewife)), the words indicating organization (店 (shop) and 病院 (hospital)) and the proper names (こま (Koma) and カーブス (Curves)). Since there are 96 words which appeared once in the whole corpus and 24 words which appeared twice, many words

	Anaphora	Exophora	Total
GA	1703	2488	4191
WO	594	100	694
NI	409	388	797
GA2	72	116	188
Total	2778	3092	5870

Table 8: Number of zero anaphora/exophora

	Author	Reader	Others	Total
GA	602	176	925	1703
WO	8	4	582	594
NI	78	44	287	409
GA2	23	8	41	72
Total	711	232	1835	2778

Table 9: Breakdown of zero anaphora

become mentions of the author depending on the context. Among words that mention the reader, the frequency of 客 (customer) is the second most frequent word after 皆様 (you all). This is because many of the web pages assuming potential readers are business pages. There are the words assuming document-specific readers such as 生徒 (student), 贈り主 (giver) and 市民 (citizen). The words that are used for both author and reader includes 自分 (self).

The numbers of the annotated zero anaphora and zero exophora are shown in Table 8. In this Table, the zero anaphora/exophora occurred most frequently in GA (nominative) case and about 60% of them are zero exophora. There is not much difference between the total of the zero anaphora and the zero exophora between WO (accusative) case and NI (dative) case, but the ratio of the zero exophora of NI case is larger than that of WO case. The breakdown of the numbers of zero anaphora is shown in Table 9 and one of zero exophora is shown in Table 10. In Table 9, "Author" and "Reader" mean that the referent of zero anaphora has a coreference relation with the author and the reader. Table 9 and Table 10 indicate that the one third of the referents of GA case are the author and the one sixth is the reader. In contrast, the reader is more than the author for the referent of zero exophora in NI case. In WO case, there are few referents that refer to the author or the reader and about 80% of the referents of zero exophora is unspecified-person and unspecified-matter.

The numbers of the annotated anaphoric and exophoric relations are shown in Table 11. The breakdowns are shown in Table 12 and Table 13. Table 11

	Anaphora	Exophora	Total
=	2201	363	2564
NO	3185	201	3386
$\simeq$	757	43	800
Total	6143	607	6750

Table 11: Number of anaphoric/exophoric relations

	Author	Reader	Others	Total
=	100	29	2072	2201
NO	256	96	2833	3185
$\simeq$	31	24	702	757
Total	387	149	5607	6143

Table 12: Breakdown of anaphoric relations

indicates that most reference relations are anaphoric relations regardless of types. Since NO relations are more than $\simeq$, more bridging references can be rephrased as the form "A の B."

The inter-annotator agreements are shown in Table 14 and Table 15[7]. Only the agreement of coreference, is annotated by "=," is calculated by the MUC score (Vilain et al., 1995). For the agreement of other cases, we show only representative cases and "Total" includes cases that are omitted from the table. In Table 15, although the agreements of GA and WO are very high, that of GA2 is very low. It is because that GA2-case sometimes can be rephrased to other cases. For example, since it is possible to rephrase Example(11) to both (12) and (13), there are two annotation candidates, (11a) and (11b). We had set up a criterion that a case marker other than GA2 to which the target expression can be paraphrased is preferred to GA2. However, the judgment on such paraphrasing was not consistent between the annotators. Similarity, the judgment on paraphrasing to NO (A の B) was not stable, and this instability was a cause of the low agreement of $\simeq$.

(11) 魚は 高くて 買えない
Fish-TOP *too expensive cannot buy*
監督。
director.
'Fish are too expensive for the director to buy.'

a. (買えない ←GA2:監督, GA:魚)
b. (買えない ←GA:監督, WO:魚)

[7]A, B and C indicate each annotator

	Author	Reader	Unspecified-Person	Unspecified-Matter	Unspecified-Situation	Total
GA	930	637	734	95	92	2488
WO	3	9	32	52	4	100
NI	66	153	140	27	2	388
GA2	43	44	25	4	0	116
Total	1042	843	931	178	98	3092

Table 10: Breakdown of zero exophora

	Author	Reader	Unspecified-Person	Unspecified-Matter	Unspecified-Situation	Total
=	258	105	0	0	0	363
NO	95	52	28	26	0	201
≃	16	18	4	5	0	43
Total	369	175	32	31	0	607

Table 13: Breakdown of exophoric relations

A vs. B	A vs. C	B vs. C
0.709	0.770	0.691

Table 14: Agreement of coreference relations

	A vs. B	A vs. C	B vs. C
GA	0.852	0.823	0.865
WO	0.890	0.822	0.848
NI	0.726	0.729	0.766
GA2	0.593	0.385	0.296
NO	0.690	0.610	0.558
≃	0.483	0.375	0.375
Total	0.764	0.724	0.738

Table 15: Agreement of annotation

(12) 監督が 魚が 買えない。
director-NOM *fish*-NOM cannot buy.

(13) 監督が 魚を 買えない。
director-NOM *fish*-ACC cannot buy.

6 Conclusion

In this paper, we described the details of the semantically annotated corpus that consists of various documents in the web. In this corpus, we annotated predicate-argument structures and anaphoric relations as semantic annotation. We focused on the mentions of the author and the reader in the documents and annotated these mentions. In order to reduce the workload of each document, we annotated only the first three sentences. As a result, we built an annotated corpus that consists of 1,000 documents. Our corpus analysis revealed that the author and the reader appeared in many of the documents, these are mentioned in various expressions and have an important role in zero anaphora and zero exophora.

References

Ryu Iida, Mamoru Komachi, Kentaro Inui, and Yuji Matsumoto. 2007. Annotating a japanese text corpus with predicate-argument and coreference relations. In *Proc. of the Linguistic Annotation Workshop*, pages 132–139.

Daisuke Kawahara, Sadao Kurohashi, and Koiti Hasida. 2002. Construction of a japanese relevance-tagged corpus. In *Proc. of LREC'02*.

Kyoko Ohara. 2011. Full text annotation with japanese framenet: Study to annotation semantic frame to bccwj(in japanese). In *Proc. of the 17th Annual Meeting fo the Association for Natural Language Processing*, pages 703–704.

L. Rello and I. Ilisei. 2009. A comparative study of spanish zero pronoun distribution. In *Proc. of the International Symposium on Data and Sense Mining, Machine Translation and Controlled Languages (ISMTCL)*, pages 209–214.

Kepa Joseba Rodríguez, Francesca Delogu, Yannick Versley, Egon W. Stemle, and Massimo Poesio. 2010. Anaphoric annotation of wikipedia and blogs in the live memories corpus. In *Proc. of the Seventh conference on International Language Resources and Evaluation (LREC'10)*.

Marc Vilain, John Burger, John Aberdeen, Dennis Connolly, and Lynette Hirschman. 1995. A model-theoretic coreference scoring scheme. In *Proc. of the 6th conference on Message understanding*, pages 45–52.

Text Readability Classification of Textbooks of a Low-Resource Language

Zahurul Islam, Alexander Mehler and Rashedur Rahman
AG Texttechnology
Institut für Informatik
Goethe-Universität Frankfurt
zahurul,mehler@em.uni-frankfurt.de, kamol.sustcse@gmail.com

Abstract

There are many languages considered to be low-density languages, either because the population speaking the language is not very large, or because insufficient digitized text material is available in the language even though millions of people speak the language. Bangla is one of the latter ones. Readability classification is an important Natural Language Processing (NLP) application that can be used to judge the quality of documents and assist writers to locate possible problems. This paper presents a readability classifier of Bangla textbook documents based on information-theoretic and lexical features. The features proposed in this paper result in an *F-score* that is 50% higher than that for traditional readability formulas.

1 Introduction

The readability of a text relates to how easily human readers can process and understand a text as the writer of the text intended. There are many text related factors that influence the readability of a text. These factors include very simple features such as type face, font size, text vocabulary as well as complex features like grammatical conciseness, clarity, underlying semantics and lack of ambiguity.

Nowadays, teachers, journalists, editors and other professionals who create text for a specific audience routinely check the readability of their text. Readability classification, then, is the task of mapping text onto a scale of readability levels. We explore the task of automatically classifying documents based on their different readability levels. As input, this function operates on various statistics relating to lexical and other text features.

Automatic readability classification can be useful for many Natural Language Processing (NLP) applications. Automatic essay grading can benefit from readability classification as a guide to how good an essay actually is. Similarly, search engines can use a readability classifier to rank its generated search results. Automatically generated documents, for example documents generated by text summarization systems or machine translation systems, tend to be error-prone and less readable. In this case, a readability classification system can be used to filter out documents that are less readable. The system can also be used to evaluate machine translation output. A document of higher readability tends to be better than a document that belongs to a lower readability class.

Research in the field of readability classification started in 1920. English is the dominating language in this field although much research has been done for other languages like German, French, Chinese and so on. These languages are considered as high-density languages as many language resources and tools are available for them. However, many languages are considered to be low-density languages, either because the population speaking the language is not very large or because insufficient digitized text material is available for the language even though it is spoken by millions of people. Bangla is such a language. Bangla, an Indo-Aryan language, is spoken in Southeast Asia, specifically in present day Bangladesh and the Indian state of West Bengal.

With nearly 230 million speakers, Bangla is one of the largest spoken languages in the world, but only a very small number of linguistic tools and resources are available for it. For instance, there is no morphological analyzer, POS tagger or syntax parser available for Bangla.

To create a supervised readability classification, it is important to use a corpus that is already classified for the different levels of readers. In this work, the corpus is collected from textbooks that are used in primary and middle school in Bangladesh. The collected documents are classified according to their readability. So the extracted corpus is ideal for a readability classification task.

In this paper, we present a readability classification based on information-theoretic and lexical features. We evaluate this classifier in comparison with traditional readability formulas that, even though they were proposed in the early stages of readability classification research, are still widely used.

The paper is organized as follows: Section 2 discusses related work followed by an introduction of the corpus in Section 3. The features used for classification are described in Section 4, and our experiments in Section 5 are followed by a discussion in Section 6. Finally, we present our conclusions in Section 7.

2 Related Work

There is no standard approach to measuring text quality. According to Mullan (2008), a good readable English sentence should contain 14 to 22 words. He also stated that if the average sentence length is more than 22 words then the content is not clear. If the average sentence length is shorter than 14 then it is probable that the presentation of ideas is discontinuous.

Much work was done previously in this field and many different types of features were used. We summarize the related research grouped by type:

Lexical Features: In the early stage of readability research fairly simple features were used due to the lack of linguistic resources and computational power. *Average Sentence length* (ASL) is one of them. The ASL can be used as a measure of grammatical complexity assuming that a longer sentence has a more complex grammatical structure than a shorter one. Dale and Chall (1948; 1995) showed that reading difficulty is a linear function of the ASL of the percentage of rare words. They listed $3,000$ commonly known words for the 4th grade.

Gunning (1952) also considered the numbers of sentences and complex words to measure text readability. The formula uses similar lexical features as (Dale and Chall, 1948; Dale and Chall, 1995) with different constants. The Flesch-Kincaid readability index (Kincaid et al., 1975) considers the average number of words per sentence and the average number of syllables per words. They proposed two different formulas, one for measuring how easy a text is to read and the other one for measuring grading level. Senter and Smith (1967) also designed a readability index for the *US Air force* that uses the average number of characters in a word and the average number of words in a sentence. Many of the other readability formulas are summarized in (Dubay, 2004).

English has a long history of readability research, but there is very little previous research in Bangla text readability. Das and Roychudhury (2004; 2006) show that readability formulas proposed by (Kincaid et al., 1975) and (Gunning, 1952) work well for Bangla text. The readability formulas were tested semi-automatically on seven documents, mostly novels. Obviously this data set is small.

Petersen & Ostendorf (2009) and Feng et al. (2009) show that these traditional methods have significant drawbacks. Longer sentences are not always syntactically complex and the syllable number of a single word does not correlate with its difficulty. With recent advancements of NLP tools, a new class of text features is now available.

Language Model Based Features: Collins-Thompson and Callan (2004), Schwarm and Ostendorf (2005), Alusio et al. (2010), Kate et al. (2010) and Eickhoff et al. (2011) use statistical language models to classify texts for their readability. They show that trigrams are more informative than bigram and unigram models. Combining information from statistical language models with other features using Support Vector Machines (SVM) outperform traditional readability measures. Pitler and Nenkova (2008) also used a unigram language model and found that this feature is a strong predictor of readability.

POS-based Features: Parts of Speech (POS)-based grammatical features were shown to be useful in readability classification (Pitler and Nenkova, 2008; Feng et al., 2009; Aluisio et al., 2010; Feng et al., 2010). In the experiment of (Feng et al., 2010), these features outperform language-model-based features.

Syntax-based Features: Text readability is affected by syntactic constructions (Pitler and Nenkova, 2008; Barzilay and Lapata, 2008; Heilman et al., 2007; Heilman et al., 2008). In this line of research, Barzilay and Lapata (2008) show, for example, that multiple noun phrases in a single sentence require the reader to remember more items.

Semantic-based Features: On the semantic level, a paragraph that refers to many entities burdens the reader since he has to keep track of these entities, their semantic representations and how these entities are related. Texts that refer to many entities are extremely difficult to understand for people with intellectual disabilities (Feng et al., 2009). Noemie and Huenerfauth (2009) show how working memory limits the semantic encoding of new information by readers.

Researchers also experimented with semantic features like *lexical chains*, *discourse relations* and *entity grids* (Feng et al., 2010; Barzilay and Lapata, 2008). It has been shown that these features are useful for readability classification.

In this paper, we do not compare our work with any previous work that explores linguistic features. Due to the unavailability of a Bangla syllable identification system, we could not compare our work with readability formulas that use syllable information. We will only compare our proposed features with a baseline system that uses three traditional readability formulas proposed by Gunning (1952) , Dale and Chall (1948; 1995) and Senter and Smith (1967). These traditional formulas are widely used in many readability classification tools.

3 Corpus Extraction

The government agency *National Curriculum and Textbook Board, Bangladesh*[1] makes available textbooks that are used in public schools in Bangladesh. The textbooks cover many different subjects, including Bangla Literature, Social Science, General Science and Religious Studies. These textbooks are for students from grade one to grade ten. All of the textbooks are in Portable Document Format (PDF). Some of them are made by scanning textbooks and some of them are converted from typed text. There is a Bangla OCR (Hasnat et al., 2007) available but it is unable to extract text from the scanned PDF books. Therefore, we only considered textbooks that were converted to PDF from typed text. The *Apache PDFBox*[2] is used to extract text from PDFs. Note that 24 textbooks were extracted from class *two* to class *eight*. After text extraction, it was observed that the text was not written in Unicode Bangla. A non-standard Bangla input method called *Bijoy* is used to type the textbooks. This is an ASCII based Bangla input method that was widely used in the 1990s. The next challenge was to convert non-standard text to Bangla Unicode.

The selected text books were written using a font called *SutonnyMJ* that has many different versions, all of which differ slightly in terms of the code point of some *consonant conjuncts*. The freely available open source CRBLPConverter[3] is used to convert these non-standard Bangla texts to Unicode. To cope with the font of the text, the CRBLPConverter required some slight modifications. Text books not only contain descriptive texts but also contain questions, poems, religious hymns, texts from other languages (e.g., Arabic, Pali) and transcription of Arabic texts (e.g., Surah). Manual work was involved to clean these non-descriptive texts and extract each chapter as a document. Class *two* contains only one

[1]http://nctb.gov.bd/book.php

[2]http://pdfbox.apache.org/

[3]http://crblp.bracu.ac.bd/converter.php

Classes	Documents	Avg. Document Length	Avg. Sentence Length	Avg. Word Length
three	123	65.21	8.07	4.31
four	88	126.25	8.63	4.37
five	43	196.72	9.34	4.41
six	62	130.13	11.53	4.85

Table 1: The Bangla Readability Corpus

textbook and class *six*, *seven* and *eight* contain two textbooks each. To avoid a data sparseness problem, class *two* is merged with class *three* and class *seven* and *eight* are merged with class *six*. Each document is tokenized using a slightly modified version of the tokenizer which is freely available in[4]. Table 1 shows the details of the corpus. The *Average Document Length* shows the average number of sentences per document. The *Average Sentence Length* represents the average number of words in a sentence and *Average Word Length* displays the average number of characters in a word.

It should be noted that 80% of the corpus is used for training and the remaining 20% is used as a test set.

4 Features

4.1 Lexical Features

In this paper, we compare a lexical and information-theoretic classifier of text readability with a classifier based on traditional readability formulas. The literature explores some of the linguistic indicators of readability. This includes the avg. sentence length, avg. word length and the avg. number of difficult words (of more than 9 letters). We develop a classifier of text readability based on lexical and information-theoretic features. We first describe lexical features used by this classifier.

The *Average Sentence Length* is a quantitative measure of syntactic complexity. In most cases, the syntax of a longer sentence is more difficult than the syntax of a shorter sentence. However, children of lower grade levels are not aware of syntax. In any event, a longer sentence contains more entities and children have to remember all of these entities in order to understand the sentence, which makes a longer sentence more difficult for them. As an example, Table 1 shows that the *Average Sentence Length* rises in the text of higher readability classes. The *Average Word Length* is another lexical feature that is useful for readability classification. A longer word carries some difficulties for children at a lower grade level. For example: the word *biodegradable* will be harder to pronounce, spell and understand for children at a lower grade level. This characteristic is reflected in our readability corpus that is shown in Table 1. The *Average Word Length* will be more useful for agglutinative languages such as German, which allows concatenation of morphemes to build longer words.

The *Average Number of Complex Words* feature is related to the *Average Word Length*. The average length of English written words is 5.5 (Nádas, 1984). Table 1 shows that the average word length in our corpus is below 5. Dash (2005) showed that the average word length in the CIIL[5] corpus is 5.12. Majumder et al. (2006) claimed that the average word length in a Bangla news corpus is 8.62. They have mentioned that the average length is higher due to the presence of many hyphenated words in the news corpus. In this work, any word that contains 10 or more characters is considered a complex word. A complex word will be harder to read for children at a lower grade level. The type token ratio (TTR), which indicates the lexical density of text, has been considered as a readability feature too. Low lexical densities involve a great deal of repetition.

The term *Hapax Legomena* is widely used in linguistics referring to words which occur only once within a context or document. These are mostly content words. Kornai (2008) showed that 40% to 60% of the words in larger corpora are *Hapax Legomena*. Documents with more *Hapax Legomena* generally will contain more information. In terms of text readability, the difficulty level will be higher.

4.2 Entropy Based Features

Recently, researchers have independently made the suggestion that the entropy rate plays a role in human communication in general (Genzel and Charniak, 2002; Levy and Jaeger, 2007). The rate of

[4]http://statmt.org/wmt09/scripts.tgz

[5]http://www.elda.org/catalogue/en/text/W0037.html

information transmission per second in a human speech conversation is roughly constant, that is, transmitting a constant number of bits per second or maintaining a constant entropy rate.

Since the most efficient way to send information through a noisy channel is at a constant rate, Plotkin and Nowak (2000) have shown that this principle could be viewed as biological evidence of how human language processing evolved. Communication through a text should satisfy this principle. That is, each sentence of a text, for example, conveys roughly the same amount of information. In order to utilize this information-theoretical notion, we start from random variables and consider their entropy as indicators of readability.

Shannon (1948) introduced entropy as a measure of information. Entropy, the amount of information in a random variable, can be thought of as the average length of the message needed to have an outcome on that variable. The entropy of a random variable X is defined as

$$H(X) = -\sum_{i=1}^{n} p(x_i) \log p(x_i) \quad (1)$$

The more the outcome of X converges towards a uniform distribution, the higher $H(X)$. Our hypothesis is that the higher the entropy, the less readable the text along the feature represented by X. In our experiment, we consider the following random variables: *word probability*, *character probability*, *word length probability* and *word frequency probability* (or frequency spectrum, respectively). Note that there is a correlation between the probability distribution of words and the corresponding distribution of word frequencies. As we use Support Vector Machines (SVM) for classification, these correlations are taken into consideration.

4.3 Kullback-Leibler Divergence-based Features

The *Kullback-Leibler divergence* or *relative entropy* is a non-negative measure of the divergence of two probability distributions. Let $p(x)$ and $q(x)$ be two probability distributions of a random variable X. The relative entropy of these distributions is defined as:

$$D(p||q) = \sum_{i=1}^{n} p(x_i) \log \frac{p(x_i)}{q(x_i)} \quad (2)$$

$D(p||q)$ is an asymmetric measure that considers the number of additional bits needed to encode p, when using an optimal code for q instead of an optimal code for p. In other words: $D(p||q)$ measures how much one probability distribution is different from another distribution. More specifically, if the probability distribution of a document p is closer to q than to q' then the document has a smaller distance to q. The document belongs to the category corresponding to q.

In order to apply this method in our framework we start from a training corpus where for each target class and each random variable under consideration we compute the distribution $q(x)$. This gives a reference distribution such that for a text T whose class membership is unknown, we can compute the distribution $p(x)$ only for T in order to ask how much information we get about $p(x)$ when knowing $q(x)$. Since $q(x)$ is computed for each of the four target classes (see Table 1), this gives for any random variable X four features of *relative entropy*.

5 Experiments and Results

5.1 Baseline System

To measure accuracy of our proposed features, a baseline system is implemented that uses three traditional readability formulas, such as: *Gunning fog readability index* (Gunning, 1952), *Dale–Chall readability formula* (Dale and Chall, 1948; Dale and Chall, 1995) and *Automated readability index* (Senter and Smith, 1967). There are more traditional formulas available that use syllable information, these are not considered for this task due to unavailability of a Bangla syllable identification system. The *Gunning fog readability index* and *Dale–Chall readability formula* both use complex or difficult words. The definition of these words varies slightly. Gunning (1952) defines a complex word as a word that contains more than three syllables and Dale and Chall (1948; 1995) introduce 3000 familiar words. Any word not in the list of 3000 words is considered difficult. For this work, both types of words are defined in the same way, described in section 4.1. We consider any word that has 10 or more letters as a difficult or complex word. Table 2 shows the evaluation of the baseline system. The evaluation shows that these features do not perform well. Among

Features	Accuracy	F-Score
Gunning fog readability index	48.3%	36.5%
Dale–Chall readability formula	48.3%	45.0%
Automated readability index	51.6%	46.2%
All together	53.3%	49.6%

Table 2: Evaluation of baseline system with 3 traditional readability formulas.

Features	Accuracy	F-Score
Average sentence length	51.6%	47.3%
Type token ratio	41.6%	30.6%
Avg. word length	50.3%	46.9%
Avg. number of complex Words	46.6%	34.2%
Hapax legomena	40.0%	28.3%
All together	60.0%	56.5%

Table 3: Evaluation of lexical features.

these formulas, *Automated readability index* is the highest performing formula. Das and Roychudhury (2004; 2006) showed that these traditional features nonetheless work well for Bangla novels. Note that we have used the SMO (Platt, 1998; Keerthi et al., 2001) classifier model in WEKA (Hall et al., 2009) together with the Pearson VII function-based universal kernel PUK (Üstün et al., 2006).

5.2 System with Lexical Features

Lexical features use the same kind of surface features as the traditional readability formulas used in the baseline system (see: Section 5.1). Table 1 shows that the *average sentence length* and difficulty levels are proportional. That means that sentence length increases for higher readability classes. *Average word length* exhibits the same characteristics. These characteristics are reflected in the experiment. These two are the best performing features among all of the lexical features. Table 3 shows the evaluation of the system that uses only lexical features. Although the individual accuracy of some of these features is similar to the traditional formulas, the combination of all lexical features outperforms the baseline system.

5.3 System with Entropy Based Features

As noted earlier, entropy measures the amount of information in a document. The entropy rate is constant in human communication (see Section: 4.2).

Features	Accuracy	F-Score
Word probability	53.3%	49.3%
Character probability	48.3%	35.4%
Word length probability	50.0%	36.9%
Word frequency probability	43.3%	32.4%
Character frequency probability	53.3%	47.7%
Entropy features	61.6%	59.8%
Lexical + entropy features	73.3%	72.1%

Table 4: Evaluation of entropy based features.

The documents in this work are assumed to be a medium of communication between writers and readers. Conversely, information flow of a very readable document will differ from that of a less readable document. So, the constants for the corresponding entropy rates of the different readability classes will differ. As a single feature, these entropy based features perform similarly to lexical features. But, collectively this is the best performing feature set. Among all similar features the random variable with *Word Probability* works better than others. Table 4 shows the results of these features. Adding *lexical* features with *entropy* based features improves *accuracy* and *F-score* substantially.

5.4 System with Kullback-Leibler Divergence-based Features

Relative entropy-based features represent the distance between the test document and target classes. The target class with the lowest distance will be the class of the test document. Five different types of random variables are used in this work (see Section 4.3). The random variable based on *character probabilities* is the best performing individual feature among all features used in this work. However, this feature set performs worse than the *lexical* and *entropy* based features set. The evaluation is shown in Table 5. The combination of all, i.e., *lexical, entropy* and *relative entropy* based features, gives the best result, namely *accuracy* of 75% and *F-score* of 74.1%.

6 Discussion

Das and Roychudhury (2004; 2006) found that traditional readability formulas are useful for Bangla readability classification. However, the experimental results in this paper show that these formulas are

Features	Accuracy	F-Score
4 Word probabilities	50.0%	50.2%
4 Character probabilities	61.6%	61.1%
4 Word length probabilities	48.3%	46.5%
4 Word frequency probabilities	50.0%	45.6%
4 Character frequency probabilities	43.3%	34.2%
20 Relative entropy based features	56.6%	54.0%
Entropy + relative entropy features	68.3%	65.9%
Lexical + entropy + relative entropy based features	75.0%	74.1%

Table 5: Evaluation of Kullback-Leibler Divergence-based Features.

not useful for studies like the one presented here. This is probably due to the fact that these formulas were specially designed for English. One reason for the poor performance is that Bangla script is a syllabic script that has glyphs representing clusters and ligatures.

It also has to be noted that Bangla is an inflectional language, so that the average word length can be longer than that of many other languages.

The lexical features that are assumed to be good indicators of text difficulty did indeed perform well in classification. The respective feature set performs better than the baseline system. *Average sentence length* and *Average word length* do not perform well, as reflected in Table 1. That shows that the average word and sentence lengths are longer in higher readability classes than in lower readability classes.

As an individual feature, each *entropy* based feature performs similarly to other features. However, the combination of the *entropy* based features are the best performing features among all. The classification performance even increases when *entropy* based features are combined with *lexical* features.

Among all *relative entropy* based features, the random variable based on *character probabilities* performs best. This feature performs better than the baseline system. But the performance drops when this feature is added to other *relative entropy* based features. Although the *relative entropy* based feature set performs better than the baseline system, the *lexical* and *entropy* based feature set performs even better. The performance surpasses the baseline system by 50% when *lexical*, *entropy* based and *relative entropy* based features are combined.

7 Conclusion

In this paper, we have presented features for text readability classification of a low resource language. Altogether we have proposed 30 quantitative features. Twenty-five of them are information-theoretic based features. These features do not require any kind of linguistic processing. Recent advances in NLP tools argue that linguistic features are useful for readability classification. However, our experimental results show that lexical and information-theoretic features perform very well. There are many languages in the *Asia Pacific* region that are still considered as low resource languages. These features can be used for readability classification of these languages. As a future work, we plan to explore many other information-theoretic features like *mutual information*, *point wise mutual information* and *motifs*.

8 Acknowledgements

We would like to thank Mr. Munir Hasan from the Bangladesh Open Source Network (BdOSN) and Mr. Murshid Aktar from the National Curriculum & Textbook Board Authority, Bangladesh for their help on corpus collection. We would also like to thank Andy Lücking, Paul Warner and Armin Hoenen for their fruitful suggestions and comments. Finally, we thank three anonymous reviewers. This work is funded by the LOEWE Digital-Humanities project in the Goethe-Universität Frankfurt.

References

Ra Aluisio, Lucia Specia, Caroline Gasperin, and Carolina Scarton. 2010. Readability assessment for text simplification. In *NAACL-HLT 2010: The 5th Workshop on Innovative Use of NLP for Building Educational Applications*.

Regina Barzilay and Mirella Lapata. 2008. Modeling local coherence: An entity-based approach. *Computational Linguistics*, 21(3):285–301.

Kevyn Collins-Thompson and James P Callan. 2004. A language modeling approach to predicting reading difficulty. In *HLT-NAACL*.

Edgar Dale and Jeanne S. Chall. 1948. A formula for predicting readability. *Educational Research Bulletin*, 27(1):11–20+28.

Edgar Dale and Jeanne S. Chall. 1995. *Readability Revisited: The New Dale-Chall Readability formula*. Brookline Books.

Sreerupa Das and Rajkumar Roychoudhury. 2004. Testing level of readability in bangla novels of bankim chandra chattopodhay w.r.t the density of polysyllabic words. *Indian Journal of Linguistics*, 22:41–51.

Sreerupa Das and Rajkumar Roychoudhury. 2006. Readabilit modeling and comparison of one and two parametric fit: a case study in bangla. *Journal of Quantative Linguistics*, 13(1).

Niladri Sekher Dash. 2005. *Corpus Linguistics and Language Technology: With Reference to Indian Languages*. New Delhi: Mittal Publications.

William H. Dubay. 2004. The principles of readability. *Costa Mesa, CA: Impact Information*.

Carsten Eickhoff, Pavel Serdyukov, and Arjen P. de Vries. 2011. A combined topical/non-topical approach to identifying web sites for children. In *Proceedings of the fourth ACM international conference on Web search and data mining*.

Lijun Feng, Noémie Elhadad, and Matt Huenerfauth. 2009. Cognitively motivated features for readability assessment. In *Proceedings of the 12th Conference of the European Chapter of the ACL*.

Lijun Feng, Martin Janche, Matt Huenerfauth, and Noémie Elhadad. 2010. A comparison of features for automatic readability assessment. In *The 23rd International Conference on Computational Linguistics (COLING)*.

Dimitry Genzel and Eugene Charniak. 2002. Entropy rate constancy in text. In *Proceedings of the 40st Meeting of the Association for Computational Linguistics (ACL 2002)*.

Robert Gunning. 1952. *The Technique of clear writing*. McGraw-Hill; Fourh Printing Edition.

Mark Hall, Eibe Frank, Geoffrey Holmes, Bernhard Pfahringer, Peter Reutemann, and Ian H. Witten. 2009. The WEKA data mining software: an update. *ACM SIGKDD Explorations*, 11(1):10–18.

Md. Abul Hasnat, S M Murtoza Habib, and Mumit Khan. 2007. A high performance domain specific ocr for bangla script. In *International Joint Conferences on Computer, Information, and Systems Sciences, and Engineering (CISSE)*.

Michael Heilman, Kevyn Collins-Thompson, and Maxine Eskenazi. 2007. Combining lexical and grammatical features to improve readavility measures for first and second language text. In *Proceedings of the Human Language Technology Conference*.

Michael Heilman, Kevyn Collins-Thompson, and Maxine Eskenazi. 2008. An analysis of statistical models and features for reading difficulty prediction. In *Proceedings of the Third Workshop on Innovative Use of NLP for Building Educational Applications (EANL)*.

Rohit J. Kate, Xiaoqiang Luo, Siddharth Patwardhan, Martin Franz, Radu Florian, Raymond J. Mooney, Salim Roukos, and Chris Welty. 2010. Learning to predict readability using diverse linguistic features. In *23rd International Conference on Computational Linguistics (COLING 2010)*.

S.S. Keerthi, S. K. Shevade, C. Bhattacharyya, and K. R. K. Murthy. 2001. Improvements to Platt's SMO algorithm for SVM classifier design. *Neural Computation*, 13(3):637–649.

J. Kincaid, R. Fishburne, R. Rodegers, and B. Chissom. 1975. Derivation of new readability formulas for Navy enlisted personnel. Technical report, US Navy, Branch Report 8-75, Cheif of Naval Traning, Millington, TN.

András Kornai. 2008. *Mathematical Linguistics*. Springer.

Roger Levy and T. Florian Jaeger. 2007. Speakers optimize information density through syntactic reduction. *Advances in neural information processing systems*, pages 849–856.

Khair Md. Yeasir Arafat Majumder, Md. Zahurul Islam, and Mumit Khan. 2006. Analysis and observations from a bangla news corpus. In *9th International Conference on Computer and Information Technology (ICCIT 2006)*.

W.M.A Mullan. 2008. Dairy science and food technology improving your writing using a readability calculator.

A. Nádas. 1984. Estimation of probabilities in the language model of the ibm speech recognition system. *IEEE Transactions on Acoustics, Speech and Signal Processing*, 32(4):859–861.

Sarah E. Petersen and Mari Ostendorf. 2009. A machine learning approach to reading level assesment. *Computer Speech and Language*, 23(1):89–106.

Emily Pitler and Ani Nenkova. 2008. Revisiting readability: A unified framework for predicting text quality. In *Proceedings of the Conference on Empirical Methods in Natural Language Processing (EMNLP)*.

John C. Platt. 1998. *Fast training of support vector machines using sequential minimal optimization*. MIT Press.

Joshua B. Plotkin and Martik A. Nowak. 2000. Language evolution and information theory. *Journal of Theoretical Biology*, 205(1):147–159.

Sarah E. Schwarm and Mari Ostendorf. 2005. Reading level assessment using support vector machines and statistical language models. In *the Proceedings of the 43rd Annual Meeting on Association for Computational Linguistics(ACL 2005)*.

R.J. Senter and E. A. Smith. 1967. Automated readability index. Technical report, Wright-Patterson Air Force Base.

Claude Elwood Shannon. 1948. A mathematical theory of communication. *The Bell System Technical Journal*, 27(1):379–423.

B. Üstün, W.J. Melssen, and L.M.C. Buydens. 2006. Facilitating the application of support vector regression by using a universal Pearson VII function based kernel. *Chemometrics and Intelligent Laboratory Systems*, 81(1):29–40.

A Hybrid Approach for the Interpretation of Nominal Compounds using Ontology

Sruti Rallapalli, Soma Paul
Language Technologies Research Center
International Institute of Information Technology
Hyderabad
sruti@students.iiit.ac.in
soma@iiit.ac.in

Abstract

Understanding and interpretation of nominal compounds has been a long-standing area of interest in NLP research for various reasons. (1) Nominal compounds occur frequently in most languages. (2) Compounding is an extremely productive word formation phenomenon. (3) Compounds contain implicit semantic relations between their constituent nouns. Most approaches that have been proposed so far concentrate on building statistical models using machine learning techniques and rely on large-scale, domain-specific or open- domain knowledge bases. In this paper we present a novel approach that combines the use of lexical hierarchies such as PurposeNet and WordNet, with WordNet-based similarity measures for the interpretation of domain-specific nominal compounds. We aim at building a robust system that can handle most of the commonly occurring English bigram nominal compounds within the domain.

1 Introduction

Understanding and interpretation of nominal compounds has been a long-standing area of interest in NLP research. The main reasons that make understanding compound nouns an interesting and challenging task are: (1) Compound nouns are a frequent phenomenon in many languages, occurring in different languages with varying frequencies. English and Sanskrit are two languages that display great flexibility in compounding (Ó Séaghdha, 2008). About 3.9 % of the words in Reuters are bigram nominal compounds (Baldwin and Tanaka, 2004). (2) Compounding is a recursive process that can lead to formation of large and complex compounds, that are difficult for comprehension. (3) Compounds usually carry an implicit meaning that may sometimes differ significantly from that of the combining concepts. Consider the example of a *garden knife*. A *garden knife* is interpreted as a knife used in the garden. Here the modifier *garden* modifies the locative information of the head noun *knife*. Alternatively, consider the example of a *gamma knife*. A *gamma knife* is a device used to treat brain tumors by administering gamma radiations in a particular manner. Here, the modifier does not necessarily modify the head, instead they both combine together to denote a different concept. This understanding of the difference in the structure and purpose between *gamma knife* and other kinds of knife cannot be achieved by any means of statistical predictions or morphological and syntactic analyses of the compound.

The most common representations adopted for the interpretation of nominal compounds involve an inventory of verbs, prepositions or abstract semantic relations. Verb and preposition paraphrases bring in lexical ambiguity in the interpretation of the compound, essentially owing to the polysemous nature of verbs and prepositions. For example, *morning tea* and *bar lights* would both be paraphrased using the preposition *in*. However, the paraphrase 'tea in the morning' conveys the *temporal* aspect of the compound, while the paraphrase 'lights in the bar' describes the *location* information in the compound. Due to this polysemous behaviour of prepositions and verbs, a restricted inventory of abstract semantic relations is more favorable for the compound interpretation problem.

Most of the approaches proposed for interpreting nominal compounds fall into one of the two classes (a) supervised machine learning approaches, and (b) unsupervised data driven approaches. These approaches fail to handle the sparseness of data, which is a major issue in case of noun compounds. They collect statistics that use occurrence frequencies of the compounds. Therefore, rarely occurring compounds lead to wrong estimations of probabilities and thereby unreliable interpretations. A third and less frequently adopted alternative involves the use of large-scale, domain-independent, lexical and conceptual hierarchies that provide detailed natural language semantics. Such ontologies promise reliability and accuracy of data but fail to cover equally, lexical items and semantic relations. Moreover, construction of such ontologies is extremely time-consuming, due to which manually built ontologies are never up to date with changes in the language. This motivates us to argue that the most optimal approach to compound interpretation would be the combination of a lexical hierarchy for the frequent and idiosyncratic compounds (Johnston and Busa, 1996) and WordNet-based similarity for those that are not listed in the hierarchy. We show in this paper, that adopting our hybrid approach helps us achieve significant results (70% accuracy) in ontology-based compound interpretation, irrespective of the size, coverage and domain of the ontology. We perform all our experiments using PurposeNet (KiranMayee et al., 2008), which is a purpose-centric ontology of artifacts and semantic relations.

The rest of the paper is divided into the following sections. In section 2, we discuss some related works that use ontologies and also motivate our choice of a hybrid approach using ontology. In section 3, we discuss the architectural design of PurposeNet in brief. We then proceed to explain our hybrid approach in section 4, and discuss the preparation and analysis of data in section 5. We finally produce in section 6, the results for the compound interpretation experiments performed, and then discuss the scope of improvement and future work in section 7.

2 Related Work

The most common approaches to handle compound interpretation are broadly categorized under supervised and unsupervised approaches. The supervised approaches combine machine learning techniques with lexical taxonomies to classify the nominal compounds into one of a set of pre-defined semantic relations. The unsupervised approaches are usually data-driven probabilistic methods that collect statistics on the occurrence frequency of compounds in the corpus and use them to predict the most probable interpretation for the compounds. Other approaches have evolved which focus on the use of large, lexical and conceptual hierarchies, both domain specific and domain independent, for this task. The earliest such approach is by Johnston and Busa (1996). They make use of the Generative Lexicon model proposed by Pustejovsky (1991), that couples lexical semantic representations with mechanisms to capture the relations between those representations and their syntactic expressions. Their lexicon consists of a type, argument, event, and qualia structure for every lexical entry. Phrase structure schemata were developed to compositionally understand the links between the qualia of head nouns and their corresponding modifiers. However, this approach works only for those nouns and noun compounds whose qualia are listed in the lexicon. It also restricts the nominal compounds that can be interpreted by the type of the modifier and the action prescribed in the qualia of the head.

Most of the approaches that followed depend on supervised machine learning and domain specific lexical hierarchies. Rosario and Hearst (2001) mapped the nominal compounds into unique concept IDs and into terms in the MeSH medical ontology. They built different models based on these MeSH descriptor terms and trained artificial neural networks to classify every nominal compound into one of the different semantic relations. Kim and Baldwin (2005) introduced a machine learning approach that used WordNet for classifying compounds based on abstract semantic relations. They built a training set of 1088 manually annotated compounds, and interpreted the test cases using WordNet-based similarity. They calculated the similarity between a given test instance and every training instance in the training set, and predicted the semantic relation of the most similar training instance. They used different similarity measures such as WUP (Wu and Wu, 1994), LCH (Leacock and Chodorow, 1998), JCN (Jiang and Conrath, 1997)and LIN (Lin, 1998) and obtained a good result of 53% accuracy over open domain. The only bottleneck however, is that it requires sufficient training data distributed over the different abstract semantic relations. We therefore increase the robustness of our system by extending ontology search with a module that performs word similarity measurement for compounds.

3 PurposeNet Ontology

3.1 Architectural Design

PurposeNet is a purpose-centric ontology of artifacts, where the artifacts are organized in a multiple inheritance hierarchy. The ontology contains artifacts and relations between them. There are two types of features:

- Descriptive features
- Action features

and three types of relations:

- Subtype
- Component
- Accessory

Every artifact is expressed in terms of 20 descriptive features and 7 action features and is connected to the other artifacts via one or more of the above mentioned relations. While the descriptive features capture information pertaining to the physical nature of the artifact, the action features capture information about the actions performed on and by the artifact, such as its birth, maintenance and destruction. Table 1 shows the descriptive features for *Butter Knife* while Table 2 shows the action features for the *Car*.

Descriptive Features	**Possible Values**	**Butter Knife**
Color	Black, White, Green	any
Constituition	Metal, Plastic, Foam, Rubber	Steel,Metal
Fluidity	Fluid, Non-fluid	Non-fluid
Heaviness	Light-Weight, Moderate-Weight, Heavy-Weight	Light Weight
Inertness	Inert, Reactive, Alkaline, Acidic	Inert
Mobility	Mobile, Immobile	Immobile
Oiliness	Oily, Non-oily	Non-oily
Physical State	Solid, Liquid, Gaseous	Solid
Shape	Cubical, Cuboidal, Cylindrical, Flat	Flat
Size	Big, Small, Huge	Small
Sliminess	Slimy, Non-slimy	Non-slimy
Smell	Pleasant, Unpleasant, Odourless	Odourless
Smoothness	Smooth, Rough	Smooth
Softness	Soft, Hard	Soft
Sound	Silent, Bearable, Unbearable, Noisy	Silent
Stability	Stable, Non-stable	Stable
Subtleness	Subtle, Non-subtle	Non-subtle
Taste	Sweet, Sour, Bitter	Tasteless
Temperature	Hot, Cold, Room-temperature	Room-temperature
Transparency	Transparent, Translucent, Opaque	Opaque
Viscidity	Viscous, Non-viscous	Non-viscous

Table 1: Descriptive features for *Butter Knife*.

3.2 Schema for Handling Nominal Compounds in the Ontology

A nominal compound is a complex construction where two or more different concepts combine together to form a single concept. While on the conceptual level, a nominal compound represents a single concept, it manifests as a set of ordered lexical items, due to which representation of a nominal compound in a knowledge base becomes a challenge by itself. Compounds can be represented by a single unit or a single node in the ontology. They can also be broken into their respective constituents and the constituents be placed under appropriate classes with appropriate relations ascribed between them. We discuss in this section how compounds are handled in different ontologies, and the motivation for the schema adopted in PurposeNet.

WordNet (Fellbaum, 1998) is one of the most notable of the available, large scale, general pur-

Action Feature	Subtype	Definition	Some Values for Car
Birth		Manufacture of artifact	Fix Chassis to Body, Attach Seats, Attach Tyres
Purpose		Purpose of artifact	Transport Human
Maintenance	General Maintenance	Maintenance of artifact	Clean Car, Clean Engine
	Repair Maintenance		Repair Car, Repair Engine
Wear and Tear		Wear and tear of artifact	Burst Tyre, Overheat Engine
ProcessRel		Actions the artifact can perform	Board Passengers, Move from A to B, Alight Passengers
Set up	First time Set up	Set up the artifact for functioning	Check Ignition System, Check Brake
	General Set up		Check Tyre, Check Brake
Result On Destruction		Results on destruction of artifact	Engine recycled to metal, Seats - reused

Table 2: Action features for *Car*.

pose, domain-independent ontologies. Although it focuses mainly on the taxonomies of words, it does not attach any significance to the representation of multi-word expressions (MWEs) such as compounds. Most of the compounds listed in WordNet are represented as a single node in the lexical hierarchy. Ex : wildfire, orange juice and mailman. Such a representation is suitable only to compound nouns that are commonly occurring and in which the relationship between the constituents is unambiguous and easily comprehensible (Mahesh, 1996).

ConceptNet (Havasi, 2007) is a large-scale, commonsense knowledge base, similar in structure to WordNet, but the nodes in ConceptNet are mostly semi-structured English fragments or compound concepts connected to each other by semantic relations. Since all the compound formations are covered as individual nodes in the ontology, ConceptNet fails to explicate the relations within the constituents of the compound, much like WordNet. Further, such a representation has led to redundancy in data. Similar compound constructions are represented as different nodes in the ontology. This fails to capture the similarity between different constructions and leaves little scope for interpreting new compounds made from similar constructions. For example, ConceptNet captures *orange juice*, *lemon juice*, and *fruit juice* as different nodes. It fails to capture the information that a fruit juice is made from a fruit, and the fruit can be orange, or lemon or any other.

Yet another ontology that we have surveyed is the Brandeis Semantic Ontology (Pustejovsky et al., 2006) built on the basis of the Generative Lexicon approach (Johnston and Busa, 1996). This ontology uses a type structure, argument structure, qualia structure and an event structure for every entry, and couples them with phrase structure schemata. However, as discussed in section 2, this approach works only for nouns whose qualia are defined in the lexicon and which adhere to the type of the modifiers and the action prescribed in the qualia. The above discussed drawbacks have motivated us to adopt a new schema for representing nominal compounds in the ontology.

1. Compounds that are incomprehensible by themselves and cannot be predicted from similar constructions are defined as unique nominals. Even compounds that are significantly different from similarly constructed compounds, in terms of their physical nature or in their purpose, manufacture etc, are unique.

2. All unique nominals must be represented by a single node in the ontology hierarchy. Example : *gamma knife* and *garden knife*.

3. All similarly constructed compounds must be represented by a generic compound in such a way that the similarity between the constructions is captured while leaving scope for new constructions to be captured.

Consider the examples of *wheat bread*, *rice bread* and *ginger bread*. Compounds such as *wheat bread*, *rice bread*, *oat bread*, *barley bread* and all other similar constructions can be captured using the feature {component, cereal} in the generic class *bread*. However, gingerbread is a confectionery. It is a unique nominalisation, and must be represented by a single node in the ontology. Such a representation therefore shrinks the ontology from polynomial to linear space without any loss of information.

4 APPROACH

We propose a hybrid approach that combines the use of ontology with word similarity measures to interpret nominal compounds. The approach includes the following two phases: (1) ontology search and (2) word-similarity based interpretation. In the first phase, given an nominal compound, we search the ontology to locate the node corresponding to the head or the nominal compound, and then extract the corresponding descriptive and action features of the artifact represented by it. We use pattern matching techniques to match the modifier in these features, and then with the use of a pre-constructed mapping between the features and semantic relations, we map the feature to its corresponding semantic relation in our inventory. This phase can only interpret a compound when both its constituent nouns are covered in the ontology. It fails for the rest of the cases when the head and/or the modifier are not covered in the ontology. To increase the robustness of the system, we adopt in the second phase, a word similarity measurement technique to handle the remaining compounds where the head or the modifier are not covered in the ontology.

4.1 Pre-Processing

The first step in our approach is the pre-processing of the test data and the ontology. Pre-processing of the test instances includes stemming of constituent nouns in the given compounds using Porter Stemmer. In every compound that is made up of one or more plural constituent nouns, we modify Porter Stemmer to stem those plurals and rebuild the compound from the new constituents.

In order to access the ontology in an efficient way, we need to index the nodes in the ontology. We therefore adopt the Dewey Encoding scheme [1] to index the nodes in our ontology hierarchy. This type of indexing helps in quick accessing of the nodes and also makes it easy for traversal from one node to another within the hierarchy. We apply the indexing mechanism starting from the root node of the ontology which is 'Entity' and label it '0'. Every other node in the ontology is given an index containing the path from the root to the node, and each path uniquely identifies the absolute position of the node within the hierarchy (Tatarinov et al., 2002). Figure 1 shows a small part of the indexed PurposeNet hierarchy.

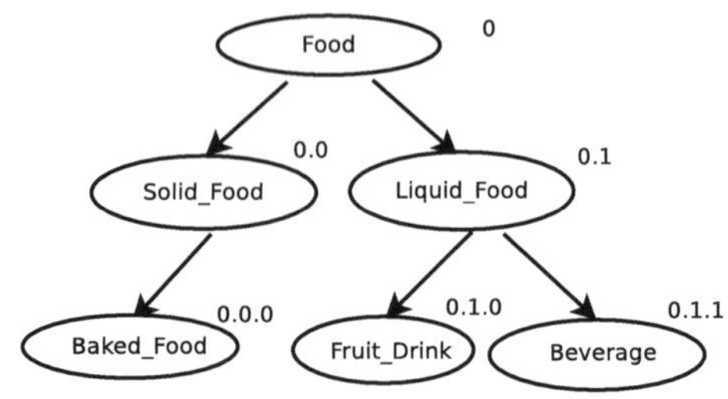

Figure 1: Dewey Order Indexing

4.2 Ontology Search

Given a compound $\langle N1N2 \rangle$ to be interpreted, we first check for the following different possibilities regarding its coverage in the ontology, each of which can be handled in our hybrid approach:

(a) the compound is unique and occurs as a single node in the ontology.

(b) the compound is non-unique and both the head (N2) and the modifier (N1) are encoded as different nodes in the ontology.

(c) the compound is non-unique and only the head (N2) is present in the ontology.

(d) the compound is non-unique and only the modifier (N1) is covered in the ontology.

Case (c) and (d) are handled in the next phase using word similarity measures. However, the case where neither of the constituents of the nominal compound are covered in our ontology is currently not handled in our hybrid approach.

Our strategy is to adopt different search traversals suited to each of the different cases, and use pattern matching to identify the right features in the ontology. For the compound $\langle N1N2 \rangle$, we first define a Left end (LE) and a Right end (RE) as boundaries of our search traversal. They are essentially the nodes representing the compound or its constituents in the ontology. We then obtain the indexes corresponding to N1 and N2 by reading from the index table. Then, we extract all the action features $\langle A \rangle$, and all the descriptive features $\langle D \rangle$ of the RE, and match the LE using simple pattern matching expressions. When the compound is unique and occurs as a single node

[1] `http://en.wikipedia.org/wiki/Dewey_Decimal_Classification`

in the ontology (case (a)), the LE is the modifier while the RE is the node that defines the compound as an artifact. In the case when both the constituents of the compound occur as different nodes in the ontology (case (b)), the LE is the modifier, while the RE is the head of the compound.

Now, given the LE and the RE, we implement a robust search mechanism between the two ends, using different search traversals postulated below:

- One level search - Consider the example of *lemon tea*, where *tea* has a feature {*component,emon*}. In such cases where the LE and the RE are directly related to each other, we perform a single level search through the features of the RE and extract that feature whose value matches the LE.

- Multi Level Search - This search is called when the one level search fails to return any non-empty feature for the compound. Consider the example of *bedroom light*. We define the family of *bedroom* as its parents and siblings, that is the immediate super class in the hierarchy(parent), and all those nodes that are sub classes of the parent (siblings). We replace the LE (*bedroom*) with each member of its family and repeat the one level search with each of the new LE. Here, we also take into consideration the super class of the LE from WordNet (Hypernym) in the family of LE. The intuition behind this multi level search is that every modifier that belongs to the same family modifies the head noun in the same way. Ex: A *lemon juice* is juice made from *lemon*, and so is a *fruit juice*, juice made from *fruit*.

- If the above search mechanisms fail to retrieve a semantic relation for the compound, we replace the RE with the values of each of its features in turn, and repeat the One level and Multi Level search with the new RE. This search mechanisms particularly holds for compositional compounds that follow the law of transitivity. If *A* is a component of *B* and *B* is a component of *C*, then *A* is a component of *C*.

When all the above search traversals fail to retrieve any feature, then ontology search fails to interpret the given compound.

4.3 Word Similarity Measurement

This phase of our experiments is built on a hypothesis that states that 'a compound can be interpreted, at least in part, by knowledge about the meanings of similar compounds' (Ó Séaghdha, 2008). Therefore, we define our experiments on the unpredicted compounds of phase 1 in such a way that by understanding and interpreting similar compounds formed by each of their constituents taken individually, we can interpret the underlying semantic relation for our target compound instance.

Most of the word similarity measures can be classified into one of the following three classes: (a) Approaches that use knowledge resources such as ontologies and thesauri for extracting information such as glosses of the lexical items, or hierarchy information such as the Is-A from WordNet. (b) Approaches that acquire context information for each of the words and check the overlap between the contexts to calculate the similarity. Here, words that occur in similar contexts are intuitively more similar. (c) Approaches that are specifically built for similarity between word pairs. These approaches consider, for each word pair, the contexts in which the constituents of the word pairs occur together. The intuition behind this approach is that when both the constituents occur together in a particular context, the context will most likely yield information about the relation between the constituents (Ó Séaghdha, 2008).

In this paper, we use the Extended gloss overlap measure that uses gloss information from WordNet (Banerjee and Pedersen, 2003). The extended gloss overlap measure calculates the relatedness between two lexical items by comparing their glosses, along with the glosses of the synsets that are related to these lexical items. As mentioned earlier, cases (c) and (d) are handled in this phase, along with other compounds that can not be predicted in phase 1 due to lack of coverage in the ontology. Our strategy consists of building a set of compounds which we call the base set, and measuring the similarity between a given test instance and each base instance. We choose the k most similar base instances, and interpret them using ontology search. We first explain the steps involved in building the base set for cases (c) and (d).

Given a nominal compound whose head is covered as a node in the ontology hierarchy, we extract all the descriptive features of the corresponding node, as well as the descriptive features of every action feature, as each of these can be potential modifiers of the head in a compound. For example, consider a nominal compound $\langle N1, N2\rangle$, where N1 and N2 are the modifier and the head respectively, and N2 is covered in the ontology. We extract the descriptive features $\langle D\rangle$ and the action features $\langle A\rangle$ of N2. However, since the action features are verbs and cannot act as modifiers in a nominal compound, we extract the descriptive features $\langle D'\rangle$ of the node corresponding to every A ϵ $\langle A\rangle$ and append $\langle D\rangle$ and $\langle D'\rangle$ to the list of potential modifiers $\langle M\rangle$. In the next step, we add the family members(parent, siblings) of every M ϵ $\langle M\rangle$. We then run a POS tagger on each of these modifiers and prune away those modifiers that are NNP or are not tagged as nouns. For each of the remaining modifiers M in $\langle M\rangle$, we construct compounds with the head N2 and form the base set of compounds.

For a compound whose modifier is covered in the ontology, we follow a similar strategy as above, building a set of base compounds based on on the occurrences of the modifier in the ontology. Consider again, a nominal compound $\langle N1, N2\rangle$, where N1 and N2 are the modifier and the head respectively and N1 is covered in the ontology. In this case, we extract all the nodes in the ontology $\langle N\rangle$ and for every N ϵ $\langle N\rangle$, we extract its descriptive features $\langle D\rangle$, and action features $\langle A\rangle$. We then check its descriptive features $\langle D\rangle$ as well as the descriptive features $\langle D'\rangle$ of every node corresponding to the action features $\langle A\rangle$ for any occurrence of the modifier N1. For every occurrence of the modifier N1, we construct a compound of N1 with that node N and add to our list of base compounds.

In the next step, we use the *WordNet::QueryData*[2] to query the different senses of the constituents for the test compound $\langle N1, N2\rangle$ and each of the base set compounds $\langle N1', N2'\rangle$. For each sense of N1 and each sense of N1', we calculate the relatedness using the extended gloss overlap measure, and obtain the most related senses. Similarly, we obtain the most similar senses of N2 and N2', and then calculate the similarity between the compounds $\langle N1, N2\rangle$ and $\langle N1', N2'\rangle$ as the product of the similarity between the most related senses of their corresponding constituents N1-N1' and N2-N2'. For example, the 3 most similar base compounds to the nominal compound *fruit custard* were found to be *fruit soup*, *fruit skin* and *fruit drink*. We show in Table 3, the relatedness measures of these base compounds with our test compound. Finally, we use the k-best method and obtain k(3 or 4) base compounds that are most similar to the test compound. We then interpret them using the ontology search. This results in a set of most probable interpretations for the test instance. Human judgement would be required to choose the most appropriate interpretation out of the most probable interpretations.

Base compound	Similarity of modifiers	Similarity of heads
Fruit Soup	5145	70
Fruit Skin	5145	40
Fruit Drink	5145	37

Table 3: Base compounds and their similarity with *Fruit custard*.

5 Preparation of Data

5.1 Extraction

In order to perform our experiments on nominal compounds that are within the tourism domain, we compiled a list of those compounds from the web, that were formed by the artifacts listed in our PurposeNet ontology. Firstly, we extracted all the artifacts that are described in the ontology. Those artifacts which are represented using noun compounds in the ontology were further split into their corresponding noun constituents and then appended to the list of nouns for web search. We then used the Bing Search API to search the web for all occurrences of the nouns representing each of the artifacts and extract compounds formed by them. The search was restricted to the top 10 web results obtained from Bing. We used a simple heuristic to identify the noun compounds, similar to that used by Lauer (1996). All those occurrences of the artifact nouns that were preceded or succeeded by nouns,

[2] http://search.cpan.org/dist/WordNet-QueryData/QueryData.pm

and which are not flanked by tokens tagged as nouns on either side were extracted as noun compounds. A list of stop words was then used to prune away compounds containing junk words. This extraction does not retrieve hyphenated noun sequences as these noun sequences need further validation before appending to the list of nominal compounds.

There are a total of 616 artifacts in the ontology. These artifacts were used to prepare a list of 400 nouns for the web search. We ran the bing web search API on each of these 400 nouns and a total of 89,578 compounds were extracted. However, this extraction mechanism also resulted in incorrect cases due to false tagging of words as nouns. Therefore, we manually identified and extracted from this list, some compounds which were restricted to our tourism domain, to form a small test set of 600 compounds for our experiment.

5.2 Semantic Relations

In our experiment, we use an inventory of 22 semantic relations proposed by Girju (2006) for interpreting the nominal compounds. We chose this list as it contains clearly defined semantic relations, with clear and well defined boundaries and sufficient coverage of the different possible semantic relations that can exist between two nouns. Moreover, most of these relations are captured as features in PurposeNet. This simplifies the task of mapping features from the ontology to these relations in the PurposeNet experiment.

5.3 Annotation

We used two human annotators for annotating the compounds. Only a list of compounds and the annotation guidelines were provided for the annotation. The compounds were allowed to be annotated with more than one semantic relation, as and when suitable. Table 4 shows the distribution of the compounds among the different relations, for each of the annotators. Rarely occurring relations (<5 times) have not been considered in the table. We observe that different semantic relations in our inventory provide different depths of interpretations for the nominal compounds. For example, the *type* relation has a very 'surfacy' nature, and most of the compounds can be classified into this class. A *wine bottle* is a type of bottle, *glass furniture* is a type of furniture, and similarly, *orange juice* is a type of juice. Alternatively, each of these compounds can be interpreted using deeper semantic relations, such as *purpose* and *source*. A *wine bottle* can be interpreted as a bottle used to serve wine, a *glass furniture* is furniture made up of glass, and *orange juice* is juice made from orange. Therefore, in case of such compounds, both *type* and *purpose*, *type* and *source* can be considered as the appropriate annotations. However, all occurrences of *purpose*, *source* and other relations cannot be replaced using *type*. Since there is no clear method of distinguishing the agreements from the disagreements in annotations involving *type*, we choose to calculate the inter annotator agreement in two ways. The first calculation counts all the mismatches between *type* and *purpose*, *type* and *source* etc as disagreements, while the second calculation counts all the mismatches containing *type* as one of the annotations as an agreement between the annotators. In the first case, the inter-annotator agreement on the 600-nominal compounds set was 65.6% with a moderate kappa score of 0.57. The second calculation, on the other hand, produced a high inter annotator agreement of 89% with a kappa score of 0.87. The ideal inter-annotator agreement can be defined as a value belonging to range bound by these two limits.

Relation	Annotator 1	Annotator 2
Part-Whole	184	90
Type	178	192
Purpose	132	122
Source	70	78
Property	25	22
Hypernymy	25	30
Location	34	30
Topic	12	8
Theme	8	8
Temporal	5	5

Table 4: Distribution of annotated data among the relations.

It is evident from analysis that *part-whole(meronymy)* and *purpose* exhibit very little agreement with each other. This can be mainly attributed to the possibility of more than one correct interpretations for a given compound. For example,

Annotation1	Annotation 2	Disagreement count
Part-Whole	Type	90
Purpose	Type	22
Source	Type	14
Hypernymy	Type	12
Part-Whole	Source	10
Property	Type	6
Part-Whole	Purpose	6
Purpose	Theme	6
Purpose	Location	6
Source	Hypernymy	6

Table 5: Distribution of the disagreements in annotation[3].

Relation	Predicted		Unpredicted
	Phase1	Phase2	
Meronymy	22.5	14	3
Purpose	16.5	3.5	6
Type	22.5	12	10
Location	0	2.5	1
Source	2.5	2.5	1
Hypernymy	6	5	2
Property	3	0	2
Beneficiary	3.5	1	0

Table 6: Distribution of the predicted and unpredicted nominal compounds.

a *glass furniture* can be interpreted as 'furniture made of glass' (*part-whole*) or 'furniture made from glass' (*source*) or 'a type of furniture' (*type*). All such instances of disagreements that occurred in our data set were solved using a third annotator whose judgement was chosen as final.

6 Experiment and Results

We conducted our experiments on the set of 600 nominal compounds extracted from web using the Bing Search API. Each nominal compound was allowed to be interpreted using more than one feature from PurposeNet. These features were in turn mapped to their corresponding semantic relations in our inventory using a set of rules that were built manually based on the definitions of the features and semantic relations. In order to evaluate the performance of the hybrid approach, we adopt a single-label evaluation method where compounds with atleast one correctly predicted label are considered to be correctly interpreted by our system. However, we disregard the less informative labels such as *hypernymy* and *type* as correct interpretations for any compound, and do not consider them in our evaluation. The results of our experiment on the 600 nominal compounds are reported in detail in Table 6. The first column lists all the semantic relations that were found in our data set. The second column reports the distribution of the compounds that were successfully interpreted by our model, with detailed contribution of each phase, for each semantic relation. The last column gives the distribution of those compounds that failed to be interpreted by our hybrid model. Compounds that were annotated with multiple labels were counted under each of the labels. We observe that our system has precision and recall values of 0.76 and 0.92 respectively, while its overall accuracy (calculated as the ratio of the number of correctly predicted compounds to the total number of compounds) is 0.70. As shown in the table, most of the uninterpreted compounds belong to *type* and *purpose* relation. We also observe that of all the nominal compounds that were predicted, 55% of the compounds were predicted in phase 1 of the approach, while the remaining 39% of the compounds were predicted at the end of phase 2. This indicates that the addition of lexical word similarity measures to our ontology search has caused a significant improvement in the results of compound interpretation.

[3]Minor disagreements (<5) have not been shown in the table.

7 Conclusion and Future Work

We have observed that most of the approaches proposed so far for understanding nominal compounds implement machine learning techniques or statistical prediction methods to classify nominal compounds into different semantic relations. In this paper, we described a hybrid, ontology-based approach for the understanding and labeling nominal compounds with semantic relations. It is a unique system that combines lexico-semantic information from a domain-specific hierarchy with gloss information from WordNet for interpreting two word nominal compounds. It implements an efficient look-up mechanism that uses minimised search space for searching nominal compounds in the ontology. To increase the robustness of the system, we use lexical similarity measures based on gloss information from WordNet to handle compounds beyond the scope of our ontology.

We presented the experimental results of our hybrid approach, and compare the contribution of each phase of our system in successfully interpreting nominal compounds. Our system has achieved an accuracy of about 70% on domain-specific nominal compouns and is comparable in its performance to Girju's state-of-the-art best performing system for domain-independent nominal compounds (Girju et al., 2005) that reports, on an average, an accuracy of 75%. This motivates us to further experiment our hybrid approach our hybrid model on different ontologies (such as ConceptNet and WordNet) and different lexical and relational word similarity measures and compare their performance for the task of compound interpretation.

References

Timothy Baldwin and Takaaki Tanaka. 2004. Translation by machine of complex nominals: Getting it right. In *Proceedings of the ACL04 Workshop on Multiword Expressions: Integrating Processing*.

Satanjeev Banerjee and Ted Pedersen. 2003. Extended gloss overlaps as a measure of semantic relatedness. In *Proceedings of the Eighteenth International Joint Conference on Artificial Intelligence*, pages 805–810.

Christiane Fellbaum, editor. 1998. *WordNet An Electronic Lexical Database*. The MIT Press, Cambridge, MA ; London, May.

Roxana Girju, Dan Moldovan, Marta Tatu, and Daniel Antohe. 2005. On the semantics of noun compounds. *Comput. Speech Lang.*, 19(4):479–496, October.

Roxana Girju. 2006. Out-of-context noun phrase semantic interpretation with cross-linguistic evidence. In *Proceedings of the 15th ACM international conference on Information and knowledge management*.

Catherine Havasi. 2007. Conceptnet 3: a flexible, multilingual semantic network for common sense knowledge. In *the 22nd Conference on Artificial Intelligence*.

Jay J. Jiang and David W. Conrath. 1997. Semantic similarity based on corpus statistics and lexical taxonomy.

Michael Johnston and Federica Busa. 1996. Qualia structure and the compositional interpretation of compounds.

Kim and Baldwin. 2005. Automatic interpretation of noun compounds using wordnet similarity. In *Proceedings of the 2nd International Joint Conference on Natural Language Processing, Jeju Island, South Korea, 11–13*, pages 945–956.

P. KiranMayee, Rajeev Sangal, Soma Paul, and Navjyoti Singh. 2008. An ontological resource organized around purpose. In *Proceedings of 6th International Conference on Natural Language Processing, Pune*.

Mark Lauer. 1996. Designing statistical language learners: Experiments on noun compounds. *CoRR*, cmp-lg/9609008.

C. Leacock and M. Chodorow, 1998. *Combining local context and WordNet similarity for word sense identification*, pages 305–332. In C. Fellbaum (Ed.), MIT Press.

Dekang Lin. 1998. An information-theoretic definition of similarity. In *Proceedings of the 15th International Conference on Machine Learning*, pages 296–304. Morgan Kaufmann.

Kavi Mahesh. 1996. Ontology development for machine translation: Ideology and methodology. Technical Report MCCS-96-292, CRL, New Mexico State University.

Diarmuid Ó Séaghdha. 2008. *Learning compound noun semantics*. Ph.D. thesis, Computer Laboratory, University of Cambridge. Published as University of Cambridge Computer Laboratory Technical Report 735.

James Pustejovsky, Catherine Havasi, Jessica Littman, Anna Rumshisky, and Marc Verhagen. 2006. Towards a generative lexical resource: The brandeis semantic ontology. In *Proceedings of the Fifth Language Resource and Evaluation Conference*.

James Pustejovsky. 1991. The generative lexicon. *Comput. Linguist.*, 17(4):409–441, December.

Barbara Rosario and Marti Hearst. 2001. Classifying the semantic relations in noun compounds via a domain-specific lexical hierarchy. In *Proceedings of the 2001 Conference on Empirical Methods in Natural Language Processing (EMNLP-01*, pages 82–90.

Igor Tatarinov, Kevin Beyer, and Jayavel Shanmugasundaram. 2002. Storing and querying ordered xml using a relational database system. In *In SIGMOD*, pages 204–215.

Zhibiao Wu and Zhibiao Wu. 1994. Verb semantics and lexical selection.

Improved Constituent Context Model with Features

Yun Huang[1,2] **Min Zhang**[1] **Chew Lim Tan**[2]
huangyun@comp.nus.edu.sg mzhang@i2r.a-star.edu.sg tancl@comp.nus.edu.sg

[1]Human Language Department
Institute for Infocomm Research
1 Fusionopolis Way, Singapore

[2]Department of Computer Science
National University of Singapore
13 Computing Drive, Singapore

Abstract

The Constituent-Context Model (CCM) achieves promising results for unsupervised grammar induction. However, its performance drops for longer sentences. In this paper, we describe a general feature-based model for CCM, in which linguistic knowledge can be easily integrated as features. Features take the log-linear form with local normalization, so the Expectation-Maximization (EM) algorithm is still applicable to estimate model parameters. The ℓ_1-norm is used to control the model complexity, leading to sparse and compact grammar. We also propose to use a separated development to perform model selection and an additional test set to evaluate the performance. Under this framework, we could automatically choose suitable model parameters rather than setting them empirically. Experiments on the English treebank demonstrate that the feature-based model achieves comparable performance on short sentences but significant improvement on longer sentences.

1 Introduction

Unsupervised grammar induction, the task to induce hierarchical structures from plain strings, has attracted research interests for a long time. The induced grammars can be used to construct large treebanks (van Zaanen, 2000), study language acquisition (Jones et al., 2010), improve machine translation (DeNero and Uszkoreit, 2011), and so on. In general, most approaches either induce the constituency grammars (Klein and Manning, 2002; Bod, 2006; Seginer, 2007; Cohn et al., 2009; Ponvert et al., 2011), or the dependency grammars (Klein and Manning, 2004; Headden III et al., 2009; Cohen and Smith, 2009; Spitkovsky et al., 2010; Blunsom and Cohn, 2010).

Among these approaches, the Constituent Context Model (CCM) (Klein and Manning, 2002; Klein, 2005) is a simple but effective generative model for unsupervised constituency grammar induction. Specifically, the sequences (the contents enclosed by spans) and contexts (the preceding and following words) are directly modelled in CCM. The Expectation-Maximization (EM) algorithm is used to estimate parameters to optimize the data likelihood. Although the CCM achieves promising results on short sentences, its performance drops for longer sentences. There are two possible reasons: (1) CCM models all constituents under only single multinomial distributions, which can not capture the detailed information of span contents; and (2) long sequences only occur a few times in the training corpus, so the probability estimation highly depends on smoothing. Another problem of original CCM and following improved unsupervised models (Smith and Eisner, 2004; Mirroshandel and Ghassem-Sani, 2008; Golland et al., 2012) is the problematic evaluation framework. The previous approaches train and evaluate models on the same dataset, so there is no reasonable way to choose model parameters unless setting them empirically.

In this paper, we focus on CCM and present a general feature-based framework in which various overlapping features could be easily added. Previous dependency induction approach (Cohen and

Smith, 2009) demonstrates enabling factored covariance between the probabilities of different derivation events could improve the induction results. The proposed feature-based model provides a simpler and more flexible way to share information between constituents, e.g. different sequences may share the same boundary words. Various features could capture rich information about span contents, which alleviates the data sparsity problem and estimation problem of CCM mentioned above. In addition, features are combined in the log-linear form with local normalization, so the EM algorithm can be adopted to estimate model parameters with minor change, without increasing the computing complexity. To avoid overfitting, we use ℓ_1-norm regularization to control the model complexity. Finally, we advocate to estimate model probabilities on training set, use a separated development set (a.k.a. the validation set) to perform model selection, and measure the generative ability of trained model on an additional test set. Under this framework, we could automatically select suitable model and parameters rather than choosing them manually. We carry out experiments on the English treebank. Compared to original CCM, the proposed feature-based model achieves comparable performance on short sentences but significant improvement on longer sentences. After examining the effect of grammar sparsity, we conclude that with good regularization parameter (tunned on the development set), the learned grammar could be both compact and accurate.

The main contributions of this paper can be summarized as follows:

(1) We present a general feature-based CCM, where knowledge can be easily incorporated.

(2) We use ℓ_1-norm to control the model complexity, leading to compact grammars.

(3) We propose to use separated development set to tune parameters instead of heuristically choosing parameters.

This paper is structured as follows. Section 2 gives an overview of the original CCM. Section 3 proposes the feature-based CCM and corresponding parameter estimation method. Section 4 lists the feature templates used in experiments. Section 5 shows the experimental results. We compare our work to related approaches in Section 6 and conclude in Section 7.

2 Constituent Context Model

The Constituent-Context Model (CCM) (Klein and Manning, 2002) is the first model achieving better performance than the trivial right branching baseline in the unsupervised English grammar induction task. Unlike many models that only deal with constituent spans, the CCM defines generative probabilistic models over all spans of a sentence, no matter whether they enclose constituents or distituents (a.k.a. the non-constituents).

In particular, let B be a boolean matrix with entries indicating whether the corresponding span encloses constituent or distituent. Note that each tree could be represented by one and only one bracketing, but some bracketings are not tree-equivalent, since they may miss the full-sentence span or have crossing spans. Define sequence σ to be the substring enclosed by span, and context γ to be the pair of preceding and following terminals[1]. The CCM generate a sentence S in two steps: first choose a bracketing B according to prior distribution, then generate the sentence given the chosen bracketing:

$$P(S, B) = P(B)P(S|B).$$

The prior $P(B)$ uniformly distributes its probability mass over all possible binary trees of the given sentence, and zero for non-tree-equivalent bracketings. The conditional probability $P(S|B)$ is further decomposed to the product of generative probability of sequence σ and context γ for each span $\langle i, j\rangle$:

$$\begin{aligned} P(S|B) &= \prod_{\langle i,j\rangle} P(\sigma_{\langle i,j\rangle}, \gamma_{\langle i,j\rangle} | B_{\langle i,j\rangle}) \\ &= \prod_{\langle i,j\rangle} P(\sigma_{\langle i,j\rangle} | B_{\langle i,j\rangle}) P(\gamma_{\langle i,j\rangle} | B_{\langle i,j\rangle}). \end{aligned} \quad (1)$$

From the above decomposition, we can see that given B, the CCM fills each span independently and generates yield and context independently.

The Expectation Maximization (EM) algorithm is used to estimate the multinomial parameters $\boldsymbol{\theta}$. In the E-step, a cubic-time dynamic programming algorithm is used to calculate the expected counts for

[1] For example, in sequence "$_0\mathtt{RB}_1\mathtt{DT}_2\mathtt{NN}_3$", we have $\sigma_{\langle 1,3\rangle} = \langle\mathtt{DT\ NN}\rangle$, and $\gamma_{\langle 1,3\rangle} = \langle\mathtt{RB}, \diamond\rangle$. Since CCM works on part-of-speech (POS) tags, only POS tags are shown here. The special symbol $\diamond$ represents the sentence boundary.

each sequence and context for both constituents and distituents according to the current $\boldsymbol{\theta}$. The detailed calculation of expectation can be found in Appendix A.1 in (Klein, 2005). In the M-Step, the model finds new $\boldsymbol{\theta}'$ to maximize the expected completed likelihood $\sum_B P(B|S, \boldsymbol{\theta}^{old}) \log P(S, B|\boldsymbol{\theta}')$ by normalizing relative frequencies.

From the probability definition (1), the CCM gives single multinomial probability distribution over all sequences. However, the number of possible sequences grows exponentially with respect to the span length, leading to severe data sparsity problem for long sentences. In the next section, we propose the feature-based model to alleviate the this problem, since overlapping features could represent small units of the span contents.

3 Feature-based CCM

3.1 Model Definition

Motivated by (Berg-Kirkpatrick et al., 2010), we define factors in the log-linear form with local normalization. Let $F_{1,\dots,K}$ be K different factors. Each factor F_k corresponds to a n_k-dimensional feature vector $\boldsymbol{f}_k$ and a n_k-dimensional weight vector $\boldsymbol{w}_k$. For the kth factor F_k, the corresponding multinomial parameter in original CCM is now treated as a function of weights $\boldsymbol{w}_k$. Define the factor category function δ_k to be $+1$ if F_k is constituent factor, and -1 otherwise. In detail, for span $\langle i, j\rangle$ in some bracketing B for sentence S, define

$$\begin{aligned} F_k(S_{\langle i,j\rangle}|\boldsymbol{w}_k) &= P_k(S_{\langle i,j\rangle}|B_{\langle i,j\rangle} = \delta_k, \boldsymbol{w}_k) \\ &= \frac{\exp(\boldsymbol{w}_k \cdot \boldsymbol{f}_k(S_{\langle i,j\rangle}))}{\sum_v \exp(\boldsymbol{w}_k \cdot \boldsymbol{f}_k(v))} \end{aligned} \quad (2)$$

where $\boldsymbol{f}_k$ returns a feature vector, $\boldsymbol{w}_k$ is the corresponding weight vector, and $(\cdot)$ denotes the inner product of vectors. The denominator sums over the unnormalized probabilities (the numerator) for all possible factor values v. We approximately calculate this summation only over values that appear in training corpus.

For factor F_k over bracketing B with corresponding tree T_B, define the active span set $\mathcal{A}_k(B)$ as

$$\mathcal{A}_k(B) = \begin{cases} \{\langle i,j\rangle \in T_B\}, & \text{if } \delta_k = +1 \\ \{\langle i,j\rangle \notin T_B\}, & \text{if } \delta_k = -1 \end{cases} \quad (3)$$

Then the joint probability of $P(S, B|\boldsymbol{w})$ can be defined:

$$\begin{aligned} P(S, B|\boldsymbol{w}) &= P(B)P(S|B) \\ &= P(B) \prod_{\langle i,j\rangle} P(S_{\langle i,j\rangle}|B_{\langle i,j\rangle}) \\ &= P(B) \prod_{\langle i,j\rangle \in \mathcal{A}_k(B)} F_k(S_{\langle i,j\rangle}|\boldsymbol{w}_k) \\ &= P(B) \prod_{\langle i,j\rangle} \prod_{k:\delta_k=-1} F_k(S_{\langle i,j\rangle}|\boldsymbol{w}_k) \\ &\quad \times \prod_{\langle i,j\rangle \in T_B} \frac{\prod_{k:\delta_k=1} F_k(S_{\langle i,j\rangle}|\boldsymbol{w}_k)}{\prod_{k:\delta_k=-1} F_k(S_{\langle i,j\rangle}|\boldsymbol{w}_k)} \\ &= K(S|\boldsymbol{w}) \prod_{\langle i,j\rangle \in T_B} \prod_k F_k^{\delta_k}(S_{\langle i,j\rangle}|\boldsymbol{w}_k) \end{aligned}$$

where $K(S|\boldsymbol{w})$ is independent of B and the following production is taken over tree spans only. One advantage of the locally normalized model is that the EM algorithm could be still used to estimate parameters, which will be described in the next subsection.

If we define the same factors of CCM (sequence and context for constituent and distituent) and set weights properly, then the probability of feature-based model is degenerated to the original CCM model. So the original CCM can be treated as a special case of the feature-based model.

3.2 Parameter Estimation

Let $\mathcal{S}$ be the set of training sentences. Under the maximum likelihood estimation, we want to find $\boldsymbol{w}$ to maximize the data log likelihood:

$$L(\mathcal{S}|\boldsymbol{w}) = \sum_{S \in \mathcal{S}} \log \sum_{B \in \mathcal{B}(S)} P(S, B|\boldsymbol{w}) \quad (4)$$

However, the summation of hidden variable B is inside the logarithm operator, resulting in the complicated expressions for the analytical solution. Instead, we use the Expectation-Maximization (EM) algorithm to solve the problem approximately.

Given current model parameters $\boldsymbol{w}^{old}$ in each iteration of EM, we seek new parameter $\boldsymbol{w}$ to maximize the expectation of the completed-data log likelihood:

$$\begin{aligned} &Q(\boldsymbol{w}, \boldsymbol{w}^{old}) \\ &= \sum_{S \in \mathcal{S}} \sum_{B \in \mathcal{B}(S)} P(B|S, \boldsymbol{w}^{old}) \log P(S, B|\boldsymbol{w}) \end{aligned} \quad (5)$$

E-Step

The E-step evaluates the posterior probability $P(B|S, \boldsymbol{w}^{old})$ given fixed $\boldsymbol{w}^{old}$. We modify the inside-outside algorithm (Lari and Young, 1990) to efficiently calculate the expected count for each factor. The original inside/outside merits are recursively calculated over binary rules. In the feature-based CCM, we recursively calculate these values over spans. To simplify following derivations, we define

$$\phi_{\langle i,j\rangle} = \prod_k F_k^{\delta_k}(S_{\langle i,j\rangle}|\boldsymbol{w}_k) \quad (6)$$

The inside probability $\text{IN}_{\langle i,j\rangle}$ can be defined recursively:

(a) Unary spans: $\text{IN}_{\langle i,j\rangle} = \phi_{\langle i,j\rangle}$, if $j - i = 1$;

(b) Other spans:

$$\text{IN}_{\langle i,j\rangle} = \sum_{k=i+1}^{j-1} \phi_{\langle i,j\rangle} \, \text{IN}_{\langle i,k\rangle} \, \text{IN}_{\langle k,j\rangle}.$$

For sentence S with length l, the outside probability can be defined as:

(a) Sentence span: $\text{OUT}_{\langle 0,l\rangle} = 1$;

(b) Other spans:

$$\text{OUT}_{\langle i,j\rangle} = \sum_{k=0}^{i-1} \phi_{\langle k,j\rangle} \, \text{OUT}_{\langle k,j\rangle} \, \text{IN}_{\langle k,i\rangle} + \sum_{k=j+1}^{l} \phi_{\langle i,k\rangle} \, \text{OUT}_{\langle i,k\rangle} \, \text{IN}_{\langle j,k\rangle}.$$

Then we calculate the expected ratio $\phi_{\langle i,j\rangle}$ for each span:

$$e[\phi_{\langle i,j\rangle}] = \text{IN}_{\langle i,j\rangle} \times \text{OUT}_{\langle i,j\rangle} \, / \, \text{IN}_{\langle 0,l\rangle} \quad (7)$$

Finally, we accumulate expected counts e and $1 - e$ constituent factors and distituent factors respectively.

We do not consider empty spans in the above calculation of inside/outside probabilities. Since the empty spans do not depend on trees, we just add expected count 1 for each distituent factor and 0 for each constituent factor over empty spans.

M-Step

In M-step, we want to tune $\boldsymbol{w}$ to maximize the expected complicated log likelihood together with the regularization terms:

$$Q(\boldsymbol{w}, \boldsymbol{w}^{old}) - \sum_{k=1}^{K} \lambda_k \|\boldsymbol{w}_k\|_1 \quad (8)$$

where λ_k is a non-negative coefficient for the ℓ_1-norm of the kth weight vector $\boldsymbol{w}_k$. Because of the high-dimensional feature space, we use ℓ_1-norm of weight vector $\boldsymbol{w}$ as regularization terms to control the model complexity. The regularization terms can serve as automatic feature selector, leading to compact models.

In original CCM, model parameters (multinomial distribution probabilities) are estimated by normalizing relative frequencies in the M-step. In the feature-based model, we use gradient-based search algorithm to optimize the above objective function numerically. Due to the ℓ_1-norm regularization, the objective is not differentiable at $\boldsymbol{w} = \mathbf{0}$. So we adopt the OWL-QN method (Andrew and Gao, 2007) to perform optimization. The open-source C++ implementation `libLBFGS`[2] is used in experiments. The optimization process needs to calculate the gradient of $Q(\boldsymbol{w}, \boldsymbol{w}^{old})$ with respect to $\boldsymbol{w}$.

Since the probabilities of factors are multiplied together, so the logarithm term in equation (5) can be decomposed into the sum of the logarithm of each factor probability. Additionally, the ℓ_1-norm term in equation (8) is the sum of ℓ_1-norm of the weights for each factor. As a result, optimizing the overall objective function is equivalent to optimize the corresponding functions for each factor.

Assuming the set $\mathcal{V}_k$ contains all values of the kth factor F_k that can be found in training corpus, then the gradient (omitting the regularization terms) of Q_k can be computed as follows:

$$\boldsymbol{\nabla}_{\boldsymbol{w}_k}(Q_k) = \sum_{v \in \mathcal{V}_k} e[F_k(v)] \times \boldsymbol{\Delta}_v(\boldsymbol{w}_k) \quad (9)$$

$$\boldsymbol{\Delta}_v(\boldsymbol{w}_k) = \boldsymbol{f}_k(v) - \sum_{v' \in \mathcal{V}_k} F_k(v')\boldsymbol{f}_k(v') \quad (10)$$

where $e[F_k(v)]$ contains the expected counts calculated in the E-step. The similar derivation can be found in (Berg-Kirkpatrick et al., 2010).

In this feature-based model, rich features can be easily incorporated. We give some useful feature templates in next section.

[2] `http://www.chokkan.org/software/liblbfgs/`

4 Feature Templates

4.1 Basic features

There are two kinds of features: constituent features, with prefix {`c:`}; and distituent features, with prefix {`d:`}. Features in the two categories are active only if the span enclose constituent or distituent respectively. The basic feature templates are listed as follows with their names and descriptions. A running example, span $\langle 1, 3\rangle$ in "$_0\text{RB}_1\text{DT}_2\text{NN}_3$", is also shown for each feature template.

• `const`: This constant feature always takes value 1 for any given span. We use this feature to measure the number of spans.

• `seq[n]`: This indicating feature is active for sequence enclosed by span with size n. If $n = 0$, then sequences with any lengths are considered.

seq2	...	DT_JJ	DT_NN	RB_DT	...
value	...	0	1	0	...

• `lx[n]/rx[n]`: The indicating feature for the preceding/following n terminals (left/right context), where ◇ represents sentence boundary.

lx2	...	◇_◇	◇_RB	RB_DT	...
value	...	0	1	0	...

rx2	...	DT_NN	NN_◇	◇_◇	...
value	...	0	0	1	...

• `lb[n]/rb[n]`: The left/right n boundary terminals inside given span. If the length of span is less than n, then this feature template is not activated.

lb2	...	RB_DT	DT_NN	TO_VB	...
value	...	0	1	0	...

rb1	...	RB	DT	NN	...
value	...	0	0	1	...

4.2 Composite features

Basic features can be composited to more complicated features. We define two composition operators: join (.), and concatenation (+). For the join operator, the composited feature space is the Cartesian product of the feature spaces of the two operands. For the concatenation operator, the composited feature space is the concatenation of the operands' feature spaces.

Here we use an example to demonstrate the difference between join operator and concatenation operator. Assuming there are three possible values {◇, RB, DT} for feature `lx1`, and three possible values {DT, NN, ◇} for feature `rx1`, then the joined feature space has $3 \times 3 = 9$ dimensions while the concatenated feature space has $3 + 3 = 6$ dimensions. The feature vectors of these two operators for span $\langle 1, 3\rangle$ in "$_0\text{RB}_1\text{DT}_2\text{NN}_3$" are shown as follows.

lx1.rx1								
◇.{DT,NN,◇}			RB.{DT,NN,◇}			DT.{DT,NN,◇}		
0	0	0	0	0	1	0	0	0

lx1			+ rx1		
◇	RB	DT	DT	NN	◇
0	1	0	0	0	1

We restrict that only join followed by concatenation is allowed. As an example, the original CCM could be represented as: {`c:seq0`, `d:seq0`, `c:lx1.rx1`, `d:lx1.rx1`}.

4.3 Summary

There are huge number of feature combinations that we can not try each of them in experiments. In experiments, we use following sets of features.

The first feature set includes the sequences with length up to 5: {`seq1`, `seq2`, `seq3`, `seq4`, `seq5`}. Note that sequences with arbitrary lengths are modelled in the original CCM, while we restrict the maximal sequence length to be 5. Since most of the longer sequences occurs only once or twice in the training corpus, we discard them to speed up training procedure and reduce memory usage.

Boundary words have been proven useful for detecting phrase boundaries in supervised learning task (Xiong et al., 2010). We introduce this idea to unsupervised grammar induction. The features used in experiments are combinations of left boundary and right boundary words with lengths up to 2: {`lb1`, `lb2`, `rb1`, `rb2`, `lb1.rb1`, `lb1.rb2`, `lb2.rb1`, `lb2.rb2`}.

The original CCM also considers the pair of preceding one word and following one word as contexts. We consider combinations of left context and right context words with lengths up to 2: {`lx1`, `lx2`, `rx1`, `rx2`, `lx1.rx1`, `lx1.rx2`, `lx2.rx1`, `lx2.rx2`}. The special token ◇ is introduced to represent sentence boundaries.

The last feature used is the constant feature {`const`}. The constant feature always takes value 1 for each span.

Overall, we define two constituent factors and two distituent factors. The first constituent/distituent factors, denoted as $F_{\mathtt{c:s}}$ and $F_{\mathtt{d:s}}$, are the concatenation of sequence features, boundary features, and constant feature. The second constituent/distituent factors ($F_{\mathtt{c:x}}$ and $F_{\mathtt{d:x}}$), are the concatenation of context features and constant feature.

5 Experiments

5.1 Datasets and Settings

We carry out experiments on the Wall Street Journal portion of the Penn English Treebank (Marcus et al., 1993). We report the unlabeled F1 score (the harmonic mean of precision and recall) as evaluation metric. Constituents which could not be gotten wrong (single words and entire sentences) are discarded. These are standard settings used in previous work (Klein, 2005).

To perform model selection and parameter tunning, we split the treebank into three parts: section 02-21 as training set, section 00 as development set, and section 23 as test set. As standard machine learning pipeline, we perform EM on training set, tune parameters on development set, and report the result of selected model on test set. We remove punctuation and null elements in treebank, as the standard preprocessing step (Klein, 2005). For comparison, we build various datasets with sentences lengths no more than 10, 20, 30, 40 words after removing punctuations. Table 1 gives the number of sentences for each dataset.

Dataset	Train	Dev	Test
PTB10	5,899	265	398
PTB20	20,243	992	1,286
PTB30	32,712	1,573	2,028
PTB40	37,561	1,809	2,338

Table 1: Data statistics

We select regularization parameters from set $\{0.03, 0.1, 0.3, 1, 3, 10\}$ for factors $F_{\mathtt{c:s}}$ and $F_{\mathtt{d:s}}$. No regularization is used for factor $F_{\mathtt{c:x}}$ and $F_{\mathtt{d:x}}$, since the number of context types are almost fixed and relatively small in datasets with different lengths. Each combinations of $\lambda_{\mathtt{c:s}}$ and $\lambda_{\mathtt{d:s}}$ are tested on the development set. The final values of λ is the one with the highest development F1 score.

5.2 Induction Results

EM algorithm is sensitive to the initial condition. We adopt the same uniform-split initialization and the same smoothing values (2 for constituents and 8 for distituents) as described in (Klein, 2005). For feature-based model (F-CCM), we still use uniform-split strategy to initialize probabilities in the first E-step, and set all weights to zero as the initial point of the gradient-based search algorithm in the M-step.

PTB10	Train	Dev	Test
LBranch	28.62	28.64	30.58
RBranch	61.58	63.59	61.00
UBound	88.20	88.35	86.80
CCM	**72.50**	**73.58**	**70.30**
F-CCM	71.66	72.95	69.75
PTB20	Train	Dev	Test
LBranch	17.22	17.43	17.21
RBranch	48.39	47.85	47.96
UBound	86.35	86.26	86.20
CCM	48.96	48.46	48.08
F-CCM	**59.86**	**59.86**	**59.10**
PTB30	Train	Dev	Test
LBranch	13.37	13.61	13.33
RBranch	42.70	42.76	42.57
UBound	85.72	86.02	85.88
CCM	43.01	43.27	42.59
F-CCM	**48.87**	**48.82**	**48.15**
PTB40	Train	Dev	Test
LBranch	12.08	12.31	11.95
RBranch	40.59	40.54	40.73
UBound	85.54	85.77	85.69
CCM	33.44	33.62	33.10
F-CCM	**45.44**	**45.46**	**45.10**

Table 2: Results on PTB10, PTB20, PTB30, PTB40

Table 2 shows the experimental results on the datasets of different length limits. LBranch and RBranch rows show the left branching and right branching binary tree baselines. As the English grammar tends to be right branched, the trivial RBranch achieves quite high F1 scores. UBound rows show the results of binarized treebank, which is the upper bound of any grammar induction systems that output binary trees. We reimplement the baseline CCM, which achieves comparable performance compared to previous reported results (Klein, 2005). The results of feature-based CCM are presented in the F-CCM rows.

From these results, we observe that the original CCM performs much better than the right branching baseline on short sentences, but the performance decreases dramatically on longer sentences, even lower than the right branching baseline. In contrast, our feature-based CCM achieves comparable performance with original CCM on PTB10, and much better performance than the original CCM and the right branching baseline on longer sentences. These experimental results demonstrate the effectiveness and robustness of the feature-based model.

5.3 Grammar sparsity

The regularization terms can serve as feature selection mechanism. In this section, we compare the sparsity of learned sequence grammars between various regularization coefficients on PTB10.

$\lambda_{\texttt{c:s}}$	$\lambda_{\texttt{d:s}}$	$F_{\texttt{c:s}}$	$F_{\texttt{d:s}}$	Dev
0	0	72,289	72,289	69.56
0.1	0.03	55,407	71,668	70.39
0.1	0.1	54,591	69,988	70.87
0.1	0.3	56,660	57,729	70.32
0.1	1	55,860	27,058	**72.95**
0.1	3	55,534	9,885	60.82
0.1	10	56,513	3,149	55.55
0.03	1	69,390	28,046	67.13
0.1	1	55,860	27,058	**72.95**
0.3	1	31,763	27,525	70.32
1	1	11,816	27,418	71.01
3	1	4,040	27,559	71.08
10	1	1,456	27,875	72.26

Table 3: Number of non-zero weights for factors $F_{\texttt{c:s}}$ and $F_{\texttt{d:s}}$. The corresponding F1 scores on the development set are shown in the last column.

As mentioned in section 5.1, we only tune regularization parameters $\lambda_{\texttt{c:s}}$ and $\lambda_{\texttt{d:s}}$. We can not report results of all combinations since there are too many of them. Instead, we report results with either $\lambda_{\texttt{c:s}}$ or $\lambda_{\texttt{d:s}}$ fixed to the best tunned value. The number of active dimensions (i.e. with non-zero weight) and the development F1 score are examined in experiments.

Table 3 shows the results of these experiments. With the increasing of regularization parameters, the model becomes more and more sparser (as measured by the number of non-zero weights). The tuned optimal parameter values are $\lambda_{\texttt{c:s}} = 0.1$ and $\lambda_{\texttt{d:s}} = 1$. It is interesting to observe that the optimal regularization value for distituent factor is greater than the one for constituent factor. This fact can be explained that since there are more distituents than constituents, the distituent weights need to be penalized more heavily. The best development F1 is 72.95, greater than the F1 score 69.56 achieved without regularization, since the unregularized model may overfit the training data.

If we compare experiments with fixed $\lambda_{\texttt{c:s}}$, the development F1 score first increases and then decreases with the increase of $\lambda_{\texttt{d:s}}$. In contrast, with fixed $\lambda_{\texttt{d:s}}$, the performance varies little for different $\lambda_{\texttt{c:s}}$. These results somehow demonstrate the distituents modelled in CCM play a more important role than the constituents.

5.4 Discussion

Experiments show that we achieve better performance than original CCM while using compact grammars. There are some issues we want to discuss here.

1. We only test a few feature templates. Other features such as words, stems may improve the results. Moreover, punctuations contain useful information in grammar induction (Spitkovsky et al., 2011b; Ponvert et al., 2011), while currently punctuations are ignored in our model.
2. In previous unsupervised constituency grammar induction, how to choose parameters is an art. While in the proposed model, we use development set to perform model selection.
3. EM algorithm could only find sub-optima. One possible solution is the Lateen EM (Spitkovsky et al., 2011a), in which multiple objective functions are an alternative optimized. Another method is the annealing technique during probability estimation process. We will investigate these in future work.
4. ℓ_1-norm regularization is used to learn sparse and compact model. Bayesian learning is an alternative framework, which can be also applied to CCM.

570

6 Related Work

The Constituent-Context Model (Klein and Manning, 2002; Klein, 2005) is the first unsupervised constituency grammar induction system that achieves better performance than the trivial right branching baseline for English. However, the performance of CCM degrades on long sentences. Following approaches improve CCM in various aspects. Smith and Eisner (2004) propose to condition the yield feature on the length of the yield and use annealing techniques to estimate parameters. Annealing techniques can be also used for the proposed F-CCM, which we plan to do in future work. Klein and Manning (2004) demonstrate the joint model of constituency and dependency could improve unsupervised grammar inference. Some other approaches also consider to use additional information such as the words (Headden III et al., 2009), the automatic induced tags (Headden III et al., 2008), or the parent information (Mirroshandel and Ghassem-Sani, 2008). These information could be easily incorporated to the proposed model as features.

Feature-based models have been widely used in many supervised tasks such as parsing (Charniak, 2000), word alignment (Moore, 2005; Liu et al., 2006), machine translation (Koehn et al., 2003), etc. For the unsupervised learning tasks, the calculation of normalization part is usually time-consuming or even impossible. Existing approaches are mainly based on the contrastive estimation (Smith and Eisner, 2005; Smith and Eisner, 2005; Dyer et al., 2011) to learn parameters. The local normalized feature-based model has been proposed in (Berg-Kirkpatrick et al., 2010), in which features are defined over generative rules and the normalization is done locally. They use the ℓ_2 regularization, while we apply the local-normalization model to CCM with ℓ_1 regularization and show improved performance could be achieved with sparse solution. Many unsupervised approaches aim to learn compact and sparse grammar, including the Bayesian models (Johnson et al., 2007; Cohn et al., 2010; Blunsom and Cohn, 2010) and posterior regularization (Ganchev et al., 2010). We use alternative (and simpler) regularization technique to obtain sparse solution.

The most related work is (Golland et al., 2012), in which a similar feature-based model for CCM is proposed. There are many differences between their work and our proposed model. (1) We use ℓ_1 regularization to learn sparse model, while they do not mention sparsity problem. (2) We propose to use a separated development set to perform model selection and an additional test set to report final results, while they directly train and evaluate their model on the same dataset, which is problematic. (3) We evaluate different feature sets from theirs. The limited lengths for sequences could reduce the memory usage for long sentences.

7 Conclusion

The constituent-context model performs well on short sentences, but the performance degrades on longer sentences. We present a feature-based model for CCM, in which linguistic knowledge can be integrated as features. Features take the log-linear form with local normalization, so the EM algorithm is still applicable to estimate model parameters. To avoid overfitting, we use the ℓ_1-norm regularization to control model complexity. We also proposed a reasonable model selection and evaluation framework. Experimental results demonstrate that the feature-based model achieves comparable performance on short sentences but significantly outperforms the original CCM on longer sentences.

Acknowledgments

We would like to thank Zhonghua Li for insightful discussion about the feature-based model and help on the numeric optimization toolkit. We also thank Xiangyu Duan for his help on the reimplementation of original CCM. Thank the anonymous reviewers for their helpful comments and suggestions.

References

Galen Andrew and Jianfeng Gao. 2007. Scalable training of l1-regularized log-linear models. In *Proceedings of the 24th International Conference on Machine Learning*, pages 33–40.

Taylor Berg-Kirkpatrick, Alexandre Bouchard-Côté, John DeNero, and Dan Klein. 2010. Painless unsupervised learning with features. In *Human Language Technologies: The 2010 Annual Conference of the North American Chapter of the Association for Computational Linguistics*, pages 582–590.

Phil Blunsom and Trevor Cohn. 2010. Unsupervised induction of tree substitution grammars for dependency parsing. In *Proceedings of the 2010 Conference on Empirical Methods in Natural Language Processing*, pages 1204–1213.

Rens Bod. 2006. An all-subtrees approach to unsupervised parsing. In *Proceedings of the 21st International Conference on Computational Linguistics and 44th Annual Meeting of the Association for Computational Linguistics*, pages 865–872.

Eugene Charniak. 2000. A maximum-entropy-inspired parser. In *Proceedings of the 1st North American chapter of the Association for Computational Linguistics conference*, pages 132–139.

Shay Cohen and Noah A. Smith. 2009. Shared logistic normal distributions for soft parameter tying in unsupervised grammar induction. In *Proceedings of Human Language Technologies: The 2009 Annual Conference of the North American Chapter of the Association for Computational Linguistics*, pages 74–82.

Trevor Cohn, Sharon Goldwater, and Phil Blunsom. 2009. Inducing compact but accurate tree-substitution grammars. In *Proceedings of Human Language Technologies: The 2009 Annual Conference of the North American Chapter of the Association for Computational Linguistics*, pages 548–556.

Trevor Cohn, Phil Blunsom, and Sharon Goldwater. 2010. Inducing Tree-Substitution grammars. *Journal of Machine Learning Research*, 11:3053–3096.

John DeNero and Jakob Uszkoreit. 2011. Inducing sentence structure from parallel corpora for reordering. In *Proceedings of the 2011 Conference on Empirical Methods in Natural Language Processing*, pages 193–203.

Chris Dyer, Jonathan H. Clark, Alon Lavie, and Noah A. Smith. 2011. Unsupervised word alignment with arbitrary features. In *Proceedings of the 49th Annual Meeting of the Association for Computational Linguistics: Human Language Technologies*, pages 409–419.

Kuzman Ganchev, João Graça, Jennifer Gillenwater, and Ben Taskar. 2010. Posterior regularization for structured latent variable models. *Journal of Machine Learning Research*, 11:2001–2049.

Dave Golland, John DeNero, and Jakob Uszkoreit. 2012. A feature-rich constituent context model for grammar induction. In *Proceedings of the 50th Annual Meeting of the Association for Computational Linguistics (Volume 2: Short Papers)*, pages 17–22.

William P. Headden III, David McClosky, and Eugene Charniak. 2008. Evaluating unsupervised part-of-speech tagging for grammar induction. In *Proceedings of the 22nd International Conference on Computational Linguistics (Coling 2008)*, pages 329–336.

William P. Headden III, Mark Johnson, and David McClosky. 2009. Improving unsupervised dependency parsing with richer contexts and smoothing. In *Proceedings of Human Language Technologies: The 2009 Annual Conference of the North American Chapter of the Association for Computational Linguistics*, pages 101–109.

Mark Johnson, Thomas L. Griffiths, and Sharon Goldwater. 2007. Adaptor grammars: A framework for specifying compositional nonparametric bayesian models. In *Advances in Neural Information Processing Systems 19*, pages 641–648.

Bevan K. Jones, Mark Johnson, and Michael C. Frank. 2010. Learning words and their meanings from unsegmented child-directed speech. In *Human Language Technologies: The 2010 Annual Conference of the North American Chapter of the Association for Computational Linguistics*, pages 501–509.

Dan Klein and Christopher D. Manning. 2002. A generative constituent-context model for improved grammar induction. In *Proceedings of 40th Annual Meeting of the Association for Computational Linguistics*, pages 128–135.

Dan Klein and Christopher Manning. 2004. Corpus-based induction of syntactic structure: Models of dependency and constituency. In *Proceedings of the 42nd Meeting of the Association for Computational Linguistics (ACL'04), Main Volume*, pages 478–485.

Dan Klein. 2005. *The Unsupervised Learning of Natural Language Structure*. Ph.D. thesis, Stanford University.

Philipp Koehn, Franz J. Och, and Daniel Marcu. 2003. Statistical phrase-based translation. In *Proceedings of the 2003 Human Language Technology Conference of the North American Chapter of the Association for Computational Linguistics*, pages 48–54.

K. Lari and S. J. Young. 1990. The estimation of stochastic context-free grammars using the Inside-Outside algorithm. *Computer Speech and Language*, 4:35–56.

Yang Liu, Qun Liu, and Shouxun Lin. 2006. Tree-to-string alignment template for statistical machine translation. In *Proceedings of the 21st International Conference on Computational Linguistics and 44th Annual Meeting of the Association for Computational Linguistics*, pages 609–616.

Mitchell P. Marcus, Mary Ann Marcinkiewicz, and Beatrice Santorini. 1993. Building a large annotated corpus of English: the Penn Treebank. *Computational Linguistics*, 19(2):313–330.

Seyed Abolghasem Mirroshandel and Gholamreza Ghassem-Sani. 2008. Unsupervised grammar induction using a parent based constituent context model. In *Proceedings of the 18th European Conference on Artificial Intelligence*, pages 293–297.

Robert C. Moore. 2005. A discriminative framework for bilingual word alignment. In *Proceedings of Human Language Technology Conference and Conference on Empirical Methods in Natural Language Processing*, pages 81–88.

Elias Ponvert, Jason Baldridge, and Katrin Erk. 2011. Simple unsupervised grammar induction from raw text with cascaded finite state models. In *Proceedings of the 49th Annual Meeting of the Association for Computational Linguistics: Human Language Technologies*, pages 1077–1086.

Yoav Seginer. 2007. Fast unsupervised incremental parsing. In *Proceedings of the 45th Annual Meeting of the Association of Computational Linguistics*, pages 384–391.

Noah A. Smith and Jason Eisner. 2004. Annealing techniques for unsupervised statistical language learning. In *Proceedings of the 42nd Meeting of the Association for Computational Linguistics (ACL'04), Main Volume*, pages 486–493.

Noah A. Smith and Jason Eisner. 2005. Contrastive estimation: Training log-linear models on unlabeled data. In *Proceedings of the 43rd Annual Meeting of the Association for Computational Linguistics (ACL'05)*, pages 354–362.

Valentin I. Spitkovsky, Hiyan Alshawi, and Daniel Jurafsky. 2010. From baby steps to leapfrog: How "less is more" in unsupervised dependency parsing. In *Human Language Technologies: The 2010 Annual Conference of the North American Chapter of the Association for Computational Linguistics*, pages 751–759.

Valentin I. Spitkovsky, Hiyan Alshawi, and Daniel Jurafsky. 2011a. Lateen EM: Unsupervised training with multiple objectives, applied to dependency grammar induction. In *Proceedings of the 2011 Conference on Empirical Methods in Natural Language Processing*, pages 1269–1280.

Valentin I. Spitkovsky, Hiyan Alshawi, and Daniel Jurafsky. 2011b. Punctuation: Making a point in unsupervised dependency parsing. In *Proceedings of the Fifteenth Conference on Computational Natural Language Learning*, pages 19–28.

Menno van Zaanen. 2000. ABL: Alignment-based learning. In *Proceedings of the 18th International Conference on Computational Linguistics (Coling 2000)*, volume 2, pages 961–967.

Deyi Xiong, Min Zhang, and Haizhou Li. 2010. Learning translation boundaries for phrase-based decoding. In *Human Language Technologies: The 2010 Annual Conference of the North American Chapter of the Association for Computational Linguistics*, pages 136–144.

Accuracy and robustness in measuring the lexical similarity of semantic role fillers for automatic semantic MT evaluation

Anand Karthik TUMULURU, Chi-kiu LO and **Dekai WU**
HKUST
Human Language Technology Center
Department of Computer Science and Engineering
Hong Kong University of Science and Technology
{jackielo,aktumuluru,dekai}@cs.ust.hk

Abstract

We present larger-scale evidence overturning previous results, showing that among the many alternative phrasal lexical similarity measures based on word vectors, the Jaccard coefficient most increases the robustness of MEANT, the recently introduced, fully-automatic, state-of-the-art semantic MT evaluation metric. MEANT critically depends on phrasal lexical similarity scores in order to automatically determine which semantic role fillers should be aligned between reference and machine translations. The robustness experiments were conducted across various data sets following NIST MetricsMaTr protocols, showing higher Kendall correlation with human adequacy judgments against BLEU, METEOR (with and without synsets), WER, PER, TER and CDER. The Jaccard coefficient is shown to be more discriminative and robust than cosine similarity, the Min/Max metric with mutual information, Jensen Shannon divergence, or the Dice's coefficient. We also show that with Jaccard coefficient as the phrasal lexical similarity metric, individual word token scores are best aggregated into phrasal segment similarity scores using the geometric mean, rather than either the arithmetic mean or competitive linking style word alignments. Furthermore, we show empirically that a context window size of 5 captures the optimal amount of information for training the word vectors. The combined results suggest a new formulation of MEANT with significantly improved robustness across data sets.

1 Introduction

We present larger-scale evidence overturning previous results, showing that the Jaccard coefficient among the alternative lexical similarity measure based on word vectors most increases the robustness of MEANT, even more than that of the Min/Max metric with mutual information metric, as used by Lo *et al.* (2012) in their formulation of MEANT that outperformed BLEU (Papineni *et al.*, 2002), NIST (Doddington, 2002), METEOR (Banerjee and Lavie, 2005), PER (Tillmann *et al.*, 1997), CDER (Leusch *et al.*, 2006), WER (Nießen *et al.*, 2000), and TER (Snover *et al.*, 2006).

MEANT, the fully-automatic, state-of-the-art semantic MT evaluation metric as introduced by Lo *et al.* (2012) uses the Min/Max metric with mutual information on word vectors as the similarity measure to score phrasal similarity of the semantic role fillers which is the matching criterion to align semantic frames. In achieving the same, word vectors are trained on a window size of 5 and use arithmetic mean to aggregate token similarity scores into segment similarity scores.

We explore the potential of alternate similarity metrics on word vectors such as the Jensen Shannon divergence, the Dice's coefficient and Jaccard coefficient apart from cosine similarity and the Min/Max metric with mutual information employed by Lo *et al.* (2012) in their work. We show that Jaccard coefficient not only outperforms the Min/Max metric with mutual information, in achieving higher Kendall correlation against human adequacy judgments, but all the other similarity measures in comparison.

In order to test the robustness of the method across various data sets, we conduct experiments across GALE-A, GALE-B and GALE-C data sets examining the Kendall correlation against human adequacy judgments following NIST MetricsMaTr protocols (Callison-Burch *et al.*, 2010). We train the weights used for computing the weighted f-score over matching role labels using a grid search and then test them on a combination of these data sets and since each data set has different average sentence length and number of sentences we identify robust metrics that perform across all the variations after thorough analysis on the quality of the weights assigned to the role labels.

The strategy used in evaluating the phrasal similarity score from the component token similarity scores is critical in deciding the overall performance of the MEANT metric, as role fillers are often phrases. In contrast to the arithmetic mean and competitive linking strategies we show that that using the geometric mean for this purpose is more reliable.

In order to examine the optimum amount of contextual information to be captured while training the word vectors, we vary the window size while training the word vectors from 3 to 13. Surprisingly, we achieve both high performance and robustness at the window size of 5 not only for Jaccard coefficient but across almost all the metrics in comparison.

Our results indicate that Jaccard coefficient on word vectors trained with a window size of 5, and using geometric mean style of aggregation as the criterion for aligning semantic frames and significantly enhances the performance in comparison to other metrics and robustness across varying data sets of MEANT.

2 Related work

Evaluating lexical similarity of phrases plays an important role in many language technology applications such as Machine Translation Evaluation, Word Sense disambiguation, Query Expansion, Information Retrieval, Question Answering etc.

BLEU (Papineni *et al.*, 2002) , NIST (Doddington, 2002), METEOR (Banerjee and Lavie, 2005), PER (Tillmann *et al.*, 1997), CDER (Leusch *et al.*, 2006), WER (Nießen *et al.*, 2000), and TER (Snover *et al.*, 2006), are some of the commonly used phrasal similarity metrics. Although lexical similarity evaluation with all the metrics can be done very quickly at low cost, they assume that a good translation shares the same lexical choices as the reference translation, which is not justified semantically.

We argue that a lexical similarity metric that reflects meaning similarity needs to be aware of the contextual similarity, and not merely flat lexical similarity.

3 Word vector models and similarity metrics

Word Vector models (Dagan, 2000) are guided by the principle that similar words occur in similar contexts. In the word vector model, each word in the lexicon is represented by a word vector, where each entry corresponds to the frequency of cooccurence with every other word in the lexicon. The definition of the cooccurence relation decides the nature of the context we capture and have been used in a wide variety of tasks, such as in word sense disambiguation by Gale *et al.* (1992) by defining the relation as the cooccurence within a distance of 50 words. Grammatical and syntactic relations were also identified, by defining the relation as the cooccurence in a relatively shorter window of 5 words, as in the work of Smadja (1993) and Dagan *et al.* (1993) . The word vector models can be readily trained on any large mono-lingual corpora and hence their utility is not constrained to resource rich languages.

In this work, we make a choice of defining the cooccurence relation as the joint cooccurence of the word within a short window of text, by the principle of occam's razor. A window size of n symmetrically encompasses word tokens at a distance of upto $\frac{(n-1)}{2}$ on both directions and hence captures not only semantic context, but but also a mixture of grammatical and topical cooccurences. We make a choice of not using any techniques such as stemming, lemmatisation or stop-word pruning as using such limit the use of the word vector models to only some languages.

The trained word vectors can be used with a variety of mathematical measures of similarity between a pair of vectors to evaluate the degree of similarity of the words that they represent. We use a diverse set of such functions, each quantifying a different aspect of the accumulated cooccurence statistics between a pair of vectors.

3.1 Cosine Similarity

Cosine measure gives the cosine of the angle between the two vectors and is commonly used in the vector space model. Since the word vectors have non-negative components, the range is between 0 and 1, where a value of 0 indicates that the vectors are orthogonal or dissimilary and a value of 1 indicates that the vectors are parallel or similar. The cosine similarity between two tokens x and y is defined as follows:

$$\begin{aligned}\overrightarrow{w_x} &= \text{context vector of word token x}\\ w_{xi} &= \text{attribute i of context vector } \overrightarrow{w_x}\end{aligned}$$

$$f(x, w_{xi}) = \frac{c(x, w_{xi})}{\sum_j c(x, w_{xj})}$$

$$\text{cosine}(x, y) = \frac{\sum_i f(x, w_{xi}) \times f(y, w_{yi})}{\sqrt{\sum_i f(x, w_{xi})^2}\sqrt{\sum_i f(y, w_{yi})^2}}$$

3.2 Min/Max metric with Mutual Information

Using the above given definition of w_{xi}, the min/max with mutual information (Cover and Thomas, 1991) similarity between two sequences of two tokens, x and y is defined as follows:

$$P(w_{xi} \mid x) = \frac{c(x, w_{xi})}{\sum_j c(x, w_{xj})}$$

$$P(w_{xi}) = \frac{\sum_y c(y, w_{xi})}{\sum_y \sum_j c(y, w_{xj})}$$

$$\text{MI}(x, w_{xi}) = \log\left(\frac{P(w_{xi} \mid x)}{P(w_{xi})}\right)$$

$$\text{MinMax-MI}(x,y) = \frac{\sum_i \min(\text{MI}(x, w_{xi}), \text{MI}(y, w_{y_i}))}{\sum_i \max(\text{MI}(x, w_{xi}), \text{MI}(y, w_{y_i}))}$$

The range of Min/Max metric with Mutual Information is 0 to 1, a value of 0 indicates that the vectors are completely dissimilar and a value of 1 indicated that they are identical.

3.3 Jensen Shannon Divergence

Using the above given definitions of w_{xi}, the Jesen Shannon divergence (Lin, 1991), (Rao, 1982) is defined as follows:

$$D(x \mid\mid \frac{x+y}{2}) = \sum_i P(w_{x_i} \mid x) \log \left(\frac{2 \times P(w_{x_i} \mid x)}{P(w_{x_i} \mid x) + P(w_{y_i} \mid y)} \right)$$

$$\text{JSD}(x,y) = D(x \mid\mid \frac{x+y}{2}) + D(y \mid\mid \frac{x+y}{2})$$

Here, $D(x \mid\mid y)$ represents the Kullback-Leibler Divergence (Cover and Thomas, 1991). The Jensen Shannon divergence addresses the problem of assymetry assosiated with KL divergence, and has a range of 0 to 1. The square root of Jensen Shannon Divergence is a metric, also with a range of 0 to 1, but since it is divergence metric, a value of 0 indicates that the vectors of x and y are similar and a value of 1 indicates that they are orthogonal.

3.4 Dice's coefficient

Dice's coefficient for two words x and y is defined as the ratio of total number of shared cooccurences of their vectors to the total number of cooccurences in both the vectors. It is formulated as follows:

$$\text{DC}(x,y) = \frac{\sum_i \min(c(x, w_{xi}), c(y, w_{y_i}))}{\sum_i (c(x, w_{xi}) + c(y, w_{y_i}))}$$

where the definitions of w_{xi} and $c(x, w_{x_i})$are the same as above. Here, $\min(a, b)$represents the minimum of the values a, b. The range of Dice's coefficient is 0 to 1, a value of 0 indicates that the vectors are completely dissimilar and a value of 1 indicated that they are identical.

3.5 Jaccard coefficient

The Jaccard coefficient for two words x and y is defined as the ratio of intersection of their cooccurences to the union of their cooccurences of their word vectors.

$$\text{JC}(x,y) = \frac{\sum_i \min(c(x, w_{xi}), c(y, w_{y_i}))}{\sum_i \max(c(x, w_{xi}), c(y, w_{y_i}))}$$

where the definitions of w_{x_i}, $c(x, w_{x_i})$ and $\min(a, b)$ are the same as above. Here, $\max(a, b)$ represents the maximum of the values a, b

The range of Jaccard coefficient is 0 to 1, a value of 0 indicates that the vectors are completely dissimilar and a value of 1 indicated that they are identical.

4 Computing phrasal similarity

In this section, we define the methods used in computing the similarity of two phrases given the degree of similarity of the component tokens. Evaluating phrasal similarity in the context of word vectors is a challenge, as we have no information about the alignment of the token pairs in the given phrases.The strategy employed must provide sufficient discriminatory power in order for MEANT to align the one pair of similar role fillers among many such pairs with mismatched lengths and word ordering. We now discuss the methods we use in computing the phrasal similarity scores from the component token similarity scores.

4.1 Arithmetic Mean

In this method, we simply assume that there is a complete alignment between the two phrases. We then compute the phrasal similarity score as the mean of similarity scores of all the component token pairs. The phrasal similarity between two sequences of word tokens $\vec{u}$ and $\vec{v}$ using the arithmetic mean method is defined as:

$$\text{AM}(\vec{u}, \vec{v}) = \frac{1}{t \times s} \sum_i \sum_j S(u_i, v_j)$$

where t is the number of word tokens in $\vec{u}$ and s is the number of word tokens in $\vec{v}$. $S(u_i, v_j)$ is the token similarity score of the ith token in $\vec{u}$ and the jth token in $\vec{v}$ obtained using any of the above mentioned token similarity metrics.

4.2 Geometric Mean

In this method, again, we assume that there a complete alignment between the two phrases. We then compute the phrasal similarity score as the geometric mean of similarity scores of all the component token pairs. The phrasal similarity between two sequences of word tokens $\vec{u}$ and $\vec{v}$ using the geometric mean method is defined as:

$$\text{GM}(\vec{u}, \vec{v}) = e^{\frac{1}{(t \times s)} \sum_j \sum_i \ln(S(u_i, v_j))}$$

where t is the number of word tokens in $\vec{u}$ and s is the number of word tokens in $\vec{v}$. $S(u_i, v_j)$is the token similarity score of the i^{th}token in $\vec{u}$and the jth token in $\vec{v}$ obtained using any of the above mentioned token similarity metrics.

4.3 Modified Competitive Linking

In this method we attempt to align the tokens in the phrases using the similarity score of the token pair as a heuristic. As in the previous methods, we avoid the danger of aligning a token in one segment to excessive numbers of tokens in the other segment, by adopting a variant of competitive linking by Melamed (1996). The competitive linking algorithm adopts a greedy best first strategy in making strictly one to one word alignments. Since we frequently encounter phrases for alignment with unequal lengths, this one to one constraint severely restricts alignments and so we modify the competitive linking strategy by allowing one to many alignments. The number of such one to many alignments must be equal to the difference in the segment lengths. Once these alignments have been made, we compute the similarity of the two phrases as the arithmetic mean of the similarity scores of the aligned tokens.

5 Jaccard coefficient outperforms other metrics

We show that the Jaccard coefficient outperforms other similarity metrics as the criterion for evaluating lexical similarity to align role fillers in MEANT.

5.1 Experimental Setup

We report the performance of all the similarity metrics - cosine similarity, Min/Max with mutual information, Jensen Shannon divergence, Jaccard coefficient and the Dice's coefficient on the word vector models as described above as criterion for aligning semantic frames in MEANT.

We train the word vector models on the uncased Gigaword corpus. We do not use techniqes such as stemming, lemmatisation or stop-word pruning. We train the word vectors on the Gigaword corpus with window sizes ranging from 3 to 13.

For our benchmark comparison, the evaluation data for our experiments is the same two sets of sentences, GALE-A and GALE-B that were used in Lo and Wu (2011), where in GALE-A is used for estimating the weight parameters of the metric by optimizing the correlation with human adequacy judgment, and then the learned weights are applied to testing on GALE-B. For the automatic semantic role labeling, we used the publicly available off-the-shelf shallow semantic parser, ASSERT (Pradhan *et al.*, 2004). Semantic frame alignment is done by applying maximum bipartite matching algorithm with the lexical similrity of predicates as edge weights. The correlation with human adequacy judgments on sentence-level system ranking is assessed by the standard NIST MetricsMaTr procedure (Callison-Burch *et al.*, 2010) using Kendall correlation coefficients.

We first run a grid search on the GALE-A data set for each of these metrics on all window sizes to obtain weights for the role labels. We then use these weights to evaluate the GALE-C data set. The Kendall correlation score is obtained using MEANT as described in Lo Wu 2012. In this experiment, we use geometric mean as the aggregation method and vary the window sizes for each metric to first identify one metric that performs robustly across all window sizes for the given dataset. We also examine the distribution of weights over the semantic role labels across all the window sizes to verify that the metric is both: performing consistently and producing the excpected distribution of weights over semantic role labels.

5.2 Results

Table 1 shows that the Jaccard coefficient performs consistently well and relatively out performs most other similarity metrics in comparision. It is surprising that the performance of all the metrics does not improve significantly and sometimes, decreases with increasing window size. For a window size of 5 for the Jaccard coefficient, we achieve close to 0.21 Kendall for testing on GALE-B, outperforming the scores reported on the same data sets MEANT in Lo *et al.* (2012). A kendall of 0.26 and 0.22 are observed for Dice's coefficient with window sizes of 3 and 11. On a closer look at the weights assigned to each role labels after training on GALE A, we observe that the weights in these cases have been abnormally chosen in the favour of matching role fillers with less important role labels, but on the contarary, in the case of Jaccard coefficient they have been distributed with relatively higher importance for predicate, agr0, arg1 and arg2 across all window sizes indicating that it is enabling the alignment of more important roles accurately.

6 Phrasal similarity best computed through geometric mean

We show that the Geometric mean method of aggregation out performs the arithmetic and competitive linking methods using Jaccard coefficient

6.1 Experimental Setup

We report the performance of the arithmetic mean and competitive linking methods of aggregation using Jaccard coefficient as the lexical similarity measure. These similarity metrics are employed on word vectors trained on the Gigaword corpus with window sizes ranging from 3 to 13. The evaluation data for our experiment is the same as described above.

6.2 Results

In tables 2 and 3, we observe that the geometric mean method of aggregation outperforms arithmetic mean and competitive linking methods of aggregation. Although we see markedly higher kendall scores with training on the GALE-A data set using the modified competitive linking method of aggregation, the resultant weights that yield such high scores are not only improperly distributed, but also perform poorly when tested on the

Table 1: Kendall correlation scores with human adequacy judgment on GALE-A (training) and GALE-B (testing) comparing MEANT integrated with various lexical similarity measures as criterion for aligning semantic role fillers: (a) cosine similarity, (b) Min/Max with mutual information (c) Jensen Shannon divergence (d) Jaccard coefficient and (e) Dice's coefficient with word vectors trained from window sizes 3-13 and using geometric mean as the aggregation method

	Training on GALE A	Testing on GALE B
window size 3	0.2702	0.2095
window size 5	0.3783	0.1523
window size 7	0.3783	0.1142
window size 9	0.3153	0.0857
window size 11	0.2972	0.180
window size 13	0.3603	0.1523
Min/Max with MI		
window size 3	0.3603	0.1333
window size 5	0.3603	0.1523
window size 7	0.2252	0.1714
window size 9	0.3333	0.2476
window size 11	0.2882	0.1523
window size 13	0.2522	0.1142
JSD		
window size 3	0.3963	0
window size 5	0.3603	0
window size 7	0.3423	0
window size 9	0.3603	0
window size 11	0.3243	0.0952
window size 13	0.3603	0.1428
Jaccard Coefficient		
window size 3	0.3783	0.1904
window size 5	0.3333	0.2095
window size 7	0.3423	0.2000
window size 9	0.3423	0.1809
window size 11	0.3513	0.0952
window size 13	0.3513	0.1142
Dice's Coefficient		
window size 3	0.3603	0.2666
window size 5	0.3603	0.1809
window size 7	0.3513	0.1904
window size 9	0.3693	0.1714
window size 11	0.3693	0.2285
window size 13	0.3603	0.1714

Table 2: Sentence-level correlation with human adequacy judgment on GALE-A (training) and GALE-B (testing) comparing MEANT integrated with Jaccard coefficient as measure of lexical similarity on word vectors trained on window sizes 3-13 between semantic role fillers using arithmetic mean as the aggregation method

	Training on GALE A	Testing on GALE B
Jaccard Coefficient		
window size 3	0.3603	0.1523
window size 5	0.3333	0.2000
window size 7	0.3603	0.1809
window size 9	0.3603	0.1619
window size 11	0.3603	0.2380
window size 13	0.3603	0.2095

Table 3: Kendall correlation scores with human adequacy judgment on GALE-A (training) and GALE-B (testing) comparing MEANT integrated with Jaccard coefficient as measure of lexical similarity on word vectors trained with window sizes 3-13 between semantic role fillers using Competitive linking as the aggregation method

	Training on GALE A	Testing on GALE B
Jaccard coefficient		
window size 3	0.3873	0.1714
window size 5	0.3963	0.1904
window size 7	0.3783	0.1333
window size 9	0.3783	0.0952
window size 11	0.3693	0.0761
window size 13	0.3693	0.0952

Table 4: Kendall correlation scores with human adequacy judgment and the corresponding role label weights on GALE-C as the training set and GALE-A as the testing set with MEANT integrated with Jaccard coefficient as measure of lexical similarity between semantic role fillers with word vectors trained on window sizes 3-13 and using Geometric Mean as the aggregation method. The role labels are pr - predicate, a0 - arg0, a1 - arg1, a2 - arg2, te - temporal, lo - locative, pu - purpose, ex - extent, ma - manner, o - other, m - model, n - negation

Jaccard Coefficient	GALE C	GALE A	pr	a0	a1	a2	te	lo	pu	ex	ma	o	m	n
window size 3	0.1443	0.1981	2	3	1	0	2	0	2	0	0	0	0	2
window size 5	0.1520	0.3243	5	3	0	0	1	0	0	1	0	1	0	1
window size 7	0.1505	0.1351	0	4	4	0	0	0	3	0	0	0	0	1
window size 9	0.1520	0.1441	1	2	0	0	3	0	1	0	0	2	0	3
window size 11	0.1505	0.1441	1	2	0	0	3	0	1	0	0	2	0	3
window size 13	0.1566	0.1441	1	2	0	0	3	0	1	0	0	2	0	3

GALE-B data set. Other variants of the competitive linking method of similar nature may also be expected to suffer from this problem of overfitting.

The arithmetic mean method performs extremely well in the case of higher window sizes - 11 and 13 in this pirticular case, where we use GALE-A as the train data set and GALE-B as the test dataset, but does not perform as well as the geometric mean over relatively larger datasets as in the case of training with GALE-C and testing on GALE-A and GALE-B, where we observe negative correlation scores.

It has been observed, the method in which we compute the phrasal similarity scores from the component token similarity scores of the role fillers impacts the overall performance at two levels - (1) In effectively handling different lengths of phrases and (2) In the distribution of weights on the roles. By out-performing arithmetic mean and competitive linking, the geometric mean method of aggregation as seen in table 1 has proven to handle both the factors robustly.

7 Jaccard coefficient is robust across various data sets

Given the positive results on the above mentioned data sets, we ask : Does Jaccard coefficient perform robustly across various data sets? The concerns with varying data sets is two fold: (1) Does Jaccard coefficient as a metric have enough discriminatory power? (2) Is the Jaccard coefficient enabling consistent distribution of weights to role labels during training.

7.1 Experimental Setup

We follow a similar setup as laid out in the previous experiments, except for our benchmark comparison, the evaluation data for our experiments we use GALE-A, GALE-B and GALE-C as used in that were used in Lo and Wu (2011), where in GALE-C is used for estimating the weight parameters of the metric by optimizing the correlation with human adequacy judgment, and then the learned weights are applied to testing on both GALE-A and GALE-B.

7.2 Results

In tables 4 and 5, we observe that Jaccard coefficient still performs very well on varying the training and testing data sets, achieving scores of 0.15, 0.32 and 0.26 on GALE-C (training), GALE-A (testing) and GALE-B (testing) respectively. This indicates robustness of Jaccard coefficient as a lexical metric and its reliability for using it across any new data sets.

Table 5: Kendall correlation scores with human adequacy judgment and the corresponding role label weights on GALE-C as the training set and GALE-B as the testing set with MEANT integrated with Jaccard coefficient as measure of lexical similarity between semantic role fillers with word vectors trained on window sizes 3-13 and using Geometric Mean as the aggregation method. The role labels are pr - predicate, a0 - arg0, a1 - arg1, a2 - arg2, te - temporal, lo - locative, pu - purpose, ex - extent, ma - manner, o - other, m - model, n - negation

Jaccard Coefficeint	GALE C	GALE B	pr	a0	a1	a2	te	lo	pu	ex	ma	o	m	n
window size 3	0.1443	0.1333	2	3	1	0	2	0	2	0	0	0	0	1
window size 5	0.1520	0.2666	5	3	0	0	1	0	0	1	0	1	0	1
window size 7	0.1505	0.0476	0	4	4	0	0	0	3	0	0	0	0	1
window size 9	0.1520	0.1904	1	2	0	0	3	0	0	0	0	2	0	4
window size 11	0.1505	0.1523	1	2	0	0	3	0	1	0	0	2	0	3
window size 13	0.1566	0.1714	1	2	0	0	3	0	0	0	0	2	0	4

7.3 What is the optimal window size?

A closer analysis at the weights assigned to the role labels on training with Jaccard coefficient across all window sizes using the geometric mean method of aggregation shows that evaluating with word vectors trained on a window size of 5 gives relatively higher importance by by concentrating the weight mass over the more important role labels. This has been observed even for the experiments with a different data set - by training on GALE-A and testing on GALE-B. We also observe relatively higher scores consistent with the weighing scheme, using this combination for all the data sets. Jaccard coefficient with word vectors trained on a window size of 5, using the geometric mean method of evaluating phrasal similarity out performs all the other methods and robustly so across various data sets.

8 Conclusion

We have shown through a broad range of comparative experiments that Jaccard coefficient as a phrasal lexical similarity metric within MEANT out performs all the other metrics and most importantly than that of the Min/Max with mutual information metric, as used by Lo *et al.* (2012) in thier formulation of MEANT that outperformed BLEU, METEOR, WER, PER, CDER and TER.

We have also shown that using a window size of 5 the word vectors is optimal to train the word vectors after analyzing the performance of Jaccard coefficent across window sizes 3 to 13. Jaccard coefficient is shown to be more discriminative using the geometric mean method of aggregation over the arithmetic mean and competitive linking methods. Through experiments across across various data sets Jaccard coeffficient as a lexical similarity metric is shown to be robust and consistently yielding high performance.

By incorporating Jaccard coefficient as the lexical similarity metric, we except that the new formulation of the MEANT metric would show improved performance and robustness.

Acknowledgments

This material is based upon work supported in part by the Defense Advanced Research Projects Agency (DARPA) under BOLT contract no. HR0011-12-C-0016, and GALE contract nos. HR0011-06-C-0022 and HR0011-06-C-0023; by the European Union under the FP7 grant agreement no. 287658; and by the Hong Kong Research Grants Council (RGC) research grants GRF621008, GRF612806, DAG03/04.EG09, RGC6256/00E, and RGC6083/99E. Any opinions, findings and conclusions or recommendations expressed in this material are those of the authors and do not necessarily reflect the views of the RGC, EU, or DARPA.

References

Satanjeev Banerjee and Alon Lavie. METEOR: An Automatic Metric for MT Evaluation with Improved Correlation with Human Judgments. In *Proceedings of the 43th Annual Meeting of the Association of Computational Linguistics (ACL-05)*, pages 65–72, 2005.

Chris Callison-Burch, Philipp Koehn, Christof Monz, Kay Peterson, Mark Pryzbocki, and Omar Zaidan. Findings of the 2010 Joint Workshop on Statistical Machine Translation and Metrics for Machine Translation. In *Proceedings of the Joint 5th Workshop on Statistical Machine Translation and MetricsMATR*, pages 17–53, Uppsala, Sweden, 15-16 July 2010.

T. Cover and J. Thomas. *Elements of information theory*. Wiley, New York, 1991.

Ido Dagan, Shaul Marcus, and Shaul Markovitch. Contextual word similarity and estimation from sparse data. In Lenhart K. Schubert, editor, *ACL*, pages 164–171. ACL, 1993.

Ido Dagan. Contextual word similarity. In Robert Dale, Herman Moisl, and Harold Somers, editors, *Handbook of Natural Language Processing*, pages 459–476. Marcel Dekker, New York, 2000.

G. Doddington. Automatic Evaluation of Machine Translation Quality using N-gram Co-occurrence Statistics. In *Proceedings of the 2nd International Conference on Human Language Technology Research (HLT-02)*, pages 138–145, San Francisco, CA, USA, 2002. Morgan Kaufmann Publishers Inc.

William A. Gale, Kenneth Ward Church, and David Yarowsky. A method for disambiguating word senses in a large corpus. *Computers and the Humanities*, 26:415–439, 1992.

Gregor Leusch, Nicola Ueffing, and Hermann Ney. CDer: Efficient MT Evaluation Using Block Movements. In *Proceedings of the 13th Conference of the European Chapter of the Association for Computational Linguistics (EACL-06)*, 2006.

J. Lin. Divergence measures based on the shannon entropy. *Information Theory, IEEE Transactions on*, 37(1):145 –151, jan 1991.

Chi-kiu Lo and Dekai Wu. Structured vs. Flat Semantic Role Representations for Machine Translation Evaluation. In *Proceedings of the 5th Workshop on Syntax and Structure in Statistical Translation (SSST-5)*, 2011.

Chi-kiu Lo, Anand Karthik Tumuluru, and Dekai Wu. Fully automatic semantic mt evaluation. In *Proceedings of the Seventh Workshop on Statistical Machine Translation*, pages 243–252, Montréal, Canada, June 2012. Association for Computational Linguistics.

I. Dan Melamed. Automatic construction of clean broad-coverage translation lexicons. In *Proceedings of the 2nd Conference of the Association for Machine Translation in the Americas (AMTA-1996)*, 1996.

Sonja Nießen, Franz Josef Och, Gregor Leusch, and Hermann Ney. A Evaluation Tool for Machine Translation: Fast Evaluation for MT Research. In *Proceedings of the 2nd International Conference on Language Resources and Evaluation (LREC-2000)*, 2000.

Kishore Papineni, Salim Roukos, Todd Ward, and Wei-Jing Zhu. BLEU: A Method for Automatic Evaluation of Machine Translation. In *Proceedings of the 40th Annual Meeting of the Association for Computational Linguistics (ACL-02)*, pages 311–318, 2002.

Sameer Pradhan, Wayne Ward, Kadri Hacioglu, James H. Martin, and Dan Jurafsky. Shallow Semantic Parsing Using Support Vector Machines. In *Proceedings of the 2004 Conference on Human Language Technology and the North American Chapter of the Association for Computational Linguistics (HLT-NAACL-04)*, 2004.

C. Radhakrishna Rao. Diversity: Its Measurement, Decomposition, Apportionment and Analysis. *Sankhy: The Indian Journal of Statistics, Series A*, 44(1):1–22, 1982.

F. Smadja. Retrieving collocations from text: Xtract. *Computational Linguistics*, 19(1):143–177, 1993.

Matthew Snover, Bonnie J. Dorr, Richard Schwartz, Linnea Micciulla, and John Makhoul. A Study of Translation Edit Rate with Targeted Human Annotation. In *Proceedings of the 7th Conference of the Association for Machine Translation in the Americas (AMTA-06)*, pages 223–231, 2006.

Christoph Tillmann, Stephan Vogel, Hermann Ney, Arkaitz Zubiaga, and Hassan Sawaf. Accelerated DP Based Search For Statistical Translation. In *Proceedings of the 5th European Conference on Speech Communication and Technology (EUROSPEECH-97)*, 1997.

Type Construction of Event Nouns in Mandarin Chinese

Shan Wang[1, 2] Chu-Ren Huang[1]

[1]Dept. of Chinese and Bilingual Studies, The Hong Kong Polytechnic University, Hung Hom, Kowloon, Hong Kong

[2] Department of Computer Science, Volen Center for Complex Systems, Brandeis University

{wangshanstar, churenhuang} @gmail.com

Abstract

Natural and non-natural kinds have significant differences. This paper explores the subclasses of each kind and establishes the type system for event nouns. These nouns are divided into natural types, artifactual types, complex types (including natural complex types and artifactual complex types). This new classification not only enriches the Generative Lexicon theory, but also helps us to capture the properties of different types of event nouns.

1 Introduction

A considerable amount of research has been condu cted into event nouns in Mandarin Chinese (Chu 2000; Han 2010a; Ma 1995; Wang & Zhu 2000; Wang & Huang 2011a, 2011b, 2011c, 2012a, 2012b, 2012c, 2012d). Previous research on the classification of these nouns is based on their semantic categories (Han 2004, 2010b; Liu 2004; Wang 2010; Zhong 2010). However, such classification conceals the shared characteristics of different categories of event nouns. Because natural and non-natural kinds have significant differences (Pustejovsky 2001, 2006; Pustejovsky & Jezek 2008), this paper explores the subclasses of each kind and establishes the type system for event nouns.

The Data in this research are collected from three sources: (a) a balanced Modern Chinese corpus *Sinica Corpus*[1], accessed through *Chinese Word Sketch Engine*[2], (b) Gigaword Corpus, also accessed through *Chinese Word Sketch Engine*, and (c) web data collected through the search engines *google* and *baidu*.

2 Related Work

Pustejovsky (2001, 2006) and Pustejovsky & Jezek (2008) establish a type system for the three upper concepts (entity, event and quality). Each concept is divided into three subtypes (natural, artifactual and complex) by using qualia structure as a typing specification. Entities are distinguished into three types: (a) Natural Types: Predication from the domain of substance, e.g., the qualia formal or constitutive. (b) Functional Types: Predication includes reference to either agentive or telic qualia. (c) Complex Types: Cartesian type formed by Dot Object Construction. Similarly, the domains of relations and properties are also partitioned into three ranks: (a) Natural Events: Arguments in the predicate or relation are only from the domain of substance, e.g., the qualia formal or constitutive. (b) Functional Events: At least one argument in the predicate or relation is a functional type, f, e.g., makes reference to either agentive or telic qualia. (c) Complex Events: At least one argument in the predicate or relation is a complex type, e.g., a type formed by Dot Object Construction.

Pustejovsky (2006) further discusses three linguistic diagnostics which motivate a fundamental distinction between natural and

[1] http://db1x.sinica.edu.tw/kiwi/mkiwi/

[2] http://wordsketch.ling.sinica.edu.tw/

unnatural kinds. These diagnostics are: (a) Nominal Predication: How the common noun behaves predicatively; (b) Adjectival Predication: How adjectives modifying the common noun can be interpreted; (c) Interpretation in Coercive Contexts: How NPs with the common noun are interpreted in coercive environments. The analysis in Pustejovsky (2006) is summarized in Table 1.

Diagnostics		Natural Kind	Non-Natural Kinds
Nominal Predication	singular predication	yes	yes
	nominal co-predication	no	yes
	and-therefore-construction	yes	yes
Adjectival Predication	adjectival modification	unambiguous in their modification of the nominal head	modify aspects of the nominal head other than the physical object; ambiguous
Interpretation in Coercive Contexts	selection of NPs in type coercive contexts	NPs carry no prior information to undergo type coercion	NPs carry their own default interpretation in coercive contexts

Table 1: Diagnostics between Natural and Non-Natural Kinds

Pustejovsky (2006) has used the three diagnostics to test entity nouns. In the following, we will use them to test event nouns, as depicted in (1)-(4).

(1) a. 這是地震。
Zhè shì dìzhèn.
this is earthquake
'This is an earthquake.'
b. ！這是地震和海嘯。
！Zhè shì dìzhèn hé h ixiào.
this is earthquake and tsunami
！'This is an earthquake and a tsunami.'
c. 這是地震，所以是自然災害。
Zhè shì dìzhèn, su y shì zìrán zāihài.
this is earthquake, therefore is natural disaster
'This is an earthquake, and therefore a natural disaster.'

(1) show cases of nominal predication of natural-kind event nouns. They permit singular predication as shown in (1a). Same with entity nouns in Pustejovsky (2006), natural event noun requires predicative uniqueness, so the nominal co-predication in (1b) is an anomaly. The predication in (1b) is contradictory. In (1c), the construction 所以是 *su y shì* 'therefore (it) is' is valid with the first noun as a subtype of the second. Since 地震 *dìzhèn* 'earthquake' is a subtype of 自然災害 *zìrán zāihài* 'natural disaster', the construction in (1c) is acceptable.

(2) a.這是婚禮。
Zhè shì hūnl .
this is wedding
'This is a wedding.'
b. 這是婚禮和宴會。
Zhè shì hūnl hé yànhuì.
this is wedding and banquet
'This is a weddings and a banquet.'
c. 這是婚禮，所以是社會活動。
Zhè shì hūnl , su y shì shèhuì huódòng.
this is wedding, therefore is social activity
'This is a wedding, and therefore a social activity.'

(2) show cases of nominal predication of non-natural kind event nouns. Non-natural kind event nouns permit both singular predication and co-predication as shown in (2a) and (2b) respectively. (2a) tells us what this activity is. (2b) shows this activity has the function of both a wedding and a banquet. In (2c), a wedding is a subtype of social

activities, so (2c) is valid when 所以是 *su y shì* 'therefore (it) is' links the two event nouns.

(3) a. 猛烈的地震
mĕngliède dìzhèn
violent earthquake
'a violent earthquake'

b. 很長的早餐
hĕn ch ng de z ocān
very long DE breakfast
'a very long breakfast'

(3) are examples of adjectival modification to both natural and non-natural event nouns. In (3a), the adjective 猛烈的 *mĕngliède* 'violent' modifies the intensity of the earthquake and is unambiguous. In (3b), the modifier 很長的 *hĕn ch ng de* 'very long' can refer to both the eating event and the food itself, so (3b) is ambiguous.

(4) a. ！他們開始了風。
! Tāmen kāish le fēng.
they begin ASP wind
! 'They began the wind.'

b. 他們開始了體操比賽。
Tāmen kāish le t cāo b sài.
They begin le gymnastics competition
'They began the gymnastics competition.'

(4) show the difference between natural and non-natural event nouns in coercive context. In (4a), the natural event noun 風 *fēng* 'wind' has no prior information to get coerced, so this sentence is odd. In (4b), however, the non-natural event noun 體操 *t cāo* 'gymnastics' is coerced to be performing gyms through agentive role exploitation.

Examples (1)-(4) indicate that event nouns display clear differences between natural and non-natural kinds. This is the similar to entity nouns.
However, the discussion on nominal co-predication and adjectival predication in Pustejovsky (2006) is not sufficient. First, let's look at cases of nominal co-predication. Though non-natural kinds permit nominal co-predication, it is impossible to co-predicate any artifacts, as shown in (5).

(5) ！這是鋼筆和桌子。
! Zhè shì gāngb hé zhuōzi.
this is pen and table
!this is a pen and a table.

A pen is a long thin object that is used for writing, while a table is a piece of furniture with a flat top that is used for putting things on. It is rarely possible that an entity can have either the form or function that both a pen and a table have. The basis for nominal co-predication of artifacts is that the artifacts describe different form (the formal role) or function (the telic role) of one entity from different perspectives. This argument also holds for event nouns, as shown in (6).

(6) ！這是戰爭和海水浴。
! Zhè shì zhànzhēng hé h ishu yù.
this is war and seawater bath
! 'This is a war and a seawater bath.'

A war is a violent fight between different parties that last long, while a seawater bath is a way that you wash yourself in seawater. The two artificial events are too divergent to be co-predicated and refer to one social event.

Second, let's turn to adjectival modification. It is not the case that all natural kinds are unambiguous when they are modified by adjectives, as shown in (7).

(7) 大雨
dà y
heavy rain
'heavy rain'

In (7), the adjective 大 *dà* 'heavy' can modify the raining event and the raindrops. This is because 雨 *y* 'rain' is a complex type and thus inherently ambiguous.

Besides, it is not true that all non-natural kinds are ambiguous when they are modified by adjectives, as shown in (8).

(8) 白色的牆
báisède qiáng
white wall
'a white wall'

In (8), the adjective 白色的 *báisède* 'white' modifies the artifact 牆 *qiáng* 'wall', which means that the wall has a white color. It is not ambiguous at all.

Based on these analyses, we made some modifications to nominal co-predication and adjectival modification in Pustejovsky (2006). a) Nominal co-predication of non-natural kinds requires that the co-predicated nouns must share a property of the item being predicated, such as the formal role or the telic role. b) When an adjective modifies a complex-type natural noun, this construction could be ambiguous, as shown in (7). When an adjective modifies an artifactual-type non-natural noun, this construction is not necessarily ambiguous, as depicted in (8).

This section has indicated that natural kind and non-natural kind event nouns have different properties. The following section will establish a classification system for event nouns based on the natural and non-natural distinction.

3 Establish a Classification System for Event Nouns

Previous research classifies event nouns according to their semantic categories (Han 2004, 2010b; Liu 2004; Wang 2010; Zhong 2010). The main categories include natural phenomenon, wars, conferences, competitions, entertainments, ceremonies, etc. These semantic categories, however, cover the shared properties of event nouns from different categories. For example, wars, conferences, and competitions are all non-natural kinds and have more features in common compared to natural kinds. This section will investigate the subclasses of natural kinds and non-natural kinds based on GL.

3.1 Natural Kinds: Natural Types and Natural Complex Types

Though intuitively all natural occurring events should have physical object manifestations, not all of them are linguistically represented. For example, 地震 *dìzhèn* 'earthquake' occurs due to seismic waves caused by a sudden release of the crust's energy. The corpus data of 地震 *dìzhèn* 'earthquake' shows that linguistically only the 'event' aspect of 地震 *dìzhèn* 'earthquake' is expressed, while the 'wave' aspect is not. This is shown from Table 2 to Table 4.

First, let's look at the classifiers of 地震 *dìzhèn* 'earthquake'.

classifier	*pīnyīn*	Translation	Frequency	Saliency
次	*cì*	once (re. frequency of event)	59	39.04
級	*jí*	magnitude	5	16.16
場	*ch ng*	a (scheduled) event (with beginning and ending)	3	9.15
起	*q*	event (especially a happening, an accident)	1	4.44

Table 2: Classifiers of 地震 *dìzhèn* 'earthquake' in Sinica Corpus (frequency ≥1)

Table 2 shows all the classifiers of 地震 *dìzhèn* 'earthquake' in Sinica Corpus. All of them are event classifiers (Huang & Ahrens 2003), so the noun they select must represent an event.

Second, the verbs that have 地震 *dìzhèn* 'earthquake' as their subject in Sinica Corpus (frequency ≥2) are illustrated in Table 3.

Subject of	*pīnyīn*	Translation	Frequency	Saliency
發生	*fāshēng*	occur	18	22.29
造成	*zàochéng*	cause	19	21.71
模擬	*món*	simulate	5	17.06
繼續	*jìxù*	continue	9	15.48
引致	*y nzhì*	lead to	2	12.47
破壞	*pòhuài*	damage	4	11.87
釋放	*shìfàng*	release	2	9.4

停止	*tíngzh*	stop	2	7.54
導致	*d ozhì*	result in	2	6.5
影響	*y ngxi n g*	affect	2	4.1
來	*lái*	come	2	2.3

Table 3: Verbs that have 地震 *dìzhèn* 'earthquake' as their subject in Sinica Corpus (frequency ≥2)

In Table 3, 地震 *dìzhèn* 'earthquake' is the subject of these verbs in Sinica Corpus. In Table 3, the first verb 發生 *fāshēng* 'occur' is the most salient predicate of 地震 *dìzhèn* 'earthquake'. It is an event-selecting verb as shown in Table 4. This table lists the words that are the subjects of 發生 *fāshēng* 'occur'. These words either represent events in themselves or are coerced to refer to events. For example, 事件 *shìjiàn* 'event', 事故 *shìgù* 'accident', and 車禍 *chēhuò* 'car accident' refer to events directly. 問題 *wèntí* 'problem' is an entity noun, but it is coerced to be an event when it is selected by 發生 *fāshēng* 'occur'. Therefore, in Table 3, the subject 地震 *dìzhèn* 'earthquake' selected by 發生 *fāshēng* 'occur' has an event reading, rather than a wave reading.

Subject	*pīnyīn*	Translation	Frequency	Saliency
事件	*shìjiàn*	event	52	27.38
地震	*dìzhèn*	earthquake	18	21.78
事故	*shìgù*	accident	13	20.53
事情	*shìqíng*	affair	27	20.36
悲劇	*bēijù*	tragedy	11	19.24
情形	*qíngxíng*	situation	23	18.39
事	*shì*	affair	29	16.42
車禍	*chēhuò*	car accident	6	14.18
意外	*yìwài*	accident	7	12.12
現象	*xiànxiàng*	phenomenon	11	11.81
情況	*qíngkuàng*	situation	11	10.49
案	*àn*	case	5	8.83
狀況	*zhuàngkuàng*	status	6	7.81
問題	*wèntí*	problem	12	6.36
行為	*xíngwéi*	behavior	5	5.96

Table 4: Subjects of 發生 *fāshēng* 'occur' in Sinica Corpus (frequency ≥5)

Similar with 發生 *fāshēng* 'occur', in Table 3, verbs 造成 *zàochéng* 'cause', 繼續 *jìxù* 'continue', 引致 *y nzhì* 'lead to', 破壞 *pòhuài* 'damage', 停止 *tíngzh* 'stop', 導致 *d ozhì* 'result in', 來 *lái* 'come' also only selects the event aspect of 地震 *dìzhèn* 'earthquake' rather than the wave aspect. Verbs 模擬 *món* 'simulate', 釋放 *shìfàng* 'release' and 影響 *y ngxi ng* 'affect' could have either the earthquake event or seismic waves as their subjects, so their selectional status is undecided.

Thirdly, the verbs that have 地震 *dìzhèn* 'earthquake' as their object in Sinica Corpus (frequency ≥2) are presented in Table 5.

Object_of	*pīnyīn*	Translation	Frequency	Saliency
發生	*fāshēng*	occur	10	19.07
觸發	*chùfā*	trigger	2	13.58
觀看	*guānkàn*	watch	2	10.58
引發	*y nfā*	cause	2	8.47
等	*děng*	wait for	2	8.09
經過	*jīngguò*	go through	2	6.93
造成	*zàochéng*	cause	2	5.75

Table 5: Verbs that have 地震 *dìzhèn* 'earthquake' as their object in Sinica Corpus (frequency ≥2)

In Table 5, 地震 *dìzhèn* 'earthquake' is the object of these verbs (frequency ≥ 2) in Sinica Corpus. Most of the verbs are event-selecting words, such as 發生 *fāshēng* 'occur', 觸發 *chùfā* 'trigger', 引發 *y nfā* 'cause', 經過 *jīngguò* 'go through', 造成 *zàochéng* 'cause'. Thus they predict that the object 地震 *dìzhèn* 'earthquake' is an event. Seismic waves are invisible, so it is impossible that the verb 觀看 *guānkàn* 'watch' selects them; this verb can only select the event aspect of 地震 *dìzhèn* 'earthquake'. The verb 等 *děng* 'wait for' could select either the event aspect of 地震 *dìzhèn* 'earthquake' or waves, so its selectional status is undecided.

In sum, three evidences have been explored to discover whether 地震 *dìzhèn* 'earthquake' has an event reading or a seismic waves reading linguistically. They are: 1) all its classifiers are event classifiers; 2) when it is a subject, most of its predicates select event-reading words, except that 模擬 *món* 'simulate' and 釋放 *shìfàng* 'release' and 影響 *y ngxi ng* 'affect' have a undecided status; 3) when it is an object, the majority of the predicates select an event, except that 等 *děng* 'wait for' has a undecided status. These evidences indicate that no verbs exclusively select the wave aspect of 地震 *dìzhèn* 'earthquake'. We know the existence of the 'wave' aspect due to our world knowledge. Linguistically 地震 *dìzhèn* 'earthquake' only has an event reading. For natural-kind nouns like 地震 *dìzhèn* 'earthquake', which only have an event reading and no physical manifestation linguistically represented, we classify them into natural types.

Different from the natural phenomenon 地震 *dìzhèn* 'earthquake', 雪 *xuě* 'snow' can be linguistically expressed as both an event and a physical object (physobj), as shown in Table 6 through Table 8.

First, all the classifiers of 雪 *xuě* 'snow' in Sinica Corpus are illustrated in Table 6.

Classifier	pīnyīn	Translation	Frequency	Saliency	雪 *xuě* 'Snow'
場	*ch ng*	a (scheduled) event (with beginning and ending)	5	16.84	event
堆	*duī*	pile	2	11.36	physobj
次	*cì*	once (re. frequency of event)	2	7.37	event
捧	*pěng*	handful	1	7.17	physobj
團	*tuán*	lump	1	6.64	physobj
把	*b*	handful	1	6.43	physobj
重	*chóng*	layer	1	6.17	physobj
層	*céng*	layer	1	5.86	physobj
片	*piàn*	chunk	1	5.36	physobj

Table 6: Classifiers of 雪 *xuě* 'snow' in Sinica Corpus (frequency ≥1)

場 *ch ng* 'a (scheduled) event (with beginning and ending)' and 次 *cì* 'once (re. frequency of event)' are event classifiers which indicate that 雪 *xuě* 'snow' is an event. Differently, 堆 *du*'pile', 捧 *pěng* 'handful', 團 *tuán* 'lump', 把 *b* 'handful', 重 *chóng* 'layer', 層 *céng* 'layer', and 片 *piàn* 'chunk' are individual classifiers, which selects entities. Hence 雪 *xuě* 'snow' is a physical object when selected by them.

Secondly, the verbs that have 雪 *xuě* 'snow' as their subject in Sinica Corpus (frequency ≥2) are depicted in Table 7.

Subject_of	pīnyīn	Translation	Frequency	Saliency	雪 *xuě* 'Snow'
紛飛	*fēnfēi*	fall in flakes	4	20.95	physobj
落下	*luòxià*	fall	3	15.8	physobj
停	*tíng*	stop	3	13.13	event
下	*xià*	fall	4	12	event
停止	*tíng zh*	stop	3	11.43	event
覆蓋	*fùgài*	cover	2	10.81	physobj
埋	*mái*	bury	2	10.36	physobj
來臨	*láilín*	advent	2	10.17	event
封	*fēng*	close	2	9.03	physobj
來	*lái*	come	3	4.83	event

Table 7: Verbs that have 雪 *xuě* 'snow' as their subject in Sinica Corpus (frequency ≥2)

紛飛 *fēnfēi* 'fall in flakes', 落下 *luòxià* 'fall', 覆蓋 *fùgài* 'cover', 埋 *mái* 'bury', and 封 *fēng* 'close' describes 雪 *xuě* 'snow' as physical objects: snowflakes. By contrast, 停 *tíng* 'stop', 停止 *tíngzh* 'stop', 下 *xià* 'fall', 來臨 *láilín* 'advent', and 來 *lái* 'come' and depicts the snowing event.

Thirdly, the verbs that have 雪 *xuě* 'snow' as their object in Sinica Corpus (frequency ≥ 2) are illustrated in Table 8.

Object_of	*pīnyīn*	translation	Frequency	Saliency	雪 *xuě* 'Snow'
賞	*sh ng*	appreciate	12	27.33	event·physobj, or physobj
下	*xià*	fall	9	19.27	event
玩	*wán*	play	6	15.74	physobj
看	*kàn*	look at	9	12.42	event·physobj, or physobj
躲避	*du bì*	avoid	2	11.43	event
夾	*jiá*	mix	2	9.89	physobj
冒	*mào*	brave	2	9.87	event
降	*jiàng*	drop	2	9.86	event
避	*bì*	avoid	2	9.82	event
落	*luò*	drop	2	9.68	event·physobj
像	*xiàng*	resemble	2	5.15	physobj
無	*wú*	not have	2	4.94	event·physobj, or physobj

Table 8: Verbs that have 雪 *xuě* 'snow' as their object in Sinica Corpus (frequency ≥2)

玩 *wán* 'play', 夾 *jiá* 'mix', and 像 *xiàng* 'resemble' treats 雪 *xuě* 'snow' as snowflakes. 下 *xià* 'fall', 躲避 *du bì* 'avoid', 冒 *mào* 'brave', 降 *jiàng* 'drop', 避 *bì* 'avoid' depict 雪 *xuě* 'snow' as an event. 落 *luò* 'drop' describes 雪 *xuě* 'snow' as a dot object event·physobj. 賞 *sh ng* 'appreciate', 看 *kàn* 'look at', and 無 *wú* 'not have' can either refer to event·physobj or simply snowflakes. Moreover, the event reading and physical object reading of 雪 *xuě* 'snow' can be represented in one sentence as shown in (9).

(9) 這場下了三天三夜的大雪覆蓋了整片森林。

Zhè ch ng xià le sān tiān sān yè de
this CL fall ASP three day three night DE
dàxuě fùgài le zhěng piàn sēnlín.
heavy snow cover ASP entire CL forest
'The snow that lasted three days and three nights covered the entire forest.'

In (9), 場 *ch ng* 'a (scheduled) event (with beginning and ending)' is an event classifier which indicates that 雪 *xuě* 'snow' is an event. 覆蓋 *fùgài* 'cover' selects a physical object as its subject as shown in (10).

(10) 豆苗被雜草覆蓋。

Dòumiáo bèi zác o fùgài.
bean seedling BEI(passive marker) weed cover
'Bean seedlings are covered by weeds.'

In (10), 雜草 *zác o* 'weed' is an entity rather than an event. Hence, 覆蓋 *fùgài* 'cover' selects the snowflakes reading of 雪 *xuě* 'snow'.

In sum, three evidences have indicated that linguistically 雪 *xuě* 'snow' can either direct at the snowing event or the physical objects *snowflakes*. They are: 1) its classifiers can be both event classifiers and individual classifiers; 2) when it is a subject, its predicates select either the event reading or the physical object reading; 3) when it is an object, its predicates select the snowing event, physical objects *snowflakes* or event·physobj. For natural-kind nouns like 雪 *xuě* 'snow', which have both an event reading and a physical object reading encoded in one lexical item, we classify them into natural complex types.

To summarize, the corpus data prove that natural phenomenon can fall into either natural types or natural complex types. 地震 *dìzhèn* 'earthquake' only refers to an event and thus it is a natural type, while 雪 *xuě* 'snow' can be either an event or a physical object and thus it is a complex type.

3.2 Non-Natural Kinds: Artifactual Types and Artifactual Complex Types

Social activities can be from either artifactual types or complex types. Some social activities such as 戰爭 *zhànzhēng* 'war' and 比賽 *b sài* 'game' are only artifactual types.

(11) 這場*曠日持久的*戰爭不僅造成嚴重的人員傷亡和財產損失，而且成為影響俄社會穩定與安寧的重要因素。

Zhè ch ng kuàngrìchíji de zhànzhēng bùj n
this CL protracted war not only
zàochéng yánzhòngde rényuánshāngwáng hé
cause serious casualties and
cáich n s nshī, érqiě chéngwéi y ngxi ng é
property loss, but also become affect Russia
shèhuì wěndìng y ānníng de zhòngyào
society stability and tranquility DE important
yīnsù.
factor.
'This protracted war not only caused serious casualties and property losses, but has also become an important factor that affects the stability and tranquility of the Russian society.'

(12) *馬拉松式的*比賽及火熱氣溫是球員體力和球技的大考驗。

M lāsōngshì de b sài jí hu rè qìwēn
Marathon-style DE game and hot temperature
shì qiúyuán t lì hé qiújì de
are player physical strength and ball skills DE
dà k oyàn.
big challenge
'Marathon-style game and high temperature are a big challenge to the physical strength and ball skills of the players.'

Both 戰爭 *zhànzhēng* 'war' and 比賽 *b sài* 'game' represent events. In (11) 戰爭 *zhànzhēng* 'war' is modified by 曠日持久的 and in (12) 比賽 *b sài* 'game' is modified by 馬拉松式 *m lāsōngshì* 'Marathon-style'. The two adjectives refer to the duration of the war and the game respectively, which indicates that both war and game are events. Some other social activities such as Event•Information (演講 *y nji ng* 'lecture'), Event•Music (音樂會 *yīnyuè huì* 'concert'), Event•Physobj (早餐 *z ocān* 'breakfast'), and Process•Result (分析 *fēnxī* 'analysis') are complex types. These event nouns refer to more than one aspect.

(13) 這場演講很有意義。

Zhè ch ng y nji ng hěn y u yìyì.
this CL speech very has meaningful
'This speech is meaningful.'

For example, in (13), 場 *ch ng* 'a (scheduled) event (with beginning and ending)' is an event classifier, which indicates that 演講 *y nji ng* 'lecture' is an event noun. 很有意義 *hěn y u yìyì* 'of great significance' states the information aspect of 演講 *y nji ng* 'lecture'.

To summarize, event nouns of non-natural kinds can be divided into artifactual types and artifactual complex types. For example, 戰爭 *zhànzhēng* 'war' only has an event reading, so it is an artifactual type. 演講 *y nji ng* 'speech' can direct at either the speaking event or the information, so it is an artifactual complex type.

4 Structures to Identify Complex Types

Pustejovsky & Jezek (2008) argues that co-predication is a property of complex types. Our research provides more syntactic patterns to identify complex types in Mandarin Chinese, such as 既……又…… *jì……yòu……* 'not only……but also……', 不但……而且…… *bùdàn……érqiě……* 'not only……but also……', (雖然)……但是…… *(suīrán)……dànshì……* '(although) …… but ……', 又……又…… *yòu……yòu……* '(both) …… and ……'.

Examples (14) and (15) illustrate complex types of natural and artifactual event nouns respectively. In (14), 密 *mì* 'dense' is about the physical object aspect of snow; 急 *jí* 'rapid' is about the event aspect of snow. The conjunctions 又……又…… *yòu……yòu……* '(both)……and……' connects both 密 *mì* 'dense' 'dense' and 急 *jí* 'rapid', which indicates that 雪 *xuě* 'snow' is a complex type. In (15), 冗長 *r ngcháng* 'tediously long' modifies the breakfast's event aspect; 好吃 *hào chī* 'good to eat' modifies its physical object aspect. They are connected by the conjunctions 雖然……但是…… *suīrán……dànshì……* 'although …… but ……', which proves that 早餐 *z ocān* 'breakfast' is a complex type.

(14) 好大的***雪***，又密又急。

H o dà de xuě, yòu mì yòu jí。
how heavy DE snow, and dense and rapid
'What a heavy snow! (It is) dense and rapid.'

(15) 這次***早餐***雖然很冗長，但是很好吃。

Zhè cì z ocān suīrán hěn
this CL breakfast although very
r ngcháng, dànshì hěn hào chī.
tediously long, but very good eat
'The breakfast, although it is tediously long, was tasty.'

Though co-predication is important property of complex type, it is not a necessary property. Example (16) is from Pustejovsky (2005).

(16) appointment (Event•Human)

a. Your next appointment is at 3:00 pm.

b. Your next appointment is a blonde.

(16a) refers to an event, while (16b) refers to a human. The event and human aspects of *appointment* cannot get co-predication.

5 Conclusions

To conclude, this paper finds that natural kinds can be divided into natural types and natural complex types; non-natural kinds fall into artifactual types or artifactual complex types. This is shown in Table 9.

<table>
<tr><td rowspan="4">Event Nouns</td><td rowspan="2">Natural Kinds</td><td>Natural Types</td></tr>
<tr><td>Natural Complex Types</td></tr>
<tr><td rowspan="2">Non-Natural Kinds</td><td>Artifactual Types</td></tr>
<tr><td>Artifactual Complex Types</td></tr>
</table>

Table 9: Event Nouns: Natural Kinds and Non-Natural Kinds

Table 9 can be re-represented in Table 10 in order to fit into the tripartite system in Pustejovsky (2001, 2006) and Pustejovsky & Jezek (2008). Event nouns are divided into natural types, artifactual types and complex types (including natural complex types and artifactual complex types).

<table>
<tr><td rowspan="4">Event Nouns</td><td colspan="2">Natural Types</td></tr>
<tr><td colspan="2">Artifactual Types</td></tr>
<tr><td rowspan="2">Complex Types</td><td>Natural Complex Types</td></tr>
<tr><td>Artifactual Complex Types</td></tr>
</table>

Table 10: A Tripartite Classification System for Event Nouns

The results indicate that event nouns of the same semantic category can be from different types. For instance, event nouns that represent natural phenomenon can either belong to natural types or natural complex types. Event nouns that represent social activities can be either from artifactual types or artifactual complex types.

This work has enriched the complex types by including both natural complex types and artifactual complex types. The new classification, which is based on types rather than semantic categories, can help to capture the characteristics of different types of event nouns.

Acknowledgements

We would like to express our gratitude to Prof. James Pustejovsky for the discussion on this paper. The remaining errors are ours.

References

Chu, Zexiang. 2000. *An Investigation on Nouns' Adaptation to Temporality.* Modern Chinese Grammar Studies that Face the Challenges of New Century: the International Conference on Modern Chinese Grammar, 1998, ed. by Jianming Lu. Jinan: Shandong Education Press.

Han, Lei. 2004. An Analysis of Event Nouns in Modern Chinese. *Journal of East China Normal University (Philosophy and Social Sciences)*, 36 (5).P106-113.

Han, Lei. 2010a. Analysing the Word Class Status of Event Nouns. *Journal of Ningxia University (Humanities & Social Sciences Edition)*, (1).P6-10.

Han, Lei. 2010b. The Definition of Event Nouns. *Paper presented at The 16th Symposium on Modern Chinese Grammar*, City University of Hong Kong, Hong Kong.

Huang, Chu-Ren & Kathleen Ahrens. 2003. Individuals, Kinds and Events: Classifier Coercion of Nouns. *Language Sciences* 25 (4).P353-373.

Liu, Shun. 2004. A Study of Temporality of Common Nouns. *Language Teaching and Linguistic Studies* (4).P25-35.

Ma, Qingzhu. 1995. *Verbs with Denotational Meaning and Nouns with Statement Meaning*. Research and Exploration of the Grammar. Beijing: The Commercial Press.

Pustejovsky, James. 2001. *Type Construction and the Logic of Concepts*. The Language of Word Meaning, ed. by Pierrette Bouillon & Federica Busa, P91-123: Cambridge University Press.

Pustejovsky, James. 2005. A Survey of Dot Objects. Brandeis University. Technical report.

Pustejovsky, James. 2006. Type Theory and Lexical Decomposition. *Journal of Cognitive Science* 7 (1).P39-76.

Pustejovsky, James & Elisabetta Jezek. 2008. Semantic Coercion in Language: Beyond Distributional Analysis. *Distributional Models of the Lexicon in Linguistics and Cognitive Science, special issue of Italian Journal of Linguistics/Rivista di Linguistica*.

Wang, Hui & Xuefeng Zhu. 2000. *Subcategorization and Quantitative Research on Modern Chinese Nouns*. Modern Chinese Grammar Studies that Face the Challenges of New Century:the International Conference on Modern Chinese Grammar,1998. Jinan: Shandong Education Press.

Wang, Shan & Chu-Ren Huang. 2011a. *Compound Event Nouns of the 'Modifier-head' Type in Mandarin Chinese*. Proceedings of The 25th Pacific Asia Conference on Language, Information and Computation (PACLIC-25), ed. by Helena Hong Gao & Minghui Dong, P511-518. Nanyang Technological University, Singapore.

Wang, Shan & Chu-Ren Huang. 2011b. Domain Relevance of Event Coercion in Compound Nouns. *Paper presented at The 6th International Conference on Contemporary Chinese Grammar (ICCCG-6)*, I-Shou University, Kaohsiung, Taiwan.

Wang, Shan & Chu-Ren Huang. 2011c. Event Classifiers and Their Selected Nouns. *Paper presented at The 19th Annual Conference of the International Association of Chinese Linguistics (IACL-19)*, Nankai University, Tianjin, China.

Wang, Shan & Chu-Ren Huang. 2012a. A Constraint-based Linguistic Model for Event Nouns. *Paper presented at Forum on 'Y. R. Chao and Linguistics', Workshop of The 20th Annual Conference of the International Association of Chinese Linguistics (IACL-20)*, The Hong Kong Institute of Education, Hong Kong.

Wang, Shan & Chu-Ren Huang. 2012b. *A Preliminary Study of An Event-based Noun Classification System*. The 13th Chinese Lexical Semantics Workshop (CLSW-13), ed. by Yanxiang He & Donghong Ji, P4-9. Wuhan University, China.

Wang, Shan & Chu-Ren Huang. 2012c. Qualia Structure of Event Nouns in Mandarin Chinese. *Paper presented at The Second International Symposium on Chinese Language and Discourse*, Nanyang Technological University, Singapore.

Wang, Shan & Chu-Ren Huang. 2012d. Temporal Properties of Event Nouns in Mandarin Chinese. *Paper presented at The 57th Annual International Linguistic Association Conference (ILA-57)*, New York, USA

Wang, Yanqing. 2010. *A Study on the Combination of the Time-quantity Phrase and the Event Noun*. Wuhan: Central China Normal University.

Zhong, Ming. 2010. *A Study on Event Nouns in Chinese and English*. Nanchang: Nanchang University.

On Interpretation of Resultative Phrases in Japanese

Tsuneko Nakazawa
Language and Information Sciences
University of Tokyo
3-8-1 Komaba, Meguro-ku, Tokyo 153-8902 Japan
tsuneko@boz.c.u-tokyo.ac.jp

Abstract

The present paper attempts to formalize the semantic interpretation of resultative phrases in Japanese in the framework of Generative Lexicon, with a focus on the semantic subject of resultative phrases, i.e. the entity which resultative phrases are predicated of. The semantic subject cannot always be identified with the direct object of transitive verbs or the subject of unaccusative verbs, as generally believed, but also is expressed as an oblique NP or not syntactically expressed at all. It poses a challenge to the interpretation of resultative phrases since it cannot be tied to a specific syntactic constituent. The interpretation of resultative phrases is encoded in terms of the FORMAL quale and its argument built through the co-composition operation.

1 General Properties of Japanese Resultatives

The resultative phrase is most generally characterized as the second predicate to describe the state of an argument, which results from the event denoted by the main verb. It is generally understood (e.g. Tsujimura, 1990; Kageyama, 1996) that resultative phrases in Japanese come in two types: object-oriented resultative phrases with transitive verbs and subject-oriented resultative phrases with unaccusative intransitive verbs. Object-oriented resultative phrases appear in a sentence headed by a transitive verb, and describe the resultant state of the referent of object NP as in (1). (In the following examples, resultative phrases are underlined while the semantic subjects of resultative phrases are in bold.)

(1) Taro-ga **kabin**-o <u>konagona-ni</u> kowasi-ta.
Taro-NOM vase-ACC pieces-NI break-PAST
'Taro broke the vase into pieces.'

In (1), the resultative phrase *konagona-ni* 'into pieces' describes the state of the object *kabin* 'vase' which results from Taro's breaking it. Subject-oriented resultative phrases, on the other hand, appear with an unaccusative intransitive verb, and describe the state of the referent of subject NP, which results from the event expressed by the verb, as in (2).

(2) **hune**-ga <u>huka-ku</u> sizun-da.
ship-NOM deep-KU sink-PAST
'A ship sank deep.'

The resultative phrase *huka-ku* 'deep' describes the resultant state of the referent of subject *hune* 'ship' after its sinking.

These resultatives conform to the general characteristics of two of the three types of resultatives in English, originally observed and analyzed by Simpson (1983). The resultative construction in Japanese, however, lacks the third type in Simpson's analysis of English resultatives with an unergative intransitive verb with 'a fake object', in which the semantic subject of resultative phrases is not an argument subcategorized by the main verb: e.g. *I cried my eyes blind*. Other types of phrases which are analyzed as resultatives by various authors are also absent in Japanese: phrases that appear with the main verbs of sound emission (e.g. *The garage door rumbles open*.) and of location change (e.g. *John danced mazurkas across the room.*). The analysis in the present paper mostly focuses on the first type of typical resultative phrases in Japanese shown in (1), i.e. the construction with a transitive verb and an object-oriented resultative phrase.

As a direct consequence of the definition that resultative phrases express the state that results from the event denoted by the verb, the verbs which appear in the construction denote a change of state either lexically or by virtue of an accompanying resultative phrase (cf. Pustejovsky, 1991 for a distinction between the true resultatives and the emphatic resultatives). Although the verbs can lexically be either telic or atelic, the result expressed by a resultative phrase provides an end point to the event, making the whole sentences descriptions of a bounded event.

The state expressed by a resultative phrase is generally a result which is predictable, or 'canonical or generic' (Wechsler, 1997), from the event denoted by the main verb. Some authors analyze resultative phrases as a syntactic realization of the description of a result which is lexically encoded in the semantic representation of the verb to start with (e.g. Green, 1972). Washio (1997) claims that resultatives in Japanese describe only a predictable result, called 'weak resultatives', while English additionally allows 'strong resultatives': for example, the sentence *The horses dragged the logs smooth* has no well-formed Japanese equivalent because, it is claimed, logs' being smooth is not a result predictable from horses' dragging them. Wechsler (1997) points out that the third type in Simpson's (1980) analysis, i.e. resultatives with an unergative intransitive verb and a non-subcategorized object, do not require the expressed result to be predictable in English, and the lack of resultatives of this type in Japanese gives an empirical justification to Washio's claim that Japanese allows only resultative phrases of a predictable result.

At the same time, in either in English or Japanese, it seems undeniable that even resultative phrases expressing a predictable result are not totally productive. That is, collocations of particular verbs and resultative phrases are to some extent conventionalized, or idiomatic, and expressions of imaginable results are not always acceptable: for example, **hutatu-ni kowasi-ta* 'broke into two pieces' is not acceptable while *konagona-ni kowasi-ta* 'broke into pieces' in (1) and *mapputatu-ni kowasi-ta* 'broke into exact halves' are.

Morphologically, the head of resultative phrases can be a noun such as *konagona-* 'pieces' in (1), an adjective such as *huka-* 'deep' in (2), or an adjectival noun such as *taira-* 'flat' in (18). Nouns and adjectival nouns are suffixed by *-ni*, and adjectives are suffixed by *-ku* in resultative phrases. These morphological forms are, however, not unique to the resultative construction, and they also mark the head of coordinate and subordinate clauses, and adverbial uses of nouns and adjectives.

As a general characteristic of sentence structures, Japanese imposes few restrictions on the ordering among coarguments and adjuncts within a clause, and allows variations in the linear order of phrases including resultative phrases. While the linear order of the nominative NP, the accusative NP, and the resultative phrase in Japanese examples (1) and (2) is the unmarked one, the other linear orders are also possible as long as the verb remains at the end of the sentence.

2 Analysis of Resultatives Cast in Generative Lexicon

The object oriented resultative in (1) can be analyzed straightforwardly in the framework of Generative Lexicon, following the analysis for English resultatives in Pustejovsky (1995). The semantic representation of the verb *kowas-* 'break' in (1) is shown in (3).

(3) the semantic representation of *kowas-*'break' in (1)

$$\begin{bmatrix} \textit{kowas-}\ \text{'break'} \\ \text{EVENTSTR} = \begin{bmatrix} E_1 = e_1\text{:process} \\ E_2 = e_2\text{:state} \\ \text{RESTR} = <_{\propto} \\ \text{HEAD} = e_1 \end{bmatrix} \\ \text{ARGSTR} = \begin{bmatrix} \text{ARG}_1 = [1] \begin{bmatrix} \text{animate-ind} \\ \text{FORMAL} = \text{physobj} \end{bmatrix} \\ \text{ARG}_2 = [2] \begin{bmatrix} \text{artifact} \\ \text{FORMAL} = \text{physobj} \end{bmatrix} \end{bmatrix} \\ \text{QUALIA} = \begin{bmatrix} \text{default-causative-lcp} \\ \text{AGENTIVE} = \text{break-act}(e_1, [1], [2]) \\ \text{FORMAL} = \text{break-result}(e_2, [2]) \end{bmatrix} \end{bmatrix}$$

The representation in (3) states that *kowas-*'break' is a transitive verb of direct causation. It takes two arguments: the first argument ARG$_1$ is an animate being which corresponds to the syntactic subject *Taro-ga* 'Taro-NOM' in (1) while the second argument ARG$_2$ is an artifact which is realized as the object NP *kabin-o* 'vase-ACC'.

The FORMAL quale in (3) indicates that the verb *kowas-* 'brake' denotes a change of state, and that it is the referent of the object NP, marked as [2], that undergoes the change. As discussed in Section 1, Japanese allows only resultative phrases of a predictable result, and a range of predictable results is lexically encoded as break-result in (3). Following the processing model proposed by Nakatani (2007), it is assumed that the semantic representation of resultative phrase *konagona-ni* 'into pieces' is conjoined into the FORMAL quale through the co-composition operation, further specifying the resultant state of the vase.

The following sections demonstrate that, unlike the typical example of object-oriented resultatives in (1), it is not always the referent of object NP that undergoes a change of state and appears in the FORMAL quale of the verb.

3 Polysemous Arguments with Resultative Phrases

It is commonly assumed that a resultative phrase can be paraphrased as a clause which describes a result: for example, the sentence *Taro broke the vase into pieces* in (1) can be paraphrased as 'Taro broke the vase, and (as a result) the vase was in pieces.' The paraphrasing captures the interpretation of the resultative phrase as a description of the state of the vase which results from the breaking event.

Some instances of the resultative construction such as (4), however, resist paraphrasing, posing a problem to the generalization that the resultative phrase with a transitive verb is object-oriented.

(4) Taro-ga mado-o ooki-ku ake-ta.
Taro-NOM window-ACC big-KU open-PAST
'lit. Taro opened the window big.'

The resultative phrase *ooki-ku* 'big' in (4) describes the window being wide-open as a result of Taro's opening it. The putative paraphrase *mado-ga ooki-i* 'The window is big', however, can only be interpreted as a description of the size of the window as a physical object, and not of the opening. Clearly, paraphrasing as a simple diagnostic tool of a resultative phrase fails due to the polysemous behavior of the noun *mado* 'window'.

As is the case of the English counterpart *window*, *mado* can refer to both a physical object and an aperture, which is often called figure/ground polysemy. The multiple senses are represented in terms of a dot object physobj·aperture in the QUALIA structure in the semantic representation of *mado* 'window' in (5).

(5) the semantic representation of *mado* 'window' in (4)

$$\left[\begin{array}{l} \textit{mado}\ \text{'window'} \\ \text{ARGSTR} = \left[\begin{array}{l} \text{ARG}_1 = [1]\text{physobj} \\ \text{ARG}_2 = [2]\text{aperture} \end{array}\right] \\ \text{QUALIA} = \left[\begin{array}{l} \text{physobj}\bullet\text{aperture-lcp} \\ \text{FORMAL} = \text{aperture-of}([2], [1]) \end{array}\right] \end{array}\right]$$

When *mado* 'window' appears as the object NP of the causative verb *ake-* 'open' as in (4), co-composition of their semantic representations gives rise to the semantic representation shown in (6).

(6) the semantic representation of *mado-o ake-* 'open a window' in (4)

$$\left[\begin{array}{l} \textit{mado-o ake-}\ \text{'open a window'} \\ \text{EVENTSTR} = \left[\begin{array}{l} \text{E}_1 = \text{e}_1\text{:process} \\ \text{E}_2 = \text{e}_2\text{:state} \\ \text{RESTR} = <_{\propto} \\ \text{HEAD} = \text{e}_1 \end{array}\right] \\ \text{ARGSTR} = \left[\begin{array}{l} \text{ARG}_1 = [3]\text{animate-ind} \\ \text{ARG}_2 = [4]\left[\begin{array}{l} \text{window} \\ \text{FORMAL} = \text{aperture-of}([2], [1]) \end{array}\right] \end{array}\right] \\ \text{QUALIA} = \left[\begin{array}{l} \text{default-causative-lcp} \\ \text{AGENTIVE} = \text{open-act}(\text{e}_1, [3], [4]) \\ \text{FORMAL} = \text{open-result}(\text{e}_2, [2]) \end{array}\right] \end{array}\right]$$

The VP *mado-o ake-* denotes an event of opening a window. The verb is a two-place predicate and takes an animate individual as the first argument ARG$_1$, which is syntactically realized as the subject NP, and the object NP *mado-o* 'window-ACC' as the second argument ARG$_2$. The FORMAL quale selects a dot element aperture, marked as [2] in both (5) and

(6), from the multiple referents of object NP. This dot element is available for modification by the resultative phrase.

Following Pustejovsky (1995), in (5), both a physical object sense and an aperture sense are analyzed to be the denotation of a single lexical item *mado* 'window', i.e. members of physobj·aperture-lcp, rather than denotations of separate homonymous nouns. Consequently, the selection of the object *mado* 'window' as the semantic subject of resultative phrase in (4) still conforms to the generalization that resultative phrases with a transitive verb are object-oriented. However, paraphrasing of the resultative phrase as a clause *mado-ga ooki-i* 'The window is big' fails because the predicative adjective *ooki-i* 'big' induces the interpretation of the subject *mado* 'window' as a physical object rather than an aperture. Although the exact aspects of linguistic environments which determine the 'sense in context' of polysemous nouns is not clear, it is clear that the explicit semantic representation of polysemous nouns as dot objects, such as in (5), is necessary to represent the exact sense of the semantic subject of resultative phrases.

4 Locative-Alternation Verbs with Resultative Phrases

The resultative construction in English is subject to the constraint, originally observed and analyzed by Simpson (1983), later dubbed Direct Object Restriction (the DOR; Levin and Rappaport Hovav, 1995), that the semantic subject of resultative phrases must be the direct object of the transitive verb, or the underlying object (surface subject) of the unaccusative intransitive verb. Accordingly, the contrast of examples such as those in (7) has repeatedly been pointed out.

(7) (Williams, 1980:204)
  a. John loaded **the wagon** <u>full</u> with hay.
  b. *John loaded the hay into **the wagon** <u>full</u>.

The resultative phrase *full* in both examples in (7) is intended to describe the state of the goal argument *the wagon*. Only (7a), however, is acceptable where the semantic subject *the wagon* of the resultative phrase is expressed as the syntactic object of the verb, as predicted by the DOR. Since the two examples in (7) are near paraphrases of each other, the nature of the DOR is clearly syntactic, rather than semantic, and it is often rephrased in terms of the syntactic structure of sentence constituents and the *c*-command relation in them (e.g. Levin and Rappaport Hovav, 1995).

Although the same constraint is generally assumed for Japanese resultatives (e.g. Takezawa, 1993; Koizumi, 1994), the examples in (8) show that the resultative phrase *aka-ku* 'red' can be predicated of not only the object NP *kabin-o* 'vase-ACC' in (8a), but also the oblique NP *kabin-ni* 'vase-LOC' in (8b) in Japanese.

(8) a. Taro-ga **kabin**-o penki-de
Taro-NOM vase-ACC paint-INSTRUMENTAL

<u>aka-ku</u> nut-ta.
red-KU cover/apply-PAST
'lit. Taro covered the vase with paint red.
(Taro painted the vase red.)'

b. Taro-ga **kabin**-ni penki-o
Taro-NOM vase-LOC paint-ACC

<u>aka-ku</u> nut-ta.
red-KU cover/apply-PAST
'lit. Taro applied paint to the vase red.
(Taro painted the vase red.)'

The argument structure of the verb *nut-* 'cover/apply' alternates in a similar way to that of the English verbs *load*, *splash* and *spray*, a phenomenon called 'locative alternation' (Levin and Rappaport Hovav, 1995): the goal argument *kabin* 'vase', i.e. the object NP in (8a), can also be expressed as an oblique NP as in (8b), in which case, the theme argument *penki* 'paint' is expressed as the object NP. The adjective *aka-*'red' describes the resultant state of the vase (the paint is red to start with) after Taro's painting it regardless of whether the vase is expressed as an object or an oblique NP.

In the semantic representation of the verb *nur-* 'cover/apply' in (9), the AGENTIVE quale is assumed to be a three-place predicate, which takes the agent, the theme, and the goal arguments.

(9) the semantic representation of *nur-*'cover/apply' in (8)

$$\left[\begin{array}{l} \text{nur- `cover/apply'} \\ \text{EVENTSTR} = \left[\begin{array}{l} E_1 = e_1\text{:process} \\ E_2 = e_2\text{:state} \\ \text{RESTR} = <_{\infty} \\ \text{HEAD} = e_1 \end{array}\right] \\ \text{ARGSTR} = \left[\begin{array}{l} \text{ARG}_1 = [1]\text{animate-ind} \\ \text{ARG}_2 = [2]\text{material} \\ \text{ARG}_3 = [3]\text{physobj} \end{array}\right] \\ \text{QUALIA} = \left[\begin{array}{l} \text{default-causative-lcp} \\ \text{AGENTIVE} = \text{put-act}(e_1, [1], [2], [3]) \\ \text{FORMAL} = \text{on}(e_2, [2], [3]) \end{array}\right] \end{array}\right]$$

When the goal argument ARG3, *kabin* 'vase', is mapped to the object NP as in (8a), it is the semantic subject of the resultative phrase as it would be in *spray the vase red with paint* in English. When the theme argument ARG2, *penki* 'paint', is mapped to the object NP as in (8b), the resultative phrase can still be predicated of the goal argument *kabin* 'vase', although English equivalent, **spray paint on the vase red*, would be unacceptable. The equal acceptability of both examples in Japanese indicate that resultative phrases in Japanese are manifestations of the FORMAL quale of the semantic representation, not constrained by its syntactic realization as is the case of English resultatives.

5 Creation Verbs with Resultative Phrases

While resultative phrases can describe the referent of an oblique NP as shown in the previous section, they can also be predicated of an entity only implied in the sentence. The examples in (10) show alternating uses of the verb *hor-* 'dig'.

(10)a. Taro-ga zimen-o <u>huka-ku</u> hot-ta.
Taro-NOM ground-ACC deep-KU dig-PAST
'lit. Taro dug the ground deep. (Taro dug a deep hole in the ground.)'

b. Taro-ga **ana**-o <u>huka-ku</u> hot-ta.
Taro-NOM hole-ACC deep-KU dig-PAST
'lit. Taro dug a hole deep. (Taro dug a deep hole.)'

In (10a), the verb *hor-* 'dig' takes the agent *Taro* 'Taro' as its subject and the theme *zimen* 'ground' as its object. Assuming the verb is lexically a simple transitive verb of state change (Pustejovsky 1991: 123), the basic semantic structure of the verb is represented as in (11).

(11)the basic semantic representation of *hor-* 'dig'

$$\left[\begin{array}{l} \textit{hor-}\text{ `dig'} \\ \text{EVENTSTR} = \left[\begin{array}{l} E_1 = e_1\text{:process} \\ \text{HEAD} = e_1 \end{array}\right] \\ \text{ARGSTR} = \left[\begin{array}{l} \text{ARG}_1 = [1]\text{animate-ind} \\ \text{ARG}_2 = [2]\text{physobj} \end{array}\right] \\ \text{QUALIA} = \left[\begin{array}{l} \text{state-change-lcp} \\ \text{AGENTIVE} = \text{dig-act}(e_1, [1], [2]) \end{array}\right] \end{array}\right]$$

The verb denotes an event of digging. It is a two-place predicate and takes an animate individual as the first argument ARG1, which carries the agent role, and some physical object as the second argument ARG2, which carries the theme role.

The instance of the verb *hor-* 'dig' in (10b), on the other hand, is a derived use of the verb as a creation verb: that is, the object *ana* 'hole' expresses the product of digging. The co-composition operation between the verb of state change in (11) and the object NP expressing the product of the process gives rise to the derived semantic representation of indirect causation for the phrase *ana-o hot-ta* 'dug a hole' in (12) for (10b).

(12)the semantic representation of *ana-o hor-*'dig a hole' in (10b)

$$\left[\begin{array}{l} \textit{ana-o hor-}\text{ `dig a hole'} \\ \text{EVENTSTR} = \left[\begin{array}{l} E_1 = e_1\text{:process} \\ E_2 = e_2\text{:state} \\ \text{RESTR} = <_{\infty} \\ \text{HEAD} = e_1 \end{array}\right] \\ \text{ARGSTR} = \left[\begin{array}{l} \text{ARG}_1 = [1]\text{animate-ind} \\ \text{D-ARG}_1 = [2]\text{physobj} \\ \text{ARG}_2 = [3]\left[\begin{array}{l} \text{hole} \\ \text{CONST} = \text{part-of}([2]) \end{array}\right] \end{array}\right] \\ \text{QUALIA} = \left[\begin{array}{l} \text{create-lcp} \\ \text{AGENTIVE} = \text{dig-act}(e_1, [1], [2]) \\ \text{FORMAL} = \text{dig-result}(e_2, [3]) \end{array}\right] \end{array}\right]$$

The second argument ARG_2 in (11), which is realized as *zimen* 'ground' in (10a), is now demoted to a default argument D-ARG_1 in (12), and no longer syntactically expressed in the sentence (10b). Instead, the third argument ARG_2 which corresponds to the product of digging is realized as the object NP *ana-o* 'hole-ACC' of the verb. It is also composed into the FORMAL quale, and modified by the resultative phrase *huka-ku* 'deep' in (10b).

The resultative phrase in (10b) is a typical instance of the object-oriented resultative construction: it describes the state of the direct object *ana-o* 'hole-ACC' which results from digging. The resultative phrase in (10a), on the other hand, lacks an expression of the semantic subject although it is still understood to describe a hole which is created by the digging event.

As shown in the basic semantic representation in (11), the verb *hor-* 'dig' is a process verb which denotes a change of state of the theme argument, i.e. *zimen* 'ground' in (10a). Aspectually, the lexical verb is atelic and the digging event denoted by *zimen-o hor-* 'dig the ground' (without a resultative phrase) does not entail any final product coming into being, which would serve as a bound of the digging event. Both the examples with resultative phrases in (10), however, express an event which is bounded by the creation of a deep hole. While it is the expression of the product, *ana* 'hole', as the object NP that brings about the derived creation sense of the verb in (10b), the example in (10a) demonstrates that obviously, the resultative phrase *huka-ku* 'deep' is sufficient to derive the creation sense of the verb and implies the product of digging as the (unexpressed) semantic subject. That is, the semantic contribution of the resultative phrase in (10a) brings about a FORMAL quale similar to that in (12), a predicate of a hole. Co-composition of the verb *hor-* 'dig' of state change in (11) and the resultative phrase derives a semantic representation similar to (12) for indirect causation, as shown in (13).

(13) the semantic representation of *zimen-o hor-*'dig the ground' with the resultative phrase in (10a)

$$
\left[\begin{array}{l}
\textit{zimen-o hor-}\ \text{`dig the ground'} \\
\text{EVENTSTR} = \left[\begin{array}{l} E_1 = e_1\text{:process} \\ E_2 = e_2\text{:state} \\ \text{RESTR} = <_{\propto} \\ \text{HEAD} = e_1 \end{array}\right] \\
\text{ARGSTR} = \left[\begin{array}{l} \text{ARG}_1 = [1]\text{animate-ind} \\ \text{ARG}_2 = [2]\text{ground} \\ \text{D-ARG}_1 = [3]\left[\begin{array}{l}\text{hole}\\ \text{CONST} = \text{part-of}([2])\end{array}\right]\end{array}\right] \\
\text{QUALIA} = \left[\begin{array}{l} \text{create-lcp} \\ \text{AGENTIVE} = \text{dig-act}(e_1, [1], [2]) \\ \text{FORMAL} = \text{dig-result}(e_2, [3]) \end{array}\right]
\end{array}\right]
$$

Unlike the derived creation verb in (12) for (10b), the second argument ARG_2 in (11) for *zimen* 'ground' remains as a true argument in (13) and is syntactically realized as the object NP. Like (12), however, the third argument for the product of digging is added as a default argument D-ARG_1 as part of the semantic contribution of the resultative phrase, and it also appears in the FORMAL quale.

6 The Shadow Argument with Resultative Phrases

Sentences like (14) and (15) have long posed a syntactic puzzle, in which resultative phrases describe a resultant state after the event expressed by the verb but concern an entity that could not constitute an argument of the verb. In (14), the resultative phrase *kata-ku* 'tight, stiff' describes the tightness of a knot of shoe laces, but not of shoe laces.

(14) (Washio, 1997:18)

kare-wa	kutu-no	himo-o
he-TOP	shoe-GEN	lace-ACC

kata-ku	musun-da.
tight-KU	tie-PAST

'He tied his shoelaces tight.'

Similarly in (15), the resultative phrase *atu-* 'thick' is naturally interpreted as describing a state of ice formed as a result of the river's freezing.

(15) (Korean equivalent is pointed out by Wechsler and Noh, 2001:409)
kawa-ga atu-ku koot-ta.
river-NOM thick-KU freeze-PAST
'lit. The river froze thick.'

Unlike previous examples in Sections 4 and 5, there is no straightforward way to incorporate the individuals predicated by the resultative phrases into the sentences using either an oblique NP or alternating argument structures of the verbs. Hence, Washio (1997) analyzes *kata-ku* 'tight' in (14) as an example of 'the spurious resultative' which describes the manner of action, rather than a resultant state of anything, and Wechsler and Noh (2001) claim that the Korean equivalent of *atu-ku* 'thick' in (15), *twukkep-key,* is not a resultative phrase but an adverbial use of the adjective which describes 'a thick manner' of the freezing event. (Note that as discussed in Section 1, the suffix *-ku* in Japanese, as well as *-key* in Korean, is attached to adjectives to mark either resultative phrases or adverbial uses of adjectives.) Aside from the fact that the sentences lack overt expressions of the semantic subject, however, there is no independent evidence to consider the examples in (14) and (15) as distinct constructions from the resultative.

Although the resultative construction in English requires the semantic subject to be expressed as the direct object of the transitive verb, there are some expressions of a result similar to (14) and (15), which Levinson (2010) calls 'resultative adverbs' following the analysis of Geuder (2000).

(16) (Levinson, 2010:137)
a. They decorated the room beautifully.
b. They loaded the cart heavily.

In these examples in (16), the suffix *-ly* of *beautifully* and *heavily* is obligatory, and hence morphologically they are clearly adverbs. However, they are distinct from typical manner adverbs in that *beautifully* does not describe the manner of their decorating the room in (16a), and it is not the manner of their loading action that is heavy in (16b). Rather, they describe an individual which undergoes a change of state as resultative phrases generally do, and through the description of the result, they describe a way the event is carried out.

While the individual that undergoes a change can be identified with the referent of the direct object *the room* in (16a), such an individual is not expressed in (16b). Nevertheless, the only possible interpretation of the sentence is that it is the load on the cart that undergoes a change of state and is described by the adverb *heavily*. Geuder (2000) proposes a function which selects such a pragmatically salient entity, not necessarily expressed in a sentence, among the participants of the event described by the main verb. In Generative Lexicon terms, the load is a necessary element of the loading event and, though not realized syntactically, constitutes a shadow argument incorporated into the lexical semantics of the verb *load* (cf. Levinson, 2010 for a semantic analysis of 'root creation verbs' such as *load*).

The examples of resultative phrases in (14) and (15) are similar to the resultative adverbs in English in (16) in that they describe an entity which is salient in the event but not expressed as an element of the sentence. A knot of shoe laces implicit in (14) and ice in (15) are incorporated into the semantics of the verbs *musub-* 'tie' and *koor-* 'freeze', and are available for modification by the adjective phrases *kata-ku* 'stiff' and *atu-ku* 'thick' respectively. While resultative adverbs in (16) are formally distinct from resultative phrases in English, in Japanese, there is no morphological evidence to consider those adjective phrases in (14) and (15) distinct from resultative phrases. They are instances of the resultative construction which pervasively exhibits a lack of syntactic expressions of the semantic subject.

The proposed semantic representation for the verb *koor-* 'freeze' in (15) is given in (17). The verb is lexically unaccusative and describes the event headed by the stative sub-event e_2. Unaccusative verbs often induce the interpretation of resultative phrases as a description of the syntactic subject as exemplified in (2). In (15), however, the resultative phrase *atu-ku* 'thick' is not predicated of the syntactic subject *kawa* 'river' of the verb but rather of the shadow argument S-ARG$_1$ which refers to the ice formed as a result of the freezing event.

(17) the semantic representation of *koor-* 'freeze' in (15)

$$\left[\begin{array}{l} \textit{koor-}\ \text{`freeze'} \\ \text{EVENTSTR} = \left[\begin{array}{l} E_1 = e_1\text{:process} \\ E_2 = e_2\text{:state} \\ \text{RESTR} = <_{\infty} \\ \text{HEAD} = e_2 \end{array}\right] \\ \text{ARGSTR} = \left[\begin{array}{l} \text{ARG}_1 = [1]\text{liquid} \\ \text{S-ARG}_1 = [2]\left[\begin{array}{l} \text{ice} \\ \text{CONST} = \text{solid-state-of}([1]) \end{array}\right] \end{array}\right] \\ \text{QUALIA} = \left[\begin{array}{l} \text{default-causative-lcp} \\ \text{AGENTIVE} = \text{freeze-act}(e_1, [1]) \\ \text{FORMAL} = \text{freeze-result}(e_2, [2]) \end{array}\right] \end{array}\right]$$

The semantic representation states that the freezing event necessarily brings about a frozen entity, which is a solid state of the argument ARG_1. While the entity does not surface in a sentence, thus encoded as a shadow argument S-ARG_1, it is still an argument of the FORMAL quale and available for modification by resultative phrases.

7 Problem: Destruction Verbs with Resultative Phrases

Unlike previous examples, some resultative phrases seem to be predicated of an entity which cannot be considered as a true argument, a default argument, or a shadow argument of the verb. The examples in (18) show resultative phrases with a transitive verb *kezur-* 'scrape'.

(18)

a.* hyoga-ga **zimen**-o taira-ni kezut-ta.
glacier-NOM ground-ACC flat-NI scrape-PAST
'lit. Glaciers scraped the ground flat.'

b. hyoga-ga **yama**-o taira-ni kezut-ta.
glacier-NOM mountain-ACC flat-NI scrape-PAST
'lit. Glaciers scraped mountains flat.'

The resultative phrase *taira-ni* 'flat' in (18a) is intended to describe the state of the referent of object *zimen* 'ground' after glaciers scraping it. The sentence is, however, unacceptable with the resultative phrase probably because the ground is generally perceived as a flat entity, and it is hard to interpret the adjective phrase as a description of the result of a change, or as an adverbial which describes the manner of scraping. On the other hand, replacing the object with *yama* 'mountain', makes the sentence acceptable as shown in (18b). In (18b), the resultative phrase *taira-ni* 'flat' describes the state resulting from glaciers' scraping mountains away. The natural interpretation, however, gives rise to a problem that the resultative phrase cannot be predicated of the object since mountains are not flat by definition of the word.

The verb *kezur-* 'scrape' is a simple causative verb as its basic use, and the direct object denotes the theme argument as in *zimen-o kezur-* 'scrape the ground' in (18a), *ki-o kezur-* 'plane wood', and *enpitu-o kezur-* 'sharpen a pencil'. In (18b) with the resultative phrase, on the other hand, the object NP refers to an entity which is destroyed as a result of the scraping event, and the use of the verb is, in a sense, an inverse of the verb *hor-* 'dig' as a creation verb discussed in Section 5: a creation verb takes an object which expresses an entity created by the event while a 'destruction verb' takes an object which expresses an entity eliminated by the event.

Assuming the instance of the verb *kezur-* 'scrape' in (18b) is a derived use of indirect causation, its semantic representation is approximated in (19), based upon the semantic representation of *hor-* 'dig' as a creation verb shown in (12).

(19) a tentative semantic representation of *yama-o kez-*'scrape mountains' in (18b)

$$\left[\begin{array}{l} \textit{yama-o kezur-}\ \text{`scrape mountains'} \\ \text{EVENTSTR} = \left[\begin{array}{l} E_1 = e_1\text{:process} \\ E_2 = e_2\text{:state} \\ \text{RESTR} = <_{\infty} \\ \text{HEAD} = e_1 \end{array}\right] \\ \text{ARGSTR} = \left[\begin{array}{l} \text{ARG}_1 = [1]\text{phyobj} \\ \text{D-ARG}_1 = [2]\text{physobj} \\ \text{ARG}_2 = [3]\left[\begin{array}{l} \text{mountain} \\ \text{CONST} = [2] \end{array}\right] \end{array}\right] \\ \text{QUALIA} = \left[\begin{array}{l} \text{destroy-lcp} \\ \text{AGENTIVE} = \text{scrape-act}(e_1, [1], [2]) \\ \text{FORMAL} = \neg\text{exist}(e_2, [3]) \end{array}\right] \end{array}\right]$$

The theme argument, which is realized as *zimen* 'ground' in (18a), is represented as a default argument D-ARG_1 in (19), and syntactically not expressed in the sentence (18b). Instead, the object *yama* 'mountain' is encoded as the second true argument ARG_2. This argument, marked as [3], corresponds to the entity eliminated as a result of the scraping event, and is also composed into the FORMAL quale, $\neg$exist(e_2, [3]). Thus, the semantic representation implies that the object would be available for modification by a resultative phrase. The resultative phrase *taira-ni* 'flat' in (18b), however, cannot be analyzed as predicated of mountains, and conjoining the semantic representation of the resultative phrase would produce a logical representation of an entity which is non-existent yet flat.

The general problem in analyzing resultative phrases with verbs of destruction is that the resultative construction in Japanese allows a resultative phrase to cooccur with an object NP whose referent is an entity to be destroyed or eliminated in the event described by the verb. The resultative phrase denotes a property which can no longer be predicated of the destroyed entity. Rather, it describes an entity which is a remnant of destruction but does not constitute an argument of the verb. The problem of representation of the semantic subject of such resultative phrases is left open for further research.

8 Conclusion

It has been demonstrated that the resultative construction in Japanese describes the resultant state of a wide range of participants of the event. Unlike the counterpart in English, the semantic subject of resultative phrases in Japanese cannot always be identified with the referent of the direct object of transitive verbs, or the subject of unaccusative intransitive verbs. Rather, interpretation of resultative phrases requires an extensive semantic context which makes it possible to identify the individual described by resultative phrases, whether it is expressed as the syntactic object as shown in Section 2, as a 'sense in context' of polysemous nouns as in Section 3, as an oblique NP as in Section 4, or not expressed at all as in Sections 5 through 7.

The argument of resultative phrases is commonly referred to as the 'affected theme' of change-of-state events, an individual which undergoes a change of state in the event expressed by the verb (e.g. Miyagawa, 1989). It is shown that such individuals are not limited to those formally encoded in the argument structure of the verb as the theme argument, but also include the goal argument of locative-alternation verbs (e.g. *nur-* 'cover/apply'), the product of creation verbs (e.g. *hor-* 'dig'), and the implied outcome of lexical causative verbs (e.g. *musub-* 'tie') and unaccusative verbs (e.g. *koor-* 'freeze'). Since the resultative construction in Japanese does not require those individuals to be expressed as part of a sentence, standard compositional semantics based upon the syntactic constituents of the surface sentence is not enough to capture the full range of individuals available for modification by resultative phrases. The proposed analysis is an attempt to encode the notion of 'affected theme' into the semantic representation through co-composition of the semantic representations of a verb, its complements or default/shadow arguments, and a resultative phrase.

A further problem of resultative phrases with verbs of destruction is pointed out, but left open. It is not clear how to compose into the semantic representation an entity which results from destruction and is described by a resultative phrase, but does not constitute an argument of the verb.

References

Geuder, Wilhelm. 2000. Oriented adverbs: Issues in the lexical semantics of event verbs. Doctoral dissertation, Universität Tübingen.

Green, Georgia M. 1972. Some observations on the syntax and semantics of instrumental verbs. *Papers from the eighth regional meeting of Chicago Linguistic Society,* ed. by Paul M. Peranteau, Judith N. Levi, and Gloria C. Pharess, 83-97. Chicago: Chicago Linguistic Society.

Kageyama, Taro. 1996. *Doshi imiron: Gengo-to ninchi-no setten* [Semantics of verbs: The interface between language and cognition]. Tokyo: Kuroshio.

Koizumi, Masatoshi. 1994. Secondary predicates. *Journal of East Asian Linguistics* 3.25-79.

Levin, Beth and Malka Rappaport Hovav. 1995. *Unaccusativity: At the syntax-lexical semantics interface*. Cambridge, Massachusetts: MIT Press.

Levinson, Lisa. 2010. Arguments for pseudo-resultative predicates. *Natural Language and Linguistic Theory*

28.135-182.

Miyagawa, Shigeru. 1989. *Structure and case marking in Japanese* (Syntax and Semantics 22). San Diego: Academic Press.

Nakatani, Kentaro. 2007. Bunshori sutoratezi-to iu kanten-kara mita kekkakobun-no ruikeiron [A typology of resultative construction from the viewpoint of sentence processing strategy]. *Kekkakobun kenkyu-no sin-siten* [A new perspective of research on the resultative construction], ed. by Naoyuki Ono, 289-317. Tokyo: Hitsuji Shobo.

Pustejovsky, James. 1991. The syntax of event structure. *Cognition* 41,47-81.

Pustejovsky, James. 1995. *The generative lexico*n. Cambridge, Massachusetts: MIT Press.

Simpson, Jane. 1983. Resultatives. *Papers in Lexical-Functional Grammar*, ed. by L. Levin, M. Rappaport, and A. Zaenen, 143-157. Bloomington, Indiana: Indiana University Linguistics Club.

Takezawa, Koichi. 1993. Secondary predication and locative/goal phrases. *Japanese syntax in comparative grammar*, ed. by Nobuko Hasegawa, 45-77. Tokyo: Kuroshio.

Tsujimura, Natsuko. 1990. Unaccusative nouns and resultatives in Japanese. *Japanese/Korean linguistics*, ed. by Hajime Hoji, 335-349. Stanford: Center for the Study of Language and Information.

Washio, Ryuichi. 1997. Resultatives, compositionality and language variation. *Journal of East Asian Linguistics* 6.1-49.

Wechsler, Stephen. 1997. Resultative predicates and control. *The syntax and semantics of predication*, ed. by R. C. Blight and M. Moosally (Texas Linguistic Forum 38), 307-321. Austin: University of Texas Department of Linguistics.

Wechsler, Stephen and Bokyung Noh. 2001. On resultative predicates and clauses: Parallels between Korean and English. *Language Sciences* 23.391-423.

Williams, Edwin. 1980. Predication. *Linguistic Inquiry* 11.203-238.

Event Coercion of Mandarin Chinese Temporal Connective *hou* 'after'

Zuoyan Song
School of Chinese Language and Literature
Beijing Normal University
Beijing, China
meszy@163.com

Abstract

Unlike its English equivalent *after*, which often takes NP complement, Chinese temporal connective *hou* tends to take VP complement. In terms of type coercion, while *after* seems to generally license event coercion, Chinese *hou* does not (with a few exceptions), as in most cases the presence of a verb is required for the *hou*-construction (and the sentence) to be correct. Rather than attributing this difference to the different lexicalization of nouns in these two languages, this paper argues that it is due to the difference between *hou* and *after*. In particular, *hou* is weaker in its coercion force than *after* because of its polysemy. It is either a temporal connective or a locative connective.

1 Introduction

Natural language often leaves many meaning facets unexpressed in the surface form, which will lead to type-mismatch, underspecification or semantic incongruity. For example, there is some covert event meaning in the sequence in (1), which must be recovered in understanding or interpretation. Type mismatch occurs because *the book* is an entity type and *begin* requires its complement to be an event type.

(1) John began the book.

The theory of Generative Lexicon (Pustejovsky,1995,2001,2006) proposes in particular that the mismatch is solved by the operation of type coercion, which is defined as follows (Pustejovsky, 1995: 111).

(2) Type Coercion
A semantic operation that converts an argument to the type which is expected by a function where it would otherwise result in a type error.

It is redefined as (3) (Pustejovsky, 2006).

(3)Type Coercion: the type a function requires is imposed on the argument type. This is accomplished by either:
①Exploitation: taking a part of the argument's type to satisfy the function;
②Introduction: wrapping the argument with the type required by the function.

In essence, it confers to the predicate the ability to change the argument type. The eventive verb *begin* in (1) coerces its argument to assume an event type (i.e. *read/write the book*) from an entity type (i.e. *the book*). *Read* and *write* are the telic role and agentive role of *book* respectively. The type coercion discussed above will be called event coercion below, which makes an entity type shift to an event type.

Similarly, some temporal connectives can coerce its complement to be an event type. Consider the following examples. Some events like *eating dessert* and *drinking coffee* can be reconstructed respectively (Pustejovsky, 1995:231).

(4) Let's leave after dessert.

(5) Let's leave after the coffee.

(6) is a case of French temporal connective *après* (Godard & Jayez, 1993).

(6) Après ce livre, je me seas fatigué.
After this book I feel tired.

Lin & Liu (2005) claim that most of the coercion mechanisms postulated by GL do not seem to work in Mandarin Chinese. While event coercion mechanism works in English as shown in (1), it does not in Mandarin Chinese as shown in (7). To obtain a grammatical expression, a verb such as 读'read' or 写'write' must be explicitly provided.

(7) *张三 开始 一 本 书。
zhangsan kaishi yi ben shu
Zhangsan begin one CL book
'Zhangsan began a book.'

However, other researches paint a different picture. According to Huang & Ahrens (2003), Liu (2005), Lin et al. (2009), Song(2011a, 2011b) , coercion is a universal linguistics mechanism and pervasive in Mandarin Chinese which is exemplified by (8) . 赶 'rush' is an eventive verb like *begin*.

(8) 我 在 赶 这 篇 论文。
wo zai gan zhe pian lunwen
I being rush the CL paper.
'I am rushing (to write) the paper'.

To my knowledge, so far no study on Chinese temporal connectives has been done from the perspective of type coercion. Based on data from bilingual corpora, this paper aims to show that event coercion of后*hou*[1] is not as pervasive as that of its English equivalent *after* and give an explanation for the phenomenon.

The rest of this paper is organized as follows. In Section 2 I first list the argument types of *hou*. Section 3 compares *hou* with *after* and shows the difference between them in the respect of type coercion through analyzing the data from Chinese-English bilingual corpora. Section 4 attempts to account for the difference. Finally, I summarize the paper in Section 5.

[1] 后 *hou* stands for 后 *hou*, 之后 *zhihou* and 以后 *yihou*, all of which have a sense equivalent to *after*.

2 Argument Type of *hou*

The argument types of *hou* can be classified into intervals, events and entities. As a temporal connective, *hou* normally selects for an interval type argument as its complement as in (9). 十点 'ten o'clock' refers to a point of time and 三天 'three days' refers to a period of time, respectively. Here the mechanism at work is pure selection since the type requirement of *hou* is satisfied directly.

(9) a. 十 点 **后**
shi dian **hou**
ten o'clock after
'after ten o'clock'

b. 三 天 **后**
san tian **hou**
three day after
'after three days'

Secondly, expressions denoting events can combine with *hou* naturally because time is the basic element of event and an event always extends over time. See the following examples.

(10) 会 **后** 有 茶点
hui **hou** you chadian
meeting after there-be refreshments
供应。
gongying
provide
'Refreshments will be served after the meeting.

(11) 写 完 论文 **后**，我 就 睡 了。
xie wan lunwen **hou** wo jiu shui le
write ASP paper after I EMP sleep ASP
'After finishing the paper, I went to sleep. '

The event-denoting expression can be an NP involving an event nominal (会*hui*'meeting') as in (10) or a VP (写完论文*xie wan lunwen* 'finishing the paper') as in (11).Here *hou* coerces an event to shift to an interval.

Finally, some nouns denoting entities such as 酒 *jiu*'wine' can be a complement of *hou* occasionally. For the case in (12), the NP 三杯马提尼 *san bei matini* 'three martinis' does not satisfy the type required by the temporal connective *hou* since it denotes entities, but the sentence is acceptable. It is because *hou* coerces the NP into obtaining an event denotation, one which is available from the NP's qualia structure. That is, an event reading such as 喝完三杯马提尼后 *he wan san bei matini hou* 'after drinking three martinis' can be reconstructed. 喝 'drink' is the telic qualia of the 酒. Type Coercion as defined in (2) and (3) makes this possible. Here an entity shifts to an event.

(12) 三 杯 马提尼 <u>后</u>，约翰 感觉 好 了。
san bei matini **<u>hou</u>** yuehan ganjue hao le
three CL martini after John feel well ASP
'After three martinis John felt well. '

In this paper, I confine my research to an analysis of the type coercion as shown in (12), i.e. event coercion. I will illustrate how *hou* and *after* are different in event coercion and further explain where the difference comes from.

3 A Comparison of *hou* and *after*

In this section I will take advantage of bilingual corpora to compare *hou* and *after*. My analysis is based on Chinese-English bilingual Corpus of Peking University and Jukuu Chinese-English bilingual Corpus. Also, a few data are collected by informants' intuition.

In section 2, I classify the kinds of complement of *hou*. At a first glance it seems that there is no significant difference between *hou* and *after* since both of them can take interval, event and entity type complement. To put it in another way, both basically select for the arguments of type interval and event, and can license event coercion whereby an entity type shifts to an event type. However, the data from bilingual corpora show that event coercion of *hou* is not so pervasive as that of *after*. *hou* tends to take VP rather than NP complement when the complement nouns are entity type. My analysis focuses on this type. In addition, the complex type of *physobj•event* will be touched on.

3.1 Entity Type Nouns

hou can't combine with entity type nouns as freely as *after* can. Data show the frequency of event coercion involving *hou* in the bilingual corpora is very low, suggesting that it is not a pervasive phenomenon. Actually, no relevant instances of [entity type noun+ *hou*] construction were found in both bilingual corpora, whereas 23 instances of [after+ entity type noun] construction were found. All the missing verbs in English sentences appear overtly in the corresponding Chinese sentences. See the following examples.

(13) ***喝*** 了 几 杯 马提尼酒 <u>后</u>，
he le ji bei matinijiu **<u>hou</u>**
drink ASP some CL martini after
他 的 表演 发挥 到 了 最佳
ta de biaoyan fahui dao le zuijia
he POSS performance develop to ASP best
状态。
zhuangtai
status
'He played best after a couple of martinis.'

(14) ***吃*** 过 中餐 <u>后</u>，来 一 杯
chi guo zhongcan **<u>hou</u>** lai yi bei
eat ASP Chinese food after come one CL
绿茶 很 棒。
lvcha hen bang
green tea very good
'after a Chinese food a cup of green tea is perfect. '

(15) ***通过*** 海关 <u>之后</u>，你 必须
tongguo haiguan **<u>zhihou</u>** ni bixu
go through customs after you must
在 移民局 出示 你 的 护照。
zai yiminju chushi ni de huzhao
at immigration show you POSS passport
'After the Customs, you must show your passport to the office at Immigration.'

In (13), the verb 喝*he*'drink' shows up although the Chinese sentence is still allowed without it. In (14) and (15), the verbs 吃*chi* 'eat' and 通过 *tongguo* 'go through' can't be absent. Otherwise the *hou*-construction (and the sentence) would be ungrammatical. In most cases, the construction of [*after* + entity type noun] can't be translated into Chinese word for word and a verb must be explicitly provided to obtain a grammatical expression. More examples are presented in (18).

(18) 大学 ***毕业*** <u>后</u>
daxue biye **<u>hou</u>**
College graduate after
'after college'

喝 *完* 茶 <u>后</u>
he wan cha **<u>hou</u>**
Drink ASP tea after
'after tea'

喝 *过* 咖啡 <u>后</u>
he guo kafei **<u>hou</u>**
drink ASP coffee after
'after coffee'

打 *完* 高尔夫 <u>后</u>
da wan gaoerfu **<u>hou</u>**
play ASP golf after
'after golf'

听到 信号 <u>后</u>
tingdao xinhao **<u>hou</u>**
hear tone after
'after the tone'

收 *过* 小麦 <u>以后</u>
shou guo xiaomai **<u>yihou</u>**
gather ASP wheat after
'after wheat'

在 *写* *了* 两 部 练笔 的
zai xie le liang bu lianbi de
at write ASP two CL apprentice MOD
小说 <u>之后</u>
xiaoshuo **<u>zhihou</u>**
novel after
'after two apprentice novels'

In the above cases, the complements of *hou* are VPs and the verbs (and aspectual markers) in italics must be present. The complements of *after*, however, are NPs.

To confirm further the frequency of [entity type noun+ *hou*] construction, I have consulted Modern Chinese corpus of Peking University which consists of more than 1.5 hundred million words. As a result, only 2 instances are found which is presented below. In these cases, coercion can facilitate type satisfaction and an event reading can be recovered from the complement nouns. The hidden verb is 烧 *shao* 'burn' in (16) and 喝 *he* 'drink' in (17) , which are the telic role of 香 *xiang* 'incense' and 酒 *jiu* 'wine' respectively.

(16) 一 炷 香 <u>后</u>，和尚 推 开 了
yi zhu xiang **<u>hou</u>** heshang tui kai le
one CL incense after monk push open ASP
门。
men
door
'After one stick of incense burnt out, the monk pushed open the door.'

(17) 于是 三 杯 酒 <u>后</u>， 就 说：
yushi san bei jiu **<u>hou</u>** jiu shuo
then three CL wine after EMP say
"你 的 太太 真 像 Nancy Caro11。"
ni de taitai zhen xiang Nancy Caro11
you POSS wife very like Nancy Caro11
'Then after three glasses of wine, (he) said "your wife is just like Nancy Caro11 "'

Note that the cardinal-classifier phrase in (16) can't be deleted, otherwise error will occur. Namely, 香后 is impossible as shown in (18c). Although 酒后is grammatical in Mandarin Chinese, it is a compound and can't combine with other words freely. It is usually used in some fixed expressions like four- character idioms, e.g.酒后驾车 *jiuhoujiache* 'drive after having drunk'. Moreover, not all the imaginable occurrences of the sequence [bare noun+*hou*] are allowed as shown in (18c-d). According to my data, only 酒后 and 茶后 are possible.

(18) a. 酒<u>后</u>*jiuhou* 'after drinking'
b.茶<u>后</u>*chahou* 'after tea'
c.*香<u>后</u>*xianghou*
literal translation: incense after
d.*咖啡<u>后</u>*kafeihou* 'after coffee'

It appears that the [cardinal ＋ CL ＋ N+*hou*] construction can license event coercion as both 一炷香 and 三杯酒are sequences of this kind of construction. However, it is not so for all the imaginable occurrences of construction. *Hou* imposes some restrictions on this construction. Firstly, the [cardinal＋classifier＋N] construction has no definite reading and only indefinite reading is available. Secondly, generally speaking, the cardinals involved in this construction are limited to 半*ban* 'half', 一*yi* 'one', 二*er* 'two' and 三*san* '*three*', and the nouns are limited to those denoting incenses, liquors and teas. (19) is acceptable but it means 'behind the three books'. Here *hou*/*zhihou* is not a temporal connective but a locative connective. 三本书exhibits a definite reading.

(19) 三 本 书 **后/之后**
san ben shu **hou/zhihou**
three CL book behind
'behind the three books'

3.2 Complex Type Nouns

It seems that some nouns denoting to other entities can be complement of *hou* as shown in (20a). 早餐 *zaocan* 'breakfast' can refer to food, so it can be a entity type. Oddly enough, (20b) is not allowed even though 中餐*zhongcan* 'Chinese food' also refers to food.

(20) a. 早餐 **以后**，我们 去 巡视
zaocan **yihou** women qu xunshi
breakfast after we go make-a-tour
柏林墙。
bolinqiang
Berlin Wall
'After breakfast we made a tour of the Wall.'

b. *中餐[2] **后**
zhongcan **hou**
Chinese food after
'after Chinese food'

It is because these two nouns belong to different types. 中餐 *zhongcan* 'Chinese food' is an artifactual type and only refers to an entity, while 早餐*zaocan* 'breakfast' is a complex type and refers to more than one aspect, an entity or an event. It identifies both an eventuality of eating and the physical manifestation of food: *event•food.* (20a) is acceptable because coercion by dot exploitation takes place (cf. Pustejovsky, 2011). In this example, it is the event manifestation of the noun meaning that is selected for by *hou*. More examples are presented in (21), all the nouns in which are typed as a dot object *event•physobj* [3]and the event aspect are selected for by *hou*.

(21) 午餐后*wucan hou* 'after lunch'
晚餐后*wancan hou* 'after supper'
雨后*yuhou* 'after the rain'
雪后*xuehou* 'after the snow'

3.3 Summary

In short, when the complement noun is an entity type, *hou* tends to take VP rather than NP complement. It is different from its English equivalent *after*, which often takes NP complement. In terms of type coercion, while *after* seems to generally license event coercion, Chinese *hou* does not (with a few exceptions), as in most cases the presence of a verb is required for the *hou*-construction (and the sentence) to be correct. In rare cases, the [cardinal+CL+N+*hou*] construction licenses coercion. Many restrictions, however, are imposed on it and therefore the examples of event coercion of *hou* are few and far between.

4 Discussion

Data from bilingual corpora prove event coercion of *hou is* much less than that of *after*. My findings are in line with the studies of Liu (2004) and Lin & Liu (2005). By comparing complement coercion in Chinese and English, they come to a conclusion that while in English some event information is left unexpressed in surface syntactic form, in Chinese it tends to be expressed directly. Lin & Liu (2005) claim that coercion involving event information (i.e. event coercion) does not work in Chinese as shown in (7). They further propose a hypothesis, which assume that being an analytical language, Chinese lexicon does not share the same degree of richness in sub-lexical event information as in a language like English. In English the primitives that carry event information are extensively incorporated into individual lexical forms, but in Mandarin Chinese they are sent directly to syntactic computation. In other words, it is because nouns in Mandarin Chinese don't have sub-lexical event information that complement coercion

[2] 中餐 *zhongcan* has another sense. In this sense, it is a synonym of 午餐 *wucan* 'lunch', which is a complex type and can combine with *hou* as shown in (21).

[3] Not all the nouns of complex type *event•physobj* can be the complement of *hou*. For example, *电影后 *dianying hou* 'after the film' is not allowed.

doesn't work. For example, (1) is acceptable but its (7) is not, because 书 *shu* 'book' doesn't have sub-lexical event information while *book* does. According to this account, it is because 中餐 *zhongcan* 'Chinese food' does not have sub-lexical event information that 中餐后 *zhongcan hou* 'after Chinese food' is impossible (cf.(20b)).

However, there is a problem with this analysis. If it is the poverty of sub-lexical event information that makes coercion inapplicable in Mandarin Chinese. 一炷香后 *yi zhu xian ghou* and 三杯酒后 *san bei jiu hou* (cf.(16) and (17)) should be unacceptable since 香 *xiang* 'incense' and 酒 *jiu* 'wine' have no sub-event information to be retrieved. But that is not the case as shown in (16) and (17).It suggests that they are not short of event information at all and instead they can provide a verb 烧 *shao* 'burn' and 喝 *he* 'drink' respectively for the reconstruction of event reading.

Rather than attributing this difference to the different lexicalization of nouns in these two languages, this paper argues that it is due to the different coercion force of the temporal connectives. *Hou* is weaker in its coercion force than its English equivalent *after*. Specifically, *after* is a temporal connective referring to time sequence and means "later in time than". *hou*, however, can be either a temporal connective or a locative connective. In particular, it is polysemous and has at least two senses. One is equivalent to *after* and refers to time sequence. The other is equivalent to *behind* and refers to location. The temporal meaning is derived metaphorically from the spatial meaning. As a locative connective, it usually selects for entity type nouns as complement. As a temporal connective, if it also combines with entity type nouns, ambiguity will arise in [entity type noun + *hou*] construction. For example, 海关之后 *haiguan zhihou* might mean either "behind the customs" or "after (going through) the customs"(cf.(17)).To avoid this ambiguity, the verb 通过 *tongguo* 'go through' must be present. This is why the temporal connective *hou* does not take an entity type complement and license event coercion.

Against the analysis above, 一炷香后 *yi zhu xian ghou* and 三杯酒后 *san bei jiu hou* can license coercion. There seem to be two reasons for such counterexamples. First, cardinal-classifier plays an important role. Despite in Chinese cardinal-classifier-noun phrases have definite explanation in certain context (cf.(19)), they have only indefinite readings in this context. Hence, the physical objects denoted by them occupy no specific position and can not be used as a reference to specify the location of the other objects. *hou* gets only the temporal meaning. But, if the cardinal-classifier-noun phrases are preceded by demonstrative pronouns such as 这 *zhe* 'this', its definite reading will be salient and *hou* will get spatial meaning other than temporal meaning. So (22) denotes some locations other than time.

(22)a. 这 一 炷 香 __之后__
zhe yi zhu xiang __**zhihou**__
this one CL incense after
'behind the incense'

b.这 三 杯 酒 __之后__
zhe san bei jiu __**zhihou**__
This three CL wine after
'behind the three glasses of wine'

Second, the sequence of [cardinal+classifier+N] such as 一炷香 *yi zhu xian* is a highly conventionalized construction and functions as [cardinal+ CL+ temporal measure word] construction, which denotes a period of time. It can be observed from the contrast between (23) and (24).

(23) a.一 炷 香 的 时间
yi zhu xiang de shijian
one CL incense MOD time
'the time that it takes for one stick of incense to burn out'

b. 一 炷 香 __**后**__
yi zhu xiang __**hou**__
one CL incense after
'After one incense burnt out

(24) a. 一 个 小时 的 时间
yi ge xiaoshi de shijian
one CL hour MOD time
'one hour'

b.一 个 小时 __**后**__
yi ge xiaoshi __**hou**__

one CL hour after
'after one hour'

In the examples above, both 一炷香 *yi zhu xian* and 一个小时 *yi ge xiao shi* can modify temporal nouns such as 时间 *shijian* 'time' and describe duration of time. Since 一个小时之后 *yi ge xiao shi zhihou* is allowed, it becomes logical for 一炷香 *yi zhu xian* to combine with *hou.* Other such NPs includes 一盏茶 *yi zhan cha* 'one cup of tea', 三杯酒 *san bei jiu* 'three glasses of wine' and so on. Without denoting a period of time, 一本书 *yi ben shu* can't modify time nouns as shown in (25a) and therefore 一本书后 *yi ben shu hou* is impossible as shown in (25b).

(25) a. *一 本 书 的 时间
yi ben shu de shijian
one CL book MOD time
'the time that it takes for one to finished one book'

b. *一 本 书 **后**[4]
yi ben shu **hou**
one CL book after

It is not difficult to conclude that only the NPs which can modify time nouns can combine with *hou*. Because of the lack of timer such as clock and watch, in ancient China, time can be measured in the duration of one stick of incense burning out, or having a cup of tea or a glass of wine. For example, it takes about one hour for one incense to burn out, so 一炷香的时间 *yi zhu xiang de shijian* is equivalent to one hour or so.

5 Conclusion

To conclude, this paper describes the difference between *hou* and its equivalent *after* in event coercion. Furthermore, an alternative account is given for the difference.

Future study is required to investigate more temporal connectives in different languages and further discuss this issue from a typological perspective.

[4] It can't mean 'behind the book', because unlike 三本书 *san ben shu* in (19), 一本书 *yi ben shu* does not have definite reading.

Acknowledgments

This study is supported by the National Social Science Foundation of China (Grant No.10CYY032) and the Fundamental Research Funds for the Central Universities. I am grateful to the three anonymous reviewers for detailed comments and suggestions.

References

Godard, Danièle, and Jacques Jayez. 1993. Towards a proper treatment of coercion phenomena. *Proceedings of the 6th Conference of the European Chapter of the ACL*, 168-177. Utrecht: OTS Utrecht.

Huang, Chu-Ren, and Kathleen Ahrens. 2003. Individuals, kinds and events: classifier coercion of nouns. *Language Sciences* 25.4:353–373.

Lin, Shu-Yen, Shu-Kai Hsieh and Yann-Jong Huang. 2009. Exploring Chinese type coercion: a web-as-corpus study. Paper presented at 5th International Conference on Generative Approaches to the Lexicon. Italy: Pisa.

Lin, T.-H. Jonah, and C.-Y. Cecilia Liu. 2005. Coercion, event structure, and syntax. *Nanzan Linguistics* 2:9-31.

Liu, Mei-chun. 2005. Lexical information and beyond: meaning coercion and constructional inferences of Mandrain verb GAN. *Journal of Chinese Linguistics.* 33.2:310-332.

Liu, Chiung-Yi. 2004. *Dynamic Generative Lexicon.* Master thesis. National Tsing Hua University, Taiwan.

Pustejovsky, James. 1995. *The Generative Lexicon.* Cambridge, MA: MIT Press.

Pustejovsky, James. 2001. Type construction and the logic of concepts. *The Syntax of Word Meanings*, ed. by Federica Busa and Pierrette Bouillon, 91-123, Cambridge: Cambridge University Press.

Pustejovsky, James. 2006. Type theory and lexical decomposition. *Journal of Cognitive Science 6:*39-76.

Pustejovsky, James. 2011. Coercion in a generative theory of argument selection. *Linguistics* 49:1401-1431.

Song, Zuoyan. 2011a. Light verb, event and complement in Mandarin Chinese. *Studies of the Chinese Language* 3:205-217.

Song, Zuoyan. 2011b. The semi-productivity and multiple interpretations of logical metonymy. *Language Teaching and Linguistic Studies*3:43-50.

To Construct the Interpretation Templates for the Chinese Noun Compounds Based on Semantic Classes and Qualia Structures

Xue wei
Dept. of Chinese Lang. & Lit., Peking University/ Research Center of Chinese Linguistics/ Ministry of Education Key Laboratory for Computational Linguistics
Ellen_wx@163.com

Yulin Yuan
Dept. of Chinese Lang. & Lit., Peking University/ Research Center of Chinese Linguistics/ Ministry of Education Key Laboratory for Computational Linguistics
yuanyl@pku.edu.cn

Abstract

This paper focuses on the semantic relations and interprations of Chinese noun compounds (mostly search terms). In light of the semantic classification from Semantic Knowledge-base of Contemporary Chinese (SKCC) and Qualia Structures introduced by Pustejovsky (1991, 1995), we analyze the combinations of the semantic classes of the noun compounds, and thus, discover the implicit predicates of the noun compounds. Based on these semantic relations of the nouns, we summarize the semantic patterns of the noun compounds and built up an interpretation template database of the paraphrasing verbs for the noun compounds. In conjunction with this database, we further develope an automatic interpreatation program of Chinese noun compounds.

1 Background

As the society is developing rapidly with a lot of new ideas and technologies, noval names sprout out to denote these new concepts, products and etc.. Many noval names are created in the form of noun-noun compound. The phrase pattern "n1+n2" is ambiguous, since it represents different syntactic constructions，such as predication construction, modifier-head construction, appositional construction, and paratactic construction. Among these constructions, the inner semantic relation of the modifier-head "n1+n2" construction is especially complicated. There is a semantic compression with an invisible predicate implied in the noun compounds. Since the predicate is invisible, the semantic relations between the head and the modifier are not quite clear[1].For example, "木头桌子"(the wood table, which means that the table is made of wood), "爱情故事"(love story, which means that the story is about love[2]), "钢材仓库"(steel warehouse, which has two different meanings: the warehouse to store

[1] Some modifier-head constructions have implicit nouns, for example, "封面女郎"(cover girl, which means that the girl whose photos are on the cover) .
[2] Cf. Yuan Yulin (1995).

steel, and the warehouse made of steel[3]). We suggest that the implicit predicate could be the paraphrase verb that reveals the semantic relations between the modifier and the head in noun compounds. Thus, the aim of this paper is to discover the implicit predicate of the noun compounds and to generate the paraphrases of the noun compounds.

The modifier-head noun compounds are basic constructions in almost all languages. As they are "derivative, easily composed but ambiguious"(Wang Meng, et al. 2010), they have aroused much interest in Theoretical Linguistics and Computational Linguistics. As Wang Meng et al. (2010) points out, the research on Chinese noun compounds interpretation can be applied in the fields like question answering, information retrieval and lexicography. We suggest that the noun compounds interpretation is crucial in information retrieval.

A basic information retrieval process contains the following steps: submiting searching request → sending the request → sorting → seaching index → selecting pages → ranking results → presentation of the results. The information retrieval appears to be a simple behavior accomplised in just a few seconds, while a lot of analysis and operations are needed after a simple query[4]. The operating procedures in information retrieval are generally divided into two parts: one part is to analyze the users' search intention which is top-down, and the other part is to analyze the structure and meaning of the searching words which is bottom-up. Both parts are important to obtain the required results.

Therefore, if we want to interprate the noun compounds automatically, we need to understand the ontological meaning of the noun compounds that submitted by the web user, and provide references of the users' search intentions as well. For example, when a user inputs "蔬菜大王"(vegetable king) as the searching word, we guess that he maybe wants to know the news about "蔬菜大王"(vegetable king). However, the noun compound "蔬菜大王"(vegetable king) happens to be an ambiguous noun compound. It might means someone who sells/buys vegetables, or someone who plants vegetables, or someone who eats vegetables. If we can decote these different meanings of the compound "蔬菜大王", we can provide the different searching results for the user. Thus, to recover the implicit predicates of the noun compounds is helpful to understand the users' search intentions.

In order to have a better understanding of the search intentions, we have collected 850 Chinese noun compounds from the daily top search terms of Baidu news[5] (2010.9 to 2011.4) and some other literature texts. Besides the basic analysis of the semantic relations and the implicit predicates of these noun compounds, we need the following steps to arrive at their semantic patterns: (1) we summarize the combination patterns according to the semantic classes of the nouns from SKCC. We thus can predict the implicit predicates according to the semantic classes of the modifier and head nouns; (2) in light of the Qualia Structures introduced by Pustejovsky (1991, 1995), we find out that most implicit verbs of the noun compounds are agentive roles or telic roles of the head noun. We thus treat them as paraphrase verbs to reveal the semantic relations of the noun compounds. (3) In the base of the paraphrase verbs, we build up a paraphrase database and an

[3] Cf. Zhou Ren (2007).

[4] Cf. Sina Reports on Science and technology, Mar. 12, 2012. http://www.sina.com.cn.

[5] http://top.baidu.com

automatic paraphrase program of the noun compounds.

2 The semantic classification of nouns

The Semantic Knowledge-base of Contemporary Chinese (SKCC) is a large scale Chinese semantic resource developed by the Institute of Computational Linguistics of Peking University. It provides a large amount of semantic information such as semantic hierarchy and collocation features for 66,539 Chinese words and their English counterparts (Wang and Yu, 2003). Because the classification of nouns is designed for the need of grammatical research (Wang Hui, et al. 2006) and is based on grammatical analysis (Wang and Yu, 2003), we adopt this classification standard as the basis to construct the interpretation templates of the noun compounds. The semantic classification of nouns in SKCC is as follows:

- 1 thing
- 1.1 entity
  - 1.1.1 organism
    - 1.1.1.1 person
      - 1.1.1.1.1 individual
        - 1.1.1.1.1.1 name
        - 1.1.1.1.1.2 profession
        - 1.1.1.1.1.3 identity
        - 1.1.1.1.1.4 relation
      - 1.1.1.1.2 group
        - 1.1.1.1.2.1 organization
        - 1.1.1.1.2.2 society
    - 1.1.1.2animal
      - 1.1.1.2.1 beast
      - 1.1.1.2.2 bird
      - 1.1.1.2.3 insect
      - 1.1.1.2.4 fish
      - 1.1.1.2.5 reptile
    - 1.1.1.3 plant
      - 1.1.1.3.1 tree
      - 1.1.1.3.2 grass
      - 1.1.1.3.3 flower
      - 1.1.1.3.4 crop
    - 1.1.1.4 microbe
  - 1.1.2 object
    - 1.1.2.1 artifact
      - 1.1.2.1.1 building
      - 1.1.2.1.2 clothes
      - 1.1.2.1.3 food
      - 1.1.2.1.4 drug
      - 1.1.2.1.5 cosmetics
      - 1.1.2.1.6 works
      - 1.1.2.1.7 software
      - 1.1.2.1.8 hardware
      - 1.1.2.1.9 asset
      - 1.1.2.1.10 bill
      - 1.1.2.1.11 certificate
      - 1.1.2.1.12 symbol
      - 1.1.2.1.13 material
      - 1.1.2.1.14 instrument
        - 1.1.2.1.14.1 tool
        - 1.1.2.1.14.2 vehicle
        - 1.1.2.1.14.3 weapon
        - 1.1.2.1.14.4 furniture
        - 1.1.2.1.14.5 musical-instrument
        - 1.1.2.1.14.6 electricity
        - 1.1.2.1.14.7 stationery
        - 1.1.2.1.14.8 sports-instrument
    - 1.1.2.2 natural object
      - 1.1.2.2.1 celestial body
      - 1.1.2.2.2 geography
        - 1.1.2.2.2.1 land
        - 1.1.2.2.2.2 water
      - 1.1.2.2.3 weather
      - 1.1.2.2.4 mineral
      - 1.1.2.2.5 element
      - 1.1.2.2.6 substance
    - 1.1.2.3 excrement
    - 1.1.2.4 shape
  - 1.1.3 part
    - 1.1.3.1 body-part
    - 1.1.3.2 object-part
- 1.2 abstraction

1.2.1 attribute
1.2.1.1 measurable
1.2.1.2 fuzzy attribute
1.2.1.2.1 property_of_human
1.2.1.2.2 description_of_event
1.2.1.2.3 property_of_object
1.2.1.3 color
1.2.2 information
1.2.3 field
1.2.4 rule
1.2.5 physiological_state
1.2.6 psycho feature
1.2.6.1 feelings
1.2.6.2 cognition
1.2.7 motivation
2 process
2.1 event
2.2 natural phenomenon
2.2.1 visible phenomenon
2.2.2 audible phenomenon
3 space
3.1 location
3.2 direction
4 time
4.1 specific time
4.2 relative time

3 The Qualia Structures of nouns: Agentive roles and Telic roles

The generative lexicon theory (here after GLT), which is proposed by Pustejovsky (1991, 1995), has a great impact in the field of linguistics and natural language processing. Based on the computation and cognition background, this theory deals with natural language semantics, in particular the semantics of words, both alone and in combination, i.e. the problem of compositionality. It aims to explain the meanings of words in the specific contexts by using a detailed description of semantics of words and building a limited semantic operation mechanism.

GLT has divided the semantics of words into four levels: argument structure, qualia structure, event structure and lexical inheritance structure. Argument structure is a specification of number and type of logical arguments, and how they are realized syntactically. Qualia structure is the modes of explanation that includes Formal, Constitutive, Telic and Agentive roles. Event structure is the definition of the event type of a lexical item and a phrase, whose sorts include State, Process, and Transition. Lexical inheritance structure is the identification of how a lexical structure is related to other structures in the type lattice, and its contribution to the global organization of a lexicon. A set of generative devices connects these four levels, providing for the compositional interpretation of words in context (Pustejovsky, 1995: 61).

The qualia structure is inspired by Aristotel's *Four Causes*. A qualia structure has four roles: constitutive role is the relation between an object and its constituents, or proper parts (including Material, Weight, Parts and Component elements); formal role is the basic category which distinguishes the object within a larger domain (including Orientation, Magnitude, Shape, Dimensionality and so on); telic role is the purpose and function of the object; agentive role is the factors involed in the origin or "bringing about" of an object. In fact, a noun's qualia structure illustrates the things, events and relationships related to the object, which is very helpful to the interpretation of noun compounds.

In light of this idea, we find that most implicit predicates of the noun compounds (n1+n2) are n1 or n2's telic roles or agentive roles. So we can use nouns' telic roles or agentive roles to build the database of interpretation templates of noun compounds[6].

4 The cognitive basis of noun compounds

From the perspective of cognition, every noun compounds (n1+n2) has a hidden event (we call it "background event"). When events in concept are expressed in the level of language，it always includes verbs and the arguments dominated by the verbs. The words of n1 and n2 are usually the arguments of the verbs. For example, "红木家具"(mahogany furniture), whose background event is making furniture by mahogany. "Mahogany" is the Material role of "make", while "furniture" is the Product role of "make". Another example is "体操奶奶"(gymnastics grandma). Its background event is that a grandma does gymnastics. "Grandma" is the Agent role of "do", while "gymnastics" is the Result role of "do".

When the speaker wants to emphasize a certain semantic role (noun) of the event in a declarative way, *de* structure , a correspondent analytic pattern of NN compound, such as "NP1+V+的+NP2" or "V+NP1+的+NP2", could also be used. In Chinese, particle *de* is ususuall considered as a marker introducing a relative clause for the head.

When the speaker use *de* structure, the the head of the noun is emphasized, while the modifiers，namely the verb and other arguments， are downgraded in the *de* structure, for example, "（用）红木制作的家具"(the furniture which is made of mahogany) and "做体操的奶奶"(the grandma who does gymnastics). When the speaker usese "n1+n2"pattern, he wants to emphasize both the head n2 and the modifier n1, while the verb connecting n1 and n2 is omitted in the phonological level. For example, we use the Material "红木"(mahogany) to be the modifier, the Product "家具"(furniture) to be the head, and get the noun compound"红木家具"(mahogany furniture). Another example is that we use the Activity "体操"(gymnastics) to be the modifier and the Agent "奶奶"(grandma) to be the head, and then we get the noun compound "体操奶奶"(gymnastics grandma).

The listener usually intends to decode the noun compounds in the background events, which is built on the basis of common sense. Therefore, we can interpret the noun compounds just in a reverse process. We need to recover the semantic roles of n1 and n2 through their semantic classes and find out the predicate that dominates them. Then we can recover the whole background event completely. Especially, to find the verb that dominates the two nouns is the key to interpret the noun compound (n1+n2)[7].

As different kinds of noun compounds have different kinds of background events and implicit verbs, we have summarized different interpretation templates that express different background events from 850 noun compounds instances (n1+n2). Among these interpretation templates, we find that most implicit verbs of the noun compounds (n1+n2) are n1 or n2's telic roles or agentive roles. For example, the explanation of "摩托妈妈"(Motorcycle Mom) is "骑/坐/造/修摩托的妈妈"("the mom who rides on/makes/repairs the motorcycle"). In this case, the semantic class pattern is "artifact+ relation". The verb "骑/坐"(ride on) is the telic role of n1"摩托"(motorcycle), and the verb "造/

[6] Song Zuoyan (2010) has pointed out that the implicit predicate of noun compounds could be gotten by n1 or n2's telic roles or agentive roles. But the details need to be further investigated and generalized.

[7] Cf. Yuan Yulin (1995).

修"(make/repair) is the agentive role of n1"摩托"(motorcycle). Another example is "司机餐馆"(drivers restaurant), whose explanation is "（专门供）司机吃饭的餐馆"(the restaurant is specially for the drivers). The semantic class pattern is "occupation+ building". The verb "吃饭"(eat) is the telic role of n2 "餐馆"(restaurant). In the interpretation templates, we indicate the roles of the verbs. Meanwhile, we add their telic roles and agentive roles in the noun knowledge database. We thus build up a data model that is based on the knowledge and approach of linguistics for the interpretation of noun compounds.

5 The computation procedures and the interaction between semantic patterns and interpretation templates

5.1 The computation procedures Electronically-available resources

Based on the analysis in the above chapters, we deal with the 850 instances of the noun compounds (n1+n2) in the following proeduress:

⑴ Use the segmentation software to split all the noun compounds (n1+n2) into n1+n2.

⑵ Find all n1s' and n2s' semantic classes in SKCC and describe the semantic class combination patterns with the semantic classes of n1 and n2. We abstract the tokens of noun compounds into types of combination patterns. We thus can predict the implicit predicates (paraphrasing verbs) according to the semantic classes of the modifier and head nouns

Since the lexicon database in SKCC is limited, we can add an unknown word's semantic class manually.

⑶ Paraphrase the interpretation template with implicit predicates for every noun compound. We also specify the roles of the verbs. Is it the role of n1 or n2, and is it an agentive role or telic role? If it is a qualia structure role of n1, we mark it as v1; if it is a qualia structure role of n2, we mark it as v2.

⑷ Every noun compound (n1+n2) has a semantic class combination pattern and an interpretation template. We sort out these semantic class patterns and interpretation templates to build up a noun-noun coordination database.

5.2 The interaction between semantic patterns and interpretation templates

We have summarized 326 semantic class patterns (here after semantic patterns) and 208 interpretation templates in total. These semantic patterns can be divided into two classes: ⑴ a sematic pattern in correspondence with one interpretation template; ⑵ a semantic pattern in correspondence with two or more interpretation templates.

⑴ a sematic pattern in correspondence with one interpretation template;

We have gotten 212 such semantic patterns, and 62 corresponding interpretation templates. We choose ten interpretation templates and the corresponding semantic patterns randomly, and list them below:

i. If the semantic class of n1 is "tool" and the semantic class of n2 is "cognition", the interpretation template is "(通过)+n1+表现+的+n2" ((through)+n1+express+De+n2). The verb "表现" (express) can be seen as the agentive role of n2. For example, "瓷器爱国主义" (china patriotism), the interpretation is "(通过)瓷器表现的爱国主义"(the patriotism which is expressed through the china).

ii. If the semantic class of n1 is

"relative time" and the semantic class of n2 is "field", the interpretation template is "n1+产生+的+n2/产生于+n1+的+n2" (n1+be produced+De+n2/Be produced in+n1+De+n2). N1 is the time when n2 is/was produced. For example, "当代文学" (contemporary literature), the interpretation is "当代产生的文学/产生于当代的文学" (the literature which is produced in contemporary age).

iii. If the semantic class of n1 is "organization" and the semantic class of n2 is "location", the interpretation template is "n1+建立+的+n2" (n1+build+De+n2). The verb "建立" (build) can be seen as the agentive role of n2. For example, "网易养猪场" (Wangyi Pig farm), the interpretation is "网易建立的养猪场" (The pig farm which is built by Wangyi).

iv. If the semantic class of n1 is "profession" and the semantic class of n2 is "organization", the interpretation template is "供+n1+v2+的+n2" (For+n1+v2+De+n2). The verb v2 is the telic role of n2. For example, "民工学校" (migrant workers school), the interpretation is "供民工读书/上学的学校" (the school for migrant workers to study).

v. If the semantic class of n1 is "physiological_state" and the semantic class of n2 is "microbe", the interpretation template is "引起+n1+的+n2" (cause+n1+De+n2). For example, "流感病毒" (flu virus), the interpretation is "引起流感的病毒" (viruses that cause flu).

vi. If the semantic pattern is "field+event[8]", or "property_of_object+abstraction", or "property_of_object+artifact", the interpretation template is "是+n1+(性+)的+n2" (is+n1+De+n2). The corresponding examples are "历史机遇" (historical opportunity), "基础项目" (basic project), "基础设施" (infrastructure construction), their corresponding interpretations are "是历史(性)的机遇" (the opportunity which is historical), "是基础(性)的项目" (the project which is basic), "是基础(性)的设施" (the installation which is basic).

vii. If the semantic pattern is "tool+artifact", or "profession+society", or "profession+group", the interpretation template is "由+n1+构成+的+n2" (by+n1+constitute+De+n2). The corresponding examples are "电脑网络" (computer network), "工人阶级" (worker class), "义工组织" (volunteer organization), their corresponding interpretations are "由电脑构成的网络" (the network which is constituted by computers), "由工人构成的阶级" (the class which is constitued by workers), "由义工构成的组织" (the organization which is constituted by volunteers).

viii. If the semantic pattern is "name+relation[9]", or "name+feelings", the interpretation template is "n1+拥有+的+n2" (n1+own+De+n2). The corresponding examples are "汪峰女儿" (WangFeng's daughter), "梁咏琪恋情" (LiangYongqi's love affair), their corresponding interpretations are "汪峰拥有的女儿" (the daughter who is owned by WangFeng), "梁咏琪拥有的恋情" (The love affair which is owned by LiangYongqi).

ix. If the semantic pattern is "building+material", or "food+drug", the interpretation template is "v1+n1+用+的+n2" (v1+n1+use+De+n2). The verb v1 is the agentive role of n1 (such as "修建" (build), "制作" (make), etc.). The corresponding examples are "建筑钢材" (building steel), "食品添加剂" (food additives), their corresponding

[8] It means that n1's semantic class is field and n2's semantic class is event. Follwings are the same.

[9] Most nouns that are n2s are monovalent nouns, and n1 is an argument of n2.

interpretations are “修建建筑用的钢材” (the steels that are used for building), “制作食品用的添加剂” (the additives that are used for food).

x. If the semantic pattern is “location+cosmetics”, or “location+excrement”, or “location+food”, or “location+tool”, the interpretation template is “产自+n1+的+n2” (produce in+n1+De+n2). N1 is n2’s place of origin. The corresponding examples are “法国香水” (French perfume), “南海珍珠” (South Sea pearls), “信阳毛尖” (Xinyang tea), “景德镇瓷器” (Jingdezhen china), their corresponding interpretations are “产自法国的香水” (the perfume which is produced in French), “产自南海的珍珠” (the pearls which are produced in South Sea), “产自信阳的毛尖” (the tea which is produced in Xinyang), “产自景德镇的瓷器” (the china which is produced in Jingdezhen).

⑵ a semantic pattern in correspondence with two or more interpretation templates.

We divided this situation into two types: ① a semantic pattern has two interpretation templates; ② a semantic pattern has three or more interpretation templates.

① a semantic pattern has two interpretation templates

We have collected 88 semantic patterns of this type, and 100 corresponding interpretation templates. We choose four interpretation templates and the corresponding semantic patterns randomly, and list them below:

i. If the semantic class of n1 is “event”, and the semantic class of n2 is “location”, the two interpretation templates are: a. “发生+n1+的+n2” (happen+n1+De+n2); b. “有+n1+的+n2” (have+n1+De+n2). N2 is the place where n1 happens. For example, “交通路口” (traffic crossing), the corresponding interpretations are: “a.发生交通的路口; b.有交通的路口” (the crossing where traffic happens).

ii. If the semantic class of n1 is “drug”, and the semantic class of n2 is “animal”, the two interpretation templates are: a. “喂了+n1+的+n2” (feed+n1+De+n2); b. “吃了+n1+的+n2” (eat+n1+De+n2)[10]. For example, “瘦肉精羊” (drug sheep), the corresponding interpretations are: “a.喂了瘦肉精的羊 (the sheep which is fed with drugs); b.吃了瘦肉精的羊 (the sheep which eats drugs)”.

iii. If the semantic pattern is “name+works”, or “name+event”, or “identity+works”, and the two interpretation templates are: a. “n1+v2+的+n2” (n1+v2+De+n2), the verb v2 is the agentive role of n2 (such as “发表” (publish),“表演” (perform),“写” (write), etc.); b. “关于+n1+的 +n2” (about+n1+De+n2). The corresponding examples are “鲁尼声明” (Rooney statement), “刘谦新魔术” (LiuQian new magic), “小学生日记” (primary school student diary), and their corresponding interpretations are: “a. 鲁尼发表的声明 (the statement which is published by Rooney), b. 关于鲁尼的声明 (the statement about Rooney)”; “a. 刘谦表演的新魔术 (the magic which is performed by Liu Qian), b. 关于刘谦的新魔术 (the magic about LiuQian)”; “a. 小学生写的日记 (the diary which is written by a primary school student), b. 关于小学生的日记 (the diary ahout a primary school student)”.

iv. If the semantic pattern is “organization+society[11]”, or

---

[10] Animals won’t take the initiative to eat medicine or additives, so if the sematic class of n1 is “drug”, and the semantic class of n2 is “animal”, the relation between n1 and n2 is not the initative to eat, but the passive feeding. Through the entailment: X feed Y Z → Y eat Z, “喂了+n1+的+n2”(feed +n1+ De+n2) can entail “吃了+n1+的+n2”(eat +n1 +De +n2). Cf. Yuan Yulin and Wang Minghua (2009, 2010).

[11] Organization is usually founded by people, and has certain social functions. So all members in the organization have the character “work”, and belong to

"organization+identity", or "group+society", the two interpretation templates are: a. "在+n1+工作+的+n2" (in+n1+work+De+n2); b. "属于+n1+的+n2" (belong+n1+De+n2). The corresponding examples are "企业员工" (enterprise employee), "委员会成员" (committee members), "消防队人员" (fire brigade staff), their corresponding interpretations are: "a. 在企业工作的员工 (the employees who work in the company), b. 属于企业的员工 (the employees who belong to the company)"; "a. 在委员会工作的成员 (the members who work in the committee), b. 属于委员会的成员 (the members who belong to the committee)"; "a. 在消防队工作的人员 (the staff who work in the fire brigade), b. 属于消防队的人员 (the staff who belong to the fire brigade)".

②a semantic pattern has three or more interpretation templates

We have gotten 26 semantic patterns of this type, and 46 corresponding interpretation templates. We choose four interpretation templates and the corresponding semantic patterns randomly, and list them below:

i. If the semantic class of n1 is "organization", and the semantic class of n2 is "abstraction", and the three interpretation templates are: a. "n1+v2+的+n2" (n1+v2+De+n2), the verb v2 is the agentive role of n2 (such as "创造" (create), "设计" (design), etc.); b. "n1+拥有+的+n2" (n1+own+De+n2); c. "供+n1+使用+的+n2" (for+n1+use+De+n2). For example, "国家财政" (state finance), the corresponding interpretations are: "a. 国家制定的财政 (the finance which is formulated by state); b. 国家拥有的财政 (the finance which is owned by state); c. 供国家使用的财政 (the finance which is used by state)".

ii. If the semantic class of n1 is "food", and the semantic class of n2 is "event", the three interpretation templates[12] are: a. "v1+n1+的+n2" (v1+n1+De+n2), the verb v1 is the telic role of n1 (such as "吃"(eat), etc.); b. "n1+引起+的+n2" (n1+cause+De+n2); c. "关于+n1+的+n2" (about+n1+De+n2). For example, "兴奋剂事件" (dope event). The corresponding interpretations are: "a. 吃兴奋剂的事件 (the event which is taking dope); b. 兴奋剂引起的事件 (the event which is caused by dope); c. 关于兴奋剂的事件 (the event which is about dope)".

iii. If the semantic pattern is "location+profession", or "space+profession", the three interpretation templates are: a. "来自+n1+的+n2" (come from+n1+De+n2); b. "在+n1+v2+的+n2" (in+n1+v2+De+n2), the verb v2 is the telic role of n2 (such as "教书" (teach), etc.); c."在+n1+工作+的+n2" (in+n1+work+De+n2). N1 can be the place where n2 comes from, or the place where n2 works. The corresponding examples are "上海工人" (Shanghai workers), "中学教师" (middle school teachers), their corresponding interpretations are "a. 来自上海的工人 (the workers who come from Shanghai), b. 在上海上班的工人 (the workers who work in Shanghai), c. 在上海工作的工人 (the workers who work in Shanghai)"; "a. 来自中学的教师 (the teachers who come from middle school), b. 在中学教书的教师 (the teachers who teach in the middle school), c. 在中学工作的教师 (the teachers who work in the middle school)".

iv. If the semantic class of n1 is

the organization.

12 These three templates express the semantic information of noun compounds from detailed or enriched to less. In the first template, we know the detail of the event by the telic role of n1; in the second template, we only know that the event is caused by n1, but don't know how it is caused; in the third template, we only know that the event is related to n1, but don't know how it is related.

"field" and the semantic class of n2 is "abstraction", the six interpretation templates are: a. "关于+n1+的+n2" (about+n1+De+n2), n1 is the content of n2. For example, "法律常识" (law commonsense). Its corresponding interpretation is "关于法律的常识" (the commonsense which is about law); b. "在+n1+领域/方面内+存在+的+n2" (in+n1+field+exist+De+n2). For example, "政治把柄" (politics handle). Its corresponding interpretation is "在政治领域/方面内存在的把柄" (the handle which exists in politics); c. "v2+n1+的+n2" (v2+n1+De+n2), the verb v2 is the telic role of n2 (such as "经营"(operate), etc.). For example, "化工行业" (chemistry industry). Its corresponding interpretation is "经营化工的行业" (the industry which is engaged in chemistry); d. "n1+（上）+使用+的+n2" (n1+(top)+use+De+n2). For example, "工业技术" (industry technology). Its corresponding interpretation is "工业上使用的技术" (the technology which is used in industry); e. "由+n1+组成+的+n2" (by+n1+compose+De+n2). For example, "社会环境" (society environment). Its corresponding interpretation is "由社会等诸因素组成的环境" (the environment which is composed of society and other factors); f. "考虑+n1+的+n2" (consider+n1+De+n2). For example, "政治头脑" (politics mind). Its corresponding interpretation is "考虑政治（方面问题）的头脑" (the mind which considers about politics). There are many meanings of this semantic pattern. That's because the meanings of nouns of filed and nouns of abstraction are very fuzzy, and it's hard to decide which verb connects the two nouns.

6 Summary

All in all, we build up an interpretation template database that contains the paraphrasing verbs for noun compounds in Chinese. Based on this database, we exploit some other language resources (such as Hownet) to generate the telic roles and agentive roles of every noun automatically. Finally, we develop a program to automatically interpret the meanings of the noun compounds. The accuracy of this program is 94.23% by manual evaluation. [13]

References

Rumshishy, Anna and James Pustejosky. 2011. Generative Lexicon Theory: Theoretical and Empirical Foundations. PPT of *Summer School* at the Center for Chinese Linguistics, Peking University.

Dong, Zhendong and Dong Qiang. *Hownet*. Website: http://www.keenage.com.

Ungerer, Friedrich and Hans-Jörg Schmid. 2006. *An Introduction to Cognitive Linguisitics—Second Edition*. Pearson Education Limited.

Pustejovsky, James. 1991. The generative lexicon. *Computational Linguistics,* 17(4): 209–441.

Pustejovsky, James. 1995. *The Generative Lexicon*, Cambridge, Massachusetts: The MIT Press.

Li, Xiaoming, Yan Hongfei and Wang Jimin. 2005. *Search Enging—Principle, Technology and System*. Beijing: Science Press.

Song, Zuoyan. 2009. *Research on the Event Coercion in Mandarin Chinese*. Ph.D. thesis, Peking University.

Song, Zuoyan. 2010. On the Affixoid Which Can Trigger Off Event Coercion. *Chinese Teaching in the World*, 24(4): 446-458.

[13] Cf. Wei Xue (2012) §7.2: The result of test and analysis.

Tan, Jingchun. 2010. Semantic relations between nouns and noun modifiers and their roles in dictionary definition. *Chinese Language*, 337: 342-355.

Wang, Hui and Yu, Shiwen. 2003. The Semantic Knowledge-base of Contemporary Chinese and its Applications in WSD. In the *Proceedings of the Second SIGHAN workshop on Chinese Language Processing*, ACL.

Wang, Hui, Yu Shiwen and Zhan Weidong. 2003. New Progress of the Semantic Knowledge-base of Contemporary Chinese(SKCC). *Language Computing and Content-based Text Processing*. Beijing: Tsinghua University Press.

Wang, Hui, Zhan Weidong and Yu Shiwen. 2003. The Specification of the Semantic Knowledge-base of Contemporary Chinese. *Journal of Chinese Language and Computing*, 13 (2): 159-176.

Wang, Hui, Zhan Weidong and Yu Shiwen. *2006*. Structure and Application of the Semantic Knowledge-base of Modern Chinese. *Applied Linguistics*, 1: 134-141.

Wang, Meng, Huang Chu-ren, Yu Shiwen and Li Bin. 2010. Chinese Noun Compound Interpretation Based on Paraphrasing Verbs. *Journal of Chinese Information Processing*, 24(6): 3-9.

Wang, Meng. 2010. *Linguistic Knowledge Acquisition of Noun for the Construction of Probablistic Lexical Knowledge-base*. Ph.D. thesis, Peking University.

Wei, Xue. 2012. *Research on Chinese Noun Compound Interpretation for Semantic-Query*. M.A. thesis, Peking University.

Yuan Yulin. 1995. On the Implicit Predicate and its Syntactic Consequences. *Chinese Language*. 4: 241-255.

Yuan, Yulin. 2008a. A Programme of Semantic Resources Oriented to Information Retrieval. *Linguistic Sciences*, 7(1): 1-11.

Yuan, Yulin. 2008b. *Cognitive-based Studies on Chinese Computational Linguistics* (Essays). Beijing: Peking University Press.

Yuan, Yulin and Wang Minghua. 2009. The Types of Textual Entailment and their Inference Mechanisms. *Chinese Linguistics*, 3: 123-138. Beijingl: Peking University Press.

Yuan, Yulin and Wang Minghua. 2010. The Inference and Identification Models for Textual Entailment. *Journal of Chinese Information Processing*, 24(2): 3-13.

Zhang, Xiusong and Zhang Ailing. 2009. An Introduction to the Generative Lexicon. *Contemporary Linguistics*, 3: 267-271.

Zhou, Ren. 2007. The Principle of Information Amount and the Rhythm Mode of Syntactic Combination in Mandarin Chinese, *Chinese Language*, 3: 208-222.

Compositional Mechanisms of Japanese Numeral Classifiers

Miho Mano
Naruto University of Education
748 Nakashima, Takashima, Naruto-cho
Naruto-shi, Tokushima, JAPAN
mmano@naruto-u.ac.jp

Abstract

This paper suggests that Generative Lexicon Theory (Pustejovsky, 1995, 2006, 2011) offers a new analysis of numeral classifiers, focusing on Japanese having various kinds of classifiers. It is often said that classifiers agree with quantified nouns, that is, the nouns have to match the semantic requirements of the classifiers. This paper examines their lexical structures and compositional mechanisms. Though Huang and Ahrens (2003) explain the compositional mechanisms between the classifiers and the quantified nouns using "coercion" instead of the agreement, this paper indicates that other mechanisms including Type Matching (Pustejovsky, 2011) also occur in Japanese depending on the type required by the classifier and the source type of the quantified noun, following Mano and Yonezawa's (to appear) suggestion.

1 Introduction

Japanese has various counters, called *josuushi* in Japanese, including so-called "numeral classifiers (Aikhenvald, 2000)," as well as other East Asian languages such as Chinese, Indonesian, Korean, and Thai. In Japanese, nouns cannot be directly modified by numerals but must be quantified by counters, as shown in (1).

(1) a. *ni-{inu/kuruma} (Japanese)
2-dog/car
'two dogs/cars'

b. ni-hiki-no inu/ ni-dai-no kuruma
2-CL-GEN dog/ 2-CL-GEN car[1]
'two dogs/two cars'

The counters are morphemes used together with numerals, and each of them has semantic restrictions on its objects. For example, a classifier -匹 *hiki* in (1b) requires its objects to be nonhuman animals, and -台 *dai* mainly selects for machines[2].

Most of the previous studies on classifiers assume that the modified nouns agree with the classifiers, because the classifiers can only count nouns which have particular meanings. Many studies have been done on the semantic restrictions of numeral classifiers (concerning Japanese, see Matsumoto (1991, 1993); Downing (1996), Iida (1999), and Nishimitsu and Mizuguchi (2004).).

Huang and Ahrens (2003), however, suggest that the classifiers do not simply agree with the quantified nouns but coerce particular meanings to them, focusing on the numeral classifiers of Mandarin Chinese. This paper shares the view that classifiers can coerce the nouns to refer to particular types, but as Mano and Yonezawa (to appear) point out, it seems that they may agree with the nouns without changing their source types.

There are some contradictory examples in Japanese, however. Taking *chuusha* 'injection,' for example, which is a polysemous noun that means a

[1] The abbreviations used in this paper are as follows: ACC= accusative case, CL=classifier, GEN=genitive case, NOM= nominative case, phys=physical object, PRES=Present tense, PROG=progressive, PST=past tense, TOP=topic marker
[2] See Matsumoto (1991, 1993) and Iida (1999) for more detailed restrictions of *-dai*.

physical object 'syringe' and also an event 'injection.' It can be counted by the classifiers, -本 *hon* and -回 *kai*. -*Hon* requires one dimensional (i.e. long and thin) physical objects (*phys*), and -*kai* is a classifier for events. Given that classifiers coerce the quantified nouns to be required types, *ni-hon-no chuusha* (2-CL-GEN injection) should be of type *phys* meaning 'two syringes,' while *ni-kai-no chuusha* should mean an event 'having injection(s) two times.' But that is not the case. The verb, *owaru* 'end,' is the predicate that selects for *event* as its complement, so it is predicted that only *ni-kai-no chuusha* is allowed. In fact, -*hon* is also allowed as in (2), however, contrary to the coercion analysis.

(2) ni-{hon/kai}-no chuusha-ga owat-ta.
2-CL/CL-GEN injection-NOM end-PST
'(I) had {two injections/injection(s) two times}.'

With regard to this issue, we examine the lexical structures of Japanese numeral classifiers and the compositional mechanisms more closely. The lexical structures of classifiers are examined in Section 2, and the compositional mechanisms are demonstrated in Section 3. Section 4 shows a conclusion and further issues.

2 Classifiers and their Lexical Structures

According to Iida (1999), there are about 360 counters in Japanese, and Kageyama et al. (2011) divide them into "numeral classifiers" and "measure specifiers" depending on their functions, which will be shown in 2.1. This paper focuses on only numeral classifiers. Their lexical structures will be examined in 2.2 and 2.3.

2.1 Classifiers and Measure Specifiers

Some categorizations of Japanese counters have been proposed (cf. Matsumoto, 1991, 1993; Downing, 1996; Iida, 1999; Nishimitsu and Mizuguchi, 2004). This paper adopts Kageyama et al.'s (2011) categorization, which divides them into "numeral classifiers" and "measure specifiers" according to their functions[3]. Numeral classifiers (classifiers, henceforth) classify and count limited and specific groups of nouns, which means their function is "categorization (cf. Bisang, 1993)" of objects. On the other hand, measure specifiers can be used as measures for a wide variety of nouns as in (4b), and their function is considered to be "individuation (cf. Bisang, 1993)" of objects. Some examples are shown in (3-4) (the simplified semantic restrictions of each classifier are in round brackets[4].).

(3) a. classifiers: -回 *kai* (events),-人 *nin* (human), -匹 *hiki* (animals), -個 *ko* (3D phys), -枚 *mai* (2D phys), -串 *kushi* (skewered foods), -台 *dai* (machines), -機 *ki* (planes), -基 *ki* (placed artifacts)
b. measure specifiers: -束 *taba* 'bundle,' -杯 *hai* 'cup,' -箱 *hako* 'box,' -切れ *kire* 'slice,' -キロ *kiro* 'kilogram'

(4) a. ni-hiki-no {ikita okiami/*himono/*su}
2-CL-GEN living.krill/dried.fish/vinegar
'two {living krills/dried fish/water}'
b. ni-{kiro/hai}-no {ikita okiami/himono/su}
2-kilogram/cup-GEN
'two kilograms/cups of {living krill/dried fish/vinegar}'

This paper focuses on classifiers because they have more semantic restrictions on the quantified nouns than measure specifiers, which enables us to examine their compositional mechanisms more clearly.

2.2 Previous studies on the Lexical Structures of Classifiers

Only a few Generative Lexicon approaches have so far been attempted on classifiers (cf. Bond and Paik, 1997; Huang and Ahrens, 2003; Kageyama et al., 2011; Mano and Yonezawa, to appear), and there seems to be still room for argument.

Bond and Paik (1997) propose a basic lexical structure for Japanese sortal classifiers, assuming that the Formal qualia are allowed to take at least two values: a sortal typing of the argument and a feature of dimensionality. (5) is a lexical structure for -個 *ko* (3D phys). There are two variables in the argument structure: one is a numeral+ (which includes numerals, quantifiers, and interrogatives), and another is a quantified noun. The latter is a

[3] Bisang (1993) suggests four functions of classifiers: individuation, categorization, referentializaion, and relationalization.

[4] See Matsumoto (1991, 1993), Downing (1996), and Iida (1999), for more information on the semantic restrictions.

default argument, because it is not necessarily expressed overtly in Japanese, as in (6).

(5) *-ko* "3D"
ARGSTR [ARG1 x: numeral+ / D-ARG1 y: inanimate / DIMEN 3D]
QUALIA [FORMAL quantifies (x, y)]
(Bond and Paik, 1997)

(6) san-ko(-no hako-ga) aru.
3-CL(-GEN box-NOM) be.PRES
'There are three (boxes).'

Huang and Ahrens (2003) and Kageyama et al. (2011) develop the idea further and show that classifiers may have some requirements also in the Constitutive, Telic, and Agentive roles in addition to the Formal role. (7) shows some examples of classifiers that have semantic requirements in the qualia structures of their objects pointed out by Kageyama et al. (2011).

(7) a. Formal role: *-人 nin* (humans), *-匹 hiki* (animals), *-本 hon* (1D phys), *-枚 mai* (2D phys), *-個 ko* (3D phys)
b. Constitutive role: *-戸 ko* (residences), *-串 kushi* (skewered foods), *-体 tai* (bodies)
c. Telic role: *-機 ki* (planes to fly), *-着 chaku* (clothing to wear), *-軒 ken* (buildings to live in)
d. Agentive role: *-揃え soroe* (coordinated ones), *-基 ki* (placed large artifacts)

2.3 Semantic Restrictions by Classifiers

Following these studies, Mano and Yonezawa (to appear) propose more detailed lexical structures for Japanese classifiers. The basic lexical structure of classifiers suggested by them is given in (8). Each classifier is considered to have specifications on the quantified noun, i.e. D-ARG1.

(8) CL *-α*
ARGSTR = [ARG1 = x: quantity[5] / D-ARG1 = y: entity]
QUALIA = [FORMAL = quantify (x, y)]
(Mano and Yonezawa, to appear)

[5] This is considered to be equivalent to "numeral+" in Bond and Paik (1997).

They assume that the most basic type of classifiers is the one that specifies the Formal role of their objects, i.e. (7a). For example, (9) shows the lexical structures of the classifiers for animates, and *-kai*, a classifier to count events, is also considered to have a similar structure, as in (10) (It should be noted that only the relevant parts of lexical structures are shown in this paper.). We agree with them with regard to this type.

(9) a. *-人 nin* D-ARG1=y: human (ibid.)
[FORMAL=human (y)]
b. *-匹 hiki* D-ARG1=y: animal
[FORMAL=animal (y)]
c. *-羽 wa* D-ARG1=y: bird
[FORMAL=bird (y)]

(10) *-回 kai* D-ARG1=y: event (ibid.)
[FORMAL = event]

Next, we will review other types, (7b-d), which have semantic requirements on the roles other than the Formal role. The lexical structure for *-串 kushi*, a classifier to count skewered foods, is shown in (11). It requires skewers to be included in the Constitutive role of the objects. They also point out that the Formal, Agentive, and Telic roles are also specified because *-kushi* counts foods only as shown in (12).

(11) *-串 kushi* ARGSTR=D-ARG1=y: food
[QL= FORMAL=food (y)
CONST=consist_of (y, {skewer...})
TELIC=eat (e, z, y)
AGENT=skewer (e, w, y)]
(ibid.)

(12) san-kushi-no {sate/*kanzashi/*nendo}
3-CL-GEN satay/hair.stick/clay
'three sticks of satay/hair stick/clay'

For *-機 ki,* a classifier to count planes focusing on the Telic role, they also assume multiple specifications as in (13).

(13) *-機 ki* ARGSTR=D-ARG1=y: machine
[QL= FORMAL=machine (y)
TELIC=fly (e, y)
AGENT=make (e, z, y)]
(ibid.)

(14) san-ki-no {hikooki/*kami-hikooki/*tori}
3-CL-GEN plane/paper-plane/bird

'three planes/paper planes/birds'

There are two problems with their analysis, however. One is that the specifications are sometimes redundant (e.g. *artifacts* must have particular Agentive and/or Telic roles), though it might be true that they have multiple specifications. Another is that they ignore the importance of the Formal role. It should be noted that all Japanese classifiers have particular type requirements on the Formal role of their objects (the animacy is strictly restricted in Japanese classifiers[6]). In addition to it, note that the Formal role is considered a head type, and the additional qualia values can be seen as structural complementation to it in Pustejovsky (2011:1409).

Following Pustejovsky (2011), we suggest the following simplified representations in (15-16) for the lexical requirements of classifiers in order to solve the problems above. These representations are consistent with the characteristics of Japanese classifiers: though some classifiers have multiple requirements, they usually focus on "one" role in addition to the Formal role (cf. (7)).

(15) a. -人 *nin* is of type *human*→t cf.(9)
b. -匹 *hiki* is of type *animal*→t
c. -羽 *wa* is of type *bird*→t
d. -回 *kai* is of type *event*→t (10)

(16) a. -串 *kushi* is of type $food \otimes_C skewer$→t (11)
b. -機 *ki* is of type $machine \otimes_T fly$→t (13)
c. -基 *ki* is of type $artifact \otimes_A place$→t

3 Compositional Mechanisms

3.1 Problems of the Previous Studies

Huang and Ahrens (2003) analyze the Mandarin classifier system and suggest that classifiers coerce nominal semantic types:

> "...classifiers can coerce nouns to have a particular individual reading depending on the information entailed in the classifier itself. The classifier can vary in the Constitutive, Formal, Telic or Agentive roles that it carries (p.361)."

The situation in Japanese, however, is considered to be more complex because there are some cases where type coercion does not seem to take place, as pointed out in Section 1. Therefore, we adapt the four mechanisms suggested by Pustejovsky (2011) and show that all of the mechanisms occur when classifiers count nouns in Japanese. Mano and Yonezawa (to appear) also take the same view, but their discussion is limited.

Pustejovsky (2011:1411) suggests the following mechanisms in (17)[7] for the selection of an argument, which allow for modulation of types during semantic composition.

(17) a. SELECTION (Type Matching): The target type for a predicate, F, is directly satisfied by the source type of its argument, A: $F(A_\alpha)_\alpha$

b. ACCOMMODATION SUBTYPING: The target type a function requires is inherited through the type of argument, A: $F(A_\beta)_\alpha$, $\beta \sqsubseteq \alpha$

c. COERCION BY INTRODUCTION: the type a function requires is imposed on the argument type. This is accomplished by wrapping the argument with the type required by the function:
$F(A_\alpha)_{\odot\sigma}$, $\alpha \sqsubseteq \beta$ (domain-preserving)
$F(A_\alpha)_\beta$, $\alpha \rightarrow \beta$ (domain-shifting)

d. COERCION BY EXPLOITATION: the type a function requires is imposed on the argument type. This is accomplished by taking a part of the argument's type to satisfy the function: $F(A_{\alpha\odot\tau})_\beta$, $\tau \sqsubseteq \beta$

3.2 Classifiers and the Compositional Mechanisms

Here we will show that all four mechanisms in (17) are observed when classifiers modify and count nouns in Japanese. What is the most crucial is whether the head type (i.e. the Formal role) of the quantified noun is changed or not.

First, Selection (Type Matching: TM) will take place when the type required by a classifier is directly satisfied by the quantified noun. It is predicted that the quantified source noun stays the same type in this case because the operation does not change the type. In (18a), the noun, *hito* 'human being,' satisfies the type required by the classifier, *-nin*, because both the source and target

[6] See Matsumoto (1991, 1993), Downing (1996), Iida (1999, 2004), and Nishimitsu and Mizuguchi (2004), for example.

[7] $\odot$ represents the disjunction of the two type constructors, $\otimes$ and $\cdot$.

types are *human* (cf. (15a))[8]. The same is true for (18b), in which both the source and target types are *event* (cf. (15d)).

(18) a. san-nin-no hito-ga iru.
3-CL-GEN human-NOM be.PRES
'There are three men.'
b. san-kai-no ensoo-ga owat-ta.
3-CL-GEN performance-NOM end-PST
'(lit.) Three performances were over.'

Second, we will show an example of Accommodation Subtyping (AS). As shown in (19), *tsubame* 'swallow' is counted by both *-wa* and *-hiki*.

(19) ni-{wa/hiki}-no tsubame-ga tondeiru.
2-CL/CL-GEN swallow-NOM fly.PROG
'Two swallows are flying.'

It is assumed that the TM applies when it is quantified by *-wa* (15c), because the Formal role of *tsubame* is typed as *bird*. The AS takes place, however, when it is counted by *-hiki* (15b), because the type *bird* is a subtype of the type *animal* (*bird* ⊑ *animal*). Actually, all the nouns counted by *-wa* can also be counted by *-hiki*, but not vice versa.

type requirement of the classifier	mechanism
-wa: *bird*→t	TM
-hiki: *animal*→t	AS

Table 1. Compositional mechanisms of *tsubame*

Third, we will see cases where coercion takes place. *Dango* 'rice dumpling,' for example, is an artificial type, and its type structure is considered to be "food$\otimes_T$ *eat*." It is not necessarily skewered, but it is interpreted to be skewered when counted by *-kushi* as in (20). As *-kushi* is of type "*food*$\otimes_C$ *skewer*→t" (16a), Coercion by Qualia Introduction (CI-Q) applies to *dango*, adding the Constitutive value *skewer*[9].

(20) san-kushi-no dango
three-CL-GEN rice.dumpling
'three sticks of rice dumpling'

Dotted objects can be good illustrations of occurrence of more than one generative mechanism. For example, *supiichi* 'speech', whose lexical structure is shown in (21), seems to be a dotted type (event·information), even though it is quantified by the classifiers, *-kai* and *-hon*. This is because its eventive meaning can be modified by *nagai* 'long,' and its content meaning (info) can be modified by *omoshiroi* 'interesting' regardless of the existence of the classifiers, as shown in (22).

(21) *supiichi* 'speech'
[event·information_lcp
QL= FORMAL=information (x)
AGENT=speak (e, z, x)
TELIC=communicate_to (e, z, x, w)]
(Mano and Yonezawa, to appear)

(22) a. nagakute omoshiroi supiichi
long interesting speech
'long and interesting speech'
b. kare-no (ni-{kai/hon}-no) supiichi-wa
3SG-GEN 2-{CL/CL}-GEN speech-TOP
dochira-mo nagakat-ta-ga omoshirokat-ta.
both-also long-PST-but interesting-PST
'Both of his speeches were long but interesting.'

Now we examine the compositional mechanisms occurring in (22b). As shown above, *supiichi* is a complex type (e·i), and the classifier, *-kai*, is a classifier for *event* as in (15d), so Coercion by Dot Exploitation (CE-·) applies. The classifier, *-hon*[10], in (22b) seems to focus on the informational aspect of *supiichi* as a way of communication. This kind of *-hon* is considered to be of type "*information*$\otimes_T$ *communicate*→t," which means that after the CE-·, CE-Q occurs in *ni-hon-no supiichi*, exploiting the Telic value *communicate*.

[8] *Kashu* 'singer' (*human*$\otimes_T$ *sing*) is also counted by *-nin*. We assume that CE occurs, making *kashu* be of type *human*. As pointed out by one reviewer, however, we should compare this with the case of *hito* and make clear whether there is any (syntactic and semantic) difference between them or not.

[9] We assume that TM applies when *-kushi* counts *sate* 'satay: grilled meat stick' as in (12), because the Constitutive value *skewer* is included in the lexical structure of *sate* as in (i).

(i) *sate* QL=FORMAL=food (y)
CONST=consist_of (y, {skewer, meat…})
TELIC=eat (e, x, y)

[10] *-Hon* is a shape classifier for inanimate one-dimensional physical objects, but it is well known to have several extended usages, counting other than physical objects: for example, hits (baseball), movies, letters, phone calls, etc. See Lakoff (1987), Matsumoto (1993), and Iida (1999).

Lastly, we will show a case in which Coercion by Introduction (CI) takes place. As shown in (23a), *supiichi* can also be counted by *-mai* which selects for a type *phys (2D)*.

(23) a. ni-mai-no supiichi-wo yabut-ta.
2-CL-GEN speech-ACC tear-PST
'(I) tore two sheets of speech.'
b. ni-{kai/hon}-*(bun)-no supiichi-wo yabutta.
2-CL-quantity-GEN
'(I) tore two speeches.'

The CI is considered to apply to *supiichi* (e·i) here, resulting in the noun being a type *phys*. This is confirmed in (23a), because it can be the argument of the predicate, *yaburu* 'tear,' which selects for *phys*. This is impossible when it is counted by *-kai* and *-hon*, as shown in (23b).

Table 2 summarizes the compositional mechanisms observed with regard to *supiichi*.

type requirement of the classifier	mechanism
-kai: *event*→t	CE-·
-hon: $information \otimes_T communicate$→t	CE-Q
-mai: *phys(2D)*→t	CI

Table 2. Compositional mechanisms of *supiichi*

It follows from what has been shown in this section that all four mechanisms are observed when classifiers select their arguments.

4 Conclusion

By using the Generative Lexicon Theory, this paper suggests the formalization of semantic requirements of classifiers in Japanese. It is also shown that all four compositional mechanisms in (17) are observed between classifiers and the quantified nouns. It is reasonable to say that the Generative Lexicon approach can propose a new analysis of classifiers.

It needs further investigation, however. As space is limited, we have concentrated on limited classifiers, but the lexical structures of other classifiers should be examined. In addition to this, I have not addressed the issues of the quantifier floating. Their syntactic structures should be more carefully examined.

Acknowledgments

I am deeply grateful to three anonymous reviewers of GLAL 2012 for their insightful comments and suggestions. All errors are, of course, my own.

References

Alexandra Y Aikhenvald. 2000. *Classifiers: A Typology of Noun Categorization Devices*. Oxford University Press, Oxford.

Walter Bisang. 1993. Classifiers, Quantifiers and Class Nouns in Hmong. *Studies in Language*, 17:1-51.

Francis Bond and Kyonghee Paik. 1997. Classifying Correspondence in Japanese and Korean. *PACLING-97*:58-67.

Pamela A Downing. 1996. *Numeral Classifier Systems: The Case of Japanese*. John Benjamins, Amsterdam.

Chu-Ren Huang and Kathleen Ahrens. 2003. Individuals, Kinds and Events: Classifier Coercion of Nouns. *Language Sciences*, 25:353-373.

Asako Iida. 1999. *Nihongo Shuyoo-josuushi-no Imi-to Yoohoo*. Ph.D. Dissertation, University of Tokyo.

Asako Iida. 2004. *Kazoekata-no Jiten*. Shoogakkan, Tokyo.

Taro Kageyama, Miho Mano, Yu Yonezawa, and Takayuki Tohno. 2011. Meishi-no Seishitsu-to Kazu-no Kazoekata. Taro Kageyama ed. *Nichi-ei-taishoo Meishi-no Imi-to Koobun*, 10-35, Taishukan, Tokyo.

George Lakoff. 1987. *Woman, Fire, and Dangerous Things*. The University of Chicago Press, Chicago.

Miho Mano and Yu Yonezawa. to appear. Lexical Semantics of Japanese Counters in the Generative Lexicon Theory. *Lexicon Forum*, 6. (In Japanese)

Yo Matsumoto. 1991. The Semantic Structures and System of Japanese Classifiers. *Gengo Kenkyu*, 99:82-106. (In Japanese)

Yo Matsumoto. 1993. Japanese Numeral Classifiers: A Study of Semantic Categories and Lexical Organization. *Linguistics*, 31:667-713.

Yoshihiro Nishimitsu and Shinobu Mizuguchi eds. 2004. *Ruibetsushi-no Taishoo*. Kuroshio, Tokyo.

James Pustejovsky. 1995. *The Generative Lexicon*. MIT Press, Cambridge, MA.

James Pustejovsky. 2006. Type Theory and Lexical Decomposition. *Journal of Cognitive Science*, 6:39-76.

James Pustejovsky. 2011. Coercion in a General Theory of Argument Selection. *Linguistics*, 49:1401-1431.

Psych-Predicates: How They Are Different

Chungmin Lee
Seoul Nat'l U
1 Gwanak-ro,
Seoul 151-742,
Korea
clee@snu.ac.kr

Abstract

This paper is concerned with characterizing psych-predicates in Korean and possibly in Japanese in the GL spirit. We focus on the the status of the Experiencer (or 'judge') in relation to other arguments and examine the first-person subjectivity data (constraint). The relevant cause and effect relation and consequent coerced event function is postulated for coherent interpretation.

Keywords: psych-predicates, experiencer, first-person (subjectivity) data, causation.

1 Introduction

We will characterize psych-predicates = experiencer-predicates and predicates of personal taste in Korean, focusing on the status of the Experiencer in relation to arguments and examining the first-person subjectivity data (constraint). The relevant cause and effect relation and consequent coerced event function is postulated for coherent interpretation. **2** will show data and raise issues; **3** will discuss issues in the GL spirit; and **4** will conclude the discussion.

2 Data and Issues

Consider (1) (Lee 2010), where description of psych state in the present tense by **the first-person** but not by the third or second person is acceptable. Here the 'judge' is the speaker. This first-person subjectivity constraint is observed in Korean and Japanese.

(1) na/?*ku/?*ne -nun ecirep-ta
I/he/you -TOP dizzy-DEC
'I am/?*he is/?*you are dizzy.'

(2) watashi-wa/?*kare-wa/?*anata-wa sabishi 'lonely' desu
'I am/?*he is/?*you are lonely.'

However, even in the present, if the psych-adjective takes a verbalizer *–e hay* 'show signs of being *psych*-Adj,' a third-person with it becomes quite acceptable, as in (2).

(3) ku-ka ecirep *–e hay*
he -NOM dizzy-E do
'He shows signs of being dizzy.'

Because the speaker sees his act of, say, turning in circles as evidence to utter (2), Tenny (2006) calls the Japanese counterpart *–garu* an evidential, which also lifts the person restriction as in Korean. In English, 'He is dizzy' may be uttered on the basis of the speaker's seeing him turn in circles or hearing from him or someone else[1] and is not distinct from 'I am dizzy.' The past form of (1) is fine with the 3rd-person subject (*Ku-nun ecirew-ess-ta* 'He was dizzy'); it may be assumed that there could have been conveyance of information from him to the speaker). With a modal (conjecture) or future marker attached to the psych-adjective, the 1st-person constraint is waived. Korean has a clearer reportative evidential, as in (4), which also lifts the first-person restriction.

(4) ku-ka ecirep *-tay* [*-tay*: reportative]
he-NOM dizzy-REPORT -DEC
'He says he is dizzy' or
'He is said to be dizzy.'

On the other hand, in an interrogative sentence in the present tense, the second person subject, not the first person subject, is acceptable, asking the hearer = the speaker-to-be about her/his psychological state. The perspective is shifted from the current speaker to the next speaker, who is the hearer, who will answer the question. At the point of answering the question, the person who answers or speaks is the one who is entitled to know her/his own internal psychological state.

(5) ne ecirewu-nya?
you dizzy -Q
'Are you dizzy?'

The cause of spins may be from drinking on an empty stomach. But utterances can appear without expressing causes and such psych-Adjectives as 'dizzy,' 'lonely' may form a sentence with just an Experiencer. In a cause adjunct clause, the Agent is typically co-referential with the 1st-person Experiencer in the main clause psych-predicate. The drinker and the one who feels dizzy must be the same person, in accordance with argument coherence in causation structure in GL (Pustejovsky 1995).

Then, let us observe the following type, which some authors call 'predicates of personal taste' (Lasersohn, 2005; Stephenson, 2007).

(6) The roller coaster is fun (for me).
(7) a. This walnut is tasty (for me/for him).
b. Walnuts are tasty.

They require the Stimulus subject/Topic unlike (1). Instead, the 1st-person Experiencer or evaluator is an optional adjunct.

Lasersohn (2005) makes use of Kaplan's (1978) distinction between *character* and *content*, and between *context* of utterance and *index* of evaluation. Lasersohn adds a *judge* to the *index* of evaluation, which becomes a triple <w,t,j> of world, time, and judge.

(8) $[[\text{fun}]]^{c;\, w,t,j} = [\lambda x_e.\ x \text{ is fun for } j \text{ in } w \text{ at } t]$

(9) $[[\text{tasty}]]^{c;\, w,t,j} = [[\text{taste good}]]^{c;\, w,t,j} = [\lambda x_e\ .\ x$ tastes good to j in w at t$]$

(10) $[[\text{This cake is tasty}]]^{c;\, w,t,j} = 1$ iff this cake is tasty to j in w at t.

However, j can shift from *me* the speaker to *him* a non-speaker, depending on a judge salient in the context in English. In Korean, the 1st-person constraint must be kept (such that j=I, if t=n ('now'/speech time) and the formalism must be adjusted conditionally accordingly. The 1st-person orientation is generally accepted. The shifting from it to attitude holder (in attitude report sentences such as, *Mary thinks this cake is tasty*)

One clear distinction between the type of (1) and that of predicates of personal taste is that the latter can have a generic statement such as (7b) but not the type of (1). See the contrast: (10a) vs. (10b).

(10) a. ???hankwukin-un ecirep-ta
Koreans –TOP dizzy
'Koreans are dizzy.'
b. hankwukin-un hwal-ul cal sso-n-ta
'Koreans are excellent archers.'

Furthermore, for predicates of personal taste, the following faultless/subjective disagreement is agreed on:

(10) a. John: This cake is tasty.
b. Mary: No, it's not tasty.

Here both speakers have said something true, so

[1] We can posit some abstract hidden evidentiality of learning about or simulating the psych state of the third-person statement.

long as each was sincere. Thus the disagreement does not seem to be one that can be resolved.

But for Experiencer-present psych-predicates, as in (1), the same disagreement is not warranted, as in (11). Other than the speaker is not entitled to disagree on the 1st-person speaker's expressed psychological state (therefore, 11b). (11c) is not relevant in the context.

(11) a. John: I am dizzy. (angry, lonely, sad)
b. Mary: ??No, you are not dizzy.
c. Mary: ??No, I am not dizzy.

There are debates between **relativists** and **contextualists**. In work on context-dependence, some authors have argued that certain types of sentences such as those of personal taste and epistemic modality give rise to a notion of relative truth: truth relative not only to a world and time of evaluation, but also to something like a "context of evaluation" (Egan et al. 2004), "context of assessment" (MacFarlane, 2005) or a "judge" (Lasersohn 2005).

An alternative contextualist approach argues that the context-dependence enters in passing from "character" in the sense of Kaplan (1989) to the actual proposition expressed ("content"): what proposition is expressed may vary from context to context, but once the proposition is fixed, its truth-conditions are not "relative", and no extra parameters need to be added to indices of evaluation (Stanley 2007). Positing implicit content, this commonly employed linguistic strategy leads to contextualism, e.g. for Kratzer's appeal to implicit "in view of" clauses providing the implicit domains of various modals. The posited implicit content becomes part of the proposition expressed (or of the semantic content). This is relevant for propositional attitude ascriptions and for sentential anaphora, etc. (Partee 2009).

Regarding (11a), Stojanovic (2011) inherits some aspect of the Kaplanian view (1989) with the following sequence (modified):

(12) a. Mary (pointing at John): He is dizzy.
b. Jane: That's what he said, too.

Based on the '*same-saying*' between (11a) and (12a) and the truth of the related report in (12b), she proposes that the content of (11a) is a function that takes an individual (with a world, a time and other things) and returns value True iff the individual is dizzy (in that world and at that time). John is asserting this content of himself. The content associated with (12a) is the very same function, and Mary is asserting this content about John. The contents are the same and the function corresponds to the property of being dizzy. By having an operator that binds the variable for the 1-st-person oriented interpretation of the sentence, the property claim makes it 'judge-free' (Pearson, forthcoming). However, there is a language-specific constraint that blocks the shift from (11a) ('I' expression) to (12a) ('he' expression) in the present tense, namely, in Korean and Japanese. "He was dizzy" in the past is acceptable. This constraint must be represented.

Psych predicates involve direct sensory/perceptual experience by the 1st-person at the core and the direct sensory/perceptual evidential marker *–te* in Korean, which Japanese lacks, also involves the 1st-person at the core and they occur, as in (13). The evidential marker *–te* implicates that the current speaker has direct sensory/perceptual evidence, acquired before speech time by default, regarding its prejacent argument proposition Φ of type < s, t >. Φ itself is a psych predicate. In (13), therefore, the Experiencer, the 1st-person, which can appear as Topic at S-initial position, coincides with the evidence holder, the 1st-person again, not realizable on the surface.

(13) a. Ku namwu-ka *po-i-**te***-ra [visual]
the tree-NOM see-PASS-
'The tree was visible to me.'
b. Kangtang-i *shikkurep-**te***-ra [hearing]
auditorium-NOM noisy- TE-DEC
'[I heard] the auditorium was noisy.'
c. Pipimpap-i *mas-iss-**te***-ra [taste]
pipimpap-NOM tasty -TE-DEC
'[I tasted] the pipimpap was tasty.'
d. Kkoch-i *hyangkirop* - ***te***-ra [smell]
flower-NOM fragrant TE-DEC
'[I smelled] the flower was fragrant.'
e. Son-i *pwuterep-**te***-ra [touch]
hand-NOM soft -TE-DEC

'[I touched] the hand was soft.'

f. Ttang-i pal-ey *tah*-**te**-ra [touch]
earth –NOM foot-at reach-TE-DEC
'[I felt] my foot touched the earth.' (in water)

g. Kapang-i *mwukep*- **te**-ra [weight]
bag -NOM heavy- TE-DEC
'[I weighed] the bag was heavy.'

h. (Na-nun) sulphu-*te*-ra [feeling]
I-TOP sad -TE-DEC
'[I felt] I was sad.'

The science of consciousness must be based on the 1st person data vs. the 3rd person data involved in this asymmetry (Chalmers 2010, 1995), with the *third-person data* about behavior and brain processes, and *first-person data* about "subjective experience." Chalmers lists first-person data as follows:

(14) a. visual experience (e.g. that of color and depth)
b. other perceptual experiences (e.g. auditory and tactile experience)
c. bodily experiences (e.g. pain and hunger)
d. mental imagery (e.g. recalled visual images)
e. emotional experience (e.g. happiness and anger)
f. occurrent thought (e.g. the experience of reflecting and deciding)

However, we have one finer distinction between outer-directed and inner-directed in evidentials and psych-predicates in Korean, which we need, even though they may be considered in the same wider subjective experience category. My volitional act, unlike psych predicates, cannot occur with the direct evidential maker *–te*. A psych sentence cannot take a non-1st-person subject if it co-occurs with the evidential maker *–te*. With *–te*, introspection is possible, as in (13), but outer-directed direct observation is odd, as in (15). A volitional act (15) with *–te* shows exact asymmetry in possible subject persons.

(15) ???Nay-ka pap-ul mek-***te***-ra
I-NOM rice-ACC eat-TE-DEC
'[I observed] I was eating rice.'

On the other hand, there occurs a very interesting contrast between (16a) and (16b). By the direct evidential marker *–te* (16a) asserts at-issue that 'he was dizzy' and implicates that I, the speaker, acquired the evidence by observing it directly at that time, which after all turn out to be odd. Rather, the past tense marking of the same psych proposition at-issue is felicitous in (16b). Because of the past tense, there could have been a time interval in which the speaker could learn about 'his being dizzy' or hear/see his saying/showing signs of or simulate 'I am dizzy.'

(16) a. ?*Ku-nun *ecirep*-***te***-ra
he-TOP dizzy-TE-DEC
'[I directly perceived] he was dizzy.'
b. Ku-nun *ecirep*-**ess**-ta
he-TOP dizzy-PAST-DEC
'He was dizzy.'

3. GL Concerns: Causation

Now in the GL concerns, the overall causation structure matters (based on Aristotelian qualia) and a coherent causal relation between the causing event (with the AGENTIVE quale) and the resulting event is considered even for psych (experiencer) predicates.

Psych predicates with a Stimulus subject or predicates of personal taste, as in (13), typically involve a metonymic reconstruction of the subject to an event (function) via agentive quale in GL. (*Mary's watching*) *the movie* frightened her, (*My seeing*) Bill's face scared me, and (*My reading*) the book bored me, are examples of coerced activity involving perception/cognition in a transitive causative sentence in English. However, inanimate subjects in a transitive causative sentence are not fully acceptable in Korean. Instead, Experiencer Topic + Stimulus Nominative + Psych predicate is typical (with the Topic alternating with a Dative+Top). Observe (14). If the Experiencer Topic is extra-ordinarily focused, it also gets a Nominative, forming a so-called a double Nominative construction.

(13) The movie <u>frightened</u> Mary.
(14) na-nun horangi-ka <u>mwusep</u>-ta
I-TOP tiger -NOM fear
'I fear a tiger.'

In GL (Pustejovsky 1995), *angry* is as follows in its qualia specification:

$$\left[\text{QUALIA} = \begin{bmatrix}\text{FORMAL} = \textbf{angry}\ (\mathbf{e_1}, <1>) \\ \text{AGENTIVE} = \textbf{psych\_act}\ ((\mathbf{e_2}, <1>, <2>)\end{bmatrix}\right]$$

1. TABLE: Attribute-Value Matrix for *angry*

Unlike in direct causation, as in *kill*, the Experiencer's psych state event $\mathbf{e_1}$ is headed instead of its causative/imchoative process $\mathbf{e_2}$, where the default second argument is not prominent. Even in the specification of the transitive causative verb *anger*, only the Experiencer argument is prominently represented regardless of the surface realization of the causing sub-event.

In Korean and English, there can be different classes of psych predicates in combination with cause event: one class such as *mianha-ta* 'sorry' that are used with a causal event of the Experiencer's own act not favorable to the other party. The English *sorry* can also be used to show the Experiencer's sympathy with the other party for her/his unfavorable event. A psych predicate *komap-ta* 'thankful/grateful' is used for the other or third party's act as agent, but not for the Experiencer's own act, in the preceding causal event. These are used as semi-performatives when uttered to the addressee in the present tence. Many psych predicates such as *boring, scaring, frightening, surprising, pleasing, amusing, fascinating,* and *fun*, and their Korean equivalents are used with the Experiencer's own perceptual or cognitive causal event. (See Nam (2009) for two classes in Korean.)

Because of the event function coming from the agentive quale of the nominal in the subject position in English and the post-Topic position in Korean, it is well explained why psych predicates, predominantly or underlyingly adjectival, are basically not an individual-level predicate such as *intelligent* and *tall* but a stage-level predicate, as exemplified in GL. Some of them are somewhat lasting, not just instantaneous, in their aroused psychological state but they may be different from real individual-level predicates. Pearson's forthcoming, however, argues that predicates of personal taste are individual-level predicates, showing **There were cakes tasty*, **There were games fun* in parallel with *There were people tall*, and associating them with genericity (the genericity claim coincides with Lee's 2011 claim). Other approaches in semantics and philosophy of language rarely touch on this event function possibility and a semantically default (logically implicated but not realized) causative/inchoative process event for psych predicates.

4. Concluding Remarks

The 1st-person (present) constraint for psych predicates in Korean and Japanese is the core and starting point of subjectivity. The science of cognition and consciousness must seek clues of evidentiality of learning (and or simulation) in the possible expression of 'Mary is dizzy' vs. the impossible expression of ?*'Mary is dizzy' in Korean and Japanese. Otherwise, we cannot secure the objective state of 'Mary is dizzy' even if we have her brain opened up and take a look at the associated physical states.

The GL principle of argument coherence in the overall psych causation structure and qualia are suggestive but their descriptive contents must be further specified to be further actively applied.

References

Chalmer, David. 2010. How Can We Construct a Science of Consciousness? In Gazzaniga, M.S. (ed.) The Cognitive Neurosciences. MIT Press, Cambridge, (4th Edition).

Egan, Andy, John Hawthorne, and Brian Weatherson. 2004. Epistemic modals in context. In *Contextualism in Philosophy*, eds. G. Preyer and G. Peter. Oxford: Oxford University Press.brian.weatherson.org/em.pdf

Kuno, Susumu. 1973. *The Structure of the Japanese Language.* Cambridge, MA: The MIT Press.

Lee, Chungmin. 1986. Cases for Psychological Verbs in Korean. *Linguistic Journal of Korea* (Eoneo) 1.1.

Lee, Chungmin. 2010. Evidentials and Epistemic Modals in Korean: Evidence from their Intractions. *Proceed's of PACLIC* 24.

Lee, Chungmin. 2011. Dynamic Perspective Shifts in Evidentials: Evidence from Korean. LENLS 8 Takamatsu, Japan.

Lee, Chungmin. Forthcoming. Evidentials and Modals: Evidence Prototypicality, Interactions and Shiftability in Korean. In Lee, C. and J. Park (eds.) *Evidentials and Modals*. CRiSPI. Emerald.

Lim, Dongsik and Chungmin Lee. 2012. Perspective Shifts in Korean Evidentials and the Effect of Contexts. *Proceed's of SALT* 22: 26-42. http://elanguage.net/journals/index.php/salt.

Kaplan, David. 1978. On the Logic of Demonstratives, *Journal of Philosophical Logic*, VIII: 81-98.

Koev, Todor. 2011. Evidentiality and temporal distance learning. *Proceed's of SALT* 21: 115-134.

Matthewson, Lisa Forthcoming. Evidence Type, Evidence Location, Evidence Strength. In Lee, C. and J. Park (eds.) *Evidentials and Modals*, CRiSPI, Emerald.

McCready, Eric. 2010. Evidential Universals. T. In P. Peterson and U. Sauerland (eds.) *UBC WPL: Evidence from Evidentials*. 105-127.

MacFarlane, John. 2005. Making sense of relative truth. *Proceedings of the Aristotelian Society* 105 321–339. http://johnmacfarlane.net/makingsense.pdf.

Moltmann, Friederike. In-press. Generalizing Detached Self-Reference and the Semantics of the Generic 'one.' *Mind and Langauge*. *http://semantics.univ-paris1.fr/pdf/one-philos.pdf*

Nam, Seungho. 2009. Event structures of Experiencer Predicates in Korean: their causal, temporal, and focal sub-structure. At the Int'l Conference on Generative Lexicon Theory, Pisa.

Partee. Brabara. 2009. Predicates of Personal Taste, Epistemic Modals, First-Person Oriented Content, and Debates about the Implicit Judge(s). Lecture Notes. UMass.

Pearson, Hazel. Forthcoming. A Judge-Free Semantics for Predicates of Personal Taste. *Journal of Semantics*.

Pustejovsky, James. 1995. *The Generative Lexicon*. Cambridge: The MIT Press.

Stanley, Jason. 2007. *Language in Context: Selected Essays*. Oxford University Press.

Tenny, C. 2006. Evidentiality, Experiencers, and the Syntax of Sentience in Japanese. *Journal of East Asian Linguistics*. 15:245–288.

The Role of Qualia Structure in Mandarin Children Acquiring Noun-modifying Constructions

Liu Zhaojing **Chan Wing-shan, Angel**

Department of Chinese & Bilingual Studies
The Hong Kong Polytechnic University
liuzhaojing@hotmail.com ctaachan@polyu.edu.hk

Abstract

This paper investigates the types and the developmental trajectory of noun modifying constructions (NMCs), in the form of [Modifier + *de* + (Noun)], attested in Mandarin-speaking children's speech from a semantic perspective based on the generative lexicon framework (Pustejovsky, 1995). Based on 1034 NMCs (including those traditionally defined as relative clauses (RCs)) produced by 135 children aged 3 to 6 from a cross-sectional naturalistic speech corpus "Zhou2" in CHILDES, we analyzed the relation between the modifier and the head noun according to the 4 major roles of qualia structure: formal, constitutive, telic and agentive.

Results suggest that (i) NMCs expressing the formal facet of the head noun's meaning are most frequently produced and acquired earliest, followed by those expressing the constitutive quale, and then those expressing the telic or the agentive quale; (ii) RC-type NMCs emerge either alongside the other non-RC type NMCs *at the same time*, or emerge *later* than the other non-RC type NMCs for the constitutive quale; and (iii) the majority of NMCs expressing the agentive and telic quales are those that fall within the traditional domain of RCs (called RC-type NMCs here), while the majority of NMCs expressing the formal and the constitutive quales are non-RC type NMCs.

These findings are consistent with: (i) the semantic nature and complexity of the four qualia relations: formal and constitutive aspects of an object (called natural type concepts in Pustejovsky 2001, 2006) are more basic attributes, while telic and agentive (called artificial type concepts in Pustejovsky 2001, 2006) are derived and often eventive (hence conceptually more complex); and (ii) the properties of their adult input: NMCs expressing the formal quale are also most frequently encountered in the adult input; followed by the constitutive quale, and then the agentive and telic quales.

The findings are also consistent with the idea that in Asian languages such as Japanese, Korean and Chinese, RCs develop from attributive constructions specifying a semantic feature of the head noun in acquisition (Diessel 2007, c.f. also Comrie 1996, 1998, 2002).

This study is probably the first of using the generative lexicon framework in the field of child language acquisition.

1 Introduction

1.1 Noun Modifying Constructions (NMCs) in Asian Languages from Semantic and Pragmatic Perspectives (Comrie 1996, 1998, 2002; Matsumoto 1997, 2007)

In typology, relative clauses (RCs) in certain Asian languages such as Japanese, Korean and Chinese have recently taken on new theoretical significance. In these Asian languages, RCs can be considered a subset of NMCs involving no syntactic operation such as gap-filling or movement (Comrie 1996, 1998, 2002). Rather, it could involve simply attaching a modifying clause to the head noun based on semantic-pragmatic relations.

Chinese has a productive NMC in which a noun is modified by a clause without there being a grammatical relation between the clause and the head noun. For example, in the Mandarin examples (1) and (2) the head nouns 'shoes' and 'sound' are not strictly arguments of the verbs 'go (to school)' and 'play', but are associated with the modifying clauses semantically and pragmatically.

(1) 上学 的 鞋子
shangxue de xiezi
go to school DE shoes
'The shoes for going to school'

(2) 我 弹 钢琴 的 声音
wo tan gangqin de shengyin
I play piano DE sound
'The sound from me playing the piano'

It proves difficult, if not impossible, to separate NMCs such as (1) and (2) from those 'conventional' RCs such as (3) and (4) below (Comrie 1996, 1998, 2002).

(3) 我 买 的 鞋子
wo mai de xiezi
I buy DE shoes
'The shoes that I bought'

(4) 我 听到 的 声音
wo tingdao de shengyin
I hear DE noise
'The sound that I heard'

Under this alternative view, Chinese and some other Asian languages such as Japanese and Korean do not have a syntactic RC distinct from other NMCs such as (1) and (2). Rather, these languages have a general NMC for attaching modifying clauses to head nouns based on semantic-pragmatic relations between the two constituents, and this construction has a range of interpretations which can be characterized as relative clause interpretations, or complement clause interpretations, or some kind of modifying clause interpretations (see also Huang 2008). As such, Chinese RCs can be analyzed as a subset of NMCs in which a modifying clause is attached to the head noun based on semantic-pragmatic relations.

If this is so, Chinese NMCs call for an approach that recognizes the role of semantics and pragmatics in accounting for the processing and acquisition of these constructions. For instance, Matsumoto (1997, 2007) developed a framework to account for NMCs in Japanese, building on ideas in existing works on frame semantics (e.g., Fillmore 1977, 1982; Fillmore & Atkins 1992). Under this frame semantic analysis of NMCs in Japanese, the construal of NMCs is described in terms of 'the relation between the concept denoted by one of the constituents of the construction (i.e. the modifying clause or the head noun) and the frame evoked by the other' (Matsumoto 1997: 166). In addition, how a specific interpretation of the construction is determined depends on the construer's world-views regarding contextual information and cultural knowledge (Matsumoto 1997: 166-167; 2007: 132). Future research could apply similar framework to consider the acquisition and processing of Chinese RCs and other NMCs from a semantic-pragmatic approach (c.f. Matsumoto 1997, 2007 on Japanese).

1.2 Semantic Relations between the Modifier and the Head Noun: Qualia Structure (Pustejovsky, 1995)

As an initial attempt to study the acquisition of NMCs in child Mandarin from a semantic perspective, we first focus on characterizing the semantic relations between the modifier and the head noun of NMCs in young children's speech across age.

Generative Lexicon (GL) Theory (Pustejovsky, 1995) has become one of the most influential theories in semantics and qualia structure is a central framework in the GL theory. The GL Theory provides us with an explanatory model for capturing the qualia modification relations in the semantic composition within a compound (Lenci et al., 2000). Similarly, Chinese NMCs are composed of a modifier and a head noun. It can be deduced that qualia modification relations also exist between the modifiers and the heads of Chinese NMCs. We therefore attempt to use qualia structure relations as a framework to analyze the semantic relations between the modifier and the head noun NMCs in this paper.

Qualia structure specifies four essential aspects of a lexical item's meaning (Pustejovsky (1995), see also Lenci et al., (2000) for further elaborations):

1) The Formal role can distinguish the object within a larger domain. Orientation, magnitude, shape, dimensionality, color, and position are its role values. For example: beautiful dancer, white paper.

2) The Constitutive role is the relation between an object and its constituents or parts. The role values include material, weight, parts and component elements. For example: glass door, heavy stone.

3) The Agentive role describes the factors involved in the origin of an object, such as creator, artifact, natural kind, and causal chain. For example: bullet hole, lemon juice.

4) The Telic role is about the purpose and function of an object. For example: hunting rifle, race car.

2 Data Analyses

2.1 The Zhou2 Corpus in the Child Language Data Exchange System (CHILDES)

The naturalistic data used in this study came from one released naturalistic child Mandarin corpus called "Zhou2" deposited at the CHILDES archive (MacWhinney, 2000) (downloadable at: http://childes.psy.cmu.edu/data/EastAsian/Chinese/). The corpus "Zhou2" was created by Zhou Jing (Eastern China Normal University) in 2007. This cross-sectional corpus consists of transcripts of naturalistic adult-to-child interactions from 140 mother-child pairs in Nanjing, China. The children, with equal numbers of girls and boys, belong to 7 age groups (see Table 2) and there are about 20 children in each age group.

2.2 NMCs Expressing Different Qualia Relations in Children's Speech

There are 1034 utterances containing NMCs, in the form of [Modifier + *de* + (Noun)] where the Head Noun can be (un)expressed, attested in the children's spontaneous speech. These NMCs include those that fall *within* the traditional domain of RCs (called RC-type NMCs here), and those that do *not* fall within the traditional domain of RCs (called non-RC NMCs here; these constructions are "gapless" because there is no grammatical relation between the head noun and the modifier, and hence there cannot be a gap co-referential with the head). In addition, the modifiers in these NMCs include both clausal and non-clausal.

We analyzed the relation between the modifier and the head noun according to the four major roles of qualia structure: formal, constitutive, telic and agentive.

Table 1 below gives examples of each type attested in the corpus.

Table 1: Examples of Each Type of NMC Attested in the Corpus

NMC type	Qualia	Examples
Non-RC	Formal	大大 的 眼睛 (Age[1]: 3;00) dada de yanjing big DE eye 'Big eyes'
		尖尖 的 嘴 (Age: 5;06) jianjian de zui pointed DE mouth 'A pointed mouth'
	Constitutive	兔子 的 脚 (Age : 3;00) tuzi de jiao Rabbit DE foot 'The rabbit's foot'
		玻璃 的 （杯子）(Age: 6;00) boli de (beizi) glass DE (cup) 'A glass cup (a cup made of glass)'
	Agentive	宝宝 的 声音 (Age: 3;06) baobao de shengyin baby DE noise 'Baby's noise (The noise made by the baby)'
		吃 跳跳糖 的 声音 (Age: 5;06) chi tiaotiaotang de shengyin eat Leaping Sweets DE noise 'The noise made from eating the Leaping Sweets'
	Telic	好 玩 的 东西 (Age: 3;06) Haowan de dongxi good-play DE thing 'The thing that is fun for playing'
		你 的 电话 (Age: 6;00) ni de dianhua you DE phone call 'Your phone call (a phone call to find you)'
RC	Formal	跟 这个 一样 的 （颜色） (Age: 3;00) gen zhege yiyang de (yanse) as this CL same DE (color) 'The color that is same as this'
		像 玩具 的 （东西） (Age: 6;00) xiang wanju de (dongxi) like toy DE (thing) 'The thing that looks like a toy'
	Constitutive	剩 下来 的 香蕉 (Age: 4;00) shengxialai de xiangjiao left-over DE banana 'The banana that is left over'
		剩下 的 一只 皮皮鼠 (Age: 6;00) shengxia de yizhi pipishu left-over DE one CL Hooded Rat 'One Hooded Rat that is left over'
	Agentive	我 搭 的 这个 球 (Age: 3;06) wo da de zhege qiu I build DE this CL ball 'This ball that I built'

[1] Age: 3;00 means 3 years and 0 month old; Age: 5;06 means 5 years and 6 months old

		我做　的楼梯　　(Age: 6;00) wo zuo de louti I make DE stairs 'The stairs that I made'
	Telic	我看过　的书　　(Age: 4;00) wo kan guo de shu I read ASP DE book 'The book that I have read'
		我最 喜欢　的玩具　　(Age: 6;00) wo zui xihuan de wanju I most like DE toy 'The toy that I like playing most'

Table 2 presents an overview of the distribution of NMCs (both non-RC type NMCs and RC-type NMCs) expressing the four major qualia roles across the seven age groups of children. In addition, we also singled out the RC-type NMCs and examined the distribution of their types expressing the four major qualia roles in children's naturalistic speech across age. See Table 3.

Table 2. The Distribution of NMCs Expressing the Four Major Qualia Roles in Children's Naturalistic Speech Across Age

Age	3;00 (20)[2]		3;06 (21)		4;00 (16)		4;06 (19)		5;00 (22)		5;06 (16)		6;00 (21)	
Qualia	Token	%	Token	%	Token	%	Token	%	Token	%	Token	%	Token	%
Formal	88	68.8	109	75.2	88	56.8	74	61.7	93	52.2	70	50.0	93	55.4
Constitutive	26	20.3	22	15.2	43	27.7	30	25.0	51	28.7	39	27.9	45	26.8
Agentive	11	8.6	4	2.8	5	3.2	5	4.2	15	8.4	24	17.1	17	10.1
Telic	3	2.3	10	6.9	19	12.3	11	9.2	19	10.7	7	5.0	13	7.7

Table 3. The Distribution of RC-type NMCs Expressing the Four Major Qualia Roles in Children's Naturalistic Speech Across Age

Age	3;00 (20)		3;06 (21)		4;00 (16)		4;06 (19)		5;00 (22)		5;06 (16)		6;00 (21)	
Qualia	Token	%	Token	%	Token	%	Token	%	Token	%	Token	%	Token	%
Formal	4	23.5	5	31.3	6	20.0	6	30.0	7	17.1	7	20.6	3	11.1
Constitutive	0	0.0	0	0.0	1	3.3	0	0.0	0	0.0	0	0.0	3	11.1
Agentive	10	58.8	3	18.7	4	16.7	3	15.0	15	36.6	21	61.8	10	37.0
Telic	3	17.7	8	50.0	18	60.0	11	55.0	19	46.3	6	17.6	11	40.8

[2] The number in parentheses indicates the number of children who have produced at least 1 NMC in that age group.

Results in Table 2 show that:

- across all the 7 age groups, NMCs expressing the formal quale are most frequently attested, accounting for more than two-third of the NMCs produced at ages 3;00 and 3;06 and at least half of the NMCs produced for the remaining 5 age groups
- NMCs expressing the constitutive quale rank consistently second for all age groups, accounting for about a quarter of the NMCs produced from age 4 to 6
- NMCs expressing the telic or agentive quale are relatively less frequently attested

Upon further examination of the data for each individual child, the developmental pattern revealed appears to be consistent with the above analyses that are based on token frequency of use of NMCs:

- By age 3;00 and consistently thereafter, more than 80% of the children in their respective age group have at least 1 NMC expressing the formal quale attested in their speech sample
- By age 3;06 and consistently thereafter, more than 50% of the children in their respective age group have at least 1 NMC expressing the constitutive quale attested in their speech sample
- By age 5;00 and consistently thereafter, more than 40% of the children in their respective age group have at least 1 NMC expressing the agentive quale attested in their speech sample
- By age 3;06 and consistently thereafter, around 40% of the children in their respective age group have at least 1 NMC expressing the telic quale attested in their speech sample

Taken together all the above facts, the findings suggest that NMCs expressing the formal quale are acquired earliest; followed by constitutive; and then telic or agentive.

Results in Table 3 show that in general, RC-type NMCs constitute only 17.8 % (184 out of 1034 NMCs) of all the NMCs attested in children's speech. RC-type NMCs emerge either *alongside* the other non-RC type NMCs at the same time, or emerge *later* than the other non-RC type NMCs for the constitutive quale.

In addition, taking the results in Tables 2 and 3 together, the majority of NMCs expressing the agentive and telic quales are RC-type NMCs; while the majority of NMCs expressing the formal and the constitutive quales are non-RC type NMCs.

3 Discussion

How do we account for the developmental patterns observed? We consider (i) the semantic nature and complexity of the four qualia relations; (ii) adult input properties; and (iii) structural complexity.

3.1 The Semantic Nature and Complexity of the Four Qualia Relations

The developmental findings are consistent with the semantic nature and complexity of the four qualia relations: formal and constitutive aspects of an object (called natural type concepts in Pustejovsky 2001, 2006) are more basic attributes, while telic and agentive (called artificial type concepts in Pustejovsky 2001, 2006) are derived and often eventive (hence conceptually more complex).

3.2 Adult Input Properties

The developmental findings appear to be also consistent with the properties of their adult input. We did a parallel analysis of the 3053 NMCs attested in the mother-to-child speech in the Zhou2 corpus. See Table 4. The adult input findings indicate that NMCs expressing the formal quale are also most frequently

Table 4. The Distribution of NMCs Expressing the Four Major Qualia Roles in Children's Adult Input (mother-to-child's naturalistic speech) Across Age

Age	3;00 (20)[1]		3;06 (21)		4;00 (16)		4;06 (19)		5;00 (22)		5;06 (16)		6;00 (21)	
Qualia	Token	%	Token	%	Token	%	Token	%	Token	%	Token	%	Token	%
Formal	307	57.2	294	56.0	256	54.1	223	51.6	218	53.0	133	55.0	190	45.9
Constitutive	148	27.6	142	27.0	118	24.9	107	24.8	101	24.6	65	26.9	119	28.7
Agentive	40	7.4	56	10.7	53	11.2	64	14.8	61	14.8	28	11.6	64	15.5
Telic	42	7.8	33	6.3	46	9.7	38	8.8	31	7.5	16	6.6	41	9.9

encountered in the adult input; followed by the constitutive quale, and then the agentive and telic quales.

3.3 Structural Complexity

The idea to consider here is that since the Telic and Agentive quales always involve some event, which is in turn expressed by a full clause, telic and agentive NMCs are structurally more complex than the formal and constitutive ones, and therefore acquired later. However, in Mandarin, telic and agentive NMCs can also be non-clausal (hence not necessarily always structurally more complex; e.g. "Baby's noise (The noise made by the baby)") and examples of these are also attested in the children's speech at an early age, although few. In addition, some NMCs expressing the formal quale with a clausal (hence structurally more complex) modifier are also noticed in the children's speech at an early age, albeit not frequently attested in the current corpus (see examples of the RC type-NMCs in Table 1).

On the other hand, to clarify, we are not claiming that structural complexity has no or only an insignificant role to play here. We need to design experimental tasks such as elicited production and imitation tasks (as future research) to systematically elicit the 4 types of NMCs (formal, constitutive, agentive and telic) within each type of which varying in structural complexity (involving both clausal and non-clausal modifiers, for instance) to fully consider and evaluate the role of structural complexity.

4 Concluding Remarks

Traditionally, RCs have often been studied from a structural perspective and with little emphasis on the relationship between RCs and other types of NMCs in the language. More recently, however, linguists such as Comrie (1996, 1998, 2002) and Matsumoto (1997, 2007) proposed that, in certain Asian languages, RCs should be analyzed as a subset of NMCs based on semantic-pragmatic relations between the head noun and its modifier.

As an initial attempt to study the acquisition of NMCs in child Mandarin from a semantic perspective, we first focus on characterizing the semantic relations between the modifier and the head noun based on the generative lexicon framework (Pustejovsky, 1995).

This attempt is probably the first of using the generative lexicon framework in the field of child language acquisition. The new data and the observed developmental patterns may serve as a basis or reference for inspiring more experimental work and more wide-ranging cross-linguistic work examining the acquisition of NMCs from a semantic approach. Such cross-linguistic findings may reveal some robust descriptive generalizations about the acquisition of NMCs from a semantic perspective.

References

Comrie B. 1996. The unity of noun-modifying clauses in Asian languages. Proceedings of the 4th International Symposium on Pan-Asiatic Linguistics, 1077-88.

Comrie B. 1998. Rethinking the typology of relative clauses. Language Design, 1: 59-85.

Comrie B. 2002. Typology and language acquisition: The case of relative clauses. In Giacalone Ramat (ed.) Typology and Second Language Acquisition. Berlin: Mouton de Gruyter.

Diessel H. 2007. A Construction-Based Analysis of the Acquisition of East Asian Relative Clauses. Studies in Second Language Acquisition. 29 (2). pp 311-320

Fillmore C. J. 1977. Topics in lexical semantics. In *Current Issues in Linguistic Theory*. R. Cole. (ed.), 76-138. Bloomington: Indiana University Press.

Fillmore C. J. 1982. Frame semantics. In *Linguistics in the Morning Calm*. C. J. Fillmore (ed.), 111-138. Linguistic Society of Korea. Seoul: Hanshin Publishing Co.

Fillmore C. J. & Atkins B. T. 1992. Toward a frame-based lexicon: the semantics of RISK and its neighbors. In *Frames, Fields, and Contrasts*. A. Lehrer and E.F. Kittay (eds), 75-102. Hillsdale, NJ: Lawrence Erlbaum Assoc.

Huang S.-F. 2008. Rethinking the relative clause construction in spoken Chinese: a typological perspective. *Talk Presented at the Department of Linguistics and Modern Languages of the Chinese University of Hong Kong*. 8 Dec 2008.

Lenci A. et al. 2000. SIMPLE Work Package 2, Linguistic Specifications, Deliverable D2.1, The Specification Group.

MacWhinney B. 2000. The CHILDES Project: Tools for Analyzing Talk. Third Edition. Mahwah, NJ: Lawrence Erlbaum Associates.

Matsumoto Y.1997.Noun-Modifying Constructions in Japanese: A Frame-Semantic Approach. Amsterdam: John Benjamins.

Matsumoto Y. 2007. Integrating Frames: Complex Noun Phrase Constructions in Japanese. In Aspects of Linguistics: In Honor of Noriko Akatsuka (Gengogaku no Syosoo: Akatsuka Noriko Kyoozyu Kinen Ronbunsyuu), S. Kuno, S. Makino & S. Strauss (eds), 131-154. Tokyo: Kurosio Publishers.

Pustejovsky J. 1995. The Generative Lexicon. Cambridge, Massachusetts: The MIT Press.

Pustejovsky J. 2001. *Type Construction and the Logic of Concepts*, in P. Bouillon and F. Busa (eds.) The Syntax of Word Meaning, Cambridge University Press, Cambridge.

Pustejovsky J. 2006. Type theory and Lexical Decomposion, Journal of Cognitive Sciience, 1, p.39

Gap in "Gapless" Relative Clauses in Korean and Other Asian Languages

Jeong-Shik Lee
Department of English Language and Literature, Wonkwang University, 344-2 Shinyong-dong, Iksan 570-749, South Korea
jslee@wku.ac.kr

Chungmin Lee
Department of Linguistics, Seoul National University, 1 Gwanak-ro, Gwanak- gu, Seoul 151-742, South Korea
clee@snu.ac.kr

Abstract

This paper attempts to argue that the so-called gapless relative clause (GRC) in Korean (Chinese and Japanese as well) can best be dealt with by the Generative Lexicon Theory (GLT) put forward in Pustejovsky (1995). There arises a superficial conflict in the construction: the GRC, with no apparent gap, contains a relative verb that does not directly relate to the head noun in terms of cause-effect relation required between the GRC and the following head noun. The paper shows that this incomplete realization of the cause-effect relation can be fully recovered from the lexical-semantic(-pragmatic) information specified under the GL framework. Thus, the qualia structure of GLT can successfully fill the meaning of the best hidden relative verb in the GRC for the correct interpretation.

Keywords: "gapless" relative clauses, Generative Lexicon Theory, qualia structure, agentive/telic role, Korean

1. Introduction

In Korean (Chinese and Japanese as well) the so-called gapless relative clauses (GRC) have been discussed in Cha (1997, 2005), J. Lee 2012, and others, representatively illustrated in (1, 2, and 3) (Adn = adnominal).

(1) *cause-effect relation with sensory head noun*
[sayngsen-i tha-nun] naymsay
fish-Nom burn-Adn smell
'the smell that comes from fish burning'

(2) *cause-effect relation with non-sensory head noun*
[thayphwung-i cinaka-n] huncek
typhoon-Nom pass-Adn trace
'the trace left after a typhoon hit'

(3) *cause-effect relation with non-natural phenomenon*
[apeci-ka so-lul phal-un] ton
father-Nom ox-Acc sell-Adn money
'the money obtained by selling an ox'

It is observed that there exists a semantic cause-effect relation holding between the GRC and its modifying head noun: the content of the adnominal GRC constitutes *cause* and the denotation of its head noun *effect*. Without the cause-effect relation, the GRC is not allowed (e.g., [*sayngsen-I tha-nun*] ?**hyangki* ('fragrance)/?**moyang* ('appearance') /**huncek* ('trace)). GRC is different from a typical relative clause (RC) like (4) containing a gap which is externally realized as a head noun.

(4) [apeci-ka △ phal-un] so (△=*so* 'ox')
father-Nom sell-Adn ox
'the ox that father sold'

Also, GRCs are different from noun complements in examples like (5) in that they are not a complement of the head noun:

(5) [apeci-ka so-lul phal-ass-ta-nun]
father-Nom ox-Acc sell-Past-Dec-Adn
somwun/ sasil/cwucang
rumor/fact/claim
'the rumor/fact/claim that father sold an ox'

Thus, GRCs in Korean are different from regular RCs, and they are not noun complements; therefore, as most researchers claim, GRCs are like gapless clausal modifiers for the following head nouns (Yoon, JH 1993, Cha 1997, 1998, 2005 in Korean and papers for Japanese and Chinese).

In this paper, we for the first time claim that for the correct, coherent interpretation in GRCs like (3), for example, the required cause-effect relation should be fully realized by the addition or coercion of a verb like *pel-* 'earn,' which comes from the agentive role in the qualia structure of *ton* 'money,' in conjunction with the main event predicate *phal-* 'sell,' as shown in (6).

(6) [apeci-ka [[so-lul phal-a] [pel]-n]]
father-Nom ox-Acc sell earn-Adn
ton
money
'the money that father earned by selling an ox'

We then argue that the meaning of the hidden verb *pel-* 'earn' in (3) can be successfully recovered from the reservoir containing the lexical-semantic (-pragmatic) information of the given lexical items specified under the GL framework. In section 2, we observe more related phenomena to claim that recovering the hidden verb has actual empirical bearing as seen in examples like (6). In section 3, we elaborate the current proposal in detail within the GLT, offering the lexical-semantic information of the elements of the GRC construction. In section 4, we briefly discuss cross-linguistic implications of the proposed GL analysis. Finally, section 5 concludes the paper.

2 Some Related Phenomena

The typical relative clause (RC) in Korean can appear in the pseudo-cleft , as in (7) (cf. (4)).

(7) [apeci-ka phal-n kes-un] so-i-ta.
father-Nom sell-Adn KES-Top ox-be-Dec
'What father sold is an ox.'

The GRC, however, cannot appear in the **pseudo-cleft**, as in (8, 9, 10) (cf. (1, 2, 3)).

(8) *[sayngsen-i tha-nun kes-un] naymsay-i--ta.
fish-Nom burn-Adn KES-Top smell-be--Dec
'What fish burns is the smell.' (Lit.)
(9) *[thayphwung-i cinaka-n kes-un] huncek-
typhoon-Nom pass-Adn KES-Top trace-
-i-ta
be-Dec
'What a typhoon passed is the trace.' (Lit.)
(10) *[apeci-ka so-lul phal-n kes-un]
father-Nom ox-Acc sell-Adn KES-Top
ton- i-ta.
money-be-Dec
'What father sold an ox is the money.'

The pseudo-cleft fact displayed in the above examples indicates that head nouns are not the elements of the GRCs, and indicates that GRCs are gapless clausal modifiers for the following head nouns.

The regular RC can appear as a predicate of the relative head noun, whatever grammatical role it may take in the RC, in the form of a topic construction (C. Lee 1973), as in (11). C. Lee argues that an RC head is realized via a topic in the relevant RC.

(11) ku so-nun [apeci-ka phal-ass-ta].
the ox-Top father-Nom sell-Past-Dec
'The ox, father sold it.'

The GRC, however, cannot form a **topic construction** in which the topic of the relative head noun and its comment predicate cohere, as in (12, 13, and 14). This is a crucial and decisive piece of evidence showing that we need a coerced predicate for compositionality and coherence.

(12) *ku naymsay-nun [sayngsen-i tha-n-ta].
the smell-Top fish-Nom burn-Pres-Dec
'As for the smell, fish burns.' (Lit.)
(13) *ku huncek-un [thayphwung-i cinaka-
the trace-Top typhoon-Nom pass-
ass-ta].
Past-Dec
'As for the trace, a typhoon passed.' (Lit.)
(14) *ku ton-un [apeci-ka so-lul phal- ass-ta].
the money-Top father-Nom ox-Acc sell Past-Dec
'As for the money, father sold an ox.' (Lit.)

We point out that the fact that relative noun heads cannot serve as topics with GRCs in (12, 13, 14), compared with regular RCs like (11), is due to the lack of additional predicate that can fully realize the aforementioned cause-effect relation in the predicative position. This is corroborated by the following representative example where this relation is fully realized.

(15) ku ton-un [apeci-ka so-lul phal-a
the money-Top father-Nom ox-Acc sell
pel-ess-ta].
earn-Past-Dec

In the above example, the verb *pel-* 'earn' is coerced from *ton* 'money' as an agentive quale and added to realize the effect fully. The same kind of saving effect is found in the pseudo-cleft, as representatively illustrated in (16).

(16) [apeci-ka so-lul phal-a pel-n
father-Nom ox-Acc sell earn-Adn
kes-un] ton-i-ta.
KES-Top money-be-Dec
'What father earned by selling an ox is money.'

Thus, overt coercion of the addition of the relevant predicate is necessary in the **topic** and **pseudo-cleft** constructions for coherence. Putting the head noun in the prominent topic position or in the highlighted focused position is a crucial test to see what is missing conceptually. Although the GRC construction may allow the addition in question by hitting on compatible verbs with no principled basis, as in (17, 18, 19), this construction does not necessarily superficially require it, as seen in (1, 2, 3).

(17) [sayngsen-i tha-a na-nun] naymsay
fish-Nom burn arise-Adn smell
'the smell that comes from fish burning'

(18) [thayphwung-i cinaka-a namki-n] huncek
typhoon-Nom pass leave-Adn trace
'the trace left after a typhoon hit'

(19) [apeci-ka so-lul phal-a pel-n] ton
father-Nom ox-Acc sell earn-And money
'the money that father earned by selling an ox'

It thus appears that in the GRC construction, the head noun and the main event predicate in the GRC are close enough to allow the cause-effect relation to be covertly coerced and recovered in the absence of the additional predicate that helps fully realize the relation. In the next section, we discuss the matter in question in some detail. We will show that GLT can serve the purpose.

Note also that in languages like English where the head noun precedes the RC, GRCs and RCs corresponding to (1, 2, 3) and (17, 18, 19), respectively, are not allowed:

(20) a. *the smell that fish burns
b. *the smell that fish burns and arises
cf. the smell that arises from fish burning

(21) a. *the trace that a typhoon passed
b. *the trace that typhoon passed and is left
cf. the trace that is left from typhoon passing

(22) a. *the money that father sold an ox
b. *the money that father sold an ox and earned
cf. the money that father earned from selling an ox

We attribute this contrast to the different word order between the relative head noun and the RC: in English type European languages, unlike in Korean type East Asian languages, the head noun and the main event predicate in the GRC or RC are not close enough, so the cause-effect relation is not allowed to be covertly coerced and recovered. The same is also found in the non-appearance of GRCs in pseudo-clefts and in the predicative position in Korean, as shown in (8, 9, 10) and (12, 13, 14). So the contrast under consideration can find a deeper reason.

3. How GL Can Account for the Gap in GRC

One might postulate the predicate *pel-* 'earn' in the underlying structure of GRCs like (3), repeated below, by taking notice of the overt presence of examples like (6), repeated below.

(3) [apeci-ka so-lul phal-n] ton
father-Nom ox-Acc sell--Adn money
'the money obtained by selling an ox'

(6) [apeci-ka [[so-lul phal-a] [pel]-n]] ton
father-Nom ox-Acc sell earn-Adn money

'the money that father earned by selling an ox'

Based on the fact that (3) and (6) have almost the same interpretation, ellipsis may be claimed to be involved in deriving (3) from (6) (J. Lee 2012).

But this analysis does not seem to have any repertoire of deep explanatory devices for the above state of affairs. On the other hand, the GL mechanism offers a fundamental answer to the question of where the verb *pel-* 'earn' comes---it is exactly the agentive quale of the (social artifact) noun head *ton* 'money,' which can be represented as follows:

(23) AGENTIVE (*ton* 'money') = $\lambda z \lambda x \lambda y \lambda eT$ [*pel-* 'earn' (eT, z, x, (by)y)]

In (23), *ton* 'money' is something (x) that an agent (z) *earns by* (causal means) doing something (y). The interpretation 'the money which father earns by selling an ox' can be easily obtained by applying this agentive quale. Thus argument coherence of identity between the agent 'father' of the ox-selling causal event that appears in the adjunct clause and the agent 'father' of the money-earning effect that appears in the event phrase or clause is well observed (Pustejovsky 1995). The temporal ordering is also kept by precedence or overlap of the causal event compared to the result event.

We assume that basically the same GL approach can extend to other head nouns like *naymsay* 'smell' and *huncek* 'trace' in the GRCs in (1, 2). These nominal heads have similar cause-effect relations with their perceptual effects. They can be represented by some verbs of arousal, being emitted (by), or result (or leaving behind), etc. to apply to (1, 2) and justify the coerced event functions that show up in (17) and (18). The connective can be the simultaneity marker *–myense* 'when,' 'while,' showing the causing event can directly or almost simultaneously emit perceptual nominals such as smell (of burning fish), sound, and shape.

In (6) a limited set of verbs can appear in place of *pel-* 'earn,' including verbs like *malyenha-* 'prepare,' *mantul-* 'make,' *pat-* 'receive'; all these verbs share the basic meaning of 'obtaining (money as a result of selling an ox in a given context).' The specific choice of a particular verb is determined in a given context. The default is *pel-* 'earn.'

We further extend our analysis to the following interesting contrast:

(24) a. [apeci-ka so-lul phal-a kaph-un]
father-Nom ox-Acc sell pay.back-Adn
ton
money
'the money that father paid back by selling an ox'

b. *[apeci-ka so-lul phal-a kkwu-/ ilh-/
father-Nom ox-Acc sell borrow-/lose-/
cwup-un] ton
find-Adn money
'the money that father borrowed/lost/ found by selling an ox'

In (24a) the cause-effect relation indirectly holds between the causing event *so-lul phala* 'selling an ox' and the following additional verb *kaph-* 'pay.back' by the mediation of the verb *pel-* 'earn,' as illustrated in (25).

(25) [apeci-ka [[so-lul phal-a] [pel-e]
father-Nom ox-Acc sell earn
[kaph-]]--un] ton
pay.back-Adn money
'the money that father paid back by selling an ox and thereby earned'

In other words, the agentive quale of the noun head *ton* 'money,' namely, the verb *pel-* 'earn,' is consistent with the verb *kaph-* 'pay.back' conjunctively as a following event, so this verb can follow the verb licensed by the agentive quale defined above. But this addition is irrelevant to the original GRC. (25) entails (⇒) (24a) but not (24b). Interestingly, example (3), reproduced at the beginning of this section, cannot be interpreted as meaning (24a). This fact confirms our proposal. Since the agentive quale of the noun head *ton* 'money' is determined as the verb *pel-* 'earn,' with the causing event (in the *–a* adjunct) accompanied, the interpretation of (3) is to be different from (24a) in which the verb *kaph-* 'pay.back' is separately added, as seen in (25).

In (24b), on the other hand, the verbs *kkwu-* 'borrow,' *ilh-* 'lose,' and *cwup-* 'find' do not constitute a natural effect of the causing event, *so-lul phal-a* 'selling an ox,' so there arises a conflict in the information structure. More specifically, the agentive quale of the noun head *ton* 'money,' namely, the verb *pel-* 'earn,' is inconsistent with the above verbs, so these verbs cannot be licensed by the agentive quale defined above.

4 Some Cross-linguistic Implications

It is reported that GRCs are also observed in Chinese (Zhang 2008, Tsai 2008, among others) and Japanese (Murasugi 1991, Matsumoto 1997, among others).

(26) Chinese
a. [Lulu tan gangqin] de shengyin
Lulu play piano DE sound
'the sound which (is produced by) Lulu's playing the piano'
b. [mama chao cai] de weidao
Mom fry vegetable DE smell
'the smell from Mom's vegetable-frying'

(27) Japanese
a. [dereka-ga doa-o tataku] oto
someone-Nom door-Acc knock sound
'the noise of someone knocking at the door'
b. [sakana-ga yakeru] nioi
fish-Nom burn smell
'the smell that a fish burns' (Lit.)

We suggest that the current proposed analysis developed from Korean exactly apply to the same GRCs in these East Asian languages. The most common previous analysis is that the GRC is a simple gapless clausal modifier for the following noun head. Murasugi (1991) and Tsai (2008), among others, claim that the so-called GRCs in Japanese and Chinese, respectively, are not really RCs but just complex noun phrases with gapless adnominal clauses.

Our GL approach, however, offers a more specific, deeper RC analysis on this phenomenon: the agentive quale of the noun heads like *sound* and *smell* above can covertly coerce or recover the appropriate relative predicates that help fully realize the required cause-effect relation. For example, *sound* is something (x) that an agent (z) *produces by* (causal means) doing something (y); *smell* is something (x) that is *produced by* (causal means) doing something (y).

Zhang (2008) proposes that the GRC is a subject and the following head noun is a predicate in Chinese. Interesting though the proposal is, we do not buy it since different morphology in Korean does not point to it, as can be seen in (1, 2, 3), in which the predicate in the GRC ending with the modifying adnominal maker –*(nu)n*, not being a nominalizer, cannot make the GRC a subject in Korean. Even if the GRC turns into a nominal with the addition of the nominal *kes* after the predicate in question, as seen in the pseudo-clefts in (8, 9, 10), the GRC cannot still function as the subject.

According to Tsai (2008: 116-118), Ning (1993) proposes the VP adjunct analysis for GRCs in Chinese, treating the overtly added or coerced verbal part as a VP adjunct containing a gap. Thus, in the following corresponding Korean examples, repeated below as (28, 29, 30), the phrase enclosed by bracelets is a VP adjunct and contains a trace left by the usual relative movement involved.

(28) [sayngsen-i tha-a {t na-nun}] naymsay
fish-Nom burn arise-And smell
'the smell that comes from fish burning'

(29) [thayphwung-i cinaka-a {t nam-un}]
typhoon-Nom pass leave-Adn
huncek
trace
'the trace left after a typhoon hit'

(30) [apeci-ka so-lul phal-a {t pel-n}]
father-Nom ox-Acc sell earn-Adn
ton
money
'the money that father earned by selling an ox'

Contrary to Ning, our analysis shows that the causing event is rather realized as an adjunct. The morphological marker *–a* (or, *–myense*) attached to the main event predicate confirms this analysis since it appears at the end of the adjunct clause. This is further syntactically evidenced by the well-known fact that extraction out of an adjunct produces a bad result. The fact that the above examples are good refutes Tsai's VP-adjunct analysis.

Notice that the clause containing the main event predicate does not involve any gap, which suggests that this main predicate clause is in turn an adjunct. Since there is no gap here, there arises no adjunct island violation. Thus, Tsai's argument against Ning's wrong adjunct approach is in fact based on false ground.

Zhaojing (2012:(6), a paper to be believed to be presented in this workshop) claims that the following noun modification construction from Chinese just involves the Formal Qualia modifier:

(31) hongse de yanjing
red eye
'red eyes'

Here we can basically agree with Zhaojing that the construction involves Formal Qualia, if the color red is meant to be an inherent property of the eyes. The question is whether this construction could involve any role like Agentive, as implicated by our analysis. The color red here seems to be meant to involve some result of inchoative change from non-red to red because of drinking or other causes. The non-change situation does not but the change situation does involve Agentivity. Nevertheless, the construction could be analyzed as containing a subject gap because it constitutes an intransitive sentence with a stative predicate. This comes from the corresponding Korean example given below.

(32) pwulk-un nwun
red-Ad eye
'red eyes'

What we note is the presence of the modifying adnominal marker *–un* attached to the attributive adjective as well as to attributive (G)RCs. Without this marker, the phrase is illicit. Thus it would not be implausible to assume the adjectival modifier here is in fact a clause, as has also been suggested in Kaynean approach.

5. Residues

5. 1 How about purpose (telic) quale?

On the other hand, we can tentatively say that the range of GRCs under discussion does not involve any purpose (telic) role. This is because of the head noun Agentive cause-effect relation required between the GRC and the head noun. However, a purpose (telic) quale does not seem to be entirely excluded in some less common contexts. Consider (33) (Prashant Pardeshi p.c.). The purpose of an artifact commercial is to draw the audience's attention intensively in a very short period of time.

(33) hwacangshil-ey mot ka-nun commercial
toilet-to not able go-Ad
'a commercial that attracts our attention so intensively that we cannot go to the toilet.'

However, if commercial interruptions in a soap opera are used to go to the toilet, the failure of their purpose must be due to the attraction of the soap opera program (Allan Kim p. c. and C. Lee share this intuition). All Agentive interpretations of our GRCs, together with the first telic interpretation of (33), can be based on the lexical-semantic content, but the second telic interpretation of (33) is heavily context-dependent and may be pragmatic. The head NP in (33) must be a subject in a causal adjunct clause in a bi-clausal structure.

An aspectual elliptical clause can form a regular RC easily, requiring a coerced purpose (telic) or Agentive role, as in (34). The coerced predicate *read* or *write* is based on the qualia structure lexical-semantic specification of the artifact nominal *book*. Suppose the subject of (34) is a goat. Then, the coerced predicate in that particular context may be *chew* or *eat*, calling for pragmatics.

(34) Mary-ka shicak-ha-n chayk
M –Nom begin-do-Ad book
'A book Mary began {to read, to write}.'

5. 2 How about in the Keenan-Comrie Hierachy?

One may well say that because the Keenan-Comrie Noun Phrase Accessibility Hierarchy treats mono-clausal relative clauses (Keenan and Comrie 1977), based on non-GRCs, the hierarchy is not relevant to the underlyingly bi-clausal and superficially gapless Asian language relative clauses. The hierarchy is about how a grammatical relation NP is accessible to relativization in competition with others in a clause. However, we can suggest that the hierarchy encompass gap-like head NPs in recovered bi-clausal relative clauses in Asian languages; the hierarchy is purported to be semantically based. From a coherent qualia based bi-clausal sentence, an NP in the main clause of the sentence can undergo a relativization operation to form a modifying relative clause with a head NP. So, GRCNP may be at the bottom of the hierarchy, as follows:

(35) Accessibility Hierarchy (AH)

SU > DO > LO > OBL > GEN > OCOMP
> GRCNP

But it is interesting to note that the same original hierarchy may work recursively in the Agentively coerced main clause within the bi-clausal structure. For that kind of recursivity, the coerced main clause verb better be an intransitive verb *na-* 'come out' for the higher SU 'smell' than the transitive verb *nay-* 'emit' for the lower DO 'smell' in (17). For the sake of causation argument coherence, however, the transitive verb treatment seems more adequate.

In sum, we found that the coerced event function has not been proposed yet, and claim that our GL qualia structure analysis can encompass GRCs in East Asian languages like Chinese, Japanese, and Korean.

6. Conclusion

We attempted for the first time to demonstrate how GL can well account for the mysterious phenomenon of "gapless" relative clauses that appear in at least three Asian languages by means of the event function coercion from the qualia structure enrichment of lexical meanings. We need further studies in the direction of incorporating pragmatic/discourse factors that should also be involved in coherent interpretations of such interesting phenomena.

References

Cha, Jong-Yul. 1997. Type-hierarchical Analysis of Gapless Relative Clauses in Korean. Paper presented at the 4th International Conference on HPSG. Cornell University.

Cha, Jong-Yul. 1998. Relative Clause or Noun Complement Clause: The Diagnoses. *Selected Papers from the Eleventh International Conference on Korean Linguistics*, 73-82. University of Hawai at Manoa.

Cha, Jong-Yul. 2005. *Constraints on Clausal Noun Phrases in Korean with the Focus on the Gapless Relative Clause Construction.* Doctoral dissertation, University at Illinois at Urbana-Champaign.

Keenan, Edward and Comrie, Bernard. 1977. Noun Phrase Accessibility and Universal Grammar, *Linguistic Inquiry* 8, 63-99.

Lee, Chungmin. 1973. *Abstract Syntax and Korean with reference to English*. Doctoral dissertation. Indiana University.

Lee, Jeong-Shik. 2012. Ellipsis in Gapless Relative Clauses in Korean, *Proceedings of the 14th Seoul International Conference on Generative Grammar*, 277-296.

Zhaojing, Liu. 2012. The role of Qualia structure in Mandarin Children Acquiring Noun-Modifying Constructions. A paper to be presented in the GLAL Workshop in 2012, Bali.

Matsumoto, Yoshiko. 1997. *Noun-modifying Constructions in Japanese: A Frame Semantics Approach*. Amsterdam: John Benjamins.

Murasugi, Keiko. 1991. *Noun phrases in Japanese and English: A Study in Syntax, Learnability and Acquisition.* Doctoral dissertation, University of Connecticut.

Ning, Chunyan. 1993. *The overt Syntax of Relativization and Topicalization in Chinese*. Doctoral dissertation. University of California, Irvine.

Pustejovsky, James. 1995. *The Generative Lexicon.* Cambridge: The MIT Press.

Tsai, Hui-Chin Joice. 2008. On gapless relative clauses in Chinese. *Nanzan Linguistics: Special Issues* 5: 109-124.

Yoon, Jae-Hak 1993. Different Semantics for Different Syntax: Relative Clauses in Korean. *Ohio State University Working Papers in Linguistics* 42: 199-226.

Zhang, Niina. 2008. Gapless relative clauses as clausal licensors of relational nouns. *Language and Semantics* 9: 1003-1026.

Author Index